The Willard J. Graham Series in Accounting

Consulting Editor ROBERT N. ANTHONY *Harvard University*

Managerial Cost Accounting

Gordon Shillinglaw

Professor of Accounting
Graduate School of Business
Columbia University

Fourth Edition

1977

RICHARD D. IRWIN, INC. Homewood, Illinois 60430
Irwin-Dorsey Limited Georgetown, Ontario L7G 4B3

Previous editions of this book were published under the title
Cost Accounting: Analysis and Control.

© RICHARD D. IRWIN, INC., 1961, 1967, 1972, and 1977

Fourth Edition

4 5 6 7 8 9 0   K 5 4 3 2 1 0

ISBN 0-256-01905-3
Library of Congress Catalog Card No. 76–47716
Printed in the United States of America

To
FRANK P. SMITH
a great teacher and a good friend,
who made his students see that accounting
is worth thinking about

Preface

THE AIM OF this book is to explain cost accounting—what it is, who needs it, and how it can be used. The coverage is comprehensive, but the emphasis is managerial. Our main interest is in what managers want or need to know and how best to provide this information.

Mastery of cost accounting techniques unaccompanied by an understanding of what they are designed to achieve is no mastery at all. For this reason I have made a particular effort to place the technical aspects of cost accounting in a sound conceptual framework. The problems, exercises, and cases are all designed with this in mind.

Most students facing this material for the first time will have completed a one- or two-semester course in financial accounting. The only prerequisite, however, is an understanding of the basic structure of financial accounting; detailed familiarity with generally accepted financial accounting principles is unnecessary. It is taken for granted that the reader knows what an income statement is and how assets are measured for public financial reporting.

Outline

This edition is divided into three parts. Part One, consisting of the first nine chapters, describes the basic structure of cost accounting, including a summary of the context in which cost accounting data are used. Chapter 1 sets the stage, Chapters 2 through 5 relate mainly to the accountant's role in managerial planning, and Chapters 6 through 9 focus for the most part on accounting's contribution to control reporting.

Part Two extends the discussion of cost accounting for planning purposes. It does this first by examining methods of activity costing not covered in Part One; second by describing a number of decision models which require cost accounting data; and third by introducing several analytical techniques that though not part of cost accounting proper are essential to the cost accountant's training.

Part Three describes and analyzes accounting systems for financial control reporting, ranging from systems designed to help first-line factory managers control their costs to those used by the top management of multiproduct, decentralized corporations to evaluate the profitability of divisional activities and the performance of the division managers.

Cost accounting techniques to develop data for corporate financial reporting are discussed at appropriate points in each part of the book. Chapters 2, 8, 10, 11, and 22 give the greatest amount of space to this topic. The requirements of contract costing are also mentioned in these chapters, as well as in Appendix B, which summarizes the first 14 contract costing standards promulgated by the new Cost Accounting Standards Board.

The Fourth Edition

This edition is in most respects a new book. It even has a new title. Although the general orientation is the same as in previous editions, a great deal of effort has been made to make the book more useful to the reader. Almost 200 new diagrams have been added, much new material has been introduced, and more than 250 new problems have been provided. A particular effort has been made to insure that each chapter lays a firm foundation for the exercises and problems that follow it.

A considerable amount of care has been taken to insure that this edition is comprehensive and up to date. The new appendix on cost accounting standards is one obvious example. Another example is the chapter on the behavioral aspects of financial control systems—I have revised it extensively to reflect the current emphasis on expectancy theory. I have also expanded the discussion of such topics as statistical regression analysis, learning curve analysis, linear programming, uncertainty analysis, and the disposition of factory cost variances for external financial reporting.

As in previous editions, one or more independent study problems are provided at the end of most chapters. Most of them are new in this edition, and I have expanded the selection to provide a more representative coverage of the subject matter in each chapter.

A new feature in this edition is the list of key terms at the end of each chapter. The purpose of this feature is to help the student review and organize the material in the chapter. Each list consists mainly of terms not listed in previous chapters. A few terms are included more than once, however, because they are extremely important and might otherwise be overlooked.

Despite these changes, the conceptual rigor that characterized the earlier editions has not been tampered with. I remain firmly convinced that this is the only sound way to approach this subject.

Study Suggestions

Each chapter is designed to help the student understand the concepts and apply them to practical problems. No accounting book reads like a detective story, however, not even this one. Understanding comes only with some effort. Many students find it useful to make their own calculations as they read the text, verifying the numbers in the illustrations and tracing the relationships among the exhibits as they are introduced.

The instructor is likely to assign one or more problems as preparation for each class session. These may be all the practice many students will need. Others will find it useful to work the independent study problems, using the captions on these problems to choose those most relevant to the topics to be covered in class. These problems should also be useful in reviewing the materials before scheduled examinations.

Acknowledgments

I owe much to many for their help and encouragement as this book has gone through four editions. It is difficult to single out some without slighting others, but I shall always be indebted to Myron J. Gordon, Carl L. Nelson, and the late Willard J. Graham for the enormous contributions they made to the success of the first three editions.

Several users of previous editions, and some nonusers as well, took the time and trouble to let me know what they liked and what they didn't like. Carl Allen, Lawrence Benninger, George Bruha, Joseph Curran, Joel Demski, Gary Fox, Sanford Gunn, and William Voss made useful comments on various parts of the third edition or on parts of the manuscript for this edition as it progressed. David Nadler, also of the Columbia faculty, helped me reorient the behavioral chapter. Mr. Nelson H. Shapiro of the Cost Accounting Standards Board staff was kind enough to read Appendix B and make a number of valuable suggestions.

My greatest thanks on this edition must go to Robert N. Anthony of Harvard University and Phyllis Barker of Indiana State University. Professor Anthony, as consulting editor of this series, read both the previous edition and the entire manuscript of this edition, making many valuable suggestions. Professor Barker undertook the monumental task of overseeing a team of students who volunteered to check every problem, every exercise, and every case. In preparation for this task, Professor Barker read the full manuscript, paragraph by paragraph. Her comments and suggestions were invaluable, and the book is far better for them.

None of these friendly critics is responsible for defects that may survive in this edition, of course. I can only hope that I have been able to take advantage of the help that has been offered me.

Harvey Babiak, Lawrence Benninger, John C. Burton, Eric Flamholtz, Michael Ginzberg, Michael Jensen, Philip Meyers, Carl L. Nelson, David Solomons, and Russell Taussig have been most generous in letting me use or modify problems or cases they have written. I am also grateful to Luigi Dusmet de Smours, director of the IMEDE Management Development Institute in Lausanne, Switzerland, for his permission to use cases that I wrote while serving on the IMEDE faculty. Charles Summer was my coauthor on the AB Thorsten (D) case, appearing at the end of Chapter 26, and I acknowledge his contribution most gratefully. I also thank the Institute of Management Accounting and the American Institute of Certified Public Accountants for letting me use or adapt materials from their professional examinations. The questions from the Institute of Management Accounting are labeled "CMA," the letters designating the recipients of the institute's certificate in management accounting.

Finally, I should like to thank my wife for her patience and understanding month after month as the clickety clack of my typewriter has disturbed the peace and given me the excuse to avoid (or postpone) doing household chores.

February 1977   GORDON SHILLINGLAW

Contents

Costs. Standard Cost Files: *Standard Materials Prices. Standard Labor Rates. Standard Materials Quantities. Standard Labor Quantities. Standard Product Costs.* Variances from Standard Cost: *Calculating Quantity Variances. Measuring Price Variances. Variances for Scorecard Reports. The Need for Dollar Variances.* A Standard Costing System: *Characteristics of the Basic Plan. Recording Materials Purchases. Isolating the Quantity Variances. Isolating the Labor Rate Variance. Basic Plan Cost Flows.* Problems with Standard Costing: *System Cost. Nonstandard Products. Behavioral Problems.*

Case
Frozen Meals, Inc., 216

7 Flexible Budgets: Controlling Overhead Costs of Responsive Activities   224

Performance Standards for Overhead Costs: *Standard Factory Overhead Costs. The Flexible Budget. Interpreting the Flexible Budget. Technical Problems in Flexible Budgeting. Behavioral Problems in Flexible Budgeting.* Reporting Departmental Overhead Costs: *Departmental Spending Variances. Frequency of Reporting. Reporting Noncontrollable Costs. Amount of Detail. Authorized Budget Changes. Price and Quantity Components of the Spending Variance. Reports for Higher Management.* Volume Variances in Factory Overhead Costs: *Calculating the Overhead Variances. Interpreting the Volume Variance. Reconciling the Variances.*

Case
Rigazio Enterprises, 252

8 Interdepartmental Cost Allocations   256

Reasons for Allocations: *Inventory Measurement. Decision Analysis. Control Reporting. Contract Costing.* Allocations in Predetermined Overhead Rates: *Allocation Procedures. A Full-Cost Allocation Plan: Sequential Allocation. Allocations under Variable Costing.* Interdepartmental Allocations for Control Reporting: *Reasons for After-the-Fact Allocations. Comparing Allocated Costs with Flexible Budget Allowances. An Allocation Illustration. Interpreting Service Department Variances. Including Allocations in Monthly Performance Reports. Full Cost versus Variable Cost Transfer Prices.* Appendix: Cross Allocations.

9 Financial Reporting to Marketing Management   295

The Marketing Function: *Order-Getting Activities. Order-Filling Activities. Marketing Administration.* Controlling Order-Getting Costs: *Inapplicability of Standard Costs and*

Flexible Budgets. The Plan as a Profit Standard. Profit Contribution Reporting: *The Case for Profit Contribution Reporting. Reporting Attributable Profit. Reporting Controllable Profit. Measuring the Cost of Goods Sold at Full Cost.* A Reporting System: *Base Level Profit Reports. Reporting to the General Sales Manager. Reporting to the Product Manager.* Interpreting Marketing Results: *Marketing Response Functions. Time Lags. Ratio Analysis.* Secondary Control Techniques.

Case
The Federal Company, 327

Calculating Product Cost: *Identifying the Production Centers. Measuring Costs. Measuring Output. Computing Unit Cost. Spoilage and Waste. Calculating Product Cost: The Final Step. Dealing with Mixed Outputs.* Process Costing on a Variable Costing Basis: *Process Costing for Wholly Variable Costs. Variable Costing with Semivariable Costs.* Integrating Process Costing into Financial Statements: *Why Special Calculations Are Needed. First-In, First-Out Method. Moving Average Method. Accounts for Process Costing.* Using Process Costing Information in Control Reporting: *Historical Costing. Standard Costing and Flexible Budgets.*

Recognizing Joint Products and Joint Costs: *Split-off Points. Joint Costs.* Joint Costs in Decision Making: *Joint Products as a Group. Individual Joint Products. Separable Costs and Joint Production Decisions.* Costing Co-Products for Financial Reporting: *Physical Unit Basis of Allocation. Market Price Basis of Allocation. Net Realization Basis of Allocation. Using the Unit Cost Figures.* The Costing of By-Products: *Defining By-Products. Illustration of By-Product Costing. Timing of By-Product Recognition. Inventory Measurement of By-Products.* Joint Costs of Variable-Yield Processes: *Measuring Incremental Costs: Variable Input Quality. Measuring Incremental Costs: Variable Input Mix. Measurement Difficulties.*

Case
The Williamson Chocolate Co., Ltd., 393

Standards. Management by Exception. The Controllability Criterion. Harmonization of Conflicting Goals. Behavioral Problems in System Administration: *Insensitivity of the Budgeting Staff. Irresponsibility of Operating Managers.*

Case
Sussex Products, Ltd., 660

Identifying and Reporting Quantity Variances: *Characteristics of the Comprehensive Plan. Comprehensive Plan Reporting to Management. Recording the Causes of Quantity Variances. Costs and Benefits of the Comprehensive Plan.* Statistical Approaches to Variance Investigation: *Statistical Control Limits. An Investigation Decision Model.* Accounts for the Comprehensive Plan: *Factorywide Work-in-Process Accounts. Four-Wall Inventory Accounting.* Appendix: Calculation of Control Limits.

Overhead Cost Variances in Standard Costing Systems: *The Total Overhead Variance. Two-Variance Analysis. Three-Variance Analysis.* Analysis of Labor Cost Variances: *Materials Yield Component of Labor Quantity Variance. Labor Mix and Substitution Variances.* Materials Mix and Yield Variances: *The Analysis. Assumptions and Interpretation. Other Analyses.*

Classifying Variances for Annual Reporting: *Taking All Variances to Income. Assigning All Variances to the Balance Sheet. Approximating Average Historical Cost. Current Practice.* Seasonal Variances: *Cost Variations. Volume Variations.* Reconciling Standard Costs with the Financial Statements: *Newly Adopted Standards. Prorated Variances. Lifo Inventory Adjustment. Prorating Materials Cost Variances.*

Project Approval: *Approval Criteria. Review of Proposals.* Detailed Scheduling: *Network Diagrams. Float Diagrams. Resource Commitment Tables and Charts. Uncertainty and PERT Time Estimates.* Progress Review: *Project Reporting. Departmental Performance Review.*

Case
Space Constructors, Inc. (B), 774

The Organizational Setting: *Profit Centers. Investment Centers. Why Companies Decentralize. Administered Centers. Service Centers.* Purposes of Divisional Profit Reporting: *Motivational Reinforcement. Operations Evaluation. Activity Evaluation. Managerial Evaluation.* Profit, Return on Investment, and Residual Income: *Income or Profit Contribution. Return on Investment (ROI). Residual Income.* Measurement Problems: *Defining the Investment Base. Allocating Centrally Administered Assets and Expenses. Choosing the Depreciation Method. Adjusting for Changes in Resource Prices.*

Case

Profit Variance Analysis: *Single-Product Firm, Variable Costing. Single-Product Firm, Absorption Costing. Two-Product Firm: Sales Mix Variance. Variances in Selling and Administrative Expenses. Multiproduct Firm: Synthetic Index of Volume. Limitations of the Analysis. Reporting Variances to Shareholders.* Profit Ratio and Trend Analysis.

Criteria for Transfer Pricing: *Divisional Resource Allocation Decisions. Evaluating Managerial Performance. Divisional Activity Evaluation. Fiscal Management.* Bases for Transfer Pricing: *Cost-Based Systems. Market Price. Combination Methods: Programmed Prices.* Transfer Pricing Mechanisms: *Dictated Transfer Prices. Negotiated Transfer Prices.* Transfer Pricing between Profit Centers: *Market-Based Negotiated Prices. Standard Full Cost. Marginal Cost. Variable Cost Plus Retainer. Market in/Cost out. Mathematically Programmed Prices.* Pricing Transfers to Administered Centers.

Cases

part one

The Basic Structure

1

The Role of
Cost Accounting

What Is Cost Accounting?

COST ACCOUNTING deals with the means used by an organization to reach individual cost objectives. A cost objective is a purposeful use of resources, and cost is the amount of resources that have been or must be sacrificed to achieve some objective. Manufacturing a product is an objective, operating an office is an objective, filling an order is an objective.

Putting these pieces together, we can see that cost accounting is the process of measuring or estimating the costs of specific objectives of individual organizations, together with the entire body of concepts, methods, procedures and record-keeping systems necessary to do this. What does it cost to make a product, operate a department, or prepare a payroll?

Cost accounting's answers to questions like these depend on the purpose for which the cost figures are to be used. Cost accounting doesn't exist for its own sake; we have it because it can contribute to managerial accounting, to financial accounting, to tax accounting, and to contract accounting. One set of costs may be relevant to management's choice of a price for a new product; a different set may be relevant to the question of how much to spend to get customers to buy it; still another may be necessary to meet the requirements of tax accounting or of financial accounting.

The purpose of this chapter is to introduce the four branches of accounting that make cost accounting necessary. Our emphasis will be on managerial accounting, the process of measuring, analyzing, estimating, and reporting to management on the costs and benefits of individual activities and segments of the organization. We'll then look more briefly at financial, tax, and contract accounting, and see how responsibility for cost accounting fits into the organization structure.

1

MANAGERIAL ACCOUNTING FOR PLANNING

Much of cost accounting is designed to help management decide how to allocate the organization's resources. Should a new product be introduced? Should the company make its own parts or buy them from others? What prices should it charge for its goods and services?

All of these decisions and many more are what planning is all about. Planning is the process of deciding how to use the resources available to the organization. It takes four forms:

1. Strategic planning.
2. Long-range periodic planning.
3. Project and situation planning.
4. Short-range periodic planning.

Strategic Planning

Strategic planning establishes the basic direction and shape top management wants the organization to take. It is an attempt to answer questions such as, What does our organization have that others don't have? What are its goals? How much risk should it expose itself to? What kinds of business should it be in? (For the nonprofit organization, what role should it play in society?)

These are all questions for top management, and top managers need to weigh very carefully the alternatives before them. Strategic planning doesn't take place on any regular schedule, only when management feels that fundamental changes may have taken place, making it desirable to review the organization's strategy.

Long-Range Periodic Planning

If strategic planning sets the course to be steered, long-range planning establishes in a preliminary way the resources that this course will require and what it is expected to accomplish, year by year. What kinds of facilities will be required and when should they be built? How much cash will be available to finance these facilities?

Long-range planning is a periodic activity, usually carried out once a year. It produces a forecast, a statement of intentions, not a firm commitment. The long-range plan typically extends three, five, or even ten years into the future.

Project and Situation Planning

Project and situation planning consists of decisions to use parts of the organization's resources in specified ways. Examples are decisions to borrow money, build a new factory, price a new product, start a research project, start an advertising campaign, or hire more people. Each of these decisions requires a choice among competing alternatives; each deals with a unique problem or opportunity.

The relationships of this form of planning to the two we have just discussed are indicated by the direction of the two arrows at the left in

EXHIBIT 1–1

Managerial Planning Processes

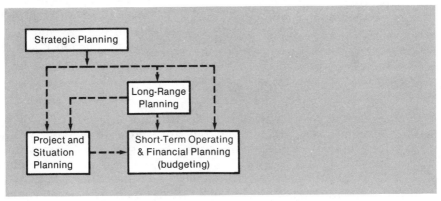

Exhibit 1–1. Strategic plans and long-range plans establish the framework; project and situation decisions translate it into action. Unlike strategic and long-range planning, each project or situation decision is a firm commitment to use some of the organization's resources in a specified way. It leads to actions here and now, not just predictions. This means that individual project and situation decisions affecting more than the current period should be consistent with the decisions implicit in the long-range plans; if not, one or the other should be changed.

Short-Range Periodic Planning

Short-range periodic planning—*budgeting,* for short—completes the planning cycle illustrated in Exhibit 1–1.[1] It is the process by which management decides how the organization's resources will be used during a specific time period, and predicts the results of those decisions. The operating and financial plan, or *budget,* shows what resources the organization has decided to use, where it plans to get them, where and how it plans to use them, and what it expects to accomplish during this specific period. Typically, it is the first year of the long-range plan.

Budgeting takes place periodically, usually once a year. It pulls together all the project and situation decisions that have already been made, makes a preliminary forecast of those to be made and implemented during the coming period, and produces an integrated plan for the period. Many of the decisions embodied in the plan can still be changed as the period goes on and more information is available,

---

[1] The term budgeting is sometimes used to describe a process almost devoid of decision content. The advantages of seeing budget preparation as a decision process are enormous, as we shall explain when we return to this topic in Chapter 5.

but inclusion in the budget is the next thing to a firm commitment.

The approved budget serves two main purposes. First, it acts as a reminder of what has been decided. The manager needs to keep his part of the plan in front of him as he[2] goes along, just as the builder has to consult the architect's drawings from time to time. Second, it serves as a benchmark with which future performance can be compared. We shall have more to say about this in the section on control.

We should emphasize that all of these types of planning are decision processes, although the term decision making is often applied only to project or situation planning. Choosing a marketing program for a new product in March is really no different from deciding in November what the whole company's marketing plan for the next year will look like. The only reason for a separate category is that the budgeting process is too cumbersome, too tied to the calendar. Price decisions and plant expansions are too important to be held up until it is time to prepare the annual operating plan as a whole.

The Role of Managerial Accounting in Planning

Managerial accounting is part of the planning mechanism. It focuses on individual activities and groups of activities because management's resource allocation decisions are keyed to the activities that resources are or might be committed to.

This relationship comes out clearly from the definition of an activity. An activity is an action or set of actions requiring the use of resources in the expectation of achieving desired results. Performing a research project is an activity; manufacturing and marketing a product is an activity; billing customers is an activity. By controlling the activity structure, management is able to control the flows of resources.

This is not always obvious. Some decisions seem to focus on organization units, as in decisions to open new branch offices or to close existing ones. On closer analysis, however, it becomes clear that the decision focus is not the organization unit itself but the activities it encompasses or the means of carrying them out. The branch's activity is the servicing of a given group of customers and prospects. The managerial question is how best to carry out this activity, or whether it is worth carrying out at all. The organization structure affects and is affected by these decisions, but it's the activity that matters.

It is too early to spell out in any detail what form cost accounting data on activities will take. For some decisions, costs must be in the form of totals; for others, estimates of unit costs are necessary. Prices, for example, are generally quoted item by item, and costs for pricing are unit costs. In deciding whether to withdraw a product from the line, however, management must focus on total cost. How total cost should be measured for this purpose will be our concern in Chapter 3.

---

[2] Here and in similar passages the masculine pronoun is used for succinctness and is understood to include both males and females.

MANAGERIAL ACCOUNTING FOR CONTROL

The second role of managerial accounting is to help management control the organization. No matter how carefully a plan is conceived or how faithfully it is carried out, many things can happen to cause it to go astray or make it obsolete. Control consists of management's efforts to prevent undesirable departures from planned actions, to keep track of what is happening, to interpret this information, and to take action in response to it.[3]

Our interest in control focuses on the kinds of control information management might be able to use profitably. These fall into three categories:

1. Yes/no controls.
2. Steering controls.
3. Scorecard controls.[4]

The relationships among these are diagrammed in Exhibit 1–2, but a few words about each are necessary.

EXHIBIT 1–2

Types of Controls

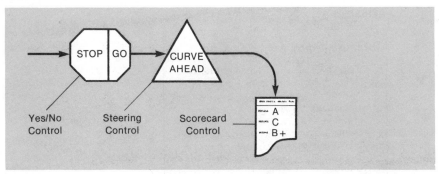

Yes/No Controls

Yes/no controls are rules that must be consulted before certain kinds of actions are taken. These rules list the conditions that must be met if the manager is to proceed. A good example is the "open to buy" allowance for department store buyers. These allowances are

---

[3] Many definitions of control are broader than this. Planning, for example, may be the most important way of influencing or controlling the organization's destiny because it determines how much money is spent and what it is spent for. Our definition reflects the usual use of the term. For a different view, see Robert N. Anthony, *Planning and Control Systems* (Boston: Harvard Graduate School of Business Administration, Division of Research, 1965).

[4] This classification is derived from an interesting book by William H. Newman, *Constructive Control* (Englewood Cliffs, N.J.: Prentice-Hall, Inc., 1975). Newman uses the term "post-action controls" where we use scorecard controls, but the meaning is the same.

reduced when the buyers place orders and are ordinarily increased as merchandise is sold. By looking at the current figures, the buyers know whether they are free to buy the quantities they have in mind.

Yes/no controls are generally defensive controls. They come into play before money is spent rather than afterward. They make it relatively safe for higher management to delegate authority because they reduce the size of the mistakes lower managers can make. Every organization has to have some of them, but bureaucratic paralysis sets in when there are too many. They stifle initiative by reducing the manager's freedom. To do something when the rule says no, managers must ask for permission or take their chances that events will prove them right. Most systems discourage actions like these.

Steering Controls

Steering controls provide signals. These signals are intended either to reassure management that its present course is satisfactory or to indicate the need for some kind of action. The producers of a Broadway play, for example, are likely to receive daily reports from the box office, perhaps containing information like that in Exhibit 1–3.

EXHIBIT 1–3

DAILY BOX OFFICE REPORT	
Date: April 13, 19x1	
	No. of Seats
Attendance:	
Matinee......................	423
Evening......................	494
Advance sales:	
Today's sales................	212
Cumulative bookings..........	4,462
Today's cash receipts..........	$3,591

To use this as a steering control, the producers would need to know whether attendance at this level was enough to cover daily operating costs. They would also need to know what level of advance sales was necessary to keep the show running. At the first sign of trouble, the producers should consider their alternatives: spend more on advertising, sell half-price tickets to students, ask the cast to accept salary cuts, or prepare to close the show as soon as revenues go below the break-even level.

The best steering controls are forecasts of what will happen if management continues to follow its present script, compared with some measure of what management wants to achieve. Few steering controls fit this specification, simply because adequate data are not available. Instead, steering control signals generally spotlight differences between actual results and planned results.

Active responses to steering control signals are of two kinds. A *corrective response* leaves the objective alone but tries to change the methods being used to reach it. An *adaptive response* is an action by management to restate its objectives and develop new plans for achieving them.

Management's decision to make a corrective response assumes three things: the original plan is still all right, the cause of the poor performance is inside the organization, and the manager can do something about it. An adaptive response, on the other hand, presumes that the cause is outside. Either the forecast was wrong or the world has changed. Since the manager doesn't have the power to change outside conditions, the only course of action is to see how best to adapt to the emerging situation. This means a new decision, or *replanning*.

Scorecard Controls

Top management can't control everything directly. It must delegate part of its authority to executives and supervisors at lower levels in

EXHIBIT 1–4

OPERATIONS REPORT		
	Month: April 19x1	
	Actual	*Budget*
Revenues....................	$104,300	$120,000
Expenses....................	92,400	90,000
Income....................	$ 11,900	$ 30,000
Cash on hand................	$ 38,000	$ 55,000

the organization. Each of these is then responsible for using resources effectively and efficiently. (Effectiveness means getting the job done as it was supposed to be done; efficiency means maintaining a satisfactory relationship between costs and benefits.)

Managers are seldom able to remain intimately familiar with the operations they have delegated to their subordinates. Instead, they rely on scorecard controls to keep them informed on progress toward the organization's goals. Scorecard controls are summary reports on the performance of various activities or organization segments and of the managers responsible for them. Our theatrical producers, for example, might get a report containing the information in Exhibit 1–4.

Management uses scorecard reports of this kind for three reasons:

1. To evaluate the effectiveness and efficiency of individual managers and groups in the organization (*managerial evaluation*).

2. To reinforce the managers' *motivation* to work toward the goals behind the agreed-upon plan.

3. To identify activities that seem to be either particularly good or particularly bad uses of the organization's resources so that top management can consider putting additional resources in or taking some out (*activity evaluation*).

The theatrical producers, for example, hope the theater manager's motivation to control costs and expand ticket sales will be reinforced by knowing that one of these reports will be issued each month. They use the report itself to summarize the manager's success in controlling costs and to judge the profitability of the current production. Are the results encouraging enough to take this play on the road? Should pricing or promotional methods be reconsidered? Finally, the theater manager uses the report to judge whether the control efforts made in the past month have been effective. If not, something else should be tried.

Scorecard controls bear very much the same relationships to planning as steering controls. These relationships are diagrammed in Exhibit 1–5. Planning produces a plan. This becomes a set of instructions to be executed. The results of these actions are then compared with the plan in a series of reports. These are interpreted to determine what kind of response is appropriate. A corrective response requires a change in the way the plan is carried out, while an adaptive response requires replanning. Each of these leads back to an earlier phase of the process and the loop is completed.

Both scorecard controls and steering controls use data on what has happened. Both use a kind of information known as "feedback," and both can be referred to as *control by feedback response*. The main differences are that steering controls typically come earlier and more

EXHIBIT 1–5

Planning and Control Loops

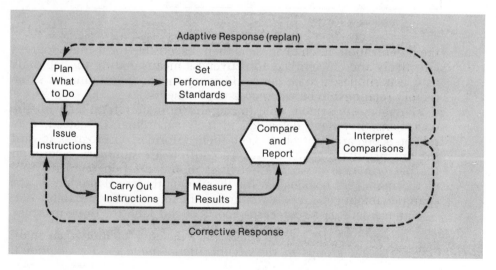

often, and the response, if any, comes sooner. The similarity becomes even more pronounced once we realize that scorecard reports on segments and activities at lower levels serve as signals (steering controls) for top management action.

One final point should be recognized. Control is not achieved by issuing feedback reports. Control is accomplished by management. All the reports in the world won't control anything or anyone unless they trigger some sort of action.

Managerial Accounting for Control Purposes

Managerial accounting makes its contribution to control mainly by measuring and reporting on various aspects of the performance of individual *responsibility centers* and their managers. A responsibility center is an organization segment headed by a single person, answerable to higher authority, and obligated to perform certain tasks.[5]

The authority/responsibility patterns in an organization are usually drawn in the shape of a pyramid, as in Exhibit 1–6. Each segment in

EXHIBIT 1–6

Organization Chart

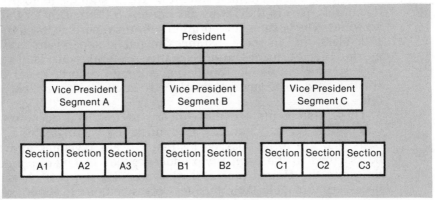

this chart represents an executive, and each of these executives is responsible for the use of the resources in that segment. He or she is also responsible for the use of resources by the executives in the segments farther down in the pyramid. The president is responsible for the whole organization. The vice president of segment A is responsible for that segment, including the activities of the people in sections A1, A2, and A3. The manager of section A1 is responsible only for what goes on in that small area.

---

[5] Responsibility for an organization segment's work may be shared by two or more persons. If the sharing is complete, they will act as a single person on all matters. In the more usual case, they divide the tasks of managing the segment between them. This effectively creates two responsibility centers within the segment.

Control information at the lowest level relates to the activities in individual responsibility centers. Costs for this purpose may be very different from costs for various kinds of planning decisions or for various nonmanagerial uses. To cite just one example, if a manager can't control the unit costs of the services provided by other parts of the organization, the control reports should not reflect variations in those unit costs. For at least some decisions, however, up-to-date unit cost data are essential.

FINANCIAL, TAX, AND CONTRACT ACCOUNTING

Cost accounting serves many masters. One of these is managerial accounting, as we have just seen. Cost accounting is also used to measure the cost of the goods in inventory. This contributes mainly to financial accounting and to tax accounting. Finally, it is the basis for calculating the amounts to be collected from outsiders who agree to pay the costs of specific goods or services. This makes it part of contract accounting.

Financial Accounting

Every organization must submit financial statements to people who do not take part in the day-by-day administration of the organization's activities. The business corporation submits reports to its shareholders, to lenders, and in some instances to public supervisory bodies such as the U.S. Securities and Exchange Commission. The symphony orchestra or charitable foundation submits reports to its board of trustees and to a governmental body such as a state corporations office.

These statements are the concern of financial accounting. Cost accounting serves financial accounting by distinguishing between costs that are to be charged against current revenues and those to be assigned to the company-produced goods in end-of-period inventories. In the United States, it also provides the cost classifications necessary to enable large business organizations to report separately the results of individual company segments ("lines of business"), as required by the accounting profession, the Securities and Exchange Commission, and other government agencies.

Financial accounting is more restrictive than managerial accounting. For managerial accounting, management is free to decide how costs are to be measured; for financial accounting the measurement criteria come from outside. We shall see in Chapter 4, for example, that for some managerial purposes the cost accountant may exclude some manufacturing costs from estimates of the costs of manufactured products. For financial accounting, all manufacturing costs must be included.

Measurement criteria for financial accounting are governed by "generally accepted accounting principles." These are based on centuries of accounting practice and are now largely embedded in formal pronouncements of various professional accounting committees and boards. The current rule-making body in the United States is the Financial Accounting Standards Board, with members chosen from the public accounting profession, industry, the universities, and government.

Tax Accounting

In some countries, inventory figures for financial accounting must be the same ones used for tax purposes; in others, different figures are permitted. When differences are allowed, as in the United States, tax rules and regulations are likely to be more detailed than financial accounting guidelines.

The cost accountants' roles in tax accounting are exactly the same as in financial accounting. They must look to the rules and regulations for guidance. These establish the limits the cost figures must fall between. Because tax accounting is so specialized and is constantly changing, we shall not attempt to deal with it in any way.

Contract Accounting

Cost-reimbursement contracts are fairly common, particularly in commercial dealings between governmental agencies and firms in the private sector. When the two parties to the contract are both outside the government, the contract itself must spell out how cost is to be measured. The less specific the contract, the more likely the two parties will be arguing the definition of cost in court before they are finished. The cost accountants' work in contract accounting is known as *contract costing*.

Government agencies are generally required to use specific sets of rules, worked out in advance to cover all contracts of a certain type. The most completely developed set of rules in the United States is embodied in the Armed Services Procurement Regulations and regulations of the General Services Administration, incorporating the standards promulgated since 1972 by the Cost Accounting Standards Board (CASB). The first 14 standards issued by the CASB are summarized in Appendix B.

ORGANIZING THE ACCOUNTING FUNCTION

The chief accounting officer, who usually has the title of controller, has responsibility for all accounting functions. The controller generally reports to the president or to a financial vice president.

Despite the title, the controller doesn't control anything outside the controller's department. He or she has a staff relationship with executives in other parts of the organization, with authority to give advice and provide help but with no direct power of enforcement. Even so, the controller is often an active and influential member of top management, gaining influence and power gradually by doing the job well and winning the respect of others in the organization.

In small organizations the functions of controllership are likely to be highly centralized. As the organization grows, first clerical employees and then members of the controller's staff are likely to be moved out of the controller's office to other locations within the organization. As the organization continues to grow, these satellite departments grow, too. Their function becomes less and less one of collecting data for processing in the home office. Instead, the outlying staff spends more and more of its time providing managerial accounting services to local management.

The cycle is complete when these people are transferred from the central controller's payroll to report directly to local management. In

EXHIBIT 1–7

Positions of Divisional and Plant Controllers

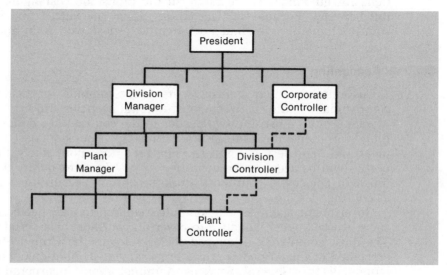

a large manufacturing corporation, for example, each operating division is likely to have its own divisional controller, reporting directly to the division manager. Within the divisions each factory is likely to have a plant controller, reporting to the plant manager.

This decentralization of the controller's organization is desirable in that it identifies the role of the controller's staff as service to management. It creates some problems, however. First, it raises the possibility that each division will go its own way in accounting matters, making it difficult for the central accounting staff to report to top management or outside investors. The usual solution to this is to have the corporate controller maintain a "dotted line" relationship with the divisional and plant controllers, providing control over the technical aspects of their work. (See Exhibit 1–7.)

Second, the divisional and plant controllers are likely to see their road to advancement along the dotted lines—that is, to other positions in controllership rather than to other kinds of managerial positions. This may lead them to sacrifice the interests of local management when conflicts arise between service to local management and the demands of the corporate controller.[6]

COST ACCOUNTING IN PERSPECTIVE

We sometimes get too close to our own systems to see their faults and their limitations. With this in mind, let us end this introductory chapter with four simple observations:

1. *The managerial accountant is not management's only source of data for planning and control.* Accounting has always focused on quantities that can be expressed in monetary terms, in dollars. Management needs other kinds of information, expressed in units of time, weight, volume, or presence. It may even call for qualitative statements of conditions or results, such as "good" or "likely to succeed." As a result, most organizations have a lot of physical data, plus a good deal of information on what is happening outside the organization. This could be made part of managerial accounting, but in most cases it is not.

2. *Accounting procedures often suffer from a confusion of purposes.* Figures that are necessary for contract costing or for financial accounting may be misleading if management tries to use them for planning or control. To cite just one example, sales are usually recorded in the accounts when goods are shipped or services are performed for clients or customers. This is done for financial accounting and for tax accounting. To the sales force, however, the sale takes place when the customer places an order. The accountant's easiest course of action is to use the figures on shipments for all purposes. This may be very misleading to management, at least in some periods.

3. *Accounting systems often measure resources at prices that have no relevance to current managerial decisions.* The data recorded in the accounts should be regarded solely as a point of departure, as a set of indicators rather than as gospel truth.

4. *All data-gathering and classification schemes are subject to the law of diminishing productivity.* This statement, in other words, means that beyond some point successive increments of data have progressively smaller managerial payoffs. Ideally, the amount of data provided should be determined from the application of a cost-benefit model, comparing the value of information with its cost. Although formal efforts to apply such models are scarce, they are always implicit in the system. Every system represents a set of decisions as to how much and what kinds of information will be productive.

---

[6] This danger was exposed and explored in a book as valid today as when it was written. Herbert A. Simon, George Kozmetsky, Harold Guetzkow, and Gordon Tyndall, *Centralization vs. Decentralization in Organizing the Controller's Department* (New York: Controllership Foundation, 1954).

SUMMARY AND REVIEW

Cost accounting serves managerial accounting, financial accounting, tax accounting, and contract costing. The emphasis in this book will be on its contributions to managerial accounting. The managerial aspects of cost accounting are inseparable from managerial accounting and, therefore, must be discussed in this broader context.

Planning is the process of deciding how to use the organization's resources. To serve management's planning needs, the managerial accountant focuses on the individual activities the organization is engaged in. Control, on the other hand, consists of observing, interpreting, and reporting what is going on and taking action in response to this information. It consists of yes/no controls, steering controls, and scorecard controls. It is exercised through the organization's responsibility structure. Managerial accounting contributes to this process by providing steering control and scorecard information to the responsible managers.

Managerial accounting and cost accounting are among the responsibilities of the chief accounting officer or controller. In large organizations each major subdivision is likely to have its own controller. This emphasizes the importance of the controller's role as adviser and servant of management. We shall reinforce this image as we go along.

With these preliminaries behind us, we can get down to business. The next eight chapters describe the basic structure of cost accounting, with major emphasis on its managerial accounting aspects. In Chapters 2 to 4 we shall be looking at four different ways of classifying operating costs: (1) by their cost objectives, the activities and organization segments that make costs necessary; (2) by their place in published financial statements; (3) by their relationships to changes in operating volume; and (4) by their relevance to managerial decisions. Chapters 5 to 9 deal mainly with the role of accounting in financial planning and control systems.

Building on this foundation, the chapters in Part Two go more deeply into methods and uses of cost measurement; Part Three explores further aspects of corporate financial control systems.

KEY TERMS

The most important terms introduced and defined in this chapter are the following:

Activity	Planning
Control	Project and situation planning
Controller	Responsibility
Cost	Responsibility center
Cost objective	Scorecard controls
Decision making	Steering controls
Managerial accounting	Strategic planning
Periodic planning	Yes/no controls

EXERCISES AND PROBLEMS

1. Different purposes of cost accounting. A company manufactures and sells 100,000 shovels a year. Some shovels are short and flat, others are rounded and have long handles. The company has 14 different kinds of shovels in all, and its annual operating costs are:

Manufacturing (including such items as the cost of steel and lumber, depreciation on equipment, and the plant manager's salary).................	$150,000
Selling (including sales commissions and showroom rentals)...	50,000
Administration (including the costs of an outside bookkeeping service and the president's salary)...	30,000
Total.......................................	$230,000

Use this information to illustrate the statement in the chapter that cost accounting must develop different sets of cost figures for different purposes. For example, which costs in the three categories in the table above might management find useful in deciding whether one shovel model should be dropped from the line, or in setting a desired price on another model, or in evaluating the plant manager's success in controlling costs, or in measuring inventories of shovels for public financial reporting? What problems do you think you would encounter in developing these figures? *Numerical answers are not expected.*

2. Planning. You are considering enrolling next term in a course in managerial economics. By itself, this is a project planning decision. Prepare a short report to relate this to your strategic educational plan, your long-range educational plan, and your short-range educational plan.

3. Steering and scorecard controls. The manager of a chain of motion-picture theaters relies on written reports to keep informed about the operations of individual theaters. Films are booked for a week at a time, with an unlimited renewal option. Runs of six to eight weeks are not uncommon, but many films are replaced at the end of one week. The film shown at one theater may also be shown at one or more others in the chain, but a separate booking decision is made at each theater each week.

Each theater has a manager, responsible for maintaining and operating the theater. Employees are hired by the local manager, but salaries must be approved by the chain manager. The chain manager selects the films to be shown, makes all the booking decisions, and hires the theater managers.

a. What reports is the chain manager likely to find useful? Indicate how each of these reports would be used and whether you regard it as a steering control or as a scorecard control.

b. What would you report to the individual theater managers, and how frequently would you report it? Indicate how the manager would use this information and whether it would be steering control or scorecard control information.

c. To what extent should the theater managers be held responsible for income from sale of refreshments? How would you evaluate their performance?

4. Steering and scorecard controls. You own a two-year-old automobile. You have been satisfied with its performance and it is still in good condition. There is no bus service or other form of public transportation where you live. You need to use an automobile to get to work; a car pool is impossible because none of your neighbors works where you do.

You ordinarily have the car serviced and repaired at a garage near your office, delivering it in the morning on your way to work and picking it up on your way home. Occasionally a neighbor can deliver you to a bus stop if your car is out of service, but he has to go several miles out of his way to do this, and you ask his help as seldom as you can.

A friend has offered, without charge, to prepare control reports you think would be useful to you as owner of the car, and to keep any records necessary to provide data for these reports.

a.   Prepare a short statement indicating the purpose(s) you would like the reports to serve.
b.   What reports would you like to receive, what would they contain, and how often would you like to receive them?
c.   Identify each report as either a steering control or a scorecard control. Indicate how you would use it and how your friend would get the data necessary to prepare it.

CASE 1–1. DEREK STEELE, GROCER
(Planning and Control System)*

"Well, I seem to manage, somehow," Derek Steele said, "But I'll have to think about it a bit before I can tell you just how I do it."

Mr. Steele was the proprietor of a small grocery store in Panbridge, England. He sold several hundred different items of packaged foods, bread, wines, and household supplies, as well as a line of fresh dairy produce— milk, cheese, butter, etc. Mr. Steele's son-in-law, a recent graduate in management studies, had asked him how he planned and controlled the inventories of the items that he offered for sale in his store.

Mr. Steele decided to make a few notes about the process. Bread and dairy produce, he noted, were delivered daily. Except for unusual items ordered for specific customers, he never placed an order for these items. Instead, he told the delivery man each day what he thought he would need until the next day's delivery. Any unsold bread could be returned the next day to the delivery man, but at a reduced price. Milk could be kept in the store for two days, and Mr. Steele was always careful to sell any milk left over from the previous day before placing the current day's delivery in the display case. Butter, cheese, and similar items could be kept a good deal longer, and Mr. Steele ordinarily ordered several days' requirements at a time.

Most other items were ordered either by telephone or from wholesalers' or manufacturers' representatives who called at the store. Three or four of these representatives would stop at Mr. Steele's store in a typical day. For some items ordered in this way, delivery was made the following day; for others, the delay was longer, sometimes as long as two weeks.

Mr. Steele knew that he could obtain lower purchase prices on some items if he would buy larger quantities in each order. To do this, however, he would have to order much farther ahead of the desired delivery date, and he would also have to prepare additional storage space behind his

* Copyright 1968 by l'Institut pour l'Etude des Méthodes de Direction de l'Entreprise (IMEDE), Lausanne, Switzerland. Reproduced by permission.

store. When his son-in-law asked him how much he could save by making purchases in larger quantities, Mr. Steele had to reply that he didn't know, but he was happy doing business as he was.

Most of Mr. Steele's customers bought only a few items at a time, things that they had forgotten during their last visit to the chain store or things that would not justify a trip to the chain store on the high street. Mr. Steele's prices were a little higher than chain store prices, but he did not feel that he would get any more business of this sort if he reduced his prices to the chain store level.

"I don't know how you'd describe my system," he said, "but I watch my shelves fairly closely. When I see that I'm running low on an item, I order it. If I buy something and it doesn't sell well, I notice that too, and the next time the salesman asks me to order it I tell him no. If he comes in with something new, I try to decide whether my customers will like it and how much shelf space it will take. Some things come in several sizes and colors, and I might have to push several items aside to make room for one new one. That new line of toilet soap, for example, comes in three sizes and each size comes in three colors. I had to drop one brand of laundry detergent to make room for all that variety, but my customers like the soap and I think I made the right choice.

"Actually, my biggest problem comes from the daily deliveries. If I order too little, my stock is exhausted before the end of the afternoon. Over-ordering is not as serious a mistake, because I can adjust the next day's order on everything but bread.

"Most of this I do myself. My clerk is a pleasant young fellow, but he's not very bright. He can follow instructions, but I have to make it quite clear what he is expected to do."

a. Describe the planning portion of the process used by Mr. Steele to plan and control his inventories. What kinds of data might he find useful at this point? Where might he expect to find these data?

b. Describe the feedback portion of the process. What kinds of data would be useful and where would they come from?

c. To what extent is Mr. Steele's planning and control system a decision-making process? How much of the work could Mr. Steele safely delegate to his clerk?

2

The Costing Structure
and Job Order Costing

THE COST ACCOUNTANT'S first job is to design a system to measure the costs of operating each part of the organization and of carrying out its activities. This chapter outlines a system of this sort for a relatively simple manufacturing firm. We shall discuss three aspects of the system:

1. Classifying operating costs as they occur, based on their traceability to specific activities or responsibilities.
2. Measuring the costs of individual activities by means of job order costing.
3. Integrating the job order costing records into the ledger account structure.

Before turning to the first of these, we wish to emphasize that although our illustration will be a manufacturing firm, everything in the first two sections and even some of the third section is directly applicable to nonmanufacturing organizations. Bank managers, hospital administrators, and even museum managers need cost information just as much as factory managers. Our only reason for using a manufacturing example is that the cost accounting system is more likely to be integrated with the general ledger in manufacturing than in service businesses, and we wish to show how this integration takes place.

THREE-DIMENSIONAL COSTING

Decision makers are interested in the effects of their decisions on the results that matter to their organizations. Decisions can't affect the past. Decision costs, in other words, are future costs. To satisfy the decision maker, therefore, the cost accountant must either provide estimates of future costs or supply data that others can use for this purpose.

It should not come as a surprise, however, to find that cost accountants spend a lot of their time preparing an analytical record of past transactions. This record is the richest source of data decision makers are likely to find anywhere, and they'd be hard put to estimate costs without it. They can sift it, dissect it, splice it, and extend it, but they can't ignore it if it has been put together well in the first place.

A record of the past is also necessary if the cost accountant is to meet management's needs for control information. Managers can't control something if they don't know whether things have been going well in the immediate past. And historical data are necessary for financial accounting, tax accounting and contract costing, too.

A good place to begin, therefore, is with the systems cost accountants use to classify operating costs as they occur. There are three ways to classify an operating cost:

1. By organization segment.
2. By object of expenditure.
3. By activity.

The first and third of these describe where the costs were used and why. The second shows what kinds of resources were used.

Classification by Organization Segment

The first dimension of the cost accounting structure parallels the organization chart. Exhibit 2–1 shows the main elements of the organization structure of the Apex Company, a small manufacturer of electrical components. Each block in this diagram represents a re-

EXHIBIT 2–1

APEX COMPANY

Partial Organization Chart and Organizational Account Codes

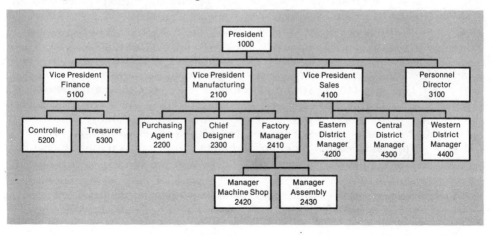

sponsibility center. The four-digit number shown beneath the title in each of the blocks is the organizational account number.

Three aspects of the organization classification need discussion:

1. Costs are matched with responsibility centers by applying the *traceability* criterion.
2. Some responsibility centers are subdivided into *cost centers*.
3. Some traceable costs are not *controllable* by the responsibility center managers.

The traceability criterion. Whenever any set of figures is divided into groups, the people doing the classifying have to have criteria to help them decide in which group any particular figure belongs. In making their initial assignments of costs to responsibility centers, the accountants use the traceability criterion—that is, they assign each cost to the lowest responsibility center it is traceable to.

A cost is traceable to a center if it is incurred entirely to support one or more of the activities of that center or the activities of two or more of the centers below it in the organization chart. The salary of the machine shop manager, for example, is traceable all the way down to the machine shop department, while the factory manager's salary is traceable only to his office, one level higher up.[1] In accounting language, the factory manager's salary is a *direct cost* of the factory, but an *indirect cost* of the first-level responsibility centers. Any cost that is traceable to a cost objective is a direct cost of that cost objective.

Subdividing the responsibility center. The organization structure sometimes doesn't subdivide costs finely enough to satisfy management's needs for data. A factory department, for example, may have both mechanized and manual operations. The costs of the mechanized operations are likely to be so different from those of the manual operations that management will expect the accountant to be able to separate them out.

One answer to this problem is to subdivide some responsibility centers into subunits known as *cost centers*. A cost center is either a whole responsibility center or part of one for which the accountant wishes to collect separate cost data. The fourth digit in Apex's organizational account code is used to identify cost centers within departments. To avoid clutter, however, Exhibit 2–1 goes down to the departmental level in only one section—the factory—and the more detailed breakdown into cost centers is omitted entirely.

The only reason for subdividing a responsibility center is to separate costs that are likely to behave differently. As a result, the costs of a cost center relate to a more limited and homogeneous set of activities than those of the responsibility center as a whole.

Subclassification by controllability. Costs are assigned to cost centers on the basis of traceability. This is not the same as *controllability*.

---

[1] In practice, the salaries of executives and department heads are recorded separately to keep the figures confidential. Wherever they are recorded, however, they are usually coded by responsibility center.

EXHIBIT 2–2

Classification of Responsibility Center Costs by Cost Center and Responsibility

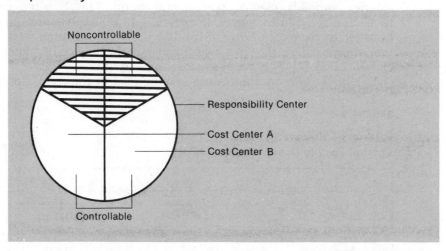

As Exhibit 2–2 shows, some of the costs traceable to a cost center are likely to be controllable by the responsibility center manager, while others are not. For example, property taxes on a factory building can be traced to the factory but the factory manager is not responsible for these taxes. Local management may be able to influence the amount of the taxes by presenting an effective case for a lower tax assessment to the local board of assessors, but responsibility lies with the executives who have the authority to decide whether to keep the plant or sell it to someone else. We shall defer any further discussion of controllability to Chapter 6.

Classification by Object of Expenditure

Management's decisions affect many things, such as the volume and location of production. Many of these decisions affect cost. Knowing the relationships between costs and the factors that determine costs therefore should help management make decisions. It should also be helpful in cost control. The manager can control cost only by acting on the determinants of cost.

This suggests that accounting data should be collected in ways that make it easier to identify the relationships between costs and their determinants. In other words, the costs in any one class should be *homogeneous*—they should all show the same pattern of response to the various determinants of cost. For example, if the costs of lubricating oil vary with the number of machine-hours and the costs of cleaning supplies vary with the number of labor hours, putting them in the same account would be likely to obscure the underlying relationships.

Dividing departments into cost centers is one way of getting more homogeneous data, as we saw just a moment ago. Another way is to classify a cost center's costs into their "natural elements," such as salaries, supplies, electric power, and so on. This is often referred to as classification by *object of expenditure*. (Supplies are the *object* obtained by the *expenditure* of funds.) If the organizational classification shows *where* the cost was incurred, the object of expenditure classification shows *what* resources were used.

Exhibit 2–3 shows the coding system used in the Apex Company's

EXHIBIT 2–3

APEX COMPANY

Chart of Factory Cost Accounts

Element	Department	2410 Factory Manager	2420 Machine Shop	2430 Assembly
01	Direct materials	2410.01	2420.01	2430.01
02	Direct labor	2410.02	2420.02	2430.02
11	Supervision	2410.11	2420.11	2430.11
12	Labor—travel time	2410.12	2420.12	2430.12
13	Labor—idle time	2410.13	2420.13	2430.13
14	Labor—clerical	2410.14	2420.14	2430.14
15	Labor—other	2410.15	2420.15	2430.15
21	Overtime premium	2410.21	2420.21	2430.21
22	Vacation and holiday pay	2410.22	2420.22	2430.22
23	Payroll taxes	2410.23	2420.23	2430.23
24	Pensions	2410.24	2420.24	2430.24
31	Travel allowances	2410.31	2420.31	2430.31
51	Tools	2410.51	2420.51	2430.51
52	Supplies	2410.52	2420.52	2430.52
53	Equipment rental	2410.53	2420.53	2430.53
54	Depreciation	2410.54	2420.54	2430.54
61	Insurance	2410.61	2420.61	2430.61
71	Other	2410.71	2420.71	2430.71

factory. The object-of-expenditure account titles and code numbers are shown at the left; the full two-dimensional account codes are shown in the three columns at the right. When a cost is incurred, it must be classified both by cost center and by object of expenditure. If John Jones works a full eight hours repairing equipment in the machine shop at an hourly rate of $8, the account 2420.15 (Machine Shop Labor—Other) will be charged with $64.

Some of these codes are unlikely to be used—assembly department personnel are unlikely to have travel allowances, for example. In concept, however, the cost structure is fully two-dimensional. We shall return later in this chapter to explain those account titles that may not be fully self-explanatory.

Limits to System Size

Increasing the number of cost centers or object-of-expenditure classifications is not an unmixed blessing. It does make each account clearer, but it increases both the cost of the accounting system and the probability that costs will be misclassified. With only one cost account, the bookkeepers can't misclassify a cost. With 2 accounts to choose between, they'll make some mistakes; with 40 they'll make a lot more.

It must be remembered that adding a new classification doesn't add accounts—it multiplies them. For example, suppose Apex decides to break the factory manager's office into two cost centers. This will add only one more column to Exhibit 2–3, but that column will contain 18 object-of-expenditure accounts of its own. In other words, the number of cells in the account structure will go from $3 \times 18 = 54$ to $4 \times 18 = 72$. With ten cost centers in this factory instead of four, the number of accounts will go up to 180. The ledger will take up more space, clerical operations will be more complicated, and more costs will be recorded in the wrong place.

As a result, the cost accountants must compromise. They must trade flexibility of the data against system cost and inaccuracy. Beyond some point the added flexibility to be obtained by expanding the classification scheme won't be worth its cost. When this point is reached, the cost accountant must combine costs that are similar but not quite identical. This means predicting which classifications will prove more useful in the future and most difficult to develop later on if the data are not recorded separately now.

Classification by Activity

The third dimension of the structure is the activity classification. Some of the business organization's activities are designed to induce customers to buy merchandise or place orders. These are known as order-getting activities. Others are undertaken to provide services to outside customers or to manufacture finished products. These are sometimes referred to as *final cost objectives;* we shall call them *end-product activities*. Finally, we have service and support activities, undertaken to support activities in the other two classes.

Accounting systems sometimes do provide for the identification of the costs of individual order-getting, service and support activities. Our concern in this chapter, however, is with the end-product activities. Most of these consist of the production of goods or services for outside clients or customers—automobiles, restaurant meals, and hospital patient care are useful examples. Other end-product activities include research projects for the organization's own future benefit, and the construction of productive facilities for the organization's own use.

The classification of costs by end-product activity is seldom as neat as the classifications by cost center and by object of expenditure. The reason is that many activities have very short lives—filling one customer's order may take only a few hours or a few days. The number of separate end-product activities in a year can be enormous.

This problem of numbers makes the activity dimension difficult to diagram in a textbook, but it is not the main problem in activity costing. The main problem is that the simple traceability test we have been using so far isn't up to the task of classifying costs by activity. Most cost centers do more than one thing. A maintenance shop does many repair jobs, an advertising department works on many different advertising campaigns, and so on.

Some of a cost center's costs can be traced to specific end-product activities, if the company is willing to spend the money to get this done. Others can't be traced, no matter what anyone does. How much of the monthly rental on a bakery store can be traced to the cakes and how much to the pies? The answer is, none to either. In the next section we shall study one method accountants use to deal with this problem.

COSTING INDIVIDUAL ACTIVITIES: JOB ORDER COSTING

The method used to assign costs to end-product activities depends in the first place on how the organization gets its work done. The simplest systems are *process costing* systems, used when a cost center's facilities turn out a single kind of product or service for long periods of time (cement, flour, electricity, and so on). We shall study process costing in Chapter 10.

The alternative to process costing is *job order costing,* or job costing. We shall use the next few pages to show how the Apex Company uses job order costing to measure the costs of the products it manufactures in its factory.

The Nature of Job Order Costing

In job order costing, the unit of production is the *job.* A job is a project, contract, or batch of products that is clearly distinguishable from other projects, contracts, or batches while processing is taking place.

Factories which work on many different jobs at the same time are known as job shops. Jobs are the end-product activities of job shops. The Apex Company's factory is a job shop. Production begins when someone in authority issues a *production order* or *job order,* calling for the manufacture of a specified quantity of one of the company's products or component parts. The production order ordinarily contains detailed instructions, specifying the materials required, the operations to be performed, and the production centers to be used. (A *production center* in a job shop is a cost center which works directly on individual job orders.)

Job order costing is a set of procedures used to assign operating costs to individual jobs in a job shop. In factory job order costing, the cost of a job is defined as the sum of the costs that are readily trace-able to that job (its *direct costs*) plus a share of the factory's operat-ing costs that are not readily traceable to individual jobs (the *indirect costs* of the job, otherwise known as *factory overhead costs*). Typical examples of factory overhead costs are depreciation on equipment, the salaries of factory executives, and the costs of lighting the factory building. Each of these is a direct cost of some cost center, but none is a direct cost of a specific job in a job shop.

Our task in this section is to see how the accountant:

1. Measures the direct materials costs of individual job orders and distinguishes them from the costs of indirect materials.
2. Measures the direct labor costs of individual job orders and dis-tinguishes them from the labor components of factory overhead costs.
3. Assigns factory overhead costs to individual job orders.

Materials Costs

One way to begin work on a job is to get some of the *direct mate-rials* that will be needed for that job. Direct materials are all raw materials and component parts that can be traced readily to individual job orders. When direct materials are *issued*—that is, transferred from a storeroom for use in the factory—the manager receiving them ordinarily must initial a form known as a *materials requisition*. Exhi-bition 2–4, for example, is a requisition for direct materials. It shows the number and description of the item, the quantity issued, the cost center it is to be used in, and the job number. Unit price and total cost figures are entered later, in the office.

EXHIBIT 2–4

Materials Requisition

APEX COMPANY
MATERIALS REQUISITION

17426
Date: 5/3/ –

Item	Quantity	Price	Total
Shell No. 14	2,100		

Cost Center: 2421
Job No.:   1234
Acct. No.: _____   Rec'd by: *F. Smith*

EXHIBIT 2–5

Job Cost Sheet

Description: Canister No. 278	Job Order No.: 1234
Date Ordered: 5/1/—	Date Completed: 5/12/—
Quantity Ordered: 2,000	Quantity Completed: 2,000

	Materials Cost				Cost Summary:		
Date	Item	Quantity	Price	Amount	Materials......... $3,538		
5/3	Shell No. 14	2,100	$1.32	$2,772	Labor............. 194		
5/4	Shell No. 14	(50)	1.32	(66)	Overhead......... 180		
5/5	Handle No. 142	2,000	0.41	820	Total.............. $3,912		
5/10	Paint	2	6.00	12			
	Total			$3,538	Unit cost.......... $1.956		

		Labor Cost			Overhead Cost		
Date	Cost Center	Hours	Rate	Amount	Hours *	Overhead Rate	Amount
5/4	2421	6	$8	$ 48	9 MH	$6	$ 54
5/6	2422	10	7	70	12 MH	6	72
5/10	2431	14	4	56	14 DLH	3	42
5/11	2431	4	5	20	4 DLH	3	12
	Total			$194			$180

* MH = machine-hours; DLH = direct labor hours.

The costs of individual jobs are accumulated in job cost sheets as shown in Exhibit 2–5. The cost of the materials covered by the requisition in Exhibit 2–4 has been entered on the first line of the materials cost section of this job cost sheet. The third and fourth entries in this section also reflect issues of direct materials.

The second item is a little different, however. The figures are in parentheses, showing that a small portion of the materials originally issued but not needed on the job were returned to the storeroom. Whenever this happens, the storeroom clerk records the quantity returned on a returned materials card, identical in format to a materials requisition. From this the information is transferred both to the storeroom inventory record cards and to the job cost sheet.

Indirect materials costs.   The Apex factory also uses many materials that it can't trace readily to any one job. These are called indirect materials, and they are part of factory overhead costs. They fall into two categories:

1. Costs of materials that are used on individual job orders in such small amounts that tracing them to job orders would be very expensive—e.g., the glue and upholstery nails used in making furniture.

2. Costs of materials used to support more than one job—e.g., floor cleaning compounds and lubricating oil.

Costs of items in the first group *could* be traced to individual jobs if management wanted to pay to have this done; costs in the second group *cannot* be traced to individual jobs. The machines need to be oiled once in a while and the accountant has no way of saying how much oil is used on one job and how much on another.

Issues of indirect materials are also recorded on materials requisitions. A requisition for indirect materials is identical to one for direct materials except that it shows an object-of-expenditure overhead cost account number in the lower left-hand corner instead of a job order number. We'll see in a moment how the costs of indirect materials enter the job costing system.

Labor Costs

Labor costs in factory production cost centers are of three kinds:

1. *Direct labor.* The time spent on individual jobs, multiplied by the workers' regular wage rates.
2. *Indirect labor.* All other labor time, multiplied by the workers' regular wage rates.
3. *Wage premiums.* Amounts paid or payable to employees in excess of their regular wage rates.

To see how labor costs are classified into these three categories and how the direct labor costs get to the job cost sheets, we need to study three questions:

1. How does the cost accountant get information on the workers' use of their time?
2. How should wage premiums, particularly overtime premiums, be handled?
3. How should the costs of payroll taxes and other fringe benefits be treated?

Labor time records. The most important means of classifying labor costs is the record of how the workers have spent their time. This information is provided by labor time tickets like the one in Exhibit 2–6. This identifies the worker, the cost center, the job, the time the worker started working on this job, and the completion time. For indirect labor the object-of-expenditure overhead account number is filled in instead of the job number. The hours shown on the time tickets are then multiplied by the appropriate hourly rates to derive the amounts to be charged to individual jobs or overhead accounts.

Returning to Exhibit 2–5, for example, we find that six hours of direct labor time were charged against job 1234 on May 4. This may mean that T. Jones returned to this job after lunch and spent an extra four and one-half hours to finish the work, or that someone else also put in some time on this job that day. In all, 34 hours of

EXHIBIT 2–6

Labor Time Ticket

```
┌──────────────────────────────────────────────────┐
│              APEX COMPANY                          │
│              TIME TICKET              # 22663      │
│                                                    │
├──────────────────────────────────────────────────┤
│  Name  T. Jones                  Date 5/4/—        │
│  Employee No.  204-46-4765                         │
│  Pay grade    6                                    │
│  Cost center   2421         Start    10:10         │
│  Job No.       1234         Finish   11:40         │
│  Acct. No.                  Elapsed   90 min.      │
└──────────────────────────────────────────────────┘
```

direct labor were entered in the labor cost section of the job cost sheet, at wage rates ranging from $4 to $8.

Overtime premiums. Employees in certain categories who work nights, weekends and holidays, or more than a specified number of hours a week are paid wage premiums in addition to their regular wages. Overtime premium, for example, is the amount added to the basic hourly wage rate for hours worked in excess of some specified number each day or each week. If the basic or straight-time wage rate is $6 an hour and the overtime rate is $9, the overtime premium is $3 for each overtime hour. Overtime hours are charged to jobs or to indirect labor in just the same way as regular time hours, and at straight-time rates. The premium is recorded separately.

Overtime premiums are assignable to individual jobs only if they were caused by work on *specific* jobs. This is true only if (1) the employees work full-time on a specific job, both on regular time and on overtime, and (2) employees can't be transferred freely to or from other duties. In all other situations overtime premiums are correctly regarded as overhead.

Many people don't agree that traceability should be defined this narrowly. Overtime, for example, is often added to meet a specific customer's rush order. Why shouldn't the overtime premiums be charged to this order? The answer is that overtime results from a *total* demand on the production facilities in excess of regular-time capacity. *All* production shares equally in the responsibility for the overtime. Whenever workers can be transferred from job to job, overtime premiums are just as much the result of sticking to the original production schedule on the first jobs scheduled as they are to speeding up the rush order.

This is not to say that accountants should never assign overtime premiums to rush orders. For example, the customer may agree to pay a premium for any overtime hours worked. These assignments don't mean much, however. Scheduling the rush order for the morning hours, pushing other work into the overtime hours at the end of the day, makes the rush order no less responsible for the overtime premiums than if all of the work were done at night.

Fringe benefits. The employees' wage rates always understate the cost of their services. The reason is the cost of fringe benefits, including paid vacations, paid holidays, company-sponsored recreation and education programs, medical insurance, and unemployment benefits (see Exhibit 2–7).

The costs of fringe benefits are often classified as overhead costs because this is the easiest way to handle them. In concept, however, the costs of these benefits are part of the hourly labor cost. If the labor time is traceable to a job, then the fringe benefits attributable

EXHIBIT 2–7

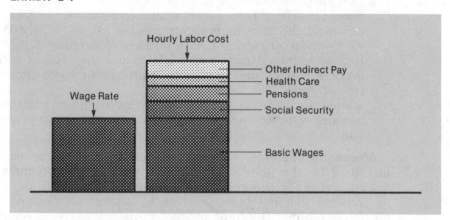

to that time should be included in the rate used to record direct labor on the job cost sheet. This kind of comprehensive labor rate is referred to as a *charging rate*.

Overhead Costing Rates

Up to now, job order costing has been straightforward. The traceability criterion has worked quite well. It has enabled us to identify the *prime costs*—that is, direct materials and direct labor—and enter these on the job cost sheets. A problem has been lurking in the background, however. What do we do with the overhead costs—indirect materials, indirect labor, overtime premiums, and others—we have been pushing aside? These costs are necessary to the production of the various job orders, and for the moment at least we shall assume this means they are part of the cost of these jobs.

The only way to get overhead costs into job cost is to use some kind of formula. The usual formula includes two elements—an overhead rate and a measure of the size of the job:

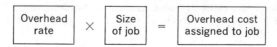

The overhead rate.[2]   An overhead rate is an average amount of overhead for a unit of operating volume, calculated by dividing overhead costs by some measure of volume. For example, the Apex Company might measure volume by the number of direct labor hours. If overhead cost is $210,000 a month and volume is 20,000 direct labor hours, then the overhead rate is:

$$\$210,000/20,000 = \$10.50 \text{ per direct labor hour}$$

If this rate is used, then a job using 100 direct labor hours will be assigned $100 \times \$10.50 = \$1,050$ in factory overhead costs.

Overhead rates really are this simple, but several issues need to be noted before we move on:

1.   How should operating volume be measured?
2.   Should overhead rates reflect actual cost experience each month or should the rates be *predetermined*—that is, calculated in advance and kept constant for a number of months?
3.   If predetermined rates are used, should they reflect estimated average cost in the immediate future or in some "normal" or typical period?
4.   Should the company use a single factorywide overhead rate or a number of rates, one for each cost center or group of cost centers?

Measuring operating volume.   Volume in a job shop cannot be measured by the number of units of product manufactured. The reason is that the overhead rate is supposed to indicate the amount of overhead that has been provided to support an average unit of operating volume. Different product units are likely to require different amounts of support. A product requiring ten minutes of machine time needs a lot less support than one that stays on the same machine for five hours. The volume figures that overhead rates are based on should reflect these differences.

The result is that overhead rates are almost always based on some measure of production input, such as direct labor hours, direct labor cost, machine-hours, or pounds of direct materials processed. Other things being equal, the choice should fall on the measure that most closely corresponds to the factors requiring overhead support. If most of the overhead cost consists of equipment depreciation and maintenance, then a machine-hour rate probably best meets this test. Only if the preferred measure would be relatively expensive to collect should an inferior measure be used. In practice, overhead rates are often based on direct labor hours or direct labor cost simply because these figures are readily available.

Predetermined overhead rates.   Overhead rates can be calculated each month, after all the overhead costs have been counted and operating volume has been measured. This is often inconvenient,

---

[2] Overhead rates are also known as *burden rates*. Because this latter term seems to imply that overhead costs are unproductive, it is gradually going out of fashion.

however—the accountant can't assign overhead costs to jobs as the work is done, but must wait until all the data have been collected.

After-the-fact overhead rates also produce inconsistent cost figures. Average overhead costs are likely to fluctuate from month to month and the amount of overhead charged to a particular job will depend on which month the work is done. The salary of the manager of a soft drink bottling plant, for example, is likely to be just as high in the winter, when volume is low, as in the peak bottling season. Other things being equal, average cost will be higher when volume is low and lower when volume is high (see Exhibit 2–8).

One way to avoid these problems is to use a predetermined overhead rate, the *estimated* average overhead cost, and stick to it for several months, usually a year. When this is done, entries to the job

EXHIBIT 2–8

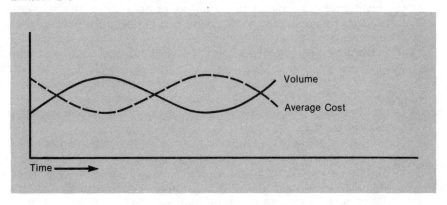

cost sheets can be made just as soon as the work is finished. Furthermore, job cost will not be affected by fluctuations in average overhead costs arising from causes entirely unrelated to the job order itself.

Rates based on normal volume. A predetermined overhead rate can reflect the conditions expected in the coming year, or it can be the estimated average overhead cost in a "normal" or typical period:

$$\text{Overhead rate} = \frac{\text{Estimated overhead costs in a normal month}}{\text{Total volume in a normal month}}$$

Our vote is for overhead rates based on normal cost experience, rather than expected cost experience in a particular year. As we said a moment ago, the overhead rate is supposed to indicate the average amount of overhead cost necessary to support a unit of operating volume. This includes the cost of a normal amount of idleness. This is because, in designing its plants, management knows that the facilities will be partly idle some of the time because market conditions don't remain constant. Total designed capacity therefore is usually greater than the average expected rate of operation. This fact is built into the definition of *normal volume,* defined as the designed capacity of the facilities less an allowance for the average amount of

EXHIBIT 2–9

APEX COMPANY

Departmental Overhead Rates

		Machine Shop	Assembly
1.	Normal volume.....................	10,000 machine-hours	4,000 direct labor hours
2.	Estimated overhead cost at normal volume...........	$60,000	$12,000
3.	Overhead rate [(2)/(1)]..............	$6/machine-hour	$3/direct labor hour

idleness management expected when it set up the facilities in the first place. Fluctuations in the amount of idle time affect average cost, but these changes in average cost don't reflect changes in the amount of necessary support costs.

Cost center overhead rates. Overhead costs are more important in some production centers than in others. Recognizing this, cost accountants often use a separate rate for each production center or for each of several groups of production centers. The purpose is to get a more accurate measure of the amount of costs attributable to individual jobs.

Although each of Apex's two production departments has more than one cost center, differences in overhead rates within departments are relatively small. For this reason the company uses a composite rate for each department, applicable to all cost centers in that department. It uses a machine-hour rate for work done in the machine shop, and a labor hour rate for assembly work. The calculation of these rates is summarized in Exhibit 2–9.

Factory overhead absorbed. The final step in measuring the cost of a job is to use the overhead rates to assign overhead costs to the job cost sheets. The overhead portion of the job cost sheet in Exhibit 2–5 is in the lower right-hand corner. It contains the following data:

Date	Cost Center	Hours	Overhead Rate	Overhead Assigned
5/4..............	2421	9 machine-hours	$6	$ 54
5/6..............	2422	12 machine-hours	6	72
5/10..............	2431	14 direct labor hours	3	42
5/11..............	2431	4 direct labor hours	3	12
Total				$180

This shows the amount of activity the job has generated in each cost center, the overhead rates, and the amount of factory overhead assigned to the job.

For example, the first line shows that job 1234 used nine machine-hours in cost center 2421. This is one of two cost centers in, the machine shop. The overhead rate for the machine shop, from Exhibit 2–9, is $6 a machine-hour. This first set of operations therefore required the accountant to charge $9 \times \$6 = \$54$ of overhead costs against job 1234. Cost center 2422, also in the machine shop, contributed 12 machine-hours, for another $72 in factory overhead. In all, $180 of the factory's overhead costs were assigned to this job. This brought the total cost of job 1234 to $3,912, for an average of $1.956 a unit.

Defective Units, Rework, and Scrap

Our illustrative job cost sheet gave no recognition to any units that may have been put in production but failed to emerge as first-quality products. Three aspects of this phenomenon need to be explored: accounting for rejected units, accounting for rework labor, and accounting for scrap.

Rejected units. The number of good units emerging from a job order is often smaller than the number placed in production. The question is whether any costs should be removed from the job cost sheet before the unit cost is calculated. Unless some clearly unusual event has occurred, all costs are ordinarily left on the job cost sheet— that is, the costs incurred on the lost or defective units are spread over the good units in the lot. Unit cost is calculated by dividing total job cost by the number of good units.

For example, the costs assigned to job 1234 amounted to $3,912. The production order called for production of 2,000 units, but only 1,956 units passed inspection tests. Unit cost is:

$$\frac{\text{Total cost}}{\text{Total good production}} = \frac{\$3,912}{1,956 \text{ units}} = \$2.00 \text{ a unit}$$

If all 2,000 units had passed inspection, average cost would have been $3,912/2,000 = $1.956. Defective production therefore added $2.00 − $1.956 = $.044 to the unit cost of this job.

This treatment is based on either of two assumption: (1) the reject percentage is small; or (2) the rejection rate depends on the characteristics of individual jobs rather than on the characteristics of the production process itself. If the rejection rate is process related, however, then the rejection rate on any particular job will depend on how good the process happens to be when that particular job is processed. In such cases, the costs incurred on defective units should be removed from the cost sheet and reclassified as overhead. The overhead rate then must include a provision for normal rejection experience. This is seldom done, however.

Rework labor. Defective units are not always destroyed or sold as second-quality items. The defects are often worth correcting. The labor costs of these corrective efforts are referred to as rework labor.

The distinction we made for the rejection rate applies to rework labor as well. Rework labor time should be classified as direct labor if it is job related and as overhead if it is process related. In practice, rework labor is generally assumed to be process related. Amounts that are readily measurable are generally classified as overhead.

Scrap. Units or materials that are disposed of as scrap often have a market value. This is almost never big enough to justify the effort to trace it to individual jobs. Instead, the net market value of scrap recovered is typically credited to overhead. The result is to overstate the cost of direct materials and understate average overhead, but the inaccuracy in product cost is likely to be immaterial.

EXHIBIT 2–10

Steps in Costing a Factory Job Order

1. Develop an overhead rate or rates.
2. Identify the job.
3. Set up a job cost sheet.
4. Identify the costs of direct labor and direct materials and enter them on the job cost sheet.
5. Multiply each overhead rate by the number of activity units used on the job—direct labor hours, pounds of materials, etc.—and enter the totals on the job cost sheet.
6. Add the costs on the job cost sheet and divide by the number of good units in the job lot.

Product-Line Classification

So far we have identified only one group of costs that can be classified all three ways—by organization segment, by object of expenditure, and by activity. These are the direct costs of individual end-product activities. The reason we could find no more is that the definition of an end-product activity focuses attention on individual projects or services or batches of products.

If we assemble related end-product activities in groups, however, we are able to classify many more costs on an activity basis. Salespeople, for example, may work full time on one product line (group of related products). Their salaries and travel expenses are definitely traceable to that product line and can be classified that way when incurred.

This illustrates a fundamental fact of cost accounting: many costs may be classified as direct to one segment or activity and indirect to another. For example, the cost of property taxes on a factory building is a direct cost of the factory but is an indirect cost of the cafeteria in that factory. Similarly, food costs are direct costs of the cafeteria but indirect costs of the individual products manufactured by the employees who use the cafeteria.

The point is that when accountants say that a cost is a direct cost, they must also specify the organization segment or activity they are talking about. "Direct" merely means "traceable"; for the term to be truly informative it must be modified to indicate what the cost is traceable to. The only virtually unambiguous terms are direct materials and direct labor, simply because they are almost always used the same way, to describe materials and labor costs traceable to individual end-product activities.

JOB COST FLOWS AND FINANCIAL STATEMENTS

As we indicated at the end of Chapter 1, the three-way classification of costs that has taken up most of this chapter is only one of a number of possible classification schemes that might be used. Another is the distinction between the costs that will remain on the statement of financial position or balance sheet (asset costs) and those that will go on the income statement in external financial reports (expenses).

Job order costing helps the accountant classify factory costs in this way. To understand how it does this, we need to look at the so-called *cost accounting cycle*, tracing the flow of factory costs through a set of ledger accounts. For this purpose we have divided the cycle into four stages:

1. Purchase and use of materials.
2. Use of labor services.
3. Overhead cost absorption.
4. Job completions and product sales.

To make the picture as clear as possible, we shall study the transactions of a factory even simpler than the one the Apex Company operates. This factory has only one overhead rate, but this is quite enough for our purposes here.

Purchase of Materials

Materials costs enter the factory accounts with the purchase of materials. For example, the company bought materials during May at a cost of $30,000 and placed them in the factory storeroom. Payment for these materials was to be made within 30 days. In summary form, the entry to record these purchases was:

(1)

Materials Inventory 30,000
    Accounts Payable   30,000

That is, the purchases increased both the assets and the liabilities by $30,000.

The Materials Inventory account is a *control account*. This means that the balance in this account is supposed to equal the sum of the balances in a set of subsidiary accounts, one for each kind of materials in the inventory. The file of subsidiary accounts is known as a *subsidiary ledger*. Each time a purchase is made, an entry is made in one or more subsidiary accounts. A summary entry in the control account is made periodically to record the total of the amounts entered in the subsidiary ledger during the period. Entry (1) is one of these summary entries.

Use of Materials

The storeroom clerk issued materials costing $22,675 to factory departments during the month. Of this sum, $22,145 represented the cost of materials issued specifically for individual jobs, to be charged as direct material on those jobs. The remaining $530 was the cost of supplies for general use in the factory, not easily traceable to any specific job. In other words, it was a factory overhead cost. The following entry summarizes these transactions:

(2)

Work-in-Process Inventory 22,145
Indirect Materials 530
    Materials Inventory 22,675

This entry records the transfer of materials costs from one asset category (Materials Inventory) to another (Work-in-Process Inventory) and to an overhead cost category (Indirect Materials). These cost flows are diagrammed in Exhibit 2–11.

EXHIBIT 2–11

Flow of Materials Costs

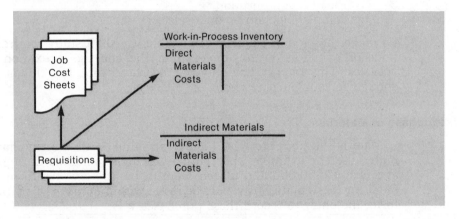

The file of job cost sheets is a type of subsidiary ledger, Work-in-Process Inventory being the control account.

In practice, each cost center has its own indirect materials cost accounts, along the lines outlined earlier in this chapter. To keep the illustration simple, we are representing these by a single, factorywide account.

Labor Costs

Payroll accounting has two sides: the first dealing with the *liability-payment* aspects of the transactions and the second having to do with the identification of the cost with various segments of activity, usually referred to as the *distribution* of labor cost.

Payroll accrual. The liability-payment aspects of payroll accounting are not part of cost accounting, and only the briefest summary is necessary here. Wage and salary liabilities are accrued on the basis of information from two sources: personnel records and attendance or production records. For each employee, a master personnel record is maintained, showing his or her employment history with the company, job classification, title, current rate of pay, and authorized deductions for hospitalization insurance, pension plans, savings plans, union dues, and so forth.

The attendance record is usually provided by an in-and-out clock card from which it is possible to compute the total elapsed time the employee has been on duty. Elapsed time is classified between regular time and overtime.

For salaried employees, the payroll liability is ordinarily taken directly from the master personnel record. For hourly employees, wage liability is computed by multiplying the rate shown on the personnel record by the number of hours worked, as shown on the clock card. If a shift differential is paid for workers on second and third shifts, the basic rate is adjusted to provide for this differential. Overtime hours are paid for at the overtime rate applicable to the particular employee and shift.

Labor cost distribution. Labor cost distributions in job order production are usually based on the individual time tickets described earlier. Because these time tickets are prepared as work is performed, the company has the option of distributing wage costs directly from the time tickets without waiting for reconciliation with the attendance records.[3]

The factory payrolls for May in our sample company totaled $19,-330. This amount included $14,225 for the portion of production workers' time that could be traced to individual jobs (the direct labor), and $5,105 for various types of indirect labor. A summary entry to record these payrolls is:

(3)

Work-in-Process Inventory	14,225	
Indirect Labor	5,105	
Payrolls Payable[4]		19,330

The direct labor costs were also entered on the individual job cost sheets. These cost flows are diagrammed in Exhibit 2–12. Not surprisingly, it looks just like Exhibit 2–11—only the names of the source documents and the title of the overhead account are different.

---

[3] Payroll accrual and cost distribution can be performed simultaneously if the payroll period and cost reporting period coincide. The procedure described here is useful if cost reports are needed more frequently or if different clerical personnel process the payrolls and distribute the costs.

[4] This liability, or most of it, was extinguished almost immediately by the payment of cash. When and how liabilities are liquidated has no bearing on cost accounting, however, and payment transactions therefore can be ignored in this illustration.

EXHIBIT 2–12

Flow of Labor Costs

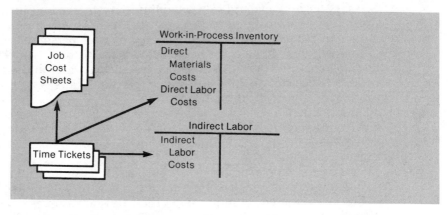

Actually, each cost center may have several object-of-expenditure accounts for indirect labor. Some of these, bearing titles such as Waiting for Materials, Waiting for Repairs, and Rework Labor, are used to accumulate the costs of various kinds of nonproductive or downtime. Use of such an account is justified whenever a particular event is likely to happen often enough and with a large enough effect to require routine feedback. For example, if machine breakdowns are likely to cause ten hours of idle time a year in a ten-employee cost center, management probably doesn't need precise data on breakdown time.

Other Factory Overhead Costs

Our sample factory had overhead costs in addition to the costs of indirect materials and indirect labor. Some of these, such as electric power and telephone charges, represented services purchased and used during the month. These totaled $4,655. Others represented amortizations of the costs of plant and equipment ($1,220) and factory property insurance ($550) purchased in previous months and years.

Entries were made in detailed cost center object-of-expenditure accounts, but once again we shall use a single account to represent them all:

(4)

Other Factory Overhead 6,425	
Accumulated Depreciation	1,220
Prepaid Insurance	550
Accounts Payable	4,655

Overhead Cost Absorption

Direct labor and direct materials costs go directly into the job cost sheets and simultaneously to the Work-in-Process account. Accountants can't do this with factory overhead costs, though, because they can't trace these costs to specific jobs. Instead, they accumulate the actual costs in overhead accounts and use overhead rates to charge overhead costs to the job cost sheets. The total of these charges to the job cost sheets is also assigned to the Work-in-Process account by a process known as *overhead absorption.* The total amount of factory overhead assigned to jobs in any period is known as the amount of *overhead absorbed.*

During May our sample factory recorded 3,500 direct labor hours. It used a single plantwide overhead rate of $3 a direct labor hour. This means that $10,500 ($3 × 3,500) was entered in the various job cost sheets. The entry to record this total in the ledger was:

(5)

Work-in-Process Inventory 10,500
    Factory Overhead Absorbed   10,500

The Factory Overhead Absorbed account is a contra account to the various factory overhead cost accounts. Whereas they accumulate the costs, this one accumulates the amounts that are soaked up by the production that actually took place. If there is no production, there is nothing to absorb the costs. These relationships are diagrammed in Exhibit 2–13.

EXHIBIT 2–13

Relationship of Factory Overhead Absorbed to Factory Overhead Cost Accounts

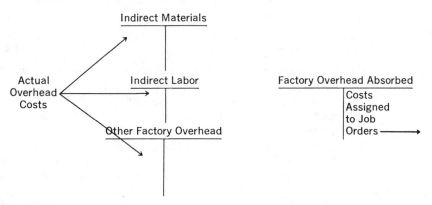

Job Completions and Sales

Two more steps remain in the cost accounting cycle. The first is the completion of job orders; the second is the sale of finished products.

Completion of a job is the signal for removing the job cost sheet from the in-process file. It also triggers an entry to record the transfer of costs from the work-in-process to the finished goods category. Our sample factory had no work-in-process at the beginning of May. It worked on four jobs during the month. The job cost sheets for these four jobs are represented in Exhibit 2–14. (The costs on these job cost

EXHIBIT 2–14

The Job Cost File

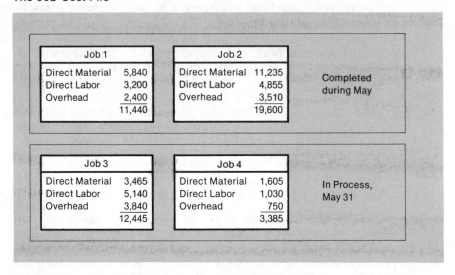

sheets add up to the amounts charged to the Work-in-Process Inventory account in entries [2], [3], and [4].)

Jobs 1 and 2 were completed during May, and were transferred to the finished goods warehouse. An entry was made to transfer the costs accumulated on these two jobs from one asset account to another:

(6)

Finished Goods Inventory 31,040
      Work-in-Process Inventory   31,040

In other factories some job orders are for the manufacture of parts or subassemblies, and these are returned to factory stockrooms rather than to finished goods inventory locations. The costs of these jobs would be transferred to a Materials Inventory account rather than to finished goods.

The final step in the cost accounting cycle is the transfer of costs to expense. An expense is any cost that is deducted from revenues on the income statement.[5] In this case the cost to be classified as expense is the cost of the goods sold during the period.

Job costs are reclassified as expenses when the revenues from the sale of finished products are recognized. Job 1, for example, was for 1,100 water pumps. All of these were sold during May, and the full cost of $11,440 was transferred from the Finished Goods Inventory account to the Cost of Goods Sold account. Job 2 consisted of 500 oil burners. With total job cost of $19,600, the unit cost was $39.20. The sales force sold 425 oil burners during the month, for a cost of goods

---

[5] The term manufacturing expense is often used in practice to refer to factory overhead costs. To avoid confusion, we shall use the term expense only to describe deductions from revenues.

sold of 425 × $39.20 = $16,660. The total cost of goods sold therefore was $11,440 + $16,660 = $28,100. The transfers of costs were summarized in the following entry:

(7)

Cost of Goods sold 28,100

    Finished Goods Inventory   28,100

This established the transfer of costs from the asset category to their new status as expenses.

The goods sold during this period brought in revenues of $42,000, all from credit sales. The summary entry to record these sales was as follows:

(8)

Accounts Receivable 42,000

    Sales Revenues   42,000

Summary of the Cost Flows

The complete cycle is summarized in Exhibit 2–15. Costs enter the factory accounts at the left of the diagram. Some are stored temporarily in inventory, fixed asset, or prepayment accounts which appear on the company's balance sheet. Others (direct labor) go directly to Work-in-Process, while others go temporarily into Factory Overhead accounts. As materials are issued and work is performed, costs move out of the accounts at the left and into work-in-process, either directly

EXHIBIT 2–15

Cost Flows for Income Determination in Manufacturing

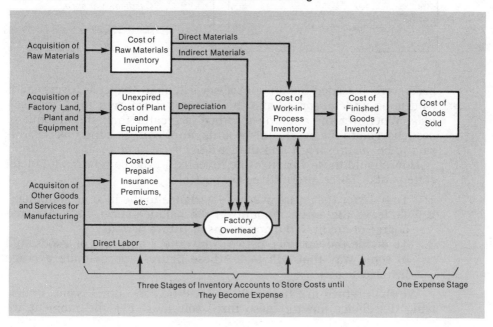

or by way of the Factory Overhead accounts. Factory overhead is charged to work-in-process by means of predetermined overhead rates.

As jobs are completed, the costs are transferred from Work-in-Process to the Finished Goods inventory account. They are still shown on the balance sheet because they are the costs of assets. Finally, as the revenues from particular goods are recognized, the costs leave the balance sheet and go to the income statement under the heading "Cost of goods sold." Some costs, in other words, go through three kinds of balance sheet accounts before being recognized as expense.

Disposing of Under- or Overabsorbed Factory Overhead

The completion of the cost accounting cycle leaves one loose end, the $1,560 difference between the actual overhead costs for the period and the amount absorbed by production. This difference is called the *overhead cost variance*, as shown in Exhibit 2–16. If the overhead

EXHIBIT 2–16

The Overhead Variance

Actual Overhead	
Indirect materials.............	$ 530
Indirect labor...............	5,105
Other overhead...........	6,425
	$12,060

Overhead Absorbed by Production	
3,500 direct labor hours × $3...............	$10,500

Overhead Variance
$12,060 − $10,500 = $1,560

costs have exceeded the amount absorbed, as in this case, overhead is said to be *underabsorbed* and the variance is referred to as *unfavorable*. Whenever the amount absorbed is greater than the amount of cost charged to the overhead accounts, on the other hand, overhead is said to be *overabsorbed* and the variance is *favorable*.

How should these variances be reflected in the company's financial statements? Three alternatives are possible:

1. To transfer the entire overhead variance to the income statement.
2. To leave the entire amount on the balance sheet, as a deferred charge or credit to the operations of future periods.
3. To divide the variance between inventory and cost of goods sold in some way that will make these figures approximate average historical cost.

We shall return in Chapter 22 to face the conceptual issues underlying the choice among these three solutions. For the moment we must be content to note that variances of U.S. corporations are likely to be taken to the income statement in their entirety unless they are material in amount. In such cases they will be split between the income statement and the balance sheet.

Summary of Factory Costs

The cost flows in our example, together with information on inventory balances, can be summarized in a table like the statement of manufacturing costs in Exhibit 2–17.

EXHIBIT 2–17

Statement of Manufacturing Costs

Direct materials:			
Materials and supplies inventory, May 1.......................			$52,485
Purchases..			30,000
			$82,485
Less: Supplies used...		$ 530	
Materials and supplies inventory, May 31..............		59,810	60,340
Direct materials used.......................................			$22,145
Direct labor...			14,225
Factory overhead:			
Indirect labor..		$ 5,105	
Supplies..		530	
Depreciation..		1,220	
Insurance...		550	
Other overhead..		4,655	
Total overhead..		$12,060	
Less: Overhead unabsorbed...............................		1,560	
Overhead applied to production..............................			10,500
Total product cost...			$46,870
Add: Work in process, May 1.................................			...
			$46,870
Less: Work in process, May 31..............................			15,830
Cost of Goods Finished..			$31,040

This statement is too cluttered to be suitable for managerial reporting, but it does show how all the figures fit together. The upper part shows the costs of operating the factory ($22,145 in direct materials, $14,225 in direct labor, and $12,060 in factory overhead). These differ from the amounts charged to jobs by the amount of the unabsorbed overhead, $1,560 in this case. The cost of goods finished is equal to the amount charged to jobs, plus or minus the change in the work-in-process inventory. Because this factory had no work in process on May 1, the cost of goods finished was equal to total product cost less the costs of the jobs still in process at the end of the month (jobs 3 and 4).

This statement can be converted into a statement of the cost of goods sold by adding or subtracting the change in the finished goods inventory.

SUMMARY

To provide data that management will find helpful in planning and controlling the organization's operations, the accountant classifies operating costs on three separate bases: by organization segment or cost center, by object of expenditure, and by activity.

The primary criterion for assigning costs to individual cost centers and individual objects of expenditure is traceability. Costs can always be traced to cost centers and objects. The accountant also uses traceability to some extent in classifying costs by activity, but not all costs can be classified in this way. In job order costing, for example, the direct materials and direct labor costs are those traced to individual jobs. Nontraceable (overhead) costs are assigned to jobs by multiplying cost averages, known as overhead rates, by some measure of the size of the job, such as the number of direct labors hours used on the job. The object is to assign to each job the amount of overhead cost that was provided to support the amount of activity the job represented. For this purpose, most overhead rates are based on estimates made at the beginning of the year, and a separate overhead rate is used for each production cost center or group of related production centers.

Management uses job cost data in evaluating the profitability of its present activities and in preparing estimates of the costs of future jobs. These data are also used to divide production costs between the income statement and balance sheet for external financial reporting. The final section of this chapter has been used to explain how this is done.

KEY TERMS

The most important terms introduced and defined in this chapter are the following:

Charging rate	Job order costing
Cost accounting cycle	Normal volume
Cost center	Object of expenditure
Direct costs	Overhead absorbed
Direct labor	Overhead costs
Direct materials	Overhead rate
End-product activities	Overtime premiums
Indirect costs	Prime costs
Indirect labor	Service and support activities
Indirect materials	Traceability criterion
Job order	

INDEPENDENT STUDY PROBLEMS
(Solutions in Appendix C)

1. Cost classification systems. The Montague Company was originally established to distribute a new type of waterproof, heat-resistant glue to shoe manufacturers. The glue was produced under contract by a large chemical company, and product sales were made by a field sales force of four sales representatives who contacted shoe manufacturers directly. These representatives were all chemical engineers and had the responsibility of training their customers' personnel in the proper method of applying the glue. The revenues and expenses of the company have been recorded in a fairly simple set of accounts:

Sales	Office Supplies
Sales Returns and Allowances	Rent
Cost of Goods Sold	Printing and Postage
Sales Salaries	Telephone and Telegraph
Sales Commissions	Retirement Expense
Travel Expenses	Insurance Expense
Office Salaries	Miscellaneous Expenses

The president of the company has just decided to expand operations in two ways: first by taking on the distribution of a line of shoe findings (miscellaneous small items used in shoe manufacture), and second by marketing the company's glue to furniture manufacturers. Two new representatives are to be added to the shoe trade sales force. The furniture trade sales force will consist initially of three new salespeople to be hired for that purpose. The president, who heretofore has also acted as sales manager and controller, has decided to promote the company's senior sales representative to the position of sales manager. The present office manager will become controller and office manager, with a new assistant to be hired.

What changes, if any, should the company make in its cost classification system? Why would these changes be desirable?

2. Job cost and overhead variance. Chailly, Inc., uses a job order costing system in its factory with a predetermined overhead rate based on direct labor hours. You are given the following information:

1. Job No. 423 was started on March 3, finished on March 28.
2. Other data:

	Job No. 423	All Jobs (in March)	Annual Budget at Normal Volume
Direct labor hours....................	60	10,000	100,000
Direct labor cost....................	$400	$ 60,000	$ 350,000
Direct materials cost...............	$800	$150,000	$1,300,000

3. Factory overhead budgeted for the entire year was $900,000; actual overhead for the month of March was $106,000.

a. Compute the cost of job No. 423.
b. Calculate the overhead variance for the month of March.

3. Unit cost and journal entries. The Basic Foundry prepares metal castings for specific orders, using a job order costing system. The following information about job No. 103 is available:

1. Materials issued: 21,000 pounds at $0.66 a pound.
2. Labor hours: 2,000 at $6.68 an hour.
3. Factory overhead charged to jobs: $4 a direct labor hour.
4. Unused material returned to storeroom: 800 pounds.
5. Castings started: 10,000.
6. Castings completed: 9,800.

a. Compute unit cost of production to the nearest cent.
b. Prepare journal entries to record these transactions.

4. Classifying labor costs.   J. Jones worked 45 hours last week, 9 hours a day for five days. His wage rate was $8 an hour, with time-and-a-half for overtime hours, in excess of 40 hours a week. Mr. Jones spent all of his time last week on job M227, except for three hours on Wednesday morning on equipment maintenance and the final hour on Friday on job M246.

Mr. Jones is one of several production workers who could have worked on job M227. Some of these earned overtime last week; others did not. A total of 50 overtime hours were recorded last week. Management authorized the overtime to avoid the necessity of hiring and training another worker to handle a seasonal peak load in the factory.

How much of Mr. Jones's wages last week should have been assigned to job M227?

5. Manufacturing cost flows.   The Ace Appliance Company had the following inventories on October 1:

Material and supplies	$12,650
Work in process	8,320
Finished goods	11,100

The following transactions took place during the month:

1. Purchased material at a cost of $4,500.
2. Issued direct material, $6,320; indirect material, $930.
3. Accrued payrolls: direct labor, $3,300; indirect labor, $1,880; selling and administrative salaries, $2,600.
4. Miscellaneous manufacturing overhead, $2,700.
5. Applied manufacturing overhead at 150 percent of direct labor cost.
6. Goods completed during the month cost $12,650.
7. Miscellaneous selling and administrative expenses, $1,835.
8. Ending inventory, finished goods, $9,250.
9. Sales revenue from goods sold, $19,350.

a. Account for the above transactions, using T-accounts, and establish the closing balances in the inventory accounts.

b. Prepare an income statement for the month, with a supporting schedule of the cost of goods manufactured and sold. (Overhead over- or under-absorbed is to be included in the cost of goods sold.)

EXERCISES AND PROBLEMS

1. Identifying end-product activities.   Which of the following activities are end-product activities?

a. In an advertising agency: writing advertising copy for a client.
b. In a factory: direct labor on a job order.
c. In a hospital: technicians operating an x-ray machine.
d. In a university: preparing a payroll.
e. In a restaurant: cooking soup.
f. On a football team: washing uniforms.
g. In a department store: issuing a charge card.
h. In a factory: issuing direct materials.

2. Direct versus indirect.   Harrow, Inc., has a single factory, with 12 departments, each one a cost center. One of these is the factory manager's office; all others perform work on specific products.

Production is on a job order basis. The factory manufactures 20 regular catalog products and a large number of specialty items to meet customers' individual needs. The regular products fall into three different product lines; specialty items are regarded as a separate product line. About 30 percent of the direct labor costs are expended on the specialty line, which brings in about 40 percent of the total revenue.

Customers are solicited and served through six branch offices, with between 5 and 12 sales representatives operating out of each branch. Each sales representative handles all of the company's products. Each branch has a full-time manager who calls on a few major customers and supervises the sales representatives in that branch. The branch managers all report to the marketing vice president.

Indicate whether each of the following costs is a direct cost of a job order, a direct cost of a product line, a direct cost of a division (marketing or manufacturing), or a direct cost of a first-level cost center (factory production department or sales branch). The cost may be direct in all, some, or none of these categories:

a.   Lubricating oil for factory machinery.
b.   Materials used on a specific job order.
c.   The factory manager's salary.
d.   The president's secretary's salary.
e.   Gasoline for sales representatives' cars.
f.   Sales commissions (3 percent of net sales).
g.   Overtime premium for worker in factory production department.
h.   Rent on San Francisco branch office.
i.   Salary of factory department head.
j.   National advertising for product X.

3. Cost classification systems.   The Ace Maintenance Company provides routine equipment maintenance service and performs equipment repairs for a large number of industrial users in the New York metropolitan area. The company will service or repair almost any factory equipment and has built a reputation for prompt, efficient service.

Ace Maintenance was founded ten years ago by Paul Mace, a highly gifted salesman and administrator. Mr. Mace is still president of the company, doing most of the direct selling himself. His vice president, Don Wynant, is responsible for hiring all service personnel and for the day-to-day operation of the service end of the business.

The company's operating cost accounts for a typical month show the following balances:

	Executive Office	Accounting	Operations
Salaries and wages	$10,000	$3,000	$26,000
Overtime premiums	—	—	1,100
Materials and supplies	500	450	1,000
Repair parts	—	—	14,000
Utilities	1,200	—	—
Payroll taxes	300	120	1,200
Pension plan	700	150	1,300
Travel	100	—	2,100
Advertising	200	—	—
Insurance	800	—	—
Taxes	900	—	—
Rent	2,500	—	—
Miscellaneous	400	30	600
Total	$17,600	$3,750	$47,300

A large industrial service company has offered to buy Mr. Mace's interest in the business. Mr. Mace would retire and his place would be taken by a president and a salaried sales manager.

a. The company's chart of accounts has three departmental codes (one each for the executive office, accounting, and operations) and the 13 object of expenditure classifications listed in the table above. In what ways, if any, will the chart of accounts have to be changed to meet the needs of the new owners and the new manager? Give reasons for your suggestions.

b. What problems would you be likely to encounter in trying to carry out your suggestions?

4. Cost classification.   The Harrell School is a nonprofit educational institution. It has both day students and boarding students enrolled in a college preparatory high school program.

The school also conducts an evening program for older children and young adults who have dropped out of high school but are now working to earn their high school diplomas on a part-time basis.

The school also sponsors various noncredit adult education courses in a variety of subjects ranging from foreign languages to home repair techniques.

Athletic fields, a dormitory, and a classroom and office building are all located on the school's campus, far from the downtown area of a medium-sized city. The dormitory contains kitchen and dining facilities, as well as rooms for the boarding students. Boarding students take all of their meals in the dining room, seven days a week; day students may either bring their lunch or eat in the dining room with the boarding students upon payment of a weekly fee. No dining service is provided to the students and faculty of the evening programs.

The school's administrative staff consists of a headmaster (who also teaches one course in the day program), an admissions director, a director of the evening programs, a guidance counselor, an administrative assistant, a bookkeeper, and two secretaries.

The dormitory staff consists of a director, a dietician, a head cook, two "residents," and a number of people who do the cooking, serving, and cleaning. Three people take care of the buildings and grounds on a full-time basis, bringing in part-time help as needed for special or evening work.

The school has a full-time faculty for the day program. The evening programs are staffed on a part-time basis, with fees negotiated separately for each course. The buildings and grounds staff are paid extra for evening work.

A small endowment fund is invested in long-term securities. The income from these investments supplements the revenues from tuition and fees and the annual gifts from foundations and alumni and friends of the school.

Textbooks are provided free to students in the evening high school program. Students in the day program and in the adult education courses buy their books from the school. All book sales are handled by the administrative assistant.

a. Draw an organization chart for the Harrell School.

b. Outline a cost classification system for this school, with organizational, object of expenditure, and activity dimensions to the extent you deem appropriate. You need not prepare a full list of accounts, but you should indicate how extensive each of the classifications should be. (You may assume that an adequate revenue classification scheme can be developed to go with your cost classifications.)

c.   What problems, if any, would you expect to encounter in classifying costs in the ways you suggest?

5. Labor charging rate. The work week of employees in the foundry department of the ABC Company ranges between 42 and 50 hours, with all hours in excess of 40 per week being paid at a rate of one and one-half times the basic hourly wage rate of $7.20 an hour. On the average, each worker works 45 hours a week.

a.   What is the foundry labor cost per hour that should be included in product unit cost for public financial reporting? How much of this should be shown as direct labor? Explain your answer.

b.   Management is trying to decide whether certain products are profitable enough to continue manufacturing. From this point of view, what is the foundry labor cost of a product that requires ten hours of foundry labor? Explain.

6. Overtime premiums; Nonmanufacturing. The firm of Rundell Associates does a number of kinds of drafting, lettering, and commercial artwork for outside clients. A system of requisitions and time sheets is used to accumulate the costs of materials and personal services consumed on individual job orders.

Although a few jobs are accepted on a flat fee basis, most jobs are priced to customers on a cost-plus-time basis. On these jobs, the customer's bill includes four elements:

Cost of materials used.
Personal service fees (at predetermined hourly rates, including markup over hourly cost).
Overtime premiums paid for work on specific jobs.
Miscellaneous out-of-pocket costs incurred on specific jobs.

Materials costs on some jobs are substantial, and occasionally a customer will complain of being charged for too many spoiled materials. In general, however, materials costs amount to less than 10 percent of the gross amount of the customer invoice.

Customers complain frequently about the size of the personal service fee, but this appears to be part of a bargaining strategy to impress on Rundell Associates the need to watch costs carefully on subsequent orders. Complaints about the overtime premiums are considerably stronger and often lead to downward revision of the invoices. During recent months these downward revisions have been large enough to cut the firm's net profit in half and the managing partners are worried.

Indicate any changes that you would make in the company's cost accounting and billing procedures, giving reasons for your changes. If you wish to leave the present system unchanged, indicate briefly why you think no improvement is called for.

7. Overhead rate and absorption. A company uses a job order costing system with a predetermined overhead rate based on normal volume. Overhead costs are budgeted at $10,000 a month plus $2 for each direct labor hour. Normal volume is 10,000 direct labor hours. Actual volume for August was 9,000 direct labor hours, and actual overhead cost totaled

$28,700. Job No. 423 was started on August 6 and completed on August 20, with the expenditure of 40 direct labor hours.

a. How much overhead was charged to Job No. 423?
b. How much overhead was charged to all jobs during August?
c. What was the total factory overhead variance for August?

8. Job costs. A factory uses a job order costing system. A careless bookkeeper has lost the file of job order cost sheets covering the work done last week, but the underlying documents are still available. You have the following data:

1. Direct labor and direct materials used:

Job Order	Direct Materials	Direct Labor Hours
498....................	$1,500	116
506....................	960	16
507....................	415	18
508....................	345	42
509....................	652	24
511....................	308	10
512....................	835	30
Total..............	$5,015	256

2. The direct labor wage rate is $4 an hour.
3. The overhead rate is $5 a direct labor hour.
4. Actual overhead costs for the week, $1,480.
5. Jobs completed: Nos. 498, 506, and 509.
6. The factory had no work in process at the beginning of the week.

a. Prepare a summary table that will show the total cost assigned to each job.
b. Compute the amount of overhead over- or underabsorbed during the week.
c. Calculate the cost of the work-in-process at the end of the week.

9. Unit cost; Spoilage. Job order X150 was placed in production in December 19x1. During December, materials costing $800 were issued for use on this job, and 60 direct labor hours were expended at an average rate of $4.40 an hour. The overhead rate in 19x1 was $2 a direct labor *dollar*.

The company's new fiscal year began on January 1, 19x2. Job order X150 was finished in January with the additional expenditure of 90 direct labor hours at an average wage rate of $4.60 an hour, and additional direct materials amounting to $250 were issued for use in this job. The overhead rate in 19x2 was set at $9 a direct labor *hour*.

The job consisted of 500 product units, but 20 of these units were spoiled and were discarded as trash. The remaining 480 units were placed in the finished goods stockroom on January 28, 19x2. The next day 100 of these units were sold and shipped to customers.

a. Enter the appropriate data in a job cost sheet.
b. Compute unit cost to the nearest cent. Explain your method of accounting for the spoiled units.
c. Prepare journal entries to record the transactions.

10. Departmental overhead rates. The Robertson Company has been using a single plantwide overhead rate in its factory. The controller has proposed using departmental overhead rates instead. You have the follow-information:

1. Three products (A, B, C) are produced in three departments (1, 2, 3).
2. Labor hours required for each unit of product are:

	Department			
Product	1	2	3	Total
A....................	2	1	1	4
B....................	0	2	2	4
C....................	2	3	3	8

3. Product produced in a normal year: A, 40,000 units; B, 40,000 units; and C, 10,000 units.
4. Overhead incurred in a normal year: department 1, $400,000; department 2, $300,000; and department 3, $100,000.
5. Sales this year: A, 20,000 units; B, 40,000 units; and C, 10,000 units.
6. The company's inventories are listed on a full cost Lifo basis, and the year-end inventories of product A were 10,000 units greater than the year-beginning quantities.

a. Estimate the effects of changing to departmental overhead rates based on direct labor hours.
b. Explain the arguments for and against making this change.

11. Spoilage. In a job order for 500 piece parts, 80 parts are damaged beyond repair in the production operation and must be junked.

Should the costs of these parts be removed from the job order cost sheet? Indicate the criteria by which you judged this question and the reasons why application of these criteria led to the course of action you have chosen.

12. Spoilage; Rework labor. Carson, Inc. manufactures a number of products. Past records indicate that about 5 percent of the units will be defective and will have to be reworked. This is true of all products. Rework labor time averages 8 percent of the amount of productive direct labor (productive time excludes rework time).

Job No. 563 consisted of 200 sole plates, of which 20 were defective. Productive direct labor on this job amounted to $500, and rework labor to correct the defects cost $65.

Would you charge the cost of rework labor cost to the job order cost sheet in this case? If not, how would you record it? Give your reasons.

13. Overhead rate: Estimated versus normal volume. The Bolt Company has been using a relatively small percentage of its capacity for the past year and this situation is likely to persist. You have the following data:

1. Estimated factory overhead cost at normal volume (10,000 machine-hours a month), $30,000.
2. Estimated factory overhead cost at estimated actual volume for this year (8,000 machine-hours a month), $28,000.
3. Actual factory overhead cost at actual volume for March (7,500 machine-hours), $28,500.

a. Calculate a predetermined overhead rate based on normal volume.
b. Calculate the amount of overhead under- or overabsorbed during March.

c. Would the amount of the overhead variance have been larger or smaller if the overhead rate had been based on estimated actual volume? How, if at all, does the size of the overhead variance affect the decision to use a rate based on normal volume instead of a rate based on estimated volume? Explain.

14. Basis for overhead rate. The Frantic Products Company manufactures a variety of fabricated metal products and sells metal castings in a variety of sizes, shapes, and specifications. The casting shop is the biggest department in the factory, and each casting order is costed separately on a job order basis.

Management is now setting an overhead costing rate for the coming year. The following data have been estimated:

	Capacity Production	Normal Volume	Anticipated Current Volume
Output (pounds).....................	10,000,000	7,000,000	6,000,000
Furnace hours........................	90,000	63,000	54,000
Direct labor hours....................	45,000	31,500	27,000
Costs:			
Direct labor........................	$225,000	$157,500	$135,000
Indirect labor......................	76,000	70,000	68,000
Other overhead costs..............	59,000	56,000	55,000

The normal volume figures represent the designed capacity of the plant —that is, the plant was designed so that operations at this volume would be at a competitive average unit cost.

The amount of labor time per furnace hour and the types of labor used vary substantially from product to product.

a. Compute overhead rates for this department on four different bases: (1) pounds, (2) furnace hours, (3) direct labor hours, and (4) direct labor costs.

b. Using each of these overhead rates in turn, compute the amount of overhead that would be assigned to two jobs with the following characteristics:

	Job No. 1	Job No. 2
Pounds.........................	10,000	10,000
Furnace hours..................	90	120
Labor hours....................	45	50
Labor dollars..................	$225	$200

c. What criteria would you use in deciding which of these four rates to use?

d. Which of these rates seems most likely to satisfy these criteria?

15. Overhead rate, nonmanufacturing firm. Franklin Associates is a management consulting firm. Each consulting engagement is covered by a contract. The contract price is negotiated in advance, sometimes as a fixed fee, sometimes as professional staff time plus traceable expenses. The billing rates for the various members of the professional staff are always fixed in advance and are expected, in the aggregate, to cover nontraceable (indirect) costs and provide a margin of profit.

The company uses a job costing system to measure the costs of each contract. All costs not directly traceable to specific contracts are recorded as indirect costs; a single predetermined overhead rate is used to assign indirect costs to contracts, based on the number of *professional staff hours*.

Budgeted time and costs for the year and actual time and costs for February were as follows:

	Annual Budget		February	
	Hours	Cost	Hours	Cost
Direct costs:				
Professional staff..............	25,000	$300,000	1800	$25,000
Secretarial staff................	6,000	36,000	550	3,300
Art work and printing...........		7,000		800
Copying.......................		2,000		200
Travel........................		35,000		2,700
Total.....................		$380,000		$32,000
Indirect costs:				
Professional staff..............	5,000	$ 60,000	600	$ 7,400
Secretarial staff................	12,000	72,000	800	3,300
Art work and printing...........		3,000		300
Copying.......................		1,000		100
Travel........................		8,000		400
Other.........................		56,000		4,700
Total.....................		$200,000		$16,200

a. Prepare a predetermined hourly rate for indirect costs.

b. The following direct cost data were recorded during February for one of the company's contracts. How much cost was assigned to this contract during February?

Professional staff (70 hours)........................ $910
Secretarial staff (10 hours)......................... 65
Art work and printing............................. 60
Copying.. 10
Travel... 280

c. Would this contract have been more profitable or less profitable if the overhead rate had been based on the company's actual cost experience in February?

16. Job costing accounts. The Simmons Company's factory uses a job costing system. Inventories at the beginning and end of 19x1 were:

	January 1	December 31
Materials......................	$50,000	$43,000
Work in process................	12,000	16,000
Finished goods.................	63,000	61,000

Transactions during the year were:

1. Purchases of materials for direct and indirect use, $169,000.
2. Unusable materials returned to suppliers, $2,000.
3. Direct labor, various job orders, $80,000.
4. Indirect labor, $7,000.
5. Indirect materials issued from materials inventories, $6,000.
6. Heat, power and light, $7,000.
7. Depreciation, $13,000.
8. Miscellaneous factory costs, $1,000.
9. Overhead absorbed, $32,000.

a. Set up the necessary operating cost and inventory accounts, enter the January 1 balances given above, and make entries to record the year's transactions, including the cost of goods sold. Use a single account for factory overhead costs.

b. Prepare a statement of the cost of goods manufactured.

17. Job costing accounts. The Apex Company uses a job order costing system in its factory. The April 1 balances in the inventory and overhead accounts were:

Raw material...$35,000
Work in process... 8,000
Finished goods... 26,000
Overhead underabsorbed to date..........................:.... 3,000

1. The following costs were incurred during the month:

Raw materials purchased...................................$23,000
Direct labor.. 14,000
Indirect labor.. 8,000
Power... 1,500
Depreciation.. 1,500
Supplies.. 2,000
Other manufacturing costs................................. 5,000
Selling and office expense................................ 9,000

2. Raw material costing $31,000 was put into process during April.
3. At the close of the month the production orders still in process, all of which had been started during the month, had been charged with the following costs: direct material, $4,000; direct labor, $1,500.
4. Overhead is charged to jobs at 140 percent of direct labor cost.
5. Finished goods inventory on April 30 amounted to $18,000.

a. Using a single account to accumulate all factory overhead costs, present journal entries to cover the transactions indicated by the above information.
b. List the balances in the inventory accounts and the amount of the over- or underabsorbed overhead as of April 30.

18. Job cost sheet; identifying direct costs. One of the jobs in the factory of the Gentry Company during June was job No. 422, calling for the manufacture of 100 Flister Blidgets, Polished, Large. The factory accountant had to record the following events, among others, during June:

June 1 Issued 200 pounds of material X for job No. 422 at $0.75 a pound.
      4 Issued 50 pounds of material Z for job No. 422 at $3.20 a pound.
      5 Expended labor during week on job No. 422—76 hours in department A at $8 an hour.
      8 Issued lubricants and cleaning compounds to department A, $100.
     11 Returned 10 pounds of material Z to storeroom—quality not up to specification for job No. 422.
     11 Issued 15 pounds of material Z for job No. 422, at $3.30 a pound.
     12 Expended labor during week on job No. 422—33 hours in department A at $8, and 10 hours in department B at $7 an hour.
     15 Discovered defects in five Flister Blidgets, which were then sent back to department A for reworking.
     16 Issued 20 pounds of material P to department B for job No. 422, at $2 a pound.
     17 Damaged five pounds of material P originally issued for job No. 422, and transferred them to scrap bin.
     18 Finished job No. 422.
     19 Expended labor during week on job No. 422—3 hours in department A (reworking defective units) at $8 an hour, and 30 hours in department B at $7 an hour.
   1–19 Overhead rates for production departments: department A, $2 a direct labor hour; department B, $5 a direct labor hour.
     30 Collected the month's scrap from both departments, 100 pounds with scrap value of 10 cents a pound (total materials processed by both departments during the month, 10,000 pounds).

a.   Prepare a job order cost sheet, enter all the pertinent costs, and compute unit costs, by element, for job No. 422. (Note: Some of the items may not be reflected directly in the job order cost sheet.)
b.   How would you use the unit cost obtained in (a)? Explain.

19. Interpreting job cost data.

Jerry Blaine is a contractor specializing in small house remodeling jobs. Most of his employees are free-lance specialists who work for other contractors as well, so that the size of his payroll rises and falls with fluctuations in the amount of work to be done. Higher wage rates are paid to the more highly skilled workers, but the average wage rate in the construction industry in Mr. Blaine's area is about $10 an hour.

Mr. Blaine recently installed a job order costing system and now has the following labor cost data:

	Estimated		Actual	
Job Number	Labor Hours	Labor Cost	Labor Hours	Labor Cost
T12	700	$7,000	680	$ 7,500
T15	300	3,000	330	3,600
T16	800	8,000	750	8,200
T18	100	1,000	90	1,000
T19	900	9,000	980	11,700
T20	400	4,000	500	5,600
T21	500	5,000	450	4,700

During the period covered by these figures, Mr. Blaine submitted bids on 18 jobs. Other contractors underbid him on 11 of these; he was the low bidder on the 7 jobs shown above. Mr. Blaine's profit margin was considerably lower than that of most of his competitors during this period.

a.   What advice can you give Mr. Blaine on the basis of these figures? Do they help explain his low profit margin? Is there anything he can do about it?
b.   What further data would you probably find in the job cost sheets or supporting documents that would throw further light on these questions?
c.   Would charging overhead costs to individual job orders provide Mr. Blaine with useful information?

20. Job costing transactions.

The Farquar Corporation uses job order costing in its factory. The inventory accounts showed the following balances on February 1:

Materials and Supplies.. 40,000
Jobs in Process.. 57,000
Finished Goods... 73,000

The job cost file showed the following details at that time:

	Materials	Labor	Overhead	Total
No. D1762	$ 600	$ 1,900	$ 2,850	$ 5,350
No. D1783	2,900	3,200	4,800	10,900
No. E0004	4,000	1,400	2,100	7,500
No. E0010	6,500	1,000	1,500	9,000
No. E0011	14,000	2,000	3,000	19,000
No. E0013	4,000	500	750	5,250
Total	$32,000	$10,000	$15,000	$57,000

The following transactions were recorded during February:

1. Materials and supplies received in the factory storeroom, $62,000.
2. Materials and supplies issued by the storeroom to factory departments:

Job No. E0004	$ 500
Job No. E0010	1,000
Job No. E0013	2,500
Job No. E0015	8,000
Job No. E0016	11,000
Job No. E0017	6,000
Job No. E0018	9,000
Indirect materials, department M	4,800
Indirect materials, department P	500
Indirect materials, department A	2,200
Total	$45,500

3. Labor performed in factory departments:

Job No.	Department	Cost
D1762	A	$ 200
D1783	M	300
D1783	P	400
E0004	M	7,200
E0010	P	3,400
E0010	A	5,300
E0011	M	12,000
E0013	M	3,100
E0013	P	1,400
E0013	A	3,300
E0015	A	3,600
E0016	P	2,500
E0016	M	6,500
E0017	A	3,800
E0017	M	8,800
E0017	P	2,400
E0018	M	3,000
Indirect	M	19,900
Indirect	P	3,100
Indirect	A	8,500
Total		$98,700

4. Other overhead costs charged to the factory:

	Department M	Department P	Department A
Supervision	$11,000	$3,200	$ 8,300
Maintenance	6,500	1,900	400
Heat, light, and power	2,400	700	1,500
Payroll taxes and pensions	12,400	2,600	5,300
Depreciation	7,800	800	900
Miscellaneous	600	400	200
Total	$40,700	$9,600	$16,600

5. Predetermined departmental overhead rates, expressed as percentages of direct labor cost, were as follows: department M, 150 percent; department P, 140 percent; department A, 180 percent.
6. Jobs completed and transferred to finished goods: Nos. D1762, D1783, E0004, E0010, E0013, E0017.
7. Cost of finished goods sold, $138,000.

a. Enter the February 1 balances in individual job cost sheets and record the month's transactions on these sheets.

b. Enter the February 1 balances in the inventory accounts and record the month's transactions. A single account may be used for each department's overhead costs.

c. Compute the amount of the under- or overabsorbed overhead in each department.

d. Prepare a statement of the cost of goods manufactured and sold. The under/overabsorbed is not to be included in the cost of goods sold.

CASE 2–1: TIPOGRAFIA STANCA, S.p.A.*

Mr. Giulio Cattani, founder and president of Tipografia Stanca, S.p.A., was worried. The company was doing more business than ever before—sales were at an annual rate of about $625,000 a year—but net income had decreased slightly during recent months and the ratio of income to sales had dropped sharply. Mr. Cattani wondered what had gone wrong and what he could do about it. He called in his chief (and only) accountant, Mr. Gaetano Pareto, and asked him to find out what was happening.

Tipografia Stanca was an Italian corporation located in Milan and doing a general printing business on a customer order basis. Mr. Cattani set the price to be charged for each job. When possible, he waited until the work was done and then quoted a price equal to 140 percent of the cost of the paper stock used, plus $12.50 for each labor hour. Straight-time wage rates in the past, adjusted for recent wage rate increases, had averaged about $4 an hour, and this formula seemed to provide an adequate margin to cover overhead costs and provide a good profit.

Most of Tipografia Stanca's work was done on the basis of predetermined contract prices. In bidding on these jobs, Mr. Cattani applied his standard pricing formula to his own estimates of the amount of labor and paper stock the job would require. He prided himself on his ability to make these estimates, but he sometimes quoted a price that was higher or lower than the formula price, depending on his judgment of the market situation.

Stanca's production procedures were fairly simple. When a customer's order was received, it was assigned a production order number and a production order was issued. The material to be printed, known as the customer's copy, was given to a copy editor who indicated on the copy the sizes and styles of type that should be used. The editor sometimes made changes in the copy, usually after telephoning the customer to discuss the changes.

Once the customer's material had been copy-edited, it was sent to the composing room, where it was set in type. A proof copy was printed by hand and returned to the copy editor, who checked the printed copy against the original. Any errors in the proof were indicated in the margin and the marked proof was sent to the customer for approval. At this point the customer might decide to make changes in the copy, and these changes, as well as corrections of type-setting errors, were made as soon as the corrected proof was returned to the composing room.

In some cases a second proof was sent to the customer for his approval, but at Tipografia Stanca most orders were sent to the pressroom as soon

---

* Copyright 1968 by l'Institut pour l'Etude des Méthodes de Direction de l'Entreprise (IMEDE), Lausanne, Switzerland, revised and updated in 1976. Published by permission. The figures have been restated in dollars for convenience.

as the customer's corrections had been made and the second proof had been approved by the copy editor.

At this point, the order was ready for production on one of the presses in the pressroom. Printing instructions were contained in the production order, which specified the particular press to be used; the number of copies to be printed; the color, size, style, weight and finish of the stock or paper to be used; and similar details. Copies were then printed, bound, and packaged for delivery to the customer.

An order could take as little as one day in the copy-editing and composing-room stages or as long as several weeks. Printing, binding, and packaging seldom took more than two days except on very large production runs of multipage booklets.

For many years the shop had had enough work to keep it busy steadily throughout the year, without serious seasonal slack. As a result, Tipografia Stanca's before-tax profit had fluctuated between 13 and 15 percent of net sales. The interim profit report for the first half of 1968 therefore came as a great shock to Mr. Cattani. Although volume was slightly greater than in the first half of 1967, profit was down to 8.8 percent of sales, an all-time low. The comparison, with all figures expressed as percentages of net sales, was as follows:

	1968	1967
Net sales	100.0%	100.0%
Production costs	77.6	72.3
Selling and administrative costs	13.6	13.9
Profit	8.8	13.8

Mr. Pareto knew that the company's problem must be either low prices or excessive costs. Unfortunately, the cost data already available told him little about the cost-price relationship for individual jobs. Tipografia Stanca's operating costs were classified routinely into 20 categories, such as salaries, pressroom wages, production materials, depreciation, and so forth. Individual job cost sheets were not used and the cost of goods in process was estimated only once a year, at the end of the fiscal year.

Detailed data were available on only two kinds of items: paper stock issued and labor time. When stock was issued, a requisition form was filled out, showing the kind of stock issued, the quantity, the unit cost, and the production order number. Similar details were reported when unused stock was returned to the stockroom.

As for labor, each employee directly engaged in working on production orders filled in a time sheet each day, on which he recorded the time he started on a given task, the time he finished it or moved on to other work, and (in the case of time spent directly on a specific production order) the order number. His department number and pay grade were recorded on the time sheet by the payroll clerk.

Mr. Pareto's first step was to establish some overall cost relationships. Employees, for example, fell into three different pay grades, with the following regular hourly wage rates:

Grade	Rate
1	$6
2	4
3	3

These rates applied to a regular work week of 44 hours a week. For work in excess of this number of hours, employees were paid an overtime premium of 50 percent of their hourly wage. Overtime premiums were negligible when the work load was light, but in a normal year they averaged about 5 percent of the total amount of hourly wages computed at the regular hourly wage rate. In a normal year this was approximately 20 cents a direct labor hour.

In addition to their wages, the employees also received various kinds of benefits, including vacation pay, health insurance, and old-age pensions. The cost of these benefits to Tipografia Stanca amounted to about 70 percent of direct labor cost, measured at regular straight-time hourly rates. The overtime premiums didn't affect the amount of fringe benefits paid or accrued.

Mr. Pareto estimated that all other shop overhead costs—that is, all copy department, composing room and pressroom costs other than direct

TABLE 1

Partial List of Materials Requisitions
(for the week of October 5–9)

Req. No.	Job No.	Amount*
4058	A-467	$150
R162	A-469	(10)
4059	A-467	30
4060	A-442	3
R163	A-455	(5)
R164	A-472	(4)
4060	A-467	18
R165	A-465	(6)
4062	A-467	48
4063	A-471	160
4064	A-473	132
4065	A-458	11
R166	A-467	(16)
4066	A-481	88

* Amounts in parentheses are returned materials.

materials, direct labor, overtime premiums, and employee benefits on direct labor payrolls—would average $2 a direct labor hour in a normal year.

Armed with these estimates of general relationships, Mr. Pareto then proceeded to determine the costs of several recent production orders. One of these was order A–467. This was received for copy editing on Monday, October 5 and delivered to the customer on Friday, October 9. Mr. Cattani had quoted a price of $900 on this job in advance, on the basis of an estimate of $240 for paper stock costs and 45 direct labor hours. All requisitions and time records relating to order A–467 are included in the lists in Tables 1 and 2. (To save space, some of the details shown on the requisitions and time tickets have been omitted from these tables.)

a.   Develop a costing rate or rates for labor costs, to be used to charge a job cost sheet or factory overhead account for an hour of labor time. You must decide whether to use a single rate for all pay grades or a separate rate for each. You must also decide whether to include various kinds of fringe benefit costs in the labor costing rates or to

TABLE 2

Partial Summary of Labor Time Sheets
(for the week of October 5–9)

Employee No.	Pay Grade	Dept.	Job No.*	Hours
14...............	2	Copy	A-463	6.6
14...............	2	Copy	A-467	1.4
15...............	1	Copy	A-467	3.3
15...............	1	Copy	—	2.7
15...............	1	Copy	A-467	8.8
18...............	3	Press	A-467	4.0
18...............	3	Press	A-472	4.6
22...............	1	Composing	A-455	3.8
22...............	1	Composing	A-467	8.4†
22...............	1	Composing	—	1.5
23...............	2	Press	A-458	3.4
23...............	2	Press	A-467	4.7
23...............	2	Press	—	1.1
23...............	2	Press	A-459	2.5†
24...............	2	Copy	A-470	7.4
28...............	1	Press	A-467	7.0
28...............	1	Press	A-458	1.0
31...............	3	Press	—	8.0
33...............	1	Composing	A-471	7.6
33...............	1	Composing	A-472	4.2
40...............	2	Press	A-469	3.6
40...............	2	Press	A-467	4.9
40...............	2	Press	—	0.2
43...............	1	Press	A-467	3.5
43...............	1	Press	A-481	5.8

* A dash indicates time spent on general work in the department
and not on any one job.
† Employee No. 22 worked six hours of overtime during the week,
none of them on job A-467, while employee No. 23 worked eight hours of
overtime, including four hours spent on job A-467.

regard these as overhead. Also develop an overhead rate for use in charging shop overhead costs to individual job orders.

b. Prepare a job order cost sheet for production order A–467, and enter the costs that would be assigned to this order, using the costing rates you developed in the answer to (a) above.

c. What conclusions might Mr. Pareto have reached on the basis of his analysis of this order? What suggestions would you make to Mr. Cattani?

d. What could be the advantages of developing product unit costs routinely for every job? Do you think that these advantages would be great enough to persuade Mr. Cattani to hire an additional clerk for this purpose at an annual cost of about $10,000?

3

Cost Behavior and Decisions

MANAGEMENT's decisions determine how the organization's resources are to be used. The cost figures supplied to management for this purpose must be estimates of the effects of those decisions on the costs that will prevail during the period affected by the decisions—that is, future costs.

Product costs assembled by the methods described in Chapter 2 are intended to measure the costs that were necessary to provide operating capacity and to manufacture the product. The same methods also can be used to prepare estimates of what individual products will cost in the future. For some decisions, however, and for some control purposes, management may need to define cost differently. To see why this is so, we need to examine two questions:

1.   What kinds of costs are relevant to management's decisions?
2.   How do costs relate to variations in the rate at which the organization's facilities are used?

COSTS FOR MANAGERIAL DECISIONS

To prepare estimates of costs for managerial decisions, the accountant needs to understand how management will use these figures. In the following pages we shall take our first look at this question. Specifically, we shall look at six decision-oriented concepts:

1.   The benchmark alternative.
2.   Cash flows.
3.   Differential costs.
4.   Different costs for different decisions.
5.   Sunk costs.
6.   Opportunity costs.

61

The Benchmark Alternative

A decision is always a choice among the alternative courses of action available to the decision maker. The effects of a decision therefore are *differential* effects—that is, the differences between the results of the chosen alternative and those of a rejected alternative.

One way to identify the differences among alternatives is to list them all, tabulate the total results anticipated under each one, and see which one seems likely to be best. There is nothing wrong with this except that it is apt to be cumbersome. Analysts at General Motors, for example, would be very unlikely to justify a proposal to rent an additional office copying machine by estimating General Motors' total profit with and without the machine.

A more manageable approach is to measure all alternatives from some common reference point. Suppose that a castaway on a desert island was deciding which sand dune to sleep on. He wanted to pick the highest dune. He found that dune A was 6 feet above the waterline. After exploring the coastline for several hours, he located dune B, which was 8 feet out of the water. He chose dune B and woke up in a foot of water. The trouble was that he measured dune A at high tide and dune B when the tide was out (see Exhibit 3–1). The moral, of course, is that measurements from different reference points are not comparable.

Although any common reference point will do, we often find it convenient to designate one alternative as the *benchmark alternative*. The figures given for each of the other alternatives then will measure differences from this benchmark. Our preference is to choose as a benchmark an action management will take if none of the others is approved. This helps make it clear what the decision is all about.

For example, Mr. David England, president of the Peerless Spring Company, was evaluating a proposal to add a newly designed window catch to his company's product line. Peerless Spring manufactured a line of household and industrial hardware products. It had a strong distribution organization, but intensified competition had cut into its sales volume, leaving the company with substantial idle productive capacity. Since the company was investor-owned, it operated with a profit objective—that is, its management was expected to take actions that would bring in more resources than they consumed. Mr. England

EXHIBIT 3–1

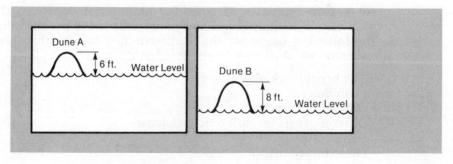

therefore had to consider the impact of his decision on the firm's profits.

Mr. England recognized three alternatives that the company might adopt:

1. Reject the offer and continue operating with the existing product line.
2. Use the company's regular sales organization to offer the new product to Peerless Spring's present customers.
3. Set up a new sales force to market the new product.

He designated the first of these as the benchmark alternative. If he rejected the proposal, in either of its forms, he was perfectly willing to continue operating with his existing product line. In other words, the profitability of the second and third alternatives was to be measured by the *differences* between the results under these alternatives and the results under the alternative of continuing the existing operation.

Using Cash Flows to Measure Decision Effects

In comparing alternatives, the most crucial question is how to measure the effects of differences between them. Since Peerless Spring had a profit objective, the logical solution would seem to be to measure differences in profit. Unfortunately, profit is an ambiguous term. It means an excess of resource inflows over resource outflows, but it doesn't tell us how to measure these quantities.

For decision analysis, profit must be defined in terms of cash flows —that is, the only resource inflows that count are receipts of cash, and the only relevant resource outflows are cash payments. *Net cash flow* is the difference between cash receipts and cash outlays, as diagrammed in Exhibit 3–2.

EXHIBIT 3–2

Cash Flows versus Other Resource Flows

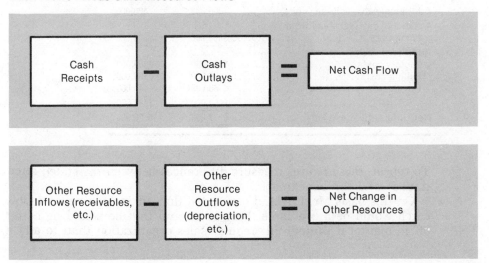

The reason for this emphasis on cash flows is simple. In most circumstances cash is the only resource management can use to get productive goods and services or to reward the shareholders. If the firm doesn't have any cash and can't get some, it can't meet its payroll, no matter how many receivables or how much equipment it has. On the other hand, if the cash is coming in, it can be used to buy materials and pay the employees. Noncash resource outflows, such as depreciation on existing equipment, reduce the income figure for financial reporting, but they don't reduce management's current purchasing power.

Fortunately, the need to use cash flows to define costs and profits for decision purposes doesn't mean we can never use the figures accountants develop for financial accounting, based on the accrual concept. Most of the time these will approximate the cash flows quite closely. We have to be alert, however, to recognize situations in which financial accounting data don't give us what we want, the effect on cash.

Estimating Differential Cash Flows

When we consider the cash flow concept in conjunction with the idea that decisions are based on differences between alternatives, we get the concept of *differential cash flow,* the difference in the company's net cash flow expected to result from choosing one alternative instead of another. This is also referred to as *differential profit* or *incremental profit.*

After choosing his benchmark alternative, for example, Mr. England's next step was to estimate what each of the other two alternatives would *add* to the cash flows from his present operation. After a good deal of study, he and his staff came up with the following estimates of the differential cash flows:

	Use Regular Sales Force	Add Special Salespeople
Additional sales volume (units)..........	300,000	400,000
Additional cash received from customers...........................	$450,000	$600,000
Additional cash payments:		
Factory costs........................	$300,000	$360,000
Selling costs........................	70,000	180,000
Royalties...........................	30,000	40,000
Total...........................	$400,000	$580,000
Net Differential Cash Flow..............	$ 50,000	$ 20,000

To repeat, these figures measure differences between the stated alternatives and the benchmark.

On this basis Mr. England concluded that adding the new window catch would be a profitable thing to do and that he would be better off to market it through his regular sales organization than to add a

EXHIBIT 3–3

Steps in Profit-Based Decision Analysis

1. Define the problem or opportunity to be examined.
2. Identify the actions that might be taken—these are known as the *alternatives.*
3. Select a *benchmark alternative* to serve as a point of reference for the others.
4. For each alternative estimate the *differences* in *net cash flows* from those likely to arise under the benchmark alternative.
5. Identify the alternative with the greatest anticipated net cash inflow (or lowest net cash outflow).

specialized sales force. The steps he followed in reaching this conclusion are summarized in Exhibit 3–3.

Notice that we have not said how much money Peerless Spring was making or losing on its existing operations. That was irrelevant. Our only concern was whether the company could improve things by taking on the new product. This was the inevitable result of Mr. England's decision to use a benchmark alternative. A benchmark alternative, *by definition,* is a course of action management is willing to take if it can find nothing better to do. The question of what to do with the existing operations was decided when management agreed to use continued operations as the benchmark alternative. If management is now unhappy with this alternative, it should reopen the issue and see whether other possible alternatives would be better.

Turning Averages into Differentials

The costs that enter the calculation of differential cash flow are *differential costs,* also known as *incremental costs.* Differential cost is the difference in total cash outflow that will result from selecting one alternative instead of another.

Differential costs are likely to be very different from the costs emerging from costing systems of the kind described in Chapter 2. For example, Peerless Spring is now operating its factory 3,000 direct labor hours a week, far less than the plant's capacity. Another firm is having difficulty fulfilling a large government contract and has asked Peerless Spring to assemble 400 door panels a month for the next six months at a price of $60 each.

The factory accountants have prepared the following estimates of manufacturing costs for the door panels:

	Unit Cost	Total Cost (400 Panels)
Direct materials................	$30	$12,000
Direct labor (3 hours per panel)........................	18	7,200
Factory overhead ($5 per direct labor hour)............	15	6,000
Total factory cost........	$63	$25,200

The $5 hourly overhead figure is the overhead rate in Peerless's assembly department, where the work will be done.

Knowing that some factory overhead costs would not increase if the door panel contract were taken on, Mr. England asked the accountants to prepare a new cost estimate, reflecting average cost at the new production volume. They came up with the following figures:

	Anticipated Volume	Anticipated Volume +400 Panels
Number of direct labor hours...........................	3,000	4,200
Total factory overhead.............	$15,000	$16,800
Average factory overhead per direct labor hour.............	$ 5	$ 4
Average factory overhead per panel......................	$15	$12

The addition of panel assembly to the present work load thus would reduce average overhead cost per hour from $5 to $4, a reduction of $1 an hour and $3 for each panel. Using this new rate, the accountants reduced their estimate of the total cost of the panels from $63 to $60, just equal to the $60 quoted price.

EXHIBIT 3–4

Differential Factory Overhead Costs of Door Panel Production

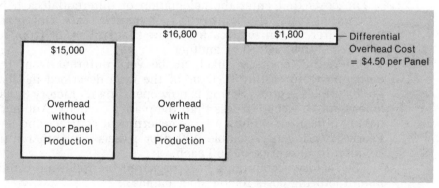

Neither of these cost figures measures the differential cost of taking on the new business. We have no reason to question the relevance of the direct labor and direct materials costs here, but differential factory overhead cost is very different from the average. It amounts to $1,800, or $4.50 a panel, as shown in Exhibit 3–4. The total differential cost thus comes to $21,000, calculated as follows:

	Total	Per Panel
Direct materials....................	$12,000	$30.00
Direct labor.......................	7,200	18.00
Factory overhead..................	1,800	4.50
Total differential cost........	$21,000	$52.50

This shows that the company can take on this business and add $60 − $52.50 = $7.50 to its profits for each panel it assembles. The differential profit from 400 panels will amount to $3,000 a month.

Different Costs for Different Purposes

The concepts of differential cost and differential profit apply to all resource allocation decisions. Should we take on more business? Should we expand the plant? Should we withdraw a product from the market? Each of these requires a different definition of what is differential, however. No part of the plant manager's salary is a differential cost in a decision to accept an order for 400 door panels, but it certainly is a differential cost if management is considering closing the plant.

Differences, in other words, relate to specific decisions and specific sets of alternatives. The motto, different costs for different purposes, should be emblazoned on every cost accountant's office wall. Accountants, when asked what something costs, should refuse to answer until they find out how the figure is to be used. They should also recognize that contract costing and inventory measurement for public financial reporting require cost figures that may be totally irrelevant to many kinds of decisions management may have to make. Still another set of figures may be needed for internal control reporting. We shall try to make these distinctions clear as we go along.

Sunk Costs

A term frequently used in decision analysis is *sunk cost*. Although some people use the term differently, we prefer to define sunk cost as any cost that will be unaffected by the decision to be made.[1] For any given decision, all costs can be divided into two classes—sunk costs and differential costs.

The amounts paid in the past to buy a plot of land are sunk costs. Nothing management can do now can change that amount. The same is true of costs that have already been incurred to develop a new product that management is now considering placing on the market.

[1] Our distinctions are derived from Joel Dean, *Managerial Economics* (Englewood Cliffs, N.J.: Prentice-Hall, Inc., 1951), chap. 5. Some accountants use the term in a narrower sense, to describe costs that represent cash flows of previous periods, but we see no need for a term to describe this class of costs. They form a special subclass of sunk costs.

Even the plant manager's salary is a sunk cost in an analysis of whether to take on another order. In other words, the term is used to identify costs that are irrelevant to a particular decision. "These costs are sunk, and we don't need to consider them."

Opportunity Cost

Proposals sometimes call for the use of resources the company already controls. No cash outlay has to be made to obtain them. They have a differential cost, however, measured by the net cash inflow that will be lost if they are diverted from their best alternative use. This differential cost is known as the *opportunity cost* of these resources. It is the value of an opportunity foregone. It belongs in the analysis because *an action that eliminates a cash inflow is exactly equivalent to an action that requires a cash outflow*. The effect on the company's cash position is identical.

For example, a variety chain paid $500,000 ten years ago for a plot of land as a site for a shopping center. Uncertainty as to state highway relocation plans forced management to postpone the project, and the land has lain idle ever since. The route of the new highway has now been established, and the company is again considering the possibility of using the land as a shopping center site.

The original purchase price of the land is a sunk cost, irrelevant to the decision. The shopping center proposal must be charged for the land, however, because building the shopping center would prevent the company from using it to generate cash in other ways. If we find that the land can be sold for a net price of $800,000, after deducting all commissions, fees, and taxes, and if the chain has no other use for the land, then $800,000 is its opportunity cost for the purpose of this decision. This amount should be included among the cash outflows required by the shopping center proposal.

We wouldn't need the opportunity cost concept if we always listed all the alternatives available to the decision maker. In the illustration we could simply have labeled one alternative "build shopping center" and another "sell land." We can't always do this easily, however, as we saw when we were discussing the benchmark alternative. The owned resources to be incorporated into a particular project are often a small part of the total project, and several such resources may be involved. A full set of alternatives would include one for each possible combination of resource uses, and the number could get so large as to be unwieldy. The better procedure ordinarily is to compute an opportunity cost for each resource.

SHORT-TERM COST-VOLUME RELATIONSHIPS

Many resource allocation decisions focus on management's efforts to use existing capacity profitably. Increasing or decreasing the amount of capacity takes time, and in the meantime management must try to do its best with what it has.

The Peerless Spring Company, for example, decided to produce door panels because this seemed more profitable than letting the factory remain partially idle. It came to this conclusion only after studying how its costs, particularly its factory overhead costs, would be affected by a decision to operate its factory more fully. Our next task is to try to find out how costs are likely to respond to decisions of this kind.

We shall begin by assuming that all costs can be divided into two categories, fixed and variable. While this oversimplifies things, the distinction is a useful one and is as good a place to start as any. With this behind us, we shall move on to a number of related concepts: (1) semivariable costs; (2) marginal costs; (3) the straight-line approximation; and (4) the relationship of cost variability to the measurement of differential cost.

Variable Costs

All organizations engage in *responsive activities*—that is, activities imposed on a responsibility center by activities outside it. Manufacturing is a responsive activity, meeting demands arising out of marketing activities. Preparing payrolls is a responsive activity, meeting demands arising out of all the firm's activities.

Some costs of responsive activities go up or down almost automatically in response to small changes in operating volume. Operating volume, or *level of activity*, is the rate at which resources are used (pounds of material per hour) or at which goods or services are produced (meals served per week). Any cost that must be increased if the firm is to achieve a small increase in the level of activity is a *variable cost*.

One possible pattern of variability is illustrated in Exhibit 3–5. The lines in both charts in this exhibit represent a cost that changes in direct proportion to changes in volume. A good example is a royalty or commission payment calculated by multiplying the number of units sold by a constant amount per unit. As the diagram in the upper portion of Exhibit 3–5 shows, this amounts to zero when volume is zero and rises in a straight line as volume increases. The average variable cost per unit remains constant, as the lower chart shows.

Another possible pattern of variation is reflected in the following figures:

Volume	Total Variable Cost
1	$ 5.00
2	9.00
3	12.00
4	15.00
5	18.00
6	21.00
7	24.50
8	29.20
9	36.00
10	46.00

EXHIBIT 3–5

Proportionately Variable Costs

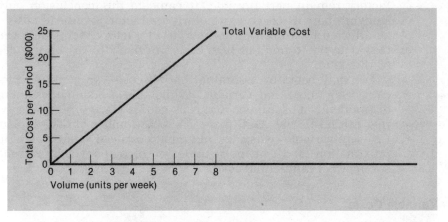

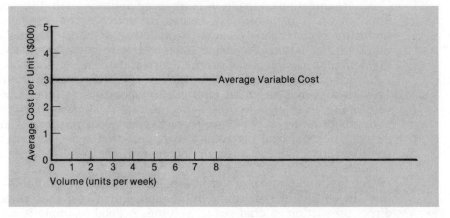

The variable cost of producing the first unit is $5. The second unit adds $4 to the total, and the third, fourth, fifth and sixth add $3 each. Total variable cost starts up more sharply again with the seventh unit, which adds $3.50 to the total. The eighth unit adds another $4.70, and so on.

This pattern is illustrated in Exhibit 3–6. The total cost rises sharply as volume moves up in the lower portion of the volume range, then rises more gradually as volume achieves normal operating levels, and finally rises sharply again as operations begin to approach the limits of existing capacity.

The diagram at the bottom shows the same set of cost estimates expressed as averages instead of as totals. Average cost is high at low volumes while total cost is rising sharply. Average cost falls as the increase in total cost becomes more gradual. Finally, after total variable cost begins to rise more steeply as volume approaches capacity, average variable cost begins to rise.

EXHIBIT 3–6

Progressively Variable Costs

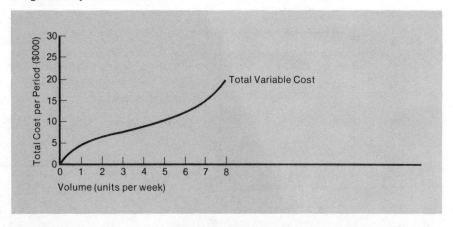

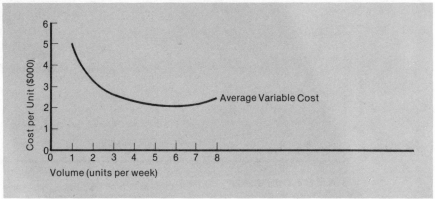

Fixed Costs: Responsive Activities

Costs that do not change as a necessary result of small changes in volume are known as *fixed costs*. Some of these are the fixed costs of responsive activities, also known as *capacity costs*. They are the costs of the resources used to provide or maintain current operating capacity. As we said at the beginning, capacity is likely to remain relatively constant during the planning period. This means that average capacity cost per unit will decline as the use of capacity increases. A cost that amounts to $4,200 a week, no matter what the operating volume, will average $2,100 a unit if volume is two units a week or $420 a unit if volume is ten units.

This is illustrated in Exhibit 3–7. With total fixed costs of $4,200 a week, average fixed cost falls from $4,200 at a weekly volume of one unit to $525 at a volume of eight units a week. In other words, average fixed cost usually falls as volume increases within capacity limits. Average variable cost, as we have already seen, is likely to remain

EXHIBIT 3–7

Fixed Costs

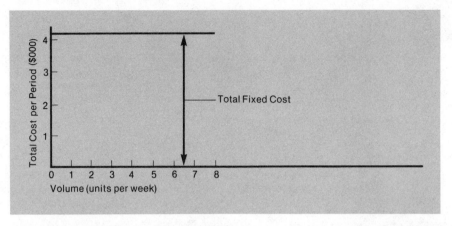

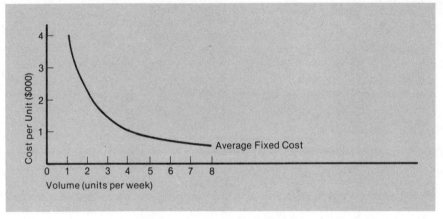

constant or increase. This means that average total cost—fixed costs plus variable costs—will fall as long as average variable cost remains constant or as long as the reduction in average fixed cost exceeds any increase in average variable cost.

Capacity costs can be classified further into standby costs and enabling costs. *Standby costs* are those that will continue to be incurred if operations or facilities are shut down temporarily. Examples are depreciation, property taxes, and some executive salaries. *Enabling costs* are those that can be avoided by a temporary shutdown but must be incurred if operations are to take place.

Some enabling costs are likely to be constant over the entire output range; others are apt to vary in steps, as diagrammed in Exhibit 3–8. For example, one departmental supervisor may be adequate for single-shift operation, but operation of a second shift will require a second supervisor.

EXHIBIT 3–8

Step-Variable Capacity Costs

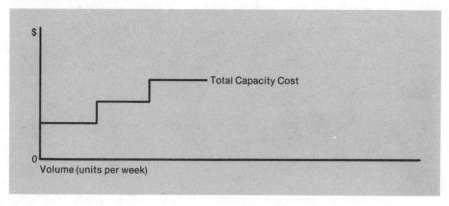

Step-variable capacity costs are classified by economists as variable costs. Executives and accountants classify them as fixed if the steps are wide, as in Exhibit 3–8. The basic block of fixed costs provides the capacity to operate at volumes up to the limit of the first step. When fixed costs move up to the next level, they provide more capacity, enough to support operating volumes up to the limit of the next step. To get still more capacity, a third batch of fixed costs must be incurred.

Some steps are narrower than these because the fixed costs are more divisible than in this diagram. The salary costs of a billing department with 15 billing clerks, for example, are divisible into at least 15 steps. If costs are this divisible, they may be averaged out for most analytical purposes and treated as part of the variable costs.

Fixed Costs: Programmed Activities

Every organization has a second group of fixed costs, fundamentally different from the first. These are the costs of *programmed activities*, undertaken at management's initiative to meet objectives other than meeting demands for service imposed on the organization from the outside. Research and development are programmed activities; so is sales promotion; so are methods improvement studies.

Programmed activities determine the organization's scope and direction. Some of them are *innovative*, designed to enable the organization to change the way it operates—by developing new products, acquiring other firms, improving operating methods, and so forth. Others are *promotional*, intended to stimulate demands for the organization's goods and services—most selling activities fall in this category.

Programmed activities are very different from responsive activities. Responsive activities are more or less imposed on the organization by

EXHIBIT 3–9

Types of Fixed Costs

Capacity costs	Provide or maintain the capacity to produce or sell
Standby costs	Continue even after temporary shutdown
Enabling costs	Necessary if facilities are operated; may vary in steps
Programmed costs (also discretionary costs, managed costs)	Carry out programmed promotional and innovative activities

the success of its programmed activities. The costs of responsive activities must adapt to changes in volume if the organization is to meet its commitments; the costs of programmed activities need not go up if responsive activities expand.

The costs of programmed activities are known by many names, including programmed costs, discretionary costs, and managed costs (see Exhibit 3–9). They tend to be budgeted at constant levels for individual time periods. Once the budget is set, programmed costs per unit will be low if volume is high and high if volume is low. The size of the programmed cost budget, however, should be determined on the basis of estimates of the effectiveness of these costs in achieving management's goals. If an increase in budgeted spending seems likely to increase volume by a larger percentage than the increase in spending, average cost will fall. If additional spending produces a less than proportional increase in volume, however, average cost will rise. This is illustrated in the following table:

Total Programmed Cost	Volume Achieved	Average Programmed Cost
$10...........	50	$0.20
20...........	125	0.16
30...........	200	0.15
40...........	250	0.16
50...........	280	0.18
60...........	300	0.20
70...........	310	0.23

Semivariable Costs

Some costs don't fit neatly into either the fixed cost or the variable cost category. We shall refer to these as semivariable costs. Many patterns of variability are possible. Three of these are illustrated in

EXHIBIT 3–10

Semivariable Costs

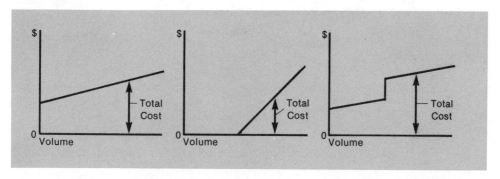

Exhibit 3–10. The first chart might represent the cost of equipment maintenance. The amount varies with the rate at which the equipment is used, but some maintenance is necessary even if the equipment is not used at all. This kind of cost has both fixed and variable components.

The second chart is a picture of the costs of overtime work. Overtime premiums are likely to be very small for large parts of the possible operating range. They begin when the operating rate starts to approach capacity and rise sharply from then on.

The third chart is a diagram of the costs of inspecting the output of an assembly line that can be run either one shift or two shifts a day. Each shift has a salaried inspector and a variable number of assistants who are paid according to the number of hours they work. As the factory moves to a second shift, the fixed component of cost (the inspectors' salaries) jumps up. Like the costs in the first chart, this cost element includes both fixed and variable components.

Marginal Cost

Accountants are interested not only in total costs but also in the change in cost as volume moves from one level to another. The increase in total cost that results from increasing the volume of activity by one unit per period is known as the *marginal cost*.

If there are no steps either in the fixed costs or in the semivariable costs, then marginal cost will be measured by the change in total variable cost. If total variable cost moves along a straight line, so that average variable cost is constant, each additional unit will have the same variable cost as the one before. In other words, marginal cost will be constant and equal to average variable cost. This is diagrammed in Exhibit 3–11. If the slope of the total cost line is flat, the marginal cost will be small. If the total cost line is steep, marginal cost will be high.

Marginal costs will not trace a straight line if fixed costs move up

EXHIBIT 3–11

Constant Marginal Cost

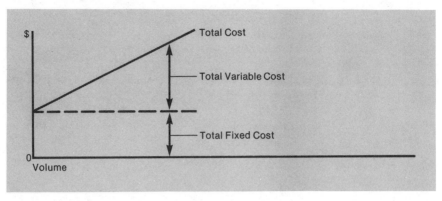

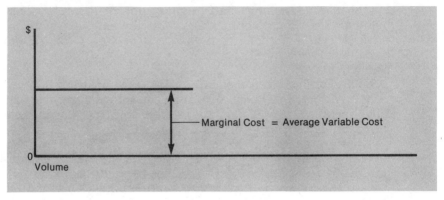

in steps or if average variable cost changes with volume. Exhibit 3–12 shows two possibilities. In the chart at the top, marginal cost remains constant for most of the output range, then begins to rise at volume X as volume begins to approach existing capacity limits. A diagram of total costs would show total costs sloping upward to the right in a straight line until volume X, then sloping upward more and more sharply as volume moved up beyond that point.

The bottom chart represents a factory that can run either one, two, or three shifts. Marginal cost remains constant through most of the output range of single-shift operations, begins to rise at volume X, and continues to rise until it gets high enough to make a second shift more economical. Marginal cost is higher for second shift operations than for the first shift, but it remains steady until volume Y is reached, when it begins another upward climb. And so on. Each of the three shifts follows the same cost pattern. A total cost curve here would rise gradually in a straight line at first, then rise more steeply through the second shift and more steeply still for third shift operations.

The concept of marginal cost has no meaning in connection with

EXHIBIT 3–12

Rising Marginal Cost

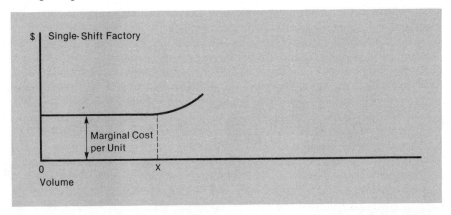

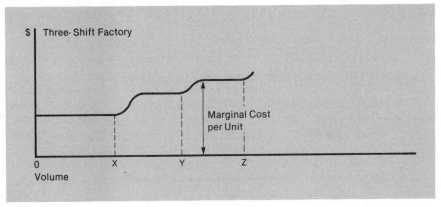

programmed costs unless they are truly contingent on sales revenues. Marginal costs measure the effects of increasing volume; most programmed costs don't change as a direct result of changes in volume. Marginal cost therefore consists of increments in the costs of responsive activities, together with any increments in the volume-contingent costs of programmed activities. The only programmed costs that are truly contingent on volume are sales commissions.

The Straight-Line Approximation

When called upon to draw a line representing total costs at various volumes, most business executives would probably draw a straight line like the one in the first diagram in Exhibit 3–11. This doesn't means that executives really believe that average variable cost will be the same at all operating volumes from zero to full capacity. They know that capacity operations are likely to put pressure on costs. They are also convinced, however, that a straight line is a reasonable

EXHIBIT 3–13

A Practical Approximation of the Cost Function

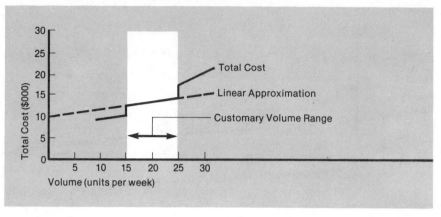

approximation to the true cost-volume relationship within the range of volume in which the company is likely to operate.

Exhibit 3–13 shows what the business executive is really doing. The solid line shows how costs are expected to vary with volume. Most of the time, however, the company will be operating somewhere in the wide portion of the range in which costs rise steadily, in a straight line. The fixed costs of operating in this range include not only the standby costs but also the enabling costs, including the step that takes place at a volume of about 15 units a week.

Rather than complicate the chart with information on expected cost behavior outside the customary range, executives are likely to draw only the dashed line. They could just as well have cut off both ends of the total cost line, leaving only the straight section in the middle. The purpose is to identify the rate at which costs are likely to vary within this crucial portion of the output range.

INTERPRETING COST BEHAVIOR FOR DIFFERENTIAL COSTING

Information about cost variability helps us convert job costing data into estimates of differential costs. This is not just a matter of separating the fixed costs from the variable costs, however. Some fixed costs may be differential costs for some decisions; some variable costs may not be differential costs for others. To emphasize this point, let's see how data from job costing records can be converted to estimates of differential cost in three different decision situations:

1.   Accepting a special order.
2.   Making or buying a component part.
3.   Rationing scarce capacity.

Special Order Decision

The variable costs are likely to be the only differential costs in decisions representing choices between two alternatives differing only slightly in the amount of capacity used. Decisions to accept or refuse one-time orders are typical examples.

For most of these decisions, differential cost can be measured by the costs of factory direct labor, direct materials, and the variable portion of factory overhead. We shall return in later chapters to other methods of estimating the variability of overhead costs. At this point we suggest listing the various elements of overhead in each cost center affected by the decision, estimating the average rate of variability for each.

For example, management is considering a possible order for 100 units of hydrogenated widgets to be manufactured in department X. The first step is to list all the overhead costs in that department in a normal month, and classify them by their estimated variability:

Supervision..........	$2,700	all fixed
Indirect labor.........	3,000	all variable
Supplies.............	500	all variable
Power...............	800	all variable
Depreciation.........	400	all fixed
Other................	600	half variable
Total..........	$8,000	

The second step is to estimate the average rate of variability. In this case, normal volume is 2,000 direct labor hours a month, and the average is calculated as follows:

Indirect labor.....................	$3,000
Supplies.........................	500
Power...........................	800
Other............................	300
Total variable..............	$4,600

$$\text{Average variable overhead} = \$4,600/2,000 = \$2.30 \text{ an hour}$$

The final step is to estimate the direct inputs and add the overhead component. Each widget requires $8 of direct materials and 0.3 direct labor hour at a wage rate of $8 an hour. For 100 widgets, the estimated incremental costs are as follows:

Direct materials..........................	$ 800
Direct labor: 30 hours at $8..............	240
Variable overhead: 30 hours at $2.30......	69
Total differential cost..............	$1,109

The average differential cost therefore is $11.09 a unit. If the estimates prove to be correct, any price higher than this will be profitable.

Four footnotes should be added very quickly, before these comments can be misunderstood:

1. Fixed costs *may* be affected, even by decisions as limited in scope as this one—for example, this order may require a great deal of special design work, beyond the capacity of the present design department.
2. Some of the variable costs may not be differential costs—for example, the order may use materials that otherwise would merely deteriorate, or it may provide work for employees who otherwise would remain on the payroll with nothing to do.
3. If many of these decisions are made in any given period, management must consider their cumulative effect—for example, accepting ten orders like this one may require hiring an additional supervisor.
4. Calculating differential cost does not mean that price should be set at or near this level—the cost figure merely gives management one element in the pricing equation, and many other factors must be considered.

We shall return to the use of costs in pricing decisions in Chapter 16.

Make or Buy Decision

The same approach can be used if the decision seems likely to affect fixed costs. For example, suppose the company in our last illustration has been buying its requirements of a certain material at a price of $3 a pound. Its consumption of this material has been going up and is expected to average 10,000 pounds a month next year. The question is whether to make this in the company's own plant.

Most make or buy decisions include decisions on investments in new production facilities, so that the cash flows are spread over several planning periods. This raises a more complex set of issues that we are not yet ready to deal with. To avoid these, let's assume here that the company has enough space and enough equipment to manufacture this material, and that the factory engineers have estimated the manufacturing cost as follows:

Direct materials...................... $0.90
Direct labor (0.2 hours)................   1.60
Factory overhead (0.2 hours × $4)......   0.80
      Total........................... $3.30

The factory overhead figure is based on the overhead rate in department S, where the material would be made. This rate was derived from the figures we presented earlier: $8,000 of overhead divided by 2,000 direct labor hours equals $4 a direct labor hour. Once again we need to break this down to estimate the differential costs:

Variable costs.................... $2.30 an hour

Fixed costs per month:
Supervision.................... $2,700
Depreciation..................   400
Other.........................   300
    Total...................... $3,400

We must be alert to the possibility that the introduction of a new operation like this will change the rate at which the variable cost elements vary. Materials handling requirements, for example, may be very different from those of the department's other products. In the present case, however, the engineers believe the $2.30 rate can be used for the new material as well.

Differential fixed overhead costs should be estimated on an element-by-element basis. In this case, supervision costs would go up by $1,200 a month because making the material would require the appointment of an additional quality control inspector. Depreciation is not a cash flow and would be unchanged by this decision anyway. Other departmental fixed overheads would not be affected. The fixed costs of factory administration, purchasing, and other corporate activities would not be affected, either. The estimated monthly differential costs therefore are as follows:

Direct materials: 10,000 × $0.90........... $ 9,000
Direct labor: 10,000 × $1.60............... 16,000
Variable overhead: 10,000 × 0.2 × $2.30....   4,600
Fixed overhead: supervision..............   1,200
    Total.............................. $30,800

> Average.............. $3.08 a pound

In this case differential cost is greater than the cost of outside purchasing. The company should continue to buy the material.

Capacity Rationing Decision

Variable costs may be sunk costs in a different kind of situation from any of those we have discussed so far. A department may not have enough capacity to handle all the work available. When this happens, management has to decide how to ration the available capacity among the various potential uses.

Whatever the decision, capacity is likely to be fully utilized. This means that total overhead costs may be the same, no matter which alternative is chosen. The choice may then depend on the size of the spread between total revenue and the total costs of materials and differential overhead costs in other departments for each alternative.

For example, an hour of direct labor in department X can be used to produce two units of product A or four units of product B. The company could sell 800 units of A and 1,600 units of B, if it had the capacity, but only 400 direct labor hours are available for these two products. At a labor rate of $8 an hour, total direct labor costs will amount to $3,200, no matter which product is manufactured. This means we can ignore them. Furthermore, since overhead costs in department X vary with the number of direct labor hours, they too will be unaffected by the decision. We can ignore them, too.

After collecting estimates of the other cost elements affected by the decision, we can compare these two alternatives as follows:

	Product A	Product B
Costs per unit:		
Direct materials................	$ 1.50	$ 1.25
Differential costs in		
other departments...........	2.00	3.75
Total differential		
cost.....................	$ 3.50	$ 5.00
Unit price.......................	9.25	8.00
Differential		
profit margin.................	$ 5.75	$ 3.00
Maximum production possible...	800 units	1,600 units
Total differential profit...........	$4,600	$4,800

Product B should be manufactured even though its average margin over differential cost (75 cents) is smaller than that of product A.

SUMMARY

Decisions should always be based on estimates of differences among the alternatives available. Only differential or incremental profits are relevant to decisions. Furthermore, the profit differences among alternatives should be measured in terms of the effects of the decisions on the flows of cash into and out of the organization. This means that the accountant must define and measure cost differently for each kind of analysis because different costs will be affected by different kinds of decisions.

One major determinant of cost is operating volume, the rate at which the organization uses its resources. Some costs respond to variations in operating volume within the limits of existing capacity; others either generate volume or maintain the organization's capacity to do business, and do not respond to variations in operating volume. Since fixed costs are assigned to activities by means of averages in job order costing, these costs must be adjusted to make them relevant to decisions in which the average doesn't conform to the increment. We shall return in the next chapter to see how accountants can adapt their methods to provide a more accurate picture of the fixed element of activity costs.

KEY TERMS

The most important terms introduced and defined in this chapter are the following:

Benchmark alternative

Capacity costs

Cash flows

Differential cost

Differential profit

Fixed costs

Incremental cost

Incremental profit

Marginal cost

Opportunity cost

Programmed activities

Responsive activities

Semivariable costs

Step-variable costs

Sunk cost

Variable costs

INDEPENDENT STUDY PROBLEMS
(Solutions in Appendix C)

1. Cost-volume relationships. From the following estimates of total cost at different volumes, compute (a) average total cost, (b) average fixed cost, (c) average variable cost, and (d) marginal cost for each volume of activity. (Note: For this problem assume that fixed cost is the same at all volumes.)

Volume (units)	Cost
0	$10
1	11
2	12
3	13
4	14
5	15
6	16
7	17
8	18
9	20
10	23

2. Using average costs in decisions. The manager of a department in a social welfare agency has proposed the inauguration of a new social service, requiring the addition of 15 social workers to his department's payroll. The costs of other departments in the agency would not be affected by the addition of this new service, except as noted below.

The director of the agency agrees that the social service would fill an important need and that providing it would be consistent with the agency's charter. She can make $200,000 available to finance this service by discontinuing one of the services now being provided by one of the agency's other departments, but will do so only if the new service can be provided for $200,000 or less.

The department head has developed the following figures:

	If the Service Is	
	Provided	Not Provided
Total number of social workers in the department....	25	10
Average cost of the department's operations......	$14,000	$15,500

Calculate differential cost. Should the proposal be approved?

3. Opportunity cost. Nancy Smith bought 100 shares in Hydrophonics, Ltd. on January 15, 19x1, paying $15 a share. She bought an additional 100 shares on March 18, 19x4, paying $20 a share. The market price of this stock fell rapidly in 19x5, reaching a low point of $6 a share. Early in 19x6 the market price had recovered to $8 a share. At that point General Enterprises, Inc., offered to buy all shares tendered to it at a price of $10 a share.

What cost figure should Ms. Smith use in evaluating this offer?

4. Make or buy decision. The purchasing agent of Planette, Inc. has just recommended that the company purchase its requirements of three machine parts that are used in repairing some of the machines in Planette's factory. These parts are now being manufactured in the company's own repair shop.

The purchasing agent has collected the following data to support the recommendation:

Part No.	Estimated Monthly Requirements	Purchase Price per Unit	Manufacturing Cost per Unit			
			Labor	Materials	Overhead	Total
104...........	120 units	$4.00	$2.00	$1.80	$1.51	$ 5.31
173...........	200 units	7.00	3.90	2.30	2.94	9.14
221...........	50 units	8.00	4.80	2.20	3.62	10.62

The factory engineer opposes the purchasing agent's proposal, pointing out that direct labor and direct materials costs are less than the purchase price for each part.

As controller of the company, you have the following additional information:

1. Full-cost overhead rates are used in each factory department, including the repair shop. These are predetermined rates, based on anticipated overhead costs at normal production volume.
2. Production volume in the repair shop is measured by the amount of direct labor cost in that department. Normal volume is $13,000 direct labor cost. If the repair shop continues to manufacture these three parts, its monthly operating volume is expected to average $11,500 in direct labor costs during the coming year.
3. If the parts are purchased, all of the direct labor of manufacturing them can be saved—that is, the total factory payroll will be reduced by this amount.
4. The repair shop's operating costs other than direct labor and direct materials are as follows:

	Direct Labor Cost per Month		
	$10,000	$11,500	$13,000
Overhead:			
Supervision........................	$ 1,200	$ 1,200	$ 1,200
Indirect labor.....................	2,000	2,300	2,600
Indirect materials..................	500	575	650
Service charges....................	3,500	3,575	3,650
Depreciation.......................	800	800	800
Other fixed charges................	900	900	900
Total overhead................	$ 8,900	$ 9,350	$ 9,800
Overhead/direct labor..............	$ 0.890	$ 0.813	$ 0.754

5. None of the present equipment in the shop will be retired if the proposal is accepted because the shop must always be in readiness to perform emergency work. Similarly, the size of the inventory will not be
   affected by this decision.
6. If the proposal is accepted, purchasing and handling costs will be increased by $100 a month for each part it decides to buy.

Prepare a recommendation on this proposal, giving figures to support
your conclusions.

EXERCISES AND PROBLEMS

1. Incremental cost: Special order. The overhead rate of a factory is
$3 a machine-hour, based on estimated costs at a normal operating volume
of 10,000 machine-hours a month. Operating volume is now running at a
rate of 9,000 machine-hours a month and overhead costs at this volume
total $28,800, an average of $3.20 an hour. No change in cost or volume
is in sight unless management accepts the following order.

A customer has offered to buy all of its requirements of a machined part
for the next year. This order would add 1,000 machine-hours a month to
the factory's volume. The price received would exceed the cost of direct
labor and direct materials by $2,900 a month.

Would you use $3.20, $3, or some other figure to estimate overhead cost
for the purpose of deciding whether to accept this order? Give your reasons.
Would you accept the order?

2. Incremental and sunk costs. Last year Mogul Movies, Inc., paid
$300,000 for the screen rights to a novel, *Virtue Is Its Own Reward*. The
film was made earlier this year at a cost of $1 million. This figure in-
cludes $100,000 for depreciation on studio facilities and $250,000 for
costumes and rental charges on equipment used during filming. This
latter amount has not yet been paid, but arrangements have been made
to pay it later this year.

The author of *Virtue Is Its Own Reward* has just been arrested and has
pleaded guilty to a charge of plagiarism. The novel actually was written by
two other people. The real authors will allow the film to be released if
Mogul Movies will pay them $500,000 in cash. Costs of insuring, advertis-
ing, and delivering the films to the theaters will amount to $50,000 if the
film is released.

Top management at Mogul Movies estimates that if the film is released
in its present form, Mogul's share of the theater receipts will be $700,000,
spread out over the next ten months.

a. Classify each of the costs described in this problem as either relevant
   or irrelevant to the decision to release the film.
b. Should the film be released? Show your calculations.

3. Differential unit cost. Franklin Enterprises can ship product A to
a customer for $40. Shipping charges for product B are $30. If both
products are packed together, the total shipping cost is $50. Only one
unit of product B may be packed with each unit of product A.

a. The customer now buys product A but not product B. What cost would
   you use in evaluating the desirability of getting the customer to buy
   product B?
b. Franklin Enterprises ships equal quantities of both products to its

warehouses near the customer at the $50 combined shipping cost. The customer buys only product B, product A being sold to other nearby customers. The customer has found a use for product A and asks for a price quotation. What shipping cost would you use in calculating the profitability of any given price?

4. Average costs in decision making. A factory's costs can be estimated accurately from the following schedule of average hourly cost:

Hours	Cost
4,000	$6.25
4,500	6.11
5,000	6.00
5,500	5.91

The company has a chance to bid on a new job that would add 500 hours a month for two months to the factory's volume. Efficient workers for this job can be obtained without difficulty or loss of efficiency. The job would have no effect on nonfactory costs.

Without this job, the factory would operate at a monthly volume of 4,000 hours. When built, the plant was expected to operate 5,000 hours a month, on the average.

What is the minimum price the company could afford to quote for this job without being worse off?

5. Differential and sunk costs. An oil company has paid a foreign government $4 million for the rights to explore for oil. If oil is found, the agreement calls for the oil company to pay the government $8 for every barrel produced.

The company has spent $3 million on the drilling operation and has just struck oil. Management estimates that it will be able to recover 10 million barrels of oil from this field. This oil can be sold for $10 a barrel and it will cost $1 a barrel to get it out of the ground.

Yesterday the government imposed an additional fee of 60 cents a barrel, to pay for insurance against damages caused by oil spills that might take place in the future.

Should the company begin producing oil? Prepare an analysis to support your recommendation.

6. Marginal cost. The line in each of the following diagrams shows how total cost for one cost element varies with volume. For each of these, indicate whether marginal cost increases with volume, decreases, remains constant, or behaves in some other way:

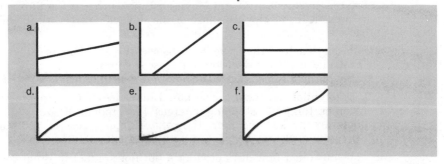

7. Average variable cost. For each of the diagrams in Problem 6, indicate whether average variable cost increases, decreases, remains constant, or follows some other pattern as volume increases.

8. Opportunity cost; special order. As a result of an expansion program, Pasabache Industries has excess capacity which is expected to be absorbed by the domestic market in a few years. Twenty-five thousand excess machine-hours are available for the next year.

It has received inquiries from two firms located abroad. One offers to buy 2 million units of product A at 3.8 cents a unit; the second offers to buy 3 million units of product B at 5 cents a unit. Management has made the following estimates:

	Product A	Product B
Unit costs:		
Variable costs......................	$0.029	$0.042
Fixed costs........................	0.009	0.012
Total costs.....................	$0.038	$0.054
Machine-hours per thousand units....	6	8

One of the two orders will be accepted. Which should it be? Why?

9. Cost-volume relationship. From the following estimates of hourly cost at different hourly volumes, compute (*a*) average total cost, (*b*) average fixed cost, (*c*) average variable cost, and (*d*) marginal cost for each volume of activity. (Note: For this problem assume that fixed cost is the same at all volumes.)

Units	Cost
0..........................	$100
1..........................	200
2..........................	250
3..........................	290
4..........................	330
5..........................	370
6..........................	410
7..........................	450
8..........................	500
9..........................	570
10..........................	670

10. Variations in fixed costs. The following letter was received from a cost accounting student:

Dear Sir:

In your book you say that fixed costs may be affected by changes in the volume of activity. I have had three economics instructors, all of whom have their doctoral degrees, tell me that this definition is incorrect. They argue that if a cost is fixed it does not change. Would you please explain to me this difference of opinion?

Sincerely,

How would you answer this letter?

11. Relevant benchmark; Adding a product. The Downtown Business Institute has two classrooms for which it pays monthly rentals of $800 each. These classrooms are adequate for the three courses that the institute now offers to its students. These three courses make the following monthly profits:

Course	Profit
Bookkeeping........................	$1,600
Typing.............................	1,300
Shorthand.........................	960

Classroom rentals and top management expenses have not been charged to these courses.

Management is thinking of offering a course in computer programming. This could be done in the existing classroom, but only if one of the three current courses were to be discontinued. Additional classroom space is available in the institute's present building, however, and management is trying to decide whether to rent this space and offer the new course.

The additional space can be rented for $1,100 a month. The expected monthly profit from the new programming course is as follows:

Tuition and fees............................		$5,000
Expenses:		
Teaching salaries.........................	$1,400	
Equipment rental........................	400	
Telephone charges.......................	300	
Books and supplies......................	600	
Other....................................	200	
Total expenses........................		2,900
Profit......................................		$2,100

What should the institute do? Cite figures to support your conclusions.

12. Differential cost; Marginal cost. A manufacturing plant operates with a single shift five days a week. It can produce up to 8,000 units of output a week without the use of overtime or extra-shift operation. Fixed costs for single-shift operation amount to $30,000 a week. Average variable cost is a constant $10 a unit at all output rates up to 8,000 units a week. The plant's output can be increased to 12,000 units a week by going on overtime or adding Saturday operations or both. This entails no increase in fixed costs, but the variable cost is $12 a unit for any output in excess of 8,000 units a week up to the 12,000-unit capacity.

The plant also operates a second shift if sales volume warrants, and if second-shift operation is more efficient than overtime or Saturday operation. The maximum capacity of the second shift is 7,000 units a week. The variable cost on the second shift is $10.50 a unit, and operation of a second shift entails additional fixed costs of $4,500 a week.

a. At what operating volume does it become economical to operate a second shift? (Assume that the product cannot be inventoried in any substantial quantities.)

b. Prepare a schedule of marginal cost for output rates ranging from 5,000 units a week to 17,000 units a week, in 1,000-unit intervals, assuming that any overtime or Saturday operations are performed by the first shift.

13. Bidding on a special order. The Argus Company has just received an invitation to quote a price for installing the electrical wiring in a new building. Mr. Jason Argus, the company's president, estimates that this job would require 250 labor hours *each month for two months*. Total materials cost of the job would be $850.

Mr. Argus says that the work force is flexible enough to let him operate at any volume between 2,000 and 2,500 labor hours a month. Volumes in excess of 2,500 labor hours are completely beyond the company's current capacity, because trained personnel are not available and the present work force will not add further to their overtime hours.

Mr. Argus estimates that the company's average operating costs, excluding materials cost, ought to be as follows:

Total Monthly Volume (No. of Labor Hours)	Average Cost per Labor Hour
2,000	$7.92
2,250	7.70
2,500	7.90

Mr. Argus also tells you that all of his other work is priced at $10 a labor hour, plus materials costs.

Assuming that these estimates are correct, calculate the minimum price the company could charge for this job without losing money on it if, without this job, the company would have enough other work to operate at a volume of:

a. 2,000 labor hours a month.
b. 2,250 labor hours a month.
c. 2,500 labor hours a month.

14. Rationing limited capacity. Overhead costs in department Z vary with the quantity of materials processed in the department. The following formula is used to derive estimates of overhead cost:

Department Z overhead cost = $10,000 per month + $1 per pound of materials.

The overhead rate used for product costing is 50 percent of direct labor cost.

The department manufactures several products and is now operating at its full physical capacity of 12,500 pounds of materials each month. The marketing manager has suggested that production of product A be discontinued, to make room for production and sale of a new product, product B. Either product would be processed completely in department Z. The following estimates of monthly costs and revenues have been presented to management:

	Product A	Product B
Materials quantity required	2,500 lbs.	2,500 lbs.
Revenues from sales	$32,000	$28,000
Production costs:		
Direct materials	$ 4,600	$ 5,000
Direct labor	13,000	9,000
Overhead (50% of direct labor)	6,500	4,500
Total production costs	$24,100	$18,500
Profit margin	$ 7,900	$ 9,500

The manufacture of product B would require additional quality control inspection. This would increase fixed factory overhead costs by $900 a month. Adequate quantities of direct labor and direct materials could be obtained for either product; the total size of the labor force can be increased or decreased without penalty.

Selling and administrative expenses will be unaffected by the choice between these two products.

Which of these two products should be manufactured? Present figures to support your conclusion.

15. Using materials on hand. The Jones Company has 2,000 yards of a plastic material on hand; 1,000 yards were purchased at an invoice price of $2 a yard and 1,000 yards were purchased later at an invoice price of $2.20 a yard.

This material deteriorates in storage and if the company does not use or sell its present inventories within the next six weeks they will become worthless.

Some of the inventory could be used to make product A. Each unit of product A requires one yard of the plastic material plus $3 in other incremental costs. A maximum of 500 units of product A could be sold at a price of $5.25 a unit.

The company is also thinking of manufacturing product B. Each unit of B requires one yard of the plastic material plus $4 in other incremental costs.

The Jones Company could sell any quantity of the plastic material for $1.80 a yard. It could also buy additional quantities of this material for $2.40 a yard.

What unit cost would you use in considering a proposal to produce and sell 500 units of product B during the next six weeks? 1,000 units? 1,500 units? 2,000 units? 2,500 units?

(From a problem by Professor Alfred Oxenfeldt)

16. Using available capacity. In March of last year, Alicia Cranshaw was trying to decide what to do. Ms. Cranshaw was the owner-president of Cranshaw Packaging Services, Inc., a small firm located in Bethlehem, Pennsylvania. The Cranshaw firm advised its clients with ideas about how to package their products, worked with clients' personnel to keep packaging equipment operating efficiently and even supplied people and equipment from time to time to do small specialty packaging jobs that clients were not equipped to do themselves.

Ms. Cranshaw's immediate concern was whether to take a job for one of the packaging machines, the AX-40. This machine had been developed by Ms. Cranshaw and one of her engineers several years earlier to provide the company with capacity to wrap regularly packed products in special gift wrappings. It had proved so successful that it was always fully booked during the months of August through mid-November, as clients prepared for the annual holiday trade. It often remained partly idle during the rest of the year, however, because few local companies needed special packaging work in the off season.

Ms. Cranshaw had worked untiringly to find more off-season jobs for the AX-40, but her efforts had been only partly successful. Now two local manufacturers who had never before been Cranshaw clients had expressed an interest in using the machine during the spring months, but only at prices lower than Cranshaw Packaging usually charged. One of these, Maurer Products, Inc., offered to pay $30,000 for the use of the equipment for a period of 35 days. The work would be done by Cranshaw employees in the Cranshaw shop. The other prospect, Franklin Packing Company, wished to use the equipment in its own plant, with its own employees. The contract would be for a 60-day period, including shipping and installation time. Franklin Packing would pay $10,000 plus all costs of transportation and installation, including transport insurance.

No other potential users were in sight, and Ms. Cranshaw thought that if she took on one of these jobs she might make some money and gain a steady customer to boot. Before going ahead, however, she asked Robert

Underwood, her assistant, to work up the costs for the two proposals. Mr. Underwood returned with the following figures:

	Maurer	Franklin
No. of days required...................	35	60
Proposed contract price..............	$30,000	$10,000
Estimated costs:		
Labor...............................	$17,500	$ 100
Supplies............................	2,000	...
Maintenance........................	500	750
Depreciation ($20/day)..............	700	1,200
Amortization of development costs		
($100/day)........................	3,500	6,000
Power..............................	2,100	...
Insurance...........................	100	250
Administrative expenses		
(5 percent of sales)................	1,500	500
Total costs.......................	$27,900	$ 8,800
Profit margin.........................	$ 2,100	$ 1,200

The maintenance cost figures in this table represent the estimated out-of-pocket cost of overhauling and adjusting the machine at the end of the contract. The insurance figures represent the cost of fire, theft, and vandalism insurance. The insurance company charged a higher premium for any day the machine was not on the Cranshaw company's property.

Mr. Underwood reminded Ms. Cranshaw that the costs of developing and building the AX-40 had not yet been completely amortized. For this reason, this machine would remain fairly costly to operate for about two more years.

Only one of these two proposals could be accepted because both customers wanted to use the machine at about the same time. What would you have recommended?

17. Special order. George Jackson operates a small machine shop. He manufactures one standard product which he sells in competition with many other similar businesses and he also manufactures products to customer order. His accountant has prepared the following summary from the annual income statement:

	Custom Sales	Standard Sales	Total
Sales revenues..........	$50,000	$25,000	$75,000
Expenses:			
Material..............	$10,000	$ 8,000	$18,000
Labor................	20,000	9,000	29,000
Depreciation..........	6,300	3,600	9,900
Power................	700	400	1,100
Rent.................	6,000	1,000	7,000
Heat and light........	600	100	700
Miscellaneous........	400	900	1,300
Total expenses....	$44,000	$23,000	$67,000
Income before taxes....	$ 6,000	$ 2,000	$ 8,000

The depreciation charges are for machines used in the respective product lines. The power charge is apportioned on estimates of the amounts of power consumed by each line. The rent is for the building space which has been leased for ten years at $7,000 a year. The rent, heat, and light are apportioned to the product lines based on the amount of floor space occupied. All other costs are directly traceable to the specific product lines.

Power costs for each product line tend to vary with the amount of materials processed for that line. Miscellaneous expenses are half fixed for each product line; the variable portion varies with the labor cost in the line.

A valued customer of custom products has asked Mr. Jackson if he would manufacture 5,000 special units for him. Mr. Jackson is working at capacity and would have to give up some other business in order to take this business. He can't renege on custom orders already agreed to but he could reduce the output of his standard product by about one half for one year while producing the specially requested custom product.

The customer is willing to pay $7 for each custom unit. The material cost would be about $2 a unit and the labor would be $3.60 a unit. Mr. Jackson would have to spend $2,000 for a special device which would be discarded when the job was done.

a. Calculate and present the following costs related to the 5,000 unit custom order:
1. The incremental cost of producing the special units.
2. The opportunity cost of taking the order.
b. Should Mr. Jackson take the order? Explain your answer.

(CMA adapted)

18. Dropping a product. The Bertles Company manufactures a number of products. You have the following data for three of these:

	Dugran	Lorgran	Pilgran
Price........................	$3.80	$6.00	$7.50
Manufacturing cost per unit:			
Direct materials.............	$1.50	$1.75	$3.00
Direct labor................	0.50	0.50	0.75
Overhead...................	1.00	1.00	1.50
Total..................	$3.00	$3.25	$5.25
Direct marketing costs........	$75,000	$775,000	$150,000
Units sold....................	100,000	250,000	50,000

All three products are manufactured with other products in a large factory. A factorywide overhead rate of 200 percent of direct labor cost is used to assign overhead costs to products. Overhead costs in this factory at a direct labor cost of $500,000 a year are as follows:

Supervision.........................	$ 130,000
Indirect labor.......................	120,000
Pensions and payroll taxes..........	150,000
Indirect materials..................	180,000
Power..............................	70,000
Heat and light......................	60,000
Depreciation.......................	50,000
Taxes and insurance................	160,000
Miscellaneous......................	80,000
Total.......................	$1,000,000

You have the following additional information:

1. Other products now use $200,000 a year in direct labor cost.
2. Factory supervision costs will be $25,000 less if total direct labor cost falls below $300,000 a year.
3. Indirect labor, indirect materials, and power costs are proportionately variable with direct labor cost.
4. Pensions and payroll taxes are calculated at 20 percent of total labor cost.
5. Heat and light, depreciation, and taxes and insurance are wholly fixed.
6. Half of the miscellaneous overhead costs at normal volume are variable.
7. Marketing and administrative costs other than those directly traceable to individual product lines amount to $300,000 a year. These costs would be the same even if none of these three products was marketed.
8. The direct marketing costs of Pilgran include $50,000 to amortize the costs incurred to develop this product initially. This cost will be completely amortized three years from now.

a. Based on the company's method of product costing, which of these products appear to be profitable?
b. Judging solely from the information provided in this problem, would you recommend that any of these three products be discontinued? Show your calculations.
c. If any product appeared to be unprofitable in your answer to (a) but worth continuing in your answer to (b), under what circumstances would you consider withdrawing it from the market?

19. Special order. More than two years ago, a large railway system decided to change its system of track control signals. This decision led to an abrupt decline in the sales volume of one of Valley Manufacturing Company's largest industrial customers, who then canceled or reduced the size of his orders for several Valley Manufacturing products. Since that time, Valley Manufacturing has been unable to keep its factory operating at normal volumes, despite a vigorous sales promotion program.

Yesterday morning, Bob Pettifogg, the company's sales manager, handed Tom Pruitt, the marketing vice president, a customer order for 12,000 foot wrinklers, to be made and delivered within the next six months. To get this order, Mr. Pettifogg had quoted a price less than the standard catalog price, which meant that Mr. Pruitt's approval was necessary.

Although the factory would have to put a number of workers on overtime for the next six months to meet the required delivery schedule, Mr. Pettifogg is convinced that the order should be accepted. "First," he said, "all of the work would be done in department 27, which we can't seem to keep busy no matter how hard we try. If we don't take this order, we'll be running only 7,000 machine-hours a month in that department, against a normal monthly volume of 10,000 machine-hours. This order will bring in 1,000 machine-hours of work each month for six months, and that's a big difference. Some of our people are now on a short workweek, and this order will let us put them back on the full-time payroll and give them some overtime pay, too.

"Second, while I'll admit that the margin is slim, the price I have quoted is greater than our cost, even after allowing for the abnormal amount of overtime. The price is $2.50 a unit and the cost is $2.40. That gives us a margin of about 4 percent of sales. That isn't much, but it's better than nothing."

Mr. Pettifogg then handed Mr. Pruitt the following cost and profit summary to back up his recommendation:

Cost per unit:
Direct materials..................................... $0.57
Direct labor (0.2 hour × $7)....................... 1.40
Factory overhead:
    Normal (0.5 mach.-hr. × $0.80)................. 0.40
    Overtime premium adjustment................ 0.03
        Total cost per unit.......................... $2.40
Selling price....................................... 2.50
Profit margin per unit............................ $0.10

"The provision for factory overhead," Mr. Pettifogg continued, "is based on the department's normal overhead rate of 80 cents for each machine-hour used, plus an allowance for extra overtime premiums that would have to be paid to get this job out on time. Normal overheads are shown in this second table, together with a monthly overhead cost forecast for the next six months at a monthly volume of 7,000 machine-hours:

	Forecast at 7,000 Hours	Normal at 10,000 Hours
Indirect labor..............................	$3,100	$4,000
Overtime premium.........................	...	800
Supplies....................................	840	1,200
Depreciation..............................	1,100	1,100
Other......................................	750	900
Total.................................	$5,790	$8,000
Average per machine-hour..............	$0.827	$0.80

"The cost accountant tells me that except for the overtime premium adjustment, we can get a reasonably good estimate of overhead cost at any volume between 7,000 and 10,000 machine-hours per month by interpolating between the figures given in this table."

"I understand the normal overhead charge," Mr. Pruitt replied, "but what is this overtime premium adjustment? I thought they didn't have enough to keep busy down there and yet they're charging us for extra overtime."

Mr. Pettifogg was ready for this question. "It's true that they have plenty of idle capacity," he said, "but it's idle machine time, not idle labor. They could increase the size of the work force by hiring people, but they won't do that unless they can see good prospects for keeping them busy for a lot longer than six months. They figure that it would be cheaper to go on overtime than to train new workers, use them, and let them go six months from now.

"This means that we have to adjust the overhead rate to allow for the unusual amount of overtime. I made the overtime premium adjustment myself, on the basis of estimates prepared by the factory scheduling department. These show that overtime premiums for department 27 as a whole would probably average 14 cents a machine-hour until this order was finished. The overhead rate already includes 8 cents for overtime premiums, so I added another 6 cents an hour, or 3 cents a unit, to allow for this factor."

Acceptance of this order would have no effect on total selling and administrative expenses, but the average ratio of selling and administrative expense to total sales would be reduced by about one fifth of one percent.

Mr. Pruitt sees no reason why acceptance of this order would lead to reductions in the prices the company would be able to get in the future for this or other products; his sole concern is whether the quoted price is a profitable one. What would you tell him?

20. Make or buy decision. The Vernom Corporation, which produces and sells to wholesalers a highly successful line of summer lotions and insect repellents, has decided to diversify in order to stabilize sales throughout the year. A natural area for the company to consider is the production of winter lotions and creams to prevent dry and chapped skin.

After considerable research, a winter products line has been developed. However, because of the conservative nature of the company management, Vernom's president has decided to introduce only one of the new products for this coming winter. If the product is a success, further expansion in future years will be initiated.

The product selected (called Chap-off) is a lip balm that will be sold in a lipstick-type tube. The product will be sold to wholesalers in boxes of 24 tubes for $8 a box. Because of available capacity, no additional fixed charges will be incurred to produce the product. However, a $100,000 fixed charge will be absorbed by the product to allocate a fair share of the company's present fixed costs to the new product.

Using the estimated sales and production of 100,000 boxes of Chap-off as the standard volume, the accounting department has developed the following cost estimates for each box of the new product (including the costs of manufacturing the tubes):

Direct labor..............	$2.00
Direct materials.........	3.00
Total overhead..........	1.50
Total..................	$6.50

Vernom has approached a cosmetics manufacturer to discuss the possibility of purchasing the tubes for Chap-off. The purchase price of the empty tubes from the cosmetics manufacturer would be $0.90 per 24 tubes. If the Vernom Corporation accepts the cosmetics firm's proposal, it is estimated that direct labor and variable overhead costs will be reduced by 10 percent and direct material costs will be reduced by 20 percent.

   a.   Should the Vernom Corporation make or buy the tubes? Show calculations to support your answer.
   b.   What would be the maximum purchase price acceptable to the Vernom Corporation for the tubes? Support your answer with an appropriate explanation.
   c.   Instead of sales of 100,000 boxes, revised estimates show sales volume at 125,000 boxes. At this new volume additional equipment, at an annual rental of $10,000, must be acquired to manufacture the tubes. However, this incremental cost would be the only additional fixed cost required even if sales increased to 300,000 boxes. (The 300,000 level is the goal for the third year of production.) Under these circumstances should the Vernom Corporation make or buy the tubes? Show calculations to support your answer.
   d.   The company has the option of making and buying at the same time. What would be your answer to part (*c*) if this alternative was considered? Show calculations to support your answer.

(CMA adapted)

4

Variable Costing and Profit Charts

THE FACTORY job costing system described in Chapter 2 is known as a *full costing* or *absorption costing system*—that is, each job absorbs a share of each of the costs of operating the factory cost centers working on that job. Cost figures used in corporate financial statements are always based on absorption costing, and management often receives cost estimates on this basis.

Unfortunately, as we saw in Chapter 3, costs calculated this way don't tell management how total company costs are likely to respond to decisions leading to increased or decreased production and sales of individual products. To answer questions of this sort, the cost accountant may use a different kind of costing system known as *variable costing*. In this chapter we shall study four related questions:

1. What variable costing is and how it is applied to job order production.
2. How management can use data from variable costing systems.
3. How charts representing cost-volume-profit relationships are drawn and how they can be used.
4. How variable costing would affect reported income if it were used for external financial reporting.

THE BASIS FOR VARIABLE COSTING

Variable costing is a method of measuring *product cost*—that is, the cost of an individual end-product activity. In variable costing, product cost includes only those factory costs that vary in response to short-run changes in the rate of production—that is, the variable costs. As Exhibit 4–1 shows, direct materials, direct labor, and the variable portion of factory overhead are product costs in a variable costing system. Fixed manufacturing overheads are not assigned to individual end-product activities—they are not classified as product costs.

EXHIBIT 4–1

Product Costs under Full Costing and under Variable Costing

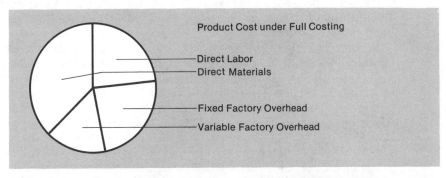

Product Cost under Full Costing

Direct Labor
Direct Materials

Fixed Factory Overhead

Variable Factory Overhead

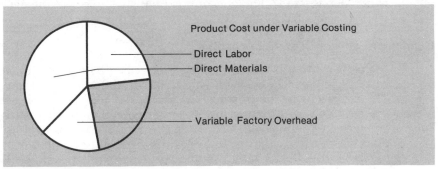

Product Cost under Variable Costing

Direct Labor
Direct Materials

Variable Factory Overhead

A Job Costing Illustration

Variable costing is not an alternative to job costing. It is simply another way of measuring the costs of individual jobs. For example, suppose departmental volume is measured in machine-hours and departmental overhead costs are expected to vary as follows:

	Fixed per Month	Variable per Machine-Hour
Supervision.....................	$1,400	....
Indirect labor...................	.....	$0.10
Indirect materials..............	.....	0.05
Maintenance...................	100	0.08
Power.........................	.....	0.02
Total........................	$1,500	$0.25

In this case the variable costing overhead rate would be 25 cents a machine hour. In variable costing, a job order requiring ten machine hours in this department would be charged $2.50 (10 hours × $0.25) for variable overhead, and no charge would be made for any portion of the $1,500 in fixed costs. In full costing, the overhead rate would include a provision for fixed costs.

Two things should be noticed in this illustration. First, overhead costs were assigned to the job by means of an overhead rate. Variable overhead is no easier to trace to individual jobs than fixed overhead. The only way to assign overhead costs to job orders is to use overhead rates.

Second, variable costing can be used even if some cost elements contain both fixed and variable components. Since the overhead rate is predetermined, all the accountants have to do is estimate the *rate* of variability. They don't have to record the fixed and variable components separately. In this case they are able to include 8 cents in the overhead rate to provide for variable maintenance costs, even though they probably have no way of labeling most maintenance expenditures as either fixed or variable when they are made. (Of two drops of oil placed on a bearing, which one is the variable drop and which one is fixed? The question is unanswerable and the accountant wisely doesn't try.)

Handling Nonlinear Cost Relationships

Cost variation is not always well described by straight lines, as we saw in Chapter 3. Two such situations are illustrated in Exhibit 4–2. The cost steps in the upper chart are not all the same size, but they are relatively small and close together. In other words, fairly small changes in volume will lead to changes in the amount of this cost. Since this is what the variable costing figures are supposed to show, the average rate of change should be included in the variable costing overhead rate. The slope of the "leveled cost" line measures the average rate of variability (40 cents a machine-hour), and this is part of variable cost.

The situation represented in the lower half of Exhibit 4–2 is not as clear-cut. For fairly large ranges of volume variation, the rate of cost variability is represented by the slope of line A. If the entire volume span from zero to capacity is included, however, the leveled cost line would be the one labeled B and the rate of cost variability would be twice as high, 20 cents a machine-hour instead of 10 cents.

Most advocates of variable costing would probably use line A in a case of this sort, on the grounds that average variable cost figures are typically applied to decisions encompassing fairly small increments in operating volume, and that averaging the step functions would cloud the meaning of unit cost when the steps are this large.

Terminology: Variable Costing versus Direct Costing

Product costing systems of the kind just described are generally referred to as *direct costing* systems. This is unfortunate. As we pointed out in Chapter 2, the term "direct" means that a cost is traceable to a specified cost objective. If the cost objective is a job order, no overhead cost is a direct cost. If the cost objective is the operation of a particular production center, many fixed costs are direct. "Direct cost," in other words, does not describe variable product costs, and that is what variable costing is all about.

EXHIBIT 4–2

Step Functions and Variable Costing Rates

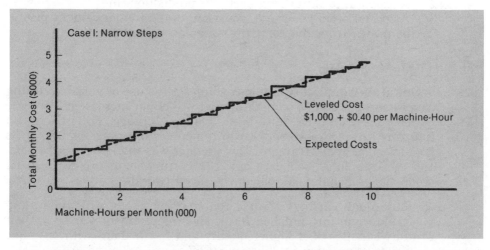

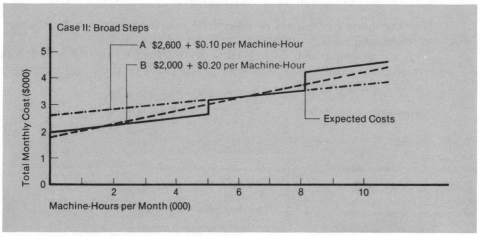

ESTIMATING COSTS FROM VARIABLE COSTING DATA

Variable costing has three main purposes, all of them related to management's needs for decision-oriented information:

1. To enable the accountant to provide estimates of short-run variable costs more quickly and efficiently.
2. To help management analyze the sensitivity of profit to variations in operating volume.
3. To give management a clearer picture of the relative profitability of different products and different marketing strategies.

This section deals with the first of these. We shall look at three situations in which variable costing data would be helpful:

1. A proposal to substitute one raw material for another, leaving total fixed costs unaffected.
2. A proposal to shut down part of a production line.
3. A special order for a product incorporating a component part to be drawn from the company's regular stockroom.

Substituting Raw Materials

One of the simplest situations calling for the use of variable costing data is a proposal to do something that will either increase or decrease the use of existing capacity by a small percentage. For instance, a company had to choose between two methods of producing one of its products. The main frame of this product was made from a casting, and the company needed to buy 100 castings a month to meet its production schedules. Management faced two alternatives:

1. Buy rough castings from a foundry, cut them, drill them, and grind them into finished form, all in department 43.
2. Buy castings of a higher quality and finish them with a simple drilling operation in department 57.

The company had plenty of capacity to do the work in either department. Fixed costs would be unaffected by the choice.

A cost comparison, using full-cost overhead rates, showed unit costs as in Exhibit 4–3. The margin in favor of the quality castings seemed quite large.

EXHIBIT 4–3

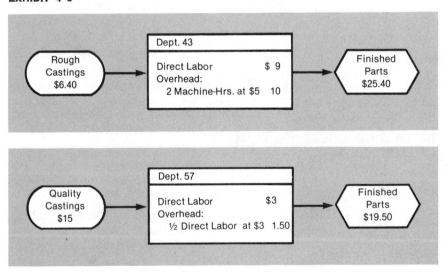

The variable costing overhead rates in this case were considerably lower than the full costing rates. Variable costs averaged only 50 cents a machine-hour in department 43 and 20 cents a direct labor hour in department 57. Using these rates, the comparison showed the following differential unit costs:

	Rough Castings	Quality Castings
Material................	$ 6.40	$15.00
Labor..................	9.00	3.00
Variable overhead:		
Dept. 43 at $0.50 per machine-hour......	1.00	
Dept. 57 at $0.20 per machine-hour......		0.10
Total............	$16.40	$18.10

Which of these analyses are we to believe? Since the amount of fixed costs in each department was not affected by the decision, they should be ignored. This means that buying the rough castings was clearly the thing to do, and the use of variable costing information pointed in that direction.

Shutting Production Facilities

The decision in the last illustration wasn't big enough to affect total fixed cost in either department. Suppose, however, that this product called for 1,000 castings a month instead of 100. Without this production department 43 could shut down one of its production units, with a $2,000 reduction in supervisors' salaries and other fixed costs each month. Department 57's fixed costs would be unaffected. The comparison now shows:

	Rough Castings	Quality Castings
Differential variable costs per unit.................	$16.40	$18.10
Number of units...........	× 1,000	× 1,000
Total differential variable costs..........	$16,400	$18,100
Differential fixed costs......	2,000	—
Total differential cost..	$18,400	$18,100

Buying the quality castings now appears to be the better alternative, by $300 a month.

The point is that even in this second situation, with changes in fixed costs as well as in the variable costs, variable costing provided data in a more manageable form than full costing. We were able to study the fixed costs separately. We did not have to disentangle them from the unit costs as we would have had to do under full costing.

Using Materials from Stock

Our third example is also designed to show that variable costing makes it easier to identify the variable component of product cost. A customer wanted to place an order with Dalton Electronics for 500 units of a new product to be used by his sales people to test the product's commercial appeal. If the test proved favorable, the customer would ask several competing manufacturers to bid on a long-term contract to supply the product on a mass-production basis.

The customer offered a price of $40 a unit for the test models. Dalton's specialty products staff wanted to accept this order if they could. They knew that unit costs for a mass-production contract would be a good deal lower than for this special order, and filling the special order would give them the experience necessary to prepare a realistic bid on the long-term contract. They were unwilling to lose money on the special order, however, and they got the following estimate of unit costs:

Direct materials	$26
Direct labor	12
Factory overhead	24
Total	$62

The staff estimated that at normal volume 25 percent of the factory overhead costs were variable—that is, one fourth of the overhead rate represented variable costs and three fourths was fixed. Their estimate of variable cost therefore showed the following:

Direct materials	$26
Direct labor	12
Variable factory overhead	6
Total differential cost	$44

This still left them with a differential cost estimate $4 over the $40 limit.

What the specialty products people overlooked in this case was that the materials for this order were fabricated parts which had been produced to stock in Dalton's factories. Each of these factories used full absorption costing. The $26 in materials costs therefore included

EXHIBIT 4–4

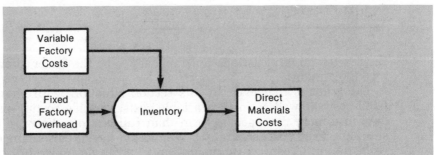

a good deal of these factories' fixed factory overhead (see Exhibit 4-4).

To dig out the differential costs of these materials, the staff had to go back and pull out the fixed component of each of the overhead rates reflected in the $26 figure. This showed that $5 of fixed factory overhead was included in the $26 materials cost figure. Excluding this amount brought the estimate of differential cost down to $39, just $1 less than the price offered. A variable costing system would have supplied the variable cost information directly.

PROFIT SENSITIVITY ANALYSIS USING PROFIT CHARTS

The second advantage of variable costing is that it can help management analyze the sensitivity of profit to variations in operating volume. We shall look at eight aspects of the accountant's approach to this task:

1. Calculating contribution margin.
2. Using charts to describe cost-volume-profit relationships.
3. Locating the break-even point.
4. Analyzing operating leverage.
5. Measuring the margin of safety.
6. Allowing for dividend coverage.
7. Delineating the customary volume range.
8. Adjusting the analysis for dynamic effects.

Contribution Margin

The first step in profit sensitivity analysis is to develop measures of relationship between product costs and product revenues. Because profit sensitivity analysis focuses on the short run, the cost relationships should show the effects on costs of variations in the use of existing capacity. Variable costing systems attempt to provide this information.

For example, product X sells for $10 and has variable manufacturing costs of $5.50 a unit. Salesmen are awarded a commission of 30 cents for each unit sold, and the variable costs of processing orders, shipping the products, and handling the paperwork amount to 20 cents a unit. The $4 difference between the $10 selling price and these variable costs is product X's *contribution margin*. It is also known as the *variable profit* or *P/V income* (P/V stands for profit/volume).

Contribution margin is typically expressed as a rate per unit, or as a percentage of the selling price. These rates or percentages are used to approximate the profit effects of changes in sales volume.

The Cost-Volume-Profit Chart

Profit sensitivity analysis usually centers on some form of profit chart. The most familiar of these is the cost-volume-profit chart. This is a diagram showing the amount of revenue, cost and profit to be expected at various sales volumes. For example, a company sells a single product at a price of $10 a unit. Fixed costs are $240,000 a year and variable costs are a flat $6 a unit. The cost-volume relationship is represented by the "Total Cost" line in Exhibit 4–3. At zero volume total cost is $240,000—i.e., no variable costs. At 10,000 units total cost is $240,000 + 10,000 × $6 = $300,000. And so on.

At a price of $10 a unit, total revenues will be zero if sales are zero, $100,000 if 10,000 units are sold, and so on. This is shown by the "Total Revenue" line. The vertical distance between the two lines at any volume is the anticipated profit or loss at that volume. If sales amount to only 10,000 units, then a loss of $300,000 − $100,000 = $200,000 is predicted.

EXHIBIT 4–5

Cost-Volume-Profit Chart

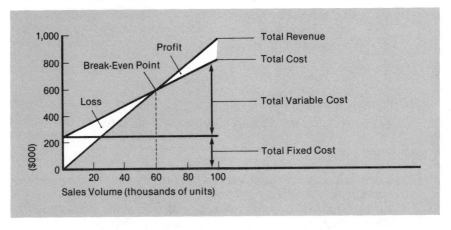

Our terminology here is slightly fuzzy. *Revenue* is an income statement term, but is used here on the assumption that in a normal period net revenues and cash receipts from customers will be identical. We don't use two other income statement terms, however— *expense* and *income*. Expenses are costs deducted from revenues on the income statement; income is the difference between revenues and expenses. These terms are not used here because we don't know whether the operating cost of any given period will equal the amount reported as expense. To cite just one example, the costs in these charts typically reflect estimates of the current purchase prices of raw materials used in production. The actual cost of goods sold, however, may include some materials prices from the preceding year (as under Fifo) or even from years far in the past (as under Lifo, in some circumstances). In general, the differences will not be great. We shall use the terms cost and profit in profit charting because everyone else uses them.

Break-Even Points

The two lines in this chart cross at a sales volume of 60,000 units. This is known as the *break-even point.* At lower volumes the company loses money; at higher volumes it makes a profit. In fact, the break-even point is so prominent that these charts are sometimes called *break-even charts.*

The break-even point can be calculated arithmetically if the cost and revenue lines are straight lines. The formula is:

$$\text{Break-even volume} = \frac{\text{Total fixed costs}}{\text{Contribution margin per unit}}$$

In this case fixed costs amount to $240,000 and the contribution margin (the difference between selling price and variable cost) is $4. The break-even volume therefore is $240,000/$4 = 60,000 units.

This makes sense. If the company sells one unit, it covers $4 of the fixed costs. If two units are sold, $8 of the fixed costs are covered. By dividing $4 into the total fixed cost we can find out how many units have to be sold to cover all of the fixed costs.

Operating Leverage

The most important feature of the cost-volume-profit chart is not the break-even point but the profit spread. This shows up better if we redraw the chart as in the lower diagram in Exhibit 4–6. The advantage of this new version is that the contribution margin is clearly visible. This makes it possible to diagram the firm's *operating leverage,* the degree to which the firm uses fixed costs to generate profit.

The most useful way to measure operating leverage is to calculate the following ratio:

$$\frac{\text{Total fixed costs}}{\text{Contribution margin per unit}}$$

Leverage can be increased by increasing fixed costs or by reducing the unit contribution margin. The purpose of leverage is to create the possibility of substantial rewards for high-volume performance.

Exhibit 4–7, for example, shows two different cost structures a firm might adopt to penetrate a new market. The diagram at the top shows a highly leveraged structure. The break-even point is relatively high, but profits grow rapidly after the break-even point has been passed. The high fixed costs provide the capacity to achieve high operating volumes.

The diagram at the bottom, Chart B, shows a situation with much less leverage. The break-even point is farther to the left, but the rewards for volume in excess of the break-even amount increase more gradually and reach a much lower ceiling.

Notice that the operating leverage ratio is nothing more than the formula for the break-even volume. A high break-even point means

EXHIBIT 4–6

Contribution Margin Chart

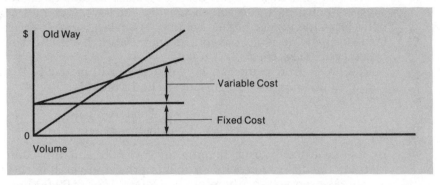

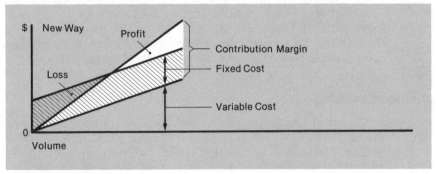

high operating leverage. We have merely looked at it from a different perspective. Its significance can be judged only in conjunction with information on the probable range of volume fluctuations. If the likely volume range is narrow, variations in the operating leverage ratio will be relatively unimportant. If the volume forecast is highly uncertain, however, the ratio will be very significant:

> If the ratio is high and volume is highly variable, the risks and potential rewards will be relatively large. (In Chart A the maximum loss is $240,000 and the maximum gain is $80,000.)
> If the ratio is low and volume is relatively stable, the risks and potential rewards will be relatively small. (In Chart B, the maximum loss is $60,000 and the maximum gain is $40,000.)

The Margin of Safety

Another aspect of profit sensitivity analysis is the calculation of the *margin of safety*, the gap between the forecasted volume and the break-even volume. Exhibit 4–8, for example, is the same chart as Exhibit 4–5 with forecasted sales of 70,000 units drawn in. With a break-even volume of 60,000 units, the margin of safety is 10,000 units, or one seventh of the forecasted sales.

EXHIBIT 4–7

Operating Leverage

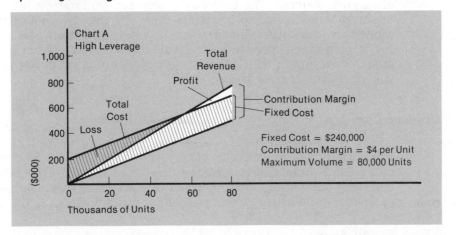

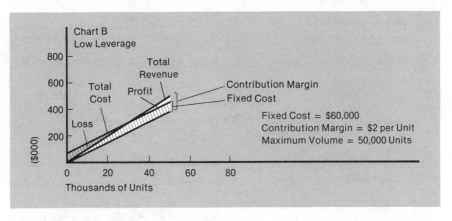

EXHIBIT 4–8

The Margin of Safety

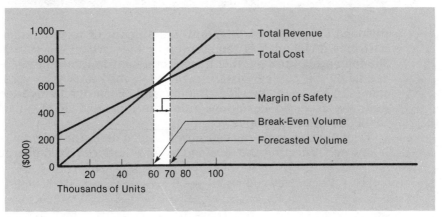

The margin of safety is used in business firms to measure risk. A firm that has a high margin of safety is less vulnerable to unexpected changes in demand. Therefore, a decision that will narrow the margin of safety is presumed to be riskier than one that will not. This is a crude way to allow for uncertainty, however, and it may be misleading. A plan may appear to have a wide margin of safety but be much riskier than one in which the margin of safety is small but the possible forecasting error is also small.

Dividend Coverage

The break-even point is seldom very significant in itself. Business firms are not in business to break even. For this reason, the basic cost-volume-profit charts are often drawn to include a specific dividend requirement or a specific profit objective as a fixed charge.

Exhibit 4–9 illustrates this possibility, using $80,000 as the annual

EXHIBIT 4–9

Cost-Volume-Profit Chart with Dividend Requirement

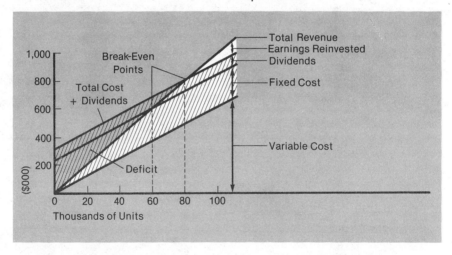

dividend figure. In this diagram, the amount of fixed charges (fixed cost plus dividends) is represented by the vertical distance between the top and bottom parallel lines. Total contribution margin is represented by the vertical distances in the shaded area. The vertical distances in the areas marked "Deficit" and "Earnings Reinvested" measure the expected deviations from the indicated dividend target of $80,000 a year at various volumes.

Two break-even points can now be calculated, the original one and a new one reflecting the dividend as an additional fixed charge:

$$\text{Break-even volume} = \frac{\$240,000 + \$80,000}{\$4} = 80,000 \text{ units}$$

The Customary Volume Range

The profit charts we have been looking at so far show the sensitivity of profit to changes in volume that are unrelated to changes in fixed costs. Costs and revenues are drawn as straight lines because the charts assume that marketing costs and selling prices will not change during the period the charts relate to, and that the costs of responsive activities will vary in a linear pattern.

The assumption that marketing costs and selling prices are fixed is not unreasonable. They are embodied in the marketing strategy management has adopted, and this strategy typically establishes the selling prices and the marketing outlays to be made during the period covered by the chart. If the strategy works well, volume will be high and so will profit. If the marketing efforts are ineffective, volume will be low and so will profit.

The assumption that factory and distribution costs will be linear is more questionable. We have already described the steps that are likely to occur in these costs as volume changes by large amounts. In addition, bottlenecks are likely to appear in the factory and in the distribution organization as the company gets close to capacity. That will increase average variable costs and may even call for some increase in fixed costs as well.

We don't deny that these nonlinearities exist, but we do assume in most cases that they lie in the portions of the volume range the company seldom operates in. The usual profit charts describe cost and profit behavior within this customary operating range, not outside it. Within this portion of the range, the lines are likely to be fairly straight, as in the center section of Exhibit 4–10. The apparent inconsistency arises because we extend these lines to the left and to the right, also as straight lines. We do this to focus attention on the amount of fixed cost and the rate of variability within the customary

EXHIBIT 4–10

Cost-Profit Behavior beyond the Customary Volume Range

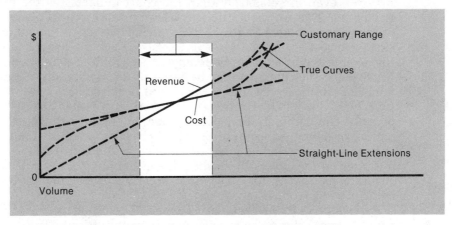

range. To be accurate, the portions of the chart outside the customary volume limits should be erased, perhaps to be replaced by the extensions labeled "True Curves" in the exhibit.

In other words, we use straight lines because management wants the chart to show the effects on profit of variations in the *effectiveness* of marketing effort, not the effects of changes in the *amount* of effort expended. Cost variations or price changes designed to produce volume variations do not appear in the chart.

Some writers have claimed that the straight-line assumption is an inescapable part of the profit chart. This is too strong. If management knows enough about cost behavior to insert steps and curves, it should put them in. If selling prices or purchase prices are automatically different at higher volumes than at lower volumes, other things being unchanged, then these should be put in, too. The only inescapable assumption is that each point on each line represents the anticipated cost or revenue for steady operation at this volume. We shall explore this assumption in the next few paragraphs.

Dynamic Effects

Profit graphs are static devices, designed to illustrate the profit normally associated with steady operation at various operating volumes, assuming no change in P/V ratios or fixed costs. Costs are not likely to follow the cost line on the profit chart all the time, for various reasons. Three situations are worth noting:

1. A rapid movement from one volume level to another.
2. A temporary shift in the level of activity.
3. A persistent shift in product demand.

Transitional effects. When volume moves rapidly from one level to another, the costs of responsive activities may respond either faster or more slowly than the chart indicates. A volume expansion may be sustained for a while without moving up to a new step in certain semivariable costs such as supervision. At the same time, variable costs may rise even more sharply than the chart indicates as the firm has to buy materials on rush orders or has to hire untrained personnel.

Temporary volume shifts. Management may choose to support an excessive cost structure for a short period if volume has declined and the decline seems likely to be temporary. Layoffs of personnel are expensive and the company may be better off to pay standby salaries for a while than to pay severance wages and train new workers when volume picks up again. By the same token, if volume increases temporarily, the company may find it more economical to resort to abnormal overtime, subcontracting or other costly practices than to add to its permanent staff. Again, actual costs will depart from the levels indicated on the chart. The dashed line in Exhibit 4–11 may be a more accurate picture of the movement of costs as volume moves temporarily away from a stable base.

Persistent shifts in demand. The usual profit charts reflect a specific economic climate, a specific management attitude. If the climate

EXHIBIT 4–11

Profit Response to Temporary Shifts in Demand

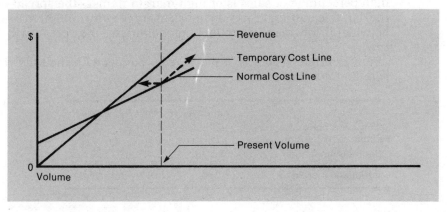

changes, management's attitudes will change, too. Cost behavior is likely to be affected.

For example, as volume moves down toward or even below the break-even point, management's attitudes toward activities it has thought of as essential are likely to change. Discretionary activities such as window washing and even some responsive activities may feel the hot breath of the cost cutter. For this reason, the actual zero-profit volume is likely to be a good deal lower than the break-even volume on the chart.

By the same token, if demand has shifted upward, fixed costs are likely to inch up, a movement sometimes referred to as "creep." Cost control seems less urgent, and fringe activities seem more attractive because "after all, the company can afford it."

PRODUCT ANALYSIS IN MULTIPRODUCT FIRMS

Most businesses have several or even thousands of products. The third purpose of variable costing is to give management a clearer picture of the relative profitability of different products and different marketing strategies in this kind of situation. It does this mainly by making it easier for the analyst to identify the effects of product-oriented decisions. Our discussion will focus on two questions:

1. The impact of the product mix on overall profit rates.
2. The use of contribution margin ratios to guide product emphasis decisions.

Impact of the Product Mix

Volume in a multiproduct firm can't be measured in physical units because units of different products vary widely in size and importance. In most cases, dollar sales must be used. Furthermore, unless all products have identical contribution margins, the overall profit-volume relationship depends on the *product mix,* the relative proportions in which the various products are sold. If the mix is rich—that is, if a high percentage of sales is of high-margin items—the spread between the variable cost and revenue lines (average contribution margin) will be wide; if low-margin products predominate, the spread will be narrow.

For example, a company has three products with the following contribution margins:

	Product A	Product B	Product C
Selling price per unit............	$20	$10	$ 5
Variable costs per unit..........	15	6	2
Contribution margin...........	$ 5	$ 4	$ 3
Contribution margin (%)........	25%	40%	60%

The company's total fixed costs amount to $627,000, and total sales volume is $3 million.

If all sales were of product A, the average contribution margin would be 25 percent and the break-even volume would be $627,000/0.25 = $2,508,000. If all sales were of product C, on the other hand, the overall contribution margin would be the margin for product C, 60 percent, and the break-even volume would be $627,000/0.6 = $1,045,000.

The company is at neither of these extremes. Sales volume is as follows:

Product	Units Sold	Revenues	Percent of Total
A..........	90,000	$1,800,000	60%
B..........	90,000	900,000	30
C..........	60,000	300,000	10
Total........		$3,000,000	100%

For convenience, we shall refer to this as a 60–30–10 product mix. The average contribution margin from this mix is 33 percent:

	Sales	Contribution Margin	
Product	Revenues	Amount	Percent
A............	$1,800,000	$450,000	25%
B............	900,000	360,000	40
C............	300,000	180,000	60
Total.........	$3,000,000	$990,000	33%

The break-even volume is $627,000/0.33 = $1.9 million. By multiplying this figure by each product's share of total sales, the accountant can calculate each product's share of the total break-even volume:

Product	Share of Total Sales	Share of Break-Even Sales
A.........	$1,800,000/$3,000,000 = 60%	$1,140,000
B.........	$ 900,000/$3,000,000 = 30%	570,000
C.........	$ 300,000/$3,000,000 = 10%	190,000
Total.......		$1,900,000

The picture would be very different if the mix could be shifted to a 40–40–20 basis, leaving total sales unchanged. The contribution margins would be:

Product	Sales Revenues	Contribution Margin
A.........	$1,200,000	$ 300,000
B.........	1,200,000	480,000
C.........	600,000	360,000
Total.......	$3,000,000	$1,140,000

The average contribution margin would be $1,140,000/$3,000,000 = 38 percent, and the break-even point would drop substantially, to $627,000/0.38 = $1,650,000.

These two product-mix assumptions are illustrated in Exhibit 4–12. The contribution margin spread is wider in Chart B than in Chart A, the break-even point is farther to the left, and the margin of safety is greater. At a $3 million sales volume, profit is $363,000 in Chart A and $513,000 in Chart B, a 41 percent increase.

The profit spread in each of the charts in Exhibit 4–12 shows what will happen to profit if volume changes with no change in mix and no change in fixed costs. The differences between the profit spreads in the two charts show how profit will be affected if mix changes on its own, with no change in marketing effort. Taken individually and together, they illustrate another form of profit sensitivity analysis.

Product Emphasis Decisions

A natural reaction to the contribution margin figures underlying these charts is to devote more effort to product C and less to product A. The contribution margin from product C, after all, is more than double the contribution margin on product A. While this may be the thing to do, management must consider at least three factors that a simple ratio comparison of this kind overlooks:

1. Effort/result ratios are unequal.
2. Changes in the product mix may require changes in the total amount spent on various forms of sales promotion.
3. Sales of some products are interdependent.

EXHIBIT 4–12

Effect of Product Mix on Profit Margins

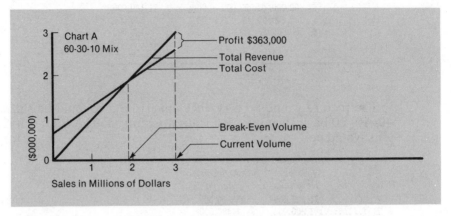

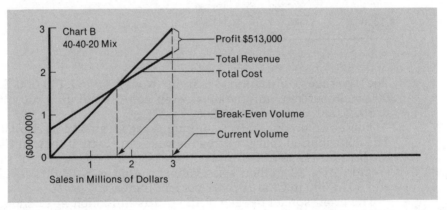

Differences in effort/result ratios. One way to influence the product mix is to shift advertising or the time of salespeople from one product to another. Shifts of this sort should not be based solely on product-to-product differences in contribution margin, however. Some products are harder to sell than others, and the response to the increased effort on these may be too small to offset the effects of lost sales of other products.

For example, if salespeople can sell $2 worth of product B in the time it would take them to sell $1 worth of product C, they should stick to product B. $2 of B yields a contribution margin of $2 × 40 percent = 80 cents, while $1 of C yields only 60 cents.

Changes in marketing expenditures. The second way to shift the product mix is to change the amounts spent to promote individual products. Analyzing the profitability of these changes is a five-step process:

1. Estimate the fixed costs required by each proposal and the pro-
    posed net selling price for each product (gross price less dis-
    counts, allowances, and uncollectible amounts).
2. Using variable costing data and the proposed net selling prices,
    calculate the estimated contribution margin per unit for each
    product.
3. For each proposal, estimate the sales of each product.
4. Multiply the estimated unit margins by the estimated sales and
    subtract the estimated fixed costs.
5. Evaluate the risks each proposal will entail and choose the pro-
    posal that offers the risk-profit combination that management
    finds most acceptable.

   For example, management has prepared the following estimates for
two different marketing proposals:

	Proposal X	Proposal Y
Total fixed cost.........	$ 627,000	$ 787,000
Product mix.............	60–30–10	40–40–20
Average contribution margin...............	33%	38%
Expected sales.........	$3,000,000	$3,300,000

The estimated profit under proposal X is:

$$(\$3,000,000 \times 0.33) - \$627,000 = \$363,000.$$

The estimated profit under proposal Y is:

$$(\$3,300,000 \times 0.38) - \$787,000 = \$467,000.$$

   This comparison clearly favors proposal Y. Management is concerned, however, because proposal Y would add $160,000 to the fixed
marketing outlays, increasing the amount of money at risk. To help
management visualize the margin of safety in the proposal, the accountant prepared the profit chart in Exhibit 4–13. This shows that
the break-even point under proposal Y is slightly higher than under
proposal X, but the margin of safety is a good deal wider. Even if sales
volume only reaches $3 million, proposal Y will generate almost as
much profit as proposal X—the spread between the lines at that volume is minimal. Management may decide that the added risk is not
so great, after all.
   This diagram uses a different kind of profit chart from those we
have been looking at. It omits the revenue and cost lines, showing
only the profit at each volume. The height of the profit line above or
below the baseline at any given volume depends on the anticipated
profit or loss at that volume. It crosses the baseline at the break-even
volume for that mix and level of fixed costs.
   This kind of chart is simpler and cleaner than the cost-volume-profit
chart. It may be more difficult to explain to the executive who is not
already familiar with profit-volume charting, however. Although the

EXHIBIT 4–13

Alternative Marketing Proposals

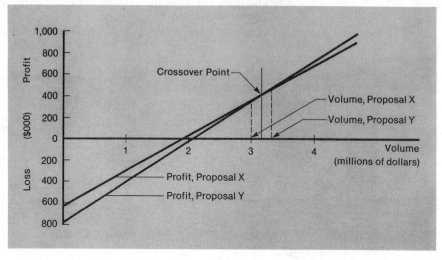

amount of fixed cost and the size of the contribution margin can be
read from this chart, they are not labeled explicitly. If this hurdle can
be crossed, this simplified format is probably the better one to use.

Interdependencies.   Contribution margin ratios don't necessarily
indicate the total effect on company profit of a change in product
volume. The reason is that some products are substitutes for each
other and others are companion products whose sales move up and
down together.

For example, the contribution margin at the present product mix is
as follows:

	Product A	Product B	Product C	Total
Units sold...........................	72,000	90,000	60,000	
Sales revenues.....................	$1,800,000	$900,000	$300,000	$3,000,000
Variable costs......................	1,350,000	540,000	120,000	2,010,000
Contribution margin..............	$ 450,000	$360,000	$180,000	$ 990,000
Contribution margin percent of sales	25%	40%	60%	33%

The company has $627,000 in fixed costs, leaving income before taxes
of $363,000.

Not satisfied with this forecast, management is considering spending an extra $20,000 a month on its efforts to sell product C. Man-
agement is convinced that this would increase sales of product C to
70,000 units a month, 10,000 more than the rate currently anticipated. If this forecast is correct, product C's contribution margin
would be:

	New Proposal	Increase over Present Proposal
Sales revenues.................	$350,000	$50,000
Variable costs (40% of sales)...	140,000	20,000
Contribution margin	$210,000	$30,000

In other words, management believes that spending the extra $20,000 would add $30,000 to the contribution margin, a net benefit of $10,000.

Management knows, however, that some of the company's customers see products B and C as possible substitutes for each other. Product B sells for $10, double the price of product C. Some customers are willing to pay this price, while others find the $10 price too high and buy product C. If the additional promotional effort succeeds in increasing sales of product C, sales of product B are likely to fall.

In fact, management estimates that 10 percent of any added sales of product C would be a direct result of customers shifting away from product B. The contribution margin on these lost sales must be subtracted in calculating the profit from the increased effort devoted to product C. In this case an additional 10,000 units of product C would divert 1,000 buyers away from product B. At a $10 price, these lost sales would add up to $10,000 a month. With a 40 percent contribution margin ratio, $4,000 in contribution margin would be lost:

Added contribution margin from product C...	$30,000
Lost contribution margin from product B.....	(4,000)
Increased promotional expenditures.........	(20,000)
Net increase in profit..................	$ 6,000

The availability of variable costing data makes analysis of these *substitution effects* just a little easier.

We are not quite finished with our illustration. Management knows that many people buy product A only because they use product C. Every sale of a unit of product C adds a tenth of a unit to the sales of product A, without any increase in the fixed selling costs of product A. Since the proposal would increase sales of product C by 10,000 units a month, product A's sales should go up by one tenth of that, or 1,000 units. At a selling price of $20 a unit and a 25 percent contribution margin, this would bring in $20,000 in revenues and $5,000 in contribution margin. The final estimates can be put together easily:

Added contribution margin from product C...	$30,000
Added contribution margin from product A...	5,000
Lost contribution margin from product B.....	(4,000)
Increased promotional expenditures.........	(20,000)
Net differential profit..................	$11,000

Products A and C are *complementary* products, not substitutes. Razors and blades, cameras and film, and pens and refills are familiar

examples. The tough part of the analysis is to estimate the relationships between sales of one product and sales of others. Once these
estimates have been made, variable costing can help by making it
easier to calculate the effects on profits.

VARIABLE COSTING AND EXTERNAL REPORTING

The objective of variable costing is to provide product unit costs for
use by management. It is not designed to provide data for public financial reporting and in fact has been specifically rejected for this purpose
by the accounting profession. Variable costing for public financial reporting does have its supporters, however, and this section will be devoted to examining the implications of this possibility.

The only factor likely to cause a material difference between variable costing income and absorption costing income is a disparity between production volume and sales volume. Suppose a company
manufactures only one product. Its costs at a normal volume of 50,000
units are as follows:

	Total	Per Unit
Variable factory costs....	$37,500	$0.75
Fixed factory costs.......	12,500	0.25
Total.............	$50,000	$1.00

The fixed costs are totally fixed, without steps, and the variable costs
are proportional to volume—that is, the factory cost total can always
be determined from the following formula:

$$\text{Total factory cost} = \$12,500 + \$0.75 \times \text{units manufactured}$$

We shall see what happens to reported income under four sets of
conditions:

1. Production equals sales at normal volume.
2. Production exceeds sales.
3. Production equals sales at subnormal volume.
4. Sales exceed production.

To avoid unnecessary complications, we shall assume that our illustrative company has no inventory of finished products at the beginning of our illustration.

Production Equals Sales at Normal Volume

In period 1, both sales and production were at the normal volume of
50,000 units. Under variable costing, all fixed factory overhead costs
are treated as period costs; they are taken directly to the income statement as expenses of the current period, without passing through product inventory accounts. Thus the income statement for period 1 would
show the following manufacturing costs:

Variable cost of goods sold (50,000 × $0.75)................. $37,500
Fixed factory costs.. 12,500
    Total costs shown as expense...................... $50,000

Under absorption costing, the cost of goods sold is determined by multiplying sales volume by the full unit cost at normal volume. In this case, during period 1:

$$\text{Cost of goods sold} = 50{,}000 \times \$1 = \$50{,}000$$

The amount of cost absorbed by production is determined by multiplying production volume by full unit cost at normal volume, in this case $1. At this rate the production volume of 50,000 units would have just absorbed the $50,000 in factory cost that was normal at this volume.

In other words, $50,000 of manufacturing costs would appear on the income statement under either system.

Production Exceeds Sales

In period 2, production rose to 55,000 units, but sales fell to 47,000 units. The remaining 8,000 units were in the finished goods inventory at the end of the period:

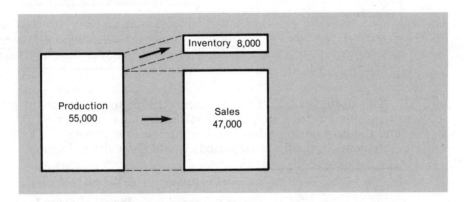

Again, production costs were at the levels anticipated for the actual volume of production:

$$\text{Total factory costs} = \$12{,}500 + 55{,}000 \times \$0.75 = \$53{,}750.$$

Under variable costing, total expense for a sales volume of 47,000 units would be:

Variable cost of goods sold (47,000 × $0.75)................. $35,250
Fixed factory costs.. 12,500
    Total expense..................................... $47,750

Under absorption costing, $55,000 would be assigned to the 55,000 units produced in period 2, $47,000 going to the cost of goods sold and

$8,000 to the inventory. The story wouldn't end there, however. Fixed factory costs would be overabsorbed by $1,250:

```
Absorbed fixed costs (55,000 × $0.25)...................... $13,750
Actual fixed costs..........................................   12,500
        Overabsorbed fixed costs..........................  $ 1,250
```

If all of this were to be reported on the current income statement, the absorption costing company would report a net expense of $45,750:

```
Cost of goods sold (47,000 × $1)............................ $47,000
Less: overabsorbed factory cost............................    1,250
        Total expense......................................  $45,750
```

This is $2,000 less than the total expense under variable costing.[1]

The $2,000 difference between the two expense figures for period 2 lies entirely in the amount of fixed cost assigned to the end-of-period inventory. Whereas variable costing would have charged the entire $12,500 as period 2 expense, absorption costing would have assigned $2,000 of this to the 8,000-unit addition to inventories (at the 25-cent burden rate), leaving only $10,500 for the income statement:

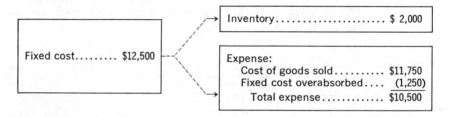

The absorption effect is even more striking in relation to the amount of income reported. Suppose that the product sells for $1.20 a unit and the firm has no selling and administrative expenses. The income statements in the first two periods would show the following:

	Absorption Costing		Variable Costing	
	Period 1	Period 2	Period 1	Period 2
Sales revenues...............	$60,000	$56,400	$60,000	$56,400
Expenses....................	50,000	45,750	50,000	47,750
Income before taxes.....	$10,000	$10,650	$10,000	$ 8,650

Despite the 3,000-unit decrease in sales, under absorption costing the company would report a $650 *increase* in reported income. Under

---

[1] If the $1,250 is regarded as "material" in amount, part of it will be subtracted from the cost of goods sold and part from the cost of the ending inventory. Assuming a zero opening inventory, the fixed costs assigned to the units sold will be 47/55 of $12,500, or $10,680. This is $1,820 less than the $12,500 fixed costs reported as expense under variable costing. In other words, regardless of whether the variance is split in this way or taken in its entirety to current income, variable costing and full costing figures are likely to differ.

variable costing, the 3,000-unit reduction in sales would be reported as a $1,350 reduction in income. This latter figure can also be calculated by multiplying 3,000 units by the product's 45 cent contribution margin ($1.20 selling price minus $0.75 variable cost).

Production Equals Sales at Subnormal Volume

We have already seen that the two costing methods produce the same income result when both production and sales are at normal volume. Let's see whether that will continue to hold true if production and sales are both less than normal volume. This happened in period 3, when production dropped to 47,000 units and sales remained at that level. Expenses under variable costing would be as follows:

Variable cost of goods sold (47,000 × $0.75)...	$35,250
Fixed factory costs..........................	12,500
Total expense........................	$47,750

Absorption costing in these circumstances would produce a cost of goods sold of $47,000:

Variable cost of goods sold (47,000 × $0.75)...	$35,250
Fixed cost of goods sold (47,000 × $0.25).....	11,750
Total cost of goods sold..............	$47,000

Fixed costs actually amounted to $12,500, however. Since only $11,-750 in fixed costs would be absorbed by production, the unabsorbed balance would be $750. This, too, would have to be treated as expense. The total expense for the period therefore would be $47,000 + $750 = $47,750. This is the same figure we calculated for variable costing. Income before income taxes would be $8,650, no matter which costing method was used in period 3:

	Absorption Costing	Variable Costing
Sales revenues..........	$56,400	$56,400
Expenses...............	47,750	47,750
Income before taxes.	$ 8,650	$ 8,650

Although the two methods yield the same income figure in period 3, they show the *change* from period 2 very differently. Under variable costing income would stay the same in period 3 as in period 2 because volume stayed the same. Under absorption costing, income would drop by $2,000, from $10,650 to $8,650 as shown in Exhibit 4–14.

The reason for this apparent inconsistency is that management did not have 8,000 units of extra unsold production in period 3 to absorb a share of fixed overhead, as it had had in period 2. So, even though sales stabilized at 47,000 units in period 3 and management took prudent action to prevent a further unwanted increase in inventory, ab-

EXHIBIT 4–14

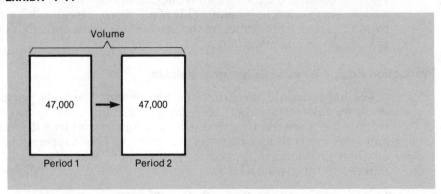

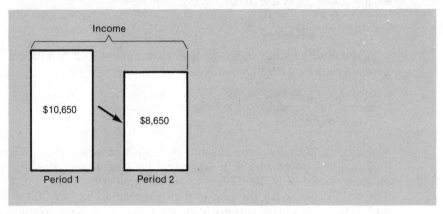

sorption costing would give a signal to investors that the company's earnings position had deteriorated in period 3.

Sales Exceed Production

The cycle was completed in period 4, when production was cut to 44,000 units while sales went up to 52,000, completely eliminating the inventory of finished units. Total expense under variable costing would be:

Variable cost of goods sold (52,000 × $0.75)...	$39,000
Fixed costs................................	12,500
Total expense........................	$51,500

Total expense under absorption costing would be:

Cost of goods sold (52,000 × $1)..............	$52,000
Unabsorbed fixed overhead (50,000 − 44,000 = 6,000 × $0.25)...........................	1,500
Total expense........................	$53,500

The income statements would show the following:

	Absorption Costing	Variable Costing
Sales revenues............	$62,400	$62,400
Expenses.................	53,500	51,500
Income before taxes...	$ 8,900	$10,900

In other words, variable costing income would be $2,000 greater than absorption costing income in period 4 because absorption costing would charge all of period 4's fixed costs against current revenues as well as $2,000 of the fixed costs of prior periods. Variable costing income would also be $2,250 greater than in periods 2 and 3, while absorption costing income would go up only $250 from the period 3 level. The income differences are summarized in Exhibit 4–15.

The Final Arguments

This comparison is the basis for the argument that variable costing should be used for income reporting. Those favoring variable costing argue that a series of income figures computed on a variable costing basis is a better index of the changes in the company's fortunes than absorption costing figures. This stems from the proposition that revenues are the source of the firm's operating income. Other things being equal, when revenues go up, income should go up; and when revenues fall, income should fall. If revenue recognition at the time of production is inappropriate, then income should not be increased by production to inventory or vice versa.

Results are reported in this way under variable costing, but not under absorption costing as we just demonstrated. Absorption costing income can be influenced significantly by the level of production, and

EXHIBIT 4–15

Effect on Income of Choice Between Absorption Costing and Variable Costing

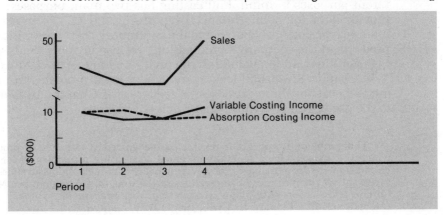

management's decisions on the rate of production can smooth or ac-
centuate period-to-period income fluctuations that are caused by
changes in the level of sales revenues.[2] This is why absorption costing
income in our example was almost constant despite large fluctuations
in revenues. The potential amount of smoothing varies inversely with
the rate of inventory turnover and with the length of the reporting
period. In other words, monthly financial statements are more vulnerable to this effect than annual statements; statements of companies
with slow-moving inventories are more vulnerable than those of high-
turnover firms.

This argument should be judged on the basis of the ability of variable costing financial statements to improve investor decisions. Lacking such evidence, the accounting profession continues to subscribe
to full costing for public financial reporting. Since all factory costs are
necessary to production, it is a generally accepted accounting principle that every factory overhead cost should be reflected in one overhead rate or another for inclusion in product cost.

VARIABLE COSTING IN PERSPECTIVE

Despite the glowing buildup we have been giving variable costing,
we must emphasize that it doesn't provide answers to all of management's costing questions. Many decisions affect fixed costs as well as
variable costs. Decisions to expand capacity or to drop products from
the line should not be made until their effects on fixed costs or even on
average variable costs have been considered.

No product, for example, should stay in the line on a continuing
basis unless the revenues it brings in are adequate to cover all of the
costs that could be saved or phased out if it were withdrawn from the
market. By the same reasoning, a company introducing a new product
needs to know what the product will cost, on the average. If the company can't charge enough to cover these costs once the product has
reached maturity, then the product doesn't belong on the market.

We can't jump from there, however, to the conclusion that full
costing is better than variable costing. The two are designed with different purposes in mind. Full costing has two main purposes: (1) to
provide data for public financial reporting; and (2) to provide estimates of the costs attributable to the continuing presence of individual
products in the company's product line, for use in some kinds of pricing decisions and in evaluating the product's long-term viability.

In Chapter 8 we shall look at some additional problems in measuring full cost for these purposes; a good part of Chapter 16 is devoted
to the use of full cost in product pricing decisions.

---

[2] This problem disappears if revenue is recognized at the time of production,
which is consistent with generally accepted accounting principles under certain
circumstances. In most cases, however, accountants lack the assurances necessary to allow them to recognize revenues at the time of production. See Myron J.
Gordon and Gordon Shillinglaw, *Accounting: A Management Approach*, 5th ed.
(Homewood, Ill.: Richard D. Irwin, Inc., 1974), chap. 5.

SUMMARY

Unit costs based on full absorption of factory overhead costs are used to measure inventories for external financial reporting. They are also likely to be used as estimates of the amount of factory costs attributable to individual manufactured products. These estimates may be used in product pricing and to identify products that lack long-term earning power.

Full costs are difficult to use in differential cost analysis, however. For this reason, factory product costs are often calculated on a variable costing basis—that is, unit cost is defined as the average variable cost of production. Fixed factory overhead costs are not included.

Variable costing also facilitates the calculation of product contribution margins. Contribution margin ratios provide ready-made estimates of profit responses to volume changes, when variable costs and revenues can be assumed to vary in proportion to volume.

Finally, variable costing facilitates the calculation of break-even points and the construction of profit-volume charts, also known as break-even charts. These charts show how rapidly profit is likely to rise or fall if the market for the company's products or services is better or poorer than anticipated.

Actual profits are apt to differ from the profit spreads in the charts, however, because profit generation is a dynamic process. Management's adjustments to changing volume, as well as actions taken to induce these changes, violate the stability assumptions on which the charts are drawn. The charts are useful mainly as pictorial devices, to dramatize forecasts of the sensitivity of profit to variations in volume or to demonstrate the effects of different marketing plans on operating leverage or product mix.

KEY TERMS

The most important terms introduced and defined in this chapter are the following:

Absorption costing	Margin of safety
Break-even point	Operating leverage
Complementary products	P/V ratio
Contribution margin	Product mix
Direct costing	Substitute products
Full costing	Variable costing

INDEPENDENT STUDY PROBLEMS
(Solutions in Appendix C)

1. Profit-volume diagrams. The Cranby Company manufactures and sells a single product. You have the following data:

Fixed costs............... $32,000 a month
Variable costs............. $3 a unit
Selling price............... $5 a unit
Anticipated sales.......... 20,000 units

a. Construct a profit-volume chart.
b. Calculate the break-even point, the margin of safety, and the anticipated profit at the anticipated sales volume.
c. The company is considering increasing the selling price to $5.50. At this price it expects to sell 18,000 units.
   (1) Recalculate the break-even point, the margin of safety, and the anticipated profit.
   (2) Redraw the profit-volume chart, showing both the old and the new profit spreads.
   (3) What effect would the price change have on the operating leverage?
   (4) How many units would have to be sold at the new price to produce a 10 percent increase in total profit before taxes?
d. The sales manager has offered a counterproposal. The price would be reduced to $4.60, and an additional $4,000 a month would be spent on advertising.
   (1) Recalculate the break-even point.
   (2) What effect would this change have on the operating leverage?
   (3) How many units would have to be sold at the new price to produce a 10 percent increase in total profit before taxes?

2. Variable costing. A company manufactures many products. Each product passes through two production departments, which have the following cost structures:

	Department A	Department B
Normal monthly volume......	5,000 direct labor hours	10,000 pounds of material
Monthly fixed costs at normal volume..........	$10,000	$40,000
Monthly variable costs at normal volume..........	15,000	20,000

Two of the job orders that went through the factory last month had the following results:

	Job 1 (Product X)		Job 2 (Product Y)	
	Quantity	Cost	Quantity	Cost
Direct inputs:				
Direct materials.........	480 lbs.	$2,400	1,500 lbs.	$4,800
Direct labor:				
Department A........	180 hrs.	1,620	100 hrs.	900
Department B........	60 hrs.	420	40 hrs.	280
Output....................	600 units		1,000 units	

a. Calculate the unit cost of each of these jobs on an absorption costing basis.
b. Recalculate unit costs on a variable costing basis.
c. Why are the relative variable costs of these two products so different from their relative full costs?

3. Effect of product mix. The Carillo Company sells two products, A and B, with contribution margin ratios of 40 and 30 percent and selling prices of $5 and $2.50 a unit. Fixed costs amount to $72,000 a month. Monthly sales average 30,000 units of product A and 40,000 units of product B.

a. Assuming that three units of product A are sold for every four units of product B, calculate the sales volume necessary to break even, in dollars and in units. Calculate the margin of safety in sales dollars.
b. If the company spends an additional $9,700 on advertising, sales of

product A can be increased to 40,000 units a month. Sales of product B will fall to 32,000 units a month if this is done. Should this proposal be accepted?

c. Recalculate the break-even point, in dollars, based on the figures in (b).

d. State the conditions that would have to hold true for the company to earn a zero profit at the break-even volume you calculated in (c).

4. Variable costing income statements. Sales and profits of the Feaster Manufacturing Company for the first two quarters of the year were:

	First	Second
Sales.....................	$300,000	$450,000
Net profit................	55,000	57,000

The directors are concerned that a 50 percent increase in sales has resulted in only a small increase in profit. The chief cost accountant explains that unabsorbed overhead was charged to second-quarter operations. His statement is based on the following data:

	First Quarter	Second Quarter
Sales—units....................................	20,000	30,000
Production—units..............................	30,000	24,000
Ending inventory—units........................	10,000	4,000
Selling price per unit...........................	$ 15	$ 15
Variable manufacturing cost per unit............	5	5
Fixed manufacturing overhead costs.............	180,000	180,000
Fixed overhead per unit (overhead rate).........	6	6
Selling and administrative expenses............	25,000	27,000

The company uses a first-in, first-out (Fifo) method for costing inventory. All underabsorbed or overabsorbed manufacturing costs are closed out to Cost of Goods Sold at the close of each period.

a. Prepare income statements for the two periods, using the method now employed by the Feaster Manufacturing Company. Indicate the book value of the ending inventory for each quarter.

b. Prepare similar statements using the variable costing method.

c. What would second-quarter net profit have been under each method if production in that period had been 30,000 units?

EXERCISES AND PROBLEMS

1. Price change; Break-even point. A company is considering a proposal to change the price of its product. The following data are available:

	Present	Proposed
Selling price...................	$ 15.00	$ 13.50
Monthly sales (in units).......	10,000	12,000
Variable costs per unit.......	$ 9.00	$ 9.00
Monthly fixed costs..........	$40,000	$42,000

The increase in fixed costs would be necessary if the factory were to increase its production volume to the new level. Selling costs would be unaffected by the proposed price change.

a. Would the price reduction be profitable? Show your calculations.

b. What would be effect of the proposed price change on the break-even point? How might knowledge of the effect on the break-even point affect the pricing decision?

c. What is the crossover volume, the minimum sales volume necessary to make the new price as profitable as the present price?

2. Product cost under variable costing. A company used a job order costing system with a factorywide predetermined overhead rate based on estimated costs at a normal volume of operations. Factory overhead costs were classified into three categories:

1. Fixed: unaffected by month-to-month changes in production volume.
2. Semivariable: affected by changes in volume, but less than proportionally.
3. Variable: proportional to volume.

Factory volume was measured by the number of direct labor hours. You are given the cost and volume expected during a normal month and actual data for the month of May:

	Normal	May
Factory overhead costs:		
Fixed.......................................	$ 50,000	$ 49,500
Semivariable...........................	30,000	32,000
Variable.................................	20,000	23,500
Total.............................	$100,000	$105,000
Factory volume (no. of direct labor hours)................................	50,000	50,000

Costs in the semivariable category are expected to vary at a rate of 50 cents a direct labor hour.

a. Prepare a predetermined overhead rate based on the variable costing concept.
b. Assuming that product costing was based on the variable costing concept, compute unit cost for a job lot of 1,000 units requiring a total of $1,000 in direct materials and 500 direct labor hours at an average wage rate of $8 an hour.
c. How much factory overhead was charged to all jobs combined during May: (1) if product costing was based on variable costing? (2) if product costing was based on full costing?

3. Profit-volume diagram. Dave's Garage has five mechanics on its payroll. They are paid $8 an hour and ordinarily work between 30 and 40 hours each week. The garage charges its customers $18 an hour for repair work. Parts are priced at cost plus 25 percent. Parts sales average 20 percent of the amounts billed customers for labor time. Fixed overhead amounts to $1,000 a week and variable overhead averages $2 an hour.

The mechanics are now working 175 repair labor hours each week.

a. Calculate the break-even volume, the margin of safety, and the current profit margin.
b. Draw a profit-volume diagram.

4. Break-even: Salaried employees. Each of the mechanics in Dave's Garage (see Problem 3) has just been put on a salary of $300 a week. This entitles Dave to 40 hours of labor time each week if enough customers can be found.

What change, if any, should be made in the break-even chart to reflect this change in Dave's payroll system? Explain your answer, using figures or a profit-volume chart.

5. Dropping unprofitable products. The Whitney Company regularly accepts a number of orders at prices that management knows will not cover their full factory costs. Last year these jobs accounted for one third of the orders processed and 20 percent of the total job costs. The costs and revenues are summarized in the following table:

	Profitable Orders	Unprofitable Orders
Direct materials............	$ 800,000	$200,000
Direct labor................	600,000	150,000
Factory overhead...........	1,000,000	250,000
Total cost of goods sold..............	$2,400,000	$600,000
Revenues.................	3,000,000	500,000
Gross margin (loss)...	$ 600,000	$(100,000)

Factory overhead for the year totaled $1,250,000. Variable overhead costs averaged 30 percent of the total factory overhead. There was no over- or underabsorption.

Most of the unprofitable orders came from customers whose orders in other years were also classified as unprofitable.

a. Was management right, in the aggregate, to accept the "unprofitable" orders?
b. Would variable costing figures be helpful in this situation?
c. Under what circumstances would you begin to refuse these orders?

6. Operating leverage. A company sells its product for $20 a unit. Materials cost $10 a unit. Direct labor costs $6 a unit; each direct labor worker produces eight units a day. Direct labor workers are employed by the day, and can be laid off indefinitely without pay if there is no work for them to do. The company now has nine direct labor workers on its payroll.

Other variable costs amount to $1 a unit; fixed costs amount to $150 a day.

a. Calculate the contribution margin per unit and the break-even volume.
b. The legislature has just required that all employees be placed on salary. Workers can be laid off for a day or longer, but an amount equal to 80 percent of their salaries must be paid to an industrial wage bank until they are rehired. Recalculate the contribution margin and the break-even volume.
c. Is operating leverage now greater or less than it was before the new legislation was passed?

7. Dividend coverage. The Argus Company sells products with an average pretax contribution margin of 40 percent of sales. Its sales volume is $2 million and its fixed costs amount to $500,000. The income tax rate is 50 percent and dividends of $80,000 are paid.

a. Calculate net income.
b. Calculate the volume at which net income equals the dividend.
c. Calculate the volume at which net income is twice the dividend.
d. The prices of the variable inputs are expected to increase by 5 percent next year. Fixed costs will also increase by 5 percent. Selling prices will remain the same. Management will maintain the dividend at its present level if net income is $126,000 next year. What volume will have to be achieved to provide this income?

8. Variable costing: Cost of materials used. A company owns two factories: factory No. 1 and factory No. 2. Costs for an output of 14,000 units of product X in factory No. 1 are:

Materials	$35,000
Labor	14,000
Variable overhead	12,600
Fixed overhead	8,400
Total	$70,000

The raw materials cost in this table is the amount charged to factory No. 1 for product A, which is manufactured in factory No. 2. Each unit of product X requires two units of product A as a raw material.

Factory No. 2 sells part of its output to factory No. 1 and part to outside customers. Its normal monthly volume is 50,000 units of product A, and the costs of producing this volume are:

Materials	$10,000
Labor	5,000
Variable overhead	2,500
Fixed overhead	45,000
Total	$62,500

Factory No. 1 uses variable costing; factory No. 2 follows the full costing concept in product costing. Personnel in one factory have no access to the other factory's cost records.

a. You are the factory controller for factory No. 1. Compute the variable unit cost of product X.

b. How would your answer to (*a*) have differed if both factories had used variable costing?

9. Variable costing: New product decision. The sales manager of Tortilla Flatware, Inc. has recommended the addition of a new deluxe model to the company's product line. The company could sell 20,000 units a month at a unit price of $22. Most of these would be sold to customers who would otherwise buy competitors' products; sales of Tortilla's regular model would be reduced by only 3,000 units a month, to 80,000 units a month.

Adequate physical capacity is available to manufacture the new model, but an additional assembly line would have to be put in operation, with additional supervisors, inspectors, and other personnel. Total fixed factory overhead costs now average $282,000 a month. Opening the new assembly line would add $38,000 a month to total fixed factory overhead. Selling and administrative costs would go up by $20,000 a month, to a new total of $180,000 a month.

The company uses variable costing with supplemental rates to cover average fixed factory overhead costs. Addition of the new model would lead the company to recalculate its supplemental rates. A new average would also be calculated for selling and administrative costs. Using these new rates, the company's accountants have prepared the following revised unit cost and profit estimates for the two products:

	Regular	Deluxe
Unit cost:		
Direct materials	$ 3.00	$10.00
Direct labor	4.50	6.00
Variable overhead	1.50	2.00
Total variable cost	$ 9.00	$18.00
Fixed factory overhead	3.00	4.00
Selling and administrative costs	1.80	1.80
Total unit cost	$13.80	$23.80
Selling price	17.00	22.00
Profit (loss) per unit	$ 3.20	$(1.80)

a. Should the new model be introduced if management accepts the sales manager's estimates? Show figures to support your answer.

b. To what extent did the company's variable costing system make your analysis easier or more difficult?

10. Overhead rates under variable costing. The management of the Leininger Company has decided to use variable costing for cost estimating purposes. Full cost figures will be entered on the job order cost sheets and in the financial accounts. The estimated overhead costs of factory department 77 at a normal volume of 4,000 direct labor hours a month are as follows:

Supervision..................	$ 4,000
Indirect labor...............	6,000
Fringe benefits..............	8,400
Supplies....................	1,200
Power......................	1,000
Depreciation................	800
Miscellaneous..............	600
Total.....................	$22,000

You have the following additional information:

1. Supervision costs remain at $4,000 a month for any volume between 3,000 and 5,000 direct labor hours. If volume drops below 3,000 hours, supervision can be cut to $2,800; if volume exceeds 5,000 hours, supervision costs will go up to $5,000 a month.
2. One third of indirect labor costs at normal volume are fixed; two thirds are proportional to the number of direct labor hours.
3. Fringe benefits amount to 20 percent of labor cost, including direct labor, supervision, and indirect labor. Direct labor wage rates average $8 an hour.
4. Supplies and power costs should be proportional to the number of direct labor hours.
5. Depreciation and miscellaneous overhead costs are entirely fixed.
6. The volume of activity ordinarily fluctuates between 3,200 and 4,600 direct labor hours.

Calculate overhead rates for this department, both for variable costing and for full costing.

11. Product cost under variable costing. A factory has four production departments. Overhead rates are calculated on both variable costing and full costing bases, as follows:

Department	Variable Cost	Full Cost
A................	$3 per direct labor hr.	$4 per direct labor hr.
B................	$3 per machine-hr.	$9 per machine-hr.
C................	$2 per direct labor hr.	$3 per direct labor hr.
D................	$1 per pound of direct materials	$2 per pound of direct materials

In scheduling three representative jobs last month, management prepared the following estimates:

	Job 1	Job 2	Job 3
Department A—direct labor hours.........................	90	20	50
Department B—machine-hours.............................	10	50	30
Department C—direct labor hours.........................	50	40	80
Department D—direct materials pounds...................	100	75	45

a. Calculate the amount of overhead to be included in the cost of each job, under variable costing and under full costing.

b. Management uses estimates of manufacturing cost in preparing bids on possible customer orders. Assuming that the full costing figures would be calculated anyway for financial reporting purposes, would calculating variable costs give management additional useful information for preparing its bids?

12. Variations in product mix. The Mossback Company manufactures and sells five products. You have the following data (all dollar figures are averages per unit):

	Prod. A	Prod. B	Prod. C	Prod. D	Prod. E
Annual sales (units).............	200,000	1,000,000	500,000	400,000	800,000
Discounts and allowances........	$0.05	$0.03	$0.12	$0.16	$0.10
Variable costs...................	1.42	0.84	2.81	3.12	5.22
Fixed costs.....................	0.84	0.46	1.95	2.42	1.46
Unit price......................	2.50	1.50	3.95	5.70	8.00

The company's productive facilities are general-purpose facilities, and all products require operations to be performed in every department of the factory.

a. Compute the break-even volume for each product.

b. Compute the break-even volume for the company as a whole at the present product mix. Explain any difference between your figure and the total of the figures derived in (*a*).

c. Prepare a profit forecast under the assumption that the product mix has changed to the following:

Product	Unit Sales
A................................	150,000
B................................	800,000
C................................	400,000
D................................	500,000
E................................	1,000,000

d. If fixed selling expenses had to be increased by $400,000 a year to effect the shift in product mix described in part (*c*), would you recommend taking this action?

13. Effect of costing method on reported income. The Sterling Company used a factory overhead rate of $2.50 a machine-hour, both in 19x4 and 19x5, based on full costing. Under- or overabsorbed factory overhead cost is closed out to the income statement at the end of each year.

In 19x5 the company recorded a total of 100,000 machine-hours. Actual overhead amounted to $275,000. Overhead costs included in inventories totaled $50,000 on January 1, 19x5 and $75,000 on December 31, 19x5, using the method followed by the company.

Budgeted variable factory overhead costs averaged $1 a machine-hour both in 19x4 and 19x5. Reported income for 19x5 was $85,000.

What would reported income have been if the company had reported income on a variable costing basis? (Ignore income taxes.)

14. Costs of transferred materials. A company has three multiproduct factories for which the following data are available:

	Factory 1	Factory 2	Factory 3
Normal monthly volume....................	50,000	30,000	100,000 lbs.
	Labor hours	Machine-hours	of product
Expected overhead costs at normal volume:			
Variable...............................	$75,000	$30,000	$20,000
Fixed..................................	25,000	90,000	80,000

All three factories use predetermined overhead rates for product unit costing.

Factory 1 makes product X, with the following input requirements per unit: materials—two and a half pounds of material A from factory 3, two units of material B from factory 2, one unit of material C from an outside vendor at $5; direct labor—three hours at $8 an hour.

Direct labor and materials costs in factory 3 average 70 cents a pound. A unit of material B has a direct labor and direct materials cost in factory 2 of $2 a unit and requires one and a half hours of machine time in factory 2.

The manager of factory 1 is also in charge of a small sales force which has the responsibility of bringing in orders to keep the factory busy. Business has been very slack lately throughout the industry. Being anxious to secure additional business, the manager of factory 1 has authorized the sales force to quote prices only slightly higher than the costs of the factory's labor, materials, and variable overhead. The factory's products are of recognizably competitive quality, but the low-price quotations haven't been low enough to get the orders. The manager has no reason to suspect that the factory is any less efficient than those of competing companies.

a. Compute the unit cost of product X following the full costing principle.
b. Compute the unit cost of product X following the variable costing principle.
c. What kind of costing system must the company be using if variable cost in factory 1 appears to be greater than competitors' prices? By how much would the manager of factory 1 be likely to overestimate the variable costs of product X, given this system?

15. Effect of costing method on reported income.   The Dowd Company operates one small factory in which it manufactures a single product for sale to customers in the chemical and plastics industries. The company's costing system is based on the full costing concept. The following results were reported for the years 19x1 and 19x2:

	19x1	19x2
Sales—units..........................	25,000	37,500
Beginning inventory—units...........	5,000	15,000
Ending inventory—units..............	15,000	7,500
Production—units....................	35,000	30,000
Fixed factory overhead costs.........	$280,000	$290,000
Selling and administrative expenses...	30,000	36,000

Although materials prices and wage rates increased during these years, the company was able to offset these increases to a large extent by a vigorous program of cost reduction. Accordingly, variable cost remained unchanged at $7 a unit during these two years. The selling price of the product also remained constant, at $20 a unit. Factory fixed costs were assigned to products in both years on the basis of an overhead rate of $8 a unit.

All underabsorbed or overabsorbed factory costs were taken to the income statement for the year in which they arose.

a. Compute reported income for the two years by (1) full costing and (2) variable costing.
b. Now assume that both production and sales in 19x2 were 37,500 units. Calculate the company's reported income for 19x2 under (1) full costing, and (2) variable costing. Assume that total fixed costs

were $290,000 and that the same overhead rates were used in both years.

16. Break-even; Effect of advertising. R. A. Ro and Company, maker of quality handmade pipes, has experienced a steady growth in sales for the past five years. However, increased competition has led Mr. Ro, the president, to believe that an aggressive advertising campaign will be necessary next year to maintain the company's present growth.

To prepare for next year's advertising campaign, the company's accountant has prepared and presented Mr. Ro with the following data for the current year, 19x2:

Variable Costs:
    Direct labor...................... $8.00 per pipe
    Direct materials.................. 3.25 per pipe
    Variable overhead................ 2.50 per pipe
        Total variable costs........... $13.75 per pipe

Fixed Costs:
    Manufacturing........................... $ 25,000
    Selling................................. 40,000
    Administrative.......................... 70,000
        Total fixed costs.................... $135,000

Selling price, per pipe..................... $25.00
Expected sales, 19x2 (20,000 units)......... $500,000
Tax rate 40%

Mr. Ro has set the sales target for 19x3 at a level of $550,000 (or 22,000 pipes.)

a.   What is the projected after-tax net income for 19x2? (The amounts shown on the tax return are the amounts on the income statement.)

b.   What is the break-even point in units for 19x2?

c.   Mr. Ro believes an additional selling expense of $11,250 for advertising in 19x3, with all other cost relationships remaining constant, will be necessary to attain the sales target. What will be the after-tax net income for 19x3 if the additional $11,250 is spent?

d.   What will be the break-even point in dollar sales for 19x3 if the additional $11,250 is spent for advertising?

e.   If the additional $11,250 is spent for advertising in 19x3, what is the required sales level in dollar sales to equal 19x2's after-tax net income?

f.   At a sales level of 22,000 units, what is the maximum amount which can be spent on advertising if an after-tax net income of $60,000 is desired?

(CMA adapted)

17. Dropping a product: Interdependencies. The Upson Company manufactures four products in a single factory. Factory volume is considerably lower than normal, and substantial unfavorable overhead variances have resulted. Sales, cost, and expense data for the four products are as follows:

	Product A	Product B	Product C	Product D	Total
Sales......................	$2,000,000	$2,500,000	$1,000,000	$500,000	$6,000,000
Cost of goods sold:					
Materials................	$ 300,000	$ 400,000	$ 200,000	$ 40,000	$ 940,000
Labor....................	500,000	600,000	400,000	100,000	1,600,000
Overhead................	600,000	800,000	500,000	100,000	2,000,000
Total cost of goods sold...............	$1,400,000	$1,800,000	$1,100,000	$240,000	$4,540,000
Gross margin............	$ 600,000	$ 700,000	$ (100,000)	$260,000	$1,460,000

	Product A	Product B	Product C	Product D	Total
Selling and administra- tive expenses (15% of sales)..............	300,000	375,000	150,000	75,000	900,000
Unadjusted income	$ 300,000	$ 325,000	$ (250,000)	$185,000	$ 560,000
Underabsorbed overhead .					300,000
Income before Taxes..............					$ 260,000

Factory overhead is approximately 40 percent variable at normal operating volumes. Variable selling and administrative expenses amount to
approximately 5 percent of sales.

The substantial losses reported for product C have led management to
consider discontinuing its manufacture, but the company's controller has
opposed any such action, saying that company profits would be even lower
without product C than with it.

a. Prepare a report that would support the controller's position and provide a better indicator of the relative profitability of each of the company's products.
b. The president of the company agrees with your figures but says that as
   soon as practical product C should be dropped. "In the long run," he
   says, "we cannot afford to retain any product that does not cover its
   costs." At what time would you consider it "practical" to drop product
   C? What information would you find useful in making such a decision?
c. Is it conceivable that even in the long run it might be profitable to
   keep product C in the line? Under what conditions?
d. A copy of your report is brought to the attention of the manager of the
   market research department, who calls you in and tells you that you
   have overlooked the following relevant facts:

   1. Fifty percent of the sales of product C are for applications in
      which product D can also be used. If product C were not available,
      sales of product D could be increased by $400,000 a year without
      any substantial change in fixed selling expenses.
   2. Twenty percent of the sales of product C are sold in conjunction
      with product A. These customers would not be able to substitute
      product D and would seek other sources of supply of product A.
      It is estimated that sales of product A would decline by 10 percent
      if product C were withdrawn from the company's line.
   3. The company's controller has also estimated that a complete
      abandonment of product C would permit a reduction of fixed
      factory, selling, and administrative costs in the amount of $100,-
      000 a year. If product C were kept in the line only as a service to
      product A customers, receiving no direct selling effort or ad-
      vertising, the reduction in fixed costs would amount to only
      $40,000 a year.

   In view of this additional information, prepare a report indicating
   whether sale of product C should be continued, or discontinued entirely, or continued only as a service to the small group of product A
   customers whose business would be lost if product C were not available.

5

Budgetary Planning

MANAGERS can manage for a while by dealing with each problem as it comes along. Even relatively small organizations, however, usually find it useful to try to fit their major decisions into an integrated, coordinated framework. The vehicle they use is annual budgetary planning. Our purpose in this chapter is to describe what budgets are, why they can be useful, and how they are prepared. The chapter has four parts:

1. A description of the major components of the budget.
2. An analysis of the advantages budgeting can have.
3. A prescription for more effective budgeting of individual activities and programs.
4. An illustration, following one firm's path through an annual budgeting cycle.

In practice, preparation of a long-range plan is part of the annual budgeting cycle. It raises no special conceptual issues, however, and to save space we have omitted this part of the cycle from our discussion.

COMPONENTS OF THE BUDGET

A budget is the quantitative expression of a plan. It reflects what management has decided to do and what it expects to accomplish by doing it. In other words, as we defined it in Chapter 1, budgeting is an integrated set of project and program decisions covering the organization as a whole and each of its many parts for a specified period of time.

We usually classify the parts of the budget into two groups, operating budgets and financial budgets. *Operating budgets* list the amounts of goods and services the organization plans to consume during the operating period and the benefits it expects these activities to produce. In most organizations the resources consumed are generally represented by cost figures as well as by physical quantities; in a profit-

EXHIBIT 5–1

Budget Components

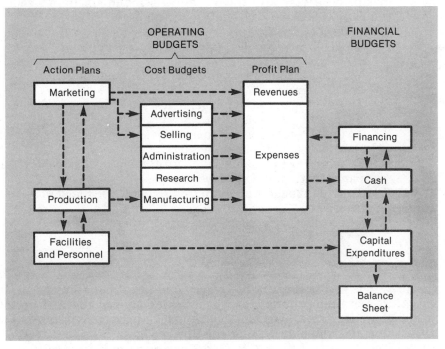

oriented company, benefits are represented by revenues. The *financial budgets*, on the other hand, show how much money the organization plans to spend during the period and where it plans to get it.

Exhibit 5–1 describes the budget of a manufacturing firm. Each block in the diagram represents one or more parts of the overall budget. For convenience, we shall refer to each part as a budget, although we find it useful to remember that these are all part of a single budgetary plan.

The budget also has an organizational dimension, not shown in this diagram. Each division, each department has its own portion of the overall plan. Departmental budgets are narrow in scope, dealing with only one or two elements. Divisional budgets are more comprehensive—divisions with both sales and production operations even have their own profit plans and may have divisional balance sheets and partial financing plans. Overall financing remains a head office responsibility, however, and most organizations control cash mainly in the head office.

THE PURPOSES OF BUDGETING

Budgeting is a lot of work. Each division manager in a large company is expected to submit a proposed operating plan and capital expenditure budget well ahead of the end of the year. Putting these proposals together may take two or three months. Reviewing them, making necessary adjustments, and assembling them in a coordinated companywide plan takes another month or two.

No one does this for fun. It must have a good payoff if management is to go to all this trouble. Six potential advantages are worth noting:

1. To force managers to *analyze* the company's activities critically and creatively.
2. To direct some of management's attention from the present to the *future*.
3. To enable management to *anticipate* problems or opportunities in time to deal with them effectively.
4. To reinforce the managers' *motivation* to work to achieve the company's goals and objectives.
5. To give managers a continuing *reminder* of the actions they have decided on.
6. To provide a *reference point* for control reporting.

Creative Analysis

The first purpose of budgeting is to force management at all levels to reexamine the company's activities periodically and consider alternative programs or methods. Budgeting is really a form of *simulation*, in which managers run the business on paper, without risk. They can try different combinations in an effort to find the one that seems likely to work best. In a large organization they may have large-scale computer programs to help them, but even back-of-the-envelope analysis can be very useful.

The result of this kind of analysis may be to shift emphasis from one product to another, to move into new market areas, or even to discontinue certain activities. It may also be to leave everything unchanged. Whatever the outcome, budgeting is intended to get the manager to remember that nothing is as constant as change. What worked yesterday won't necessarily work tomorrow. Organizations that don't figure this out tend to stagnate, lose their vitality, and eventually disappear unless someone comes along to get things moving again.

A Sense of Futurity

Management's natural tendency in most organizations is to concentrate on the pressing problems of the day—"putting out fires," this is often called. Budgeting lifts the manager's attention for a while and redirects it toward the future. What is the future apt to be like and how is it likely to affect this part of the business? The manager who can anticipate environmental changes is better prepared to deal with them when they occur or to adapt to them in advance.

Anticipation of Problems

Programs sometimes fail because of hidden flaws that come to light only when management tries to execute them. No one can ever guarantee that this won't happen, but a good budgeting procedure forces all managers to set down in a good deal of detail just what they plan to do and how they plan to do it. This makes it less likely that some vital ingredient will be forgotten, some step overlooked.

Higher management, too, must submit to budget discipline. As proposals come up to headquarters, management must try to fit them together. This is known as *coordination*. Inconsistencies and bottlenecks are apt to show up at this point. Finding them now, while everything is still on paper, is a lot better than trying to cope with them under pressure later on.

Motivation

Given the amount of work it requires, budgeting may not seem to be a very useful vehicle for motivating managers. Furthermore, the budget itself is not a motivating force. It is just a piece of paper. The motivation comes, if at all, from the process of producing the budget, not from the end product. Put another way, the objective is to use the process to *reinforce* the manager's motivation to work to achieve the company's goals. It is only one of several motivational elements and will work only if the others are also active.

Budgeting works in part because in working on the budget the managers are constantly reminded of the goals of their own sections of the organization. They are asked to judge each budgeting decision by its likely effect on progress toward these goals. Furthermore, by participating in preparing it, the managers are expected to make personal commitments to the successful execution of the plan. It becomes their plan, not something imposed on them from above. We'll have a good deal more to say about this in Chapter 19.

Action Reminder

The first four purposes of budgeting were advantages of the budgeting *process*. The final two items in the list are advantages of the budget documents themselves. The budget serves the managers as a constant reminder of the plan they have adopted. As such, it provides a blueprint they can consult from time to time as they work to implement the plan. The contractor who ignores the blueprint is prone to build a shack, not a house. The manager who ignores the budget is in the same position.

A Reference Point

The final purpose of the budget is to serve as a benchmark against which actual performance can be measured. This is an essential element in control reporting. Since we shall devote several chapters to this, beginning in Chapter 6, we need not explore this point further now.

THE ACTIVITY DIMENSION IN BUDGETING

Management must make many difficult decisions at budget time. We shall examine some of these in the next section, as we trace the steps in a typical budgeting cycle. Before we begin, however, we need to see what some of the difficulties are and how management can structure the budget and the budgeting process to help resolve these difficulties. This section will explore two questions:

1. How the budget can be structured to reflect both organizational responsibilities and the activity focus of budgeting decisions.
2. How management might deal with problems arising from the organization's inability to measure the benefits of individual activities.

Organizational and Program Budgeting

The budget typically follows the organization chart—that is, a budget is prepared for each responsibility center on the chart. The budgets for responsibility centers at higher organization levels summarize the budgets for the responsibility centers below them. This is called *organizational budgeting*.

Organizational budgeting is essential because it identifies the resources individual managers are expected to use and the objectives they are expected to achieve. This may not be enough, however. The budget for each responsibility center covers all of that center's activities. When the center is engaged in more than one activity, the part each is to play is not clear unless the budget is subdivided by activity. In a research department, for example, a separate budget is likely to be prepared for each research project and for departmental administrative activities.

Developing budgets for individual activities or for groups of related activities has two main advantages. First, it makes the plan itself a lot clearer. This makes it a better guide for the manager and a better basis for comparison with actual results. Second, it gives management a better foundation for decision making. The best way to review budget proposals is to calculate the costs and benefits of individual activities. Subdividing the budget by activity makes this feasible.

Program budgeting is the name for the process of building the activity dimension into the budget. In concept, it applies to any kind of activity, but in practice the term generally refers to the budgets for major groups of related activities, or programs. These may cut across organizational lines as shown in Exhibit 5–2. Each of the responsibility centers in this exhibit has two activities. Three of these activities are independent, while three are part of an integrated program. In a research organization, for example, these might all relate to a new product or customer service. In a book publishing company

EXHIBIT 5–2

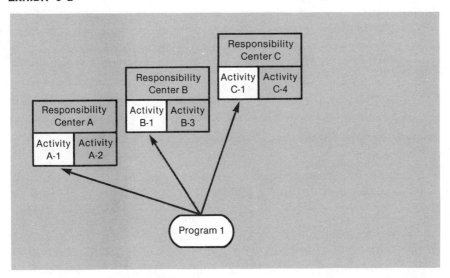

they might relate to a coordinated set of study materials. In such cases the main decision focus is on the larger program rather than on the individual activities within the responsibility centers.

Budget Review

Responsibility for developing the budget ordinarily falls in the first instance on the responsibility center managers. In some organizations top management starts the process by establishing the broad limits within which it expects each center's budget proposals to fall. In others, each of the first-line responsibility center managers is expected to prepare a set of budget proposals. In either situation, higher management needs to review the proposals for feasibility and for desirability.

Budget proposals may be reviewed in two different ways. One is to ask whether the anticipated benefits from each proposed activity are great enough to justify the proposed expenditures. For this kind of analysis, each proposal can be examined more or less independently of the others.

The second kind of review focuses on the *relative* merits of different proposals. This is necessary because no organization has unlimited resources. It may lack money, it may lack equipment, or it may lack skilled personnel. Whatever the reason, most organizations find it necessary to reject some proposals for lack of resources, even though the proposals themselves seem to have favorable benefit/cost ratios.

For either kind of review, management needs to estimate the benefits to be realized from each proposal. The benefits of many kinds of proposals cannot be measured in terms of their direct monetary benefits to the organization, however. This makes it impossible to compare costs and benefits directly. Attempts to get around this difficulty were a central feature of a massive effort in the 1960s to introduce program planning and budgeting systems (PPBS) in governmental departments and agencies.[1] Government executives were asked to classify their budget requests by activity (program budgeting or program planning) and to estimate the benefits arising from each activity. In an effort to put costs and benefits on a comparable plane, efforts were made to measure benefits in dollars.

The main reason for seeking dollar measures of benefits is that having these would make it easier to compare budget requests from different agencies. Without these, requests can be ranked only on an ordinal scale—this proposal is better than that one, which is better than another, and so on.

Business firms have these same problems. Proposals to pay dividends are not directly comparable to proposals to sponsor employee recreation activities because benefits are not measured in comparable terms. These problems must be solved, and the solutions must reflect management's judgment. To help management apply its judgment, some authorities suggest a systematized approach known as zero-base budgeting.[2] Zero-base budgeting has three main features:

1. The activities of individual responsibility centers are divided into a series of incremental "packages."
2. Each package is ranked ordinally.
3. Managers at higher levels consolidate the proposals submitted by their subordinates, providing their own ordinal rankings.

For example, suppose a manager of a community relations department has submitted a proposed budget of $300,000. Under zero-base budgeting, this would be subdivided into packages, perhaps as follows:

	Packages	Amount	Rating
1.	Base package: department's manager and secretary, adult job training	$150,000	6
2.	Summer youth sports program	70,000	5
3.	Winter youth sports program	40,000	4
4.	College scholarships	20,000	3
5.	Educational television	20,000	3

The manager's superior must combine this set of proposals with those submitted by the other department heads. This isn't easy, because the ordinal scales used by the various managers aren't comparable. Should the community relations manager's 3 be given the same priority as a 3 from the personnel manager?

Easy or not, sooner or later these proposals must be merged. In the

---

[1] See David Novick, *Program Budgeting*, 2d ed. (New York: Holt, Rinehart & Winston, Inc., 1969).

[2] See Peter A. Pyhrr, "Zero-Base Budgeting," *Harvard Business Review*, November–December 1970, pp. 111–21.

end, higher management will probably have to reject some spending proposals; to do this it will have to identify certain proposals as less desirable than others. By definition, the proposals management rejects are those management classifies as least desirable. Zero-base budgeting merely systematizes the process by which this classification is made.

Zero-base budgeting is not a panacea. Managers are reluctant to admit that all of their activities are not of the highest priority. They are also likely to define activity packages broadly enough to attach pet projects to the coattails of other, more easily justified activities. These tendencies are difficult to control. Furthermore, the process may seem so mechanistic that managers may come to regard it as a meaningless exercise.

The concepts it is based on are worth implementing, however. Few activities are indivisible, and managers should be encouraged to evaluate the incremental costs and benefits of each subactivity they are responsible for. The use of ordinal rankings is also to be encouraged, particularly for discretionary programmed activities such as support of philanthropic and cultural activities.

Ordinal rankings can also be used for certain kinds of responsive activities, those for which the technological relationship between volume and response is weak. For example, a company can probably hire employees without a hiring manager. The more people it needs to hire, the more awkward it becomes not to have someone in charge of the logistics of the hiring function. The benefits of having a hiring manager, however, are difficult to estimate in dollars. A possible solution is to rank this proposal with others on an ordinal scale.

AN ANNUAL BUDGETING CYCLE

Each organization has its own way of trying to reap the benefits budgeting can provide, but most systems have a great deal in.common. In this final section we shall study a fairly typical system, the one used by the Caldwell Company, a small manufacturer of hand drills.

This company has two products, the Drillmaster and the Handyman. Both products are made in the same factory and sold by the same sales force, working out of a network of company-owned branch offices. The branch managers supervise the salespeople and try to keep on top of developments in their territories. They report directly to the marketing vice president. These relationships are shown in Exhibit 5–3. (To keep the illustration manageable, most blocks in the organization chart have been omitted from the diagram.)

The budgeting process at the Caldwell Company can be broken down into six major steps:

1. Setting top management's objectives.
2. Preparing the marketing plan.
3. Developing the production plan.
4. Assembling the capital budget.
5. Preparing the cash budget.
6. Working out further details.

EXHIBIT 5–3

CALDWELL COMPANY
Partial Organization Chart

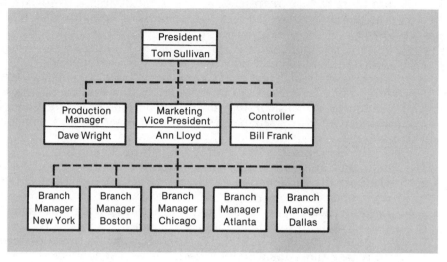

Top Management's Objectives

Tom Sullivan, the company's president, started the budgeting process in 19x1 with a meeting in his office just after Labor Day. Looking at the company's performance for the first eight months of the year and forecasts of economic activity prepared by the company's bankers, he suggested that 19x2 ought to be a good year. He asked his division managers to work toward a 15 percent increase in sales and a 25 percent increase in net income.

Ann Lloyd, the marketing vice president, and Dave Wright, the production manager, thought these targets were too high. They cited the narrow product line, old factory equipment, and intense foreign competition, particularly for the Handyman drill. Mr. Sullivan said he was looking at merger possibilities, but none of these could be negotiated before the end of 19x2. "For the time being, we'll have to stick with what we have," he said. "Maybe you can't meet the objectives I have in mind, but I think they're within reach. Give it a try and see what you can come up with."

This is a very common practice. Most systems start with a set of common forecasts of what the environment will be like and some statement of broad objectives by top management. In larger companies these objectives are based on intensive analysis of industries and markets by headquarters staff; in smaller firms they are often semi-intuitive, like Mr. Sullivan's.

The Marketing Plan

Bill Frank, the controller, was responsible for administering the budget—that is, it was his job to collect budget proposals from Ms.

Lloyd and Mr. Wright, review them, and assemble them in a coordinated package.

The logical place to start was the marketing plan. Marketing is the largest and most important of Caldwell's programmed activities, as it is in most business firms. The marketing plan determines how many orders will be received and for what. This then determines how busy the factory will be, how much warehouse space will be necessary, and how large the clerical staff should be. Ms. Lloyd took the following steps, with Mr. Frank's help:

1. She estimated the average variable cost of manufacturing each product.
2. She estimated the contribution margin from the sale of one unit of each product.
3. She had the branch managers estimate sales and branch expenses under at least two alternative marketing plans.
4. She reviewed the estimates and developed a tentative consolidated marketing plan.
5. She tested the plan for feasibility.
6. She prepared a revised proposal.

Estimating product cost.   Many marketing decisions call for estimates of the costs of individual products. Ms. Lloyd asked Mr. Frank to work with Mr. Wright on the factory cost estimates for 19x2. (In practice, management would work with a preliminary set of estimates at this point, revising them later. We'll save space by describing the entire process in detail now.)

Direct materials costs.   The specification sheets for each product list the materials to be used. Combining these lists with estimates of materials prices, Mr. Wright made the following estimates of direct materials costs per unit:

	Drillmaster	Handyman
Direct materials costs...............	$6.00	$5.14

Direct labor costs.   The Caldwell factory had two production departments, machining and assembly. The estimated wage rate was $8 an hour in machining and $4 an hour in assembly. The estimated direct labor requirements for a unit of each of the company's products were as follows:

	Drillmaster	Handyman
Direct labor hours per drill:		
Machining..............................	0.8	0.6
Assembly..............................	1.0	.9
Direct-labor cost:		
Machining at $8 per direct labor hour.......	$ 6.40	$4.80
Assembly at $4 per direct labor hour.......	4.00	3.60
Total.................................	$10.40	$8.40

Variable overhead costs. Mr. Wright's next step was to estimate variable overhead cost. To do this, he had to develop a variable overhead costing rate for each department. He worked with his department heads and with Mr. Frank to develop the cost estimates summarized in Exhibit 5–4.

EXHIBIT 5–4

CALDWELL COMPANY
Estimated Variable Factory Overhead Costs
for 19x2

	Machining	*Assembly*
Indirect labor.................	$138,000	$22,900
Maintenance.................	27,600	7,000
Supplies......................	46,000	45,800
Power.......................	55,200	14,300
Miscellaneous................	3,200	800
Total variable overhead......	$270,000	$90,800
Direct labor hours............	180,000	227,000
Variable overhead costing rate................	$1.50/direct labor hour	$0.40/direct labor hour

Dividing estimated variable overhead costs by the estimated number of direct labor hours in each department yielded the variable overhead rates shown at the bottom of Exhibit 5–4. These were then multiplied by the estimated direct labor hours required to manufacture each product. The entire variable product cost calculation is summarized in Exhibit 5–5.

EXHIBIT 5–5

CALDWELL COMPANY
Estimated Variable Product Costs

	Drillmaster	*Handyman*
Direct materials............................	$ 6.00	$ 5.14
Direct labor:		
Machining at $8 per direct labor hour......	6.40	4.80
Assembly at $4 per direct labor hour.......	4.00	3.60
Variable overhead:		
Machining at $1.50 per direct labor hour.....	1.20	0.90
Assembly at $0.40 per direct labor hour......	0.40	0.36
Total................................	$18.00	$14.80

Estimating contribution margin. The second step was to estimate the contribution margin provided by one unit of each product. To do this, Mr. Frank had to estimate the net amount the company would realize from each unit sold.

The Drillmaster units were priced at $40 each, to be competitive with comparable products of other manufacturers. The Handyman units sold for $20 each. Discounts and allowances were expected to average 5 percent of gross sales for Drillmasters and 6 percent of gross sales for Handyman units. Mr. Frank used these percentages to derive the following estimates of net revenue per unit:

	Drillmaster	Handyman
Gross price...........................	$40.00	$20.00
Discounts and allowances.............	2.00	1.20
Net revenue......................	$38.00	$18.80

Putting these figures together with the estimates of variable factory cost, Mr. Frank got the following estimates of contribution margin per unit:

	Drillmaster	Handyman
Net revenue..........................	$38.00	$18.80
Variable factory cost.................	18.00	14.80
Contribution margin..............	$20.00	$ 4.00

These figures were to help Ms. Lloyd decide how much to spend on marketing each product and how much to spend in each region.

Estimating branch sales and expenses. Ms. Lloyd next asked her branch managers to estimate sales and branch expenses on the assumption that the same marketing strategy would be used in 19x2 as in 19x1, the same selling prices and the same sales force. Second, do this again on the assumption that the price of the Handyman would be raised to $25. She reminded them that the Drillmaster was a much more profitable model and should be emphasized whenever possible. She also asked them to suggest ways headquarters could help them market the company's products more effectively.

Caldwell's approach to sales forecasting is a *grass-roots approach,* with the line selling organization preparing its own sales forecasts. The company has two reasons for doing it this way. First, the salespeople know more about their own customers than a central market research department could hope to know. In other words, Ms. Lloyd believes that she gets a better sales forecast by relying on the sales force. Second, by helping set their own budgets, the salespeople become more fully committed to them. This means a stronger motivation and presumably better performance.

This is not to deny the value of central sales forecasting or market research. Even if the basic forecasts are made in the field, the market research staff can be of material assistance. It can conduct qualitative research to reveal market potentialities, environmental trends, and competitive activities. It can engage in quantitative research to estimate how much can be sold, by product and by territory or by other major categories of the company's business. These estimates can be checked against the field estimates to reveal any wide discrepancies that can then be traced further. Market research can also perform a service function to the field sales force, analyzing data supplied from the field and advising sales managers in reviewing sales forecasts made by individual salespeople.

No matter which of these approaches is used, most companies will find it impossible to prepare a separate forecast for each product as the Caldwell Company was able to do. Resources simply can't be spared for this detailed an analysis. Instead, products are classified into closely related groups and forecasts are made for each group as a whole. Typically, this means dollar forecasts or forecasts of some common denominator such as tonnage.

We should also emphasize that sales forecasting is not the same as sales budgeting. Forecasting is essentially a passive activity; budgeting is more active. Sales volume depends on the amount and kinds of marketing effort, and a separate forecast has to be made for each marketing program management wants to consider.

Review, revise, and consolidate the estimates.   Ms. Lloyd found that only one of the five branch managers believed that the Handyman prices could be raised without reducing sales severely. This model competed directly with low-priced imported models and their prices were unlikely to go up. Ms. Lloyd agreed the price should remain at $20.

On reviewing the proposals from the branches, Ms. Lloyd found that the manager in Atlanta was budgeting 1,000 fewer Drillmasters in 19x2 than in 19x1, even though this seemed to be a growing market. The manager explained that his sales force could not cover the growing suburban markets effectively without losing their old customers in the cities in the Atlanta region. At Ms. Lloyd's suggestion, he drew up a new plan calling for the hiring of an additional sales representative.

Ms. Lloyd also found that the Dallas branch was forecasting a 25 percent increase in unit sales, mostly in the Handyman line. This was far greater than in any of the other branches and much larger than the growth rates in the Southwest would suggest. The branch manager explained that the Handyman drills he had placed in a local supermarket chain in August were selling very well. He suggested using the supermarket channel in other areas as well, with someone from headquarters to work closely with the branch sales force on the supermarket accounts. The other branch managers were enthusiastic, and Ms. Lloyd tentatively agreed to move one of the more experienced salespeople into the head office to help in supermarket sales.

Test for feasibility.   New sales forecasts were made on this basis and the total came to 255,000 units. Ms. Lloyd checked with Dave Wright, the production manager, and found that no more than 240,-000 units could be delivered in 19x2. The factory had enough capacity to make more, but the supplier of a patented ratchet that went into each drill had limited Caldwell to 20,000 ratchets a month for the next year while its own plant expansion program was under way. This is known as a *constraint,* defined as a limit to action set by law, policy, custom, or shortage.

The presence of a shortage-based constraint requires management to allocate the resource that is in short supply among the activities that need it. To do this in a profit-oriented organization, management needs to estimate how much profit a unit of the scarce resource can contribute in each of its possible uses.

Contribution for this purpose is defined as the net revenue from the sale of a unit, less all the variable costs except the cost of the scarce resource itself. (Since the total amount of this resource will be used under any likely solution, its total cost will be the same under all of them and therefore can be ignored.) We saw earlier that the variable cost of a Drillmaster was $18, against $14.80 for a Handyman. Each of these figures included $1 to cover the cost of a ratchet. The contribution of each ratchet therefore was calculated as follows:

	Drillmaster	Handyman
Total variable cost	$18.00	$14.80
Less: ratchet costs	1.00	1.00
Other variable costs	$17.00	$13.80
Net revenues	38.00	18.80
Contribution of each rachet	$21.00	$ 5.00

The difference between these two contribution figures was so great that Ms. Lloyd cut 15,000 Handyman drills out of the tentative sales plan to bring sales and production into balance. She decided to go ahead with the supermarket venture, however, because this would absorb 60,000 drills in 19x2, even after the cutback, with a promise of substantial growth and profit in later years.

Assemble the final proposal. Once these decisions were made, Ms. Lloyd was ready to prepare the tentative marketing budget. This budget was to use a *profit contribution* format. The profit contribution from any revenue segment is the total contribution margin of that segment, less the fixed costs traceable to that segment, as shown in Exhibit 5–6.

EXHIBIT 5–6

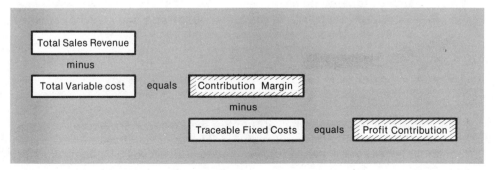

EXHIBIT 5–7

CALDWELL COMPANY
Proposed Marketing Budget

	Drillmaster	Handyman	Total
Units sold............................	110,000	130,000	240,000
Gross sales...........................	$4,400,000	$2,600,000	$7,000,000
Discounts and allowances.............	220,000	156,000	376,000
Net sales.............................	$4,180,000	$2,444,000	$6,624,000
Variable cost of goods sold...........	1,980,000	1,924,000	3,904,000
Contribution margin...................	$2,200,000	$ 520,000	$2,720,000
Direct product marketing expenses....	80,000	100,000	180,000
Product profit contribution..............	$2,120,000	$ 420,000	$2,540,000
General marketing expenses:			
Branch offices........................			620,000
Headquarters.........................			140,000
Marketing Profit Contribution............			$1,780,000

Profit contribution figures are usually stated as monthly totals. They show how much each segment of the firm's business (product, territory, and so forth) contributes to the common kitty to help pay for the general costs of administering the company and serving its customers. These costs are necessary to support operations, but they are not traceable to individual segments.

The proposed marketing budget is shown in Exhibit 5–7. The profit contribution concept has been applied at two levels:

1. The costs traceable to each product have been subtracted from the product's contribution margin to get a profit contribution figure for that product.
2. The general expenses traceable to the marketing division but not to individual products have been subtracted to get the divisional profit contribution figure.

Notice all the things that happened after Ms. Lloyd got the first tentative proposals from the branches:

1. Pricing policy was reviewed.
2. One branch proposal was sent back for revision.
3. A strategic decision was made in the head office to make a major move affecting all branches.
4. The entire plan was found to be unfeasible due to production restrictions; the sales budgets were reduced.

In other words, this was not a sterile exercise in filling out forms. It was a highly dynamic, creative process.

The Production Plan

Once the tentative marketing plan was ready, Mr. Wright was able to put the production plan in shape. The top executives agreed that if the supermarket venture was successful, the Caldwell Company would want to go into 19x3 prepared to increase its deliveries of Handyman drills substantially. Additional ratchets were expected to be available by that time to enable a substantial expansion in volume.

To prepare for this, Mr. Wright proposed to build an inventory of component parts for 10,000 Drillmasters and 10,000 Handyman drills, fitting them into the machining department's schedule whenever convenient. They would be assembled in 19x3, when additional ratchets were expected to become available. Mr. Wright took six steps to get his budget proposal in shape:

1. He estimated direct materials requirements.
2. He estimated direct labor requirements.
3. He estimated factory overhead requirements.
4. He prepared a summary of the estimated manufacturing costs.
5. He prepared physical resource plans.
6. He prepared tentative production schedules, in detail, for the first three months of 19x2.

Estimating direct materials requirements. The first step was to multiply direct materials costs per unit by estimated production quan-

EXHIBIT 5–8

CALDWELL COMPANY
Direct Materials Cost Budget

	Drillmaster	Handyman	Total
Units placed in production..................	120,000	140,000	260,000
Units finished............................	110,000	130,000	240,000
Direct materials costs per drill:			
Ratchet......................................	$ 1.00	$ 1.00	
Other materials..........................	5.00	4.14	
Total.................................	$ 6.00	$ 5.14	
Total materials costs:			
Ratchets (units finished).................	$110,000	$130,000	$ 240,000
Other materials (units placed in			
production)...........................	600,000	579,600	1,179,600
Total.............................	$710,000	$709,600	$1,419,600

tities. These calculations are summarized in Exhibit 5–8. Separate estimates were made for ratchet costs (based on total production of 240,000 finished units) and for other materials, enough to produce the 240,000 finished units and add 20,000 units to the inventory of partly processed drills.

Estimating direct labor requirements. Mr. Wright then used his estimates of the number of direct labor hours required for a unit of each product to calculate total direct labor hours. For example, we see in the first column of Exhibit 5–9 that each drillmaster would require 0.8 of an hour of labor time in the machining department. Since machining work was to be performed for 120,000 Drillmasters in 19x2, production of Drillmasters would require 96,000

EXHIBIT 5–9

CALDWELL COMPANY
Direct Labor Budget

	Drillmaster	Handyman	Total
Direct labor hours per drill:			
Machining.............................	0.8	0.6	
Assembly.............................	1.0	0.9	
Production requirements (no. of drills):			
Machining.............................	120,000	140,000	260,000
Assembly.............................	110,000	130,000	240,000
Total direct labor hours:			
Machining.............................	96,000	84,000	180,000
Assembly.............................	110,000	117,000	227,000
Total direct labor cost:			
Machining at $8 per direct labor hour....	$ 768,000	$ 672,000	$1,440,000
Assembly at $4 per direct labor hour.....	440,000	468,000	908,000
Total.............................	$1,208,000	$1,140,000	$2,348,000

direct labor hours in 19x2. Multiplying the direct labor hour totals by
the estimated direct labor wage rates then yielded the estimates of
direct labor costs shown at the bottom of Exhibit 5–9.

Mr. Wright's budgeting job was relatively easy because the company
had only two products. He could move directly from the tentative sales
budget to a detailed list of production requirements. This may not be
feasible if the product line is extremely broad. One company deals
with this problem by developing three separate tentative sales budgets,
one for each of the following product groups:

1. Major catalog products, budgeted in both physical units and sales
    dollars.
2. Minor catalog products, budgeted in dollars only.
3. Custom products, also budgeted in dollars.

The sales mix in the minor catalog products tends to remain relatively
stable and historical mix ratios can be used to predict product output
requirements. Custom products, on the other hand, are so diverse that
common output units cannot be found. Instead, materials and labor
requirements are based on average historical relationships between the
sales value of production and labor and materials inputs.

Estimating factory overhead requirements. Mr. Wright had already
done most of the work on this phase when he developed the estimates
of variable factory overhead costs (Exhibit 5–4). He reviewed those
earlier estimates and also worked with his department heads to estimate the amount of fixed factory overhead costs necessary to support
the anticipated volume of production. His estimates are summarized
in Exhibit 5–10. (To make the illustration easier to trace, we have designed the illustration so that all overheads can be classified as wholly
variable or wholly fixed.)

Preparing a summary of manufacturing costs. Mr. Wright summarized all of the factory cost data in the statement of budgeted

EXHIBIT 5–10

CALDWELL COMPANY
Factory Overhead Cost Budget

	Machining	Assembly	Factory Administration	Total
Variable overhead:				
Indirect labor..................	$138,000	$ 22,900	—	
Maintenance....................	27,600	7,000	—	
Supplies.......................	46,000	45,800	—	
Power.........................	55,200	14,300	—	
Miscellaneous.................	3,200	800	—	
Total variable................	$270,000	$ 90,800	$ —	$ 360,800
Fixed overhead:				
Supervision....................	$175,000	$ 70,000	$ 90,000	
Clerical.......................	—	—	42,000	
Maintenance....................	—	—	3,000	
Supplies.......................	—	—	6,000	
Heat and light.................	—	—	66,000	
Depreciation...................	205,000	15,000	75,000	
Property tax...................	—	—	60,000	
Property insurance.............	—	—	30,000	
Miscellaneous.................	—	—	3,000	
Total fixed...................	$380,000	$ 85,000	$375,000	840,000
Total overhead...........	$650,000	$175,800	$375,000	$1,200,800

manufacturing costs shown in Exhibit 5–11. This exhibit contains only one new bit of information, the provision for an increase in raw materials inventories. If the plan was approved, production levels in 19x2 would be considerably higher than in 19x1. This would require a greater inventory of materials and purchased parts, calculated as follows:

Inventory, January 1, 19x2..............	$155,400
Inventory, December 31, 19x2...........	230,000
Increase in materials inventory.......	$ 74,600

Prepare physical resource plans. This has been a very sketchy summary of the production planning process. To make the illustration easier to follow, we left out vast quantities of detail that the production plan had to have. Labor, for example, is not a homogeneous commodity. Each department requires people with different skills, both for direct labor and for indirect labor operations. These requirements must be spelled out in detail so that the personnel department can complete a personal plan. The purchasing department will also have to prepare a detailed budget for purchases of materials.

Prepare production schedules. Mr. Wright's final step was to prepare production schedules for the first three months of 19x2. Production schedules are not really part of the production plan. They provide immediate instructions to first-line production personnel.

EXHIBIT 5–11

CALDWELL COMPANY
Budgeted Manufacturing Costs

Product costs:	
Direct materials:	
Inventory, January 1, 19x2...................	$ 155,400
Purchases................................	1,494,200
Total.....................................	$1,649,600
Inventory, December 31, 19x2..............	230,000
Direct materials issued (Exhibit 5–8).......	$1,419,600
Direct labor (Exhibit 5–9).....................	2,348,000
Variable overhead (Exhibit 5–10)..............	360,800
Total product costs......................	$4,128,400
Fixed factory overhead (Exhibit 5–10)...........	840,000
Total manufacturing costs................	$4,968,400

Which products are to be manufactured in which departments by which personnel on which machines on what days?

Production schedules are seldom prepared more than a few months in advance, and are frequently revised from day to day as conditions change. The production plan, on the other hand, typically covers the entire year and is not revised. Its main purpose is to show how sales plans will be implemented, thereby giving production management a chance to evaluate alternative production methods and select the combination that seems to meet planned delivery requirements at minimum cost. In the process, it may identify the lack of adequate labor force, materials, or facilities to support the tentative sales plans. If production capacity can't be increased rapidly enough at reasonable cost, then the sales plan will have to be cut back.

The Profit Plan

The proposed marketing plans, production plans, and proposals to spend money for administrative support, engineering and other operating purposes come to the budget director or controller for review and consolidation into a proposed profit plan. In the larger company, each division will do its own consolidating and central management will get an integrated set of proposals from each. The Caldwell Company isn't big enough for that, however, and it is the controller's job to pull everything together.

Putting the components together. Mr. Frank had worked closely with Ms. Lloyd and Mr. Wright throughout the budgeting process and was thoroughly familiar with their figures. Before putting the tentative profit plan in finished form, however, he had to estimate how much of the manufacturing costs would be reported as the cost of goods sold and how much would be added to the cost of the inventories during the year.

Variable costs. The company's internal accounting records were kept on a variable costing basis. Mr. Frank's first step was to estimate

EXHIBIT 5–12

CALDWELL COMPANY
Variable Cost of Inventory Increment

	Drillmaster	Handyman	Total
Unit costs (from Exhibit 5–5):			
Direct materials, except ratchets...............	$ 5.00	$ 4.14	
Machining direct labor.........................	6.40	4.80	
Machining variable overhead...................	1.20	0.90	
Total unit cost............................	$12.60	$ 9.84	
Units added to inventory........................	10,000	10,000	
Costs of units added to inventory...............	$126,000	$98,400	$224,400

the increment in the variable cost of the inventories of work-in-process and finished goods expected to be on hand at the end of 19x2.

All factory inventories were measured on a last in, first out (Lifo) basis. This means that the 20,000-unit increase in semiprocessed products would be measured at the 19x2 costs of the machining operations, including all materials except the ratchets. These calculations are summarized in Exhibit 5–12.

The quantities of finished goods on hand were not expected to change in 19x2. These, too, were accounted for on a Lifo basis, and the reported cost of the ending inventory therefore was expected to be the same as the reported cost of the beginning inventory.

Fixed costs. Variable costing is not an acceptable method of measuring inventory costs for external financial reporting, as we pointed out in Chapter 4. Since the work-in-process inventory was expected to increase in 19x2, the amount of fixed costs assigned to the work-in-process inventory would also have to go up.

Normal volume in the machining department was 200,000 direct labor hours. Budgeted fixed costs totaled 380,000 (from Exhibit 5–10). The supplemental overhead rate for 19x2 therefore was $380,000/200,000 = $1.90 per direct labor hour. The increment in the amount of fixed overhead costs assigned to the inventories was calculated as follows:

	Machining Hours per Unit	Units	Total Machining Hours	Total Fixed Overhead at $1.90
Drillmaster...........	0.8	10,000	8,000	$15,200
Handyman..........	0.6	10,000	6,000	11,400
Total........			14,000	$26,600

Small though this amount was, Mr. Frank decided to reflect it in the budget for 19x2. He rounded the dollar figure to $27,000 and made the following calculations:

	Variable	Fixed
Total manufacturing costs (Exhibit 5–11).....................	$4,128,400	$840,000
Less: Increases in work-in-process inventories...............	224,400	27,000
Amounts to be entered in tentative profit plan.........	$3,904,000	$813,000

Mr. Frank then assembled the budget proposals from the head office administrative departments (including his own), calculated interest and income tax expenses, and prepared the tentative profit plan shown in Exhibit 5–13.

Reviewing the tentative plan.   The controller's usual options at this point are diagrammed in Exhibit 5–14. If the plan seems inconsistent or unfeasible, it can be sent back for revision. It can also be sent back if it passes this first test but appears unlikely to meet top management's goals. If the controller is satisfied with the proposed plan, or if the division managers reject the controller's suggestions, the plan goes to top management, which will then have to decide whether any further improvement is possible. If not, the plan becomes final.

Top management often has reason to be dissatisfied with the plan proposed for one of the product lines or for one of the company's divisions. The controller is expected to anticipate this kind of reaction so that the revisions can be made before formal review at the top. By keeping the communications channels open in both directions, the controller usually can work things out with the division managers so that the final request for approval is a mere formality.

EXHIBIT 5–13

CALDWELL COMPANY
Tentative Profit Plan

	Drillmaster	Handyman	Total
Gross sales....................................	$4,400,000	$2,600,000	$7,000,000
Discounts and allowances...................	220,000	156,000	376,000
Net sales......................................	$4,180,000	$2,444,000	$6,624,000
Variable cost of goods sold..................	1,980,000	1,924,000	3,904,000
Contribution margin..........................	$2,200,000	$ 520,000	$2,720,000
Product-traceable fixed costs................	80,000	100,000	180,000
Profit contribution...........................	$2,120,000	$ 420,000	$2,540,000
General expenses:			
Fixed factory overhead......................			$ 813,000
Marketing....................................			760,000
Administration..............................			320,000
Interest......................................			80,000
Income taxes.................................			289,000
Total general expenses....................			$2,262,000
Net income...................................			$ 278,000

EXHIBIT 5–14

Responses to Budget Proposals

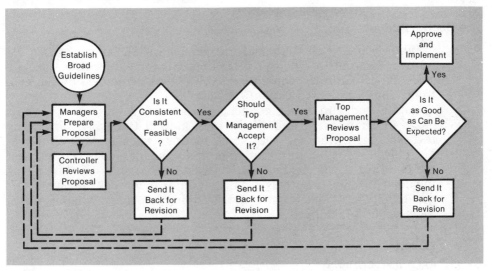

Sometimes top management has no quarrel with any specific component of the plan, but is unwilling to accept the overall result. Then managers in all departments have to review their proposals and come up with something better. Ideally, this would lead managers at lower levels to redouble their efforts to find ways to reduce costs or market their products more effectively.

In practice, a different result is more likely. Most operating budget proposals include many programmed activities that are not expected to provide substantial cash benefits in the immediate future. Research and community service activities are good examples. Budgets also include provisions for activities that are responsive to service demands, but only after a delay. Preventive maintenance is an example —it can be deferred, although at a cost. To meet a current profit target, management may choose to cut down on activities like these, despite the unfavorable future consequences of doing this.

Returning to the Caldwell Company, we find that Mr. Frank knew the president would be very unhappy with a net income of only $278,-000 and with the $420,000 profit contribution of the Handyman drill. The high cost of manufacturing the Handyman made this a marginal product at best, but it accounted for more than half the unit sales. Without it, the company would show a loss in 19x2.

Ms. Lloyd reminded Mr. Frank that the budgeted profit contribution from the Handyman drill was up substantially from the 19x1 level, thanks to the new supermarket venture. Mr. Wright maintained that the best way to reduce production costs would be to simplify the product. He saw no way of putting the redesigned product into production before the end of 19x2, but he did decide to prepare a proposal to buy automated assembly equipment that would be needed for the redesigned product.

The Capital Budget

While working on the operating plan, each of the company's executives also put together a set of proposals for the purchase or construction of plant and equipment. These were assembled by the controller into a proposed *capital budget.*

Capital budgeting is a complicated process. We'll discuss it in some depth in Chapters 14 and 15. At the Caldwell Company, Mr. Frank reviewed each proposal, sent some of them back to Mr. Wright or Ms. Lloyd for further information or analysis, and finally put together the tentative capital budget summarized in Exhibit 5–15. Mr. Frank included all these proposals because each of them met the company's profitability tests on its own, but he didn't know yet whether all of them could be financed.

EXHIBIT 5–15

CALDWELL COMPANY
Tentative Capital Budget

| | Payments to Be Made in | |
	19x2	19x3
Projects approved in 19x1, to be completed in 19x2.............	$ 70,000	—
New projects:		
Automatic assembly equipment.....	260,000	$ 40,000
Machinery department equipment replacements..........	240,000	—
Factory extension...................	600,000	200,000
Office equipment....................	50,000	—
Total..........................	$1,220,000	$240,000

The Cash Budget

The final link in the chain is the cash budget. Not until this is put together can management decide whether the firm has enough cash to do everything that is being proposed. Cash budgeting is essentially a five-step process:

1. Estimate cash receipts from operations.
2. Estimate operating cash payments.
3. Estimate other cash receipts and disbursements.
4. Identify expenditure limits.
5. Ration scarce cash.

Mr. Frank and his staff were responsible for the first four steps; the fifth was the president's job.

1. *Estimate cash receipts from operations.* The company's main continuing source of cash is its collections from its customers. Collections may be either less or greater than revenues, but in a growing company collections usually lag behind the growth in revenues. Mr. Frank estimated that in this case the increase in budgeted sales would require a $112,000 increase in accounts receivable. This reduced anticipated receipts to $6,512,000:

Net sales (Exhibit 5–13)...............	$6,624,000
Less: Increase in receivables........	112,000
Collections from customers.....	$6,512,000

2. *Estimate operating cash payments.* Increases in revenues usually require increases in inventories as well as increases in expenses. The first approximation to the amount of cash required to pay for operations therefore is the sum of expenses and inventory changes. Several things may interfere, however. Depreciation charges, for example, do not represent current cash payments, and these must be subtracted from the total. Similarly, any increases in accounts payable, wages payable, or taxes payable will reduce the amounts to be paid currently in cash. They, too, must be subtracted. Any decreases in these items of course must be added.

In this case, Mr. Frank estimated that accounts payable would increase by $21,000, while taxes payable would increase by $40,000, a natural result of the company's anticipated growth in 19x2. Budgeted operating cash payments amounted to $6,316,000, as calculated in the following table:

Expenses (Exhibit 5–13):		
Variable cost of goods sold..................	$3,904,000	
Product-traceable fixed costs................	180,000	
General expenses..........................	2,262,000	$6,346,000
Inventory increases:		
Materials (Exhibit 5–11)......................	$ 74,600	
Work-in-process (Exhibit 5–12)...............	224,400	
Fixed costs in inventories....................	27,000	326,000
Total operating expenditures...........		$6,672,000
Adjustments:		
Depreciation (Exhibit 5–10)..................	$ (295,000)	
Increase in accounts payable...............	(21,000)	
Increase in taxes payable...................	(40,000)	(356,000)
Payments to employees and suppliers...		$6,316,000

Cash generated by operations therefore amounted to $196,000:

Collections from customers.................	$6,512,000
Payments to employees and suppliers......	6,316,000
Cash generated by operations.........	$ 196,000

3. *Estimate other cash receipts and disbursements.* To complete the tentative cash budget, management must estimate the amounts to be received from such sources as planned borrowing, the sale of shares of stock, and the sale of long-term assets or plant and equipment. In this case, Mr. Frank anticipated no asset sales, no long-term borrowing or debt retirement, and no sales of stock. He included dividends in the tentative cash budget at the same amount as in 19x1, $200,000, along with the $1,220,000 current portion of the tentative capital budget (Exhibit 5–15).

4. *Identify expenditure limits.* Caldwell's practice in the past had been to finance all its capital expenditures either from current operating funds or from long-term sources. Interest rates were expected to remain at very high levels throughout 19x2, however, and the stock market was depressed. Mr. Frank knew that the board of directors would go to the long-term financial markets only if the company's survival seemed to depend on it. Any financing in 19x2 would have to be from short-term sources.

Mr. Frank's discussions with the company's bankers and with Mr. Sullivan convinced him that the maximum amount the company either could obtain or was willing to obtain by short-term borrowing in 19x2 was $800,000. This set a tentative expenditure limit of $996,000 for 19x2:

Cash from operations......................	$196,000
Maximum borrowing........................	800,000
Expenditure limit.......................	$996,000

5. *Ration scarce cash.* The tentative estimate of cash inflows and outflows are summarized in Exhibit 5–16. From this it is clear that Caldwell could not finance all the activities included in the tentative operating plan and capital budget. Cutbacks improving cash flows by at least $424,000 would have to be made.

EXHIBIT 5–16

CALDWELL COMPANY
Tentative Cash Budget

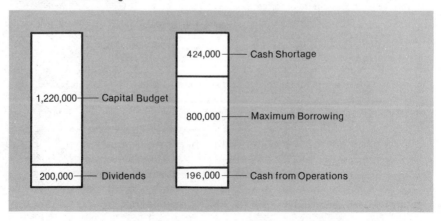

What were management's alternatives at this point? Mr. Frank listed six items for Mr. Sullivan to consider:

1. Reduce the dividend.
2. Revise the profit plan.
3. Eliminate the increase in the inventory of semiprocessed drills.
4. Defer the equipment replacements.
5. Defer the assembly automation project.
6. Defer the plant expansion.

The most obvious of these might seem to be the dividend. Mr. Sullivan knew, however, that the board of directors would take this route only as a last resort. Cutting the dividend would depress the price of the company's stock and make raising new funds in the future much more difficult.

Mr. Sullivan had worked with his division managers quite closely as they worked on the profit plan. He saw no way to change this that would not hurt the company in the future. He decided to leave that untouched. He also decided to keep the proposed inventory buildup. Without this, a substantial and profitable market expansion in 19x3 would be impossible.

Turning to the items in the capital budget, Mr. Sullivan decided to keep all the equipment replacement proposals. Without these, meeting production cost and delivery targets would be impossible. He finally decided to make ends meet by postponing the plant expansion and automation proposals until the company had more experience with the supermarket venture. He left the automation proposal and equivalent financing in the budget but ruled out any expenditure on the project until more data on supermarket sales were available toward the middle of the year.

We must emphasize that these decisions were highly subjective. The rankings made by Caldwell's management have no relevance to the decisions to be made by other managers in other situations. The solution in each case will reflect the judgment of the managers on the spot.

Further Details

Mr. Frank discussed the cash situation with Mr. Sullivan and got the decision on the plant expansion proposal before putting the budget in final form. At that time he prepared an estimated end-of-year balance sheet and redid the cash budget on a monthly basis to reveal any seasonal patterns in cash flows. The cash budget may be in surplus for the year as a whole, but deep in deficit for part of the year, as in Exhibit 5–17.

Management must forecast these seasonal patterns, so that it can adjust the timing of enough receipts and disbursements to keep the cash balance at an adequate level. It can borrow seasonally, shift the timing of discretionary expenditures such as purchases of equipment, or invest temporarily idle cash in short-term securities.

Monthly profit plans are also useful, mainly to serve as bases of

EXHIBIT 5–17

Seasonal Imbalances in Cash Flows

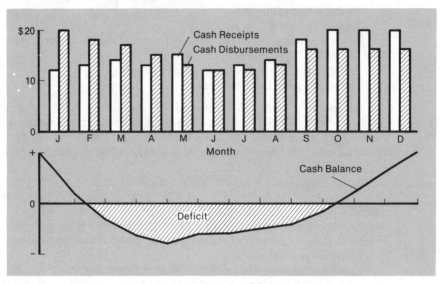

comparison with actual performance as the year goes on. Important though these seasonal translations are, however, they raise no new conceptual problems that require further discussion here.

One final point should be emphasized. Budgeting is an *iterative* process, in which budget proposals move haltingly, level by level, up through the organization to the top. Budget proposals are prepared, submitted to the next management level, sent back for revision or further evidence, resubmitted, approved and passed up to the next level, reviewed there and sent back down, revised again and resubmitted, and so on.

The process is not as inefficient as it may seem, however. In a well-designed system, people talk to each other as they go along. It is ideas and suggestions, rather than formal documents, that are most likely to go up and down the chain of command. Furthermore, both top management and division management have staff assistants to handle analytical problems and keep the process moving.

SUMMARY

Budgeting is a form of decision making. It has many purposes—to force managers to consider alternatives, to reinforce their motivation to work toward the organization's goals, to identify emerging problems and opportunities, to coordinate the organization's activities, and to produce a set of documents that will guide managers and serve as a benchmark for later control reporting.

We have tried to convey a feeling for the complexity and dynamism of the budgeting process. Budget preparation starts at the top, with the formulation of broad statements of policy and the establishment of the basic framework. The next step is taken at the grass-roots level, as local managers work on their marketing plans, translate these into production plans, and back them up with proposals for capital investment. These plans are reviewed, revised, and consolidated as they move up the organizational ladder toward final top management approval. They all come together eventually in a series of profit plans and cash budgets that are both feasible and acceptable to top management.

As this would imply, budgeting is a responsibility of line management; the controller or budget director administers the system and provides useful advice and assistance. When finally completed, the budget becomes a managerial commitment and a benchmark against which future performance can be measured.

KEY TERMS

The most important terms introduced and defined in this chapter are the following:

Capital budget	Production plan
Cash flow from operations	Production schedule
Constraint	Profit contribution
Financial budgets	Profit plan
Marketing plan	Program planning and budgeting
Motivation	system
Operating budgets	Zero-base budgeting

INDEPENDENT STUDY PROBLEM
(Solution in Appendix C)

1. Profit planning and cash budgeting. The Darnell Company is organized in three divisions, each with a division manager, a small office staff, and its own sales force. The various divisions sell different kinds of products and deal with different groups of customers.

The company's budget director has received the following proposals and estimates for next year from the division managers:

	Division A	Division B	Division C
Divisional marketing costs amounting to..................	$ 150	$ 500	$ 300
Will produce revenues of........	1,000	3,000	2,100
And cost of goods sold of........	650	1,650	1,260
Administrative expenses to support these activities will total......................	150	300	200
Accounts receivable will increase by....................	10	200	50
Inventories will exceed this year's ending balance by.......	50	100	50
Accounts payable will increase by....................	15	50	80

The expenses of the company's central management are tentatively budgeted at $400 for the year, to be paid in cash. Cash purchases of equipment amounting to $130 and cash dividends of $350 are also proposed. Of the equipment purchases, $60 is to replace existing equipment and $70 is for expansion. The expansion proposals, which management has approved in principle, will have no effect on next year's income statement.

Depreciation is included in the administrative expense figures above as follows: central management, $10; Division A, $5; Division B, $15: Division C, $20.

a. Prepare a tentative profit plan and cash budget for next year, on the assumption that all of these proposals are approved.
b. The company will start next year with a cash balance of $290 and an unused line of bank credit of $100. The minimum cash balance is 5 percent of sales. Is the tentative plan feasible?

EXERCISES AND PROBLEMS

1. Cash budgeting; Constraints. The management of Salisbury Products Company at the beginning of 19x1 anticipated (1) a decrease in sales as compared with 19x0 because of production time lost in converting to new products, and (2) a considerably smaller profit margin due to higher material and labor costs. You have the following forecasts:

Change in accounts receivable.............. $	50,000 decrease
Change in accounts payable................	10,000 decrease
Inventories.................................	15,000 decrease
Sales revenues ($200,000 less than in 19x0)...	2,000,000
Additions to plant and equipment (gross)...	150,000
Depreciation, 19x1..........................	110,000
Income before taxes, 19x1..................	100,000
Income tax expense, 19x1 (payable in 19x2)..	40,000
Dividend payments (at 19x0 rates)..........	45,000

The cash balance on January 1, 19x1 was $54,000, about $25,000 less than management felt was necessary to ensure prompt payment of bills and maintain the company's credit rating. The accrued tax liability on January 1, 19x1, arising from 19x0 taxable income, amounted to $93,000. The company had no bank loans outstanding.

a. Assuming that any balance sheet items not listed above would be unchanged, prepare a schedule of forecasted cash receipts and cash disbursements for 19x1 and determine the expected cash balance on December 31, 19x1.
b. What action would you expect management to take when it sees the cash flow estimates for the year?

2. Profit planning. Canyon, Inc. operates two stores that sell and install automobile seat covers and a few automotive supplies such as upholstery cleaner and auto washing compounds. The company's president has heard that budgetary planning is a good thing and has decided that a profit plan should be prepared for the coming year. The managers of the two stores have submitted the following tentative budgets:

	Downtown Store	Suburban Store
Sales revenue:		
Seat covers......................	$400,000	$720,000
Auto supplies....................	72,000	160,000
Total........................	$472,000	$880,000
Store expenses:.....................		
Supervisory & clerical salaries......	$ 47,200	$ 47,600
Installers' wages..................	40,800	80,000
Store clerks' wages................	18,400	18,800
Rent...........................	38,400	35,200
Utilities..........................	6,000	8,400
Other............................	2,800	5,200
Total........................	$153,600	$195,200

During the coming year, the purchase cost of seat covers is expected to average 55 percent of selling prices, while the selling prices of auto supplies will be about twice their purchase cost. The president has prepared a tentative head office budget for the coming year:

Executive salaries..........................	$100,000
Clerical salaries...........................	48,000
Advertising................................	40,000
Rent.......................................	24,000
Office supplies.............................	4,000
Utilities...................................	4,800
Legal and consultants' fees................	6,800
Other......................................	2,000
Total................................	$229,600

a. Assemble these data into a tentative profit plan for the coming year. Use a profit contribution format.
b. What problems do you think the president and the store managers encountered in preparing their tentative sales and expense plans? What were their principal sources of information?
c. What criteria would you use in reviewing these proposals?
d. Prepare a revised profit plan, using additional data that your instructor will provide.

3. Profit contribution budget. The PDQ Company manufactures a line of high-quality office furniture which it sells to dealers in the northeast. Its sales force is divided into two divisions, each headed by a division manager. The preliminary profit plan for next year shows the following (in thousands of dollars):

	Atlantic	New England	Total
Sales..	$900	$1,200	$2,100
Expenses:			
Variable cost of goods sold...............	$540	660	$1,200
Sales commissions (5% of sales)..........	45	60	105
Fixed expenses:			
Manufacturing.........................	108	132	240
Marketing.............................	71	106	177
Administration.........................	36	42	78
Head office...........................	30	40	70
Total expenses.....................	$830	$1,040	$1,870
Income before taxes.......................	$ 70	$ 160	$ 230
Income taxes at 50%.....................	35	80	115
Net income...........................	$ 35	$ 80	$ 115

You have the following additional information on these figures:

1. All products are manufactured in a single factory and product costs are calculated on a variable costing basis.
2. Fixed factory overhead costs are divided between the divisions in proportion to the cost of goods sold.
3. Division marketing and administrative expenses are completely traceable to the individual divisions.
4. Head office expenses are divided between the divisions in proportion to sales.
5. The company's factory has ample capacity to increase production by 40 percent without increasing the variable costing rate.

Top management is not satisfied with this proposal. Although economic conditions next year are expected to be considerably better than this year, the proposed budget shows virtually no change from this year's budget.

Top management has told the manager of the Atlantic Division that the division's marketing expenses must be reduced by $4,000 and administrative expenses reduced by $6,000 unless the division can come up with a better proposal. These reductions would not affect sales next year but might make future marketing more difficult.

As a result of this prodding, the manager of the Atlantic Division has proposed that sales promotion in this region be increased materially by adding a merchandising manager and two more sales representatives to the staff and by additional advertising. The annual fixed cost of these additional efforts would amount to $80,000. Sales would increase 20 percent if this were done, with no change in selling prices and no change in the product mix. If this is accepted, the order to cut $10,000 out of the current expense budget will be rescinded.

The manager of the New England Division believes that physical sales volume can be increased by 15 percent if prices are reduced selectively, to large customers who are particularly sensitive to price. List prices would be unchanged, but the average price realized in the division would be about 5 percent less than in the initial budget proposal. The product mix would not be affected, and no additional marketing or administrative expenses would be necessary. In fact, the manager has agreed to reduce the proposed divisional marketing expenses by $4,000, whether the price reductions are approved or not.

Executives in the head office have agreed to reduce their proposed operating expenditures by 5 percent. The factory manager has convinced top management that no further reduction in factory fixed costs is possible.

a. Recast the original budget proposals in a profit contribution format.
b. Calculate the anticipated profit contribution for each division if its revised proposal is accepted. Which of these proposals would you endorse?
c. Prepare a revised profit plan, in a profit contribution format, reflecting your answer to (b).

4. Budgeting discretionary expenditures. After examining all the feasible alternatives, the management of a sporting goods company has decided on a set of marketing, production, and administrative plans for next year that meet feasibility and profitability tests. The budget director has given management the following summary of the anticipated cash flows implicit in these tentative plans for next year:

Maximum net cash flow.......... +$580,000
Expected net cash flow........... + 400,000
Minimum net cash flow.......... + 180,000

You have the following additional information:

1. Some additional seasonal financing will be available for seasonal
    needs next year; otherwise, all expenditures must be financed from
    the company's cash flows.
2. The cash dividend to the company's shareholders has totaled $100,000
    for each of the last three years. Earnings per share increased this year
    and is expected to increase again in the coming year. Management
    would like to increase the dividend to $120,000 next year.
3. The corporate relations department has proposed that the company
    engage in three new activities that have not yet been included in the
    budget for next year.

Summer street recreation program for
  children in a large eastern city............ $100,000
Grant to public television to support
  broadcasts of figure skating contests.....   80,000
Grant to support student scholarships at a
  graduate business school at which the
  company recruits actively.................   20,000

4. Capital expenditure proposals received from various departments:

New extruding machine to permit manufacture
  of components now purchased outside...... $ 70,000
Replacements for various factory machines....   100,000
Replacements of office equipment............   10,000

5. Depreciation for next year is expected to total $30,000 on buildings
    and $90,000 for equipment.

Decisions on all these expenditures will be made by top management
next week when it meets to adopt the final budget for next year. The budget
director has time to talk to the various executives responsible for these
proposals, and even to get further written justification for each, but
no one will be able to gather any data not already presented in support
of the individual proposals.

a. Indicate what the budget director can and should do to facilitate
    management's task. In your answer, indicate how the proposals should
    be presented to management, and what information should and proba-
    bly can be supplied. *You cannot and should not try to recommend
    acceptance or rejection of any of these proposals.*
b. Describe the choices management must make next week and recom-
    mend a procedure which management might use in making these
    choices. In other words, given the data supplied by the budget di-
    rector, what should management do next?

5. Monthly budget schedules.   The Grumball Company sells merchandise on credit. You have the following data:

1. Budgeted gross sales (at list prices) for the first quarter of the coming year are:

January.................. $260,000
February.................   243,000
March....................   293,000

2.   Customers are required to pay for their purchases within 30 days, and the Grumball Company offers a 2 percent cash discount from list price if payment is made within 10 days.

3. Past experience indicates that customers' accounts are settled according to the following timetable:

	Percent
Month of sale..............	65%
Next month................	33
Third month................	1

The remaining 1 percent eventually prove uncollectible.

4. Accounts receivable on January 1 are expected to amount to $130,-000. Of this amount, $105,000 will have arisen from December sales, $6,000 from November sales, the $19,000 from sales made prior to November. No accounts have been written off as uncollectible so far this year, but a number of the accounts now on the books are doubtful, and management sees no reason to change its estimate of the average rate of customer defaults.

5. Of the customer accounts settled in any month, 90 percent are settled within the discount period and the customers take the discount.

6. The cost of goods sold is budgeted at 60 percent of gross sales. Sales commissions amount to 3 percent of gross sales. Other operating expenses will amount to $60,000 a month, including $5,000 a month for depreciation. Sales commissions are paid the month following the month they are earned. Cash payments arising from other operating expenses are paid 70 percent immediately and the remainder in the following month.

7.   Budgeted purchases of merchandise for the three months are $150,-000, $175,000, and $160,000, respectively. Purchases are paid for 30 days after the date of purchase.

8. Accounts, sales commissions, and wages payable on January 1 are expected to be as follows:

Accounts payable for merchandise.........	$139,500
Sales commissions payable.................	9,000
Other accounts and wages payable.........	16,500

9. The capital budget calls for the purchase of equipment in February for $100,000. Payment is to be made in March, with $60,000 of this amount to be covered by new bank borrowing at that time.

10. A $50,000 cash dividend is to be paid in January.

11. Income taxes are accrued monthly at 40 percent of pretax income. The only tax payment to be made in this three-month period is a payment of $40,000 in January.

a.   Prepare a schedule of revenues and expenses for each of the three months.
b.   Prepare a schedule of cash flows for each of the three months, with a line for the cumulative effect on the cash balance.

6. Reviewing an operating budget proposal.   Frank Thomas is reviewing the tentative operating budgets his department heads have just submitted. Mr. Thomas is the administrative vice president of a food-processing company, a job he has held for the last three years.

Mr. Thomas has found it difficult to deal intelligently with his subordinates' annual budget proposals. Last year was a good one for the company and he felt little pressure to come in with a low budget proposal. He made few changes in his subordinates' proposals, merely endorsing most of them and including them in the divisional budget proposal submitted to the budget director. The year before, the heat was on, and he cut many of the proposals back sharply. The most persuasive and persistent department heads were cut back less than the others, however, and this made Mr. Thomas uneasy.

A particularly difficult budget to deal with is the budget for the personnel department. Jean Carlisle, the personnel manager, has requested a 23 percent increase over the budget for this year. About a fifth of this increase is to pay higher salaries and cover increased prices of supplies and other cost elements; the rest is to pay the salaries and expenses of a new professional development office. Ms. Carlisle is convinced that the company's management development efforts have been uneven and uncoordinated, but neither she nor anyone on her staff has been able to find time to do the job right.

In addition to management development, the personnel department is responsible for a number of activities, mainly recruiting and hiring new employees; maintaining personnel records; administering an annual performance review program; maintaining records of the company's antidiscrimination program; maintaining a personal skills inventory and suggesting candidates for promotion; administering the company's employee benefits program; supervising the job rating and salary administration program; operating a grievance procedure; and supervising an on-the-job training program for office personnel. This year's budget and the proposal for next year are as follows:

	This Year	Proposed, Next Year
No. of employees..................	20	23
Salaries...........................	$325,000	$382,000
Employee benefits.................	71,500	86,000
Consultants and contractors.......	2,900	41,100
Travel.............................	17,800	18,500
Computer.........................	23,700	24,500
Advertising	14,200	14,900
Rent..............................	36,000	36,000
Heat, light and power.............	5,300	6,100
Postage and supplies..............	8,900	12,800
Other.............................	2,100	2,500
Total........................	$507,400	$624,400

Mr. Thomas and Ms. Carlisle have often discussed the need for a better approach to management development and he wants to support the proposal for a professional development office. All of the other departments in Mr. Thomas's division are proposing increased spending, however, ranging from a low of 10 percent to a high of 20 percent. Mr. Thomas knows that he will never be able to get the top management budget committee to approve a 15 percent increase in his division's budget, no matter how eloquent he is or how convincing his case. Therefore, if personnel gets 23 percent, some other departments in the division will probably get little or nothing.

a. Knowing that the key to the proposed budget is in the salary line, Mr. Thomas has asked your help in evaluating this item. How would you proceed?

b. What further information should Mr. Thomas ask Ms. Carlisle to provide before he reviews her proposed budget? (Limit your suggestions to data she might reasonably be expected to be able to assemble fairly quickly.) How would Mr. Thomas use this additional information?

7. Profit plan. The Erskine Sales Corporation serves as a manufacturers' representative for several manufacturers of automotive replacement parts. It has sales branches in each of the three major eastern cities. Sales and expense data for the current fiscal year are expected to show the following totals (in thousands):

	Boston	New York	Philadelphia	Head Office	Totals
Sales..........................	$4,000	$10,000	$6,000	—	$20,000
Cost of goods sold.........	2,700	6,750	4,050	—	13,500
Gross profit..................	$1,300	$ 3,250	$1,950	—	$ 6,500
Expenses:					
Salaries and commissions..	$ 900	$ 1,600	$1,200	$ 300	$ 4,000
Rent........................	20	60	40	50	170
Travel expense.............	100	120	110	40	370
Advertising.................	10	20	20	30	80
Other expenses............	5	15	10	20	50
Total expenses.........	$1,035	$ 1,815	$1,380	$ 440	$ 4,670
Income before taxes.........	$ 265	$ 1,435	$ 570	$(440)	$ 1,830
Income taxes................					950
Net income................					$ 880

In planning for the coming year, the company's budget director obtained the following information:

1. Expected automobile "population" in the region, classified by make and age of car, was obtained from the company's suppliers and was distributed to the branch managers.

2. The company's suppliers announced their intention to raise list prices (charged by Erskine Sales to its customers) by 5 percent. Prices paid by Erskine Sales will be increased by 4 percent.

3. Salaries and commissions per employee will be 3 percent higher next year.

4. Sales forecasts received from the branches anticipate the following increases in physical sales volume: Boston, 6 percent; New York, 10 percent; and Philadelphia, 8 percent. The product mix, or relative proportions of total sales represented by each of the company's products, is expected to be the same next year as this year.

5. To handle the increased sales volume, the following increases in personnel are anticipated: Boston, 2 percent; New York, 4 percent; Philadelphia, 3 percent; and head office, 2 percent. (These increases will occur in the indicated proportions at all salary levels.)

6. Rent will be the same at all locations except New York, where a $30,000 increase is expected on lease renewals.

7. Travel expenses will be $10,000 greater in each of the branches and $5,000 greater in the head office.

8. The New York office has asked for an increase in its advertising appropriation to $40,000. All other advertising appropriations are to remain at this year's level.

9. Other expenses are expected to increase next year by 5 percent at all locations.

10. Income taxes are budgeted at 30 percent for the first $25,000 of income and 50 percent for all income in excess of that figure.

a. Prepare a tentative operating budget for each branch office, for the head office, and for the company as a whole for the coming year.

b. Each of the three branches has indicated that it could expand sales by an additional 10 percent next year (that is, 10 percent of *this year's* physical sales volume) if it were permitted to add to its sales force and clerical staff. The added salaries and commissions, in excess of those already budgeted for next year, would be $120,000 at any branch for which such additional hiring is approved. Travel, advertising, and other expenses would be increased by $30,000 for any such branch. Head office expenses would be increased by $10,000 for each branch for which expansion approval is granted. Prepare calculations to indicate which branch or branches, if any, should be permitted to make the requested additions to their sales forces.

8. Budget: Nonprofit organization. DeMars College has asked your help in developing its budget for the coming academic year. You are supplied with the following data for the current year for the lower (freshman-sophomore) and upper (junior-senior) divisions:

	Lower	Upper
Average number of students per class...........	25	20
Average salary of faculty member................	$15,000	$15,000
Average number of credit hours carried each year by each student.........................	33	30
Enrollment (including scholarship students).......	2,500	1,700
Average faculty teaching load in credit hours a year (10 classes of 3 credit hours)..............	30	30

Lower division enrollment in the coming year is expected to increase by 10 percent, while the upper division's enrollment is expected to remain at the current year's level. Faculty salaries will be increased by a standard 5 percent, and additional merit increases to be awarded to individual faculty members will be $90,750 for the lower division and $85,000 for the upper division.

The current budget is $210,000 for operation and maintenance of plant and equipment; this includes $90,000 for salaries and wages. Experience of the past three months suggests that the current budget is realistic, but that expected increases for the coming year are 5 percent in salaries and wages and $9,000 in other expenditures for operation and maintenance of plant and equipment.

The budget for the remaining expenditures for the coming year contains the following:

Administrative and general................	$440,000
Library.....................................	160,000
Health and recreation......................	75,000
Athletics...................................	320,000
Insurance and retirement...................	365,000
Interest....................................	48,000
Capital outlay.............................	300,000

The college expects to award 25 tuition-free scholarships to lower division students and 15 to upper division students. Tuition is $31 per credit hour and no other fees are charged.

The college has a small unrestricted endowment which has been invested in securities which now have a market value of approximately $2 million. In addition, commercial bank account balances total $50,000, but this amount is necessary to support the college's normal operations.

Budgeted revenues for the coming year from sources other than tuition are as follows:

From endowment.................... $114,000
From auxiliary services............. 235,000
From athletics...................... 280,000

The college's only other source of funds is an annual support campaign held during the spring.

a. Prepare a schedule computing (1) the anticipated enrollment, (2) the total credit hours to be carried by students, and (3) the number of faculty members needed for each division.

b. Calculate tuition revenues and faculty salaries for each division and for the school as a whole. Combine these with estimates of other revenues, other expenses, and capital outlays to form a tentative budget proposal for the coming year. Indicate how much money will have to be raised during the annual support campaign to cover all expenditures if this budget proposal is approved.

c. In what ways should the structure of the available budget information be changed to facilitate periodic planning?

d. The college's president is concerned about the effect on the college's finances if enrollments fall below the budgeted levels. Prepare an alternative budget on the basis of a 6 percent reduction in enrollment below the budgeted level in each division. The number of scholarships would not be reduced. In what ways would you use this additional information? What other analyses would you want to carry out?

(CPA adapted)

9. Cash and profit budgets. The Airtight Company prepares its cash and profit budgets one quarter in advance. The following data are relevant to the budgets for the fourth quarter of the current year:

1. The cash balance is expected to amount to $60,000 on October 1. Accounts receivable on that date are expected to total $220,000.

2. The company's product is sold at a price of $2.50 a unit. Sales are made on terms of net 30 days, and customer remittances are typically received 30 days after the merchandise is shipped.

3. Tentative sales and production schedules for the next four months are as follows (in units):

	Produced	Sold
October.....................	100,000	80,000
November....................	100,000	90,000
December....................	100,000	100,000
January.....................	110,000	110,000

4. For budgeting purposes, the company classifies its manufacturing costs into seven groups:

	Budgeted Amount
Direct materials.....................	$0.87 per unit produced
Direct labor........................	$0.35 per unit produced
Indirect labor......................	$0.08 per unit produced + $20,000 per month
Royalties...........................	$0.05 per unit produced
Property taxes and insurance........	$2,000 per month
Other cash costs....................	$0.12 per unit produced + $3,000 per month
Depreciation........................	$5,000 per month

5. Manufacturing overhead costs (all manufacturing costs other than direct materials and direct labor) are assigned to products by means of a

predetermined overhead rate based on budgeted full cost at a normal volume of 100,000 units a month.

6. Direct materials are paid for in the month *prior* to the month in which they are used in production.

7. Factory direct and indirect labor payrolls are generally paid in the month in which the work takes place, subject to accrued but unpaid balances, as follows:

October 1............... $3,000
November 1............. $0.10 per unit produced in October
December 1............. None
December 31............ $0.10 per unit produced in December

8. Royalty payments are made monthly on production during the preceding month. Production during September is expected to total 80,000 units.

9. Property taxes and insurance are paid at irregular intervals during the year. Payments for these items during the fourth quarter are expected to amount to $5,000 in November and $2,000 in December.

10. Other cash manufacturing costs are paid 80 percent during the month of production and 20 percent in the following month.

11. Cash dividends of $25,000 are to be paid to Airtight's stockholders in December. Budgeted expenditures on capital equipment amount to $15,000 in October and $10,000 in December. The effect of these capital expenditures on the monthly depreciation charge is to be ignored.

12. Selling and administrative expenses amount to $50,000 a month, all paid in cash. Income taxes are accrued at 52 percent of income before taxes each month, but no income tax payments are to be made during the fourth quarter.

a. Prepare a tentative profit budget for each of the next three months.
b. Prepare a tentative schedule of cash receipts, cash disbursements, and cash balances for each of the next three months.

CASE 5–1: CYCLE WORLD, INC.

Dave Burke, president of Cycle World, Inc., has been working on next year's budget for the past several weeks. The company, a retailer of bicycles and motorcycles, has managed to pay dividends to its shareholders ever since it was incorporated ten years ago. At that time it moved into its present quarters, a one-story, concrete block structure with a showroom in front and a parts storeroom and repair shop in the rear. Sales volume increased rapidly at first, but the growth rate has been very small for the past five years. Rising operating costs have kept net income at about the same level it reached five years ago. The cash flow from operations has been about equal to the sum of net income and depreciation.

This pattern seems likely to continue for the next few years, and Mr. Burke sees little chance of increasing the size of the cash dividend on the company's stock, now running at $12,000 a year, unless he can come up with some new money-making ideas. "If we just go on as we have been going," he said, "we'll make about $14,000 a year. That will cover the dividend, but without much to spare."

A tentative profit budget drawn up on this basis is summarized in Table 1. Three items need some explanation: (1) product warranty reimbursements; (2) salaries; and (3) depreciation. Product warranty reimbursements are the amounts recovered from the manufacturers to cover Cycle World's costs of repairing defective merchandise under the terms of the manufacturers' warranties to purchasers of their bicycles and motorcycles. The amount shown for salaries includes Mr. Burke's $30,000 a year, together with the salaries of a salesperson and a bookkeeper-typist. Depreciation covers the building, various pieces of repair equipment, a typewriter, and storage cabinets for the company's inventories of spare parts. (A zero income tax rate has been assumed to eliminate unnecessary complexity in the case.)

Mr. Burke has always viewed budget preparation as an occasion for reviewing operations and discussing the firm's financial position with his banker. He has not hesitated to make major decisions at other times, as he did when he added a line of light motorcycles shortly after the firm moved into its present location, but many of the innovations he has made have emerged from his annual wrestling match with the budget.

TABLE 1

CYCLE WORLD, INC.
Preliminary Projection of Net Income from Present Operations

Revenues:			
Product sales.................................			$150,000
Repair services..............................			100,000
Less: uncollectible accounts..............			(3,000)
Net revenues...........................			$247,000
Expenses:			
Cost of goods sold..........................		$ 85,000	
Mechanics' wages...........................		43,000	
Salaries.....................................		55,000	
Repair supplies.............................		20,000	
Heat and light..............................		5,500	
Advertising.................................	$10,000		
Less: reimbursements from Sussex Bicycles....................	5,000	5,000	
Depreciation................................		6,000	
Property taxes..............................		9,000	
Interest.....................................		2,000	
Other.......................................		6,000	
Total expenses........................		$236,500	
Less: product warranty reimbursements....		3,500	
Total expenses........................			233,000
Net Income...........................			$ 14,000

"Maybe I'd better see what would happen if I took on that Ivrea line of motor scooters," he continued. "I've never sold scooters before, but I've been servicing the Ivreas for years and I know they're a good product. Dom Bosco (Ivrea's regional manager) has been pushing me to take on an exclusive dealership for this area. He started working on me two years ago, and his terms have gotten better and better. Now he says it's time to fish or cut bait; they'll set up their own sales branch if we don't accept this final offer."

Taking on the Ivrea line would require Cycle World to invest $20,000 in an inventory of scooters and repair parts. Adequate space is available to carry these added inventories. Ivrea would finance one half of this requirement with a permanent credit line of $10,000 and with no interest charge, but Cycle World would have to finance the remainder from other sources. Cycle World would also have to hire an additional full-time mechanic, who would be trained at Ivrea's expense before being transferred to the Cycle World payroll.

Judging from data provided by Mr. Bosco, combined with his own experience in introducing new lines in the past, and with some help from the bank, Mr. Burke has drawn up the forecasts for the Ivrea line summarized in Table 2. All of these figures represent increments to the figures arising from Cycle World's present business. According to Mr. Burke, the figures given for the second year seem likely to be representative of what later years would bring.

TABLE 2

CYCLE WORLD, INC.
Projection of Income from Introduction of Ivrea Motor Scooters

	First Year	Second Year
Revenues:		
Product sales...........................	$50,000	$75,000
Repair services........................	11,000	13,000
Less: uncollectible accounts............	(1,000)	(1,500)
Net revenues......................	$60,000	$86,500
Expenses:		
Cost of goods sold.....................	$33,000	$49,500
Mechanics' wages......................	14,500	14,800
Repair supplies........................	1,000	2,100
Advertising...........................	4,000	4,000
Other.................................	500	750
Total..............................	$53,000	$71,150
Less: product warranty reimbursements..........................	1,500	2,000
Total expenses.....................	$51,500	$69,150
Incremental Income.............	$ 8,500	$17,350

If the Ivrea line is taken on, Mr. Burke expects net accounts receivable (after deducting the allowance for uncollectible amounts) to go up by $30,000 during the first year and by another $20,000 in the second.

While he was thinking about this proposition, Mr. Burke had a call from the Sussex Bicycle Company, one of Cycle World's major suppliers. Sussex has been reimbursing Cycle World for the full cost of local advertising of Sussex bicycles, up to a $5,000 annual limit. Sussex has now offered to pay half of the cost of local advertising, with a $2,500 limit on its contribution. "We could cut this advertising out completely," Mr. Burke said, "but I know it has brought in quite a few customers in the past. Sussex is a good name, and it brings people into the store. We're selling about $30,000 worth of Sussex bikes now, at a 45 percent gross margin. I'd hate to take a chance of losing any of that."

Whether he takes on the Ivrea line or cuts back on Sussex advertising, Mr. Burke has a number of other projects under consideration for next year. For one thing, his chief mechanic has put in a request for $2,000 to buy several pieces of shop equipment to replace equipment which no longer functions reliably. The annual depreciation expense will go up by $100 if the replacements are made. If the replacements are not made, depreciation charges will remain at $6,000 a year, but other shop expenses will exceed the amounts in Table 1 by about $300 next year, mainly in increased equipment maintenance costs. During the past five years replacement expenditures have ranged from $1,000 to $2,000, averaging about $1,800 a year.

Another possible expenditure is $3,200 to modernize the showroom with better lighting, a new front window, and new interior decoration. This would be accounted for as a current expense.

A third proposal is to spend $1,900 to renovate the lavatory. It is difficult to keep clean, one of the units is permanently out of service, and the mechanics have been grumbling that they'd rather use the facilities in the gasoline station across the street. This expenditure would also be treated as an expense.

Finally, Mr. Burke is considering a request from the local Chamber of Commerce for $3,000 for the Chamber's municipal improvement fund, to be used to attract more business to stores and shops in the downtown area. Mr. Burke is one of the Chamber's directors this year. Cycle World itself is not located in the downtown area, but Mr. Burke is convinced that a decaying business center would eventually affect business in the outlying districts as well.

Cycle World has little access to capital other than the amounts it can generate by its own operations. When the business was incorporated ten years ago, Mr. Burke and eight other people bought shares of stock in the new corporation. "I'm related to most of them in one way or another," Mr. Burke commented. "None of them has any extra money to invest, and they wouldn't give it to me if they did. We've paid their dividends regularly, but they all expected more than we've been able to cough up so far. I still own a controlling interest, but I'd sure get a lot of flak if I got the board to cut the dividend next year.

"The picture on borrowed money is a little brighter. We've got all the bank loans we can get on the basis of our present operations. I play golf with the president of the bank and he's really laid it on the line. I showed him our projections on the Ivrea line, though, and he and his chief loan officer have agreed to a new $20,000 term loan at 8 percent interest if we go through with the deal. But that's it; they won't go any farther." This loan would be made at the beginning of the year.

a. Prepare estimates of the incremental income and incremental cash flows associated with the Ivrea line for each of the first three years. Based on these figures, should Cycle World accept the Ivrea offer if enough funds can be found to finance it?

b. Prepare tentative cash flow statements for each of the next three years and a tentative income statement for next year, assuming that the Ivrea line is taken on and that all the requested expenditures are made this year. By what amounts are the company's cash resources inadequate to finance all the requested expenditures? (Ignore income taxes.)

c. List the major actions Mr. Burke might take to close the gap between anticipated receipts and anticipated disbursements. Choose the set of actions you would recommend and prepare a revised cash budget and profit plan reflecting these recommendations. Attach a brief explanation of the reasons for your recommendations.

CASE 5–2: VERLIES & WINST, N.V.*

During the first nine months of 1976, Verlies & Winst, N.V. operated its only factory two shifts a day plus a good deal of overtime work, and expected to continue at this production rate through the end of the year. At this rate, it was unable to meet the growing demand for its products, and inventories of finished products had been reduced during 1976 to amounts that the management felt were inadequate in view of the company's reputation for delivering its products promptly on the dates promised.

To correct this situation and to satisfy customer's demands, the company's executives in November 1976 decided to consider the desirability of moving to three-shift operations. To provide data useful for this decision, Mr. J. C. Verlies, the company's controller, was to prepare a profit plan and cash budget for 1977.

The Verlies & Winst product line consisted of two items of unusual design, both invented by the company's president, Mr. H. L. Winst. One product was a desk calendar holder of unusual design called "Dagmat"; the other was a desk-size device in which to list frequently called telephone numbers, sold under the name "Telemat."

In addition to Mr. Winst, the company's management consisted of Mr. Verlies and two product managers, one for each of the two products. Because the company was small, Mr. Winst performed the duties of general sales manager and production manager, in addition to his functions as president.

Using an economic forecast supplied by the company's bank, together with reports of dealer sales and inventories gathered by the company's salesmen, the two product managers gave Mr. Verlies the tentative budgets for 1977 shown in Table 1.

Mr. Winst's estimates of maximum production capacity and "general factory costs" (all factory costs except materials, labor, and depreciation) were:

	Production Capacity (machine-hours)	General Factory Costs at Capacity Operating Rates
Two-shift operations..................	91,450	$ 90,000
Three-shift operations...............	122,900	118,000

These estimates included allowances for labor overtime and also provided for a normal amount of time lost due to machine breakdowns and other kinds of work interruptions. Factory personnel for the third shift could be obtained without difficulty, and new people required almost no training.

The increases in sales promotion expenditures in excess of 1976 levels would consist mostly of increases in local newspaper advertising and point-of-sale promotional displays. The projected increases in sales could not be obtained without these increased expenditures. No increase in the number of salesmen was anticipated.

---

* Copyright 1967, 1977 by l'Institut pour l'Etude des Méthodes de Direction de l'Entreprise (IMEDE), Lausanne, Switzerland. Reprinted by permission. The monetary amounts have been restated as dollar amounts.

TABLE 1

VERLIES & WINST, N.V.
Product Managers' Budget Proposals for the Year 1977

	Dagmat	Telemat
1977 sales (in units)...............................	400,000	300,000
Increase over 1976................................	+ 100,000	+ 90,000
Price per unit (both years).........................	$ 1.00	$ 3.00
1977 production costs per unit:		
Material cost......................................	$ 0.25	$ 0.55
Labor cost...	$ 0.15	$ 0.45
Machine-hours required............................	0.10	0.30
1977 product promotion expense....................	$ 50,000	$ 60,000
Increase over 1976................................	+$ 12,500	+$ 18,000
Increase in finished goods inventories required if sales remain at 1976 levels (units)............	5,000	4,500
Additional increase in assets because of increased sales over 1976:		
Accounts receivable..............................	+$ 20,000	+$ 54,000
Materials inventories............................	+$ 2,500	+$ 4,950
Finished goods inventories (units)................	+ 5,000	+ 3,500
Work in process inventories......................	Negligible	Negligible
Increase in accounts payable accompanying increased sales..................................	+$ 2,500	+$ 4,950

Other estimates and budget proposals that were submitted to Mr. Verlies were:

General sales and administrative expenses (except depreciation)....	$210,000
Depreciation:	
Factory and factory equipment..................................	50,000
Office and sales facilities..	25,000
Interest on long-term debt (maturing in 1985)......................	50,000
Dividends on common stock..	30,000
Research and development expenditures...........................	100,000
Equipment replacement expenditures.............................	90,000
Plant expansion expenditures (these additional facilities would not be completed in 1977)...	300,000
Interest to be paid in 1977 on short-term bank loans was at a rate of 8% on the balance of the bank loans outstanding at the end of 1976.	
Income taxes were computed at a rate of 47% of taxable income and were due in the first six months of the year following.	
Minimum cash balance..	140,000

Research and development expenditures are charged to expense as incurred. Depreciation for 1977 would not be affected by replacement expenditure decisions for 1977. Taxable income and reported income before taxes are identical in this company.

Mr. Verlies estimated that working capital balances would be as follows on January 1, 1977:

Cash...		$160,000
Accounts receivable...............................		186,000
Inventories..		33,350
Total current assets........................		$379,350
Less current liabilities:		
Bank loan payable............................	$30,000	
Accounts and interest payable.................	19,050	
Income taxes payable.........................	54,000	103,050
Working capital...................................		$276,300

Mr. Verlies was convinced that the company would be unable to obtain any new long-term capital during 1977. Cash had to be paid for all assets and services purchased except that trade credit (i.e., accounts payable) was available to finance increases in raw materials inventories. In addition, bank credit was available up to 50 percent of the sum of the face amount of accounts receivable and the total cost of all inventories. (Finished goods were costed at their materials and labor costs only, general factory costs being considered an expense). Bank credit was available in units of $10,000. For budgeting purposes, it was assumed that any amounts borrowed during the year would be borrowed on July 1, 1977. Interest on bank loans in force during 1977 would be paid in cash during January, 1978.

a. Did the company have adequate production capacity to service the tentative sales budget? What criteria would you use to allocate productive capacity between the two product lines whenever total capacity is inadequate to meet all demands?

b. Prepare a *factory cost* and *production volume* plan for 1977 that would have been technically feasible. Factory capacity should be assigned to the products in such a way as to maximize company profits, subject to the following restrictions: (1) the sales of each product are to be at least as large as they were the preceding year; and (2) inventories of finished goods must be built up to the minimum established for the level of sales anticipated in your *revised* sales plan for 1977.

c. Prepare a tentative cash budget for 1977, reflecting your factory cost and production volume plan and all the other estimates and budget proposals listed above. Is this budget feasible? In case of a shortage of cash, how should management decide which expenditures to cut back?

d. Prepare a profit plan for the year that is both technically and financially feasible, and which meets the restrictions listed under (b) above. Would this plan be accepted automatically, or would management be likely to subject it to further tests?

6

Standard Costing for Control of Labor and Materials Costs

THE LAST FOUR CHAPTERS have focused on the ways accounting can help management plan—that is, decide how to use the organization's resources. We now turn our attention to *control,* the process of keeping an organization's behavior consistent with its objectives.

Control may be viewed as an 11-step process, as summarized in Exhibit 6–1. Accountants are likely to participate in each of these

EXHIBIT 6–1

Steps in the Control Process

1. Decide what to control.
2. Decide what purposes the control information is expected to serve.
3. Identify or assign responsibility for control.
4. Decide what measurements will be useful.
5. Set performance standards.
6. Measure results.
7. Compare results with performance standards.
8. Report these comparisons to the responsible executives.
9. Interpret derivatives of results from standards.
10. Take responsive action, wherever appropriate.
11. Review the effects of these responsive actions.

steps, but their main contribution is to collect data on various aspects of the organization's activities and summarize these data in reports to management.

We shall approach this topic from the bottom, by examining the kinds of data the accountant can generate to monitor factory direct materials and direct labor costs. Our discussion will focus on five questions:

1. Why are standard costs the appropriate performance standards for factory direct labor and direct materials costs?
2. What kinds of data do the standard cost files contain?
3. How can variances from standard costs be classified?
4. How might a simple standard costing system work?
5. What major problems are likely to arise from the use of standard costing systems?

With this behind us, we shall turn in Chapter 7 to factory overhead costs and in Chapter 9 to profit-oriented marketing costs. In Chapter 8 we shall examine the problems of measuring and reporting the costs of service and support centers.

PERFORMANCE STANDARDS AND STANDARD COSTS

Good control information is comparative. The idea is to direct management's attention to conditions that are not what they ought to be. This calls for a *performance standard,* defined as a statement of the level of results management regards as appropriate under a specified set of circumstances. It may be stated as a rate per period of time, as a ratio of input to output (or output to input), or as a ratio of one input to another. (An *input* is any material or service used in a process. An *output* is any useful result of a process. Output is also referred to as the amount of *work done.*)

The Exception Principle

Performance standards are essential to a management principle known as *management by exception,* which states that management should devote its scarce time only to operations in which results depart significantly from the performance standards. Operations in which results are close to the performance standard are presumed to be under control.

A simple exception-based report is illustrated in Exhibit 6–2. Each district total less than $100,000 and each deviation greater than 7 percent is highlighted. An explanation of each figure designated by an arrow must be made within three days.

Historical Performance Standards

Many cost reporting systems use historical performance standards —that is, control information consists of comparisons of actual costs with those of previous periods. This lets management see how rapidly costs are rising or falling. The accountant can analyze these data to find out how much of the change in cost is due to changes in such factors as materials prices and wage rates. This information may help management decide what action to take, if any.

Historical performance standards have one main shortcoming. Comparisons with the costs of prior periods don't show whether costs

EXHIBIT 6–2

Exception Report: Actual Sales versus
Planned Sales

District	Actual Sales This Month	Deviation from Plan (percent)
Boston..................	$ 140,000	− 3%
New York...............	263,000	+ 2
Atlanta..................	202,000	−11◄—
Pittsburgh.............	105,000	− 4
Cleveland..............	306,000	+ 5
Chicago................	183,000	+ 3
Minneapolis............	58,000◄—	+ 1
St. Louis...............	125,000	−18◄—
New Orleans...........	95,000◄—	− 4
Dallas..................	274,000	+ 1
Denver.................	198,000	+ 6
Seattle.................	102,000	− 7
San Francisco..........	161,000	+ 1
Los Angeles...........	423,000	+15◄—
Total.............	$2,635,000	+ 1%

are higher or lower than they ought to be. Performance may be better than in the past but still very bad—or worse than in the past but still very good.

Standard Costs

This shortcoming of historical performance standards has led many companies to seek an alternative. In evaluating profit performance, for example, management usually starts by comparing actual results with the profit plan. We'll look at those comparisons in Chapter 9.

The profit plan is a poor performance standard for the costs of responsive activities, however. Many of these costs are expected to vary with the volume of work done, and the performance standard must reflect this. For factory direct materials and direct labor costs, the most suitable performance standards are provided by *standard costs*. A standard cost is management's estimate, prepared in advance, of the costs of the inputs that should be necessary to obtain a specific material, product, or service. It takes three forms:

1. *Standard price.* The price that management estimates should be necessary to obtain a unit of material or an hour of labor services of a specific grade or quality. The standard price of labor time is known as a *standard labor rate*.
2. *Standard operations cost.* The quantities of the various inputs that management estimates should be necessary to perform each production operation within the factory's capability, multiplied by their standard prices.

3. *Standard product cost.* The quantities of the various inputs that management estimates should be necessary to manufacture one unit of a particular product in production lots of a specified size, multiplied by their standard prices.

The remainder of this chapter will be devoted to a discussion of the use of standard costs as performance standards for factory direct labor and direct materials inputs.

STANDARD COST FILES

The standard cost file is likely to contain five different kinds of data:

1. Standard materials prices.
2. Standard labor rates.
3. Standard materials quantities—the bill of materials.
4. Standard labor quantities—the operations flow sheet.
5. Standard product costs—the standard cost sheet.

Standard Materials Prices

Standard materials prices should represent management's best estimates of the delivered costs of materials during the period covered by the standards. The standard for any particular item should include a provision for freight-in, variable handling costs, and expected discounts. For example, the standard price of a metal stamping might be determined as follows:

```
Purchase price, in 500-piece quantities........ $6.00
Freight from supplier's plant.................   0.40
Receiving and stacking.......................    0.20
Less: purchase discounts.....................   (0.12)
        Standard materials price...............  $6.48
```

Some companies treat freight-in, discounts, and variable handling costs in other ways, but they are inescapable components of materials price and should be accounted for as such unless the clerical costs are prohibitive.

Standard Labor Rates

Standard labor rates should include provisions for the costs of fringe benefits that vary with the size of the total payroll, along the lines we suggested in Chapter 2. For bookkeeping convenience, however, many companies limit the standard labor rate to the regular-time wage rate, classifying fringe benefit costs as overhead costs.

Once this issue has been decided, management still has another choice to make: a single standard labor rate for the factory as a whole, a single rate for each department, or separate standard rates for each pay grade. Separate rates are the most accurate, but they are slightly more expensive to use. If different operations call for operators with very different degrees of skill and therefore very different labor rates, separate rate standards probably should be used. An hour of floor sweeping time simply cannot be equated with an hour of highly skilled machinists' time.

Standard Materials Quantities

Materials quantity standards start from product specifications as to size, shape, appearance, desired performance characteristics, and permissible tolerance limits. These are reflected in the bill of materials, which lists the quantity required of each of the various materials and parts that will go into the creation of the finished product. A sample bill of materials, for a product known as a base plate, is shown in Exhibit 6–3.

Notice that the standard allows for more than one anchor and brace for each base plate. Standards are expected to show what will happen when conditions are normal and costs are under control. Since some wastage of materials is inevitable in most processes, standard costs include allowances for normal wastage. In manufacturing these base plates, for example, the company expects the factory to spoil or lose

EXHIBIT 6–3

Bill of Materials

STANDARD MATERIALS REQUIREMENTS							
Item: Base Plate No. 423					Drawing No.: 9463		
Standard Quantity: 1,000					Date: 11/14/—		
Materials					Remarks		
No.	Description		Required for Standard Lot				
176	Steel plate		4,200 lbs.				
Parts							
Part No.	Description	Specs. per Unit	Required for Lot	Part No.	Description	Specs. per Unit	Required for Lot
201	Anchor	1	1,010				
217	Brace	2	2,080				

EXHIBIT 6–4
Variations in Materials Usage

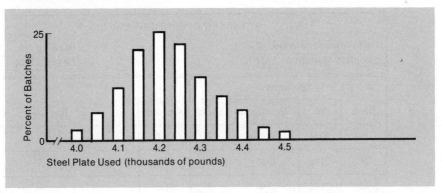

about 1 percent of the anchors issued and about 4 percent of the braces.

Even with these allowances, actual quantities will seldom be exactly equal to standard quantities. No matter how well standardized the operation or how simple the product, some variation in materials usage is inevitable. If a large number of batches of Base Plate No. 423 were manufactured, for example, the amount of steel plate used might very well fit the pattern described in Exhibit 6–4. The average is about 4,200 pounds, but the process sometimes uses as little as 4,000 pounds, sometimes as much as 4,500.

Standard quantities typically reflect management's estimates of "attainable good performance," the level an average experienced worker can be expected to achieve under standardized conditions. Attainable good performance is usually slightly better than management actually expects to achieve. We shall study the behavioral implications of this practice in Chapter 19. For the moment we should merely note that in preparing cost estimates for decisions management should adjust the standard quantities for any bias introduced by the application of the attainable good performance concept.

Standard Labor Quantities

Labor quantity standards also start from product specifications, which determine the factory operations necessary to manufacture the product. These operations are summarized on a flow sheet such as the one shown in Exhibit 6–5. This flow sheet specifies the operations to be performed and the labor quantities required for each. The column headed "Job Class" specifies the kind of employee who normally should be assigned to each operation. The form may also specify the equipment to be used and the amount of machine time required.

These labor time standards are usually slightly greater than the amount of time the operations themselves are expected to take. Workers cannot be expected to work at peak efficiency at all times. They

EXHIBIT 6–5

Operations Flow Sheet

STANDARD OPERATIONS LIST					
Item: Base Plate No. 423				Drawing No.: 9463	
Standard Quantity: 1,000				Date: 11/14/—	

Dept.	No.	Description	Job Class	Hours Allowed	Remarks
P	1731	Setup	1	2.0	
M	2146	Cut	2	5.5	
M	2172	Drill	2	21.0	
M	2175	Bevel	3	6.0	
M	2304	Polish	3	14.5	
A	2903	Press	5	2.5	
A	2905	Slip	5	2.5	

take coffee breaks, attend to their personal needs, wait for someone to supply them with materials, or fix their equipment. Since it is reasonable to expect that the amount of time spent in these ways should be proportional to the amount of productive time, labor standards ordinarily include a provision for the normal amount of nonproductive time.

Labor time, like materials quantities, can't be predicted with pinpoint accuracy. Sometimes it will be less than standard; sometimes it will be greater. Management's task is to pick a point in this range that skilled operators should be expected to achieve, on the average.

One possible approach is to consult with engineers or other technical people. An experienced garment cutter, for example, usually can estimate quite accurately the number of men's suits that can be cut from a given quantity of cloth, because this job is so familiar. In other cases, industrial engineers can synthesize data from commercially available tables of time standards for individual work elements of specific operations (methods time measurement). Alternatively, a time study engineer can obtain data by observing a series of test runs (time studies and yield studies).

This approach is relatively expensive and time consuming. As a result, controlled test runs are seldom undertaken except to meet other objectives, such as work standardization and methods improvement.

When studies are made for these purposes, accurate quantity standards can be obtained as a by-product at little additional cost. When a company is first introducing standard costing, however, it may very well get an adequate set of initial standards by analyzing the quantity data in the historical cost records.

Standard Product Costs

Standard product costs are computed by entering the data from the bill of materials and the operations flow sheet, together with standard materials prices and wage rates, on a standard product cost sheet such as the one shown in Exhibit 6–6. This lists the operations, materials, and costs deemed reasonably necessary for a lot of 1,000 base plates. The first column specifies the types of materials required and the operations to be performed, while the second identifies the departments responsible. The next six columns list the quantities and costs of these various inputs. The last four columns identify the standard overhead costs.

VARIANCES FROM STANDARD COST

As we have already pointed out, accounting control reports emphasize the differences between actual results and the results embodied in performance standards. These differences, or any subdivisions of them, are known as variances. For example, the direct labor cost variance is the difference between the actual cost of direct labor and the standard direct labor cost of the work done.

Many events lead to direct materials and direct labor cost variances. Some of these lead the company to use either more or fewer units of materials or labor than the standards call for:

> The portion of the total variance attributable to these causes is the *quantity variance,* defined as the difference between actual and standard input quantities for the output actually achieved.

Others affect the prices the company pays for materials or the wage rates of its employees:

> A variance arising in this way is known as a *price variance* or a *rate variance,* defined as the difference between actual and standard input prices for a specified quantity of resource inputs.

In this section we shall see how to (1) calculate quantity variances, (2) measure price variances, and (3) decide which variances to report to management.

Calculating Quantity Variances

Quantity variances are indexes of physical efficiency. They show the relationships between the quantities of resources used and the quantities of the outputs derived from them.

EXHIBIT 6–6

Standard Cost Sheet

STANDARD COST SHEET

Description: Base Plate No. 423
Batch Quantity: 1,000 pieces

Standard Cost per Batch: $1,864
Standard Cost per Unit: $1,864

Operation or Item	Dept.	Materials			Labor			Overhead			
		Quantity	Price	Cost	Hours	Rate	Cost	Base*	Quantity	Rate	Cost
Setup	P				2.0	10.00	20.00	LH	2.0	4.00	8.00
Steel plate	M	4,200	0.10	420.00							
Cut	M				5.5	8.00	44.00	MH	5.5	5.00	27.50
Drill	M				21.0	8.00	168.00	MH	32.0	5.00	160.00
Bevel	M				6.0	8.00	48.00	MH	5.0	5.00	25.00
Polish	M				14.5	8.00	116.00	MH	41.5	5.00	207.50
Anchor	A	1,010	0.24	242.40							
Press	A				2.5	6.00	15.00	LH	2.5	2.00	5.00
Brace	A	2,080	0.07	145.60							
Slip	A				2.5	6.00	15.00	LH	2.5	2.00	5.00
Total		—	—	808.00	—	—	426.00	—	—	—	438.00

*LH = Standard direct labor hours; MH = standard machine hours.

Physical measures of variances. Given enough data, we can always measure the quantity variances in physical units. For example, suppose that combining 1.2 pounds of material A with 0.3 hours of labor is expected to yield one unit of product Y. This relationship can be expressed in a formula:

$$1.2 \text{ pounds } A + 0.3 \text{ labor hours} \rightarrow 1 \text{ unit } Y$$

Suppose further that on April 18, a batch of ten units of Y was produced from 14 pounds of material A and required four labor hours. In schematic terms:

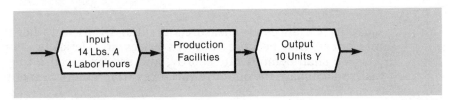

But ten units of product Y can also be expressed in terms of their *standard input* content of 12 pounds of A (10 times 1.2) and three hours of labor (10 times 0.3). Substituting these equivalents and separating the materials from the labor, we have:

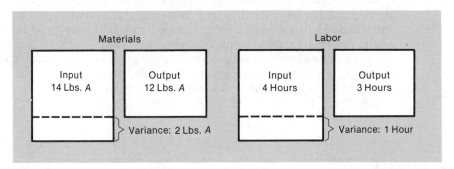

The quantity variances are the differences between actual input quantities (14 pounds and 4 hours) and the standard input quantities for the work that has been done (12 pounds and 3 hours). In this example, the company used more materials (2 pounds) and more labor (1 hour) than the standards called for. These are called *unfavorable* variances. If the actual input quantities had been less than the standard quantities, we would refer to the differences as *favorable* variances.

Stating quantity variances in dollars. Although quantity variances represent physical quantities, they are usually measured in dollars. To get these dollar figures, the accountant multiplies the physical quantities by standard prices. If the standard price of material A is $7 a pound, the materials quantity variance can be calculated in dollars as follows:

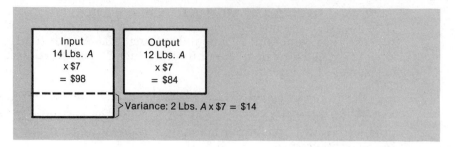

Quantity variances are measured at standard prices rather than at actual prices, first because standard prices are clerically simpler to use, as we shall demonstrate shortly, and second because they make it easier to compare the quantity variances from month to month.

Measuring Price Variances

Direct materials and direct labor cost variances also arise because actual purchase prices or actual wage rates differ from standard prices or wage rates. Since the wage rate is the price of labor services, both of these can be classified as price variances.

We generally calculate price variances by multiplying the actual input quantity by the difference between the actual input price and the standard input price. For example, our batch of product Y was produced by a factory employee who was paid $5.25 an hour to do the work. The standard wage rate was $5 an hour. The price variance for labor is called the labor rate variance, and amounted in this instance to 25 cents an hour for four hours, or $1 in total.

Schematically, the labor variances on this operation can be summarized as follows.[1]

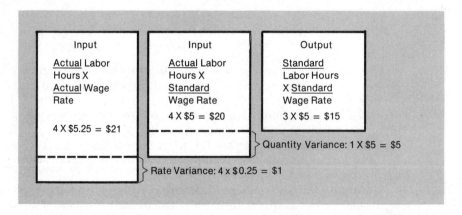

---

[1] The rate variance could be divided into two parts: the variance on the standard input quantity (in this case, three hours times $0.25, or $0.75) and

Again the variance is unfavorable, in that the company paid more than the standard allowed for. The following table should make it easy to distinguish between favorable and unfavorable variances:

	Unfavorable	Favorable
Quantity variances	Actual quantities greater than standard quantities	Actual quantities less than standard quantities
Price variances	Actual prices greater than standard prices	Actual prices less than standard prices

Variances for Scorecard Reports

Quantity variance data on individual operations may be very useful for steering controls, as we shall see in Chapter 20. Scorecard controls, on the other hand, call for a certain amount of aggregation. The success of the production center manager's control efforts is not measured by how large a variance is recorded on any one job or operation. The real test is the center's efficiency over a period of time. To measure this, we must cumulate the production center's variances, usually for a week or a month.

In deciding which variances to report to a particular manager, we generally apply the *controllability criterion*, that managers should be assigned only those variances they are expected to control. The managers of production centers are expected to control quantity variances; price variances are usually outside their jurisdiction and therefore are not reported to them.

Cumulative quantity variances measure the differences between the actual quantities of inputs used in the department with the department's output for the period.[2] We need to see how these two sets of quantities are measured.

Measuring inputs. Input figures for variance calculations should measure the actual quantities of resources used, multiplied by their standard prices. For example, suppose the forming department in the Galahad Company's factory used the following direct materials and direct labor inputs during July:

Material A.................... 4,500 pounds
Material B.................... 1,100 pounds
Direct labor.................... 3,500 hours

the variance on the excess input quantity (one hour times $0.25, or $0.25). The latter component is the joint product of price and quantity variation. The conventional procedure, however, is to measure the rate variance as a single quantity, as in the diagram: actual input quantity times the difference between actual and standard input prices.

[2] To simplify our terminology from here on, we shall refer to production centers as departments, reflecting an assumption that each department consists of one production center only. In practice, separate reports may be prepared for each production center in multicenter departments.

The standard prices of these three inputs were $7 a pound for material A, $2 a pound for material B, and $5 an hour for labor. At these prices, the total standard cost of the materials and labor used during the month was as follows:

Material A: 4,500 × $7............ $31,500
Material B: 1,100 × $2............ 2,200
    Total materials............... $33,700
Direct labor: 3,500 × $5........... $17,500

Measuring outputs.   The output of any department during any period of time consists of the products it completes plus any increase (or minus any decrease) in the amount of work in process in the department during the period. These relationships are diagrammed in Exhibit 6–7. The blocks at the left of the equal sign represent the total amount of output in the department at some time during the period, including some of the output contributed by last month's operations (opening work in process); the blocks at the right show how much of this output went out of the department and how much remained in process at the end. In this diagram the ending work in process is larger than the beginning work in process—therefore the *total* amount of work done (the output) is greater than the amount of work done on the jobs *completed* during the period.

In standard costing calculations, all of the quantities in this diagram are measured by their standard costs—that is, the standard input quantities multiplied by their standard prices. The relationships among them can also be expressed in an equation:

Output = Standard cost of units completed
        + Standard cost of work in process at end of period
        − Standard cost of work in process at beginning of period

Galahad's forming department worked on only two products during July. It completed 900 units of product P and 2,000 units of product

EXHIBIT 6–7

Output, Product Completions, and Work in Process

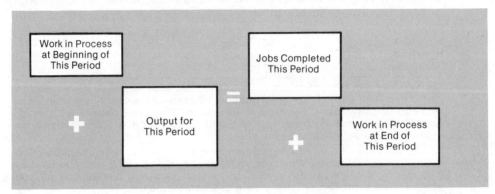

Q during the month and transferred them to the factory assembly department. The standard forming department input quantities for these two products were:

> 1.2 pounds of A + 0.8 hour of labor → 1 unit of P
>
> 1.5 pounds of A + 0.6 pound of B + 1.3 hours of labor → 1 unit of Q

At standard prices, the two products had the following standard costs:

	Materials	Labor
Product P.........	1.2 lbs. × $7 = $ 8.40	0.8 hrs. × $5 = $4.00
Product Q.........	1.5 lbs. × $7 = $10.50	1.3 hrs. × $5 = $6.50
	0.6 lbs. × $2 = 1.20	
	$11.70	

The total standard materials cost of the units completed was 900 × $8.40 = $7,560 for product P and 2,000 × $11.70 = $23,400 for product Q. The standard labor costs were 900 × $4 = $3,600 and 2,000 × $6.50 = $13,000.

To complete our equation, we need to know how much work was in process at the beginning and at the end of the month. Upon investigation, we find that the beginning inventory consisted of 200 units of product P. Forty percent of the labor operations had been performed on these units in June, with a standard labor cost of $1.60 a unit. All of the materials necessary to complete these units had already been applied. The standard cost of this beginning inventory therefore was as follows:

> Materials: 200 units × $8.40 = $1,680
> Labor: 200 units × $1.60 = $ 320

The inventory in process at the end of the month was even greater, consisting of 300 partly processed units of product P. Sixty percent of the work on these units had been completed, with a standard labor cost of $2.40 each; again the full complement of materials had already been applied, with a standard cost of $8.40 a unit. The standard cost of this ending inventory therefore was:

> Materials: 300 units × $8.40 = $2,520
> Labor: 300 units × $2.40 = $ 720

Substituting these figures in the output formula, we get the output figures shown at the bottom of Exhibit 6–8. As this shows, the department accomplished more than it would have accomplished if all it had done was process the 900 units completed during this period. It added to the work in process, and this is an accomplishment the department should get credit for.

EXHIBIT 6-8

Forming Department, Standard Cost of Departmental Output

	Number of Units	Standard Materials Cost	Standard Labor Cost
Products completed and trans- ferred out:			
Product P (Materials at $8.40, Labor at $4)......................	900	$ 7,560	$ 3,600
Product Q (Materials at $11.70, Labor at $6.50)....................	2,000	23,400	13,000
Total.........................		$30,960	$16,600
Add: Work in process, July 31:			
Product P.........................	300	2,520	720
		$33,480	$17,320
Less: Work in process, July 1:			
Product P.........................	200	1,680	320
Standard cost of departmental output..............................		$31,800	$17,000

Calculating the variances. When this information on output is combined with the input figures from page 192, calculating the quantity variances is simple arithmetic:

	Input (Standard Cost of Resources Used)	Output (Standard Cost of Work Done)	Quantity Variance
Materials.........	$33,700	$31,800	$1,900 Unfavorable
Labor.............	17,500	17,000	500 Unfavorable

As the first line shows, the standard cost of the actual materials used exceeded the standard materials cost of the actual output by $1,900; this was the materials quantity variance for the month, and was unfavorable. The standard labor cost of the work done was also less than the standard cost of the amount of labor actually used, by $500. This means that the workers in the forming department turned out less production per hour than the standards called for. In other words, the labor quantity variance for the month amounted to $500 and was unfavorable.

The Need for Dollar Variances

If production processes were all as simple as in this illustration, standard costing systems would be almost unnecessary. All quantity variances could be stated in physical units, which often have a more direct meaning to the first-line supervisor. In the real world, however, each department is likely to use many different kinds of inputs, instead of just one, and to process many different products. The result is that statements of variances in physical terms become unwieldy; often only the dollar variances are reported.

This should not be thought of as a sacrifice of information, however. For one thing, the dollar totals are merely a convenient way of summarizing the underlying physical deviations from standard performance. Second, dollar variance information serves an important purpose in its own right, even when inputs and outputs are few in number. Expressing the variance in monetary terms gives management a measure of its relative importance, and a basis for deciding how much control effort is worthwhile.

A STANDARD COSTING SYSTEM

An accounting system consists of a set of accounts, procedures, files, and reports, together with the concepts underlying them. When standard costs are included in this set, the system is said to be a *standard costing system.*

Standard costing systems differ from each other in many ways. Each one has its own distinguishing characteristics; each uses its own account structure to accumulate data. In this section we shall look at four aspects of a simple system that we call a *basic plan* system:

1. The main characteristics of the basic plan.
2. Recording purchases of materials.
3. Using accounts to isolate quantity variances.
4. Accounting for labor rate variances.

Characteristics of the Basic Plan

Standard costing systems built on the basic plan have the five main characteristics list in Exhibit 6–9. The last two of these are the most important and the most controversial. Quantity variances calculated in this way cannot be reported frequently or in great detail. This means that the first-line supervisors can use basic plan variance reports only as scorecard controls; they must supply their own steering control information by keeping a close watch on what is going on in their departments. If the first-line supervisors have to rely on the standard costing system to provide steering controls, a more elaborate

EXHIBIT 6–9

Characteristics of the Basic Plan

1. Materials price variances are identified and segregated when the materials are purchased; actual prices are not used in accounting for inventory costs.
2. Production centers are charged for the actual direct labor and materials quantities used, multiplied by standard materials prices and wage rates.
3. Production centers are credited for the standard costs of the work done—i.e., standard direct labor and materials quantities, multiplied by standard materials prices and wage rates.
4. Labor and materials quantity variances are identified at the end of the period, on the basis of a physical count of the work in process.
5. Labor and materials quantity variances are identified as production center totals for the time period as a whole; they are not computed for individual job orders or individual operators.

system may be appropriate. We shall describe one such system in Chapter 20.

Recording Materials Purchases

The first characteristic of a basic plan system, and of some other types of systems as well, is that materials price variances are identified when the materials are purchased. The amounts entered in the materials inventory accounts are the actual quantities of goods received multiplied by their standard purchase prices. Differences between the standard prices and the actual prices of the items bought are recorded in separate price variance accounts.

The Galahad Company, for example, uses one materials inventory account, entitled Materials and Parts, and one materials price variance account. During July, the company bought materials and parts from outside suppliers in a number of separate transactions. The total of the invoice prices was $35,000, less discounts of $1,500. The standard costs of these goods totaled $42,700, including provision for standard freight charges and discounts. Each invoice was recorded separately, of course, but we can summarize them all in a single entry:

(1a)

Materials and Parts	42,700	
Materials Price Variance		9,200
Accounts Payable		33,500

In other words, the asset was recorded at standard prices, the liability was recorded at net actual prices (after deducting the discounts allowable) and the difference was placed in the variance account.

The purchase price variance was not actually this large, however. The standard prices for the materials and parts included a provision for freight charges, but the actual purchase prices did not always cover freight charges. Separate freight charges on Galahad's July purchases amounted to $7,500. This amount was charged to the variance account because the amounts already charged to the inventory account contained a standard provision for these costs:

(1b)

Materials Price Variance	7,500	
Accounts Payable		7,500

Actual delivered cost, in other words, was $35,000 − $1,500 + $7,500 = $41,000. This was $1,700 less than the total standard cost of the materials purchased:

Actual quantity purchased × actual prices
$41,000

Actual quantity purchased × standard prices
$42,700

Materials price variance:
actual quantity purchased ×
(actual prices − standard prices)

$1,700 Favorable

This same $1,700 variance appeared as a credit balance in the Materials Price Variance account after all the purchase-related transactions had been analyzed and recorded:

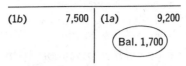

Materials Price Variance

(1b)	7,500	(1a)	9,200
		Bal. 1,700	

This conforms to a very simple rule:

> Favorable cost variances appear as credit balances.
> Unfavorable cost variances appear as debit balances.

Calculating price variances at the time of purchase lets the accountant report them to management soon after they arise, not weeks or months later when the materials are finally used. It also permits substantial savings in the cost of materials bookkeeping, in that all materials inventories are measured at standard prices which remain unchanged for a year or longer. Detailed inventory records can be maintained in physical units only; when dollar totals are desired, the physical quantities can be multiplied by standard prices.

Aggregate price variances, even when reported separately for each broad class of materials, ordinarily provide little information for the purchasing agent. Purchasing decisions center on the item, not on the class of materials, and the purchasing agent can identify the variance when he places an order or at least when the order is confirmed by the vendor. Total price variance information is useful mainly in cash and profit planning, and has few other applications.

Isolating the Quantity Variances

Quantity variances in the basic plan are computed by comparing total production inputs with total production outputs for specified periods of time. Input and output data are accumulated in departmental Work-in-Process accounts, and the variances are extracted at the end of the period. The process can be described as a sequence of four steps:

1. Establish the account structure.
2. Charge input quantities to the accounts at standard prices.
3. Credit completed output quantities to the accounts at standard costs.
4. Identify the variances.

Step 1. Set up a separate Work-in-Process Inventory account for each direct labor and direct materials cost element in each responsibility center. Since the Work-in-Process accounts are the means by which variances for management's use are to be generated, they should correspond both to the responsibility structure and to the cost categories management finds relevant for control. The Galahad Company's factory has four in-process inventory accounts, two for each department:

1.   Materials in Process—Forming.
2.   Labor in Process—Forming.
3.   Materials in Process—Assembly.
4.   Labor in Process—Assembly.

Step 2.   Charge each department with the actual input quantities used, multiplied by standard input prices.   This is designed to implement the controllability criterion. Charging department heads for the quantities they use identifies the amounts they are accountable for. The controllability criterion also requires that these quantities be measured at their standard prices. The best way to keep price variances out of the departmental reports is to keep them out of the department's accounts.

For example, Galahad's forming department requisitioned several batches of materials during July. A clerk in the factory office multiplied each of these quantities by the standard price of that material. The resulting total, $33,700, was the standard cost of the materials actually used during the month. This amount was charged to the departmental Materials in Process account:

(2)

Materials in Process—Forming 33,700
    Materials and Parts   33,700

This entry identified the amounts for which the forming department was accountable and reduced the balance in the stockroom's inventory account.

Aside from updating the records of physical stocks in the storeroom each time goods are received, issued, or returned, Galahad makes no materials entries other than the summary entries illustrated above. A job cost sheet is prepared for each job at the time the job order is issued, but this job cost sheet is completely filled in at that time with the standard quantities and prices of labor and materials for the specific quantity of parts or products to be manufactured to fill the order. Actual quantities of labor and materials used on the job are not recorded on the job cost sheet.

Labor costs are charged to the departmental accounts in the same way—that is, these charges reflect the actual number of labor hours used, multiplied by standard wage rates. Indirect labor time is charged to departmental overhead accounts, also at standard wage rates. During July, the forming department was charged the following amounts:

	Actual Hours	Actual Hours × Standard Rate
Direct work on production orders.	3,500	$17,500
Indirect work.	340	1,700
Total.	3,840	$19,200

The charges to the departmental accounts can be represented by the following entry:

(3)

Labor in Process—Forming	17,500	
Indirect Labor—Forming	1,700	
Payroll Cost Summary—Forming		19,200

The indirect labor is part of overhead and does not figure further in this illustration. Payroll Cost Summary—Forming is a temporary account known as a clearing account, serving as a temporary proxy for a wages payable account. Its full purpose will become clear in a moment.

Step 3.   Credit each responsibility center with the total standard cost of the products that have been finished and transferred out of the department.   This is accomplished by finding the total number of units of each product finished during the period and multiplying this total by the standard cost of each unit. We calculated these figures earlier in this chapter:

	No. of Units Finished	Standard Materials Cost	Standard Labor Cost
Product P......	900	$ 7,560	$ 3,600
Product O......	2,000	23,400	13,000
Total.......		$30,960	$16,600

All of the units completed in July were transferred directly to the assembly department for use in production there. The entries recording these transfers are summarized in entry (4):

(4)

Materials in Process—Assembly	47,560	
Materials in Process—Forming		30,960
Labor in Process—Forming		16,600

The credit entries to the forming department accounts indicate that these goods are no longer in inventory in this department and the manager is no longer responsible for their costs. The charge to Materials in Process—Assembly records the assembly department manager's responsibility for controlling their use.

Notice that the standard labor costs of the forming operation became part of the materials costs of the assembly department. The assembly department manager sees only the physical units, not the materials and labor from which they were made. The cost of forming labor is the responsibility of the forming department manager; all the assembly manager can do is control the number of units wasted in the assembly operation. When the department wastes a unit of product P, for example, it wastes both the materials and the labor that were used in the forming department to make that unit—the manager can't control one without controlling the other. For this reason, the entire standard cost of units received from forming is treated as a materials cost in the assembly department.

Step 4. Estimate the standard cost of the inventories in process at the end of the period and make any entries necessary to bring the account balances to their correct levels. The balances in the Work-in-Process accounts after the routine bookkeeping entries have been posted represent a mixture of (*a*) the standard costs of the inventories still in process at the end of the period, and (*b*) any quantity variances that arose during the period. By counting the inventories in process and measuring their standard cost, the accountant can identify the variances and prepare entries to remove them from the inventory accounts.

For example, after entries (2), (3), and (4) were posted to the ledger, the forming department's work in process accounts showed the following:

Materials in Process—Forming				Labor in Process—Forming			
Bal. 7/1	1,680	(4)	30,960	Bal. 7/1	320	(4)	16,600
(2)	33,700			(3)	17,500		
	35,380				17,820		
Bal. 4,420				Bal. 1,220			

The opening balances in these accounts represented the standard costs of the work in process at the beginning of July, determined on the basis of a physical count at that time; the other entries were described on the preceding pages.

The inventories in process were counted again at the end of July, revealing work in process in the forming department with a standard materials cost of $2,520 and a standard labor cost of $720. These figures differed substantially from the balances in the inventory accounts:

	Materials in Process	Labor in Process
Account balance............	$4,420	$1,220
Standard inventory cost.....	2,520	720
Difference..............	$1,900	$ 500

The differences were the quantity variances for the month. They appeared in the Work-in-Process accounts because these accounts were charged with *actual* input quantities and were credited with the *standard* input quantities required by the work done during the month. Any difference between actual and standard input quantities will throw the inventory account balance off.

Once the standard cost of the ending inventory is determined, it is a simple matter to adjust the accounts. Galahad's accountants, for example, credited Materials in Process—Forming by $1,900 to reduce the balance in this account to its correct level. The accompanying debit was to a variance account:

(5)

Materials Quantity Variance—Forming 1,900
    Materials in Process—Forming   1,900

The debit to the variance account indicated that this variance was unfavorable.

The Labor in Process—Forming account also had to be credited to bring its balance down to standard at the end of the month. Again a variance account was debited, reflecting the unfavorable labor quantity variance:

(6)

Labor Quantity Variance—Forming 500
    Labor in Process—Forming   500

Isolating the Labor Rate Variance

By using standard wages rates, Galahad's accountants were able to process the labor time tickets as they came in. The labor rate variances could not be calculated, however, until the month's payrolls were prepared, establishing the actual labor cost for the month. The July payrolls for the forming department totaled $20,500, divided as follows:

Straight-time wages................	$19,500
Overtime premiums................	1,000
Total payroll..................	$20,500

$4,000 of this had to be withheld for social security and income tax payments on the employees' behalf; the remaining $16,500 was payable directly to the employees. The entry to record this information was:

(7)

Overtime Premium—Forming 1,000
Payroll Cost Summary—Forming 19,500
    Wages Payable   16,500
    Taxes Withheld   4,000

Since overtime premium costs are treated as departmental overhead costs (see Chapter 2), the amounts shown in the overtime premium accounts appear in the departmental overhead cost reports that we shall discuss in Chapter 7. Our interest at the moment centers on the Payroll Cost Summary account. It will be recalled that in entry (3) Galahad credited $19,200 to this account, representing 3,840 hours of labor at a standard wage rate of $5 an hour. Now we find that in entry (7) Galahad charged $19,500 to this account, representing the actual wages earned by employees for these 3,840 hours at straight-time wage rates (i.e., excluding overtime premiums). The account thus showed the following:

Payroll Cost Summary—Forming

(5) Actual labor hours × actual basic hourly wage rates...... 19,500	(3) Actual labor hours × standard hourly wage rates........... 19,200
(Bal. 300)	

Since the amounts on both sides of the account were based on the same number of labor hours (3,840), the $300 difference in the total could only be due to difference between actual and standard wage rates—that is, it was the labor rate variance. A credit balance would have shown up if actual wage rates had been lower than standard.

The procedure could end here, with the balance in the Payroll Cost Summary account interpreted as a rate variance for internal reporting purposes. Galahad's accountants liked to clear this account each month, however, and made the following entry at the end of July:

(8)
```
Labor Rate Variance—Forming  ....................  300
     Payroll Cost Summary—Forming  .............         300
```

After this entry was posted, the payroll cost summary account had a zero balance, ready to receive payroll data for the month of August.

Notice that the Galahad system did not distinguish the rate variance on direct labor from that on indirect labor. Obtaining this breakdown would complicate the bookkeeping process, and with no discernible managerial benefit.

Basic Plan Cost Flows

Exhibit 6–10 summarizes the mechanics of the basic plan by tracing the flow of materials costs through the Galahad Company's factory accounts. Materials costs enter the diagram at the left, at the time of purchase. They move to the Materials in Process account at the right as the materials are issued, and move off the diagram completely as the department finishes its work and transfers the goods elsewhere. Finally, the net quantity variance for the period is moved to a variance account and the inventory account is ready for the next month's transactions.

Successful application of the basic plan hinges on management's ability to measure work-in-process inventories quickly and cheaply. Fortunately, in-process inventories in many processes can safely be assumed to be constant, so that output can be measured directly by the standard cost of the units completed during the period. In other cases, only a very few jobs are in process in any department at any time, and measurement is very simple. The simpler the solution to this measurement problem, the more frequently variance information can be reported. In some cases, daily reporting would be entirely feasible.

EXHIBIT 6–10

Materials Cost Flows under the Basic Plan

Materials and Parts		Materials in Process—Forming	
Beginning Balance: Actual quantity × standard prices 130,000	Actual quantity issued × standard prices: 33,700	Beginning Balance: Actual quantity at standard cost (standard quantity × standard price) 1,680	Actual quantity of goods finished at standard cost (standard materials quantity × standard price) 30,960
Actual quantity purchased × standard prices 42,700		Actual quantity received × standard prices 33,700	
			Excess of actual quantity used over standard usage × standard price 1,900
Ending Balance: Actual quantity × standard prices 139,000		Ending Balance: Actual quantity at standard cost 2,520	

Issues (↓ between Materials and Parts and Materials in Process)
Purchases (↓ left side)
Completions (↓ right side)

Materials Price Variance		Materials Quantity Variance—Forming	
Excess of actual over standard prices of materials purchased ...	Excess of standard over actual prices of materials purchased 1,700	Excess of actual quantity used over standard usage × standard prices 1,900	Excess of standard quantity used over actual usage × standard prices ...

PROBLEMS WITH STANDARD COSTING

Standard costing systems may be very useful, but they are not without problems. The three main problems are system cost, the difficulty of developing standards for all operations, and the danger of unfavorable employee reactions to the standards.

System Cost

Standard costing systems can provide useful information, but getting this information may cost more than it is worth. We have already suggested that the cost of preparing detailed engineered cost standards for all products and all operations may exceed the value of the benefits they will generate. Developing standards of this kind also takes time, and management may not be willing to wait a year or more to get the standard costing system going.

One way to get the system going quickly and at a low cost is to develop preliminary standards from historical data already on file. These standards can then be refined as further information becomes available. Variance data in the early periods will be used more to identify standards that may be out of line than to evaluate operating performance.

Operating the standard costing system offers some cost-saving opportunities over historical costing systems, mainly by eliminating the need to use actual materials prices and wage rates to record the use of resources inputs. Individual inventory records can be kept in physical units only—total standard cost can always be calculated by multiplying the physical quantities on hand by their standard prices.

Whether operating costs will be greater or less than in historical costing systems depends in large measure on the kind of standard costing system used. Many systems are designed to provide information frequently and in great detail. These systems tend to be relatively expensive because getting the extra detail calls for a more elaborate data collecting system. We shall look at one such system in Chapter 20.

Basic plan systems deliberately sacrifice information in the interest of reducing clerical costs. Timekeeping procedures can be simplified and job order cost sheets can be eliminated. The main clerical costs peculiar to the basic plan are the costs of recording interdepartmental transfers and the costs of measuring the work in process at the end of each period. The use of standard product costs keeps the first of these within bounds, however, and stock-taking costs should not be great. In some cases, in-process inventories are either negligible or do not change materially from period to period. In others, the standard cost of the inventories can be approximated easily.

Since the basic plan is not designed to provide large quantities of steering control information, it can be justified only if it can be installed and operated at a relatively low cost. In most cases it can pass this test.

Nonstandard Products

Some portion of each month's output in job order production is typically of new products or product modifications for which no standards have been set. Most of these are merely new combinations of operations and materials already listed in the standard cost file, and standards can be derived fairly easily. When this is not the case, two solutions are possible. First, new standards might be developed for the new operations. If accuracy is attempted, the establishment of new standards is costly and could even delay production. Using rough approximations avoids these problems but may cloud the meaning of overall departmental variances.

The widely used alternative is to grant actual time allowances for unrated work. Actual costs can be accumulated on time tickets and totaled either for each job order or for each department in total. Job order totals can be compared with estimates, if desired, but the latter are not used as the basis for departmental reports. Departmental variances therefore pertain only to that portion of total production represented by input-rated operations.

Behavioral Problems

Most problems in employee relations under standard costing arise from poor execution or a basic misunderstanding of the system. The purpose of standard costing is to help management control costs, but management may try to use it as a means of inducing employees to reduce costs. Cost reduction is a laudable objective, and it may be achieved as a result of the development of standards, but it is not an automatic result. Cost reduction generally requires methods changes, and it cannot be assumed that employees will change their methods simply because someone tells them that they are not performing up to standard. We shall examine these problems more closely in Chapter 19.

SUMMARY

Control reports compare actual results with performance standards. For factory direct materials and direct labor costs, standard costs can be the performance standards. Differences between standard costs and actual costs are known as cost variances, and the accountant uses standard costing systems to generate variance information for management. Variances due to differences between actual and standard input quantities are referred to as quantity variances; price and rate variances reflect differences between actual and standard materials prices or wage rates.

Standard costing systems differ from each other in many ways, but the most significant differences are in when and how variances are isolated. The simplest standard costing systems are basic plan systems, and the quantity variances produced under these systems are in the form of departmental totals—the differences between the actual quantities of the inputs consumed in the department and the standard input equivalents of the department's actual output in each time period. When these physical quantities are multiplied by standard input prices, the result is the dollar quantity variance that appears on the periodic performance report.

The basic plan is relatively inexpensive. It identifies the departments in which quantity variances occur and provides management with a summary measure of cost control effectiveness in each department. It is appropriate when the department head relies on the standard costing system for scorecard control information only. Its main weakness is that it fails to provide detailed information from which management can identify the products, operators, machines, or operations in which the bulk of the variances occur. If management needs this information, a more expensive system may be justified. We shall examine one such system in Chapter 20.

KEY TERMS

The most important terms introduced and defined in this chapter are the following:

Basic plan standard costing   Price variances
Controllability criterion   Quantity variances
Exception principle   Rate variances
Input   Standard costing system
Output   Standard costs
Performance standards

INDEPENDENT STUDY PROBLEMS
(Solutions in Appendix C)

1. Calculating standard cost. The Egbert Company buys a powder, dissolves it in water, concentrates the solution by boiling, adds sugar, and then packages the final product in pint jars. In the initial mix, one pound of raw material added to 0.95 gallons of water yields one gallon of mix. In the boiling operation, a 25 percent reduction in volume takes place.

Addition of one-half pound of sugar per gallon of concentrate completes the blending operation, and the mixture is allowed to cool. The addition of sugar and the cooling operation do not affect the total liquid volume. A loss of 2 percent of volume is expected during the filling operation due to spilling, evaporation, overfilling of some jars, and residue left in the blending kettles. Due to breakage and defective materials, 1,005 jars must be issued for every 1,000 jars filled.

The powder costs 80 cents a pound, sugar has a standard price of 25 cents a pound, and jars cost $2.40 a dozen.

a.   Diagram the flows of materials through this process.
b.   Calculate the standard quantity of powder and the standard quantity of sugar for a pint jar of finished product.
c.   Calculate the standard materials cost of the product.

2. Labor and materials variances. A company operates a factory with only one production department. It adopted standard costing on January 1, 19x1. Standard materials prices were set equal to the average historical cost of the materials in inventory at that time. You have the following information for the month of January:

1.   Beginning work in process, none.
2.   Beginning materials inventory, $1,000.
3.   Materials purchased, $320 (standard cost, $300).
4.   Standard cost of direct materials issued, $500.
5.   Direct labor, $760 ($720 at standard wage rates).
6.   Standard cost of jobs completed and transferred to finished goods: direct materials, $490; direct labor, $650.
7.   Standard cost of ending work in process: materials, $40; labor $20.

a.   Calculate the labor rate variance, the materials price variance, the labor quantity variance, and the materials quantity variance.
b.   How would you change your answer if you found that the work in process on January 1 had a standard materials cost of $100 and a standard labor cost of $10?

3. Basic plan cost flows. The company in Problem 2 uses the basic plan of standard costing.

a.   Set up T-accounts, enter the opening balance for the materials inventory, record the transactions for the month, and make any entries
     necessary to transfer all variances to a variance summary account.
b.   Set up T-accounts and record the transactions as they would be
     recorded in a job order costing system, without standard costs. You
     may assume that the actual costs of the ending inventories were:
     materials, $802; materials in process, $43; labor in process, $21.

EXERCISES AND PROBLEMS

1. Labor quantity variances. Standard costs in the XYZ Company remain unchanged throughout the year. You have the following labor cost
data for department 16:

	May	June
Actual direct labor hours..........................	9,000	11,000
Actual direct labor wages.........................	$72,900	$91,300
Standard direct labor rate per hour...............	$ 8.20	$ 8.20
Standard direct labor cost of production..........	$71,240	$88,600

Was the labor quantity variance better or worse in June than in May? How
much better or worse? Show and explain your calculations.

2. Labor variances. Standard direct labor cost was $5 a unit for product
A and $6 a unit for product B. The standard labor cost of work in process
was $10,000 on September 1 and $5,000 on September 30. The standard
wage rate was $8 an hour, and 7,500 direct labor hours were recorded during September. The direct labor payroll for September totaled $61,000, and
4,000 units of product A and 7,000 units of Product B were completed
during the month.

a.   Compute the standard direct labor cost of the month's output.
b.   Compute the direct labor quantity variance, in dollars. How else could
     this same information be reported?
c.   Compute the direct labor rate variance.

3. Sequential variance exercises. Follow the instructions for each of
the four exercises presented below:

Exercise A.   Quantity Variances

Luceri, Inc., reports factory materials and labor quantity variances to
management monthly. It has two products, for which the following data
are available.

	Materials Required per Unit	Labor Required per Unit	Units Produced during March
Product A.......................	4 lbs.	1.5 hrs.	1,000
Product B.......................	5	4.0	2,000

Usage of materials and labor during March was as follows: materials,
13,000 pounds; labor, 10,000 hours.

a.   Compute materials and labor quantity variances for the month in
     terms of pounds of materials and labor hours. Indicate whether each
     variance is favorable or unfavorable.

b. The standard materials price is $5 a pound. The standard wage rate is $8 an hour. (1) Compute standard unit cost for each product in dollars. (2) Restate your quantity variances (from *a*) in monetary terms.

Exercise B.   *Variances, No Work-in-Process*

A. B. See, Inc., uses a basic plan standard costing system. It had no inventory of materials on December 1 and no work in process either on December 1 or on December 31. The following information was collected for the month of December:

1.   Materials:
     Standard price: $12 a pound.
     Purchased 10,000 pounds at a cost of $115,000.
     Used during December: 8,000 pounds.
2.   Labor:
     Standard wage rate: $7.50 an hour.
     Used during December: 2,700 hours at a cost of $20,000.
3.   Product output:
     Standard cost per unit of product:
        Materials: 3.9 pounds.
        Labor: 1.5 hours.
     Products manufactured during December: 1,900 units.

a. Compute labor and materials variances, in dollars, in whatever detail you think is appropriate.
b. Indicate to whom each of your variances should be reported.

Exercise C.   *Variances, Work-in-Process*

Herren, Inc., uses a standard cost system. The following information was collected for one department for the month of December:

1.   Inventory of work in process, December 1 (at standard cost):
     Materials cost: $13,000.
     Labor cost: $8,000.
2.   Used during month:
     Materials (at standard prices): $30,000.
     Labor:
        At actual wage rates, $15,000.
        At standard wage rates, $16,000.
3.   Products finished and transferred out of the department during month
        (at standard cost):
     Materials cost: $31,200.
     Labor cost: $15,700.
4.   Inventory of work in process, December 31 (at standard cost):
     Materials cost: $9,000.
     Labor cost: $9,000.

Compute labor and materials variances in whatever detail you think is appropriate.

Exercise D.   *Variances, Interdepartmental Transfers*

Smythe, Ltd. has a factory with four production departments. Department Baker receives partly processed products from department Able, adds component materials to them, and then transfers them to department Charlie for further work. A standard cost system is in use. The following data are available for department Baker for the month of February:

1. Received from department Able during February:
   Product units received, 5,000.
   Unit cost in department Able:

	Standard	Actual
Materials..........................	$1.00	$1.10
Labor..............................	6.00	6.90

2. Received component materials from stock room during month, at standard prices, $2,100; standard cost of these materials, 40 cents per product unit.
3. Used 1,100 labor hours during February, $8,250 at standard wage rates; standard cost of department Baker labor was $1.80 per product unit.
4. Transferred to department Charlie during February, 4,800 product units.
5. Work in process inventories in department Baker were negligible both on February 1 and on February 28.
6. Damaged 200 product units in processing operations; these units were not usable and had no salvage value. About half of the processing labor operations had been performed on these units before they were damaged. All of the component materials had been applied prior to the damage.

a. Compute labor and materials quantity variances for department Baker for the month of February.
b. Standard cost per product unit includes no allowances for losses of products during processing. How much of each of the variances computed in (a) was attributable to product losses? What do the remaining portions of the variances mean?

4. Quantity variances: Actual versus standard rates. A department recorded the following data during three recent months:

	May	June	July
Actual direct labor cost............................	$4,200	$4,675	$3,871
Actual direct labor hours...........................	800	850	790
Standard wage rate.................................	$ 5	$ 5	$ 5
Standard labor cost of actual production............	$4,500	$3,750	$3,400

a. Compute and analyze the variance of actual labor cost from standard labor cost for each month. The standard wage rate should be used to measure the size of the quantity variance component of this total variance each month.
b. Measure the labor quantity variance for each month using actual wage rates.
c. Measure any differences between your two sets of quantity variance figures. Give your reasons for preferring one to the other or for being indifferent to the choice.

5. Materials variances. Product X is manufactured from material A in department 1. Material A has a standard price of $4 a gallon, delivered. The standard bill of materials for product X calls for 1.2 gallons of material A for every gallon of finished product. The following transactions took place during August:

1. Purchased 10,000 gallons of material A at an invoice price of $3.80 a gallon, less a 2 percent discount for prompt payment.

2. Paid freight charges on this shipment, $3,200.
3. Issued 8,000 gallons of material A to department 1.
4. Produced 7,000 gallons of product X.

a. Compute and analyze the materials cost variances for the month.
b. The total direct labor cost variance in any period is the difference be-
    tween actual labor cost and the standard labor cost of the work done.
    Would you calculate the total materials cost variance the same way?
    If so, how would you define actual materials cost? If not, explain how
    your method differs from the method applied to direct labor.

6. Materials variances.   Materials price variances are identified at the
time of purchase. Materials inventories are costed at standard purchase
prices.

Material X is the raw material for product A. Product A is the only output of department 1. The standard materials quantity is 0.38 pounds of
material X for a gallon of product A. If the price of material X gets too
high, the plant manager will convert the process so that product A can be
manufactured from soybeans instead of material X.

Material X has a standard purchase price of $8 a pound. The company
purchased 3,000 pounds during January at a cost of $25,100. These
materials were placed in warehouse W.

Department 1 used 4,000 pounds of material X during January. All of
these came from warehouse H. They had been purchased six months
earlier at a price of $7.50.

Department 1 produced 9,900 gallons of product A during the month of
January.

a. Compute the materials price and materials quantity variances for the
    month.
b. What managerially significant information on January operations
    would you report: (1) to the supervisor of department 1; (2) to the
    plant manager?

7. Physical unit comparisons.   Art Dangerfield had been department
supervisor for 30 years. "All I want are a few key figures," he said. "The rest
of the accounting figures are rubbish. I want to know my scrap percentage
[pounds of scrap, divided by pounds of materials] and the materials yield
[pounds of product divided by pounds of materials]. If scrap is less than 5
percent and the materials yield is better than 80 percent, I've got it made."

The department processes a number of different materials and a certain
amount of waste is inherent in the process. Some materials are lost in the
process itself; some take the form of recoverable scrap. Mr. Dangerfield
retired last month and his longtime assistant, Dorothy Hellman, was
promoted to take his place. The first report she saw contained the following statistics:

Scrap.......................... 3%
Materials yield.................. 84%
Materials quantity variance
  (% of standard)............... 10% unfavorable

"Art's formula doesn't seem to be working," she observed. "I'm well within
his limits, but how did that quantity variance get so big?" She asked the
plant controller to look into the matter.

The controller analyzed the materials requisitions and production
records and came up with the following figures:

	Standard Price (per pound)	Standard Quantity (in pounds)	Quantity Used (in pounds)
Material A...........	$ 0.10	4,000	3,700
Material B...........	1.00	600	630
Material C...........	10.00	400	450
Total..........		5,000	4,780

The percentage statistics were correct: the output weighed 4,015 pounds, 84 percent of the weight of the materials used, and 143 pounds of scrap were recovered.

a. Analyze the controller's figures and provide an explanation for Ms. Hellman.
b. Does your analysis indicate that the standards should be changed? What other suggestions would you make?

8. Calculating departmental output. Department T produces several products. You have the following statistics for the month of May:

	Standard Quantity per Unit			Units in Process	
Product	Materials (in pounds)	Labor (in hours)	Units Completed	May 1	May 31
A..........	4	2	1,000	100	200
B.........	2	5	300	80	100
C.........	6	1	2,000	300	200

Materials have a standard price of $3 a pound; the standard labor rate is $8 an hour. Units in process on any date already include all the materials required; half of the labor operations have been performed.

a. Calculate total standard labor cost and total standard materials cost for the month.
b. How would you get the data you would need to estimate the standard cost of the work in process on any date?

9. Basic plan accounts. Using a basic plan of standard costing and carrying materials inventories at standard net delivered prices, record the following transactions in appropriate T-accounts. You should include an account for each variance that you wish to identify separately.

Actual cost of materials purchased:
Gross invoice price....................................... $50,000
Discounts received on purchases......................... 800
Freight and delivery charges on materials purchased...... 2,300
Standard cost of materials purchased..................... 51,000
Materials issued (at standard prices)..................... 47,000
Direct labor:
At actual wage rates...................................... 30,000
At standard wage rates.................................... 28,000
Cost of goods finished (at standard):
Materials.. 40,000
Labor... 26,000
Cost of goods in process, end of month (at standard):
Materials.. 5,200
Labor... 5,100

There was no work in process at the beginning of the month.

10. Measuring variances. Department T makes two products, X and Y, with the following standard inputs:

	Product X	Product Y	Standard Price
Direct materials:			
A....................	1 pound	3 pounds	$5 a pound
B....................	2 pounds	—	3 a pound
C....................	—	1 pound	6 a pound
Direct labor..........	0.5 hour	0.7 hour	7 an hour

You have the following additional information:

1. A basic plan of standard costing is in use.
2. The standard costs of inventories on hand were:

	May 1	May 31
Materials....................................	$47,340	$56,490
Materials in process—department T.......	2,370	1,920
Labor in process—department T..........	332	378

3. The following materials were purchased during May—A: 6,000 pounds, $31,300; B: 6,000 pounds, $19,800; C: none.
4. Materials issued to department T during May: A, 4,800 pounds; B, 3,050 pounds; C, 950 pounds.
5. No materials were issued to any other department.
6. Direct labor for the month was 1,650 hours, $11,500.
7. Products completed and transferred to finished goods inventory in the home office—X, 1,600 units; Y, 1,000 units.

a. Calculate the materials price variance, the labor rate variance, the materials quantity variance, and the labor quantity variance for department T.
b. Explain how the standard materials costs of the work in process could be lower on May 31 than on May 1, while the standard labor cost was greater at the end of the month than at the beginning.
c. How would your answer to (a) have differed if the May 31 materials inventory had been $56,000 instead of $56,490?
d. Why isn't this a good way to get steering control information for the manager of department T?

11. Basic plan accounts. The company in Problem 10 uses a single account for materials inventories and separate accounts for materials in process and labor in process in each department.

a. Set up T-accounts representing these and any other accounts you find necessary. Enter the opening account balances from Problem 10.
b. Record in these T-accounts your analyses of the month's transactions.
c. Make whatever entries are necessary at the end of the month to transfer any variances to a separate variance summary account and restore the accounts to their correct balances, ready to receive the record of the June transactions.

12. Supplying missing information. A basic plan standard costing system is in use in each of the Harrison Company's factories. You have the following data on direct materials and direct labor for three of these factories:

		Factory A	Factory B	Factory C
	Inventories, June 1, at standard cost:			
1.	Materials.........................	$ 93,000	?	$163,000
2.	Materials in process...............	17,000	$ 9,500	21,000
3.	Labor in process...................	12,000	6,000	?
4.	Finished goods*....................	125,000	?	212,000
	Inventories, June 30, at standard cost:			
5.	Materials.........................	?	128,000	139,000
6.	Materials in process...............	14,600	14,900	?
7.	Labor in process...................	9,200	?	3,500
8.	Finished goods*....................	?	104,000	229,000
	Totals for the month of June:			
9.	Materials purchased, at standard prices..........................	?	72,000	51,000
10.	Materials purchased, at actual prices..........................	38,400	?	49,800
11.	Materials issued, at standard prices..........................	47,000	?	?
12.	Standard materials cost of jobs finished.........................	?	46,200	80,400
13.	Standard materials cost of the work done...........................	49,200	?	71,700
14.	Actual labor hours used............	?	10,000 hours	7,000 hours
15.	Actual labor cost..................	$ 63,200	?	$ 65,100
16.	Standard wage rate................	$8/hour	$7/hour	?
17.	Standard labor cost of the work done...........................	$ 59,200	?	$ 60,500
18.	Standard labor cost of the jobs finished.........................	?	69,000	66,000
19.	Standard labor and materials cost of the goods sold.................	131,600	107,200	?
20.	Materials price variance...........	2,400 U.	300 U.	?
21.	Labor rate variance................	800 F.	1,300 U.	?
22.	Materials quantity variance........	?	4,400 U.	?
23.	Labor quantity variance...........	?	1,000 F.	2,500 U.
24.	Total labor cost variance..........	4,000 U.	300 U.	?

* = Materials and labor costs only

Make the necessary calculations and fill in the blanks identified by question marks in this table.

13. Basic plan accounts. Eiseman, Inc. manufactures a line of children's sleds. It has a basic plan standard costing system in its factory. Materials price variances are separated at the time of purchase, and all materials inventories are costed at standard prices.

Factory overheads are regarded as wholly fixed and are charged to expense as incurred, without passing through the product inventory accounts. Factory overhead is expected to total $69,000 a month.

Standard costs and production and inventory data for the four models manufactured in the sled department during September were:

	Model 3	Model 5	Model 22	Model 30
Standard cost per unit:				
Materials..................	$0.80	$1.20	$1.50	$ 2.00
Labor.....................	2.00	4.00	6.00	10.00
Total..................	$2.80	$5.20	$7.50	$12.00
Units completed.............	5,000	10,000	4,000	2,000
Units in process, Sept. 1......	None	1,000	100	200
Units in process, Sept. 30.....	None	800	300	None

Units in process on any given date are assumed to be 100 percent complete as to materials and 50 percent complete as to labor.

The following transactions relate to the sled department during the month of September:

1. Purchased materials on account (standard cost, $35,000), $35,400.
2. Issued materials:
   Direct materials, at inventory cost, $24,500.
   Indirect materials, at inventory cost, $3,000.
3. Accrued payrolls for the month (including indirect labor), $111,800.
4. Direct labor hours (standard wage rate, $3 an hour), 11,900 hours.
5. Indirect labor, $20,000.
6. Other factory overhead, paid in cash, $50,000.

a. Prepare a schedule or schedules showing the standard costs of the inventories and of the goods completed during the month. What were the standard direct materials and standard direct labor costs of the work done during the month?

b. Record the above information in appropriate T-accounts. Be sure to enter the opening balances. Include entries that will bring the inventory accounts to their correct ending balances. A separate account should be provided for each variance that you wish to identify.

14. Variance analysis. Ross Shirts, Inc., manufactures short- and long-sleeved men's shirts for large stores. Ross produces a single quality shirt in lots to each customer's order and attaches the store's label to each. The standard direct costs for a dozen long-sleeved shirts are:

Direct materials, 24 yards at $0.75................. $18.00
Direct labor, 3 hours at $7.45..................... 22.35

During October Ross Shirts worked on three orders for long-sleeved shirts. Job cost records for the month disclose the following:

Lot	Units in Lot	Material Used	Hours Worked
30.................	1,000 dozen	24,100 yards	2,980
31.................	1,700 dozen	40,440 yards	5,130
32.................	1,200 dozen	28,825 yards	2,890

The following information is also available:
1. Ross purchased 95,000 yards of material during the month at a cost of $72,200. The materials price variance is recorded when goods are purchased and all inventories are carried at standard cost.
2. Direct labor incurred amounted to $82,500 during October.
3. There was no work in process at October 1. During October, lots 30 and 31 were completed. All material was issued for lot 32 and it was 80 percent completed as to labor on October 31.

a. Compute the materials price variance for October and indicate whether it was favorable or unfavorable.

b. Compute the total amount of each of the following variances and indicate in each case whether the variance was favorable or unfavorable: (1) materials quantity variance in yards and dollars; (2) labor quantity variance in hours and dollars; (3) labor rate variance in dollars.

c. Identify, for each production lot, the variances that resulted directly from the production of that lot. Would you expect this information to be available in a basic plan system? Explain how it would be derived.

(CPA adapted)

15. Variances and cost flows. Alacazam, Inc. has a small factory which performs three different kinds of operations. Production is on a job order basis. To fill a job order, the factory performs one or more of the three operations, using one or more kinds of materials. For some jobs, the same operation must be performed more than once on each unit. (For example, one operation may be to drill a hole—if the product is to have two holes in it, that operation must be performed twice.)

The three operations, with their standard labor requirements, are as follows:

	Operation 1	Operation 2	Operation 3
Standard labor hours per operation...	2	3	4
Standard labor rate per labor hour........	$10	$8	$7

Each operation is the responsibility of a separate factory department. Operation 1 is performed in department 1, operation 2 in department 2, and operation 3 in department 3. Jobs pass through the departments in numerical order—department 1 first, then department 2, and finally department 3.

Labor and materials variances are calculated and reported weekly by means of a basic plan system. Standard product cost provides for some wastage of raw materials, but no allowance is made for the loss of units of semiprocessed products in departments 2 and 3.

You have the following information about the operations of the factory during the week of August 16:

1. The factory completed work on four job orders during the week, one for each of four products: A, B, C, and D. The operations required, the standard materials required by these four products, and the number of units produced were as follows:

	Product				Standard Price
	A	B	C	D	
Operations required	1	1	1 (twice)	1 (twice)	
	2	3	3 (twice)	2	
	3 (twice)			3 (three times)	
Standard materials per unit:					
Material X...........	6 lbs.	6 lbs.	8 lbs.	10 lbs.	$2 per lb.
Material Y...........	4 ft.	—	—	6 ft.	$4 per ft.
Material Z...........	4 pieces	2 pieces	4 pieces	6 pieces	$1 per piece
No. of units in job.....	100	150	50	125	

Material X is used in operation 1, material Y is used in operation 2, and material Z is used in operation 3.

2. Operation 1 had been performed the previous week on product A; operations 1 and 2 had been performed the previous week on product D

All jobs were completed during the week. There was no work in process in any department at the end of the week.

3. Materials issued:

Material X: 1,500 pounds, to department 1.
Material Y: 525 feet, to department 2.
Material Z: 1,660 pieces, to department 3.

No department had any inventory of these materials either at the beginning or at the end of the week.

4. Direct labor costs for the week:

	Hours	Cost
Department 1.............	480	$ 5,000
Department 2.............	360	3,000
Department 3.............	3,000	20,700

5. Work completed and transferred:

From department 1 to department 3:   products B and C.
From department 2 to department 3:   product A.
From department 3 to finished goods: products A, B, C, and D.

6. Overhead costs are not covered by the standard costing system and do not enter this problem.

a. Calculate the standard cost of each product, listing each element and each material separately.
b. Calculate the standard cost of the work in process at the beginning of the week. Set up two Work-in-Process accounts for each department and other accounts, as appropriate. Enter the opening balances.
c. Calculate each department's standard direct materials cost and standard direct labor cost for the week. Remember that this is a basic plan system, with interdepartmental transfers.
d. Record the effects of the week's transactions, using whatever accounts you find necessary. (Check figures: the total standard direct labor cost of the work finished by department 2 during the week was $2,400; the total standard direct materials cost of goods finished by department 3 during the week was $29,950.)
e. Prepare a summary of the week's variances.
f. Suppose 10 units of product A had been lost in department 2, so that only 90 units were placed in finished goods inventory. Indicate which variances would be different and by how much.

CASE 6–1: FROZEN MEALS, INC.*

Frozen Meals, Inc., is a small but rapidly growing manufacturer of frozen tray dinners. The company processes and freezes the meals at a central plant and ships them to regional distribution centers where they are stored in refrigerated warehouses on a consignment basis. Sales are made principally to large wholesale grocery distributors, mostly in the

---

* Adapted with permission from an article written by Patrick J. McCullagh, published by the National Association of Accountants.

western half of the United States. The company sold more than 4 million tray dinners last year and this year's total is likely to approach 6 million.

When the firm was first founded, top management was able to keep close tabs on the manufacturing operation. Elaborate cost control or even cost reporting systems did not seem necessary. The firm grew rapidly, however, and top management realized that it needed an accounting information system. Arthur Hesse, the company's president, saw the problem this way: "This is a low-margin business. Prices are generally set by competition and our profits are extremely vulnerable to small variations in unit costs. This means that reliable and timely cost information is vital. This information must include accurate manufacturing costs for each menu, accurate distribution costs for each major sales area, and information on which to base local and general advertising budgets. We also need to know when our costs are getting out of line—even a penny or two on each meal can put a real dent in our profits. Even worse, our growth gives us an insatiable appetite for funds to finance our working capital requirements, and we can't afford mistakes that cut down our cash flow."

To design and install the new accounting system, Mr. Hesse hired Margaret Bonomi, a business school graduate with five years of experience on the controller's staff of a large mail-order house. Ms. Bonomi was given the title of controller and was assigned responsibility for all accounting and clerical operations.

"I knew from the beginning," Ms. Bonomi said, "that I had to get the system going very quickly. Art Hesse no longer had the time to keep tabs on the factory on a daily basis. When he hired me, he also hired Ted Crawford as plant manager. The factory is Ted's baby. He expects the managers of the three production departments—preparation, assembly, and wrapping—to meet delivery schedules and keep costs under control. Ted does most of the production planning and helps the department heads out when problems arise, and this keeps him too busy to know everything that's going on all the time. He's been a great help to me in getting the system started. Fortunately, since we had no information system at all before I came, I could start fresh and really move. I hired an assistant and an accounting clerk and we had the new system working in about three months. We even did something with our distribution and warehousing costs, but I know you're not interested in those right now."

Materials Costs

Because materials costs bulk so large in the overall cost structure, Ms. Bonomi began by concentrating on developing cost standards and reporting procedures for materials costs. She found that the number of raw materials was relatively small, fewer than 100 kinds of items. She classified these into three major groups:

1. Entree items (meat, fish, etc.).
2. Vegetables.
3. Other ingredients and condiments.

She found that some items of raw materials are received daily, such as fresh meat, fresh vegetables, eggs and butter. These are held for short periods under normal refrigeration before going into production. Other items, mainly vegetables, are received frozen and are stored in freezers until they are needed. Finally, nonperishable items such as flour, sugar, and salt are stored at normal temperature in an enclosed area in the factory.

The product unit for costing purposes is the "menu," the company's term for its tray dinners. The company now has ten different menus and will probably add more in the near future. Ms. Bonomi's first step in developing a system for reporting materials costs was to establish a standard quantity of each item used for each thousand meals. This information was developed by production personnel from the recipes used for each menu. These materials usage figures were recorded on a Cost Reference Sheet like the one in Exhibit 1. The physical quantities were then extended at standard prices supplied by the purchasing department to get total cost and cost per meal figures. These became the standard materials costs, different for each menu.

The Cost Reference Sheet also includes a section for packaging supplies. These fall into two categories: (1) aluminum trays and foil overwrap, and (2) cartons and labels. Since packaging is similar for each meal, the same standard cost is used for all menus.

The next step was to design a procedure for recording the purchase and use of materials and supplies. Because seasonal price fluctuations in this industry are the rule rather than the exception, Ms. Bonomi decided to extend all materials invoices at the standard unit prices developed by the purchasing department. Four inventory accounts are maintained in the general ledger—one each for fresh, frozen, and dry ingredients and one for packaging supplies. The standard costs of the items purchased are entered in these four accounts whenever materials are received.

EXHIBIT 1

COST REFERENCE SHEET

Menu No.:   6   Date:
Meals Produced: 1,000

Ingredient		Quantity		Cost Analysis		
	Unit	Raw	Cooked	Unit Cost	Total Cost	Cost per Meal
Beef	Lb.	400#	330#	$ 1.48	$592.00	$.59200
Potatoes	Lb.	230#		.12	27.60	.02760
Lima Beans	Lb.	150#		.36	54.00	.05400
Butter	Lb.	11#		.76	8.36	.00836
Etc.	—	—		—	—	—
						$.xxxxx

Packaging Supplies					
		Quantity			
Aluminum Trays		1,009 M	$120.00	$121.08	$.12108
Aluminum Overwrap		1,013 M	24.00	24.31	.02431
Etc.		—	—	—	—
					$.xxxxx

Direct Labor	
Preparation	$.14268
Assembly Line	.07284
Wrapping	.04280
Total	$.25832
Total	$.xxxxx

EXHIBIT 2

MATERIAL RECORD CARD

Item:	Grade:	Unit:	Standard Cost:
Lima Beans	"A"	Lb.	$.36

Standard consumption	Menu #1 —	Menu #3 200#	Menu #5 ___
per 1,000 meals	Menu #2 ___	Menu #4 ___	Menu #6 150#

Vendors: A. *Grow Pak, Inc.*   B. *Freeze Fresh Corp.*

Received			Production		Consumption		
Date	*Vendor*	*Quantity*	*Menu*	*Meals*	*Standard*	*Actual*	*Variance*
1/1	Inventory	6,500	3	62,000	12,400		
1/5	B	30,000	6	45,000	6,750		
1/31	Total	36,500			19,150	19,500	Plus 350#
2/1	Inventory	17,000					

The general ledger accounts are backed up by a file of Material Record Cards, one for each item, as illustrated in Exhibit 2. When a shipment of materials is received, the physical quantity received is recorded in the column at the left of this card. Issues of materials to production departments are not recorded as they occur. Instead, a complete physical inventory is taken monthly to determine the quantity of each item on hand at the end of the month. This information is entered in the lower left-hand corner of the Material Record Cards (17,000 pounds of this item). Subtracting the ending inventory from the total material available for use (36,500 pounds) provides a measure of actual consumption for the month (19,500 pounds, in this case). This is entered at the right.

The final step is to calculate the standard consumption of each kind of materials. The daily production reports list the number of meals produced each day. These are summarized at the end of the month and the total quantities are entered on the Material Record Cards, as in the center columns of Exhibit 2. Standard consumption for the month is determined by multiplying the standard quantity figures in the upper half of the Material Record Card by the number of meals produced.

With this information, a usage variance can be calculated immediately for each kind of ingredient, measured in physical quantities only. Significant variances are identified by the controller's staff and reported to Mr. Crawford immediately. No attempt is made to classify these variances by menu, because actual usage is not recorded on this basis. "We've found these variance figures very useful," Ms. Bonomi said. "The system has been in use for less than a year, but we've already made a number of improvements in processing methods after the variance reports have shown excessive consumption of some of the ingredients."

Labor Costs

Unit cost standards have also been developed for direct and indirect labor costs. All direct labor employees are paid on an hourly basis. They are grouped into three wage categories:

Category A. $3.20 or less
Category B. $3.25 to $3.95
Category C.   More than $3.95

The standard direct labor costs of operations in the preparation department have been based on performance data collected by production personnel during a test period. An example of one of these test observations is shown in Exhibit 3. The manager of the preparation department listed the preparation steps for each menu, noted the time taken for each step in each menu, and used these data to derive a set of standard time allowances. Ms. Bonomi's assistant extended these times at the average wage rate for workers in each wage category, thereby deriving a standard labor cost for each operation and a total standard labor cost for each menu.

EXHIBIT 3

DIRECT LABOR REPORT

Department: Preparation   Date: _____

Operation: ___Breading Veal___   Menu: _#2_   Meals Prepared: 1,830

Class of Labor	Number of Employees	Time From	To	Hours	Total Hours	Average Rate	Cost
A	2	8:00A.M.	10:00A.M.	2	4	$3.00	$12.00
B	3	8:00A.M.	11:00A.M.	3	9	3.60	32.40
C	2	10:00A.M.	11:30A.M.	1½	3	4.20	12.60
							$57.00

Unit Cost of Operation per Meal $ .031

A similar procedure was followed for the assembly and wrapping departments, except that a single standard direct labor cost was developed for all menus. All menus receive identical treatment during the operations performed in these two departments.

A standard is also used for indirect labor cost—the wages of all hourly workers other than those classified as direct labor. Indirect labor is not classified by department, however, and a single rate is used to cover all kinds of indirect labor. This rate is the estimated percentage of indirect labor to direct labor cost for the factory as a whole. Standard indirect labor cost for each menu is obtained by multiplying the standard direct labor cost by this estimated percentage.

At the beginning of each week production personnel supply the payroll clerk with a schedule showing the number of employees in each category assigned to each department for the week. One week's schedule, for example, showed the following:

Wage Category	Number of Direct Labor Employees			
	Preparation	Assembly	Wrapping	Total
A................	12	35	10	57
B................	3	4	3	10
C................	10	2	2	14
				81

Any midweek changes of assignment, which occur infrequently, are reported to the payroll clerk as they occur.

The payroll clerk then distributes the total direct labor payroll (including overtime premiums) to the departments in direct proportion to the number of employees. In the week described in the table above, for example, the assembly department was charged 35/57 of the total direct labor cost of all category A employees, 4/10 of the total direct labor cost of all category B employees, and so on.

Once the direct labor costs have been distributed in this way, they are compared with the standard direct labor cost of the work done in each department during the week. This information is reported to Mr. Crawford in a weekly labor cost report. This shows the net variance from standard direct labor cost for each department during the preceding week, together with the overall ratio of indirect to direct labor and the amount of the overtime premiums in the factory as a whole.

Factory Overhead Costs

Ms. Bonomi classified all factory costs other than direct materials, direct labor, and indirect labor as factory overhead costs. Because few of these are traceable to specific departments, the overhead costs are not departmentalized.

Using statistical techniques, Ms. Bonomi's assistant tried to find relationships between various overhead costs and the volume of production. Since he was able to find none, these costs are budgeted as fixed. Standard overhead costs have not yet been developed for the company's individual products.

Monthly Control Reports

Ms. Bonomi's assistant prepares a summary factory cost variance report at the end of each month. This report is based on a tally of the month's production. The number of each menu produced is multiplied by the standard cost per unit, using the form illustrated in Exhibit 4. The figures in

EXHIBIT 4

	STANDARD COST SUMMARY		
Menu No.: _____		Month: _____ 19 __	
Item	Standard Unit Cost	Total Units Produced	Total Standard Materials & Labor
1. Entree item	$.XXXX		$
2. Vegetables	.XXXX		
3. Other ingredients	.XXXX		
4. Trays and foil	.XXXX		
5. Packaging	.XXXX		
6. Direct labor	.XXXX		
7. Indirect labor	.XXXX		
Total	$.XXXX		$

the right-hand column are then cross-totaled for all menus to determine the total standard costs of meals completed during the month.

Before these totals are compared with actual costs for the month, the inventory of work in process is checked. Production personnel count the work in process at the close of business on the last working day of the month. This generally takes only a few minutes. A clerk extends these quantities at their standard cost. Actual costs and standard costs for the factory as a whole are then summarized in the Monthly Variance Summary illustrated in Exhibit 5. For factory overhead, the figure shown in the "standard" column is one twelfth of the annual budget; for all other items it is the standard cost of meals completed, plus or minus the change in the standard cost of the work in process inventory.

EXHIBIT 5

MONTHLY VARIANCE SUMMARY				
	Standard	Price Variance	Use Variance	Actual
Raw Materials Consumed	$ —	$ —	$ —	$ —
Packaging Supplies	—	—	—	—
Direct Labor	—		—	—
Indirect Labor	—		—	—
Factory Overhead	—			—
Cost of Goods Manufactured	$ —			$ —

The first two lines on this report summarize the three categories of ingredients and two categories of packaging supplies tabulated in Exhibit 4. "We decided," Ms. Bonomi said, "that a report with too many figures would only make it more difficult for management to focus on the essentials. We can always bring these five items in as supplementary information if we need to. We can also show labor usage variances by department, but this extra detail goes only to factory management; top management wants only the broad picture, with an explanation of what is being done to correct unfavorable usage variances. We calculate the cost of goods sold each month by multiplying the number of cases sold by the standard cost per case. This means that we can put the monthly operating statement in management's hands three working days after the end of the month. The only variances we calculate weekly are the labor cost variances I described earlier; the others come out only once a month. Top management never sees the weekly labor cost reports."

Ms. Bonomi makes no effort to reconcile the monthly variance summaries with the variance information on the Materials Record Cards and on the weekly labor summaries. "The procedure we use gets the monthly variance summary out faster than if we tried to work from the detailed records. Besides, our method makes sure that the amounts shown in the inventory accounts represent the amounts actually on hand. If we've overlooked anything in the bookkeeping routine, we can pick it up here.

"We're still working on the system, but we think it has achieved its primary purpose—supplying timely information essential to profitable expansion and doing it at minimum cost and during a vital phase of growth."

Cost Bookkeeping

The cost bookkeeping procedures at Frozen Meals, Inc., are designed to minimize the number of bookkeeping entries in the inventory accounts. Six inventory accounts are maintained; four for materials and supplies (as described earlier), one for work in process, and one for finished goods.

The standard costs of the materials and supplies are charged to the materials and supplies inventory control accounts at the time of purchase. These accounts are credited once a month for the standard materials and supplies costs of meals produced, on the basis of the data in the standard cost summaries (Exhibit 4); the accompanying debits are to the work in process account.

Actual labor costs are charged to direct and indirect labor cost control accounts as payrolls are accrued. Standard labor costs, again taken from the standard cost summaries, are credited to these accounts and charged to work in process.

Overhead costs are accumulated in a set of overhead cost accounts. The balances in these accounts are closed into the work-in-process account at the end of each month.

These overhead accounts are charged each month for the actual overhead costs incurred, with two exceptions—repairs and maintenance and vacation pay. The company expends substantial amounts for repairs and maintenance, partly to keep machinery and refrigeration equipment in good working order, and partly to ensure that sanitary conditions in the plant meet government health standards at all times. Expenditures for these purposes vary considerably from month to month, but these variations are not the result of variations in the volume of production. Vacation pay is also treated separately because it is concentrated almost entirely in the summer months and at the end of the year. For each of these kinds of costs, one twelfth of the budgeted amount for the year is charged to the appropriate overhead cost account each month, with a corresponding credit to an accrual account. The actual expenditures are charged against the accrual account, which is closed out to the cost of goods sold at the end of the year.

As soon as the clerk calculates the standard cost of the work in process at the end of the month, an entry is made to transfer to the finished goods account the amount necessary to reduce the balance in the work in process account to standard cost. Finished goods inventories are also counted and a transfer to cost of goods sold is made to bring the balance in the finished goods account down to the standard cost of the meals on hand at the end of the month.

Variances in the materials and labor cost control accounts are also transferred to the cost of goods sold account at the end of the month. The balances in all inventory accounts therefore represent the standard costs of the inventories on hand at the end of the month.

a.   What were the specifications Ms. Bonomi had to meet in designing and installing the new system?

b.   How well did the new system meet these specifications? What changes, if any, would you make at this time?

7

Flexible Budgets:
Controlling Overhead Costs
of Responsive Activities

DIRECT LABOR and direct materials are not the only costs the manager needs to control. In fact, control of overhead costs—all costs not classified as direct labor or direct materials—may be even more important.

The purpose of this chapter is to see what tools the cost accountant might use to help management control one kind of overhead costs, the overhead costs of responsive activities. We shall study three sets of questions:

1. What kinds of performance standards are appropriate and how they can be developed.
2. What a set of overhead cost control reports might include.
3. How the figures in the overhead cost control reports can be reconciled with the amount of overhead cost absorbed by production.

To avoid confusion, we shall look only at the overhead costs of factory production departments. The discussion of the first two sets of questions applies with equal force, however, to the costs of any activity whose scope is determined by the total volume of work it supports—that is, any responsive activity.

PERFORMANCE STANDARDS
FOR OVERHEAD COSTS

A good control standard will tell management what ought to be happening at the moment. The so-called flexible budget comes closer to meeting this test than standard overhead cost. In this section we shall see what standard overhead cost is, what flexible budgets are and why they are better than standard overhead costs as performance standards, and what technical and behavioral problems are likely to arise in flexible budgeting.

224

Standard Factory Overhead Costs

Standard factory overhead costs are like the overhead costs assigned to products by means of predetermined overhead rates. The only difference is that standard overhead cost depends on some *standard* direct input quantity rather than the actual input quantity.

For example, suppose the overhead rate is $5 a direct labor hour. The standard direct labor time for product X is 2 hours. The standard overhead costs for this product, as shown in Exhibit 7–1, is $10. This figure is not affected by the number of direct labor hours actually used to manufacture the product. The *amount of overhead absorbed,* in other words, depends on the number of units produced, not the number of direct labor hours used.

Management can't use standard overhead cost figures to control factory overhead, for two reasons. First, overhead costs are common costs, incurred to support or facilitate all of the department's work, not traceable to individual lots or units of specific products. For this reason, control standards must be derived from departmental figures rather than from data relating to specific products or operations.

Second, overhead costs include elements that do not vary in strict proportion to changes in production volume. If a significant proportion of total cost is fixed, standard overhead cost per unit will be too restrictive a control standard at low production volumes and too lenient at high volumes.

For example, suppose the overhead rate of $5 a direct labor hour in Exhibit 7–1 covers $2 of fixed costs and $3 of variable costs. Total fixed costs at the normal volume of 2,500 units are expected to amount to $10,000 and the department head is expected to hold them at that level. Now, what happens if the department processes 2,000 units of product? The standard fixed cost of one unit is 2 direct labor hours × $2 = $4. The total standard fixed cost of 2,000 units is $8,000. This is the height of point P in Exhibit 7–2. If fixed costs are really expected to amount to $10,000 a month, this $8,000 figure would

EXHIBIT 7–1

Calculating a Product's Standard Overhead Cost

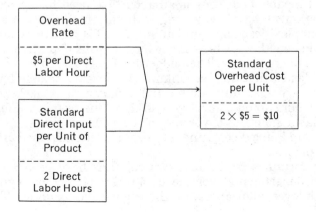

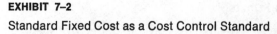

EXHIBIT 7–2

Standard Fixed Cost as a Cost Control Standard

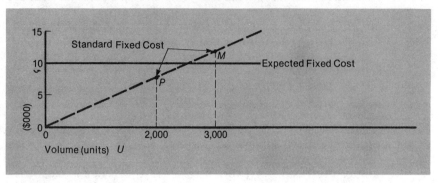

provide a pretty poor basis for a control report. The department will be $2,000 over the total standard fixed cost for the month even if it does exactly what it is expected to do.

Standard overhead cost provides just as poor a control standard at high volumes. At a volume of 3,000 units a month, total standard overhead cost will include 3,000 × $4 = $12,000 for fixed costs, point M in Exhibit 7–2. This is $2,000 greater than the amount the manager ought to be spending. Only at a normal volume of 2,500 units a month will total standard fixed cost equal the amount the manager is expected to spend, $10,000.

The Flexible Budget

What this says is that overhead cost control standards for responsive activities should consist of departmental totals, adjusted to levels of cost appropriate to the actual volume of operations. Standards of this sort come from the flexible budget. The flexible budget consists either of a cost-volume formula (such as $10,000 + $3 a direct labor hour) or a set of fixed budgets, one for each of a number of alternative production volumes.

To see what flexible budgeting is all about, we need to replace the simple illustration we have been using with one that brings in a few more of the complexities to be found in practice. The first two columns of Exhibit 7–3 show the flexible budget for the drills department of a small metal products factory. The budget in this case is presented as a set of formulas so that the accountant can develop flexible budget allowances for any operating volume the department is likely to record. It could be drawn on a chart as a straight line from a volume of 3,000 direct labor hours to a volume of 4,500 labor hours. At that point both a jump in fixed costs and a ten-cent increase in the variable cost rate take place.

The budget formulas in the first two columns have been applied to the normal departmental volume of 4,000 direct labor hours to produce the budget allowances in the right-hand column. These

EXHIBIT 7-3

Monthly Overhead Cost Budget, Drills Department
(DLH = direct labor hour)

Cost Element	Budgeted Monthly Fixed Cost	Budgeted Variable Cost per DLH	Budgeted Cost at Normal Volume (4,000 DLH)
Supervision:			
Less than 3,000 DLH................	$2,000	...	
3,000–4,499 DLH....................	2,800	...	} $ 2,800
4,500 DLH and more...............	3,500	...	
Materials handling labor..............	....	$0.12	480
Idle or lost time......................	....	0.06	240
Other indirect labor...................	....	0.32	1,280
Overtime premium....................	....	*	....
Supplies.............................	....	0.14	560
Power...............................	....	0.20	800
Maintenance.........................	600	0.10	1,000
Tools................................	....	0.21	840
Floor space..........................	800	...	800
Equipment depreciation..............	600	...	600
General factory overhead.............	2,600	...	2,600
Total..........................	$7,400†	$1.15†	$12,000

* Ten cents for each direct labor hour in excess of 4,500 hours a month.
† Totals apply only to normal operating range of from 3,000 to 4,499 direct labor hours.

figures are used both to calculate the overhead rate and to provide the control standard if volume in a particular month actually happens to be 4,000 direct labor hours. For any other volume a different set of figures has to be developed.

Interpreting the Flexible Budget

Flexible budget figures reflect the amount of overhead cost that is reasonably necessary to sustain a given volume of activity, on the assumption that production is stabilized at that volume. As long as production activity in the drills department is relatively constant at a volume of 4,000 direct labor hours a month, departmental overhead cost should amount to about $12,000 (the total of the figures in the right-hand column of Exhibit 7–3). If volume is stable at 3,500 hours, total overhead cost should be $7,400 + $1.15 × 3,500 = $11,425.

We should point out right now that the flexible budget derived in this way may not show how much cost management is willing to incur in a particular period. Even discounting the possibility that the formula was wrong to start with, two other things may have occurred to throw it off:

1. Volume may have changed so rapidly that overhead costs have not had time to settle down at amounts appropriate to the new level.

2. Volume may have fallen temporarily and management has decided to reduce organizational stress by continuing to spend at the old level for a while.

For example, if volume moves down suddenly, as from Y to X in Exhibit 7–4, the cost standard on which the department head's performance should be judged may be at level A, not the height of the normal flexible budget line at the new volume. Similarly, if volume rises suddenly from Y to Z, the correct short-term standard may be level B (if rapid expansion leads to short-term cost penalties) or level C (if the existing overhead structure can support the new volume for a short period without breaking down).[1]

What the regular flexible budget figures do is highlight *all* departures from efficient performance at the actual volume achieved. Whether anything should be done to correct these is another question.

EXHIBIT 7–4

Dynamic Budget Effects

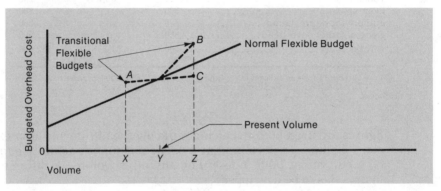

Technical Problems in Flexible Budgeting

In installing a flexible budgeting system and developing departmental flexible budgets, management must solve both technical and behavioral problems. The two most important technical problems are closely related to each other:

1. Developing good estimates of cost-volume relationships.
2. Deciding how to measure volume.

Estimating cost-volume relationships. In discussing cost behavior in Chapters 3 and 4, we made the simplifying assumption that the relationship between volume and cost could be described with perfect accuracy by drawing a single line on a cost-volume chart. Few relationships in the real world are this definite. In fact, the one illustrated in Exhibit 7–5, though far from perfect, is better than many. Each of the dots in this diagram represents the costs actually incurred

---

[1] These possibilities were discussed in more detail in Chapter 4.

EXHIBIT 7–5

Positioning the Flexible Budget

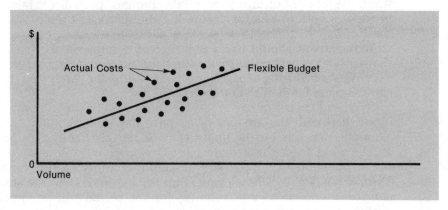

during some period when costs were under control and volume was stable. The line through the center of the diagram represents management's best effort to summarize the relationship traced by this past cost experience. This line has been drawn so that the actual observations cluster around it in a symmetrical pattern, with those below the line just balancing those above it.

Locating a set of flexible budget formulas that actually have these characteristics is not easy. One approach is to analyze historical data by a statistical technique known as least squares regression analysis. We shall discuss this method in some detail in Chapter 18.

A much simpler approach is to go down the chart of accounts for each department, classifying each cost element as wholly fixed, wholly variable, or a mixture of both. This is known as the *judgment* method or *inspection of accounts* method. Having made this classification, the analyst estimates the monthly amount for each fixed cost element and the average unit cost for each proportionally variable element. The estimate of variable cost is often based on average historical cost per unit of activity adjusted for any changes in prices, wage rates, or other conditions that may have occurred or are expected to occur.

It may also be possible to budget step functions largely by the inspection of accounts method. For example, the number of supervisors required in a responsibility unit is likely to vary only with fairly substantial changes in volume. Without going to the trouble of detailed cost analysis, the department head should be able to specify the volume level at which additional supervisors will be required.

Deciding how to measure volume. The second technical problem is to select a measure or measures of the volume of activity in each department. Only three factors need enter into this decision:

1. How closely does the measure correlate with overhead cost?
2. Is the measure readily available?
3. Can the manager understand it?

Of these, the first is the most important. If overhead costs are more likely to move up and down when direct labor hours change than when the amount of direct materials changes, then direct labor hours provides a better basis for evaluating the manager's ability to control these costs.

Management should use a measure of volume other than the one that correlates best only if collecting the preferred data would be too expensive or if the department head finds the preferred measure confusing and difficult to interpret.

Overhead costs are likely to vary more closely with the amount of input than with the amount of output. Materials handling labor, for example, depends on the quantity of materials handled rather than on the yield from these materials. This creates a problem. Suppose the flexible budget is based on the actual quantity of direct materials used. If the department uses more direct materials than the standards call for, the flexible budget figures for the period will be larger than if they were based on standard direct materials quantities. The department head will find it easier to keep overhead costs within these larger flexible budget allowances.

Management may feel that in this situation, using actual direct materials quantities to calculate flexible budget allowances condones inefficiency by giving the department heads looser control standards. This misses the point. Flexible budget figures are intended to help the managers find out whether they have controlled their *overhead* costs. They already have the materials quantity variances to let them know whether they have controlled direct materials costs.

The increased flexible budget allowance in this case is really an additional component of the materials quantity variance rather than a measure of inefficiency in controlling overhead costs. In Exhibit 7–6, it is shown as a movement upward as the materials quantity variance moves the volume index to the right. We shall explore this effect at greater length in Chapter 21.

Some departments should use more than one index of volume be-

EXHIBIT 7–6

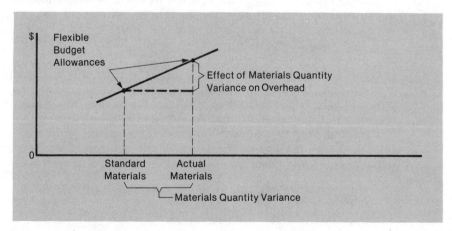

cause different costs vary with different input elements. This makes the system more expensive, of course, and may make it seem more complex than it really is. The additional cost is likely to be small, however, and if the relationships show up clearly, the extra indexes probably are worth using.

Behavioral Problems in Flexible Budgeting

The best technical apparatus in the world won't produce a good flexible budgeting system if the reactions of the people affected by the system are not considered very carefully. In fact, the most difficult part of the job of installing a new system is to get the department heads to cooperate. Some may see flexible budgeting as an effort by top management to exert pressure down the line and make their lives more difficult. Others will see it simply as extra work, extra responsibility with no personal benefits and no extra pay.

One part of the usual solution is to include both operating people and financial people in the groups responsible for getting the system going in the first place. In one company a team of supervisors, factory accountants, engineers, and headquarters staff people spent six months planning the first flexible budgeting cycle. The members of the team met frequently with the other first-line supervisors in the plant to identify and overcome technical problems and to explain the purposes of flexible budgeting. Even so, only slightly more than half of the first-line supervisors had made any real commitment to the program by the time the first budgeting cycle began. It wasn't until two years later that virtually all the supervisors and assistant supervisors were really convinced that flexible budgeting offered them more than it asked from them.

This presumes that the best way to introduce and operate a flexible budgeting system is to secure the active *participation* of the managers for whom the budgets will serve as performance standards. This is the common pattern for budgeting in the United States. The presumption is that participation leads the department heads to accept budgetary goals as their own, thereby increasing their motivation to try to reach them. The participation requirement, for example, would mean that the supervisors could override the conclusions of regression analyses of the costs if they could present logical arguments against them. A regression line may fit the data very well, but still may not describe the current situation because the data are biased or out of date.

The argument for participation is supported by the findings of a substantial body of empirical research. It raises a number of issues, however, that require a more complete discussion than we have room for here. We shall discuss this and other behavioral questions in Chapter 19.

REPORTING DEPARTMENTAL OVERHEAD COSTS

Although preparation of the flexible budget has merit for its own sake, the primary payoff comes in periodic cost performance reporting. In this section we shall look at a factory overhead cost reporting system. We shall begin by calculating the variances between the drills department's actual overhead costs and its flexible budget for one period. Given these figures, we can examine several questions:

1. How frequently should overhead costs be reported?
2. To what extent should variances in noncontrollable costs be reported to the department head?
3. How much detail should be shown in the overhead cost control reports?
4. How should authorized departures from the flexible budget be reflected in the control reports?
5. How can price variances in overhead cost elements be reported?

The section concludes with a brief comment on overhead cost reporting to higher management.

Departmental Spending Variances

The most important overhead cost report issued for the drills department is the monthly overhead summary, comparing actual costs with the appropriate flexible budget allowances. The report for the month of May is reproduced in Exhibit 7–7. The first column at the left lists the costs assigned to the department during the month, determined mainly on the basis of documents such as requisitions, time tickets, and pay slips. The second column shows the comparable flexible budget allowances. These were obtained by applying the budget formula in Exhibit 7–3 to the department's operating volume for the month, 3,500 direct labor hours. The maintenance budget, for example, was calculated as follows:

$$\$600 + \$0.10 \times 3,500 = \$950.$$

The third column then lists the differences between the figures in the first two. These are usually referred to as *spending variances*. In this case the department spent $635 more in May than the flexible budget at 3,500 direct labor hours provided for.

The year-to-date columns at the right show the actual costs for the first five months of the year and the total spending variances for the same period. These figures provide a useful perspective on the current month's figures. The current variance in overtime premium, for example, was only slightly lower than the average for the previous four months, indicating a continuing situation that might need attention. The unfavorable variance in current maintenance costs, on the other hand, accounted for most of the cumulative variance in that item. The department head would probably look into this, but the manager at the next higher level would probably be undisturbed by a single month's departure from the norm.

Frequency of Reporting

The report illustrated in Exhibit 7-7 is issued monthly. Other overhead cost reports are issued daily, and some are issued weekly. How

EXHIBIT 7–7

Drills Department, Departmental Overhead Cost Report

	DEPARTMENTAL OVERHEAD					
Department: 10—Drills					Period: May 19xx	
					Volume: 3,500 hours	
Current Month					Year to Date	
Actual	Budget	(Over) Under			Actual	(Over) Under
			Controllable:			
			Materials			
$ 410	$ 420	$ 10	handling labor		$ 2,450	$ (218)
190	210	20	Idle or lost time		1,754	(638)
			Other indirect			
1,125	1,120	(5)	labor		5,340	612
280	—	(280)	Overtime premium		1,545	(1,545)
1,070	950	(120)	Maintenance		5,027	(167)
530	490	(40)	Supplies		2,298	306
680	700	20	Power		3,620	100
610	735	125	Tools		3,815	91
			Total control-			
$ 4,895	$ 4,625	$(270)	lable		$25,849	$(1,459)
			Noncontrollable:			
$ 3,100	$ 2,800	$(300)	Supervision		$14,600	$ (600)
785	800	15	Floor space		3,990	10
			Equipment			
625	600	(25)	depreciation		3,050	(50)
			General factory			
2,655	2,600	(55)	overhead		13,519	(519)
			Total departmental			
$12,060	$11,425	$(635)	overhead		$61,008	$(2,618)

frequently performance is reported should depend on the relative strengths of two opposing sets of forces. The first of these is management's need for timely information. The sooner management gets a meaningful control report, the sooner it can respond to the information it contains. These responses presumably improve the company's cash flows. This argues for frequent, prompt reporting.

The more frequently the report is issued, however, the more it costs. Furthermore, the results in short periods are likely to be strongly influenced by random forces or by irregularities in the timing of some cost elements, such as factory supplies, recorded when they are issued rather than when they are used. This means that deviations from control standards for short periods are likely to fluctuate widely, obscuring the fundamental underlying movements in the key variables.

After considering both of these influences, most companies go to monthly reporting of their departmental overheads, limiting more frequent reporting to items of particular importance, such as scrap or rework labor or overtime premiums.

Reporting Noncontrollable Costs

The departmental overhead cost summary serves both to direct the department heads' attention to costs that appear to be out of line and to provide their immediate superiors with scorecard information on their performance. The distinction in Exhibit 7–7 between controllable and noncontrollable costs is important for both of these purposes. Department heads are interested only in the costs they can do something about, and all of these are listed "above the line" as controllable costs. These same items are the only ones that should enter into any evaluation of their performance. If they can exert no influence on the cost of supervision, then they can't be held responsible for any variances in these charges.

Whether a cost should be classified as controllable is a matter of judgment. The amount of overtime premium, for example, depends in part on the size of the work force assigned to the department. The department head can affect the amount of the overtime premium, however, by dealing with the causes of delays as they arise, helping workers who are falling behind schedule, and so forth. Controllability means the ability of the manager to influence the cost, and this should be recognized even if responsibility is shared with others.

A good way to deal with noncontrollable costs is to take them out of the report entirely. This has several advantages:

1. It reduces the size of the report and heightens its visual impact.
2. It reduces the number of disputes about amounts charged to the department.
3. It keeps the manager's cost control efforts in perspective—when the noncontrollable variances grow large, they may make the controllable items look small by contrast, and the department head may conclude that control efforts are not very important.

A second possible approach is to report the noncontrollable costs at their budgeted amounts. Even if the introduction of new equipment has increased the drills department's equipment depreciation charges from $600 to $625 a month, for example, only the $600 originally budgeted would be reported to the department head.

This has two advantages. First, it assures higher management that the noncontrollable costs will not be overlooked. Second, and more importantly, it keeps variances in noncontrollable costs out of the departmental control reports. We shall explore this idea more thoroughly in the next chapter.

Amount of Detail

The third aspect of Exhibit 7–7 worth noting is the number of line items in the report. In the final analysis, this has to be decided by management. "Idle or lost time," for example, includes time spent waiting for materials to arrive, for help from the supervisor, for equipment to be repaired, and for various other things to happen. Management could replace this one category with two lines on the report, or three, or even more.

Again we must deal with two conflicting ideas. The first is that each line on the report should identify a variable that has a unique meaning. If control of the time spent waiting for materials requires different actions from those necessary to control the time spent waiting for repairs, then two separate objects of expenditure should be recognized. This is the homogeneity principle we identified in Chapter 2.

More categories mean more bookkeeping, however. This costs money and slows down the recording and reporting process. It also makes the reports bigger and harder to read. Management has to use its judgment to decide how far along this road to go, the point at which the added detail isn't worth the added cost and confusion.

This question is not completely resolved when management decides how many overhead cost elements to recognize. It still has the option of reporting fewer figures than it collects. In some companies, for example, the computer is programmed to print only variances exceeding specified amounts or percentages, leaving all the other spaces on the report blank. A more typical solution is to itemize only the variances that are large enough to raise questions, reporting the others as a single lump sum. Exhibit 7–8 shows one way this might be done.

EXHIBIT 7–8

Highlight Report

	Amount	(Over) Under Budget
OVERHEAD COST SUMMARY		
Department: 10—Drills Period: May 19xx		
This month:		
Overtime premium...........	$ 280	$ (280)
Maintenance.................	1,070	(120)
Tools.......................	610	125
Other.......................	2,935	5
Total....................	$ 4,895	$ (270)
Year to date:		
Idle or lost time..............	$ 1,754	$ (638)
Overtime premium...........	1,545	(1,545)
Other.......................	22,550	724
Total....................	$25,849	$(1,459)

Comments:
  1. Idle time was brought into line this month.
  2. Overtime premiums are still running high.
  3. Maintenance costs were high this month only.

Other systems use charts and diagrams to give the reports more appeal. In any case, a complete report can be attached for reference if management decides this will be helpful.

Authorized Budget Changes

Many causes other than lack of control can produce spending variances. When management knows about these causes in advance, it may authorize the department head to make off-budget expenditures. Our fourth question is how to reflect these adjustments in the overhead cost reports.

Exhibit 7–9 illustrates one answer to this question. This shows that management authorized the department head to incur up to $200 in overtime premiums for a volume of 3,500 direct labor hours. The department head also agreed to reductions of $60 and $75 in the budgets for other indirect labor and tools, respectively. These changes gave the department a new set of rules to go by. As a result, the figures in the right-hand column of Exhibit 7–9 are a better measure of cost performance than those in Exhibit 7–7.

To reduce clutter, only the three rightmost columns may be reported to the department head. The full report should be accessible, however, in case anyone wants to question how the budget figures were calculated.

Price and Quantity Components of the Spending Variance

Our fifth and final question is how to handle variations in the prices of various overhead inputs. Overhead spending variances are not

EXHIBIT 7–9

Authorized Budget Changes

CURRENT OVERHEAD COST SUMMARY					
Department: 10—Drills				Period: May 19xx	
				Volume: 3,500 hours	
	Original Budget	Authorized Changes	Adjusted Budget	Actual Cost	(Over)/Under Adj. Budget
Controllable:					
Materials handling labor	$ 420	—	$ 420	$ 410	$ 10
Idle or lost time........	210	—	210	190	20
Other indirect labor.....	1,120	$(60)	1,060	1,125	(65)
Overtime premium......	—	200	200	280	(80)
Maintenance..........	950	—	950	1,070	(120)
Supplies..............	490	—	490	530	(40)
Power................	700	—	700	680	20
Tools.................	735	(75)	660	610	50
Total controllable.....	$4,625	$ 65	$4,690	$4,895	$(205)

EXHIBIT 7–10

Decomposition of Spending Variance into Price and Quantity Components

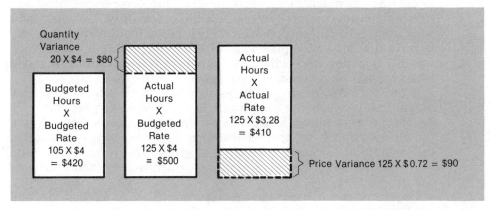

quite the same thing as the labor and materials quantity variances we described in Chapter 6 unless the accountant has designed the system to make them the same. If supplies, electric power, and indirect labor are charged to the department at actual prices and wage rates, then the spending variances will actually be a combination of quantity and price variances.

With enough information, the accountants can separate the spending variances into these two components, using exactly the same methods they use for direct labor and direct materials. For example, suppose the standard wage rate for materials handling labor was $4 an hour. The $420 budget allowance thus represented 105 labor hours for this activity. The actual wages paid for materials handling in May, however, averaged only $3.28. This means that the $410 charged to the department represented $410/$3.28 = 125 labor hours, or 20 more than the budget allowed.

With this information we can make the analysis diagrammed in Exhibit 7–10. This shows that excessive use of labor added $80 to materials handling costs, but that the availability of low-paid workers for these tasks led to a saving of $90.

Price effects can be removed in advance by using standard prices to measure the overhead costs charged to the various departments. When this is done, the spending variances will be quantity variances, pure and simple. The use of standard prices is likely to be impractical for some overhead costs, but it can be done for most indirect labor and indirect materials without adding to clerical costs if standard prices and wage rates are already being used for direct materials and direct labor.

Reports for Higher Management

Monthly reports on departmental materials quantity and labor quantity variances generally serve the first-line manager as scorecard controls. They come too late and contain too little detail to be very useful as steering controls at that level. The monthly overhead report, in contrast, is much more likely to serve the department head as a steering control, mainly because spending variances are less visible when they occur. Recorded overhead costs fluctuate from day to day in ways that may have little to do with the day-to-day fluctuations in volume. It is not clear whether a cost is reasonable until after both total cost and total volume information is available.

Scorecard and steering controls fuse into each other at the next managerial level. Higher level managers are not very interested in the details of departmental performance—they are concerned mainly with the total spending variance. This helps them decide where to direct their attention (steering control) and gives them a partial measure of the performance of the various department heads (scorecard control).

Following this reasoning, the reports issued to higher levels of management are likely to be more condensed than those issued to the department heads. It would not be unusual for each department to be represented by a single line on an overhead summary report for the factory as a whole. Copies of the more detailed departmental reports may be attached for information, but the section manager or plant manager should resist the temptation to get too far into these details. Only if the overall departmental spending variance is large and persists from month to month should higher management intervene.

The plant manager, like the department head, may get a condensed highlight report instead of a full listing of all the departments' results. Alternatively, or in addition, the plant manager may get a series of charts, perhaps like the one in Exhibit 7–11. If properly drawn, these can be used to identify the important areas quickly and with little effort.

EXHIBIT 7–11

Drills Department, Overhead Cost Performance Chart

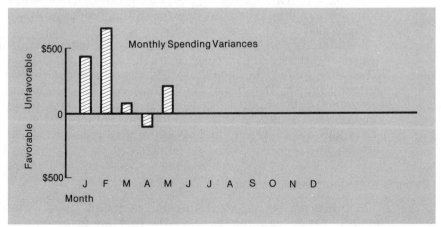

VOLUME VARIANCES IN FACTORY OVERHEAD COSTS

Most factory costing systems are integrated into the company's regular historical accounting records. In these, as we saw in Chapter 2, the factory is charged for its actual overhead costs and is given credit for the amounts charged to individual products, referred to as *absorbed overhead*. The difference between total overhead cost and the amount of overhead absorbed is known as the *total overhead variance*.

Spending variances account for only part of the total. The purpose of this final section is to bridge the gap between the spending variance and the total overhead variance in a factory which uses predetermined overhead rates on a full costing basis but does not use standard costing. We shall extend this analysis to standard costing systems in Chapter 21.

Calculating the Overhead Variances

In the absence of a standard costing system, the total amount charged to individual products (absorbed) is the overhead rate times the total amount of the input factor on which the overhead rate is based. For the drills department:

1. The overhead rate is $12,000/4,000 = $3 a direct labor hour (from Exhibit 7–3).
2. Production during May consumed 3,500 direct labor hours.
3. The amount absorbed was 3,500 × $3 = $10,500.

The actual overhead costs of the drills department during May amounted to $12,060, as we saw in Exhibit 7–7. The total overhead variance therefore amounted to $1,560 and was unfavorable (see Exhibit 7–12). We already know from Exhibit 7–7 that $635 of this was a spending variance; the question is where the other $925 came from.

The explanation is quite simple. The amount of fixed overhead absorbed in a full absorption costing system is proportional to volume.

EXHIBIT 7–12

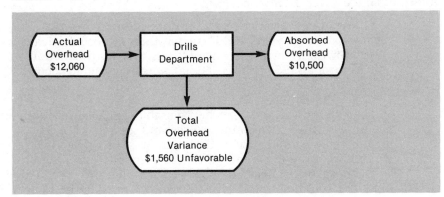

The overhead rate in this case included $1.85 to absorb fixed costs. This figure can be calculated from the data in Exhibit 7–3:

$$\frac{\text{Total fixed cost}}{\text{Normal volume}} = \frac{\$7,400}{4,000 \text{ hours}} = \$1.85 \text{ an hour.}$$

If volume had reached 4,000 hours, then all the budgeted fixed costs would have been absorbed, as Exhibit 7–13 shows. Instead, actual volume was 500 direct labor hours less than normal. This means that the fixed costs that would have been absorbed by these 500 hours had no place to go, no product to absorb them. Low volume therefore accounted for 500 × $1.85 = $925 of the unabsorbed fixed overhead. We call this a *volume variance*.

The volume variance arises only when an overhead rate is used to absorb costs that do not vary in direct proportion to variations in overall operating volume. It will appear in a variable costing system only if total variable overhead costs do not trace a straight line rising from the origin on a cost-volume chart.

EXHIBIT 7–13

The Overhead Volume Variance

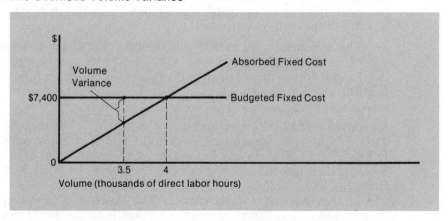

Interpreting the Volume Variance

The volume variance must be interpreted carefully. It does not mean that costs were $925 greater than expected because volume was lower than normal. It merely says that no production was available to absorb $925 of the costs that were expected to occur. Expressed differently, $925 was spent to provide production capacity that the company did not use.

The volume variance can be favorable, because normal volume is usually less than maximum volume and actual volume is sometimes greater than normal. Under these circumstances, production volume will absorb more fixed costs than the company expects to incur.

The department heads do not establish their own production schedules. The volume of activity is determined outside the factory, on the basis of the number of customer orders in hand or anticipated. This being so, volume variances are not controllable by the department head or even by the plant manager. They should not be included in the departmental control reports. They should be reported to plant managers only to help them explain the total overhead variance to higher management.

Reconciling the Variances

The overall variance computation can be summarized in the following manner:

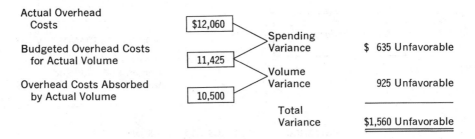

Actual Overhead Costs	$12,060
	Spending Variance $ 635 Unfavorable
Budgeted Overhead Costs for Actual Volume	11,425
	Volume Variance 925 Unfavorable
Overhead Costs Absorbed by Actual Volume	10,500
	Total Variance $1,560 Unfavorable

Exhibit 7–14 presents this same information in graphic form. This is like Exhibit 7–13 except that it includes the variable overhead costs as well as the fixed overheads. The amounts of overhead absorbed are shown by the height of the straight line rising from the lower left-hand corner of the chart. The amounts budgeted are shown by the height of the other line. Because some of the department's costs are fixed, this line has a gentler slope than the Absorbed Overhead line. Variable costs in this case are proportional to volume—$1.15 in budgeted variable costs for each direct labor hour—and thus the flexible budget is shown as a straight line.

EXHIBIT 7–14

Overhead Cost Variances

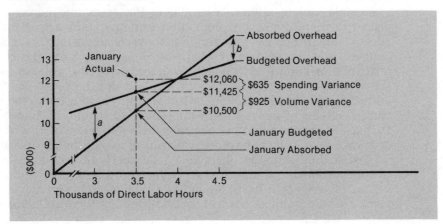

The amounts budgeted and absorbed at this month's volume of 3,500 hours are shown as large dots on these two lines. The actual amount spent is shown by another dot. By measuring the vertical distances between dots, we are able to identify the total variance and its two components parts:

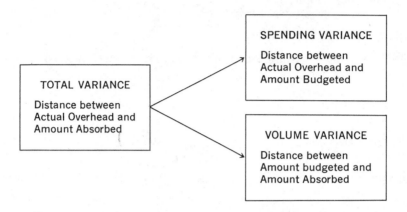

Volume variances at volumes in excess of normal volume, such as that marked *b* in Exhibit 7–14, represent overabsorption and are classified as favorable. Volume variances at volumes lower than normal, in the zone to the left of the intersection of the lines in the exhibit, represent underutilization of capacity and are referred to as unfavorable.

SUMMARY

Product standard costs are not relevant to the control of factory overhead costs because factory overheads are neither wholly variable nor traceable to individual products. Instead, control standards are reflected in departmental flexible budgets, consisting of a series of budget allowance schedules for various volume levels within the normal operating range.

Flexible budget allowances indicate the costs the manager is expected to maintain when production remains stable. Spending variances—the differences between actual overhead costs and the flexible budget—are intended to highlight all departures from the cost performance originally established as normal for the volume actually achieved. The flexible budget may not be valid, however, for periods immediately after sharp changes in volume. These transitional effects and the effects of management's decisions to sustain off-budget costs during temporary slack periods may be segregated in the cost performance reports if management is willing to pay the extra cost.

Flexible budgeting is likely to encounter both technical and behavioral problems. If the flexible budget is to help the managers as well as to serve as a basis for judging their performance, it must be developed and applied in ways that will induce them to use it to improve their performance. Questions of this sort will be discussed more fully in Chapter 19. In any case, the spending variances reported to the department heads should be the variances over which they have some control.

Spending variances only account for part of the total amount of under- or overabsorbed overhead in full absorption costing systems. The other major component is the volume variance, representing the cost of providing capacity that remains idle or is used at a supernormal level. Volume variances are not a responsibility of the department heads and should not be shown on their control reports.

KEY TERMS

The most important terms introduced and defined in this chapter are the following:

Budgeted overhead cost	Spending variance
Controllability	Standard overhead cost
Flexible budget	Total overhead variance
Inspection of accounts	Volume variance
Participation	

INDEPENDENT STUDY PROBLEMS
(Solutions in Appendix C)

1. Exercises. A department's fixed overhead cost at normal volume is expected to be $12,000 a month. Other overhead costs, amounting to $8,000 a month at normal volume, are expected to vary with the amount of direct materials processed. The department is expected to use 10,000 pounds of direct materials a month to manufacture 2,500 units of product.

The department used 9,000 pounds of direct materials during the month of August and manufactured 2,000 units of product. Overhead costs totaled $21,700.

a. Derive a predetermined, full-cost overhead rate, calculate the total overhead variance for the month, and divide it into spending and volume components.

b. Fixed costs consist entirely of building and equipment rentals. Variable costs consist entirely of indirect labor. Wage rates have increased by 5 percent since the flexible budget was developed; rentals have increased by 2 percent. Use this information to subdivide the spending variance into input price and quantity components.

c. Instead of the situation described in (b), you find that half of the fixed costs consist of the wages of employees engaged in cleaning the equipment once an hour and performing similar tasks; the other half is equipment depreciation. Half of the variable costs consist of the royalty to be paid to the inventor of the equipment used in the department, the other half is the labor cost of moving materials into the department and moving finished work to the next department. Royalty payments are proportional to the number of pounds of materials processed. Which of these are controllable costs at the departmental level? Would your answer differ if the royalty payments were based on the number of units of product manufactured?

2. Periodic performance reporting. The Riptide Company uses full-cost overhead rates and departmental flexible budgets for cost reporting. The fiscal year is divided into 13 "months" of four weeks each. Department T has a normal production volume of 4,000 direct labor hours a month and the following flexible budget, valid for volumes between 3,000 and 4,500 direct labor hours a month:

	Fixed per Month	Variable per Direct Labor Hour
Nonproductive time, machine operators......	—	$0.25
Other indirect labor.......	$2,000	0.50
Operating supplies........	—	0.15
Depreciation..............	2,000	—
Rent.....................	700	—
Total...............	$4,700	$0.90

Actual costs and volumes in two successive months were as follows:

	Month 4	Month 5
Direct labor hours..........	4,000	3,000
Nonproductive time........	$ 800	$1 200
Other indirect labor........	3,700	3,600
Operating supplies.........	650	430
Depreciation..............	2,100	2,150
Rent.....................	770	730

a. Calculate budget allowances and prepare a cost performance report for each of these months. This report should include each of the five overhead cost elements, arranged in any way you find appropriate.
b. Comment on the various items in these reports, indicating which items are likely to be of greatest significance in evaluating the cost control performance of the department supervisor.
c. Looking only at those items for which cost performance was poorer in month 5 than in month 4, what would be your reaction to the statement that the manager of this department had been lax in enforcing cost control during month 5? What remedial action would you suggest, if any?
d. Calculate the volume variances for these two months. What is the significance of the volume variance? Would it have arisen if the company had been using variable costing?

EXERCISES AND PROBLEMS

1. Overhead performance report. The monthly flexible budget allowances for the assembly department of the Boyce Furniture Company for various numbers of direct labor hours are shown in the following table:

	Direct Labor Hours				
	10,000	*10,500*	*11,000*	*11,500*	*12,000*
Supervision..................	$ 1,800	$ 1,800	$ 1,800	$ 1,800	$ 1,800
Indirect labor................	7,000	7,350	7,700	8,050	8,400
Supplies.....................	4,000	4,200	4,400	4,600	4,800
Power, fuel, and water........	1,000	1,050	1,100	1,150	1,200
Depreciation.................	2,000	2,000	2,000	2,000	2,000
Space occupancy.............	3,000	3,000	3,000	3,000	3,000
General plant overhead.......	2,800	2,800	2,800	2,800	2,800
Total...................	$21,600	$22,200	$22,800	$23,400	$24,000

Actual charges to the department for the month of March were as follows:

Supervision......................................	$ 1,900
Indirect labor...................................	7,700
Supplies..	4,020
Power, fuel, and water...........................	930
Depreciation....................................	1,950
Space occupancy................................	3,000
General plant overhead..........................	3,000
Total......................................	$22,500

The actual volume of production during March totaled 10,500 direct labor hours.

a. How much of the budgeted overhead cost would you classify as fixed? What is the average budgeted variable cost per direct labor hour?

b. Prepare a departmental overhead cost report for the month.

c. Comment on the possible causes of each of the variances shown on the report.

2. Validity of flexible budgeting. Each factory department in the Balch Company has a monthly budget, agreed upon at the beginning of the year, and a set of flexible budget formulas, used for monthly performance reporting. The formulas for the finishing department are:

Supervision....................	$1,200 a month
Indirect labor.................	$800 a month + $1 per direct labor hour
Overtime premium.............	$0.50 for each direct labor hour in excess of 2,400 direct labor hours a month
Supplies......................	$0.40 a direct labor hour
Power.........................	$200 a month + $0.15 a direct labor hour
Depreciation..................	$500 a month
Other overhead................	$0.10 a direct labor hour

Normal volume in this department is 3,000 direct labor hours a month and planned volume for this year averages 2,700 hours a month. Volume in May was 2,500 direct labor hours. The actual costs for the month were as follows:

Supervision......................	$1,260
Indirect labor....................	3,340
Overtime premium................	140
Supplies.........................	860
Power...........................	600
Depreciation.....................	500
Other............................	300
Total......................	$7,000

a. Prepare a performance report for the month of May, using the
    flexible budget.
b. The company's president is not sure that flexible budgeting is a good
    idea because it may make department heads look good even though
    average cost keeps going up. The president prefers to compare average
    actual cost with average planned cost. Prepare the figures for a report
    on this basis and draft a reply to the president's argument.

3. Overhead variance analysis. The Balch Company (Problem 2) calculates product cost on a full costing basis. It uses predetermined overhead
rates based on normal volume.

a. Using the data in Problem 2, calculate a predetermined overhead rate
    for the finishing department.
b. Calculate the total overhead variance for May, the total spending
    variance, and the volume variance.
c. Was this volume variance larger or smaller than the amount reflected
    in the annual profit plan? To whom should this information be re-
    ported? Should management focus its attention on the volume
    variance itself, on the difference between this and the planned volume
    variance for the month, or on both of them?
d. It was suggested in this chapter that the volume variance can be
    calculated by multiplying average fixed cost by the difference between
    normal volume and actual volume. Test this suggestion here and
    explain your findings.

4. Significance of spending variances. Some indirect labor in the Balch
Company (Problem 2) is performed by regular bench operators who normally perform direct labor operations. Management is reluctant to lay these
operators off for short periods of time. Instead, some of the indirect labor
work, such as cleaning and adjusting machines, is deferred until the
production schedule is light.

The manager of the finishing department thinks this should be built
into the flexible budget, with larger flexible budget allowances when
volume is low, and vice versa. This would eliminate erratic fluctuations in
the indirect labor spending variances. The plant controller disagrees,
arguing that production creates the need for indirect labor services, even
though these services may not be performed when production takes place.

Prepare a brief report on this issue, stating your position and indicating
how management should interpret and use the spending variances arising
under the solution you are recommending.

5. Overhead variances. The Tinpot Company's factory has a job order
costing system. It uses predetermined full cost overhead rates. It classifies
its manufacturing overhead cost accounts into two categories: class A
(wholly fixed), and class B (partly fixed and partly variable). The following data are available:

1. Normal volume, 20,000 direct labor hours.
2. Class A costs:
    a. Budget at normal volume, $20,000.
    b. Variable costs, none.
    c. Actual costs for July, $21,100.
    d. Volume variance in Class A costs for July, $1,400, favorable.
3. Class B costs:
    a. Budget at normal volume, $30,000.
    b. Variable costs included in (a), $1.10 per direct labor hour.
    c. Actual costs for July, $34,000.

a. What was the actual operating volume for July?
b. How much of the cost in each class was assigned to products during the month?
c. Prepare a variance summary for the month, in as much detail as you can derive.

6. Supplying missing information. The Wilson Company's factory has three production departments. Standard costs are not used, but each department has a predetermined overhead rate and a flexible budget, based on actual direct labor hours. You have the following data:

		Department A	Department B	Department C
1.	Actual overhead, July..................	$20,000	17,000	?
2.	Budgeted fixed cost per month........	?	?	$5,000
3.	Budgeted variable overhead cost per direct labor hour.....................	?	$3	$2
4.	Actual volume (direct labor hours), July.....................................	4,000	3,000	?
5.	Normal volume (direct labor hours).....	5,000	?	?
6.	Predetermined overhead rate per direct labor hour at normal volume.............................	?	?	$3
7.	Absorbed overhead, July...............	$19,600	?	?
8.	Budgeted overhead at actual volume, July.....................................	?	?	?
9.	Total overhead variance, July..........	?	2,000 U.	4,000 U.
10.	Overhead spending variance, July......	500 F.	?	1,000 U.
11.	Overhead volume variance, July........	?	1,000 F.	?

Make the necessary calculations and fill in the blanks identified by question marks in this table.

7. Overhead variances. The Dandy Wagon Company uses predetermined overhead rates based on normal volume. Volume in the axle department is measured by the number of axles manufactured. The budget formula for overhead costs in this department is as follows:

$6,000 a month + $2 an axle + $1 for each axle in excess of 2,000 in any month

You have the following additional information:

1. Normal volume is 2,500 axles a month.
2. Budgeted volume for the current year is 2,200 axles a month.
3. Actual overhead costs for April totaled $11,100.
4. The volume variance for April was $160, unfavorable.

a. Prepare a diagram showing the amounts budgeted and absorbed at volumes ranging from 1,500 to 3,000 axles a month.
b. Calculate the operating volume for the month.
c. Calculate the spending variance.
d. Enter operating volume, the volume variance and the spending variance on the diagram you prepared in answer to (a).
e. Should management be pleased with performance in this department during April? Explain your answer.

8. Choosing the measure of volume. Overhead costs vary with the number of machine-hours used. Production output is measured by the number of standard machine-hours required by the goods manufactured.

The overhead rate is $10 a machine-hour, of which $8 is fixed and $2 is proportionally variable. Normal volume is 800 machine-hours a month.

During October, production volume amounted to 1,000 standard machine-hours. The goods produced during the month actually required 1,100 machine-hours. Actual overhead cost amounted to $8,700.

a.   Calculate the spending variance for the month.
b.   List an alternative calculation you might have made, using these data, and explain why you chose the method you used in (a).

9. Choosing the measure of volume.   The following data were recorded during ten recent periods:

Period	Overhead Cost	Direct Labor Hours	Standard Direct Labor Hours	Machine-Hours
1................	$2,010	3,000	3,100	5,000
2................	2,270	3,500	3,400	5,100
3................	2,050	3,100	3,000	5,400
4................	2,100	3,200	3,300	4,800
5................	2,200	3,400	3,500	5,200
6................	2,300	3,600	3,700	6,000
7................	2,420	3,800	3,900	5,700
8................	2,390	3,700	3,600	5,300
9................	2,140	3,300	3,200	5,500
10................	2,460	3,900	3,800	5,600

a.   Plot cost against each of the three measures of volume, one on each of three separate diagrams.
b.   Which of these measures of volume would you select as the basis of a flexible budget formula? Explain your choice.

10. Analysis of the spending variance.   The flexible budget provides for the following relationships:

	Fixed per Month	Variable per Direct Labor Hour
Supervision........................	$1,650	—
Indirect labor......................	800	$0.60
Vacation pay.......................	197	0.54
Supplies...........................	—	0.80
Power..............................	—	0.40

Normal volume is 2,000 direct labor hours a month. Actual volume for the month of July amounted to 1,500 direct labor hours, and the following costs were charged to the department:

Supervision........................	$2,598
Indirect labor.....................	1,750
Vacation pay......................	7,250
Supplies...........................	1,310
Power.............................	715

You have the following additional information, not reflected in the budget data above:

1. Wage rates for direct and indirect labor were increased 5 percent by a union contract negotiated in April. Supervisory salaries were also increased 5 percent at the same time.
2. Vacation pay was budgeted originally at 9 percent of supervisory pay and 6 percent of the cost of direct and indirect labor. Vacation pay is charged to departments as employees take their vacations.
3. Power costs were budgeted at a rate of 8 cents a kilowatt-hour; the rate in July was 9 cents.
4. Supplies costs were budgeted on the basis of prices prevailing at the beginning of the year. Inventory is costed on a Fifo basis. Actual purchase prices in July were 10 percent higher than the amounts at the beginning of the year. An eight-month inventory of supplies is maintained at all times.
5. The plant manager authorized the department head to borrow an additional half-time supervisor from another department to help with the installation of a new piece of equipment during July and August. The department was charged for the amount of time this supervisor spent in the department.

Prepare a fully detailed report on the department's cost control performance during July. Indicate the amounts that should be reported to the department head and the amounts that should be reported only to higher management.

11. Reporting controllable and noncontrollable variances. Production volume in department X of factory Alpha is measured by the number of direct labor hours. Normal volume is 10,000 direct labor hours a month (each "month" consists of four consecutive weeks), and the flexible budget allowances for this volume of activity are:

Supervision—fixed.................................	$ 2,000
Indirect labor—variable...........................	16,000
Supplies—variable................................	12,000
Maintenance—variable portion....................	2,000
Maintenance—fixed portion......................	2,000
Depreciation—fixed..............................	10,000
Floor space charges—fixed......................	8,000

All variable cost elements are expected to vary in direct proportion to departmental direct labor hours.

The department used 11,250 direct labor hours during the month of March 2–March 29. The following costs were charged to the department during the month:

Supervision.......................................	$ 2,100
Indirect labor....................................	19,000
Supplies..	13,200
Maintenance......................................	3,900
Overtime premiums...............................	500
Depreciation.....................................	10,000
Floor space charges..............................	8,500

The manager of factory Alpha receives a copy of each departmental overhead cost performance report each month, with the volume variance printed on a separate line at the bottom. The manufacturing vice president, with four factories to worry about, receives a one-page summary report each month. One line on this report shows the total volume variance for each of the four factories.

The controller explains that the volume variance figures on the plant manager's reports are intended to show how fully each department's capacity is being utilized. This information can be used in decisions on staffing the various departments and to some extent in decisions on work schedules for the factory. The volume variance figures on the manufacturing vice president's reports are intended to serve the same purposes at the factory level. They are also used to demonstrate to top management and to marketing management how much cost is unabsorbed or overabsorbed, to establish the relative need for additional volume.

a. Compute the month's flexible budget allowances and cost variances for each of these seven items. (Use the letters U and F to denote unfavorable and favorable variances.)
b. For each of the seven cost items listed above, indicate whether any variances are likely to be wholly or partly controllable by the department head. How might variances arise in the noncontrollable items?
c. Calculate an overhead rate based on normal volume and use this to measure the overhead volume variance for the month.
d. How likely are the volume variance figures in the plant manager's and marketing vice president's reports to serve their intended purposes? Try to suggest other ways of serving these purposes. Which would you prefer?

12. Performance report and variance analysis. Overhead budget allowances for department 23 in the Broken Bend Manufacturing Company's main factory are prepared on the following basis:

Cost Element	Fixed	Variable per Direct Labor Hour
		Monthly Budget Allowance
Indirect labor:		
Inspection............................	$ 800	$0.23
Helpers..............................	1,200	1.00
Rework labor..........................	—	0.30
Labor downtime........................	—	0.40
Other indirect labor...................	—	0.07
Total indirect labor.................	$2,000	$2.00
Supervision...........................	2,000	—
Overtime premiums......................	—	0.60
Vacation and holiday pay...............	300	0.60
Payroll taxes..........................	430	1.12
Pensions..............................	200	0.50
Total labor..........................	$4,930	$4.82
Supplies..............................	—	0.50
Power.................................	500	0.06
Other charges.........................	1,830	—
Total overhead......................	$7,260	$5.38

During November, department 23 used 3,300 direct labor hours (DLH). The following transactions took place during the month:

1. Labor time tickets, extended at actual wage rates:

Direct labor..........................	$28,620
Inspection..........................	1,610
Helpers............................	5,235
Rework labor.......................	1,250
Labor downtime....................	845
Other indirect labor.................	315

2.   Additional charges to department 23 from the factory payrolls for the month:

Supervision.........................	$2,160
Overtime premiums.................	3,120

3.   Supplies issued, $1,425.
4.   Power consumed, $775.
5.   Other charges, $1,850.

You have the following additional information:

1.   All vacation pay, holiday pay, overtime premiums, payroll taxes, and pensions attributable to direct labor are classified as departmental overhead.
2.   Vacation and holiday pay, payroll taxes, and pensions are charged to the department monthly on the basis of the following percentages:

Vacation and holiday pay: 9 percent of supervisory payrolls, 6 percent of all other departmental wages and salaries except overtime premiums.
Payroll taxes: 10 percent of departmental wages and salaries, including amounts accrued for vacation and holiday pay.
Pensions: 5 percent of departmental wages and salaries except overtime premiums and holiday and vacation pay.

3.   The budgeted wage rate for direct labor was $8 an hour.
4.   Normal volume is 3,000 direct labor hours a month.
5.   A 7 percent increase in salaries and wage rates was negotiated after the flexible budget formulas were established: the fringe benefit formulas were left unchanged.
6.   Inventories of materials and supplies are measured at standard prices.
7.   Power rates increased 10 percent after the flexible budget formulas were drawn up.
8.   All of the costs in the department's budget except "other charges" are classified as controllable by the department head.

a.   Prepare a list of overhead cost elements and enter the amounts charged to department 23 in November.
b.   Using the formulas quoted in the table at the beginning of this problem, calculate the overhead rate for this department based on normal volume and use this to determine the total overhead variance for the month.
c.   Using these same formulas, calculate the flexible budget allowances for the month and use these to calculate the spending variances.
d.   Subdivide the spending variances into input price and quantity components. Should the department head be concerned about his cost control performance during November?
e.   Calculate the volume variance for the month. Was this affected by the adjustments you made in (d)?

 f. What changes, if any, would you suggest in the basis on which costs are charged to the department or reported to management? State the reasons for your recommendations.

CASE 7–1: RIGAZIO ENTERPRISES*
(Flexible budgeting)

 Rigazio Enterprises manufactures a wide variety of metal products for industrial users in Italy and other European countries. Its head office is located in Milan and its mills in northern Italy provide about 80 percent of the company's production volume. The remaining 20 percent is produced in two factories—one in Lyon, France, and the other in Linz, Austria—both serving local markets exclusively through their own sales organizations.

 Until 1964 the methods used by the Milan headquarters to review subsidiary operations were highly informal. The managing director of each subsidiary visited Milan twice a year, in October and in April, to review his subsidiary's performance and discuss his plans for the future. At other times the managing director would call or visit Milan to report on current developments or to request funds for specified purposes. These latter requests were usually submitted as a group, however, as part of the October meeting in Milan. By and large, if sales showed an increase over those of the previous year and if local profit margins did not decline, the directors in Milan were satisfied and did nothing to interfere with the subsidiary manager's freedom to manage his business as he saw fit.

 During 1963, the company found itself for the first time in 12 years with falling sales volume, excess production capacity, rising costs, and a shortage of funds to finance new investments. In analyzing this situation, the Milan top management decided that one thing that was needed was a more detailed system of cost control in its mills, including flexible budgets for the overhead costs of each factory.

 The Lyon mill was selected as a "pilot plant" for the development of the new system. Because the Lyon mill produced a wide variety of products in many production departments, it was not possible to prepare a single flexible budget for the entire mill. In fact, Mr. Spreafico, the company's controller, found that the work done in most of the production departments was so varied that useful cost-volume relationships could not even be developed on a departmental basis. He began, therefore, by dividing many of the departments into cost centers so that a valid single measure of work performed could be found for each one. Thus a department with both automatic and hand-fed cutting machines might be divided into two cost centers, each with a group of highly similar machines doing approximately the same kind of work.

 The establishment of the cost centers did not change the responsibility pattern in the factory. Each department had a foreman who reported to one of two production supervisors; the latter were responsible directly to Mr. Forclas, the plant manager. Each foreman continued to be responsible for the operations of all the cost centers in his department. In some cases a cost center embraced an entire department, but most departments contained between two and five cost centers.

---

 * Copyright 1965 by l'Institut pour l'Etude des Méthodes de Direction de l'Entreprise (IMEDE), Lausanne, Switzerland. Published by permission. Monetary amounts have been restated in dollars for convenience.

Once he had completed this task, Mr. Spreafico turned to the development of flexible budgets. For each cost center he selected the measure or measures of volume that seemed most closely related to cost (e.g., machine-hours) and decided what volume was normal for that cost center (e.g., 1,000 machine-hours per month). The budget allowance at the normal level of operations was to be used later as an element of standard product costs, but the budget allowance against which the foremen's performance was to be judged each month was to be the allowance for the volume actually achieved during that particular month.

Under the new system, a detailed report of overhead cost variances would be prepared in Lyon for the foreman in charge of a particular cost center and for his immediate superior, the production supervisor; a summary report, giving the total overhead variance for each cost center would be sent to the plant manager and to Mr. Duclos, the managing director of Rigazio France, S.A., in Lyon. The Milan top management would not receive copies of these reports but would receive a monthly profit and loss summary, with comments explaining major deviations from the subsidiary's planned profit for the period.

The preparation of the budget formulas had progressed far enough by mid-1964 to persuade Mr. Spreafico to try them out on the September cost data. A top management meeting was then scheduled in Milan to discuss the new system on the basis of the September reports. Mr. Duclos and Mr. Forclas flew to Milan to attend this meeting, accompanied by the controller to Rigazio France and a production supervisor responsible for some 30 cost centers in the Lyon factory.

Mr. Enrico Montevani, managing director of Rigazio Enterprises, opened the meeting by asking Mr. Spreafico to explain how the budget allowances were prepared. Mr. Spreafico began by saying that the new system was just in its trial stages and that many changes would undoubtedly be necessary before everyone was satisfied with it. "We started with the idea that the standard had to be adjusted each month to reflect the actual volume of production," he continued, "even though that might mean we would tell the factory they were doing all right when in fact we had large amounts of underabsorbed overhead. In that case the problem would be that we had failed to provide enough volume to keep the plant busy, and you can't blame the foremen for that. When you have fixed costs, you just can't use a single standard cost per hour or per ton or per unit, because that would be too high when we're operating near capacity and too low when we're underutilized. Our problem, then, was to find out how overhead cost varies with volume so that we could get more accurate budget allowances for overhead costs at different production volumes.

"To get answers to this question, we first made some preliminary estimates at headquarters, based on historical data in the accounting records both here and in Lyon. We used data on wage rates and purchase prices from the personnel and purchasing departments to adjust our data to current conditions. Whenever we could, we used a mathematical formula known as a 'least squares' formula to get an accurate measure of cost variability in relation to changing volume, but sometimes we just had to use our judgment and decide whether to classify a cost as fixed or variable. I might add that in picking our formulas we tried various measures of volume and generally took the one that seemed to match up most closely with cost. In some cost centers we actually used two different measures of volume, such as direct labor hours and product tonnage, and based some of our budget allowances on one and some on the other. These estimates were then discussed with Mr. Forclas and his people at Lyon, and the revised budget formulas were punched into tabulating cards for use in monthly report preparation.

"Although you have a complete set of the cost center reports, perhaps we might focus on the one for cost center 2122 [Table 1]. You can see that we have used two measures of volume in this cost center, direct labor hours and product tonnage. During September we were operating at less than standard volume, which meant that we had to reduce the budget allowance to $2,666, which averaged out at $115.91 a ton. Our actual costs were almost exactly 10 percent higher than this, giving us an overall unfavorable performance variance of $226, or $9.83 a ton.

TABLE 1

Overhead Cost Summary, Cost Center 2122, September

	Standard Allowance at Normal Volume (500 hours, 25 tons)	Budgeted at Actual Volume (430 hours, 23 tons)	Actual, Month of September	(Over) Under Budget
Supervision.........................	$ 180	$ 180	$ 145	$ 35
Indirect labor........................	300	272	322	(50)
Waiting time.........................	21	17	35	(18)
Hourly wage guarantee..............	14	13	6	7
Payroll taxes, etc....................	321	282	301	(19)
Materials and supplies..............	30	26	28	(2)
Tools................................	150	129	128	1
Maintenance........................	320	307	375	(68)
Scrap loss..........................	422	388	491	(103)
Allocated costs.....................	1,052	1,052	1,061	(9)
Total.........................	$ 2,810	$ 2,666	$ 2,892	$ (226)
Per ton.......................	$112.40	$115.91	$125.74	$(9.83)

"I know that Mr. Duclos and Mr. Forclas will want to comment on this, but I'll be glad to answer any questions that any of you may have. Incidentally, I have brought along some extra copies of the formulas I used in figuring the September overhead allowances for cost center 2122, just in case you'd like to look them over." [See Table 2.]

a.   Do you agree with Mr. Spreafico that $115.91 a ton (see Table 1) is a more meaningful standard for cost control than the "normal" cost of $112.40?

b.   Comment on the variances in Table 1. Which of these are likely to be controllable by the foreman? What do you think the production supervisor should have done on the basis of this report?

c.   What changes, if any, would you make in the format of this report or in the basis on which the budget allowances are computed?

d.   In developing the budget allowances, did Mr. Spreafico make any mistakes that you think he could have avoided? Does his system contain any features that you particularly like?

TABLE 2

Flexible Budget Formula, Cost Center 2122

	Allowance Factors		
	Fixed Amount per Month	Variable Rate	Remarks
Supervision......................	$ 180	—	Percent of foreman's time spent in cost center
Indirect labor....................	100	$0.40/DLH*	—
Waiting time.....................	—	0.04/DLH	Wages of direct labor workers for time spent waiting for work
Hourly wage guarantee..........	—	0.03/DLH	Supplement to wages of workers paid by the piece to give them guaranteed minimum hourly wage
Payroll taxes, etc................	41	0.56/DLH	Payroll taxes and allowances at 30% of total payroll, including direct labor payroll
Materials and supplies..........	—	0.06/DLH	—
Tools............................	—	0.30/DLH	—
Maintenance....................	160	6.40/ton	Actual maintenance hours used at predetermined rate per hour, plus maintenance materials used
Scrap loss......................	—	16.88/ton	Actual scrap multiplied by difference between materials cost and estimated scrap value per ton
Allocated costs.................	1,052	—	Actual cost per month, allocated on basis of floor space occupied

* Note: DLH = direct labor hours.

8

Interdepartmental
Cost Allocations

Cost accounting systems usually assign costs initially to the cost centers they are traceable to, as described in Chapter 2. Every operating cost is traceable to some cost center. We have already seen, however, that traceability isn't a good enough criterion to solve every costing problem. That's why we have overhead rates. Now it is time to look at another feature of the cost structure that makes us go beyond traceability to get the kinds of cost figures we want. This feature is the presence of cost centers other than the production centers that are engaged directly in end-product activities.

In Exhibit 8–1, for example, only 8 of the 18 blocks in the diagram represent production centers. These are marked by diagonal shading. The others are either *service centers,* providing services to other cost centers, or *support centers*, providing either facilities or administrative support and direction to two or more cost centers. Some typical examples are:

Maintenance shop.	Toolroom.
Power and steam plants.	Building services.
Personnel.	General supervision.
Computer center.	Cost accounting.
Production scheduling.	Production methods.

The costs of service and support centers are often assigned to other cost centers by a process known as interdepartmental cost allocation. The central issues in this chapter are why and how this might be done. We shall deal specifically with three questions:

1. Why companies make interdepartmental allocations.
2. How allocations can be used to get service and support center costs into production center overhead rates.
3. What kinds of allocations might be suitable for control reporting.

EXHIBIT 8–1

Production versus Service and Support Centers

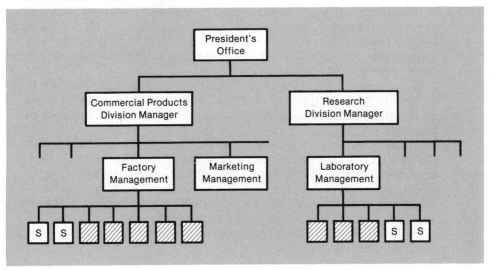

To keep the chapter to a reasonable length, we shall focus on service and support costs within a single factory, leaving other kinds of cost centers to later chapters.

TERMINOLOGY REMINDER

A cost that is traceable to a product, activity, or organization segment is a *direct cost* of that product, activity, or organization segment. A cost traceable to a service or support center is a direct cost of that center. The costs of service or support centers that are allocated to other cost centers are *indirect costs* of those other centers.

REASONS FOR ALLOCATIONS

Costs may be allocated or *redistributed* from one cost center to another for any or all of four reasons:

1. To include service and support center costs in product costs for external financial reporting.
2. To produce more accurate estimates of costs for managerial decision making.
3. To emphasize the responsibility of department heads to control the use of other departments' services.
4. To provide the cost data necessary to calculate cost-based prices.

Inventory Measurement

Generally accepted accounting principles require that inventories of manufactured goods be measured in published financial statements at their full factory cost. Full cost includes a share of all costs necessary to manufacture the product—factory overhead costs as well as prime costs, the costs of service and support centers as well as the costs of production centers.

The overhead component of factory cost is assigned to products by means of departmental overhead rates, as we saw in Chapter 2. As a job goes from department to department, it accumulates overhead costs based on the work done in each department. Products do not pass through service and support centers, however. Exhibit 8–2 shows a simplified version of a typical situation, with products flowing through the two production centers, picking up prime costs (i.e., direct labor and direct materials) and overhead costs as they go. The other two centers serve the two production centers and each other, but they do no work on the products themselves.

To get service and support costs into product cost, the accountant has two methods to choose between:

1. Direct apportionment.
2. Allocation-absorption.

Direct apportionment. Under the direct apportionment method, the accountant calculates a separate overhead rate for each group or

EXHIBIT 8–2

Product Flows versus Service and Support Flows

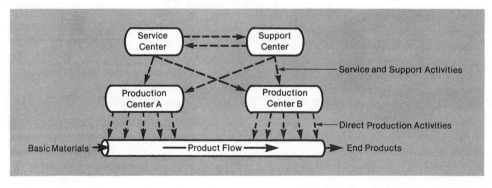

pool of service or support center costs. For example, suppose that service overheads amount to $7,000 a month, production center A operates at 5,000 direct labor hours a month, and production center B has 2,000 direct labor hours a month. A plantwide direct apportionment rate based on direct labor would be $1 a direct labor hour. A product needing 10 direct labor hours would be charged $10 for service overhead.

Allocation-absorption.   Many accountants argue that direct apportionment is not accurate enough. They point out what we saw in Exhibit 8–2, that the service and support centers serve other cost centers, not products, and that some cost centers need much more service or support than others. A direct labor hour in a machining department ordinarily will be supported by much more maintenance cost than a direct labor hour in assembly, where the ratio of equipment to people is much smaller.

To reflect these differences, most cost accountants would suggest taking the allocation-absorption route. This is a three-stage method:

1. Allocate service and support center costs to production centers.
2. Include the amounts allocated to each production center in that production center's overhead rate.
3. Use these overhead rates to assign overhead costs to products, including allocated overheads as well as the overhead costs directly traceable to the production centers.

For example, suppose production center A uses three sevenths of the total amount of service and production center B uses four sevenths. Under the allocation approach, production center A would be assigned $3,000 in service overheads, or 60 cents a direct labor hour; production center B would get $4,000 of the service costs, or $2 a direct labor hour. Now two products, each needing 10 direct labor hours, might be assigned very different amounts of service costs:

	Product X		Product Y	
	Direct Labor Hours	Service Costs Assigned	Direct Labor Hours	Service Costs Assigned
Production center A...............	9	$5.40	1	$ 0.60
Production center B...............	1	2.00	9	18.00
Total.......................		$7.40		$18.60

Whether this added accuracy justifies the added cost of the allocation approach is a question that must be answered separately in each case.

Decision Analysis

The second possible reason for interdepartmental cost allocations is to help management estimate the effects of choosing one alternative course of action instead of another. The primary effects of these choices are on the production centers. These, in turn, affect the need for services or support, leading to changes in these costs. Allocations can be used to estimate these effects.

Different kinds of decisions, of course, have different effects on service cost. For short-run decisions on how best to use existing ca-

short time frame v. long time frame

pacity, average variable service cost multiplied by the change in services needed should approximate the cost effect reasonably well. For decisions with a longer time horizon, calling for changes in the amount of service *capacity,* the estimates should include estimates of the changes in the fixed costs of the service and support centers affected.

The service cost figures relevant to long-term decisions—adding or dropping a product, for example—are the *attributable costs* of providing service or support. The attributable cost of any activity is the cost that could be eliminated, in time, if that activity were discontinued and capacity were to be reduced accordingly. If a product is withdrawn from the line, service and support capacity can be reduced. If the allocation scheme is designed to help management make decisions that will have major long-term effects on the scope of the firm's operations, the amount of service cost allocated to the product should include a share of those capacity costs that are divisible enough so that increases or decreases in normal volume will be accompanied, in time, by proportional increases or decreases in capacity costs.

Control Reporting

The third reason to allocate the costs of service centers is to encourage managers to control the amount of service they use. Department heads are expected to control their use of services provided by other departments, just as they are expected to control their use of indirect labor and supplies. To emphasize this responsibility, the department heads' budgets should include provisions for controllable service costs, and they should be charged periodically for the services they use. The accountant uses interdepartmental allocations to accomplish this objective.

The allocations for this purpose differ from those for the first two. Allocations used to calculate overhead rates or help management make decisions are allocations of estimated costs. Allocations for control reflect the amounts of services that have actually been used. We must recognize this difference in working out allocation systems.

Contract Costing

Contracts specifying that the prices of goods or services will be determined on the basis of the costs actually incurred in producing them usually provide that the costs of at least some of the contractor's service and support activities be included in the costs assignable to the work done under the contracts.

The accountants have the same options here that they have for inventory measurement—direct apportionment or interdepartmental allocation. The choice may be dictated by the contract or, in the case of government contracts, by the statutes and regulations governing the specific class of contracts. Because this is a highly specialized topic, we shall defer any major discussion of it to Appendix B.

> ### TERMINOLOGY AGAIN
>
> Overhead is any cost not directly traceable to individual batches or flows of specific products. It includes *all* of the costs of service and support centers, but only part of the costs of production centers.
>
> This definition may be modified if the accountant's interest shifts to the individual service or support center. In this case the costs traceable to the tasks that are the center's own end-product activities, such as maintenance job orders, are direct costs of those activities; all other departmental costs are overhead.

ALLOCATIONS IN PREDETERMINED OVERHEAD RATES

The overhead costs calculated for inventory measurement typically are derived from predetermined overhead rates. Predetermined overhead rates are also used to estimate the effects of some kinds of decisions on overhead costs. Our purpose in this section is to see how these before-the-fact allocations can be made. We shall deal with three aspects of this topic:

1. The various allocation procedures the accountant might use.
2. The use of one of these procedures to achieve a full allocation of all budgeted service and support center costs to production centers.
3. A set of allocations limited to variable service costs.

Allocation Procedures

Interdepartmental cost allocations may follow any of three procedures:

1. One-step allocations.
2. Sequential allocations.
3. Cross allocations.

One-step allocations.   In a one-step allocation procedure, the direct costs of a service or support center are allocated to production centers only. None of these costs is assigned to other service or support centers. This is the simplest and cheapest of the three procedures, but it is also the least accurate. Service and support centers often serve or support each other as well as the production centers, and substantial portions of their costs may be incurred for that purpose.

Sequential allocations.   In sequential allocation, the costs of the center providing the most universally used services or facilities are distributed first, those of the center next most widely used are allocated next, and so on. Once a center's costs have been allocated, it ceases to figure in any subsequent steps in the procedure.

This method is illustrated in Exhibit 8–3. In this case, service centers Y and Z and the two production centers A and B all receive support from support center X. X's costs are distributed on some basis to these four cost centers. Service center Y serves support center X as well as the other three cost centers, but X can't receive any allocation after its costs have been allocated. The costs of service center Y, including its share of the costs of X, go only to Z, A, and B. The costs of service center Z, including its allocations from X and Y, are allocated to the two production centers, with nothing going back to X and Y.

EXHIBIT 8–3

Sequential Cost Allocation

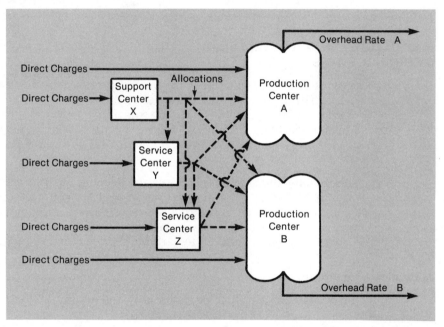

Cross allocations. The third procedure, cross allocations, recognizes the interdependence of the various cost centers. Each service or support center is charged with a portion of the costs of *each* of the others from which it receives services or support. The allocations are determined simultaneously.

The allocations here are illustrated in Exhibit 8–4. Each service or support center receives costs from each of the others; each allocates to each of the others and to the two production centers. Each of these charges covers both the direct costs of the service or support center and allocations from the other two.

This is the most accurate procedure of all, but it is also likely to be the most expensive. In any situation more complex than the one illustrated in this chapter, the only feasible way to make this procedure work is to solve the allocation equations by computer.

The allocation process is most clearly visible when sequential allocation procedures are used. For this reason, we shall use a sequential procedure to illustrate how allocations might be made to derive predetermined departmental overhead rates, first under full costing and then under variable costing. An illustration of cross allocations can be found in the Appendix at the end of this chapter.

EXHIBIT 8–4

Cross Allocation of Service Center Costs

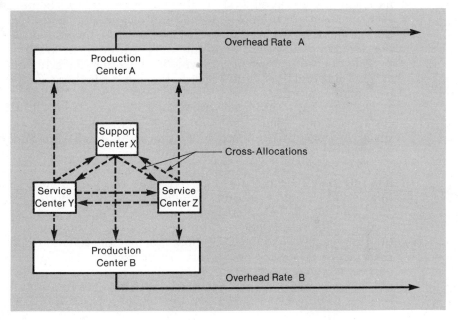

A Full-Cost Allocation Plan: Sequential Allocation

The Standoff Company, a small manufacturer of metal products, uses a sequential allocation procedure in preparing annual overhead rates for each of the three production departments in its factory. Four other factory departments provide service or support. Each of these seven departments consists of a single cost center; to save space, we shall refer to the service and support departments simply as service departments from here on.

In 19x1, the budgeted overhead costs of the Standoff Company's factory at normal volume amounted to $67,100 a month. The amounts traceable to the various departments (direct overhead) were as follows:

Service departments:
Building services...................... $ 8,000
Executive services..................... 10,320
Clerical services......................   5,540
Maintenance services..................   8,040
Production departments:
Machining.............................   15,520
Welding and plating...................   13,100
Assembly..............................   6,580
        Total........................... $67,100

Building services costs. The building services department receives relatively few services from the other departments. For this reason its costs are allocated first in the Standoff factory. Some building services costs are the costs of building ownership, such as depreciation, property taxes, and insurance. Others are the costs of maintaining and protecting the factory building. All of them are incurred to provide operating capacity, to enable the other departments to operate. Total building service cost is the same whether the building is used a lot or a little.

The Standoff Company assigns budgeted factory building services costs to the other departments in proportion to the amount of factory space they occupy. Building services costs in 19x1 were budgeted at $8,000 a month, as the preceding table shows. The factory contained 50,000 square feet of usable floor space. This made the average monthly cost 16 cents a square foot. The company's controller used this as the charging rate for including building services costs in the 19x1 budgets of the other departments. (A charging rate is a dollar amount to be multipled by a number of physical, temporal, or monetary units such as square feet, hours, or payroll dollars, to determine the amount of service or support center cost to be assigned to other cost centers.)

The amounts of space occupied and the allocations of building services costs were:

	Floor Space (sq. ft.)	Building Services Costs Allocated
Executive services.................	3,000	$ 480
Clerical services....................	2,000	320
Maintenance services..............	3,000	480
Machining.........................	20,000	3,200
Welding and plating................	7,000	1,120
Assembly..........................	15,000	2,400
Total......................	50,000	$8,000

Each of these allocations was a *capacity charge*, defined as a fee to cover one department's share of another department's costs of providing service or support capacity. To use capacity charges, we have to find a way to measure the relative amount of *capacity pro-*

vided to each other department. Because capacity costs are fixed costs, capacity charges should be used to allocate service departments' fixed costs.

Executive services costs. The second group of costs to be allocated by the Standoff Company were the costs of executive services. Executive services is the name for the office of the plant manager and its staff. Their job is to direct, schedule, and coordinate factory activities. Their work supports the activities of all the other departments and therefore the costs of this office should be allocated before the costs of clerical and maintenance services, which are narrower in scope.

The direct costs of executive services were expected to average $10,320 a month at normal volume. Adding to this the $480 in normal building services costs allocated to this cost center, we get $10,800, the amount to be allocated to the remaining two service centers and the three production centers.

These costs consist mainly of executive salaries. Again they are fixed costs, and again a capacity charge is appropriate. Although administrative capacity is impossible to measure, the Standoff Company's controller thought of it as an ability to handle the greatest number of problems that might arise. Since it seemed likely that the number of problems was apt to be proportional to the number of people employed in the factory, the controller decided to measure each department's occupancy of the factory's administrative capacity by the number of full-time employees it was authorized to have when operating at full capacity. The numbers of authorized employees and the allocations of the $10,800 in normal executive services costs were as follows:

	Number of Authorized Employees	Percent of Total	Allocated Cost (% × $10,800)
Clerical services.........................	6	5%	$ 540
Maintenance services..................	12	10	1,080
Machining.............................	42	35	3,780
Welding and plating....................	12	10	1,080
Assembly.............................	48	40	4,320
Total..........................	120	100%	$10,800

No allocation was made to the building services department because its costs had already been distributed.

Clerical services costs. The second administrative cost center covers the costs of routine bookkeeping and other clerical operations in the factory. Its costs at normal volume amounted to $5,540 in direct overheads and $860 in allocated overheads ($320 for building services and $540 for executive services), or $6,400 in all.

In any short period, these costs are likely to be fixed. As overall factory volume moves up or down by a substantial amount, however, the costs will move up or down, too, along the stepped line shown in Exhibit 8–5. The controller felt that in this case the steps in the budget were close enough together to justify drawing the straight line in Exhibit 8–5 to approximate the cost relationship.

As this line shows, the budgeted fixed costs of clerical services amounted to $2,400 a month, including the $860 in service department fixed costs allocated to this department. Variable costs at normal volume totaled $4,000 and the rate of cost variability, represented by the slope of the line, was 25 cents an operating labor hour. (Operating labor was defined as the time of hourly paid employees in maintenance and the three production departments.)

EXHIBIT 8–5

Budgeted Clerical Services Costs

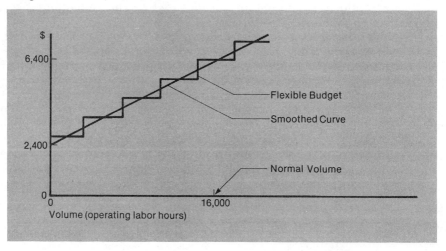

activity charge

This allocation is our first illustration of an *activity charge*. An activity charge is a rate per unit of activity in the departments receiving service or support. In this case the level of activity was measured by the number of operating labor hours. An activity charge should be used when the amount of service provided is difficult to measure but service department costs correlate with the total activity of the departments receiving the services.

The $2,400 in budgeted fixed costs was allocated by means of a capacity charge. A capacity charge is ordinarily determined by dividing the total cost of providing capacity by the amount of capacity provided. In this case the amount of clerical capacity wasn't measurable, but management decided it was likely to be proportional to budgeted operating labor hours at the normal volume of 16,000 hours. This indicated a capacity charge of $2,400/16,000 = 15 cents an hour.

The allocations of the normal costs of the clerical services department, using these rates, were as follows:

	Operating Labor Hours at Normal Volume	Cost Allocations		
		Variable Costs at 25 Cents	Fixed Costs at 15 Cents	Total
Maintenance services.......	1,000	$ 250	$ 150	$ 400
Machining...................	5,000	1,250	750	2,000
Welding and plating..........	2,000	500	300	800
Assembly....................	8,000	2,000	1,200	3,200
Total.................	16,000	$4,000	$2,400	$6,400

Maintenance service costs. Maintenance costs were allocated last, because this department only provided services to the three production departments. The maintenance department budget at normal volume totaled $10,000 ($8,040 in costs directly traceable to the department, $480 in allocated building services charges, $1,080 in allocated executive services costs, and $400 in allocated clerical services costs). With these costs the department was expected to provide 1,000 hours of maintenance service to the three production departments in a normal month. The average cost was thus $10 a maintenance hour. Using this figure, the allocation of the $10,000 in maintenance costs was as follows:

	Number of Maintenance Hours	Allocated Costs at ($10 × Maintenance Hours)
Machining........................	750	$ 7,500
Welding and plating..............	150	1,500
Assembly........................	100	1,000
Total.....................	1,000	$10,000

The allocations in this case were *usage charges,* and the $10 figure was a *transfer price.* A transfer price is a unit price used to record transfers of goods or services within an organization. It should be used for interdepartmental allocations whenever the amount of services can be measured readily and service costs vary with the amount of service provided.

To be consistent with the treatment of clerical services costs, the controller should have split this allocation into two parts, a usage charge to cover the variable costs and a capacity charge for the fixed costs. The department heads in this factory were expected to control their use of maintenance services, however, and the controller planned to charge them for the average full cost of the services they used. To get the managers used to this, a single rate was used in the budgeted allocations, too.

EXHIBIT 8–6

STANDOFF COMPANY
Sequential Allocation Sheet for Budgeted Monthly Service
Department Costs at Normal Volume

	Building Services	Execu-tive Services	Clerical Services	Mainte-nance Services	Ma-chining	Welding and Plating	Assembly
Direct overhead............	$8,000	$10,320	$5,540	$ 8,040	$15,520	$13,100	$ 6,580
Allocations:							
Building services.........	(8,000)	480	320	480	3,200	1,120	2,400
		$10,800					
Executive services.......		(10,800)	540	1,080	3,780	1,080	4,320
			$6,400				
Clerical services:							
Variable...............			(4,000)	250	1,250	500	2,000
Fixed..................			(2,400)	150	750	300	1,200
				$10,000			
Maintenance services....				(10,000)	7,500	1,500	1,000
Allocated total............					$32,000	$17,600	$17,500
Normal volume............					4,000*	1,600†	7,000†
Overhead rate.............					$8.00	$11.00	$2.50

* Volume in machine-hours, overhead rate per machine-hour.
† Volume in direct labor hours, overhead rate per direct labor hour.

Completed allocation sheet. The completed factory overhead cost budget at normal volume is shown in Exhibit 8–6. The sequential procedure shows clearly in this exhibit, and at the end of the process all normal factory overhead costs, $67,100 in all, have been assigned to one or another of the three production departments. The production totals are then used to establish the departmental overhead rates for the year, shown at the bottom of the exhibit.

Limitations of full-cost rates. The overhead rates developed in this fashion are entirely appropriate for use in inventory measurements for financial accounting. They may also be helpful in product pricing decisions, as we shall see in Chapter 16. They may not be very helpful for other kinds of decision analysis, however. First, and most obvious, full-cost rates do not help anyone estimate the effects of short-term, utilization-of-capacity decisions. If data are needed for this purpose, variable costing, not full costing, should be used. We shall see in the next subsection how the accountant can make allocations to fit into a variable costing system.

A second limitation is probably less obvious. If full cost is to have any bearing on decisions at all, it should approximate attributable cost. Unfortunately, it often does not. Many fixed costs of providing service or support are highly indivisible, meaning that the total need for service or support can go up or down a great deal without any change in the total amount of capacity cost required. The result is that full-cost allocations have to be regarded skeptically by the decision analyst.

Allocations under Variable Costing

Interdepartmental cost allocations are not restricted to full-costing systems. Factory costing systems based on variable costing also call for allocations if the variable component of service department costs is significant. Let us see how this would work in the Standoff Company's factory.

First, none of the costs of building services or executive services would be allocated. These are entirely fixed. Second, only the variable portion of clerical services costs would be allocated. Third, the fixed costs of the maintenance department would have to be taken out of the charging rate for that department.

For example, suppose $6,250 of the normal direct costs of the maintenance service department vary proportionately with that department's output, measured by the number of maintenance hours. The total variable cost of maintenance services at normal volume therefore would be $6,250 plus the $250 in variable clerical services costs allocated to the maintenance services department. This works out to $6.50 a maintenance hour. Using this rate and some assumed figures for the direct variable costs of the three production departments, we have the following distribution of variable costs:

	Maintenance	Machining	Welding and Plating	Assembly
Direct..............................	$ 6,250	$5,100	$3,650	$4,325
Clerical services...................	250	1,250	500	2,000
Maintenance services.............	$(6,500)	4,875	975	650

A note of caution should be sounded at this point, before we total the three production department columns. Although the variable cost of maintenance work amounts to $6.50 a maintenance hour, this does not necessarily make maintenance a variable production cost. If the amount of maintenance work done in the production departments is unaffected by volume, then it is a fixed cost of production operations in those departments.

Suppose, for example, that routine maintenance work, totally insensitive to volume fluctuations, amounted to 250 hours in the machining department and 50 hours each in welding and plating and in assembly. This would leave 500 hours of variable maintenance time in machining, 100 hours in welding and plating, and 50 hours in assembly. Applying the $6.50 variable-cost transfer price to these figures, we get the following amounts to be incorporated in variable costing overhead rates:

	Machining	Welding and Plating	Assembly
Variable direct overhead......	$5,100	$3,650	$4,325
Variable clerical services costs.....................	1,250	500	2,000
Variable maintenance costs...	3,250	650	325
Total..................	$9,600	$4,800	$6,650
Variable costing overhead rates.	$2.40 per machine hour	$3.00 per direct labor hour	$0.95 per direct labor hour

The variable service costs in this case are big enough to make a difference for each production department.

INTERDEPARTMENTAL ALLOCATIONS FOR CONTROL REPORTING

The cost allocations in the preceding section were all made before the fact, to get service and support costs into departmental overhead rates for product costing. Allocations are also made in many cases after the fact—that is, all or part of the costs of service departments are charged each month to other service departments and to production departments. The purpose of this final section is to see why and how such charges may be made. We shall examine six questions:

1. Why management may need after-the-fact allocations.
2. How after-the-fact allocations should be made if they are to facilitate comparisons with flexible budget allowances.
3. What a set of allocations reflecting these principles will look like.
4. What under- or overdistributed service department costs mean.
5. How allocations can be included in the production center's monthly overhead cost control reports.
6. Whether interdepartmental transfer prices should reflect full costs or variable costs only.

Once again, we shall limit our discussion to the allocation of the costs of factory service and support centers, leaving other kinds of allocations to later chapters.

Reasons for After-the-Fact Allocations

After-the-fact allocations may be made for either or both of two control purposes:

1. To help department heads control their consumption of services and to evaluate their success in doing so.
2. To let higher management or staff managers know where service consumption is high, so they can take action, if appropriate.

Department heads can't control the cost of the services provided to them, but they may be able to control the amounts of service they use. For example, the workers in a machining department have nothing to do with the amount of fuel burned in the company's power plant, but they may be able to do something about the amount of power used in the department. In such cases, charging the department can help motivate the manager to control service usage and provide a record of the department's success or failure in doing this.

A record of usage may be valuable even if the department head can't control the use of service. Factory supervisors, for example, ordinarily have no control over the amount of work done for them by the factory methods department. Factory management, however, may want to know where most of the methods work is done to help it appraise proposals for new equipment, additional staffing, and so forth.

Comparing Allocated Costs with Flexible Budget Allowances

The amounts allocated to a department for control reporting will be compared with amounts drawn from the flexible budget for the actual volume of activity. This process is illustrated in Exhibit 8–7. The two sets of blocks shown at the left represent flexible budget schedules for four possible operating volumes. One set of schedules applies to a service department, the other to a production department.

The cross-hatched block for the service department represents its flexible budget for a normal volume of operations, and from this a charging rate is calculated. This charging rate is used for the budget allocation to the production department—this allocation may be the same for all production volumes (a capacity charge) or differ (activity or usage charge).

The diagonally shaded blocks represent the flexible budgets for the two departments for the month of January, each appropriate to that month's volume. These amounts are then compared with the actual costs for the month; the production department's actual costs include one line for its allocated share of the service department's costs.

The reason for reviewing this process in such detail is to show that after-the-fact allocations for control reporting have to fit into the flexible budget system and that the departments being charged may report variances from the flexible budget allowances for service costs. Ideally, any such variances should reflect amounts the department head is expected to control. To see how this can be done, let us look first at allocations based on usage charges and then see what allocation methods should be used for any activity and capacity charges management may choose to impose.

Usage charges. The only allocations that provide control information are usage charges, based on transfer prices. If the department heads are expected to control the amount of service they use, then variances from the flexible budget should be reported as controllable items. If they can't control usage, as in the methods department example we used earlier, the variance should be measured but classified as noncontrollable.

EXHIBIT 8-7

Flexible Budget Allowances for Allocated Costs

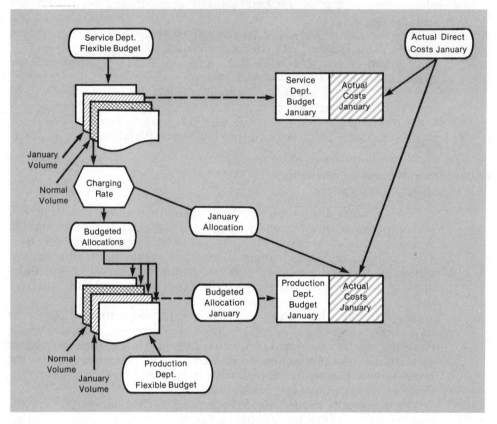

What kinds of transfer prices best meet management's needs for control information? One possibility is to charge the department for the actual amount of service used, multiplied by the average cost of operating the service department during the same period of time.

Suppose, for example, that during January 19x1, the Standoff Company's maintenance department provided 800 hours of service at an average cost of $12 an hour. The machining department operated at a volume of 3,600 machine-hours and used 650 maintenance hours. Earlier we saw that the machining department needs 250 maintenance hours a month plus variable maintenance time of 500 hours at the normal volume of 4,000 machine hours, or ⅛ maintenance hour for each machine hour. Machining's January flexible budget for maintenance was 250 + ⅛ × 3,600 = 700 hours, stated in dollars at 700 × $10 = $7,000, because only the budgeted transfer price of $20 an hour was known when the budget formula was prepared. The actual allocation for the month was 650 × $12 = $7,800, leaving a fairly substantial unfavorable spending variance of $800:

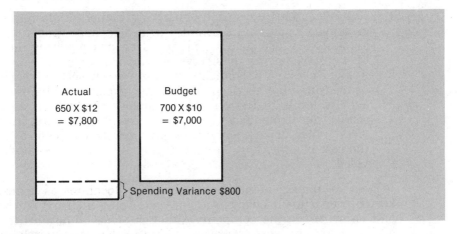

The weakness of this method may be apparent. The spending variance results both from a variance in the amount of service used and from a variance in the price charged for it. This price variance may mean any or all of three things:

1. Maintenance department volume was down, increasing average fixed cost.
2. Maintenance department costs were not well controlled.
3. Wages or supplies paid by the maintenance department went up.

None of these is controllable by the people in the machining department and they should not be penalized when one of them takes place.

A logical solution is to use a *predetermined* transfer price. If the charge for January were calculated at $10 an hour, the total charge would be 650 × $10 = $6,500 and a $500 favorable spending variance would show up in the machining department's control reports. Since the manager used 50 fewer hours of maintenance service than the flexible budget called for, the control signal now corresponds to the facts.

A maintenance department illustration was used here for simplicity and because maintenance costs are usually allocated by transfer prices. It is not always clear, however, just how much responsibility production department managers have for the amount of maintenance work performed. Directly they may have none, with responsibility for both preventive maintenance and repairs lodged in the maintenance manager or managers. Even so, the operating manager often can do much to affect the amount of maintenance required, and this is therefore often regarded as an item to be controlled jointly by the maintenance and operating managers.

Capacity and activity charges. Capacity charges and activity charges have served their purpose once the overhead rates have been calculated. After-the-fact allocations provide no control information:

1. Cost allocations by capacity charges are appropriate for services or support capacities that are provided in fixed amounts. These amounts are not changed by any decisions made by the heads of the departments they serve or support.

2. Activity charges presumably are used when service usage can't be measured but service costs vary in response to changes in the activity levels in the other departments. Only the head of the service department can control the cost of providing these services; other department heads presumably can control neither the cost of providing the service nor the amount of service provided.

Even so, management often insists on allocations as a means of keeping department heads aware of costs being incurred on their behalf elsewhere in the company. Although some authorities feel that allocations of this sort are self-defeating in that they merely distract the managers' attention from the items they can control, demands for them are so widespread that the accountant must be prepared to devise schemes that will afford the least possible danger of misinterpretation.

The solution to this problem is simple. Capacity charges should be made at their budgeted *amounts*, activity charges should be made at their budgeted *rates*. The capacity charge will remain constant from month to month; the activity charge will fluctuate by amounts equal to the fluctuations in the budget allowances. Under this system no variance from the flexible budget will appear for either of these.

PREFERRED ALLOCATION METHODS FOR CONTROL REPORTING		
Service Characteristics	*Allocation Method*	*Allocation Criterion*
Usage measurable, service volume variable	Predetermined transfer prices	Service usage
Service volume variable, no measurable output	Predetermined activity rates or no allocation	Activity in departments served
Service or support volume fixed	Predetermined capacity charges or no allocation	Percentage of service capacity needed

An Allocation Illustration

The direct overheads of the various departments in the Standoff Company's factory for the month of January, 19x1, were as follows:

Building services....................	$ 9,800
Executive services...................	10,460
Clerical services....................	5,380
Maintenance services................	7,690
Machining...........................	15,220
Welding and plating.................	13,310
Assembly............................	6,490
Total...........................	$68,350

None of these figures entered into the calculation of the allocations for the month, however. Instead, Standoff's controller used a set of predetermined rates and amounts.

Buildings services and executive services costs were both fixed and noncontrollable by the other department heads. The January allocations therefore were lump-sum capacity charges, equal to the amounts budgeted at the beginning of the year. These amounts were listed in Exhibit 8–6, but deserve repeating here:

	Buildings Services	Executive Services
Allocated to:		
Executive services.................	$ 480	—
Clerical services..................	320	540
Maintenance services.............	480	1,080
Machining........................	3,200	3,780
Welding and plating..............	1,120	1,080
Assembly........................	2,400	4,320
Total........................	$8,000	$10,800

The allocations for clerical services costs were calculated in two stages: (1) a set of capacity charges, calculated at the budgeted rate of 15 cents for each operating labor hour at normal operating volume and equal to the amounts budgeted at normal volume; and (2) a set of actual charges, calculated by multiplying the predetermined rate of 25 cents by the actual number of operating labor hours in January. These allocations were:

	Operating Labor Hours	Activity Charge	Capacity Charge	Total Charge
Allocated to:				
Maintenance services.....................	800	$ 200	$ 150	$ 350
Machining.............................	4,500	1,125	750	1,875
Welding and plating.....................	1,900	475	300	775
Assembly..............................	8,000	2,000	1,200	3,200
Total.............................	15,200	$3,800	$2,400	$6,200

We can verify the totals by going back to the budget calculations made at the beginning of the year:

Total capacity charges—total normal costs (the total amount of the
  budgeted allocations in the table on page 267)................... $2,400
Total activity charges — 15,200 operating labor hours × $0.25 (the
  rate used in calculating the budgeted allocations in the table on
  page 267)... 3,800
        Total allocation.. $6,200

Finally, the $10 predetermined transfer price was used to calculate usage charges for maintenance services:

	Maintenance Hours	Usage Charge
Machining............................	650	$6,500
Welding and plating...................	120	1,200
Assembly.............................	30	300
Total............................	800	$8,000

Interpreting Service Department Variances

The cost distribution sheet for the month is shown in Exhibit 8–8. Since predetermined charging rates were used, all four service departments showed differences between actual overhead costs and the amounts distributed. In this case, all four departments had undistributed balances.

EXHIBIT 8–8

STANDOFF COMPANY
Overhead Distribution Sheet, January 19x1

	Building Services	Executive Services	Clerical Services	Maintenance Services	Machining	Welding and Plating	Assembly
Direct overhead...........	$ 9,800	$10,460	$5,380	$ 7,690	$15,220	$13,310	$ 6,490
Allocations:							
Building services........	(8,000)	480	320	480	3,200	1,120	2,400
		$10,940					
Executive services.......		(10,800)	540	1,080	3,780	1,080	4,320
			$6,240				
Clerical services:							
Variable..............			(3,800)	200	1,125	475	2,000
Fixed.................			(2,400)	150	750	300	1,200
				$ 9,600			
Maintenance services...				(8,000)	6,500	1,200	300
Allocated total...........					$30,575	$17,485	$16,710
Absorbed................					28,800*	16,500*	17,500*
(Under)/overdistributed...	$(1,800)	$ (140)	$ (40)	$(1,600)			
(Under)/overabsorbed....					$(1,775)	$ (985)	$ 790

* Calculation of absorbed overhead:
  Machining: 3,600 machine-hours × $8 = $28,800.
  Welding and plating: 1,500 direct labor hours × $11 = $16,500.
  Assembly: 7,000 direct labor hours × $2.50 = $17,500.

Cost performance reports are issued for each of the service departments as well as for the production departments. The process is exactly the same. And just as underabsorbed overhead in a production department may not mean that the department head failed to control costs, undistributed service department balances do not necessarily indicate unfavorable performance by the department heads. Building services costs, for example, may have exceeded the average monthly budget by $1,800 simply because January is a month of very high heating and lighting costs. The $1,600 in undistributed maintenance costs may have arisen because the wage rates of maintenance employees went up sharply at the beginning of the month or because maintenance department volume was 20 percent less than normal. These factors should be analyzed as part of the process of reporting cost performance to the managers of these departments.

Including Allocations in Monthly Performance Reports

Each of the seven factory departments has a set of flexible budget schedules for the current year. Exhibit 8–9 shows the January report for the machining department. The budget allowances appropriate to a monthly volume of 3,600 machine hours in the machining department are shown in the second column, while the actual charges for the month, taken from Exhibit 8–8, are shown at the left. Supplies costs ran substantially over budget this month, but this was more than offset by the substantial favorable variances in maintenance costs and miscellaneous direct overheads.

No variances appeared below the line because the Standoff Company's system was designed to exclude them. The departmental volume variance did not appear for the same reason. The total

EXHIBIT 8–9

STANDOFF COMPANY
Machining Department, Departmental Overhead Cost Report,
January 19x1

	Actual	Budget	(Over)/Under Budget
Controllable:			
Indirect labor	$ 7,870	$ 7,760	$(110)
Supplies	580	540	(40)
Electric power	930	810	(120)
Maintenance	6,500	7,000	500
Miscellaneous	240	450	210
Total controllable	$16,120	$16,560	$ 440
Noncontrollable:			
Salaries	3,200	3,200	—
Equipment depreciation	2,400	2,400	—
Building services	3,200	3,200	—
Executive services	3,780	3,780	—
Clerical services	1,875	1,875	—
Total overhead cost	$30,575	$31,015	$ 440

variance was $1,775, as shown on the bottom line of Exhibit 8–8. With a favorable spending variance of $440 (Exhibit 8–9), the volume variance must have been $2,215, unfavorable. This was not controllable by the machining manager, however, and therefore was excluded from the departmental performance report for the month.

Full Cost versus Variable Cost Transfer Prices

Full-cost transfer prices overstate the short-run cost variability of service costs. Usage charges computed in this way in some cases lead department heads to decide not to use the services when in fact the company would be better off if the services were used.

A possible remedy for this problem is to use variable-cost charging rates. In our example, the three production department managers would be charged $6.50 instead of $10 an hour for maintenance services. This would be a more relevant figure for short-run utilization-of-capacity decisions.

The difficulty with this solution, at least in some cases, is that it might encourage managers to use so much service that additional service capacity would have to be provided to meet these demands. This additional capacity could be costly, and this cost ought somehow to get back to the managers using the services.

Although we shall explore the transfer pricing problem in some depth in Chapter 26, we shall mention now two devices a company might use to try to discourage managers from using costly services too freely. One is to charge each manager one amount for the variable costs of the services actually used and another amount, determined at the beginning of the year, for a share of the capacity costs of the service department. This capacity charge would not change during the year, but any manager who used the services heavily would get a bigger share of total capacity costs in the next year's budget.

A more conventional possibility is to use a transfer price that encompasses both variable costs and fixed costs. This may measure current average full cost, as in our illustration, or may be an estimate of the incremental cost of providing and using additional capacity— that is, attributable cost.

SUMMARY

Every organization has departments that exist to serve or support the activities of other parts of the organization. Most organizations allocate at least some of the costs of these departments to the departments they serve or support. Some of these allocations take place before the fact, to place factory service costs in a position to be included in departmental overhead rates for product costing or to notify department heads of their responsibility to control their use of the services. Other allocations are after the fact, to provide a record of the department head's success in controlling service usage or to provide necessary data for contract costing.

If the department provides measurable services, the best allocation *transfer price*

activity charge

capacity charge

device is a transfer price. If service outputs are not measurable but service costs nevertheless vary with the amount of activity in other departments, allocations should be made by activity charges. Finally, if the service load is not a function of current volume, capacity charges should be used for any allocations to be made.

Allocation rates based on a detailed analysis of the organization's costs may be developed either by a sequential procedure or by cross allocations. Cross allocations are regarded as more accurate, but the presence of fixed costs makes it doubtful that any real increase in accuracy has occurred.

The use of separate charging rates for fixed and variable costs is likely to be a useful refinement in before-the-fact allocations, although it will add to the complexity of the system.

The only variances the department heads should see on their performance reports are those reporting departures from the amounts of services included in the departments' flexible budgets for measurable services the department heads are expected to control. For this purpose it is important to use predetermined transfer prices.

Capacity charges and activity charges can be omitted in performance reporting, but if they are included they should be reported at predetermined amounts (capacity charges) or predetermined rates (activity charges) to keep noncontrollable variances out of the performance reports.

KEY TERMS

The most important terms introduced and defined in this chapter are the following:

Activity charge	Production center
Allocations	Sequential allocation
Attributable cost	Service center
Capacity charge	Support center
Charging rate	Transfer price
Cross allocations	Usage charge
Direct apportionment	

APPENDIX: Cross Allocations

Cross allocations are calculated by solving a set of equations simultaneously. In practice there will be so many equations that a computer must be used. The Standoff Company's factory is simple enough, however, to let us demonstrate the method using simple algebra.

The first step is to write a set of equations, each one showing the resources used by one service center. The building services department has direct charges of $8,000 and five authorized employees. (This last figure was not supplied earlier, and it raises the total number of authorized employees from 120 to 125.) Buildings services, with 5/125 or 4 percent of the authorized employees, is entitled to 4 percent of the costs of executive services. None of its five employees is classified as operating labor, however, so no clerical services costs are allocated to it. It uses no maintenance services, either. The equation is:

$$B = \$8,000 + 0.04\ E \tag{1}$$

in which

> B = Budgeted building services costs
> E = Budgeted executive services costs

The budgeted costs of the executive services department also cover two elements. Direct costs amount to $10,320 and the department occupies 6 percent of the floor space. Its costs are expressed in equation (2):

$$E = \$10,320 + 0.06\ B \tag{2}$$

The equation for the clerical services department (C) is as follows:

$$C = \$5,540 + 0.04B + 0.048\ E \tag{3}$$

For the maintenance department (M), the equation is:

$$M = \$8,040 + 0.06B + 0.096E + 0.0625\ C$$

If all four departments appeared in all four equations, we would have to solve all four equations simultaneously, Even with as few as four equations, a computer would be very handy. Fortunately, only equations (1) and (2) are interdependent here—that is, B depends on E and E depends on B. This means that we have to solve only these two simultaneously.

Solution of these equations is a simple exercise in algebra. Multiplying equation (1) by 25 gives us the following:

$$25B = \$200,000 + E \tag{1a}$$

We can substitute the value of E from equation (2) to get the following:

$$\$10,320 + 0.06B = 25B - \$200,000$$

When we simplify this equation we find that $B = \$8,433$. Substituting this figure in equation (2), we find that $E = \$10,826$.

The next step is to use these figures to solve equations (3) and (4), the budgeted costs of the other two service departments. Equation (3) becomes:

$$C = \$5,540 + 0.04 \times \$8,433 + 0.048 \times \$10,826 \tag{3a}$$
$$C = \$6,397$$

And equation (4) becomes:

$$M = \$8,040 + 0.06 \times \$8,433 + 0.096 \times \$10,826 + 0.0625 \times \$6,397 \tag{4a}$$
$$M = \$9,985$$

The four budget totals from these four equations can now be multiplied by the allocation factors we developed earlier. These allocations are shown in Exhibit 8–10. The overhead rates in this case are

EXHIBIT 8–10

STANDOFF COMPANY
Cross Allocations

	Building Services $8,000	Executive Services $10,320	Clerical Services $5,540	Maintenance Services $8,040	Machining $15,520	Welding and Plating $13,100	Assembly $6,580
Direct overhead..........	$8,000	$10,320	$5,540	$8,040	$15,520	$13,100	$6,580
Allocations:							
Building services..........	($8,433)	0.06 × $8,433 = $506	0.04 × $8,433 = $337	0.06 × $8,433 = $506	0.40 × $8,433 = $3,373	0.14 × $8,433 = $1,181	0.30 × $8,433 = $2,530
Executive services..........	0.04 × $10,826 = $433	($10,826)	0.048 × $10,826 = $520	0.096 × $10,826 = $1,039	0.336 × $10,826 = $3,638	0.096 × $10,826 = $1,039	0.384 × $10,826 = $4,157
Clerical services..........	—	—	($6,397)	0.0625 × $6,397 = $400	0.3125 × $6,397 = $1,999	0.125 × $6,397 = $800	0.50 × $6,397 = $3,198
Maintenance services..........	—	—	—	($9,985)	0.75 × $9,985 = $7,489	0.15 × $9,985 = $1,498	0.10 × $9,985 = $998
Allocated total..........	—	—	—	—	$32,019	$17,618	$17,463
Normal volume..........					4,000 hrs.	1,600 hrs.	7,000 hrs.
Overhead rate..........					$8.00 per hr.	$11.01 per hr.	$2.50 per hr.

virtually identical to those we derived by sequential allocation, but with more interdependencies the differences probably would be greater. On thing is true in all cases, however: *the costs assigned to the three production departments add up to the total budgeted factory cost:*

$$\$32,019 + \$17,618 + \$17,463 = \$67,100$$

No cost is added, none is overlooked.

Cross allocations are clearly able to deal with interdependent departments. Furthermore, the cost of doing this on the computer may not be very great. The problem is that these allocations are likely to look more accurate without being any more relevant to decisions than sequential allocations. The relationships expressed in most of the equations are very imprecise. Furthermore, many service and support costs are fixed over wide volume ranges. Allocating part of one of these to another department implies incorrectly that this amount could be saved if the department receiving the charge were disbanded. In other words, cross allocations may warm the mathematician's heart but they are unlikely to be more useful to management than sequential allocations.

INDEPENDENT STUDY PROBLEMS
(Solutions in Appendix C)

1. Allocations for product costing.   A factory has four direct production departments and three service departments. One of these service departments, department S, has costs of $2,000 a month plus $0.20 for each unit of department S service provided to other departments.

Monthly service unit consumption and volume of production activity in the factory's four direct production departments are normally as follows:

Department	Service Units	Production Volume
1......................	1,000	10,000 direct labor hours
2......................	5,000	8,000 direct labor hours
3......................	8,000	20,000 machine-hours
4......................	6,000	15,000 direct labor hours
Total..............	20,000	

Service consumption is wholly fixed in department 1 and proportionally variable with volume in the other three departments.

Each batch of 1,000 units of product A requires 10 direct labor hours in department 1, 20 direct labor hours in department 2, 100 machine-hours in department 3, and 5 direct labor hours in department 4. Overhead is charged to products on the basis of predetermined departmental overhead rates, including provisions for service department costs.

a.   How much department S cost would be included in the cost of a batch of product A if costing is on a full costing basis?

b.   How much department S cost should be included in the cost of a batch of product A if costing is on a variable costing basis?

2. Cost distribution sheet.   A factory has two production departments (Able and Baker), and four service departments (building, office, storeroom, and maintenance). The company uses predetermined departmental overhead rates for product costing on a full costing basis.

To develop these overhead costing rates, the company allocates normal service department costs to the two production departments sequentially, using the following statistics for operations at normal volume:

	Direct Labor Hours	Total Labor Hours	Percent of Floor Space	Main- tenance Hours	Percent of Requi- sitions	Direct Overhead Costs
Building........................	—	500	—	—	—	$ 5,000
Office...........................	—	600	15	10	—	6,370
Storeroom......................	—	300	10	—	—	2,260
Maintenance..................	—	500	5	—	5	6,000
Able............................	5,000	5,600	40	150	35	2,770
Baker..........................	2,000	2,500	30	250	60	3,100
						$25,500

a. Prepare a cost distribution sheet and develop departmental fixed and variable overhead rates for Able and Baker, based on direct labor hours. You should distribute the service department costs in the following sequence and on the following bases:

Building..................... Percent of floor space
Office....................... Total labor hours
Storeroom................... Percent of requisitions
Maintenance................ Maintenance hours

b. Calculate full cost departmental overhead rates that would be used under direct apportionment, using direct labor hours as the absorption base for all overhead costs. Three rates should be developed, one for each production department and one for all service departments combined.

c. Calculate the amount of overhead assigned to the following two jobs, first using the allocated rates you developed in (a), then using the direct apportionment rates you developed in (b):

	Job 123	Job 321
Direct labor hours—Able.............	5	2
Direct labor hours—Baker...........	2	5

3. Cross allocations. The Tisket Tasket Casket Company, manufacturers of burial caskets and morticians' equipment, has three service departments and eight production departments. The company has decided to use predetermined rates as the basis for service department cost allocation. The budgeted direct departmental charges for the three service departments for the current years are as follows:

Department A................ $12,000 a month
Department B................ 18,000 a month
Department C................ 20,000 a month

The estimated numbers of service units budgeted for this year are as follows:

Department Providing the Service	Budgeted Monthly Service Consumption by Departments				
	A	B	C	Production	Total
A.................	—	1,200	800	6,000	8,000
B.................	600	—	1,400	8,000	10,000
C.................	2,000	1,000	—	12,000	15,000

This table should be read as follows: service department A provides 1,200 units of service to service department B, 800 units of service to service department C, and 6,000 units of service to various production departments.

a.   Compute, for each of the three service departments, a charging rate per service unit that covers only the costs directly traceable to that department (direct departmental charges). In other words, the charging rate will not include any provision for the costs of other service departments, nor will service departments be charged for their use of other service departments' services.

b.   Compute charging rates by sequential allocation, taking the service departments in alphabetical order.

c.   Compute charging rates which give full recognition to the interdependence of the three service departments, using cross-allocations. Three equations must be solved simultaneously, one for each service department. The equation for department A is:

$$\text{Charging rate } A = \frac{\$12{,}000 + 600 \times \text{charging rate } B + 2{,}000 \times \text{charging rate } C}{8{,}000 \text{ total service units consumed}}$$

4. Flexible budget comparisons. Service department S provides services to other departments of the company's manufacturing division. The amount of service provided depends on the needs of the other manufacturing departments, as determined by their respective managers.

The normal operating volume for department S is 10,000 service hours a month. Budgeted cost is $20,000 plus $2.50 per service hour. Actual department S cost for February was $42,000, at a volume of 8,000 service hours, including 1,100 service hours performed in production department M.

The normal operating volume for department M is 15,000 direct labor hours a month. At this volume, department M's budget allows for the consumption of 1,000 department S hours. During February, department M operated at a volume of 12,500 direct labor hours, and at this volume it had a budget allowance of 900 department S hours.

a.   How much should department M be charged for department S services for the month of February? State your reasons.

b.   Compute the variance in the charge for department S services that would appear on department M's cost performance report for the month, using the allocation method you developed in (a). Give a one-sentence explanation of the meaning of this variance.

c.   Compute the variance in departmental costs that would appear on department S's cost control reports for the month.

EXERCISES AND PROBLEMS

1. Predetermined allocations: Full costing, variable costing, and attributable costing. The Calnan Company's Elmira factory has seven production and four service departments. One of the service departments, department S, has the following monthly budget at its normal monthly volume of 1,400 service hours:

Service labor............................	$ 9,800
Supervision..............................	1,400
Supplies.................................	280
Depreciation.............................	1,750
Other costs..............................	70
Total.................................	$13,300

All of these except supervision and depreciation are proportionately variable with volume. Supervision costs represent the salary of the department head. Depreciation is the straight-line amortization of the cost of the equipment used in department S (seven identical service machines).

Raw materials for product X are processed in department 1 and then transferred to department 2 for finishing. Product X is only one of the many products that these two production departments work on every month.

Normal monthly operating statistics for these two departments are as follows:

	Department 1	Department 2
Normal monthly operating volume........	25,000 pounds of output	10,000 direct labor hours
Normal monthly consumption of department S services.........................	300 service hours	200 service hours

Consumption of department S services in these two departments varies in direct proportion to changes in operating volume.

One unit of product X weighs 10 pounds and requires five direct labor hours in department 2.

a. How much department S cost should be included in the cost of a unit of product X on a full cost basis?
b. How much department S cost should be included in the cost of a unit of product X on a variable costing basis?
c. How much department S cost should be included in the cost of a unit of product X on an attributable costing basis?

2. Predetermined allocations: Fixed and variable service consumption. Department 3 is another production department in the Calnan Company's Elmira factory (see Problem 1). It uses a good deal of department S service. Under normal conditions, it will use 100 hours of service each month for routine work plus one service hour for every 100 direct labor hours in department 3.

Normal volume in department 3 is 10,000 direct labor hours a month, and a departmental overhead rate is computed on that basis.

Department 3 uses an outside company, Goodbody, Inc., to do some work that Calnan's own service departments are not equipped to do. Goodbody has now offered to expand its services by doing the work now done by department S in department 3. The price would be a flat fee of $1,400 a month. The decision on this proposal is to be made by the manager of the Elmira factory. Department S will continue to service the factory's other departments in any case.

a. How large a provision for the costs of department S should be included in a variable costing overhead rate for department 3?
b. How large a provision for the costs of department S should be included in the overhead rate for department 3 if this is to reflect department 3's attributable costs?
c. Analyze the Goodbody proposal and recommend a course of action, giving reasons for your recommendation.

3. Direct apportionment. The Calnan Company's management (see Problem 1) may change from an allocation system to the direct apportionment method for assigning department S's costs to individual products. The Elmira factory completes 1,400 jobs in an average month, weighing a total of 84,000 pounds and requiring 28,000 direct labor hours.

a. What are the arguments for and against this change?

b. Suppose management has decided to make the change. How would the accountants implement this decision? What decisions would they have to make and what criteria would they use in making them? Illustrate your answer with Elmira factory data.

4. Capacity, activity, and usage charges. A factory has a number of departments, including the following:

1. The personnel department recruits prospective employees, organizes on-the-job training programs, conducts personal performance reviews, maintains the personnel files, and carries out other personnel-related work. Ninety percent of the department's direct costs consist of salaries and fringe benefits. This department has ten employees.

2. The steam plant provides steam to heat the building and drive production equipment in several factory departments. Sixty percent of the department's direct costs are for fuel, another 20 percent is for depreciation and equipment maintenance. The department has eight employees.

3. The scheduling department prepares production schedules, coordinates materials flows, and keeps track of the progress of individual jobs. Ninety percent of its direct costs are salaries and fringe benefits of its five employees.

4. The building service department is responsible for keeping the factory building clean, attractive, and in good working condition. Eighty percent of the department's direct costs consist of salaries and fringe benefits. The department has nine employees.

a. For each of these departments, indicate whether allocations should be based on capacity charges, activity charges, or usage charges. Explain your reasoning in each case.

b. In each case, indicate whether monthly allocations would serve a control purpose. If so, explain how the allocated amounts should be interpreted.

5. Direct apportionment, one-step allocation, and sequential allocation. The Parker Manufacturing Company has two production departments (fabrication and assembly) and three service departments (factory administration, factory maintenance, and factory cafeteria). A summary of budgeted costs and other data is as follows:

	Fabrication	Assembly	Factory Adminis-tration	Factory Mainte-nance	Factory Cafeteria
Direct labor costs...........	$3,840,000	$3,120,000	$168,000	$243,000	$210,000
Direct material costs........	3,130,000	950,000	—	65,000	180,000
Factory overhead costs.......	1,154,000	986,000	132,000	112,000	110,000
Direct labor hours...........	480,000	520,000	31,000	27,000	42,000
Number of employees........	240	240	12	8	20
Square footage occupied.....	90,000	60,000	10,000	4,000	6,000

The costs of the factory administration department, factory maintenance department, and factory cafeteria are allocated on the basis of direct labor hours, square footage occupied, and number of employees, respectively. For allocation purposes, labor and materials expended in a service department on that department's major service-producing activities are referred to as direct labor and direct materials in those departments. For product costing, however, all the costs of these three departments are classified as factory overhead costs. Product cost is to be calculated on a full-cost basis.

a. Allocate the service department costs by the one-step allocation method and calculate an overhead rate for each of the production departments, based on direct labor hours.
b. Allocate the service department costs by the sequential method, starting with the service department with the greatest costs, and calculate an overhead rate for each of the production departments, based on direct labor hours.
c. Management is considering using the direct apportionment method, based on direct labor hours. Calculate the total amount of overhead costs assignable to a job requiring 100 direct labor hours in fabrication and 50 direct labor hours in assembly. Compare this amount with the amounts assignable to this job under the methods prescribed in (a) and (b). Is one of these clearly more accurate than the others? Explain.

(CPA, adapted)

6. Cross allocations.   A factory has four departments, two production departments (A and B) and two service departments (C and D). Volume in each production department is measured in direct labor hours (DLH). Costs are shown in the following table:

Department	Traceable Fixed Overhead Costs	Traceable Variable Overhead Costs		Units of C's Services Required	Units of D's Services Required
		Per DLH	Per Unit of Service		
A............	$50,000	$2.00	—	0.010 per DLH	—
B..........	30,000	1.50	—	0.035 per DLH	0.0475 per DLH
C..........	19,350	—	$2.00	—	0.050 per unit of C's services
D..........	9,780	—	3.00	0.010 per unit of D's services	—

Each line in this table shows the inputs required by one department. The line for department A, for example, shows that the traceable fixed costs of this department are $50,000, direct variable overhead costs are $2 per direct labor hour, and 0.01 of a unit of service provided by department C is needed for each direct labor hour in department A.

Normal production volume is 29,000 direct labor hours in department A and 20,000 direct labor hours in department B.

a. Compute a full cost overhead rate for each production department to the nearest tenth of a cent. (Note: This requires cross allocations.)
b. Compute overhead rates for use in a variable costing system.

7. Flexible budget allowances for allocated costs.   Service department S provides services to a number of production departments. The cost budget for the department at a normal volume of 5,000 service hours per month, together with actual departmental charges for the month of March, is as follows (4,000 hours of service were provided to production departments during March):

	Budget at Normal Volume		
	Amount	*Fixed or Variable*	*March Actual*
Service labor........................	$15,000	V	$14,000
Supervision.........................	2,000	F	2,000
Indirect labor......................	4,000	V	3,000
Supplies............................	1,000	V	1,100
Depreciation........................	5,500	F	5,600
Rent................................	2,500	F	2,900
Total........................	$30,000		$28,600

Depreciation charged each month is 1 percent of the original cost of equipment installed in the service department. The rental charge is based on the department's pro rata share, based on floor space occupied, of the costs charged to the building service department's accounts during the month.

Production department M uses department S services, and the supervisor in charge of department M is expected to control use of these services. Normal production volume in department M is 10,000 machine-hours. Department M's use of department S services is budgeted at one service hour for every ten machine-hours. A full cost charging rate is used.

Service hours are charged to production departments on the basis of average actual service department cost for the month multiplied by the number of service hours used during the month. During March department M operated a total of 11,000 machine-hours and used 900 hours of department S service.

a.   Express department M's cost budget for its use of department S services as a mathematical formula.

b.   Compute department M's budget allowance for department S service: (1) at normal volume, (2) at 11,000 machine-hours.

c.   Compute the service charge to department M for March.

d.   Calculate the spending variance for department M's use of department S services during March.

e.   Analyze department M's March spending variance in department S charges, showing a breakdown between the variance due to factors over which department M had some control and the variance due to other causes.

8. Monthly allocations: Interpretation of variance.   The costs of a factory service department, such as maintenance, are frequently distributed to other departments by multiplying a "charging rate" by the number of units of service provided to each other department. The charging rate is computed so as to provide for a complete distribution of service department costs, using the following formula:

$$\frac{\text{Actual direct service dept. costs} + \text{actual costs allocated to service dept.}}{\text{Total units of service provided to all other departments}}$$

The factory of Green, Inc., uses a system of this kind. The milling department in this factory has a budget allowance of 50 maintenance hours a month plus one maintenance hour for every 100 milling department machine-hours in excess of 8,000 hours a month.

During April, the milling department operated at a volume of 11,000 machine-hours and used 70 maintenance hours. The departmental overhead cost report for the month included the following line:

	Budget	Actual	Variance
Maintenance labor.................	$720	$735	$(15)

a.   What conclusions can you draw from this unfavorable variance? How well did the milling department manager control maintenance costs this month? What other factors are likely to have contributed to the $15 variance?

b.   What changes, if any, would you suggest in the company's interdepartmental cost allocation system? Give your reasons either for your suggested changes or for your satisfaction with the present system.

9. Selecting a basis for monthly allocations.   The budgeted costs of the power service department amount to $9,520 a month; of this amount $2,500 is considered to be a fixed cost. Costs during April amounted to $9,300.

Power consumption in this factory is measured by the number of horsepower hours. The monthly power requirements of the factory's four other departments, in horsepower hours, are as follows:

	Producing Departments		Service Departments	
	A	B	X	Y
Needed at capacity production..............	10,000	20,000	12,000	8,000
Budgeted...................................	8,000	15,000	8,000	5,000
Used during April........................	8,000	13,000	7,000	6,000

What dollar amounts of power service department costs should be allocated to each of these four departments for the month of April?

(CPA adapted)

10. Departmental performance report.   The following information has been taken from the overhead cost budget for a direct production department and from the accounting records of this department for the month of December:

	Budgeted		Actual
	At Normal Volume	At Actual Volume	Actual Cost
Cleanup labor......................	$ 400	$ 400	$ 550
Indirect labor......................	3,000	3,600	3,400
Overtime premium..................	300	500	750
Steam............................	1,500	1,800	1,700
Heat, light, depreciation, and			
insurance.......................	2,000	2,000	2,400
Factory administration..............	800	800	800

All budgeted figures are at standard prices and standard wage rates. Indirect labor and cleanup labor are charged to the department at standard wage rates. Steam is purchased from a local utility at a price which varies with the price of fuel; steam costs are charged to the departments on the basis of the average steam price for the month multiplied by consumption determined on the basis of meter readings. Heat, light, depreciation, and insurance costs are charged to the departments on the basis of the percentage of the factory's floor space occupied at the beginning of the year.

Indicate what figures you would report to the department head, how you would arrange these figures on the department head's report, and what further data you would like to obtain to make the report more useful to the department head and managers at higher levels. Give your reasons.

11. Choosing bases for control allocations.   The management of Blake-Emmich wants to have departmental cost statements that will be all-inclusive so that the department heads will be cognizant of their shares of the total costs of operating the factory, but which will be used primarily for control purposes. The monthly budget of the machining department includes the following categories of costs:

1. Fixed costs which are distributed among the factory's departments on a "fair and equitable" basis: the machining department's share of these costs is $12,000 a month.
2. Fixed costs which are direct to the department, the amount of the cost being determined by the factory superintendent: $2,000 a month.
3. Fixed costs which are direct to the department, the amount of the cost being determined by the department head: $600 a month.
4. Variable direct costs for which the department head determines the amount of inputs used but not input prices: $4 a standard direct labor hour.
5. Variable costs of service departments for which the machining department head determines the amount of service used: five units of service per standard direct labor hour, at an average variable service department cost of $0.20 a unit.
6. Variable costs of service departments for which the service department head or the factory superintendent determines the amount of service used: four units of service per standard direct labor hour at $0.30 a unit.

The machining department's output for July was the equivalent of 2,000 standard direct labor hours.

a.   Compute a machining department flexible budget allowance for July for each of the six cost categories listed above.
b.   Comparisons between these flexible budget allowances and the "actual costs" charged to the department for July will be embodied in a monthly departmental cost report. Indicate for each category how "actual cost" should be measured and reported. Remember that the report is to be used for control purposes.

12. Impact of increasing allocations.   "I get overcharged by the graphics department every month, and I'm getting pretty tired of it," Patrick Denning said. Mr. Denning was the manager of his company's advertising department.

"I know we use a lot of graphics," he continued, "but the amount they charge me has gone up a lot faster than my usage. Besides, I know that most of the costs down there are fixed costs. It seems to me that incremental cost would be a better basis for the charge."

Janet MacKenzie, the controller, admitted that Mr. Denning's charges had gone up, but cited figures to show that the increases were justified. "We have worked out an hourly rate," she said, "and everyone is treated alike. The hourly cost has gone up every year as we have expanded the system and gotten more sophisticated equipment. We don't raise the rate within the year, though. The rate is based on the budget for the year and each department has a budgeted allocation. If they don't use more time, they don't get charged more.

"The annual rate covers all of the costs that have been budgeted for operating the department during the year. We divide this by the number of hours we expect to devote to productive work, and this gives us the rate. We don't attach any of the costs to idle time or to the time we use for training purposes within the department. These are necessary and we feel that everyone should bear a fair share of the total.

"Actually, Pat Denning has kept pretty well within his budget limits over the years. I don't know what he's complaining about. Besides, his department's jobs use more of the expensive equipment than the rest of our work put together. If anything, we should charge him more than we do now."

a. Why is Mr. Denning upset? Does he have reason to worry?
b. What should Ms. MacKenzie do in response to Mr. Denning's complaints?

13. Incremental allocation rates. The General Student Corporation of America purchased in December 19x4, a Comprox Sigma 1102 electronic data processing machine. The machine was bought primarily for department A, which began using about half of its capacity.

After the machine was installed, four other departments (B, C, D, and E) decided they, too, would like to use it. They claimed, however, that they should pay for the direct costs of use only, and that the total overhead should be carried by department A. This arrangement would be fair, they claimed, because the purchase of the Sigma 1102 could be justified on the basis of its use in department A alone. Moreover, the opportunity cost of letting other departments use the machine would be nil,[1] because if the machine were not used-it would just stand idle. Renting the machine to outsiders on a part-time basis was not considered appropriate.

The arrangement proposed by the four departments was put into force, to everyone's satisfaction. By January 19x5, the machine time was fully booked. At that point a sixth department, F, also found ways to use the machine. The controller decided that machine time should be used where its benefits were the greatest. To accomplish this, a new system was devised, whereby each department would have to pay a share of the overhead, the cost being divided in proportion to the time used.

This new system reduced the hourly charges to department A, which then increased its usage to about half of the time available. Department B took one quarter of the machine time, but the other departments decided the system was too costly and took their work off the machine. The machine, therefore, remained idle one fourth of the time.

Criticize the two methods used to charge for machine time. Describe the method you would use, state what you would expect it to accomplish, and why you prefer it.

(Prepared by Professor Michael Jensen)

14. Cost distribution sheet, monthly allocations, and departmental variances. The Premier Company's factory has four production departments and four service departments—office, buildings, maintenance, and logistics.

All accounting, personnel, and plant management functions are performed in the office department. The buildings department is responsible for heating, lighting, and maintaining the factory building and grounds. The maintenance department handles repairs of all equipment except

---

[1] This assumption is made only to simplify the analysis of this problem. In general, this is a highly inaccurate characterization of this technology.

office equipment, the latter being serviced on contract by an outside firm. The logistics department handles all incoming shipments of materials and parts and operates the stock room.

At normal volume, the factory overhead costs traceable to factory departments would be budgeted at the following levels:

Shaping........................	$ 29,584
Drilling.........................	24,624
Finishing.......................	109,012
Assembly.......................	5,200
Office..........................	73,040
Buildings......................	34,000
Maintenance...................	19,860
Logistics.......................	8,680
Total.....................	$304,000

The budgets for the service departments show the following detailed breakdown of these figures:

	Office	Buildings	Mainte-nance	Logistics
Supervision.......................	$ 4,000	$ 1,000	$ 1,800	$ 800
Other salaries.....................	24,000	—	—	—
Indirect labor.....................	—	7,000	12,400	3,000
Supplies..........................	9,000	2,000	1,840	3,800
Depreciation—building.............	—	5,000	—	—
Depreciation—equipment..........	200	200	420	—
Heat and light.....................	—	12,000	—	—
Other direct charges...............	35,840	6,800	3,400	1,080
Total direct charges.........	$73,040	$34,000	$19,860	$8,680

Budgeted operating data at normal monthly volume are:

	Direct Labor Hours	Floor Space (square feet)	Employees	Maintenance Labor Hours	No. of Requisitions
Shaping............	6,000	18,000	50	560	400
Drilling.............	5,000	16,000	40	610	600
Finishing...........	14,000	33,000	100	930	800
Assembly..........	9,000	20,000	60	500	500
Office..............	—	10,000	34	—	—
Buildings..........	—	1,000	11	—	—
Maintenance.......	—	1,000	17	—	—
Logistics...........	—	2,000	6	—	—
Total.........	34,000	101,000	318	2,600	2,300

Monthly cost reports are issued to the managers of each of the company's departments. These reports are to be used primarily in reviewing the effectiveness of cost control in each department. Production department managers are presumed to share responsibility with the maintenance department manager for the number of maintenance labor hours used.

The following operating and overhead cost data were recorded for the month of November:

	Direct Labor Hours	Direct Departmental Overhead	Employees	Maintenance Labor Hours	Logistics
Shaping............	6,500	$ 31,600	54	600	410
Drilling.............	5,500	25,720	42	650	650
Finishing...........	13,000	106,070	96	900	790
Assembly..........	7,500	4,950	50	550	400
Office..............	—	70,600	33	—	—
Buildings..........	—	38,400	11	—	—
Maintenance.......	—	21,000	18	—	—
Logistics..........	—	9,400	6	—	—
Total........	32,500	$307,740	310	2,700	2,250

a. Prepare an overhead cost distribution sheet, allocating the full costs of service departments in the following sequence and on the following bases: (1) buildings—floor space; (2) office—number of employees; (c) maintenance—maintenance labor hours; and (4) logistics—number of requisitions. In each case indicate whether you are using capacity charges, activity charges, or usage charges. No distinction between fixed and variable costs need be made.

b. Prepare a full-cost overhead rate for each production department.

c. Using charging rates developed in (a), prepare an overhead cost distribution sheet for the month of November.

d. Calculate the amount over- or underabsorbed in each production department and the amount over- or underdistributed in each service department. Enter these amounts at the bottom of your cost distribution sheet.

15. Departmental reporting. The flexible budgets of the Premier Company's finishing and maintenance departments (see Problem 14) are calculated from the following formulas:

	Finishing	Maintenance
Direct overhead:		
Supervision.........................	$2,200 + $1,800 for each 5,000 direct labor hours (or major portion thereof)	Fixed
Other salaries......................	Fixed, $2,500	None
Indirect labor......................	$2.50 for each direct labor hour	$4.80 for each maintenance labor hour
Supplies............................	$0.70 for each direct labor hour	$150 + $0.65 for each maintenance labor hour
Depreciation—equipment............	Fixed, $12,000	Fixed
Other direct charges................	$14,112 + $2 for each direct labor hour	$20 + $1.30 for each maintenance labor hour
Allocated overhead statistics:		
No. of employees...................	3 + 1 for each 150 direct labor hours + 1 for each 5,000 direct labor hours	1 for each 150 maintenance labor hours
Floor space........................	Fixed	Fixed
Maintenance hours.................	230 + 5 for each 100 direct labor hours	None
Requisitions.......................	5.71 for each 100 direct labor hours	None

Part-time employees are not used, and the flexible budget allowances reflect the notion that if more than half an employee is required, a full-time employee will be hired.

Actual direct overhead costs for these two departments were as follows in November:

	Finishing	Maintenance
Supervision........................	$ 7,790	$ 1,860
Other salaries.....................	2,550	—
Indirect labor......................	36,100	13,050
Supplies...........................	8,230	1,760
Depreciation.......................	12,000	420
Other direct charges...............	39,400	3,910
Total direct overhead........	$106,070	$21,000

a. Prepare flexible budget allowances for November for each of these departments.

b. Prepare an overhead cost performance report for each department, including all allocated costs. You may assume that all direct overhead costs are controllable except supervision, other salaries, and equipment depreciation.

9

Financial Reporting to Marketing Management

Marketing executives, unlike manufacturing managers, have responsibility for revenues as well as for costs. The control reports must reflect this difference. Our purpose in this chapter is to see how this can be done. We shall deal with four topics:

1. The nature of the marketing function.
2. Measurement of marketing profit performance—the profit contribution approach.
3. Interpretation of marketing results.
4. Secondary control techniques.

THE MARKETING FUNCTION

Three kinds of activities are usually or at least frequently associated with the marketing function:

1. Order getting.
2. Order filling.
3. Marketing administration.

The first and third are inescapable parts of the marketing function; the second will be part of marketing if top management wants to put it there.

Order-Getting Activities

When we think of marketing, we usually think of activities leading to the sale of the company's goods and services. These are the order-getting activities, mainly market research, advertising, and direct selling. They are what we have referred to as programmed activities—that is, their scope depends on management's estimates of the benefits they will yield and the costs of obtaining them.

EXHIBIT 9–1

Volume Determining versus Volume-Determined Activities

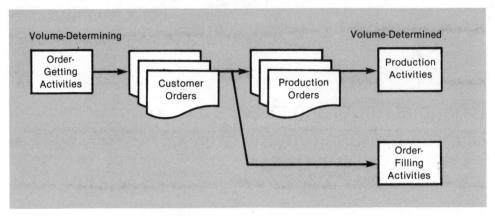

Order-getting costs differ from manufacturing costs in that they are volume determining rather than volume determined. The arrows in Exhibit 9–1 all point from left to right. Order-getting activities produce customer orders; production and order-filling activities are scaled to respond to the level of orders received. Production can't go on very long unless customers are buying.

Market research is a step or two removed from sales solicitation, the main activity in direct selling. Even so, it should be classified as an order-getting activity. Its main purpose is to try to make sure that the company's products will appeal to its customers. This affects the volume and composition of the orders received. In other words, it is a volume-determining activity and its costs have the same characteristics as other volume-determining activities.

Order-Filling Activities

Many marketing organizations are responsible not only for volume-determining activities but also for the physical movement of products to the firm's customers and for various clerical operations initiated by the filing of customer orders. These are sometimes referred to as order-filling activities. They include reviewing customers' credit-worthiness, warehousing, assembling goods to be shipped ("picking and packing"), preparing shipping documents, shipping, billing, maintaining the customer ledger, and collecting amounts due from customers.

These order-filling activities aren't really part of the marketing function, but describing them here puts the characteristics of order-getting costs in sharper relief. Order-filling activities are responsive activities, necessary to service the volume of business generated by the order-getting activities. As such, they have the same general characteristics as manufacturing activities. The work tends to be

EXHIBIT 9-2

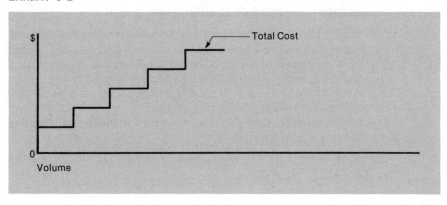

reasonably well structured and repetitive. This means that standard costs and flexible budgets are entirely applicable.

Putting this into practice is not as easy as it may sound. The costs of most order-filling activities move up in the step pattern familiar to us from previous chapters (see Exhibit 9–2). This chart doesn't describe short-term cost variability very well, however. Staffing for the year is largely determined at budget time. Most clerical personnel are on salary, and layoffs are uncommon. This means that when business is slow, their work load is light. When volume is high, management is slow to hire more people and the clerks' work load is heavy. As a result, cost variances are likely to fluctuate as volume fluctuates.

The usual solution is to use estimates of work loads to establish fixed budget allowances for the year and then compare actual costs with these budget allowances as the year goes on. We shall return to an analysis of these costs in Chapter 12.

Marketing Administration

Every marketing organization has an administrative superstructure, designed to provide direction and logistical support to both order-getting and order-filling personnel. Some administrative personnel are located at marketing headquarters; others are at regional and branch locations.

Some administrative costs that arise from order-filling operations may vary with the volume of orders received, but more are pure capacity costs, determined by the volume of business the organization plans to generate and serve.

CONTROLLING ORDER-GETTING COSTS

The immediate aim of periodic control reports is to enable the manager to compare actual results with a performance standard. This is just as true in marketing as in manufacturing. To see how control reports for order-getting activities differ from those for manufacturing activities, we need to examine four questions:

1. Why performance standards for order-getting activities should be based on profits, not on standard costs and flexible budgets.
2. Why planned profit is a better performance standard than the profit earned in a previous period or periods.
3. Why the profit contribution format should be used in periodic control reports to marketing managers.
4. What modifications of the profit contribution format might be worth considering.

We shall look at the first two of these in this section and at the others in the section that follows.

Inapplicability of Standard Costs and Flexible Budgets

Until now we have derived cost control standards by finding the amount of cost that ought to be necessary to produce the output actually achieved. The greater the output, the larger the cost standard.

This can't be done for order-getting costs. True, marketing output can be measured—by the number of orders, the dollar value of the orders received, or some measure of the total profit these orders generate. But order-getting costs don't vary in response to changes in any of these. This means that neither standard costs nor flexible budgets can be used to establish the amount that should have been spent to achieve the volume recorded in any period. In fact, a low ratio of cost to volume may be very undesirable because it means the marketing organization has limited itself to the easiest market sector, leaving more difficult but still profitable sectors to competitors.

For example, marketing expenses make up only 2 percent of total sales in the diagram at the top of Exhibit 9–3, as opposed to 10 percent in the lower diagram. Sales in the lower diagram are so much larger, however, that profit is substantially higher, even after allowing for the added marketing costs.

This is just another way of saying that minimizing costs is not what the marketing manager is expected to do. A favorable variance in order-getting costs may be just as bad or worse than an unfavorable variance. What other alternatives are available? Sales volume is one. The marketing managers' effectiveness may be measured by the total volume of sales or share of the market they have been able to achieve. Effectiveness doesn't mean efficiency, however. Some products sell at prices much closer to cost than others; this means that some product mixes are more desirable than others. Furthermore, some marketing segments—that is, territories or product markets or customer groups —are more expensive to serve than others. Sales in a high-cost segment are worth less than sales in a low-cost segment. These differences are illustrated in Exhibit 9–4 for two segments equal in sales but very different in the cost of goods sold and in selling expenses.

This leaves us with profit. Profit is the only measure that encom-

EXHIBIT 9–3

Ratios versus Amounts as Marketing Standards

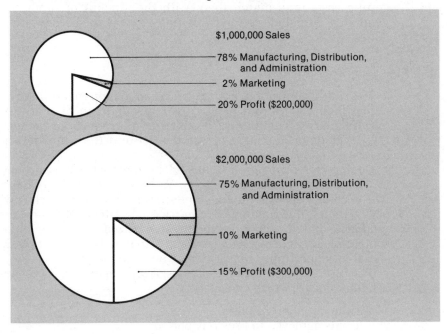

EXHIBIT 9–4

Impact of Variations in Expense Ratios

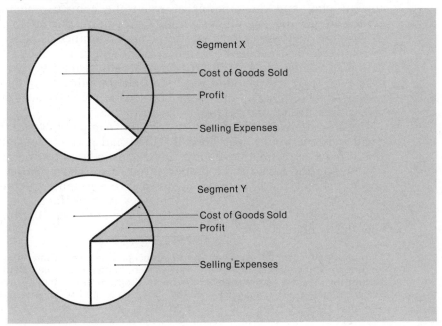

passes both the managers' responsibility for revenues and their responsibility for costs. In other words, the only way to evaluate order-getting costs is to match them with the amount of profit they have generated. We shall use most of this chapter to see how this can be done.

The Plan as a Profit Standard

Marketing control reports are designed to help marketing managers adjust their tactics and deploy their resources to take advantage of current market conditions. To do this, they need someone to send them signals on the state of the market and the company's position in it.

Comparisons with profit plans. The most widely used benchmark for this purpose is the profit plan. We described this in Chapter 5 as both a commitment by management and a forecast of what will happen if the planned actions are carried out effectively and efficiently. Evidence that the plan is not being realized is a clear signal that something has gone wrong; evidence that it is being exceeded may signal an opportunity management ought to seize.

The profit plan is not the only possibility, however. Two alternative benchmarks are worth considering:

1. An updated profit plan.
2. Profits achieved in previous periods.

Comparisons with updated plans. Conditions do change and forecasts do turn out to be wrong. To get around this problem, the accountant might compare actual profits with two benchmarks—the current plan and the amount of profit the company *should have earned* under the conditions actually prevailing during the period.

This two-way breakdown of the overall variance is diagrammed in Exhibit 9–5. The overall variance at the top of the diagram would help management figure out how large an adjustment to make in the cash budget, the production plan, and all the other elements linked closely to the original profit plan. The second comparison would provide a measure of management's performance.

Unfortunately, to make this work, the company would have to decide what it would have done if it had had perfect foresight. This would require a whole new budgeting cycle, focused on the past, and no one has the time or the money to do this.[1] The accountant can, however, break the total variance down into a number of component parts, representing the effects of changes in such factors as selling prices, product mix, and sales volume. We shall see in Chapter 25 how this is done.

---

[1] For a pioneering effort to apply this concept to an operation in which the condition-result relationships were fairly well known, see Joel Demski, "An Accounting System Structured on a Linear Programming Model," *Accounting Review*, October 1967, pp. 701–12, and "Predictive Ability of Alternative Performance Measurement Models," *Journal of Accounting Research*, Spring 1969, pp. 96–115.

EXHIBIT 9–5

Two-Way Profit Comparisons

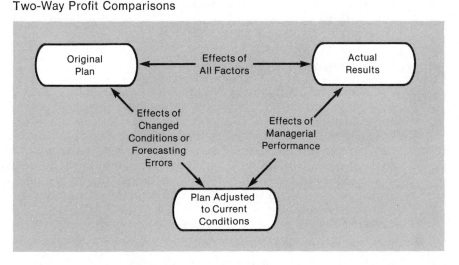

Prior year comparisons. Some managers prefer comparisons with actual results in some previous period or periods, usually the identical period of the preceding year. Probably the main reason for this is that the past is a known quantity, whereas planned results are always a guess. Comparing this year with last year therefore seems to give a more solid measure of progress than any comparison with the plan.

We have strong reasons for urging that historical comparisons be used mainly at the planning stage, not in control reporting. First, other interlocking activities are predicated on the activities and results embodied in the current plan. If results follow the plan, then no adjustments need be made in these other activities, no matter what the comparisons with last year or last month show.

The second argument against prior year comparison reporting is that last year's experience may be totally irrelevant under this year's conditions.

Item. Automobile sales in the United States in the first quarter of 1975 were up by large percentages over their 1974 levels. This didn't mean that 1975 sales were good; it merely emphasized how bad 1974 had been, and that was no news to anyone.

Item. Profits reported by the major oil companies in 1975 were much lower than in 1974. This didn't mean that 1975 was a bad year; it simply meant that the phenomenal 1974 results were a poor basis for evaluating performance in 1975.

As we have already seen, the profit plan is not a perfect benchmark for profit reporting, but it has two advantages. First, it reflects a set of interrelated decisions that management presumably has been implementing. Thus it means more than a set of past results which no one is using to guide his or her current actions. Second, it represents a managerial commitment, and management has the right to know how well that commitment is being met. Use of prior period comparisons diverts attention from these commitments and dilutes whatever motivational impact they may have.

PROFIT CONTRIBUTION REPORTING

Control reports in marketing are issued to the managers responsible for specific marketing segments. In deciding how to report profits to these managers, the accountant must try to reconcile two partially conflicting objectives. One is to identify all the costs and revenues *attributable* to a given set of marketing activities, to help management make decisions affecting these activities. The other is to identify the costs and revenues *controllable* by particular marketing managers to help them and their superiors evaluate their performance.

EXHIBIT 9–6

Dividing the Segment Revenue Dollar

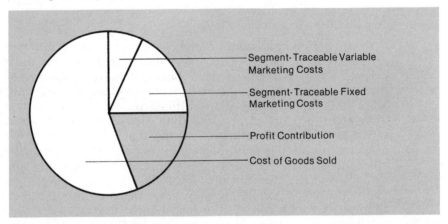

The usual solution doesn't do either of these things perfectly. It is to report profit contribution, the amount *traceable* to the specific marketing segment in question. Exhibit 9–6 illustrates the relationship between segment revenues and profit contribution. In the rest of this section we shall see how profit contribution reports can be used, how they relate to attributable profit, and how they can be tied into the controllability criterion.

The Case for Profit Contribution Reporting

The main advantage of the profit contribution approach is that it eliminates arbitrary, potentially misleading cost allocations. It gives marketing managers a clearer picture of the impact of their decisions on company profit than segment net income and doesn't saddle them with charges for things that don't concern them.

For example, suppose a branch is charged 20 percent of sales for divisional and corporate administrative services. The branch manager is comparing two possible ways of deploying the branch's sales force. One strategy will expand sales of product A, the other will sacrifice A for sales of B. Product A has a higher price but a lower contribution margin per unit than product B. The manager makes the following comparison:

	First Strategy	Second Strategy
Sales...............................	$1,000	$800
Cost of goods sold....................	650	480
Contribution margin................	$ 350	$320
Branch expenses.....................	80	80
Profit contribution..............	**$ 270**	**$240**
Allocated expenses..................	200	160
Income before taxes...............	$ 70	$ 80

The allocation makes the second strategy appear better, even though the first strategy will produce a much larger total profit contribution. The first strategy is clearly superior to the second.

Reporting Attributable Profit

This argument for profit contribution reporting has one major flaw. It ignores the effects of the segment's activities on costs that are not traceable to it. Management may wish to show these effects in the segment profit reports.

The profit figure meeting this specification is *attributable profit,* the amount of the firm's income contributed directly by this segment. It is calculated by deducting from profit contribution estimates of the nontraceable costs that could be eliminated, in time, if the company were to withdraw from the segment and reduce its capacity accordingly. As we saw in Chapter 8, any cost that could be eliminated, in time, by withdrawing from a segment is an attributable cost of that segment.

To get attributable profit, we must allocate some of the nontraceable costs. These allocations fall into the three classes we first identified in Chapter 8:

1. *Usage charges.*   For measurable services specifically used to support the segment's activities.
2. *Activity charges.*   For costs that, though nontraceable, are likely to vary with changes in the volume of activity in the segment.
3. *Capacity charges.*   For the amount of nontraceable fixed costs that could be eliminated if the company were to withdraw from the segment and reduce operating capacity accordingly.

Many companies try to approximate attributable profit by allocating *all* nontraceable costs to segments. To do this, they can't avoid making some allocations for which no clear cost-activity relationships can be found. Allocating the marketing vice president's salary among the various product lines, for example, is likely to be a job for a meta-physicist, not an accountant. If allocations of this kind are numerous, segment net profit becomes meaningless.

Although we believe we have a clear conceptual basis for calculating attributable profit, we have some misgivings about suggesting that it be included in routine profit reports. The attributable portion of nontraceable fixed costs is difficult to estimate for routine profit reporting. Crude approximations may cast a cloud of doubt on the whole reporting system. Our vote, therefore, is to go no further than usage charges, allocating other nontraceable costs only as part of special profitability studies, aimed at specific managerial decisions.

Reporting Controllable Profit

The second flaw in using profit contribution to measure marketing performance is that it may not be fully consistent with the controllability criterion. Some costs may be fully traceable but not controllable at all. Some may be controllable but not fully traceable.

We have four ways of dealing with these problems:

1. *Exclude noncontrollable costs from the profit report.* Management is likely to reject this because it would make the reports less useful in evaluating the segment's activities as a whole. We'll discuss this at length in Chapter 24.

2. *Use predetermined charges.* In other words, report all cost elements but report the noncontrollable elements at their budgeted amounts. This is a useful solution for any cost that is totally non-controllable, such as property taxes.

3. *Report the items, with variances, as noncontrollable.* This is the usual solution. Higher management must be careful to remember, however, that variances "below the line" are noncontrollable.

4. *Use predetermined input prices.* This should be adopted when input quantities are controllable but input prices are not. We made this suggestion in Chapter 8 in connection with cost allocations. It is just as valid for such items as the cost of goods sold. When the marketing manager has no control over the prices of the merchandise sold, the cost of goods sold should be measured at budgeted prices. In a manufacturing company, this usually means standard costs. Factory cost variances shouldn't be charged to marketing segments unless they clearly result from specific marketing activities.

Marketing managers should be charged for variances that arise because they mark orders for rush service or submit design changes after production operations have begun. Unfortunately, these are difficult to separate from variances due to other causes, and the marketing manager can always claim that they should have been much smaller. The best solution is to calculate the charge in advance. If this is done, the marketing managers will know what they are getting into when they ask for special treatment. The cost can then be classified as controllable.

Measuring the Cost of Goods Sold at Full Cost

In discussing contribution margin in Chapter 4, we suggested that only variable manufacturing costs be used to measure the cost of goods sold. Some internal profit reporting systems do this; others use full manufacturing cost. One reason full cost is used is that top management wants to keep its variable cost figures to itself. Another is that it wants its own marketing managers to develop only those markets they can sustain profitably on a continuing basis.

A possible compromise solution is to use a so-called two-part tariff —that is, measure product cost at standard variable cost but charge each marketing segment a flat fee to cover the costs of a certain portion of manufacturing capacity, as in the third column of Exhibit 9–7.

EXHIBIT 9–7

Alternative Measures of Cost of Goods Sold

	Cost of Goods Sold at Variable Cost	Cost of Goods Sold at Full Cost	Cost of Goods Sold at Variable Cost Plus Capacity Charge
Sales..............................	$100	$100	$100
Cost of goods sold....................	55	70	55
Contribution margin................	$ 45	$ 30	$ 45
Less: Traceable selling expenses......	20	20	20
Factory capacity charge...........	—	—	15
Profit contribution....................	$ 25	$ 10	$ 10

The two-part tariff is worth more attention than it usually gets, and we'll spend more time on it in Chapter 26. Our point here is that the profit contribution approach can be used no matter whether product cost is measured at variable cost or at full cost. The essential feature of profit contribution reporting is the absence of arbitrary allocations of outside support costs.

A REPORTING SYSTEM

Probably the best way to understand what we have been talking about and to raise one or two other issues is to see how one company's system works. Ormsby, Inc., a diversified manufacturer of plastic films and powders, chemicals, food products, and industrial textiles, has a typical reporting system for a company of its size. The company is organized in four major product divisions, as shown in the upper part of Exhibit 9–8. The division managers have extensive authority over the selection, design, manufacture, and marketing of their divisions' products.

EXHIBIT 9–8

ORMSBY, INC.
Division Structure

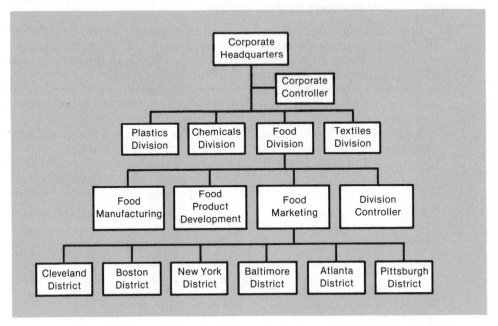

The lower half of Exhibit 9–8 shows part of the internal structure of one of these divisions, the Food Division. We shall examine four aspects of this division's reporting system:

1. The reports issued to the district managers.
2. The reports prepared for the general sales manager.
3. The reports received by the division's product managers.
4. Possible improvements in the measurement system.

Base Level Profit Reports

Each of the district sales managers in this division receives a set of profit reports each month. The district-wide summary report for the Boston district is shown in Exhibit 9–9. Four features of this report should be noted:

1. The report is limited to the district's profit contribution. No charge is made for corporate or divisional overhead costs.
2. The report emphasizes deviations from the profit plan.
3. Cost of sales is measured at standard cost.
4. The district has no variable costs other than the standard cost of goods sold.

A glance at this report will tell the district manager that the actual sales volume was $514,000, that this produced a gross margin $8,000

EXHIBIT 9–9

FOOD DIVISION
District Profit Report

DISTRICT SALES AND EXPENSE SUMMARY				
District: Boston				Month: March
	Budget	Actual	Deviation	Actual % of Sales
Net sales billed	$500,000	$514,000	$14,000	100.0
Standard cost of sales	280,000	286,000	(6,000)	55.6
Contribution margin	$220,000	$228,000	$ 8,000	44.4
District operating expenses:				
Branch salaries	$ 2,800	$ 2,800	—	0.5
Sales salaries	25,200	25,900	(700)	5.0
Travel	7,900	6,800	1,100	1.3
Entertainment	800	1,300	(500)	0.2
Local advertising	1,000	1,000	—	0.1
Storage and delivery	6,500	6,800	(300)	1.4
Branch office expense	700	1,100	(400)	0.2
Other	100	300	(200)	0.1
Total district operating expenses	$ 45,000	$ 46,000	$(1,000)	8.9
District profit contribution	$175,000	$182,000	$ 7,000	35.4

larger than the profit plan called for, and that the district profit contribution for the month was $7,000 greater than its profit objective. It also shows that most of the costs of running the branch exceeded the budgeted figures for the month, and some of these variances may have needed investigation.

Summary profit charts. Nonaccountants often find columns of figures tedious. Even some accountants don't like them. One way to avoid this reaction is to present reports containing only information management is likely to find significant. The report in Exhibit 9–9, for example, could be replaced by one containing only actual sales, actual profit contribution, the total deviation from the planned district profit contribution, and details on any variances large enough to deserve management's attention. The rest of the spaces would be blank. The computer can be programmed to exclude any variances smaller than predetermined amounts or percentages.

Another possibility is to use charts instead of tables. Exhibit 9–10 shows one way the Boston district's performance might be diagrammed. This shows the current month's performance (better than the plan) as well as the performance for previous months and the cumulative performance for the year to date (poorer than planned performance). Most tabular reports also present cumulative data, but we omitted them from Exhibit 9–9 for lack of space. Including them

EXHIBIT 9–10

FOOD DIVISION
District Profit Report

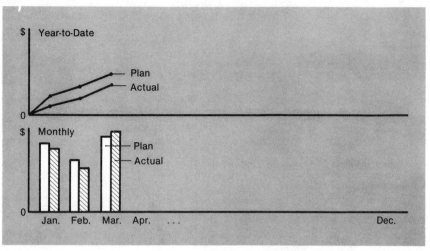

doubles the number of figures in the report and makes finding the significant items more difficult.

Sales force performance reports.   Districtwide totals fail to give the district manager any explanation of the sources of the main deviations from the profit plan. For this reason, the accountant might prepare another report like the one in Exhibit 9–11. This shows the five items traceable to individual salespeople—sales, cost of goods sold, sales salaries, travel and entertainment—and calculates the deviation from planned profit performance for each sales representative.

Charging the sales representatives with the direct expenses of their own operations, as in this report, is a very useful feature. Kelly, for example, sold $4,000 more than Williams but when all the costs traceable to these sales were deducted, Kelly's profit contribution was $800 less than Williams's. Kelly more than met the planned profit contribution, though, while Williams and three others fell short of theirs.

Product-line reports.   Since some products or services are usually more profitable than others, an essential feature of the profit plan is usually an estimate of the product mix, as we saw in Chapter 5. The packaging division has three product lines—White Shield, Red Label, and Commercial. The White Shield line has a much larger contribution margin than the other two. Management quite naturally is interested in how well the product mix holds up in the market.

Exhibit 9–11 gave the district manager no information on product mix, but Exhibit 9–12 does. The Red Label line was much poorer than had been planned, down $50,000 in sales and $11,000 in profit contribution. Both the White Shield and the Commercial lines showed improvements, however, and the overall effect was a substantial gain in the quality of the product mix.

EXHIBIT 9–11

FOOD DIVISION
District Sales Report

SALES FORCE PERFORMANCE SUMMARY						
District: Boston					Month: March	
Sales Representatives	Net Sales Billed	Standard Cost of Sales	Salary and Direct Expenses	Profit Contribution		
				Amount	Budget Deviation	% of Sales
Brown	$ 40,000	$ 21,900	$ 2,500	$ 15,600	$ (800)	39.0
Cannon	31,000	18,300	3,200	9,500	(1,900)	30.6
Evars	63,000	32,000	4,300	26,700	3,700	42.4
Johnson	30,000	18,100	2,900	9,000	(2,400)	30.0
Kelly	54,000	30,600	4,200	19,200	400	35.6
Lusso	47,000	25,800	3,100	18,100	2,800	38.5
McGregor	76,000	42,200	3,800	30,000	4,000	39.5
Nelson	55,000	31,400	3,400	20,200	1,500	36.7
Stern	68,000	38,700	3,600	25,700	2,200	37.8
Williams	50,000	27,000	3,000	20,000	(1,600)	40.0
Total	$514,000	$286,000	$34,000	$194,000	$ 7,900	37.7
General branch expenses				12,000	(900)	2.3
District profit contribution				$182,000	$ 7,000	35.4

EXHIBIT 9–12

FOOD DIVISION
District Product Line Summary

PRODUCT CONTRIBUTION REPORT						
District: Boston					Month: March	
Product Line	Net Sales Billed		Standard Cost of Sales	Other Product Expenses	Profit Contribution	
	Actual	Variance			Actual	Variance
White Shield	$204,000	$26,000	$102,000	$1,000	$101,000	$14,000
Red Label	133,000	(50,000)	77,000	—	56,000	(11,000)
Commercial	177,000	38,000	107,000	—	70,000	5,000
Total	$514,000	$14,000	$286,000	$1,000	$227,000	$ 8,000
Other branch expenses					45,000	(1,000)
District profit contribution					$182,000	$ 7,000

Notice that in this exhibit a much smaller percentage of expenses is assigned to individual segments of the district's business than in the sales force report. Sales salaries and traveling expenses are traceable to individual salespeople, but not to individual product lines. The only product-traceable district costs are the costs of local advertising for the White Shield line, amounting only to $1,000.

Reporting to the General Sales Manager

The district managers in the Food Division all report to the division's general sales manager. Managers at this level are farther removed from the day-to-day operations of individual sales branches, and therefore are less likely to be aware of problems and opportunities as they emerge. As a result, they must rely heavily on accounting reports to direct their attention in the right directions. A scorecard report for a district manager becomes a steering control device for the general sales manager.

The general sales manager's needs might be met by preparing a set of district profit contribution reports, together with a short report on the costs of operating the central office. This would have two disad-

EXHIBIT 9–13

FOOD DIVISION
Marketing Department Profit Summary

MARKETING DEPARTMENT PROFIT PERFORMANCE SUMMARY (000 omitted)			
			Month: March
	Net Sales	Profit Contribution		Contribution Margin: Ratio to Operating Expenses
		Amount	Variance	
Boston	$ 514	$ 182	$ 7	5.0
New York	946	409	25	5.9
Baltimore	472	134	(33)	3.5
Atlanta	348	109	15	3.6
Pittsburgh	588	197	3	4.1
Cleveland	627	210	(2)	4.6
Total	$3,495	$1,241	$15	
Central marketing expense:				
Administration		$ 40	$ 1	
Market research		26	(1)	
Advertising		103	10	
Other		23	(3)	
Total		$ 192	$ 7	
Profit contribution		$1,049	$22	

vantages. First, important figures might be lost in a welter of detail. Second, the general sales manager might be tempted to run individual branches by remote control, undermining the authority and motivation of the district managers.

The usual solution is to give the middle manager a more condensed set of reports. One such report is illustrated in Exhibit 9–13. Again the profit contribution format is used. Each district's results are summarized on a single line. Net sales, profit contribution, and the variance in profit contribution for each branch are taken directly from the District Sales and Expense Summary, illustrated for the Boston district in Exhibit 9–9. The ratio of the district's total contribution margin to its operating expenses is also calculated from this report. For the Boston district, total contribution was $228,000 and district operating expenses totaled $46,000, for a 5.0 ratio.

General selling expenses for the marketing department as a whole and the costs of administering the general sales manager's office are grouped together in the lower half of the departmental report, but are not charged to individual districts. The bottom line in Exhibit 9–13 shows the amounts left to cover divisional and corporate overheads and to provide a profit for the company.

Reporting to the Product Manager

Marketing management often has a two-way organization structure. The sales force has a geographical structure, with branch managers, regional managers, and a headquarters sales manager. These managers have direct responsibility for building and maintaining the company's market position, getting customer orders, and keeping informed on what customers and competitors are doing. So far, all of our discussion of Ormsby's reporting system has related to the needs of these managers.

This structure may be all the company needs, particularly if it sells only a few products and if the differences from region to region are more important than the differences between one product market and another. When the characteristics of individual products are extremely important, however, and the company can't afford to set up a separate sales force for each, management may appoint *product managers*, one for each major product or group of products handled by the common sales force. For example, Ormsby's Food Division has three product managers, working out of division headquarters, each responsible for one of the division's three product lines. Their position in the organization is diagrammed in Exhibit 9–14.

The reason for having product managers is to give the company's operations a program orientation, so that product design, manufacturing, and marketing will be seen as an integrated whole rather than as separate, independent activities. The product managers are expected to come up with marketing plans for their products, dealing with such matters as package design, distribution channels, advertising, pricing, and promotional tactics. They are also expected to do everything they can to see that the plan is carried out and that its goals are achieved.

EXHIBIT 9–14

FOOD DIVISION
Product Managers

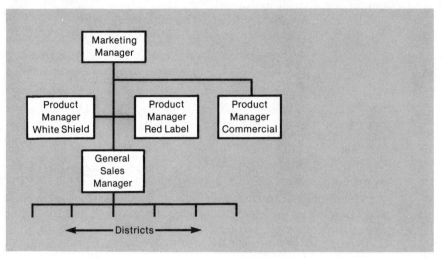

Product managers are in a very peculiar position to do all this. They have no direct authority over the sales force, but they are responsible for developing the market for the product or products under their wings. They have no authority over the production manager, but they have to see to it that their products come out of the factory on time, in the right quantities, and at the right quality. Anyone who can do all this well under these conditions is likely to go far.

Each product manager in the Ormsby Food Division gets monthly profit contribution reports like the one in Exhibit 9–15. White Label sales were well ahead of plan everywhere but in Baltimore. The favorable profit variances were about half as big as the sales variances everywhere except in Cleveland. The product manager would probably concentrate on these two districts to see why performance was out of line.

INTERPRETING MARKETING RESULTS

Evaluating marketing performance requires a great deal of insight into the market and the marketing process. The accounting reports can help the marketing manager identify important behavioral patterns. We need to devote a few paragraphs to three aspects of this task:

1. Identifying marketing response functions.
2. The importance of time lags.
3. The analysis of marketing ratios.

EXHIBIT 9–15

FOOD DIVISION
Product Manager's Summary Report

PRODUCT LINE SUMMARY (000 omitted)					
Product Line: White Label				Month: March	
	Sales		Local Product Expenses	Profit Contribution	
	Actual	Variance		Actual	Variance
Boston	$ 204	$ 26	$ 1	$101	$ 14
New York	589	85	4	307	41
Baltimore	126	(22)	—	60	(17)
Atlanta	162	58	1	81	29
Pittsburgh	264	63	2	135	30
Cleveland	274	79	2	142	29
Total	$1,619	$289	$10	$826	$126
Product management expenses:					
Administration				$ 12	—
Advertising				48	—
Total				$ 60	—
Profit contribution				$766	$126

Marketing Response Functions

The Food Division's profit contribution reports do very little to help the marketing managers identify a set of relationships that they would probably find more useful than any other information the accounting system might provide. These relationships are known as *marketing response functions,* the underlying relationships among marketing inputs, sales, and profits.

Ormsby's accountants make some effort to provide response function information. The ratios in the right-hand column of Exhibit 9–13 are intended to reflect the sensitivity of contribution margin to marketing effort in each district. For example, the contribution margin in New York was 5.9 times the operating expenses of the New York district. In other words, a dollar spent in New York brought in $5.90 of contribution margin, on the average, while a dollar in Baltimore produced only $3.50.

If the general sales manager were to interpret these figures literally, more money would be spent in Boston and New York and less in Baltimore and Atlanta. Unfortunately, the ratios in the table are averages, not increments. What the manager would really like to know is what would happen if the company spent a little more in New York, or what would happen if it spent less in Baltimore.

EXHIBIT 9–16

A Simple Marketing Response Function

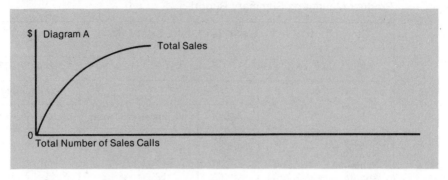

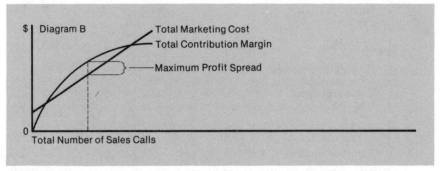

This information is difficult to generate because the marketing response functions are likely to be nonlinear. To get volume, the company has to find new customers or get its present customers to buy more. This costs money. The bigger the share of the market it already has, the harder it has to work to increase it. Each additional percentage point of market share will cost more than the one before, either through additional marketing expenditures or through direct or indirect price reductions.

Diagram A in Exhibit 9–16, for example, shows one possible response function, reflecting a simple relationship between the number of calls made on potential customers and the total volume of sales. Sales increase as the number of calls is increased, but the sales increment gets smaller and smaller as customer offices get more and more saturated with visiting salespeople.

This information would be extremely valuable to management. By combining it with estimates of the contribution margin from sales and of the cost of increasing the number of calls, as in diagram B, management could determine the optimal number of calls to be made.

One way to get information on marketing response functions is to experiment. New consumer products, for example, are almost always launched in test markets before being placed in national distribution. Sales in these markets can be measured and the margins compared with the costs of marketing. Mail-order houses are even more ideally situated to identify response functions. Many of their sales can be traced back to specific mail lists and even to specific mailings or catalogs.

Even in these cases, however, most of the information reflects average relationships. It shows what a given set of marketing inputs have produced, not how many sales were obtained for each additional dollar of marketing effort.

Another possible approach is to relate the *change* in contribution margin from one period to another to the changes in marketing inputs. A comparison for the Boston district might show the following:

	Period 1	Period 2	Change
Contribution margin........	$228	$273	+$45
Selling expenses..........	46	56	+ 10
Response ratio............	5.0	4.9	4.5

These data must be interpreted very cautiously. Many conditions change from one period to another, and the change in contribution margin is the net result of many of these changes, not just one.

A final difficulty is that response functions are very complex. The effect of spending on samples depends not only on the total number of samples provided but also on the accompanying program for advertising the product and calling on customers. It also depends on the actions competitors take. A direct competitor who starts distributing reduced-price coupons will make Ormsby's sales less responsive to its own marketing efforts.

Time Lags

Sales/expense and contribution margin/expense ratios may be misleading for another reason, too. Promotional effort is often made before the company recognizes the revenues it leads to. Sometimes this is due to a time lag between effort and results (orders); sometimes it is due to a time lag between results and accounting recognition of these results (revenues). These lags are illustrated in Exhibit 9–17.

EXHIBIT 9–17

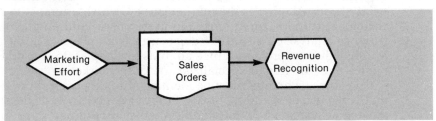

Most accounting systems are content to overlook these time lags, trusting in the good judgment of marketing executives and top management to make due mental allowances when reviewing reported results. Another possibility is to recognize revenues for internal reporting purposes on the basis of orders received, no matter what basis is used for external reporting. This would not solve the problem raised by the first kind of time lag, but it would adjust for the second.

The main obstacle to this solution is its cost. It requires entries in the factory ledger when the orders come in and another set of entries in the general ledger later on, when revenues are recognized. If the lag is short and stable, the extra cost probably isn't worthwhile.

Ratio Analysis

The study of marketing response functions is a particularly sophisticated type of ratio analysis. A number of simpler ratios are also available, and many marketing managers use these to help them understand what is going on. Some typical ratios and what they are supposed to represent are:

Ratio	Intended Meaning
Sales/calls	Response function
Contribution margin/calls	Response function
Selling expenses/sales	Response function
Sales/orders	Sales efficiency
Calls/days	Sales effort
Travel expense/days	Cost consciousness

None of these is more than a crude approximation of what it is supposed to measure. None is likely to be very useful by itself. Their main value is in helping management identify important patterns, and for this it is the overall picture that is important rather than the absolute size of any one ratio. For example, one sales representative may have a high cost per call and few calls per day but a much larger sales volume and a higher profit contribution than others on the sales force have. If the sales territories are comparable, this may indicate the greater effectiveness of a policy of selective selling.

SECONDARY CONTROL TECHNIQUES

Marketing managers have many other tools to help them keep abreast of the markets they operate in. One of these is sales analysis, the study of orders received to determine who is buying what and by what means. Another is the market survey, which attempts to identify customer attitudes, intentions, and preferences. Still another is profit variance analysis, the study of departures from planned profit results. We shall discuss profit variance analysis in Chapter 25; the other techniques must be left to specialized works in marketing.

One other technique must be mentioned at this point, however, and that is the use of spending limits. Profit variance analysis doesn't give the manager much help in judging whether subordinates are spending money unproductively. Were the increases in travel and entertainment costs necessary to serve the market, or was the sales force living it up at the company's expense? By setting spending limits in advance, the marketing manager hopes to avoid having to try to answer these questions.

Spending limits are useful, but they are difficult to establish and enforce, mainly because these costs depend so heavily on the specific market situation. Hotel room prices, for example, may vary as much as $20 or $30 from one city to another. In the small organization, managers can cope with these differences on an individual basis, relying on their own judgment of their subordinates to identify unproductive outlays. The large organization, however, is likely to use formulas for this purpose, simply because it has too many employees to deal with each one individually.

Formulas are probably necessary, but they do create problems. Even if allowances are made for differences in costs from territory to territory—and many large organizations try to make such allowances—the adjustment process is usually slow. It is very difficult, probably impossible, to develop formulas that everyone will accept as fair.

SUMMARY

Marketing costs can be divided into order-getting costs, order-filling costs, and administrative costs. Order-filling costs are responsive costs, much like manufacturing costs. Order-getting costs are programmed costs, controlled primarily by the profit-oriented decisions that set them up in the first place and adjust them in the light of information flowing to management while the programs are in force. Administrative costs are incurred to support the other two.

Reports to marketing managers contain many kinds of information. Much of this information describes what customers and competitors are doing, who is buying which products, and so on. The main financial reports are likely to be profit contribution reports, identifying the amount of profit traceable to individual marketing segments. Since order-getting costs do not vary as a result of fluctuations in volume, the profit contribution reports must replace standard costs and flexible budgets as the primary means of conveying cost control information. Profit contribution reports give marketing managers a picture of the effects of their marketing decisions, unobscured by the frequently arbitrary cost allocations necessary to derive net profit.

Profit contribution reports may focus on individual responsibilities or individual product lines or programs. Most reporting systems are pyramidal, with marketing executives at successively higher levels receiving reports that are more and more condensed. Marketing managers may try to identify marketing response ratios from these reports in an attempt to direct marketing resources where they can be used most profitably. They may also use various ratios to gain additional insight into what is going on, but in the final analysis they must place their main reliance on their knowledge of the market and of their own segments' profit performance.

KEY TERMS

The most important terms introduced and defined in this chapter are the following:

Attributable profit   Order-filling cost
Controllable profit   Order-getting cost
Marketing response function   Product manager
Marketing segment

INDEPENDENT STUDY PROBLEM
(Solution in Appendix C)

1. Profit contribution reporting. The Talcott Company manufactures and sells two products. It has one factory, and all departments perform production operations on both products.

Each month a report is prepared summarizing the profit performance of each product. A similar set of reports is prepared for individual sales districts. The marketing vice president uses these reports to evaluate the performance of the branch managers and the two product managers and to monitor progress toward achievement of the goals of the current marketing plan. Major variances signal the presence of problems or opportunities to be investigated.

The marketing manager is concerned with product A at the moment. Sales are up but profit is down, as the following report for last month shows:

	Budget	Actual	Variance
Cost of goods sold (at standard).........	$350	$385	$(35)
Factory cost variances...................	4	22	(18)
Sales commissions......................	10	11	(1)
Delivery expenses......................	14	16	(2)
Product advertising.....................	11	11	—
Sales salaries..........................	8	10	(2)
Other marketing expenses..............	12	15	(3)
Administrative expenses................	9	12	(3)
Total expenses...................	$418	$482	
Net sales.............................	500	550	50
Income before taxes..............	$ 82	$ 68	$(14)

You have the following additional information:

1. All of the company's operating expenses are distributed to one product or the other each month.

2. The budgeted amounts in the monthly reports are the amounts budgeted at the beginning of the year, not flexible budget allowances.

3. Approximately $290 of the budgeted standard cost of goods sold for product A was regarded as proportionally variable with volume. None of the fixed factory overhead is traceable to individual products.

4. The budgeted cost of goods sold for product A included $250 in standard direct labor and materials and $100 in standard factory overhead cost. The budget called for product B to absorb $150 in factory overhead costs. Budgeted sales equaled budgeted production in both lines, and no volume variance was budgeted.

5. Last month, manufacture of product A absorbed $110 in factory over-

head, while product B absorbed only $90. The total factory overhead volume variance for the month was $30, unfavorable. Other factory variances totaled $10, none of them traceable to an individual product.

6. Factory cast variances are assigned to the two products in proportion to their standard costs of goods sold.

7. Sales commissions and delivery expenses are regarded as proportionally variable with sales.

8. Product advertising costs are traceable to the individual products.

9. Sales salaries, other marketing expenses, and administrative expenses are allocated in proportion to sales volume.

a. Develop a profit contribution statement for product A for last month, showing both actual and budgeted figures.
b. Should any portion of the volume variance be assigned to product A?
c. Would your answer to (b) differ if you found that management insisted on retaining the full costing format?
d. What changes would you suggest in the methods of allocating nontraceable costs to individual products, again assuming that management insists on full allocation?
e. Comment on product A's profit performance last month. Does the product need top management's attention?

EXERCISES AND PROBLEMS

1. Profit performance standard. The marketing vice president was looking at the following report for one of the sales branches:

	Budget	Actual	Variance
Sales.....................................	$1,000	$1,100	$100
Cost of goods sold....................	$ 600	650	(50)
Management salaries.................	40	40	—
Sales salaries.........................	70	75	(5)
Advertising............................	20	25	(5)
Delivery................................	30	40	(10)
Rent.....................................	10	10	—
Total expense..................	$ 770	$ 840	
Profit contribution..................	$ 230	$ 260	$ 30

"It looks good to me," the vice president said, "but I wonder whether it's as good as it should be. I wonder if we could apply flexible budgeting here."

Prepare a response to the vice president's suggestion, illustrating your answer with figures from the branch sales report.

2. Controlling travel expenses with a budget. The travel expense budget for the Winchell Company's New Orleans branch amounts to $8,500. It is now the last month of the fiscal year, and $8,473 has already been charged to New Orleans branch travel expense. Travel expense vouchers received from the New Orleans branch manager in this morning's mail amount to $286.

a. As controller of the company, would you refuse to honor the vouchers, notify the president, ask the branch manager for an explanation, charge the amount in excess of budget to another account that has an unexpended balance, or take some other action?

b. If the New Orleans branch manager had consulted you at the beginning of the month, before the travel expenses had been incurred, what action would you have taken?

3. Interpreting a profit contribution report. The marketing vice president of a consumer goods company received the following summary report on the operations in the company's sales regions last month (in thousands of dollars):

	Sales		Profit Contribution	
	Amount	Over/(Under) Budget	Amount	Over/(Under) Budget
Atlanta....................	$ 680	$ 40	$182	$ 12
Boston....................	440	(20)	118	8
Chicago...................	420	(80)	92	(18)
Dallas....................	240	—	42	22
Denver....................	180	(60)	20	—
Los Angeles..............	580	(20)	132	12
New Orleans..............	280	(20)	36	(12)
New York.................	760	(40)	220	2
Pittsburgh................	340	(60)	48	(32)
Seattle...................	260	(60)	50	(30)
Total..............	$4,180	$(320)	$940	$(36)

The marketing manager's own performance is judged on the division's success in reaching budgeted goals. Another aspect of performance is the manager's success in directing sales efforts where they will do the most good. Central marketing division expenses amounted to $340,000 last month and another $190,000 was spent on central administrative and research activities. As the marketing vice president has said, "it's the bottom line that counts."

a. Calculate the profit contribution/sales ratio for each region.
b. How would you expect the marketing vice president to use this report? What significant facts does it reveal? Which regions seem to be the strongest? Which are the weakest?

4. Attributable profit and controllable profit. The following monthly profit contribution report was received by the manager of the Marston Company's Memphis branch:

	Budget		Actual		Variance
Sales......................		$200		$205	$ 5
Expenses:					
Cost of goods sold.................	$125		$130		(5)
Sales salaries......................	10		10		—
Other salaries.....................	5		5		—
Travel............................	2		3		(1)
Advertising.......................	6		9		(3)
Depreciation......................	2		2		—
Property taxes.....................	3		5		(2)
Insurance.........................	1		2		(1)
Utilities..........................	1	155	1	167	—
Profit contribution....................		$ 45		$ 38	$(7)

You have the following additional information:

1. Salaries, insurance, and advertising expenditures are determined in the head office, not at the branch.
2. The branch office building was reassessed earlier in the year, resulting in a substantial increase in property taxes.
3. The head office investigates credit, prepares bills and payrolls, and collects the amounts due from customers. The cost of performing these activities for the Memphis branch and its customers is $6.

a.   Using this information, distinguish among controllable profit, profit contribution, and attributable profit. Prepare a profit report reflecting the concept of controllable profit.
b.   Comment on the performance of the Memphis branch. What seems to have happened?

5. Profit contribution statements: Product profitability.   Stream and Fall, Inc. has two products, known by the trade names Slip and Slide. Slide was introduced several years ago to compete on a price basis in a mass market, leaving Slip to serve customers interested in a product of high quality and willing to pay for it.

The original forecasts called for Slide's sales to reach 300,000 units a month this year. This year's budget established a more modest objective of 250,000 units a month. Actual volume was only 200,000 units last month, while sales of Slip were at their budgeted level of 50,000 units. At this volume, revenues don't even cover costs.

Management has asked you to study the desirability of dropping Slide. If this is done, Stream and Fall, Inc. will become a one-product company again. You have decided to begin by drawing up a profit contribution statement for each product. Because top management is not used to profit contribution statements, you want to draw them up with a section below the line for noncontrollable fixed costs. You have the following data:

1. Product data:

	Slip	Slide
Selling price	$ 5.00	$ 2.00
Manufacturing cost:		
Direct materials	$ 0.50	$ 0.30
Direct labor	1.00	0.50
Overhead	1.50	0.75
Total	$ 3.00	$ 1.55
Sales discounts and allowances (percent of gross sales)	5%	1%
Sales commission per unit	$ 0.25	$ 0.05
Advertising and other direct selling costs (per month)	$20,000	$40,000

2. The two products are manufactured in the same factory building, but on separate production lines. Each line has its own overhead rate, covering the following costs:

	Slip	Slide
Variable	$0.75	$0.30
Traceable fixed	0.60	0.30
Allocated fixed	0.15	0.15
Total	$1.50	$0.75
Volume base (units)	50,000	250,000

3. Production volume was equal to sales volume last month and there were no spending variances in factory overhead costs. Unabsorbed nontraceable factory overhead is allocated between the two products each month on the basis of the relative direct labor cost of production in that month.
4. There were no variances in direct materials and direct labor costs last month.
5. Depreciation charges account for $5,000 of Slip's traceable fixed factory overhead costs and $25,000 of Slide's. $4,000 of the nontraceable fixed factory overhead costs could be eliminated if either production line were closed down while the production line for the other product remained in operation.
6. Costs of sales promotion, general company administration, and so forth not otherwise specified above are regarded as fixed and are not traceable to either product. They amount to $78,000 a month and are allocated between the two products each month on the basis of relative gross sales dollars that month. Elimination of either product while the other product remained in the company's line would permit a reduction in these costs of $10,000 a month.
7. Sales discounts and allowances were at their normal rates last month.
8. Advertising and other direct selling costs were at their budgeted levels last month.

a. Prepare a monthly profit contribution budget for each product for the current year, including an "allocated charges" section at the bottom to bring each product down to a fully allocated income before taxes, using the company's allocation formulas.
b. Prepare a performance report for last month in a profit contribution format, using the company's absorption and allocation formulas. Report separately on each product as well as for the total of the two.
c. What does this report reveal about the performance of Slide? How would you interpret the report on Slip?
d. What additional information would management reasonably expect to have before deciding what to do about Slide?

6. Evaluating sales representatives.   Sherman Products, Inc., manufactures and sells laundry detergents, floor wax, tooth paste, and a wide variety of related products throughout the United States and Canada. To facilitate sales management, the market is divided into 12 major sales regions, each with its own regional manager. Each region is subdivided into territories, each territory being the exclusive province of a single sales representative.

The controller's staff have developed a highly detailed reporting system that most regional managers have adopted for their own use. This system focuses on monthly measurements of performance in four key areas: orders received, calls made, initial orders received, and net profit. Orders received are classified by size, measured in dollars. Calls are classified by customer group, as follows:

Group A: regular customers, annual sales volume at least $10,000.
Group B: prospects, no purchases during previous fiscal year.
Group C: regular customers, annual sales less than $10,000.

"Initial orders" are the first orders of the year from group B customers.
One of these monthly reports, for salesman Jones, is shown in the following table:

	Last Month				This Territory, Same Month Last Year
	Jones Actual		Jones, Planned	Average, All Salespeople	
	No.	Amount			
Orders received (sales):					
$ 0– 250..................	45	$ 3,000	.....	$ 3,100	.....
251– 500..................	20	7,000	.....	8,100	.....
501–1,000..................	8	6,000	.....	11,200	.....
1,001–2,000..................	4	5,000	.....	7,800	.....
2,001–5,000..................	2	8,000	.....	6,300	.....
More than $5,000..............	1	6,000	.....	3,500	.....
Total......................	80	$35,000	$32,000	$40,000	$33,000
Cost of goods sold (at standard).....		$26,000	$22,500	$28,000	$23,000
Direct expenses...................		2,200	2,250	2,300	2,100
Marketing overhead (5% of sales)...		1,750	1,600	2,000	1,650
Administrative overhead (8% of sales)........................		2,800	2,560	3,200	2,640
Net profit........................		$ 2,250	$ 3,090	$ 4,500	$ 3,610
Initial orders received..............	5	$ 1,000	$ 1,500	$ 2,500	$ 1,200
Calls made:					
Group A customers..............	30		40		25
Group B customers..............	20		20		26
Group C customers..............	50		30		45
Total Calls...................	100		90	100	96

This report goes to the regional manager, who uses it to identify ways in which Jones can improve his performance. In addition, these reports help differentiate the better sales representatives from the poorer ones.

Marketing and administrative overheads are almost entirely fixed costs.

a. Compute the following: (1) sales and expense variances for the month; (2) Mr. Jones's contribution to company profits for the month; (3) cost per call—actual and planned for Mr. Jones, all-sales representatives average, and same territory last year; (4) sales per call, as in (3); (5) profit to sales ratios, as in (3).

b. Using the figures from (a), whenever pertinent, and any others that you deem appropriate, analyze Mr. Jones's performance for the month.

7. Monitoring marketing program performance. Robinson Enterprises, Inc., shifted to a profit contribution approach to internal profit reporting several years ago. The profit contribution format is used in budgeting and in the company's monthly profit reports for individual product lines and for regional and branch offices.

The company's Western Division has three groups of products, all manufactured in a large factory located in Valejo, California. Profit contribution reports are issued monthly to the division manager, Ms. Jane Andrews. She reviews these carefully, looking for signs that changes in the marketing mix may be appropriate.

The profit contribution reports show three groups of expenses:

1. Variable costs.
2. Segment-traceable fixed costs.
3. Allocated costs.

The variable factory cost of goods sold includes direct materials (standard direct manufacturing cost, adjusted by the ratio of actual purchase prices to standard purchase prices during the month), direct labor (standard direct labor cost, adjusted by the ratio of actual wage rates to standard wage rates during the month), and standard variable factory overhead.

Nontraceable costs are allocated each month on the basis of that month's sales. They include budgeted fixed factory overhead, materials and labor quantity variances, factory overhead spending variances, and divisional selling and administrative expenses not traceable to individual product lines.

The company's main product line, known as the Premium line, has its own sales force and a substantial product-centered advertising campaign. Four months ago, at the beginning of August, Ms. Andrews put into effect a new marketing plan, calling for substantial increases in the amount of promotional effort devoted to the Premium line. The plan called for an $8 increase in monthly direct selling costs to increase sales to $160 a month, up $60 from the $100 previously planned. Seasonal factors were not important.

The expenditures were made, and results for this product were as follows:

	July	August	September	October	November
Sales revenues	$100	$100	$120	$120	$140
Variable expenses:					
Variable factory cost of goods sold	$ 55	$ 57	$ 67	$ 69	$ 77
Sales commissions	3	3	3.0	3.6	4.2
Shipping and handling	2	2	2.4	2.4	2.8
Total variable expenses	$ 60	$ 62	$ 73	$ 75	$ 84
Contribution margin	$ 40	$ 38	$ 47	$ 45	$ 56
Direct product selling costs	10	14	14	16	18
Profit Contribution	$ 30	$ 24	$ 33	$ 29	$ 38
Fixed overhead costs (allocated)	20	18	24	26	28
Income before taxes	$ 10	$ 6	$ 9	$ 3	$ 10
Order backlog (at selling prices)	$200	$220	$215	$240	$270

Noting that "Income before Taxes" has just recovered to the level prevailing just before the new plan went into effect, despite a 40 percent increase in sales volume, Ms. Andrews has asked you to analyze these figures and report back to her.

a. Prepare a brief report in response to this request, including some comment on the apparent results of the new promotional effort. You need not make a complete analysis of the numerical data, but incorporation of some numerical calculations in your report will be desirable.
b. Suggest ways of improving the profit report.

8. Monitoring marketing program performance. "I don't understand it. My sales were 10 percent higher than the budget, but I still didn't make the budgeted profit!" lamented Cathy Goldman, manager of the housewares department in a large California department store.

The report from the store's accounting department which prompted Ms. Goldman's comments is reproduced below.

	Budget	Actual	Variance
Sales.....................................	$120,000	$132,000	$12,000
Cost of goods sold......................	$ 84,000	$ 92,400	(8,400)
Salaries.................................	2,400	2,420	(20)
Employee benefits and taxes............	960	1,210	(250)
Billing and accounting..................	3,600	5,445	(1,845)
Warehousing and receiving.............	2,000	3,045	(1,045)
Occupancy charge.......................	13,750	13,875	(125)
General overhead.......................	5,800	6,400	(600)
Departmental income...................	$ 7,490	$ 7,205	($285)

The department managers have considerable responsibility, including staffing the department, selecting and ordering merchandise, setting prices, and deciding how much floor space they will use for merchandise display. Hence, the store's management believes that department managers should be responsible for the profit generated by their departments.

A number of the items in the profit statement deserve some explanation. Salaries includes the salaries of all full-time personnel in the department, including the manager. Employee benefits and taxes were budgeted as a percentage of salaries. After the budget was prepared, however, there was a change in the employee benefit plan which resulted in an increase in the percentage charge from 40 percent to 50 percent.

Billing and accounting costs are charged to the department as its share of the customer credit office's expenses. The budgeted amount was based on the assumption that 75 percent of the department's sales would be credit sales, and that the costs of running the customer credit office would be 4 percent of total credit sales. Housewares' credit sales for August were 75 percent of their total sales.

The warehousing and receiving charge is based on the average number of cubic feet of storage space in the store's warehouse used by the department. Housewares was budgeted to use 8,000 cubic feet but actually used 8,700.

The occupancy charge includes building rental, heat, light, maintenance, and property taxes. This charge is based on the square feet of floor space used by the department for merchandise display during the month. Housewares was budgeted to use 11,000 square feet during August, but actually used 11,100.

General overhead is an allocation of the costs of general store management. Costs are allocated to departments on the basis of their gross sales revenues.

a. Comment on the likely cause (or causes) of each of the variances shown in the August profit statement.
b. Do you believe that the $285 unfavorable profit variance adequately reflects Ms. Goldman's department's performance during August? Briefly defend your position.
c. How would you restructure the profit statement to provide more useful information for evaluating Ms. Goldman's efforts to control costs in her department? (You need not calculate all the numbers in this statement; just lay out its structure and explain briefly your reasons for selecting that structure.)

(Prepared by Professor Michael Ginzberg)

9. Profit contribution reporting system. A company reports income for its various product lines on a net profit basis. A full absorption costing system is used in the factory.

The company's new controller has suggested that the profits from each product line be reported on a profit contribution basis. To help management evaluate his proposal, he has measured the profit performance of one of the product lines both ways, as follows:

	Net Profit	Profit Contribution
Revenue......................................	$80,000	$80,000
Standard cost of goods sold:		
Materials.....................................	$10,000	$10,000
Labor..	21,000	21,000
Overhead....................................	18,000	6,000
Total....................................	$49,000	$37,000
Gross margin.................................	$31,000	$43,000
Other expenses:		
Variable distribution costs....................		$ 4,000
Fixed direct selling and administration costs.......................	$10,000	6,000
Allocated fixed selling and administration costs........................	9,000	—
Fixed direct factory overhead.................	—	3,000
Production volume variances.................	3,000	—
Other factory cost variances..................	1,000	—
Total other expenses....................	$23,000	$13,000
Product profit...............................	$ 8,000	$30,000

As this shows, product contribution was $22,000 greater than product net profit. The marketing vice president has expressed enthusiasm for this proposal; the president, who once served as controller, is dubious. "You're just kidding yourself," he said. "You can't just wipe out $22,000 in costs with a stroke of the pen. Those costs have to be covered somehow."

The controller countered by saying that his objective was to let marketing management see how profit responded to marketing effort and that the profit contribution report did this better than the net profit report. "For example," he said, "if sales and production volume were to increase by 25 percent, all other things being equal, the profit figure would look like this:

	Net Profit	Profit Contribution
Revenues.....................................	$100,000	$100,000
Standard cost of goods sold...................	61,250	46,250
Gross margin.................................	$ 38,750	$ 53,750
Other expenses:		
Variable distribution costs....................		$ 5,000
Fixed direct selling and administration costs.......................	$ 11,000	6,000
Allocated selling and administration costs........................	11,000	—
Fixed direct factory overhead.................	—	3,000
Production volume variances.................	2,000	—
Other factory cost variances..................	1,000	—
Total other expenses....................	$ 25,000	$ 14,000
Product profit...............................	$ 13,750	$ 39,750

"Profit contribution at this volume would be $9,750 greater than at the actual volume. Net profit would be only $5,750 greater. The $9,750 increase in profit contribution is a much better measure of the increment in company profit than the $5,750 increase in apparent net profit, because it isn't obscured by changes in the amount of fixed costs allocated to the product. We can use the profit contribution figures in deciding where we should spend our promotional dollars."

"Nonsense!" the president sputtered. "You can't make money unless all of your costs are covered. I'm only interested in the bottom line."

Draft a report to be presented to the president. You may take either side of this argument or a position at variance with both. You must support your position with a reasoned analysis, however, including an analysis of the arguments advanced by the president and controller. Your answer should consider the following questions, among others:

1. What are the objectives of profit reporting in this situation?
2. Are the controller and the president both focusing on the same objectives?
3. Would a change to profit contribution reporting lead to a better or poorer realization of those objectives? Would anything be lost in the process?

CASE 9–1: THE FEDERAL COMPANY

The Federal Company was a medium-sized manufacturer of consumer soft goods. The headquarters marketing staff in Cleveland was responsible for overall planning and direction of all marketing activities, while responsibility for field selling activities was assigned to the managers of the company's six regional branch offices.

David Halsey, Federal's marketing vice president, was experimenting with a new financial reporting format that he hoped would help him make better promotional expenditure decisions. "Our move to profit contribution reporting several years ago was a step in the right direction," he said, "but it didn't go far enough. For one thing, sales are still reported several months after the promotional activity takes place. This makes for some pretty funny profit contribution figures sometimes.

"For another, they still don't tell me whether I'm spending the right amount in each market area. For example, I was pretty sure that we were spending too much in the Atlanta branch, but I couldn't prove it. I couldn't put the squeeze on the branch manager, either, because he was turning in a larger profit contribution than any of the other branches. I want the system to help me answer this kind of question."

The new reporting system had been worked out by Jack McClendon, Federal's controller. "We made a special study," he said, "trying to find out how long it takes before promotional effort pays off. Frankly, the results aren't very clear, but they have given us something to think about. For instance, we found that calling on a customer more frequently seemed to increase the average order size as well as the total sales volume. I don't know how far we can carry that, but we're certainly going to follow up on it.

"We did find that the orders received in a month correlate pretty well with the current month's field selling and local advertising expenses. I've talked this over with Dave (Halsey) and we've agreed to report sales and cost of goods sold internally on the basis of orders received. That will mean a little more bookkeeping—the company's financial statements will still show revenues from shipments—but I think the benefits are worth it."

Mr. Halsey explained his experimental report structure to the case writer. "The main feature of these reports is that they focus on month-to-month changes rather than on departures from the budget. We still get monthly reports of variances from the profit plan for control purposes, but they don't help us much in decision making.

"Let me show you what I mean. Here is last month's report for the Atlanta branch [Table 1]. The figures in the right-hand column show the

TABLE 1

THE FEDERAL COMPANY
Profit Performance Report, Atlanta Branch (dollar figures in thousands)

	This Month	Change from Same Month Last Year
Sales (net orders received).........................	$5,000	+$450
Standard variable manufacturing cost...............	$2,010	+$181
Standard variable distribution cost..................	253	+ 22
Contribution margin...........................	$2,737	+$247
Field selling expenses.............................	$ 669	+$ 71
Local advertising..................................	523	+ 65
Administration....................................	128	+ 4
Total branch expenses.......................	$1,320	+$140
Branch Profit.....................................	$1,417	+$107
Effectiveness Ratios:		
Gross margin to sales............................	0.55	—
Field selling and advertising to sales..............	0.24	—
Branch profit to sales............................	0.28	—
Branch profit to field selling and advertising.......	1.19	0.79

changes from the same month a year ago. I'm not sure that that's the right way to go, but we felt that it would be better than a comparison of two successive months.

"Our real emphasis is on the ratios at the bottom of the report. The ratios in the left-hand column are conventional percentage figures. Every company uses these. Our big interest is in the ratio to the right, and I don't know of anyone else who calculates this one. It shows the relationship of the *change* in profit or the *change* in sales to the change that has taken place in marketing costs. We call this our 'response function.' At Atlanta, for example, we got 79 cents for every extra dollar that we spent on field selling and advertising. This is the $107,000 change in branch profit divided by the $136,000 change in field selling and advertising costs."

"That means that you didn't get your money back, doesn't it?"

"No, it's a net figure. We've already deducted the $136,000 from the profit figure, so that we're okay as long as the ratio is positive."

"I'm not sure how much good that ratio will do you," said the case writer. "A lot of other things could have happened, and you can't assume that the increase in sales was all due to the added marketing costs."

"I can't argue with you on that, but we don't take the ratios one by one. What we really want to do is compare the branches, as we do here [in Table 2]. This shows that we were wrong about Atlanta. With a profit ratio of 0.79, it is now giving us more for our added promotional dollar than we get in any other branch. In fact, we're considering spending more money in Atlanta rather than less. Seattle and Denver are at the other extreme. Both of them have negative ratios, and we may decide to cut back on our efforts there."

"I don't understand what the negative ratios mean. Why should they lead you to reduce your promotional outlays in those branches?"

"Well, look at Seattle, for instance. We put an extra $70,000 in there, but our branch profit went down by $7,000. That's a negative response to our effort. The extra $70,000 wasn't a very good investment, in my opinion."

TABLE 2

THE FEDERAL COMPANY
Branch Profit Comparison (dollar figures in thousands)

	Atlanta	Cleveland	Houston	Boston	Denver	Seattle
Results						
Sales:						
This year......................	$5,000	$4,560	$3,076	$3,249	$1,865	$2,722
Change from last year.........	+ 450	+ 333	+ 243	+ 390	− 67	+ 132
Promotional expense:						
This year......................	1,192	684	369	520	375	599
Change from last year.........	+ 136	+ 107	+ 90	+ 135	− 44	+ 70
Branch profit:						
This year......................	1,417	1,280	831	1,007	634	517
Change from last year.........	+ 107	+ 76	+ 40	+ 72	+ 5	− 7
Effectiveness Ratios						
Current period:						
Gross margin to sales.........	0.55	0.52	0.42	0.49	0.58	0.46
Promotional expenses						
to sales......................	0.24	0.18	0.12	0.16	0.20	0.22
Branch profit to sales..........	0.28	0.28	0.27	0.31	0.34	0.19
Response function (change						
in branch profit to change						
in promotional expenses)....	+0.79	+0.71	+0.44	+0.54	−0.11	−0.10

"I can understand the minus figures for Seattle, but what about Denver? There your profit actually went up."

"That's right. We spent less than last year, and we lost some business as a result—sales were down by $67,000. Fortunately, the gross margin on the lost sales was less than the amount we saved in marketing expense. That's what a negative ratio means. Whenever I see a minus sign, it tells me that I can make money by spending less on marketing. With a plus sign, I figure that the market isn't saturated yet, so I should put in a little more money. It doesn't tell me how much more or less to spend, but it gives me the direction."

"How do you allow for changes in general economic conditions? It seems to me that these could have such huge effects on the changes that your ratios would lose all their validity."

"We haven't figured out how to grapple with that one yet. One way is to deal with quarterly data instead of monthly data and compare each quarter with the one before instead of the one a year earlier. The drawback there is that seasonal influences are important in our business, and I don't think the figures would be very useful. Another possibility is to adjust the figures in some way for changes in the gross national product or some other index of the volume of business generally. Even without these changes, though, I think we can use the ratios productively. Don't forget that a change in business conditions is likely to affect all of our markets. Other things being equal, a change of this kind would produce either minus signs in all branches or plus signs in all branches. We're looking for differences, knowing that the ratios aren't precise and that all they can do is suggest directions we might want to move."

a. Do you agree that Federal should spend more money in Atlanta and less in Denver and Seattle?
b. Do you think that the new reporting system will provide Mr. Halsey with better information for decision making? What changes, if any, would you make in the system to make it more useful?

part two

Further Topics in Activity Costing and Decisions

10

Process Costing

THE METHOD used to measure the cost of a product or service (product cost) depends on the methods used to produce that product or service. Job order costing, as we saw in Chapter 2, is appropriate when individual production centers work on a number of different jobs. Process costing, on the other hand, is called for when a particular product or service is needed in large enough volumes to require the full-time use of production or service facilities for considerable periods of time.

Our objective in this chapter is to explain what process costing is and how process costing information can be used. We shall cover four topics:

1. Using process costing to calculate the costs of individual products or services.
2. Using variable costing in process production.
3. Integrating process costing calculations into the financial statements.
4. Using process costing information for control reporting.

CALCULATING PRODUCT COST

Process costing can be used either in cost estimation before production takes place or in cost measurement after the fact. In either case, the procedure for calculating or estimating product cost consists of six steps:

1. Identify the production centers.
2. Accumulate or estimate each production center's operating costs for a specified period of time.
3. Measure or estimate each production center's output for this same time period.
4. Divide cost by output to obtain average unit cost.

5. Adjust for the effects of spoilage.
6. Add the unit costs of various production centers to obtain the unit costs of individual products.

Identifying the Production Centers

Because unit cost is to be obtained by dividing cost by a single output figure, each production center's output must be homogeneous—that is, the work it does must be repetitive enough to permit production to be measured by a simple count of the number, weight, area, or volume of the units processed.

A production process may be split up into two or more production centers, all processing the same product, if they perform different kinds of operations on that product. This is typical of straight sequential processes like the one illustrated in Exhibit 10–1. Here the

EXHIBIT 10–1

Product Flows in Straight Sequential Processing

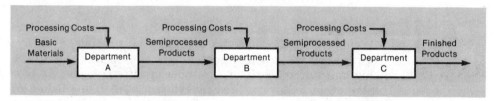

physical flows move steadily from left to right, but the work done consists of three separate operations, each requiring the exclusive use of a specific portion of the company's productive facilities. (For simplicity, the terms production center and department will be used interchangeably in this discussion.)

Recognition of separate production centers in situations like this permits management to see where costs are going up, where they are going down, and which operations are the most costly. In general, the decision of how many process centers to recognize in a given production sequence can be made on the basis of the criteria set forth in Chapter 2 for the identification of cost centers.

Production need not always flow in a single, straight-line sequence through the factory. Sequences such as those shown in Exhibit 10–2 are also fully adaptable to process costing. In the topmost panel, the output of one process center is split between two subsequent production centers for separate processing into two different products. Thus, even though the factory's output consists of two products rather than one, the output of each of the three departments is homogeneous and process costing can be used.

In the center panel, the outputs of two separate processing operations are combined in a third to yield a single product, while in the bottom panel part of the output of department B goes to department D

EXHIBIT 10–2

Product Flows in Parallel Processing

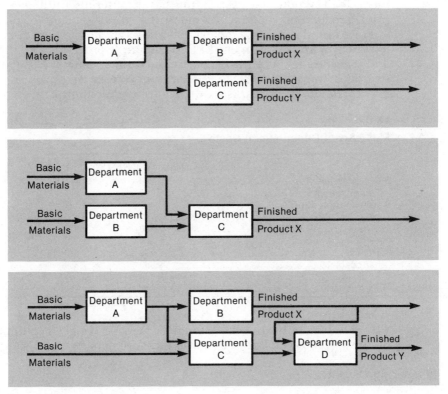

for further processing (e.g., assembly) while the rest goes into the finished stockroom (e.g., replacement parts). Process costing is applicable in all three situations; the only requirement is that output at each stage must be homogeneous.

Measuring Costs

The measurement of product cost in process costing is simpler than in job order costing. Costs need to be identified by productions center only; since each production center's output is homogeneous, this serves to identify them by product as well.

Notice that the direct materials–direct labor–overhead breakdown used in job order costing is not appropriate here. Because the product costing unit in process costing is the production center's output for a period of time, *any* cost traced to the production center can be referred to as a direct cost. The line is thus no longer between direct and indirect materials but between different classes of direct materials.

Process costing has one cost measurement problem that is not met in job order costing. Costs are transferred from production center to production center, following the flow of semifinished products through the factory. This means that the manager of one of the later departments can't know the cost of the basic materials until the costs of prior production centers are measured at the end of each period.

For example, a small factory has only two production centers, department A and department B. Department A processes raw materials and transfers its output to department B for finishing. Costs of these two departments for the month of June are summarized in Exhibit 10–3. The question marks in the right-hand column can be replaced

EXHIBIT 10–3

Summary of Departmental Costs

	Department A	Department B
Basic materials............................	$54,000	$ —
Finishing materials.........................	5,100	—
Materials from dept. A.....................	—	??
Productive labor...........................	20,700	8,700
Idle time..................................	1,800	870
Overtime premiums........................	900	870
Supplies..................................	2,700	3,480
Other costs...............................	9,900	7,830
Total...............................	$95,100	$??

with numbers only after department A's costs have been computed. To do this, we must first decide how to measure department A's output.

Measuring Output

The purpose of computing output is to get a figure that can be divided into the costs of the resources put into a production center during a particular measurement period. It should represent, therefore, the results achieved by these inputs.

Output measurement is complicated by the presence of work in process. Four situations can be distinguished:

Situation 1. The production center has no work in process either at the beginning or at the end of the measurement period. In this situation, all inputs (and therefore all costs) relate to the units *completed* during the period:

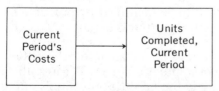

Output here must be measured by the number of units completed.

Situation 2. The production center had some work in process at the beginning of the period. Some of the inputs needed to produce some of the units completed during the period were consumed in the preceding period:

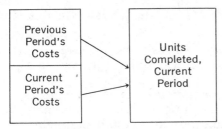

In other words, the number of units completed overstates the amount of output produced by this period's inputs. In this situation, output must be measured by the difference between the number of units completed and the amount of the work in process at the beginning of the period.

Situation 3. The production center has work in process at the end of the period but none at the beginning. The current period's inputs, in other words, created both completed and incomplete units:

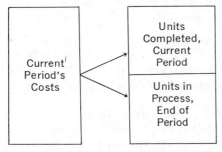

Output here must include both the number of units completed and the amount of work in process at the end of the period.

Department A was in this position in June. It started the month with no inventory in process, completed operations on 85,000 pounds of product during the month, and had 15,000 pounds of product in process at the end of the month. At first glance, the calculation of output seems easy:

Units completed.............................	85,000
Units still in process, end of month..........	15,000
Total..................................	100,000

Unfortunately, this is incorrect. The units in process are not fully equivalent to completed units because some costs will still have to be incurred to complete them in the next period. Uncompleted units, in other words, should be counted only in proportion to the percentage of the required inputs that have already been expended on them.

Department A has three kinds of inputs: basic materials, finishing materials, and processing costs. Basic materials are put in process in their entirety at the beginning of processing. Finishing materials are applied at the end of processing, just before the product is transferred to department B. Processing inputs are applied at a steady rate. For example, suppose the units in process at the end of June had been through one third of the process, on the average. In this situation, we know the following:

1. With respect to *basic materials costs*, each pound of work in process at the end of the month was fully equivalent to a pound of finished product.
2. With respect to *finishing materials costs*, units in process counted for nothing because the finishing materials had been applied only to the units completed and transferred to department B.
3. With respect to *processing costs*, each pound of work in process was equivalent to one third of a pound of finished product.

The cost divisor for basic materials costs therefore was 100,000 pounds, as calculated above, and the cost divisor for finishing materials was 85,000 pounds. The correct divisor for processing costs was 90,000 pounds:

Units completed (pounds)...............................	85,000
Equivalent units in ending inventory (⅓ of 15,000 pounds)......	5,000
Unit cost divisor (pounds)...............................	90,000

This 90,000-pound figure is also known as *equivalent production.*

In deciding how many cost divisors to use, we need to classify the production center's cost elements on the basis of their timing, as in this example. In general, two or three divisors will be adequate. Sometimes we can get by with one.

Situation 4.   The production center has work in process both at the beginning and at the end of the period. This is a combination of situations 2 and 3, and is the situation department B was in in June. This department completed work on 89,000 pounds of product during the month and transferred this amount to the finished goods warehouse. It also had 6,000 pounds of half-completed product in process at the end of the month. Unlike department A, however, department B began the month with an inventory of 10,000 pounds of product, half-processed in this department.

Department B uses two kinds of materials: (1) semifinished units received from department A; and (2) processing materials, used at a steady rate throughout the processing operation. Semifinished units are to department B what basic materials are to department A, and are often referred to as "materials." They are put into process in their entirety when department B starts its production operations. Each unit of work in process therefore contains all of these materials it will ever have. The cost divisor is obtained by adding the number of units still in process at the end of the month to the number of units completed during the month and subtracting the number of units in beginning inventory:

Units completed (pounds).......................................	89,000
Units in ending inventory (pounds).............................	6,000
	95,000
Less: Units in beginning inventory (pounds)....................	10,000
Materials cost divisor (pounds)................................	85,000

The divisor for processing costs in department B (including the costs of processing materials) is calculated in the same way, except that the inventory figures must be converted to their equivalent in finished units:

Units completed (pounds).. 89,000
Equivalent units in ending inventory (½ of 6,000 pounds)......... 3,000
                                                                 92,000
   Less: Equivalent of work done in prior period on beginning
        inventory (½ of 10,000 pounds)............................. 5,000
Equivalent production (pounds)................................. 87,000

This is actually less than the number of units completed during the month because the amount of work in process decreased between the beginning and the end of the month. Another way of stating the same thing is that equivalent production equals the number of units completed plus or minus the change in work in process.

EXHIBIT 10–4

Calculation of Equivalent Production

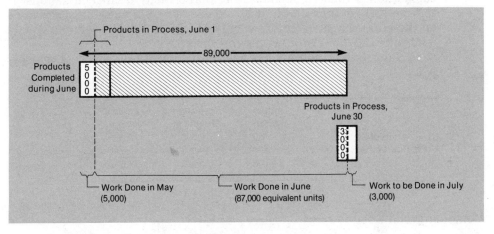

The rationale for this calculation is diagrammed in Exhibit 10–4. Of the 89,000 pounds completed during the month (upper block in the diagram), the equivalent of 5,000 pounds was actually produced during the previous month, and thus must be subtracted (unshaded area at the left of the block). This indicates that the work actually done during June on the units completed during the month was the equivalent of complete processing of 84,000 pounds of finished product (shaded area in the upper block). To this must be added the 3,000-pound equivalent of the inventory still in process at the end of the month, represented by the shaded area in the lower block of the exhibit. The total of these figures is equivalent production.

Anticipated shrinkage or growth. The calculation of cost divisors is sometimes complicated by changes in the size or form of the physical unit as it moves through a process:

> *Normal shrinkage:* a unit of work in process will yield less than a unit of finished product.

> *Normal accretion:* a unit of work in process will yield more than a unit of finished product (for example, through the addition of water).

> *Change of form:* the finished product may be measured one way (by weight or unit count, for example), in-process inventory another (by volume or length).

In any of these situations, the in-process inventories must be converted to their normal equivalent in finished units. For example, suppose a production center finishes work on 120,000 gallons of product during the month and has 40,000 gallons of semiprocessed product in process at the end of the month. Under normal circumstances, inventory at this stage is expected to shrink by 25 percent before processing is completed. The appropriate figure to enter into the output calculation is thus 75 percent of 40,000 or 30,000 finished gallons. If the company figures that half of the department's work has been done on these in-process inventories, only 15,000 equivalent gallons should enter into the divisor for processing costs.

In summary, assuming no beginning inventory, the cost divisors would be:

	Actual Gallons	Equivalent Materials	Equivalent Processing
Units completed.............	120,000	120,000	120,000
Units in process.............	40,000	30,000	15,000
Total..................	160,000	150,000	135,000

Computing Unit Cost

Calculating unit cost is a simple matter once the cost divisors have been computed. For example, department A's costs (from Exhibit 10–3) need only be divided by the divisors computed above:

	Total Cost	Divisor	Unit Cost
Basic materials.......................	$54,000	100,000	$0.54
Finishing materials...................	5,100	85,000	0.06
Productive labor......................	20,700	90,000	0.23
Idle time.............................	1,800	90,000	0.02
Overtime premiums..................	900	90,000	0.01
Supplies.............................	2,700	90,000	0.03
Other costs..........................	9,900	90,000	0.11
Total........................	$95,100		$1.00

The unit cost computation in department B is just as simple. This company charges department B at the full unit cost of $1 a pound for all products transferred to it. Once this has been done, unit costs in department B can be determined:

	Total Cost	Divisor	Unit Cost
Materials from dept. A..............	$ 85,000	85,000	$1.00
Productive labor....................	8,700	87,000	0.10
Idle time...........................	870	87,000	0.01
Overtime premiums.................	870	87,000	0.01
Supplies...........................	3,480	87,000	0.04
Other costs........................	7,830	87,000	0.09
Total........................	$106,750		$1.25

Notice that materials, labor, and other processing costs of department A are merged in a single figure in department B. To department B's manager, these are just like the costs of any other materials. If a unit is spoiled, the entire cost of that unit is lost. It doesn't matter whether prior departments' labor costs amounted to 10 percent or 90 percent of the total.

Spoilage and Waste

Few processes are so tightly conceived that all productive inputs emerge as good products ready for sale or further processing. Leakages occur through spoilage, evaporation, on-premises consumption, and other factors. Much of this leakage is unavoidable, a necessary part of the cost of producing units of good product. In standard costing systems, the standards typically allow for normal spoilage; deviations from normal show up as variances. In the absence of standard costing, one of the following two methods is usually used:

1. Adjust unit cost by spreading the cost spoiled units over all good production.
2. Identify the costs of spoiled units and report them separately.

Method 1. Adjusting unit cost for spoiled units. The easiest solution is to average the cost of lost or spoiled units into the cost of the remaining units of good product. For example, suppose department B had 10,000 pounds of product in process on January 1 and 6,000 pounds in process on January 31, half processed in each case. It received 85,000 pounds of product during June, but finished only 72,000 pounds. The remaining 17,000 pounds were spoiled, the spoilage occurring just before processing in department B was half completed. (In other words, the units in process are assumed to be subject to no further spoilage.)

The number of equivalent units of good product is calculated as follows:

	Prior Dept. Costs	Processing Costs
Units finished..........................	72,000	72,000
Work in process, January 31.............	6,000	3,000
Moving average divisors...............	78,000	75,000
Work in process, January 1..............	10,000	5,000
Equivalent production.................	68,000	70,000

The number of units spoiled didn't enter this calculation; we looked only at outputs (units finished plus the change in work in process), not at the inputs.

Once this calculation has been made, the average cost of the good units can be calculated in the usual way:

	Prior Dept. Cost	Processing Cost	Total Cost
Total cost........................	$85,000	$21,750	$106,750
Equivalent production...........	68,000	70,000	
Average cost....................	$1.250	$.311	$1.561

Any scrap recovery under this method is taken as a reduction of unit cost. For example, suppose the 17,000 spoiled units had an immediate scrap value of 10 cents each, or $1,700 in total. This amount could be deducted either from prior department costs or from departmental processing costs. If we treat it as a negative component of departmental processing cost, we get the following unit costs:

	Prior Dept. Costs	Processing Costs	Total Costs
Total cost........................	$85,000	$21,750	$106,750
Less: salvage....................	—	1,700	1,700
Net cost..................	$85,000	$20,050	$105,050
Equivalent production...........	68,000	70,000	
Average unit cost..............	$1.250	$.286	$1.536

Method 2. Separating the costs of spoiled units. The second method of accounting for the costs of spoiled units is to transfer their costs to a separate overhead or expense category. To do this, we need to recalculate the cost divisors to include spoiled units as well as good units. The procedure is simple:

1. Calculate the number of equivalent units spoiled, element by element.
2. Add these figures to the equivalent production figures.[1]
3. Divide total cost by the revised cost divisors to get average cost.
4. Multiply these average costs by the number of equivalent units spoiled.

In this case spoiled units are half processed in the department but complete as to prior department costs. The revised cost divisors are:

	Prior Dept. Costs	Processing Costs
Equivalent production....................	68,000	70,000
Equivalent units spoiled................	17,000	8,500
Cost divisors, including spoiled units.........................	85,000	78,500

Using these divisors, we get the following average unit costs:

Prior department costs.............	$85,000/85,000 =	$1.000
Processing costs..................	$21,750/78,500 =	.277
Total.......................		$1.277

The total cost of the spoiled units is:

Materials: 17,000 × $1.00...............................	$17,000
Processing: 17,000 × ½ × $0.277......................	2,355
Total..	$19,355

These costs are not averaged into the costs of the good units. The average materials cost of the good units, for example, remains at $1, not $1.25.

Under this approach, the salvage value of the spoiled units should be deducted from their cost to determine the net cost of spoilage. Since the spoiled units in our example were sold for 10 cents each, the net cost of spoilage was reduced to $19,355 − $1,700 = $17,655 (see Exhibit 10–5). This $17,655 would appear on the income statement as an expense of the current period.

The main advantage of this treatment is that it places a dollar amount on the spoiled quantities and thereby calls attention to the dollar effect of spoilage. Its main disadvantage is that it ignores the fact of normal or standard spoilage. For inventory measurement and decisions, product cost should reflect this normal experience. For control, too, what we want is the deviation from normal rather than the

---

[1] If unit costs are calculated by the moving average method for cost bookkeeping purposes, equivalent spoiled units should be added to the moving average divisors calculated by method 1.

EXHIBIT 10-5

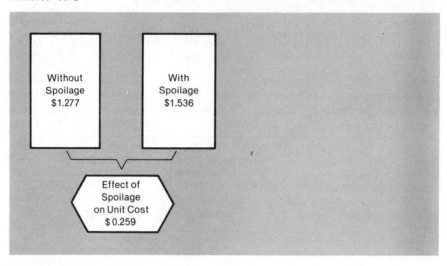

EXHIBIT 10-6

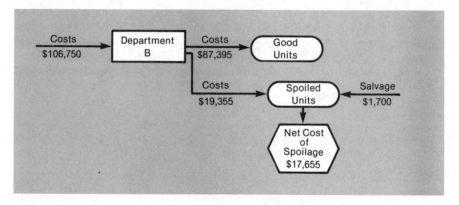

normal cost. This is also a disadvantage of the first method, but since that method is cheaper it is more likely to be used.

Effect of spoilage on unit cost. Management may choose to use method 1, but ask the accountant to calculate the effect of spoilage on average unit cost each period. We can do this by comparing the unit costs derived by method 1 with those derived by method 2 (Exhibit 10-6).

Calculating Product Cost: The Final Step

The unit cost of a product is the sum of the unit costs of the processes it passes through. This means that process costing can be used if different products pass through a process—the only requirement is that the production center performs the same *operation* on all the products that pass through it.

When a process center operates this way, the prior department costs of each product must be kept separate. For example, if 50,000 units of product X and 40,000 units of product Y are processed in department C and then sent on their separate ways, department C's costs might be summarized in the following way:

	Total Cost	Unit Cost Product X	Unit Cost Product Y
Costs from prior departments:			
Product X............................	$ 80,000	$1.60	...
Product Y............................	96,000	...	$2.40
Labor..................................	72,000	0.80	0.80
Other processing costs...............	108,000	1.20	1.20
Total..........................	$356,000	$3.60	$4.40

Processing cost is the same for each product, but total unit cost differs because the unit costs of prior departments' work were different.

Dealing with Mixed Outputs

Although process costing is strictly applicable only when departmental output is homogeneous with respect to departmental operations, it may be used even though this condition is not quite met. For example, process costing would probably be used in a production center engaged in filling pint, quart, and gallon containers with three different types of liquids. The output in this case is not homogeneous, but it is close enough to it to justify the simplifying assumption that it is. Output can be measured either in gallons or in numbers of containers filled, depending on whether costs are more likely to be related to gallons or to the container count.

Whether the homogeneity assumption can be applied is of course a matter of judgment, and the tolerable limit of heterogeneity cannot be specified precisely. The main criterion is whether management loses significant information by not computing separate unit costs for separate products, information which cannot be obtained more cheaply in other ways. For the container-filling operation, for example, an inexpensive engineering study could probably provide adequate estimates of the differences in cost per gallon resulting from different container sizes or different liquid inputs. In other cases, subdivision of the production center into smaller, more homogeneous cost centers will be the answer. Job order costing should be adopted only as a last resort, because of its higher clerical cost and more complicated paperwork.

PROCESS COSTING ON A VARIABLE COSTING BASIS

The illustration in the last section was based on the full-costing principle. Process costing can also be applied to variable costing, perhaps in modified form. Two situations need to be distinguished:

1. All of the production center's costs can be classified as either wholly fixed or wholly and proportionately variable.
2. Some of the production center's costs are semivariable.

Process Costing for Wholly Variable Costs

Variable costing is simple if a production center's costs can be classified as wholly fixed or wholly variable. In such cases each variable cost element can be divided by an appropriate cost divisor; the fixed costs do not enter the unit cost calculation.

Exhibit 10–7 shows the calculation of unit cost in the Mixing and

EXHIBIT 10–7

MIXING AND GRINDING DEPARTMENT
Variable Costing, Month of November

	Total Cost	Unit Cost
Variable costs:		
Direct labor...........................	$ 6,541	$0.0327
Indirect labor*.......................	303	0.0015
Payroll charges.......................	1,298	0.0065
Fuel and water.......................	2,527	0.0126
Light and power......................	9,806	0.0490
Grinding supplies....................	953	0.0048
Dust collector.......................	427	0.0021
Total variable....................	$21,855	$0.1090
Fixed costs:		
Supervision..........................	$ 712	
Maintenance labor....................	2,299	
Maintenance materials...............	1,956	
Total fixed.......................	$ 4,967	

* All labor is traceable to the department and thus is direct labor, as that term has been defined here. This company uses the term to identify those classes of work performed directly in production, while indirect labor is identified as the costs of miscellaneous departmental chores such as cleaning and messenger work.

Grinding Department of a cement mill. Eight cost elements are classified as variable, and an average unit cost is computed for each element each month. The fixed costs, however, are not averaged over the units produced.

The output figures used in this kind of calculation are measured in the way described in the last section. The only difference is that the cost divisors are applied solely to the variable cost elements.

Variable Costing with Semivariable Costs

The main defect with the method just described is that it doesn't provide for semivariable costs. When these are material in amount, the correct approach is to use a predetermined overhead rate, at least for those components of cost that cannot reasonably be assumed to be completely and proportionately variable.

EXHIBIT 10–8

MIXING AND GRINDING DEPARTMENT
Variable Costing Using Predetermined Rates for
Semivariable Cost Elements

	Total Cost	Unit Cost
Variable costs:		
Direct labor	$ 6,541	$0.0327
Indirect labor	303	0.0015
Payroll charges	1,298	0.0065
Fuel and water	2,527	0.0126
Grinding supplies	953	0.0048
Dust collector	427	0.0021
Total variable	$12,049	$0.0602
Semivariable costs:		
Light and power	$ 9,806	$0.042*
Maintenance labor	2,299	0.005*
Maintenance materials	1,956	0.009*
Total semivariable	$14,061	$0.056*
Total product cost	xxx	$0.116
Fixed costs:		
Supervision	$ 712	

* Predetermined rates for variable component only.

Exhibit 10–8 illustrates how this change might affect unit costing in the cement mill's Mixing and Grinding Department. One item previously classified as variable has now been reclassified as semivariable on the ground that it includes a fixed cost component, while two items not previously included in product cost have been moved from the fixed to the semivariable category. For each element, actual costs for the month are shown for the information of the department head, but the unit cost figures shown in the semivariable cost section of the exhibit are predetermined and represent the variable component only. They do not reflect the current month's cost experience in any way.

The unit cost figure of $0.116 a barrel is a hybrid: partly predetermined and partly based on cost performance for the month. This makes it very similar to unit cost under job order costing, in which actual direct labor and materials costs are mingled with overhead applied on the basis of predetermined overhead rates.

INTEGRATING PROCESS COSTING INTO
FINANCIAL STATEMENTS

The unit costing procedures described above can be applied either to historical costs or to estimates of future costs. Slightly different procedures may be used for cost bookkeeping and for financial accounting, however, to assign costs to units transferred from department to department, to finished goods inventory, and to the cost of goods sold. In this final section we shall study four questions:

1. Why special calculations are needed for this purpose.
2. What happens when first-in, first-out inventory costing is used.
3. What effect the use of the moving average method has on process costing.
4. The accounting entries needed to implement process costing.

Why Special Calculations Are Needed

The reason why the above procedures may be modified for this purpose can be seen from a simple example. Suppose that department B's 10,000-pound opening inventory had a total materials cost of $10,500, based on the department's cost experience during the previous month. The total cost in this department's materials account would thus be as follows:

Costs of opening inventory....................................	$10,500
Costs transferred from department A...........................	85,000
Total cost to be accounted for...........................	$95,500

If the $1 a pound cost computed for the month of June were to be applied both to the ending inventory and to the units finished during the month, only $95,000 would be accounted for:

Units finished (at $1 each).....................................	$89,000
Units in ending inventory (at $1 each).........................	6,000
Total cost accounted for.................................	$95,000

The $500 discrepancy between these two figures arises because the cost of the opening inventory was ignored in the unit cost calculation for June; yet these costs entered into the cost pool that had to be distributed.

The accountant has three main alternative ways of dealing with this problem:

1. Use a method of inventory bookkeeping that takes the beginning inventory into consideration.
2. Transfer the $500 to the income statement as an expense of the period.
3. Measure all inventories and transfers at standard cost, and take all variances to the income statement.

The second and third of these are more convenient than the first and should be used unless the undistributed amounts would be too large to pass the materiality test. To see why they are more convenient, let us look briefly at two methods that do take opening inventory costs into consideration—the Fifo and moving average methods.

First-In, First-Out Method

Under Fifo inventory costing, beginning-of-month inventory cost balances are transferred to the next department as part of the cost of the first units completed during the month. For example, the cost of the 10,000-pound initial inventory in department B was $11,600, made up as follows.

	Per Unit	Total Cost
Materials*............................	$1.05	$10,500
Processing.........................	0.11	1,100
Total........................	$1.16	$11,600

* The correct title here would be "Semiprocessed Products Received from Department A," but because these semiprocessed products are really department B's materials, we shall use the simpler title.

Completion of these units in June added another $1,250 to this total (the 10,000 pounds were half processed at June's average cost of $0.25 a pound). Thus under Fifo the first 10,000 units completed would lead to a transfer of $11,600 plus $1,250, or $12,850, to the Finished Goods Inventory account.

The other 79,000 units completed would then be costed at the average cost for the month, or $1.25. The total cost of output transferred to finished goods therefore would be:

	First 10,000	Next 79,000	Total
Materials.................	$10,500	$79,000	$ 89,500
Processing...............	2,350	19,750	22,100
Total...............	$12,850	$98,750	$111,600

For convenience, no distinction would be made in finished goods inventories between the first 10,000 and the next 79,000 pounds of product. They would all be entered at an average cost of approximately $1.254 a pound ($111,600 divided by 89,000). This simplification would also be made if the work were transferred to another department rather than to finished inventories.

The inventory remaining in department B on June 30 would then be Fifo-costed at average cost for the month:

Materials: 6,000 lbs. at $1...............................		$6,000
Processing: 6,000 lbs., half processed, at $0.125...........		750
Total...		$6,750

The cost distribution of department B could then be summarized as in Exhibit 10–9.

EXHIBIT 10–9

Distribution of Department B's Costs: Fifo Method

	Total Amount	Per Equiva- lent Pound
Costs in department:		
Materials:		
In process, 6/1........................	$ 10,500	$1.05
Received.............................	85,000	1.00
Total.............................	$ 95,500	xxx
Processing costs:		
In process, 6/1........................	$ 1,100	$0.22
Labor.................................	8,700	0.10
Other.................................	13,050	0.15
Total.............................	$ 22,850	xxx
Total departmental cost.................	$118,350	xxx
Cost distribution:		
To finished products:		
Materials.............................	$ 89,500	$1.006
Processing...........................	22,100	0.248
Total finished products............	$111,600	$1.254
In process, 6/30:		
Materials.............................	$ 6,000	$1.000
Processing...........................	750	0.125
Total in process, 6/30..............	$ 6,750	$1.125
Total cost distributed...................	$118,350	xxx

Moving Average Method

The calculation procedure can be simplified slightly by using a single average cost (referred to as a moving average) to apply to all product units in a department during a particular period of time.

For example, the total cost of materials in process in department B during June was $95,500 (opening balance plus $85,000 for materials received from department A during the month). The units available to absorb these costs included the 89,000 units finished and transferred out of the department during the month and the 6,000 units still in process at the end of the month, a total of 95,000 units.

The average materials cost for these 95,000 units was $95,500/ 95,000 = $1.00526 a pound. (Carrying the answer to this many decimal places is both meaningless and unnecessary; we have done it here simply to remove the rounding errors from the illustration.) This average would be used to measure the materials cost of the units in process at the end of the month as well as the materials cost of the units finished during the month.

This cost distribution is illustrated in the following diagram:

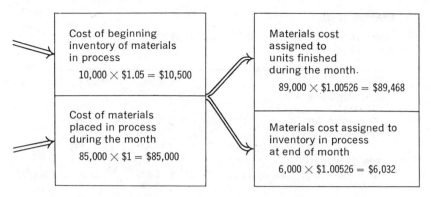

The figures in each side of this diagram add up to $95,500, the total materials cost within the department's responsibility during the month.

A similar calculation can be made to distribute the $22,850 in departmental processing costs ($1,100 from the beginning work in process, $8,700 in labor cost for the month, and $13,050 in other processing costs). The unit cost divisor in this case would be 92,000 pounds, because the ending inventory was only half processed (89,-000 pounds of fully completed products plus the equivalent of 3,000 pounds in the ending inventory). Average cost would be $22,850/92,000 = $.24837 a pound.

The processing cost to be transferred therefore would be $22,105 (89,000 pounds × $.24837), leaving $745 (3,000 equivalent pounds × $.24837) as the cost of the ending inventory in process. These calculations are summarized in Exhibit 10–10. (Unit costs in the right hand column have been rounded to the nearest tenth of a cent.)

The unit cost divisor under the moving average approach differs from equivalent production by the number of equivalent units in the opening inventory:

	Materials	Processing
Units completed during period................	89,000	89,000
Plus: In process, end of period.............	6,000	3,000
Cost divisor, moving average.................	95,000	92,000
Less: In process, start of period............	10,000	5,000
Equivalent production......................	85,000	87,000

The peculiarity of the average cost calculation is that the sum of the number of units finished and the number of those still in process at the *end* of the period is divided into the sum of the costs incurred during the period and the costs in process at the *beginning* of the period. The reason for this is that the latter sum reflects all of the

EXHIBIT 10–10

Distribution of Department B's Costs: Moving
Average Method

	Total	Per Pound
Costs in department:		
Materials:		
In process, 6/1..........................	$ 10,500	$1.05
Received.............................	85,000	1.00
Total.............................	$ 95,500	$1.005
Processing costs:		
In process, 6/1..........................	$ 1,100	$0.22
Labor.................................	8,700	0.10
Other.................................	13,050	0.15
Total.............................	$ 22,850	$0.248
Total Department Cost...................	$118,350	$1.253
Cost distribution:		
To finished products:		
Materials.............................	$ 89,468	$1.005
Processing............................	22,105	0.248
Total finished products............	$111,573	$1.253
In process, 6/30:		
Materials.............................	$ 6,032	$1.005
Processing............................	745	0.124
Total in process, 6/30..............	$ 6,777	$1.129
Total Cost Distributed...................	$118,350	xxx

costs while the former sum represents all of the *units* available to absorb these costs. Equivalent production, on the other hand, is used as a divisor for the current month's costs only, and this requires the subtraction of the opening inventory.

The differences between the moving average and Fifo methods should not be overstressed. The resultant unit costs will not depart materially from each other unless the production cycle is particularly long and monthly cost per unit of equivalent production changes rapidly. For this reason, the choice between the two ordinarily can be made on the basis of convenience. *In any case, equivalent production is the only legitimate divisor in calculating current unit cost because it is the only one that measures the amount of work done, the amount for which the current period's costs were incurred.*

Accounts for Process Costing

Because the processing department is the basis for product costing as well as for control reporting, the account structure for process costing is relatively simple. It consists of (1) a set of object of expenditure accounts for each department, and (2) a set of work-in-process accounts, one for each group of cost elements calling for a separate cost divisor.

For example, department B has seven object of expenditure accounts and two work-in-process accounts:

Object of Expenditure	*Work in Process*
Materials from Department A	Materials in Process—B
Productive labor	Processing Costs in Process—B
Idle time	
Overtime premium	
Supplies	
Other costs	
Scrap recovery	

Each of the object of expenditure accounts has a departmental code number, omitted here for simplicity.

The two work-in-process accounts had June 1 balances of $10,500 and $1,100, respectively. The journal entries to record the month's transactions are not difficult and can be summarized quickly:

1. Receipt of materials

Materials from Department A—B	85,000	
Basic Materials in Process—A		45,900
Finishing Materials in Process—A		5,100
Processing Costs in Process—A		34,000

Three work-in-process accounts are used in department A because three different cost divisors are used there.

2. Labor costs

Productive Labor—B	8,700	
Idle Time—B	870	
Overtime Premium—B	870	
Wages Payable		10,440

3. Receipt of indirect materials

Supplies—B	3,480	
Materials Inventory		3,480

4. Miscellaneous inputs used

Other Costs—B	7,830	
Accounts Payable		
Accumulated Depreciation		7,830
Etc.		

5. Scrap. No scrap was recovered in June in department B. The entry to record it would have taken the following form:

Scrap Inventory (at market value)	xxx	
Scrap Recovery—B		xxx

6. Transferring monthly costs to work-in-process accounts. Once the object of expenditure accounts have served their cost classification purposes, their balances can be closed into the inventory accounts:

Materials in Process—B 85,000
Processing Costs in Process—B 21,750
    Materials from Department A—B   85,000
    Productive Labor—B   8,700
    Idle Time—B   870
    Overtime Premium—B   870
    Supplies—B   3,480
    Other Costs—B   7,830

7. Product completions (moving average method)

Finished Goods Inventory 112,295
    Materials in Process—B   89,468
    Processing Cost in Process—B   22,105

This should bring the work-in-process account balances down to the amounts assigned to the units on hand at the end of the month:

Materials in Process—B				Processing Costs in Process—B		
Bal.	10,500			Bal.	1,100	
(6)	85,000	(7)	89,468	(6)	21,750	(7)	22,105
Bal.	6,032			Bal.	745	

These are the balances shown in Exhibit 10–10.

8. Spoilage. If the costs of good products are to include the net costs of spoiled units, no entry is required to record spoilage. If the costs of spoiled units are to be treated as operating losses, however, then the costs assigned to the spoiled units must be credited to the work-in-process accounts in an entry of the following form:

Spoiled Units—B xxx
    Materials in Process—B   xxx
    Processing Costs in Process—B   xxx

If the spoiled units have a salvage value, this too should be recorded:

Spoiled Units Inventory xxx
    Scrap Recovery—B   xxx

Department B had no spoilage in June, however, so none of these entries had to be made.

USING PROCESS COSTING INFORMATION IN CONTROL REPORTING

Management has the same need for control information in process production as in job order production. In this section we shall see how both historical process costing and standard process costing might be used for this purpose.

Historical Costing

Product cost in process costing is also departmental cost. For this reason, unit product cost is often used to provide departmental con-

EXHIBIT 10–11

Departmental Cost Report: Process Production

Cost Center: 5116—Coke Batteries					Month: October	
	Current Month, 44,000 Tons		Last Month, 40,000 Tons	Year Ago, 43,000 Tons	Year to Date	
					This Year	Last Year
Cost Item	Cost	Per Unit	Per Unit	Per Unit	Per Unit	Per Unit
Direct materials	$981,200	$22.30	$22.38	$21.98	$22.54	$21.65
Recoveries	(230,121)	(5.23)	(5.22)	(5.26)	5.58	5.41
Net direct materials	$751,079	$17.07	$17.16	$16.72	$16.96	$16.24
Indirect materials	1,463	0.03	0.03	0.03	0.03	0.03
Fuels	79,538	1.81	1.77	1.75	1.76	1.68
Labor	13,251	0.30	0.31	0.26	0.31	0.27
Utilities	2,604	0.06	0.06	0.07	0.06	0.06
Services	41,623	0.95	1.05	0.88	1.03	0.85
Maintenance	5,190	0.12	0.13	0.16	0.11	0.12
Administrative	8,095	0.18	0.22	0.17	0.19	0.17
Total	$902,843	$20.52	$20.73	$20.04	$20.45	$19.42

trol information. An example of a production center control report is shown in Exhibit 10–11.

In this exhibit, departmental costs are classified into several descriptive categories and a unit cost is computed for each. Extra columns are provided to show last-month, year-to-date, and prior-year figures. Space is usually added for explanations of important changes in the figures.

Reports of this kind are attention-getting devices. They may lead immediately to corrective action or eventually to decisions on changes in methods, equipment used, and so forth. They have a number of shortcomings, however:

1. Comparison is with the past, not with what was expected or what should have happened.
2. Average fixed cost varies with volume, and the manager doesn't control volume.
3. Input prices vary, and the manager doesn't control prices.

Standard costs and flexible budgets can be used to eliminate all three of these objections, as we shall see in a moment. Historical comparisons can be made cheaply, however, and may be good enough if volume and input prices remain relatively constant.

Standard Costing and Flexible Budgets

Standard costing is much easier to apply to process production than to job order production. In fact, the parallels between historical process costing and basic plan standard costing (Chapter 6) are startling (see Exhibit 10–12).

EXHIBIT 10–12

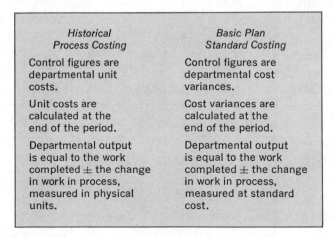

Historical Process Costing	*Basic Plan Standard Costing*
Control figures are departmental unit costs.	Control figures are departmental cost variances.
Unit costs are calculated at the end of the period.	Cost variances are calculated at the end of the period.
Departmental output is equal to the work completed ± the change in work in process, measured in physical units.	Departmental output is equal to the work completed ± the change in work in process, measured at standard cost.

All that is necessary to convert a historical process costing system to a standard costing system is to use standard prices to measure departmental inputs and standard costs to measure departmental outputs. The variances drop out as in the following diagram:

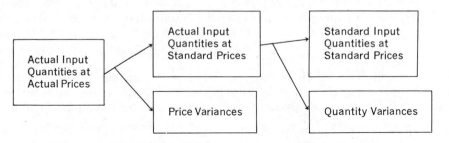

Take department B in our earlier illustration, for example. Suppose we have the following standards:

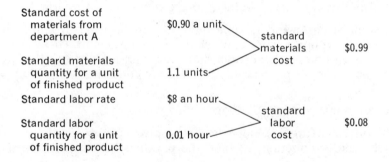

The inventory in process on August 1 had a standard materials cost of $4,950 and a standard labor cost of $250. During August the department received 90,000 units from department A, used 850 productive labor hours, and completed work on 80,000 units. The departmental work-in-process accounts showed the following:

Materials in Process—B		Labor in Process—B	
Bal. 4,950	80,000 × 0.99	Bal. 250	80,000 × 0.08
90,000 × 0.90	= 79,200	850 × 8 = 6,800	= 6,400
= 81,000			
(Bal. 6,750)		(Bal. 650)	

At the end of the month 10,000 units of product remained in process. All of the anticipated shrinkage had already taken place in these units, and half the necessary productive labor had been applied. Their standard cost, in other words, was:

Materials: 10,000 × $0.99............. $9,900
Labor: 10,000 × ½ × $0.08........   400

With these figures we can calculate the standard cost of the month's output and determine the variances:

	Materials from Department A	Productive Labor
Standard cost of output:		
Units completed.............	$79,200	$6,400
Ending inventory............	9,900	400
	$89,100	$6,800
Beginning inventory.........	4,950	250
Standard cost...........	$84,150	$6,550
Standard cost of inputs........	81,000	6,800
Quantity variances..... $ 3,150 Favorable	$ 250 Unfavorable	

The elements in the calculation of the standard cost of the output are exactly the same as those we used to calculate equivalent production earlier in this chapter:

Units completed + equivalent units in ending inventory − equivalent units in beginning inventory = equivalent production.

The only difference is that we are now measuring equivalent production in dollars of standard cost rather than in physical units.

Calculations like these can be made for every cost element expected to vary proportionally with volume. This can also be done in job order production—variances can be accumulated separately for different classes of direct labor or direct materials, if management finds these distinctions useful enough to justify spending the extra money to make them. *The basic plan of standard costing is fully and ideally suited to process production.*

The basic plan doesn't provide control information for fixed and semivariable cost elements, however. Just as in job order production, cost standards for these elements must be provided by flexible budgets. Overtime premium, for example, may average 1 cent a unit when volume is 90,000 units, but may rise to 2 cents when volume goes up to 100,000 units a month.

Since both the basic plan and flexible budgeting are identical in all essentials, whether applied to job order production or to process production, no further discussion is necessary here.

SUMMARY

Whenever the output of a production center is sufficiently homogeneous to be measured in physical product units, unit cost can be determined by the process costing method. In process costing, unit cost is determined by dividing each production center's costs by its output for a specified period of time.

The only difficult question is how to calculate output for this purpose. The solution is to group resource inputs into classes selected so that inputs in each class are applied at approximately the same stage of the production process. For each class, output is equal to the number of units finished by the production center during the period plus or minus the change in the number of equivalent finished units in process. If in-process inventories increase, then output is greater than the number of units finished, and vice versa.

Unit costs calculated in this way are sometimes used for control reporting. Care needs to be taken, however, to analyze the effects of changing volume and to use standard cost benchmarks rather than the average cost in some previous period. Process costing can also be used to generate unit costs on a variable costing basis.

Finally, process costing figures can be integrated quite easily into the financial accounting records. The last illustration in this chapter showed how this could be done, using both first-in, first-out and moving average inventory cost bookkeeping.

KEY TERMS

The most important terms introduced and defined in this chapter are the following:

Cost divisor	Process Costing
Equivalent production	Sequential Processing
Parallel processing	

INDEPENDENT STUDY PROBLEMS
(Solutions in Appendix C)

1. Unit costs, two departments, no spoilage. The Butts Company has a two-process factory in which all materials are placed in process in department A at the start of processing and semifinished products are transferred to department B for completion. No additional materials are introduced in department B. The following data relate to the month of June:

Department A:
  Beginning inventory (50 units, 30 percent completed): materials, $45, processing costs, $41.
  Raw materials received during month (100 units), $105.
  Processing costs incurred during month, $399.
  Ending inventory: 60 units, one-third completed.

Department B:
  Beginning inventory (40 units, one-half completed): materials, $213; processing costs, $150.
  Processing costs incurred during month, $570.
  Ending inventory: 45 units, two-thirds completed.

No product units were lost in either department during the month.

a. For department A, calculate unit costs for the unit, then calculate the cost of the work in process on June 30 and the cost of goods transferred to department B during the month, using the moving average basis for the transfer calculation.

b. Repeat these calculations for department B, using the Fifo basis to calculate the cost of the work in process on June 30 and the cost of goods transferred out of the department during the month.

2. Unit costs, one department, spoilage. The Stanley Chemical Company uses a process costing system of unit cost determination. The company's factory consists of two departments: raw materials are first mixed in the mixing department and then transferred to the refining department for completion. Units of product still in process in a department at the end of a month are assumed to be 100 percent complete as to materials and 50 percent complete as to processing costs in that department. You are given the following data for the refining department for the month of January:

Quantities:
  In process, January 1................... 4,000
  Transferred in......................... 93,000
  Transferred out........................ 82,000
  In process, January 31................. 10,000
Costs:
  In process, January 1:
    Materials (from Mixing)............. $ 2,800
    Processing.......................... 1,650
  Materials received from Mixing......... 81,840
  Labor.................................. 61,200
  Other processing costs................. 45,900
    Total costs........................ $193,390

Units of product lost in production are assumed to be fully processed; their cost is to be spread evenly over the equivalent good production.

a. Calculate the cost divisors for the month.
b. Calculate a separate unit cost for each cost element in the month of January.
c. Calculate the effect of the lost units on unit costs.
d. Calculate the costs assigned to the goods finished and the costs of the ending in-process inventory, using the moving average method.

EXERCISES AND PROBLEMS

1. Cost divisor exercise. Department A finished work on 50,000 units during April and transferred them to department B. On April 1, department A's inventory consisted of 15,000 units complete as to materials but only one third processed. During April it received 59,000 unprocessed units from the storeroom, and on April 30, it had 24,000 units still in process, complete as to materials but only one-half processed.

Calculate the equivalent production for the month for materials and for processing costs.

2. Cost divisor exercises. The following three exercises present situations of progressively greater complexity.

Exercise A

Department Alpha takes raw materials from the stockroom and shapes them into blanks for widgets. On January 1, it had 20,000 partly processed widget blanks on hand, half processed in the department. During January, it received 40 tons of materials and delivered 200,000 widget blanks to department Beta. On January 31, it had 50,000 widget blanks on hand, half processed in the department.

a. Calculate two cost divisors, one for materials and one for processing costs, to measure equivalent production during the month.
b. Explain why the 40 ton figure was irrelevant to your calculations.

Exercise B

Department Gamma polishes discs, coats them with plastic, and transfers them to department Delta. The plastic coating is placed on the polished discs by opening a pipeline valve just before the polished discs are transferred to department Delta.

Department Gamma received 200,000 unpolished discs from the storeroom during January and delivered 210,000 coated discs to department Delta. It had 60,000 discs in process on January 1 and 50,000 discs in process on January 31. Work in process inventories are always regarded as complete as to prior department costs and half processed in the department.

a. Calculate three cost divisors, one for discs, one for plastic coating material, and one for processing costs, to measure the department's equivalent production during January.
b. Calculate the moving average cost divisors for each of these three cost elements.
c. Explain the rationale behind the assumption that the inventories were half processed in the department.

Exercise C

The finishing department receives assembled products from the assembly department, performs a number of operations on them, and transfers the finished units to the shipping platform. A certain amount of spoilage is expected, and spoilage can take place at any point in the finishing process. Spoiled units have no value.

The finishing department had 18,000 units of product in process on January 1, received 300,000 units of product from the assembly department during January, spoiled 73,000 units during the month, transferred 200,000 units to the shipping platform, and had 45,000 units in process on January 31.

Units in process at any time are assumed to be complete as to prior department costs and half processed by the finishing department; half of the eventual spoilage is assumed to have taken place. In calculating the number of equivalent units in the work in process inventory, management makes the assumption that 20 percent of the units entering the department will be spoiled between the time they enter and the time the units are finished.

a. Calculate two divisors, one for prior department costs and one for finishing department costs, to measure the month's equivalent production.
b. Recalculate the divisors on the assumption that costs are to be assigned to the spoiled units. Assume that the spoilage took place when the spoiled units were half processed.

3. Unit cost exercises. The following three exercises are of progressively greater complexity.

Exercise A

Department Able produces doodads. It started the month of May with no doodads in process, completed 16,000 doodads during the month, and ended the month with 4,000 doodads in process, complete as to materials and half processed on the average.

The department's costs for the month consisted of 15,000 pounds of materials at $3 a pound, and $29,700 in processing costs.

a. Calculate unit costs for the month.
b. Calculate the cost of the ending work in process inventory.
c. Calculate the cost of the goods finished during May.

Exercise B

Ardway Corporation sells products in reusable containers. When containers are returned by customers, the shipping department selects those suitable for immediate reuse and sends the rest to department Baker. Department Baker inspects the containers and recycles those worth salvaging.

On June 1, department Baker had 5,000 containers in process. It received 20,000 containers during the month, 2,000 of which were unsuitable for recycling and had to be sold to a scrap dealer for $100. It completed work on 22,000 containers during the month and had 1,000 containers in process on June 30. Inventory costs are determined on a moving average basis. Containers in process on any date are assumed to be half processed.

The beginning inventory had a materials cost (containers) of $4,800 and a processing cost of $3,000. Department Baker was charged $21,000 for the 20,000 containers received in the department, this being the depreciated book value of these containers. Processing costs amounted to $14,640.

a. Calculate the average cost of the work done in department Baker during the month, with separate calculations for materials and processing costs. Explain how you handled the 2,000 scrapped containers and your reasons for choosing this method.
b. Does the average cost this month appear to have been higher or lower or the same as in May? Explain how you figured this out.
c. Calculate the cost of the ending inventory.

Exercise C

Department Charlie processes flanges. It started the month of July with no flanges in process. It received 2,400 unprocessed flanges at a cost of $7.92 each, used 2,100 hours of processing labor at a labor rate of $7 an hour, and spent $13,860 on other processing inputs. Processing labor is regarded as completely variable with the number of flanges processed; $6,300 of the other processing costs in July were fixed, while the other $7,560 were variable with production.

Department Charlie completed work on 1,800 flanges during the month and ruined 200 half-processed flanges due to a severe malfunctioning of a major piece of equipment. The ruined flanges were sold immediately for scrap at a price of $1 each. This amount was credited to department Charlie as a deduction from its processing costs. The department had 400 semiprocessed flanges in process at the end of the month.

a. Assuming that the cost of the spoiled units is to be averaged into the cost of the good units produced, and that product costing is on a full-costing basis, calculate the unit cost of the flanges completed during the month.
b. Perform the same calculations, but assuming that the cost of spoiled units is to be reported separately, as a loss occurring during the period.
c. What was the effect of spoilage on the unit cost of the good units? Use figures from your answer to (b) to calculate the net loss from spoilage during July.
d. Perform the same calculations as in (a), (b), and (c), but on a variable costing basis.
e. Does the figure you calculated in answer to (d) provide a more accurate measure of the net spoilage loss than the figure you calculated in answer (c)? Explain your answer.

4. Unit cost; Journal entry. The Tawny Company's Albany factory has two departments, mixing and curing. Costs are accumulated in departmental accounts, and at the end of each month the goods transferred from mixing to curing and from curing to finished goods are costed at average cost for the month. The following information is available for the month of July:

	Mixing	Curing
Pounds of materials received:		
From storeroom (at $0.50 a pound).......	40,000	...
From mixing department.................	...	35,000
Pounds of product transferred out.........	35,000	25,000
Pounds of product in process, July 31......	5,000	10,000
Processing costs.........................	$15,500	$ 9,150

The ending inventory in the mixing department was three-quarters processed; the ending inventory in curing was half processed. Neither department had inventory in process on July 1.

a. Compute (1) materials cost per unit and (2) processing costs per unit for each department.
b. Prepare a table showing the costs to be accounted for in each department and how you would distribute these costs between the work completed and the work still in process at the end of the month.
c. Prepare a journal entry to record the transfer of costs from the mixing department to the curing department. Each department has two work-in-process accounts, one for the materials it receives and the other for its own processing costs.

5. Unit Cost, Fifo cost, and moving average cost. The following costs were charged to process 2 of the H Company during July:

Costs transferred from process 1................. $184,000
Materials added in process 2.....................   34,000
Processing costs................................. 104,000

Production figures for the month for process 2 were:

Work in process, July 1.................... 2,000 pounds, 60% completed
Finished during July....................... 20,000 pounds
Work in process, July 31................... 5,000 pounds, 40% completed

Process 2 materials are not added to the semifinished product received from process 1 until the very end of processing in process 2. The work in process in process 2 on July 1 had a cost of $22,500. Of this, $17,050 was the cost of materials transferred from process 1, and $5,450 was processing cost in process 2.

a. Calculate the cost divisors.
b. Calculate unit costs for the month.
c. Calculate the July 31 cost of the work in process and the cost of units transferred out of the process during July, using the Fifo method.
d. Calculate the July 31 cost of the work in process and the cost of units transferred out of the process during July, using the moving average method.
e. Explain why you did or did not use the figures you calculated in (b) to answer parts (c) and (d).

6. Unit cost: Anticipated shrinkage. Materials are received in department A, processed, and then transferred to department B, where final processing takes place. The following data relate to the operations of department A for December:

	Quantity	Cost
Inventory in process, December 1:		
Materials..................................... 95 {		$ 228
Processing costs...........................		72
Materials added from stockroom........................	520	1,242
Processing costs...	...	528
Units completed and transferred to department B........	310	?
Inventory in process, December 31:		
Materials..................................... }190 {		?
Processing costs...........................		?

All materials are placed in process at the start of processing—thus all work in process is complete as to materials. A total shrinkage of 10 percent is regarded as normal in department A, however, and it is assumed that half of the expected shrinkage has already taken place in the inventory in process at any time.

Inventory in process is assumed to be half processed in the department, and the costs of lost units are to be spread over all equivalent good units produced.

a. What is equivalent production for the month with respect to (1) materials and (2) processing costs?

b. Compute the unit costs that you would report to management to reflect the efficiency of the department's operations for the month.

c. Using the moving average method, compute the costs to be transferred to department B and the costs of work still in process in department A at the end of December.

7. Unit costs; Journal entries. Thermal Products, Inc., uses a process costing system to account for manufacturing costs in one of its plants. The Pical department in this plant is devoted to the manufacture of a product known as Pical. Two materials are used in the manufacture of this product: Corex, brought from outside suppliers and issued to the Pical department from materials inventory, and Formula 42X, supplied by another department in the plant, the Forming department. Completed units of Pical are transferred to finished goods inventory.

The following labor and materials costs were incurred by the Pical department during the month of October:

1. Materials issued: Corex, 10,000 pounds at $0.55 a pound; Formula 42X, 2,000 gallons—cost in the Forming department was materials $1 a gallon, labor $0.32 a gallon.

2. Labor costs: leader, 168 hours at $10 an hour; operators, 350 hours at $9 an hour; and lifters, 840 hours at $7 an hour.

Costs other than labor and materials may be ignored for this problem. Each department has two inventory accounts—Materials in Process and Labor in Process. The Pical department has three object of expenditure accounts for labor costs, one for each class of labor; a single account is used for materials.

The department completed work on 10,000 pounds of Pical during the month and transferred this quantity to finished goods. An additional 1,000 pounds of semiprocessed product remained in inventory at the end of the month, complete as to materials but only half-processed in the department.

a. Calculate the unit cost of each class of materials and each class of labor.

b. Calculate the cost of materials finished and the cost of the work in process at the end of October.

c. Prepare summary journal entries to record the department's transactions for the month.

8. Control reporting. Operating volume in the Bayou Refinery of the Bipex Petroleum Company is measured by the number of barrels of crude oil processed. Operating efficiency is measured by the average processing cost per barrel. Each month the factors leading to major increases in operating costs are identified and their effects are estimated.

These figures are summarized in a monthly cost report, prepared for the refinery manager. The controller of the Bayou Refinery prepared the following summary of operating costs, exclusive of the cost of crude oil and other product ingredients, for the month of December:

	This December		Increase/(Decrease) Over Last December	
	Amount	Per Barrel	Amount	Change Percent
Barrels per calendar day............	51,791		3,268	6.7
Controllable costs:				
Salaries and wages:				
Operating......................	$ 448,536	$0.2794	$ 32,838	7.9
Maintenance...................	87,946	0.0546	5,830	7.1
Other.........................	64,142	0.0400	2,476	4.0
Total......................	$ 600,624	$0.3740	$ 41,144	7.4
Employee benefits..............	45,104	0.0280	7,446	19.8
Operating material..............	53,894	0.0336	14,458	36.7
Maintenance material...........	78,842	0.0492	11,874	17.7
Catalyst.......................	109,678	0.0684	56,276	105.4
Fuel...........................	390,538	0.2432	31,226	8.7
Other controllable..............	402,506	0.2508	26,894	7.0
Total controllable............	$1,681,186	$1.0472	$189,318	12.7
Noncontrollable costs.............	573,378	0.3570	38,354	7.2
Total operating cost.........	$2,254,564	$1.4042	$227,672	11.2
Increase (decrease) over cost per barrel last year..............		$0.0284		

Analysis of Major Increases:

Payrolls:
Increased salaries and wage rates...................	$24,844
Increased work force..............................	10,304
Increased overtime................................	2,110
Increased vacation and holiday pay................	2,156
Increased sickness and accident pay..............	1,730
Total increase in payrolls........................	$41,144

Operating material:
Low value items formerly charged to warehouse, now charged to refinery when purchased...........	$11,538
Other increases......................................	2,920
Total increase in operating material..............	$14,458

Catalyst:
Reformer Unit No. 1—catalyst change................	$12,426
Reformer Unit No. 2—initial batch for start-up........	35,776
Desulfurizer—initial batch for start-up................	6,836
Increased requirements..............................	1,238
Total increase in catalyst........................	$56,276

Fuel:
Increased price of fuel gas...........................	$11,730
Increased quantity consumed........................	19,496
Total increase in fuel............................	$31,226

a. How did the controller identify the effects of individual cost determining factors? (You are not expected to go into this in detail, but you should comment on at least four different items in the analytical section of the report.)

b. How does this report differ from one based on standard costing and flexible budgeting?

c. Is this report likely to be as useful to management as one based on standard costing and flexible budgeting? Would you recommend a change to that basis?

9. Control comparisons; Anticipated shrinkage. The Andrews Metals Company operates two refining units of equal size, with identical equipment, paying identical wage rates. The following data relate to the operations of these two units during the month of September:

	Selby Mill	Franklin Mill
Quantities:		
Pounds in process, Sept. 1 (half completed)............................	9,800	8,400
Pounds received.........................	78,000	52,000
Pounds refined, completed..............	60,000	37,500
Pounds in process, Sept. 30 (half completed)............................	7,700	9,800
Costs:		
Materials in process, Sept. 1..............	$ 8,000	$ 6,400
Processing costs in process, Sept. 1......	7,000	5,600
Materials.................................	75,311	49,536
Supervision..............................	5,965	5,805
Operating labor..........................	60,843	36,765
Depreciation.............................	31,018	30,960
Scrap credit.............................	(1,779)	(1,161)

A certain amount of shrinkage is expected in the refining process, inasmuch as the refined metal weighs less than the ore concentrate from which it is refined. This weight loss takes place continuously during processing and is assumed to be proportionate to the percentage of completion. For the purpose of costing materials in processs, it is assumed that the refined metal constitutes 75 percent of the ore concentrate, by weight.

Prepare an analysis that will assist management in comparing the relative efficiency of the two plant managers in controlling operating costs. Indicate what additional information you would like to have, if any.

10. Operating costs: Effects of new equipment. Factory department 67 makes an industrial chemical known as Monite. Monite's standard cost is $12 a gallon ($5.25 for materials, $4.25 for labor, and $2.50 for other processing costs), but these figures are obsolete and must be changed. The reason is that department 67 was recently closed down to permit the installation of new equipment which was expected to reduce costs substantially.

The new equipment was put into operation on a trial basis two months ago, but last month was the first full month under normal working conditions. Management is anxious to find out whether the anticipated reduction in operating costs was achieved. The following information is available:

1. Inventory in process, beginning of month: 2,000 gallons, complete as to materials, half of processing work completed. Materials cost was $11,400; labor cost, $3,300; and other processing costs, $5,600.

2. Operating costs charged to department 67 during the month: materials, $130,000; labor, $48,300; and other processing costs, $73,600.

3. Amount of Monite finished during the month: 20,000 gallons.

4. Inventory in process, end of month: 8,000 gallons, complete as to materials but only half of processing work completed.

a. If last month's costs were typical, did the introduction of the new equipment lead to lower unit cost? Compute unit cost for each group of costs to document your answer.
b. One of the company's cost analysts believes that this month's unit cost will be less than last month's. What good reasons can you advance to support this belief?

11. Standard costs; Spoilage. The molding department delivers molded products to the coating department, where they are coated and moved to the heat treating department for further processing. Coating is charged for the standard materials, labor and variable overhead costs of the molded units: $8.10 for material, $3.60 for molding labor, and $1.80 for variable overhead costs. Fixed overhead costs are not included in product costs.

Standard costs in the coating department are based on the assumptions that (1) 10 percent of the molded units will be spoiled in coating; and (2) the recovery value of the spoiled units will be $1 each. Standard labor cost is 0.9 labor hours for each unit of good product at a standard labor rate of $8 an hour. Processing costs amount to $1 a labor hour plus $40,-950 a month. Spoilage is identified when the products are inspected at the end of the coating process. The value of scrap recovered is credited to the department as a separate item at the time the spoiled units are sold.

You have the following information on the coating department for the month of March:

1. Work in process, March 1: 4,000 units, half processed in the coating department.
2. Molded products received from the molding department: 18,600 units.
3. Products finished and transferred to heat treating: 19,800 units.
4. Labor cost: 15,750 hours at $8.10.
5. Scrap recovered and sold for cash: 1,980 units at $8 each.
6. Other processing costs: $59,535
7. Work in process, March 31: 2,000 units, half processed.

a. Calculate the standard variable cost of a unit of coated product.
b. Calculate the necessary cost divisors, calculate unit costs for each cost element in the coating department for the month of March, and determine the differences between actual unit costs and standard unit costs. (For this purpose, standard unit costs for "other processing costs" should be defined as the average flexible budget at the actual labor volume.)
c. Calculate the materials quantity variance, the labor quantity variance, the overhead spending variance, and the scrap recovery variance for the month. What interpretation do you make of the scrap recovery variance?

12. Cost distribution sheet; Usefulness of unit costs. Dashing Dachshund Dippers are made in two sequential processes, bristle toning and assembly. The bristle toning department manufacturers bristle sets, while the assembly department assembles the final product. The data are:

Bristle toning department:
Opening inventory: 400 units, 100 percent complete as to materials ($1,900) and 50 percent complete as to processing costs (1,860).

Units started during month: 3,150.

Bristle sets completed and transferred to assembly: 3,000.

Units spoiled: 50. This is considered normal; scrap recovery of $75 is credited against current period material cost.

Closing inventory: 100 percent complete as to materials, 40 percent complete as to processing costs.

Costs for the current period: materials, $9,375 (before credit for scrap recovery); labor, $6,000; other processing costs (variable), $4,500; other processing costs (fixed), $3,000.

Unit costs are determined by the moving average method.

Assembly department:

Opening inventory: 200 units, 100 percent complete as to materials ($5,300) and 25 percent complete as to processing costs ($975).

Materials required in this process (per finished unit): two bristle sets from bristle toning; óne bristle holder, at $3 (required at start of process).

Units started: 1,500.

Units transferred to finished goods: 1,500.

Units spoiled: none.

Closing inventory: 100 percent complete as to materials, 75 percent complete as to processing costs.

Costs for the current period: materials, to be computed from data given above; labor, $8,000; other processing costs (variable), $6,400; other processing costs (fixed), $4,800.

Ending inventories and transfers to finished goods are costed on a Fifo basis.

a. Prepare a production cost summary and distribution sheet, distributing the full costs of each department by the method specified.

b. What unit costs should be reported to management as the costs of operations for the month? Should any distinction be made between fixed and variable costs in such calculations?

c. What are the shortcomings of these unit cost figures for managerial decision making?

(Adapted from a problem by Professor John C. Burton.)

13. Interpreting unit costs.   In recent months, the Vyberg Company has been unable to satisfy all of its customers' demands for Vylac, an industrial chemical manufactured in the company's Rochester plant. To meet these demands, a second set of Vylac processing facilities is now under construction at the company's Chicago factory, and these facilities are expected to go on stream in six or seven months.

The new facilities will give the company more production capacity than Vylac's present users can possibly take. In fact, management's decision to build the new facilities was predicated on the marketing director's assurance that she could find and develop additional profitable markets for this product. She has now come up with several suggestions, and you have been asked to assist management by estimating Vylac's unit cost.

Vylac is now manufactured in department 423 in the Rochester plant. Production facilities in this department are used exclusively for the manufacture of this product. Vylac is produced by mixing three materials (designated A, B, and C for easy reference here), heating the mixture under pressure in the presence of a catalyst, cooling it, and filtering out impurities. The finished product is then pumped into storage tanks for later packaging or shipment in bulk containers.

You have begun your investigation by collecting cost and output data from the Rochester plant records. Because the several steps in the manufacturing process take place in a continuous sequence, the process has always been treated as a single operation for product costing purposes. The following information on last month's operations has been made available to you:

Costs charged to department:

Material A, 10,000 pounds.....................	$ 20,800
Material B, 1,000 gallons.......................	5,200
Material C, 4,000 gallons.......................	27,300
Labor and other processing costs..............	48,000
Total input costs................................	$101,300

Quantities (gallons of Vylac):

In process, beginning of month.................	4,000
Finished and pumped into storage tanks.......	48,000
In process, end of month......................	8,000

Because processing starts when the raw materials are put into the mixing tanks, no additional materials are ever needed to complete the units that are in process in this department at any time. You also find that approximately half of the processing work had already been performed on the units in process in this department at the beginning and end of last month. Finally, a check of the accounts reveals that the work in process in this department at the beginning of last month was carried at a total materials cost of $4,000 and a total processing cost of $1,800.

The facilities at Chicago will be almost identical to those at Rochester, and the engineers see no reason why costs in the two plants should be very far apart once the new plant has gone through the shakedown stage, as long as production volumes are comparable.

a.   Compute unit cost for last month.
b.   Indicate how you think management might use these unit cost figures. Identify any additional information that you think would make the unit cost figures more useful. How, if at all, would you change the unit cost calculations?

14. Comprehensive unit cost problem; Journal entries.   The King Process Company manufacturers one product, putting it through two processes—No. 1 and No. 2.

For each pound of process No. 1 output, two units of raw material X are put in at the start of processing. For each gallon of process No. 2 output, three cans of raw material Y are put in at the end of processing. Two pounds of process No. 1 output are placed at the start of process No. 2 for each gallon of finished goods started. Spoilage occurs in process No. 2 just before processing is 50 percent complete. The costs of the spoiled units are assigned to the equivalent good units produced during the period or in process at the end of the period.

The company uses Fifo for inventory costing for process No. 1 and finished goods, and moving average cost for inventory costing for process No. 2. Separate accounts are maintained for each process for (1) raw materials, (2) processing costs, and (3) prior department costs (costs of semiprocessed products received by process No. 2 from process No. 1). The recovery value of spoiled units is deducted from prior department costs.

Data for March:

1. Units transferred:
   From process No. 1 to process No. 2: 2,200 pounds.
   From Process No. 2 to finished goods: 900 gallons.
   From finished goods to cost of goods sold: 600 gallons.
2. Raw material unit costs: X, $1.51 per unit; Y, $2 per can.
3. Processing costs: process No. 1, $3,344; process No. 2, $4,010.
4. Spoilage recovery, $100.
5. Inventory data:

	Process No. 1		Process No. 2		Finished Goods	
	Initial	Final	Initial	Final	Initial	Final
Units of product......	200 lbs.	300 lbs.	200 gal.	300 gal.	700 gal.	1,000 gal.
Fraction complete, processing costs....	½	⅓	½	⅔		
Cost:					$13,300	
Materials..........	$560		0			
Processing costs....	$108		$ 390			
Prior department costs............	0		$2,200			

a. Calculate the cost, element by element, of each unit of equivalent production in process No. 1 during March. Then calculate the total cost assigned to the March 31 inventory in process No. 1 and to the units transferred to process No. 2.

b. Calculate the cost, element by element, of each unit of equivalent production in process No. 2 during March. Then calculate the total cost assigned to the March 31 inventory in process No. 2 and to the units transferred to the finished goods inventory. Calculate the cost of goods sold and the cost of the March 31 inventory of finished goods.

c. Compute the effect of spoilage on unit cost in process No. 2. Do you agree with the company's practice of including the cost of spoiled units in the cost of the good units produced? Give your reasons.

(CPA adapted)

11

Costing Joint Products

(two products produced at once)

THE ILLUSTRATIONS of job order and process costing in previous chapters all dealt with manufacturing operations in which processing a given set of materials yielded only one kind of product. Job order and process costing can also be used when the processing of a single input or set of inputs yields two or more products simultaneously. These are known as joint products. Examples are gasoline and heating oil, cowhides and beef carcasses.

Unfortunately, job order or process costing can only measure the cost of the joint products as a group. If costs are to be assigned to individual joint products, an additional set of calculations must be made. This chapter is concerned with four aspects of this process, in the following sequence:

1. Recognizing joint products and the joint costs of producing them.
2. Analyzing the joint costs of fixed-yield processes to identify the costs relevant to managerial decisions.
3. Distributing joint costs among the various joint products for financial accounting purposes.
4. Analyzing joint costs when management can influence the relative yields of the various joint products.

RECOGNIZING JOINT PRODUCTS AND JOINT COSTS

Some joint products emerge from the joint production process quickly; others do not appear until a substantial number of processing steps have taken place. Once a joint product does emerge, it may either be offered for sale or be sent elsewhere for further processing.

371

Split-off Points

The stage of production at which the joint products are separated for further independent processing or sale is commonly referred to as the *split-off point*. At this point the individual products have separate identities for the first time. These identifiable products, whatever their form, are the joint products of the processing operations prior to the split-off point.

EXHIBIT 11–1

Split-off Points in Joint Production

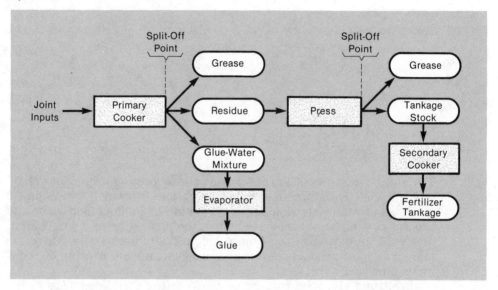

Exhibit 11–1 shows a process with two split-off points. Raw materials are first cooked, after which three separate products are split off: grease, a glue and water mixture, and a residue. Both the glue-water mixture and the residue are subjected to separate processing. Processing the mixture yields one product only: glue. Processing the residue, on the other hand, yields two products: grease and tankage stock. The latter is then cooked once again to yield fertilizer tankage.

Notice that all three outputs of the first production process are joint products, even though only one of them is in final salable condition. Joint production ends at the split-off point; therefore, the joint products are the products that emerge at this point. We may seem to be splitting hairs to say so, but the third joint product of this first process is the glue-water mixture, not the glue. The glue is the output of a separate process. It is not a joint product.

Joint Costs

This distinction has a strong bearing on the classification of costs. *Joint costs* are the costs of those input factors that are necessary for the manufacture of all the joint products as a group. They are not traceable to any one of the various joint products. The costs of operating the primary cooker are joint costs of all the outputs of that process.

Separable costs, on the other hand, are the costs that are traceable to the processing of a single joint product after the split-off point. The costs of operating the evaporator are separable costs of glue manufacture. These are also referred to as *specific costs*.

In some cases, the classification of a cost as either joint or separable depends on which product or products are being discussed. The costs of operating the press, for example, are separable costs of processing the residue, but they are joint costs of the grease and tankage stock emerging from that process.

JOINT COSTS IN DECISION MAKING

Joint costs are worth studying in the first instance because they need to be handled carefully in analyses designed to help management make decisions. To emphasize this point, we need to consider two kinds of decisions:

1. Decisions relating to the joint products as a group—e.g., discontinue total production or expand total production.
2. Decisions relating to the depth of additional processing to be applied to individual joint products—e.g., sell the product as it stands or process it further before sale.

To keep the discussion simple, we shall assume for the moment that the joint production process is a fixed-yield process—that is, each joint product's percentage of the total physical output is fixed by formula, as in certain chemical reactions.

Joint Products as a Group

For the group of joint products as a whole, the question is whether the total revenue to be derived from the sale of all joint products, less any processing and distribution costs necessary to place these products in marketable form, is adequate to cover the incremental costs of the joint inputs. For example, the decision to work a mine which produces ore containing gold, zinc, and lead must be based on consideration of the market prices of all three metals.

Individual Joint Products

Once it has been determined that joint production is profitable, the next question is how far to process each of the joint products. For example, should cowhides be tanned or should they be sold on the market untanned? For this kind of decision, the question is whether the sale value of the product can be increased by more than the incremental separable costs.

The cost of the steer no longer has any meaning for this decision.

What is relevant is opportunity cost, in this case the amount that could be realized from the sale of the untanned hides. If hides can be sold untanned for 40 cents a pound, then 40 cents a pound is the opportunity cost of any hides that are retained for further processing. (Not selling the hides at 40 cents requires the same economic sacrifice as buying hides at 40 cents; this the meaning of opportunity cost.) The relevant comparison is:

Market value of tanned hides............................		$0.50
Less: Market value of untanned hides.................	$0.40	
Incremental separate processing cost...........	0.08	0.48
Incremental processing profit............................		$0.02

This kind of comparison is valid even if the joint product in question is totally valueless and unmarketable at the split-off point. The absence of a market for one of the joint products merely means that opportunity cost for that product is zero. The desirability of processing this product further, therefore, can be determined by comparing the costs of further processing with the net market proceeds from the product after processing. No allocation of the joint costs will assist in this decision.[1]

Separable Costs and Joint Production Decisions

The separable costs of further processing and distribution of individual products may in some cases have a bearing on the decision as to whether to manufacture the joint products as a group. In making this decision, the incremental profit from further processing should be considered but processing losses from further processing should be ignored.

For example, suppose processing a certain material will yield 2,000 tons of product A and 500 tons of product B a week at a total joint cost of $60,000 a week. Product A can be sold for $40 a ton, but product B is unsalable without further processing. After further processing, product B can be sold for $15 a ton, but incremental separable processing costs total $6,000 a week. The decision to continue joint production should be based on the following comparison:

	A	B	Total
Sales...	$80,000	$7,500	$87,500
Incremental separable processing cost......	—	6,000	6,000
Product contribution.........................	$80,000	$1,500	$81,500
Joint processing cost.......................			60,000
Joint profit...................................			$21,500

---

[1] This analysis ignores the possibility of placing individual joint products in inventory until market conditions improve. For some observations on this possibility, see Ronald V. Hartley, "Decision Making when Joint Products are Involved," *The Accounting Review,* October 1971, pp. 746–55.

But suppose product B can be sold for only $10 a ton, or total revenues of only $5,000. Unprocessed units of product B must be trucked away at a cost of $1 a ton. In this case further processing of B cannot be justified, and the joint production decision must be based on the revenue for product A alone. Product B will be obtained along with A, but management is under no compulsion to process it further. In this case the comparison might take the following form:

Sales, product A..................................		$80,000
Less: Joint processing costs..................	$60,000	
Removal costs, product B..............	500	60,500
Joint profit.......................................		$19,500

Any costs of disposing of the unwanted by-product must be charged against product A revenues, but any losses that would occur if the by-product were processed further can be disregarded because further processing is not an acceptable course of action.

COSTING CO-PRODUCTS FOR FINANCIAL REPORTING

For decision purposes, each joint product should be costed at its opportunity cost. The accountant cannot use opportunity cost to measure the costs of individual joint products for financial accounting purposes, however, because the total of the opportunity costs will almost never equal the total cost of production.

Unfortunately, the historical cost of a joint product is not a measurable quantity—historical costs can be measured only for the group of joint products as a whole. As a result, the accountant has to use a formula of some sort to allocate the joint costs to the various joint products. In this section we shall discuss several of the formulas that might be used when each of the joint products is a *co-product,* contributing a significant percentage of the total market value of the joint products as a group. These formulas are built on three different bases:

1. Physical unit basis.
2. Market price basis.
3. Net realization basis.

Physical Unit Basis of Allocation

The simplest method of allocation is to count the number of units of each of the joint products, add these figures together, and then divide the total number of units into the total joint cost to get an average unit cost. Under this method, all products have the same unit cost.

For example, suppose that it costs a lumber mill $10,000 to produce 100,000 board feet of lumber. This lumber is inspected and divided into five different quality grades, in the following proportions:

Grade	Board Feet
Clear.............................	10,000
Industrial..........................	20,000
No. 1.............................	40,000
No. 2.............................	20,000
No. 3.............................	10,000
Total.......................	100,000

In this case the average cost of $10,000 divided by 100,000, or $100 per thousand board feet, would be used to measure the cost of each of the five grades of lumber.

If this method is used, the various joint products will have different apparent profit rates. Suppose, for instance, that the various grades of lumber can be sold at the following prices per thousand feet:

Grade	Price
Clear..............................	$240
Industrial..........................	180
No. 1.............................	150
No. 2.............................	120
No. 3.............................	60

If each grade is assigned a cost of $100 per thousand feet, some grades will appear to be very profitable and one grade will even show a loss, as illustrated in Exhibit 11–2.

main defect – ignores cost-value relationship

The main defect of this method is that it ignores the cost-value relationship implicit in accounting measurements of nonmonetary assets. The purpose of costs is to create values. The use of cost to measure assets is based on the assumption that a prudent manager will not incur costs unless the value created is likely to exceed the costs. If the value of the group is greater than the cost of producing it, then no portion of the joint cost can be said to be unproductive. Use of the $100 figure for all grades implies that some of the joint costs are more productive than others, an economic impossibility. When applied to the poorest grade of lumber, it produces an even

EXHIBIT 11–2

Profit Margins Reflecting the Physical Unit Basis of Allocation

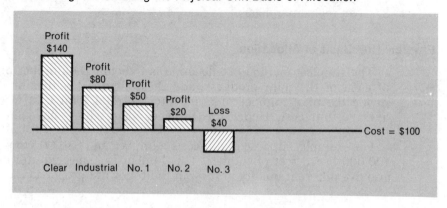

more absurd result—an apparent loss on production. If this were true, the company could avoid the loss by not producing No. 3 lumber; since this can't be done without sacrificing the other grades as well, the cost figure must be wrong.

Support for this conclusion can be found in another quarter as well. Clear evidence that outputs are not equally costly is provided by the premiums that ordinarily must be paid for higher quality inputs. For example, if a given stand of timber is expected to yield a high proportion of the higher valued grades of lumber, the timber rights will command a higher price than if the lower grades predominate. Therefore, since output value affects input cost, it would seem reasonable to reflect value differences in the cost allocation.

Market Price Basis of Allocation

One alternative to the physical unit basis is the relative market price basis. When this basis is used, costs are allocated to each joint product in proportion to its percentage of the total of the market prices of all the joint products (see Exhibit 11–3).

EXHIBIT 11–3

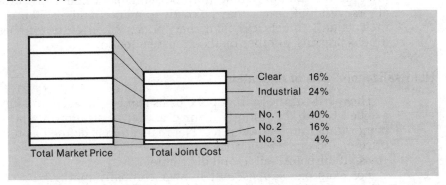

The allocation of lumber costs on this basis is illustrated in Exhibit 11–4. The prices in column (2) are the market prices of the joint products at the split-off point. Based on these prices, the total market price of the joint outputs totals $15,000, as shown at the bottom of column (3). Each product's percentage of this total is then multiplied by the $10,000 total joint cost to yield the cost allocations in column (5).

Since clear lumber has 16 percent of the total market value, it gets 16 percent of the joint costs, or $1,600. Dividing this by the output figure in column (1) yields a unit cost of $160 per thousand board feet. (The unit cost figures can also be determined by multiplying the market prices in column (2) by the cost-value ratio: $10,000/$15,000 = 2/3.)

This method does succeed in allocating all of the joint costs. Furthermore, unit cost can never be greater than market price unless

EXHIBIT 11–4

Joint Cost Allocated on Relative Market Price Basis

	(1)	(2)	(3)	(4)	(5)	(6)
			Total	Percent		Allocated
	M Feet		Market	of Total	Total Cost	Cost per
	Pro-	Price per	Price	Market	Allocated	M Feet
Grade	duced	M Feet	(1) × (2)	Price	(4) × $10,000	(5) ÷ (1)
Clear..............	10	$240	$ 2,400	16%	$ 1,600	$160
Industrial.........	20	180	3,600	24	2,400	120
No. 1..............	40	150	6,000	40	4,000	100
No. 2..............	20	120	2,400	16	1,600	80
No. 3..............	10	60	600	4	400	40
Total........	100	xxx	$15,000	100%	$10,000	xxx

market prices are too low to cover the joint costs in total. Paradoxically, however, the method doesn't necessarily ensure that the allocated cost will always be less than market value, nor that cost figures will be proportional to value. The reason is that price is not always a good measure of value. Some products that have no market price at the split-off point may be valuable when fully processed; others with high prices may be costly to market and distribute, so that their value is much less than their price. When either of these conditions prevails, another method must be found.

Net Realization Basis of Allocation

The merits of the market price basis can be salvaged and its defects avoided if market value is defined as net realization at the split-off point rather than market price. Net realization is defined as the selling price of the *end product* less any costs necessary to process it after the split-off point, sell it, and distribute it.

For example, suppose our lumber company markets its output of clear and industrial grades without further processing, but sells the other three grades only after processing each of them separately.

EXHIBIT 11–5

Calculation of Net Realization

	(1)	(2)	(3)	(4)	(5)
		End-		Separate	
		Product	End-Product	Processing	Net
	M Feet	Selling	Sales Value	and Mar-	Realization
Grade	Produced	Price	(1) × (2)	keting Costs	(3) − (4)
Clear..............	10	$240	$ 2,400	—	$ 2,400
Industrial...........	20	180	3,600	$ 80	3,520
No. 1..............	40	190	7,600	1,200	6,400
No. 2..............	20	160	3,200	640	2,560
No. 3..............	10	150	1,500	380	1,120
Total........	100	xxx	$18,300	$2,300	$16,000

Clear lumber can be sold without any additional marketing costs, and industrial grade lumber requires very little marketing effort. The products made from the other three grades are costly to produce and distribute, but the net realization is greater than the unprocessed lumber would generate if sold without processing.

The necessary data are shown in Exhibit 11–5. The selling prices of the finished products are shown in column (2). Column (4) shows the separate costs of processing and marketing the various products, and column (5) shows the net realization from each.

Cost allocations can now be based on these net realization figures, as in Exhibit 11–6. Each product's percentage of the total net realization of all five products combined, from column (3), is applied to the total joint cost of $10,000 to determine the amount to be allocated to each, shown in column (4). These amounts are then divided by the outputs of the various joint products to derive the unit cost figures

EXHIBIT 11–6

Cost Allocation on a Net Realization Basis

Grade	(1) M Feet Produced	(2) Net Realization	(3) Percent of Total Net Realization	(4) Joint Cost Allocated (3) × $10,000	(5) Allocated Unit Cost (4) ÷ (1)
Clear.............	10	$ 2,400	15%	$ 1,500	$150
Industrial.........	20	3,520	22	2,200	110
No. 1.............	40	6,400	40	4,000	100
No. 2.............	20	2,560	16	1,600	80
No. 3.............	10	1,120	7	700	70
Total.......	100	$16,000	100%	$10,000	xxx

in column (5). Thus clear lumber provides 15 percent of the net realization and is allocated 15 percent of the joint cost, or $1,500. This amounts to $150 for each thousand board feet.

Using the Unit Cost Figures

The net realization method is widely used because it provides unit costs for inventory measurement that are less than the net realizable value of the units in inventory. For example, inventories of lumber in the illustration would be measured by the unit cost figures in column (5). Inventories of processed lumber would be measured by these amounts plus the average separable costs of processing the lumber. If the separable costs of No. 3 lumber are $20 for processing and $10 for marketing, inventories of the processed product will be measured at $70, their share of the joint costs, plus $20 (marketing costs are not included in the cost of unmarketed inventories).

Unit costs also enter into profit calculations. Product profit margins under the uniform net realization method are proportional to net realization, however, and no product will show a loss as long as all products as a group are profitable. It should be apparent that unit costs and profit margins determined in this way have no relevance to management decision making. The decision maker needs measures of the sacrifices that the company must make to secure units of the individual products. No method designed to allocate all of the joint costs to the various joint products will provide this information.

By the same token, the unit costs of individual products should not be used in depth-of-processing decisions. For example, suppose that the clear lumber can be converted into cabinets at an incremental cost of $100 per thousand square feet. The cabinets can be sold at a price of $300. If the lumber is charged against this proposal at the $150 unit cost derived in Exhibit 11–6, the proposal will look quite profitable:

Revenue..		$300
Less: Joint processing cost.........................	$150	
Separable processing cost....................	100	250
Operating margin.....................................		$ 50

In view of the opportunity costs, however, the proposal is clearly unprofitable:

Incremental revenue:	
Revenue from sale of cabinets............................	$300
Less: Revenue from sale of lumber.......................	240
Incremental revenue.................................	$ 60
Separable costs...	100
Processing loss...	$(40)

Since the total joint cost will be $10,000 whether the lumber is processed or sold "as is," the accountant's unit cost is a sunk cost and irrelevant to this decision.

THE COSTING OF BY-PRODUCTS

In principle, the relative net realization basis can be used in any joint cost situation to derive cost figures for financial accounting purposes. This method is modified in practice, however, when one or more of the joint products is classified as a by-product. In this section we shall see how by-products differ from co-products and illustrate how by-products are treated in the cost allocation procedure.

Defining By-Products

Although the distinction between by-products and co-products or main products is inevitably imprecise, a reasonable working definition is that a by-product is a joint product for which the market value is an immaterial proportion of the total market value of all the joint products.

Any distinction between co-products and by-products must be regarded as strictly temporary, to be reconsidered as conditions change.

Gasoline, for example, was originally thought of as a by-product in the manufacture of kerosene. With the growth of the automobile and electric lighting, kerosene became the by-product; but the jet airliner brought kerosene back into the picture as a major product once more.

Illustration of By-Product Costing

The costing method known as the by-product method consists of subtracting the net realizable value of the by-products from the total of the joint costs. The residual is then divided among the main products.

For example, suppose that a process yields three products, A, B, and C. Product C is to be treated as a by-product, A and B as main products. The total cost of processing a 1,000-pound batch of products is $934. Yield and market value data are as follows:

Product	Yield (Pounds)	Market Value per Pound	Total Market Value
A....................	200	$1.90	$ 380
B....................	500	1.50	750
C....................	300	0.10	30
Total.........	1,000	xxx	$1,160

The first step in the by-product method is to subtract the market value of the by-product from the total joint cost:

Joint cost.................................	$934
Less: Value of by-product................	30
Cost assigned to main product.............	$904

The remainder of the joint cost is then apportioned between the main products by one of the methods described earlier. A relative market value distribution is as follows:

Product	Percent of Total Market Value	Total Cost Allocated	Allocated Cost per Pound
A....................	33.6	$304	$1.52
B....................	66.4	600	1.20
Total.........	100.0	$904	xxx

byproduct - no profit. Cost = rev.

This method assigns to the by-product a cost equal to its anticipated value. In the example, joint cost amounts to $934, but only $904 of this is assigned to the main products. The remaining $30 goes to product C, which then shows neither a profit nor a loss.

Timing of By-Product Recognition

By-product revenues may be recognized in the accounts either at the time of split-off or at the time the by-products are sold. Deferral until point of sale has the advantage of avoiding the need to estimate sale value. It has the distadvantage of introducing into the accounts irregularities that have nothing to do with the production operations in the periods in which the by-products are sold. Unless the total value of all of the by-products is immaterial, by-product values should be recognized in the periods in which they are produced.

Inventory Measurement of By-Products

The selection of the time for recognizing the value of by-products carries with it an implicit assumption as to the method of measuring by-product inventories. Delay in recognition to the time of sale implies that by-products will be carried as memorandum quantities only. Recognition of value at the time of split-off implies measurement at market value. This violates the cost basis for inventory measurement in general, but the effect on net income is likely to be immaterial.

JOINT COSTS OF VARIABLE-YIELD PROCESSES

Until now, we have dealt only with fixed-yield processes, in which each product's percentage of the total physical output is fixed by formula. Now we shall turn briefly to two kinds of variable-yield situations:

1. *Materials-determined yields:* the percentage yield of each of the joint products depends on the quality or composition of the joint materials inputs.
2. *Processing-determined yields:* the relative yields of the various joint products can be varied by alterations in the processing methods employed.

In each case, variations in yield are accompanied by variations in cost. This means that accountants can calculate the incremental cost of producing individual joint products, something they can't do when yields are fixed. In this section we shall see how this can be done and what problems are likely to be encountered. Product costs for financial accounting purposes are no different from those used in fixed-yield situations.

Measuring Incremental Costs: Variable Input Quality

Measuring incremental cost is relatively simple when the yield depends on the kind of materials used. To illustrate, suppose that materials costing $100 can be processed for $50 to yield 20 units of X and 50 units of Y. If higher quality materials costing $120 are used instead, the output of X will go up to 25 units; the output of Y will remain at 50 units. The increments therefore are as follows:

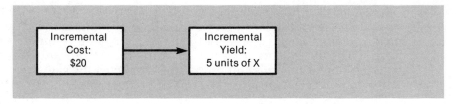

The average incremental cost of product X is $20/5 = $4 a unit.

A related problem is to determine the maximum price that the company can afford to pay for joint inputs of a given grade or specification. For example, in buying raw materials that vary in quality, the price that can be paid will be higher on grades that yield a greater proportion of high-value products. The maximum purchase price is a function of the total value of all the joint products less all the joint costs of processing or conversion.

Measuring Incremental Costs: Variable Input Mix

The same idea can be applied to more complex situations in which yields can be influenced by the processing methods used. For example, assume that a department produces two products, X and Y, from a single process. Product X sells for $5 a pound; product Y is priced at $2 a pound. Production of these two products is currently in the ratio of 40 percent product X and 60 percent product Y, but by varying production techniques the yield of X can be increased to a maximum of 60 percent if conditions warrant.

This may be treated as a problem in the desirability of further processing. First, let us assume that the increased yield of product X results from subjecting product Y to an additional processing operation (as in subjecting gas-oil distillates to catalytic cracking to increase the gasoline yield). If 60 pounds of product Y can be processed further to yield 20 additional pounds of product X and only 40 pounds of product Y, at an incremental processing cost of $0.75 a pound, we get the following comparison:

Revenues after processing:
Product X, 20 pounds at $5...............................		$100
Product Y, 40 pounds at $2...............................		80
Total..		$180
Less: Processing cost, 60 pounds at $0.75....................	$ 45	
Market value of Y before processing (60 pounds at $2).	120	165
Incremental profit..		$ 15

Phrasing this in another way, the incremental cost of another 20 pounds of product X is the sum of $45 processing cost and $40 in lost revenues from the sale of 20 pounds of product Y, or $85. The average incremental cost of product X is thus $4.25 a pound. Incremental revenue is $5 a pound, and incremental profit is $5.00 − $4.25 = $0.75 a pound, or $15 for a twenty-pound batch.

A similar set of calculations can be prepared if the increased yield results, not from further processing of one of the original joint products, but from modifications in the basic processing techniques themselves. The incremental cost of increasing the yield of any product is still the sum of incremental processing costs plus the sale value of the other joint products lost by the shift in product mix.

Measurement Difficulties

Two major difficulties hamper efforts to apply this approach in practice. First, incremental cost is not a constant but varies, depending on relative yields. If the crude run is yielding 35 percent gasoline, the cost of increasing the yield to 36 percent will probably be less than it would be to increase the yield from 40 to 41 percent. This requires the development of a schedule or table of incremental costs, one for each assumed product mix.

Second, the opportunity cost of products sacrificed to increase the yield of others is the net revenue lost by this sacrifice. This is not necessarily equal to the product price. For example, if existing market prices are rigid and increased output of product Y will merely result in increased inventories of product Y, then the opportunity cost component of the incremental cost of product X is zero. (It may even be negative to allow for inventory carrying costs.) Even if market prices are flexible, if the company's share of the market is so large that increases in sales volume can be achieved only by price reductions or greater promotional effort or both, the opportunity cost of product Y will almost certainly be less than its market price.

Calculations of this sort are made routinely in industries such as oil refining in which production operations are highly automated and technically advanced. The usefulness of the results, however, depends on the quality of the estimates of the relationships between costs and yields. If the quality of these estimates is low, the estimates of incremental costs will be unreliable.

SUMMARY

When products are manufactured independently, a large number of costs can be attributed clearly to one product or another. When two or more products are produced jointly from a single set of inputs, however, the joint costs cannot be attributed clearly to individual products.

Faced with this problem, the accountant has developed several methods of allocating joint costs among the various joint products. One of these, the relative net realization method, allocates joint costs in proportion to their share of the total value of the ultimate end products, less any costs necessary to convert joint products into end products. This method yields unit costs that are adequate for public financial reporting and possibly also for other purposes such as contract costing, insuring inventories, and calculating taxes.

No method that routinely allocates all the joint costs to one joint product or another produces product costs that are relevant to decisions. Products that emerge from fixed-yield processes should be measured for decision purposes by their opportunity costs; those emerging from variable-yield processes should be measured either at opportunity cost or at the incremental cost of increasing the relative yield of each individual joint product, the choice depending on the decision to be made. Opportunity cost is used routinely only for joint products classified as by-products; incremental cost is calculated only in highly sophisticated systems which are able to deal with changes in incremental cost as the relative product mix varies.

KEY TERMS

The most important terms introduced and defined in this chapter are the following:

By-products	Net realization method
Co-products	Separable costs
Fixed-yield process	Split-off point
Joint cost	Variable-yield process
Joint product	

INDEPENDENT STUDY PROBLEMS
(Solutions in Appendix C)

1. Unit cost for inventory measurement. The Zandrum Company processes a group of raw materials in a single processing operation. The output of this operation consists of three products destined for further processing in the company's factory and one by-product that is sold "as is" to fertilizer manufacturers. None of the three products that are processed further is salable in the form in which it emerges from joint production.

The company's policy is to treat by-product values as reductions of joint cost and to allocate net joint cost among the main products by the net realization method. During July, the costs of raw materials and joint processing amounted to $21,500. Other data were as follows:

Product	Quantity Produced (units)	Final Selling Price	Estimated Cost per Unit to Complete
A......................	1,000	$ 6.20	$0.90
B......................	2,000	3.80	0.80
C......................	2,500	10.00	2.52
D......................	10,000	0.05	—

a. Calculate the unit costs of the three joint products by the net realization method. How much cost is assigned to the by-product?
b. Recalculate unit costs by the physical unit method. Is this method likely to be acceptable for financial reporting? Explain your reasoning.

2. Joint costs in decision making. A factory processes 300,000 pounds of material X each month to produce 100,000 pounds of Y and 200,000 pounds of Z. Product Y sells for $0.60 a pound; product Z sells for $0.45. The costs of this process are as follows:

Materials: 300,000 × $0.20.............. $ 60,000
Variable processing..................... 30,000
Fixed processing.......................   10,000
    Total............................. $100,000

These costs are divided between the two products in proportion to their relative market values. The unit cost of Y is $0.40; Z has a unit cost of $0.30.

A proposal has just been made to subject product Y to further processing by mixing it with other purchased materials. This would take the entire current output of product Y. The new product, known as Y-Plus, would sell at a price of $1.30 a package. Each package of Y-Plus would require one pound of product Y as raw material. Additional costs of other materials, labor and overhead to process Y into Y-Plus would total $80,000 a month. The effects of the changeover on selling and administrative costs and on revenues from the sale of product Z would be negligible.

a. Should the proposal be accepted? Show your calculations. How useful was the $0.40 unit cost figure in this calculation?

b. Assume that the Y-Plus proposal has been rejected. An opportunity has arisen to sell an additional 20,000 pounds of Z at a price of 35 cents a pound. The existing market for Z would not be affected by acceptance of this proposal. All units of Y would be sold at a uniform price. What is the minimum price of Y that would make this a profitable proposal?

c. Assume that both the Y-Plus and Z proposals have been rejected. A new material has just become available. Processing costs would remain the same, but the process would yield two pounds of Y for every three pounds of Z. Total volume would be limited to 300,000 pounds of material, as at present. What is the maximum price the company could afford to pay for the new material?

EXERCISES AND PROBLEMS

1. Determining unit cost.   Joint costs amount to $19,200. The process yields two products in fixed proportions: 10,000 pounds of product A and 6,000 pounds of product B. Product A sells for $2.10 a unit, product B sells for 50 cents. All production is sold and the process has no excess capacity.

a. Calculate unit costs by the physical unit method.
b. Calculate unit costs by the relative market price method.
c. Which of these methods would you use? For what purpose?

2. Costing inventories of processed products.   The Emilia Company allocates joint costs between first-quality and second-quality products on the basis of their relative market value at the split-off point.
    Selling prices and allocated unit costs are as follows:

	Price	Cost
Firsts....................	$1.75	$1.50
Seconds..................	1.40	1.20

The seconds are reworked at a cost of 33 cents a unit. They are then sold as first-quality products. What unit cost would you assign to any of these reworked units that remain in the inventory at the end of the period?

3. Costing inventories; Separate processing. During the past year the Atom Chemical Company converted raw materials into 500,000 pounds of material A and 1 million gallons of liquid B. The total joint cost of production was $388,000. After separation, material A was further processed and converted into material C at an additional cost of 3 cents a pound. The sale price of material C was 40 cents a pound and that of liquid B 30 cents a gallon.

a. Prepare a physical flow diagram of these processes. Enter cost, quantity, and price data on this diagram.
b. Compute the unit cost that you would use to measure each of these products for public financial reporting.

4. Separate processing decision; Relevance of unit cost. A company processes soybeans. The initial process separates soybean oil and leaves a cakelike residue. The cake is then ground and moisturized to form soybean meal.

Last week the company processed 10,000 bushels of soybeans to yield 90,000 pounds of soybean oil and 450,000 pounds of cake. Further processing of the cake yielded 500,000 pounds (250 tons) of meal, the increase in weight resulting from added moisture.

The cost of the beans was $6 a bushel, the costs of joint processing were $14,400 and the costs of processing the cake into meal amounted to $2,500. The market price of meal was $150 a ton, and the market price of oil was 50 cents a pound.

a. Compute unit costs for the week using the net realization method of cost allocation.
b. Compute unit costs allocating joint costs on a physical unit basis.
c. The company has an opportunity to sell 50,000 pounds of cake. What figure would you use as the cost of cake for the purpose of deciding whether to take advantage of this opportunity?

5. Classifying a product as a by-product. The Jensen Chemical Company has a plant which produces two chemicals, borine and selinate, in a single joint process. The total cost incurred to the split-off point is $864,000 a month. Monthly production is 2 million gallons of borine and 300,000 pounds of selinate.

Borine is processed further to make one of the company's branded products, Tri-Bor. The net realization from sales of Tri-Bor, after deducting separate processing costs, is equivalent to 45 cents a gallon of borine. The average selling price of selinate is 20 cents a pound.

a. Compute the total cost and unit cost of borine on the assumption that selinate is a coproduct.
b. Compute the total cost and unit cost of borine on the assumption that selinate is a by-product.
c. Would you classify selinate as a by-product or as a co-product? Defend your recommendation.

6. Costing a by-product. Products A, B, and C are joint products. Products A and B are treated as main products; product C is treated as a by-product, its market value of $20 a pound being subtracted from joint costs at the time of split-off. The remaining joint costs are allocated between the main products on the basis of relative market values less completion costs.

During July, joint product costs amounted to $85,000 and costs of separate processing of product B totaled $10,000. The month's production was as follows:

Product A..................... 30,000 lbs.
Product B..................... 10,000 lbs.
Product C.....................   200 lbs.

Product A sells at a net price of $2 a pound; product B is sold at a price of $4 a pound.

a. How much of the joint cost is assigned to each unit of product C?
b. How much of the joint cost is assigned to each unit of product A?
c. In view of its high price per pound, do you agree with the company's decision to treat product C as a by-product? Explain briefly.
d. A proposal has been made to cost inventories of product A at $2 a pound and unprocessed product B at zero, on the ground that these figures represent their opportunity costs. Comment briefly on this proposal.

7. Profitability of a processed joint product. Product X and material Y are produced at a joint cost of $105,000 a month. Material Y is then processed further at a cost of $20,000 a month to become product Z.

Both X and Z are sold outright to a chain of grocery stores and the company incurs no selling expenses on these products. Material Y cannot be sold without further processing and cannot be obtained from other sources outside the company.

In a normal month, output consists of the following quantities and prices:

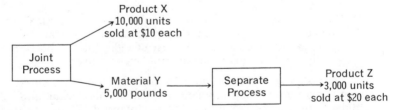

a. How much profit does the company earn on sales of product Z?
b. This company has 100 units of product X in its inventory. Given only the information above, at what amount would you expect the company to report this inventory on its balance sheet? Explain your calculations and your reasons for selecting the method you used.

8. Maximum purchase price. A company processes a raw material to yield two products, Dip and Nod. A unit of Dip sells for $0.50, a Nod brings in $0.40.

The process is now operating at full capacity, processing 10,000 pounds of raw materials each week to yield 20,000 units of Dip and 10,000 units of Nod. The company could sell more at these prices, but the existing equipment can't be used to process more than 10,000 pounds a month.

Weekly processing costs (excluding the costs of the raw materials) are as follows:

Fixed..................... $3,000
Variable.................   5,000

The fixed costs include $1,000 of depreciation, salaries of security guards, taxes, insurance, and other costs that would continue even if the process were to shut down entirely for a time; the remaining fixed costs are necessary to support any level of production up to full capacity. The variable costs vary in proportion to the number of pounds of materials processed.

a. What is the maximum price the company could pay for its raw materials without reporting a loss on this operation?

b. What is the maximum price the company could pay for its raw materials without finding it more profitable to shut the process down temporarily?

c. How would you change your answer to (b) if you found that the output of Nod could be converted into Snooze at a cost of $1,500? Snooze sells for $0.60 a unit.

d. How would you change your answer to (b) if you found that Dip could be converted into Plunge at a cost of $3,500. Plunge sells for $0.65 a unit.

9. Expanding production of joint products. A department processes 10,000 pounds of materials a month to manufacture two products, alpha and beta. Materials cost $0.40 a pound, and processing 10,000 pounds costs $2,300. The yield is 6,000 pounds of alpha and 4,000 pounds of beta. Alpha sells for $1 a pound; beta sells for $0.25. The allocation of joint costs, based on the net realization method, produces unit costs of 90 cents a pound for alpha and 22.5 cents a pound for beta.

The market for alpha is very strong and the company could sell an additional 3,000 units of this product each month at the current price. The present facilities are inadequate to process more than 10,000 pounds of materials, but the company can rent additional equipment for $500 a month to process an additional 5,000 pounds of materials. Other additional processing costs would be $1,000 a month.

a. How can the company afford to sell beta for $0.25 when the materials alone cost $0.40 a pound?

b. What is the company's profit or loss from beta?

c. Would you recommend renting the additional equipment?

10. Effect of materials quality on product cost. A substitute material for the raw material described in Problem 9 costs 48.4 cents a pound. Processing 10,000 pounds of this material would yield 8,000 pounds of alpha and 2,000 pounds of beta. Processing costs would not be affected by the substitution.

a. Recalculate product cost by the net realization method.

b. Calculate the cost of alpha on an incremental basis.

c. Should the substitution be made? Show your calculations.

11. Inclusion of separable costs in costing joint products. The Stendahl Company has used the net realization method to allocate joint costs between two products, A and B. Product A has a sale value of $10 a unit, while product B has no sale value without further processing. After separate processing, product B is sold for $6 a pound.

The company has just hired a new chief accountant, who feels that the net realization method assigns too much cost to product B. "We need both of these products to make the process pay," he said recently. "This means that every dollar we spend processing product B makes just as great a contribution to earnings as a dollar spent on the main process."

Production in a typical month amounts to 5,000 units of product A and 10,000 units of product B. The costs of the joint process amount to $67,-000 and separate processing of product B costs $10,000. The chief accountant's proposal is to place all costs in a single pool and allocate them on the basis of the relative sales value of the two products. The ratio is:

$$\frac{\text{Cost}}{\text{Sales value}} = \frac{\$67,000 + \$10,000}{5,000 \times \$10 + 10,000 \times \$6} = 70 \text{ percent}$$

a. What unit costs would emerge if the chief accountant's proposal were adopted?
b. What unit costs would be derived from the net realization method?
c. Which allocation method would you support? Give the reasons for your choice.

(Based on a suggestion by Professor Lawrence Benninger)

12. Joint costs and decisions. The ABC Company uses raw materials A and B in a process which yields two products, X and Y, in fixed proportions. The company has no other operations. The following figures are forecasted for an average month during the coming year:

1. Materials used: A, 5,000 pounds, $29,800; B, 500 gallons, $11,000.
2. Product output: X, 4,000 pounds; Y, 2,000 pounds; waste, 1,000 pounds.
3. Processing costs: variable, $8,000; fixed, $9,600. Fixed costs include the salary of the department head, straight-line depreciation on building and equipment, and amortization of the costs of developing the process some years ago.
4. Product selling prices: X, $15 a pound; Y, $40 a pound.
5. Direct product selling expenses: X, $16,000; Y, $44,000.
6. General selling and administrative expenses (not allocated to individual products), $14,000.
7. The company pays Ace Disposal Company a flat fee of $3,200 a month to remove and dispose of all waste produced by this process.
8. All selling and administrative expenses are fixed, and are paid in cash.

a. On the basis of this information, prepare an estimate of average factory cost per unit for each product.
b. Explain and defend the method you used in (a) to allocate joint costs.
c. By treating the waste, the ABC Company can convert it into a product selling for $4 a pound. Unfortunately, the incremental cost of processing the waste in this manner would be $5 a pound. Should the company process the waste? What is the highest cost per pound the company could afford to pay for processing the waste?
d. The sales manager says that increasing direct selling cost by $2,000 a month would increase sales of product X by 10 percent, without reducing the price. Assuming that the cost figures are correct, make calculations to determine the conditions necessary to justify accepting this proposal. What contribution did the unit cost figure you developed in answering (a) make to your analysis of this question?

13. Measuring departmental average cost. The Wilde Corporation operates a factory with two production departments. Materials first pass through department I, where a substantial loss in weight takes place at the start of processing. The semiprocessed materials pass on to department II, where they are processed further to form two separate products, Elong and Ulong, together with a waste material known as "tailings." The following data refer to the month of April:

	Department I	Department II
Quantities (pounds):		
Materials received..........................	100,000	80,000 (from Dept. I)
Work in process, April 1 (materials 100% complete, one half processed in department)..	20,000	None
Work completed...........................	80,000	20,000 Elong 50,000 Ulong 8,000 tailings
Work in process, April 30 (materials 100% complete, one third processed in department).	15,000	None
Costs:		
Costs in process, April 1:		
Materials................................	$ 8,100	None
Processing costs.........................	6,000	None
Materials received.......................	28,000	?
Processing costs incurred..................	46,700	$31,050

Sales and selling costs during April were as follows:

	Elong	Ulong	Tailings
Selling price per pound.......................	$ 3.00	$ 2.00	$0.10
Units sold (pounds)..........................	18,000	70,000	8,000
Traceable costs of packing and delivery.......	$2,700	$14,000	0

The traceable costs of packing and delivery were wholly variable with the number of pounds sold. In addition, fixed selling and administrative costs, not traceable to any product, amounted to $40,000 for the month.

The company uses the moving average method of inventory costing. Joint cost is allocated on the basis of the net realization method. Tailings are to be treated as a by-product.

a. Compute the total cost and cost per unit of department I inventory in process on April 30.

b. Compute the unit costs that would be used in recording the transfer to finished goods inventory of Elong, Ulong, and tailings, respectively.

c. Prepare unit cost figures for department I, based on equivalent production for the month. Suggest and describe at least one way to derive analogous figures for department II.

14. Using joint product inventories. The Wilde Corporation (Problem 13) in recent months has been unable to sell all its production of Elong at a price of $3 a pound. Rather than accept a lower price, management has increased the company's inventories quite substantially. This situation seems likely to continue. Management now believes it will not be able to sell more than 18,000 pounds of Elong a month, but sales of Ulong are expected to average 50,000 pounds a month. Two pounds of Elong are produced for every five pounds of Ulong, and these proportions can't be altered.

The production manager has recently figured out a way of treating Elong to make it acceptable to a few customers who use a competing product. Approximately 2,000 pounds of treated Elong can be sold each month to these customers, at a price of $2.50 a pound. The costs of treatment would be $0.50 a pound, and the costs of selling the product would be $0.20 a pound.

a. Should the 2,000 pounds of Elong be treated in this way? Support your conclusion with figures from this problem and a concise statement of your reasoning.
b. Recalculate unit costs on the assumption that this pattern of production and sales will continue. Is the new unit cost figure for Elong likely to encourage the manager to accept proposals like the one described in this problem?

15. Accepting a special order; Usefulness of standard joint cost. The management of Lincoln Products Company is considering a customer's request for a monthly shipment of 10,000 pounds of Awlcon, an industrial chemical, at a selling price of 70 cents a pound. This is considerably less than its current list price of 90 cents, but higher than its standard manufacturing cost (66 cents). Management would like to accept this contract, but only if it will increase the company's profits.

Awlcon is a specialty product, not available from other manufacturers. It is used as a processing chemical in several industries; the largest present user buys about 5,000 pounds a month. The proposed contract would be the company's first breakthrough into the rubber products industry. Because the end uses are so different, management has little fear that lower prices to the rubber manufacturers would spread to its other customers. In any case, management is convinced that it will never penetrate this industry without some price concessions.

Awlcon is manufactured in two stages. In the first stage, raw materials are processed to produce two intermediates, in fixed proportions. One of these intermediates is then processed further to yield a product called Tincon; the other intermediate is converted into Awlcon in a separate finishing operation.

The Awlcon finishing process yields both finished Awlcon and a waste material. This waste material has no market value, but the company is able to convert it into a salable product called Griscon. The company can sell as much Griscon as it can produce, at a price of 30 cents a pound.

The relationships between these production processes can be seen in the following diagram:

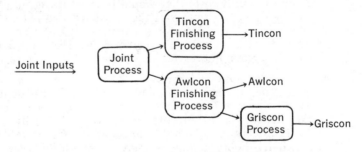

The company has a standard costing system which yields the following total standard cost per pound for each product, based on the net realization method:

Tincon........................ $0.38
Awlcon........................ 0.66
Griscon....................... 0.30

Volume, costs, and prices are expected to be at normal levels for the next year. Production quantity, market price per pound, and sales volume are as follows in a normal month:

	Quantity (Pounds)	Market Price	Market Value
Tincon	400,000	variable	$194,000
Awlcon	100,000	$0.90	90,000
Griscon	10,000	0.30	3,000
Total			$287,000

At these normal volumes, materials and processing costs are expected to total as follows:

	Basic Process	Separate Finishing Processes		
		Tincon	Awlcon	Griscon
Materials	$ 64,000	$22,000	$ 3,000	$ 200
Labor	30,000	45,000	18,000	1,100
Variable overhead	6,000	10,000	5,000	100
Fixed overhead	10,000	5,000	1,000	600
Total	$110,000	$82,000	$27,000	$2,000

Output can be increased or decreased fairly easily by as much as 25 percent of normal volume. Any larger increase would require an expansion of plant capacity. Within these limits, materials, labor, and variable overhead costs tend to vary directly and proportionately with volume, while fixed costs remain fairly stable. Selling and administrative costs are entirely fixed and none of them can be traced to any of the three products.

a. Verify the calculation of the standard cost figures. Griscon is treated as a by-product.
b. Under what conditions, if any, would you recommend acceptance of this order? Quantify your answer insofar as you are able.
c. For what purpose or purposes, if any, would you find the company's standard unit cost figures useful?

CASE 11–1: THE WILLIAMSON CHOCOLATE CO., LTD.*

The Williamson Chocolate Co., Ltd., which has its headquarters and principal factory in Leicester, England, has been engaged in the production of chocolate and cocoa products since the beginning of this century. Subsidiary companies have been established in Canada, Australia, and South Africa, and each of the subsidiaries manufactures the more important of the company's products and markets them in its home market.

The Australian company is located in Melbourne, where all of its manufacturing activities take place. Warehouses for local distribution are also maintained in Sydney, Adelaide, and Perth. The main output at the factory is chocolate in bars. Cocoa beans, the principal raw material for the manufacture of chocolate, are imported from abroad. As a rule, the

* This case was written by Professor David Solomons. Copyright by l'Institut pour l'Etude des Méthodes de Direction de l'Entreprise (IMEDE), Lausanne, Switzerland. Reproduced by permission. Places and dates have been disguised.

beans are cleaned, roasted, ground, and then passed through a press. In the press, cocoa butter is separated from cocoa powder, which comes out of the press in the form of cocoa cake. The cocoa butter leaves the press in liquid form because of the heat that is generated during the press operation. The cocoa butter is then stored in large tanks, ready for use in the current production of chocolate.

The Melbourne factory was a net user of cocoa butter, i.e., its chocolate production called for more cocoa butter than could be obtained from the pressing of cocoa beans for powder manufacture. This extra cocoa butter could have been imported but it was subject to a heavy import duty, and the local management believed that it was cheaper to import beans and extract the cocoa butter from them. As a result of implementing this policy the factory found itself with a steadily mounting stock of cocoa powder.

The following figures show how the stock of cocoa powder (in pounds) increased during the period 1968–70:

1968:
Stock at January 1, 1968.............................		30,500
Output of press....................................		416,975
		447,475
Less: Usage in 1968...............................		324,500
Stock at December 31, 1968.........................		122,975

1969:
Output of press....................................		638,750
		761,725
Less: Usage in 1969...............................	506,420	
Sales in 1969...............................	35,500	541,920
Stock at December 31, 1969.........................		219,805

1970:
Output of press....................................		792,125
		1,011,930
Less: Usage in 1970...............................	641,600	
Sales in 1970...............................	43,385	684,985
Stock of cocoa powder, December 31, 1970..........		326,945

These large stocks of cocoa powder held at the factory caused a serious storage problem, and the local management made continuous efforts to find profitable outlets for the excess cocoa powder. However, the sale of this powder on the Australian market raised a question as to its proper valuation. In accordance with accounting instructions issued by the head office in London some time before the last war, the cost of the cocoa beans purchased, together with the labor and overhead costs of the pressing process had to be allocated between the cocoa butter and the cocoa cake on the basis of the fat content remaining in these two products after the pressing operations. This gave a cost for cocoa powder of about $0.23 a pound or about 50 percent above its current market price at the end of 1970. The company was therefore unable to dispose of its excess stock of cocoa cake without incurring a considerable loss. For balance sheet purposes, however, the company made a provision in its accounts in order to bring the book value of its stock of cocoa down to the market value.

During 1971, cocoa prices fell further and the subsidiary was unable to sell any large quantities of its excess stocks, because its costs were too high. There was practically no market in Australia for cocoa cake. Williamson Chocolate did succeed, however, in exchanging 13,000 pounds of cake against 2,000 pounds of cocoa butter with another manufacturer.

In the middle of 1971, Mr. Cannon, the marketing manager, brought forward a scheme to market a new cocoa preparation for making a hot chocolate drink. The marketing pospects seemed good so long as the selling price could be kept low enough. This new product offered a promising means of disposing of the excess stocks of cocoa powder but only if they were costed out at substantially less than the cost allocated to them in the books.

The production manager, Mr. Parker, supported this proposal with enthusiasm. He had repeatedly drawn the attention of the subsidiary's managing director, Mr. Woodstock, to the storage problem created by the cocoa stocks, and he welcomed the possibility which now opened up of dealing with this problem once for all. Besides, he said, he had never been able to see the logic of basing the cost of cocoa powder on its fat content. It was its flavor which was important, and fat content had little to do with flavor.

Both Cannon and Parker were surprised to find that Mr. Woodstock was not unreservedly enthusiastic about Cannon's proposal. He pointed out that if cocoa powder were charged to the new product at present cost levels, the product would never show a profit; and without a drop in the price of cocoa beans greater than anyone could at present foresee, the only way to reduce the cost of cocoa powder would be to change the basis of cost allocation between cocoa powder and cocoa butter. This could not be done without permission from London and he was by no means certain that such permission would be given unless some basis of cost allocation which was clearly better than the present one could be proposed. It was all very well to attack the present basis of allocation, as Mr. Parker had done. But unless he or somebody else could suggest a better one, why should London agree to a change?

Mr. Woodstock went on to point out that there was another aspect of the matter which made him reluctant to approach London. If the allocation of costs to cocoa powder were reduced, with a consequent increase in the cost of cocoa butter, the calculation which had been supplied to London in 1967 to support the expenditure of $40,000 on a new cocoa press would be completely undermined. Only on the basis of the present cost of producing cocoa butter as compared with the cost of importing it could investment in the press be justified. If more cost were to be allocated to cocoa butter, it might be shown that it ought to be imported after all, and the investment in the press would be shown to have been misguided.

a. What alternative methods of eliminating the surplus cocoa powder are available to Mr. Woodstock? What figures would he want to consider?
b. What should Mr. Woodstock tell London? Should he recommend a change in the allocation method?

12

Costing Marketing and Service Activities

MOST OPERATING costs in manufacturing firms can be placed in one of four categories: manufacturing, marketing and merchandising, research and development, and administrative service and support. In Chapter 2 we saw how costs in all four areas can be classified by organization segment and object of expenditure. Except for that brief discussion and some attention to marketing costs in Chapter 9, our interest has focused almost exclusively on the costs of manufacturing tangible products, omitting the other three categories.

This chapter will attempt to fill this gap. The first four sections deal with the marketing and administrative service costs of manufacturing concerns:

1. *Functional cost analysis*—measuring the costs of individual marketing and administrative service functions.
2. *Segment cost analysis*—assigning functional costs to individual marketing segments.
3. Using segment cost analysis to measure the costs of servicing individual *product lines*.
4. Using segment cost analysis to measure the costs of filling customer *orders of different sizes*.

The final section illustrates the application of these methods of analysis to the task of measuring the costs of end-product activities in *service businesses*—that is, those that are in the business of providing services rather than tangible goods to their customers.

FUNCTIONAL COST ANALYSIS

The first stage in costing marketing and administrative service activities is to measure or estimate the costs of individual *functions*. A function is any activity of one or more marketing or administrative service centers. In this section we shall see why management may be interested in measuring functional cost and explore two measurement techniques—time recording and engineering analysis.

Reasons for Functional Cost Analysis

Management may wish to measure or estimate the costs of performing individual functions to help answer five questions:

1. Does the function cost more than it's worth?   Benefits may be hard to measure, but cost/benefit analysis is impossible without estimates of costs.

2. Can the function be performed more cheaply by outside contractors?   This question doesn't arise for all functions, but it needs to be asked from time to time.

3. How many people and how much equipment are needed to perform the function?   This can be especially important at budget time.

4. Is the cost center performing efficiently?   This is a continuing concern, in the office no less than in the factory.

5. How much functional cost does a marketing segment require? Functional cost centers serve or contribute to programs. Program evaluation requires knowledge of functional cost.

Approaches to Functional Cost Analysis

Functional cost analysis is very simple when a cost center is devoted exclusively to a single function, such as payroll preparation. The techniques of process costing are directly applicable.

Many functions, however, share one or more cost centers. For example, a study of the operations of a billing and order processing department might reveal the following separate processes:

1.   Order recording.
2.   Credit reviewing.
3.   Invoicing—headings.
4.   Invoicing—line items.
5.   Order file maintenance.
6.   Correspondence.

Process costing is impractical in this situation because the output of the cost center is not homogeneous. Job order costing is out of the question because the typical task is so small that task-oriented time-keeping and requisitioning procedures would be uneconomical and counterproductive. Furthermore, even when work is done in batches, data on the costs of individual batches have little meaning. Unlike work in a factory job shop, every batch is much like every other batch, except perhaps for its length. The function, in other words, comprises many repetitions of the same operation, not a unique combination of different operations.

As a result, the costs of marketing and administrative service functions are measured, if they are measured at all, in the following ways:

1. If employees or equipment are assigned exclusively to one function for significant, clearly measurable time periods	Time records are used to allocate labor and equipment costs to individual functions, but not to specific batches or work orders.
2. If these conditions are not present	Labor and equipment costs are either assigned to functions by statistical or engineering techniques or left unassigned.
3. In most situations	The costs of materials (office supplies, for the most part) are classified as cost center overheads and are allocated to functions, if at all, as part of some broadly conceived average of all overhead costs.

To see why the first two of these statements are true, let's see how time recording and engineering analysis techniques can be applied here.

Time Recording

Time records can be kept for people or for equipment. Computer use, for example, is usually very closely monitored. If computer jobs can be traced to specific functions, then equipment time and cost also can be traced to functions.

Labor time recording is more spotty. Time clocks are seldom used because at least one of the following three conditions is present:

1. Employees don't work on one function long enough at a stretch —a payroll clerk, for example, may be engaged in information retrieval 20 times a day, but never spend more than a few minutes at any one time.
2. Work done off-premises is beyond the reach of the company's time clocks—sales functions, for example.
3. Office workers lack a timekeeping tradition—this has been one way they have differentiated themselves from factory workers, a differentiation they like to retain.

Whatever the reason, the most common method of timekeeping off the factory floor is the honor system. The employees fill in their own time cards at the end of each day, basing their entries on whatever record-keeping systems seem appropriate. Most employees keep no records at all, but estimate at the end of each day how they have spent their time. An example of a weekly time card for a clerk in credit and collections is shown in Exhibit 12–1.

Honor system time records are obviously inaccurate, but their main weakness has nothing to do with the method used to collect the data. The weakness is that certain kinds of time are not traceable to specific

EXHIBIT 12–1

Name: P. Jones					Week: June 5	
Dept.: Credit						

	M	T	W	T	F	Total
Credit check	1	2	4	S	3	10
Collection	4	4	3	I	2	13
Inquiries	2	1	–	C	2	5
				K		
Total	7	7	7		7	28

production functions. For example, suppose management decides that all sales force activities are either direct selling or market research functions. At each call the sales representatives perform both functions—and they are also likely to have to wait. The waiting time is seldom traceable to one function or the other. The same is true of time spent traveling from one prospective buyer's office to another.

This brings us back to our concept of *attributable cost*. As applied here, it has the following definition:

> *Attributable cost:* the amount of cost that could be eliminated if the company were to discontinue a specific function, given enough time to reduce functional capacity to zero.

Any allocation of such elements as travel and waiting time should reflect this concept. The result almost inevitably will be a pool of costs attributable to no one function but common to them all. Allocation of these costs would have no analytical significance.

Engineering Techniques

The second major approach to functional cost measurement is an industrial engineering approach. Two kinds of engineering techniques are used:

Engineered standards | To establish how much time each activity *ought* to take—applicable only to standardized, repetitive activities.

Work sampling | To establish how much time each activity *has taken*—applicable only to on-premises activities.

Engineered standards call for careful investigation of the input requirements of each function. The engineering method most commonly used today is some variant of the Methods Time Measurement (MTM) technique. Under this approach, the operations are first studied to identify the major tasks to be performed. Standard time allowances for each task are then obtained from commercially available tables.

Work sampling consists largely of recording what people are doing at particular instants of time, selected at random, during some longer time period. For example, the sampling plan may require the recording of the activities being performed by each clerk in the office at 9:12, 10:34, and so on. From a number of such samples taken at various times, a percentage time distribution can be obtained, and the estimated times to perform the various repetitive service activities can be derived from this.

The work sampling and engineering methods of deriving cost standards are applicable primarily or exclusively to labor costs. Work sampling has both the advantage and the disadvantage of indicating what the costs are rather than what they should be. The disadvantage in this approach is that it gives management little assurance that its costs are reasonable. The advantage is that it provides management with information as to what its money is buying. Furthermore, these studies can indicate trends in functional cost if they are carried out periodically.

These methods are expensive and they ordinarily cannot be justified except as a by-product of a program of work simplification and methods improvement. In other words, the added accuracy of the data derived from engineered standards is ordinarily insufficient by itself to justify the cost and disruption entailed in developing the standards.

Control of Functional Activities

One of our five reasons for studying functional cost is to estimate functional efficiency. For example, a control report prepared for a cost center preparing invoices and payrolls might show the following:

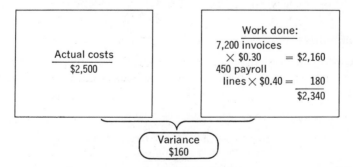

This kind of comparison is useful, but its benefits should not be overstressed. It doesn't measure short-term cost control performance. Most marketing and administrative costs are fixed in the short run, as we explained in Chapter 9. For this reason, variances of this sort are more likely to reflect variations in the overall demand for functional services than functional efficiency or inefficiency.

SEGMENT COST ANALYSIS

One reason for identifying the costs of individual functions is to provide a basis for segment cost analysis—that is, for estimating the amount of cost attributable to individual marketing segments. This section sets forth the methods used for this purpose in a general way; the remainder of the chapter will then see how these methods can be used to estimate the costs of different kinds of marketing segments.

EXHIBIT 12–2

Relationship between Functional Costs and Segment Costs

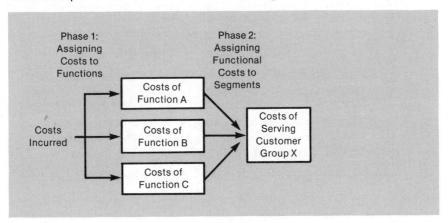

The relationship between functional costs and segments is illustrated in Exhibit 12–2. Assigning costs to functions is the first phase; reassigning them to segments is the second. This second phase consists of four stages:

1. Identify the marketing segments to be studied.
2. Identify any functional costs traceable to individual segments.
3. Identify any other costs of responsive functions that are attributable to individual segments.
4. Identify any costs of programmed functions that are attributable to individual segments.

Stage 1. Identifying Marketing Segments

The first stage in the analysis is to identify the marketing segments to be studied. Typical bases for marketing segmentation are the product line, the region, the customer group, the order size, and the channel of distribution.

The choice of the revenue segments to be studied depends on the purpose of the analysis. Product-line segments will be selected if the question is whether a given product line is pulling its own weight. Geographical segments will be used if the problem is whether a specific sales branch is profitable enough to keep open.

Stage 2.   Identifying Segment-Traceable Costs

As always, the primary basis for cost assignment is traceability. Some costs can be classified directly by segment as well as by function. These should be treated as direct costs of the segments unless doing so would add substantially to the cost of data processing.

Most segment-traceable costs are the costs of programmed activities —advertising, direct selling, and so forth—but they may include some responsive activities as well. The costs of a fleet of delivery trucks, for example, can often be traced entirely to retail sales or wholesale

---

TERMINOLOGY REMINDER

Responsive activities: undertaken by a cost center to provide necessary service or support to activities centered elsewhere in the organization.

Programmed activities: undertaken at management's initiative to meet objectives other than meeting demands for service imposed on the organization unit from outside.

---

sales, or to one region or another, if those are the revenue segments management is interested in.

Stage 3.   Assigning the Costs of Responsive Functions

When the traceability criterion fails, some other method must be used to assign functional costs to segments. For responsive functions, we can adapt the allocation procedures used in manufacturing. This is a five-step process:

1. Identify the main determinants of functional cost—referred to as governing factors or, in some cases, as work units.
2. Identify those functional costs that are divisible enough to vary with the demand for functional services.
3. Calculate functional unit cost.
4. Calculate the number of governing factors or work units required by each segment.
5. Multiply the number of governing factors or work units by functional unit costs.

Only the first two of these require discussion; the three final steps are routine.

Step 1. Selecting governing factors and work units. The criteria for selecting an allocation base for a given function are simple:

1. Does it correlate well with variations in the total cost of the function?
2. Can it be measured easily for each segment?

The measure that best meets the first of these criteria is a measure of the influences that determine how much cost will be incurred to perform the function. We shall refer to these cost determinants as *governing factors*. The governing factors for functional costs are those aspects of segment activity that determine the need for functional services. Examples are the number of customer orders obtained and the number of deliveries to be made.

These governing factors determine the need for services, but the services themselves may have other names. The demand for payroll services, for example, may depend on the total number of employee-hours, but the output of the payroll department is measured by the number of payroll lines written. These output units are known as *work units:*

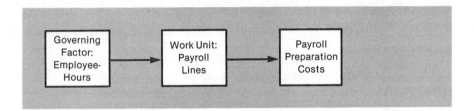

Whether the analysis is based on governing factors or on work units depends to some extent on the nature of the activity. For this purpose we recognize two kinds of functions:

1. Repetitive service functions.
2. Diversified service functions.

Repetitive service functions are those for which output is relatively homogeneous—for example, one payroll line is very much like another payroll line. Work units usually can be established for these. For an order processing department, the work units might be:

Task	Work Unit
Order recording	Total orders received
Credit reviewing	Charge orders received
Invoicing—headings	Invoices ⎫ or line items
Invoicing—line items	Line items ⎭
Order file maintenance	Total orders received
Correspondence	Letters written

Different work units might be appropriate for different cost elements if they have different variability patterns. For example, in the delivery department:

Element	Work Unit
Loading labor................................	Total pounds loaded
Gas, oil, and maintenance.....................	Miles
Bulk delivery labor...........................	Miles
Route delivery labor..........................	Deliveries
Bulk unloading labor.........................	Deliveries

Even here, the work unit is not entirely homogeneous—for example, bulk delivery labor costs will vary with traffic conditions as well as with miles traveled—but the unit selected is a fairly reliable index of the output requirement.

The work unit is not always a good basis for assigning functional costs to segments. For example, the payroll line is generally a good measure of the output of payroll preparation. It may be a very poor assignment base, however, because payroll lines can't be traced to segments. In other words, payroll lines does not meet the second of our two selection criteria. In this situation, the accountant must either fall back on the governing factor as the allocation base, or, as a last resort, find a substitute measure of the volume of segment activity that can be identified easily with the segments and also correlates well in total with the total demand for functional service. If no such measure can be found, then the functional cost should not be allocated to the segment.

Diversified service functions differ from repetitive service functions only in that the units of output are many, nonstandardized, and constantly changing. Examples include the duties of a good part of the executive force, office management, secretarial work, telephone switchboard operation, and similar tasks. Secretarial output could possibly be measured in terms of the number of telephone calls made, number of letters typed, number of visitors received, and so forth, but there is so little homogeneity within any one of these measures that they offer very little promise for standardization.

Service volume for diversified service activities has to be measured indirectly, in units of some governing factor or factors. For example, the governing factor for an employee recreation function might well be the number of company employees. Selection of such units is ordinarily not very difficult, the only practical problem being that so many different factors may be selected for the various functions that obtaining statistics would become a massive job. The typical solution is to try to reduce the number of measuring rods so that one index will serve a number of functions.

Step 2. Identifying attributable cost. The second step in assigning the costs of responsive functions to segments is to decide how much of the cost of the function is assignable. Short-run variable cost is a poor concept for this purpose. First, short-run variability is likely to be insignificant. Second, the decisions for which this kind of costing is relevant are not short-run decisions. They attempt to resolve questions such as:

1. Should we abandon product line A?
2. Should we accept small orders and, if so, should we impose a surcharge on orders smaller than a certain size?

3. Should we distribute our products directly to retail outlets or channel them through wholesalers?

In each case the choice affects a substantial volume of business, enough to have a significant impact on the amount of functional service capacity needed.

The fixed costs of responsive functions are often highly divisible, and this provides the basis for estimates of attributable cost. The usefulness of segment cost analysis, therefore, depends on the ability of attributable cost to approximate incremental cost for the alternatives being evaluated. The rule throughout this chapter will be to include in functional unit cost only those cost elements that seem sufficiently divisible to justify the assumption of proportionate changes in response to substantial changes in the total volume of functional activity.

Notice that the attributable cost concept has been applied twice, first to measure the amount of cost attributable to the performance of individual functions, and then to measure how much of this is attributable to individual marketing segments. As this suggests, not all costs attributable to specific functions can be attributed to specific marketing segments; some functional costs therefore should not be redistributed to segments. Our objective is to find out how much cost the segment makes necessary, not to find a segment for every cost.[1]

Stage 4. Nontraceable, Attributable Programmed Costs

The final stage in the analysis is to estimate the amount of nontraceable programmed costs, if any, that can be attributed to individual marketing segments. Probably the best estimates will be judgmental estimates by marketing management, supported by such data as the time records in sales representatives' call reports. The accountant should resist the temptation, however, to make sure that these allocations distribute nontraceable costs in full. To repeat, it is highly unlikely that the total of the attributable costs for the various segments will equal total functional cost.

PRODUCT-LINE ANALYSIS

The most obvious illustration of segment cost analysis is in the analysis of the profitability of individual product lines. Suppose, for example, that a company wishes to decide which of its three product lines deserves the most short-run promotional effort, as well as which of them appear to have weaknesses that if not corrected will endanger their long-run survival. Estimated sales volume and factory costs for the coming year are as follows:

---

[1] Contract costing usually requires a complete distribution of all administrative service and support costs. Cost allocations for this purpose are described in Appendix B.

	Line A	Line B	Line C
Gross sales....................	$1,000,000	$800,000	$750,000
Variable factory cost..........	500,000	450,000	350,000
Variable factory margin........	$ 500,000	$350,000	$400,000
Attributable fixed factory cost.	50,000	30,000	—
Attributable factory margin....	$ 450,000	$320,000	$400,000

Choosing the segment constituted stage 1 of our analytical routine. The other three stages are:

1. Identify traceable costs.
2. Identify other attributable costs of product-related service activities.
3. Identify other attributable costs of programmed activities.

Traceable Costs

Three groups of cost elements—sales commissions, product management costs, and the costs of samples and product sales brochures—are completely traceable to individual product lines in our illustration. Sales commissions are calculated at a rate of 1 percent of gross sales. The other two cost elements are expected to be as follows:

	Line A	Line B	Line C
Product management..........	$23,000	$21,000	$22,000
Samples and brochures......	8,000	7,000	10,500

Product-Related Service Costs

Our second task is to identify any other product-related nonmanufacturing functions and calculate their unit costs. Our illustrative company has found the following (the number of functions has been reduced to simplify the presentation):

	Variable Costs	Attributable Fixed Costs
Product handling.......	$0.02 × pounds of product	$0.0075 × pounds of product
Storage value.........	—	$0.0230 per year × average inventory cost
Storage space........	—	$1.40 per year × square feet required
Inspection...........	$7.20 × inspection hours	—

To use these rates, we need to collect the necessary governing factor or work unit data on a product-line basis:

	Line A	Line B	Line C
Average inventory..................	$ 300,000	$182,000	$160,000
Product weight (lbs.)...............	2,000,000	400,000	300,000
Warehouse space required (sq. ft.)..	50,000	6,500	5,000
Inspection hours...................	10,000	1,000	1,250

The allocations based on these statistics and the unit costs given above are:

	Line A	Line B	Line C
Variable costs:			
Product handling...................	$ 40,000	$ 8,000	$ 6,000
Inspection.........................	72,000	7,200	9,000
Total variable product cost........	$112,000	$15,200	$15,000
Attributable fixed costs:			
Product handling...................	$ 15,000	$ 3,000	$ 2,250
Storage value......................	6,900	4,186	3,680
Storage space......................	70,000	9,100	7,000
Total attributable fixed cost......	$ 91,900	$16,286	$12,930

Three aspects of these allocations deserve a special note at this point:

Space costs. A charge of $1.40 was made for each square foot of warehouse space required by each product line. This represented opportunity cost, not the average internal cost of the company's warehouses. Average internal cost is highly unlikely to measure the opportunity cost of space occupied and almost never should be used for decision purposes.

Depreciation. Depreciation charges on existing equipment are allocations of sunk costs and therefore should not be assigned to revenue segments for short-term decision making. Any assignments of depreciation to revenue segments should approximate the incremental cash flow attributable to a major expansion or contraction of the segment. Current annual replacement expenditures ordinarily measure the incremental cash flow better than average historical cost. Furthermore, these figures should be used only if the facilities are divisible enough so that elimination of one product line would have a significant effect on the size of the annual capital budget.

Customer-related service costs. The allocations in our illustration didn't include the costs of any customer-related service functions, such as order processing, billing, and customer bookkeeping. The amount of these costs is determined by such customer characteristics as the number of orders per year. These costs should be included in product-line analysis only if clear relationships between functional activities and product-related governing factors can be found.

For example, do buyers of line A place fewer orders per year than buyers of line B or line C? If so, then differences in order-processing costs should be reflected in the analysis.

Nontraceable Programmed Costs

Few nontraceable programmed costs can be attributed to individual product lines. The major candidate for this honor is the cost of the field sales force. The difficulty, as we indicated earlier, is that much of the time of individual sales representatives is common to two or more product lines. Attributability can't be approximated very well by multiplying average hourly cost by the amount of time recorded on the sales force call reports. In the absence of specific estimates of the number of sales representatives to become redundant if a product line were dropped, we are better off to leave these unallocated.

The Profitability Estimates

Application of the unit cost factors to these estimates yielded the product-line profit forecasts shown in Exhibit 12–3. Notice how the

EXHIBIT 12–3

Product-Line Profit Forecasts

	Product Line A		Product Line B		Product Line C	
	Amount	Percent	Amount	Percent	Amount	Percent
Gross sales....................	$1,000,000	100.0	$800,000	100.0	$750,000	100.0
Variable product costs:						
Factory........................	$ 500,000	50.0	$450,000	56.2	$350,000	46.7
Product handling................	40,000	4.0	8,000	1.0	6,000	0.8
Inspection.....................	72,000	7.2	7,200	0.9	9,000	1.2
Sales commissions..............	10,000	1.0	8,000	1.0	7,500	1.0
Total variable product cost....	$ 622,000	62.2	$473,200	59.1	$372,500	49.7
Contribution margin..............	$ 378,000	37.8	$326,800	40.9	$377,500	50.3
Attributable fixed costs:						
Factory........................	$ 50,000		$ 30,000		—	
Product management...........	23,000		21,000		$ 22,000	
Samples and brochures.........	8,000		7,000		10,500	
Product handling................	15,000		3,000		2,250	
Storage value..................	6,900		4,186		3,680	
Storage space..................	70,000		9,100		7,000	
Total attributable fixed cost..	$ 172,800	17.3	$ 74,286	9.3	$ 45,430	6.0
Product margin...................	$ 205,200	20.5	$252,514	31.6	$332,070	44.3

ranking of product line A has been changed by the introduction of nonmanufacturing costs into the analysis. Just looking at manufacturing costs would give the impression that product line A would have a contribution margin ratio of 50 percent of sales and an attributable profit ratio of 45 percent. Comparable ratios for product line B would be 43.8 and 40 percent. Product line A is a heavy consumer of nonmanufacturing services, however, and recognition of these shows that product line A's contribution margin ratio is slightly lower than that of product line B, and its attributable profit or product margin is substantially lower.

Consistency with Incremental Approach

If carried out as described here, product cost analysis is in no sense inconsistent with the incremental approach to decision making advocated in preceding chapters. The methods outlined in this chapter are designed to get better data on cost increments. The introduction of attributable cost figures is intended to serve the purposes for which many accountants have computed full cost in the past, but for which full cost figures are inappropriate.

No one should pretend that this approach contains the magic formula that will automatically produce the right cost for every situation. Routine cost analysis of this sort is always a substitute for a detailed item-by-item estimate of incremental cost, and is almost inevitably inferior to the latter.

The advantage of the attributable cost figures is that they can be prepared in advance and at less cost than custom-tailored estimates. In a medium-sized office with 20 cost centers and 10 cost elements in each, for example, 200 separate estimates would have to be made for each decision, and this would be prohibitively expensive. What routine cost analysis does is provide a reasonable approximation to incremental cost. As long as the analyst avoids the full cost fallacy, this can be accurate enough for the purpose.

COST ANALYSIS BY SIZE OF ORDER

A product-line classification was chosen as the first illustration of distribution cost analysis because product-line analysis was already familiar from earlier chapters. In a sense, it was a poor starting point, however, because most problems calling for distribution cost analysis relate to some dimension of the customer mix.

One important form of customer-related analysis is the estimation of the costs of handling orders of different sizes. This "unit of sale" analysis can be used by management in such matters as setting minimum order sizes, establishing a quantity discount structure, or altering methods of promoting and distributing products to small-order customers.

Basic Method

Estimates of the costs of handling orders of different sizes can be obtained from the functional cost totals, derived by the methods described earlier. Every functional cost element which has a governing factor that depends on the number, size, or other dimension of customer orders is germane to the analysis. Other items should be rigorously excluded. The cost of writing a customer invoice, for example, is clearly an order-related cost; the salary of the marketing vice president just as clearly is not.

A thorough example would have so many cost elements that a whole chapter would be required to discuss it. To illustrate the method, however, let us assume that functional cost analyses have revealed the following unit cost totals:

Governing Factor	Unit Cost
Number of orders.....................................	$1.00 per order
Value of orders.......................................	0.001 per dollar
Number of product units ordered.....................	0.03 per unit
Number of order lines................................	0.01 per line

This table, of course, represents the summation of all of the functional cost elements governed by each of the factors listed; a full example would have to list each function separately.

The next step is to find out how many units of each of these governing factors are associated with orders of various sizes. For example, a sample of orders might yield the following statistics:

Order Size	Orders	Number of Governing Factor Units		
		Order Value	Product Units	Order Lines
$ 1–$ 99....................	50,000	$ 1,000,000	200,000	100,000
100– 199.....................	20,000	2,600,000	500,000	60,000
200– 499.....................	20,000	5,600,000	1,100,000	80,000
500 and up..................	10,000	6,000,000	1,200,000	50,000
Total..................	100,000	$15,200,000	3,000,000	290,000

Because the question in this case is how much it costs to obtain and service an order, these statistics next should be restated as averages, as follows:

Order Size	Orders	Average Number of Governing Factor Units per Order		
		Order Value	Product Units	Order Lines
$ 1–$ 99.....................	1	$ 20	4	2.0
100– 199.....................	1	130	25	3.0
200– 499.....................	1	280	55	4.0
500 and up..................	1	600	120	5.0
Average..............	1	$152	30	2.9

The final step is to multiply these statistics by the unit cost figures cited earlier. The end result is the unit cost of an order, as summarized below:

		Costs Attributed to			
Order Size	Each Order	Value of the Order	Number of Units in Order	Number of Order Lines	Total Cost per Order
$ 1–$ 99.........	$1.00	$0.02	$0.12	$0.02	$1.16
100– 199.........	1.00	0.13	0.75	0.03	1.91
200– 499.........	1.00	0.28	1.65	0.04	2.97
500 and up......	1.00	0.60	3.60	0.05	5.25
Average...	$1.00	$0.152	$0.90	$0.029	$2.08

Orders that contribute less product contribution margin or attributable profit than the amounts shown in the right-hand column are not covering their costs.

In practice, this analysis could be further simplified by consolidating two or more governing factors that are highly correlated. In this example, for instance, the number of units in each order correlated very closely with the value of the order. This can be checked by computing average value per unit, which in this case is virtually constant. Another simplification would be to omit insignificant variables, in this case the number of order lines.

The Quantity Discount Problem

The preceding analysis could serve as a basis for the establishment of a quantity discount schedule. From an economic point of view, the quantity discount structure is a means of discriminating among different segments of the market to obtain a greater total revenue from a given physical sales volume than could be derived from a one-price policy.

This form of price discrimination has long been accepted practice in the regulated electric power industry. Outside the public utility field, however, public policy has been to discourage systematic discrimination of this sort, principally through the provisions of the Robinson-Patman Act. The Robinson-Patman Act was enacted by the U.S. Congress in 1936 and is enforced by the Federal Trade Commission. It prohibits quoting different prices to different customers who compete with each other, if interstate commerce is affected. A seller accused of violating the Robinson-Patman Act has five possible defenses:

1. Interstate commerce is not affected.
2. Competition is not affected.
3. Quoting a lower price to one customer than to another is necessary to meet an equally low price quoted by a competitor.
4. The products sold at different prices are very different from each other.
5. The price difference is fully justified by differences in the cost of serving the different customers.

The fifth of these is known as the cost justification defense. Although it can be applied to any kind of price differential, it has been used most often in attempts to defend published discount schedules for purchases in quantities larger than some minimum amount. To illustrate briefly how cost data might be used in justifying quantity discounts, suppose that the company in the previous illustration has offered quantity discounts as follows:

Size of Order	Discount
1–$ 99	None
100– 199	3%
200– 499	5
500 and up	7

If this structure is to be justified, the cost differential per dollar of order value must be at least as great as the percentages indicated. In other words, if it costs 10 percent less per order dollar to process a $600 order than to process a $20 order, then any discount of 10 percent or less is justifiable on a cost basis. The computed cost differentials in this example are:

Order Size	(1) Average Order Value	(2) Average Cost per Order	(3) Average Cost per Order Dollar (2) ÷ (1)	(4) Cost Differential from Base Class $0.0580 − (3)
$ 1–$ 99	$ 20	$1.16	$0.0580	—
100– 199	130	1.91	0.0147	$0.0433
200– 499	280	2.97	0.0106	0.0474
500 and up	600	5.25	0.0088	0.0492

This table shows that the 3 percent discount offered to customers purchasing in $100–$199 quantities is more than justified by the cost savings attributable to these larger orders $(0.0580 − 0.0147 = 4.33$ percent). The discounts offered to customers buying in larger quantities cannot be justified in this way, however. The 5 percent discount offered to the third class of invoices is 0.26 of a percentage point greater than the cost differential $(0.0580 − 0.0106 = 4.74$ percent), and the gap is even wider in the case of the top discount category.

A moment's reflection will indicate that these cost differentials per order dollar are not created by those functional cost elements that vary directly with order dollars. These average 60 cents for a $600 order and 2 cents for a $20 order, or 0.1 cent per order dollar in both cases. In more general terms, *the costs that are relevant to the quantity discount structure are those that are order-related but do not vary proportionately with the size of the order.* When order size is measured in dollars, the relevant costs are those that do not vary in proportion to the dollar value of the individual order but do vary with the number of orders or order elements.

Calculations of the costs of processing orders should measure the attributable costs of orders of different sizes if the figures are to be used by management in making order size decisions. The Federal Trade Commission, however, accepts only full-cost calculations for Robinson-Patman purposes. If $1 is the attributable cost of processing an order, full cost might be $1.05 or $1.25. Full-cost order-size differentials are likely to be slightly greater than attributable cost differentials.[2]

Exclusion of Manufacturing Cost Differentials

No mention has been made thus far of possible differentials in manufacturing costs for orders of different sizes. The reason is that in most cases manufacturing cost per unit is a function of the total volume of production rather than of the volume generated by any one order.

For example, suppose a company usually sells its products in batches of 50 units each. It is considering offering a discount to anyone ordering the product in batches of 100 units. It has the following estimates of manufacturing costs:

Size of Batch	Total Cost	Unit Cost
50	$ 6,000	$120
100	10,000	100

These figures seem to support a discount of up to $20 for the larger order, because a batch of 100 units can be manufactured for an average of $20 a unit less than a batch of 50 units.

This analysis would be valid if each customer's order were always produced separately. If this is not the case, then two customer orders for 50 units each could be combined; they, too, would then enjoy the $100 average cost.

Manufacturing cost differentials can be relevant to the quantity discount question, if the Robinson-Patman Act doesn't apply. The question is a different one, however. The question is whether the incremental costs of serving a larger *total* volume are smaller than the price differential that must be granted to large customers to get their business.

Suppose the total business of customers buying in batches larger than 50 units amounts to 400 units a month. Without a $10 discount these customers won't buy. The total business of the company's smaller customers amounts to 600 units a month. The relevant cost figures are:

---

[2] For an exhaustive study of this question, see Herbert F. Taggart, *Cost Justification, Michigan Business Studies, Vol. XIV, No. 3* (Ann Arbor: Bureau of Business Research, University of Michigan, 1959). Supplements to this volume were issued in 1964 and 1967.

	(1)	(2)	(3)
			Unit
	Monthly	Monthly	Cost
	Volume	Cost	(2) ÷ (1)
Without discounts....................	600	$48,000	$80.00
With quantity discounts..............	1,000	75,000	75.00
Difference.....................	400	$27,000	$67.50

This shows that the differential manufacturing cost of selling the large orders is only $67.50; this is $12.50 less than the average manufacturing cost of filling the small orders. On commercial grounds, therefore, it can be argued that a $10 discount is justified.

EXHIBIT 12–4

Effect of Order-Ranking on Attribution of Incremental Costs

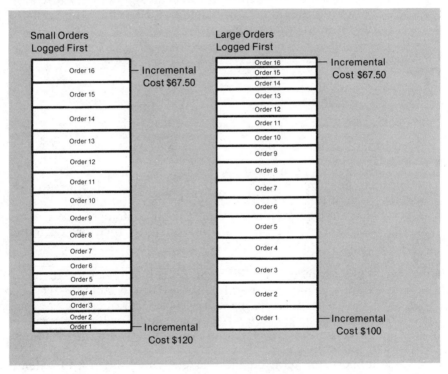

This is a correct analysis, but *it has nothing to do with order size.* The real question is what has to be done to keep enough price-sensitive orders coming in to keep the order level at 1,000 units a month. The analysis so far has treated the larger orders as the marginal orders, the ones to which the lower incremental costs should be assigned, as in the left-hand diagram in Exhibit 12–4. We could just as well array the orders with the little orders on top, as in the right-hand diagram. In other words, the $67.50 cost figure really applies to *each* order in the house. Any customers who have to be given a $10 discount to keep their orders coming in should get it. For any order that will come in without a discount, management has no reason to give one.

APPLICATIONS IN SERVICE BUSINESSES

Job order costing and process costing can be used to cost the service outputs of some kinds of service businesses. Advertising agencies and automobile repair shops are good examples of job order applications.

Many service businesses, however, carry out their end-product activities much as the manufacturing business carries out its internal service activities: each cost center provides more than one kind of service; individual service batches are either too small to make job order costing feasible or too similar to make it worthwhile. It shouldn't be surprising to find, therefore, that the methods we have been describing in this chapter have also been found useful in service businesses. Three brief illustrations should demonstrate the similarities.

Commercial Banking

One of the most familiar service businesses is the commercial bank. The costs of servicing a checking account depend on the number of deposits, the number of checks written, and the complexity of the statements issued to the depositor. The bank usually asks the depositor to pay for these services, either directly or by maintaining a large balance in the account at all times.

Banking, in general, is a highly competitive business. A bank whose fees are substantially in excess of cost is likely to lose deposits; fees that don't cover costs are unprofitable. Good service information can help management steer a course between these two dangers.

Once again the appropriate approach is to develop estimated or standard costs of performing various functions, and then use these rates to determine the costs of serving various segments of the bank's business. The functions related to depositors' accounts can be classified into two groups:

1. One-time functions—opening and closing accounts, handling stop-payment orders, etc.
2. Continuing functions—accepting deposits, cashing checks, transferring funds, insuring deposits, issuing statements, etc.

The costs of each function can be related to one or more governing factors or work units. By identifying the amount of each governing factor arising from a given class of depositors, the bank's management can identify cost-price relationships that are out of line. It can then take whatever action it deems appropriate.

Intercity Trucking

Transportation businesses have cost structures even more complicated than those of commercial banking. The extreme example is the U.S. Postal Service, with hundreds of thousands of employees, millions of shipping and destination points, tens of thousands of processing and transfer points. The costing problem is staggering.

The problems faced by a typical intercity trucking company are similar, but somewhat simpler. Exhibit 12–5 is a simplified diagram

EXHIBIT 12–5

Flows of Shipments in Intercity Trucking

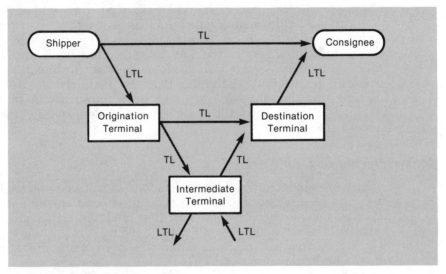

TL = truckload shipments.
LTL = less-than-truckload shipments.

of the flow of trucking services in one such firm. In this firm shipments big enough to preempt a truck's full capacity are loaded at the shipper's premises and delivered directly to the consignee. Other shipments are consolidated in the origination terminal into truckload lots. Some of these are trucked directly to a destination terminal; others are taken to an intermediate terminal for reloading and reshipment.

Management's main interest in costing centers on questions such as the profitability of individual traffic lanes (e.g., New York to Cleveland, Houston to Denver), the profitability of shipments of different sizes, the profitability of shipments going different distances, and the productivity of different responsibility centers within the organization. The main functional groupings are pickup and delivery, platform operations, line-haul, and billing and collecting.

In general, pickup and delivery functions cost proportionately more per unit for small shipments than for large ones. Small shipments are also more likely to pass through intermediate terminals, requiring reloading and reshipment expenditures. Traffic lanes without intermediate terminals are cheaper than lanes of equal length but containing one or more intermediate terminals. And so on.

It is feasible in this kind of operation to accumulate certain kinds of functional data by detailed input recording schemes—crew time, gasoline and diesel fuel consumption, for example. These data can't be used directly, however, to estimate the cost of, say, a 500-pound shipment, picked up from a shipper at point A, moved through terminals at points B, C, and D, transported a total of 800 miles, and delivered to the consignee at point E. What is necessary is a set of cost figures for each function at each location or in each lane segment. At least some of these can be derived from analyses of the kind described in this chapter; others call for statistical regression analyses like those covered in Chapter 18.

Vending Machine Company

Our third and final example of the use of service cost analysis in a service business is provided by a company in the vending machine business. It sells and services vending machines of many types in a wide variety of locations.

This company recently undertook a study to determine the costs associated with four of its most important types of equipment. The machines were further grouped by type of location—e.g., offices, light industrial factories, heavy industrial factories, supervised public locations, and unsupervised public locations. The company's study recognized eight major classes of activities:

Selling.
Delivery and installation.
Financing.
Field maintenance.
Shop maintenance.
Repainting and reconditioning.
Bookkeeping.
Repossession.

Using some sample data and some data drawn from the routine historical accounting records, the company developed unit costs for activities in each of these classes, as well as records of functional consumption for each of the 20 machine-type–location combinations (Type A—Offices, Type B—Offices, Type A—Light Industrial Factories, and so on).

This analysis provided the company's management with information on which to base its machine rental charges. (The company's objective was to break even on the machine, relying for its profits on products sold in the machine.) Such a study might also reveal that certain types of equipment are more suitable than others in given kinds of locations or that some kinds of locations are so hard on the machines that the profitable course of action is to withdraw from those locations altogether.

Feasibility: Using the Computer

Most organizations use a large number of service centers to perform an even larger number of service functions. This complexity probably kept many companies from doing very much with functional and segment cost analysis in the past. The benefits simply weren't worth the costs.

The advance of computer technology in recent years has changed the economics of this comparison drastically. Computer time, storage capacity, programming and access devices are vastly less expensive and more versatile than they used to be. This has already increased the use of functional and segment cost analysis and is likely to have an even greater effect in the future.

The quality of segment cost analysis still depends on the quality of the data fed into the computer, however. Full-cost allocations are no better when made by the computer than when made by hand. Attributable costing still requires the accountant's judgment, no matter what computational facilities are available or how little they cost.

SUMMARY

Job order and process costing are often too expensive to use in costing marketing and service activities. When this is true, the accountant can use another technique, functional and segment cost analysis. This is still not cheap, even with the computer, but it can be used to develop cost estimates at lower cost than would otherwise be possible.

The costs of a marketing or service function are measured in two stages. The first stage is to identify any costs traceable to the function; the second is to use engineering techniques or managerial judgment to identify any other costs attributable to the function.

Although functional costs are useful in themselves, they also enter into the calculation of the costs attributable to individual marketing segments. To make these calculations, the accountant has to relate functional costs to measures of the forces leading to functional costs. These measures are referred to as governing factors. The costs of service functions assignable to a marketing segment are then obtained by multiplying the unit costs of service functions by estimates of the number of each governing factor associated with that segment.

The governing factors for programmed activities in marketing cannot be used to assign the costs of these activities to segments, however. The governing factors arise from the firm's profit objectives, not from the characteristics of the individual segments. This is just another way of making a point we first raised in Chapter 9, that unit cost has no analytical meaning for programmed activities. The attributability of cost must be estimated in other ways.

This chapter has described two applications of segment cost analysis in some detail—analysis by product line and analysis by size of order. Other typical examples are analysis by channel of distribution, analysis by customer industry, and analysis by region. The method also can be used in costing the main revenue-producing activities of service businesses. Three of these applications have been described briefly here.

Analyses of this kind are costly enough to make management think twice about asking for one. And when they are made, an effort should be made to resist the temptation to distribute all functional costs to individual segments. Marketing costs, in particular, are difficult to assign to segments unless they can be traced directly to them. All allocations should reflect the concept of attributable cost, and this provides for leaving some costs in a common, unallocated pool. Only in this way will segment cost have the meaning attributed to it.

KEY TERMS

The most important terms introduced and defined in this chapter are the following:

Diversified services function	Robinson-Patman Act
Function	Segment cost analysis
Functional cost analysis	Work sampling
Governing factor	Work unit
Repetitive service function	

INDEPENDENT STUDY PROBLEM
(Solution in Appendix C)

1. Segment cost analysis: Sales regions. Blandish Mills, Inc., manufactures and sells three products. Its market is divided into three sales regions for which the following monthly data are typical:

	Region A	Region B	Region C
Orders:			
Number of orders..........................	800	900	1,500
Number of units:			
Product X................................	2,000	1,000	10,000
Product Y................................	8,000	14,000	7,000
Product Z................................	5,000	5,000	10,000
Shipments (pounds)..........................	25,000	30,000	55,000
Number of customers..........................	2,000	2,200	3,000
Number of new customers......................	50	55	100
Number of employees..........................	15	16	20
Sales discounts and allowances..................	$ 1,000	$ 2,000	$ 4,000
Sales salaries..................................	5,000	6,000	8,000
Sales travel expense..........................	3,000	3,000	2,000
Regional office expenses......................	4,000	4,500	5,000

Factory cost, selling price, and sales commissions on each of the three products are:

	Selling Price	Standard Factory Cost	Sales Commissions
Product X..................	$ 5	$4	$0.25
Product Y..................	10	6	0.50
Product Z..................	2	1	0.10

Customer defaults ("bad debts") are expected to average one half of 1 percent of gross sales.

Variable factory costs represent 75 percent of total factory cost at normal volume. Sixty percent of the fixed factory costs are reasonably divisible.

Unit costs have been developed for a number of the activities performed in the head office, as follows:

Payroll.............................	$12.00 per employee per month
Order processing...................	2.40 per order
Packing and shipping...............	0.06 per pound
Credit review......................	24.00 per new customer
Cashier............................	0.50 per customer
General accounting.................	0.70 per customer

These unit costs represent cost elements that are almost entirely fixed in the short run but are divisible and thus variable in response to large changes in volume. They do not include highly indivisible costs such as space rental.

Divisional and corporate expenses, other than those already listed, are as follows:

Marketing division management salaries..........	$10,000
Freight and delivery..............................	6,050
Advertising.......................................	8,000
Other marketing division expenses................	12,000
Corporate management expenses.................	20,000

Marketing division management consists of the division manager ($3,000 a month), a director of market research ($2,000), a staff assistant ($1,400), and three secretaries. The division manager and staff assistant spend about half of their time in general analytical and policy work, one quarter in region C, and the remainder divided equally between the other two regions. The director of market research does no work on a regional basis.

Freight and delivery costs amount to 8 cents a pound in regions A and B and 3 cents a pound in region C.

Advertising costs consist of $5,000 in national media and $1,000 in local media in each of the sales regions.

Other marketing division expenses consist of office rent, executive travel expense, office supplies, utilities, computer rentals, and so forth.

Corporate management expenses consist of salaries and expenses of the company's president and corporate staffs, depreciation, taxes and insurance on the headquarters building, and similar charges.

Prepare a statement that will best indicate the relative profitability of the three sales regions. Think carefully about how you want to handle fixed factory costs and the costs of marketing and corporate management.

EXERCISES AND PROBLEMS

1. Assigning functional costs to order-size segments. The Angel Meat Company has studied its selling and administrative expenses to determine the costs attributable to different segments of the company's business. It has found that some of these expenses are fixed, but the bulk of the expenses can be related to one of the following three indicators of sales volume: (1) number of orders, (2) number of items, and (3) number of hundredweights. Classification of expenses on these bases yields the following totals:

	Selling	Packing	Delivery	Adminis-trative	Total
Fixed per month.............	$20,000	$1,000	$ 3,000	$15,000	$ 39,000
Variable according to:					
Number of orders...........	46,200	1,200	4,000	23,400	74,800
Number of items............	21,600	1,400	5,000	11,600	39,600
Number of cwts.............	4,200	2,400	10,000	6,800	23,400
Total.......................	$92,000	$6,000	$22,000	$56,800	$176,800

Analysis of orders received during the analysis period shows the following data:

Size of Order	Orders	Items	Total Cwt.
Less than 50 lbs...................	56,000	81,800	14,000
50–199 lbs.........................	58,000	168,200	52,200
200–499 lbs........................	12,000	45,600	37,200
500–999 lbs........................	8,000	48,000	56,000
1,000 lbs. and over................	2,000	16,400	20,600
All orders.........................	136,000	360,000	180,000

Compute the cost per hundredweight for each order size, to the nearest 100th of a cent. Defend your method of dealing with fixed costs.

2. Assigning functional costs to sales territories. The Montgomery Company sells its products in three territories. Management has established the following standard administrative expenses to be used in preparing profit and loss statements for each territory:

Credit...	$ 5.00 per new account
Collection.....................................	10.00 per overdue account
Bookkeeping...................................	0.35 per transaction
Stenographic..................................	0.60 per letter
Other clerical.................................	1.00 per customer account
Executive salaries.............................	0.03 per sales dollar
Other administrative expense..................	0.02 per sales dollar

The following data were recorded for the month of October:

	Territory A	Territory B	Territory C
New accounts.......................	80	140	100
Overdue accounts...................	50	60	60
Transactions.......................	10,000	18,000	16,000
Letters............................	400	500	600
Customer accounts..................	500	1,000	800
Sales..............................	$200,000	$300,000	$250,000

a. Compute the amount of head office administration cost per dollar of sales in each territory for the month of October.

b. Comment on the usefulness of the comparison of these costs among territories.

3. Order-size analysis; Engineering approach. As part of the preparation for its defense in a Robinson-Patman case, C. E. Niehoff & Company conducted a series of time and motion studies of order-processing operations. Seventeen orders of varying sizes were selected for study, and the processing times were obtained for each of these by a time-study engineer. The engineer then added 25 percent to these observed times to allow for personal needs and fatigue. The total processing times, priced at standard wage rates for individual operations, are listed in the table below:

Order No.	No. of Items	No. of Packages	Net Billing	Processing Cost	Cost per Dollar
44524..........................	1	2	$ 12.00	$ 1.1909	9.92¢
44525..........................	6	23	37.66	1.3141	3.49
44576..........................	20	29	45.14	1.9457	4.31
44575..........................	8	49	56.51	2.0506	3.66
45968..........................	33	69	125.20	2.6529	2.11
44572..........................	25	116	134.47	3.2335	2.33
46162..........................	37	171	206.79	3.6094	1.74
44577..........................	36	86	﹐ 208.64	3.3236	1.59
44573..........................	63	163	223.76	4.7155	2.11
45969..........................	49	110	259.60	3.8108	1.47
45945..........................	56	163	305.01	5.4135	1.77
46161..........................	49	236	341.79	4.4516	1.30
44991..........................	68	391	496.98	7.1486	1.44
45078..........................	81	334	523.22	8.6659	1.66
45301..........................	101	623	785.80	10.7736	1.36
45079..........................	94	598	811.57	11.4696	1.41
44993..........................	89	469	846.66	10.3696	1.23

Source: Herbert F. Taggart, *Cost Justification* (Ann Arbor: University of Michigan, Graduate School of Business Administration, Bureau of Business Research, 1959), p. 408.

a. On a sheet of graph paper, plot processing costs per dollar of net billing against size of order (measured by net billings) and draw a line of relationship freehand, as accurately as you can.
b. Assuming that these are the best data available, indicate how you would use these figures in: (1) setting a minimum order size; (2) estimating the profitability of different customer groups.
c. Comment on the methods used to obtain the data and their adequacy for the purposes outlined in (b).

4. Determining functional cost. The personnel department of Mansdowne Manufacturing Company has the following costs:

Salaries....................................	$17,000
Advertising.............................	1,200
Rent.......................................	1,000
Postage and supplies....................	400
Telephone...............................	200
Depreciation............................	100
Computer services......................	300
Total.............................	$20,200

Five personnel functions have been identified:

Personnel records.
Recruiting.
Management development.
Labor relations.
Wage and salary administration.

You have the following additional information:

1. The salaries of the department's ten employees are classified as follows:

	No. of Employees	Total Salaries
Director................................	1	$ 2,800
Assistant director.....................	1	2,200
Recruiting.............................	2	3,600
Labor relations........................	1	2,400
Personnel records.....................	2	2,000
General clerical.......................	3	4,000
Total...........................	10	$17,000

2. The director has made the following estimates for five employees who work on more than one function:

	Director	Assistant	Clerical
Personnel records........................	—	10%	20%
Recruiting...............................	10%	40	30
Management development...............	50	30	20
Labor relations..........................	10	10	10
Wage and salary administration...........	30	10	20

3. All advertising costs relate to the recruiting function.
4. The department is charged rent for the space it occupies in the company's headquarters building. The rental charge is based on the average cost of owning and operating the building. Comparable space in the building is now being rented to other tenants at $1,500 a month, but a considerable amount of rentable space is now vacant. The amount of work space occupied by individual employees varies only slightly from employee to employee.
5. The director estimates that half of the postage and supplies and half of the telephone charges relate to recruiting; another 20 percent relates to management development; the rest is unidentified.
6. Computer services are 90 percent for personnel records, 10 percent for wage and salary administration.
7. Depreciation is for office furniture and equipment and is approximately equal to average replacement expenditures.

a. Prepare estimates of the costs of each of the five functions. Explain each of your allocations in a word or a phrase. You should allocate only those costs that seem relevant to managerial decisions relating to individual functions.
b. What are the most likely uses of this functional cost information?
c. Which of these functions should be allocated to segments for purposes of product-line analysis?

5. Interpreting service department variances. A company charges the managers of its three product divisions for head office services, using the following charging rates:

Head Office Department	Charging Rate
Credit department....................... $	0.30 per order
Billing department......................	0.95 per order
Payroll department......................	2.50 per employee
Accounts receivable department.........	0.40 per order
General accounting department.........	0.30 per entry
Treasurer...............................	0.35 per customer remittance
General sales manager..................	2,000.00 per month to each product division
Legal department.......................	3,000.00 per month to each product division
Executive management.................	10,000.00 per month to each product division

Statistics for the month of February were as follows:

No. of orders received...	3,900
No. of employees..	860
No. of entries...	9,300
No. of customer remittances.................................	4,600

Head office expenses and volume-adjusted budget allowances for February were:

Department	Actual	Budget
Credit..................................	$ 1,350	$ 1,400
Billing.................................	4,150	4,000
Payroll.................................	2,400	2,200
Accounts receivable....................	1,730	1,800
General accounting.....................	2,910	2,850
Treasurer..............................	1,680	1,700
General sales manager.................	5,630	6,000
Legal..................................	6,200	9,000
Executive management.................	30,400	30,000

a. Compute the undistributed cost for each head office department for the month of February, and divide it into volume and spending variance components.

b. How would you expect management to respond to large variances in the head office departments? How, if at all, do they differ from factory overhead variances?

6. Segment cost analysis; Channels of distribution. The Henlo Company has separate sales divisons for each of its product lines. The company's factories are not specialized by product lines but serve all divisions to varying degrees.

The Hardy Products Division is one of the company's oldest sales divisions. Its products are marketed through a network of 900 retail stores. Of these, 400 are served directly and the remaining 500 are served by 25 wholesalers.

This divided distribution network was not really planned. Hardy Products originally distributed its products in a relatively small geographical region, close to the company's main factories. No wholesalers were used in this region. When management decided to expand into other areas, it decided that wholesalers would provide the fastest and most effective means of penetrating those areas.

Retailers in the areas served by the wholesalers are very similar to those in the company's older areas, but their average gross sales are slightly lower. This disparity has led management to consider the possibility of hiring additional sales representatives so that all retailers could be dealt with directly, replacing the wholesalers entirely.

The following data can be regarded as typical of a full year's activity in the Hardy Products Division:

	Wholesale	Retail
Revenue from sales	$500,000	$700,000
Cost of goods sold	$420,000	$420,000
Number of sales representatives' calls	500	4,500
Number of invoice lines	45,000	255,000

Wholesalers pay lower prices than retailers to compensate them for warehousing and other sales-related functions that Hardy Products performs in connection with its directly served retail customers.

The division's six sales representatives are all on salary. When adjusted for changes in salary rates and outside price levels, the cost of sales solicitation per sales representative (salaries, travel, and samples) has remained roughly constant from year to year. The number of salespeople has been increased from three to six in the past few years as Henlo's business volume has expanded. The solicitation costs of obtaining the sales listed in the preceding table total $126,000 a year.

A call on a wholesaler takes approximately one and a half times as long as a call on a retailer. Wholesalers are also farther apart than retailers, and in an experiment conducted two years ago, the company found that a sales representative assigned full time to wholesale accounts made calls at an average annual rate of 450 calls a year, whereas a sales representative working full time on retail accounts made calls at the rate of 900 calls a year.

Costs of inventory record keeping, order receiving and filling, invoicing, accounts receivable bookkeeping, and collecting total $138,000 a year. These are regarded as fixed but have increased from year to year in parallel with the increase in the number of invoice lines.

Advertising expenditures amount to $62,000 a year, covering advertisements aimed at the ultimate consumers of the company's products.

Inventory storage costs which are incurred exclusively to service retailers amount to $24,000 a year. Storage costs consist entirely of warehouse rent, based on the amount of space used. These costs tend to increase from year to year, roughly in proportion to increases in the standard cost of goods sold.

The cost of goods sold is approximately 30 percent fixed and 70 percent variable. Factory fixed costs are largely indivisible.

Management's objective is to use the channel of distribution that will maximize the profit of the company as a whole.

a. Calculate the profit attributable (1) to the average wholesale customer, and (2) to the average direct retail customer.
b. Do these figures tend to support the proposal to expand the direct sales force to deal directly with the more distant retailers, thereby eliminating the wholesalers in these areas? Quantify your answer insofar as you can. What additional data would you want to collect before making a final recommendation on this question?

7. Functional cost analysis; Service department. The mimeograph room in the head office of David Metrics, Inc. was a busy place. David Metrics was a large management consulting firm with headquarters in New York and branch offices in 14 other cities in various parts of the United States. Using several high-speed mimeograph machines, a high-speed copying machine, and a small copier, the mimeograph room staff reproduced a large volume of internal memoranda, working drafts, and reports to the company's clients, and did a significant amount of work for other tenants of the office building in which the company's headquarters were located. No typing was done in the mimeograph room; all mimeograph stencils and master copies for the copying machines were prepared by the departments or outside customers from whom the work orders were received.

Jonathan David, the firm's administrative vice president and brother of the president, felt that the mimeograph room's costs were getting out of hand. "This doesn't tell me much," he said, pointing to the department's cost summary for the preceding month. "I know we've been doing a lot more copying work since we put in the high-speed copier, but I can't believe that one new machine has been responsible for the big cost increases we have had in this department."

Jane Rogers, the office manager in the New York headquarters, agreed to pull together some better figures for Mr. David. With the help of one of the firm's consulting engineers, Ms. Rogers carried out a quick work sampling study of the mimeograph room's machine operators. This study showed that the operators' time was divided in the following proportions:

Operating mimeograph machines	20 percent
Operating copying machines	29
Out of room	10
Telephoning	5
Writing	2
Collating mimeograph work	17
Collating copying work	8
Waiting	6
Wrapping	3

The routine cost report for the mimeograph room during this same period showed the following breakdown:

Supervisor's salary	$ 2,000
Clerical salaries	8,400
Paper and supplies	4,928
Maintenance, mimeograph machines	160
Rentals, copying machines	5,800
Depreciation, mimeograph machines	120
Space charge	480
Total	$21,888

The work load during this period was:

	Mimeograph	Copying
Number of work orders	5,000	20,000
Number of stencils processed	25,000	n.a.
Number of copies made	500,000	58,000

Ms. Rogers pointed out that most writing and telephoning was in connection with inquiries about the status of individual work orders. Virtually all wrapping time was spent on mimeographing work. Wrapping time is a function of the number of copies in the order.

After observing a number of representative operations, Ms. Rogers estimated that paper and supplies for copying work cost about twice as much per copy as the paper and supplies for mimeograph work. Copying machine rentals are based on the number of copies made.

a. Assuming that these data are typical, prepare cost estimates for each of the two classes of work done in this department. Be prepared to explain how you derived these estimates.

b. Stencils cost approximately 30 cents each. Adding these costs to those of the mimeograph room itself, calculate the cost of a 50-copy run of a 40-page report (1) by mimeograph machine, and (2) by copier. In either case the finished copies would be wrapped for delivery.

c. How else might Mr. David use the figures derived in (*a*)?

8. Product-line analysis. The Lucky Products Company manufactures and sells a line of electronics components to government contractors, telephone companies, and manufacturers of radio and television receivers and transmitters. Sales for the current year are expected to total $5 million, distributed as follows:

	Government	Telephone	Radio-TV
Sales..................................	$1,200,000	$3,000,000	$800,000
Standard cost of goods sold...........	1,000,000	2,400,000	500,000
Gross margin....................	$ 200,000	$ 600,000	$300,000

Concerned by the low margin on its government business, management has initiated a study of the profitability of the three classes of its business. The following information has been collected.

Standard cost is based on the full costing principle. Supplementary variable cost figures indicate the following ratios of variable cost to full cost at standard volume:

Government........................	70 percent
Telephone...........................	75
Radio-television......................	80

No factory department is devoted solely to any one class of business.

The following amounts of out-of-pocket fixed factory costs could be eliminated each year if one class of business were to be dropped, the others remaining in service:

Government...........................	$100,000
Telephone............................	500,000
Radio-television......................	200,000

Bookkeeping costs—that is, the costs of inventory record keeping, order receiving and filling, invoicing, accounts receivable bookkeeping, and collecting—total $150,000 a year. These are regarded as fixed, but have increased from year to year in parallel with the increase in the number of invoice lines. A sample of the invoices prepared this year indicates the following numbers of invoice lines for the three classes of business:

Government...........................	4,000
Telephone............................	6,000
Radio-television......................	20,000

Warehousing costs amount to $58,000 a year, almost entirely in wages and salaries of warehouse and storeroom personnel. Warehouse costs tend to vary from year to year, roughly in proportion to the standard cost of goods sold to telephone companies and radio-television manufacturers. Government products are transferred immediately to government supply depots and do not enter the Lucky Products warehouse space.

The costs of central administration, including executive salaries, amount to $240,000 a year. These are almost completely unaffected by the volume of business done.

The company's research and development department has operating costs of $100,000 a year. The department consists of two research engineers, three technicians, and a variety of test equipment. The two engineers specialize in different fields, and both fields provide essential support for all three classes of business.

The costs of field selling total $250,000 a year. None of this is accepted by the government as a cost of the government products, but it includes $50,000 a year to cover the salary and expenses of a sales engineer to work full-time on identifying sales opportunities and preparing bids and proposals in this market. The only other information on these costs is the number of calls made by the other salespeople in the course of a year: 500 on telephone companies and 2,500 on radio-television manufacturers. The sales manager estimates that a call at a telephone company is likely to take about three times as long as a call on a radio-television manufacturer. All the salespeople are paid on a straight salary basis, with no commissions.

Advertising accounts for $100,000 a year. Of this, $70,000 is directed specifically to manufacturers of radio-television equipment and $30,000 is for advertisements in engineering journals read by engineers in all industries.

All of the company's operations are contained in a single building. Fixed costs of providing this space amount to $120,000 a year. These costs are included in factory overhead cost—that is, no space costs are allocated to other company divisions. Space occupancy is as follows:

Executive offices........................ 10 percent
Factory................................. 68
Sales................................... 5
Warehouse............................. 10
Bookkeeping........................... 5
Research and development............. 2

The location and layout of the building make it virtually impossible to sublet any space that might become idle.

a. Prepare a revised estimate of profitability for each class of business and explain the methods and assumptions that you used in the process. (Suggestion: start by listing the total cost in each category; then decide how much to allocate to each class of business.)
b. What course(s) of action or further investigation would you suggest on the basis of this information?

9. District profitability analysis. The Western Appliances, Ltd. income statement for the year ended December 31, 19x1 appears below:

Sales (1,900,000 units)....................................			$3,800,000
Cost of goods sold....................................		$2,280,000	
Bad debts...		11,500	2,291,500
Gross profit..			$1,508,500
Packing and shipping:			
Shipping containers....................................		$ 91,750	
Packing and shipping labor expenses...................		221,250	
Freight-out...		375,750	$688,750
Selling expenses (excluding advertising):			
Sales manager's salary................................		$ 15,200	
Sales representatives' salaries........................		32,000	
Sales representatives' commissions....................		24,000	
Agency commissions..................................		30,000	101,200

Advertising:
Local newspapers	$ 43,500		
National magazines	57,000	100,500	
Administrative expenses (fixed)		64,750	966,700
Net Operating Profit			$ 533,300

The company distributes a single product in a variety of colors. The selling price is $2 a unit.

The product is distributed in four market areas—A, B, C, and D.

District A is the district in which the company's distribution center and offices are located. No salespeople are employed. Orders are received through the mail and by telephone, and customers send their trucks to the distribution center to pick up their orders when ready.

District B is located 100 miles from the distribution center. The company employs four sales representatives in this area, each on a commission basis. The company also places a quarter-page advertisement once each week in the local newspaper.

District C is located 200 miles from the distribution center. The company employs eight sales representatives in the area, each on a salary basis. The company takes one quarter of a page of advertising three times a week in the local paper in district C; the cost per insertion is twice as much as that in district B.

District D is an agency. It is 400 miles distant from the distribution center. The company shares with the agency the cost of a quarter-page weekly advertisement in the local paper on a 1:3 ratio, the space cost being the same as in district B.

The product is packaged in containers of three different sizes: namely, 16s (small), 32s (medium), and 48s (large), and shipments are made in case lots only. It is assumed that each order calls for one case.

Sales and agency commissions are paid on a flat percentage of sales basis.

The following unit costs per case have been determined:

	Small	Medium	Large
Container	$1	$1.50	$2
Packing and shipping labor expenses	3	3.50	4
Freight-out (cost per 100 miles)	2	3.50	5

A statistical analysis of the marketing operation during 19x1 shows the following, in total and by districts:

	Total	A	B	C	D
Number of orders:					
Small cases	22,500	2,500	—	20,000	—
Medium cases	30,500	5,000	7,500	15,000	3,000
Large cases	11,750	—	7,500	—	4,250
Estimated bad debts—					
% of sales		¼ of 1%	⅛ of 1%	⅜ of 1%	½ of 1%

a. Prepare a set of statements showing the profitability of each sales district. Describe and defend the basis on which costs were assigned to each district.

b. Calculate the total profit attributable to each case size, and from these figures calculate profit per case and per unit in each case size. Describe and defend the basis on which costs were assigned to each size group.

c. It has been proposed that an additional $50,000 a year be spent on local advertising in district C. By how much must the sales volume of the district increase to warrant such an expenditure?

(SICA adapted)

10. Regional profitability analysis. The Scent Company sells men's toiletries to retail stores throughout the United States. For planning and control purposes the Scent Company is organized into 12 geographic regions with two to six territories within each region. One salesperson is assigned to each territory and has exclusive rights to all sales made in that territory. Merchandise is shipped from the manufacturing plant to the 12 regional warehouses, and the sales in each territory are shipped from the regional warehouse. National headquarters allocates a specific amount at the beginning of the year for regional advertising.

The net sales for the Scent Company for the year ended September 30, 1974 totaled $10 million. Costs incurred by national headquarters for national administration, advertising and warehousing are summarized as follows:

National administration............................	$250,000
National advertising................................	125,000
National warehousing..............................	175,000
	$550,000

The results of operations for the South Atlantic Region for the year ended September 30, 1974 are presented below.

Net Sales...		$900,000
Deductions:		
Advertising..	$ 54,700	
Bad debts...	3,600	
Cost of goods sold................................	460,000	
Freight out..	22,600	
Insurance...	10,000	
Salaries and employee benefits...................	81,600	
Sales commissions...............................	36,000	
Supplies..	12,000	
Travel and entertainment.........................	14,100	
Wages and employee benefits....................	36,000	
Warehouse depreciation..........................	8,000	
Warehouse operating costs.......................	15,000	
Total Deductions..............................		753,600
Regional Contribution..............................		$146,400

The South Atlantic Region consists of two territories—Green and Purple. The following cost analyses and statistics for the current year are representative of past experience and are representative of expected future operations:

	Green	Purple	Total
Sales.....................................	$300,000	$600,000	$900,000
Cost of goods sold......................	184,000	276,000	460,000
Advertising.............................	21,800	32,900	54,700
Travel and entertainment...............	6,300	7,800	14,100
Freight out.............................	9,000	13,600	22,600
Units sold..............................	150,000	350,000	500,000
Pounds shipped.........................	210,000	390,000	600,000
Sales force miles traveled..............	21,600	38,400	60,000

Other information on the items in the statement of operations:

1. Bad debts have averaged 0.4 percent of net sales in the past.

2. 30 percent of the insurance is for protection of the inventory while it is in the regional warehouse; the remainder is on the warehouse itself.

3. Salaries and employee benefits consist of the following items:

Regional vice president..	$24,000
Regional marketing manager..............................	15,000
Regional warehouse manager.............................	13,400
Salespeople (one for each territory with each	
receiving the same salary base).........................	15,600
Employee benefits (20 percent)............................	13,600
	$81,600

4. Each sales representative receives a base salary [item (3) above] plus a 4 percent commission on all items sold in the territory. No employee benefit costs arise in connection with sales commissions.

5. Supplies are used in the warehouse for packing the merchandise that is shipped.

6. Travel and entertainment costs are incurred by the salespeople calling on their customers.

7. Wages and employee benefits relate to the hourly paid employees who fill orders in the warehouse.

8. The warehouse operating costs cover heat, light, maintenance, and so forth.

a. Prepare a cost schedule for the South Atlantic Region, separating the operating costs into the fixed and variable components of order-getting, order-filling, and administration, using the following format:

	Territory Costs		Regional	Total
	Green	Purple	Costs	Costs
Order-getting...........				
Order-filling.............				
Administration..........				

b. Suppose top management is considering splitting the Purple territory into two separate territories (Red and Blue). Which of the data supplied would be relevant to this decision? What other data would you collect to aid top management in this decision?

c. If Scent Company keeps its records in accordance with the classifications required in (a), can standards and flexible budgets be used in planning and controlling marketing costs?

(CMA, adapted)

CASE 12–1: ROBSON, LTD.*
(Profitability of small orders)

"Sorry to be late, John," Alan Thurston said. "I had a customer in my office and I just couldn't get rid of him."

"That's okay, Alan. I just got here myself. I hope you made a big sale."

* Copyright 1967, 1977 by l'Institut pour l'Etude des Méthodes de Direction de l'Entreprise (IMEDE), Lausanne, Switzerland. Published by permission.

"No such luck. I'll bet this customer has never done more than $100 worth of business with us and yet he sat in my office asking questions for an hour. We have too many customers like him."

Mr. Thurston was the sales manager of Robson, Ltd., a small Australian manufacturer of industrial supplies. He made the statement quoted above as he sat down to lunch with Mr. John Axelson, the company's controller. After they had ordered their lunch, Mr. Thurston returned to the subject. "I know how my sales stack up," he said, "but I have no idea how much money we make on the big customers or how much we lose on the little ones. Could you put some figures together for me on this?"

"I can't get at it myself right now," said Mr. Axelson, "but why don't we put Peter on it? It would be good experience for him and I don't have anything else important for him to do at the moment." Peter Halford was Mr. Thurston's nephew and was working at Robson, Ltd. during his summer holidays from the university. This was his second summer with Robson, and Mr. Axelson felt that he knew enough about the company to be able to get the figures Mr. Thurston wanted.

Mr. Halford first collected the statistics shown in Table 1. He started

TABLE 1

ROBSON, LTD.
Customer Statistics

	Group					
	A	B	C	D	E	F
Annual sales to each customer.....	$ 10,000 or more	$ 2,000– $ 9,999	$ 1,000– $ 1,999	200– 999	$1–$199	$0
Number of customers............	46	117	234	420	2,521	1,872
Total annual sales................	$800,000	$500,000	$300,000	$200,000	$200,000	—
Total gross margin...............	160,000	110,000	75,000	48,000	49,000	—
Total variable manufacturing profit..........................	280,000	190,000	120,000	79,000	81,000	—
Sales calls per year..............	230	585	940	1,680	4,575	3,740
Customer orders per year.........	700	800	1,000	2,000	5,000	—
Average sales per customer.......	$ 17,391	$ 4,274	$ 1,282	$ 476	$ 79	—
Average sales per order..........	1,143	625	300	100	40	—

by classifying all the company's customers and active prospects on the basis of the total amount of business they had done with Robson in the last complete fiscal year. At one extreme, he found that 46 customers had bought more than $10,000 each during the previous year, while 1,872 customers and prospects (all referred to by the company as "customers") had bought absolutely nothing.

Fortunately for Mr. Halford, the company's sales records were quite complete, and he was able to identify the gross margin (sales minus the cost of goods sold) for each customer. As a result of some work he had been doing that summer, he was also able to make an estimate of the variable component of the cost of goods sold, and this permitted him to assemble the set of figures identified in Table 1 as "total variable manufacturing profit" (sales minus variable manufacturing cost of goods sold).

The profit-sales ratios varied slightly from group to group, mainly because of differences in the discounts granted to different customers.

The statistics on sales calls and customer orders were readily available in the files, although Mr. Halford had to work fairly hard to dig them out.

Next Mr. Halford turned to the task of identifying the cost of serving individual customers. At his request, Mr. Thurston got all of his salespeople to keep a record of their time for one week. This showed the following breakdown:

Call time (waiting for and talking to customers)........	50 percent
Travel time...	30
Office time (preparing reports, following up on orders, etc.).......................................	20
Total...	100 percent

The ten-person sales force was organized regionally, the individual representatives having their own sales territories. Some territories were relatively compact, while others required a good deal of traveling. Each representative was responsible for promoting all of the company's products.

Mr. Halford summarized the annual costs of the sales department and computed the average cost per sales call, as follows:

	Amount	Per Call
Sales supervision...............................	$ 18,800	$ 1.60
Sales salaries and benefits.......................	122,200	10.40
Clerical salaries.................................	8,460	0.72
Sales travel.....................................	79,900	6.80
Customer entertainment.........................	14,100	1.20
Samples..	7,050	0.60
Rent...	2,350	0.20
Other..	2,820	0.24
Total.....................................	$255,680	$21.76

This was the estimated cost of the sales department for the current year. The only omission was $4,230 of clerical salaries which Mr. Halford excluded from the total above on the basis of Mr. Thurston's estimate that the office staff devoted only two thirds of its time to matters related to the sales force (typing expense accounts, preparing payrolls, etc.). The remaining one third of office clerical time was spent processing customer orders and thus should not be included in the cost per call figures. Instead, Mr. Halford included this amount in a rough estimate of the clerical cost of processing an order. Orders came both through the sales force and directly from the customers, by mail or telephone. The office procedure was the same in either case and Mr. Halford estimated that the total cost of clerical salaries and benefits averaged about $2.40 an order. He thought that he could get a more accurate figure if he tried, but he didn't have enough time to study the costs of other items such as depreciation on office equipment, office supplies, and office rent.

On the basis of these figures, Mr. Halford prepared the analysis of customer profitability shown in Table 2. "This will really make Uncle Alan sit up and take notice," he said. "Even on the most favorable calculation, we still lose $30,000 a year on our small customers and pour more than $80,000 down the drain on customers who don't buy anything at all. I'll bet he changes his sales policy now." He walked confidently toward Mr. Axelson's office to show him the results of the analysis.

Do these data mean that Robson, Ltd. would be able to increase its profits by discontinuing sales calls on the customers in groups E and F?

TABLE 2

ROBSON, LTD.
Statement of Customer Profitability

	Groups					
	A	B	C	D	E	F
Selling costs (no. of calls × $21.76).........................	$ 5,005	$ 12,730	$20,454	$36,557	$ 99,552	$ 81,382
Order-filling costs (no. of orders × $2.40).................	1,680	1,920	2,400	4,800	12,000	—
Total expense...................	$ 6,685	$ 14,650	$22,854	$41,357	$111,552	$ 81,382
Excess of gross margin over expense......................	$153,315	$ 95,350	$52,146	$ 6,643	$(62,552)	$(81,382)
Excess of variable manufacturing profit over expense............	273,315	175,350	97,146	37,643	(30,552)	(81,382)

Indicate how you would interpret the data. Also describe any changes in analytical method that you would recommend. Remember that this is a small company and that Mr. Halford had only a few weeks, at most, to study this problem.

13

Short-Run Optimization Models

DECIDING how to allocate the organization's resources is far more difficult than some of our earlier illustrations may have implied. To deal with these complexities more effectively, management can use formal *decision models*. A decision model is a description of the relationships presumed to exist between the possible courses of action and the other variables in the real situation the model represents, together with a set of rules and procedures to be used in comparing alternatives and developing a recommended course of action.

The purpose of this chapter is to explain how two relatively simple decision models work and what kinds of data they call for. The two models are:

1. Linear programming, for rationing capacity when two or more resources are scarce.
2. An inventory decision model, for setting the inventory level and the size of production or purchase orders.

These are both short-term decision models, to help management decide how to use its existing facilities. We shall look at capacity determining decisions in Chapters 14 and 15 and at some of the implications of uncertainty in Chapter 17.

The first model we shall examine is a linear programming model. To lead into this discussion, however, we shall try to demonstrate the logic of linear programming by examining a trial-and-error procedure for allocating scarce resources.

RATIONING CAPACITY:
A TRIAL-AND-ERROR SOLUTION

Most of the decision situations we described in previous chapters were excess-capacity situations—that is, the question was whether to

435

use capacity or let it remain idle. When we did encounter full capacity, as in Chapter 5, we were always able to measure capacity by a single number, such as a specified number of labor hours or machine-hours. Now we shall see what happens when we introduce a second scarce resource. The question is how two scarce resources should be allocated among various possible uses of these resources.

The procedure we'll follow in this section reflects the assumption that the decision rule is to adopt the alternative that promises to generate the greatest amount of profit. This procedure is designed to find out which alternative does this, and it consists of three steps:

1. Estimate the relationships among the various variables.
2. Estimate the results to be achieved by one possible resource allocation pattern.
3. Try other possible patterns until no further improvement of results can be found.

Estimating the Relationships

Three sets of relationships must be estimated in a capacity-rationing situation:

1. The profitability of each of the competing uses of capacity.
2. The amount of capacity each competing use requires.
3. The total amount of capacity available.

For example, a company manufactures two products, each of which is processed in the same two production departments. The company has received more orders than it can fill with its existing facilities and needs to decide how much of each product to produce. Capacity in each department is measured by the number of machine-hours available for production—4,500 hours in department X and 7,500 hours in department Y.

Since the total capacity will remain constant, no matter which solution is chosen, capacity costs will be unaffected by the decision and can be ignored. This means that the profitability of each product can be measured by its contribution margin. The estimated contribution margins and the capacity required per unit are shown in Exhibit 13–1.

EXHIBIT 13–1

	Product A	Product B
Contribution margin per unit:		
Selling price..............................	$45	$15
Variable costs...........................	35	9
Contribution margin..................	$10	$ 6
Machine-hours required per unit:		
In department X..........................	4	1
In department Y...........................	2	3
Sales orders (units)........................	1,000	2,500

The First Trial Solution

The first step in the analysis is to relate the contribution margin to the amount of capacity required. If one product has a higher contribution margin per unit of capacity in *each* department, then it is clearly preferable to the other. Unfortunately, this is not the case here:

	Product A	Product B
Contribution per hour:		
In department X........................	$2.50	$6
In department Y........................	5.00	2

In other words, product A is a more profitable use of department Y's resources than product B, while product B uses department X's resources more profitably than product A does.

These contribution margin figures don't give us much help in deciding which possible solution to try first. One is as logical as another. Fortunately, it doesn't matter—we'll come to the same conclusion no matter where we start. So let's be arbitrary and start by seeing what would happen if the company were to devote as much capacity to product A as it would need to manufacture 1,000 units of this product, filling in with product B only if some capacity were left over after the entire demand for product A was filled.

From Exhibit 13–1 we find that a unit of product A requires four hours of machine time in department X and 2 hours in department Y. Production of 1,000 units therefore would take up 4,000 hours of department X's capacity, plus 2,000 hours in department Y. This would leave 500 hours of unused capacity in department X and 5,500 hours in department Y, available for the production of product B. Since each unit of B needs one hour of department X's time, that department's capacity would be exhausted by the production of 500 units of product B. The results under this solution would be as follows:

Product	Units of Output	Capacity Utilized Dept. X	Capacity Utilized Dept. Y	Contribution Margin
A........................	1,000	4,000	2,000	$10,000
B........................	500	500	1,500	3,000
Total.................		4,500	3,500	$13,000
Capacity available.........		4,500	7,500	
Idle capacity.............		0	4,000	

The Second Trial Solution

The first trial solution would leave 4,000 hours of department Y's capacity unused. Product B uses department Y more intensively than product A does. This suggests that the company might find it profitable to shift at least some resources from A to B.

To implement this idea, we might try a second solution in which the company would produce as much of product B as department Y could handle. Since one unit of B requires three hours in department Y (from Exhibit 13–1), this department's capacity would be completely absorbed by 2,500 units of product B:

Product	Units of Output	Capacity Utilized		Contribution Margin
		Dept. X	Dept. Y	
A.......................	0	0	0	0
B.......................	2,500	2,500	7,500	$15,000
Total.................		2,500	7,500	$15,000
Capacity available........		4,500	7,500	
Idle capacity.............		2,000	0	

Product B's contribution margin is $6 a unit, and the total contribution would be $15,000. This is better than the results under the first solution, but this time some of department X's capacity would be idle.

The Optimal Solution

To see whether any other solution would improve the anticipated results still further, we need to calculate the net gain or loss from reducing the output of product B by one unit, while increasing the output of product A. In this case, reducing product B's output by one unit would release enough capacity in department Y (three hours) to make one and a half units of product A (at two hours a unit). In other words, the company would lose the profit on one unit of B and gain the profit on one and a half units of A:

Gain: 1.5 × $10................ $15
Loss: 1.0 × $6................. 6
     Net gain.................... $ 9

Notice what we have just discovered. When department X is underutilized, management can increase its profits by substituting product A for product B. Similarly, when department Y is underutilized, profit can be increased by substituting product B for product A. This suggests that the optimal solution will be reached when both departments are fully utilized, with capacity allocations somewhere between those in our own trial solutions.

To move from the second solution to the optimal solution, we need to substitute production of product A for production of product B until department X's idle capacity is fully utilized. As we just saw, the company can substitute one and a half units of A for one unit of B without changing the total number of hours used in department Y. Each such substitution uses up five hours of department X's idle capacity:

Added production of A: 1½ × 4............................ 6 hours
Less: Reduced production of B: 1 × 1.................... 1 hour
     Net increase in use of department X................ 5 hours

Because department X had an idle capacity of 2,000 hours in the second trial solution, both departments will be operating at capacity if $2,000/5 = 400$ units of B are subtracted from that solution. This will bring production of B down from 2,500 units to 2,100 and will release enough capacity to produce 600 units of A:

		Hours Required	
Product	Units Produced	Dept. X	Dept. Y
A.........................	600	2,400	1,200
B.........................	2,100	2,100	6,300
Total.................		4,500	7,500

The solution is feasible and capacity is fully utilized in each department.
     The total contribution under this optimal solution is:

$$600 \times \$10 + 2,100 \times \$6 = \$18,600$$

This is $3,600 greater than the better of the two trial solutions. The amount of the improvement could have been predicted: the benefit from substituting one and a half units of A for one unit of B was $9, and we made 400 of these substitutions.

EXHIBIT 13–2

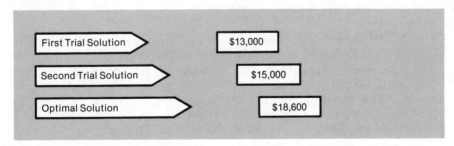

RATIONING CAPACITY BY LINEAR PROGRAMMING

     The technique we have just described is a special case of a widely used technique known as linear programming. Linear programming consists of a set of mathematical procedures by which management finds the capacity-occupancy pattern that will maximize or minimize a performance measure that management has selected. In this section we shall see how a formal linear programming technique can be applied to an illustrative capacity-rationing problem. The discussion has five parts:

1. Constructing the program.
2. Solving the problem graphically.
3. Calculating the value of changes in the amount of productive capacity (shadow prices).
4. Using the program in sensitivity analysis.
5. Specifying the accounting data to be used.

Constructing the Program

To construct a linear program, we need to take three steps:

1. Identify the decision variables.
2. Identify the relationship between these variables and the measure to be maximized or minimized.
3. Identify the constraints.

The decision variables. The first step is to identify the decision variables, the ones management can influence directly. We have identified two decision variables in our simple illustration:

$$A = \text{Number of units of product A to be manufactured.}$$
$$B = \text{Number of units of product B to be manufactured.}$$

The relationships. The next step is to identify the relationship between these variables and the measure to be maximized or minimized. This relationship is known as the *objective function*, because it shows the relationship (function, in mathematical terms) between the decision variables and the measuring units in which management expresses its objective. In this case the objective is profit maximization and the objective function is:

$$\text{Total contribution margin} = \$10 \times A + \$6 \times B$$

We could add fixed costs to this equation to express the objective function as a net profit function. The decision will affect only the number of units of A and B produced, however, not the fixed costs, and no purpose would be served by putting the fixed costs in.

The constraints. The third step is to identify the conditions that an acceptable solution must meet. These are referred to as the *constraints*. The constraints in the illustration are:

1. The capacity of department X is 4,500 hours.
2. The capacity of department Y is 7,500 hours.
3. Output of product A cannot be negative.
4. Output of product B cannot be negative.

The first constraint can be expressed mathematically as an inequality—that is, production of the two products must use no more than 4,500 hours in total. Mathematically:

Hours used for A + hours used for $B \leq 4,500$

(The symbol $\leq$ means "is less than or equal to.") Since we know that each unit of product A requires four hours of department X time and each unit of product B requires one hour, we can restate the inequality as follows:

$$4A + 1B \leq 4,500 \qquad \text{(Department X capacity constraint)} \qquad (1)$$

A similar translation of the capacity constraint for department Y yields the following inequality:

$$2A + 3B \leq 7,500 \qquad \text{(Department Y capacity constraint)} \qquad (2)$$

The third and fourth constraints may seem superfluous, but they must be introduced to rule out nonsensical solutions that might otherwise emerge from a mechanistic application of the mathematical problem-solving technique. The mathematical expression of the constraints is as follows:

$$A \geq 0 \qquad\qquad\qquad (3)$$
$$B \geq 0 \qquad\qquad\qquad (4)$$

(The symbol $\geq$ means "is greater than or equal to.")

Graphic Solution

This problem can be solved by a number of different linear programming techniques. One of these, the graphic method, is the clearest way to show the logic underlying them all. This form of analysis takes place in three stages:

1. Diagramming the constraints.
2. Diagramming the objective function.
3. Identifying the profit-maximizing output combination.

Diagramming the constraints. The first task is to prepare a sheet of graph paper and draw in the constraints. Exhibit 13–3 shows a graph with a line representing the first constraint drawn in. Drawing this line is a three-step process:

1. Find what value of B just satisfies the first constraint when the output of A is zero:

$$4 \times 0 + 1 \times B \leq 4,500 \qquad (1)$$

That is, when $A = 0$, B must be less than or equal to 4,500 units. The point labeled P identifies The $A = 0$, $B = 4,500$ output combination.

2. Find what value of A just satisfies the first constraint when the output of B is zero:

$$4 \times A + 1 \times 0 \leq 4,500 \qquad (1)$$

This shows that the output of A can't be greater than $4,500/4 = 1,125$ units when B's output is zero. This output combination is labeled point Q.

EXHIBIT 13–3

Graph Showing First Constraint

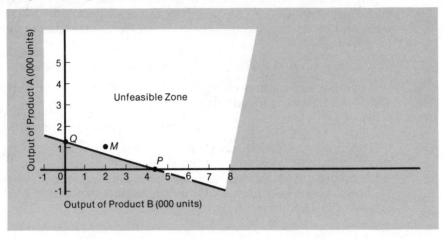

3.   Draw a straight line through these two points.

None of the output combinations in the unshaded area in the diagram is feasible because department X's capacity is too small to handle
any combination in this area. Suppose we tried to schedule 1,000 units
of A and 2,000 units of B, for example—point M in the diagram. This
would require the following amounts of time in department X:

Product A   1,000 × 4................ 4,000 hours
Product B   2,000 × 1................ 2,000 hours
    Total.......................... 6,000 hours

This is clearly impossible because department X has only 4,500 hours
available.

A line representing the second constraint can be located by the
same method, by solving inequality (2) for two different pairs of
values:

1.   When $A = 0$:

$$2 \times 0 + 3 \times B \leq 7{,}500 \qquad\qquad (2)$$
$$B \leq 2{,}500$$

2.   When $B = 0$:

$$2 \times A + 3 \times 0 \leq 7{,}500 \qquad\qquad (2)$$
$$A \leq 3{,}750$$

These two combinations are identified as points R and S in Exhibit
13–4. The line connecting these two points establishes the maximum
output of department Y. Every output combination in the unshaded
area to the right of the SR line calls for more time than department Y
has available.

The third and fourth constraints are also shown in Exhibit 13–4.
The white space to the left of the vertical axis indicates that negative

outputs of product B are impossible. Similarly, the white space below the base line shows that negative outputs of product A are impossible.

Diagramming the objective function. Once all the constraints have been drawn in, we can see that only a few possible output combinations are feasible. These are the combinations in the shaded area of Exhibit 13–4. These combinations are not all equally profitable. To find the best one, we have to find some way of putting the objective function into the diagram.

This is the most difficult step to visualize, but the procedure is basically very simple. We start by picking any output combination and computing the anticipated profit from that combination. An easy combination to plot is the combination of no units of A and 2,000 units of B. The contribution margin for this combination is:

$$\text{Contribution margin} = 0 + 2{,}000 \times \$6 = \$12{,}000.$$

The next step is to find another output combination that provides this same $12,000 contribution margin. This time the easiest solution is to let B equal zero, so that the output of A can be calculated from the following equation:

$$\$12{,}000 = \$10 \times A + 0.$$

From this it is easy to see that it takes 1,200 units of A to generate a $12,000 contribution margin.

These two points, labeled T and V, have been plotted in Exhibit 13–5 and a straight line has been drawn between them. (Ignore the other dashed lines for the moment and concentrate on the one joining points T and V.) Because the profit relationship in the objective function is linear, every point on this line represents an output combination that will produce a $12,000 contribution margin. We call this an "isoprofit" line.

EXHIBIT 13–4

Graph Showing All Constraints

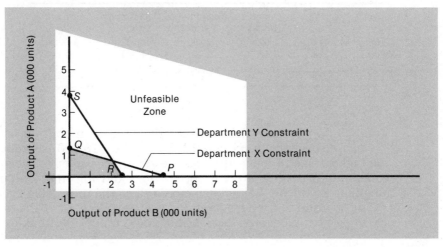

EXHIBIT 13–5

Linear Programming: Graphic Solution

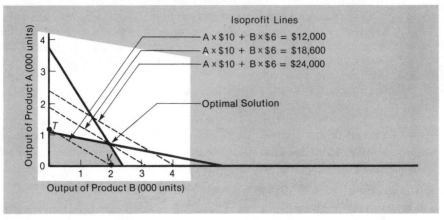

Even more important, all points to the "northeast" of this line represent output combinations that will yield more than $12,000. Since many of the points to the northeast of the $12,000 line are in the feasible region of the chart, it is clear that the company can find a combination with a contribution margin greater than $12,000.

Identifying the profit-maximizing solution. The third step is to draw other isoprofit lines parallel to the first, moving progressively outward. Each line stands for a higher profit total than the one before, as shown in the exhibit. The maximum profit solution is found when an isoprofit line crosses the last outer edge of the feasible output zone, the shaded area in the diagram.

In this case, the maximum possible contribution margin is $18,600, obtainable when the output of A is 600 units and the output of B is 2,100 units:

	Output (Units)	Department X Hours	Department Y Hours	Contribution Margin
Product A............	600	2,400	1,200	$ 6,000
Product B............	2,100	2,100	6,300	12,600
Total.............		4,500	7,500	$18,600

This solution just uses up all the available time in both departments. We can also see from Exhibit 13–5 that the $18,600 isoprofit line is the highest one to touch the feasible zone. Any other feasible output combination is on a lower isoprofit line, and all other output combinations producing $18,600 or more fall in the unfeasible zone.

The solution to a linear program is always located at the point of an angle at the edge of the feasible zone, unless the maximum isoprofit line coincides with one of the constraint boundaries. In that limiting case, a number of combinations will be equally desirable.

In summary: (1) the capacity constraints define the feasible region; (2) the best combination of outputs is found by moving the isoprofit line out until it reaches the farthest limit of the feasible region; and (3) this combination normally will be at the intersection of two of the constraint lines.

Developing Shadow Prices

The constraints in linear programs are ordinarily less rigid than the mathematical formulation would imply. If the payoff is great enough, management often can find a way to alter the constraint. The linear program can be used to identify the constraints that are most worth changing.

For example, suppose department X's capacity could be increased by one hour, to 4,501 hours. Suppose also that fractional outputs are feasible. The question is how much the company would be willing to pay to get an additional hour of capacity in department X. Department Y's capacity is to remain unchanged.

We saw earlier that if the company has five hours of idle time in department X and no idle time in department Y, the best way to use this is to reduce production of product B by one unit and increase output of product A by one and a half units. If only one hour of time is idle, each of these figures should be reduced to one fifth. This means that one additional hour of time in department X would permit the following adjustment:

$$\text{Product A: } +0.2 \times 1.5 = +0.3 \text{ unit}$$
$$\text{Product B: } -0.2 \times 1.0 = -0.2 \text{ unit}$$

The profit contribution of a unit of product A is \$10; that of product B is \$6. The extra hour of capacity therefore would increase total company profit by $0.3 \times \$10 - 0.2 \times \$6 = \$1.80$. In other words, an hour of department X capacity is worth \$1.80. This is referred to as department X's *shadow price*.

A similar calculation can be made for department Y. Additional capacity in department Y, unaccompanied by an increase in the capacity of department X, can be used only by substituting some units of product B for product A. Since a unit of A requires four hours in department X and a unit of B takes only one hour, the substitution would be in a four-to-one ratio. Adding four units of B would increase usage of department Y by 12 hours, less the 2 hours saved by the cutback in production of A there, a net increase of 10 hours. Since we are only adding one hour of capacity, we can handle only one tenth of this substitution, permitting the following adjustment:

$$\text{Product A: } -0.1 \times 1 = -0.1 \text{ unit}$$
$$\text{Product B: } +0.1 \times 4 = +0.4 \text{ unit}$$

The addition of an hour of department Y capacity therefore would be worth $0.4 \times \$6 - 0.1 \times \$10 = \$1.40$. This means that the capacity constraint in department Y is $0.40 an hour less costly than the one in department X. Management should be willing to pay up to $0.40 more for an extra department X hour than for a department Y hour.

Sensitivity Analysis

The calculation of shadow prices is a simple example of sensitivity analysis. Sensitivity analysis is any procedure designed to test the responsiveness of the action recommendation or of the amount of any variable to changes or errors in any of the other variables in a decision model.

Since the action recommendations are the main reason for applying decision models, we shall focus on this aspect of sensitivity analysis. Some recommendations are relatively sensitive to changes in decision variables, as in the left-hand diagram of Exhibit 13–6. This

EXHIBIT 13–6

Sensitivity of Action Recommendation to Variations in a Decision Variable

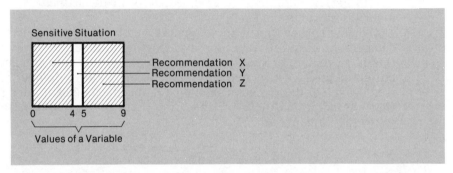

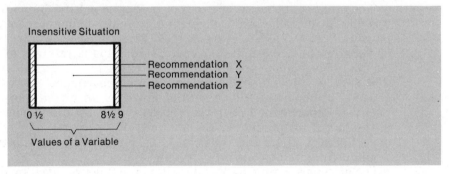

shows that recommendation Y is valid only if the variable has a value between 4 and 5. The right-hand diagram, in contrast, shows a highly insensitive situation in which recommendation Y is valid for any value of the variable from one half to eight and a half.

In our illustration, the action recommendation (how much of A and how much of B to produce) is highly sensitive to changes in the constraints. We saw this in our analysis of shadow prices. The action recommendation is highly insensitive, however, to changes in the relative contribution margins of the two products. The action recommendation will not change at all unless the ratio of one contribution margin to the other changes substantially.

For example, remember that each unit of product B requires as much of department X's capacity as four units of product A. Suppose product A's contribution margin is $27, while product B's contribution margin remains at $6. The objective function is now:

$$\text{Contribution margin} = \$27 \text{ A} + \$6 \text{ B}.$$

If all of department X's capacity is used to produce product A, the company will be able to manufacture 1,125 units:

$$\frac{\text{Total department X capacity}}{\text{Hours in department X for a unit of product A}} = \frac{4,500 \text{ hours}}{4 \text{ hours}}$$
$$= 1,125 \text{ units}.$$

If this is done, the situation will be as follows:

Total contribution margin   1,125 × $27   = $30,375
Department Y hours required   1,125 × 2   = 2,250 hours
Idle capacity in department Y 7,500 − 2,250 = 5,250 hours

In these circumstances, the total contribution margin can't be increased by substituting product B for product A, even though that substitution would use some of department Y's idle capacity. Remember that product B requires one hour in department X, while product A needs 4 hours. This means that reducing production of A by one unit would provide enough capacity to produce 4 units of B. The effect on profit would be:

Add	4 units of B at $6	+$24
Subtract	1 unit of A at $27	− 27
	Loss from substitution	−$ 3

This new objective function is shown in the new isoprofit line in Exhibit 13–7. The slope of the isoprofit line is now flatter than the slope of the constraint for department X. The company can reach the highest feasible isoprofit line ($30,375) only by devoting all of department X's capacity to product A. This is the solution indicated by the point at which the $30,375 isoproduct line touches the left-hand edge of the diagram. This is the only output combination in the feasible zone that will produce a total contribution margin as large as $30,375.

What does this have to do with sensitivity analysis? It shows that the output combination decision will not be shifted toward product A unless the contribution margin of product A is more than 4 times the contribution margin of product B. (With contribution margins of $24 for A and $6 for B, each product would return the same contribution margin per department X hour.)

EXHIBIT 13–7

Effect of Change in Relative Profit Ratio

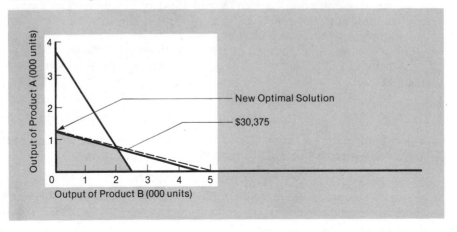

This analysis revealed department X's capacity as the more important scarce resource. If product B is much more profitable than product A, however, the company may be able to justify using all of department Y's capacity to produce product B, leaving product A out in the cold. Again the point at which this change would be made is determined by the ratio of the contribution margin of a unit of product B to the contribution margin of a unit of product A. Since department Y needs 3 hours to produce a unit of B and 2 hours to produce a unit of A, the contribution margin of B would have to be at least 3/2 of the contribution margin of A to justify the extreme solution of producing all B and no A.

In other words, the action recommendation will be the same for any ratio of the two contribution margin figures falling between the following limits:

$$\left(\frac{P_A}{P_B} = \frac{4}{1}\right) \geq \text{Actual ratio} \geq \left(\frac{P_A}{P_B} = \frac{2}{3}\right)$$

(P_A is the contribution margin of product A; P_B is the contribution margin of product B.) The estimated ratio in our illustration was $10/\$6 = 5/3$, far from either end of the range.

The reason for this application of sensitivity analysis is uncertainty. Management probably doesn't know the contribution margin figures with certainty, and this analysis indicates how serious this lack of knowledge is likely to be. In our example, it wasn't serious at all because the error would have had to be very great to affect management's decision.

Accounting Data Required

Accountants need to be able to construct and solve linear programs because they may have to recommend actions in decision situations.

For this purpose they should study linear programming in far greater depth than we have room for here.

Our main reason for introducing linear programming in this text is to examine a question that most descriptions of the method overlook or pass over very lightly—how to measure the costs of different uses of the organization's capacity. We start with the requirement that the cost figures used in the contribution margin multipliers in the objective function should measure the response of cost to changes in volume within the range affected by the decision. Three cost questions remain to be resolved:

1. Steps in the cost function.
2. Changes in rates of variability.
3. Variable costs that are unaffected by the operations mix at full capacity.

Steps in the cost function. The easiest of these to deal with is the question of how to handle steps in the cost-volume relationship. We have given this question enough attention in previous chapters to make any lengthy discussion unnecessary. Since linear programming can deal only with linear relationships, increments or steps in fixed costs must be either excluded or averaged. If the steps are relatively close together, they should be averaged into the variable costing figure. Otherwise they should be excluded.

Changes in rates of variability. A second question is how to deal with changes in rates of variability. For example, capacity operations may require the use of high-cost suppliers for 10 percent of total materials. In this situation, the full penalty price—that is, the price paid to high-cost suppliers—should be used to cost all the materials used, on the grounds that this approximates marginal cost. This will give products with low materials requirements a larger share of the optimal product mix.

The only flaw in this approach is that if the cost penalty is big enough, it may increase the production of products with low materials requirements so far that the need for high-cost purchases disappears. If the adjustment is this large, then models of greater complexity must be developed.

Variable costs unaffected by product mix. The final question is how to deal with costs that vary with the degree of utilization of capacity but are not affected by the product mix once capacity is reached. For example, suppose that capacity in department X is measured in labor hours and that when the department is operating at capacity, it has 16 employees, no more and no less. This means that total labor cost will be the same no matter which products are manufactured, as long as all of the capacity is used.

Although this would seem to describe a typical sunk cost situation, department X's labor cost should not be left out of the objective function. The reason is that linear programming does not preclude solutions that do not use all of the available capacity. Consider, for example, the following set of figures:

	Product A	Product B
Labor hours in department X........	4	1
Labor cost in department X at $5 an hour.....................	$20	$ 5
Other variable costs.................	35	9
Total variable cost............	$55	$14
Selling price........................	45	15
Contribution margin..........	−$10	$ 1

The objective function, in other words, is:

$$\text{Contribution margin} = -\$10 \times A + \$1 \times B.$$

Since production of even one unit of product A would be unprofitable, it is clear that the best decision in this case would be to produce no product A at all. Department Y's capacity would limit output of product B to 2,500 units and these would use only 2,500 hours of department X time, leaving 2,000 hours of idle capacity. The labor cost of these 2,000 hours is a variable cost and is incremental to any decision between full utilization and less than full utilization. Only those costs that will be the same whether capacity is used or not should be excluded from the objective function.

Solutions by the Simplex Method

The graphic method of solving linear programs has two major limitations: (1) it cannot be used if management has more than two decision variables to manipulate; and (2) it is time consuming because each program has to be solved manually in its entirety. To get around either or both of these limitations, the analyst is likely to use a method that works directly from the mathematical relationships to a solution. The most popular of these methods is the simplex method.

We don't have enough room here to describe and illustrate the simplex method.[1] In essence, however, it is a trial-and-error method in which the successive trials are rigidly prescribed and mechanistically applied. This makes it ideally suited for solution by computer, and most problems in linear programming can be solved quickly with the help of readily available computer programs.

INVENTORY DECISION MODELS

One of the most frequent routine actions is the placing of production or purchase orders. Management must decide what to produce or buy, when, and in what quantity. A number of decision models have

---

[1] For a description of the simplex method, consult a good textbook in quantitative analysis, linear mathematics, or operations research. A specialized work is by Saul I. Gass, *Linear Programming: Methods and Applications*, 4th ed. (New York: McGraw-Hill Book Co., 1975).

been developed to take the judgment out of many of these decisions so that management can delegate the authority to lower level managers or clerical personnel. In this section we shall study three aspects of one of these models:

1. Calculating the economic order quantity.
2. Calculating desired safety stocks and reorder points.
3. Identifying the data needed.

The Economic Order Quantity

Most inventory models represent a systematic, programmed method of making purchase or production order decisions. The key relationship in most if not all of these models is between the size of the order and the average amount of inventory on hand. At a given usage rate, the average inventory quantity will vary directly with the size of the order.

For example, a company needs ten units of a certain item each week. It now buys a week's requirements at a time—that is, each order is for ten units. The inventory on hand varies from ten units (just after the receipt of the latest order quantity) to zero (just before the receipt of the next order quantity). If the consumpion rate is steady during the week, the average inventory will be halfway between ten and zero, or five units.

This behavior pattern is illustrated in the left-hand panel of Exhibit 13–8. Inventory quantity starts at ten, falls gradually to zero, and then bounces back to ten when the new shipment is received. The inventory level in the right-hand panel shows the same pattern, but the purchase quantity is doubled, to 20 units. This means that orders have to be placed only every other week, but the average inventory goes up to 10 units.

This relationship is significant because costs are ordinarily affected by the number of orders placed in a given time period and by the average inventory quantity. Weekly purchases, for example, require 50 times as many orders as annual purchases, and therefore approximately 50 times as much clerical time, 50 times as many forms, and 50 times as much postage. The average inventory is only one 50th as large, however, which means that less storage space will have to be provided, less insurance will be carried, less capital will be tied up, and fewer units will deteriorate or become obsolete.

The other major variable that is common to all inventory models is the rate at which the item is used, usually referred to as the *demand rate* or *demand*. Other things being equal, both order size and average inventory will be large if the demand is great and small if it is small.

The decision rule in the simplest inventory decision models is to minimize total inventory cost, given a stable level of demand that is known with absolute certainty. The objective function is:

$$TC = N \times C_o + I \times C_c$$

in which

TC = The annual inventory cost.
N = The number of orders per year.
I = The average inventory quantity.
C_o = The cost of processing an average order.
C_c = The cost of carrying a unit of inventory for a year.

Since inventory carrying costs at a given demand level vary directly with order size and purchase costs vary inversely, cost minimization is a matter of increasing the order quantity until the marginal carrying cost of further increases in inventory would exceed the marginal

EXHIBIT 13–8

Effect of Order Quantity on Average Inventory

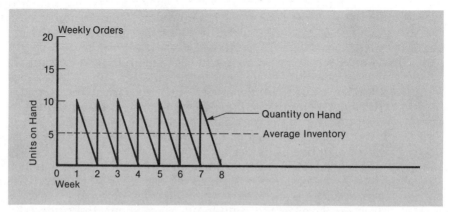

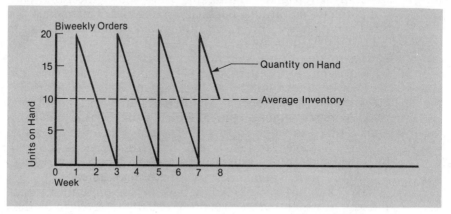

reduction in ordering cost. The simplest formula used to calculate this point is:[2]

---

[2] This is derived by differentiating the total cost equation with respect to order quantity, setting the derivative equal to zero, and solving for EOQ. For a simple derivation of this formula, see Martin K. Starr, *Production Management: Systems and Synthesis*, 2d ed.; (Englewood Cliffs, N.J.: Prentice-Hall, Inc., 1972), pp. 280–81.

$$EOQ = \sqrt{\frac{2DC_o}{C_c}}$$

where EOQ is the economic order quantity and D is the number of units used per year.

For example, suppose the annual demand (D) is 10,000 units and the order processing cost (C_o) is \$16. The purchase price is \$5 and the annual carrying cost per dollar of inventory is 40 cents. Carrying cost per unit (C_c) therefore is \$5 $\times$ 0.40 = \$2. The economic order quantity is:

$$EOQ = \sqrt{\frac{2 \times 10,000 \times \$16}{\$2}} = 400 \text{ units}$$

The purchasing and inventory costs associated with this purchase quantity can be summarized as shown in Exhibit 13–9.

EXHIBIT 13–9

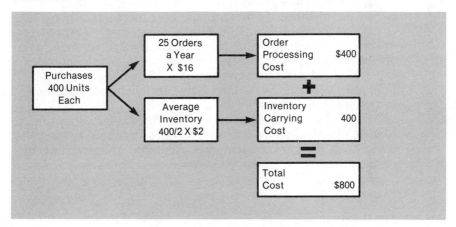

The total merchandise-based cost, including the cost of the merchandise itself, is \$50,800. No other purchase quantity would produce a total merchandise-based cost as low as this.

Safety Stocks and Reorder Points

Orders typically must be given to suppliers many days or weeks before delivery is desired. This interval is known as the *lead time*, and an essential element of any inventory decision model is the *reorder point*, identified by the model as the signal to place a new purchase order.

Lead time would pose no problem if an order placed when the quantity on hand was just equal to the quantity that would be used during the lead time would arrive just as the existing stock was exhausted. The real world is not this simple. Both the rate of use and the length of the lead time are uncertain. This means that *stock-outs* can occur.

A stock-out is a failure to fill a customer's order or a materials requisition on the desired delivery date because the goods ordered are not available.

Management can reduce the number of stock-outs by providing a *safety stock*, that is, extra inventory to allow for the possibility that demand will increase or replenishment will be delayed. The problem is to adjust the size of the safety stock so that the carrying cost of the last unit in the inventory is just equal to the stock-out cost avoided by having that unit in stock. The solution can be reached in four steps:

1. Formulating the basic model.
2. Calculating the stock-out costs.
3. Calculating the costs of the safety stock.
4. Calculating the optimal safety stock.

The basic model. Suppose the economic order quantity for a part used in the factory is 200 units, with an average usage of 20 units a week. The lead time is four weeks. This means that if no safety stock is carried, a reorder will be placed when the inventory reaches 80 units (four weeks' supply). Since both the lead time and the demand are uncertain quantities, the company will be out of stock some of the time if it carries no safety stock. This will happen whenever more than 80 units are demanded between the time of reorder and the time the goods are received.

To avoid overcomplicating the arithmetic, let us assume that lead time is certain but that demand varies between 10 and 30 units a week, with the various demands occurring at the following frequencies:

Weekly Demand (units)	Percentage Probability
10	5
15	10
20	70
25	10
30	5

In other words, demand is expected to exceed the 80-unit reorder date inventory during 15 percent of the reorder intervals, when weekly demand is more than 20 units.

Management has several options here. One is to carry a zero safety stock and accept the likelihood of being out of stock 15 percent of the time. Another is to reduce the stock-out frequency to 5 percent by carrying a 20-unit safety stock—that is, by placing the order while five weeks' supply is on hand instead of four. Finally, the stock-out probability can be reduced to zero by increasing the safety stock to 40 units, a two-week normal supply, reordering when 120 units are in inventory.

To choose among these alternatives, management needs two sets of estimates: (1) how the stock-out costs are associated with each safety stock level, and (2) the inventory level corresponding to each safety stock level.

Stock-out costs. Stock-out costs can be costly. If the result is the loss of a customer order, at least part of the cost is the opportunity cost of the lost order. If the result is an outside purchase to fill the customer's order, the cost is the penalty paid for prompt delivery. If the result is deferred delivery to the customer, the cost is the value of repeat orders that will be lost because of failure to deliver on time this time. In all three cases, the stock-out may increase the amount of idle time and disrupt production flows, thereby increasing factory costs for the volume of work done.

The calculation of the stock-out costs associated with different safety stock levels requires a merging of the stock-out probabilities with the costs of individual stock-outs. This calculation is illustrated in Exhibit 13–10. Starting on the first line, we see that with a zero

EXHIBIT 13–10

Calculation of Stock-Out Costs

(1)	(2)	(3)	(4)	(5)	(6)
				Expected	Expected
Safety	Units	Order		Units Short	Annual
Stock	Short per	Periods	Prob-	per Year	Stock-Out Cost
(units)	Order Period	per Year	ability	(2) × (3) × (4)	(5) × $18
0	20	5	0.10	10	
	40	5	0.05	10	
				20	$360
20	20	5	0.05	5	90
40	0	5	0.00	0	0

safety stock the company will be 20 units short 10 percent of the time. Since orders are placed every 10 weeks, on the average, and the factory operates 50 weeks a year, five orders will be placed in an average year. This means that ten units will be out of stock on an annual basis ($20 \times 10\% \times 5$ times a year).

The next line in the exhibit shows that the zero safety stock will lead to a few 40-unit stock-outs as well as the 20-unit stock-outs covered on the first line. This will happen 5 percent of the time, or 10 units a year. If stock-out costs amount to $18 a unit, annual stock-out costs of a zero safety stock will be $360. Similar calculations for two other safety stock levels are summarized on the final two lines.

Safety-stock costs. Safety stocks are also costly. By increasing the average inventory quantity, they increase inventory carrying costs. The next step in the analysis, therefore, is to calculate the carrying costs of different levels of safety stocks.

The carrying cost of the safety stocks is determined by multiplying the increase in the average inventory by the carrying cost per unit. If the safety stock is 20 units and the carrying cost is $6 a unit, the carrying cost of the safety stock will be $120 a year. If the safety stock is 40 units, the carrying cost will be $240.

The optimal safety stock. With these figures, calculating the optimal safety stock is simple:

Safety Stock	Carrying Cost	Stock-Out Cost	Total Cost
0	$ 0	$360	$360
20	120	90	210
40	240	0	240

In other words, the company can minimize the cost of its safety stock by providing a safety stock of 20 units and a reorder level of 100 units (the safety stock plus the normal consumption during the four-week lead time).

Data Requirements

Many other inventory decision models have been developed, most of them more complex than the one described above. Most of them require the same kinds of data, however, and discussion of the data requirements of one will serve them all.

Order quantity models call for three kinds of physical unit data: demand, out-of-stock, and inventory quantities. Although many companies fail to record out-of-stock data, measurement of these quantities poses no conceptual problems. The main task is to make sure that information is available in usable form.

Cost data are more difficult to prescribe. Three cost factors must be estimated:

1. Order cost.
2. Carrying cost.
3. Stock-out cost.

Order costs. Order processing costs consist mainly of clerical salaries and equipment rentals. Although these are fixed costs, most of them should be included in the order cost function. The reason is that total order cost depends on the joint outcome of thousands of order quantity decisions. Although a single extra order will cost little more than a few cents for paper and postage, a 10 percent increase is likely to require an additional order clerk and a 20 percent increase may call for another purchasing officer.

The fixed costs to be included in the estimated cost of placing an order should be those that vary in steps as anticipated volume goes up or down. We have referred to these earlier as attributable fixed costs.

Carrying costs. Carrying costs are of two different kinds: those that vary with the cost or value of the average inventory, and those that vary with the physical quantity of the average inventory. Insurance, financing, and spoilage costs are in the former category; the cost of warehouse space may vary with the latter.

Once again, and for the same reason as for order costs, carrying costs should be based on the attributable cost concept. If the company can adjust the amount of storage space it occupies and if the amount of space and the number of storage personnel are sensitive to changes in the inventory level, their costs should be included in the carrying cost multiplier.

The largest component of the carrying cost figure is likely to be one that doesn't appear in the historical accounting records at all. This is a charge for the amount of capital needed to finance the inventory. This charge is necessary whether the capital is supplied by the owners of the company or by lenders—both of them provide capital only if they can reasonably expect to be paid for doing so. The lender receives interest, the owner gets dividends and appreciation in the market value of his investment.

The figure used to charge for the use of capital is known as the cost of capital. It is a key figure in decision models designed to help management decide whether to spend money in one period to obtain benefits in others. This will be our topic in the next chapter.

Stock-out costs.   Stock-out costs are the most difficult to measure and estimate. As we noted earlier, the cost depends on the consequences of the stock-out—loss of current sales, premium payments for rush delivery, loss of future sales, extra factory costs, or some combination of these.

If the result of the stock-out is lost sales, the cost ordinarily can be measured by the product's contribution margin. In most cases standard variable manufacturing cost will be a reasonable approximation of the marginal cost of production. Variable sales commissions and other short-run variable selling and administrative costs should also be entered at average variable cost. Step-function increments in fixed costs should be excluded, because the aggregate volume of stock-outs is likely to be insufficient to permit significant reductions in divisional fixed costs.

If stock-outs lead to rush orders and subcontracting rather than lost sales, the stock-out cost is the difference between the internal variable cost of manufacture and the costs of dealing outside. The latter should include such hidden penalties as the costs of extra telephone calls, the costs of preparing specifications and choosing among suppliers, and the costs of expediting delivery.

The costs of idle labor time, including allowances for fringe benefits and other related costs, must also be included in the stock-out cost. This refers to idleness of wage-related employees, not salaried personnel; again on the grounds that the volume differential seldom will be large enough and last long enough to permit any significant adjustment of salary costs to lower aggregate volume. For this reason, idle time costs are likely to be considerably smaller in connection with models governing reorder points of purchased merchandise than for goods purchased for processing or internal consumption.

SUMMARY

Management now has an almost bewildering number of quantitative decision models to choose among. Each of these has its own data requirements. This chapter has attempted to throw some light on these requirements by discussing two different kinds of optimization models.

The first section of the chapter dealt with a linear programming model, designed to help management decide how to ration available capacity among various potential uses of that capacity. For linear programming, incremental costs must fit a linear formula—that is, a single-unit cost figure must be used for each product or other potential use of capacity. This usually means average short-run variable costs. If steps in fixed costs are small enough to be affected by the outcome of the program, however, they should be averaged into the variable cost figures.

One short section was also devoted to an introduction to sensitivity analysis. Although linear programming lends itself very easily to sensitivity analysis, any decision model can be examined for sensitivity, both to examine the impact of uncertainty on the quality of the decision and to explore the desirability of altering, adding, or eliminating constraints.

The final section introduced a simple inventory decision model, by which economic order quantities and reorder points can be determined if management is willing to make certain simplifying assumptions about the behavior of product demand. For these models the appropriate cost concept is attributable cost, because the aggregate effect of the decisions to be based on the model is likely to introduce changes in fixed costs.

These same ideas can be applied to other decision models as well, including those that recognize uncertainty. The main problem is to determine the scope of the choices to be made. The wider the scope, the larger the cost increment. Determination of the scope therefore serves to specify the cost definition that should be used.

We have not attempted to delve very deeply into the models themselves, nor have we discussed the practical limitations of simple models like the ones described. Our objective was merely to go far enough to identify the data requirements of the models and indicate the criteria by which data choices can be made.

KEY TERMS

The most important terms introduced and defined in this chapter are the following:

Carrying cost	Order cost
Constraint	Reorder point
Decision model	Safety stock
Decision variable	Sensitivity analysis
Economic order quantity	Shadow price
Linear programming	Stock-out

INDEPENDENT STUDY PROBLEMS
(Solutions in Appendix C)

1. Linear programming; Graphic solution. Product A has a contribution margin of $5 a unit, while product B's margin is $8. The company can sell as many as 2,000 units of each product without reducing the unit contribution margin.

A unit of product A requires two hours in department X and two hours in department Y. A unit of product B requires one hour in department X and four hours in department Y.

Department X has 3,000 hours available for these two products, while department Y has 6,000 hours available.

a.   Construct the objective function and formulate the constraints.
b.   What is the optimal production schedule? What is the anticipated total contribution margin at this level of production?
c.   How sensitive is the scheduling decision to variations in the contribution margin of product A?

2. Economic order quantity. The cost of processing a purchase order is $36. Carrying costs average 20 percent of average inventory cost. The company expects to use 10,000 units of material X during the next year. The purchase price is expected to be $2.50 a unit.

a.   Determine the economic order quantity, using the formula supplied in this chapter.
b.   Calculate the total annual cost of processing purchase orders and carrying inventories, assuming a zero safety stock.
c.   Assuming a certain lead time of three weeks and a constant rate of usage, calculate the inventory reorder point. (For convenience, the year is assumed to consist of 50 weeks.)

3. Safety stocks. Stock-out costs for material X (Problem 2) are measured by the cost of idle labor time plus penalty costs for emergency deliveries. Management estimates that these amount to $1 for each unit not on hand when it is needed. The usage of this material during the three-week reorder period is expected to correspond to the following pattern:

Usage During Three-Week Period	Probability of This Usage
400	.10
500	.20
600	.40
700	.20
800	.10

a.   What safety stock should be carried? (You should consider only multiples of 100 units.) Show your calculations.
b.   How would your answer change if the stock-out cost were $0.75 a unit instead of $1? $0.50? $0.10?

EXERCISES AND PROBLEMS

1. Linear programming: Multiple choice. The Random Company manufactures two products, Zeta and Beta. Each product must pass through two processing operations. All materials are introduced at the start of Process No. 1. There are no work-in-process inventories. Random may produce either one product exclusively or various combinations of both products subject to the following constraints:

	Process No. 1	Process No. 2	Contribution Margin Per Unit
Hours required to produce one unit of:			
Zeta.........................	1 hour	1 hour	$4.00
Beta.........................	2 hours	3 hours	5.25
Total capacity in hours per day.........................	1,000 hours	1,275 hours	

A shortage of technical labor has limited Beta production to 400 units per day. There are *no* constraints in the above schedule. Assume that all relationships between capacity and production are linear, and that all of the above data and relationships are deterministic rather than probabilistic.

1. Given the objective to maximize total contribution margin, what is the production constraint for Process No. 1?
   a. Zeta + Beta ≤ 1,000.
   b. Zeta + 2Beta ≤ 1,000.
   c. Zeta + Beta ≥ 1,000.
   d. Zeta + 2Beta ≥ 1,000.
2. Given the objective to maximize total contribution margin, what is the labor constraint for production of Beta?
   a. Beta ≤ 400.
   b. Beta ≥ 400.
   c. Beta ≤ 425.
   d. Beta ≥ 425.
3. What is the objective function of the data presented?
   a. Zeta + 2Beta = $9.25.
   b. $4.00 Zeta + 3($5.25) Beta = Total contribution margin.
   c. $4.00 Zeta + $5.25 Beta = Total contribution margin.
   d. 2($4.00) Zeta + 3($5.25) Beta = Total contribution margin.
                                                                    (CPA)

2. Linear programming: Multiple choice. Patsy, Inc., manufactures two products, X and Y. Each product must be processed in each of three departments: machining, assembling, and finishing. The hours needed to produce one unit of product per department and the maximum possible hours per department follow:

	Production Hours Per Unit		Maximum Capacity In Hours
Department	X	Y	
Machining.........	2	1	420
Assembling.......	2	2	500
Finishing..........	2	3	600

Other restrictions follow:

X ≥ 50
Y ≥ 50

The objective function is to maximize profits where profit = \$4X + \$2Y. Given the objective and constraints, what is the most profitable number of units of X and Y, respectively, to manufacture?
a.   150 and 100.
b.   165 and 90.
c.   170 and 80.
d.   200 and 50.

(CPA)

3. Linear programming: Multiple choice. A company markets two products, Alpha and Gamma. The marginal contributions per gallon are \$5 for Alpha and \$4 for Gamma. Both products consist of two ingredients, D and K. Alpha contains 80 percent D and 20 percent K, while the proportions of the same ingredients in Gamma are 40 percent and 60 percent, respectively. The current inventory is 16,000 gallons of D and 6,000 gallons of K. The only company producing D and K is on strike and will neither deliver nor produce them in the foreseeable future. The company wishes to know the numbers of gallons of Alpha and Gamma that it should produce with its present stock of raw materials in order to maximize its total contribution.

1. The objective function for this problem could be expressed as
    a. $f \max = 0X_1 + 0X_2 + 5X_3 + 5X_4$
    b. $f \min = 5X_1 + 4X_2 + 0X_3 + 0X_4$
    c. $f \max = 5X_1 + 4X_2 + 0X_3 + 0X_4$
    d. $f \max = X_1 + X_2 + 5X_3 + 4X_4$
    e. $f \max = 4X_1 + 5X_2 + X_3 + X_4$
2. The constraint imposed by the quantity of D on hand could be expressed as:
    a. $X_1 + X_2 \geq 16,000$
    b. $X_1 + X_2 \leq 16,000$
    c. $.4X_1 + .6X_2 \leq 16,000$
    d. $.8X_1 + .4X_2 \geq 16,000$
    e. $.8X_1 + .4X_2 \leq 16,000$
3. The constraint imposed by the quantity of K on hand could be expressed as
    a. $X_1 + X_2 \geq 6,000$
    b. $X_1 + X_2 \leq 6,000$
    c. $.8X_1 + .2X_2 \leq 6,000$
    d. $.8X_1 + .2X_2 \geq 6,000$
    e. $.2X_1 + .6X_2 \leq 6,000$
4. To maximize total contribution the company should produce and market
    a.   106,000 gallons of Alpha only.
    b.   90,000 gallons of Alpha and 16,000 gallons of Gamma.
    c.   16,000 gallons of Alpha and 90,000 gallons of Gamma.
    d.   18,000 gallons of Alpha and 4,000 gallons of Gamma.
    e.   4,000 gallons of Alpha and 18,000 gallons of Gamma.
5. Assuming that the marginal contributions per gallon are \$7 for Alpha and \$9 for Gamma, the company should produce and market
    a.   106,000 gallons of Alpha only.
    b.   90,000 gallons of Alpha and 16,000 gallons of Gamma.
    c.   16,000 gallons of Alpha and 90,000 gallons of Gamma.
    d.   18,000 gallons of Alpha and 4,000 gallons of Gamma.
    e.   4,000 gallons of Alpha and 18,000 gallons of Gamma.

(CPA)

4. Economic order quantity: Multiple choice. A company places orders for inventory with its suppliers for a certain item for which the order size is determined in advance as

$$\text{Order size} = \sqrt{\frac{2 \times \frac{\text{Cost to place}}{\text{one order}} \times \frac{\text{Demand per}}{\text{period}}}{\frac{\text{Cost to hold one unit}}{\text{for one period}}}}$$

All orders are the same size. When the policy is implemented, demand per period is only one-half what was expected when order size was computed. Consequently, actual total inventory cost will be

a. Larger than if the expected demand per period had occurred and larger than if the actual demand per period had been used to calculate order size.
b. Larger than if the expected demand per period had occurred and smaller than if the actual demand per period had been used to calculate order size.
c. Smaller than if the expected demand per period had occurred and larger than if the actual demand per period had been used to calculate order size.
d. Smaller than if the expected demand per period had occurred and smaller than if the actual demand per period had been used to calculate order size.

(CPA)

5. Inventory decision model: Multiple choice. A manufacturer expects to produce 200,000 widgets during the year to supply a demand which is uniform throughout the year. The setup cost for each production run of widgets is $144 and the variable cost of producing each widget is $5. The cost of carrying one widget in inventory is $0.20 a year. After a batch of widgets is produced and placed in inventory, it is sold at a uniform rate, and inventory is exhausted when the next batch of widgets is completed.

Management wishes an equation to describe the above situation and determine the optimal quantity of widgets to produce in each run so as to minimize total production and inventory carrying costs.
Let

c = Total annual cost of producing and carrying widgets.
X = Number of widgets to be produced in each production run.

1. The number of production runs to be made during the year should be expressed as:
    a. $200,000 + 144X$
    b. $200,000 + X$
    c. $200,000$
    d. $200,000/X$
    e. $X/200,000$
2. Total setup costs for the year can be expressed as:
    a. $144(200,000/X)$
    b. $200,000/X$
    c. $144X$
    d. $144X/200,000$
    e. $144/200,000 + X

3. Total cost of carrying inventory during the fiscal year can be expressed as:
   a. $0.20($144X)$
   b. $$.20X$
   c. $0.20(200,000/X)$
   d. $0.20(X/2)$
   e. $0.20($144X/200,000)$
4. The quantity of widgets which should be produced in each run to minimize total costs is:
   a. 19,060
   b. 16,970
   c. 16,000
   d. 12,480
   e. 12,000

(CPA adapted)

6. Objective function and constraints. The Witchell Corporation manufactures and sells three grades, A, B, and C, of a single wood product. Each grade must be processed through three phases—cutting, fitting, and finishing—before it is sold.

The following unit information is provided:

	A	B	C
Selling price...................	$10.00	$15.00	$20.00
Direct labor....................	5.00	6.00	9.00
Direct materials................	.70	.70	1.00
Variable overhead...............	1.00	1.20	1.80
Fixed overhead..................	.60	.72	1.08
Materials requirements in			
board feet....................	7.	7	10
Labor requirements in hours:			
Cutting......................	3/6	3/6	4/6
Fitting......................	1/6	1/6	2/6
Finishing....................	1/6	2/6	3/6

Only 5,000 board feet per week can be obtained.

The cutting department has 180 hours of labor available each week. The fitting and finishing departments each have 120 hours of labor available each week. No overtime is allowed.

Contract commitments require the company to make 50 units of A per week. In addition, company policy is to produce at least 50 additional units of A and 50 units of B and 50 units of C each week to remain active in each of the three markets. Because of competition only 130 units of C can be sold each week.

Formulate and label the linear objective function and the constraint functions necessary to maximize the contribution margin.

(CMA adapted)

7. Production schedule: Graphic solution. The graph (page 464) presents the constraint functions for a chair manufacturing company whose production problem can be solved by linear programming. The company earns $8 for each kitchen chair and $5 for each office chair sold.

a. What is the profit-maximizing production schedule?
b. How did you select this production schedule?
c. Would your answer to (a) have been different if the office chairs had earned $1 each instead of $5? Explain.

(CMA adapted)

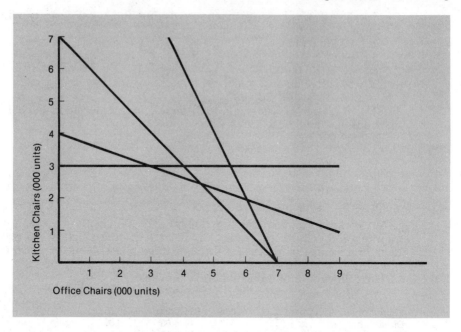

8. Calculating setup costs: Inventory decision model.

A single large machine is the only equipment used in one of the Beaman Company's factory departments. Quite a few different products are processed on the machine, and management is interested in finding the most economical lot size in which each product should be manufactured.

One cost that must be considered in determining the most economical lot size is the cost of changing the machine over from one product to another—the setup cost. The following information has been obtained for use in computing the setup cost for product A:

1. Two workers from the maintenance department have to spend four hours each to set up the equipment, which is located in department P. Maintenance department employees have a basic wage rate of $7 an hour. It is the company's policy to provide its maintenance force with a 40-hour week, adjusting the size of the maintenance staff only if changes in the size of the work load are substantial and likely to persist.

2. Department P's machine is operated by a crew of six, each with a basic wage rate of $6 an hour. While the machine is being set up, the members of the crew perform minor finishing operations and carry out other productive tasks to the extent that such work is available. Experience indicates that they are idle approximately 60 percent of the time required for machine setup.

3. Department P's costs other than direct materials, the wages of the operating crew, and setup labor are expected to average the following monthly amounts:

Depreciation	$ 760
Power	280
Space	160
Payroll taxes and insurance	592
Maintenance labor	440
Supervisors	1,200
Operating supplies	300

4. All payroll taxes and insurance costs on both direct and indirect labor are classified as overhead. They average approximately 16 percent of the gross payroll. Payroll taxes and insurance on setup and maintenance labor are not charged to department P but remain in maintenance department overhead accounts.

5. Operating supplies and maintenance labor costs charged to department P (as in the table above) are expected to be roughly proportional to the number of productive hours of the operating crew.

6. Department P's depreciation, power, space, and supervisory costs are regarded as fixed costs.

7. Maintenance department costs other than labor and payroll taxes and insurance are completely fixed.

8. A typical month has 20 producing days of eight hours each.

Establish the cost of setting up the machines and explain how you derived your figures.

9. Linear programming model: Estimating unit costs. Inventory carrying costs in the Youngblood Company are very large, so management ordinarily tries to produce each month only as much of each product as it expects to sell in the following month.

Unfortunately, some departments aren't big enough to fill all customer orders in months of peak demand, and departmental capacity must be rationed on the basis of the relative profitability of the various products. Department 17, for example, is now fully utilized, producing several products. It is operating two shifts a day, with 4,000 labor hours a month on the first shift and 3,000 labor hours a month on the second shift. Third-shift and overtime operations are not feasible.

Labor costs of the second shift are recorded separately from those of the first shift. Output statistics are also recorded separately. Materials, supplies, utilities, and all other nonlabor costs are not assignable to individual shifts.

Output in department 17 is measured by the number of standard direct labor hours (standard hours) for the work done. Costs and output in a normal month are as follows:

	First Shift	Second Shift	Total
Output (standard hours).............	4,200	2,800	7,000
Actual direct labor hours.............	4,000	3,000	7,000
Direct labor.........................	$20,000	$15,000	$35,000
Indirect labor.......................	4,000	3,000	7,000
Supervision.........................	4,500	3,200	7,700
Shift differential (on direct and indirect labor)....................	...	1,800	1,800
Labor benefits and payroll taxes......	5,700	4,600	10,300
Supplies............................			3,500
Power..............................			4,200
Other costs.........................			14,000

Direct labor performance is poorer on the second shift than on the first shift because the best workers are assigned to the first shift and because the employees work less efficiently during evening hours than during the daytime.

Analysis of historical data indicates that cost variability in this department is as follows:

Item	Variability Pattern
Direct labor..................	100% variable with direct labor hours
Indirect labor................	70% variable with direct labor hours
Supervision..................	100% fixed and indivisible for each shift
Shift differential............	Proportional to second-shift direct and indirect labor
Labor benefits and payroll taxes......................	Proportional to total gross wages and salaries
Supplies.....................	100% variable with weight of materials used
Power........................	100% variable with weight of materials used
Other costs..................	10% variable with direct labor hours

On the average, products processed in department 17 require one standard direct labor hour for every four pounds of materials.

How much of department 17's costs should be inserted in the objective function as part of the unit cost of a product requiring four pounds of materials and two standard direct labor hours in this department?

10. Inventory decision model. The Robney Company is a restaurant supplier. One of its products is a special meatcutter with a disposable blade. The blades are sold in packages of 12 blades for $20 a package.

After a number of years, it has been determined that the demand for replacement blades is at a constant rate of 2,000 packages a month. The Robney Company buys the packages from a manufacturer for $10 each. The manufacturer requires a three-day lead time from date of order to date of delivery. The ordering cost is $1.20 per order and the carrying cost is at an annual rate of 10 percent. Robney has adopted the order quantity formula described in this chapter.

a. Calculate:
   1. The economic order quantity.
   2. The number of orders needed per year.
   3. The total cost of buying and carrying blades for a year.
b. Assuming there is no safety stock and that the present inventory level is 200 packages, when should the next order be placed? (Use 360 days equals one year.)
c. Suppose the number of units sold in a three-day period is uncertain. It shows the following pattern:

Usage	Probability
170.........................	.05
180.........................	.10
190.........................	.20
200.........................	.30
210.........................	.20
220.........................	.10
230.........................	.05

What level of safety stock (in a multiple of ten units) would you recommend if the stockout cost is 20 cents for each unit out of stock when it is needed?
d. Discuss the problems most firms would have in attempting to apply these formulas to their inventory problems.

(CMA adapted)

11. Objective function and constraints: Multiple variables. A company manufactures three products, A, B, and C. These three products have been well received in the market, and at current selling prices the company can sell all that it can produce. Data for these three products are as follows:

	A	B	C
Selling price.............................	$15	$19	$24
Materials cost...........................	5	10	13
Other variable costs (paid when incurred)...............................	6	4	7
Portion of selling price collected in month of sale........................	$\frac{1}{3}$	0	0

Each product requires one unit of its own special raw material. These materials are not interchangeable—that is, A's material may not be used for B or C, B's may not be used for A or C, and so on. The raw materials inventories will be as follows on January 1:

200 units of material for A at $5................... $1,000
120 units of material for B at $10................. 1,200
50 units of material for C at $13................. 650

Additional quantities of these materials can be acquired from nearby suppliers on a few hours' notice. Materials are always paid for in cash when they are received.

The products pass through two departments. The maximum machine time available during January is 400 hours in department 1 and 800 hours in department 2. Machine time for processing a unit in each department is:

	Hours Required by a Unit of		
	A	B	C
Department 1...................	$\frac{1}{2}$	1	$\frac{1}{4}$
Department 2...................	1	1	$4\frac{1}{2}$

Departmental fixed costs (for both departments) will be $900 in January. This includes $200 in depreciation charges; the balance will be paid when incurred.

The January 1 cash balance is expected to be $6,660. The ending cash balance cannot be less than $3,000. Due to a seasonal shutdown, the company will have no outstanding accounts receivable on January 1.

Formulate an objective function to maximize profits and specify the constraints this function is subject to.

12. Production decision: Sensitivity analysis. The management of Danielson, Inc. is preparing its production schedule for the next three months. The company sells two products, A and B, which it manufactures in two departments, X and Y. Department X has a total capacity of 2,700 labor hours a month, while department Y has a monthly capacity of 3,000 machine-hours.

Danielson is now entering its busy season. Orders are flowing in at a record rate, and management knows that it will not be able to fill all of them. Fortunately, the two products are bought by different customers, so that refusal of orders for one product will not lead to cancellation of orders for the other.

The company's accountants have gathered the following information on unit costs, prices, and input requirements for the two products:

	A	B
Materials used (lbs.)..............	2	1
Labor hours, department X..........	1	3
Machine-hours, department Y........	2	3
Selling price.....................	$47	$53
Sales commissions.................	2	1
Direct labor cost:		
Department X....................	5	15
Department Y....................	6	12

The Danielson company has 5,400 pounds of materials in inventory. More materials are on order, but will not be delivered in time for use during the next quarter. The materials now on hand cost $7 a pound; the units on order will cost $8 a pound when delivered.

Overhead costs in department X vary with the number of direct labor hours used, at a rate of $1 per direct labor hour. Variable overhead costs in department Y amount to one third of departmental direct labor cost.

a. Develop the objective function and express the constraints in a form suitable for the use of linear programming.

b. Prepare a recommended production schedule for each of the next three months. The production level will be the same each month.

c. How, if at all, would your recommendation change if you found that two former company employees, now in retirement, would be willing to return to work in department X for a few months on a part-time basis at regular wage rates? These employees would be willing to put in a total of 200 hours a month during the next three months.

d. Danielson, Inc. could increase the price of product A by $7 a unit without losing a significant number of orders. How, if at all, would such a change affect your recommendation?

13. Inventory decision: Calculating the parameters. The Acme Belt Company has decided to determine purchase order quantities on the basis of the formula described in this chapter. The cost parameters are to reflect the following elements:

Purchase price: *Storage cost:*
  Invoice price   Insurance
  Freight and carting   Taxes
                                Interest
Purchase order cost: Breakage and spoilage
  Forms and supplies   Space rental
  Order preparation   Warehouse operation
  Processing payments
  Receiving and inspection

You have the following information:

The invoice price of product X is $10 a unit, with a 5 percent discount on purchase orders of 1,000 units or more. Annual consumption of product X averages 10,000 units.

Freight charges on product X amount to $2.50 a unit.

The purchasing department is responsible for preparing all purchase orders. It processes approximately 2,000 purchase orders a month. Its costs consist of the salaries of the purchasing agent and assistant ($2,500 a month, including fringe benefits); salaries of six order clerks ($4,000 a month, including fringe benefits); and the costs of forms, supplies, and other variable inputs ($200 a month).

Payments are processed in the accounting department. Work sampling studies indicate that the labor cost of processing an order, including fringe benefits, averages $4 an order. The rental cost of the data processing equipment for the time used to process an average order amounts to $1. Electricity and other variable costs of data processing amount to 20 cents an order.

All purchased items are inspected in the shipping and receiving department. Wages in this department amount to $6,000 a month, plus $1,200 for the supervisor. Approximately one third of the workers' time is devoted to receiving and inspecting incoming goods, with the remainder being devoted to shipping finished products. The supervisor's time is not included in this percentage.

Annual insurance and personal property taxes amount to 7 percent of the cost of the average amount of inventory on hand.

The company has a small amount of short-term, seasonal bank debt at an interest rate of 8 percent a year. Capital expenditure proposals are expected to produce a return on investment of at least 20 percent before taxes.

Breakage and spoilage each month amount to 0.0833 percent of the items in storage.

The company rents one warehouse on a 20-year lease at an average annual cost of $2 a square foot. Comparable warehouse space in the area now rents for $3 a square foot. The company's warehouse can be sublet only in its entirety. A unit of product X requires one fifth of a square foot of space, but space must be available for twice the anticipated average inventory quantity. One fifth of the total floor space must be reserved for aisles, etc.

All warehouse labor costs are incurred to move goods into and out of the warehouse. They average 10 percent of the average inventory cost in an average year.

a. Calculate purchasing cost per order and carrying cost per inventory dollar. Explain your treatment of each item.
b. Should the company take advantage of the discount? What order size should it establish?
c. To what extent would historical records help you provide the data from which these cost parameters could be derived? What information sources would you use to supplement or replace historical records for this purpose? What analytical methods would you apply to your basic data?

14. Profit planning; Shadow prices; Minimum sales requirements. In November 19x4, the Springfield Manufacturing Company was preparing its budget for 19x5. As the first step it prepared the following pro forma income statement for 19x4 based on the first ten months' operations and revised plans for the last two months.

Sales.....................................		$3,000,000
Materials................................	$1,105,000	
Labor....................................	310,000	
Factory overhead.........................	775,000	
Selling and administrative................	450,000	2,640,000
Income before Income Taxes..........		$ 360,000

These results were better than had been expected and operations were close to capacity, but Springfield's management was not convinced that demand would remain at present levels and hence had not planned any increase in plant capacity. Its equipment was specialized and made to its order; a lead time in excess of one year was necessary on all plant additions.

Springfield produced three products with the following annual sales volumes:

100,000 units of product A at $20....................... $2,000,000
 40,000 units of product B at $10.......................   400,000
 20,000 units of product C at $30.......................   600,000
    Total sales...................................... $3,000,000

Management had ordered a profit analysis for each product and had the following information:

	A	B	C
Material.....................	$ 6	$ 4.00	$17.25
Labor........................	2	1.00	3.50
Factory overhead.............	5	2.50	8.75
Selling and administrative...	3	1.50	4.50
Total costs..................	$16	$ 9.00	$34.00
Selling price................	20	10.00	30.00
Profit/(Loss)................	$ 4	$ 1.00	$(4.00)

Factory overhead was applied on the basis of direct labor cost at a rate of 250 percent; approximately 20 percent of the overhead was variable and did vary with labor costs. Selling and administrative costs were allocated on the basis of sales at the rate of 15 percent; approximately one half of this was variable and did vary with sales in dollars.

As the next step in the planning process, the sales department was asked to make estimates of what it could sell. These estimates were reviewed and accepted by the firm's consulting economist and by top management. They were as follows:

Product A.................. 130,000 units
Product B.................. 50,000
Product C.................. 50,000

Production of these quantities was immediately recognized as being impossible. Practical capacity was 66,000 machine-hours in department 1 and 63,000 machine-hours in department 2. The industrial engineering department reported that these limits could not be increased without the purchase of additional equipment. Anticipated sales for 19x5 would require operating department 1 at 136 percent of capacity and department 2 at 121 percent. Standard costs for the three products, each of which required activity in both departments, were based on the following production rates:

	A	B	C
Department 1...........	2 per hour	4 per hour	4 per hour
Department 2...........	4 per hour	8 per hour	1⅓ per hour

Four solutions to the problem of limited capacity were rejected. First, subcontracting the production out to other firms was considered to be unprofitable because of problems of maintaining quality. Second, operating a second shift was impossible because of shortage of labor. Third, operating overtime would have created problems because a large number of employees were "moonlighting" and would therefore have refused to work more than the normal 40-hour week. Finally, price increases were ruled out. Although they would result in higher profits in 19x5, the long-run competitive position of the firm would be weakened, resulting in lower profits in the future.

The treasurer, Molly Pitcher, then suggested that product C had been carried at a loss too long and that it was time to eliminate it from the product line. She argued that if all facilities were used to produce A and B, profits would be increased.

Paul Jones, the sales manager, objected to this solution because of the need to carry a full line. In addition he maintained that the firm's regular customers had provided and would continue to provide a solid base for the firm's activities and that these customers' needs must be met. He provided a list of these customers and their estimated purchases (in units) which totaled as follows:

Product A...................... 80,000
Product B...................... 32,000
Product C...................... 12,000

It was impossible to verify these contentions, but they appeared to be reasonable, and therefore the president concurred.

Ms. Pitcher acquiesced reluctantly, but she maintained that the remaining capacity should be used to produce A and B. Because A produced four times as much profit as B, she suggested that the production of A (that is, the amount in excess of the 80,000 minimum set by the sales manager) be four times that of B (that is, the amount in excess of the 32,000 minimum set by the sales manager).

David Farragut, the production manager, made some quick calculations and said that this would result in budgeted production and sales of:

Product A...................... 106,666 units
Product B...................... 38,667
Product C...................... 12,000

On this basis Ms. Pitcher made the following profit forecast:

Product A: 106,666 at $4...................... $426,664
Product B: 38,667 at $1......................   38,667
Product C: 12,000 at −$4..................... (48,000)
Total.. $417,331

As this would represent an increase of more than 15 percent over the current year, there was a general feeling of self-satisfaction. Before final approval was given, however, the president, Alfred LeGrand, said he would like to have his new assistant check over the figures. Somewhat piqued, Ms. Pitcher agreed and at that point the group adjourned.

The president has just asked you to review the above information and report to him tomorrow. Prepare this report, using nontechnical language and indicating how much of each product should be produced and what the income before taxes is likely to be.

(Prepared by Professor Carl L. Nelson)

15. Shadow Prices; Effect of constraints. The president of Springfield Manufacturing Company (Problem 14) is impressed with your report but believes that a more formal structuring of the relationships would be useful.

a.   Formulate this as a linear programming problem.
b.   Calculate the shadow prices by finding the optimal product mix and

addition to profit if one hour is added to the capacity of each department, the capacity of the other being held constant.

c. How much profit, if any, is lost in the short run as a result of the imposition of the minimum sales constraints? Show your calculations.

14

Capital Expenditure
Decision Models

THE CAPACITY RATIONING and economic order quantity models we described in Chapter 13 are single period models—that is, costs and benefits are so close to each other in time that they can be assumed to occur simultaneously. We now turn to a different class of decisions, identified as *investment problems*. An investment problem is a situation requiring management to decide whether to expend cash in one or more time periods to obtain cash inflows in another time period or periods. The cash flow patterns in two investment problems look like Exhibit 14–1.

In the upper diagram, management pays cash now for the right to a series of cash receipts in the next few years. In the lower diagram, management will pay cash later to get a cash inflow now. In both cases, management must decide whether the benefits to be derived from the cash inflows are big enough to justify the cash outflows.

One group of investment problems is important enough to be singled out for special treatment. These are the problems embodied in proposals to buy or build land, buildings, and equipment, referred to as *capital expenditure* proposals. In this chapter we shall outline a capital expenditure decision model based on the concept of present value, compare it briefly with two alternative models, study the administrative structure necessary to make it work, and see how it can be applied to disinvestment problems. Chapter 15 will then examine the problems of developing the estimates these models require.

THE PRESENT VALUE DECISION MODEL

Investment problems differ from other decision problems because decision makers place a lower value on future cash than on present cash. Money, in other words, has a time value. In this section we shall

EXHIBIT 14–1

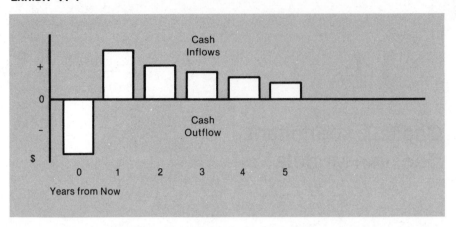

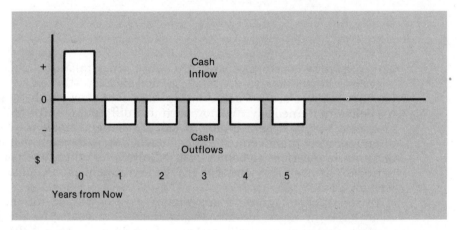

explain the time value of money and outline a decision model built around this concept.

The Time Value of Money

Other things being equal, dollars expected to be available in the future are worth less than the same number of dollars now. One reason is that the future is uncertain. In most cases, the longer the wait, the greater the possibility that conditions will change and the dollar never will be received. The primary reason, however, is that the dollar received today can be invested to grow to more than a dollar a year from now. This future amount is known as the *future value* of today's dollar.

Future value. If a bank will pay $1,050 one year from now in return for a $1,000 deposit today, it is paying interest at the rate of 5 percent a year. This relationship can be expressed mathematically in the following expression:

$$F_1 = P(1 + r) \tag{1}$$

in which P = the present outlay or deposit in the bank, r = the rate of interest, and F_1 = future value. If $P = \$1,000$ and $r = 0.05$, then $F_1 = \$1,050$.

Continuing the example, if the $1,050 is left in the bank for a second year, it will build up by the end of the two years to a balance of $1,050 + ($1,050 × 0.05) = $1,102.50. Interest in this second year amounts to $52.50 and is greater than the first year's interest because the bank is now paying interest not only on the original investment but also on the interest earned during the first year. The mathematical formula for computing the future value of a present sum two years later is:

$$F_2 = F_1(1 + r) = P(1 + r)(1 + r) = P(1 + r)^2 \tag{2}$$

If $r = 0.05$, $(1 + r)^2$ will be 1.1025 and the future value of $1,000 now will be $1,102.50.

Extending these calculations beyond two years reveals the relationships shown graphically in Exhibit 14–2. Starting with $1,000, the

EXHIBIT 14–2

Future Values Equivalent to a Present Value of $1,000
(annual compounding at 5 percent a year)

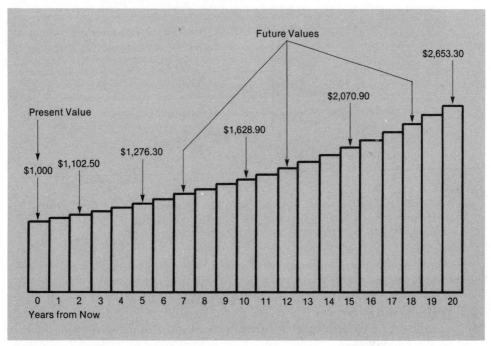

Source: Myron J. Gordon and Gordon Shillinglaw, *Accounting: A Management Approach,* 5th ed. (Homewood, Ill.: Richard D. Irwin, Inc., 1974), Appendix A.

depositor's account will build at 5 percent to $1,050 in one year, $1,102.50 in two years, and so on, up to $2,653.30 at the end of 20 years.

This form of interest calculation, in which interest is earned on previously earned interest, is known as *compounding*. In this case interest has been compounded annually, meaning that interest is added to the bank balance only once a year. In general, it can be shown that if an amount P is put out at interest of r percent a year, compounded annually, at the end of n years it will have grown to a future value (F_n) of the following amount:

$$F_n = P(1 + r)^n \tag{3}$$

Present value. This relationship can also be inverted, to focus attention on the *present value* of a future amount. The present value of a future sum is the amount which, if invested now at compound interest at the specified rate, will grow to an amount equal to the future sum at the specified future date. Present value and future value, in other words, are just two ends of the same relationship (see Exhibit 14–3). Since all of the bars in Exhibit 14–2 are future values of $1,000, it follows that all of them have the same present value, $1,000. An investor who considers 5 percent annual compound interest as a satisfactory return on money should regard each of these amounts as fully equivalent to each of the others.

EXHIBIT 14–3

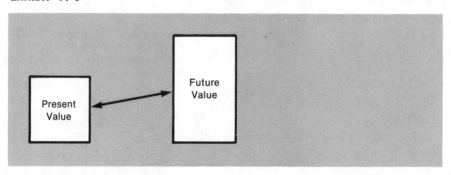

The formula for computing present value from known or estimated future values can be found by turning equation (3) around. Since $F_n = P(1 + r)^n$, then

$$P = F_n(1 + r)^{-n} \tag{4}$$

This shows that the present value of any future sum can be determined by multiplying the latter by $(1 + r)^{-n}$ or by dividing it by $(1 + r)^n$. If n is two years, r is 5 percent, and an asset is expected to yield a cash inflow of $1,000 two years from now, then the present value of this asset today is:

$$P = \$1,000/(1.05)^2 = \$1,000/1.1025 = \$907.03.$$

In other words, $907.03 will grow to $1,000 in two years if it is invested now at 5 percent interest, compounded annually; it is therefore the present value of that future amount.

Net present value. Knowledge of the time value of money permits us to deal with decision problems in which differences in the timing of cash flows are important. The interest rate is, in a sense, the transfer price that would be applied to the exchange of cash at one point in time for cash at another. The use of this transfer price makes it possible to add or subtract sums that occur at different points in time.

For example, suppose that an investor decides that 10 percent is an adequate return on any investments he may make. An entrepreneur offers to pay $1,000 one year from now if the investor will invest $925 now in a scheme the entrepreneur is interested in. From formula (4), we can calculate the present value of $1 at 10 percent:

$$P = \$1/(1 + 0.10) = \$1/1.1 = \$0.909$$

The present value of the $1,000 therefore is $1,000 × 0.909 = $909.

This process of multiplying a future sum by a present value multiplier is known as *discounting*. For this reason, present values are also known as *discounted cash flows*. The discounted cash flows for this proposal are shown in the right-hand column of the following table:

Date	Cash Inflow (+) or Outflow (−)	Present Value at 10 Percent	
		Multiplier	Amount
Immediately..............	−$ 925	1.000*	−$925
One year from now........	+ 1,000	0.909	+ 909
Net present value......			−$ 16

*The present value multiplier for an immediate payment or receipt is always 1.000. A dollar tomorrow is worth less than a dollar today, but a dollar today is a dollar. (Mathematically, if $n = 0$, then $(1 + r)^n = 1$.)

This array is known as a *timetable* of cash flows. Inflows are identified by plus signs; outflows are listed as minuses. The total of the present value figures is known as *net present value*, the difference between the present values of the cash outlays and the present values of the cash receipts.

The investor would find this proposal unattractive. The present value of the cash he would receive from this investment is $16 less than the $925 he would have to pay now to get this benefit. Another way of saying this is that if he requires a 10 percent return on investment, the future cash receipt of $1,000 is not big enough to repay the original investment ($925) plus a return on investment at an annual rate of 10 percent ($925 × 0.10 = $92.50).

The Minimum Acceptable Rate of Return

Business firms, too, must be careful to make investments that will produce an adequate rate of return. The money they have to invest comes from their stockholders and from lenders. These investors expect to be rewarded for letting the firm use their money.

The percentage yield investors demand as a minimum reward for investing money in the firm is referred to as the firm's *cost of capital.* Risky firms have high capital costs; low-risk firms have low capital costs. If the expected reward is lower than the cost of capital, management will not find enough investors willing to invest their money in the firm. Management, therefore, should not make investments that will earn less than the cost of capital.

This proposition also has a corollary: all proposals that are expected to earn more than the cost of capital should be accepted. This is valid as long as the firm can get enough money to finance all proposals in this class. We shall come back in a moment to see what can be done when this assumption can't be made.

Calculating Net Present Value

The most direct way to find out whether a proposal will generate a rate of return in excess of the minimum acceptable rate is to discount all the anticipated cash flows to their present values at the minimum acceptable rate. If the rate of return is greater than the minimum rate, net present value will be positive. If the rate of return is too low, net present value will be negative.

To illustrate, suppose the company is considering a proposal to invest $34,000 (proposal A). Net present value can be calculated in three steps:

Step 1. Estimate the cash flows.   The cash flows associated with this proposal are as follows:

Years from Now	Cash Flow
0	−$34,000
1	+ 10,000
2	+ 10,000
3	+ 10,000
4	+ 10,000
5	+ 10,000

Step 2. Discount the cash flows.   This company regards 10 percent as the minimum acceptable rate of return. Present value multipliers could be derived by solving equation (4) for $n = 1, 2, 3, 4, 5$. Fortunately, this work has already been done, and the multipliers are listed in Appendix A. The multipliers in Table 1 of Appendix A are for single cash flows; those in Table 2 are for series of identical cash flows.

The multipliers and the present values of the cash flows for proposal A are:

	(1)	(2)	(3)
		Present Value at 10 Percent	
Years from Now	Cash Flow	Multiplier (Table 1)	Amount (1) × (2)
0.........	−$34,000	1.000	−$34,000
1.........	+ 10,000	0.909	+ 9,090
2.........	+ 10,000	0.826	+ 8,260
3.........	+ 10,000	0.751	+ 7,510
4.........	+ 10,000	0.683	+ 6,830
5.........	+ 10,000	0.621	+ 6,210
Net present value..................			+$ 3,900

Step 3. Apply the decision rule. The decision rule implicit in the discounted cash flow method is to accept any proposal that promises a positive net present value. Other things being equal, proposal A should be accepted. It offers a net present value of $3,900, indicating that the anticipated cash flows are more than adequate to provide a 10 percent return on investment.

Step 4. Verify the results. Although the decision itself requires the managers to go beyond the raw figures and apply their judgment, the basic calculations need go no farther than step 3. It may be useful this time, however, to check the truth of the statement that proposal A will yield a rate of return greater than 10 percent.

To do this, we need to examine the process from the other end. The initial investment is $34,000. The first year's interest at 10 percent, therefore, would amount to $3,400. Since $10,000 in cash is received, the remaining $6,600 can be treated as a partial recovery of the original investment. This leaves an unrecovered balance of $27,-400 at the end of the first year. Interest on that in the second year is $2,740, leaving $7,260 of the second year's cash receipts to be treated as a recovery of another portion of the initial outlay. Continuing these calculations for three more years produces the following table:

Principle of unrecovered investment

	(1)	(2)	(3)	(4)
	Unrecovered Investment, Beginning	Interest	Amortization of Investment	Unrecovered Investment, End of Year
Year	of Year	at 10 Percent	[$10,000 − (2)]	(1) − (3)
1..........	$34,000	$3,400	$6,600	$27,400
2..........	27,400	2,740	7,260	20,140
3..........	20,140	2,014	7,986	12,154
4..........	12,154	1,215	8,785	3,369
5..........	3,369	337	9,663	(6,294)

By the end of the fifth year, the entire investment has been recovered, despite annual interest payments at a 10 percent rate, and the firm still has $6,294 left over (see Exhibit 14–4). In other words, the com-

EXHIBIT 14–4

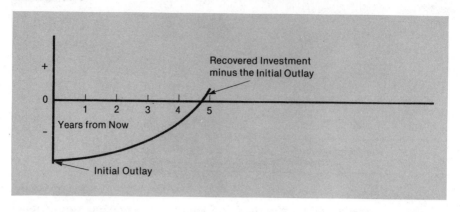

pany could have paid more than 10 percent interest from the cash flows from this investment.[1]

The Internal Rate of Return

Net present value is sometimes an awkward figure to use in discussing the merits of individual capital expenditure proposals. For this reason some companies prefer to use the *internal rate of return,* defined as that rate of discount at which the net present value is zero. Calculating the internal rate of return is a three-step, trial-and-error process:

Step 1. Discount all cash flows at a trial rate. We have already performed this step. The net present value of the cash flows at 10 percent is $3,900. This indicates that the rate of return is greater than 10 percent, but it doesn't show how much greater.

Step 2. Discount all cash flows at a second trial rate. Since we know that the internal rate of return is higher than 10 percent, a reasonable second trial rate is 15 percent. To simplify the calculations, we can use the present value multiplier from Table 2 in Appendix A; this is simply the sum of the multipliers in Table 1 for the first five years. The multipliers and present values at this rate are:

Years from Now	Cash Flow	Present Value at 15 Percent	
		Multiplier	Amount
0......................	−$34,000	1.000	−$34,000
1–5.....................	+ 10,000 per year	3.352	+ 33,520
Net present value...			−$ 480

---

[1] The $6,294 residual is the future value of $3,900 five years later, compounded annually at 10 percent.

EXHIBIT 14–5

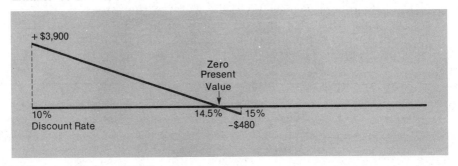

The present value of the cash receipts at a 15 percent discount rate is only $33,520, producing a negative net present value. This means that the cash flows are not big enough to produce a rate of return as high as 15 percent.

Step 3. Interpolate. The true rate of return is somewhere between 10 percent and 15 percent. It is the rate of return at which net present value equals zero. We can approximate this by interpolating between two points on a graph, as shown in Exhibit 14–5. We can do the same thing algebraically, again rounding the answer to the nearest tenth of a percent.

$$\text{Approximate rate} = 10\% + \frac{\$3,900}{\$3,900 + \$480} \times (15\% - 10\%) = 14.5\%$$

($3,900 + $480 = $4,380 is the total distance between +$3,900 and −$480.)

The Argument for Net Present Value

The advantage of the present value model is that it is the only one sensitive both to the timing of the anticipated cash flows and to the cost of capital. For example, a company can invest in any or all of the following proposals:

Years from Now	Net Cash Receipts (+) or Cash Outlays (−)		
	Proposal X	Proposal Y	Proposal Z
0...............................	−$13,000	−$13,000	−$13,000
1...............................	+ 1,000	+ 5,000	+ 9,000
2...............................	+ 5,000	+ 5,000	+ 5,000
3...............................	+ 9,000	+ 5,000	+ 1,000
Total cash flow...............	+$ 2,000	+$ 2,000	+$ 2,000

These three proposals have identical lifetime total cash flows, but they are far from equally desirable. Proposal Z is the best proposal because cash is received earlier under this proposal than under either of the others. Proposal X is the worst of the three.

This difference appears clearly in present value calculations. Assuming an 8 percent cost of capital, the present values of these proposals are:

Years from Now	Present Value Multipliers	Proposal X	Proposal Y	Proposal Z
0	1.000	−$13,000	−$13,000	−$13,000
1	0.926	+ 926	+ 4,630	+ 8,333
2	0.857	+ 4,285	+ 4,285	+ 4,285
3	0.794	+ 7,146	+ 3,970	+ 794
Net present value		−$ 645	−$ 115	+$ 413

The present value multipliers in this table came from the 8 percent column of Table 1 in Appendix A.

In this case, proposals X and Y promise a return on investment of less than 8 percent; only proposal Z promises a return in excess of 8 percent. Only proposal Z should be accepted. The present value measure, in other words, permits management to compare proposals that differ in the timing of their cash flows. Present value is the means by which all cash flows of all proposals can be restated at their equivalent values at a common point in time. These proposals, therefore, can be compared directly with each other.

Opportunity Cost of Capital

The main assumption in the present value model is that the firm can obtain all the funds it needs to finance projects promising to earn more than the cost of capital. When this isn't true, proposals must be tested against the *opportunity cost of capital.* The opportunity cost of capital applicable to a specific proposal is the rate of return on the project that would have to be rejected to permit the proposal to be accepted.

For example, suppose the firm has only $1 million to invest and can get no more until next year. It has five proposals, each requiring a $250,000 investment and each good enough to pass the company's cost of capital test. The internal rates of return on these proposals are:

Proposal	Investment Required	Rate of Return (percent)	
1	$ 250,000	40%	
2	250,000	30	
3	250,000	25	
4	250,000	20	
	$1,000,000	←	cutoff point
5	250,000	15	

The opportunity cost of capital is 20 percent because this is the amount to be sacrificed if a substitute proposal is accepted in place of proposal 4.

use ext.
cost of capital
The rule, in other words, is to use the external cost of capital or the opportunity cost of capital, whichever is greater. In practice, this is often accomplished by calculating the *profitability index,* the ratio of

or
opport. cost,
whatever is
greater
the present value of a proposal's future cash flows to the present outlay required. Proposal A, for example, with anticipated cash receipts of $10,000 a year and an investment outlay of $34,000, has a profitability index of 1.11:

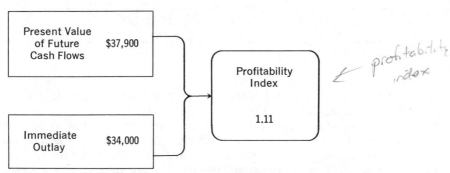

← profitability index

By accepting the proposals with the highest profitability index first and going down the list until the money is all gone, management can maximize the present value obtainable from the money at its disposal.

Multiple Alternatives

So far we have assumed that the decision maker has only two alternatives: accept the proposal or reject it. This is not always true. A proposal to build a new factory, for example, is ordinarily justified by the net present value of the differences between the company's total cash flows with the new factory and total cash flows without it. The company may actually be better off, however, to use idle capacity in other factories, or add small amounts of capacity in several of the company's present factories. For major capital expenditure proposals, management should insist that a real effort be made to identify one or more substitute proposals that might fill the same needs in different ways.

This means that the present value decision rule has to be modified slightly. When enough money is available to finance all projects that promise to earn a net present value, and the company must choose among mutually exclusive proposals, *management should select the proposal with the greatest positive net present value; if none of the proposals has a positive net present value, all should be rejected.*

An illustration. If management rejects proposal A, it can accept either proposal B, or proposal C, but not both. If it accepts B or C, it cannot accept A. The cash flows and multipliers for proposals B and C are as follows:

Years from Now	(1) Present Value Multiplier at 10 Percent	(2) Proposal B Cash Flow	(3) Present Value (1) × (2)	(4) Proposal C Cash Flow	(5) Present Value (4) × (1)
0	1.000	−$56,000	−$56,000	−$45,000	−$45,000
1	0.909	+ 16,000	+ 14,544	+ 15,000	+ 13,635
2	0.826	+ 16,000	+ 13,216	+ 15,000	+ 12,390
3	0.751	+ 16,000	+ 12,016	+ 15,000	+ 11,265
4	0.683	+ 16,000	+ 10,928	+ 10,000	+ 6,830
5	0.621	+ 16,000	+ 9,936	+ 5,000	+ 3,105
Net present value			+$ 4,640		+$ 2,225

Proposal B offers a higher net present value than proposal A; the net present value of proposal C is lower than that of either of the other two. Proposal B therefore should be chosen.

Incremental rate of return. The same conclusion can be reached by internal rate of return calculations, but the path is slightly more difficult. To begin with, we know that the internal rate of return for proposal B is better than 10 percent because it has a positive net present value at that rate. If we try 15 percent, we get a negative net present value:

Years from Now	Cash Flow	Multiplier at 15 Percent	Present Value
0	−$56,000	1.000	−$56,000
1–5	+ 16,000 per year	3.352	+ 53,632
Net present value			−$ 2,368

Interpolating, we find that the internal rate of return for proposal B is 13.3 percent. Earlier we found that the internal rate of return for proposal A is approximately 14.5 percent. Here is the paradox: proposal B has a lower internal rate of return than proposal A, but proposal B has a greater net present value at 10 percent than proposal A (+$4,640 instead of +$3,900).

The way out of this dilemma is to calculate the *incremental* internal rate of return. What is the additional return from the additional investment proposal B requires? The increments are as follows:

Years from Now	Proposal A	Proposal B	Increment (B − A)
0	−$34,000	−$56,000	−$22,000
1–5	+ 10,000 per year	+ 16,000 per year	+ 6,000 per year

At a discount rate of 10 percent, the increments have a net present value of $6,000 × 3.791 − $22,000 = +$746. At a 15 percent rate, net present value is −$1,888. The approximate rate of return is 11.4 percent.

Now we can see that the additional $22,000, while not producing a rate of return as high as that of the first $34,000, still does better than 10 percent. (If a baseball analogy can be allowed, this is like a shortstop hitting two for four the second day of the season, but still lowering his batting average from .750 to .625 because he hit three for four on opening day. Two for four is still good for a shortstop or for anyone else, even if it does reduce the average.) What is important is not the average but the contribution each incremental outlay can make.

This illustration explains why we prefer the net present value approach. Net present value provides a clearer basis for comparing mutually exclusive proposals as long as the firm has enough money to finance all the proposals that produce rates of return greater than the minimum acceptable rate. The rate of return can still be calculated to reassure those who are uneasy with net present value figures that the overall rate of return is higher than the cost of capital.

STEPS IN PRESENT VALUE ANALYSIS

1. Identify the alternatives management is willing to consider.
2. Estimate the amount and timing of the cash flows resulting from each alternative under consideration.
3. For each alternative, calculate the present value of each cash inflow and each cash outflow.
4. Calculate the net present value for each alternative.
5. Select the alternative with the greatest positive net present value; if each alternative has a negative net present value, reject them all.

ALTERNATIVES TO PRESENT VALUE

Present value has been part of the economist's vocabulary for more than a century. It has also been used for a long time in industrial engineering and in long-term construction accounting. Discounted cash flow models for capital expenditure decisions have been in general use only since the mid 1950s, however, and two of the models in use before then are still found in practice:

1. Payback period.
2. Average book return on investment.

A brief look at these models will be useful.

Payback Period

The most widely known alternative to present value is the payback period, the time that will elapse before future net cash receipts will equal the initial outlay. The shorter the payback period, the better the project, or so it is assumed.

If cash flows are uneven, the payback period should be calculated by adding cash flows until the total equals the initial outlay. Otherwise it can be calculated by applying the following formula:

$$\text{Payback period (years)} = \frac{\text{Investment outlay}}{\text{Average annual cash receipts}}$$

For example, if the installed cost of a piece of equipment is $50,000 and it will produce cash operating savings of $10,000 a year, it has a payback period of five years:

$$\frac{\text{Investment}}{\text{Annual cash receipts}} = \frac{\$50,000}{\$10,000} = 5 \text{ years}$$

The main defect of payback period is that it ignores the estimated useful life of the proposed facilities. If the facilities will have to be replaced five years from now, the project will have achieved no net earnings for the company. The company will have invested $50,000 at a zero rate of return. Or, if a large portion of the investment outlay is for working capital with a high end-of-life recovery value, the project may be more desirable than another with a lower payback period but no end-of-life salvage value.

The most valuable way to use payback period is as a shortcut to the calculation of more refined figures. For projects with cash flows in well-defined patterns, tables can be constructed showing the relationships among payback period, project life, and internal rate of return or net present value. For example, the figures in the cells of the following table show the approximate rates of return for a few of the many possible combinations of life and payback period, assuming equal annual cash receipts and no salvage value:

Payback Period \ Life	5	10	15	20	25	Reciprocal of Payback Period
5	0	15%	18%	19%	20%	20 %
10	negative	0	5.5	8	9	10
15	negative	negative	0	3	4.5	6.7

The figures in the right-hand column, headed Reciprocal of Payback Period, aren't strictly part of a table of this sort, but we have put them in to show the limits the rate of return percentages will approach as life gets longer and longer. If the anticipated economic life of an investment is infinitely long, no deduction for depreciation will have to be made (investments in land usually fall in this category). In such cases the internal rate of return will be equal to the reciprocal of the payback period:

for long term
IRR ≅ payback

Internal Rate of Return	*Payback Period*
$\dfrac{\text{Annual cash flow} - \text{Zero depreciation}}{\text{Initial investment outlay}}$	$\dfrac{\text{Initial investment outlay}}{\text{Annual cash flow}}$

$$\text{Internal rate} = 1/\text{payback period}$$

The longer the life of the investment, the closer the rate of return gets to this limiting value. As the project's life gets longer, the internal rate of return gets closer and closer to the reciprocal of the payback period. This suggests that when management faces projects with very long lives, the reciprocals can be used to approximate the internal rates of return. In most cases, however, a direct approach based on present value is preferable.

Average Return on Investment

A second method is to compute for each project the expected average return on investment. This may be defined in many ways, perhaps the most common being expressed by the following formula:

$$\text{Average return} = \frac{\text{Average cash receipts} - \text{average annual depreciation}}{\text{Average lifetime investment}}$$

The average lifetime investment figure depends on the method used to calculate depreciation. The use of straight-line depreciation for accounting purposes presumes that investment declines in a linear fashion as facilities age, as shown in Exhibit 14–6. The average in-

EXHIBIT 14–6

Average Investment: Straight-Line Depreciation

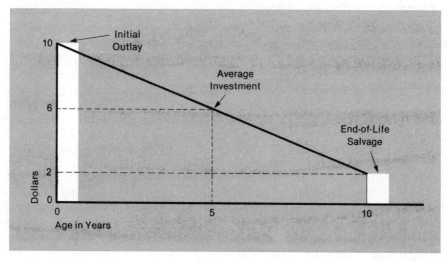

vestment under this assumption is halfway between the amount of the initial outlay and the residual investment at the end of the project's life, measured by the recoverable value of the facilities and working capital at that time.

For example, the project for which payback period was computed earlier required an initial outlay of $50,000 and had no end-of-life salvage value. Average investment is thus $25,000. Assuming that the life of this project is expected to be ten years, average annual depreciation is $5,000, and the average before-tax return on investment is 20 percent:

$$\frac{\text{Average net earnings}}{\text{Average investment}} = \frac{\$10,000 - \$5,000}{\$25,000} = 20\%$$

This method does consider the expected life of the facilities, and it does consider the amount of end-of-life salvage. It fails, however, to allow for differences in timing of outlays and receipts. By this method a project in which no receipts appear until the tenth year will appear to be just as profitable as a project in which most of the cash is received in the first few years of the project's life, as long as the average is the same.

ADMINISTERING THE CAPITAL EXPENDITURE PROGRAM

The methods used to administer a capital expenditure program may be almost as important as the evaluative techniques. Four aspects of the administrative structure deserve a brief description:

1. Preparing the annual capital budget.
2. Preparing appropriation requests.
3. Delegating authority to approve proposals.
4. Implementing capital expenditure decisions.

Preparing the Capital Budget

At the time of annual budget preparation, the division managers or department heads are asked to submit a tentative list of the proposals they plan to make during the coming year, together with a brief justification of each. These lists are combined with schedules of planned expenditures on projects that will already be approved and under way at the beginning of the year. The result is a budget schedule like the one in Exhibit 14–7. In this case the company plans to spend $4.8 million this year on projects approved and started in previous years, plus another $3.8 million on new projects. Future outlays necessary to complete these projects will amount to another $9.3 million.

The consolidated expenditure schedule is presented to the top management budget committee. If the estimated supply of funds falls short of the demand, the committee will have to assign the funds to

EXHIBIT 14-7

Capital Budget Summary (in 000s)

Project	Expenditures Required		
	Previous Years	This Year	Future Years
Prior approvals:			
Headquarters building..........................	$6,100	$1,000	
Sayville plant.................................	2,400	3,800	$1,200
Subtotal.................................	$8,500	$4,800	$1,200
Current approvals:			
Middlebury plant...............................	—	1,500	8,000
Jonesboro plant modernization.................	—	500	100
Factory equipment.............................	—	800	—
Delivery equipment............................	—	700	—
Office equipment..............................	—	300	—
Total planned approvals....................		$8,600	$9,300

the more profitable projects or explore alternative ways of raising additional funds. If the supply of funds exceeds the demand, management may raise the dividend or use the excess funds to improve its financial position. It may also inaugurate a vigorous program of seeking out new investment opportunities, taking the company into new products, increasing expenditures on research and development, or acquiring other companies.

Appropriation Requests

Budget approval seldom serves as the final authorization to undertake a capital expenditure project. Most systems require the submission of a written appropriation request for each proposal at the time the sponsor is ready to begin committing funds to it. The main purpose is to give the sponsor more time to plan as well as an opportunity to consider events that have occurred since the budget was prepared. It also gives the firm more flexibility in that all of its resources are not fully committed at the start of the year. If an emergency or an extraordinarily profitable opportunity arises during the year, projects can be initiated at once without upsetting the overall budget figure. It is only necessary to delay or cancel other projects if additional investment funds cannot be obtained on short notice from other sources.

Each appropriation request must show the reasons why the sponsor believes it should be undertaken. For many projects, this is a detailed estimate of future cash flows, either from reduced costs or expansion of capacity. For others the justification is more qualitative, with the sponsor's assertion that the benefits will be substantial even though presently unmeasurable. One part of good capital budget administration is to encourage efforts to estimate benefits as well as costs.

Approval Authority

While proposals may originate anywhere in the organization, the manager who will be responsible for the results of a project is usually expected to sponsor the request. Typically, each proposal must be approved by each person in the sponsor's chain of command, up to the level at which final approval authority is lodged.

In larger firms, final approval authority is usually delegated to managers at lower levels. Department heads may approve individual projects smaller than, say, $10,000; division managers may have authority to approve projects up to some higher amount, such as $100,000; and the president may be able to approve projects up to amounts as large as $500,000 or even $1 million, the limit depending on the size of the company and its past history. Final decisions on the largest projects are almost always made or ratified by the board of directors.

Delegated approval authority is almost always limited and subject to audit. Lower level managers are still expected to apply company profitability standards to proposals within their authority limits, and they are usually subject to limits on the total amounts that they can approve.

Project Implementation

Once an appropriation request is approved, someone must be assigned the responsibility for implementing the project. For small projects, this is usually the task of the manager who will be responsible for managing the new facilities. For major expenditures, it may be a full-time assignment lasting many months.

After the full project expenditure has been made, the actual and budgeted outlays are reported to the capital budget committee or controller's department. If the actual expenditure has exceeded the budget by a significant amount, the person in charge of the project will have to submit an explanation, usually in writing.

Some firms have experimented with post-completion audits of capital expenditures. A year after the project has been placed in operation, or longer if necessary, a study is made to ascertain whether the project realized the anticipated benefits. Unfortunately, these audits have seldom been very successful. Typically, the assumptions under which the proposal was made no longer hold, and the opportunity costs are not recorded in the accounts. Furthermore, except for very large projects, the portion of the company's profit stemming from a specific capital investment is very difficult to isolate.

The best control devices in any case are careful scrutiny of individual proposals and incorporation of the estimated results into departmental operating budgets. Although the results of individual projects cannot be isolated, their combined effects can be examined as part of the conventional periodic performance review.

DISINVESTMENT DECISIONS

All the investment problems we have looked at so far have focused on proposals to tie up company funds in plant, equipment, and working capital. A similar kind of problem arises when someone proposes to sell a factory, withdraw from a market area, or discontinue selling a product, converting the amounts invested in those activities into ready cash. These are *disinvestment problems.*

For example, a company has an opportunity to realize $500,000 in cash by closing and selling one of its factories. It can refuse this offer and continue to operate the plant, but cash flows from the sale of the products made in the plant will decline rapidly, and the resale value of the land, building, and equipment will fall even faster.

Again the best way to start is to set up a timetable of cash flows, this time with one column for each of the two alternatives and another for the differential cash flows:

(1) Years from Now	(2) Cash Flows from Abandoning the Plant	(3) Cash Flows from Keeping the Plant	(4) Differential Cash Flows (2) – (3)
0	+$500,000	0	+$500,000
0–1	0	+$250,000	− 250,000
1–2	0	+ 200,000	− 200,000
2–3	0	+ 150,000	− 150,000
3–4	0	+ 100,000	− 100,000
4–5	0	+ 50,000	− 50,000
Total	+$500,000	+$750,000	+$250,000

This problem is no different from any of the other problems we have been looking at. To see why this is true, let's turn the problem around. Instead of thinking of this as a proposal to sell the plant, we can think of it as a proposal to keep it in operation. To do that, the company must forgo an immediate cash inflow of $500,000. Doing that is just like investing $500,000 to keep the plant going. If we look at it this way, we get the following timetable:

Years from Now	Differential Cash Flows
0	−$500,000
0–1	+ 250,000
1–2	+ 200,000
2–3	+ 150,000
3–4	+ 100,000
4–5	+ 50,000

This table has exactly the same format as the other timetables we have looked at. A decision to forgo the receipt of cash to get future benefits is no different from a decision to pay out cash now to get future benefits.

If the minimum acceptable rate of return is 10 percent, and if we assume that cash flows are concentrated at the end of each year, the present value is as follows:

Time	Cash Flow	Multiplier	Present Value
0..................	−$500,000	1.000	−$500,000
1..................	+ 250,000	0.909	+ 227,250
2..................	+ 200,000	0.826	+ 165,200
3..................	+ 150,000	0.751	+ 112,650
4..................	+ 100,000	0.683	+ 68,300
5..................	+ 50,000	0.621	+ 31,050
Net present value			+$104,450

The same calculation can be made each year until it finally gives the signal to disinvest.

SUMMARY

Many of management's resource allocation problems can be classified as investment problems. Decision models for investment problems must provide a mechanism for comparing incremental cash outflows in one or more time periods with the incremental cash inflows in another time period or periods.

The model that does this most satisfactorily is the present value model, in which all anticipated incremental cash flows are discounted to their present equivalents at a discount rate based on the cost of capital. Other things being equal, the alternative with the greatest positive net present value should be selected; proposals with negative net present values should be rejected. A related technique is the calculation of each project's internal rate of return, which can then be compared directly with the cost of capital.

An administrative structure is necessary to coordinate the review of capital expenditure proposals and implement capital expenditure decisions. The main control instruments are budget review and project approval. Here as elsewhere, the decision models are only useful if management has the control mechanisms to back them up.

KEY TERMS

The most important terms introduced and defined in this chapter are the following:

Appropriation request	Capital expenditure
Approval limits	Cost of capital
Capital budget	Discounted cash flow

Economic life	Payback period
Future value	Present value
End-of-life salvage value	Return on investment
Internal rate of return	Time value of money

APPENDIX: The Cost of Capital

For any given company at any given time, the price that the company must pay to obtain funds through the issuance of a given type of security is determined by market forces. Generally speaking, this price can be expressed as the percentage expected yield that investors in that type of security demand as a reward for investing their money. From these data on demanded yields, the company can estimate its cost of capital, the cost of attracting funds into the company. This cost has two components: (1) the cost of debt capital; and (2) the cost of equity capital.

Cost of debt capital. The cost of debt capital is the rate of interest that equates the present value of the future stream of interest payments (after allowing for income tax effects) and maturity date repayment of face value to the current net proceeds from sale of the debt instruments. For example, assume that bonds with a coupon rate of 9 percent and a 20-year maturity can be sold at their face value. After providing for the tax deductibility of interest at a tax rate of 50 percent, the after-tax cost of this debt offering is 4.5 percent.

Cost of equity capital. The concept of the cost of equity capital is an unfamiliar one. Traditional terminology refers to the *cost* of debt and the *return* on equity. In financial accounting, interest is deducted as an expense in computing net income, but dividends are regarded as distributions of previously retained earnings. These distinctions, however, result from the nature of the legal relationships between the firm and the suppliers of capital, not from any inherent differences in the basic objectives of those who provide capital funds. Stockholders are just as interested in reward as bondholders or other lenders; only the form and legal status of the rewards are different.

The cost of equity capital is far more difficult to estimate because funds obtained from stockholders require no firm contractual commitment to future payments. Stockholders do have expectations, however, and the cost of equity capital can be defined as the rate of discount that stockholders apply to the expected future receipts from stock ownership to determine the price they are willing to pay. To determine this rate, we need data on the market price of the stock and the stockholders' future expectations. The latter information being unavailable, the analyst typically falls back on a study of past relationships between market prices, dividends, and capital appreciation.

As a simple illustration of the concept, if a stock is selling for $50 per share and the company's earnings are stable at $5 a share, this is some evidence that the marginal stockholders in the company are willing to pay $10 for each dollar of earnings. To attract additional funds into the firm, therefore, the company must be able to communicate an expectation that these funds will also earn a return of at least 10 percent on investment, and perhaps more.

The cost of equity capital for any company includes a risk premium in addition to the cost of risk-free capital. The size of this premium depends on the perceived risks of investing in that company relative to the risks of investing in the market generally. The so-called capital asset pricing model links the size of the risk premium to the contribution the stock makes to the variability of a diversified portfolio. Companies whose stock prices are very sensitive to movements in the stock market will have high-risk premiums, and vice versa.[2]

Weighted average cost of capital. Most companies use both debt and equity capital. Utility companies have a high proportion of debt, mining companies relatively little. A company's average cost of capital will depend not only on the costs of the two kinds of capital but also on the proportions in which they are to be used.

What this means is that the minimum acceptable rate of return should be based on a weighted average of the costs of debt and equity capital. The weights should represent the relative place each has in the company's financing plans:

	After-Tax Capital Cost	Weight	Weighted Cost
Debt....................	4.5%	40%	1.8%
Equity..................	12.0	60	7.2
Total.............			9.0%

If the company's investments do not yield a rate of return at least as great as the cost of capital, they will dilute the company's earnings and impair its ability to secure funds on a balanced basis in the future.

INDEPENDENT STUDY PROBLEMS
(Solutions in Appendix C)

1. Present value exercises. Calculate net present value at 10 percent, internal rate of return, payback period, and average return on investment for each of the following capital expenditure proposals. You should assume that each cash flow after the initial outlay occurs at the end of the year.

a. Initial outlay...................................... $10,000
   Annual cash receipts............................ $ 1,750
   Estimated life.................................... 10 years
   Salvage.. None

---

[2] James H. Lorie and Mary T. Hamilton, *The Stock Market: Theories and Evidence* (Homewood, Ill.: Richard D. Irwin, Inc., 1973).

    b. Initial outlay.................................... $10,000
        Annual cash receipts:
            First five years .... $ 2,000
            Second five years .... $ 1,500
        Estimated life................................. 10 years
        Salvage....................................... None

    c. Initial outlay.................................... $10,000
        Annual cash receipts:
            First five years .... $ 1,500
            Second five years .... $ 2,000
         Estimated life................................. 10 years
        Salvage....................................... None

    d. Initial outlay.................................... $10,000
        Annual cash receipts .... $ 1,350
        Estimated life................................. 10 years
        Salvage....................................... $ 4,000

    e. Initial outlay.................................... $10,000
        Annual cash receipts........................... $ 1,750
        Estimated life................................. 15 years
        Salvage....................................... None

2. Equivalent annuity: Retirement fund. Alpha Company has just signed a contract with its research manager. The manager will receive a salary for the next five years. Five years from today the manager will retire. The contract provides for five more annual payments to the manager, the first payment to be made one year after the retirement date. The amount will be $20,000 a year.

Alpha's president regards all these payments as payments for the research manager's services in the five years prior to retirement and wants to have the retirement payments fully funded on the retirement date. Payments are to be made to a trustee once a year. They are to be equal in amount. The first payment to the trustee is to be made immediately; the last payment is to be made the day the manager retires.

Calculate the amount of each payment to the trustee if the trustee compounds interest at 8 percent a year.

EXERCISES AND PROBLEMS

1. Present value exercises. Prepare a timetable of cash flows for each of the following independent proposals, calculate the net present value, and indicate whether the outlay should be made. You may decide to accept some, all, or none of these proposals. The minimum acceptable rate of return is 10 percent.

    a. Immediate outlay, $100; cash to be received at one year intervals for ten years, the first to be received exactly one year after the immediate outlay, $15 a year.
    b. Immediate outlay, $67; cash receipts, $20 a year for five years, starting one year after the immediate outlay.
    c. Immediate outlay, $100; cash receipts $15 a year for five years, starting one year after the immediate outlay, plus one additional receipt of $75 ten years after the immediate outlay.
    d. Immediate outlay, $67; cash receipts: $35 one year later, $30 two years later, $20 three years later, $10 four years later, and $5 five years later.

  e. Immediate outlay, $67; cash receipts: $5 one year later, $10 two
      years later, $20 three years later, $30 four years later, and $35 five
      years later.

2. Mutually exclusive proposals. The company can accept only one of
the proposals described in Problem 1. Which one would you recommend?
Why would you recommend it?

3. Internal rate of return. Calculate the internal rate of return for each
of the exercises in Problem 1. Do these calculations point to the same
recommendations you made in answer to Problems 1 and 2? Does this
seem reasonable?

4. Payback period and average return on investment. Calculate the payback period and the average return on investment for each of the situations described in Problem 1. Assume straight-line depreciation. How
satisfactory is each of these measures as a device for ranking investment
proposals? In your analysis of this question, you should use net present
value and the internal rate of return as comparison standards.

5. Payback period reciprocal. Payback period is easier to calculate
than net present value or internal rate of return. To take advantage of this
fact, some have suggested that the reciprocal of the payback period be
interpreted as an approximation of the internal rate of return and that it
be used to measure the profitability of investment proposals.

  Under what circumstances would you regard this as an acceptable approximation? (Suggestion: calculate payback period and internal rate of
return for three or four different sets of cash flows, varying such factors
as the ratio of the annual cash receipt to the initial outlay and the length
of the cash flow stream.)

6. Amortization schedule. A machine costs $4,100, payable immedi-
ately in cash. Use of this machine is expected to reduce cash outflows by
$1,000 a year for five years. The controller has calculated that the internal
rate of return from the purchase of this machine would be 7 percent. Cash
flows take place at one year intervals and interest is compounded annually.

  Without using the interest tables, prepare a schedule showing the
amount of each annual cash flow that can be regarded as a recovery of
part of the $4,100 investment in the machine, and the amount to be
regarded as a return on investment.

7. Maximum purchase price. Frank Destry has been offered the opportunity to submit a bid for the right to provide catering services in a
private club. The contract would run for eight years, and Mr. Destry estimates that his net cash receipts from the catering business would amount
to approximately $12,000 a year. If he accepts the contract, he will have
to make an initial investment of $2,000 in equipment.

  What is the maximum price that Mr. Destry can afford to bid for the
catering privilege, assuming that he requires a 14 percent return on his
investment?

8. Equipment purchase decision. The ABC Company is considering a
proposal to buy materials handling equipment to achieve economies in its
warehousing operation. The total cost of the equipment, together with
auxiliary investments in pallets and supplies, is $30,000. The equipment is
expected to be useful for seven years before replacement becomes economical. Scrap value is expected to be negligible. Annual cash savings are

expected to be $5,000 the first year, $7,000 the second year, and $8,000 in each subsequent year as the warehouse reaches full-capacity operation.

The ABC Company requires a minimum return on investment of 20 percent a year before taxes. Assuming that the decision is to be based on before-tax cash flows, should this proposal be accepted?

9. Present value; Internal rate of return. A capital expenditure proposal is expected to produce the following cash flows:

Outlays:
Two years before operations commence..................	$10,000
One year before operations commence...................	30,000
One day before operations commence....................	20,000
Ten years after operations begin.......................	20,000

Receipts:
Each year for the first three years of operations	5,000
Each year for the next ten years........................	10,000
Each year for the next five years	8,000
18 years after operations begin.........................	12,000

a. Prepare a timetable of cash flows. Each year's receipts can be assumed to come in at the end of the year.
b. Compute the net present value of this proposal at a discount rate of 15 percent.
c. Calculate the internal rate of return.

10. Business purchase decision. Henrietta Brown has an opportunity to buy a certain business, paying $50,000 immediately and $20,000 at the end of each of the next five years. It is anticipated that the net cash receipts from the operation of this business will amount to $35,000 a year for the next 15 years and $25,000 a year for the 5 years after that. Ms. Brown wishes to retire 20 years from now and believes that she will be able to sell the business at that time for $30,000. If she buys the business, she expects to spend $2,000 a year on capital replacements and improvements during the first five years, $3,000 a year during the next five years, $4,000 a year during the third five years, and nothing thereafter.

The above figures do not provide for any compensation for Ms. Brown's services. If she buys the business, she must leave her present job, in which she is earning $18,000 a year. Furthermore, if she buys the new business, she must liquidate certain investments of comparable risk that now yield a return on investment of 10 percent before taxes.

Would you advise Ms. Brown to make the purchase? Show your calculations. You may assume that all cash flows take place at the end of the year in which they arise.

11. Equivalent annuity: Minimum annual rental. A pension fund is considering the purchase of a machine for $100,000. This machine would be leased to a manufacturing firm at a fixed annual rental. The lease would be noncancellable and would run for ten years. The annual rentals would be received at the beginning of each year.

a. If the minimum acceptable rate of return is 10 percent, what is the lowest rental that should be accepted?
b. The pension fund bought and paid for the machine but the intended lessee went out of business. The machine's manufacturer will not buy it back and the fund is now seeking a new lessee. How does this situation differ from the original one? How would you establish a minimum annual rental? Would it be the same as before?

12. Equivalent annuity; Financing college fees. Barbara and Daniel
Porges both work. Barbara is an account executive with an advertising
agency, Daniel is an assistant vice president of a bank. They have three
children. The oldest child will begin her high school sophomore year next
month, the second child is two years behind the first, and the third child
is one year behind the second.

All three children have done well in school and Mr. and Mrs. Porges
expect all three to attend four-year colleges after graduation from high
school. Annual college expenses will average $6,000 for each child, pay-
able at the beginning of the college year.

Mr. and Mrs. Porges have decided to put aside a fixed amount of money
each year to provide a college fund for their children. The first payment
into the fund will be made a year from now; the last will be made a year
before the payment is made for the youngest child's senior college year.
No provision will be made for graduate school.

The fund will consist of a bank savings account, paying interest at
6 percent, compounded annually.

a. Set up a timetable showing the deposits in the fund and the amounts
    to be withdrawn for college expenses, year by year. The zero date
    should be the date of the first deposit in the fund. (The amount of
    the annual deposit is unknown and should be represented by a sym-
    bol.)
b. Calculate the amount Mr. and Mrs. Porges should deposit in the fund
    each year.
c. Verify your answer to (b) by preparing a schedule of deposits, in-
    terest, and fee payments, year by year.

13. Immediate versus deferred payment. Stanley Baker worked in research and development at the General Corporation for 35 years, retiring
as vice president 10 years ago at the age of 60. When he retired, he bought
the rights to several ideas management had decided not to commercialize.
Working in his garage, he developed a laboratory model incorporating one
of these ideas. He sold the invention to the American Company seven years
ago. This company then spent several hundred thousand dollars to perfect
the device and make it commercially feasible.

During the negotiations for the purchase of the invention, American
offered to pay Mr. Baker $200,000 for the rights to his invention. The pay-
ment was to be made exactly seven years ago. Mr. Baker refused this offer
and made a counterproposal that American pay him $10,000 a year for
five years, followed by $50,000 for each of the next three years, and
$100,000 for each of the three years after that. He reasoned that Ameri-
can placed less value on distant cash than on cash to be paid in the
near future, and would pay him more on that basis. He also knew the
company would have to spend a substantial amount to develop the invention and make it marketable, and his proposal would reduce the immediate strain on the company's cash flow. American's management
agreed, the contract was signed, and the first $10,000 payment was made
seven years ago tomorrow.

American at that time used 15 percent as its minimum acceptable return on investment. Mr. Baker was a conservative investor and placed
any idle funds in savings accounts earning 6 percent interest. Annual
compounding is appropriate in each case.

a. Was American justified in accepting Mr. Baker's counterproposal?

b. Mr. Baker is still convinced he made a good deal. Do you agree? What
    are your arguments?
c. Mr. Baker has the right to sell or assign his interest in the deferred pay-
    ment agreement. He is due to receive this year's payment tomorrow. A
    local businessman in need of ready cash has offered to buy the re-
    mainder of this contract, including this year's payment, promising to
    pay Mr. Baker or his heirs $40,000 a year for ten years, the first pay-
    ment to be made a year from now. Should Mr. Baker accept? What
    factors should he consider?

14. Unprofitable business: Multiple alternatives. National Corporation
bought Summit Corporation five years ago. Summit is a franchiser of
restaurants operating under the name Omar's Tent and serving items with
a middle eastern flavor. The franchise business has been depressed for the
past two years, so depressed that Summit has had a $10,000 operating
cash deficit each year. This seems likely to continue unless something is
done.

Gerald Avakian, Summit's founder and former owner, has offered to
buy the company back for $125,000 any time National wants to sell.
National paid him $3 million for Summit's stock five years ago, however,
and none of this has been amortized.

Summit's management has submitted three proposals to improve the
division's cash flows:

Proposal A. Invest $100,000 in a new dough-making facility to supply
the franchisees with bread dough to be baked on the premises. Management estimates this would bring a cash inflow of $40,000 a year.

Proposal B. Invest $400,000 in a new baking and packaging facility
to supply the franchisees with frozen bread to be served in the restaurants
and also sold there in packages under the brand name Omar's Loaf. This
would bring in cash flows, rising from $50,000 in the first year to $75,000
in the second and $100,000 in each year after the second.

Proposal C. Invest $300,000 in a new baking facility to supply suitably
located franchisees with freshly baked bread daily. This would produce
annual cash inflows of $70,000.

In each case management expects the facilities to be economically
productive for ten years and to have no salvage value at the end of that
time. The company has a minimum acceptable rate of return on investment of 12 percent.

Assuming that all the cash flow estimates are valid, what action would
you recommend? Explain your reasons for rejecting each of the other
alternatives. (Taxes should be ignored. Operating cash flows should be
assumed to occur at the end of the year.) As part of your answer, calculate the incremental rate of return of your recommended alternative over
the next best alternative.

15

Data for Capital
Expenditure Decisions

CHAPTER 14 pointed out that the present value capital expenditure decision model calls for estimates of the effects of accepting individual proposals on the company's cash flows. As we emphasized in Chapter 3, cash inflows give management financial power, cash outflows take it away. Management can't take advantage of the time value of money unless it has cash to invest.

This chapter shows how the components of the cash flow stream should be measured. We shall begin by examining the most pervasive of all the cash flows, income taxes. The next five sections examine the after-tax cash flows arising from a plant modernization investment—the initial outlay, secondary outlays, annual operating receipts and disbursements, and end-of-life residual values—and their translation into a set of present value estimates. The section explores the difficult task of estimating the economic life of individual investments. The final section then deals with four questions that often arise in applying the concepts described in these two chapters.

ALLOWING FOR INCOME TAXES

Income taxes are cash flows. Like any other cash flows, their amount and timing can affect the desirability of capital expenditure proposals. We shall study two questions in this section:

1. How taxes can affect an investment decision.
2. How depreciation and similar charges can shield cash flows from current taxation.

The Impact of Taxation on Cash Flows

The amount of income taxes due and payable each year depends partly on the results of the firm's activities and partly on the provi-

500

sions Congress and state legislatures have built into the tax laws. Some tax provisions actually affect the total amount of taxes to be paid during the life of an investment—we shall look at one of these, the so-called investment credit, in the next section. For the most part, however, the only question is whether taxes will be paid sooner or later—that is, they affect the desirability of investing by affecting the timing of the after-tax cash flows.

For example, a company has two proposals, X and Y, identical except for their income tax effects:

Initial outlay......................	$60,000
Annual pretax cash flow...........	25,000 a year
Life...............................	3 years
End-of-life salvage................	zero
Tax rate*..........................	40%

* The effective tax rate varies slightly from state to state and is subject to change. For simplicity, a rate of 40 percent will be used throughout this section. Although actual rates are ordinarily in the neighborhood of 50 percent, for illustrative purposes it is clearer to use the 40 percent rate, which is a round number and also produces different figures for income tax and after-tax net income.

On proposal X, the $60,000 cost can be depreciated for tax purposes at $20,000 a year for three years. On proposal Y, the $60,000 cost can be charged as a tax deduction immediately.

Proposal X. The calculation of the net present value of the after-tax cash flows is a four-step process:

Step 1. Calculate taxable income for each year. For proposal X:

Initial outlay........................	No tax impact
Annual operating earnings:	
Pretax cash flow..................	$25,000
Tax depreciation.................	20,000
Taxable income..............	$ 5,000

Step 2. Calculate the tax effects. For proposal X, the tax is 40 percent of $5,000, or $2,000 a year.

Step 3. Deduct the taxes from the pretax cash flows. For proposal X, this is $25,000 minus $2,000. The after-tax cash flow is $23,000 a year. This calculation reflects the assumption that taxes are paid as the pretax cash flows take place. This assumption is not quite accurate, but it is convenient and is usually accurate enough for the purpose. The time lag is relatively short.

Step 4. Prepare a timetable and calculate the net present value of the after-tax cash flows. In this case the timetable shows an immediate outlay of $60,000 and receipts of $23,000 one, two, and three years later. If the discount rate is 10 percent, the net present value is −$2,799:

Years from Zero Date	After-Tax Cash Flow	Present Value At 10 Percent	
		Multiplier	Amount
0..................	−$60,000	1.000	−$60,000
1..................	+ 23,000		
2..................	+ 23,000	2.487*	+ 57,201
3..................	+ 23,000		
Net present value.......			−$ 2,799

* From Table 2, Appendix A.

Since net present value is negative, the proposal should be rejected.

Proposal Y. Applying the same procedure to proposal Y, we get the figures shown in Exhibit 15–1. The initial outlay under this proposal is fully deductible in calculating taxable income at time 0. If the company has enough taxable income from other sources, this will

---

PREPARING THE TIMETABLE

Few cash flows take the form of lump-sum receipts or payments at one-year intervals. A year's operating cash receipts, for example, are likely to come in throughout the year, not all at one time. Even so, cash flows are usually assumed in capital expenditure analysis to come in or go out only once a year, on the last day of the year, and present value is calculated on the basis of annual compounding. We have conformed to customary practice by using the following conventions:

1. The zero date is the date on which the first significant cash flow takes place.
2. Operating cash flows take place as lump sums at year-end.
3. Each investment outlay is dated at the year-end nearest to the date of the anticipated cash outlay.
4. Salvage value is dated at the end of the year in which the assets become available for liquidation—usually at the end of the last year of operations.
5. Taxes are dated at the same time as the operating cash flows, investment outlays or salvage values to which they are related.

The reason for this admittedly inaccurate treatment is that it simplifies the analysis. The resulting errors in the present value calculations will be too small to affect the action recommendation, except in very rare circumstances. The errors inherent in the estimates of future cash flows are almost always much larger and therefore more important.

EXHIBIT 15–1

Calculation of Present Value after Taxes, Proposal Y

(1)	(2)	(3)	(4)	(5)	(6)	(7)
			Income	After-Tax	Present Value	
	Before-Tax	Taxable	Tax	Cash Flow		
Time	Cash Flow	Income	40% of (3)	(2) – (4)	Factor	Amount
0........	−$60,000	−$60,000	−$24,000	−$36,000	1.000	−36,000
1........	+ 25,000	+ 25,000	+ 10,000	+ 15,000		
2........	+ 25,000	+ 25,000	+ 10,000	+ 15,000	2.487*	+37,305
3........	+ 25,000	+ 25,000	+ 10,000	+ 15,000		
Net present value						+ 1,305

* From Table 2, Appendix A.

reduce the taxes on this other income by $60,000 × 40% = $24,000. The after-tax initial cash outflow required by this proposal therefore is only $60,000 − $24,000 = $36,000, the amount shown in column (5) of the exhibit.

Writing off the full investment outlay right away deprives the company of the right to write it off in the future. This means that the operating cash inflows from proposal Y will be fully taxable, with no depreciation deductions to shield them. Their after-tax amounts therefore are only $15,000 a year [column (5)].

When both of these effects are considered, the net present value of the cash flows in proposal Y is +$1,305. This means that the after-tax rate of return on the proposed investment is greater than 10 percent. Proposal Y should be accepted.

Comparing the proposals. Comparing the income tax figures for these two proposals shows why the difference in the tax treatment of the asset's cost makes proposal Y profitable and proposal X unprofitable:

Time	Income Tax Proposal X	Income Tax Proposal Y	Differential Cash Flow
0...........	—	$(24,000)	+$24,000
1...........	$2,000	10,000	− 8,000
2...........	2,000	10,000	− 8,000
3...........	2,000	10,000	− 8,000
Total.......	$6,000	$ 6,000	$ 0

In each case the government nets $6,000 in taxes. With proposal Y, however, the company gets $24,000 from the government initially (in the form of reduced taxes on its other income) and then pays $10,000 a year. Under proposal X, the company gets nothing initially and then pays $2,000 a year. This is like receiving an interest-free loan of $24,000 and paying it back in three installments of $8,000 each.

The Tax Shield

Some analysts prefer a different format for these calculations. They divide the tax calculation into two parts: (1) the immediate tax effects of the cash flows themselves; and (2) the tax effects of the tax shields—the noncash items on the tax return.

Step 1. Apply the tax rate to the pretax cash flows. For proposal X:

Pretax cash flow.........................	$25,000
Tax at 40%...............................	10,000
After-tax contribution..................	$15,000

Step 2. Calculate the present value of these amounts: 2.487 × $15,000 = $37,305. (The 2.487 multiplier comes from the 10 percent column of Table 2 in Appendix A.)

Step 3. Calculate the tax effect of the tax deductions. These deductions are called the tax shield because they shield the cash flows from current taxation. For proposal X the only tax shield comes from the annual tax depreciation deduction:

Annual tax depreciation.................	$20,000
Tax effect at 40%	8,000

Step 4. Calculate the present value of the tax shield: 2.487 × $8,000 = $19,896.

Step 5. Determine the net present value of the proposal:

Initial outlay............................	−$60,000
Pretax annual cash flow...............	+ 37,305
Tax shield.............................	+ 19,896
Net present value...............	−$ 2,799

The one danger in the tax shield approach is that the term will be misinterpreted. The tax shield is not a way of cheating the government. The tax shield arises in this case because certain outlays lead to tax reductions or refunds later on, not when the outlays are made. In other words, the firm has to pay for any tax shields it may have— the government doesn't give them away.

That objection aside, the two approaches to tax flow calculation are interchangeable because they produce the same end result. We shall use the approach summarized in Exhibit 15–1 because we find it clearer and more compact. Others prefer the tax shield approach, presumably for the same reasons.

THE INITIAL INVESTMENT OUTLAY

Investment projects affect taxes only because they alter the amount and timing of the company's cash flows. In the next four sections we shall see how a facilities modernization investment affects a company's cash flows. The pretax cash flows follow the pattern shown in Exhibit 15–2: initial outlay, level annual operating cash receipts, secondary outlay at the end of five years, and an end-of-life residual or salvage value.

The first of these, the initial outlay, includes all outlays necessary

EXHIBIT 15–2

Pretax Cash Flows in Plant Modernization Proposal

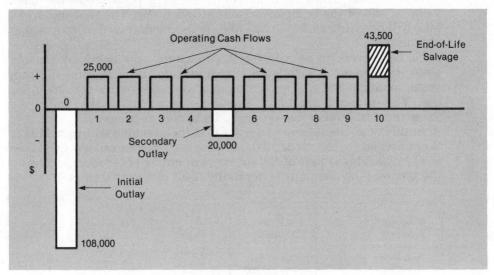

to carry out the proposal, whether for plant and equipment or for research and development, whether capitalized on the balance sheet or written off immediately for external financial reporting or for tax purposes. It consists of some or all of the following:

1. Cash outlays for plant and equipment.
2. Opportunity costs of existing facilities to be incorporated in the proposal.
3. Outlays for working capital.
4. Disposal values of facilities to be displaced by the proposal.
5. Immediate income tax effects.

Outlays for Plant and Equipment

For most proposals, the major outlays are for the acquisition and installation of physical facilities. For example, a proposal to modernize a factory is expected to require the following outlays before the investment begins to bring in cash receipts:

Equipment............................	$80,000
Installation............................	10,000
Training and test runs..................	7,000
Total............................	$97,000

If these outlays are spread over a period longer than six months, they should be divided and dated at the nearest year-end. In most cases it is accurate enough to assume that all these cash flows take place at one time.

Existing Facilities Used

The second pretax item in our illustrative proposal is the cash value of one of the company's present machines. The machine, now idle, will be put back in service only if the modernization proposal is approved.

No cash needs to be paid for this machine—the company already owns it. Even so, it belongs in the timetable. By accepting the proposal, management will make this machine unavailable for any other use. This proposal therefore should be charged for the machine's value in its best other use—that is, its opportunity cost.

In this case, management agrees that the machine will be sold if it is not needed for the modernization proposal. The estimated sale price is $12,000. This is part of the investment outlay because in accepting the proposal the company is depriving itself of $12,000 in cash:

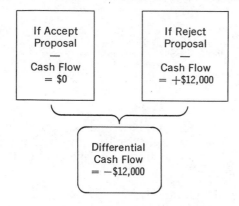

 A cash receipt forgone is always equivalent to a cash outlay. The book value of the equipment doesn't measure either current or future cash flows, of course, and therefore should be ignored.

Working Capital

Once the new equipment is in operation, management expects it will support a larger volume of sales. These will require additional working capital which should be reflected in the timetable:

Inventories: the amount spent to increase the size of the average inventory $10,000

Receivables: the difference between net revenues and collections in the first year (inserted as part of the initial outlay because estimates of operating cash flows usually reflect revenues rather than collections) 4,000

Cash: any additional balances immobilized because they are necessary to support the additional volume of activity resulting from the proposal 2,000

> *Trade payables and other short-term, noninterest-bearing liabilities:* any increments in these items arising from the additional volume of activity 11,000

These amounts should be entered in the timetable as they occur. Because the net increase in this case is small ($10,000 + $4,000 + $2,000 − $11,000 = $5,000), management has decided to simplify the calculation by putting the entire amount in the timetable as a cash outlay at zero date.

Displaced Facilities

The cash flows we have mentioned already overstate the amount of investment that will be necessary. If the proposal is accepted, a machine now serving a standby purpose can be disposed of. This machine has a tax basis (book value) of only $1,000, but once again opportunity cost, not book value, is the right measure of the cash flow. Opportunity cost is measured by the machine's scrap value, $6,000. The displaced machine, in other words, can finance $6,000 of the gross pretax outlays the proposal will require.

This may become clearer if we point out once again that we are really comparing two alternatives in our cash flow estimates:

A Accept the Proposal and Dispose of Existing Standby Equipment +$6,000	B Reject the Proposal and keep the Standby Equipment +$0

The only way to get the $6,000 cash inflow is to accept this proposal. It therefore becomes a cash inflow attributable to the proposal and must be included in the timetable.

Tax Effects of the Initial Outlay

The net incremental pretax initial outlay amounts to $108,000, the sum of the six items we just discussed:

New equipment............................... $ 80,000
Installation..................................... 10,000
Training and test runs..........................   7,000
Existing equipment............................ 12,000
Working capital................................   5,000
Less: Disposal of displaced machine.......... (6,000)
    Net pretax outlay........................ $108,000

Some of these amounts will affect the company's income taxes immediately. In fact, we have designed the illustration to include four separate tax effects: a tax credit, a tax deduction, a tax-deductible loss, and a taxable gain. (A tax credit is a direct reduction in the amount of tax due; a tax deduction is a reduction in the amount of taxable income.)

Tax credit. Many governments offer tax credits to induce business firms to invest in facilities or to increase their inventories, thereby providing jobs and stimulating the economy. In our illustration, the $80,000 outlay for new equipment is eligible for a 10 percent tax credit. This will reduce the tax by $8,000, and this amount should be deducted in calculating the initial outlay.

Tax deduction. Both the purchase price and the installation cost of the new equipment will be capitalized and depreciated for tax purposes over a period of years. The $7,000 in training and test-run costs, however, will be fully deductible from taxable revenues right away. At a 40 percent tax rate, this will reduce current taxes by $2,800. The after-tax outlay for these items therefore is $7,000 − $2,800 = $4,200.

Tax-deductible loss. The idle machine to be used in the proposal also has a tax impact. We have already seen that accepting the proposal will deprive the company of the $12,000 cash flow from selling this machine. It will also deprive the company of the right to enter the loss from the sale of the machine on the current income tax return. The loss for tax purposes is the difference between the proceeds from the sale and book value for tax purposes (the "tax basis"), which in this case happens to be $20,000:

Sale value...................................	$12,000
Tax basis....................................	20,000
Tax-deductible loss.........................	$ 8,000

Since this would reduce taxable income, it would also reduce taxes. Using the machine will deprive the company of this tax reduction. It thus becomes another cash outflow arising from the proposed investment. At a tax rate of 40 percent, the tax effect is $3,200. The after-tax cash flow is:

Sale value.............................	$12,000
Tax reduction due to loss...............	3,200
After-tax cash flow.................	$15,200

Taxable gain. The final element in the initial outlay calculation, the sale of the displaced machine, also has a tax effect. The market value of this machine is $6,000, and the tax basis is $1,000, so the taxable gain is $5,000. The cash flows are:

Market value.............................	$6,000
Tax on the gain: 40% × $5,000.............	2,000
After-tax cash flow.................	$4,000

The after-tax investment outlay. All these figures are summarized in Exhibit 15–3. In this case the net difference between the pretax

EXHIBIT 15–3

Calculation of After-Tax Initial Outlay

Item	Outlay before Tax	Tax Effect	Outlay after Tax
Equipment, installed................	$ 90,000	$(8,000)	$ 82,000
Working capital.....................	5,000	0	5,000
Training and test runs..............	7,000	(2,800)	4,200
Surplus equipment used............	12,000	3,200	15,200
Equipment displaced...............	(6,000)	2,000	(4,000)
Total..........................	$108,000	$(5,600)	$102,400

and after-tax amounts is relatively small, less than 6 percent; in other cases it will be much higher.

SECONDARY INVESTMENT OUTLAYS

Management can often predict special outlays that will have to be made in later time periods to keep the investment alive. These, too, may be for equipment or for additional working capital. Each has to be examined for its tax implications.

Secondary investment outlays of this sort are no different in concept from the initial outlay, and need no further discussion here. The only secondary investment outlay management anticipates for the plant modernization proposal is $20,000 to replace equipment at the end of the fifth year. This will have no immediate impact on taxes, and $20,000 is the after-tax cash flow.

OPERATING CASH FLOWS

The benefits from most investments come from increased revenues or from lower operating costs. Two of the many possible cash flow patterns are illustrated in Exhibit 15–4. In the upper diagram, initial operating outflows are followed by several years of positive cash flows, rising to a flat peak in the fifth and sixth years, then declining slowly. Negative cash flows (net outflows) during the first year or so are typical of investments in new products or new markets. The lower diagram depicts a mining investment with a high immediate payoff but declining cash flows as the resources become more and more difficult to exploit.

Modernization Proposal: Pretax Cash Flows

The benefit pattern in our modernization proposal is much simpler. The main benefits are expected to take the form of reduced operating costs. Although the cash costs of operating the plant will undoubtedly rise as the facilities grow older, the difference between the before-tax

EXHIBIT 15–4

Operating Cash Flow Patterns

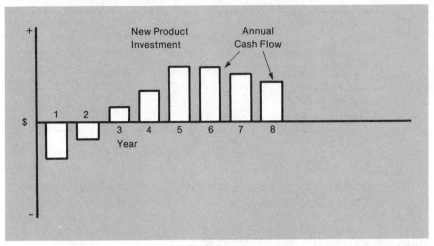

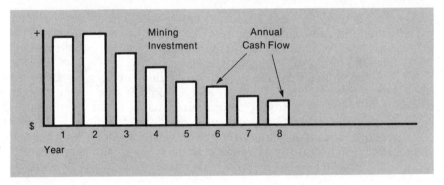

cash flows associated with the company's current facilities and those
incurred in operating the renovated facilities will be relatively constant at $25,000 a year.

Taxes on the Operating Cash Flows

The next step in the analysis is to calculate the effect of the project
on income taxes. To do this, we have to identify two sets of figures:

1. Incremental cash flows not appearing on the current tax return.
2. Incremental accounting charges and credits appearing on the current tax return but unaccompanied by current pretax cash flows.

In this case incremental taxable income is equal to the pretax cash
flow less the incremental tax depreciation. Incremental depreciation
is the difference between two amounts:

	Tax Basis	Depreciation
Depreciation on property required by the project	New equipment....... $90,000 Existing machine...... 20,000 Secondary investment.......... 20,000	20% of declining balance

	Tax Basis	Depreciation
Depreciation on property displaced by the project	Displaced machine.... $1,000	$500 a year for two years

REMINDER: TAX DEPRECIATION METHODS

Straight-line

Equal amount each year, determined as follows:

$$\frac{\text{Original cost} - \text{Estimated salvage}}{\text{Tax life}}$$

Sum-of-the-years'-digits (SYD)

Decreasing amount each year, determined as follows:

1. Number each year of the asset's anticipated life (1, 2, 3, etc.).
2. Total these numbers (sum-of-the-digits).
3. Divide this sum into the individual digits arranged in reverse order (e.g., for five-year life, year 1 is assigned digit 5 and $5/(5 + 4 + 3 + 2 + 1) = \frac{1}{3}$ of the depreciable amount).
4. Multiply these ratios by the depreciable amount: original cost − estimated end-of-life salvage.

Double rate, declining balance (DDB)

Decreasing amount each year, determined as follows:

1. Take the reciprocal of the estimated life, in years.
2. Double this.
3. Multiply this each year by the undepreciated balance at the beginning of the year.
4. Switch to straight-line amortization when straight-line amortization of remaining depreciable amount is greater than DDB amortization.

The calculation of depreciation on the equipment required by the project is summarized in Exhibit 15–5. The initial tax basis of this equipment is $110,000, as shown at the top of column (1). The first year's depreciation is 20 percent of this, or $22,000. This reduces the tax basis to $88,000 (the second figure in column [1]), and the tax depreciation for the second year is 20 percent of $88,000, or $17,600.

For simplicity, we have used a single declining-balance calculation

EXHIBIT 15–5

Tax Depreciation on New and Retained Facilities

Year	(1) Tax Basis, Start of Year	(2) Additions	(3) Tax Depreciation 20% × [(1) + (2)]	(4) Tax Basis, End of Year (1) + (2) − (3)
1	$110,000	—	$22,000	$88,000
2	88,000	—	17,600	70,400
3	70,400	—	14,080	56,320
4	56,320	—	11,264	45,056
5	45,056	—	9,012	36,044
6	36,044	$20,000	11,209	44,835
7	44,835	—	8,967	35,868
8	35,868	—	7,174	28,694
9	28,694	—	5,739	22,955
10	22,955	—	4,591	18,364

for all three types of costs in all years. In practice, tax depreciation would be converted to a straight-line write-off for each of the costs at different times. We have also assumed that retirements of equipment will be zero prior to the end of the ten years.

The tax depreciation figures in Exhibit 15–5 do not measure incremental tax depreciation. If the proposal is rejected, the equipment it would displace will be kept. Tax depreciation of $500 a year will be recorded for the first two years, until the equipment is fully depreciated. This means that *incremental* tax depreciation for each of the first two years is $500 less than the figures shown in Exhibit 15–5:

Year	Depreciation if Proposal Is Accepted	Depreciation if Proposal Is Rejected	Incremental Depreciation
1	$22,000	$500	$21,500
2	17,600	500	17,100
3	14,080	—	14,080

This last calculation may be easier to understand if it is recognized as a simple time shift. If the proposal is accepted, the equipment will be replaced and $1,000 will be deducted immediately from taxable income. If the proposal is rejected, on the other hand, the equipment will be retained and the $1,000 will be deducted from taxable income during the next two years.

Given the before-tax cash flows and the tax depreciation figures, it is a simple matter to calculate taxable income, income tax effects, and after-tax cash flows. Exhibit 15–6 summarizes these calculations

EXHIBIT 15–6

Calculation of After-Tax Operating Cash Flows

Year	(1) Cash Flow before Taxes	(2) Tax Depreciation*	(3) Taxable Income (1) − (2)	(4) Income Tax 40% × (3)	(5) Cash Flow after Taxes (1) − (4)
1	$ 25,000	$ 21,500	$ 3,500	$ 1,400	$ 23,600
2	25,000	17,100	7,900	3,160	21,840
3	25,000	14,080	10,920	4,368	20,632
4	25,000	11,264	13,736	5,494	19,506
5	25,000	9,012	15,988	6,395	18,605
6	25,000	11,209	13,791	5,516	19,484
7	25,000	8,967	16,033	6,413	18,587
8	25,000	7,174	17,826	7,130	17,870
9	25,000	5,739	19,261	7,704	17,296
10	25,000	4,591	20,409	8,164	16,836
Total	$250,000	$110,636	$139,364	$55,744	$194,256

* The figure for each of the first two years differs from that shown in Exhibit 15–5 by $500, placing it on an incremental basis, as explained in the text.

for the plant modernization proposal. With the before-tax figures in the left-hand column, the three middle columns are used to compute the income tax effect. The after-tax cash flow is then found by deducting the tax from the before-tax cash flow.

Notice how the declining-charge depreciation has changed the constant annual before-tax cash flow into a stream of gradually declining amounts. This makes this proposal more valuable than if only the straight-line method were available.

END-OF-LIFE SALVAGE VALUES

The final cash flow associated with a capital expenditure proposal is the cash value of the facilities and working capital remaining when the project's life comes to an end. This value is usually referred to as the residual value or, less elegantly, salvage value. Salvage values are quite important for short-lived investments, less so for projects with long lives. To find out whether salvage values are important, we should always prepare rough estimates except for extremely long-lived projects.

Pretax Salvage Values

The plant modernization expenditures are expected to be productive for ten years. The expected incremental salvage value is as follows:

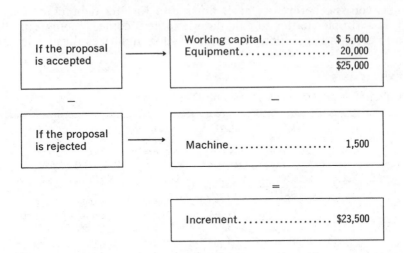

The $1,500 deduction needs some explanation. If the proposal is rejected, the company will keep its standby machine instead of selling it now. The estimated sale value of the equipment ten years from now is $1,500. The current salvage value of this machine, $6,000, was entered into the timetable through Exhibit 15–3 as a cash receipt (deduction from the initial cash outlay); its value ten years from now should be classified as an outlay (deduction from the end-of-life salvage value), as in the following table:

Years from Now	If Proposal Is Accepted	If Proposal Is Rejected	Incremental Cash Flows
0..................	+$6,000		+$6,000
10.................	—	+$1,500	− 1,500

Taxes on the Salvage Values

The estimated liquidation value of the incremental working capital, $5,000, is equal to its book value. The equipment required by the proposal, however, will have a tax basis of $18,364 at the end of ten years, as we can see in the bottom line of Exhibit 15–5. This is $1,636 less than the market value, and this amount is taxable. At a tax rate of 40 percent, the tax will be $654.

The standby machine the company will still have if the proposal is rejected will be fully depreciated ten years from now. The $1,500 liquidation value therefore will be fully taxable. The tax will be $600. The incremental after-tax salvage value is $23,446:

	Pre-tax Cash Flow	Income Tax	After-tax Cash Flow
Working capital.........	$ 5,000		$ 5,000
Equipment.............	20,000	$ 654	19,346
Standby equipment......	(1,500)	(600)	(900)
Net salvage value..	$23,500	$ 54	$23,446

The net tax impact in this case is negligible.

EVALUATING THE PROPOSAL

Once the cash flow estimates have been made, three stages of the evaluation process remain:

1. Calculating the net present value of the proposal.
2. Verifying the benchmark and revising the analysis, if appropriate.
3. Adjusting for uncertainty.

We shall summarize the first two of these in the next few paragraphs; uncertainty adjustments are discussed in Chapter 17.

Calculating Present Value

Once the cash flows have been estimated, calculating present value is a simple matter. The first step is to enter the cash flows in a time-table, as in the first three columns of Exhibit 15–7. The first column shows the initial outlay, the renovation outlay five years later, and the end-of-life salvage value. These are added to the operating cash flows to get the total cash flow figures in column (3).

EXHIBIT 15–7

Calculation of Present Value

Years from Now	(1) Investment Cash Flow after Taxes	(2) Operating Cash Flow after Taxes	(3) Total Cash Flow after Taxes (1) + (2)	(4) Present Value at 10% Multiplier*	(5) Present Value at 10% Amount (3) × (4)
0................	−$102,400	—	−$102,400	1.000	−$102,400
1................	—	+$23,600	+ 23,600	0.909	+ 21,452
2................	—	+ 21,840	+ 21,840	0.826	+ 18,040
3................	—	+ 20,632	+ 20,632	0.751	+ 15,495
4................	—	+ 19,506	+ 19,506	0.683	+ 13,323
5................	− 20,000	+ 18,605	− 1,395	0.621	− 866
6................	—	+ 19,484	+ 19,484	0.564	+ 10,989
7................	—	+ 18,587	+ 18,587	0.513	+ 9,535
8................	—	+ 17,870	+ 17,870	0.467	+ 8,345
9................	—	+ 17,296	+ 17,296	0.424	+ 7,334
10................	+ 23,446	+ 16,836	+ 40,282	0.386	+ 15,549
Total...........					+$ 16,796

* From Table 1, Appendix A.

The second step is to calculate the minimum acceptable rate of return. For our illustrative company, this is 10 percent after taxes.

The third step is to take present value multipliers from present value tables and apply these to the cash flows. The result of this step is shown in the right-hand column of the exhibit.

These calculations show that the present value of the modernization proposal is $16,796, the total of the figures in the right-hand column. This means that, if the estimates are correct, the future operating cash receipts will be big enough to pay back the amounts invested ($102,400 and $20,000) and pay interest on these amounts at an annual rate of 10 percent after taxes, with enough left over to increase the company's value now by $16,796. Other things being equal, the proposal should be accepted.

Verifying the Benchmark

The second stage in the evaluation process is making sure the proposal has been compared with the right benchmark. Two possibilities are worth noting:

1. The benefits sought can be achieved with a smaller investment outlay.
2. The benefits sought are inadequate to cover both the new investment and the continuing investment in existing facilities and working capital.

Same benefit; smaller investment. Many investment proposals are designed to provide capacity to handle new products or move into new markets. The cash flow estimates assign all the benefits from the new product or market to the proposed investment outlay. This may be a mistake.

A proposal to build a new warehouse, for example, may show a high net present value because warehouse space is necessary to support the sales of a new product. It may be, however, that some of the present warehouse space used to store low-margin items would be just as suitable for the new product as the new warehouse. Recognizing this can put the proposal in an entirely different light because it redefines the benchmark (see Exhibit 15–8).

Suppose the products with the lowest profit contributions provide total cash flows of $100,000, before deducting warehouse costs. The new product, requiring the same amount of space, would have total cash flows of $500,000. The company can improve its cash position by $400,000 without one penny of additional investment in warehouse space. This means that the new warehouse is really being built to enable the company to continue to sell its present low-margin products. The question is whether the investment in the new warehouse can be justified by annual cash flows of $100,000, not $500,000.

The disinvestment benchmark. Investments that appear worth making if the analysis is based on an invest/don't invest comparison may be totally unjustified if they are in support of unprofitable activities. The company might be better off to discontinue the activity en-

EXHIBIT 15–8

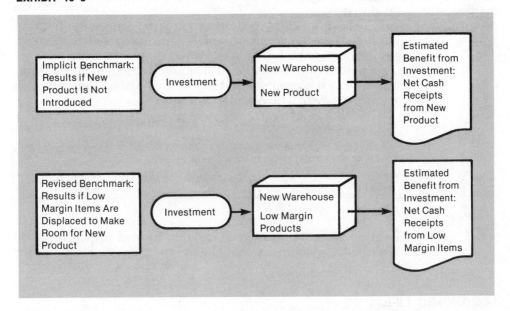

tirely than to continue on its present course. If this is so, then the cash inflows from the new investment proposal must be large enough to support both the new investment and the liquidation value of the present investment as well.

For example, suppose the company facing our plant modernization proposal could liquidate the present plant, equipment, and working capital now for $500,000 after taxes. If the plant were kept open but not modernized, its annual operating cash flow after taxes would be about $60,000, but routine replacement expenditures would run about $40,000 a year. At the end of ten years the plant, equipment, and working capital would bring in about $400,000, again after taxes. These figures are summarized in Exhibit 15–9. It is clear that unless

EXHIBIT 15–9

Present Value of Continuing the Present Operation

Years from Now	Cash Flow after Taxes			Present Value at 10 Percent	
	If Sell Now	If Keep	Difference	Multiplier	Amount
0..................	+$500,000	—	−$500,000	1.000	−$500,000
1 to 10.............	—	+$ 20,000 a year	+ 20,000 a year	6.145*	+ 122,900
10.................	—	+ 400,000	+ 400,000	0.386†	+ 154,400
Total..........					−$222,700

* From Table 2, Appendix A.
† From Table 1, Appendix A.

something drastic can be done to improve the cash flows, the plant should be closed.

This being the case, continued operation is no longer the relevant benchmark. The question now is whether the proposed modernization is good enough to restore this operation to health. If not, the additional expenditure would be wasted. The comparison, in other words, should be between the proposal and the best available alternative, in this case to close down. The calculation is:

Present value if operated in present condition (Exhibit 15–9)............ −$222,700
Present value of contribution from renovation (Exhibit 15–7)............. +   16,796
   Net present value... −$205,904

The renovation proposal is not good enough. Instead of pouring good money after bad, the company should close the plant and reinvest the proceeds elsewhere.

ECONOMIC LIFE

In principle, cash flows should be estimated for the period known as the economic life of the investment. The economic life of any asset is the time elapsing between the time of acquisition and the time at which the combined forces of obsolescence and deterioration justify replacing it or withdrawing it from service. The economic life of any tangible asset is the *shortest* of the following three figures:

1. Physical life.
2. Technological life.
3. Market life of the asset's output.

Comparison of the concepts. Although many assets can be repaired and kept in service almost indefinitely, physical life generally comes to an end when replacing an asset is cheaper than continuing to repair it. Physical life is seldom the measure of economic life in a rapidly changing economy, however. New processes and new equipment often make existing equipment obsolete long before physical life comes to an end—that is, the spread between the cash flows from operating the asset and the cash flows from operating a new asset may become wide enough to justify replacement even if the old asset's operating costs have not risen at all.

Finally, the product market may change even before this happens, so that the company can no longer sell the asset's output at a profitable price. When this happens, life comes to an end even though technological obsolescence has not yet taken its toll.

Life of an individual asset. As in human life expectancy calculations, economic life is a probabilistic notion. Of any group of similar depreciating assets, death will come to some soon after birth; others may have very long lives. Exhibit 15–10 shows one company's experi-

EXHIBIT 15–10

Survival Curve for Industrial Equipment

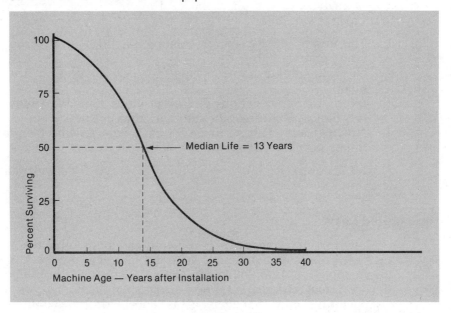

ence with the mortality of one type of industrial equipment. In this case the median historical life expectancy was approximately 13 years, meaning that half of the machines lived longer and half were retired before the end of 13 years.

Project life. Historical data of this sort may be useful in estimating the economic lives of the facilities provided for specific investment proposals, particularly when the proposals are for the replacement of existing equipment. The economic life of an investment project, however, may be very different from the life of any one of the assets required by the project. It may include buildings with a life of 50 years, production equipment with a life of 15 years, test equipment with a 3-year life, and working capital with an infinite life.

The estimated life of such a project is determined not so much by the lives of the physical facilities as by the expected duration of the stream of cash flows generated by the project. The life of the investment, in other words, will end when the present value of the remaining cash flows has fallen below the recovery value of the facilities and working capital.

SOME RECURRING QUESTIONS

The measures of costs or of revenues and expenses prepared for financial reporting sometimes affect investment decisions even though they don't measure current cash flows. Similarly, some cash flows, though not project related, are sometimes incorrectly included in cash flow timetables.

Our analysis of the plant modernization proposal has dealt with four of these situations:

1. The unamortized costs of existing facilities or programs have been ignored.
2. No deductions have been made for depreciation on new equipment.
3. Internal cost allocations and absorptions have been ignored unless they approximate the differential cash flows.
4. No provision has been made for cash flows arising from borrowing or debt repayment transactions.

A brief review of each of these should help avoid misunderstandings later on.

Unamortized Costs

Management often finds it difficult to ignore amounts spent in the past to provide equipment or to develop new products. Suppose, for example, an automobile company has spent $400 million to design, test, tool, and market a new automobile model. Sales have been disappointing and management is considering discontinuing the model. Only $220 million of the development and marketing costs have been amortized, however, leaving $180 million in tooling costs to be written off now if the company decides to drop the model from the line (see Exhibit 15–11).

The $180 million in unamortized costs is irrelevant to the decision to discontinue the model—it is not a cash flow. Even so, it may influence the decision:

1. Money is always spent to create value. Belief that a value has been created is slow to die, and managers are often reluctant to terminate an old project. ("It's a shame to write off all that money. If we just put in another $100 million, the model is sure to take hold.")
2. Managers often think of costs as amounts to be recovered. If not recovered as originally intended, they have to be charged against something else. ("We can't accept that proposal. It won't cover amortization of the costs of tooling we already have.") Result: proposals that don't bring in enough cash to cover depreciation of past outlays as well as future cash outlays may be turned down.

These are two examples of the *sunk cost fallacy*, the notion that costs not yet amortized are somehow relevant to decision making. One of these makes it harder to get rid of old projects; the other makes it harder to adopt new ones. The relevant concept in both cases is opportunity cost: What is the present salvage value of the investment, and by how much will that salvage value decline if the investment is not liquidated now? The amounts invested in the past are sunk costs; neither they nor amortization of them are relevant to today's decisions.

EXHIBIT 15–11

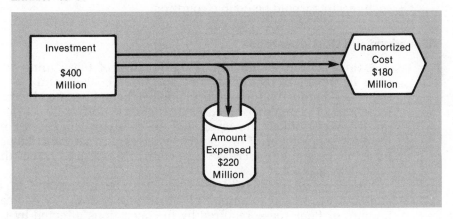

Depreciation on New Facilities

Annual depreciation charges on the equipment required by the plant modernization proposal were not reflected in the $25,000 annual cash flow. Depreciation charges don't measure cash flows. This doesn't mean that present value calculations overlook depreciation, however. Depreciation is real and can't be ignored. It is the difference between the initial outlay and the end-of-life salvage value:

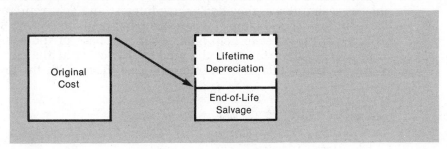

Accountants recognize depreciation for financial reporting by spreading it in some fashion over the assets' estimated lives. They reflect it in present value analysis by entering two amounts in the cash flow timetable—the initial outlay and the end-of-life salvage value—at the times these cash flows take place.

For example, on an investment proposal calling for an outlay of $60,000 now and a residual value of $3,000 in three years, the lifetime depreciation amounts to $57,000. This enters the timetable in the following way:

Time	Cash Flow
0.........................	−$60,000
3.........................	+ 3,000
Total......................	−$57,000

Entering depreciation again in the form of annual deductions from cash receipts would be double counting.

Allocations and Cost Absorption

A third source of difficulty is the practice of reassigning overhead costs by means of overhead rates and interdepartmental cost allocations. One company, for instance, applies factory overhead to products by means of a predetermined overhead rate of $2 a direct labor dollar. It is very unlikely, however, that the company will save $2 in overhead for every dollar of direct labor it saves. In fact, most laborsaving investments actually increase total company overhead rather than the other way around.

Interdepartmental cost allocations can be misleading in a very similar way. In our example, plant modernization will decrease the amount of floor space required by the operations affected by the proposal. This will reduce the amount of building occupancy costs allocated to these operations. The opportunity cost of the space saved is zero, however, because the company has no way of using it or renting it out. The cash flow estimates must ignore this apparent difference in costs.

Specific Borrowing and Interest Costs

Timetables for capital expenditure proposals don't show borrowings as cash inflows; they don't show interest and debt retirements as cash outflows. For example, if our company plans to borrow $50,000 at 8 percent interest to help finance the purchase of the equipment, with an obligation to repay the amount borrowed at the end of five years, we might identify the following cash flows with the proposal:

Years from Now	Cash Flow
0	+$50,000
1–5	− 4,000
5	− 50,000

We didn't do this, for a very simple reason. The cost of capital is used to discount the anticipated cash flows generated by capital expenditure proposals. Interest is one of the costs of the company's long-term capital. The discounting process charges interest as well as the other components of the cost of capital against project cash flows. A project with a zero net present value is one that just covers its cost of capital. To deduct interest again as a cash flow therefore would be to count it twice. Neither interest nor the amortization of long-term debt should be deducted explicitly from project cash flows even when the project is financed specifically by a particular issue of long-term debt.

Nonseasonal short-term interest-bearing debt should be classified as long-term debt for this purpose, because it provides part of the long-term capital to finance the project. Interest on seasonal short-term debt, on the other hand, is an explicit cash outlay that is not provided for by the discounting process. It should be deducted in computing annual cash flows. Similarly, interest on any seasonal investments of project funds can be regarded as a cash inflow for the project.

SUMMARY

This chapter has applied the measurement concepts we developed in Chapter 3 to the requirements of capital expenditure decision models. In calculating net present value or the internal rate of return, the analyst has to estimate the economic life of the investment, the amount and timing of the investment outlays, the amount and timing of the operating cash flows, and the end-of-life salvage value attributable to the proposal.

All of these estimates should reflect differential or incremental cash flows, not accounting allocations made for other purposes. Sunk costs should be ignored. Finally, all cash flows should be adjusted for the impact of income taxes.

Once the analysis has been completed, management still has to evaluate the proposal. For one thing, the sponsors of the proposal may have based their analysis on the wrong benchmark—the company may be better off to discontinue an activity completely than to pour more money into it. Another problem is that the cash flows are uncertain. We shall look at this aspect of the problem in Chapter 17.

KEY TERMS

The key terms in this chapter are all drawn from Chapters 3 and 14. The reader may wish to review the lists in those chapters at this point.

INDEPENDENT STUDY PROBLEMS
(Solutions in Appendix C)

1. **Estimating cash flows.** A proposal is made to purchase and install a new machine to replace an existing machine. The existing machine has a book value of $20,000, current salvage value of $8,000, and annual depreciation of $3,000. Annual out-of-pocket operating cost is now $10,000.

The replacement machine would cost $50,000 delivered. It would cost $10,000 to train employees to operate the machine, and this amount can be written off immediately for tax purposes. An immediate tax credit of 7 percent of the capitalizable outlay is available as an investment credit to reduce current taxes. Annual out-of-pocket operating cost of the new machine would be $3,200.

The first year's tax depreciation on the new machine would be 30 percent of the amount capitalized. The income tax rate is 40 percent.

a. Compute the net incremental after-tax investment outlay required by this proposal.

  b. Compute the after-tax net cash operating savings for the first year
        of operation of the replacement machine.

  2. Equipment replacement. The expected life of a proposed new facility
is ten years, the installed cost will be $50,000, and the expected end-of-life
salvage value is zero. The equipment will replace facilities now in use that
have a book value of $30,000 and a market value of $10,000. The remaining tax life of the old facilities is eight years.
  Double-rate, declining-balance depreciation will be used on the new
facilities. The undepreciated balance remaining at the end of five years
will be depreciated on a straight-line basis over the next five years. The
present facilities are being depreciated by the straight-line method down
to an end-of-line salvage value of zero.
  Estimated before-tax, before-depreciation cash savings amount to
$20,000 per year. The tax rate is 50 percent, and all savings are assumed
to take place at the end of each year.

  a. Compute the incremental after-tax present value of this proposal at
        10 percent.
  b. Compute the incremental after-tax internal rate of return on this pro-
        posal.

EXERCISES AND PROBLEMS

  1. Exercises in after-tax investment analysis. The initial investment is
$30,000. The before-tax annual cash inflow is $10,000 and will last for
six years. Depreciation for tax purposes is by the straight-line method,
based on a six-year life and no salvage value. The income tax rate is 40
percent and taxes are to be paid at the same time as the cash flows to
which they relate. The minimum acceptable rate of return is 15 percent.
Annual cash flows occur at the end of the year.

  a. Prepare a timetable of the after-tax cash flows.
  b. Calculate the reciprocal of the after-tax payback period.
  c. Calculate the after-tax net present value.
  d. Calculate the after-tax internal rate of return.
  e. Calculate the effect on net present value of changing to sum-of-the-
        years'-digits depreciation for tax purposes.
  f. Calculate the effect on net present value of expensing the entire in-
        vestment outlay immediately for tax purposes.

                                                                  (CPA adapted)

  2. Cost-reducing investment. An investment in equipment would reduce factory labor costs by $20,000 a year for five years. Factory overhead
costs are assigned to products by means of a predetermined overhead rate
of 75 percent of direct labor cost. Forty percent of factory overhead costs
at normal volume are proportionally variable with volume. Maintenance
and energy requirements of the new machine would increase fixed factory
overhead costs by $2,000 a year.
  The equipment would cost $72,000 and would be depreciated for tax
purposes on a sum-of-the-years'-digits basis over a five-year period, with
zero salvage anticipated. The company has a minimum acceptable after-
tax return on investment of 10 percent. The tax rate is 40 percent. All
operating and tax cash flows are assumed to occur at year-end.

  a. Prepare a table of cash flows for this proposal.

b. Calculate net present value. Should the investment be made?

3. Estimating after-tax cash flows. Company X is considering a proposal to increase the degree of automation in one of its manufacturing departments. The following estimates have been made:

1. Initial outlay, $100,000, of which $20,000 would be expensed immediately for tax purposes. No investment credit would be applicable.
2. The capitalized portion of the initial outlay would be depreciated for tax purposes at a straight-line rate of 10 percent a year, starting the first year.
3. The net annual before-tax cash savings would be $22,000, starting immediately after installation.
4. The facilities would be obsolete at the end of six years of operation, at which time they would be dismantled at a cash cost of $5,000 and sold for scrap. Scrap recovery at that time would be $1,000.
5. The company's effective income tax rate is expected to be 50 percent.
6. All cash flows after the initial outlay are expected to take place at year-end.

a. Calculate the after-tax initial outlay.
b. Calculate the expected after-tax cash inflow for the second year.
c. Calculate the anticipated effect of this proposal on the company's net income for the third year.
d. Calculate the after-tax cash flow from dismantling and scrap recovery at the end of six years.

4. Special order: Pretax cash flows. Dailey Company makes door locks. A mail-order house has asked Dailey to supply 400,000 locks during the next year at a price of $3 each. Payment for 300,000 locks would be received next year; payment for the remainder would be received a year later.

The locks would be made in the company's regular production departments, but a new machine costing $100,000 would have to be bought and paid for immediately. Depreciation of $20,000 a year would be included in the factory overhead rate.

The estimated manufacturing cost of one of these locks is expected to be as follows:

Materials.....................	$0.70
Labor........................	1.20
Overhead (50% of	
labor cost)..................	0.60
Total....................	$2.50

Half of the normal overhead costs are classified as variable. Work on this contract would lead to an increase in fixed factory overhead costs amounting to $50,000 a year, including the depreciation on the new machine.

A commission of 5 cents a lock would be paid to the sales representative in charge of the mail-order house account. Other selling and administrative expenses would be unaffected.

Materials costing $70,000 would have to be bought and paid for in advance. The remaining materials would be bought during the year and paid for immediately, as payments were received from the mail-order house. The new equipment would be worth $50,000 at the end of the year.

Prepare a schedule of pretax cash flows for this proposal.

5. Estimating necessary cash receipts. Orville Iron Nerves has been offered the opportunity to provide catering services at a private golf club. The contract would run for eight years and would require a payment of $7,000 a year at the end of each year.

Mr. Iron Nerves estimates that $8,000 would have to be paid in cash immediately to buy the necessary equipment. The equipment would have an eight-year life, zero salvage value, and would be depreciated on a straight-line basis for tax purposes. He also estimates a 40 percent contribution margin from sales resulting from the catering service.

If Mr. Iron Nerves wants to earn a 14 percent return after taxes on his investment, if the income tax rate is 50 percent, and if receipts from sales are the same for each of the eight years, how many dollars of sales receipts must the catering services provide each year? You should assume that cash flows always take place at the end of the year.

(Prepared by Professor Philip Meyers)

6. Pretax versus after-tax analysis. You have the following figures relating to a proposal to purchase and install new factory equipment:

1. The company's cost of capital is 10 percent after taxes; this is assumed to be equivalent to 20 percent before taxes.

2. Initial investment outlays amount to $80,000, of which $30,000 can be expensed immediately for tax purposes.

3. The capitalized portion of the initial outlay is subject to special amortization treatment. Fifty percent of the capitalized cost can be written off in equal annual installments during the first five years. The remainder is subject to depreciation at the normal straight-line rate of 6 percent per year, including the first five years.

4. The investment is expected to produce net cash receipts (before taxes) of $16,500 a year for the first five years, $11,500 a year for the next five years, and $6,500 a year for the third five years.

5. It is expected that the facilities will be retired at the end of 15 years and that salvage value will be $5,000.

6. All taxes are to be computed on the basis of a 50 percent tax rate.

Analyze this proposal on both a before-tax and an after-tax basis. How, if at all, would your recommendation to management be different if you used the before-tax basis instead of the after-tax basis?

7. Tax shield. It is sometimes useful to separate the after-tax cash flows into two parts: (1) the pretax cash flows, less the taxes that would accrue to these cash flows in the absence of depreciation charges and other items on the tax return not representing current cash flows; and (2) the effects of these other items on taxes. This second component is known as the tax shield.

Make this separation for the proposal described in Problem 6 and calculate the present value of each of these two components.

8. Investment in new facilities: Relevant benchmark. The Artling Corporation manufactures four products in four identical processing operations. The only differences among the four products are in the raw materials used. The facilities are completely interchangeable, although they differ slightly, with newer machines having higher depreciation and generally lower operating costs than older machines. Processing costs (that is, all costs other than material costs) are determined by the machines used, not by the product being manufactured.

The company is now considering a proposal to acquire a fifth set of processing facilities to manufacture a new, higher grade of product, using a more expensive raw material that has just come on the market. All machines, new as well as old, would still be completely interchangeable but the new machine would probably be used to make the new product.

The following table shows the selling prices of the five products and all of the costs per pound that would be incurred in the factory to operate the machines:

Product	Machine Used	Selling Price	Materials Cost	Depreciation Cost	Other Factory Costs	Gross Margin
A........... 1		$0.60	$0.15	$0.12	$0.31	$0.02
B.......... 2		0.66	0.20	0.12	0.30	0.04
C.......... 3		0.73	0.25	0.13	0.28	0.07
D.......... 4		0.81	0.30	0.13	0.29	0.09
E*......... 5*		0.90	0.35	0.14	0.29	0.12

* Proposed.

Depreciation cost per pound is based on estimated annual production of 200,000 pounds of each product and an estimated life of ten years. Estimated salvage value of the production equipment is zero; in fact, once the facilities are installed, their only market value is their scrap value.

In support of the proposal to add the fifth product and corresponding facilities, the sales manager of the Artling Company has pointed out that this would increase the company's gross margin by $24,000 ($0.12 a pound on an added sales volume of 200,000 pounds annually). Variable selling and administrative costs amount to 5 percent of sales.

Compute the incremental annual cash flow that you would use in deciding whether the proposed investment is adequately profitable. State your reasoning. Ignore income taxes.

9. Special order: Pretax cash flows. Lochinvar Company has an opportunity to manufacture 100,000 custom-designed wafflestands on contract for Greeley Corporation. The contract price would be $10. Deliveries would begin 6 months from now and continue for about 27 months. Production would take place in a building rented especially for the purpose.

Under the terms of the contract, Greeley would pay Lochinvar $100,000 immediately to help Lochinvar tool up for this special order. It would pay $8 for each of the first 50,000 units delivered plus $10 for each of the next 50,000 units. Deliveries would be 15,000 units this year, 45,000 units next year, and 40,000 units the third year. Greeley's payments for these units would be made at the time of delivery.

Lochinvar would need to buy special equipment for $80,000 immediately, spend $30,000 to get it installed, and pay $50,000 in cash for the initial materials inventory. Manufacturing costs would be as follows:

Materials..................... $2 a unit
Labor........................ $3 a unit
Overhead.................... $60,000 a year

The annual overhead costs would include $20,000 in depreciation on the new equipment. Total overhead would be only $50,000 the first year because the new facilities would not be in operation for the whole year. A full year's depreciation would be taken, however. No allocations of divisional or corporate overhead costs are included in these figures.

Materials inventories would remain constant until early in the third year. They would be completely used up by the time work on the contract

was completed. There would be no work in process at the end of any year.
   Additional selling and administrative costs of $45,000 would be in-
curred in each of the next three years.
   Lochinvar's management estimates that the new equipment would have
a $10,000 market value at the end of the third year. It seems very unlikely
to have any usefulness to Lochinvar after that time.

   Prepare a timetable of the pretax cash flows associated with this proposal. Operating cash flows should be assumed to take place in each case
at the end of the year.

10. Special order: Tax effects. Lochinvar's management (Problem 9)
evaluates all capital expenditure proposals by discounting the after-tax
cash flows to their present value at 8 percent. The income tax rate is 55
percent. Equipment installation costs are capitalized for tax purposes. Depreciation for tax purposes would be based on the straight-line method
over a five-year period, with zero net salvage value.
   Taxable revenue would be $10 a unit. For tax purposes all manufactur-
ing costs would be assigned to the cost of goods sold in the year in which
they would be incurred. Income taxes would be paid at the end of the year
in which they were accrued.

a.   Calculate the after-tax cash flows.
b.   Calculate the net present value of this proposal. Should the contract
       be signed?

11. Introduce a new product; Rent or buy equipment. Edwards Corporation is a manufacturing concern that produces and sells a wide range of
products. The company not only mass produces a number of products and
equipment components but also is capable of producing special-purpose
manufacturing equipment to customer specifications.
   The firm is considering adding a new stapler to one of its product lines.
More equipment will be required to produce the new stapler. There are
three alternative ways to acquire the needed equipment: (1) purchase
general-purpose equipment, (2) lease general-purpose equipment, (3)
build special-purpose equipment. A fourth alternative, purchase of the
special-purpose equipment, has been ruled out because it would be prohibitively expensive.
   The general-purpose equipment can be purchased for $125,000. The
equipment has an estimated salvage of $15,000 at the end of its useful life
of ten years. At the end of five years the equipment can be used elsewhere
in the plant or be sold for $40,000.
   Alternatively, the general-purpose equipment can be acquired by a five-
year lease for $40,000 annual rent. The lessor will assume all responsi-
bility for taxes, insurance, and maintenance.
   Finally, special-purpose equipment can be constructed by the contract
equipment department of the Edwards Corporation. While the department
is operating at a level which is normal for the time of year, it is below full
capacity. The department could produce the equipment without interfer-
ing with its regular revenue-producing activities.
   The estimated departmental costs for the construction of the special-
purpose equipment are

Materials and parts...	$ 75,000
Direct labor..	60,000
Variable overhead (50 percent of direct labor dollars).........	30,000
Fixed overhead (25 percent of direct labor dollars)...........	15,000
Total..	$180,000

Corporation general and administrative costs are fixed, averaging 20 percent of the direct labor dollar content of factory production.

Additional working capital of $60,000 will have to be provided if any of these three alternatives is selected. Half the increase in working capital will be required immediately, the other half by the end of the first year. This working capital can be recovered at any time if the company decides to discontinue manufacture and sale of the new stapler.

Engineering and management studies provide the following revenue and cost estimates (excluding lease payments and depreciation) for producing the new stapler depending upon the equipment used:

	General-Purpose Equipment		Self Constructed Equipment
	Leased	Purchased	
Unit selling price............................	$ 5.00	$ 5.00	$ 5.00
Unit production costs:			
Materials.................................	$ 1.80	$ 1.80	$ 1.70
Conversion costs........................	1.60	1.60	1.40
Total unit production costs..........	$ 3.40	$ 3.40	$ 3.10
Unit contribution margin...................	$ 1.60	$ 1.60	$ 1.90
Estimated unit volume.....................	40,000	40,000	40,000
Estimated total contribution margin........	$64,000	$64,000	$76,000
Other costs:			
Supervision.............................	$16,000	$16,000	$18,000
Taxes and insurance.....................	—	3,000	5,000
Maintenance............................	—	3,000	2,000
Total................................	$16,000	$22,000	$25,000

The company will depreciate the general-purpose machine over ten years on the sum-of-the-years-digits (SYD) method for tax purposes. At the end of five years the accumulated depreciation will total $80,000. The special-purpose machine will be depreciated over five years on the SYD method. Its salvage value at the end of that time is estimated to be $30,-000.

The company uses an after-tax cost of capital of 10 percent. Its marginal tax rate is 40 percent.

a. Calculate the net present value for each of the three alternatives that Edwards Corporation has at its disposal.
b. Should Edwards Corporation select any of the three options, and if so, which one? Explain your answer.

(CMA adapted)

12. Dropping a product from the line. The Weatherall Company is thinking of discontinuing manufacture and sale of product A. You are given the following information:

1. The projected monthly income statement for product A as is follows:

Sales...		$80,000
Less:		
Cost of goods sold (standard)....................	$64,000	
Selling and administrative expenses.............	25,000	89,000
Net Income (Loss)...............................		$(9,000)

2. Product A is manufactured in two departments, and its standard unit cost is as follows:

	Dept. X	Dept. Y	Total
Materials..................	$1.00	$0.50	$1.50
Labor.....................	1.50	0.75	2.25
Overhead.................	3.00	1.25	4.25
Total..............	$5.50	$2.50	$8.00

3. The budgeted overhead cost structure in the two departments is as follows ("DL$" stands for "direct labor dollars"). Before using these figures, see items (4) and (5) below.

	Dept. X	Dept. Y
Traceable fixed overhead.........	$40,000 per mo.	$20,000 per mo.
Traceable variable overhead......	$ 0.80 per DL$	$ 0.60 per DL$
Allocated costs..................	{ $20,000 per mo. { +$0.20 per DL$	{ $ 6,000 per mo. { +$0.20 per DL$
Standard monthly volume........	60,000 DL$	30,000 DL$

4. A study reveals that traceable fixed costs in department Y include a $2,000 step function for each 6,000 direct labor dollars—that is, fixed costs increase by $2,000 a month any time that monthly departmental production volume increases by a full 6,000 direct labor dollars. (If volume increases by 11,000 direct labor dollars a month, the fixed cost increase is still $2,000; but if the increase is 12,000 direct labor dollars, the fixed cost goes up by $4,000 a month.) Traceable fixed costs in department X have no step function.

5. Of the allocated costs, the only items likely to be eliminated by the discontinuation of product A amount to $500 a month in department X and 6 cents a direct labor dollar in department Y.

6. Selling and administrative costs charged to product A include (a) $5,000 a month for product advertising, free samples, product display material, etc.; (b) 10 cents per sales dollar for sales commissions and patent royalty payments; (c) 4 cents per sales dollar as an allocation of field selling expenses, market research, etc.; and (d) 11 cents per sales dollar for the product's share of head office expenses. Total company costs in these latter two categories would be unaffected by the discontinuation of product A.

7. The sales force estimates that sales of substitute products in the company's line could be increased by $10,000 a month if product A were abandoned. The average ratio of contribution margin to selling price for these products is 40 percent, and the increased volume in these lines would not affect fixed costs in any way.

8. It is estimated that the only investment that would be released by withdrawal of product A from the market would be working capital with a book value of $300,000. This figure includes inventories at their book value of $150,000; before-tax proceeds from liquidation of these inventories would total about $110,000. Other elements of working capital would be fully recoverable.

9. The income tax rate is 50 percent and the required minimum rate of return on capital expenditure proposals is 8 percent after taxes.

10. Remember that all figures except those given in terms (8) and (9) are *monthly* figures.

Should product A be withdrawn from the market? Show and label your calculations, explaining your reasoning if necessary.

13. Closing a branch office. The Barnstable Company manufactures and distributes through retail outlets a line of electrical products and appliances. Distribution of the company's products is accomplished through 12 regional branch offices, each of which has responsibility for maintaining adequate inventories, granting customer credit, and for collecting accounts receivable. List prices are established in the head office of the Barnstable Company, but each branch manager has authority to set the policy on discounts, returns, and allowances to meet competitive conditions in the region served by that branch.

For a number of years the company has followed the practice of preparing income statements for each branch. The San Francisco branch profit has declined from approximately $50,000 a year five years ago to a loss of $38,000 last year. Last year's income statements for this branch and a somewhat larger branch at Los Angeles were as follows (in thousands):

	San Francisco	Los Angeles
Gross sales (at list prices)......................................	$488	$675
Discounts, freight, returns, and allowances....................	72	58
Net sales...	$416	$617
Manufacturing cost of goods sold (at standard)..............	293	367.
Gross margin...	$123	$250
Branch expenses:		
Salaries and commissions......................................	$ 73	$104
Travel and entertainment......................................	15	16
Office expense...	12	13
Bad debt losses...	5	3
Miscellaneous...	6	5
Total branch expenses.....................................	$111	$141
Branch margin...	$ 12	$109
Home office charges...	50	74
Branch Net Profit (Loss).......................................	$(38)	$ 35

Capital invested at the branch consists of $90,000 in receivables (after deducting a provision for uncollectible accounts) and $50,000 in inventories. Because the branch has no depreciable assets, no depreciation charges are included in the branch expenses.

The controller of the Barnstable Company has undertaken an analysis to determine whether it would be profitable to close the San Francisco branch and serve the region from Los Angeles. Analysis of costs and expenses has produced the following estimates:

1. If the San Francisco branch remains in operation, branch margins at both the San Francisco and Los Angeles branches are likely to remain at last year's levels for the foreseeable future.

2. If the San Francisco branch were closed, approximately $400,000 in gross sales could be retained by sales people working out of Los Angeles. Discounts, freight, returns, and allowances on these sales would total $60,000 a year. The product mix in the San Francisco area would be the same at this lower volume as at the current sales volume.

3. An analysis of the company's factory costs indicate that manufacturing costs are approximately 70 percent variable and 30 percent fixed at standard volumes.

4. The San Francisco branch has five sales representatives on its payroll. Each sales representative is paid a salary of $2,000 a year plus a

sales commission. Sales commissions are computed at 12 percent of net sales. If the San Francisco office were closed, two of its sales people would be added to the Los Angeles sales force at the same salary and commission rates. The other three San Francisco sales people would be transferred to other positions in the company, as replacements for other employees who are retiring or leaving the company.

5. Closing of the San Francisco office would eliminate completely all other San Francisco branch expenses, but it is estimated that expenses of the Los Angeles office would be increased by $36,000 a year in addition to the specific items mentioned above.

6. Home office administrative expense is distributed to the branches at 12 percent of net sales. Past experience has indicated, however, that the variable portion of these expenses is only 4 percent of net sales.

7. The Los Angeles investment in inventory and receivables would increase by $20,000 and $80,000, respectively, if the San Francisco branch were closed and the San Francisco area were served from Los Angeles.

8. After taxes at 50 percent, the company's minimum acceptable return on investment is 8 percent.

a. If you had to choose between operating the San Francisco branch and abandoning the territory entirely, what would you do? Show your calculations.

b. Given the added choice of serving the territory from Los Angeles, which of the three alternatives would you recommend? Show your calculations.

CASE 15–1: SOVAD, S.A.* (Expansion Proposal)

Mr. Walter Weber, general manager of Sovad, S.A., looked across his desk at Mr. Karl Huber, the company's sales manager. Mr. Huber had just suggested that Sovad increase its capacity to manufacture automatic timing devices.

"All right," said Mr. Weber, "let's see if the profits from the increased sales will give us a big enough return on investment. As soon as you're ready, give Mr. Berner (the company's controller) your estimates of sales and what you'll need for advertising and sales promotion. He can work with purchasing and manufacturing to get the rest of the data he needs. I'll ask him to give me a recommendation on your proposal sometime next week."

Sovad, S.A. was a manufacturer of industrial controls and precision instruments, with headquarters and manufacturing facilities in Winterthur, Switzerland. Its manufacturing operations in 1967 were conducted entirely in Winterthur, but more than half of its 1967 sales were made in other countries.

First introduced in 1964, the company's automatic timers had been well received by Sovad's customers both at home and abroad. By 1967 Sovad was selling all that it could manufacture. Mr. Huber was convinced that he could expand his sales in Switzerland by large amounts if adequate factory capacity could be provided.

---

* Copyright by l'Institut pour l'Etude des Méthodes de Direction de l'Entreprise (IMEDE), Lausanne, Switzerland. Reprinted by permission. Amounts have been restated in dollars.

Before coming to Mr. Weber with his suggestion, Mr. Huber had discussed the idea of expansion with Mr. Gluck, the company's director of manufacturing. "Our Winterthur factory is already crowded," Mr. Gluck told him. "The authorities won't give us a building permit to expand it, but I know of some vacant space that we can rent in Zurich for $50,000 a year. We could put all the timer operations in there." Zurich is only 15 miles from Winterthur and Mr. Gluck was confident that he could supervise manufacturing operations in both places without difficulty.

TABLE 1

ZURICH TIMER FACTORY
Preliminary Profitability Estimate

Sales (300,000 units at $5)		$1,500,000
Out of pocket expenses:		
Factory labor and materials (300,000 units at $2.84)..	$852,000	
Rent.....................................	50,000	
Other factory costs (not including depreciation).......	70,000	
Marketing expenses...............................	160,000	
Total expenses....................................		1,132,000
Profit contribution.....................................		$ 368,000
Equipment required:		
New equipment to be purchased....................	$250,000	
Old equipment, to be moved from Winterthur.......	0	
Cost of moving old equipment from Winterthur and installing it at Zurich........................	5,000	
Total...		$ 255,000

$$\text{Payback period} = \frac{\$255,000}{\$368,000} = 0.69 \text{ years} = 8.3 \text{ months.}$$

Working with Mr. Gluck, Mr. Huber prepared the preliminary estimates shown in Table 1. As he gave this exhibit to Mr. Berner, Mr. Huber remarked that an eight-month payback period was hard to beat. He hoped that Mr. Berner wouldn't take too long to pass the proposal on to Mr. Weber for approval.

In the course of his examination of these figures, Mr. Berner discovered two things. First, the sales and expense figures given in Table 1 were not expected to be achieved until the third year of the new factory's operation. Second, they represented the *total* sales and expenses of the timers. Since the company was already selling 100,000 timers a year, Mr. Berner did not believe that the profit on these units should be used to justify the opening of the new factory. As he put it, "The data that we need are differential or incremental figures, the differences between having the new factory and not having it." Mr. Huber estimated that he would be able to sell 300,000 timers a year after a two-year introductory period. His detailed estimates of annual sales and marketing expenses are summarized in Table 2.

Mr. Berner knew that these volumes of sales would require sizable investments in working capital which Mr. Huber had omitted from Table 1. On the basis of the company's past experience, he estimated that the cumulative balance of working capital required at the beginning of each year would be as follows:

If timers are manufactured in Zurich:

Year 1	$700,000
Year 2	750,000
Year 3	800,000
If timers are not manufactured in Zurich	$300,000

When questioned about the manufacturing cost estimates in Table 1, Mr. Gluck gave Mr. Berner the figures shown in Table 3. Mr. Gluck explained that if the Zurich factory were opened, all automatic timer production would be shifted to Zurich. If the expansion proposal were to be rejected, however, the cost of producing 100,000 timers a year at Winterthur would be $3.10 a unit plus $20,000 a year. All of these costs could be eliminated if operations were transferred to Zurich.

TABLE 2

ZURICH TIMER FACTORY
Estimated Annual Timer Sales and Marketing Expenses

	Annual Sales		Annual Marketing Costs
	Units	Value	
If all timers are manufactured in Zurich:			
Year 1	200,000	$1,000,000	$260,000
Year 2	250,000	1,250,000	260,000
Year 3 and after	300,000	1,500,000	160,000
If timers are not manufactured in Zurich	100,000	$ 500,000	$ 60,000

TABLE 3

ZURICH TIMER FACTORY
Estimated Factory Costs

	Variable Costs per Unit	Fixed Costs per Year		
		Rental	Depreciation	Other
Year 1	$2.96	$50,000	$25,000	$70,000
Year 2	2.88	50,000	25,000	70,000
Year 3 and after	2.84	50,000	25,000	70,000

Mr. Berner also questioned Mr. Gluck about the equipment that would be moved from Winterthur to Zurich. "That is the old test equipment that we are now replacing here in Winterthur," he replied. "It's perfectly adequate for the timers, and it saves us from buying new equipment for the new location. It's fully depreciated on our books, but it's in perfect condition and I see no reason why it wouldn't last for years.

"If we don't open up in Zurich, we'll sell this old equipment locally for about $10,000. If we keep it, our only cost will be about $5,000 to get it from Winterthur to Zurich. We can subtract this $5,000 from the taxable income from our other operations right away, even before we start operating at Zurich."

For purposes of analysis, Mr. Berner and Mr. Huber agreed that the new Zurich plant should be able to operate for at least ten years and that the company's investment in working capital would be a reasonable measure of the value of the Zurich assets at the end of that time.

In evaluating capital expenditure proposals, Mr. Berner used an income tax rate of 30 percent of ordinary taxable income. Gains on the sale of equipment were also taxed at a 30 percent rate. Depreciation for tax purposes on the new equipment to be purchased for the Zurich plant would be $50,000 a year for five years.

a. Prepare a timetable of the before-tax cash flows that are relevant to the evaluation of this expansion proposal. Do you agree with Mr. Berner that these should be differential figures?

b. If Sovad required at least a 20 percent return on investment before income taxes, should Sovad have opened the Zurich factory?

c. How would your analysis differ if you were to use after-tax cash flows and a minimum acceptable rate of return of 14 percent?

16

Costs for Pricing Decisions

DECIDING how much to charge for products or services can be very simple or very complex. Sometimes the choice is obvious—match the price of a major competitor or competitors and concentrate on other things. In general, however, management can choose, and the wisdom of these choices may determine whether the company will succeed or fail.

One short chapter can't hope to cover all aspects of the pricing decision. For this reason, we shall limit ourselves to four topics that relate most closely to the use of cost accounting data in pricing:

1. Pricing strategy.
2. A short-run profit-maximizing model.
3. Cost-based pricing formulas.
4. Price differentiation.

PRICING STRATEGIES

A key element in product pricing is the underlying pricing strategy. The pricing strategy establishes the role price is expected to play in the marketing mix and what it is expected to accomplish. Two basic strategies are available:

1. *Skimming pricing* is a short-run profit-maximizing strategy. It calls for relatively high prices, reflecting a decision that marketing effort should be directed toward exploiting those portions of the market that are relatively insensitive to price.
2. *Penetration pricing* is a strategy for mass marketing. It calls for relatively low prices as a means of gaining rapid acceptance of the product in the price-sensitive sections of the market.

In this section we shall try to see how management can choose between these strategies in the first place and how it might decide

536

to change from skimming to penetration pricing after the product has been on the market.

Choosing a Pricing Strategy

The initial pricing strategy for a new product depends on two factors: (1) the sensitivity of sales to variations in price; and (2) the ability of other companies to introduce satisfactory competing products.

The price charged for a product or service will affect the number of units sold. Other things being equal, the lower the price the bigger the volume of sales. The economist refers to one of these price-quantity relationships as a *demand schedule*. When diagrammed, it

EXHIBIT 16–1

Demand Curve

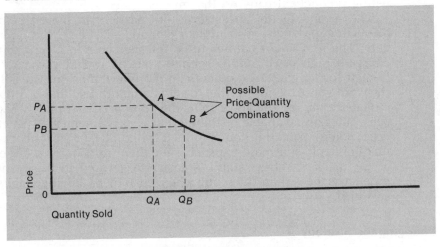

becomes a *demand curve*, as in Exhibit 16–1. Points A and B are only two of the many possible price combinations. They indicate that at a price of P_A, the quantity sold will be Q_A, while a price of P_B will increase the number of units sold to Q_B.

The sensitivity of sales to price, referred to by economists as the *price-elasticity of demand*, depends on the value customers place on the product and on their ability to meet their needs by using other products already on the market. If substitutes are very close, or if the customer doesn't value the product highly, the elasticity of demand will be high. Under the opposite conditions, elasticity will be low—that is, it will be *inelastic*.

A skimming price attempts to take advantage of the relatively inelastic portion of the demand schedule. For example, high initial prices may be a profitable way to capitalize on the novelty appeal of a new product when the responsiveness of sales to lower prices is slight.

Automobiles, television sets, ball-point pens, and pocket calculators all went through a skimming pricing stage when they were first placed on the market.

Skimming pricing may also provide a form of insurance against unexpected costs of manufacturing or distribution. It is easier to lower prices than it is to raise them, and manufacturing or engineering difficulties may raise product cost substantially above the estimates during the early shakedown period.

Skimming pricing is bad strategy, however, if the potential market is large and the product has to compete with close substitutes already familiar to the customer, or if potential competitors can enter the market quickly and cheaply. The first of these conditions makes for a highly elastic demand curve, meaning that small price premiums over the prices of competing products will reduce sales enormously. A new dishwashing product, for example, will be difficult to market if its price is significantly higher than the prices of the many competing products already on the market.

The second factor, the size of the barriers to the entry of new competing products, also affects demand elasticity, but at a later date. The first house painter to go into business in a new town can charge a high price for his services, but he probably won't be able to do it for long because others can get into the business easily once the word gets around. All they need is a paintbrush and a drop cloth.

Penetration pricing is apt to be the appropriate strategy when close substitutes are available or the market is easy to enter. A penetration price denies potential competitors a price advantage and makes it more difficult and more expensive for them to acquire a large share of the market. Market share is easier to get and to keep when the product is new than later on, when customers' buying habits have solidified.

Changing the Strategy

Deciding when to reduce a skimming price is more difficult than deciding to skim in the first place. By keeping the price high, the innovator offers potential competitors a tempting opportunity, a chance to enter the market with the competitive advantage of a low selling price. Whether they can take advantage of this opportunity depends on the strength of the barriers to the entry of competitors. The main barrier may be patent protection, the need for massive amounts of capital investment, or the power of a highly advertised, strongly entrenched brand name.

One pattern prices are likely to follow if entry barriers are weak is shown in the upper diagram in Exhibit 16–2. The price remains high for a short time as the innovator exploits the product's initial advantage. As the market expands, others see its potential and prepare to enter. To anticipate this, the innovator reduces the price. This leads to even greater volume and lower production costs. Knowing that competitors can also achieve low costs through mass production, the innovator continues to reduce the price until the economies of scale have been fully exploited. At this point the price can be said to have reached maturity.

The picture is very different when entry barriers are high, as in the lower diagram of Exhibit 16–2. Price is likely to stay at the skimming level for some time, until the innovator concludes that the upper portions of the market are becoming saturated, making it at-

EXHIBIT 16–2

Effect of Entry Barriers on Pricing Patterns

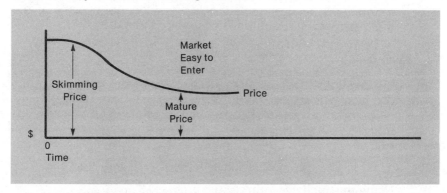

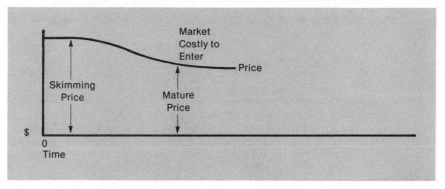

tractive to reduce the price to tap a part of the market that is more sensitive than the first. This may take a good deal of time. Another stimulus to price reductions is the emergence of new partial substitutes for the innovator's product. Competitors who can't climb the entry barrier may be able to go around it. The closer the substitute, the greater the pressure on price.

Management's job, in other words, is to judge the strentgh of the entry barriers and to estimate when they will be breached. Reducing price too soon reduces profits needlessly; reducing them too late leads to losses of market share which are likely to be accompanied by reductions in profit.

A SHORT-RUN ECONOMIC PRICING MODEL

Whether management skims or tries to penetrate the market on a mass basis, it must estimate the effect of price on volume. The only difference is that in setting a skimming price management is interested in short-run elasticity; for penetration pricing its focus is on the longer term.

Estimated or assumed price-volume relationships are central features of the models economists have developed to explain how prices and output are likely to behave. In this section we shall describe one of these models, discuss the methods management might use to estimate price-volume relationships, and examine some of the factors that often make it difficult to use the model directly in pricing.

The Basic Model

The central feature of this economic model is the assumption that the firm will try to set the price that will maximize its profits, the difference between total revenue and total cost. We can convert this into a managerial decision model by adopting this as the decision rule:

Maximize: Profit = Total Revenue − total cost

Using this model is a three-step process:

1. Estimate total quantity sold and total revenue at each of several possible prices.
2. Estimate total cost at each of these quantities.
3. Subtract total cost from total revenue at each price and select the price that maximizes the difference between them.

Estimating total revenue. If the demand curve has the shape of the one in Exhibit 16–1, price must be reduced to increase the quantity sold. If a large increase in volume results from a small decrease in price, total revenue will increase as volume increases. If a large price cut is necessary to increase total volume, total revenue may even fall as total volume goes up.

For example, suppose management estimates that ten units can be sold if the price is $20, for a total revenue of $200, as shown in the first line of the following table:

Price	Units Sold	Total Revenue	Effect of Added Volume on Total Revenue
$20	10	$200	xx
19	11	209	+$9
18	12	216	+ 7
17	13	221	+ 5
16	14	224	+ 3
15	15	225	+ 1
14	16	224	− 1

Reducing the price from $20 to $19 increases total revenue by $9, as shown in the second line. Each successive price reduction is less effective in increasing total revenue than the one before. Reducing the price from $15 to $14 actually reduces total revenue.

Estimating total cost. Total cost is also different for different volumes. The costs of responsive activities are bound to increase as volume goes up, as we have indicated many times. In our example, these are as follows:

Units Sold	Total Cost
10	$180
11	182
12	185
13	189
14	194
15	200
16	207

In this version of the model, programmed costs are the same at all volumes. If increases in volume are to be achieved by increases in the costs of programmed activities, these must be included in the model.

EXHIBIT 16–3

The Profit-Maximizing Volume

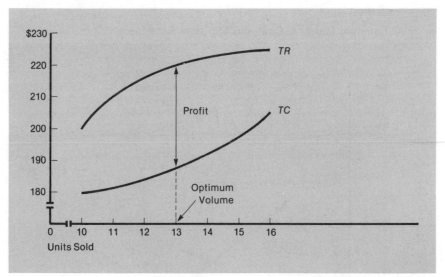

Finding the profit-maximizing price. The final step in this model is to calculate the profit at each volume and select the most profitable price-volume combination. This step is diagrammed in Exhibit 16–3. As this shows, the spread between total revenue (*TR*) and total cost (*TC*) increases as long as total revenue is climbing more rapidly than total cost. When total cost is climbing more rapidly than total revenue, actions that increase the number of units sold actually narrow the profit spread.

As this suggests, profit is at its maximum when the two rates of increase are equal—that is, when the two lines are parallel. This occurs in this case at a volume of 13 units. The price needed to get to this volume is $17, and this is the price management should choose.

Marginal cost and marginal revenue. These relationships can also be expressed in terms of marginal revenue and marginal cost. Marginal cost was defined in Chapter 3 as the increment in total cost as the result of increasing volume by one unit. Marginal revenue is the increase in total revenue that results from the sale of one additional unit of product.

Marginal revenue (MR) and marginal cost (MC) at any volume are determined by measuring the rates of climb or slopes of the total revenue and total cost curves at that volume. The usual assumptions are that the slope of the total revenue curve will decrease and that the slope of the total cost curve will increase as volume expands. If this is so, a line representing marginal revenue will slope downward to the right as volume expands and the marginal cost line will slope upward to the right.

These curves are shown in Exhibit 16–4. To move from sales of 10 units to sales of 11, management would have to reduce the price

EXHIBIT 16–4

Equating Marginal Cost and Marginal Revenue

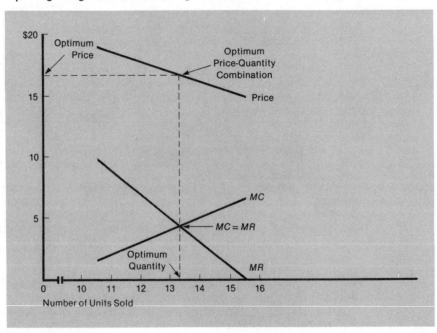

from \$20 to \$19, as we have already seen. This would increase total revenue from \$200 to \$209, an increase of \$9. This is the marginal revenue of the 11th unit, shown on the diagram as the height of the *MR* line at that point. The marginal revenue of the 12th unit is \$7, of the 13th is \$5, and so on.

Marginal cost can also be calculated by comparing total cost at successive volume levels. The marginal cost of the 11th unit is \$2, of the twelfth unit is \$3, and so on.

The optimal price-quantity combination is determined by the intersection of the marginal revenue and marginal cost curves. Lowering the price below this level would increase revenues by less than it would increase costs. Raising the price above the optimum would decrease revenues by more than it would decrease costs. In this case the two lines intersect just to the right of the 13-unit point. Since fractional units can't be sold, the optimal volume is the whole-unit output closest to the intersection point, 13 units, to be sold at a price of \$17 each.

Estimating Price-Volume Relationships

Management can use any of four techniques to estimate the impact of price on sales volume:

1.   Informed judgment.
2.   Statistical analysis of historical data.
3.   Price experimentation.
4.   Product value analysis.

Informed judgment. Marketing personnel, familiar with their customers and the prices of competing products, are likely to have some idea of the price range within which a new product will be competitive. For products already on the market, they may also be able to estimate the impact of modest increases or decreases in product price.

Management can get these estimates quickly and cheaply, and in many cases the analysis goes no farther. This approach is difficult to extend very far, however. Few managers are likely to be able to estimate sales at prices outside a limited range; and for new products the forecasting errors are apt to be extremely high.

Statistical analysis. Economists have had some success in applying statistical tests to historical data to identify apparent price-volume relationships in some industries. The technique is worth considering, but it is unlikely to prove very useful in forecasting the demand curve for specific products in specific firms. Too many factors other than price affect sales. For new products the situation is no better because historical data are not available. This means that management's best means of getting data on which to base its judgment must come from one of the other two methods.

Pricing experiments. Some companies have used experimental techniques with a great deal of success to produce more reliable estimates of the effect of price on sales. For example, one company recently placed a new product on sale in three representative regional markets before launching it nationally.

1. Every attempt was made to ensure the comparability of the three regions.
2. Three prices were selected for testing, one in each market.

Analysis of the sales responses in the three markets indicated that although profit per unit was highest at the highest of the three prices, total profit was the greatest at the medium price. These figures are shown in Exhibit 16–5.

EXHIBIT 16–5

Estimated Profit-Price Relationship

	At $1.95	At $2.45	At $2.95
Estimated unit sales.............	800,000	600,000	300,000
Price to dealers.................	$1.17	$1.47	$1.77
Estimated revenues...............	$936,000	$882,000	$531,000
Variable costs:			
Variable manufacturing costs.....	$504,000	$378,000	$189,000
Variable selling costs...........	80,160	70,920	40,860
Traceable fixed costs............	135,000	135,000	120,000
Total costs..................	$719,160	$583,920	$349,860
Product profit...................	$216,840	$298,080	$181,140

At a retail price of $2.45, the product was expected to return $54,000 less in sales than at a $1.95 retail price, but the contribution toward fixed costs and profits was expected to be the greatest at the $2.45 price.

Pricing experiments are not always feasible or reliable. For one thing, comparable test markets for some products are hard to find. Second, even if the markets are comparable, something may happen in one or more of them during the test to make the results less useful. For example, the distributors of a substitute product may launch a major promotional campaign in one of the test markets, cutting substantially into the company's sales.

Third, markets for industrial products are difficult to keep separate. Purchasing agents in the high-priced areas are bound to find out and demand equal treatment. Fourth, price-sensitive customers take longer to reach, and management may be unwilling to delay the pricing decision until the results are in.

For all these reasons, price experimentation is usually limited to low-priced consumer products of short life and little technical complexity. One or more of the other methods has to be used for products not meeting these specifications.

Product value analysis. People buy a product or a service because it has value to them. If management can figure out how many people are likely to value the product highly and how many will place a low value on it, costly and time-consuming experiments will be unnecessary.

For example, a machinery manufacturer has a file of detailed estimates of the costs of operations in its customers' factories. When a new product is developed, experienced engineers estimate the potential cost savings for large and small customers. A rough estimate of the demand schedule is prepared from these data—sales of 100 machines if the price is $20,000, sales of 250 machines if the price is $15,000, and so on. Matching this against cost estimates points toward the optimum price.

Product value analysis ordinarily enters into pricing implicitly rather than explicitly. Although few companies have the kinds of value estimates described above, they are seldom completely in the dark. Experienced executives may be able to tailor prices to customer values without even realizing that they are doing anything so systematic.

Limitations of the Model

Although this model illustrates the general nature of the economic approach to product pricing, it is seldom used in practice. This can be explained by one or more of the following:

1. Adequate data are not available.
2. Other aspects of the marketing mix are more important than price.
3. The market is oligopolistic.
4. Short-run profit maximization may have harmful long-run consequences.

Lack of data. Usable estimates of the relationship between volume and cost are usually available. Data on price-quantity relationships are much harder to get, however, as we indicated a moment ago. If management is unwilling to rely on the data it has from informed judgment, price experiments, or product value analysis, the model can't be used.

Nonprice competition. A second explanation of management's failure to use the short-run profit-maximization model is that price is only one element in the marketing mix. The marketing mix consists of all the devices the company uses to market its products more effectively and efficiently—the amounts and kinds of selling effort, the design of the product and its packaging, the price charged, the credit terms offered, and the channels of distribution used. What management does with one of these has an impact on the effectiveness of the others. Low prices will bring in big volume, for example, only if the company uses the right tools to let customers know about them.

As a result, management looks for an optimal marketing mix rather than an optimal price. This adds a third dimension to the analysis, ruling out any simplistic application of the two-dimensional model.

Oligopolistic markets. Revenues depend on many factors other than the company's own price. For example, a company can seldom assume that management's decisions as to price will not induce retaliatory pricing decisions by competing manufacturers. The circumstances under which this assumption is largely valid are those of *monopoly* (no directly competing product in the market) or *monopolistic competition* (many sellers of similar but not necessarily identical products, with no single seller having a large enough share of the market to permit competitors to identify the effects of other individual sellers' pricing decisions on their sales).

EXHIBIT 16–6

Oligopolistic Kinked Demand Curve

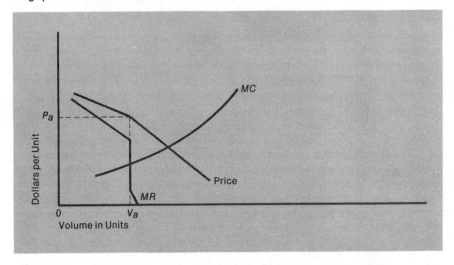

In the intermediate situation, known as *oligopoly* (a market in which a few large sellers occupy a large share of the market), the marginal revenue curve of the individual seller depends on the reactions of competitors to changes in the seller's prices. If the oligopolistic seller finds that competitors will raise their prices in response to a price increase and lower their prices in response to a price cut, then the seller's demand curve takes the same general shape as the demand curve for the market as a whole, except insofar as product differentiation affects the price sensitivity of sales.

A different situation arises if competitors will match price reductions but will not follow price increases. Sellers who try to raise their prices will find that their sales will fall off sharply as customers shift their purchases to other firms whose prices have not risen. If they lower their prices, on the other hand, their competitors will follow suit and the only source of increased revenue will be a share of any general expansion of total industry sales.

This effect is shown in Exhibit 16–6. Both the demand curve and the marginal revenue curve are interrupted or "kinked" at the sales volume (V_a) expected at the existing price (P_a). Although marginal revenue at this volume may be greater than marginal cost (as in Exhibit 16–6), any attempt to expand volume by price reductions will produce a substantial drop in marginal revenue. In this illustration the reduced marginal revenue is less than marginal cost, and thus the price reduction would be unprofitable.

A kink of this sort is likely to appear immediately only if most other firms in the industry are not operating at the limits of practical capacity. If capacity is fully utilized, competitors might find it profitable to meet any price rises, which would eliminate the kink. If they do not raise their prices but cannot absorb any additional volume immediately, the kink effect will not be felt by the high-priced seller until outside capacity has grown sufficiently to permit competitors to take advantage of all the orders that are forthcoming at existing prices. If most sellers suspect the existence of a kink of the kind illustrated here, and if they also assume that total industry sales are inelastic (relatively insensitive to price reductions), this is enough to explain why prices in many oligopolistic industries do not decline significantly during periods of idle capacity.

Long-run consequences. The fourth reason why management may not set prices on the basis of a short-run profit-maximization model is that today's prices may have consequences extending far beyond the present period. Charging a high price today may bar the company from the market tomorrow.

This objection really applies only to skimming pricing; if the model is applied to a product for which a penetration pricing strategy has been adopted, the cost and demand curves presumably reflect longer term relationships. If the skimming price appears likely to have unfavorable long-term consequences, then the decision to adopt skimming pricing should be reversed.

COST-BASED PRICING FORMULAS

Probably the most popular approach to pricing is to tie the price to an estimate of the cost of the product or service to be sold. This method applies both to *catalog products,* those offered to all potential customers on the basis of specifications and designs established prior to the solicitation of customer orders, and to *custom products,* manufactured to order on the customer's specifications or to meet a specific customer requirement. The main difference is that prices on custom products apply to individual orders only, whereas prices on catalog products are set in advance and generally remain unchanged for several months, a year, or even longer.[1]

In this section we shall examine cost-based pricing formulas from four angles:

---

[1] Many contracts specify that price will depend on the costs of fulfilling the contract. Costing for this purpose is examined briefly in Appendix B.

1. How they are used.
2. Why managers use them.
3. How cost should be determined.
4. How the formulas are used in reverse, to place a limit on product cost.

Steps in Cost-Based Pricing

Cost-based formula pricing is generally a four-step process:

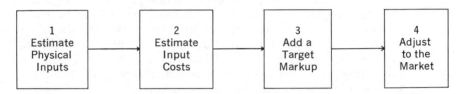

Step 1.   Estimate physical input requirements.   For a retailer, this is simply a matter of describing the item to be sold. For a service organization, such as a consulting firm, it calls for estimating the amounts of various kinds of direct time and the amounts of other direct inputs, such as photographic services and printing.

The process is the same in a manufacturing company, just a little more complicated. Starting with the product specifications, the methods department or industrial engineering staff prepares a bill of materials and a list of operations. For catalog products, these may already be summarized on a standard cost sheet. For the large number of custom products that are specialized combinations of fairly standard operations, most operating times and materials quantities can also be taken from the standard cost files if these are kept reasonably current. Otherwise, detailed estimates of operating times need to be prepared by the engineering or manufacturing staff.

Step 2.   Estimate input costs.   Given the list of estimated inputs, the cost accountant can use price lists and wage rate schedules to estimate the costs of direct product inputs. At this point the formulas diverge. Some include nonmanufacturing costs; others do not. Some include only short-run variable costs, some approximate average full cost, and some may even approximate attributable cost. The choice among these possibilities is important enough to entitle it to a separate discussion in a later section.

Step 3.   Add a target markup percentage.   A company's long-term survival depends on its ability to obtain prices for its products that will cover all costs and leave a satisfactory margin of profit, adequate to compensate investors for the use of their funds. This doesn't mean, however, that the markup percentage has to be the same on every product. Different products face different competitive conditions, and management must adapt its pricing policy to fit each market.

Finding the right markup percentage for each product isn't easy.

Sometimes the markups correspond to well-established differences in custom or competitive position. Department stores, for example, typically vary the markup from department to department. Cosmetics may carry an 80 percent markup on cost, while the markup on major appliances may be only 30 percent.

Another approach is to estimate the amount of investment attributable to the new product and set the price to achieve a specified return on investment at a given volume. For example, suppose that cost is $10 a unit at an assumed annual volume of 100,000 units. If $1 million in investment is required and the target rate of return is 20 percent, the target markup will be:

$$\frac{20\% \times \$1,000,000}{100,000} = \$2 \text{ a unit}$$

The target price is $10 + $2 = $12.

The use of customary markups is not a permanent guarantee of success in pricing. Feasible markups don't remain constant forever. The markups that have been normal for the past 20 years may suddenly turn out to be unobtainable. The neighborhood grocer found this out in the 30s, when the supermarket established a new pattern in food retailing by reducing costs and increasing turnover, thereby building an adequate profit margin at lower prices than the neighborhood grocer's. The same fate befell the full-service department store with the growth of discount retailing in the 50s. Managers who spot these possibilities early can grab a big share of the market; those who wait until the change takes place may be sorry.

Step 4. *Allow for temporary market conditions.* Prices set in this way are *target prices*. Actual prices may be either higher or lower. Managers are paid to exercise their judgment, not solve equations. If the target price is much lower than the product ought to be worth to its intended customers, the manager may add something to the target. If competing products are selling at prices well below the target, the company may have to accept a lower than normal markup unless the product offers valuable features the competitors don't have. In other words, it is reasonable to expect some prices to be higher than the target and some to be lower, as in the diagram in Exhibit 16–7.

In fact, negative markups are not unknown—that is, some products may sell at prices lower than the costs assigned to them. Even at these low prices these products yield incremental cash inflows—the company is better off to sell them than to drop them from the line.

Prices of custom products or unique services are likely to be even more sensitive to economic conditions than the prices of catalog items. For these, pricing is largely a matter of bidding or negotiating with individuals customers, order by order. In other words, a separate pricing decision has to be made for each sale.

The bid price is likely to depend on the number of orders already accepted and on the company's recent bidding experience. If the company is already using most of its capacity, the pricer will not do much price shading except possibly on orders that appear likely to lead to repeat business when greater available capacity exists. If recent bids

EXHIBIT 16–7

Variations in Actual Markups

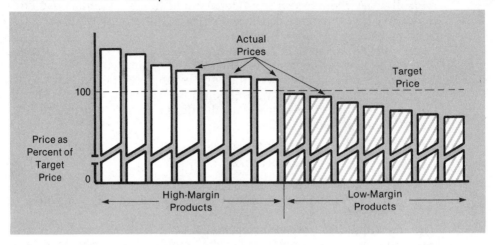

at normal levels have found ready acceptance, the company will feel justified in increasing the provision for profit on bids for new work. If substantial idle capacity exists, however, and full cost bidding has been failing to secure orders, the pricing executive faced with the choice of losing the order or quoting a price that is lower than the normal level is likely to accept the latter course and bid at some point intermediate between the estimated specific cost of the order and the normal price.

This description should provide ample support for the statement that pricing is an art rather than a science. The pricing executive must be alert to general market conditions and to differences among customers in their willingness to pay higher prices. Even when substantial idle capacity exists, it is not uncommon to find many orders priced at or above normal levels because all sections of the company's markets are not subject to the same competitive conditions.

Reasons for Cost-Based Formula Pricing

A legitimate question at this point is why cost should be used at all if the executive is going to vary the margin so freely. A quick answer often is that cost serves as a pricing "floor," shielding the seller from the risk of loss. Unfortunately, the protection it offers is illusory. It is entirely possible for the company to lose money even though every product is priced higher than cost. The reason is that many costs are fixed, so that unit cost depends on volume. A high price can drive customers away, reducing sales volume so far below the estimated volume that average cost is greater than price (see Exhibit 16–8).

Taken by itself, the need for a pricing floor can't explain the popularity of cost in pricing. Four other arguments provide a lot more of the explanation in one circumstance or another:

1. Cost-based pricing is a method of uncertainty absorption.
2. Cost-based pricing may be the only apparent path to survival.
3. Cost estimates may help management predict competitors' long-term pricing goals.
4. Cost-based formulas permit management to delegate pricing authority to their subordinates.

EXHIBIT 16–8

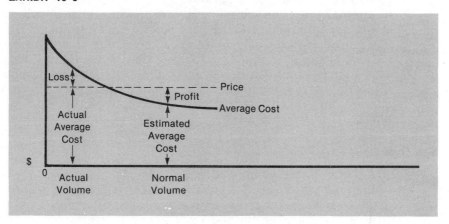

Uncertainty absorption.   One valid explanation of the popularity of cost-plus pricing is that the decision makers must make decisions in the face of a host of uncertainties. They can't possibly cope with all of these uncertainties, and to keep their sanity. They have to find some way of ignoring some of them or of getting others to accept responsibility for dealing with them. This is known as uncertainty absorption. One such device is to accept a pricing formula that seems reasonable on the surface. By accepting this, the manager feels free to ignore this source of uncertainty.

Survival pricing.   The second explanation is closely related to the first. In some situations, the alternative to product success is liquidation of all or part of the organization. Rather than liquidate, management may set a price that will assure a profit if a specified volume can be achieved. If the volume materializes, the organization survives; if not, liquidation may be the only way out. Private schools' tuition decisions very often fall in this category.

Competitive costing. The third explanation of the popularity of cost-based pricing is that estimates of the company's own costs may help the decision makers predict either their competitors' costs or a competitive price. For example, if the company has been operating for some time in a market in which markups over cost average 50 percent, management may be able to assume that the same relationships will hold on new products.

This kind of thinking is particularly valid in oligopolistic industries. Recognizing that price competition is likely to be self-defeating, price-setting executives may set a price that they feel will not attract competitors unduly and then focus their competitive efforts on other factors such as delivery, credit terms, and so forth. If every company uses cost as a basis for pricing standard products, a substantial measure of price stability can be achieved even under conditions of idle capacity.

Routinizing the pricing decision. The fourth reason for formula pricing is that many firms have so many products they cannot afford to analyze the price-volume relationships for them all. Department stores, supermarkets, and discount houses can't hope to apply a profit-maximization model to each of their thousands of pricing decisions.

Once again, by using a pricing rule that seems to work reasonably well, management can devote more time to other dimensions of the marketing mix. Management is not unaware that price affects volume and volume affects average cost—it merely has to cope with this phenomenon in other ways.

The Cost Base

Although some pricing formulas include allowances for average selling and administrative costs, these are seldom worked out in any detail. A typical cost estimate in this form is shown in Exhibit 16–9. In this example, the normal fixed manufacturing cost is $1.20 per machine-hour, fixed selling and administrative cost is applied at a

EXHIBIT 16–9

Product Cost Estimate Sheet

COST ESTIMATE SUMMARY

Product No.: 172–41-B   Prepared by: _____
Quantity: 1,000   Date: _____

Materials		Direct Labor and Machine Time			
Tooling	$ 507.00				
Fixtures, etc.	—	*Dept.*	*Setup*	*Operating*	*Machine-Hours*
Process	728.00	12	$ 6.25	$ 450.00	200
Total	$1,235.00	14	1.25	175.00	110
		17	2.50	130.00	150
		22	3.00	650.00	300
		24	1.25	85.00	20
		Total	$14.25	$1,490.00	780

Direct materials and direct labor	$2,739.25
Variable manufacturing overhead	548.00
Variable administrative costs	54.80
Total specific cost	$3,342.05
Fixed manufacturing overhead at $1.20 per machine-hour	936.00
Fixed selling and administrative at 15% of manufacturing cost	641.71
Normal profit at 12% of cost	590.37
Target price	$5,510.13

rate of 15 percent of total manufacturing cost, and the profit necessary to produce a target return on investment of 20 percent before
taxes is applied at 12 percent of total product cost.

Separate estimates of selling and administrative costs in these
formulas add little, if anything, to the price calculation. They could
just as well be treated as part of the markup percentage since they
are based on companywide or divisional averages. Manufacturing
costs, however, and the costs of product development are usually estimated in more detail. In general, they include allowances for all factory costs, fixed and variable, in production centers and service
centers. Because the cost structure is complex, we need to consider
the definition of cost quite carefully.

We suggest that target price calculations be based on the concept
of attributable cost, the cost that could be avoided, in time, if the
product were not in the line and capacity were reduced accordingly.
We also suggest that the cost figures be presented in enough detail to
help management respond to short-term departures from normal economic conditions.

The main argument for this approach is that the purpose of the cost
element in the pricing formula is to supply guidance to what a competitive price is likely to be. Empirical evidence is lacking on the relationship between average cost and competitive or "normal" prices,
but it might be presumed that long-run normal prices will bear some
relation to attributable cost. If a company is unlikely to cover the costs
attributable to a product, then it ordinarily will not introduce it. If the
product is already on the market, it will be withdrawn as soon as other
uses of capacity become available or as capacity wears out and needs
replacement.

Cost-Based Product Design

Until now, we have assumed that cost-based formulas are used to
set prices on products that have been developed and are ready for
commercialization. In many cases, however, selling price is known
and the question is what kind of product can be offered at this price.

For example, automobile manufacturers often start with a tentative
price at which they want a particular model to sell. Each proposed
design is costed, element by element, to test its feasibility at this target
price. Features are then added or subtracted, components are redesigned, or new price quotations are sought from parts suppliers, until
target cost levels are achieved. Clothing manufacturers typically follow a very similar procedure.

The cost estimates used in these calculations are of the same order
as those described above, although here the presumption in favor of
attributable costing is ordinarily even stronger.

PRICE DIFFERENTIATION

So far we haven't admitted that the same product might be sold to
different customers at different prices, but some price differentiation

has crept in nevertheless. For one thing, some skimming price strategies result in price differentiation based on the time of purchase—those buying early pay more than those buying late. Also, some pricing of custom products may be a subtle form of price differentiation—the products or services may be virtually the same, but their prices may be very different. Finally, the quantity discounts we discussed in Chapter 12 certainly produce price differentials.

Price differentiation may go beyond these examples. In this final section we shall explain why price differentiation may be desirable, see what the seller has to do to make it work, and look at the forces that limit the firm's ability to differentiate its prices.

The Benefits of Price Differentiation

Price differentiation can have both private and public benefits. The private benefit is probably obvious. Suppose an appliance dealer has two potential customers for television sets. One customer will buy a set if the price is no higher than $200; the other will buy only if the price is $110 or lower. The cost of each set is $80.

In this situation, the dealer can make $90 more if it can sell the two sets at each buyer's maximum price than if it has to adhere to a one-price policy:

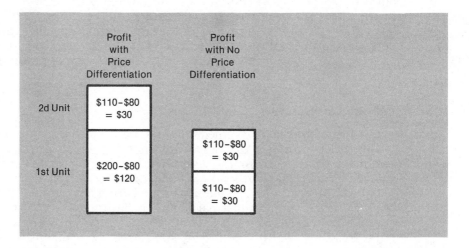

The seller, of course, needs to consider the likelihood that a price concession now will spoil the market for future sales. Fortunately, this danger is often more imagined than real. If excess capacity exists in the future, the company will probably be happy to grant the same kind of price concessions it finds profitable now. If, on the other hand, the excess capacity disappears in the future, the company will not be willing to grant price concessions in order to obtain added sales, and therefore the possibility of spoiling future markets may not be a serious objection.

The public benefit from price differentiation is less obvious. It arises when a one-price policy would fail to cover total costs, resulting in the product's withdrawal from the market. For example, suppose it costs $60 to buy each television set, plus $150 in fixed costs to run the store. Again only two customers are in the market, one willing to pay $200, the other willing to pay only $110. By differentiating the price, the dealer can sell two sets and make a profit:

Revenues: $200 + $110.............. $310
Costs: $150 + 2 × $60.............. 270
    Profit....................... $ 40

If the dealer has to quote the same price to both customers, the store will lose money, no matter what price is quoted. The result: the store will close and neither customer will have a chance to buy the product.

A more complicated situation is reflected in Exhibit 16–10. Average

EXHIBIT 16–10

Price Differentiation to Make Production Feasible

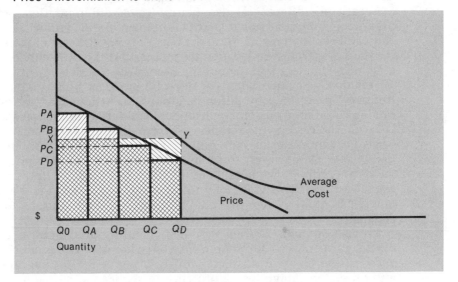

cost is greater than price at every possible volume. Without price differentiation, this product will not be offered on the market. Suppose the market can be divided into four segments, however, with a separate price in each. The price in segment A is P_A, and the quantity sold is $(Q_A - Q_0)$. The total revenue from segment A is $P_A \times (Q_A - Q_0)$, the area of the first block at the left of the diagram. The price in segment B is P_B, the quantity sold is $Q_B - Q_A$, and the revenue is $P_B \times (Q_B - Q_A)$. If the total area of the four revenue blocks is greater than the total cost (the area of the rectangle Q_0Q_DYX), the company will cover its costs and consumers will be able to satisfy their wants. (The lower fare quoted by a transit agency for off-peak travel is one familiar application of this idea.)

Bases for Price Differentiation

The markets for personal services (medicine or law, for example) are relatively easy to segment because customers in one segment can't resell the services to potential customers in another segment. Segmenting the market for tangible goods requires something more, however. We have already mentioned two methods of market segmentation—by time of purchase (skimming) and by order quantity (quantity discounts). Three other possible segmentation bases are worth mentioning: location, function, and product content.

Location. Sellers of products subject to high transportation costs may charge different prices to customers located in different regions. Products sold at low prices to customers on the West Coast, for example, can't filter back to the East Coast unless the price differential is greater than the cost of shipping and handling.

Locational differences also permit price differentiation between urban and suburban stores, between uptown and downtown, between slum and vacation resort. Here the barrier is not the cost of reshipping merchandise from one location to another but the unlikelihood of individual customers' seeking out the lower priced outlets.

Function. Segmentation can also be based on differences in the functions performed by different groups of customers. Wholesalers, retailers, and final customers usually pay different prices, presumably because wholesalers and retailers perform different functions. If these price differences depart materially from the costs of performing functional services, however, the company's prices in the high-priced segments (e.g., final customers) are likely to be eroded. Putative wholesalers can begin to sell directly to consumers at lower prices than retailers can quote. When this happens, the whole structure is likely to collapse.

Product content. A final way of segmenting the market is to offer different products to different groups of customers. The product difference can be physical—a better finish, a better fabric, more chrome and tinsel. Or it might be a difference in service—carpeted showroom floors, attentive salesclerks, faster delivery, and so forth. The only requirement is that enough customers value the differences highly enough to buy the higher priced product.

Limitations on Price Differentiation

The main limitation on the seller's ability to differentiate his prices is the customer's ability to cross segment lines. If enough purchasers decide that a product sold under a discount label is just as good as a nationally advertised product, this form of price differentiation will no longer be workable. The easier it is to move from one segment to another, the narrower the feasible price spread. And the narrower the spread, the less likely that price differentiation will be profitable.

A second limitation is the ability of competitors to underprice the seller in the high-priced segments. Successful price differentiation implies some weakness in the strength of competition. In fact, price differentiation is probably most widespread in regulated industries in which competition is restricted by law and by high investment barriers to the entry of competing sellers.

Laws of one kind or another may also prevent or limit price differentiation. We have already mentioned the Robinson-Patman Act (see Chapter 12, above). Other examples are state regulation of milk and liquor prices, and so-called fair trade laws. Public consumer agencies and private consumer groups may also have an impact. The main restriction, however, is the force of competition. When this is strong, price differentiation will be very limited.

SUMMARY

In some situations, pricing is simply a question of matching the prices of competing products already on the market. These situations are relatively rare, however. Management usually has some leeway, and often it has a great deal. This chapter relates to these situations.

Product prices should reflect consciously selected pricing strategies. Skimming pricing is a short-run, profit-maximizing strategy; penetration pricing may also maximize short-run profit, but its main focus is on the longer term. The ability to skim the market depends on the strength of the barriers to the entry of competing products—the weaker the barrier, the greater the argument for penetration pricing.

Some pricing models require data on price-volume and cost-volume relationships. These models are difficult to apply, for several reasons. As a result, management often resorts to pricing formulas, mostly based on estimates of product cost. These cost estimates are most logically based on the attributable cost concept, although the real question is which formula provides the best indication of the normal price. If attributable cost or its conceptually weaker cousin, full cost, is used, it should be supplemented by data on variable cost for use in decisions with shorter time horizons.

The main variable in a cost-based pricing formula is the markup over cost. These markups will differ from product to product and from time to time. Management may use standard markups to calculate target prices or even to quote actual prices in some circumstances. It must be alert, however, to differences in competitive conditions which make departures from target prices desirable.

Management may even be able to increase its profits by quoting different prices to different buyers of the same product. To do this, it must be able to divide its market into segments, each separate from the others and each with its own degree of price sensitivity. Price differentiation may also be the only feasible method of covering costs and therefore the only way of assuring that the market will be served.

KEY TERMS

The most important terms introduced and defined in this chapter are the following:

Demand curve

Entry barrier

Marginal revenue

Market segmentation

Oligopoly

Penetration pricing

Price differentiation

Price-volume relationships

Product differentiation

Skimming pricing

Target price

INDEPENDENT STUDY PROBLEMS
(Solutions in Appendix C)

1. The short-run economic pricing model. The Magellan Company has been selling its product at a price of $0.80 and has decided to investigate the profitability of increasing the price to compensate the company for recent increases in operating cost. The controller of the company has analyzed the company's costs, and has derived the following cost estimates:

Monthly Output (Units)	Operating Costs Fixed Cost	Marginal Cost per Unit
50,000 and less................	$10,000	$0.60
50,001–60,000...................	10,000	0.61
60,001–70,000...................	10,000	0.62
70,001–80,000...................	11,000	0.64
80,001–90,000...................	11,000	0.67
90,001–100,000..................	11,000	0.71
100,001–110,000.................	12,000	0.75
110,001–120,000.................	12,000	0.79
120,001–130,000.................	13,000	0.85

The market research department has recently studied prices and performance of competitive products and has derived an estimate of the effect of price on sales volume. The manager of market research has presented the following figures to the controller hesitantly, saying that she doesn't know how reliable they are but that they are the best she can do. She adds that in good years sales would exceed these figures, but on the average she thinks her estimate would be borne out.

Price per Unit	Monthly Unit Sales
$0.75..........................	100,000
0.80..........................	90,000
0.85..........................	80,000
0.90..........................	70,000
0.95..........................	60,000
1.00..........................	50,000

Prepare a statement that will indicate the most profitable price at which the product might be sold.

2. Price differentiation. The Hammer Company manufactures a product that it distributes through its own sales branches in the midwestern United States. The company's president, Mr. Martin, was recently approached by a West Coast distributor who was interested in obtaining a franchise for distribution of the product in seven western states not now served by the company. The distributor proposed that he purchase the product from Hammer at a price of $32.50 f.o.b. the Hammer factory and offer it for sale to retailers at a price of $42.50. He would pay freight charges to the West Coast, averaging $3.50 a unit. No sales commissions would have to be paid on these sales. Mr. Martin promised that he would consider the offer.

The product is now sold to retailers in Hammer's present market area at a price of $44 delivered. Sales commissions are computed at 5 percent of sales. Freight averages $1.50 a unit. Other selling and administrative costs are regarded as fixed and amount to $4.50 a unit. Manufacturing cost amounts to $29.50 a unit, as follows:

Materials...............................	$18.70
Labor....................................	3.00
Variable overhead........................	3.30
Fixed overhead..........................	4.50
Total...............................	$29.50

Manufacturing capacity is adequate to handle the increased volume, which Mr. Martin estimates would amount to 1,000 units a month, but fixed factory overhead would probably increase by $1,500 a month.

a. Would you advise Mr. Martin to accept the arrangement suggested by the West Coast distributor?

b. What factors other than those mentioned above should be considered in making this decision?

3. Pricing strategy. Macronaut, Inc. was founded to supply a unique electronic component for use in the U.S. aerospace program. The company has been highly successful, and even when expenditures on the space program were reduced, Macronaut's sales held up surprisingly well because of the high reliability of its product.

Macronaut has a few minor products, but it is essentially a one-product company. More than 90 percent of its revenues come from variants of its major product, and all of its revenues come either directly or indirectly from the U.S. government. Revenues now fluctuate in the neighborhood of $2 million a year and management sees little chance of getting much above that level.

Macronaut sees the automobile industry as a natural source of a new period of growth; heating and air conditioning are another. The company's product can be used directly in control mechanisms in automobiles and in heating and air-conditioning units, with no new design problems to overcome. Potential customers in these industries are interested in the Macronaut product, but only at prices half those now charged to the government. As one automobile company purchasing agent put it, "We like your product, but we're not adding anything that will increase the costs of the cars we make. Your product is too good for us. Putting it on every one of our models would cost us an extra $10 million a year, and it wouldn't sell one additional car or truck. Come back and see us when you have a competitive price."

Macronaut's net income now averages 6 percent of sales. Fixed costs account for 20 percent of manufacturing costs, and the factory is running quite close to capacity. Any major expansion would mean buying or leasing a vacant factory building nearby and equipping it with new machinery. Average costs would be reduced by about 5 percent in the expanded facility, but would still be far in excess of the prices regarded as acceptable by the auto makers.

The company's engineers can design some of the quality features out of the product and the redesigned product could be manufactured on high-speed equipment now available in the market. The equipment is very expensive, however, and buying it would be justified only if enough contracts came in to keep it busy for two shifts most of the year.

What are the main factors influencing pricing strategy in this situation? What is the role of cost?

EXERCISES AND PROBLEMS

1. Economic pricing model. Daniel Seder Associates is a market research firm, specializing in testing consumer reactions to new products. Its methods are slightly different from its competitors, and it has built a good reputation.

Prices in this industry are ordinarily quoted on the basis of a flat fee, the amount depending on the size of the job. In preparing his bids, Mr. Seder has been using a flat price of $20 an hour, and has gotten all the work he could handle at that price.

Mr. Seder decided a few months ago to experiment with different bidding formulas to see whether he could increase his earnings by putting in higher bids on new work. The results were interesting; at various prices per hour, the percentage of bids accepted was:

$30.00	32%
27.50	42
25.00	50
22.50	56
20.00	60

The total volume of work available for bidding calls for about 5,000 professional hours in an average month. Mr. Seder figures that he can handle up to 2,800 hours of work a month, which would give him about half of the local market. In fact, this is the level at which he has been operating for many months.

The costs of the professional staff are approximately constant from month to month. The bulk of the field work is done by a regular staff of part-time employees, but a few smaller firms are available to fill in (at higher prices) when the Seder load gets too heavy. Based on his past experience, Mr. Seder estimates that his monthly costs will be as follows:

Volume (Hours)	Total Cost
1,500	$33,500
1,700	34,900
1,900	36,300
2,100	38,700
2,300	40,300
2,500	41,900
2,700	43,900
2,800	44,100

What hourly price should Mr. Seder use in bidding? Present an analysis to back up your recommendations.

2. Price differentiation. The Weiss Company manufactures a highly machined precision part that is used in the manufacture of certain kinds of industrial equipment. The selling price is $350. Standard cost is as follows:

Material, 30 pounds at $2.................	$ 60
Direct labor, 15 hours at $5..............	75
Variable overhead.......................	30
Fixed overhead..........................	40
Total standard cost per unit.........	$205

The company was recently offered an order by a Canadian concern for 200 units at a price of $250 each. Freight charges and Canadian import duty, to be paid by the seller, would total $15,000. There was no danger that units shipped to Canada would be reshipped to Weiss's domestic customers because of high U.S. tariffs on imports of this product.

The Canadian company had never done business with the Weiss Company, and the sales manager pressed strongly for the sale on the ground that this was an opportunity to expand into a new market. The controller was out of town when this offer came in and was not consulted. The president turned down the sales manager's recommendation and rejected the offer.

Labor and materials quantity variances are expected to be negligible, but the standards do not reflect recent increases in materials purchases prices and wage rates. Materials prices have increased 3 percent above standard, and wage rates have increased 5 percent. Due to a number of factors, unabsorbed fixed overhead amounting to $5 a unit has been budgeted for the coming year. Wage and price changes affecting overhead costs account for $1 of this amount.

a. Do you agree with the president's decision? Support your position with arguments based on data provided above.
b. Are there any considerations that might justify a course of action other than that which you have supported?

3. Bidding with idle capacity. The Aybec Foundry Company is feeling the effects of a general overexpansion of the foundry industry in the Boston area. Its monthly production cost budget for the next six months is based on an output of only 500 tons of castings a month, which is less than half of practical capacity. The prices of castings vary with the composition of the metal and the shape of the mold, but they average $250 a ton. The condensed monthly production cost budget at the 500-ton level is as follows:

	Core Making	Melting and Pouring	Molding	Cleaning and Grinding
Labor............................	$18,000	$28,000	$10,500	$7,500
Variable overhead................	3,000	1,000	1,000	1,000
Fixed overhead...................	5,000	9,000	2,000	1,000
Total labor and overhead......	$26,000	$38,000	$13,500	$9,500
Labor and overhead per direct labor hour......................	$13.00	$9.50	$9.00	$7.60

Operation at this level has brought the company very close to the break-even point. The lack of work also means that some of the most highly skilled workers will probably have to be laid off, and if this happens they may not be available when volume picks up later on. Accordingly, when a customer asked for bids on a large casting order, the plant manager asked the plant accountant to prepare a bid "at cost."

The order is for 90,000 castings, each weighing about 30 pounds, to be delivered on a regular schedule during the next six months. Materials required would cost $1 per casting after deducting scrap credits. The direct labor hours per casting required for each department would be:

Core making............................ 0.09
Melting and pouring.................... 0.15
Molding................................ 0.06
Cleaning and grinding.................. 0.06

Variable overhead would bear a normal relationship to labor cost in the melting and pouring department and in the molding department. In core making and cleaning and grinding, however, the extra labor requirements would not be accompanied by proportionate increases in variable overhead. Total variable overhead would increase by $1.20 for every additional labor hour in core making and by 30 cents for every additional labor hour in cleaning and grinding. Standard wage rates are in effect in each department, and no labor variances are anticipated.

To handle an order as large as this, certain increases in fixed factory overhead would be necessary, amounting to $1,000 a month for all departments combined. No increases in selling and administrative expense are anticipated, but the company uses a standard selling and administrative expense rate of $12 per ton of castings in its pricing work. Production for this order would be spread evenly over the six-month period.

a. Prepare a revised monthly factory cost budget, reflecting the addition of this order.
b. What is the lowest price that the plant manager could quote without selling at a loss? Show your calculations.

4. Full-cost formula pricing. Aberdeen Appliances, Inc., is bringing out its 19x1 line of household appliances. Sales during 19x0 were at record levels and an equally good year is forecast for 19x1. Disposable consumer income is expected to be at all-time record levels, and the entire appliance industry is booming.

The appliance business has always been highly competitive, and Aberdeen feels that at least part of its success has lain in its ability to keep its costs at competitive levels. The contract that has just been negotiated with the labor union representing the company's factory employees has raised wage rates by 10 percent for next year, however, and management is worried about the effects on the profit margin.

The old and new standard costs for Aberdeen's electric buffet grill–deep fryer combination are shown in table on page 563. The new standard costs reflect the new wage rates, changes in model design, and changes in manufacturing methods.

The 19x0 model was sold to dealers at $25. In view of the higher costs of the new model, management is considering setting the price on the 19x1 model at $27. This would keep the percentage markup over standard cost at 35 percent, the level prevailing for the 19x0 model.

	19x0	19x1
Materials and parts..............	$ 8.50	$ 9.10
Labor...........................	4.00	4.30
Factory overhead................	6.00	6.50
Total........................	$18.50	$19.90

Standard overhead costs are based on estimated costs at normal volume. Factory cost variances on this product in 19x0 amounted to about 10 cents, mostly unfavorable materials price variances. The introduction of new production equipment has created difficulties with the local labor union, however, and Aberdeen Appliances is now budgeting an unfavorable labor quantity variance of 50 cents a unit on the grill-fryer combination. Other variances are expected to be minimal.

No estimates of the sensitivity of sales volume to changes in price have been made, and none can be made before management must reach a decision on the price for the new model.

To the extent that you can judge from the data given, should the price on the new model be set at $27, lower than this, or higher than this? Give reasons for your answer.

5. Timing of price increase; Response to cost increase. Dave Seeberger, president of Olympic Instruments, Ltd., feels that the time has come for a price increase on the company's most important product. "Our costs on this line have gone up 32 percent since our last price increase," he said, "and I think that justifies a price hike now. We're almost down to the break-even level and for the first time in 20 years we can't pay a dividend to the stockholders. It's a good thing that we have a higher margin on most of our other products. Without those we'd really be in the soup!"

The product is sold directly to industrial users at a price of $160. The factory cost estimates at the time of the last price increase and at present are shown in the following table:

	Then	Now
Materials........................	$ 17.50	$ 20.40
Labor...........................	32.50	40.00
Factory overhead...............	65.00	91.60
Total factory cost..........	$115.00	$152.00

The product specifications have not been changed since the previous price increase. Wage rates have gone up by 30 percent, but some labor has been saved as a result of methods changes that have been effected during this period.

Factory overhead is assigned to products on the basis of a plantwide overhead rate, reflecting estimated costs at current volume. The rate is brought up to date once a year. The overhead cost files at the time of the increase and at present show the following:

	Then	Now
Overhead rate (per direct labor dollar)......	$2.00	$2.29
Estimated monthly volume (direct labor dollars)...........................	$120,000	$110,000
Variable overhead cost....................	$ 36,000	$ 31,900

All of the company's salespeople are on salary and all selling and administrative costs are regarded as fixed. Even so, they have gone up in total from $70,000 a month to $75,000 a month. Sales have dropped from about $700,000 a month to $550,000, despite price increases on some other products.

Brad Pierce, Olympic's sales manager, is against any price increase. "We have a tough enough time now," he said. "Our competitors' list prices are about the same as ours, but my guess is that they're doing a little unofficial price cutting. Everybody in the industry has cut back, but we've been hit harder than most. Our market share on this product has fallen from about 50 percent to maybe 40 percent. If anything, we should be offering a few deals of our own, not raising prices."

a. Calculate this product's contribution margin, then and now.
b. Which elements have had the greatest impact on unit cost in this period?
c. Which kinds of cost increases is the company most likely to be able to pass along to its customers? Should the price be increased at this time? If not, what should Mr. Seeberger do?

6. Contribution margin figures in pricing. E. Berg and Sons build custom-made pleasure boats ranging in price from $10,000 to $250,000. For the past 30 years, Mr. Berg, Sr., has determined the selling price of each boat by estimating the costs of material, labor, and a prorated portion of overhead, then adding 20 percent to these estimated costs to provide a profit margin.

For example, a recent price quotation was determined as follows:

Direct materials	$ 5,000
Direct labor	8,000
Overhead	2,000
Estimated cost	$15,000
Plus 20 percent	3,000
Selling price	$18,000

The overhead figure was determined by estimating average overhead costs per direct labor dollar during the year ahead, including selling and administrative costs as well as boatyard overheads.

The customer in this case rejected the $18,000 quotation. Since the work was to be done during a slack period, Mr. Berg reduced the markup to 5 percent and submitted a second bid of $15,750. Mr. Berg often does this during slack periods, and as a result the average markup for the year is expected to be about 15 percent. Even so, the customer in this case rejected the second offer and countered with a $15,000 offer of his own.

Mr. Ed Berg, Jr., has just completed a course on pricing and believes the firm could use some of the techniques discussed in the course. The course emphasized using contribution margin figures in pricing, and Mr. Berg, Jr., feels such an approach would be helpful in determining the selling prices of the company's boats. He has estimated that $90,000 of the $150,000 estimated overhead cost for the year is fixed; the remainder is variable in direct proportion to direct labor.

a. What is the difference in net income for the year between accepting or rejecting the customer's offer? Are fixed costs likely to be affected?
b. What is the minimum selling price Mr. Berg could have quoted without reducing net income?
c. What advantages does the contribution margin approach to pricing have over the approach used by Mr. Berg, Sr.?
d. What pitfalls are there, if any, in contribution margin pricing?

(CMA adapted)

7. Formula pricing; Product value analysis. "We price to achieve a target return on investment," Al Doherty said. "First, we estimate the amount of facilities and working capital necessary to support each product. Eighteen percent is our target return on investment, before taxes, and this gives us the amount of profit we have to achieve. Then we figure out what it will cost us to operate at normal volume. Adding this to the target return gives us the price to set."

"Don't you consider the effect of price on volume?"

"Not directly. We figure that if we can't reach normal volume at a price that gives us our target return, then we don't want the product."

Mr. Doherty is the marketing vice president of Usher Enterprises, Inc., a medium-sized manufacturer of adhesives, abrasives, and industrial chemicals. He is responsible for the entire marketing program, including the establishment of product selling prices. For major pricing decisions he has a price advisory committee made up of the controller, the production manager, the industrial engineer, and himself, but the final decision is his because his performance is judged on the basis of return on investment.

At the moment Mr. Doherty is wrestling with the problem of setting a price on a new product for use in the paper processing industries. Usher's major competitor, Hinden Products, Inc., has a product with characteristics that have given it an enormous competitive advantage in paper processing industries. It sells for $3, and at this price has forced all competing products out of this market.

The only problem with the Hinden product is that it is costly to use. Users have to spend between $0.50 and $2 for auxiliary materials for every pound of the Hinden product they use. Mr. Doherty estimates that the cost penalties for using Hinden's product are as follows:

Cost Penalty	Pounds Sold (Monthly)
$0.50	40,000
1.00	80,000
1.50	120,000
2.00	160,000
Total	400,000

Usher's new product would eliminate these cost penalties.

Paper industries' consumption of the Hinden product has been growing at a rate of about 100,000 pounds a year, or 8,300 pounds a month. Hinden sells the same product to other industries in which it does not have a cost penalty, but Usher's sales organization is inadequate to cover these other industries. The decision on Usher's new product will be based solely on its performance in the paper processing industries.

Introduction of the new product would be fairly easy. Investment in plant and equipment and working capital would amount to $5 million plus $10 for each pound of product sold in an average month. Introductory promotional costs would be negligible because Usher's sales force is already in regular contact with customers in the paper processing industries, and no large initial burst of media advertising would be required.

All cost estimates have been prepared on the basis of a normal volume of 200,000 pounds a month. Factory costs for the new product would amount to $200,000 a month plus $2 a pound, up to a volume ceiling of about 250,000 pounds a month. Beyond that, cost penalties would begin to increase rather rapidly and would quickly become prohibitive. Rather than go above 250,000 pounds a month, management would either limit sales or begin the construction of additional facilities.

Selling and product management costs for the new product would aver-age $60,000 a month. These costs would be classified as fixed.

The company's central administration costs average 6 percent of factory cost at normal volume. These are fixed costs and would not change im-mediately if the new product were introduced. They would probably creep up gradually, however, for an eventual increase of about $20,000 a month.

Engineering and research and development costs to date have totaled $600,000. This amount has been expensed for external financial reporting, but it has been capitalized for internal reporting of product profitability. If Usher introduces the new product, the $600,000 will be charged against operations on a straight-line basis over the next 60 months. If Usher de-cides not to introduce the product, the entire amount will be expensed im-mediately.

a.   What price would be set if the company's pricing formula were used? Show your calculations.

b.   Do the data indicate that the price should be set at the target level? Make calculations that you think would help management decide what price to set and indicate how they might be used.

8. Pricing strategy: New product.   The Oppenheim Company is just completing the construction of a new facility to manufacture a new prod-uct. This product is intended for sale to manufacterers of a wide variety of products in which it would be used as a component part, ordinarily hidden from the view of the ultimate consumer.

Competing products sell at prices ranging from $3.80 to $4.80, but dif-ferences in product specifications and design make direct comparisons difficult. Furthermore, the company believes that there is some price shad-ing for large volume customers, but has thus far been unable to determine its extent.

Sales in this market are quite difficult to forecast, at least in part be-cause individual orders tend to be fairly large and the loss of one order can make the difference between a good forecast and a highly inaccurate one.

In making the decision to enter this market, the Oppenheim manage-ment believed that it would be able to sell 150,000 units a month within three years after commencing operations if its prices were competitive. Market conditions have changed materially since the initial decision was made, and even with heavy promotional outlays at the outset, the com-pany is not confident that it can meet the original sales target.

The company's reputation for product quality and delivery performance is such, however, that the sales manager has suggested setting a premium price of $5 a unit. The sales force is quite confident that it can sell 80,000 units a month in the first year at that price. Management thinks it unlikely, however, that the company could sell more than 80,000 units a month in the first year no matter how low a price was set. Buyers in this market try out new components in their less popular lines, often waiting two or three years before incorporating components of improved design into their major products, and this latter portion of the market tends to be highly price-sensitive.

It is estimated that materials will cost 80 cents a unit at monthly vol-umes of 100,000 units or less and 70 cents a unit if monthly volume is in excess of that figure. Labor costs will amount to $1.40 a unit. Factory overhead is to be budgeted at $90,000 per month plus 42 cents a unit. By-products from the process are expected to yield 24 cents for each unit of the main product manufactured. The plant's output can be increased to

250,000 units a month, but for all output in excess of 200,000 units a month labor cost will increase to $1.70 a unit and variable overhead will rise to 65 cents a unit.

An intensive sales promotion campaign is now being prepared to launch the new product. Advertising and special promotion activities costing $750,000 will be spread over the first year of the new product in addition to sales commissions of 5 percent of sales. Thereafter it is expected that selling costs attributable to the new product will be $20,000 a month plus commissions. No change in administrative or other nonmanufacturing expenses is expected to accompany the introduction of the new product.

The company's selling and administrative expenses (including advertising and sales representatives' commissions), together with its reported net income before taxes, have in the past averaged about 40 percent of manufacturing cost. This comes very close to a pricing formula that the company has used on many occasions: budgeted manufacturing cost at normal volume plus 45 percent.

a.   Compute unit cost on whatever basis you feel would be most helpful to management in setting an initial price on this product. Prepare a summary report to present this figure and any others that you would want management to see, including any charts or diagrams that you would find useful in getting your analysis across.

b.   Would you recommend skimming pricing or penetration pricing in this situation? You should interpret a skimming price as a price in excess of the target price based on average cost at normal volume. State the arguments for and against your recommendation, and suggest a price for management to consider.

9. Pricing strategy; New product.   Joan Robinson, president of Gregson Products, Ltd., makes all the product pricing decisions. She is now trying to decide on a price to be placed on a new type of floor wax, called "Flow-On," that has just been perfected by the company's research department. Although a number of competing brands of liquid floor wax are now on the market, the company has not previously marketed any kind of floor wax. The company's products are distributed in a seven-state regional market, rather than nationally.

Labor, materials, and manufacturing overhead costs per gallon at different volumes (gallons per week) are expected to average as follows:

	10,000	15,000	20,000	25,000	30,000
Materials	$1.00	$1.00	$0.95	$0.95	$0.95
Labor	0.50	0.45	0.40	0.40	0.43
Factory overhead	1.55	1.05	0.80	0.69	0.68
Total	$3.05	$2.50	$2.15	$2.04	$2.06

These costs are also typical of those facing the company's major competitors.

The manufacturing process is such that it requires 24-hour, three-shift operation of the production facilities. Changes in the rate of output are achieved by increasing or decreasing the number of processing units in service. In designing the facilities, the company's engineers were asked to design for efficiency at a "normal" operating level of 25,000 gallons a week, or 80 percent of maximum physical capacity. The company's efficient competitors are able to achieve about an 80 percent utilization, on the average.

The company's sales representatives are paid on a flat salary basis. Introduction of this new product, however, would require the permanent addition of two new representatives at an average salary of $360 a week each. Sales travel, advertising and other marketing costs would increase by about $500 a week if "Flow-On" were to be introduced. Administrative costs would be unchanged by the introduction of this new product. On a companywide basis, the selling and administrative cost averages about 30 percent of manufacturing cost. If the company's profitability targets were met, company net income would be approximately 20 percent of manufacturing cost, but in the past few years the reported net income has averaged about 15 percent of factory cost.

The company's research people are convinced that "Flow-On" is superior to any existing liquid floor wax. The leading competing product sells at a retail price of $5 per gallon. At the prevailing trade discount of 40 percent off list, the manufacturer's realization at this price is $3 a gallon. The other five brands in the company's market area are less popular and sell at retail prices ranging from $3.95 to $5.35. No quality product is marketed at a price of less than $4.75, and sales of the $5.35 product have been rather small, although it is marketed by a well-established manufacturer of branded household products.

Bruce Thompson, the company's sales manager, is planning an extensive promotional campaign to launch the new product. He would devote a good deal of his time to "Flow-On" during the six months prior to its introduction and the first six months after it was launched. The work of the new sales representatives would be backed up by local advertising and distribution of free samples, mostly during the first six months the product was on the market.

Mr. Thompson is convinced that if this were done he could sell 25,000 gallons of "Flow-On" per week once the product was established, as long as the price was no higher than that of the leading competitor. This would represent a market share of about 15 percent, but the impact on competitors would be lessened considerably by expansion of total sales of floor waxes in this area as a result of the extra promotion of the new brand.

Ms. Robinson is less optimistic than the sales manager. She, too, hopes for a sales volume of 25,000 gallons a week, but does not expect to reach this level of operations until normal growth of the market expands industry sales sufficiently several years hence. She thinks that 20,000 gallons a week is more likely as long as prices are competitive, and that sales might even be as low as 15,000 gallons a week.

a.   As controller of Gregson Products, you have been asked to supply the president with a figure representing the cost per gallon of "Flow-On." Prepare a short report, providing the figure(s) that you think is (are) most likely to be relevant in this situation and explaining to the president what your figures mean and why you selected them.

b.   There is no time for experiments that would test the price elasticity of demand. No one in the company can give you any information other than that supplied above. Would you recommend skimming pricing or penetration pricing in this situation? What price would you establish, and why?

10. Cost data for pricing decisions; Different costs for different decisions. The Lundstrom Company's factory consists of three production departments and two service departments, with the following normal monthly overhead costs:

	Production Departments			Service Departments	
	A	B	C	M	N
Direct overhead:					
Variable.........................	$ 5,200	$16,000	$10,500	$ 7,500	—
Fixed—divisible..................	6,000	4,500	2,000	—	—
Fixed—indivisible...............	800	1,500	3,000	2,000	$10,000
Allocated (full cost basis):					
General factory..................	2,000	2,000	2,000	—	—
Department M....................	1,000	4,000	5,000	—	—
Department N....................	5,000	2,000	2,500	500	—
Total........................	$20,000	$30,000	$25,000	$10,000	$10,000
Normal volume....................	20,000 dir. lab. hours	10,000 dir. lab. hours	12,500 machine-hours	2,000 service-hours	100,000 sq. ft.

Consumption of service department M's services is regarded as a divisible fixed cost in department A and as proportionately variable with volume in departments B and C. General factory overheads are entirely fixed and largely indivisible.

Product X has just been developed by the Lundstrom Company and is now ready for commercialization. It will be listed in the company's next product catalog, and orders will be taken for immediate or deferred delivery at list price.

Product X will compete with more than 100 products offered by 36 competing companies in the Lundstrom market area. Its biggest competition will come from the Deane Company's product P, which now sells 5,000 units a month, about 35 percent of the potential market for product X, at a unit price of $59. Lundstrom's market share in other product lines in its own region ranges from 5 to 35 percent, with most products between 10 and 15 percent. Prices in this market have been relatively stable for several years.

Product X has a number of significant advantages over product P and other competing products already on the market, and competitors will not be able to match these distinctive features for at least a year. The Lundstrom sales department is enthusiastic about the new product and feels that at a competitive price product X could achieve a good share of the market, perhaps as much as 15 percent, during the first year. Whether it could keep or increase its market share in subsequent years would depend in part on customers' experience with the product and in part on competitors' responses to product X.

The company's development engineers estimate that after an initial six-month learning period, production inputs for a unit of product X will be: direct materials, $5; direct labor, $25; department A, three direct labor hours, department B, one and a half direct labor hours; and department C, two machine-hours. Errors in the engineers' estimates at this stage of product development have generally been within 10 percent of actual costs in the past, and underestimates have been just as frequent as overestimates.

Markups over factory cost on the company's other regular products average about 40 percent of full factory cost and generally range between 25 and 45 percent.

Most selling and administrative expenses will be the same no matter what price is set on product X. Selling costs attributable to this product are expected to amount to about $5,000 a month, not counting any special price deals that might be made to stimulate sales during the introductory period.

a.   Prepare a unit cost estimate or estimates that you feel would help management arrive at a price for product X. Discuss your reasoning.

b.   Recommend a selling price for product X. Support your recommendation, using figures from the problem to whatever extent you deem appropriate.

c.   How, if at all, would your answer to (a) differ if the decision were whether to accept a single order for 100 units of product X to be shipped to a customer outside Lundstrom's ordinary sales area at a time when factory capacity in each department was only 75 percent utilized?

d.   Assuming that product X is now in the line, selling 500 units a month, and that factory production capacity is not fully utilized, what unit cost figure would you use in a rough test of the desirability of discontinuing production and sale of product X? Explain.

CASE 16–1: SANDERS COMPANY (Contract bidding)

Pierre Malin was adamant. "I know the competition is rough, he said, "but if we can't get enough out of this to cover our costs then we have no business going in."

"I couldn't agree more," George Riley replied, "but you're measuring costs the wrong way."

Pierre was the general manager and George was the controller of the Sanders Company, a small manufacturer of molded plastics products. At issue was the price to be quoted in a sealed bid that the company was submitting for a large order of drinking cups to be supplied to a local school board.

The company's molding department consists of a group of injection molding machines with interchangeable dies. Each die has a number of openings or "cavities" in the shape of the product to be molded. The molding operation consists of closing the machine, whereupon melted polystyrene is forced under pressure into the die. There it is cooled into solid form by the circulation of cold water until it reaches a predetermined temperature, at which point the die opens and the molded products are ejected. The operator then closes the machine, and the process is repeated.

The drinking cups were a relatively new product for the Sanders Company, but orders for this product had been coming in at a fairly steady rate. The reason for Mr. Riley's enthusiasm was that this was the first opportunity to penetrate the large institutional market in the area. The initial contract was for 500 gross (6,000 dozen), but the potential market was many times this amount every year.

Standard product cost was based on engineering studies of physical input requirements and cost estimates prepared by the accounting department. Standard cost was as follows:

	Cents per Dozen Cups
Materials.............	12.0
Labor.................	5.5
Overhead..............	2.2
Total standard cost...	19.7

The standard cost of the plastic powder used as raw material is $9 per thousand cups, reflecting normal wastage. Standard materials cost also includes $1 a thousand to amortize the cost of the dies used.

The labor cost of the molding operation is a function of (1) the number of cavities per die, (2) the length of the molding cycle (interval between closings), and (3) the number and compensation of operators tending each machine. The number of cavities per die is determined largely by the size and shape of the molded product, although the number of cavities actually in use may be reduced by blocking off one or more cavities that have developed defects that would lead to the rejection of finished products. Because of the high costs of die removal and setup, a die may be kept in operation with a fairly substantial number of its cavities blocked off.

The length of the molding cycle depends on how quickly the operator responds to the opening of the die. While the die is closed, the operator inspects the molded products and separates them from the plastic framework to which they are attached when ejected. An operator may delay clearing and closing the machine if these tasks haven't been finished when the machine opens.

The Sanders Company typically assigns one worker to a machine, with a reliever for each ten machines. This reliever also keeps the machines supplied with raw material. The machine operators and relievers are paid at the rate of $7.25 an hour, with time and a half for overtime. Each worker is entitled to a 15-minute rest period each morning and afternoon and a half-hour lunch period, as part of a normal eight-hour shift. The machine is operated by the reliever during the smoking period, but it remains idle during the lunch period. A study of recent experience revealed that each operator was idle for an average of 15 minutes a day while minor repairs or adjustments were being made to the machine. This idle time is not recorded separately on a routine basis. If a machine is to be out of operation for a half-hour or more, the operator is assigned to other tasks, such as correcting minor defects in rejected products.

The standard labor cost of an hour of machine time is $8.80, computed as follows:

Machine-hours per day: 10 machines at 7.25 hours each
  (total time less lunch and normal waiting time)........ 72.5

Daily labor cost for 10 machines:
  10 operators, 8 hours at $7.25 an hour................. $580.00
  1 reliever, 8 hours at $7.25 an hour....................   58.00

  Total... $638.00

Labor cost per machine-hour........................... $ 8.80

If the operator acts immediately, the complete cycle time is 25 seconds, but standards reflect an average cycle time of 30 seconds. The dies for the cups contain 20 cavities, but standard cost reflects the assumption that 20 percent of the cavities will be blocked. This would indicate a standard production rate of 1,920 cups an hour, and a standard labor cost of 5.5 cents a dozen.

Overhead cost was based on full absorption costing at normal volume. Variable costs account for approximately 30 percent of overhead cost at normal volume. The variation is in proportion to changes in labor cost.

Mr. Malin felt that standard cost was a poor basis for cost estimation in this case. "Our work force is very green," he said, "and I expect that cycle time will be 20 percent longer than standard. Overall volume is down, too, and this means that we can't take advantage of quantity discounts on our purchases. This will add 11 percent to the purchase prices of plastic powder. Besides, the lower volume means that we'll probably have to add 10 percent to our standard overhead cost to carry the cost of idle capacity. All of these things bring our costs up close to 22 cents a dozen, without any allowance for profit. I don't think we can win the contract on that basis."

"You're probably right on that score," George answered. "My guess is that we'll have to put in a bid of 21 cents a dozen if we really want this order. With standard cost at 19.7 cents a dozen, this shaves the margin pretty thin, but I think we ought to go ahead. This is a big market, and I think that standard cost gives us a better guideline than your expected actual cost figure. We can't expect our customers to pay for our inefficiencies."

Would you use standard costs, expected actual costs, or some other cost figure in this situation? Explain your reasoning.

CASE 16–2: CLOVIS, S.A.* (Price differentiation)

Clovis, S.A. manufactures a line of roller skates which it sells in France and other European countries. The company has just received a proposal from Empire Importing Company of New York to introduce Clovis skates into the U.S. market, but at lower net prices than the company now receives on its European sales.

Clovis has no foreign subsidiaries, all foreign sales being made through independent wholesale distributors in the various countries. The company sells seven different models, all manufactured in the company's plant at Lyon, France.

Annual sales volume is now approximately 3.5 million pairs. Sales of the most expensive models have remained approximately constant for the past several years, but unit sales of the moderately priced models have declined about 25 percent from the levels of a few years ago, despite successive price reductions in most European markets, as competitors have increased their shares of the market at Clovis's expense. The overall European market is about the same size as it was a few years ago.

Empire Importing is convinced that it can market three of the Clovis models in the United States as high-quality items. Typical cost and price data for one of these, Model TM-5, are shown in Table 1. The other two models have cost-price relationships similar to those in the three countries listed in the table. Markups over manufacturing cost in other European countries are less than in Switzerland but greater than in Italy.

The proposal is to offer the products for sale through department stores and discount houses in the eastern part of the United States. Empire Importing would sell Model TM-5 to retailers at a price of $17.15 a pair plus freight from New York. Empire would pay Clovis $9.20 a pair, plus all shipping charges and U.S. import duties, estimated at $4.50 a pair for the TM-5. It would be responsible for all advertising and sales promotion in the United States, would bear all U.S. credit risks, and would have exclusive rights to market Clovis skates east of the Mississippi River for a period of five years.

---

* Copyright 1965, 1976 by l'Institut pour l'Etude des Méthodes de Direction de l'Entreprise (IMEDE), Lausanne, Switzerland. Reproduced by permission. Costs and prices have been converted to dollar amounts.

TABLE 1

Selected Price and Cost Data (dollars per pair)

	France	Switzerland	Italy
Price data			
Retail price................................	$24.00	$30.08	$24.30
Wholesale price...........................	18.00	22.00	18.10
Factory price.............................	13.80	15.12	10.35
Cost data			
Manufacturing cost:			
Variable cost...........................	6.70	6.70	6.70
Fixed cost..............................	2.10	2.10	2.10
Selling and administrative expense—			
fixed....................................	1.50	1.50	1.50
Average shipping costs*...................	1.50	1.80	2.10
Import tariff*.............................	—	1.51	1.65
Approximate retail price range:			
Competing products.......................	20.50–34.00	22.13–42.56	9.41–23.52
All Clovis models.........................	20.50–30.50	26.67–36.89	18.82–24.30†

* Paid by wholesale distributor; factory prices do not cover shipping costs or import duties.
† Model TM-6, Clovis's most expensive model, is not marketed in Italy.

Mr. J. R. Martell, Clovis's sales manager, is strongly attracted by this proposal. Empire executives are convinced that they can sell 100,000 pairs of skates this year and that within three years they will be able to increase their U.S. volume to 300,000 pairs a year. Manufacturing overhead is now underabsorbed, and capacity exists in the Lyon factory to manufacture more than the 300,000 pairs per year required to supply Empire Importing. The overhead rates from which the unit cost figures in Table 1 were derived were based on an annual volume of about 4,100,000 pairs of skates. Most fixed overheads are not traceable to any one product, but represent capacity costs for the combined production of skates and skate parts.

The present level of fixed costs could probably be maintained if sales were to increase by 100,000 pairs a year, but additional supervisory and clerical personnel would be required to handle a larger increase. Clovis's accounting department has assembled estimates that the accompanying increases in total fixed costs would average approximately $180,000 a year from the second year onward. Variable manufacturing cost per pair would be approximately as shown in Table 1.

Mr. Pepincourt, Clovis's president, is not entirely convinced of the wisdom of entering the U.S. market on this basis. The company's policy has been to market no product at less than full cost, although in some countries such as Italy the profit margin above full cost has been very thin. Furthermore, expansion into the U.S. market would mean that Clovis would have to spend approximately $150,000 three or four years from now to replace certain items of factory equipment now in use. If the company does not accept the Empire Importing proposal or find other ways to increase volume, production lines can be reorganized at negligible cost, thereby making it possible to dispose of this equipment now. Thus the Empire proposal would commit Clovis to an investment which Mr. Pepincourt is reluctant to make. On the other hand, the working capital necessary to support the company's entry into the United States would be negligible.

The equipment referred to in the previous paragraph has no salvage value at the present time, but depreciation on it is included in factory fixed costs at $15,000 a year. Other fixed costs associated with this equipment amount to approximately $60,000 a year.

Shipping charges and European tariffs are high enough so that re-exportation of Clovis skates from New York to Europe would not be feasible, but Mr. Pepincourt is worried nevertheless that if he agrees to this proposal his sales manager will begin to propose major price concessions in other markets as well.

Should Clovis skates be introduced in the United States at the price proposed by Empire Importing Company? Be sure to consider the arguments advanced both by Mr. Martell and by Mr. Pepincourt.

17

Adjusting for Uncertainty

ALL THE MODELS we have dealt with so far have been deterministic—that is, they have reflected the assumption that all estimates are perfect. Only in calculating safety stocks did we admit to any uncertainty about the future.

Deterministic models are very reassuring. With perfect knowledge, the decision maker can identify the alternative with the greatest present value. The optimal decision is clearly signaled. Unfortunately, very few decisions are made with perfect or even near perfect knowledge of the consequences. It's not surprising, therefore, that more and more attention is being directed to models in which uncertainty is recognized explicitly.

We lack the space to cover these models in any detail. We can, however, examine four ways data on uncertainty can be organized:

1. Payoff tables and expected values.
2. Probability adjusted profit charts.
3. Decision trees.
4. Capital expenditures simulation charts.

PAYOFF TABLES AND EXPECTED VALUE

Forecasts of cash flows are uncertain for two reasons. First, cash flows will be affected by the conditions prevailing in the future (*events* or *states of nature*), and these conditions can't be known with certainty. Second, cash flows are affected by many factors other than the state of nature, and these relationships are uncertain.

One way of summarizing the decision maker's uncertainties from the first of these sources is to construct a payoff table. In this section we shall use the payoff table to illustrate several important concepts:

1. Outcomes and payoffs.
2. Probabilities.

3. Expected values.
4. Decision rules.

Outcomes and Payoffs

Decision making is the process of selecting from a number of ·possible managerial actions. As we have already seen, it requires estimates of the results likely to be achieved by each of these actions. The payoff table is simply a means of displaying the results to be expected under each possible combination of managerial action and state of nature.

Results can be stated either by describing what will happen or by listing the net benefits to be derived. A description of a result is known technically as an *outcome;* the net benefit is known as the *payoff.* (Net benefit is the difference between total benefit and total cost, measured by the present value of the cash flows.) Since decisions focus on costs and benefits, the payoff table focuses on payoffs.

The first step in drawing a payoff table is to identify as many managerial actions as management is willing to examine. These are listed at the left of the table. A manager deciding whether to introduce a new product, for example, might list two possible actions:

1. Add the product to the line carried by the regular sales force.
2. Set up a specialized sales force to promote the new product.

The second step is to list as many states of nature as might influence the decision. These are listed across the top of the table. Sales of our illustrative new product, for example, may depend mainly on the availability of a government subsidy to potential buyers, the subject of a bill now being debated in Congress. The manager might identify three possible states of nature:

1. The bill is rejected in its entirety.
2. The bill is passed in its present form.
3. The bill is passed with an amendment doubling the size of the subsidy.

The result so far is a two-dimensional table with six empty boxes or cells.

State of Nature Managerial Action	No Bill	Present Bill	Amended Bill
Regular sales force			
Specialized sales force			

Each of these cells represent a unique combination of actions and states of nature. With two possible actions and three possible states of nature, we have $2 \times 3 = 6$ cells. The figure to be placed in each cell is the anticipated payoff for that action/state of nature combination.

The third step, therefore, is to estimate these payoffs. The introduction of a specialized sales force would increase the fixed costs of the company's operations. The purpose would be to increase the total sales potential. If successful, the specialized sales force would produce a high net cash inflow; if unsuccessful, the high fixed costs would lead to a high cash outflow. This is the operating leverage phenomenon we described in Chapter 3. Using the regular sales force would produce less leverage, a smaller possible loss and a smaller possible gain.

The result is the set of differential cash flows (the difference between the anticipated cash flow with the new product and the anticipated cash flow without it) in the accompanying table. The figure in

State of Nature Managerial Action	No Bill	Present Bill	Amended Bill
Regular sales force	−$250	+$500	+$1,200
Specialized sales force	−$400	+$200	+$2,000

each cell shows what the payoff will be under the action shown if the state of nature listed at the head of the column turns out to be the real one. Thus if management chooses to set up a specialized sales force, only to find that Congress has defeated the bill, the payoff is a $400 cash outflow.

Probabilities

This payoff table would be a useful way of demonstrating the sensitivity of the payoff to variations in the state of nature. It ignores one crucial element, however, the likelihood that each of the states of nature will occur. This is important information. If the manager is convinced the bill will pass in its present form, the table points to using the regular sales force to market the new product. This will produce a larger cash flow than the alternatives. If the bill is likely to be defeated, however, the new product should not be introduced at all.

The likelihood that an event will occur is known as its *probability*, expressed as a percentage or as a decimal with a value between 0.0 and 1.0. A probability of 0.3, for example, means that this event will occur three times out of ten. The total of the probabilities for all the possible events or states of nature is 1.0. For example, a weather forecaster is likely to say that the probability of rain tomorrow is 20 percent ($= 0.2$). This means:

Event	Probability
Rain...............................	0.2
No rain............................	0.8
Total...........................	1.0

Some probability figures are known as *objective probabilities* because they can be established by logical reasoning, by analysis of historical data, or by experimentation. The probabilities in coin-tossing exercises and dice games are objective probabilities. We know, for example, that a tossed coin can come down either head up or tail up. Logically, we have no reason to assume the coin will come up heads either more or less often than it comes up tails. The probability of each outcome is 0.5, established by logical reasoning. We can test this empirically, if we wish, by tossing a coin or coins a number of times and recording the results. If the coins are unbiased, they will come up heads half the time.

The probabilities applicable to managerial decisions are likely to differ from these. They are more likely to represent managerial judgment than historical or experimental averages. Subjective probabilities are based on the managers' past experience, combined with information about the current state of the market and current happenings, and sometimes reflecting forecasts of various key variables made by others.

Subjective probabilities are likely to have large error factors. The issue is not whether such probabilities will be used, however. The only issue is whether they will be stated explicitly. Any managerial decision reflects, either explicitly or implicitly, management's judgment of the likelihood of different states of nature. The manager may decide to set up a specialized sales force, for example, on the grounds that this will yield a greater cash flow than marketing the product through the regular sales force. If so, this decision reflects a judgment that the amended bill has a very high probability of passage.

Expected Value

Once we have drawn a payoff table, we realize that we don't know which alternative will maximize cash flow. In our example, we have

EXHIBIT 17–1

State of Nature	Cash Flow Maximizing Action
The bill is defeated	Keep the new product off the market.
The bill is passed	Market the new product through the regular sales force.
The amended bill is passed	Set up a specialized sales force to market the new product.

three different ways of maximizing cash flow, depending on the circumstances (see Exhibit 17–1).

Before examining some of the possible ways to resolve this dilemma, we must introduce one more concept, *expected value*. The expected value of a managerial action is the average payoff, determined by weighting each possible payoff by its associated probability. For example, suppose our manager assigned probabilities of 0.2, 0.5, and 0.3 to the three states of nature. The expected value of using the regular sales force is:

State of Nature	(1) Payoff	(2) Probability	(3) Weighted Payoff (1) × (2)
No bill..........................	−$ 200	0.2	−$ 40
Present bill....................	+ 500	0.5	+ 250
Amended bill..................	+ 1,200	0.3	+ 360
Expected value............			+$570

Performing the same calculations for the specialized sales force alternative, we get an expected value of $620:

No bill: −$ 400 × 0.2................ −$ 80
Present bill: +   200 × 0.5................ + 100
Amended bill: + 2,000 × 0.3................ + 600
        Expected value........................ +$620

These figures have been inserted in the completed payoff table shown in Exhibit 17–2.

EXHIBIT 17–2

Payoff Table, with Expected Value

State of nature Action	Probability			
	0.2	0.5	0.3	
	No Bill	Present Bill	Amended Bill	Expected Value
Regular sales force	−$250	+$500	+$1,200	+$570
Specialized sales force	−$400	+$200	+$2,000	+$620

Decision Rules

The meaning of expected value is that if the probabilities are right and if management makes many decisions of this sort, management can maximize its cash flows by consistently taking actions with the greatest expected values. If our manager had 100 identical decisions, for example, and chose in each case to set up a specialized sales force (the alternative with the greater expected value), the result would be as follows:

State of Nature	Number of Times the State of Nature Occurred	Cash Flow Each Time	Total Cash Flow
No bill...........................	20	−$ 400	−$ 8,000
Present bill......................	50	+ 200	+ 10,000
Amended bill....................	30	+ 2,000	+ 60,000
Total cash flow..............			+$62,000

This of course is just the calculation of expected value with the probabilities multiplied by 100.

Maximizing expected value is one possible decision rule, but not the only one. (We defined a decision rule earlier as a set of instructions for choosing a managerial action consistent with management's objectives.) Most decision rules begin with the word *maximize* or *minimize*. Here are three other possibilities:

1. Minimize the possible loss.   Management could minimize the possible loss by not introducing the product at all. Each of the other alternatives would lead to a worse result in the worst state of nature (no bill). This is probably the most pessimistic decision rule of all— always assume the worst.

2. Maximize the possbile gain.   To do this, management should set up the specialized sales force because in no other way does it have a chance of gaining a $2,000 cash flow. This is the inveterate optimist's decision rule—always assume the best.

3. Maximize the most likely gain.   This means ignoring the extremes, going with the state of nature management thinks most likely to occur. In the present case, it leads to the use of the regular sales force because management expects the bill to pass (probability = 0.5) and in this state of nature the regular sales force brings in the greatest cash flows.

Maximizing the most likely gain is the decision rule implicit in most of the decision models we discussed in earlier chapters. For example, the budgeting model in Chapter 5 was a deterministic model. To apply the budgeting model to our current problem of deciding whether to introduce the new product and how to market it, we would (1) forecast the differential cash outlays required by each marketing plan; (2) forecast the differential cost receipts from each plan; and (3) subtract the first set of forecasts from the second. The figures might be as follows:

	Most Likely Cash Outlay	Most Likely Cash Receipts	Most Likely Net Cash Flow
Regular sales force................	$ 800	$1,300	+$500
Specialized sales force............	2,300	2,500	+ 200

Each of these six figures is single valued. It implies that choosing the marketing plan determines the outcome, with no uncertainty.

Two conditions must be present if maximizing the most likely gain is to lead to the same decisions as a decision rule calling for the maximization of expected value: (1) the possible payoffs must be distributed symmetrically around the most likely value; and (2) the probabilities of the various states of nature must be distributed symmetrically around the probability of the most likely state of nature.

Suppose our marketing manager made the following estimates:

	.2 No Bill	.6 Present Bill	.2 Amended Bill	Expected Value
Regular sales force...............	−$250	+$500	+$1,250	+$500
Specialized sales force............	− 400	+ 200	+ 800	+ 200

Notice what we had to do to make the payoffs from the specialized sales force symmetrical. We had to reduce the optimistic payoff from $2,000 to $800. Given our original estimates, maximizing the most likely payoff would be a very poor decision rule, on the average; only when the payoffs and probabilities are symmetrically distributed does it make sense.

Utility

Maximizing the expected value of the cash flows is a sensible decision rule as long as the decision maker regards each dollar of anticipated gain or loss as equal in utility. For example, if the company has 250 other products, generating $100,000 in cash flows, the manager is likely to regard a possible gain of $2,000 as five times as important as a $400 loss. Suppose the new product is only the second, however, and the first now generates only $100 in cash flows. In this situation a $2,000 gain is likely to be enticing but a $400 loss would be a disaster. The gain means more meat on the table; the loss means the table will be repossessed.

This asymmetrical attitude toward possible gains and losses is an illustration of a phenomenon known as a *nonlinear utility function*. Exhibit 17–3 shows one of these functions. This depicts a common assumption in economic theory, that the more money consumers have, the less they will value a single dollar. The $10 necessary to buy a theater ticket has much less value to rich people than to the poor. The reason is that buying a ticket might force a wealthy person to eat a $30 meal instead of a $40 meal after the theater; a poor person might have to go without lunch for a week.

The value people place on money is impossible to measure except in special situations. Economists have a name for it, however—they call it *utility*. A utility function is linear if doubling the amount of money will double the amount of utility, or value placed on the money. A linear utility function in Exhibit 17–3, for example, would be a

EXHIBIT 17–3

Nonlinear Utility Function

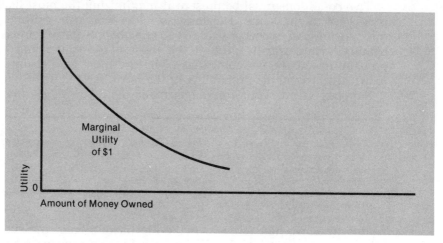

horizontal straight line. Each dollar would have the same value, no matter how many dollars the owner had.

In large organizations the utility function ordinarily can be assumed to be linear for most of the decision situations the managers find themselves in. They may not make 100 identical decisions, but they do make 100 decisions with roughly similar potential impacts. Using the expected value rule consistently over a period of time should lead to a greater cash flow than could be reached with some other decision rule. In such cases it doesn't even matter whether the utility function is linear because the manager's decisions can be evaluated as a group, not one by one. The mistakes will be more than covered by the brilliant successes.

PROBABILITY-ADJUSTED PROFIT CHARTS

The presence of uncertainty can be recognized in many ways other than in payoff tables. Another possibility is to apply them to the profit charts we described in Chapter 3.

The simplest way to do this is to superimpose a probability distribution on a conventional profit chart, as in Exhibit 17–4. The height of the bell-shaped curve represents management's estimate of the probabilities of achieving various possible sales volumes. The unshaded area under the curve represents the total probability that profit will be positive but less than the planned amount. The shaded area under the curve at the left shows the probability of reporting a loss; the shaded area under the curve at the right shows the probability of exceeding planned profit.

Conventional profit charts are designed to show the sensitivity of profits to variations in volume. Superimposing the probability distribution on one of these charts, as in Exhibit 17–4, doesn't interfere

EXHIBIT 17–4

Profit Chart with Probability Distribution

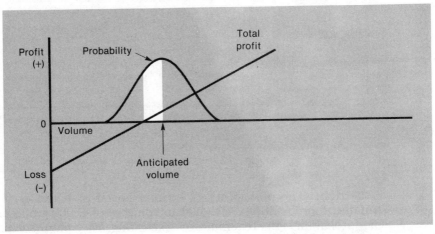

with their use for this purpose. A different kind of chart may be a better way of indicating the likelihood that the company's profit objectives will be met, however. To prepare this other chart, we need to match the *profitability* at any volume with the *probability* of getting there (see Exhibit 17–5). This is the same probability curve we had in Exhibit 17–4, but with a different scale along the base. Volume no longer appears as an independent variable—it has been factored into the profit figure. The unshaded area under the curve this time represents the total probability of meeting or exceeding the planned profit.

Management seldom has probability estimates for each possible volume level. At best, the probability-rated forecasts might show the following:

Weekly Volume (units)	Profit (Loss)	Probability
4,000	$(20,000)	0.05
5,000	(10,000)	0.1
6,000	0	0.2
7,000	10,000	0.3
8,000	20,000	0.2
9,000	30,000	0.1
10,000	40,000	0.05

The clearest way to chart these probabilities is in cumulative form. Exhibit 17–6 is in this form. For example, there is no chance whatsoever of a loss greater than $20,000—therefore, the probability that the profit level will be no worse than this is 100 percent. The probability of doing as well as or better than a $10,000 loss is only a little less than this, 0.95, so the curve dips slightly as it makes this first move

EXHIBIT 17–5

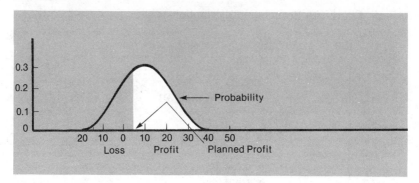

to the right. The probability of breaking even or better is 0.85, the sum of the probabilities assigned to volumes of 6,000 units or more. The probability of reaching or exceeding the planned profit of $10,000 is 0.65.

Management's main concern will be with the height of the line in the vicinity of the planned profit and with its slope in that zone. A steep slope indicates sharply decreasing probabilities of doing better, high probability of doing worse. A flat curve, on the other hand, shows that the probability of doing slightly better or worse is almost as good as the probability of reaching the objective. The combination of a low cumulative profitability level and a steep slope indicates the attainment of the planned profit is very doubtful.

EXHIBIT 17–6

Cumulative Profit Probabilities

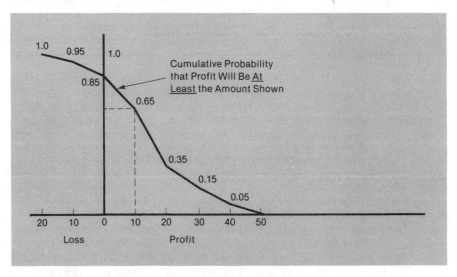

DECISION TREE ANALYSIS

Payoff tables and probability-adjusted profit charts can deal with one level of probability only. The payoff associated with a given outcome is often uncertain in itself, however. It may depend on a second set of states of nature or on a second level of decisions.

Dealing with these complexities is far from simple. In general, only the computer offers any hope of a successful analysis. The structure of the problem can be demonstrated fairly easily, however, by drawing a decision tree, a diagram of the relationships among decisions, states of nature, and outcomes or payoffs.

EXHIBIT 17–7

Decision Tree with One Decision Point

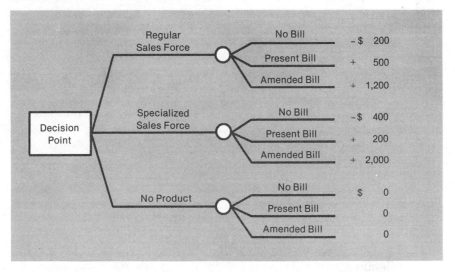

Our earlier payoff table, for example, has been redrawn as a decision tree in Exhibit 17–7. The three alternative actions are shown as three separate *decision branches* spreading out from the single *decision point*. Each of these branches is branched in its turn at what we call an *event node*. The smaller branches spreading out from the event nodes are known as *event branches* and each ends in a payoff.

To get a better picture of a decision tree, we have to use a slightly more complicated example. Suppose management is considering whether to continue a research project now in progress. If it does, the project may fail or it may succeed. If it succeeds, in the sense that it yields a new product that is capable of satisfying consumers' needs, management will have to decide either to produce and sell the product or to hold it off the market. If it decides to sell, competitors may enter, or they may not.

EXHIBIT 17–8

Decision Tree with Two Decision Points

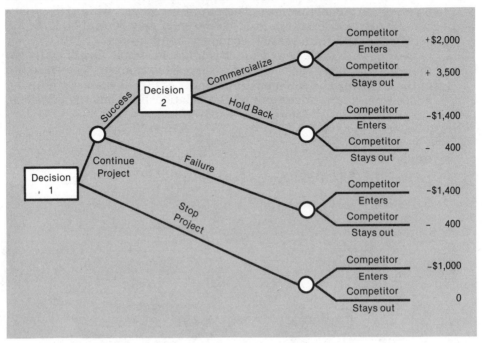

These possibilities are diagrammed in Exhibit 17–8. The squares again identify decision points; the circles are event nodes. Each final event node leads to two branches (events) labeled "competitor enters" or "competitor stays out." Each has a separate and distinct payoff.

The payoffs are shown at the right, one at the end of each branch of the tree. They are based on the following estimates:

1. Continuing the project will cost $400 that could be avoided by canceling the project now.
2. If the company decides not to commercialize the product but a competitor enters the market, the competitor will take some of the company's present business away. This lost business is now generating a $1,000 net cash inflow.
3. If the research is successful, the company decides to commercialize the product, and competitors stay out, the new product will generate cash flows of $3,500 over and above the cost of the project itself; if a competitor also enters the market, the net payoff will be only $2,000.

Several characteristics of the decision tree can be identified from this diagram:

1. Each decision point leads to two or more decision branches.
2. Each decision branch ends in an event node.
3. Each event node leads to two or more event branches.
4. Each event branch ends in (a) a decision point, (b) an event node, or (c) a payoff.
5. The tree is fully grown when all the end branches have led to payoffs.

Although the decision tree now has all its branches, it still has no leaves, in the form of probability estimates. We could use the tree without these, as a way of laying out the range of possible consequences, but this array can be difficult to understand once it gets beyond eight or ten final branches. In the more general case, the main purpose of the tree is to collect the probability figures in a form suitable for a computerized solution.

What we have to do is estimate the probabilities at each event node. A set of these probabilities has been inserted in Exhibit 17–9. Once this has been done, the expected values of each decision branch can be calculated by working backward.

The expected value of the decision to commercialize, for example, is calculated as follows:

State of Nature	Payoff	Probability	Contribution to Expected Value
Competitor enters....................	+$2,000	0.7	+$1,400
Competitor stays out................	+ 3,500	0.3	+ 1,050
Expected value................			+$2,450

This expected value figure has been entered in Exhibit 17–9 just above the last event node in the top branch. Similar calculations were made to derive the expected values of each of the other event nodes at the right. Comparison of the first two of these shows that, once the project has succeeded, commercializing the product is a much better alternative (expected value = $2,450) than holding it off the market (expected value = −$900).

We need to go through the same procedure again to calculate the expected value of the first event node in the upper branch—that is, the expected value of the decision to continue the project. We can ignore the rejected limb on this upper branch because we won't take this route if the project is successful. The expected value of continuing the project, therefore, is calculated by treating the expected values of the next event nodes as payoffs:

State of Nature	Derived Payoff	Probability	Contribution to Expected Value
Success............................	+$2,450	0.6	+$1,470
Failure.............................	− 600	0.4	− 240
Expected value.................			+$1,230

This is far better than the −$500 expected payoff from killing the project now. The project should be continued.

EXHIBIT 17–9

Decision Tree with Probabilities and Expected Values

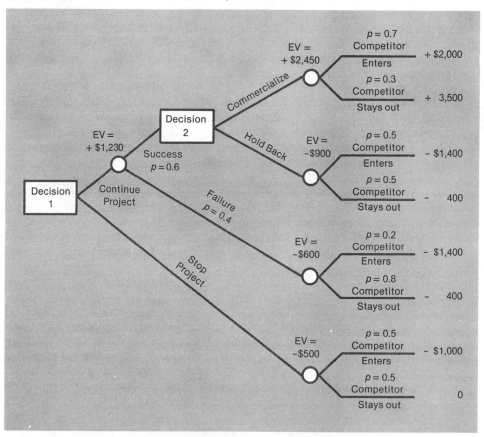

Notice that the only decision to be made now is the decision to go ahead with the project. The company is in no way committed to commercialize the product if the project is successful. We need to forecast that future decision, however, to make our present decision. If we forecast that we won't commercialize the new product even if we are successful in developing it, this forecast will reflect itself in an unfavorable expected value of the decision to continue.

CAPITAL EXPENDITURE SIMULATION CHARTS

The last method of recognizing uncertainty to be discussed here is the construction of simulation charts for capital expenditure proposals. The calculations are complex and can be performed satisfactorily only on the computer, but we can describe the basic idea.

In our discussion of capital expenditure analysis in Chapters 14 and 15, we used deterministic decision models—that is, each value was assumed to be known with certainty. In fact, each of the determinants of net present value—market size, wage rates, economic life, selling prices, and so on—is better described by a probability distribution than by a single value. The number of combinations of possible values is enormous, completely beyond our ability to calculate or digest.

One way out of this is to calculate limit values, by bracketing anticipated cash flows with pessimistic and optimistic estimates. A project with an anticipated net present value of $250,000, for example, might actually have a negative present value if events turn out to be worse than anticipated, or have a net present value of $1 million if the situation proves better than management now anticipates. This can be very useful information. Decision making is a judgmental process and these bracketing calculations can give management a better feel for the variability of the end result.

The weakness of this approach is that it ignores the probabilities. Should the pessimistic estimates reflect the worst conceivable values of the variables or values somewhere in the lowest quartile of the probability distribution? The apparent variability of the net present value or rate of return will depend on how this question is answered.

An alternative approach is to *simulate* the results, using a five-step process known as the Monte Carlo method:

1. Estimate the probability distribution for each important variable.
2. Select combinations of these values at random, giving each possible value a chance of being selected proportional to its probability.
3. Calculate net present value or rate of return for each of these combinations.
4. List the results of all the combinations tested, showing how many indicated a net present value of, say, −$10,000, how many had a net present value of −$5,000, and so on. This is known as a frequency distribution.
5. Plot this frequency distribution on a chart or charts.[1]

---

[1] An explanation of this approach published some years ago but still the clearest explanation around is by David B. Hertz, "Risk Analysis in Capital Investment," *Harvard Business Review*, January–February 1964, pp. 95–106. See also his "Investment Policies That Pay Off," *Harvard Business Review*, January–February 1968, pp. 96–108.

EXHIBIT 17–10

Capital Expenditure Simulation Charts

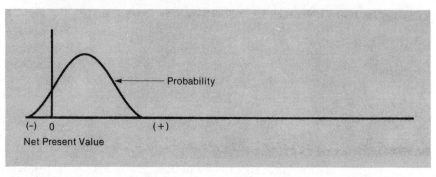

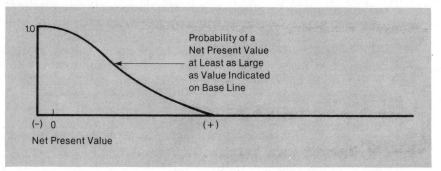

The end product may take either of the forms illustrated in Exhibit 17–10. This looks just like some of the other charts we drew earlier (Exhibits 17–4 and 17–5, for example), but the data were developed in a different way, by simulating the results under various possible combinations of conditions.

The main advantage of this approach is to help management differentiate proposals with different degrees of uncertainty. The diagram in Exhibit 17–11, derived from Hertz's work, shows two different proposals. Management can accept only one of these. The probabilities of different payoffs are symmetrically distributed for each proposal. Proposal A has a lower expected value than proposal B—50 percent of the simulations had a net present value of less than $10,000, as opposed to $15,000 for proposal B. Proposal A is much more certain, however. Almost all the simulated combinations for this proposal had present values between $5,000 and $15,000, while proposal B had quite a few with negative net present values and some with net present values in excess of $30,000.

If the decision makers' utility function is linear, they will take proposal B because it offers the higher net present value. The decision makers may weight a possible loss more heavily than a possible gain, however. If so, they may favor proposal A because it has a much

EXHIBIT 17–11

Simulation Charts for Competing Proposals

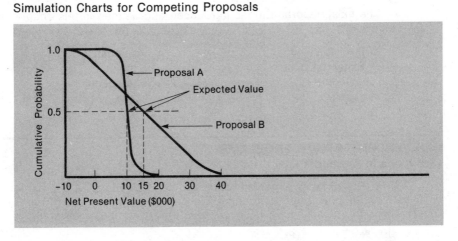

smaller probability of producing a loss. The capital expenditure simulation chart will help them make this kind of comparison.

SUMMARY

Uncertainty surrounds all decisions. Cash flows and present values are uncertain because:

1. The future values of important independent variables (e.g., the spendable income of the company's customers) are uncertain.
2. The relationship between the independent variable and the dependent variable (e.g., product sales) is uncertain.

These uncertainties become much more visible if they are displayed in payoff tables or decision trees. Decision trees can encompass whole series of uncertainties; payoff tables can deal with only one at a time.

Displays of the range of possible values can be strengthened if probabilities can be assigned to different possible states of nature. These probabilities can be used to combine the estimates into expected values, in which the various possible payoffs are weighted according to their likelihood of occurrence. The decision maker can use maximization of the expected value as the decision rule if it can be assumed that the utility of the payoffs is proportional to their amount.

Probability factors also can be used to construct probability-adjusted profit charts or, with the aid of computer simulation techniques, capital expenditure simulation charts. These can provide the decision makers with a broader foundation on which to base the exercise of their judgment. This is important because decision making, in the final analysis, is a judgmental process.

KEY TERMS

The most important terms introduced and defined in this chapter are the following:

Decision tree	Probability
Expected value	Simulation
Outcome	State of nature
Payoff	Utility

INDEPENDENT STUDY PROBLEMS
(Solutions in Appendix C)

1. Payoff table, expected value, and decision rules. A company is trying to decide how much to produce. Unsold units must be destroyed. Each unit costs $2 and sells for $3. The probabilities of various sales volumes are:

Units Sold	Probability
10................	0.1
11................	0.2
12................	0.3
13................	0.2
14................	0.15
15................	0.05

a.   Set up a payoff table.
b.   What level of production would maximize the expected value of the payoffs?
c.   How much should be produced if the company decides to maximize the possible gain? Minimize the possible loss?

2. Decision tree analysis. Loreen Green commutes to work in a large city. She can take a No. 33 bus to the end of the No. 1 subway line and take that subway to her office. Alternatively, she can take the train to the city and then take either a No. 66 bus or a No. 5 subway to the office.

The first of these is slightly more expensive than the second, but it is also slightly more comfortable. These two factors balance out, and Ms. Green will choose the combination that seems most likely to minimize her travel time. If everything is on time, the train-bus combination is the fastest, but the train is sometimes late and so is the No. 66 bus.

She has made the following estimates of commuting time (probability figures are given in parentheses):
1.   If she takes the bus to the end of the subway line:
    a.   40 minutes if everything is on time (0.5).
    b.   55 minutes if either bus or subway is late (0.3).
    c.   70 minutes if both bus and subway are late (0.2).
2.   If she takes the train but the train is late; and if she then takes the No. 66 bus:
    a.   50 minutes if the bus is on time (0.7).
    b.   65 minutes if the bus is late (0.3).
3.   If she takes the train but the train is late; and if she takes the No. 5 subway from the train station:
    a.   55 minutes if the subway is on time (0.8).
    b.   60 minutes if the subway is late (0.2).

4. If she takes the train and the train is on time; and if she then takes the No. 66 bus:
   a. 35 minutes if the bus is on time (0.7).
   b. 50 minutes if the bus is late (0.3).
5. If she takes the train and the train is on time; and if she takes the No. 5 subway from the train station:
   a. 40 minutes if the subway is on time (0.8).
   b. 45 minutes if the subway is late (0.2).
6. The probability of the train being on time is 0.7.

a. Draw a decision tree and enter the payoffs and probabilities.
b. Calculate the expected values. How should Ms. Green travel to work?
c. If the work day starts at 9 A.M. and Ms. Green's boss is willing to allow her to be late as often as 10 percent of the days without penalty, at what time should she leave home each day? You may assume that transportation is always available.

EXERCISES AND PROBLEMS

1. Payoff table and decision rules. Your automobile battery is very old, and you are afraid it will go dead during the coming winter if you don't replace it now. If you buy a new battery now, you can buy it at a price of $30. If you wait and the battery dies, you will have to pay $40 for a replacement.

Cold weather is approaching, and you believe that the probability of the battery dying during the winter is 70 percent.

a. Construct a payoff table.
b. Describe the decision rule that you would apply in this situation and indicate what decision you would make.

2. Capital expenditure simulation chart. Kendall Enterprises is considering two alternative investment proposals. Each of these calls for an initial investment outlay of $1 million. Probabilities were assigned to various values of the determinants of the rate of return, 20 sets of values were selected at random for each proposal, and the internal rate of return was calculated for each set. These calculated rates of return were as follows:

Proposal A		Proposal B	
15.0	18.6	14.4	14.9
14.7	13.5	15.6	13.5
14.0	15.3	15.0	14.6
16.0	16.5	13.9	15.0
10.5	15.1	14.8	14.2
14.9	11.4	15.0	15.8
17.1	15.6	15.0	15.1
19.5	15.0	15.4	15.2
12.2	17.8	15.1	16.1
14.4	12.9	16.5	14.9

a. Prepare a capital expenditure simulation chart.
b. Which of these two proposals would you recommend to management? Indicate the criterion or criteria you based your recommendation on. If you are unable to make a recommendation, explain why.

3. Payoff table; Bidding on a special order. The sales manager of the Franglais Company has been asked to submit a price quotation for 100,000 units of a product used by one of the Franglais customers.

The out-of-pocket cost of filling the order, if it can be obtained, is $90,000. Three possible prices are being considered, $1, $1.25, and $1.50. The sales manager is not certain how busy competitors' factories are, but in the light of their bids on recent jobs he thinks that the chance of their operating at a rate as high as 80 percent of capacity or higher is only 20 percent. Similarly, he believes that the probability that competitors are operating at 60 percent of capacity or less is 30 percent.

He estimates that if competitors' operating rates are 80 percent or higher, he can secure the order at any bid up to and including $1.50. If competitors are operating between 61 and 79 percent of capacity, a price of $1.25 or less will secure the bid, but if competitors' operating rates are 60 percent or less it will take a bid of $1 to land the order.

a. Prepare a payoff table to reflect these data.
b. Assuming that the decision rule is to maximize the expected value of the monetary return, which bid should be submitted?

4. Decision tree. Draw a decision tree to display the data in Problem 3. In a situation as simple as this, would you prefer the decision tree or the payoff table? What are the advantages of each?

5. Payoff table and expected value: Direct mailing. A direct mail company would charge you $2,000 to print and mail to a list of 10,000 selected executives a brochure describing your new "exec-o-mat" desk calendar. You buy these from a manufacturer for $15 and sell them for $30. An incremental cost of $1 is incurred to pack and ship each exec-o-mat. Your annual profit from other sources is $3,000, and your bank balance is now $2,500.

Your previous experience with mailings of this kind has indicated that any sales made in response to the mailing will be made in the three months immediately following the mailing. Your experience also leads you to expect a 3 percent response to the mailing (in this case, 300 units sold). The probabilities that you assign to the various possible outcomes are:

Percent Response		
Range	Average	Probability
0.51–1.5.................	1.0	0.10
1.51–2.5.................	2.0	0.25
2.51–3.5.................	3.0	0.50
3.51–4.5.................	4.0	0.10
4.51 or more...........	5.0	0.05

If you decide to undertake the mailing, you will increase your inventory and hire an additional stock clerk, so as to be prepared for any orders that come in. The stock clerk's wages and added inventory carrying costs on the additional inventory would amount to $500 a month. Costs of carrying the current levels of inventory and operating the stockroom total $3,000 a month.

The carrying cost figures included in the estimates quoted in the preceding paragraph apply only if sales made in response to the mailing total at least 300 units. In addition to these, extra incremental carrying costs of $0.50 would be incurred for each unit sold less than 300. (For example, if 200 units were sold, the extra carrying costs resulting from the failure to meet the 300-unit minimum would total $0.50 × (300 − 200) = $50. This figure covers the entire three-month period—it is not a cost per month.)

a. Prepare a profitability estimate on the basis of the forecasted 3 percent response.
b. Prepare a payoff table, with five states of nature.
c. Compute the expected value under each alternative management action.
d. Is this a situation in which the decision maker would be likely to use a decision rule that departs materially from maximum expected value? Comment.

6. Probability-adjusted profit charts. You have the following probability-adjusted profit charts for two different companies:

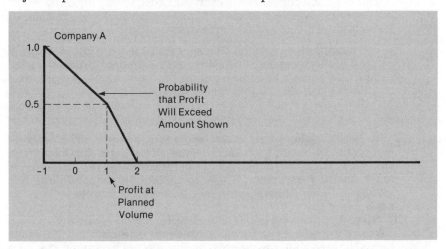

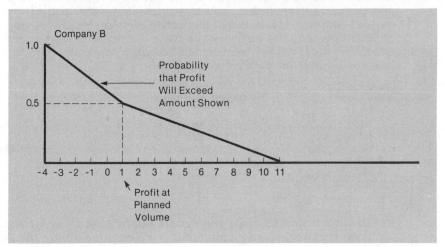

How do these two situations differ? Which situation would you prefer to be in? Explain.

7. Payoff table; Purchasing decision. Vendo, Inc., has been operating the concession stands at the University football stadium. The University has had successful football teams for many years; as a result the stadium is always full. The University is located in an area which suffers no rain during the football season. From time to time, Vendo has found itself very short of hot dogs and at other times it has had many left. A review of the records of sales of the past five seasons revealed the following frequency of hot dogs sold.

                          Total Games

10,000 hot dogs.................	5 times
20,000 hot dogs.................	10 times
30,000 hot dogs.................	20 times
40,000 hot dogs.................	15 times
	50 total games

Hot dogs sell for 50 cents each and cost Vendo 30 cents each. Unsold hot dogs are given to a local orphanage without charge. Hot dogs are paid for with the proceeds of the day's sales.

a. Assuming that only the four quantities listed were ever sold and that the occurrences were random events, prepare a payoff table (ignore income taxes) to represent the four possible strategies of ordering 10,000; 20,000; 30,000; or 40,000 hot dogs.

b. Using the expected value decision rule determine the best strategy.

(CMA adapted)

8. Payoff table; Safety stock and reorder point. The Starr Company manufactures several products. One of its main products requires an electric motor. The management of Starr Company uses the economic order quantity formula (EOQ) to determine the optimum number of motors to order. Management now wants to determine how much safety stock to order.

Starr Company uses 30,000 electric motors annually (300 working days). Using the EOQ formula, the company orders 3,000 motors at a time. The lead time for an order is five days. The annual cost of carrying one motor in safety stock is $10. Management has also estimated that the cost of being out of stock is $20 for each motor the company is short.

Starr Company has analyzed the usage during past reorder periods by examining the inventory records. The records indicate the following usage patterns during the past reorder periods:

Usage During *Lead Time*	*Number of Times* *Quantity Was Used*
440.............................	6
460.............................	12
480.............................	16
500.............................	130
520.............................	20
540.............................	10
560.............................	6
	200

a. Construct a payoff table and determine the level of safety stock that Starr Company should maintain if it wishes to minimize the expected value of its costs.

b. Calculate the reorder point on this basis.

(CMA adapted)

9. Size of batch: Expected value and parameters. A company sells product Y to retailers. Product Y is manufactured in batches in a factory that makes many other products. The labor cost of preparing the production equipment is substantial, and management tries to produce Product Y in large batches, if possible. To ensure that retailers always get fresh stock, however, the company never manufactures more in a batch than it expects to deliver in the next month. The product has a limited shelf life, and any units unsold at the end of the month must be destroyed.

The estimated labor and materials cost of product Y is $1.50 for direct materials and $3 for direct labor, when manufactured in batches of 1,000 units each. The direct labor cost figure includes $1 for the labor cost of preparing the production equipment for each batch (setup labor). Factory overhead costs in the factory as a whole, supporting production of all the company's products, are expected to amount to $10,000 plus 50 percent of direct labor cost. The full-cost factory overhead rate for product costing is 100 percent of direct labor cost.

The sales forecast for next month contains the following estimates for product Y:

Sales Volume (units)	Probability
750	0.1
1,000	0.4
1,250	0.3
1,500	0.2

The product is sold to retailers at a price of $10 a unit. Selling and administrative costs are unaffected by variations in the sales of product Y.

a. Ignoring inventory carrying costs, how large a batch of product Y should be produced to meet next month's demand if the decision rule is to maximize the expected value of the cash flows? For simplicity, you may assume that all costs are paid in cash and that cash is collected from customers on delivery.

b. Inventory carrying costs amount to $0.45 for each unit in the average inventory plus 10 percent of the incremental cost of the average inventory. Calculate the incremental carrying costs for an average inventory of 500 units. Explain your calculations.

c. Calculate the average inventory, in units, for a production volume of 1,000 units a month.

10. Probability-adjusted profit charts. The Stafford Company makes and sells cleaning fluid. It owns one large factory, located in Cincinnati, Ohio, which manufactures all the cleaning fluid the sales force can sell. This factory has a good deal of idle capacity, but seems to be operating efficiently.

The company's cleaning fluid is sold to wholesalers at a price of $2 a gallon. Stanley Jones, the company's president, asked Polly Ortner, the marketing vice president, to develop a tentative marketing plan for the coming year. Knowing Ms. Ortner's enthusiastic attitude, he asked her to use the same marketing mix and the same amount of order-getting activity, or less, as in the current year.

Working within these guidelines, Ms. Ortner submitted a proposed expense budget and estimated that expenses at this level would produce sales between 5 and 12 million gallons, the most likely volume being 8.5 million. She developed the following table of probabilities:

Volume Range (million gallons)	Probability
11–12	0.05
10–11	0.10
9–10	0.30
8– 9	0.25
7– 8	0.15
6– 7	0.10
5– 6	0.05

Management has made the following estimates of operating costs at various volumes:

Volume (million gallons)	Cost (millions of dollars)
12	$20.7
11	19.2
10	17.8
9	16.5
8	15.3
7	14.1
6	12.9
5	11.7

Estimates of cost at volumes between the levels shown in this table can be derived by linear interpolation.

Not satisfied with the original proposal, Ms. Ortner has developed an entirely different marketing plan, to present to Mr. Jones as an alternative to the first. It would increase spending on order-getting activities by $500,000, but it would increase anticipated sales volume to 9.5 million gallons. The new probability distribution is as follows:

Volume Range (million gallons)	Probability
11–12	0.10
10–11	0.20
9–10	0.30
8– 9	0.25
7– 8	0.10
6– 7	0.05
5– 6	—

a. Prepare profit-volume charts in conventional form to represent the two proposed plans. Locate and label the anticipated profit-volume combination for each. (You should draw both charts on the same sheet of graph paper.)

b. Prepare probability-adjusted profit charts for each plan, using the cumulative probabilities.

c. Using the charts only, decide which proposal management should approve. Prepare a brief list of the arguments for and against your recommendation.

11. Decision tree: Product development. The Premier Company has already spent $1,100,000 to develop a new product. Laboratory tests have been completed satisfactorily, and the next step is to set up and operate an experimental production line on a small scale to test the feasibility of manufacturing the product in commercial quantities. The cost of this experimental production will be $200,000.

The knowledgeable managers agree that the following outcomes of the production experiment are likely:

1. There is a 0.1 probability that the test will show that the product should be dropped.

2. There is a 0.7 probability that the test will show that the product can be manufactured in a standard plant costing $2 million.

3. There is a 0.2 probability that the test will show that the product can be manufactured only in a complex plant costing $4 million.

Once the plant has been built, the product faces an uncertain market:

1. There is a 0.2 probability that substantial sales will be made to chain stores. If this happens, the present value of the operating cash inflows will be $5 million.

2. There is a 0.8 probability that the market will be limited to independent retailers and institutional customers. If this happens, the present value of the operating cash inflows will be $3.5 million.

a. Draw a decision tree and enter the probabilities and payoffs.
b. Calculate the expected value of each managerial action. Should the experimental production line be set up?

(Prepared by Professor Alexander A. Robichek)

12. Decision tree: Product development. You are general manager of the Technical Products Corporation. Your chief designer is 90 percent certain of developing a new gas measuring instrument if you will allocate $100,000. He's a skilled designer but also an optimist, in your judgment, so you set these probabilities:

0.7 that he will develop the instrument for $100,000.
0.3 that he will spend the $100,000 without success and then come back saying, "I need $100,000 more."
0.4 that, if not successful at first and if given the additional $100,000 (total $200,000), he will be successful.
0.6 that, if not successful at first and if given the additional $100,000 (total $200,000), he will be unsuccessful.

You consult next with your sales manager about expected sales of the instrument and you both agree that if the design of the instrument is successful you can expect the following:

1. A one-third probability that manufacture and sale of the gas measuring instrument will break even, but with no contribution to repay development costs and provide a profit.
2. A two-thirds probability that the contribution to development costs and profit will be $300,000.

a. Draw the decision tree.
b. Calculate the expected values. Should the $100,000 be allocated?

(Prepared by Professor Alexander A. Robichek)

13. Decision tree: Investment decision. The Alps Paper Company has agreed to give an answer by Tuesday on an offer by Lavaux Lumber Company to sell Alps a pulp facility for $4 million.

The managers of Alps Paper estimate that the present value of the future cash flows from the pulp facility will be somewhere between −$1 million and +$5.5 million, before deducting the cost of the facility itself. The probabilities are:

Present Value	Probability
−$1,000,000	0.1
+ 4,000,000	0.2
+ 4,500,000	0.5
+ 5,500,000	0.2

The managers of Alps Paper are uncertain what will happen if they turn the offer down, but their best guess is that (with a 0.5 probability) Lavaux Lumber Company will reoffer the pulp facility to Alps within two weeks at a reduced price of $2.5 million.

If Alps Paper doesn't buy the facility, two other things may happen, and both are considered equally likely:

Lavaux Lumber will continue to operate the pulp facility; this will represent a zero cash flow for Alps Paper.

The pulp facility will be sold to another aggressive paper company; this will cost Alps Paper cash flows with a present value of $1 million.

a. Draw the decision tree.
b. Calculate the expected values. What should Alps Paper do now?

(Prepared by Professor Alexander A. Robichek)

14. Uncertain estimates; Sensitivity analysis. Samuel Telford is a promoter. He invests capital for short periods in new ventures in the expectation of selling out at a profit after the ventures have been fully financed. Through a privately owned corporation, Plexco, Inc., he also markets a constantly changing line of gadgets, games, novelty gifts, and office accessories. Few of these products remain on the market for more than a few months. "My products have very short life cycles," he said recently. "Once in a while I get one that catches on, like the felt-tip pen, but when that happens I look for a buyer and sell out. I'd rather get my money back and move on to something new."

Plexco has a small sales force for products that are marketed through retail outlets. Most production is either subcontracted or turned out on temporary production lines, although the company does have a small-scale manufacturing facility of its own.

Mr. Telford recently considered marketing a new wall decoration for use in executive offices, reception rooms, and so on. This product would be sold entirely by mail. A "direct mail" company would charge $20,000 to print and mail a descriptive brochure to a list of about 100,000 selected executives. Plexco's previous experience with mailings of this kind indicated a likely response percentage of about 3 percent—that is, about 3,000 units would be sold as a result of the mailing.

The wall decorations would be sold at a price of $20 each. A small assembly line would be set up for a one-month production run. The project was expected to produce a net cash inflow of $6,000, reflecting the following incremental costs and revenues:

	Unit Amount	Total
Sales	$20	$60,000
Costs:		
Materials	$ 8	$24,000
Labor (½-hour per unit)	2	6,000
Manufacturing overhead	—	4,000
Mailing	—	20,000
Total cost	xx	$54,000
Incremental cash flow	xx	$ 6,000

All of the incremental manufacturing overhead costs would be fixed costs.

Mr. Telford was not wholly convinced. "I can't argue with your estimates of materials costs, wage rates and overhead costs," he said, "but the labor time figure and response percentage could be way off. The foreman says that he can turn out a unit in 15 minutes if everything goes right, but if we get hit with a slowdown as we did last year, average time could even go up to an hour."

a. Errors in forecasting the response percentage are seldom greater than 33.33 percent of the forecasted percentage, labor time may be off by the amounts indicated above, but forecasting errors in the other profit determinants are generally 10 percent or less. For which of the parameters is the decision sensitive to forecasting errors of these magnitudes?

b. How large would the forecasting error have to be to make the decision sensitive to errors in forecasting the response percentage, materials cost, or labor time?

c. The possible response percentages range from about 0.5 percent to a little more than 5 percent. Prepare a table showing the incremental profit or loss for response rates of 0.5, 1.5, 2.5, 3.5, 4.5, and 5.5 percent.

d. The probabilities of the various response rates are approximately as follows:

Percent Response		
Range	Average	Probability
0.51–1.5.........................	1.0	0.10
1.51–2.5.........................	2.0	0.25
2.51–3.5.........................	3.0	0.50
3.51–4.5.........................	4.0	0.10
4.51 or more	5.0	0.05

Add a column to the table you prepared in answer to (c), showing the cumulative probabilities of response rates and incremental profits less than the amounts indicated in the first two columns.

e. Plot profit or loss and cumulative probability on a sheet of graph paper, draw a smooth line through the plotted points, and use this line to estimate the probability that introducing the new product will be profitable.

18

Statistical Cost Estimation

ESTIMATES of the relationships between costs and other variables are needed both in flexible budgeting and in most managerial decision models. Management uses many different techniques to identify these relationships. This chapter will examine some of the methods used in this kind of analysis. It consists of three parts:

1. A review of nonmathematical methods of estimating relationships between costs and other variables.
2. A study of mathematical methods of estimating these relationships.
3. An examination of a particular kind of cost relationship, the effect of experience on cost, referred to as the learning curve.

NONMATHEMATICAL METHODS

Some estimated relationships are based on engineers' analyses of technological relationships. Methods study and work sampling are two engineering techniques we have already mentioned. Other estimated relationships are the products of rigorous mathematical techniques that we shall examine in the next two sections. Before moving into this new ground, however, we need to review two other techniques we introduced earlier—the judgment method and graphic curve fitting. These are often used by themselves, often in conjunction with mathematical techniques, and should not be ignored. We shall also have a few words to say about a third method, the high-low points method.

Judgment Method

In the final analysis, all cost estimation is judgmental. No matter how rigorous the mathematical technique, it cannot capture all the influences on cost, many of them operating in subtle ways. Nor can it capture the future, which is usually what the analyst is interested in. Managers have to decide whether to bet the company's fortunes on the relationships turned up by their technicians or to modify these figures. The responsibility is always the manager's.

In the judgment method, also known as the *inspection of accounts* method, the manager and the accountant classify the costs in each object-of-expenditure account as wholly fixed, wholly variable, or a mixture of the two. For wholly variable cost elements, a single average cost figure is selected; for wholly fixed elements, a total cost for the time period is called for; and for mixed cost elements, the manager provides any cost formula that seems to describe the relationship best.

This approach seldom appeals to the technician, but it has several advantages:

1. It permits managers to specify relationships that are difficult to establish statistically—e.g., step functions.
2. It requires managers to participate actively in cost analysis, increasing their understanding of the ways costs behave.
3. It is not restricted to historical data, but can be used directly to identify estimated future relationships.

At its worst, the judgment method is pure guesswork; at its best, it provides estimated relationships with qualitative as well as quantitative dimensions. The main disadvantage of the judgment method is that it fails to use relevant data that are readily available. As a result, most managers will use some historical data in preparing judgmental estimates—the more data they use, the more technical analysis they are likely to need to support their judgment.

Graphic Method

The judgment method relies mainly on historical experience, supplemented in most cases by at least some historical data. Engineering methods also draw heavily from the past. The graphic method goes even further, relying exclusively on past data. Before describing this method, however, we need to define a few terms. A *regression equation* identifies an estimated relationship between a dependent variable (cost) and one or more independent variables (production volume, air temperature, and so on), based on historical or experimental observations. If the equation includes only one independent variable, it is referred to as a *simple regression,* and the regression equation can be traced on an ordinary sheet of graph paper as a *regression line.*

If the dependent variable is cost, the independent variable is volume, and the relationship is assumed to be linear, the regression line can be described by the equation for a straight line:

$$y = a + bx$$

in which

x = Volume per period.
y = Total cost per period at that volume.
a = Total fixed cost per period.
b = Average variable cost per unit of volume.[1]

If fixed costs amount to $3,000 a month and variable costs average 50 cents a direct labor hour, the equation for the regression line is:

$$\text{Cost} = \$3,000 + \$0.50 \times \text{direct labor hours}$$

(As we explained in Chapter 3, the constant, a, may not be a good estimate of costs at zero volume. It is simply a residual, determined by extending the regression line from the experienced volume range in a straight line back to the zero-volume level. To simplify the termi-

EXHIBIT 18–1

A Regression Line Fitted by the Graphic Method

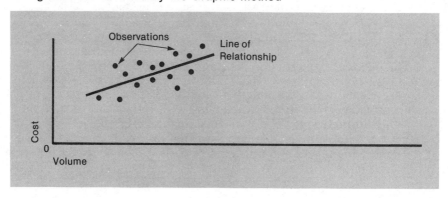

nology, however, we shall refer to this amount as total fixed cost.)

Regression analysis is the process by which a regression equation is derived. In the graphic method, the analyst draws a line ("fits a curve") on a sheet of graph paper to approximate the relationship revealed by a series of past cost-volume observations plotted on the same graph.[2] One of these is shown in Exhibit 18–1.

This may seem like a haphazard way of drawing a regression line, but it often produces results very close to those emerging from more rigorous mathematical techniques. Two skilled statisticians, looking independently at the observations plotted in Exhibit 18–1, are likely to come up with very similar estimates of relationship.

---

[1] The symbol C and V would more clearly identify cost and volume, but standard statistical notation uses x and y. Since this notation will be convenient later on, we shall use it now.

[2] The graphic method may also be used in *multiple regression analysis* (two or more independent variables). See William A. Spurr and Charles P. Bonini, *Statistical Analysis for Business Decisions*, rev. ed. (Homewood, Ill.: Richard D. Irwin, Inc., 1973), pp. 499–503.

Computer programs for regression analysis are now so widely available and so easy to use that the advantage the graphic method once had—it was cheaper to use—has evaporated. Drawing the scatter diagram—that is, plotting the observations on graph paper—is often useful, however, even if a mathematical curve-fitting technique is used. It provides a visual impression of the relationship and of the dispersion of the estimates.

High-Low Points Method

An even simpler method of estimating cost-volume relationships from historical data is the high-low points method. This consists of selecting the periods of highest and lowest volumes in the past and relating the difference in volume to the difference in cost between these two volumes. For example:

	Volume (Direct Labor Hours)	Indirect Labor Cost
High volume....................	9,500	$2,900
Low volume...................	5,000	2,000
Difference.............	4,500	$ 900

$$\frac{\$900}{4,500} = \$0.20 \text{ a direct labor hour.}$$

The $0.20 is interpreted as the average variable cost within this range.

The high-low points method uses a two-step calculation to derive an estimate of total fixed cost:

1. Multiply the average variable cost by the low volume ($0.20 × 5,000 direct labor hours = $1,000).
2. Subtract this figure from the observed total cost at the low volume ($2,000 − $1,000 = $1,000).

This method is extremely vulnerable to random variations in cost. Even if the highs and the lows are based on averages of several high points and several low points, the fact remains that the relationship is estimated solely from data at the extremes, ignoring all the observations in between. For this reason it should be used seldom, if at all.

THE LEAST SQUARES METHOD: SIMPLE LINEAR REGRESSION

Most technical analysis of cost relationships is done mathematically, for two reasons:

1. It can be done quickly and routinely on the computer.
2. It permits numerical measures of the reliability of the estimated relationship.

The mathematical method most commonly used for this purpose is least squares regression analysis. In this section we shall see how this method can be used to develop linear estimates of relationships between two variables.[3] Four stages in the analysis need to be identified:

1. Preparing the data.
2. Calculating the regression equation.
3. Testing the reliability of the equation.
4. Evaluating the results.

Preparing the Data

The first step in a regression analysis is to collect the necessary observations. Six guidelines should be noted:

1. Each observation should cover a time period long enough to smooth out major random fluctuations in cost, but not so long that the output rate varies substantially within the period.
2. Enough observations should be provided to produce a substantial number of degrees of freedom. (This term is explained later in this section.)
3. The period within which the observations are made shouldn't be so long that major changes in cost structure have taken place within it, affecting some of the observations but not all of them. (Installation of major new equipment after half the observations have been made, for example, would destroy the relevance of the pre-installation observations.)
4. Observations should cover all portions of the likely output range; the regression equation should be regarded as valid only for the covered portion of the range.
5. Data collection routines should ensure that costs are recorded as resources are used or committed; volume should be recorded as it occurs. (Unofficial inventorying of issued supplies on the shop floor and failure to consider changes in work in process are two common collection errors.)
6. Each observation must provide a value of each of the variables.

Meeting these specifications is often difficult. To get enough observations (the second guideline) we may be tempted to shorten each observation period (violating the first guideline) or to accept observations made during very early time periods (violating the third guideline). We must be careful, therefore, to inspect the data to detect

---

[3] We can do no more than review the fundamentals of mathematical regression analysis in the few pages available here. For example, we don't show the mathematical derivations of the formulas the analysis is based on. Anyone needing to apply this method independently should study a standard statistics text such as the one by Spurr and Bonini, *Statistical Analysis for Business Decisions*, chaps. 16–17; for a more advanced treatment, see Edmond Malinvaud, *Statistical Methods of Econometrics*, 2d rev. ed. (New York: American Elsevier Publishing Co., 1970), chaps. 3–10.

extreme items, changes in input prices, changes in operating methods, and spurious cost relationships. These can be handled as follows:

1.   Observations should be corrected for changes in input prices— e.g., labor costs recorded before a 5 percent wage increase should be multiplied by 1.05.
2.   If operating methods have changed, observations made prior to the change should be dropped from the analysis. If the effect of the methods change can be estimated reliably, the data may be adjusted to allow for it, but this is a risky step.
3.   Observations affected by extraordinary events (strikes, floods, and so on) should be excluded from the analysis. These often show up in a scatter diagram as extreme items, far outside the pattern traced by the other observations.
4.   Cost variations produced by accounting allocation and absorption techniques should be ignored; accounting allocations in some cases should be based on regression equations rather than the other way around. (Cost distributions based on time or usage records should not be excluded on these grounds if they measure the attributable cost of the resources used.)

Calculating the Regression Equation

The least squares method is based on a mathematical idea that the line that fits a set of data best has the following property:

> The sum of the squares of the vertical deviations of the actual observations from this line is less than the sum of the squares of the vertical deviations from any other line that might be drawn on the chart.

This is illustrated in Exhibit 18–2. Each of the observed values of y is labeled y_o; the corresponding point on the regression line is y_c. The

EXHIBIT 18–2

Property of a Least Squares Regression Line

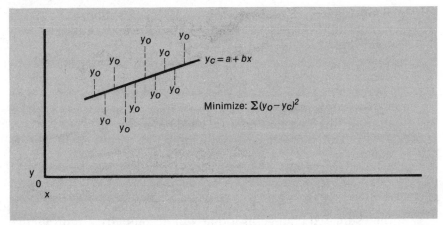

difference between the two is the vertical distance between y_o and y_c at the observed volume. Σ is the mathematical symbol for a sum.

The regression equation for a straight line with this property and representing the relationship between y and x can be found by calculating the sums required by the following two equations, known as the *normal equations*, and solving for a and b:

$$\Sigma y = an + b\Sigma x$$
$$\Sigma xy = a\Sigma x + b\Sigma x^2$$

in which $n =$ the number of observations of cost and volume.

To make these normal equations easier to work with, we can translate them into the following form:

$$a = \frac{\Sigma y}{n} - \frac{b\Sigma x}{n}$$

$$b = \frac{n\Sigma xy - \Sigma x\Sigma y}{n\Sigma x^2 - (\Sigma x)^2}$$

(1)

To illustrate the method without unnecessary arithmetic, let us suppose we have six cost/volume observations from which we wish to estimate the relationship between cost and volume. The observations and the computational quantities required by the two normal equations are as follows:

Volume	Cost		
x	y	xy	x²
3	5	15	9
4	6	24	16
5	6	30	25
6	9	54	36
7	9	63	49
8	10	80	64
$\Sigma = 33$	45	266	199

n, of course, is 6 because we have six observations.

Substituting these amounts in the normal equations, we get the following:

$$a = 45/6 - (33/6)b \tag{1}$$
$$b = (6 \times 266 - 33 \times 45)/(6 \times 199 - (33)^2) \tag{2}$$

Solving equation (2), we find that b equals $111/105 = 1.057$. Putting this in equation (1) yields a value of $a = 7.500 - 5.814 = 1.686$. The regression line therefore is described by the following equation:

$$y = \$1.686 + \$1.057\, x.$$

The value for b is known as a *regression coefficient*. It indicates the estimated change in y that will accompany a unit change in x if

EXHIBIT 18-3

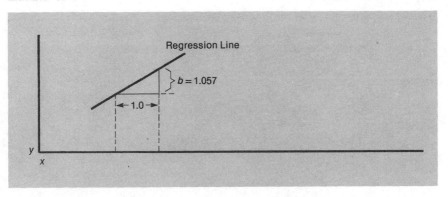

there is no change in any of the influences on y other than x (see Exhibit 18–3).

We can use this formula to predict the cost that will be incurred at any volume. At a volume of 3, for example, cost should be $1.686 + 3 \times 1.057 = 4.857$. This is $0.143 less than the amount observed at that volume. Repeating this calculation for each of the other observed volumes, we get the following comparison:

	Observed Cost	Calculated Cost	Deviation	Deviation^2
Volume x	y_o	y_c	$(y_o - y_c)$	$(y_o - y_c)^2$
3	$ 5	$ 4.857	+$0.143	0.0204
4	6	5.914	+ 0.086	0.0074
5	6	6.971	− 0.971	0.9428
6	9	8.028	+ 0.972	0.9448
7	9	9.085	− 0.085	0.0072
8	10	10.142	− 0.142	0.0202
$\Sigma =$				1.9428

These observations, predictions, and deviations are diagrammed in Exhibit 18–4. Because we had no observations at volumes less than 3, this part of the regression line is shown as a dashed line.

This regression line has the property required by the least squares method: it minimizes the sum of the squares of the cost deviations from the line. If we were to alter either a or b, the sum of the squared deviations would be greater than 1.9428.

Tests of Reliability

Although most of the observed values of y were virtually identical to the predicted values, two of them were not. In other cases, the fit will be even worse. The line in the following diagram, for example, is

EXHIBIT 18–4

Mathematically Fitted Regression Line

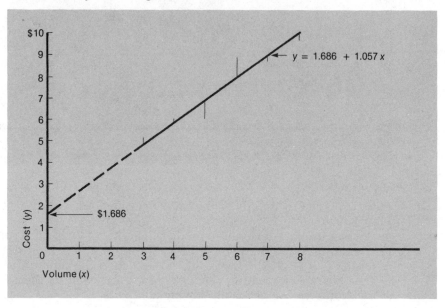

a very bad fit because the observations are scattered so widely around it (see Exhibit 18–5).

Before a regression equation can be used, the manager needs to know how closely it has fit the observed facts in the past. We shall look at three measures of reliability:

1. The coefficient of determination.
2. The standard error of the estimate.
3. The standard error of the coefficient.

EXHIBIT 18–5

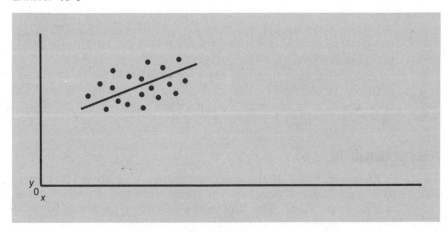

The coefficient of determination. If the regression line were to fit the actual observations perfectly, all of the observed points would lie on the line. This suggests that reliability is related to the size of the deviations of the actual observations (y_o) from the calculated values (y_c). These figures are captured in the *residual variation*, defined as the average of the sum of the squared deviations. Its symbol is s_e^2:

$$s_e^2 = \Sigma(y_o - y_c)^2/n = 1.9428/6 = 0.324$$

The smaller this figure, the better the fit.

The next question, however, is how much better a fit the regression equation is than something simpler. It may be that we could predict costs almost as well by assuming they will be equal to the average of all the observations. In other words, how much predictive ability did we gain by introducing volume (x) as an independent variable?

We can answer this by calculating the deviations of the individual cost observations (y_o) from the average of the six figures $(\bar{y})$:

Observed Cost (y)	Average Cost $(\bar{y})$	Deviation $(y_o - \bar{y})$	Deviation² $(y_o - \bar{y})^2$
5	7.5	−2.5	6.25
6	7.5	−1.5	2.25
6	7.5	−1.5	2.25
9	7.5	+1.5	2.25
9	7.5	+1.5	2.25
10	7.5	+2.5	6.25
$\Sigma =$			21.50

The statistician's measure of the size of the dispersion of a set of figures around their mean is known as the *variance*. Its symbol is s^2. To try to reduce the danger of confusing this with our term for deviations from standard cost, we shall refer to the statistical variance as the *variation*. It is defined as the average of the sum of the squared deviations from the mean:

$$s^2 = \Sigma(y_o - \bar{y})^2/n.$$

In this case the total variation is $21.50/6 = 3{:}583$.

Now we can see the significance of the residual variation we calculated earlier. By introducing variations in volume as a possible way of predicting variations in cost, we accounted for all but 0.324 of the total variation of 3.583. In other words, volume variations accounted for more than 90 percent of the variation of cost around its mean. This relationship is summarized in the *coefficient of determination* (r^2):

$$r^2 = 1 - \frac{\Sigma(y_o - y_c)^2}{\Sigma(y_o - \bar{y})^2}$$
$$= 1 - 1.9428/21.5 = 1 - 0.09 = 0.91$$

The general term for the degree of association between variables is *correlation*. If all the observations fall on the regression line, $\Sigma (y_o - y_c)^2$ will be zero, and r^2 will be equal to 1. This is known as *perfect correlation*. On the other hand, if the deviations from the predicted values are as great as the deviations from the mean, then $\Sigma(y_o - y_c)^2/\Sigma(y_o - \bar{y})^2$ will equal 1, and r^2 will equal zero. This is known as no correlation or *zero correlation*.

Standard error of the estimate.   Although the coefficient of determination says something about the reliability of estimates of the dependent variable based on the regression equation, it doesn't measure the absolute size of the probable deviations from the line. This is the role of the standard error of the estimate (s_e). For any set of observations, the standard error of the estimate can be calculated from the following formula:

$$s_e = \sqrt{\Sigma(y_o - y_c)^2/n}$$

In this case, the calculation is:

$$s_e = \sqrt{1.9428/6} = 0.569$$

This is not the only set of observations that might be collected, however. It is usually a sample from some larger "population." The population in this case consists of all combinations of cost and volume that might occur in the present operation. Our six observations may reflect the characteristics of the population perfectly—or they may be very unusual, not representative of the population at all.

If our objective is to calculate the expected amount of variation around the true line of relationship—the one that would emerge if the entire population were included—then we have to allow for the possibility that the standard error of the line drawn from the sample may not be the same as the standard error of a line drawn from the population as a whole.

The way to do this is to adjust the formula to conform to the number of *degrees of freedom* allowed by the observations. The revised formula is:

$$s_e = \sqrt{\Sigma(y_o - y_c)^2/(n - m)}$$

in which m = the number of constants and regression coefficients, and $(n - m)$ is the number of degrees of freedom. In our example, $m = 2$, leaving four degrees of freedom.[4] The standard error of the estimate therefore is:

$$s_e = \sqrt{1.9428/4} = 0.697$$

We don't have the space to explain this adjustment in full, but a few words about degrees of freedom may help. Each observation in a

---

[4] To avoid calculating all the values of y_c, we can use the following formula to calculate the standard error of the estimate for a linear regression equation with one independent variable:

$$s_e = \sqrt{\frac{\Sigma y^2 - a\Sigma y - b\Sigma xy}{n - 2}}$$

EXHIBIT 18–6

A 95 Percent Confidence Interval

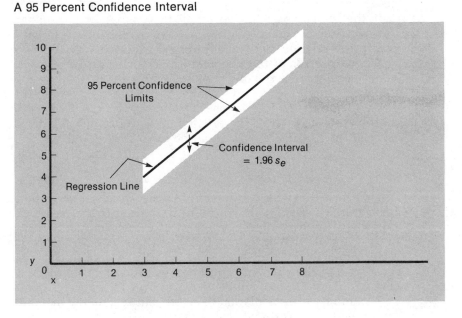

sample is free to take any value in the possible range. Once a coefficient has been calculated from a set of observations, however, at least one of them is no longer free to vary. With six observations, five can vary but the sixth must take whatever value is necessary to keep the coefficient at its calculated value. If two coefficients are calculated, two restrictions are imposed on the set of observations.

The number of degrees of freedom is important because it is one determinant of the reliability of a sample. The larger the number of degrees of freedom, the more likely the coefficients from the sample will be close to the coefficients in the population as a whole.

Confidence intervals. Our main reason for calculating the standard error of the estimate is to use it to establish *confidence intervals*. A confidence interval is a range of values of the dependent variable within which we may have some degree of confidence the true value lies. Different confidence intervals can be calculated for different degrees of confidence.

Statisticians can demonstrate, for example, that there are two chances out of three that the interval specified by $(y_c \pm s_e)$ will include the true value of y if the observations are distributed normally about the line.[5] For $x = 5$, the calculated value of y is $1.686 + 1.057 \times 5 = 6.971$. Since $s_e = 0.697$, we can state that the chances

---

[5] The observations in our illustration were not distributed normally. To eliminate this objection we would have had to use a larger, more complex set of numbers. Since our only purpose was to illustrate the method, we chose numerical simplicity over technical precision.

are two out of three that cost will be between 6.274 and 7.668 (6.971 ± 0.697).

If the interval is widened to $(y_c \pm 1.96\ s_e)$, the confidence level goes up to 95 percent. A 95 percent confidence interval for our illustrative relationship is diagrammed in Exhibit 18–6.

Standard error of the coefficient. The standard error of the estimate measures the reliability of the estimates of total cost. Another important question is how reliable the regression coefficient is, because the analysis often focuses on the *rate of variability* rather than on the absolute level of the prediction. The formula for the standard error of the b coefficient (s_b) can be expressed as follows:

$$s_b = \frac{s_e}{\sqrt{\Sigma(x_o - \bar{x})^2}}$$

This measures the relationship of the standard error of the estimate to the variation in x around its mean. If the xs cover a wide range, s_b will be small; if the values of x cover only a narrow portion of the range, s_b will be large. (In the extreme case, if all the values of x are equal to their mean, $(x_o - \bar{x})^2$ will be zero and s_b will be infinitely large. Putting this another way, you can't measure a regression coefficient if your sample doesn't cover the range.)

To simplify the calculation of s_b, we can restate the denominator in quantities we have already calculated:

$$s_b = \frac{s_e}{\sqrt{\Sigma x_o^2 - \bar{x}\Sigma x_o}}$$

In this case:

$$s_b = 0.697/\sqrt{199 - 5.5 \times 33} = 0.697/4.1833 = 0.167$$

This says that the b value of 1.057 has a standard error of 0.167. The question is whether this is big enough to cast doubt on the proposition that the b in the population as a whole is something other than zero.

To answer this question, we can calculate the ratio of the coefficient to its standard error. This is called its *t-value*. The calculation in this case is:

$$t\text{-value} = b/s_b = 1.057/0.167 = 6.329$$

This says that the b in the sample is 6.329 standard errors from zero. Intuitively, we can say that it doesn't seem likely that b would be this far from zero even if the sample wasn't representative. Statisticians don't like intuition, however. Instead, they use a table showing how many multiples of the standard error of the regression coefficient are reasonable, given a specified number of degrees of freedom and a given probability level.

A partial set of these values of t is given in Exhibit 18–7. To interpret this, let's pick one figure from the table, the figure for 4 degrees of freedom in the column headed 0.95. This says that there are only five chances in 100 that a sample would turn up a b coefficient greater than 2.776 s_b if the b coefficient for the population as a whole were

EXHIBIT 18–7

Partial Table of t-Values*

Degrees of Freedom	Maximum Values of t Consistent with Confidence Interval with Probability of		
	0.90	0.95	0.99
1...............	6.314	12.706	63.657
2...............	2.920	4.303	9.925
3...............	2.353	3.182	5.841
4...............	2.132	2.776	4.604
5...............	2.015	2.571	4.032
6...............	1.943	2.447	3.707
7...............	1.895	2.365	3.499
8...............	1.860	2.305	3.355
9...............	1.833	2.262	3.250
10...............	1.812	2.228	3.169
11...............	1.796	2.201	3.106
12...............	1.782	2.179	3.055
13...............	1.771	2.160	3.012
14...............	1.761	2.145	2.977
15...............	1.753	2.131	2.947
Infinite............	1.645	1.960	2.576

* The headings of t-tables usually identify the probabilities of values falling in one tail of a bell-shaped distribution. We have reversed the legend for greater clarity, emphasizing the probabilities of the value falling in the main body of the distribution, not in the tail. The probability 0.95, for example, is the ratio of the unshaded area in the diagram at the right to half the area under the curve. This column in a typical t-table is headed $t_{.025}$, indicating that 2.5 percent of the area under the whole curve lies in the shaded area under the curve at the extreme right. This is 5 percent of the area under the right-hand side of the bell; the unshaded area thus occupies 95 percent of that total.

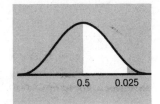

zero. The 2.776 s_b is known as the confidence interval—if the value of the coefficient is larger than this, we can be 95 percent confident that it reflects a real relationship in the population.

The 95 percent confidence interval for the b coefficient in our illustration is

$$1.057 \pm 2.776 \times 0.167$$
$$= 1.057 \pm 0.464.$$

In other words, we can be 95 percent confident that the true value of the variable cost coefficient is somewhere between 0.593 and 1.521. From a similar set of calculations, we can also be 90 percent confident that the true value is within ± 0.356 of 1.057.

These ranges are quite large, despite the high r^2 we derived earlier. The reason is that we used an example with few observations, leaving few degrees of freedom. The greater the number of degrees of freedom, the more confident we can be that the sample is representative. The farther down in Exhibit 18–7 we go, the smaller the t-values are.

Regression equation summary
$$y = 1.9428 + (1.057 \pm 0.462)x$$
$$s_b = 0.167$$
$$t_{.95} = 2.776$$
$$r^2 = 0.91$$

Technical Assumptions

So far we have assumed that if enough usable observations can be found, management can rely on the regression equations within the stated confidence intervals. This is true only if a number of technical assumptions are valid. The main technical assumptions underlying simple linear regression analysis can be summarized in two sentences:

1. The relationship between the variables in the population is linear.
2. The values of the "disturbance term" $(y_o - y_c)$ are normally distributed, independent of each other, and with constant variance.

The significance of these assumptions and what to do when they are violated are questions that must be left to books on statistical methods.[6] We mention them here merely to sound a note of caution. Although the standard errors may produce relatively narrow confidence intervals, they may not mean much if the analytical assumptions are invalid.

Evaluating the Equation

Once the equation has been calculated, management has to decide what to do with it. This is not just a matter of testing the statistical reliability of the equation and the validity of the technical assumptions. Management may find the estimates adequate for some purposes even if their statistical reliability is low. In other cases, management may decide to repeat the analysis, perhaps with a different combination of variables, perhaps with a revised set of data, in the hope of improving the reliability of the results.

Even if management decides the results are good enough, the analysis isn't necessarily finished. The least squares method is designed to estimate the relationships that *have existed* between cost and other variables in the past. To use these estimated relationships to predict the future or to establish performance standards, the manager must decide how closely the future is likely to reproduce the conditions that prevailed in the past. At a minimum, price increases and

---

[6] For example, Malinvaud, *Statistical Methods of Econometrics;* a brief explanation of these assumptions in nontechnical language can be found in George J. Benston, "Multiple Regression Analysis of Cost Behavior," *Accounting Review,* October 1966, pp. 657–72, and in Spurr and Bonini, *Statistical Analysis for Business Decisions,* pp. 469–70.

methods changes have to be allowed for specifically, both in the fixed cost and in the b coefficient.

Management always has the option of rejecting the findings out of hand, of course. Sometimes the results of a regression analysis just don't ring true. We are not saying that management's accumulated knowledge is always superior to mathematically derived estimates. Far from it. Figures can be wrong, however, and management should not shrink from using its judgment if it has good reason to doubt the figures. Regression analysis is a tool to help management, not replace it.

OTHER LEAST SQUARES REGRESSIONS

A regression analysis based on simple pairings of observations of two variables may not be good enough. In this section we shall look briefly at three possible extensions of the method:

1. Multiple regression analysis.
2. Nonlinear regression analysis.
3. Lagged regression analysis.

Multiple Regression Analysis

Cost is seldom determined by one variable only. For example, in a plant which generates its own steam and uses this steam both for heating and for motive power, two of the important determinants of cost are likely to be the number of "degree-days" (65°F. minus average outside temperature for each day) and the number of machine-hours.

A simple regression of cost on machine-hours is likely to have a relatively low coefficient of determination because the b coefficient will not capture the effects of variations in outside temperature. This suggests that one way to account for more of the total variation is to add one or more additional independent variables. Each additional variable should add a little more to our ability to understand how costs behave.

An analysis with two or more independent variables is known as multiple regression analysis. If there are two independent variables and the relationship is assumed to be linear, the regression equation will take the following form:

$$y = a + b_1 x_1 + b_2 x_2$$

in which

y = Total cost.
a = Total fixed cost.
x_1 = The number of machine-hours.
b_1 = The regression coefficient for machine-hours.
x_2 = The number of degree-days.
b_2 = The regression coefficient for degree-days.

Once again, the constant, a, doesn't necessarily measure the amount of cost that will be incurred at zero volume; it is a synthetic figure, derived by extending the relationships within the customary range of the independent variables, for which we have data, down to the zero level, for which we have no data. The important figures are b_1 and b_2: b_1 is supposed to show how y will change with a unit change in x_1, assuming that x_2 *and all unidentified variables remain constant;* similarly, b_2 measures the estimated change in y for a unit change in x_2, if x_1 remains constant.

To illustrate, suppose we have the following observations:[7]

x_1	x_2	y
1	3	11
2	5	23
3	1	5
4	2	12
5	3	19
6	5	31
7	8	48
8	6	40
$\Sigma = 36$	33	189

The normal equations for a regression equation with two independent variables are as follows:[8]

$$\Sigma y = an + b_1 \Sigma x_1 + b_2 \Sigma x_2$$
$$\Sigma x_1 y = a\Sigma x_1 + b_1 \Sigma(x_1^2) + b_2 \Sigma x_1 x_2$$
$$\Sigma x_2 y = a\Sigma x_2 + b_1 \Sigma x_1 x_2 + b_2 \Sigma(x_2^2)$$

The required sums are:

$$\Sigma x_1^2 = 204$$
$$\Sigma x_2^2 = 173$$
$$\Sigma x_1 x_2 = 173$$
$$\Sigma x_1 y = 1,057$$
$$\Sigma x_2 y = 1,013$$

The solution, for those who want to try a hand at it, is as follows:

$$y = -6 + 2x_1 + 5x_2$$

This indicates that y will go up \$2 for every additional unit of x_1 and \$5 for each additional unit of x_2. The -6 value for a seems to indicate that costs would be negative at $x_1 = x_2 = 0$, but as we have said before this merely indicates that the relationship summarized in the equation doesn't go as far as the origin.

The coefficient of multiple determination and the standard errors of the individual regression coefficients can be calculated with the aid of

---

[7] This illustration has been borrowed from Clifford H. Springer, Robert E. Herlihy, and Robert I. Beggs, *Advanced Methods and Models* (Homewood, Ill.: Richard D. Irwin, Inc., 1965), pp. 249–50.

[8] Springer, Herlihy, and Beggs, pp. 246–48, offer a simple but extremely clear explanation of the logic behind these equations.

formulas similar to those we used in our discussion of simple regression, but a good deal more complicated.[9] Many multiple regression analyses go even further, including the calculation of the so-called beta coefficients (β). These are the b coefficients, adjusted to units of comparable size. (b_1, for example, might be stated in hours and b_2 in pounds.) The betas show the *relative* impact on y of variations in each of the xs. In this way they can help management see which variables are the most important and which are the least.

Even for a set of data as simple as those in our illustration, hand calculation of the coefficients and standard errors is tedious and costly. Fortunately, standard computer programs are available to do this more efficiently and more quickly. These programs generate most of the important quantities automatically, and include them routinely in the printed results.

Multiple regression analysis rests on the same technical assumptions that underlie simple regression analysis, plus one more. It assumes that the independent variations are not related to each other. Any such relationship is known as *colinearity*. If two independent variables move up and down together, the regression coefficients won't measure what happens when one moves up or down while the other stays constant. The introduction of additional variables may produce a higher coefficient of determination, and this is likely to be desirable, but if colinearity is high it will reduce the reliability of the individual regression coefficients.

Nonlinear Regression

Regression analysis can also be used to develop nonlinear cost equations. This is seldom done, partly because nonlinearities are not large enough to show up clearly, partly because cost behavior in the usual volume range is likely to be fairly linear, and partly because nonlinear analysis is more complicated.

One way to deal with the complexity problem is to try to fit a nonlinear expression that can be translated into a linear format. For example, Sidney Davidson and Robert Roy found that a line based on the logarithms of a set of observations described a newspaper's composing room costs much better than a line based on the raw data.[10] The relationship took the following form:

$$\log C = a + b \log X + c \log Z$$

in which

---

[9] The formulas and an explanation of their meaning can be found in statistics texts such as Spurr and Bonini, *Statistical Analysis for Business Decisions*, chap. 17; for a discussion of the problems of using this method in cost analysis, see Benston, "Multiple Regression Analysis of Cost Behavior," and Robert Jensen, "Multiple Regression Models for Cost Control—Assumptions and Limitations," *Accounting Review*, April 1967, pp. 265–72.

[10] Sidney Davidson and Robert H. Roy, "A Case Study in Newspaper Operations," in Robert H. Roy (ed.), *Operations Research and Systems Engineering* (Baltimore, Md.: Johns Hopkins University Press, 1960).

C = Composing room time.
X = The number of "assembly units" (a measure of the
difficulty of the job).
Z = The amount of newspaper space used.

In other words, the analysts identified linear relationships between the logarithm of cost and the logarithms of the other variables. This represents a nonlinear relationship in terms of the raw data, but because the relationship was linear in terms of the logarithms the statistical problems were no greater than those the investigators would have encountered in fitting a linear equation to the raw data.

Lagged Regression

In some processes, cost may relate to variables identified with earlier or later periods. This can be dealt with, to some extent, by more effective data collection procedures. In other cases, the regression equation should relate the cost in one period to an independent variable one or more periods earlier or later.

For example, inspection costs and the costs of rework (repairing defective units) are likely to vary with the amount of production in a previous period or periods. The analyst might try a one-month lag, regressing cost in period t on production in period $t - 1$, or a two-month lag, regressing cost on production in period $t - 2$. Improvement in the coefficient of determination when this is done is evidence of a lagged relationship.

LEARNING CURVE ANALYSIS

One of the problems encountered in regression analysis is serial correlation—that is, the quantities observed in one period depend in part on the quantities experienced in a previous period. When this happens, the statistician has an additional task—to try to identify systematic patterns in period-to-period movements in cost.

Analysis of seasonal patterns, cyclical movements, and long-term trends, for example, has long been part of the statistician's stock in trade. In more recent years another pattern of relationship has been discovered—a reduction in cost resulting from repetitive performance of the same task. Patterns of this kind are referred to as learning curves. In this section we shall explain what they are and how they relate to accounting.

Nature of the Learning Curve

The first time a new operation is performed, both the personnel and the operating procedures are untried. As the operation is repeated, the work goes more smoothly and labor costs go down. This is likely to continue for some time. In fact, the pattern is so regular that the rate of decline established at the outset can be used in predicting operating labor costs well in advance.

The effect of experience on cost is summarized in the *learning ratio* or improvement ratio. This is usually defined by the following equation:

$$\text{Learning ratio} = \frac{\text{Average labor cost for the first } 2X \text{ units}}{\text{Average labor cost for the first } X \text{ units}}$$

If the average labor cost for the first 500 units is \$12.50 and the average labor cost for the first 1,000 units is \$10, the learning ratio is 80 percent:

$$\text{Learning ratio} = \$10/\$12.50 = 80 \text{ percent}$$

In other words, every time cumulative output doubles, average cost declines to 80 percent of the previous amount. Since the average cost of the first 1,000 units was \$10, the average cost of the first 2,000 units will be expected to be 20 percent less, or \$8 a unit.

Learning curve diagrams. The effect of learning shows up clearly in a diagram known as a learning curve. An 80 percent learning ratio is translated into an 80 percent learning curve in Exhibit 18–8. The diagram at the top is plotted on ordinary graph paper. It shows costs declining rapidly at first, then more slowly. If the curve were extended, further reductions would eventually become small enough to be ignored. The lower diagram shows the same relationship on logarithmic paper. It is a straight line because the *rate* of decrease is constant.

Learning curve equations. Mathematicians have been able to express the learning relationship in equations. The basic equation is:

$$Y = KX^s \tag{1}$$

in which Y is the cumulative average labor cost, K the labor cost of the first unit, X the cumulative production, and s the improvement exponent. The improvement exponent is calculated as follows:

$$s = \frac{\text{Logarithm of the learning ratio}}{\text{Logarithm of 2}}$$

The improvement exponent can take any value between -1 and zero. The exponent for an 80 percent learning curve, for example, is -0.322.

Equation (1) can be restated in logarithmic form:

$$\log Y = \log K + s \log X \tag{2}$$

This is identical in form to the general formula for a straight line, which is why the relationship shows up as a straight line on logarithmic paper.

Cumulative total cost. Each of the first two equations defines cumulative *average* cost. Either of them can be converted easily to a formula for the total labor cost of all units produced up to a given point. Total cost can always be calculated from a known average cost by multiplying the average by the total number of units. When we do this to equation (1), we get the following formula:

$$\text{Total cost} = XY = X(KX^s) = KX^{s+1} \tag{3}$$

EXHIBIT 18–8

An 80 Percent Learning Curve

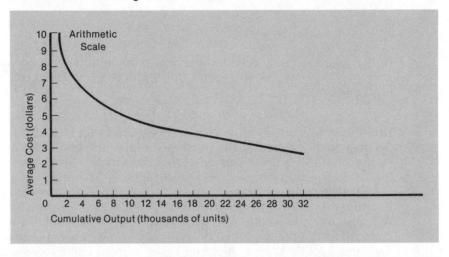

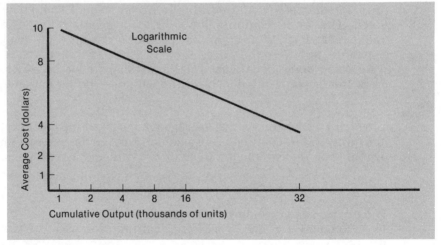

Incremental cost. If producing a second 1,000 units is to reduce cumulative average cost from $10 to $8, the cost of the second 1,000 units will have to be only $6,000, or $6 each:

	Total Cost	No. of Units	Average Cost
First 1,000 units................	$10,000	1,000	$10
Second 1,000 units............	6,000	1,000	6
Total.....................	$16,000	2,000	$ 8

Defining the learning curve in terms of this incremental relationship would be useful, but the mathematical formula is more difficult to work with. As a result, learning curve improvement ratios are usually stated as percentage reductions in cumulative average labor cost. Incremental cost can be calculated by solving equation (3) for two different cumulative production totals, then subtracting one from the other.

Although most processes improve as the company gains experience with them, learning curves can be observed mainly in processes that can be thought of as new. Most of them are based on companies' experiences with new products or new models, but the same pattern can be found in new factories as well. All that is necessary is repetitive production over an extended period of time.

Learning Curve Applications

Knowledge of the learning curve can be useful both in planning and in control. Standard costs for new operations, for example, should be revised frequently to reflect the anticipated learning pattern. For well-established operations, of course, the learning effect is likely to be negligible and can be ignored.

The main impact of learning curve analysis is likely to be on the data collected for use in decision making.

Suppose, for example, that a company is asked to bid on an order for 4,000 units of a product which has already had a run of 4,000 units at an average labor cost of $64 and an 80 percent improvement curve. The incremental labor cost of the next 4,000 units can then be computed as follows:

New average cost:	80 percent of $64....		$51.20
New total cost:	8,000 × $51.20	$409,600	
Old total cost:	4,000 × $64	256,000	
Total incremental cost		$153,600	
Average incremental cost: $153,600/4,000			$38.40

An ability to forecast this cost reduction may make the difference between landing and losing a profitable order.

Locating the Learning Curve

Learning curves are not theoretical abstractions. They are based on observations of actual events. When a historical record exists, the relationship between cost and experience can be estimated by applying regression analysis to the first differences of the historical observations—that is, the *changes* in cumulative average cost as volume increases.

In new situations, for which historical data are few or nonexistent, the curves for previous products or processes with known improvement factors can be used if management can identify similarities with the new situations. Estimates prepared in this way are subject to error, but they are likely to be better than estimates predicated on a zero improvement factor. Ironically, the shape of the improvement function may be much more accurately predictable than the cost of the initial units, and it is these that most cost estimation techniques focus on.

SUMMARY

Cost accounting is concerned not only with identifying costs with activities but also with estimating how costs will respond to changes in volume or other variables. Some of these estimates are based on the judgment of experienced managers and accountants; some are prepared by engineers on the basis of past experience, theoretical calculations, or experimental observations; and still others are based on statistical analyses of historical data.

This chapter has focused for the most part on a statistical technique known as regression analysis, in which a line or plane of relationship is fitted to observed contributions of cost and one or more independent variables. Simple linear regression analysis is used to estimate a straight-line relationship between cost and one independent variable; multiple regression analysis is used when two or more independent variables are considered simultaneously.

These analyses can be performed graphically for either one or two independent variables. It is generally more convenient, however, to fit the regression line by solving a set of regression equations, using what is known as the method of least squares. These analyses can be performed quickly and cheaply on the computer. Computer programs include tests of the statistical reliability of the calculated relationships, and the results of any such tests are printed automatically with the regression equation. The main caution to be observed is that least squares regression analysis is based on a number of technical assumptions; if these are invalid, some or all of the tests of reliability will also be invalid.

Another statistical technique is the derivation and use of learning curves, reflecting the improvement in labor performance in successive iterations of a new task. These are generally identified through regression analysis, and their main importance is in predicting future costs for decision purposes.

KEY TERMS

The most important terms introduced and defined in this chapter are the following:

Coefficient of determination	Correlation
Colinearity	Degrees of freedom
Confidence intervals	Improvement ratio

Inspection of accounts

Learning curve

Least squares method

Multiple regression

Regression coefficient

Serial correlation

Simple regression

Standard error of the coefficient

Standard error of the estimate

t-value

INDEPENDENT STUDY PROBLEMS
(Solutions in Appendix C)

1. Least squares regression analysis. Monthly power cost and machine-hour data for the Shelby Company for the 12 months of 19x0 were as follows:

Month	Machine-Hours	Cost
January	3,500	$1,000
February	4,200	1,100
March	4,900	1,300
April	4,400	1,200
May	4,300	1,200
June	3,800	1,100
July	3,300	1,090
August	4,100	1,280
September	4,700	1,400
October	3,800	1,210
November	3,000	1,080
December	4,000	1,230

Power costs during 19x0 were affected by a 10 percent increase in power rates (prices paid for power). This rate increase was effective on July 1, 19x0. No further increase is expected during 19x1.

a. Prepare the data and develop a line of relationship between power cost and machine-hours, using the least squares method.

b. Calculate the coefficient of determination and the standard error of the estimate.

c. Use the relationship you derived in (*a*) to estimate costs at 2,500, 4,000, and 5,500 machine-hours.

d. How much confidence would you have in these cost estimates?

2. Preparing a bid: Learning curve analyis. A customer has asked your company to prepare a bid on supplying 800 units of a new product. Production will be in batches of 100 units. You estimate that costs for the first batch of 100 units will average $100 a unit. You also expect that a 90 percent learning curve will apply to the cumulative labor costs on this contract.

a. Prepare an estimate of the labor costs of fulfilling this contract.

b. Estimate the incremental labor cost of extending the production run to produce an additional 800 units.

c. Estimate the incremental labor cost of extending the production run from 800 to 900 units. (Note: you may use either the formula or a graph to derive this estimate.)

EXERCISES AND PROBLEMS

1. Least squares regression exercises. MacKenzie Park manufactures and sells trivets. Labor hours and production costs for the last four months of last year, when conditions were similar to those prevailing this year, were as follows:

Month	Labor Hours	Production Costs
September.....................	2,500	$ 20,000
October........................	3,500	25,000
November.....................	4,500	30,000
December.....................	3,500	25,000
	14,000	$100,000

Let

a = Fixed production costs per month.
b = Variable production costs per labor hour.
n = Number of months.
x = Labor hours per month.
y = Total monthly production costs.

Based on the above information, select the best answer to each of the following questions:

1. Monthly production costs could be expressed by
   a. $y = ax + b$.
   b. $y = a + bx$.
   c. $y = b + ax$.
   d. $y = a + bx$.
2. According to the least squares method of computation, the fixed monthly production cost of trivets is approximately
   a. $10,000.
   b. $9,500.
   c. $7,500.
   d. $5,000.
3. The variable production cost per labor hour based on the least squares method of computation, is
   a. $6.00.
   b. $5.00.
   c. $3.00.
   d. $2.00.
4. The usefulness of the estimating equation based on these observations is very limited because it has
   a. A high covariance.
   b. Few degrees of freedom.
   c. A high beta coefficient.
   d. A low coefficient of determination.

(CPA adapted)

2. Learning curve exercise. The average number of minutes required to assemble trivets is predictable based on an 80 percent learning curve. The trivets are produced in lots of 300 units and 60 minutes of labor are required to assemble each first lot.

Let

MT = Marginal time for the xth lot.

M = Marginal time for the first lot.

X = Lots produced.

b = Exponent expressing the improvement; b has the range $-1 \le b \le 0$.

1. A normal graph, i.e., not a log or log-log graph, of average minutes per lot of production where cumulative lots are represented by the x-axis and average minutes per lot are represented by the y-axis, would produce a
   a. Linear function sloping downward to the right.
   b. Linear function sloping upward to the right.
   c. Curvilinear function sloping upward to the right at an increasing rate.
   d. Curvilinear function sloping downward to the right at a decreasing rate.
2. A log-log graph of average minutes per lot of production, where cumulative lots are represented by the x-axis and average minutes per lot are represented by the y-axis, would produce a
   a. Linear function sloping downward to the right.
   b. Linear function sloping upward to the right.
   c. Curvilinear function sloping upward to the right at a decreasing rate.
   d. Curvilinear function sloping downward to the right at a decreasing rate.
3. The average number of minutes required per lot to complete four lots is approximately
   a. 60.0
   b. 48.5.
   c. 38.4.
   d. 30.7.
4. Average time to produce X lots of trivets could be expressed
   a. MX^{b+1}
   b. MX^b
   c. MT^{b+1}
   d. MX^{b-1}
5. Assuming that $b = -0.322$, the average number of minutes required to produce X lots of trivets could be expressed
   a. $40.08X^{.678}$
   b. $40.08X$
   c. $60X^{-.322}$
   d. $60X^{1.322}$

(CPA)

3. Flexible budget allowance. Carbo Electronics Company is installing a flexible budgeting system in its factory. As part of this effort, the controller has prepared least squares regression equations for each of the major cost elements for each factory department. The estimating equation for indirect labor in the assembly department is:

Indirect labor cost = $2,000 a month + $1 an assembly labor hour

The coefficient of correlation is .62.

The assembly department manager has refused to accept this equation, saying the amount of indirect labor is determined by the number of people on the payroll, not by any formula.

How would you respond? What should the manager be asked to do?

4. Simple regression exercise. Lotus Corporation makes aluminum windows and doors. Prices are calculated on the basis of the size of the window or door, in square feet. You have the following data for ten different orders, each for 100 windows:

Window Size (sq. ft.)	Materials Cost
3	$210
8	450
4	260
6	340
4	240
7	380
5	300
7	410
5	320
6	370

a. Calculate a linear regression equation by the method of least squares.
b. Calculate the coefficient of determination and the standard error of the estimate.
c. What conclusions might management draw from this analysis?

5. Determining variable costs. The management of Johnson Brothers has an opportunity to sign a contract with a customer for all of the customer's requirements for plastic caps for the next year. The customer would pay $2,000 a month plus $4 for each thousand caps delivered.

A least squares analysis of historical data has produced an estimated average variable cost of $3.50 a unit. The process is well established and no noticeable learning effect is likely, but management is concerned that the $3.50 figure may be too low. The quantity ordered could be very large, as many as 1 million caps a month, and Johnson Brothers is not in a position to absorb substantial losses.

The regression equation was based on an analysis of cost-volume data for 15 two-week periods when operating conditions were not affected by major identifiable events. These data were adjusted for changes in materials prices and wage rates. A staff assistant has made the following calculations:
1. Sum of the squared deviations of costs from the regression line: 187,200.
2. Sum of the squared deviations of costs from their mean: 748,800.
3. Sum of the squared deviations of volume from mean volume: 90,000.

Prepare an analysis that will help management assess the reliability of the variable cost estimate.

6. Regression analysis. The manager of department X is developing a flexible budget for the next year. In the past, indirect materials costs have been budgeted as proportionally variable costs, but the factory controller wants to test this assumption.

The following are the hourly volume and the indirect materials cost totals:

Hours	Cost
3,000	$3,300
2,130	2,070
2,700	2,730
2,610	2,550
2,880	2,760
2,670	2,400
2,820	2,820
2,640	2,070
2,850	2,400
2,730	2,340
2,670	2,430
2,700	2,370

The factory controller derived the following regression equation from these observations:

$$\text{Indirect materials cost} = -\$604 + \$1.157 \times \text{labor hours}$$

a. Plot the observations on a scatter chart.
b. Calculate the coefficient of determination and the standard error of the estimate. (For this calculation you should round the y_c values to the nearest dollar.)
c. How would you interpret the negative constant in the regression equation? What figures would you establish for the coming year's flexible budget?

7. Effect of lot size on cost.   The management of the Portage Corporation has found that labor cost variances in the factory are more likely to be favorable when overall production volume is high and unfavorable when overall production volume is low. (Volume is measured by the amount of standard labor cost.) To check this, labor time was recorded in a recent period, job by job and department by department. Data for jobs of an unusual nature were discarded, leaving the following job totals:

Job	Standard Labor Cost	Actual Labor Cost
426	$1,050	$ 990
428	440	460
433	610	600
434	420	440
437	770	740
445	780	760
446	870	850
447	310	330
450	1,030	1,000
454	840	810
461	530	540
465	400	430
467	560	560
469	370	390
472	690	670
473	930	890

a. Calculate the regression equation.
b. How reliable is this equation? Calculate the coefficient of determination and the standard error of the estimate.
c. What is the meaning of the constant term in this equation?
d. How would you use the findings of this analysis?

8. Regression analysis: Production decision. The Johnstar Company makes a very expensive chemical product. The costs average about $1,000 a pound and the material sells for $2,500 a pound. The material is very dangerous; therefore, it is made each day to fill the customer orders for the day. Failure to deliver the quantity required results in a shutdown for the customers and high cost penalty for Johnstar (plus customer ill will).

Predicting the final weight of a batch of the chemical being processed has been a serious problem. This is critical because of the serious cost of failure to meet customer needs.

The company's consultants recommended that the batches be weighed one-half way through the six-hour processing period. They proposed that linear regression be used to predict the final weight from the midpoint weight. If the prediction indicated that too little of the chemical would be available, then a new batch could be started and still delivered in time to satisfy customers' needs for the day.

Included in the report of a study made by the consultants during a one-week period were the following items:

Observation No.	Weight 3 hrs.	Final Weight	Observation No.	Weight 3 hrs.	Final Weight
1	55	90	11	60	80
2	45	75	12	35	60
3	40	80	13	35	80
4	60	80	14	55	60
5	40	45	15	35	75
6	60	80	16	50	90
7	50	80	17	30	60
8	55	95	18	60	105
9	50	100	19	50	60
10	35	75	20	20	30

Data from the regression analysis:
Coefficient of determination............................ 0.4126
Coefficient of correlation................................ 0.6424
Coefficients of the regression equation
  Constant... +28.6
  Independent variable................................. + 1.008
Standard error of the estimate.......................... 14.2
Standard error of the regression coefficient for the
  independent variable................................. 0.2796
The t-statistic for a 95 percent confidence interval
  (18 degrees of freedom)................................ 2.101

a. Using the results of the regression analysis by the consultants, estimate the final weight of today's first batch which weighs 42 pounds at the end of three hours processing time.

b. Customer orders for today total 68 pounds. The nature of the process is such that the smallest batch that can be started will weigh at least 20 pounds at the end of six hours. Using only the data from the regression analysis, would you start another batch? (Remember that today's first batch weighed 42 pounds at the end of three hours.)

c. Is the relationship between the variables such that this regression analysis provides an adequate prediction model for the Johnstar Co.? Explain your answer.

(CMA)

9. Regression analysis: Choice of methods. The Ramon Company manufactures a wide range of products at several different plant locations. The Franklin plant, which manufactures electrical components, has been experiencing difficulties with fluctuating monthly overhead costs. The fluctuations have made it difficult to estimate the level of overhead that will be incurred for any one month.

Management wants to be able to estimate overhead costs accurately in order to plan its operation and financial needs better. A trade association publication to which Ramon Co. subscribes indicates that, for companies manufacturing electrical components, overhead tends to vary with direct labor hours.

One member of the accounting staff has proposed that the cost behavior pattern of the overhead costs be determined. Then overhead costs could be predicted from the budgeted direct labor hours.

Another member of the accounting staff suggested that a good starting place for determining the cost behavior pattern of overhead costs would be an analysis of historical data. The historical cost behavior pattern would provide a basis for estimating future overhead costs. The methods proposed for determining the cost behavior pattern included the high-low method, the scattergraph method, simple linear regression, multiple regression, and exponential smoothing. Of these methods Ramon Co. decided to employ the high-low method, the scattergraph method, and simple linear regression. Data on direct labor hours and the respective overhead costs incurred were collected for the past two years. The raw data are as follows:

	19 x 3		19 x 4	
Month	Direct Labor Hours	Overhead Costs	Direct Labor Hours	Overhead Costs
January..................	20,000	$84,000	21,000	$86,000
February................	25,000	99,000	24,000	93,000
March...................	22,000	89,500	23,000	93,000
April....................	23,000	90,000	22,000	87,000
May......................	20,000	81,500	20,000	80,000
June.....................	19,000	75,500	18,000	76,500
July......................	14,000	70,500	12,000	67,500
August...................	10,000	64,500	13,000	71,000
September...............	12,000	69,000	15,000	73,500
October..................	17,000	75,000	17,000	72,500
November................	16,000	71,500	15,000	71,000
December................	19,000	78,000	18,000	75,000

Using linear regression, the following data were obtained:
1. Coefficient of determination   .9109
2. Coefficient of correlation   .9544
3. Coefficients of regression equation:
   Constant   39,859
   Independent variable   2.1549
4. Standard error of the estimate   2,840
5. Standard error of the regression coefficient
   for the independent variable   .1437
6. True t-statistic for a 95 percent confidence
   interval (22 degrees of freedom)   2.074

a. Plot the observations on a scatter diagram and draw a line of relationship freehand.
b. Using the high-low points method, determine the cost behavior pattern of the overhead costs for the Franklin plant.
c. Using the results of the regression analysis, estimate the overhead costs for 22,500 direct labor hours. Do the same for the other two methods.
d. Of the three proposed methods, which one should Ramon Company use to determine the historical cost behavior pattern of Franklin plant's overhead costs? Explain your answer completely, indicating the reasons why the other methods are less desirable.

(CMA adapted)

10. Regression analysis: Preparing the data. The Wyman Company has been working for several months on the development of cost estimates for its Rutherford factory. One department's principal labor cost is the cost of processing labor. All other labor costs are classified as "indirect" labor.

Operating volume in this department is measured by the number of processing labor hours. Processing labor hours and indirect labor costs for the past two years were:

	19 x 1		19 x 2	
Month	Processing Labor Hours	Indirect Labor Costs	Processing Labor Hours	Indirect Labor Costs
January.	9,000	$12,820	12,000	$18,800
February.	8,000	11,290	10,000	14,730
March.	6,000	12,400	11,000	17,050
April.	7,000	13,100	10,000	15,220
May.	8,000	11,540	11,000	16,350
June.	7,000	10,600	12,000	17,900
July.	8,000	11,580	12,000	15,700
August.	9,000	12,600	9,000	11,860
September.	7,000	9,820	10,000	13,050
October.	6,000	8,800	8,000	10,120
November.	7,000	9,680	6,000	7,960
December.	9,000	12,430	7,000	9,180

Additional information:
1. Rearrangement of the department's machines on July 1, 19x2, made it possible to reduce materials handling time. The factory's industrial engineer estimates that this reduction has led to a saving in indirect labor costs of approximately 20 cents a processing labor hour every month since that time. The rearrangement has had no effect on the amount of overtime worked.
2. Employees are paid a premium of 50 percent of their regular hourly wage rate for each hour of overtime work. Overtime premiums are classified as overhead costs, but management doesn't segregate them in separate accounts. As a result, the overtime premiums paid on processing labor and indirect labor time in this department have been included in the indirect labor cost figures given above. Analysis of payroll documents shows that overtime premiums were as follows during the two years:

Month	19 x 1	19 x 2
January............................	$520	$2,400
February...........................	290	930
March..............................	0	1,750
April...............................	0	920
May...............................	340	1,250
June...............................	100	1,800
July...............................	280	1,500
August............................	600	560
September.........................	120	1,150
October...........................	0	320
November.........................	80	0
December.........................	630	80

3. Wage rates were 5 percent higher in 19x2 than in 19x1. Wage rates will remain at their 19x2 level throughout the current year.
4. A fire destroyed a machine in March, 19x1. Employees whose wages would otherwise have been identified as processing labor costs were assigned to other tasks classified as indirect labor until the replacement machine was ready for operation on April 10, 19x1.

Separate overtime premiums from other components of indirect labor costs, make any other adjustments that seem appropriate, and prepare separate estimating equations for overtime premiums and for the other components of indirect labor cost.

11. Learning curve: Annual model changeover.   Serkin Corporation is in an industry with an annual model changeover. Standard labor costs in the assembly department for this year were based on a 90 percent learning curve and production of 640,000 units during the model year. The labor costs of the first 10,000 units assembled this year were expected to average $2 a unit.

Production in the first three months of the model year totaled 160,000 units. Production in the fourth month totaled 80,000 units and required $94,000 in assembly labor, at standard wage rates.

a. Calculate the labor quantity variance for the fourth month, to the nearest tenth of a cent.
b. Was assembly labor performance at an acceptable level in the fourth month? Show your calculations.
c. If total production for the year is to total 640,000 units, and if the costs of units produced after the fourth month are at the levels specified by the original learning curve, would you expect production of the final 320,000 units to lead to favorable or unfavorable labor quantity variances? Show calculations to support your conclusions.

12. Learning curve: Contract bidding.   Technologics, Inc. manufactures products that incorporate advanced technological features. Each new product is virtually unique, and the effect of learning on cost is very pronounced.

A customer has asked for a price quotation on an order for 512 sensometers. They would be produced in series, one at a time. Technologics' engineers estimate that the initial setup costs would total $10,000, production labor costs of the first unit would amount to $4,000, and an 80 percent cumulative learning curve would apply to production labor costs. Production would be spread over an eight-month period.

a. Using the formula provided in the chapter, estimate the labor cost of the entire order.

b. The customer feels that the bid based on your estimate in (a) is too high. You are unwilling to reduce your bid for this quantity, but the customer has suggested that you rebid on the basis of a total production run of 750 units, spread over 12 months. Prepare a new cost estimate.

c. The customer changed his mind and accepted your original bid for the 512-unit contract. Midway through that contract he asks you to bid on extending the contract to cover an additional 238 units. Prepare an estimate of labor costs that would be useful to management in the evaluation of this possibility.

13. Learning curve: Cost forecasting. The Amdur Company recently completed development work on a new product and commenced production on a limited scale. The product has found favor with the company's customers, and the company intends to expand production to a rate of 1,000 units a week.

Labor costs for the first 2,000 units have totaled $20,000. Judging from past experience, the company's industrial engineers have estimated that a 90 percent learning curve will be applicable to this product.

a. Compute cumulative total labor cost and cumulative average labor cost for the first 128,000 units.

b. On a sheet of graph paper, prepare a diagram showing cumulative total cost for various cumulative volumes between 2,000 and 128,000 units.

c. From the diagram in (b), prepare a schedule showing the additional labor costs of producing each additional 4,000 units of product from zero to 128,000 cumulative units.

d. Much of the company's business consists of providing customers with specially selected combinations of the company's products. Each customer's package is different from the others, and competition is very keen. Cost estimates for each package are prepared by combining the product cost figures shown in the standard cost file. What labor cost standard would you establish for the first year for use in this way?

14. Learning curve: Preparing bids: Effect on cash flow. Famous Aircraft Company has developed a new short-hop jet airplane which is scheduled to go into production in about six months. Management is now reviewing its tentative pricing decision, and will seek firm purchase commitments from the airlines as soon as a final decision is reached.

The plane will be manufactured in the company's San Fernando factory. The first production run of ten planes will take about 12 months to complete, at a variable cost of $700,000 a plane, and the company's controller estimates that the cumulative average variable cost will follow an 80 percent learning curve thereafter.

The out-of-pocket fixed costs of operating the factory are expected to amount to $200,000 a month, regardless of the number of planes manufactured. Without the new plane, Famous Aircraft would have no need for this factory.

If the plane gains acceptance, orders will come in quickly for delivery one, two, and three years later. On the basis of the interest expressed by various commercial airlines, Famous Aircraft's management believes that it can sell about 250 of these planes, with deliveries spread over a six-year period on the following schedule:

Year	No. of Planes
1	10
2	30
3	60
4	60
5	60
6	30
Total	250

Competition with British and French aircraft manufacturers is intense, however, and Famous Aircraft is worried that it will lose its foreign markets if it sets too high a price on the new plane.

The company's market research department estimates that the total world market for this type of plane will amount to about 450 planes during the next six years. Both Boeing and British Aircraft are known to have somewhat similar planes in development, but the Famous management believes that it is at least six months closer to actual production than either of these competitors. In each past generation of airplanes, the manufacturer to get a plane in production first has been able to capture more than half of the market.

a. Construct a curve for use in cost forecasting.
b. Prepare production cost estimates for total production runs of 160 planes and 250 planes.
c. What pricing strategy would you follow in this situation? Indicate how you might use cost figures in arriving at a price.
d. Useful information on the demand schedule seldom can be obtained by asking potential customers how much they would be likely to buy at different prices. Market experimentation is also impractical in capital goods markets of this type. Suggest an alternative way of trying to obtain this kind of information for Famous Aircraft's management. (Suggestion: examine the motives that lead airline companies to buy new planes.)
e. It is now two years after the new plane went into production. A price of $450,000 was set, and a total of 40 planes was produced during the first two years at the costs estimated in advance. A temporary decline in the volume of air travel has led to a stretch-out in delivery schedules, so that only 40 additional planes are to be produced and delivered this year instead of the 60 originally planned. Compute the effect of the stretch-out on the company's income for the year.

part three

Further Topics in Periodic Planning and Control

19

Behavioral Aspects of
Responsibility Accounting

THIS final group of eight chapters takes us back to responsibility accounting, accounting's contribution to managerial control processes. Some of this discussion will focus on technical matters, some will deal with the interpretations management should place on the accounting figures. A planning and control system is useful, however, only if it affects the actions taken by the people who make up the organization. Before going farther, therefore, we need to look at the behavioral side of systems design—how do behavioral factors enter into the design of a system and how do they affect the likelihood the system will be successful?

For convenience, we have divided the chapter into two parts. The first part deals with the interactions between the accounting system and other aspects of management's systems for planning and controlling the organization's activities. The second part focuses on some of the behavioral problems encountered in the administration of managerial accounting systems, particularly those parts we have referred to as responsibility accounting—that is, the preparation of performance standards and the reporting of results.

BEHAVIORAL FACTORS IN SYSTEM DESIGN

A responsibility accounting system is part of the larger system designed by management to help it achieve the organization's goals. This larger system includes such elements as the leadership styles adopted by the various executives, the communications channels within the organization, and the structure of rewards and penalties for good and poor performance.

All of these elements have behavioral implications, some of them deliberate, some unintentional. Most responsibility accounting systems have the following implicit behavioral assumptions:

639

1. Other elements of the managerial system will be effective in inducing managers to strive to reach or surpass budgeted performance levels—the budgeted standards by themselves are not motivational.
2. The participation of subordinate managers in setting standards is necessary to the success of the managerial system.
3. Performance standards should be set at levels described as "tight but attainable."
4. The system is to facilitate *management by exception*—that is, management relies on the reporting of variances to ration its time effectively.
5. Management will apply the *controllability criterion*—that is, managers are expected to respond only to variances arising within their own jurisdictions.
6. When the organization has two or more explicit goals, conflicts between these goals must be resolved outside the accounting system.

We shall consider each of these in this section.

Other Elements as Motivating Forces

The first assumption underlying managerial reporting systems is that other elements, not the budgets or standards themselves, will be effective in motivating managers to strive to reach or surpass budgeted performance levels. This doesn't come automatically. Individual motivation is determined by the needs of the individuals themselves and their perception that performance (e.g., achieving budgeted performance) will lead to the satisfaction of these needs.[1] It is management's task to bring the goals of the individual and those of the organization together. If management is successful, then we say that *goal congruence* has been achieved. Achieving goal congruence is the way to validate this first assumption of responsibility accounting.

Goals of the organization and of the individuals in it are said to be congruent if the individuals have accepted the organization's goals as their own. This is known as *internalizing* the organization's goals. For individuals to internalize a goal, they must believe that achieving it will satisfy their needs better than not achieving it. Goals that individuals have internalized are known as *aspiration levels*, the performance levels they undertake to reach.

Several factors affect the probability that individuals will internalize budgeted goals as their aspiration levels. One of these is past experience—success or failure in reaching budgeted goals in previous periods. Another is the priority they assign to their own needs for personal achievement. A third is the likelihood that meeting the budget will

---

[1] Edward E. Lawler, III, *Motivation in Work Organizations* (Monterey, Calif.: Brooks/Cole, 1973). The relationships between control systems and individual needs are summarized in an excellent book by Edward E. Lawler, III and John Grant Rhode, *Information and Control in Organizations* (Pacific Palisades, Calif.: Goodyear Publishing Co., 1976), especially chap. 2.

EXHIBIT 19–1

Influences on Personal Aspiration Levels

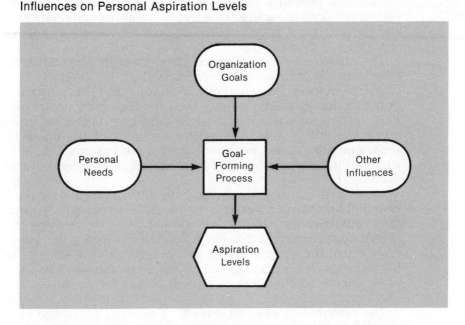

provide this sense of achievement. Still another is what they expect to be able to achieve under expected conditions.[2]

The relationships among these factors are diagrammed in Exhibit 19–1. What goes on in the box in the middle is not always clear, but it does depend on the social environment in which the aspiration levels are set. This social environment is the subject of our second assumption.

Participation

Processes are often more influential in determining outcomes than the specific contents of the various inputs to those processes. This is nowhere truer than in the process of achieving goal congruence. One way to achieve goal congruence is to have subordinate managers participate in the process of setting performance standards. We need to discuss five aspects of the role of participation in this process:

1. What participation means.
2. What contribution it can make.
3. How it can be affected by group dynamics.
4. The impact of managerial style and cultural background.
5. The necessary conditions for successful participation.

---

[2] For a more extended discussion of the factors that influence performance, see L. W. Porter, E. E. Lawler, and J. R. Hackman, *Behavior in Organizations* (New York: McGraw-Hill Book Company, 1975).

The nature of participation. Participation was an integral part of the periodic planning process described in Chapter 5. That description emphasized the subordinate's responsibility to originate proposals and the superior's responsibility to evaluate, question, and suggest changes.

These roles can also be reversed, at least in part. Superiors can propose, while their subordinates respond. If the system is to be participative, however, both parties must understand that proposals made by higher management provide a basis for discussion, not instructions. Participation means that decisions affecting individual managers' operations are to some extent joint decisions of the managers and their superiors. It is thus more than mere consultation, by which superiors inform themselves of their subordinates' views but make the decisions themselves.

Participation doesn't mean that both subordinate and superior must be in full agreement on every decision. In some cases the superior will try to influence the decision but will not go as far as using the veto, even though convinced that the subordinate is taking the wrong tack. More often, the superior's view will prevail and the subordinate will have to approve a plan regarded as less than optimal. When this happens, something else must be present if goal congruence is not to be lost.

The contribution of participation. The main advantage of participation is to help managers perceive that the objectives or performance standards are reasonable. This in turn will help them internalize the standards, which is important to what is known as *intrinsic* motivation. (Intrinsic motivation is motivation arising from within the individual, rather than from the need for praise or tangible reward.)[3]

Participation accomplishes this result in part because it requires a great deal of communication between superior and subordinates. This helps everyone get a clearer picture of the requirements of the job and of how difficult it will be to achieve different objectives. Subordinates are more likely to internalize objectives that they perceive to be reasonable, and participation may be a good way to establish the reasonableness of the objectives.

These same results sometimes can be achieved without participation. Lawler and Rhode, for example, conclude that the main problem is to get subordinates to perceive standards as reasonable. This can be done without participation, if the subordinates can be led to trust those who set the standards.[4] The main argument for participation, however, is that it is a necessary mechanism to create this feeling of trust. If this is so, then subordinate managers will be more likely to strive to achieve the planned results if they have participated actively and influentially in the development of the plan and have agreed with their superiors that it is feasible.

---

[3] Lawler and Rhode, *Information and Control in Organizations*, p. 69.

[4] For a discussion of the situations in which participation is most appropriate, see V. H. Vroom and P. W. Yetton, *Leadership and Decision Making* (Pittsburgh: University of Pittsburgh Press, 1973).

EXHIBIT 19–2

Position of the Manager in the Social Network
of the Organization

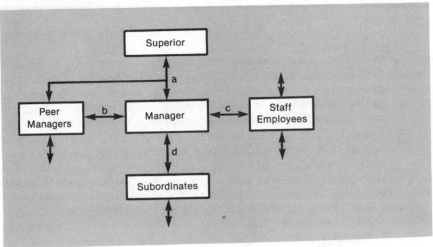

Group dynamics. Participation may be a useful way of using the individual's membership in groups to increase the acceptability of the organization's goals. Every individual belongs to many groups—the family, the neighborhood, the work group, and so on. The effectiveness of participation in securing goal congruence depends to a large extent on the values and attitudes held by the various groups the individual manager belongs to and on the strength of the manager's commitment to each group. The forces operating within the group and affecting the positions taken by individuals in the group are known as *group dynamics.*

Group dynamics in work-related groups can have a significant effect on job-related aspiration levels and group member behavior.[5] Individual managers belong to at least four intersecting groups in connection with their work, as illustrated in Exhibit 19–2.[6] Here the organization is viewed as a network, with the manager at the center. The manager shares one group with a superior (labeled as group *a*), another with subordinates (*d*), another with managers in similar positions elsewhere in the organization (*b*), and still another with the organization's staff (*c*). The dynamics of each of these groups will influence the manager's own goals, although not all to the same extent.

---

[5] J. R. Hackman, "Group Influences on Individuals," in M. D. Dunnette, ed., *Handbook of Industrial and Organizational Psychology* (Chicago: Rand McNally & Company, 1976).

[6] This diagram is from G. H. Hofstede, *The Game of Budget Control* (Assen, The Netherlands: Koninklijke Van Gorcum & Comp., 1967), p. 57. Two groups are said to intersect if some but not all members belong to both groups.

The amount of influence that group membership will have on the individuals' aspiration levels depends on how strongly they are attracted to that group. The strength of the attraction determines the *cohesiveness* of the group, the degree to which individual members value their group membership.

Individuals join or remain in a group mainly because they believe that it will help them attain their own individual goals. The greater the value placed on membership, the greater will be the likelihood that different members will have similar goals. In fact, conforming to the goals of the other members is a way of ensuring continued membership in the group. ("Membership" here means social acceptance rather than nominal affiliation in a formally constituted group). Valuing their own membership and anxious to keep it, individuals will tend to reject goals they believe conflict with the goals prevailing in the group. They will tend to accept goals that seem to be consistent with those of others in the group. The more strongly the available information seems to indicate acceptance by others in a cohesive group, the greater the likelihood that individuals will adopt the goal as their own.

Group dynamics may also work against acceptance of the organization's objectives, of course. If the group is strong and the group leaders have rejected the organization's goals, they will be able to reduce the likelihood that others will accept them. We shall say more about these situations in a moment.

Managerial style and cultural influences. The patterns and effects of group dynamics are not the same at all times and in all situations. Different managers, for example, find that different managerial styles are suited to their different personalities. Similarly, different styles may be appropriate for different kinds of tasks or in different cultural environments. A democratic style may be completely inappropriate, at least in the short run, if subordinates have never experienced it in situations they regard as comparable.

> *Example.* The introduction of participative budgeting in a large electrical equipment factory some years ago was received very coldly by most of the first-level supervisors, despite enthusiastic support from their superiors and the presence of a highly sensitive, multifunctional installation team in the factory for a period of many months. The reason seemed to be that the supervisors were reluctant to accept the risk of censure for failure to achieve targets they had set themselves. Without participation, blame could always be assigned elsewhere, at least in the supervisors' minds. It took many months to rid most of them of this fear.

> *Example.* In a series of case writing sessions, the top managers of a number of Europe-based multinational companies reported that their managers in some countries, even at fairly high levels, were reluctant to participate in budgetary planning. Those in other countries, given the same top management environment, were both ready and eager for greater autonomy.

Conditions for successful participation. Several conditions are likely to be necessary to allow participation to achieve its objective, managerial motivation. One is that the initial gap between the individual's goals and those of the organization shouldn't be so large that it can't be bridged. Another is that the managers' cultural background and environment permit them to participate in substance as well as in form. Participation is unnecessary and ineffective if lower management is conditioned to accept orders; it won't work if higher management is unwilling to compromise on details to gain acceptance of the fundamentals. Citing Lawler and Rhode again, ". . . in an autocratically run organization it is unlikely that meaningful participation can develop since it requires a climate of openness and trust."[7] Participation must be to some extent a give-and-take process.

Perhaps the most important of all the necessary conditions is that higher managers participating in the decisions should play an active, constructive leadership role. Group cohesiveness can be a constructive force; it can also be destructive. Strong individuals may use their groups to mobilize support for their personal grievances or as springboards to political power. If managerial leadership is weak, the participation process can be turned against the organization's goals.

Reasonably Attainable Standards

The third behavioral assumption underlying most responsibility accounting systems is that performance standards should be set at levels described as "tight but attainable" or "reasonably attainable." The argument for this assumption is that as long as performance standards do not exceed amounts that are reasonably attainable, managers will internalize them. If standards are set tighter than this, the managers and their subordinates will regard them as unrealistic and will cease to be motivated by them. In short, loose standards (in comparison with the reasonably attainable level) will lead to a slackening of effort and a drop in performance; tighter standards will have the same effect.

There is fairly general agreement that tight but attainable standards can improve performance if they can be internalized. Acceptance of this conclusion is not the last word, however. Two questions remain:

1. How can the tight but attainable performance level be identified?
2. Is there a valid alternative to participation as a motivating force?

Identifying the attainable level. The task of identifying the performance level that is tight but attainable can be approached either analytically or judgmentally.

The analytical approach. One analytical method is to select a level that has been achieved often in the past but is still slightly higher than the average the company's experienced employees have been able to achieve.

For example, the chart in Exhibit 19–3 shows the results of an

---

[7] Lawler and Rhode, *Information and Control in Organizations*, p. 61.

EXHIBIT 19–3

Setting Tight but Attainable Standards by Historical Analysis

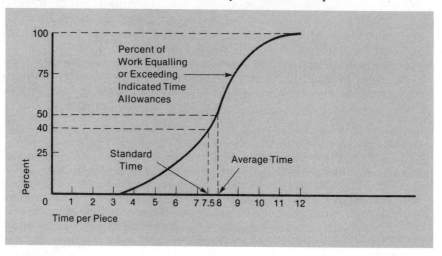

analysis of a sample of 100 time tickets. None of these time tickets showed a time less than 4 or more than 12 minutes per piece. The time of 8 minutes was met or bettered 50 percent of the time, the midpoint on the curve. The company might choose to set the standard at 7.5 minutes, however, because this time was met or bettered 40 percent of the time. A standard at this level is tighter than a standard equal to the average, but workers' success in meeting it or doing better 40 percent of the time demonstrates that it is not an unreasonable standard.[8]

If satisfactory historical data are not available for this purpose, management might turn to the engineers to develop comparable data by methods study techniques. As we mentioned in Chapter 6, however, the costs of applying these techniques generally rule them out unless they are undertaken as part of a methods improvement or work standardization program.

Analytical techniques are applicable mainly to responsive activities of a highly repetitive nature. Assembling television sets or processing bank checks are two possible examples. The historical approach may also be applied to repetitive programmed activities, such as order solicitation. For example, the number of orders sales representatives have brought in in the past may be used to establish a performance standard for the future. The number of calls salespeople have been able to make in the past may be used in a similar way.

Performance standards set in this way for programmed activities must be applied very carefully. For one thing, future conditions are

---

[8] Lawler and Rhode cite a number of empirical studies to conclude that "intrinsic motivation is most likely to be present when standards or budgets . . . have *somewhat less than a 50/50 chance* of being attained." Ibid., p. 71 (italics added). Forty percent is somewhat less than a 50/50 chance.

likely to be different from those of the past. For another, they may be inconsistent with the decision rules management goes by. Expanding the sales force may be highly profitable because the *incremental* profit contribution is substantial, but the *average* profit contribution may fall. This will put the standard based on past performance out of reach—that is, it will become tight but unattainable.

The judgmental approach. Even if the historical and engineering methods are used everywhere they are feasible, they are still unlikely to supply more than a small fraction of the number of performance standards management needs. As a result, the performance level that is tight but attainable is more likely to be established judgmentally, by management rather than by technicians. Past experience may help, industry averages may be useful, but the final result will reflect management's judgment that the standard is "about right," not too easy but attainable if the right kind of effort is made.

Motivating performance. The main problem is not to establish the performance level that is tight but attainable. Workers and managers themselves often have a good idea of what these levels are. Whether they will make the effort to achieve them is an entirely different question. The main problem, therefore, is to design a package of techniques to motivate the affected personnel to perform better than they would in the absence of the standards.

In a pioneering work done some time ago, Stedry questioned the need to achieve goal congruence. He suggested that management might manipulate standards to influence aspiration levels without worrying whether the standards themselves were internalized.[9] He suggested that standards be adapted to reflect each individual's aspiration level. The standard would be raised in an attempt to pull the aspiration level upward; this, in turn would improve performance. If actual performance still remained so far short of the aspiration level that the aspiration level would be reduced, the standard would be reduced, too. Later, when the performance gap had been narrowed, the standard would be raised again.

It can be argued that Stedry's suggestion was mainly an effort to establish the tight but attainable level of performance, because he recognized that the gap between the standard and the level individuals perceive to be attainable can't be allowed to get too wide. The main objections to his suggestion, however, are that it calls for a separate standard for each individual and that it ignores deferred effects of manipulative activities.

The first of these objections rules out applying this approach to repetitive activities in which different individuals can see that they have been assigned different standards. This objection shouldn't apply, however, to programmed activities that are likely to be unique to each manager. Managers can't really compare standards if their activities are very different. Therefore they are less likely than work-

---

[9] Andrew Stedry, *Budget Control and Cost Behavior* (Englewood Cliffs, N.J.: Prentice-Hall, Inc., 1960); and Andrew Stedry and E. Kay, *The Effects of Goal Difficulty on Performance: A Field Experiment* (Cambridge, Mass.: Sloan School of Management, Massachusetts Institute of Technology, 1964).

ers doing similar tasks on a production line to spot a discriminatory application of standards.

The second objection to an approach that deliberately rejects goal congruence as a means to an end is that it may lead to counterproductive behavior. Supervisors react to pressure in various but predictable ways. One response is to internalize the pressure by working harder, checking on subordinates more often—in effect, trying to transmit the pressure to the next level. Tensions tend to mount under these circumstances, as management has to work harder to keep the gains that have already been made. Grievances mount and the relationships between supervisors and subordinates deteriorate.

The supervisor's capacity for internalization is limited, particularly when it ceases to lead to improved results. At this point, and even before, supervisors are likely to seek ways of relieving the pressure. One way is to unite with their subordinates against "the boss." That is, pressure may lead them to identify more with the manager-subordinate group (group d in Exhibit 19–2) and less with the manager-superior group. By doing this, they can create problems for the superior and thereby transmit the pressure back up the line where it came from.

Another way of relieving pressure is to seek ways of beating the system. To avoid a subsequent tightening of standards, methods improvements will not be disclosed to staff or higher management. Materials will be hoarded for use when variances are unfavorable. Records will be falsified by misclassifying costs or misrepresenting output.

This brings us back to our earlier discussion of participation and motivation. Our conclusions are presented in an integrated format in Exhibit 19–4. This is in the form of a decision tree, and identifies a managerial control strategy appropriate to various combinations of factors.

Management by Exception

The fourth behavioral assumption of responsibility accounting is that reports emphasizing significantly large variances will induce managers to devote their time to those aspects of their operations worthy of their attention. We have referred to this before as the principle of management by exception.

The reports themselves aren't expected to motivate managers, of course. Managers can ignore exception reports just as easily as any other kind if they don't believe that paying attention to them will satisfy their needs. It is reasonable to assume, however, that the motivation is provided by other components of the managerial control structure. Our responsibility is to try to adapt the report structure to the managers' needs and to help explain how the reports are expected to help meet those needs.

The alternatives to exception reporting are so unsatisfactory that the exception reporting assumption is very difficult to deny. Omitting reports altogether, for example, is not a realistic alternative. The

EXHIBIT 19–4

Style, Climate, and Cultural Influences on Control Behavior*

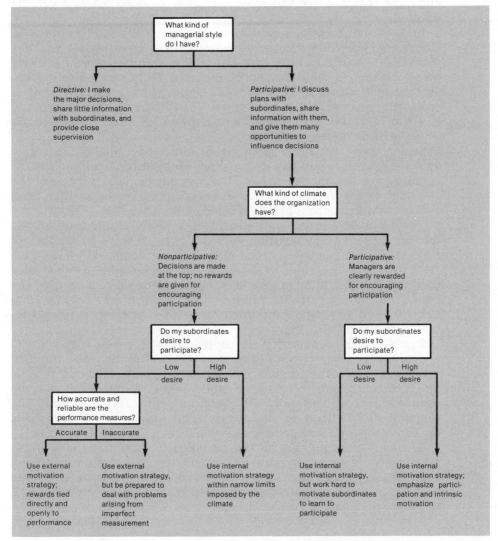

* Derived from Cortlandt Cammann and David A. Nadler, "Fit Control Systems to Your Managerial Style," *Harvard Business Review*, January–February 1976, pp. 65–72, with an assist from Lawler and Rhode, p. 185.

importance of feedback information to reinforce individuals' commitments to their goals is too well documented to allow us to doubt the desirability of a reporting mechanism of some kind.[10]

A more serious alternative might be to report absolute results only, with no explicit performance standards. This will be satisfactory if

[10] A. Zander, *Motives and Goals in Groups* (New York: Academic Press, 1971).

management can supply its own implicit standards. This becomes more and more difficult, however, as the organization becomes larger and more complex. For this reason it has to be ruled out as a general solution.

In short, the exception reporting assumption seems solidly grounded. One danger should be recognized, however. The reporting system may seem to emphasize failure, with only failures and extraordinary successes coming to the attention of higher management. Meeting the performance standard is successful performance, after all, but it ordinarily gets very little recognition. Furthermore, the recognition given to favorable variances often seems to be weaker than the response to unfavorable variances.

Seeing these evidences of apparent bias, subordinates are led to view the system as punitive rather than informative. A common result is that people become defensive. They may question the fairness of the standard or use various devices to cover up variances as they arise and prevent them from being reported.

The focus on failures can also place a premium on cautious behavior. This may be consistent with the organization's goals, but not necessarily. For example, a food manufacturer cannot allow a supervisor to try to reduce cost by departing from the standard procedures used to kill bacteria, no matter how big the potential cost saving. The penalty to the company for failure of this experiment could be catastrophic, and any such experiment must take place in a formal research context.

In a research organization, in contrast, management may want to encourage the research staff to try new approaches that raise immediate costs but offer the possibility of completing projects ahead of time. Since these approaches may not work, however, the result may be unfavorable cost variances. If these are emphasized unduly, the research staff is likely to play it safe. This may have serious effects on the company's competitive position.[11]

This suggests that care should be taken to minimize the punitive role of the reporting system and emphasize its usefulness to the subordinate. Furthermore, major efforts should be made to emphasize positive as well as negative aspects of performance, to provide "positive reinforcement."

The Controllability Criterion

The fifth behavioral assumption of responsibility accounting is that managers are expected to respond only to variances arising within their own jurisdiction. Again the assumption itself seems inescapable, but two possible side effects should be guarded against:

---

[11] In their study of large research organizations, Sayles and Chandler found a good deal of evidence of these tendencies. Leonard R. Sayles and Margaret K. Chandler, *Managing Large Systems: Organizations for the Future* (New York: Harper & Row, 1971), p. 299.

1. Managers may attempt to shift responsibility—getting unfavorable variances assigned to others is one way of getting a better performance rating.
2. Overemphasis on controllability may lead to a greater compartmentalization of the organization.

The second of these is the more subtle of the two. By failing to recognize organizational interdependence, the responsibility accounting structure may add fuel to interdepartmental conflicts as the various managers seek to keep evidences of failure out of their own reports.

For example, sales and production ordinarily take place in different departments in a manufacturing firm. One department gets the orders; the other fills them. The sales force wants to be able to offer its customers the widest possible choice of products and features, all for prompt delivery. The task of the production manager, on the other hand, is a lot easier with long production runs and a steady delivery schedule. This requires fewer products, long lead times, and few or no special modifications to meet individual customer's needs. The production manager complains that the sales manager accepts orders that are very expensive to fill; the sales manager objects to the production manager's inflexibility and insensitivity to marketing problems. Both are right; the problem is how to get each manager to consider the other's point of view.

Cooperation is also important within a single functional area such as marketing or production or research. Sayles and Chandler, for example, found that an emphasis on departmental responsibility in a large research organization seemed to be incompatible with the need for cooperation.[12]

Many companies have attempted to obtain the necessary coordination among production, sales, and other functions by appointing product managers, one for each product. The product manager sees the interrelationships and attempts to reconcile the needs of the various parties. The project manager in a research organization has the same job, although usually with more authority than most product managers have.

Accountants haven't tried to attack this problem to any significant extent. One possibility is to issue reports on a project, product or program basis rather than for individual departments. Thus a factory manager might get several reports, one for each product manufactured. Each of these reports would include sales figures as well as engineering and production costs. The implication would be that responsibility is shared rather than divided. Similarly, each department supervisor might get a report or reports showing total performance in a group of departments as well as a separate report for the supervisor's own department.

The impact of the controllability criterion is not primarily an accounting problem. The partial solution suggested in the last para-

---

[12] Sayles and Chandler, *Managing Large Systems*, pp. 299–304.

graph is really an organizational solution; the accountant cannot make this change unless line management has decided to enlarge the boundary of the responsibility center itself and introduce group responsibility.

It may even be that the positive benefits of interdepartmental conflict make it undesirable to try to eliminate it entirely, even if that were possible. Interdepartmental conflict may be better than intradepartmental conflict, for example, and may be a relatively harmless way of letting the manager let off steam. It may also be a way of getting problems out in the open where they can at least be attacked, and maybe even solved.

Management's problem is to decide how much conflict is desirable. The accountant's problem is to design the reporting system so that it doesn't produce more conflict than management wants.

Harmonization of Conflicting Goals

Our final assumption is that when a responsibility segment has more than one goal, any conflicts between goals must be resolved outside the accounting system. Pollution abatement and current profit, for example, may be conflicting goals. Delivery speed and cost minimization may be another. The accounting system can report progress toward each of these goals, and may help management analyze the trade-offs between them, but the eventual resolution of any such conflicts is left outside the routine responsibility accounting system.

To reconcile conflicting organizational goals, the accounting system would have to measure all of them in monetary terms. Penalties for late delivery could be built into the responsibility reporting structure, for example; so could the cost of continuing pollution. If this were done, then both costs and benefits would be reflected in the responsible manager's control reports. Any conflict could be resolved by a simple comparison process.

Efforts to make major movements in this direction have generally foundered on measurement difficulties. One reaction to these difficulties has been to avoid measuring certain aspects of performance at all:

> *Example.* When asked what his company was doing to present its side of the argument to the public by demonstrating its progress toward pollution abatement, the financial officer of a large electric utility admitted that the only figures he had were summaries of expenditures. Further attempts at measurement were made only under pressure from governmental bodies.

The danger in this is that managers may be moved to emphasize those variables that are measured to the neglect of variables that are not. For example, the managers of staff departments may be led to concentrate exclusively on minimizing the current cost of performing their current functions. By ignoring the development of personnel in their departments, however, they may be depleting human capital. This may not show up in the accounting reports for several years.

Many control systems do measure variables that aren't reflected immediately in reports on financial performance. Variables such as market share, emission of pollutants, product reliability, absenteeism, and community activity are included—both in budgetary planning and in periodic feedback reporting. Nonmonetary measures are used because monetary equivalents are essentially unmeasurable.

Even as further progress is made in this direction, however, the resolution of conflicts between organizational goals must remain outside the responsibility accounting structure. Composite weighting systems, with performance on each variable weighted in proportion to its relative importance, just won't work. Managerial weighting systems are implicit rather than explicit, and extremely difficult to translate into numerical form. Even more fundamentally, the implicit weights refuse to stay constant. Market share may be the watchword today, but a share-oriented composite measure of performance will be obsolete when cost-cutting becomes the order of the day.

In short, no final solution to this problem has yet been found. A useful first step is to identify the major dimensions of performance, whether measurable or not. If this has been done, each of these can be incorporated into the performance review process. The accountant can contribute by seeking ways of measuring the nonfinancial aspects; higher management can help by trying to make the managerial reward structure more visible. In the final analysis, however, the process has to remain fluid, somewhat subjective, and the individual manager can never wholly escape the task of estimating the weights implicit in the structure.

BEHAVIORAL PROBLEMS IN SYSTEM ADMINISTRATION

Undesired behavioral responses to budgetary control systems sometimes arise from the methods of implementation rather than from any inherent defects. Two possible sources of such responses are:

1. Insensitivity on the part of the budgeting staff.
2. Irresponsibility of operating managers.

Insensitivity of the Budgeting Staff

A frequent complaint is that accountants and people on the budget director's staff are insensitive to operating problems and to the needs of operating managers. In many of their contacts with operating managers, the accountants appear as adversaries. Their job is to *criticize* budget proposals, to *investigate* variances, to *enforce* compliance with prescribed procedures, and to *keep higher management informed.* In short, they are paid to find fault with the operating manager—the more fault they find, the more successful they are apt to be.

Furthermore, accountants are likely to report their findings in the first instance to their boss or to higher levels of operating management rather than to the executives immediately concerned. These executives are likely to resent this and react by obstructing the accountants' work if they can.

As a consequence, accountants sometimes encounter defensiveness, hostility, and conflict. Accountants who are aware of these problems can avoid them or at least minimize their impact. One way is by changing their attitudes toward the job and toward the operating executives. By reporting their findings in the first place to the managers who have the responsibility to act, for example, the accountants can help these managers do their job. Doing this should help the accountants build more effective relationships.

A closely related possibility is to change most accountants' formal role to that of facilitators. In this way, most of the accounting people would spend their time providing feedback and working with the line managers on their problems and decisions. For example, the accountants can try to make sure that the operating managers have enough technical help before budgetary plans are submitted, thereby reducing the number of defects to be uncovered during the review process. Similarly, if they are engaged in postmortem investigations, they can incorporate in their reports the steps the managers are taking to respond to variances that have arisen.[13]

Irresponsibility of Operating Managers

Budgeting and performance review are stressful activities. Operating managers needing to relieve pressure at such times may be inclined to strike out at the accountants, both because they are visible participants in these activities and because manager-accountant groups are less crucial than the other groupings in Exhibit 19–2. Fighting with the boss or with subordinates is dangerous business; fighting with accountants may seem safer.

Another result of this same problem is a tendency for managers to improve their relationships with their subordinates by citing the accountant or the budgeting system as the sources of burdensome requirements. For example, rather than ask a subordinate to do something because it is worth doing, the manager may justify the request on the grounds that the accountants insist on it. By making the accountants, the budget director, or even the system itself as the villain of the piece, the manager hopes to avoid unpleasant conflicts with subordinates. This also cuts down the amount of time spent explaining why something must be done.

This kind of behavior can make it difficult for the controller's staff to get their work done. The easiest solution to these difficulties is to play the same game—"I don't like this any better than you do, but

---

[13] The results of a pioneering study of the relationships between accountants and operating personnel were summarized in a perceptive research report by Herbert A. Simon, George Kozmetsky, Harold Guetzkow, and Gordon Tyndall, *Centralization vs. Decentralization in Organizing the Controller's Department* (New York: Controllership Foundation, 1954).

top management says it has to be done." A better approach in the long run is to keep explaining the process and, even better, keep producing useful results. Managers who find the responsibility accounting system helpful are likely to cooperate with the accountants much more readily than those who don't.[14]

SUMMARY

The responsibility accounting structure is based on a number of implicit assumptions about the behavior of individuals and groups making up the organization. The most fundamental of these is that individuals will strive to achieve the performance levels represented in the current operating budget. The mechanism that is relied upon to accomplish this is participation in managerial decision making by managers at all operating levels. Participation is designed to get the managers to internalize the budgetary standards, thereby converting them into personal aspiration levels. Participation works best when the superior's personal style is open, when the organizational climate is favorable to participation, and when the subordinates have a strong desire to participate. Participation in these situations can harness the forces leading to intrinsic motivation.

Participation is unlikely to have much effect when the superior manager's style is autocratic, the climate is restrictive, and the subordinate manager would rather receive orders than participate. In intermediate situations, management may try to use the positive aspects of group dynamics to secure some of the motivational benefits of participation. If a group can be induced to accept performance standards, each member of the group will find it easier to accept them as well.

The accounting structure also contains potentially destructive elements. Management by exception and the concept of controllability, for example, can lead to excessive departmentalization of effort and counterproductive efforts to shift blame or the chance of being blamed. Furthermore, the very nature of the accountant's job creates opportunities for conflict with operating personnel. If senior management tries to use the budget as a pressure device, these opportunities multiply and lead eventually to counterproductive behavior.

Solutions to most of the behavioral problems that arise in connection with the budgetary control system lie outside the accounting area. The accountant can contribute to these solutions, however: first, by being more sensitive to the needs and attitudes of operating personnel; and second, by devising methods of measurement and reporting that will further the control objectives of operating management.

---

[14] David A. Nadler, Philip H. Mirvis, and Cortlandt Cammann, "The Ongoing Feedback System: Experimenting with a New Managerial Tool," *Organizational Dynamics*, Spring 1976, pp. 63–80.

KEY TERMS

The most important terms introduced and defined in this chapter are the following:

Cohesion   Intrinsic motivation
Goal congruence   Level of aspiration
Group dynamics   Motivation
Internalization   Participation

EXERCISES AND PROBLEMS

1. Setting the standard performance level. Alpha Company is installing a standard costing system in its factory for the first time. You have been asked to choose among four possible bases for setting standards. To help you choose, management has given the following data on container costs for one of the company's products:

1. Each unit of product requires one container.
2. Average performance last year: 1,050 containers used per 1,000 units of product.
3. Average performance of engineering department test run using average experienced workers: 1,030 containers used per 1,000 units of product.
4. Best performance found by engineering department: 1,015 containers used per 1,000 units of product.

a. Taking each of these four standards in turn, indicate what the materials quantity variance would mean and whether it is more likely to be favorable or unfavorable.
b. Taking behavioral factors into account, which of these standards would you choose? How would you introduce it? Give the reasons for your choice.

2. Group dynamics. Bert Jackson got a summer job. He worked in an office with three other people, all of whom had been on the job for about a month when Bert was hired. Bert had just finished his freshman year in college; Carl Martin, the team leader and the oldest member of the team, had just graduated from college and planned to enroll as a part-time law student in the fall.

Carl reported to Janet Davis, the office manager. Janet was a woman in her late 30s and had been with the company for more than 15 years. She supervised a staff of six full-time employees in addition to Carl's team of temporary workers. She also used part-time employees for peak clerical loads.

The team's assignment was to convert the office's master customer file into a form suitable for computerization. The worker first took the customer's folder from the file and copied data from it onto a special form. He or she obtained additional data from one or more directories; occasionally a subsidiary file was consulted, and on rare occasions Janet was asked to supply some missing information.

The completed forms were assembled in batches of 50. Each week the team was expected to deliver seven batches to the keypunch operators in the computer center. Once a month the forms and a computer printout were returned to the office for vertification. The team had been complimented several times on the accuracy of its work.

Each member of the team, including Carl and Bert, did the same work; none of them specialized in any one phase of it. Once or twice a day Janet asked Carl to send someone on an errand. These assignments usually went to Bert, who welcomed the change of pace.

Bert learned the job quickly and by the second day was completing as many forms as each of the others. His first Friday on the job he reported to his family that the team had completed 430 forms that week but had turned in only seven batches of 50 forms each. The reason was to have a reserve for next week, in case the team didn't meet the 350 unit quota then. "After all," Bert said, "we don't want them to raise our quota. If we turned in eight batches this week, they'd expect us to do that every week."

At the end of the second week Carl reported to Janet that Bert was working out very well and should be moved from probationary status with a raise of 10 cents an hour. Seven batches of forms were turned in, with 60 forms held back for the next week.

a.   Comment on the group processes observed here.
b.   What action, if any, should Janet take after accidentally discovering that the team occasionally holds back part of its production. What alternatives did you consider and why did you reject them?

3. Production standards; Interdepartmental conflict. Campo Motor Parts, Inc. manufactures a wide variety of automotive parts and supplies. A basic plan standard costing system is in use in each of its factories.

One of the company's lines is a line of windshield wipers for trucks and passenger vehicles. The windshield wiper consists of four principal mechanical parts: the blade, the blade holder, the wiper arm, and a mounting bracket. The blade holders and wiper arms are made in the metal shop, the mounting brackets are made in the casting department, and the blades are purchased from a rubber manufacturer.

Holders, arms, brackets and blades are assembled in the assembly department. The blades, blade holders, and arms are brought together in a subassembly. This is then fitted on a mounting bracket. If the subassembly fits, the assembled mechanism is placed in a box and readied for transfer to the shipping room, where it is mated with an electrical actuating mechanism that is produced elsewhere in the factory.

Each batch of parts is inspected before delivery to the assembly department. Slight flaws are difficult to detect, however, and often show up only as the units are being assembled. A particularly common problem is a poor fit between the arm and blade assembly and the mounting bracket. This can be corrected by the assembler, but the correction takes from 10 to 60 seconds.

The standard assembly time includes provision for a normal percentage of defective parts and subassemblies. Whenever a sizable unfavorable labor quantity variance arises, however, the chief of assembly is inclined to claim that defective parts were the cause. The head of the castings department says that process control in that department is so tight that the mounting brackets cannot be at fault. The metal shop supervisor believes that the chief of assembly is merely trying to pass the buck. If excessive defects do occur, however, they must come from the casting process.

The plant manager has learned to live with this kind of bickering, but lately the problem has become much worse. Several months ago the company introduced a new type of wiper, requiring much tighter fitting parts. Engineered standard times were established for the new model on the basis of time studies. Labor variances in the castings department and the metal shop have been negligible; in the assembly department they have been large and unfavorable. The product manager insists that if these cost problems cannot be licked the work will be subcontracted to an outside firm. The plant manager doesn't want this to happen and has asked your advice.

a.   Is it likely that the standard costing system is partly responsible for the high costs of the new model? Give reasons to support your point of view.

b.   What changes, if any, would you make in the measurement and reporting system to alleviate the problems that have arisen? Give reasons for the position you have taken.

4. Setting a standard performance level. The Alton Company is expanding its punch press department. It is about to purchase three new punch presses from Equipment Manufacturers, Inc. Equipment Manufacturers' engineers report that their mechanical studies indicate that for Alton's intended use, the output rate for one press should be 1,000 pieces an hour.

Alton has similar presses now in operation. Production from these presses averaged 600 pieces an hour last month, based on the following record of performance:

Worker	Daily Output
L. Jones	750
J. Green	750
R. Smith	600
H. Brown	500
R. Alters	550
G. Hoag	450
Total	3,600
Average	600

Alton's management also plans to institute a standard cost accounting system in the near future. The company's engineers are supporting a standard based on 1,000 pieces an hour, the accounting department is arguing for 750 pieces an hour, and the production department supervisor is arguing for 600 pieces an hour.

a.   What arguments would the various proponents be likely to use to support their recommendations?

b.   Which alternative best reconciles the needs of cost control and the motivation of improved performance? Explain why you made that choice.

(CMA adapted)

5. Performance standards for motivation. Ray Carlson, president of Scientific Equipment Manufacturing Company, wants to introduce standard costing into his company's factory. As a result of his participation in a two-week management development course at a nearby university, Mr. Carlson is convinced that some kind of standard costing system is just what he needs to strengthen his control over factory cost. The factory now has a simple job order costing system, and no one has ever attempted to establish standard costs.

Scientific Equipment makes and sells a line of highly technical equipment for industrial users. The company is located in a small midwestern city with a population of 80,000 people. Quality, or the supplier's ability to meet exacting technical specifications, is a major consideration for most of the company's customers when deciding where to place an order.

Production is organized on a job order basis, and orders are typically manufactured to customer specifications. Most of the orders can be filled by producing items of standard design and specifications, or items which require only minor modifications of the standard designs. Jobs requiring major redesign and the use of nonstandardized production techniques amount to 30 percent of the total. The cost estimates that Mr. Carlson uses in developing price bids for this kind of nonstandardized business have been close to the actual costs of filling the orders in most cases, or at least close enough to satisfy Mr. Carlson.

Scientific Equipment is a small company, with about 75 employees. The two largest segments of the work force are 30 machine operators and 20 assemblers. The machine operators are all men. Their jobs require a considerable degree of skill and experience. The assemblers, on the other hand, are all women. Their jobs are relatively routine but require a good deal of concentration to avoid costly assembly defects. The employees generally lunch together in a nearby cafeteria. Many of the men socialize off the job, and so do several of the women.

Mr. Carlson is considering engaging a consulting firm to develop and install a standard costing system. A letter from the managing partner of the consulting firm contained the following key paragraphs:

"In order to motivate people to their maximum productivity, standards must be based upon the company's best workers and what they can achieve. If the standard were lower, the high performers could meet it too easily and it wouldn't offer sufficient motivation for the low performers. I'd set the standard at the level of performance of the top 10 to 15 percent of your employees. This would establish a high aspiration level for your people and, therefore, motivate their best efforts.

"I also suggest that superior performance be well rewarded. This means that employees who exceed standard should receive a substantial bonus, while those who do not exceed standard should receive no bonus."

Since Mr. Carlson doesn't feel qualified to evaluate this kind of statement, he has contracted the faculty member who conducted the sessions on standard costing at the local university (you), asking what you think of the philosophy underlying the proposed system.

a. Prepare a reply to Mr. Carlson. Should he engage the consultant?
b. If you agree with the consultant's basic approach, outline how you would implement it at Scientific Equipment Manufacturing Company. If you disagree with the consultant, state the basic principles underlying an alternative system and outline how you would go about developing a standard costing system for this company.

(Prepared by Professor Eric Flamholtz)

6. Separate standards for motivation and for control. Harden Company has experienced increased production costs. The primary area of concern identified by management is direct labor. The company is considering adopting a standard cost system to help control labor and other costs. Useful historical data are not available because detailed production records have not been maintained.

Harden Company has retained Finch & Associates, an engineering consulting firm, to establish labor standards. After a complete study of the work process, the engineers recommended a labor standard of 1 unit of production every 30 minutes or 16 units a day for each worker. Finch further advised that Harden's wage rates were below the prevailing rate of $6 an hour.

Harden's production vice president thought this labor standard was too tight and the employees would be unable to attain it. From his experience with the labor force, he believed a labor standard of 40 minutes a unit or 12 units a day for each worker would be more reasonable.

Dan Jones, Harden's president, believed the standard should be set at a high level to motivate the workers, but he also recognized the standard should be set at a level to provide adequate information for control and reasonable cost comparisons. After much discussion, the management decided to use a dual standard. The labor standard recommended by the engineering firm of one unit every 30 minutes would be employed in the plant as a motivation device, and a cost standard of 40 minutes a unit would be used in reporting. Management also concluded that the workers would not be informed of the cost standard used for reporting purposes. The production vice president conducted several sessions prior to implementation in the plant informing the workers of the new standard cost system and answering questions. The new standards were not related to incentive pay but were introduced at the time wages were increased to $6 an hour.

The new standard cost system was implemented on January 1. At the end of six months of operation, the following statistics on labor performance were presented to top management:

	Jan.	Feb.	Mar.	Apr.	May	June
Production (units)	5,100	5,000	4,700	4,500	4,300	4,400
Direct labor hours	3,000	2,900	2,900	3,000	3,000	3,100
Variance from labor standard	$2,700U	$2,400U	$3,300U	$4,500U	$5,100U	$5,400U
Variance from cost standard	$2,400F	$2,600F	$1,400F	$ 0	$ 800U	$1,000U

Raw material quality, labor mix, and plant facilities and conditions have not changed to any great extent during the six-month period.

a.   Discuss the impact of different types of standards on motivation, and specifically discuss the effect on motivation in Harden Company's plant of adopting the labor standard recommended by the engineering firm.

b.   Evaluate Harden Company's decision to employ dual standards in its standard cost system.

(CMA)

CASE 19–1: SUSSEX PRODUCTS, LTD.*
(Staff/line relationships)

Sussex Products, Ltd. is a manufacturer of a diversified line of industrial cleaning compounds, disinfectants, and pesticides located in Lower

---

* Copyright by l'Institut pour l'Etude des Méthodes de Direction de l'Entreprise (IMEDE), Lausanne, Switzerland. Reproduced by permission.

Grinling, Sussex, England. Its production division consists of six manu-facturing plants and a small divisional headquarters staff.

The exchange of letters given below relates to an internal audit carried out at the company's Leatherslade plant early in 1974. A partial organi-zation chart, showing the formal organizational relationships among the persons mentioned in this case is as follows:

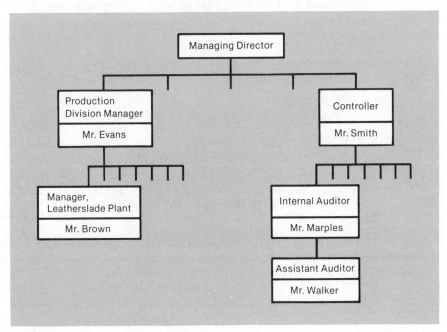

Questions

a. Whose side would you take in this dispute?
b. What, if anything, could Messrs. Evans, Smith, and Marples have done to avoid the difficulties which arose?

Exchange of Letters

FROM: P. J. Evans, Manager   To: T. P. E. Brown, Manager
Production Division   Leatherslade Plant

cc: Controller
Internal Audit Dept.   3d September, 1973

Dear Mr. Brown:

Internal Control

We draw your attention to the following section of our regulations for internal control (ACC/17—12/6/69):

"The allocation of duties and responsibilities within a plant shall be designed in such a way that there will be a system of checks and bal-ances whereby the work of one employee shall always be checked by the work of another employee, working independently."

We are, of course, of the opinion that plant managers should do their utmost to avoid loss to the company from fraud by employees. On the other hand, we are also particularly anxious to keep paperwork in our productive units to a strict minimum. We therefore point out that there should be no duplication of work merely for the sake of control, and that control systems should be devised in such a way that the work of one clerk can be checked with the work that another clerk would have done anyway.

Yours very truly,

FROM: P. J. Evans, Manager   To: T. P. E. Brown, Manager .
       Production Division   Leatherslade Plant

cc: Controller
       Internal Audit Dept.   13th January 1974

Dear Mr. Brown:

Internal Audit

This letter serves to introduce the bearer, Mr. Marples, who has been charged by management to undertake an internal audit of your plant.

The scope of his audit is determined by accepted auditing practice and will include in particular an examination of control procedures in the light of the company's regulations for internal control (ACC/17—12/6/69).

Mr. Marples is to have access to all the books of account and records necessary to complete his audit and we are sure we can rely on you to see that he is provided with all the explanations of which he stands in need.

He will discuss with you the findings of his audit before he leaves your plant.

Yours very truly,

FROM: T. P. E. Brown, Manager   To: P. J. Evans, Manager
       Leatherslade Plant   Production Division

CONFIDENTIAL   22nd January 1974

Dear Mr. Evans:

Internal Audit

This is to confirm my phone call to you today during which I informed you of the unfortunate happenings of last week.

As I explained, I find it difficult to hold myself responsible for the re-actions of my people to the internal auditors' attitude to their task. Quite apart from the auditors' inability to observe the common forms of politeness and business etiquette with supervisory staff and their attempts to brow-beat employees with many years' service with the company, matters were brought to a head this week when Mr. Marples' assistant was discovered after the normal closing hours hiding behind the stocks in the finished goods warehouse. I can only assume that the purpose of this subterfuge was to spy on warehouse staff who were having to work overtime as a re-sult of the delay occasioned in their work by the lengthy checking and re-checking of finished goods stocks insisted on by the auditors.

As you know, our union is becoming particularly militant in prepara-tion for our negotiations with them which are due this spring. I therefore requested that the audit at present be discontinued and resumed later in the year.

You, however, stated that for head office reasons the audit must go on.

Yours very truly,

FROM: F. G. Marples   TO: B. W. Smith
                Internal Auditor   Controller

CONFIDENTIAL   22nd January 1974

Dear Mr. Smith:

Leatherslade Plant Audit 1974

This is to confirm my telephone call of yesterday evening, during which I reported on the first week of our audit here.

As this is a first audit, one naturally expects some difficulties to arise, but I very much regret to report that in this instance there seems to be some definite ill will in the reaction of plant management.

I had the usual discussion with the plant manager on the second day we were here and explained to him the purpose and scope of our audit, but unfortunately was unable to elicit any positive reaction from him. In the following days the atmosphere rapidly degenerated to the point where both Mr. Walker and I were followed whenever we left the office to check anything in the plant.

The day before yesterday Mr. Walker returned to the finished goods warehouse to recover some notes which he had inadvertently left there, whereupon he was grasped by both arms by one of the factory foremen who had followed him there and was taken by force to the manager's office.

I would not normally bother you with the details of such rather childish behavior were it not for veiled threats subsequently issued by Mr. Brown that this incident, which I consider to have been rigged, was to be used for political purposes at head office.

Yours very truly,

17th February 1974

REPORT ON INTERNAL AUDIT
Leatherslade Plant

Period of Audit

13th January, 1974 to 3rd February 1974.

Conclusions

We found that most of the clerical routines in the plant were performed conscientiously, accurately, and on time, although certain recording functions could, we felt, be improved. We also found, however, that the internal control system in the areas of labor payroll, raw materials, and finished goods was defective and have made recommendations that the allocation of tasks amongst employees should be changed.

*   *   *   *   *

Cash and Stamps

At the time of our cash check the cash book had not been written up for four days. There was some evidence of subsequent alterations to entries in the cash book and some entries were not easily legible.

We recommend that the cash book be kept up to date at all times and that faulty entries be corrected in the orthodox manner.

* * * * *

Accounts Payable

We found the recording of creditors accounts up to date and correct insofar as our verifications could determine. We noted, however, that the creditors' accounts clerk orders certain technical materials, checks them on arrival, and signs for them having been received. From the point of view of internal control, the person keeping creditors' accounts records should not participate either in the ordering or reception of supplies and in any event supplies should not be ordered and vouched for upon receipt by the same person.

* * * * *

Manufacturing Account

Weekly manufacturing losses for raw materials showed the following variations during November and December:

Week 1.......... 2.0%	Week 4.......... 2.1%	Week 7.......... 2.0%
Week 2.......... 1.9	Week 5.......... 1.8	Week 8.......... 5.2
Week 3.......... 4.8	Week 6.......... 1.9	Week 9.......... 1.8

Average: 1972–73:................ 2.0%

No satisfactory explanation was given for the extraordinarily high losses of week 3 and week 8.

The final check on quantities produced is afforded by the quantities shown as entering to the finished goods warehouse. The quantities produced are recorded under the supervision of the manufacturing foreman; the quantities entering the warehouse are recorded by the warehousman. The manufacturing foreman and the warehouseman are, however, related by marriage. We feel that to ensure adequate control, the recording of goods produced should be made entirely independently of the recording of goods entering the warehouse.

* * * * *

Labor Payroll

Our check of the labor payroll for the first week of December revealed two errors in the calculation of overtime pay. These errors were rectified during our audit.

We noted that the employee who calculates the labor payroll also pays out wages to the employees. Although the payroll calculations are checked by another person, we nevertheless recommend that the payout of wages be made by someone in no way connected with the calculation of the payroll—preferably the cashier.

* * * * *

We wish to extend our thanks to Mr. Brown and his staff for the assistance rendered to us during our audit.

Respectfully submitted,

F. G. Marples
Internal Auditor

FROM: T. P. E. Brown, Manager   To: P. J. Evans, Manager
         Leatherslade Plant   Production Division

cc: Controller
        Internal Audit Dept.   2d March 1974

Dear Mr. Evans:

Internal Audit

I have for comment the report on January's audit.

Although the tone of the report would seem to be unfavorable, the substance of it seems to me to be a commendation, particularly of our office staff. The only mistakes the auditors could find were a few corrections in the cash book (the cash balance agreed with cash on hand), 7p. missing in the stamps (which even the auditors did not think worth mentioning), and two minor errors in our large payroll (which even the workers concerned had not noticed).

Failing to find anything seriously wrong with our accounting, they therefore had to comment on theoretical weaknesses and on matters outside the scope of their audit.

No comment was made to the auditors on the manufacturing losses they mention, as these had already been discussed with you in correspondence and as such manufacturing matters are clearly not the concern of auditors.

Nor can I admit that auditors should attempt to reassign jobs amongst plant employees. The payroll clerk orders and checks certain technical supplies as he previously worked in the fitter's shop and is the only office employee qualified to do so.

I fail to see how our warehouseman's marriage last summer to the manufacturing foreman's younger sister has anything whatsoever to do with his trustworthiness.

The remarks concerning Mr. Thompson, who is in charge of the payroll, seem particularly misplaced. He has worked for us now for 27 years and is known and respected by all our employees. To entrust the payout to Miss Allen, our cashier, who has been with us only 18 months and who is now only 22 years of age, just does not seem to me to be a feasible proposition.

I fully realize that our auditors are young, zealous, and without a great deal of experience of business, and I hope that the coming years will temper their theories with reality.

Yours very truly,

20

Standard Costing on the Comprehensive Plan

THE standard costing system we outlined in Chapter 6 (referred to as a *basic plan* system) was relatively simple. It was designed to provide scorecard information only. The purpose of this chapter is to examine

---

BASIC PLAN: A REMINDER

Materials price variances are identified and segregated when the materials are purchased; actual prices are not used in accounting for inventory costs.

Production centers are charged for the actual direct labor and materials quantities they use, multiplied by standard materials prices and wage rates.

Production centers are credited for the standard costs of the work done—i.e., standard direct labor and materials quantities, multiplied by standard materials prices and wage rates.

Labor and materials quantity variances are identified at the end of the period, on the basis of a physical count of the work-in-process.

Labor and materials quantity variances are identified as production center totals for the time period as a whole; they are not computed for individual job orders or individual operators.

The work-in-process account balances measure the standard costs of the inventories in process only at the end of each reporting period, after the variances have been identified and segregated in the accounts.

---

a more comprehensive kind of standard costing system, one management can use to provide steering control information as well as scorecard information. We call this the comprehensive plan, and we shall look at three of its aspects:

1. The methods used to identify quantity variances, classify them, and report them to management.
2. Statistical tools and decision models that might be used to help management interpret quantity variances.
3. The record-keeping routines that can be used to integrate comprehensive plan data into the ledger.

IDENTIFYING AND REPORTING QUANTITY VARIANCES

Management is most likely to consider adopting the comprehensive plan of standard costing when the first-level managers must rely on quantity variance information to signal the need for action. To see why this is so, we need to examine four questions:

1. What the comprehensive plan is and how it differs from the basic plan.
2. What kinds of reports can be generated from data derived under the comprehensive plan.
3. How the causes of individual variances are likely to be identified and reported.
4. What benefits and costs are likely to appear under the comprehensive plan.

Since the methods used to isolate price variances are the same as in the basic plan, we can ignore them here.

Characteristics of the Comprehensive Plan

The comprehensive plan has three main characteristics that distinguish it from the basic plan:[1]

1. Direct labor and materials quantity variances are identified as the work is performed. (In basic plan systems these variances are identified at the end of the reporting period.)
2. Direct labor and materials quantity variances are available in great detail and can be classified on many different bases. (In basic plan systems these variances are available only as production center totals for the reporting period as a whole.)
3. Work-in-Process account balances are stated at standard cost at all times. (In the basic plan the Work-in-Process account balances are stated at standard cost only at the end of each period.)

---

[1] "Comprehensive plan" and "basic plan" are terms used here to describe the main features of two different kinds of standard costing systems. Specific details of these systems will vary widely from company to company, but their main characteristics can be recognized quite easily.

All of these differences hinge on the ability of the system to identify the quantity variances as they occur. This is done by putting more data on the labor time tickets and materials requisitions than they carry in a basic plan.

Labor time tickets.   Under the basic plan, direct labor time merely needs to be classified by production center. For the comprehensive plan, a separate time ticket must be prepared for each separate labor operation. At a minimum, it must show the standard time for that operation and the actual time spent. It may also show the name of the operator, the equipment used, and the job or product on which the operation was performed.

A sample time ticket is shown in Exhibit 20–1. Each ticket is a record of the work done and of the variance arising from it. Time is recorded in this case in tenths of hours. All the data on this form can be written or punched in in advance except the actual time and the vairance time. Data from the file of standard wage rates can then be used to restate these figures in dollars and cents.

EXHIBIT 20–1

Comprehensive Plan Labor Time Ticket

Item: Base plate No. 423	Date *4/7/x1*
Batch quantity: 1,000 pieces	
	Actual hours:
Operation: 472—Press	Finish *11.1*
Department: A	Start *8.1*
Operator: P. Jones	Difference *3.0*
Job No.: X4474	Standard hours: *2.5*
	Variance hours *0.5*

Materials requisitions.   When materials usage is recorded by flow meters, as in some chemical operations, materials usage forms similar to the labor time tickets can be used. When materials go to the factory floor in batches, however, the variance calculation is likely to be made at the time the materials are issued.

One way to do this is to classify the materials requisitions into two categories: standard and supplemental. At the time a production order is prepared, a separate requisition card is prepared for the standard quantity of each material shown on the standard cost sheet. When a department begins work on the job, the department head exchanges the cards for the standard quantities shown on them.

Whenever additional materials are issued to cover excessive spoilage as the job progresses, a supplemental requisition card of a different color and with a distinctive code number is prepared, showing the quantity and code number of each of the supplemental materials. Similarly, if a job is completed without consuming all of the materials issued, the excess materials are returned to the stockroom,

EXHIBIT 20–2

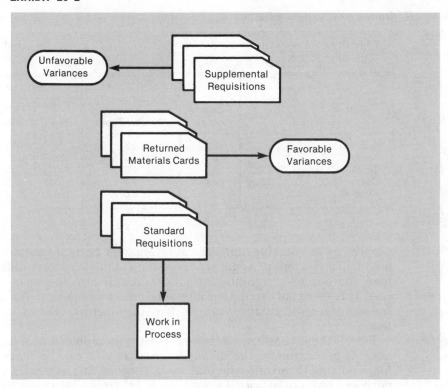

where a returned materials card is filled out with the quantity of each material returned.

Each supplemental requisition and each returned materials card represents a variance. Each standard requisition measures the amount of work done (see Exhibit 20–2). The file of standard materials prices can be used to restate all these figures in monetary terms.

Comprehensive Plan Reporting to Management

The comprehensive plan allows the accountant to prepare variance reports in great detail. In many factories, for example, a printout of the previous day's labor performance is placed on each supervisor's desk at the start of each workday, with a separate line or lines for each operator. A truncated example of such a report is shown in Exhibit 20–3.

Reports of this kind are appropriate if they are to be used as steering controls. They are tremendously detailed and are issued soon after the work takes place. They may help the manager identify problems, trace them to their source, and do somthing about them before they have done much damage.

Daily labor reports like the one in Exhibit 20–3 are not always desirable, however. Too frequent reporting may actually defeat its own

EXHIBIT 20–3

Daily Labor Variance Report

			Variance	
Operator	Standard Hours	Actual Direct Hours (Including Personal Time)	Hours	Percent of Standard
Brown, P..............	8.2	8.0	0.2	2.4
Conrad, T. T.............	8.6	8.0	0.6	7.0
Ennis, J..............	3.3	4.0	(0.7)	(21.2)
Gordon, L.............	8.4	9.5	(1.1)	(13.1)
King, M..............	7.9	8.0	(0.1)	(1.3)

Department: Machining   Date: 3/6
Supervisor: P. B. Naum

purpose by not making sufficient allowance for normal fluctuations in productive efficiency. Additional detail also makes reports difficult to read and obscures significant relationships. It also increases system cost. It is especially inappropriate when the manager's main need is for scorecard information rather than for steering control information.

For all these reasons, selective reporting is probably a better solution. At one extreme, the detailed variance data can be placed in a file, available to anyone who may need a special analysis for a specific purpose, but not reported routinely to anyone. Alternatively, only variances larger than specified amounts or percentages might be reported, all others remaining on file for later summarization and analysis. We shall explore this latter idea in the next section.

Recording the Causes of Quantity Variances

The variance report serves a steering control purpose by spotting potential problems as they emerge. Management ordinarily can then identify the causes with little difficulty and take action accordingly. Only when the cause is not obvious must management decide whether to spend time and money to try to find out what happened.

Even though the department head may be able to identify the causes of variances as they occur, higher management cannot. The system may be designed, therefore, to keep track of the most important causes of variances, not for steering controls, but to provide scorecard information on the control efforts of the production center managers. The report form illustrated in Exhibit 20–4 was used in this way. Someone close to the operation had to identify the cause of each quantity variance larger than 10 percent of standard and enter this explanation on the time ticket. The amounts in each category were then summarized and reported to management each month.

Causal identification systems as comprehensive as this are extremely rare. Management usually does ask, however, that variances

EXHIBIT 20–4

Summary Report of Causes of Quantity Variances

Code	Reason for Variance	Control-ability	Month of			Year to Date		
			Actual Hours	Variance Hours	Cost	Actual Hours	Variance Hours	Cost
0	No reason. Variances less than 10 percent.	C						
1	Estimated running time too high. Reported to standards department.	N						
2	Estimated setup time too high. Reported to standards department.	N						
3	Men's effort and/or ability above average.	C						
5	New machine, standard has not been changed.	N						
6	Change in methods, standard has not been changed.	N						
7	New or improved tools, standard has not been changed.	N						
8	Used setup from previous jobs.	C						
9	Time set for man operating one machine. Ran two.	C						
10	Time clock registers to 0.1 hour only.	N						
11	Work done under special supervision.	C						
	TOTAL GAINS							
0	No reason. Variances less than 10 percent.	C						
51	Standard too low. Reported to standards department.	N						
52	First time job was made.	C						
53	Slow or obsolete machine used.	N						
54	Planning not correct. Was changed. Standards department notified.	N						
55	Could not follow operation as planned, delivery requirements.	N						
56	Operations in previous departments not performed as planned.	C						
57	Time set for man operating two machines. One available.	N						
58	Quantity too small.	N						
59	Extra setup result of machine break down.	N						
60	Extra work.	N						
61	Two men had to be assigned to job due to nature of job.	N						
62	Learner, apprentice, or student.	N						
63	Man inexperienced. Undergoing instructions.	N						
64	Different operators used due to difficulty of job.	C						
65	Assisting inexperienced operator on another machine.	N						
66	Man's effort and/or ability below average.	C						
67	Operation not performed correctly. Additional time required.	C						
68	Parts spoiled. Had to make additional parts.	C						
69	Tools not available at time job was started.	N						
70	Trying out new tools.	N						
71	Tools not correct when job was started. Had to be corrected.	N						
72	Broke tool. Time lost redressing and sharpening.	C						
73	Oversized material used.	N						
74	Castings warped, but are within foundry tolerances.	N						
75	Casting not to dimensions. Time lost waiting for instructions.	N						
76	Material too hard. Frequent sharpening of tools required.	N						
77	Improper supervision.	C						
79	Illegible blue prints.	N						
80	Blowholes and porous casting.	N						
81	Sheet stock—secondary material or scrap ends used.	N						
99	Full quantity or operations not complete.	N						
	TOTAL LOSSES							
	GRAND TOTAL							
	Efficiency % Controllable by Foreman	C						
	Efficiency % Noncontrollable	N						
	Efficiency % Overall							

Reproduced by permission from "The Analysis of Manufacturing Cost Variances, Research Series No. 22," *N.A.(C.)A. Bulletin*, August 1952, pp. 1545–84.

due to some specific causes be identified routinely and reported periodically. These are causes that are likely to occur frequently if they are not kept under control. When this is done, the quantity variances will be reported in two sections—those due to the specified causes, one by one, and those due to all other causes combined.

We can illustrate this practice by looking at two causes of quantity variances that are often singled out for special attention:

1. Spoilage, rejection, and rework.
2. Equipment substitution.

Spoilage, rejection and rework. Quantity variances may arise because some units of output do not meet quality standards. The defective units may be destroyed, sold as scrap, or recycled; others are set aside for reprocessing, a process known as *rework*. Management may wish to identify the quantity variances arising from these causes.

If the defective units are destroyed, sold, or recycled, the appropriate procedure is to record the number of defective units and multiply this quantity by the standard cost per unit. Losses of this kind create both materials quantity variances and labor quantity variances. Because both of these arise from the same cause, they should be combined for variance reporting:

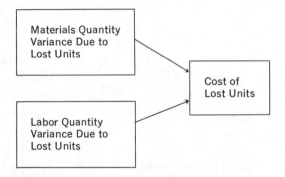

This is likely to be treated as an element of factory overhead costs, with a flexible budget allowance of its own. Scrap recoveries, if any, are typically recorded as negative items of overhead cost.

A slightly different treatment is appropriate if the defective units are repaired or reworked. In these cases, the rework labor time is recorded separately, either as a component of the labor quantity variance or as an overhead cost. The only requirement is to code the time tickets as rework labor instead of as regular labor time.

Equipment substitution. Product cost standards are generally based on the use of a particular type of machine to do each operation. Scheduling difficulties may cause the use of substitute equipment to meet delivery schedules when the preferred equipment is fully utilized by other work. This substitute equipment is likely to require more labor time than the preferred equipment; it may also call for different labor skills. In either case, a labor quantity variance will arise.

The simplest way to handle this in a comprehensive plan system is to classify the entire variance between standard labor cost and actual labor cost as the effect of the equipment substitution. This can be treated as a subdivision of the labor quantity variance or as an element of overhead cost, attributed to the work of the scheduling staff.

A variance identified in this way is only partly the result of equipment substitution, however. Other factors may also have affected the amount of labor time used. To isolate these other effects, the methods staff may prepare alternative cost standards, one for each frequently used machine type. When a substitution is made, the total variance from standard cost can be split into two parts, one the result of the substitution, the other the result of all other causes combined.

For example, a drilling operation on a certain piece part is normally assigned to a new drill press with a standard time of 21 hours for a standard lot size. It can also be performed on a slower machine in 25 hours. The actual operating time last week was 27 hours, 6 hours more than the standard time. With this information, the breakdown of the variance is simple:

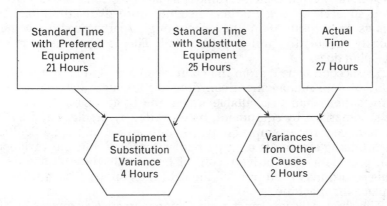

At a standard wage rate of $8 an hour, a $32 equipment substitution variance would be reported. The unexplained labor quantity variance would be $2 \times \$8 = \$16$.

This is an expensive technique. The methods staff must estimate not one standard cost for each operation, but two or even more. This effort ordinarily can't be justified by the value of the control information it provides; alternative standards typically will be available only if they are developed to help the scheduling staff decide which operations to put on each machine.

Costs and Benefits of the Comprehensive Plan

Many factors enter into the design of a standard costing system. Factors such as the availability of competent people, the strength of management's commitment to standard costing, and the amount of time the accountants have to get the system installed must be considered.

The two most important considerations are the benefits management hopes to gain from the system and the costs of installing and operating it. Comprehensive plan systems are likely to be more costly than the basic plan systems we described in Chapter 6. System costs depend largely on the number of documents to be processed, the amount of data to be extracted from them, the amount of processing to be done, the size and accessibility of the files, and the number and complexity of the reports to be issued. All of these factors relate to the amount of detail to be provided and the frequency of the control reports. The greater the detail and the more frequent the reports, the higher the cost. Since these are characteristics of the comprehensive plan, it is likely to be more costly than a basic plan system.

This being the case, what benefits can be expected from the comprehensive plan? The answer depends on how management intends to use the output of the system. Comprehensive plan systems are not ordinarily needed for scorecard reporting to higher management—this calls for condensed, periodic summaries, and the basic plan can provide these. The benefits of comprehensive plan systems, if any, arise mainly from their usefulness as steering controls, to alert first-level supervisors to situations needing immediate attention. When this is important, then the accounting reports need to come out quickly, frequently, and in great detail. This is what the comprehensive plan does.

The second benefit from the comprehensive plan is that it provides a file of data management can draw on for more detailed scorecard information than is available under the basic plan. Variances can be summarized by equipment, by operator, by product, and so forth. A manager, for example, may be fully aware of the difficulties of maintaining standards on a particular machine, but the variance file will provide a cumulative record of how costly these difficulties are. This record may even provide the necessary support for a proposal to replace the machine.

The final decision must reflect management's comparison of the added costs of the comprehensive plan with the benefits to be gained. This is likely to be a judgmental decision because the benefits are difficult to quantify. The important thing is to pose the question in this form, to avoid elaborating the system when a simpler system would do the job management has in mind.

STATISTICAL APPROACHES TO VARIANCE INVESTIGATION

Routine classification of the quantity variances generated by a comprehensive plan system is cumbersome and costly, as we have just seen. An alternative approach is to use statistical techniques to decide when a variance is big enough and important enough to warrant investigation. This section deals with two related techniques: (1) the development and use of statistical control limits; and (2) a cost/benefit investigation decision model.

Statistical Control Limits

No process is likely to be so rigidly programmed that no deviation is possible as long as the process is in control. A certain amount of random variation around the standard is expected.

This notion is embodied in *statistical control charts*, like the one illustrated in Exhibit 20–5. The line running across the middle of this chart represents the expected average time required for a specific operation on a specific machine. The lines above and below it represent the limits within which actual operating times would normally

EXHIBIT 20–5

Statistical Control Chart

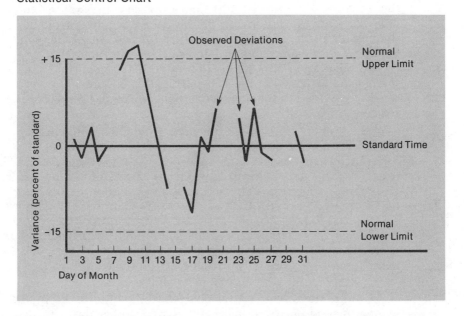

be expected to fall. If actual performance remains within these limits, the variance is presumed to result from noncontrollable, random forces; if an observation falls outside the limits it is presumed to be the result of some event or condition out of the ordinary.

The control chart in Exhibit 20–5 was used by the managers of a machine shop to monitor the operating performance of a hand-operated polishing machine. Five time tickets were chosen at random each day and the average variance percentage was plotted on the chart. When the upper limit was breached on the 10th of the month, an investigation was made. By the 12th of the month, performance was well down in the normal range again.

Whether an observation outside the limits is significant depends on how the limits were chosen and how stable the process is. Ideally, the limits should be based on the variation found in a set of historical observations, made when the operation presumably was in a state of control. If these observations distributed themselves normally around their mean, then statistical confidence intervals can be calculated from the standard deviation(s) of the observations. The standard deviation is calculated from the following formula:

$$s = \sqrt{\frac{\Sigma(y - \bar{y})^2}{n - 1}}$$

in which

y = Observed value.
$\bar{y}$ = Mean of the observed values.
n = Number of observations.

As long as operating conditions remain unchanged, we can be confident (for reasons explained in the appendix to this chapter) that there is only 1 chance in 100 that an observation falling more than 2.58 standard deviations from the mean resulted from a random fluctuation in the process.[2] The other 99 percent of the time it will be the result of some nonrandom event or condition.

The calculation and application of statistical control limits by this method is illustrated in the appendix to this chapter. The applicability of this technique to cost control is highly limited, however, for several reasons:

1. Few operations are duplicated frequently enough to make it possible to develop and apply the statistical limits.

2. Historical observations reflect a variety of conditions. If the operation was not in control when an observation was made, that observation should not be used in the calculation of the distribution of the normal range of observations. Deciding which observations represented experience under controlled conditions is very difficult.

3. Each observation is a statistical sample which should include more than one measurement so that the range of variability in the sample can be tested. This further restricts the technique to operations in which this kind of sampling is feasible.

In short, statistical control charts are likely to be highly useful in evaluating the purity of successive batches of aspirin, turned out by the millions in a repetitive operation. They are less likely to be useful in controlling the costs of direct materials and direct labor whenever production methods and output are not homogeneous.

An Investigation Decision Model

Even if all the conditions necessary for the development of statistical control limits are present, investigation of a large observed variance may not be worthwhile:

1. Investigation costs money, and the penalty for not correcting the problem may not be big enough to warrant spending this money.
2. There is a very small chance (1 in 100 with ±2.58 standard deviation limits) that the extreme observation may have been the result of a random fluctuation. Paying for an investigation here is completely fruitless.
3. The investigation may reveal that the cause of the variance is uncorrectible and that the company's best action is to continue to operate at the higher cost. Again, the costs of investigation are unproductive.

A number of decision models have been developed to deal with these variables.[3] The simplest of these is diagrammed in Exhibit 20–6.

---

[2] If the standard is not equal to the mean of these observations, the standard will not fall in the middle of the control range.

[3] For example, see Joel Demski, *Information Analysis* (Reading, Mass.: Addison-Wesley Publishing Co., 1972), chap. 6; and Thomas R. Dyckman, "The Investigation of Cost Variances." *Journal of Accounting Research*, Fall 1969, pp. 215–44.

EXHIBIT 20–6

Costs and Benefits of Variance Investigation

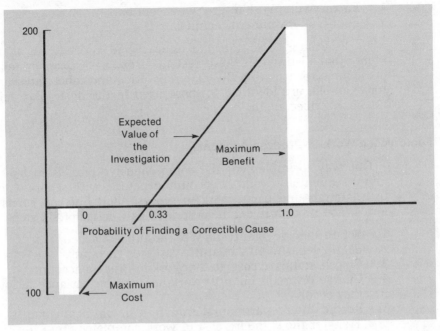

The investigation in this case will cost $100, the penalty for not find-ing a correctible cause is $300. If the money is spent and nothing is found, the company is $100 worse off. This is represented by the "maximum cost" bar at the left. If the money is spent and the cause is found and corrected, the company is $300 − $100 = $200 better off. This is the meaning of the "maximum benefit" bar at the right. If the probability of finding a correctible cause is, say, 0.25, then the expected value of the investigation is as follows:

```
Expected benefit: 0.25 × $200.......................   $50
Expected cost:    0.75 × $100.......................    75
  Expected value of investigation...................  −$25
```

In other words, if the company made 100 of these investigations it would spend 100 × $100 = $10,000 and would benefit 25 × $300 = $7,500. It would lose $2,500 by investigating, or $25 per investigation.

In this case it should spend the money to investigate only if the probability of finding a correctible cause is greater than 0.33.

ACCOUNTS FOR THE COMPREHENSIVE PLAN

The basic plan uses departmental Work-in-Process accounts be-cause they facilitate the calculation of the quantity variances. Since comprehensive plan systems isolate the quantity variances directly from the input documents, departmental Work-in-Process accounts are unnecessary. Instead, the company can simplify its bookkeeping by using either of the following:

1. Factorywide Work-in-Process accounts.
2. Four-wall inventory accounts.

In discussing these alternatives, we shall concentrate on the elements that distinguish these systems from basic plan systems. The procedures for isolating the materials price and labor rate variances, for example, are identical to those used in the basic plan and need not be described again.

Factorywide Work-in-Process Accounts

One way to implement the comprehensive plan is to use the familiar sequential inventory account structure, with separate accounts for materials and parts, work in process, and finished goods inventories. The procedure can be described as a series of six steps:

1. Set up a single, plantwide Work-in-Process account.
2. Set up departmental quantity variance accounts.
3. Charge standard costs to the Work-in-Process account.
4. Charge or credit quantity variances to the variance accounts as they occur.
5. Record interdepartmental transfers in physical quantities only.
6. Transfer the standard cost of work completed from the Work-in-Process account.

Step 1. Set up a single Work-in-Process account for the entire factory and enter the standard cost of the inventory in process at the beginning of the period. The Colson Company's work in process at the beginning of September had a standard materials cost of $4,290 and a standard labor cost of $2,110, for a total of $6,400. The account therefore showed the following:

Work-in-Process

Bal. 9/1 6,400	

No segregation of the material content from the labor content is necessary because this account will not be used to isolate any variance information. (The Work-in-Process account would also include the standard overhead cost of these inventories. We shall deal with standard overhead costs in Chapter 21.)

Step 2. Set up a quantity variance account for each direct materials and each direct labor cost element in each production center. The Colson Company uses two such accounts for each department, one for labor and one for materials. In the machining department, therefore, the two quantity variances have the following titles:

Materials Quantity Variance—Machining
Labor Quantity Variance—Machining

Step 3. Charge the Work-in-Process account for the standard labor and materials costs of the operations performed during the period. During September the machining department used standard requisitions to draw materials with a total standard materials cost of $31,800. The entry summarizing these requisitions was:

(1)

Work-in-Process 31,800
  Materials and Parts   31,800

This traced the movement of the materials from the storeroom to the factory floor.

Step 4. Charge or credit the departmental quantity variance accounts for all differences between actual and standard quantities used, measured at standard prices or wage rates. Separate materials requisitions are prepared for materials required in excess of the standard quantities. The entry summarizing the standard cost of the materials issued on these supplemental requisitions during the month of September was:

(2)

Materials Quantity Variance—Machining 2,350
  Materials and Parts   2,350

Conversely, returned materials cards are evidence of less than standard usage and lead to credits to the variance account. The standard cost of the returned materials in this case was $450, summarized in the following entry:

(3)

Materials and Parts 450
  Materials Quantity Variance—Machining   450

Because the amounts shown on the supplemental requisitions exceeded the total amounts shown on the returned materials cards, the net materials quantity variance for the period was unfavorable. It was shown directly by the balance in the quantity variance account at the end of the period:

Materials Quantity Variance—Machining

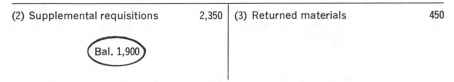

(2) Supplemental requisitions	2,350	(3) Returned materials	450
Bal. 1,900			

The individual supplemental requisitions and returned materials cards then provided a basis for detailed analysis of the overall variance by job or product or type of materials.

The Colson Company's procedures for recording labor time are similar, except that both the standard time and the variance from standard are recorded on the time ticket, not on separate documents. The standard costs shown on the time tickets are debited to the

Work-in-Process account, while the differences between these amounts and the actual times recorded on the tickets are either debited or credited to the variance accounts.

In this case, the standard labor cost of the work done during the month totaled $17,000. This amount was charged to work-in-process. An additional $930 in direct labor costs, again at the standard wage rates, was charged directly to the quantity variance account because actual time on some of the time tickets was greater than the standard time. This was partially offset by favorable variances on other jobs, however, and these totaled $430. These figures can all be summarized in a single entry:

(4)

Work-in-Process	17,000	
Labor Quantity Variance—Machining	930	
Labor Quantity Variance—Machining		430
Payroll Cost Summary		17,500

The Labor Quantity Variance—Machining account now has a debit balance of $500, reflecting labor performance slightly poorer than standard:

Labor Quantity Variance—Machining

(4) (Actual hours −
    standard hours) ×
    standard rates
	930	(4) (Standard hours −
		    actual hours) ×
		    standard rates
			430	

Bal. 500				

One other entry was made this month. The operations performed on these castings before the spoilage occurred had a standard cost of $5. These castings had a standard cost of $80. The standard labor cost of the work already done had also been included in the amounts charged to the Work in Process account. It had to be removed, too. Since the materials cost had been charged to work-in-process when the materials were requisitioned, it had to be removed from that account. The labor time, however, had been recorded in the variance account as part of the difference between the actual and standard hours of processing the remaining castings in the lot. The entry therefore was as follows:

(5)

Cost of Spoiled Work	85	
Work-in-Process		85

The spoiled work account was an overhead account.

Step 5. Make no entry to record the transfer of semiprocessed work from production center to production center; records of departmental inventories in process are maintained in physical quantities only. Once the decision has been made to use a single work-in-process account for the entire factory, transfers of partially processed goods from one department to another neither increase nor decrease the amounts covered by this account. The only possible entry would consist of simultaneous debits and credits to the same account, a clearly unnecessary bit of bookkeeping.

Step 6. Credit the Work-in-Process account and charge the Finished Goods account for the actual quantities of goods finished during the period. The final transfer of products to the finished goods warehouse is the signal to the accounting department to transfer the entire standard cost of the completed products from Work-in-Process to the Finished Goods Inventory account. The summary entry for product completions by the Colson Company's factory in September was:

(5)

Finished Goods	118,000	
Work-in-Process		118,000

This included the standard costs of all operations performed and all materials required in all departments, not just the department in which final processing took place. (If the completed units are component parts, delivered to the parts storeroom for later use in production, the charge will be to a materials and parts inventory account.)

Four-Wall Inventory Accounting

Observing that all three inventory accounts in the conventional three-stage system are measured at the standard cost of the actual quantities on hand, we sometimes take a further step to reduce cost bookkeeping. This is to replace the conventional inventory accounts, which segregate inventories by their completion status (unprocessed, in process, and finished), with comprehensive inventory accounts encompassing inventories at all three stages. These are known as "four-wall" inventory accounts because the costs remain in the same account from the time they enter to the time they leave the factory's four walls.

For example, the purchase of materials with a standard cost of $500 and actual cost of $540 occasions the following entry:

Inventory	500	
Materials Price Variance	40	
Accounts Payable		540

The issuance of standard materials quantities requires no entry at all, because the items are still in inventory. For the same reason, transfer of finished production to the finished goods warehouse requires no ledger entry. Only when the products are sold or transferred to other jurisdictions within the company is an entry made. This entry takes the following form:

Cost of Goods Sold	xxx	
Inventory		xxx

Issuance of materials on supplemental requisitions, returned materials, or loss of items from inventory are the only other reasons for credits or charges to the inventory account.[4]

The main advantage of this system is that it reduces the number of transfer entires. This reduces clerical cost and reduces the chance of bookkeeping error. It has no advantage in variance calculation, however, and is identical in substance to the more conventional three-stage inventory approach described earlier.

SUMMARY

Basic plan standard costing systems are inadequate if management relies on standard costing to generate steering control information. Comprehensive plan systems are designed to meet this need. In comprehensive plan systems, quantity variances are identified as they occur and are reported promptly to the first-level supervisor, usually in considerable detail.

Scorecard variance summaries can be prepared on several bases if the comprehensive plan is used—by operator, by operation, by machine, and by product are all possibilities. These reports can't show the causes of the variances, however, unless someone identifies the cause as each variance arises. Systems don't ordinarily go this far, but they may provide for identifying the variances due to a few major causes, such as equipment substitution or waiting for materials. Variances identified in this way are often reclassified as overhead costs.

The first-level supervisors can usually explain each variance as it occurs, if they are asked soon enough. When they can't explain the variance, statistical control charts or variance investigation decision models may be useful. The main barrier to the use of these techniques is lack of adequate data, but they do indicate the thought patterns management should adopt in deciding whether to investigate the causes of any large variances that may arise.

All this costs money. The extra costs may even be great enough to persuade management that the basic plan is a better solution. Comprehensive plan systems do permit some simplification of the account structure and the accounting routine, however. The final section of this chapter has been devoted to a discussion of how this might be done.

KEY TERMS

The most important terms introduced and defined in this chapter are the following:

Comprehensive plan	Standard requisition
Equipment substitution variance	Statistical control limits
Four-wall inventory	Supplemental requisition

[4] For a detailed description of this kind of system, see Robert L. Beyer and Donald J. Trawicki, *Profitability Accounting for Planning and Control,* 2d ed. (New York: Ronald Press, 1972).

APPENDIX: Calculation of Control Limits

Statistical control charts are based on the assumption that the number of times any given value of a variable will arise in a controlled system can be predicted from the so-called *normal curve*. The normal curve describes the number of times a given value will be observed if the mean value is known and all departures from the mean are due to purely random forces.

If we know the mean and the standard deviation of any normal distribution, we can predict the number of times the observed value will be a certain distance from the mean—say, two standard deviations away. If we observe a value outside that limit, we can calculate the probability that the difference between the observed value and the mean was due to random causes. The farther from the mean, the greater the probability that the cause was something other than random.

Calculating control limits for any process, based on the assumption that departures from the mean can be predicted from the normal curve, is a seven step procedure:

Step 1. Select a number of samples of actual experience under controlled conditions. The Aurora Company took 20 samples of five observations each of the operation of its No. 2 machine. Each observation recorded the time spent processing a single batch of products. Although the product varied from batch to batch, all batches were of the same size (100 units) and the operation was identical for each batch. The machine was in perfect adjustment for each batch and the supervisor was present and active. The observed values are shown in Exhibit 20–7.

Step 2. For each sample, calculate the mean $(\overline{X})$ and the range (R) of the observed values. The observations in the first sample had values of 42, 50, 48, 54, and 51 minutes. The mean was 49 minutes and the range (the distance between the highest and lowest values) was 12 minutes. These figures are shown in the two right-hand columns of Exhibit 20–7.

Step 3. Calculate the mean $(\overline{X})$ of the sample means. For the Aurora Company's machine, this was 50 minutes.

Step 4. Calculate the mean $(\overline{R})$ of the ranges in the various samples. The mean range here was 7.05 minutes.

Step 5. With the aid of statistical tables, calculate upper and lower control limits for the sample mean. The formula for these limits is:

$$\text{Control Limit } (CL)_{\overline{x}} = \overline{X} \pm A_2\overline{R},$$

in which A_2 is taken from a statistical table. The size of A_2 depends on the desired width of the control interval and the number of observations in the sample. For a control interval of ± 3 standard deviations and five observations in each sample, $A_2 = 0.58$.[5] The control limits are:

---

[5] These factors are taken from Eugene L. Grant and Richard S. Leavenworth, *Statistical Quality Control*, 4th ed. (New York: McGraw-Hill Book Company, 1972), Table C.

Upper control limit $(UCL_{\bar{x}}) = 50.0 + 0.58 \times 7.05 = 54.1$ minutes
Lower control limit $(LCL_{\bar{x}}) = 50.0 - 0.58 \times 7.05 = 45.9$ minutes

Step 6. With the aid of statistical tables, calculate upper and lower control limits for the range of values in the sample. The formulas as:

$$UCL_R = D_4 \bar{R}$$
$$LCL_R = D_3 \bar{R}$$

D_4 and D_3 are statistical values, taken from a table. For a control interval of ± 3 standard deviations and five observations in each sample, $D_4 = 2.11$ and $D_3 = 0$. For the Aurora Company's machine, the limits are:

$$UCL_R = 2.11 \times 7.05 = 14.9 \text{ minutes}$$
$$LCL_R = 0 \text{ minutes}$$

Step 7. Plot the means and control limits on two control charts, one for the sample mean and one for the range. The means and ranges in subsequent samples can be plotted on these charts to see whether the operation is still in control.

EXHIBIT 20–7

Sample Observations of Machine Operation

	Labor Time (minutes)						
Sample	Batch 1	Batch 2	Batch 3	Batch 4	Batch 5	Mean (X)	Range (R)
1................	42	50	48	54	51	49.0	12
2................	50	49	56	51	50	51.2	7
3................	45	51	50	46	49	48.2	6
4................	50	49	52	48	49	49.6	4
5................	43	51	47	51	50	48.4	8
6................	47	54	48	52	52	50.6	7
7................	50	49	53	52	44	49.6	9
8................	46	53	60	55	48	52.4	14
9................	46	51	49	53	52	50.2	7
10................	52	47	48	47	51	49.0	5
11................	49	51	50	52	49	50.2	3
12................	50	48	53	49	53	50.6	5
13................	54	51	56	48	52	52.2	8
14................	49	50	45	49	51	48.8	6
15................	46	55	50	47	53	50.2	9
16................	50	47	54	48	55	50.8	8
17................	49	51	50	54	53	51.4	5
18................	52	48	47	45	46	47.6	7
19................	47	51	49	52	50	49.8	5
20................	52	53	51	47	48	50.2	6

INDEPENDENT STUDY PROBLEMS
(Solutions in Appendix C)

1. Accounts for the comprehensive plan. The Irwin Seating Company manufactures a line of metal and wooden chairs for sale to large industrial buyers. Its standard costing system follows the comprehensive plan, with separate accounts for raw materials, materials in process, labor in process, and finished goods inventories.

The following events took place in the wooden chair department last September:

Materials purchased and placed in inventory:
Standard prices....................................	$123,000
Actual prices.....................................	131,000

Direct materials (at standard prices):
Standard requisitions..............................	140,000
Supplemental requisitions..........................	12,000
Returned to storeroom.............................	8,000

Direct labor:
Standard hours at standard wage rates..............	80,000
Actual hours at standard wage rates................	85,600

Direct labor payrolls:
Accrued wages payable, September 1................	8,200
September payrolls, covering period of August 30– September 24, inclusive (paid entirely in cash)......	79,500
Accrued wages payable, September 30...............	16,300

Standard cost of chairs finished:
Direct materials....................................	122,400
Direct labor.......................................	76,500

Standard cost of chairs sold:
Direct materials....................................	115,200
Direct labor.......................................	68,300

a. Account for the month's transactions, using journal entries and T-accounts, with a separate account for each cost variance you are able to identify.

b. Prepare T-accounts for a four-wall inventory system and record the month's transactions. Use separate accounts for the materials and labor elements in the inventories.

c. What could be done to trace the major causes of the materials quantity variances?

2. Statistical control limits. Yesterday the Aurora Company's No. 2 machine was used to manufacture five batches of products. The labor times were 57, 62, 49, 68, and 59 minutes.

a. Using the control limits developed in the Appendix to this chapter, determine whether the operation was in control yesterday.

b. Does the illustration in the Appendix seem realistic? What conditions must be present to make this approach feasible?

EXERCISES AND PROBLEMS

1. Comprehensive plan. Babiak Enterprises has a comprehensive plan standard costing system. Its factory has two departments, machining and finishing. Units spoiled in production are sold as scrap.

The factory records for the month of August showed the following data for the machining department:

1. Inventory in process, August 1: standard materials, $4,000; standard labor, $3,200.

2. Standard cost of materials received from storeroom: standard requisitions, $8,200; supplemental requisitions, $1,100.
3. Standard cost of materials returned to storeroom, $300.
4. Direct labor, $9,700 (at standard wage rates); standard labor cost of work done, $9,900.
5. Standard cost of goods completed and transferred to finishing: materials, $7,600; labor, $9,500.
6. Standard cost of the work done on goods spoiled in production: materials, $400; labor, $800.
7. Inventory in process, August 31: standard materials, $4,200; standard labor, $2,800.

a. Prepare a list showing all the differences between actual and standard costs for materials and labor, classified in as much detail as you can identify. Label each component clearly.
b. Prepare journal entries to record the month's transactions. Separate accounts are kept for materials, work-in-process, and finished goods.
c. How would you modify your answer to (a) if you found that the inventory in process on August 31 had a standard materials cost of $4,000 and a standard labor cost of $2,700?

2. Comprehensive plan: Spoilage. The finishing department in Babiak Enterprises (Problem 1) often spoils semiprocessed materials received from the machining department. Sometimes it requisitions additional materials the machining department has already processed and placed in the storeroom. In other cases it delivers a smaller lot to the finished goods warehouse than it received from the machining department.

One of the company's products is a polished sensometer plate. This plate has a standard machining cost of $2 for materials and $5 for labor. Standard finishing labor is $3 a unit. Last month the finishing department spoiled 100 of these after all finishing labor had been applied.

a. Would you expect the quantity variances in the finishing department to be affected by management's choice between delivering a short batch and requisitioning additional materials to bring the lot back up to the lot size specified in the production order? Explain.
b. Explain how the variances resulting from spoilage would be calculated in each of the two situations described in (a) and how it would be reflected in the accounts. Illustrate your answer with the figures supplied in this problem.
c. Suppose the company used a basic plan of standard costing. How, if at all, would you change your answers to (a) and (b)?

3. Comprehensive plan versus basic plan. Frances Thompson manages an assembly department with 40 employees, 34 of them engaged directly in the assembly of finished products. Parts are delivered to the line in rolling carts and are distributed to the individual work stations as needed.

The workers on the assembly line are divided into three groups. The members of each group perform a number of related operations and place their finished output on trays to be moved to a work station in the next group. The output of the third group is placed on a conveyor belt for final inspection and delivery to the packaging department. Total assembly time averages 13 minutes a unit. All employees are paid on an hourly basis.

Each assembled unit is inspected. A few defective units are scrapped each day, but most of them are delivered to a rework station in the assembly department, where two workers do nothing but replace defective parts or correct defective assembly work. Each of these workers has a small supply of replacement parts. Rework labor time is classified as direct labor.

Ms. Thompson has two assistants who work as roving supervisors and deal with problems arising on the line. Two employees work full time keeping the various work stations supplied with parts and partly assembled units.

Labor variances are most likely to arise from defective parts or from incorrectly performed assembly operations. Because assembled units are seldom scrapped, materials variances reflect mainly the departures from standard percentages of defective parts and standard parts usage. (If workers are careful, no parts will be damaged in assembly, but standard times are set low enough to make some mishandling inevitable, as workers strive to achieve standard performance.) Parts damaged in this way are dropped in scrap bins.

a. Would you recommend comprehensive plan or basic plan standard costing for this department? How often should quantity variances be reported to Ms. Thompson? State your reasons.
b. What would you suggest doing to identify the amount of the variance arising from each major cause. How expensive is your suggestion likely to be? Will management agree to spend this much?

4. Comprehensive plan: Two departments.   The Balfour Company's factory has two departments: forming and assembly. A comprehensive plan standard costing system is in use. You have the following data for the month of July:
1. Materials inventory, July 1 (at standard prices), $70,000.
2. Materials purchased: standard prices, $48,000; actual prices, $51,-200.
3. Standard cost of the finished goods inventory, July 1: materials, $121,800; labor, $47,600.
4. Standard cost of goods sold: materials, $72,600; labor, $28,200.

	Forming	Assembly
5. Work-in-process, July 1 (at standard cost):		
Prior department costs:		
Materials	—	3,400
Labor	—	1,600
Departmental direct materials	$4,200	7,100
Departmental direct labor	1,100	1,900
6. Direct materials issued, at standard prices:		
Standard requisitions	12,300	53,900
Supplemental requisitions	300	2,800
7. Direct materials returned to storeroom, at standard prices	500	200
8. Direct labor, at actual wage rates	6,200	22,000
9. Direct labor, at standard wage rates:		
Actual time	6,100	21,000
Standard time, actual equipment used	5,700	19,200
Standard time, standard equipment	5,400	19,200
10. Standard cost of units scrapped:		
Prior department costs:		
Materials	—	700
Labor	—	400

Department direct materials	400	1,900
Department direct labor	200	800

11. Standard cost of work transferred to assembly:

Materials	11,500	—
Labor	5,100	—

12. Standard cost of work transferred to finished goods:

Prior department costs:		
Materials	—	12,100
Labor	—	5,500
Departmental direct materials	—	53,900
Departmental direct labor	—	18,800

a. The factory uses three inventory accounts, Materials, Work-in-Process, and Finished Goods. Set up appropriate T-accounts, enter the opening balances, record the month's transactions, and calculate the ending balances.

b. Prepare a list of the variances for the month, in as much detail as you can provide.

c. Which of the variances you identified in (*b*) is likely to be available in greater detail than the data in this problem permitted you to provide? How valuable is this additional detail likely to be?

5. Comprehensive plan: Four-wall inventory accounts. The Balfour Company (Problem 4) is considering a recommendation to adopt a four-wall inventory bookkeeping system for its inventories of direct materials and direct labor costs. Two inventory accounts would be used:

Standard Materials Costs in Inventory
Standard Labor Costs in Inventory

a. Using the data supplied in Problem 4, set up the T-accounts for a four-wall inventory bookkeeping system, enter the opening balances, record the month's transactions, and calculate the ending balances.

b. Explain why the variances generated by this system are or are not the same as those in your solution to Problem 4.

6. Comprehensive plan: Reporting to management. Department A had six direct production workers on July 26, with the following hourly wage rates:

J. Cooley.................................	$8.00
R. Donaldson.............................	8.20
F. George.................................	7.80
T. Sugarman.............................	8.40
S. Taussig.................................	8.00
L. Young.................................	8.40

The standard wage rate for all workers in this department is $8 an hour. All have identical job descriptions; wage rates differ because of differences in seniority.

The time tickets for work in this department on July 26 showed the following details:

Name	Job No.	Indirect Acct. No.	Machine No.	Actual Hours	Standard Hours
Cooley............	7762		X12	3.2	3.0
Cooley............	7915		X12	1.4	0.9
Cooley............		A14		0.6	—
Cooley............	7915		X12	2.2	2.2
Cooley............	7185		T44	0.8	0.6
Donaldson........	8044		T44	1.4	1.8
Donaldson........		A12		2.8	—
Donaldson........	7918		L95	4.8	4.3
George............		A16		0.8	—
George............		A14		0.4	—
George............	7511		X16	2.0	1.2
George............	7716		X16	1.1	0.5
George............		A14		0.2	—
George............		A17		3.5	—
Sugarman.........	8345		X22	6.0	5.6
Sugarman.........		A15		0.3	—
Sugarman.........	7996		X16	2.2	2.3
Taussig...........	8212		L95	1.5	1.3
Taussig...........	7694		T44	2.3	2.5
Taussig...........		A14		0.6	—
Taussig...........	7694		T44	1.6	1.7
Taussig...........	7819		X22	3.0	2.8
Young............		A12		1.0	—
Young............	8076		X45	4.4	4.7
Young............		A12		0.8	—
Young............	8015		X45	1.1	1.3
Young............	7995		X45	1.4	1.6

a. A comprehensive plan system is in use. Summarize these data and present a report of variances, in dollars, in any way you think might be suitable. Be sure to distinguish variances that are likely to be controllable from those that are not.

b. Compute the variances showing only the amount of detail that would be available in a basic plan system. For this purpose you may assume that all the jobs referred to above were started and finished on July 26, leaving no work in process at the end of the day.

7. Reporting variances to management. Consolidated Industries operates several large factories in various parts of the world. Its factory in Rapperswil, Switzerland manufactures industrial machinery and parts for customers in several countries. Most of the products are custom-designed, and all production is on a job order basis. Standard labor costs have been established for the most frequently performed operations in the factory, however.

Hans Hassenpfeffer is a department foreman in the Rapperswil factory. Each morning he receives a labor report listing the previous day's performance of each worker in his department. This report contains one line for each task performed by each worker during the day. Below is an excerpt from the report for January 23 listing all tasks performed on that day by Anna Buri and Jorg Staub, two workers in Mr. Hasenpfeffer's department:

Employee Name	Job or Acct. No.	Rated Work				Other Actual Hours	
		Operation No.	Actual Hours	Standard Hours	Gain (Loss)	Nonrated Work	Nonproductive
Buri, Anna	J75008	179–32	8.0	7.8	(0.2)		
Staub, Jorg	J75006	176–40	2.2	1.4	(0.8)		
Staub, Jorg	A1406						0.5
Staub, Jorg	J75012					2.4	
Staub, Jorg	J75023	179–32	2.9	2.0	(0.9)		

Nonrated work consists of all productive tasks for which no standards have been prepared. Nonproductive time is time spent waiting for materials, waiting for machine repair, etc. The twice-daily coffee breaks are not recorded as nonproductive time, however. Instead, standard labor hours include a provision for this factor.

Mr. Hasenpfeffer has 12 workers in his department, and the typical daily report consists of approximately 40 lines. All workers in this department are paid a fixed hourly wage, which varies considerably from worker to worker.

a. This report is part of a much broader standard costing system that has been used in this factory for a number of years. Would you guess that this system is a basic plan system or a comprehensive plan system? Why do you think so?

b. Would you recommend that this report be prepared and given to Mr. Hasenpfeffer each morning? State the assumptions or reasons behind your recommendation.

c. Assume that the company's management has answered (b) in the negative. Would you recommend that the information necessary to prepare the daily report should continue to be collected and stored for possible future use? Give your reasons or, if you are not ready to make a recommendation without further data, describe how you would analyze this question.

d. Assume that the company's management has answered (b) in the affirmative, but that it wants a departmental labor performance summary report prepared each month. What information now likely to be available in this system would you recommend presenting on this monthly report? Give your reasons.

e. If you were Mr. Hasenpfeffer, what action, if any, would you probably take on the basis of the portion of the report dealing with Ms. Buri and Mr. Staub? Is Ms. Buri a better worker than Mr. Staub?

8. Statistical control limits. Control charts used to evaluate the quality of batches of manufactured products generally describe the normal distributions of the means and ranges of the observations in individual samples. To test the quality of a batch, several samples are drawn from the batch and the mean and range are calculated for the attribute being tested.

When applied to cost control, the procedure is sometimes modified to test individual observations against control charts based on the variability of individual observations.

a. Calculate control limits within ± 3 standard deviations of the mean, based on the individual observations in Exhibit 20–7 in the Appendix to this chapter.

b. Are these control limits wider or narrower than the control limits for

the sample means calculated in the Appendix? What explanation
can you offer for this?

c. Why is it difficult to develop control limits for costs based on the
distribution of sample means and ranges? Would it be easier to do
this for overhead costs than for direct labor costs? Explain.

9. Variance investigation decision. The Youngblood Company uses a
basic plan standard costing system in its factory. Unfavorable variances in
a process have been about $2,000 a month. If the cause of the variance
can be found, and if that cause is correctible, it will take two months to
correct it. The correction, if made, would be effective for two months.

Investigation of the variance will cost $500. Correcting the cause, if a
correctible cost is found, will cost $1,000. Management believes the proba-
bility of finding a correctible cause is 0.6.

a. Would you recommend launching an investigation?
b. What is the minimum probability of finding a correctible cause that
would justify an investigation?
c. Would conversion to a comprehensive plan standard costing system
eliminate the need for investigation decisions of this sort? Explain.

10. Alternatives to variance investigation. The Pettit Corporation has a
comprehensive plan standard costing system in which variances are identified in detail, but with no effort to identify the causes of individual variances. The department heads are asked to explain any unfavorable variances exceeding 10 percent of standard. An explanation is always found.

One thousand of these situations arise each month, with an average
variance of $20 each. In 30 percent of these situations, a correctible cause
is identified and the department head's report states, "Steps have been
taken to correct this problem."

The costs of investigating and correcting the causes of variances are of
two kinds:

1. Two people are employed to help the department heads identify the
causes of variances, at a total cost of $40,000 a year.

2. Hourly employees spend time and use supplies to correct unsatisfactory conditions—the cost of a correction is often zero, but enough of
them require the use of labor time and supplies to bring the average
correction cost to $5.

Management is now considering a proposal to identify the cause of
each variance on the cost document—time ticket or requisition—when the
variance occurs. This would reduce the cost of the investigation staff to
$21,000 a year, but would increase the cost of timekeeping and data
processing by $30,000 a year. Management expects that an additional
100 correctible variances would be found each month, averaging $10 each.
The cost of correction would average $2 for each of these additional cor-
rectible variances.

a. Do these figures indicate the proposal should be accepted? Show your
calculations.
b. The managers say they know the causes of two thirds of the correctible variances even before the variances are reported to them.
How productive is the investigation staff?

11. Comprehensive plan: Causal classification of variances. A company's factory has two departments and uses a comprehensive plan
standard costing system. Separate accounts are maintained for (1) raw

materials and parts, (2) work in process, and (3) finished goods inventories. The following data relate to the month of January:

1. Direct materials issued and returned (at standard prices):

	Department A	Department B
Standard requisitions...................	$30,000	$45,000
Supplemental requisitions..............	4,800	2,700
Returns................................	2,500	3,100

2. Direct labor distribution (at standard wage rates):

	Department A	Department B
Actual time............................	$21,000	$18,000
Standard time.........................	21,700	20,600

3. Work completed:

	Department A		Department B	
	Standard Materials Cost	Standard Labor Cost	Standard Materials Cost	Standard Labor Cost
Transferred to department A......	—	—	$ 2,200	$ 1,000
Transferred to department B......	$18,000	$12,000	—	—
Transferred to materials and parts inventory.................	4,200	3,000	9,300	5,000
Transferred to finished goods inventory......................	6,900	5,500	35,000	15,000

4. Standard cost of goods sold: materials, $42,000; labor, $23,000.
5. Direct labor payrolls, $42,000, including $750 overtime premiums in department A and $1,400 overtime premiums in department B.

a. Prepare a list of variances for the month in as much detail as the data permit.
b. Prepare journal entries to record the transactions.
c. Prepare the journal entries that would be appropriate if the company replaced its present inventory accounts with the following two accounts: Materials Costs in Inventories and Labor Costs in Inventories.
d. A run of the month's labor time tickets in department A showed that the following amounts, among others, were included in the labor quantity variance for the month (the department has a single standard wage rate of $7 an hour): (1) defective setup, 15 hours; (2) inferior materials, 25 hours; (3) standby machine used, 50 hours; (4) inexperienced operator, 40 hours; (5) one operator on two machines, 125 hours (favorable); (6) new machine, 60 hours (favorable). Prepare a revised list of labor variances for department A.

12. Comprehensive plan: Effect of machine substitution.   The Cottrell Company uses a comprehensive plan standard costing system in its factory. Some variances are identified with their causes at the time they arise; others are merely identified with the department, machine, operator, and job order number.

One department has two kinds of machines, model X and model Y. These machines are interchangeable but not equally efficient. Standard labor hours per unit of product on each type of machine are:

Product	Model X	Model Y
A....................	1.0	1.2
B....................	2.0	2.6
C....................	3.0	2.8
D....................	4.0	5.0

Standard product cost is based, in each case, on the more efficient machine model for that product—that is, C's standard cost is based on model Y machine time, while standard cost for the other three products presumes the use of model X machines. The data for March are:

1. Actual labor hours, including items (4) and (5) below, 2,200.
2. Standard wage rate, $7 an hour.
3. Actual wages, $16,000.
4. Labor hours waiting for machine repair, 40 hours.
5. Labor hours correcting defects in products rejected in inspection; product B, 50 hours; product C, 30 hours.
6. Production (units of product) on each type of machine:

Product	Model X	Model Y
A....................	500	—
B....................	200	100
C....................	—	150
D....................	140	50

a. Compute and analyze the labor variance for the month in as much detail as the data permit. Explain the meaning of each variance component that you identify.

b. Prepare a journal entry or entries to record labor transactions for the month.

c. Assuming that a maximum of 1,460 hours on model X machines and 1,200 hours on model Y machines was available for production during the month, after subtracting waiting and rework time and allowing an adequate margin for variations in efficiency, did the department achieve the most efficient scheduling of its equipment? How is any scheduling inefficiency reflected in the labor variance? Explain and quantify if possible.

21

Analysis of Factory
Cost Variances

VARIANCES from standard costs arise for a number of reasons. Some of these reasons can be recorded as the variances occur, as we saw in the last chapter. For others, the only feasible approach is to try to separate the variances into their component parts analytically, on the basis of known or presumed relationships between variables. In this chapter we shall study how the analytical approach can be used to identify the following:

1. The effects of variations in input efficiency and production volume on overhead cost variances.
2. The effects of variations in materials yields and labor mix on labor cost variances.
3. The effects of variations in materials mix on materials cost variances.

OVERHEAD COST VARIANCES IN
STANDARD COSTING SYSTEMS

We made no mention of standard overhead costs when we discussed standard costing systems in Chapters 6 and 20. The reason was that standard overhead costs are not designed to be cost control standards. Standard product cost ordinarily includes a standard overhead cost component, however, both for identifying target prices and for measuring inventories and the cost of goods sold for financial reporting. In this section we shall examine three questions arising in this connection:

1. How is the total factory overhead cost variance calculated when standard overhead cost appears in the ledger accounts?
2. Under what circumstances can a two-variance method be used to separate this total variance into two components: spending and volume?

694

3. Under what circumstances can a three-variance method be used to separate this total variance into three components: spending, efficiency, and volume?

The Total Overhead Variance

In discussing overhead variances in Chapter 7, we found that the amount of overhead cost absorbed in any period is often determined by multiplying an overhead costing rate by the number of direct *input* units used in that period. Under standard costing, the amount of overhead absorbed (charged to products) is determined by the *output* achieved during the period. The total overhead cost variance is then the difference between the actual overhead cost and the standard overhead cost of the output.

Calculating standard overhead cost. Standard overhead cost can be derived in either of two ways. One way is to count the number of equivalent units manufactured and multiply this by the standard overhead cost per unit:

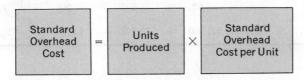

The other way is to calculate the standard quantity of the direct inputs required during the period and multiply this by the standard overhead rate. For example, if the standard overhead rate is based on direct labor hours, then standard overhead cost in any period is:

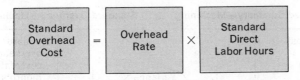

Standard direct labor hours is a measure of output because it depends on the amount of production and is unaffected by variations in the number of actual direct labor hours.

Generating the variance. The total overhead variance enters the accounting system because standard overhead cost is recorded in the accounts. This being the case, an illustration using T-accounts may be the best way to show how the total overhead variance arises. Suppose we have the following data for a machining department for a month:

1. Actual overhead costs for the month totaled $12,060.
2. The standard overhead rate was $3 a standard direct labor hour.
3. The work-in-process at the beginning of the month had 900 standard direct labor hours and a standard overhead cost of $900 \times \$3 = \$2,700$.

4. The standard overhead cost of the jobs completed by the department and placed in finished goods inventory during the month was $11,400 (3,800 standard direct labor hours).
5. The work-in-process at the end of the month had 500 standard direct labor hours and a standard overhead cost of $1,500.
6. Three overhead accounts were used: one for the standard cost of the inventory, one for the actual overhead costs, and the other for the standard overhead costs absorbed by production.

(Notice the terminology: *absorbed* refers to the amount charged to products; *standard overhead cost* is the way this is measured in a standard costing system.)

As we learned in Chapter 6, the output of any period is measured by the amount of work completed ± the change in work-in-process. In this case we can measure it two ways:

	Jobs Completed		Ending Inventory		Beginning Inventory		Output
Standard direct labor hours......................	3,800	+	500	−	900	=	3,400
Standard overhead cost.............................	$11,400	+	$1,500	−	$2,700	=	$10,200

Once the company had finished recording the month's transactions, the accounts contained the figures shown in Exhibit 21–1. The re-

EXHIBIT 21–1

Overhead Cost Flows in Standard Costing

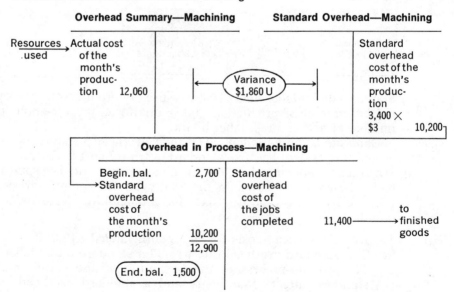

sources flowed into the department at the upper left; finished goods flowed out at the lower right. The entries were:

1. To identify the department's overhead costs:

    Overhead Summary—Machining 12,060
        Accounts Payable, etc.   12,060

2. To record absorption of overhead costs:

    Overhead in Process—Machining 10,200
        Standard Overhead—Machining   10,200

(The debit in this entry placed the cost in an inventory account; the credit identified the absorption.)

3. To transfer costs of completed jobs out of the department:

    Finished Goods Inventory 11,400
        Overhead in Process—Machining   11,400

The total overhead variance in this case was $1,860—the difference between the actual cost and the standard cost of the month's production. The ending balance in the Overhead-in-Process account was the standard overhead cost of the work-in-process at the end of the month. Since the standard overhead cost of the jobs completed was $1,200 greater than the standard overhead cost of the month's output, it shouldn't be surprising that the inventory balance decreased by this amount.

Two-Variance Analysis

In a two-variance analysis, the total overhead variance is subdivided into two parts, a spending variance and a volume variance. The calculation is as shown in Exhibit 21–2. Both variances in this diagram happen to be unfavorable; either or both can also be favorable.

To see what these variances mean and how they can be derived, suppose overhead costs in the machining department are expected to vary with the amount of output, as in the following formula:

Overhead costs = $7,400 + $1.15 × standard direct labor hours

Normal volume is 4,000 standard direct labor hours. At this volume the overhead rate includes $7,400/4,000 = $1.85 an hour for fixed costs and $1.15 for variable costs.

The total overhead variance during the month was $1,860, and volume was 3,400 standard direct labor hours. At this volume the flexible budget allowances added up to $7,400 + 3,400 × $1.15 = $11,310. This figure can be used to calculate the two variances, as described in the next two paragraphs.

Spending variance is the difference between the actual overhead cost for the period and the total of the flexible budget allowances for

EXHIBIT 21–2

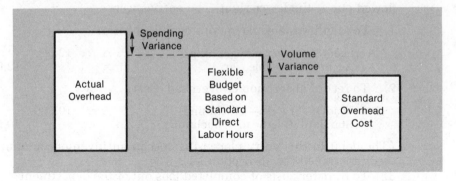

the actual volume, measured by the number of standard direct labor hours actually recorded:

Spending variance = $12,060 − $11,310 = $750 Unfavorable

This is broken down by object-of-expenditure accounts for reporting to the department head, with separate lines for indirect labor, indirect materials, etc.

Volume variance is the budgeted fixed cost of the number of hours of idle or overused capacity. Capacity in this department is measured by the number of standard direct labor hours. The department used only 3,400 standard hours instead of the normal 4,000. Since the overhead rate included $1.85 an hour for fixed costs, the idle capacity left $1,110 fixed costs unabsorbed:

Volume variance = 600 × $1.85 = $1,110 Unfavorable

The volume variance can also be calculated another way, by subtracting the amount budgeted at 3,400 hours from the amount absorbed at this volume, as in the following table:

	Budgeted at 3,400 Standard Hours	Absorbed at 3,400 Standard Hours	Volume Variance
Variable overhead at $1.15	$ 3,910	$ 3,910	—
Fixed overhead	7,400	6,290	$(1,110)
Total	$11,310	$10,200	$(1,110)

If the overhead rate had been based on a volume of 3,400 hours, $11,310 would have been absorbed in May. The difference between this and the amount actually absorbed is the portion of the total variance due to the failure to achieve normal volume.

This analysis is diagrammed in Exhibit 21–3. The calculations are almost identical to those we made in Chapter 7 to subdivide the total overhead variance in a nonstandard costing system. The only difference is that both the flexible budget allowances and the amount absorbed are now based on *standard* direct labor hours instead of actual direct labor hours. The actual number of direct labor hours does not enter into the analysis at all.

The reason is that according to the budget formula, overhead costs will rise or fall with changes in standard labor' hours but will be entirely unaffected by variations in the amount of labor actually used to produce a given output. As a result, the three points delineating the variances are located at 3,400 hours instead of at the actual number of direct labor hours, 3,500.

The results of the two-variance analysis can be summarized in the accompanying table. This is another illustration of a fundamental rule in variance analysis: *the variances in any detailed list should always add up to the total variance being analyzed.*

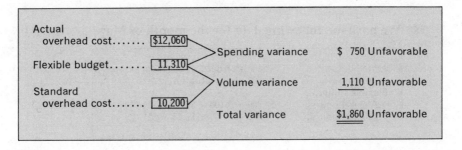

Three-Variance Analysis

A two-variance analysis is appropriate if overhead costs are expected to vary with production *output.* If overhead costs are expected to vary with production *inputs,* a three-variance analysis should be used. The three parts are illustrated in Exhibit 21–4.

Here for the first time we meet the *labor efficiency variance,* defined as the estimated effect of the labor quantity variance on overhead cost. To see how this fits into the overall picture, let's go back to our illustration. Once again, overhead absorption is based on production output, at an overhead rate of $3 a standard direct labor hour. The flexible budget formula is slightly different, however, because it is based on the *actual* number of direct labor hours rather than on standard labor time:

Overhead cost = $7,400 + $1.15 × actual direct labor hours

EXHIBIT 21–3

Two-Variance Analysis of Overhead Costs

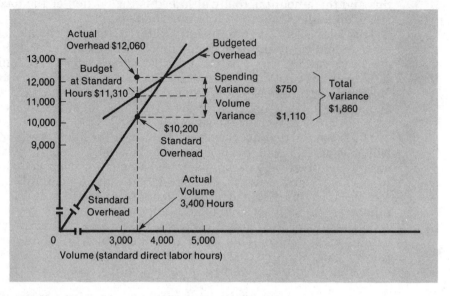

We have the following data for the month of May:

Actual output:	3,400 standard direct labor hours.
Actual input:	3,500 direct labor hours.
Flexible budget:	
At 3,400 hours:	$7,400 + 3,400 × $1.15 = $11,310
At 3,500 hours:	$7,400 + 3,500 × $1.15 = $11,425

The spending variance in this situation is $635, calculated as follows:

Actual overhead costs...........................	$12,060
Flexible budget at 3,500 hours..................	11,425
Spending variance.......................	$ 635 Unfavorable

This is $115 smaller than the spending variance we calculated under the two-variance method. The reason, of course, is that the flexible budget allowance for 3,500 hours is $115 greater than the allowance for 3,400 hours.

This $115 is the labor efficiency variance. It arose because the production center used 100 direct labor hours more than the standard called for. The flexible budget predicts that overhead costs will increase by $1.15 for every additional hour of direct labor. Labor inefficiency therefore added 100 × $1.15 = $115 to overhead costs.[1]

---

[1] In more general terms, this is an *input* efficiency variance. If overhead costs vary with materials quantities, it is a materials efficiency variance. If overhead costs vary with machine-hours, it is a machine efficiency variance.

EXHIBIT 21–4

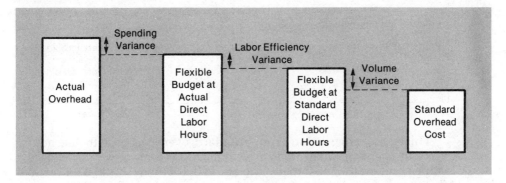

It shows up as the increase in the budget allowance as volume moves up from 3,400 to 3,500 direct labor hours (see Exhibit 21–5).

The third component of the overhead variance is the volume variance. This is exactly the same as in the two-variance analysis:

Budgeted at 3,400 standard direct labor hours..........	$11,310
Absorbed overhead.....................................	10,200
Volume variance................................	$ 1,110 Unfavorable

The labor efficiency variance does not indicate how effectively the department has controlled overhead costs. Instead, it is another component of the labor quantity variance. If the standard wage rate for direct labor in this production center was $8 an hour, for example, the full cost of an hour of lost time was $8 plus $1.15, or $9.15. In other words, the $115 labor efficiency variance for May ought to be reported as part of the labor quantity variance.

EXHIBIT 21–5

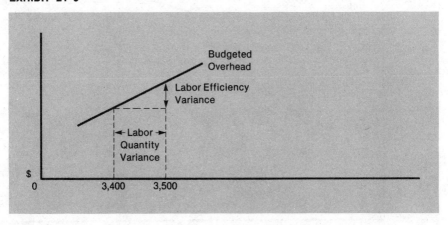

In summary, the three-variance method divides the total overhead variance into the following three parts:

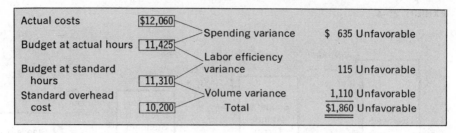

This same progression from standard overhead cost to the actual amount spent in illustrated in Exhibit 21–6. Standard overhead cost is the point on the "absorbed" line at the 3,400-hour mark. The vertical distance between this point and the point on the budgeted line above is the volume variance. The labor efficiency variance is shown by the vertical distance traveled by a movement along the "budgeted" line from 3,400 to 3,500 hours. Finally, the spending variance is shown by the distance between the budget allowance for 3,500 hours and actual overhead cost for the month.

Whether the spending variance is $635 or $750 depends on the underlying pattern of cost variation. If overhead costs vary with labor inputs, then $635 is correct. If overhead depends on the rate of output, however, the answer is $750. *In other words, the size of the spending variance depends on the determinants of overhead cost and*

EXHIBIT 21–6

Three-Variance Analysis of Overhead Costs

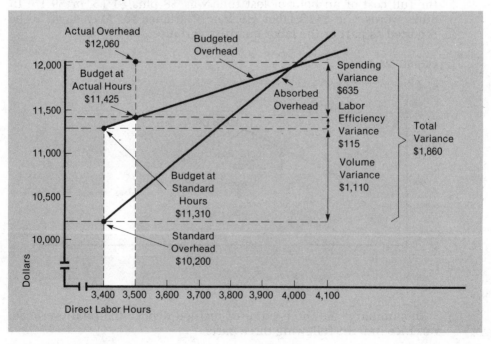

not on the method of analysis; in any given situation, only one method is appropriate.

ANALYSIS OF LABOR COST VARIANCES

The labor efficiency variance in factory overhead cost was our first example of a variance identified analytically, on the basis of an estimated relationship between cost and some factor or factors other than output. This same approach can be used to analyze direct materials and direct labor cost variances, and in this section we shall use it to identify two kinds of variances:

1. Effect of materials yields on the labor quantity variance.
2. Effect of labor substitution and variations in labor mix on the direct labor variance.

Our task in each case is to estimate the amount of the total variance resulting from this particular cause. When this is removed, the residual indicates the amount to be attributed to other causes.

Materials Yield Component of Labor Quantity Variance

In process production and other materials-paced operations, the amount of labor required is a function of the quantity of materials used rather than a function of output. For this reason, an unfavorable materials quantity variance will normally be accompanied by an unfavorable labor quantity variance. Favorable materials yields should lead to favorable labor performance.

For example, suppose three pounds of direct materials and two hours of direct labor are the standard inputs for a unit of product X:

$$\left(\begin{array}{c} \text{3 Pounds} \\ \text{Materials} \end{array}\right) \longrightarrow \left(\begin{array}{c} \text{2 Hours} \\ \text{Labor} \end{array}\right) \longrightarrow \left(\begin{array}{c} \text{1 Unit} \\ \text{Product X} \end{array}\right)$$

The standard wage rate is $5 an hour. The standard direct labor cost of product X therefore is $2 \times \$5 = \$10$. We have the following data for the month of June:

Direct materials processed................ 3,000 pounds
Direct labor............................... 1,950 hours
Product output........................... 900 units

The labor quantity variance for the month is $750, unfavorable:

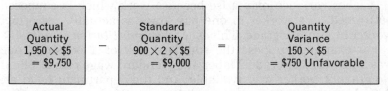

Actual Quantity $1,950 \times \$5$ $= \$9,750$	−	Standard Quantity $900 \times 2 \times \$5$ $= \$9,000$	=	Quantity Variance $150 \times \$5$ $= \$750$ Unfavorable

The question is how much of this was due to the materials quantity variance.

To answer this, we must first find out how big the materials quantity variance was. In this case, the calculation is simple:

> Standard materials quantity = 900 units × 3 pounds = 2,700 pounds

Since 3,000 pounds of materials were processed, the materials quantity variance was 300 pounds, unfavorable.

This is a materials-paced operation, and two hours of labor are necessary to process three pounds of materials. Processing an extra 300 pounds of materials therefore required an extra 200 hours of direct labor. Other things being equal, the labor quantity variance should have been 200 × $5 = $1,000, and unfavorable. It was actually only $750. This means that the labor quantity variance also had a favorable component of some kind, amounting to 50 hours × $5 = $250. This we call the *labor performance variance*, the portion of the quantity variance due to all causes other than the ones we have been able to account for.

In other words, whenever labor costs are governed by materials input flows rather than by output quantities, two components of the labor quantity variance can be identified:

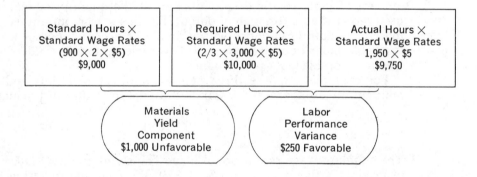

The term *required hours* refers to the standard hours required by the given quantity of materials inputs.

Labor Mix and Substitution Variances

A labor variance may arise because work which is supposed to be performed by a worker in one pay grade is actually performed by a worker in another grade. This is a *labor substitution variance*.

For example, suppose the standard cost of a polishing operation was 14.5 hours of grade 2 labor at a standard wage rate of $8 an hour. No grade 2 worker was available, and the department head assigned the job to a grade 1 operator, with a standard wage rate of $10 an hour. The operator spent 16 hours on the job. The effect of the substitution can be separated as follows:

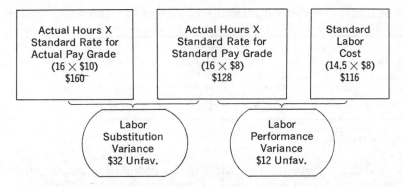

The term labor performance variance is used to identify the part of the labor quantity variance we haven't attributed to specific causes.

To get the figures required by this illustration, someone would have to identify the labor substitution when it arose. This is expensive. Management may prefer to estimate the effects of labor substitutions analytically, from statistics for the period as a whole. The variance emerging from this analysis is usually referred to as a *labor mix variance*.

Before we illustrate the calculation of the labor mix variance, we should emphasize that it has to be based on an assumption about the relative productivity of the workers in different pay grades. If the assumption is wrong, the analysis will be wrong, too.

To illustrate the analysis, suppose a department performed work on three products during July. Standard cost and production data for these three products were as follows:

Product	Output (units)	Standard Labor Hours per Unit		Total Standard Labor Hours	
		Grade 1	Grade 2	Grade 1	Grade 2
A............................	500	2	1	1,000	500
B............................	300	2	3	600	900
C............................	100	2	4	200	400
Total hours.................				1,800	1,800
Standard wage rate...........				$10	$8
Standard labor cost..........				$18,000	$14,400
				$32,400	

The department's actual labor cost was $32,600, distributed as follows:

Pay Grade	Hours	Wages
1..........................	1,900	$19,500
2..........................	1,600	13,100
Total......................	3,500	$32,600

The total labor cost variance therefore was as follows:

Pay Grade	Actual Labor Cost	Standard Labor Cost	Variance
1...................	$19,500	$18,000	$1,500 U.
2...................	13,100	14,400	1,300 F.
Total................	$32,600	$32,400	$ 200 U.

U. = Unfavorable.
F. = Favorable.

We can remove the rate variance by calculating the standard labor cost of the actual hours used, in their actual proportions:

Pay Grade	Number of Hours	Standard Rate	Standard Wages	Actual Wages
1...............	1,900	$10	$19,000	$19,500
2...............	1,600	8	12,800	13,100
Total............	3,500		$31,800	$32,600

Labor Rate
Variance
$800 Unfavorable

To isolate the labor mix variance, we shall assume that grade 1 employees can substitute for grade 2 workers with neither a gain nor a loss in efficiency. The standard costs of the three products manufactured this month called for a labor mix of 1,800 grade 1 employees and 1,800 grade 2 employees. If actual labor quantities had been in these proportions, the average standard wage rate would have been $9, just halfway between $10 and $8. The actual number of labor hours, multiplied by this rate, is:

$$3,500 \times \$9 = \$31,500$$

The actual average for the month was $31,800/3,500 = $9.09, indicating that the department used a larger proportion of grade 1 employees than the standards called for.

With this information, we can separate the mix variance from the rest of the labor cost variance:

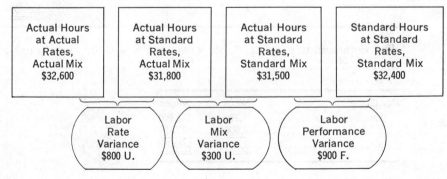

Actual Hours at Actual Rates, Actual Mix	Actual Hours at Standard Rates, Actual Mix	Actual Hours at Standard Rates, Standard Mix	Standard Hours at Standard Rates, Standard Mix
$32,600	$31,800	$31,500	$32,400

Labor Rate Variance $800 U.	Labor Mix Variance $300 U.	Labor Performance Variance $900 F.

Again the labor performance variance measures the portion of the labor variance we have not been able to attribute to specific influences. It reflects the use of 100 hours less than the standard labor quantity, at an average standard wage rate of $9 an hour.

We repeat that this separation is only as valid as our assumption that all workers are equally efficient in the work they are assigned to. All this kind of analysis can do is call management's attention to the variation in mix; management still has to decide what this means and what to do about it.

The remaining question is where the variances are likely to be located. This will depend on the design of the internal costing system. We shall examine two different situations:

1. Labor is charged to departments at the standard wage rate for each individual pay grade—the labor mix variance will be part of the departmental labor quantity variance.
2. Labor is charged to departments at a single standard wage rate for all pay grades—the labor mix variance will be part of the labor rate variance.

The T-accounts in the first situation will show the following:

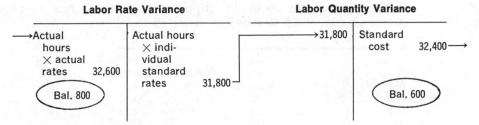

The balance in the quantity variance account is the difference between the $900 favorable labor performance variance and the $300 unfavorable labor mix variance.

The T-accounts in the second situation will show the following:

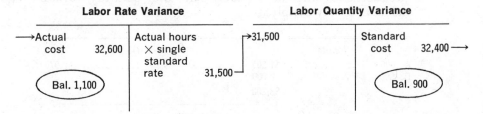

Now the balance in the quantity variance accounts shows only the labor performance variance—the other two are intermingled in the rate variance account.

No matter where the mix variance is located, it needs to be identified and reported to the responsible executives. When multiple charging rates are used, responsibility for the labor mix may lie either inside or outside the department; use of a single charging rate generally means that responsibility is lodged outside. Each situation must be examined on its own.

In a technical sense, a labor substitution variance arises when a specific substitution is made and a labor mix variance arises when the composition of the work force changes. The boundary between these two categories is very imprecise, however, and we doubt the distinction is necessary. We shall use the terms interchangeably unless the situation clearly calls for one or the other.

MATERIALS MIX AND YIELD VARIANCES

Materials inputs also may be partially interchangeable. For example, suppose a process combines two materials into a finished product. The production standard calls for these two materials to be used in equal proportions, but the proportions are difficult to control precisely. In these circumstances, management may wish to subdivide the materials variance, using the same method we just applied to labor inputs.

The Analysis

To continue the example, suppose the product has a standard materials cost of $3.30 a unit, calculated as follows:

Material	Standard Quantity (pounds)	Standard Price	Standard Cost
A..........................	.55	$2	$1.10
B..........................	.55	4	2.20
Total.....................	1.10		$3.30

In May, the process used 600 pounds of A and 500 pounds of B to produce 900 units of product. The total quantity variance can be calculated very simply:

Inputs	Output
A 600 × $2.............. $1,200	900 × $3.30.............. $2,970
B 500 × $4.............. 2,000	
$3,200	

Materials quantity
variance
$230 Unfavorable

This can be subdivided into materials mix and materials yield components by the following procedure:

1. Calculate the average standard cost per unit of *input* at the standard input mix:

$$\$3.30/1.1 \text{ pounds} = \$3 \text{ a pound}$$

2. Multiply this average standard cost by the actual quantity of materials used:

$$1,100 \times \$3 = \$3,300$$

3. Calculate the *materials mix variance* by comparing this quantity with the standard cost of the materials actually used:

$$\$3,300 - \$3,200 = \$100 \text{ Favorable}$$

4. Calculate the *materials yield variance* by comparing the quantity calculated in (2) with the standard cost of the actual output:

$$\$2,970 - \$3,300 = \$330 \text{ Unfavorable}$$

[The yield variance can also be calculated by comparing the amount of product 1,100 pounds of materials ought to have yielded (1,100/ 1.1 = 1,000 units) with the actual yield (900 units), each measured at standard cost ($3.30).]

Assumptions and Interpretation

This analysis is just as artificial as the calculation of the labor mix variance. It assumes that materials mix is a controllable variable and that the different kinds of materials are interchangeable within limits. In other words, management's task is to use no more of the more expensive materials than is absolutely necessary.

If these assumptions are true, isolation of the mix variance will give management some useful information. If they are not true, the analysis will simply be another technical exercise, ingenious but meaningless.

Other Analyses

The analyses illustrated in this section are not the only possibilities. If management can identify a factor whose influence it wants to measure, the accountant can measure it by holding everything constant except that one factor, as we have done throughout.

Usage of material X, for example, may affect the amount of labor required, as we saw earlier, but it may also affect the quantity of material Y used. If management wants to separate the quantity variance in material Y into the portion due to the variance in material X and the portion due to other factors, this can be done. The only rule in this analyses is to move in sequence, varying only one element at a time. The final list of variances should always add up to the total variance being analyzed.

SUMMARY

Variances from standard cost can often be divided into a number of component parts analytically rather than by classifying the costs as they occur. Factory overhead cost variances can be divided into volume and spending variances by this technique; if overhead costs vary with labor inputs, the effects of labor efficiency can also be separated.

Labor and materials variances, too, can be divided into two or more parts: the effects of materials usage on labor cost and the effects of variations in materials mix are two common examples. The classifications used will depend on how much management knows about the underlying causal relationships and how large an effect the individual factor is likely to have.

KEY TERMS

The most important terms introduced and defined in this chapter are the following:

Labor efficiency variance   Overhead spending variance
Labor mix variance   Overhead volume variance
Labor performance variance   Required hours
Labor substitution variance   Standard overhead cost
Materials mix variance   Three-variance method
Materials yield variance   Total overhead variance
                                     Two-variance method

INDEPENDENT STUDY PROBLEMS
(Solutions in Appendix C)

1. Overhead variance analysis. Standard costs and budget allowances in a machining department are as follows:

Flexible budget:

Machine-Hours	Manufacturing Overhead Costs
8,000	$20,000
10,000	22,000
12,000	24,000
14,000	26,000

Overhead rate = $2 per standard machine-hour.
Standard manufacturing overhead cost:
Product A............ 1 machine-hour per unit = $2 per unit.
Product B........... 1.5 machine-hours per unit = $3 per unit.

During April the department produced 4,000 units of product A and 4,000 units of product B. A total of 9,500 machine-hours was recorded during April, and actual manufacturing overhead costs totaled $21,750.

a. Compute and analyze the factory overhead cost variance.
b. Reanalyze the variance on the assumption that factory overhead varies with standard machine-hours.

2. Labor variance analysis. A department's employees are grouped into three pay grades, with standard hourly wage rates as follows:

Grade	Rate
1	$5.50
2	6.00
3	7.00

A single departmentwide standard wage rate of $6.50 an hour is used for product costing. Data for October are: (1) actual department wages, $57,000; (2) standard labor cost of the month's output, $59,000; (3) actual labor hours: grade 1—2,000; grade 2—4,000; grade 3—3,000.

Analyze the department's labor variances for the month.

3. Labor and overhead variance analysis. A factory department produces only one product. This product has a standard materials cost of 2 pounds of materials at a standard price of $4 a pound, or $8 a unit. Each pound of direct materials requires one and a half direct labor hours of processing time. The standard wage rate is $5 an hour, so the standard labor cost in this department is $15 for each unit of product.

The product's standard overhead cost in this department is $9 a unit. Overhead costs in this department are expected to bear the following relationship to the number of direct labor hours actually used:

Budgeted overhead cost = $7,200/month + $1 × direct labor hours

The department produced 1,000 units of this product in December, with the following costs:

	Standard Cost per Unit	Actual Input Quantities	Actual Cost, December
Direct materials	$ 8	2,300 lbs.	$ 9,200
Direct labor	15	3,200 hrs.	16,800
Overhead	9	—	11,100

a. Calculate the total direct labor variance for the month and break it down into as many component parts as you are able to identify.

b. Calculate the total factory overhead variance for the month and break it down into as many component parts as you are able to identify.

4. Materials, labor, and overhead variances. The Abel Company manufactures three products in two factory departments. It uses a full cost, basic plan factory standard costing system. You have the following data for department I (DLH is direct labor hours):

	Product A	Product B	Product C
Standard unit cost:			
Department I materials	$ 3	$ 6	$ 9
Department I labor (at $4 an hour)	8	12	10
Department I overhead (at $6 per DLH)	12	18	15
Inventory and production (units):			
Department I work in process, March 1	—	100	200
Completed and transferred to department II,			
March	300	500	400
Department I work in process, March 31	200	100	—

Work-in-process at both beginning and end of the month was complete as to materials and half-processed. Other data for the month were:

Materials inventories, March 1 (at standard prices)......... $11,400
Materials purchased ($5,400 at standard prices).............. 5,850
Materials issued to department I (at standard prices)....... 6,000
Actual direct labor payroll, department I (3,500 DLH)........ 14,200
Actual overhead, department I............................. 25,500

At normal operating volume and with actual DLH equal to standard DLH, variable overhead totals $8,000 and fixed overhead amounts to $16,000. It is assumed that variable overhead varies in direct proportion to variations in the number of direct labor hours used.

a. Enter these data, including the opening inventory balances, in appropriate T-accounts. Try to set up accounts that will help you identify the variances.
b. Prepare a list of variances for department I for the month of March. Be sure to label each variance clearly.

EXERCISES AND PROBLEMS

1. Exercises in overhead variance analysis. Each of the following exercises covers a different aspect of standard costing for factory overhead.

Exercise A. Standard cost; accounts
Darlon, Inc., manufactures wire goods, using a basic plan standard costing system. Overhead costs in the coating department are assigned to products at $5 a standard coating hour. The company calculates the number of standard coating hours by multiplying the standard processing time for each unit for each stage in the coating process by the number of units processed in that stage. The coating process has five stages. Because each worker can process many products at the same time, the number of standard direct labor hours is only a fraction of the number of standard coating hours.

During December the department completed work on products with 12,500 standard coating hours, standard materials costs of $128,000, and standard coating direct labor cost of $9,500. These products were transferred immediately to the assembly department. The work-in-process in this department on December 1 had passed through three stages of the coating process; the work already done on these products amounted to 2,200 standard coating hours. The work-in-process at the end of the month had passed through four stages of the coating process, with 3,400 standard coating hours already required.

a. Calculate the standard overhead cost of the work done in December.
b. Prepare journal entries to record (1) overhead cost absorption, and (2) the standard cost of products transferred to assembly.

Exercise B. Two variance analysis
The overhead costs in one department are budgeted on the basis of the following formula:

$$\text{Overhead costs} = \$100,000 + \$3 \times \text{standard direct labor hours}$$

Other data are: (1) normal volume, 50,000 standard direct labor hours; (2) actual overhead cost in June, $225,000; (3) actual direct labor hours in June, 40,000; and (4) standard direct labor hours in June, 39,000.

a. Calculate standard overhead cost for the month.
b. Calculate the total variance from standard overhead cost.
c. Use a two-variance analysis to separate the variance into component parts. Why is a two-variance analysis appropriate here instead of a three-variance analysis?

Exercise C. Three variance analysis
    The facts are the same as in Exercise B except that the overhead cost formula is as follows:

$$\text{Overhead costs} = \$100,000 + \$3 \times \text{actual direct labor hours}$$

a. Prepare a three-variance analysis of the total overhead variance.
b. What managerial use, if any, would be made of each of the variances you have calculated (i.e., who is being evaluated and in what connection)?

2. Effects of labor and materials variances on overhead. The facts are the same as in Exercise C of Problem 1, with the additional information that standard direct labor time is 0.3 direct labor hours for each kilogram of materials processed. The department processed 120,000 kilograms of materials during the month.
    Divide the total overhead variance into four parts: volume variance, effect of materials quantity variance, effect of labor performance variance, and spending variance.

3. Overhead variance analysis. Given the following data, calculate and analyze the overhead cost variance:

Actual factory overhead...........................	$29,000
Standard overhead cost of goods finished.........	27,000
Standard overhead cost of goods in process:	
Beginning of month............................	5,000
End of month..................................	7,700
Standard overhead cost.........................	$ 3 per standard direct labor hour
Flexible budget..................................	$15,000 + $1.50 per actual direct labor hour
Actual direct labor hours........................	9,500

4. Three variance analysis of overhead variance. Overhead costs vary with the number of pounds of materials processed. The overhead cost allowances for any month can be derived from the following formula:

$$\text{Overhead} = \$4,000 + \$0.02 \times \text{pounds of materials processed}$$

Standard overhead cost, based on a standard operating volume of 50,000 pounds of materials a month, is 10 cents a pound.
    The following data were recorded during the month of November:

1. Actual materials processed, 60,000 pounds.
2. Standard materials content of the month's production, 55,000 pounds.
3. Actual overhead cost, $5,700.

a. Calculate the total overhead variance for the month.
b. Analyze this variance into three parts, and indicate clearly the meaning of each.

5. Controllability of labor and overhead variances. A department's overhead cost budget is $48,000 a month plus $2 for each actual direct labor hour. Actual direct labor cost during September was $69,000 (15,000 hours at $4.60 an hour). Actual overhead was $77,500. The department's output for the month had a standard cost of:

Labor, 15,500 hours at $4.50............. $ 69,750
Overhead, 15,500 hours at $5.:.......... 77,500
   Total................................ $147,250

Materials cost variances for the month were negligible.

Departmental variances are classified as controllable or noncontrollable, favorable or unfavorable. The controllable variances are then totaled, and if the total of the favorable controllable variances exceeds the total of the unfavorable controllable variances the supervisor is paid a bonus amounting to 5 percent of the difference (the "net favorable controllable variance"). If the net controllable variance is zero or unfavorable, the supervisor receives no bonus. The supervisor has no control over wage rates or volume, but all of the overhead costs are controllable.

Prepare a list of the variances you can compute from the above data; indicate for each whether it is controllable or noncontrollable, favorable or unfavorable; and compute the amount of the supervisor's bonus, if any.

6. Overhead variance analysis. A factory processes a single product. You have the following information for this department for the month of August:

Standard materials cost: 5 pounds at $2 = $10 per unit
Standard overhead cost: 0.4 × standard materials cost
                          = 0.4 × $10 = $4 per unit
Overhead cost budget: $5,000 + $0.20 × pounds of materials
Standard overhead cost of the work in process:
  Beginning of month, $2,000
  End of month, $3,500
Materials processed during the month: 10,000 pounds
Actual overhead cost for the month: $8,200
Units of product completed during the month: 1,500 units

Identify and analyze the overhead variance for each month, indicating as clearly as possible the meaning of each component you have identified.

7. Overhead variances: Supplying missing figures. A factory has three departments. Standard overhead cost in each department is based on standard direct labor hours. You have the following information related to overhead cost in November:

	Dept. A	Dept. B	Dept. C
Budgeted fixed overhead............	$100	$150	?
Budgeted variable overhead:			
Per actual direct labor hour.........	1	0	$ 1
Per standard direct labor hour......	0	2	0
Normal output (standard direct labor			
hours).............................	50	50	100
Actual output (standard direct			
labor hours).......................	?	?	90
Overhead absorbed.................	$120	?	?
Actual overhead.....................	145	$225	?
Actual direct labor hours.............	42	43	?
Volume variance....................	?	$ 30 U.	$ 40 U.
Spending variance...................	?	?	8 U.
Labor efficiency variance.............	?	?	6 U.
Total overhead variance..............	?	?	?

Make the necessary calculations to supply the missing figures in the table.

(Prepared by Professor Carl L. Nelson)

8. Overhead variances: Two independent variables. Bob Richards is the plant manager. He has a number of departmental supervisors who are responsible for labor and materials quantity variances, but he alone is responsible for factory overhead costs. Factory overhead cost is budgeted on the basis of the following formula:

Overhead = $50,000 + $2 per labor hour used + 20% of actual labor cost

Standard product costs are based on a standard labor rate of $5 an hour and a standard overhead cost of $7 a labor hour.

Actual overhead cost in June was $84,500. The total standard cost of the June output was $192,000, made up of the following:

Materials..................	$ 60,000
Labor......................	55,000
Overhead..................	77,000
Total....................	$192,000

Materials variances were negligible in June, but there was an unfavorable labor quantity variance of $2,000 and an unfavorable labor rate variance of $5,700, the latter caused by a 10 percent wage increase due to a new labor union contract.

Mr. Richards has asked you to tell him whether his control efforts were effective.

9. Overhead variances; Itemized analysis. The Schuyler Corporation uses a standard costing system in its factory. Statistical studies have shown that variation in overhead costs in department X is more closely correlated with direct labor input than with product output. The departmental overhead rate is $2 per direct labor hour, and 15,000 direct labor hours were recorded during November. Additional data are:

	Budget		
	Fixed per Month	Variable per Direct Labor Hour	Actual, November
Supervision.....................	$ 5,600	—	$ 5,900
Indirect labor..................	500	$0.60	10,200
Supplies.......................	—	0.25	3,400
Department S service..........	—	0.10	1,750
Building service...............	6,500	—	7,600
Total....................	$12,600	$0.95	$28,850

The standard overhead cost content of work in process was $8,000 on November 1 and $10,000 on November 30. The standard overhead cost content of the work completed and transferred out of the department during the month was $29,500. Production departments are charged for department S service at a rate of $5 per service hour. Production department managers have responsibility for controlling the amount of department S service used. Building service costs are allocated to production departments on the basis of floor space occupied. The actual costs of department S for November averaged $5.20 per service hour.

a. What is the normal volume of activity in department X?
b. Calculate total standard direct labor hours for November.
c. What was the effect on total departmental overhead cost of the variation from standard direct labor efficiency during November?
d. What was the total overhead variance for November?
e. What is the meaning of the variance in building service costs for department X?
f. Prepare a brief summary of actual overhead costs and budget allowances for the month reflecting only those variances attributable in whole or in part to *overhead* cost control in department X (i.e., exclude those variances due to variations from standard direct labor efficiency).
g. Prepare a summary table showing the various components of the total variance you calculated in (d). You need not break this down by object of expenditure account.

10. Labor variance analysis: Effect of materials usage. A department processes two products at the following standard costs:

	Materials	Labor	
	(pounds)	Hours	Cost
Product A.................	10	5	$30
Product B.................	20	10	60

The amount of labor actually used depends on the weight of material processed rather than the number of units of product completed.

During January the following data were registered in this department:

Materials used:	25,000 pounds
Labor used:	12,000 hours, $74,000
Products produced:	Product A, 1,000 units
	Product B, 600 units

a. Calculate the total labor variance for this department for the month of January.
b. Analyze this variance, labeling each component clearly. Does it appear that the manager exercised adequate control over departmental labor costs during the month?

11. Labor mix variance. Actual wages total $15,000. The standard wage rate used for product costing is $4 an hour. Actual labor time totals 4,000 hours: 2,500 hours of grade A labor, with a standard wage rate of $5 an hour, and 1,500 hours of grade B labor, with a standard wage rate of $3.50 an hour. The month's output has a standard labor cost of $15,800.

a. What are the standard proportions of grade A and grade B labor implicit in the $4 standard wage rate used for product costing?
b. Compute and analyze the variances.

12. Labor variance analysis. The Dade Corporation operates a single plant, manufacturing molded plastic products. Production in the molding department is performed by crews of workers in three separate wage rate classifications. A "standard crew hour" consists of ten labor hours, distributed among the pay grades as follows:

Pay Grade	Hours	Standard Rate	Standard Cost
FA-1.............	2	$700	$14.00
FA-2.............	3	560	16.80
FA-3.............	5	480	24.00
Total.........	10	xxx	$54.80

Standard output is 1,000 pounds of finished product per standard crew hour, and on this basis standard labor cost per 1,000 pounds of product is $54.80.

During February charges to the molding department included 650 hours of FA-1 labor, 1,000 hours of FA-2 labor, and 1,600 hours of FA-3 labor. Output of the molding department totaled 330,000 pounds of finished product. There were no in-process inventories either at the beginning or at the end of the month. The department operated 160 hours during February, using two production crews throughout the period. All of this was classified as productive time except for five hours of idle time recorded by one crew while machinery was being repaired. The departmental payroll for the month totaled $18,000.

a.   Calculate the total labor variance for the month.
b.   Subdivide the variance into five component parts, in the following sequence: labor rate variance, labor mix variance, crew size variance, idle time variance, labor performance variance.

13. Labor variance analysis.   Barbizon, Inc., operates a 12-department factory in Tucson, Arizona. One of these departments, known as the granulating department, has three kinds of employees on its direct labor payroll, classified as pay grades A, B, and C. They work in ten-person crews, in the following proportions:

Pay Grade	No. of Workers in Standard Crew	Standard Hourly Wage Rate	Standard Cost per Crew Hour
A..................	6	$4	$24
B..................	3	6	18
C..................	1	8	8
Total..............	10		$50

The work crews can't work short-handed. To keep a unit operating when one of the regular crew members is absent, the head of the granulating department first tries to reassign one of the department's other workers from indirect labor operations. Grade C indirect workers can fill in anywhere on the crew, grade B workers can fill in for grades B and A, and grade A workers can fill in for absent grade A crew members. These replacement workers are as efficient as those they replace, and learning curve effects on performance are negligible.

If no one in the granulating department is able to step in, plant management will pull maintenance department workers off their regular work if possible and assign them temporarily to the granulating department. These maintenance workers are all classified as grade D employees, with a standard wage rate of $10 an hour. Highly trained in all aspects of the factory's operations, they can substitute for any of the regular crew with neither a loss nor a gain in hourly output.

The following data relate to the operations of the granulating department during the month of May:

1.   Actual work time, 1,000 crew hours.
2.   Actual direct labor hours:
        Grade A, 5,400 hours.
        Grade B, 3,200 hours.
        Grade C, 1,300 hours.
        Grade D, 100 hours.

3. Total direct labor payroll (excluding overtime premiums), $53,000.
4. Standard crew hours for actual output, 980.

Standard product cost is based on the number of crew hours required. The department is charged for the actual wages of employees performing work in the department.

a. Calculate the granulating department's total direct labor cost variance for the month of May.
b. How much of this amount was due to off-standard composition of the direct work crews?
c. What explanation(s) can you offer for the portion of the total direct labor cost variance not accounted for by your answer to (b)?
d. After completing the analysis above, you find that the number of crew hours is determined largely by the amount of material placed in process. At standard, one crew hour is necessary for every 20 pounds of materials processed. During May, the department processed 21,000 pounds of materials, but some of these materials were of poor quality, leading to a slight reduction in the quantity of product output per pound of materials. Modify your answer to (c) to reflect this additional information. Was the department head effective in controlling labor costs in the granulating department?

14. Labor variance analysis.   Joe is concerned about the large unfavorable labor quantity variance that arose in his department last month. He has had a small favorable variance for several months, and he thinks his crew worked just as effectively last month as in previous months. This makes him believe that something must be wrong with the calculations, but he admits he doesn't understand them. The variance was reported as follows:

Standard labor cost of output (120,000 pounds at 6.45 cents)........ $7,740
Actual labor hours at standard wage rate..........................   8,585
    Labor quantity variance.. $ (845)

The product is made in batches which start with 1,200 pounds of material. The standard calls for the following labor quantities for each batch:

Labor Class	Standard Wage Rate	Standard Labor Hours	Standard Labor Cost
Class 6...............	$4.50	3	$13.50
Class 5...............	4.00	6	24.00
Class 3...............	3.00	9	27.00
Total...............		18	$64.50

The raw material is of uneven quality, and the product yield from a batch varies with the quality of the raw materials used. The standard output is 1,000 pounds, resulting in a standard labor cost of 6.45 cents a pound.

Joe's work force is a crew of 12 workers. The standard crew consists of two class 6 workers, four class 5 workers, and six class 3 workers. Lower rated employees cannot do the work of the higher rated employees, but the reverse is possible with some slight loss in efficiency and a resulting increase in labor hours.

The standard work day is nine hours. Last month had 23 working days, for a total of 207 standard working hours. Premiums for overtime hours are charged to overhead accounts and do not enter this problem.

Last month, 165,000 pounds of material were used to produce 120,000 pounds of product. The actual amounts of labor used were as follows:

Labor Class	Labor Hours	Labor Rate	Labor Cost
Class 6..............	390	$4.50	$1,755
Class 5..............	980	4.00	3,920
Class 3..............	970	3.00	2,910
Total.............	2,340		$8,585

Joe's work force last month, assigned to him by the personnel department, consisted of two class 6 workers, five class 5 workers, and five class 3 workers.

What would you tell Joe? Can you get him "off the hook" with the plant manager. (Suggestion: try to separate the effects of crew mix, labor performance, and materials yield.)

(Prepared by Professor Carl L. Nelson)

15. Materials mix variance. The Rushby Chemical Company manufactures a certain product by mixing three kinds of materials in large batches. The blendmaster has the responsibility for maintaining the quality of the product, and this often requires altering the proportions of the various ingredients. Standard costs are used to provide materials control information. The standard materials inputs per batch are:

	Quantity (pounds)	Price (per pound)	Standard Cost of Materials
Bulk material.................	420	$0.06	$25.20
Coloring material..............	70	0.12	8.40
Setting material...............	10	0.25	2.50
Total batch................	500		$36.10

The finished product is packed in 50-pound boxes; the standard materials cost of each box is therefore $3.61.

During January, the following materials were put in process:

Bulk material........................	181,000 lbs.
Coloring material....................	33,000
Setting material.....................	6,000
Total............................	220,000 lbs.

Inventories in process totaled 5,000 pounds at the beginning of the month and 8,000 pounds at the end of the month. It is assumed that these inventories consisted of materials in their standard proportions. Finished output during January amounted to 4,100 boxes.

a. Compute the total materials quantity variance for the month and break it down into mix and yield components.
b. Who, if anyone, in the management of the company would be interested in seeing this breakdown of the quantity variance?

REVIEW PROBLEMS

The problems in this section are designed to integrate the materials covered in this chapter with those in previous chapters on standard costing, flexible budgeting, and cost allocation.

16. Labor, materials, and overhead variances; T-accounts. The Mooseheart Company uses a basic plan system of standard costing in its factory.

The factory has only one processing department. Inventory balances, all priced at standard cost, were as follows on March 1:

Materials................................ $1,500
Materials in process..................... 600
Labor in process......................... 200
Overhead in process...................... 180

The following transactions occurred during March:

1. Materials received from vendors: actual price, $1,290; standard price, $1,200.
2. Materials issued (at standard prices): direct materials, $1,150; indirect materials, $100.
3. Summary of labor time tickets for the month (at standard wage rates): direct labor, $2,020; indirect labor, $340.
4. Actual payroll for the month, $2,450—includes overtime premium, $60, and apprentice pay, $15, to be charged to overhead; these two amounts are not included in the figures given in item (3).
5. Other overhead charges for the month, $1,300.
6. Goods completed during March, and standard product costs:

		Standard Cost per Unit			
Product	Units Completed	Materials	Labor	Overhead	Total
X.................... 100		$1.00	$2.00	$1.80	$4.80
Y.................... 200		1.50	4.00	3.50	9.00
Z.................... 300		3.00	2.50	2.00	7.50

7. The month's flexible budget allowances for factory overhead can be calculated from the following formula:

Overhead costs = $1,000 + 0.4 × standard direct labor cost

8. Standard costs of work in process on March 31:

Materials in process.................. $500
Labor in process...................... 400
Overhead in process................... 350

a. Enter the opening inventory balances and record the transactions described in items (1) through (6) in approximately titled T-accounts.
b. Compute aggregate variances for materials, labor, and overhead, and subdivide these in any way you deem appropriate. Indicate for each variance whether it is favorable or unfavorable.

17. Direct labor, materials, and overhead variances; Profit variability. Milner Manufacturing Company uses a standard costing system. It manufactures one product. Standard unit manufacturing costs and budgeted average selling, general, and administrative expenses at normal volume are as follows:

Materials: 20 yards at $0.90 a yard......................... $18
Direct labor: 4 hours at $6 an hour............................ 24
Total factory
  overhead: Applied at five-sixths of direct labor (the ratio of
                 variable costs to fixed costs is 3 to 1)............. 20
Variable selling, general, and administrative expenses.......... 12
Fixed selling, general, and administrative expenses.............   7
    Total unit cost.. $81

Normal volume is 2,400 standard direct labor hours a month.
Actual activity for the month of October was as follows:

Materials purchased:	18,000 yards at $0.92 a yard.........	$16,560
Materials used:	9,500 yards	
Direct labor:	2,100 hours at $6.10 an hour........	12,810
Total factory overhead:	....	11,100
Units actually produced: 500		

a. Based on the standard costs and budget estimates, compute the in-
ventoriable unit cost for internal reporting purposes under variable
costing.

b. Based on the standard costs and budget estimates, a certain selling
price and number of units sold will yield an operating profit of $5,200.
Increasing this selling price by 4 percent will increase the operating
profit to $6,800. Neither the costs nor the number of units sold will
be affected by the price increase. Compute the selling price per unit
and the number of units to yield an operating profit of $5,200.

c. Compute the variable factory overhead rate per standard direct labor
hour and the total fixed factory overhead.

d. The company actually uses absorption costing for factory cost reporting. Prepare a schedule computing the following variances for
the month of October, indicating for each whether it is favorable or
unfavorable: (1) materials price variance; (2) materials usage
variance; (3) labor rate variance; (4) labor usage (quantity or efficiency) variance; (5) overhead spending (budget) variance; and (6)
overhead volume (capacity) variance.

(CPA adapted)

18. Labor, materials, and overhead variances. A company has two
products, with the following standard costs and the following production
for the month of March:

	Product A	Product B
Standard cost per unit:		
Materials..	$ 1	$ 2
Labor...	4	3
Overhead..	8	6
Total..	$13	$11
Units in process (all materials applied, but only one half		
of labor operations performed and one half of standard		
overhead absorbed):		
Beginning of month..................................	1,000	3,000
End of month.......................................	2,000	3,000
Units completed during month........................	4,000	5,000

Factory overhead costs for the month were budgeted from the following
formula:

Overhead = $60,000 + 0.5 (actual direct labor hours × standard wage rates)

The following costs were recorded during the month:

1. Materials purchased: standard cost, $20,000; actual cost, $21,200.
2. Direct materials issued (at standard prices): $17,000.
3. Direct labor payrolls, actual hours worked: at standard wage rates,
$31,600; at actual wage rates, $34,000.
4. Miscellaneous overhead costs: $75,000.

a. Prepare a list of variances for the month. Indicate for each whether
    it was favorable or unfavorable. Show your calculations.
b. Compute the standard cost of work in process at the end of the month.

19. Detailed variance analysis. The Poquette Corporation uses standard costing systems in all its plants. Departmental flexible budget allowances are computed monthly, based on standard direct labor hours earned
in each department. Each department has three work-in-process accounts,
one each for materials, labor and overhead. Materials and labor are
charged to their respective work-in-process accounts at standard prices and
wage rates. Marketable or reusable scrap is credited to departmental mate-
rials-in-process accounts at standard prices. Factory overhead costs are
accumulated in departmental overhead summary accounts, and at the
end of the month a charge is made to overhead in process on the basis of
standard direct labor hours for the month. Completed production is
credited to the departmental work-in-process accounts as finished work is
transferred out of the department.

The refining department of the Poquette Corporation's Minneapolis
plant processes a certain raw material for use in a number of the company's products. The standard cost of a ton of the refined material is:

Raw materials:
3,400 pounds of concentrate at $0.05	$170	
500 pounds of processing chemical at $0.15	75	
Less: 1,800 pounds of recoverable residue at $0.02	(36)	$209
Labor, 3 crew hours at $25 per crew hour		75
Overhead, 3 crew hours at $65 per crew hour		195
Total standard cost per ton		$479

The following data summarize the refining department's operations for
the month of October:

Materials received in department:
Concentrate	665 tons
Processing chemical	94 tons
Recoverable residue	370 tons
Actual crew wages	$30,000
Actual crew labor at standard wage rates for actual crew members	$29,200
Actual crew hours	1,180 crew hours
Actual overhead cost	$79,200
Refined materials completed	380 tons

Actual crew hours include ten crew hours of unproductive time. Standard
product cost includes no provision for this kind of unproductive time. The
amount of work in process was unchanged during the month.

The number of labor crew hours varies with the number of tons of concentrate used, in the proportions reflected in the standard cost sheet.
Overhead varies with the number of actual crew hours, and the flexible
budget for the department can be computed from the following formula:

$$\text{Budget} = \$30,000 + \$33.75 \times \text{actual crew hours}$$

Analyze all variances for the month in as much detail as you can. Use
any method of analyzing and classifying the labor and overhead variances
that seems appropriate.

20. Complete costing/reporting cycle: Departmental overhead rates, allocations, labor, materials, and overhead variances. The King Supply Company's factory has four production departments and three service departments. A full cost, basic plan standard costing system is in use.

Budgeted overhead costs for the current year, at normal volume, together with other pertinent data, are as follows (DLH is direct labor hours):

Department	Floor Space	No. of Employees	Dept. 23 Hours Used	Normal Volume per Month	Budgeted Direct Dept. Overhead
Production 11.......	20%	80	600	10,000 DLH	$30,000
Production 12.......	25	120	900	15,000 DLH	50,000
Production 13.......	35	60	1,200	20,000 machine-hours	59,300
Production 14.......	9	50	300	5,000 DLH	20,000
Service 21..........	—	6	—	—	10,000
Service 22..........	8	24	—	—	19,000
Service 23..........	3	20	—	3,000 hours	22,500

For the purpose of developing departmental predetermined overhead rates, budgeted service department costs are distributed in sequence as follows:

Department	Basis
Service 21........................	Floor space
Service 22........................	Number of employees
Service 23........................	Service 23 hours

Service department costs are distributed monthly on the following bases:

Service 21: To all departments on basis of budgeted monthly cost of floor space occupied.

Service 22: To all departments except service 21 on basis of budgeted rate per employee.

Service 23: To production departments on basis of budgeted rate per department 23 hour.

The following data relating to factory overhead costs were recorded during April:

Department	Volume of Activity	No. of Employees	Dept. 23 Hours Used	Standard Overhead Cost Absorbed	Direct Dept. Overhead Cost
11........	9,000 DLH	75	500	$38,000	$29,000
12........	16,000 DLH	125	500	70,000	55,000
13........	21,000 machine-hours	58	1,200	82,000	61,000
14........	6,500 DLH	60	300	to be calculated	23,000
21........	—	6	—	—	8,800
22........	—	22	—	—	19,200
23........	2,500 hours	16	—	—	19,000

You have the following additional information for production department 14 only (for the month of April):

1. Direct materials issued (at standard prices): $4,200.
2. Standard cost of work received from other departments: $214,800.
3. Direct labor payrolls ($39,000 at standard wage rates): $40,300.
4. Work in process April 1 (at standard cost): materials in process, $106,900; labor in process, $12,000; overhead in process (2,000 standard direct labor hours), __?__.
5. Work in process April 30 (at standard cost); materials in process, $87,200; labor in process, $4,800; overhead in process (800 standard direct labor hours), __?__.
6. Standard cost of goods finished: materials, $230,000; labor, $44,400; overhead (7,400 standard direct labor hours), __?__.
7. From the flexible budget:

	3,500 DLH	6,500 DLH
Direct departmental overhead	$17,000	$23,000
Number of employees	38	62
Department 23 hours used	250	350

Direct departmental overhead, number of employees, and department 23 hours used are expected to vary as the number of direct hours varies within this range. The variations are expected to be in proportion to the variations in the number of direct labor hours, except that the number of employees must be a whole number. If a fraction of an employee is needed, a whole employee will be provided in the department.

a. Distribute budgeted service department costs and compute predetermined overhead rates for each of the four production departments for the current year.
b. Prepare an overhead cost distribution sheet for the month of April.
c. Compute the total overhead cost variance for the month for each of the four production departments and the total amount over- or underdistributed for each of the three service departments.
d. Prepare a complete variance summary for department 14.

22

Cost Variances in
Financial Reporting

WHEN standard costs or predetermined overhead rates are used, variances accumulate in the accounts. These must be reflected in the financial statements prepared for the use of outside investors. This raises three kinds of questions:

1. How the variances should be classified for annual financial reporting.
2. How seasonal factors can be handled in interim financial reporting.
3. How differences between the standard costs of the inventories and the amounts reported on the balance sheet can be reconciled.

CLASSIFYING VARIANCES FOR
ANNUAL REPORTING

Three methods of reflecting variances in the annual financial statements need to be considered:

1. Take the entire variance to the income statement for the current year.
2. Assign the entire variance to the balance sheet, to be offset in later periods by variances in the opposite direction.
3. Divide the variance between the balance sheet and the income statement so that the inventory figures will approximate average historical cost.

Taking All Variances to Income

The argument for taking a variance immediately to the income statement is that standard cost represents the commitment implicit in management's decision to manufacture the product. If cost is greater than this, the excess represents waste. Waste should not be inventoried. Unfavorable volume variances, for example, represent the costs of idle capacity. They are attributable not to the products manufactured but to those that were not produced.

Clearing favorable variances to the income statement is harder to justify. The argument is that each product should be assigned its full share of the costs of providing capacity. Overutilization of capacity is due to currently favorable conditions which change the profitability of the company's products rather than their costs. Just as the costs of idle capacity are assignable to products not produced, so the benefits from supernormal output accrue to the extra products rather than to the normal output.

The main drawback of this latter position is that the volume variance that accompanies supernormal production volume could provide a misleading indicator of income if the production represented a speculative buildup of inventory. Similarly, taking favorable price variances immediately to the income statement would represent income recognition at the time of acquisition, in violation of generally accepted accounting principles.

Assigning All Variances to the Balance Sheet

The second possible approach also accepts normal cost as the best measure of product cost but maintains that departures from normal are temporary and will cancel themselves out if a long enough time period is permitted. Therefore, all variances should remain on the balance sheet until offset in later periods by variances in the opposite direction.

This viewpoint would be valid if variances could all be regarded as the result of random forces. Random fluctuations affect totals during a short period, but the longer the reporting period the greater is the likelihood that residual variances are nonrandom. The presumption that 12 months is a long enough time for random variances other than volume variances to cancel each other, together with uncertainty as to the length and average level of business fluctuations, has generally ruled out any extensive support for this second alternative in annual reporting.

Approximating Average Historical Cost

A third possible point of view is that inventory cost should approximate the average historical cost of production. In this view, the variances should be allocated pro rata to the inventories and to the cost of goods sold. If labor variances, for example, average 10 percent of the standard labor cost of the work done, then 10 percent should be added to the standard labor costs placed in inventory during the period; the rest would go to the income statement.

Current Practice

No recent statistics on actual practice are available. If variances are classified as immaterial, presumably any of the three solutions is acceptable. In these circumstances, most companies are likely to clear all variances to the income statement. If standards are up to date, variances are likely to be relatively small, small enough to qualify as immaterial. For this reason it is likely that many companies write off all variances immediately, assigning no portion of them to the inventories.

Favorable variances large enough to be classified as material in amount probably will be divided between the income statement and the balance sheet. The treatment of unfavorable variances is less clear.[1] These, too, may be prorated, but some of them are likely to be taken to the income statement in their entirety. It is generally accepted that unrecoverable costs should not be assigned to the inventories. Large unfavorable volume variances and large unfavorable spending variances arising during the start-up phase of new facilities are examples of variances that may be placed in this category. If so, they will be deducted from revenues in the year they take place. Unfavorable price variances and other unfavorable variances classified as material in amount but not classified as unrecoverable will be split between the balance sheet and the income statement.

SEASONAL VARIANCES

All businesses are affected in some way by seasonal patterns of cost or volume or both. There is general agreement that sales revenues should be reported on the interim financial statements for the periods in which the revenues are recognized. There is less agreement on how cost variances ought to be handled. In this section we shall take a brief look at this question.

Cost Variations

Although average variable cost may be affected by seasonal factors, their main effect is likely to be on the fixed costs. Heating and air-conditioning costs are typical examples.

We can allow for seasonal variations in these costs in either of two ways. First, we can build the seasonal pattern into the monthly budget allowances. Second, we can normalize the cost, prorating it in equal monthly installments or as a predetermined percentage of some operating variable such as direct labor hours.

Adjusting the monthly budget allowances. Building the seasonal pattern into the monthly budget allowances leads to a transfer of costs between the spending and volume variances. We can demonstrate this by expanding the overhead cost illustration we used in Chapter

---

[1] Neither the Accounting Principles Board nor the Financial Accounting Standards Board has spoken on this question. The Cost Accounting Standards Board requires full allocation of all variances for contract costing but has no jurisdiction over cost classifications for external financial reporting. (Cost Accounting Standard 407. See Appendix B at the end of this book.)

21. In that illustration the budget allowances for overhead costs were derived from the following formula:

$$\text{Overhead cost} = \$7,400 + \$1.15 \times \text{direct labor hours}$$

Standard overhead cost was $3 a standard direct labor hour. We have the following information for January:

Actual direct labor time.............. 3,500 direct labor hours
Actual overhead cost................. $12,060
Standard overhead cost (3,400
  standard direct labor hours × $3.... $10,200

Since variable overhead costs are expected to vary with the actual number of direct labor hours, we should use a three-variance method to analyze the variance, for the reasons outlined in Chapter 21. The analysis shows the following breakdown:

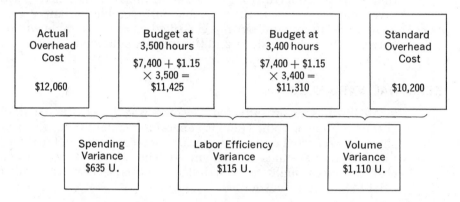

Suppose we now find that January is expected to have $1,000 more in fixed costs than an average month. The flexible budget formula for January therefore would be:

$$\text{Overhead cost} = \$7,400 + \$1,000 + \$1.15 \times \text{actual direct labor hours}$$

The spending variance can be calculated two ways:

	Original Budget Formula	Seasonally Adjusted Formula
Actual.................................	$12,060	$12,060
Budget at 3,500 hours..................	11,425	12,425
Spending variance..................	$ 635 U	$ 365 F

U = Unfavorable.
F = Favorable.

The volume variance also can be calculated two ways:

	Original Budget Formula	Seasonally Adjusted Formula
Budget at 3,400 standard hours..........	$11,310	$12,310
Standard cost.........................	10,200	10,200
Volume variance...................	$ 1,110 U	$ 2,110 U

U = Unfavorable.

Adjusting the budget shifts $1,000 from the spending variance to the volume variance.

Normalizing the seasonal variation in cost. A second method of dealing with seasonal variations in costs is to normalize them. In this case $1,000 of the costs actually incurred in January would be transferred to a suspense account. In some later month or months, when actual overhead costs are expected to be $1,000 less than the average amount, the $1,000 would be transferred from the suspense account to the departmental overhead cost account.

This method is awkward and may lead the manager to doubt the validity of the figures. This will reduce the credibility of the entire system. For this reason, this method probably shouldn't be used.

Volume Variations

Seasonal variations in volume require a different form of analysis. If volume is seasonal, the volume variance is really made up of two elements, one reflecting the seasonal influence and the other the departure of actual volume from the volume budgeted for the month.

Continuing the example, suppose the volume normally budgeted for January is 3,800 standard hours instead of the 3,400 standard hours actually achieved. The amount of overhead absorbed at this volume would be $3,800 \times \$3 = \$11,400$. The amount budgeted, including the $1,000 in extra fixed costs, would be:

Budget $= \$8,400 + \$1.15 \times 3,800 = \$12,770$

The budgeted volume variance therefore would be $1,370:

Absorbed at 3,800 standard hours...................	$11,400
Budgeted at 3,800 standard hours.................	12,770
Budgeted volume variance....................	$ 1,370 Unfavorable

Remember that we just calculated the actual volume variance for January to be $2,110:

Absorbed at 3,400 standard hours...............	$10,200
Budgeted at 3,400 standard hours (using seasonally adjusted formula).................	12,310
Actual volume variance....................	$ 2,110 U.

This was $740 greater than the $1,370 budgeted volume variance for the month, indicating that volume was substantially smaller than management had budgeted for January.

The question for financial reporting is whether the volume variance included in the interim financial statements should be $740 or the full $2,110. This depends on the outcome of the argument whether each interim period should be regarded as a separate financial period or as a fractional part of an annual financial period. For managerial reporting it seems clear that each month is part of a longer period for which current plans and forecasts have been prepared. Management needs to distinguish between anticipated seasonal patterns and variations due to other factors.

It can also be argued that management should include the results of this sort of analysis in its interim financial reports to outsiders. A comment such as the following might be appropriate:

> "Production volume in the first quarter of this year was X% smaller than the amount budgeted for this period. We anticipated a $Y million charge against revenues in the first quarter, the costs of sustaining idle facilities during the quarter. The actual cost of carrying idle facilities was $Z million during this quarter."

RECONCILING STANDARD COSTS WITH THE FINANCIAL STATEMENTS

Under most procedures, up-to-date inventory account balances represent the standard costs of the items on hand. These totals may differ from the inventory figures shown on the company's balance sheet, however, in three different situations:

1. Newly adopted standards measure anticipated costs and differ substantially from historical cost.
2. Variances are so large that generally accepted accounting principles require them to be reflected pro rata in the reported inventory totals.
3. Inventories are reported on a Lifo basis.

In all three situations, the accountant uses an *Inventory Adjustment account* or accounts to bridge the gap between the inventories at standard costs and the amounts reported in the outside financial statements.

Newly Adopted Standards

The balance in the Inventory Adjustment account on any balance sheet date is simply the difference between total standard cost of the inventory on hand and its average historical cost. It can be either a debit or a credit balance.

For example, a company adopted a standard costing system, effective January 1, 19x1. The inventories on hand at that time had the following standard direct labor costs:

Standard labor cost of the work in process..... $ 300,000
Standard labor cost of the finished goods
  inventory.................................... 1,000,000
    Total.................................... $1,300,000

The Fifo historical cost of these inventories, as shown on the December 31, 19x0 balance sheet, was $1,378,000.

When the standard costing system was introduced, on January 1, 19x1, two new inventory accounts were set up, one to receive the standard labor costs of all the inventories (both in-process and finished goods), the other to reflect the difference between standard labor cost and the Fifo historical labor cost of the inventories. Similar accounts were set up for the materials and factory overhead costs of the inventories.

The labor cost accounts had the following balances at the beginning of 19x1:

Standard Labor Costs in Inventories		Inventory Adjustment—Labor	
Bal. 1/1	1,300,000	Bal.	78,000

Together the balances in these two accounts accounted for the Fifo historical cost of the opening inventory. If the standards had been set at $1,400,000, then the Inventory Adjustment account would have had a credit balance of $22,000. The adoption of standard costing didn't affect the historical cost figures used for financial reporting.

Prorated Variances

Reported inventories also depart from standard cost if variances are large enough to be assigned, in part, to the ending inventory.

For example, Exhibit 22–1 summarizes the data in the labor cost accounts at the end of 19x1. All entries in the inventory account during the year were at standard cost, the amounts charged to the cost of goods sold were at standard, and no entries were made in the Inventory Adjustment account. Inventories were to be reported to investors on a Fifo historical cost basis.

Labor cost variances for the year averaged 8 percent of the standard labor cost of the work done ($400,000/$5,000,000). This was classified as material in amount—that is, large enough to be spread on a pro rata basis. Of the $5,000,000 standard labor cost of the work done during the year, $1,550,000 remained in the Fifo inventory at the end of the year; the remaining $3,450,000 went to the cost of goods sold. The variance was split proportionally:[2]

---

[2] The ending inventories amounted to $1,550,000/$5,000,000 = 31 percent of the work done during the year. The amount assigned to the inventories therefore should have been the variances arising during the final 31 percent of the year's production. If the variances were not spread evenly throughout the year, the approximation in the illustration would not have been appropriate.

	Standard Labor Cost	Labor Cost Variance (8%)	Adjusted Labor Cost
To ending inventory..................	$1,550,000	$124,000	$1,674,000
To cost of goods sold................	3,450,000	276,000	3,726,000
Total.........................	$5,000,000	$400,000	$5,400,000

The Fifo cost of goods sold therefore was as follows:

	Standard Labor Cost	Variance	Adjusted Labor Cost
From opening inventory....................	$1,300,000	$ 78,000	$1,378,000
From current production...................	3,450,000	276,000	3,726,000
Total...............................	$4,750,000	$354,000	$5,104,000

Two adjusting entries were appropriate. The first of these was to transfer the opening balance in the inventory adjustment account to the cost of goods sold:

Labor Cost of Goods Sold 78,000
        Inventory Adjustment—Labor 78,000

The second entry was to close the variance account:

Labor Cost of Goods Sold 276,000
Inventory Adjustment—Labor 124,000
        Labor Cost Variance 400,000

As a result, the ending balance in the inventory adjustment account was $124,000, the amount necessary to bridge the gap between the

EXHIBIT 22–1

Labor Cost Accounts, 19x1

Standard Labor Costs in Inventories

Bal. 1/1	1,300,000	Standard labor cost of goods sold	4,750,000
Standard labor cost of work done	5,000,000		
Bal. 12/31	1,550,000		

Inventory Adjustment—Labor

| Bal. 1/1 | 78,000 | | |

Labor Cost of Goods Sold

| Standard labor cost of goods sold | 4,750,000 | | |

Labor Cost Variances

| Unfavorable | 500,000 | Favorable | 100,000 |
| Bal. 400,000 | | | |

standard labor cost of the ending inventory and the Fifo inventory figure.

Lifo Inventory Adjustment

The use of Lifo is the third reason for the standard cost of the inventory to depart from the amount reported to the public. Lifo inventory costing requires (1) the separate identification of the layer of inventory coming from each year's increment; (2) the measurement of the physical inventory increment or decrement for the current year; and (3) the estimation of the unit cost applicable to the increments or decrements.

For example, suppose our company adopted Lifo on January 1, 19x1, when its inventory had an historical cost of $1,378,000. This was the *Lifo base quantity*, the Lifo cost of the initial inventory layer. The accounts at that time had the following balances (from Exhibit 22–1):

Standard Labor Costs in Inventories	Inventory Adjustment—Labor
Bal. 1/1 1,300,000	Bal. 1/1 78,000

The second step is to calculate the physical inventory increment for 19x1. We can do this by comparing the standard costs of the beginning and ending inventories:

Ending Inventory $1,550,000	−	Beginning Inventory $1,300,000	=	Inventory Increment $250,000

Since each inventory figure represented a set of physical quantities multiplied by the same set of standard prices, the difference between the two can be interpreted as an increase in the physical quantity of goods on hand.

The third step is to estimate the actual cost of the 19x1 increment. Again we might use the 8 percent average variance for the year:

$$\text{Increment} = \$250,000 \times 1.08 = \$270,000$$

The year-end Lifo inventory therefore would be as follows:

Base quantity	$1,378,000
19x1 layer	270,000
Total Lifo cost	$1,648,000

The $250,000 standard cost was already in the inventory account. (Referring back to Exhibit 22–1, we can see that the standard cost of the inventories increased from $1,300,000 at the beginning of the year to $1,550,000 at the end, an increase of $250,000.) This leaves just $20,000 of the variance for 19x1 to add to the inventory adjustment account. The entry was:

Inventory Adjustment—Labor 20,000
Labor Cost of Goods Sold 380,000
    Labor Cost Variances   400,000

This produced the flow of costs illustrated in the following diagram:

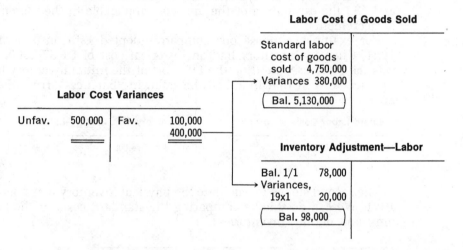

Lifo inventory liquidation. The calculations for an inventory liquidation or decrement are more complicated, but tie right back to the average variances arising in the years in which the various layers were added to the inventory. For example, suppose the standard labor cost of the inventory at the end of 19x2 was $1,400,000, just $150,000 less than the opening balance. This $150,000 came from the 19x1 layer, the last layer added to the inventory. As we just saw, the actual cost of the 19x1 layer was 108 percent of standard cost. The 19x2 Lifo decrement therefore was $150,000 × 1.08 = $162,000. This was $12,000 greater than the standard labor cost of the decrement, and the entry to adjust the accounts was:

Labor Cost of Goods Sold 12,000
    Inventory Adjustment—Labor   12,000

The ending balances in the inventory accounts were as follows:

Standard Labor Costs in Inventories		Inventory Adjustment–Labor	
Bal. 1/1 1,550,000		Bal. 1/1 98,000	
	To cost of goods sold 150,000		To cost of goods sold 12,000
Bal. 1,400,000		Bal. 86,000	

The Lifo cost of the inventory was $1,400,000 + $86,000 = $1,486,-000, covering the base quantity ($1,378,000) and the remaining two fifths of the 19x1 layer ($108,000).

Prorating Materials Cost Variances

Variances from standard materials and standard overhead costs also must be prorated if they are material in amount. The method is essentially the same as for labor cost variances and an extended illustration is therefore unnecessary. Materials variances do pose one additional problem which needs to be discussed, however—the price variances relate to the quantity *purchased*, while the quantity variances relate to the standard materials cost of the *work done*.

For example, suppose a company's inventories had the following standard materials costs on January 1, 19x1:

Raw materials........................	$ 80,000
Work in process......................	10,000
Finished goods.......................	30,000
Total............................	$120,000

The Fifo historical cost of these inventories was equal to their standard costs—in other words, the inventory adjustment account started the year with a zero balance.

We have the following information on the company's transactions in 19x1:

Standard cost of materials purchased..........	$200,000
Materials price variance.......................	20,000 U.
Standard materials cost of the work done......	220,000
Materials quantity variance....................	33,000 U.

The standard materials costs of the inventories on hand at the end of 19x1 were as follows:

Raw materials.................................	$ 27,000
Work in pricess...............................	25,000
Finished goods................................	60,000
Total materials cost in inventory...........	$112,000

The flow of materials costs is summarized in Exhibit 22–2.

To divide the variances between the inventories and the cost of goods sold, we need to calculate the average variance percentages:

> Average price variance = $20,000/$200,000 = 10%.
> Average quantity variance = $33,000/$220,000 = 15%.

Under Fifo, the first costs to be assigned to the goods sold are the costs of the opening inventories. In this case the standard cost of goods sold was greater than the standard cost of the beginning inventory. This means that all of the beginning inventory costs flowed to the income statement for the year; the year-end inventory was measured at the average historical cost of the current year (or, if

EXHIBIT 22-2

Statement of Material Costs, at Standard Prices

Standard cost of materials issued:		
Materials inventory, January 1, 19x1....................		$ 80,000
Purchases (at standard prices)........................		200,000
Total..		$280,000
Materials inventory, December 31, 19x1...............		27,000
Standard cost of materials issued....................		$253,000
Less: materials quantity variance.....................		33,000
Standard materials cost of work done...............		$220,000
Add: Standard materials cost of work in process,		
January 1, 19x1...................................	$10,000	
Less: Standard materials cost of work in process,		
December 31, 19x1...............................	25,000	15,000
Standard materials cost of products finished........		$205,000
Add: Standard materials cost of finished goods		
inventory, January 1, 19x1.........................	$30,000	
Less: Standard materials cost of finished goods		
inventory, December 31, 19x1.....................	60,000	30,000
Standard materials cost of goods sold...............		$175,000

greater refinement is desired, at the prices paid during the final weeks or months of the year).

Adjusting standard raw materials costs. The quantity variance applies only to the work done, not to the materials still in inventory in an unprocessed state. For this reason we can ignore the quantity variance in calculating the historical cost of raw materials. The Fifo historical cost of the raw materials inventory was derived by multiplying the standard cost of the ending inventory by a factor reflecting the average price variance alone:

	Standard Cost		Adjustment Ratio		Approximate Fifo Historical Cost
Raw materials.............	$27,000	$\times$	110%	=	$29,700

The $29,700 is only an approximation of historical cost because it was calculated from average relationships. The actual inventories on hand at the end of the year may have been made up of items subject to price movements either greater or less than the 10 percent average annual rate of price increase.

Adjusting standard materials costs of work in process and finished goods. The adjustment ratio for work in process and finished goods is more complicated, because it includes both price and quantity variances.[3] Since the actual quantity used was $33,000/$220,000 = 15 percent greater than the standard quantity, standard cost must be

---

[3] A case can be made for expensing unfavorable quantity variances, on the grounds that they represent unrecoverable costs due to production inefficiencies. If this approach is followed, only price variances and favorable quantity variances will be reflected in the adjustment ratios.

multiplied by 1.15. This yields the standard cost of the actual quantities used. To restate this latter figure at actual historical prices, we need to multiply it by 1.10. These two calculations are combined in the adjustments summarized in the following table:

	Standard Cost	Adjustment Ratio (percent)	Approximate Fifo Historical Cost
Raw materials...........	$ 27,000	110	$ 29,700
Work in process.........	25,000	110 × 115	31,625
Finished goods..........	60,000	110 × 115	75,900
Total...............	$112,000		$137,225

Closing the variance accounts. The difference between the standard cost and the approximate Fifo historical cost was $137,225 − $112,000 = $25,225. This was the portion of the variances for the year to be assigned to the inventory. The remainder—$20,000 + $33,000 − $25,255 = $27,745—was classified as part of the cost of goods sold. The variance accounts were closed out by the following journal entry at the end of the year:

Materials Cost of Goods Sold	27,745	
Inventory Adjustment—Materials	25,255	
Materials Price Variance		20,000
Materials Quantity Variance		33,000

SUMMARY

It can be argued that all variances should be taken to the income statement in the year in which they arise. The argument is that variances reflect departures from the conditions on which current plans were based. Unfavorable variances reflect unrecoverable costs; favorable variances reflect unanticipated gains.

This treatment is widely used for variances classified as immaterial. If variances are material in amount, however, they generally must be spread pro rata over the goods sold and the goods on hand. Large unfavorable variances due to idle capacity or gross inefficiency are the exceptions, to be reported as part of the current expenses, on the grounds that they represent unrecoverable waste.

These rules may not apply to interim financial reporting. Cost variances resulting from seasonal factors may be kept out of the income statement on the grounds that they will be offset in later interim periods. In fact, cost variances in later periods may even be anticipated by normalizing them over the full 12 months.

In any case, when the inventory figures reported on the published financial statements differ from current standard costs, a reconciling account or accounts must be set up to keep track of the differences. The final section of this chapter showed how this can be done without maintaining dual records of actual and standard costs on a product-by-product basis.

INDEPENDENT STUDY PROBLEM
(Solution in Appendix C)

1. Prorating current variances. The Weston Company's inventory accounts show the standard costs of the items on hand. For public financial reporting the year's variances are spread proportionately between the cost of goods sold and balance sheet amounts. You are given the following data:

1. Inventories (at standard):

	January 1	December 31
Raw materials..	$10,000	$15,000
Materials in process...................................	6,100	5,000
Materials in finished goods...........................	8,000	7,000

2. Materials issued, at standard cost, $30,000.
3. Materials quantity variance for the year, $5,000, unfavorable.
4. January 1 balance in the Materials Quantity Variance in Inventory account, $900 Cr. No entries were made in this account during the year.

a. Compute the Fifo cost of goods sold for the year.

b. Prepare an end-of-period entry to close out the Materials Quantity Variance account and adjust the Materials Quantity Variance in Inventory account to its appropriate year-end balance.

EXERCISES AND PROBLEMS

1. Prorating variances: Effect on income. The predetermined overhead rate in the Marston Company was $2 a machine-hour in 19x1. Product costs for this year included the following factory overhead costs, based on this rate:

Inventory, January 1.........................	$ 30,000
Goods manufactured this year...............	100,000
Inventory, December 31.....................	30,000

Unabsorbed factory overhead for 19x1 amounted to $20,000. This entire amount was deducted from revenues on the company's income statement for the year 19x1.

a. What effect did the use of a predetermined overhead rate for product costing in 19x1 instead of actual overhead cost for the year have on income before taxes for 19x1 and 19x2, assuming that inventory cost flows follow the Fifo principle?

b. How would your answer differ if Lifo were in use, assuming that physical inventories were the same at the end of 19x1 as at the beginning?

2. Disposing of factory cost variances. The trial balances of the Andrews Company included the following figures at the beginning and end of the year 19x1:

	January 1	December 31
Sales revenue......................................		$1,500,000
Direct labor cost of goods sold....................		200,000
Direct materials cost of goods sold...............		600,000
Overhead cost of goods sold......................		400,000
Overhead in process..............................	$ 50,000	80,000
Overhead in finished goods.......................	100,000	120,000
Factory overhead (debit)..........................		594,000
Factory overhead absorbed (credit)...............		450,000
Selling and administrative expenses..............		250,000

You have the following additional information:

1. The company's inventories were costed on a Fifo basis.
2. Standard costs were not used, but a predetermined rate of 200 percent of direct labor cost was used to absorb factory overhead costs.
3. The factory overhead variance in 19x0 was very small and was deducted in full on the 19x0 income statement.
4. Factory overhead costs in 19x1 were expected to conform to the following estimated relationship:

$$\text{Annual overhead} = \$360,000 + 80\% \text{ of direct labor cost}$$

a. Compute reported income before taxes for the year, on the assumption that the cost of inventories to be reported on the year-end balance sheet is to approximate actual cost rather than normal cost.
b. Recalculate income before taxes on the assumption that unfavorable overhead volume variances are to be taken to the current income statement in their entirety, but other variances are to be prorated.
c. Compare the effects of these two methods on income before taxes for 19x1 and 19x2. Which of these methods would you choose, or would you recommend writing off the entire overhead variance against income in 19x1? Give your reasons.

3. Prorating materials variances. Artemis Publications publishes books. Unlike most publishers, it has its own printing plant. Its inventories of materials (paper stock, ink, and bookbinding supplies) and unsold books were costed on a Fifo basis, including a pro rata share of applicable variances. You have the following data for the year 19x1:

1. Inventory balances:

	January 1	December 31
Materials inventory (at standard)...............	$390	$500
Materials in process............................	0	0
Materials in finished goods (at standard)........	300	400

2. Materials purchased: actual cost $2,200, standard cost, $2,000.
3. Materials quantity variances: $90 (unfavorable).
4. The Materials Variances in Inventories account had a $20 debit balance on January 1. No entries were made in the account during 19x1.

a. Calculate the standard cost of materials issued during the year.
b. Calculate the standard materials cost of goods finished during the year.
c. Calculate the standard materials cost of goods sold during the year.
d. Calculate the Fifo historical materials cost of goods sold during the year, including a prorated share of price and quantity variances.
e. Calculate the correct end-of-year balance in the Materials Variances in Inventories account.
f. What entry should be made to bring the Materials Variances in Inventories account to its correct balance at the end of the year? You may assume that separate accounts were used to accumulate the materials price and materials quantity variances during the year.

4. Prorating labor cost variances: Fifo and Lifo. A company maintains three separate accounts for the materials, labor, and overhead content of inventories, plus accompanying accounts for the inventoried portion of cost variances. A standard costing system is in use, and inventories for public financial reporting are costed on a Fifo basis. Data for 19x1 are:

1. The standard labor costs of the inventories:

	January 1	December 31
Labor in process..........................	$ 8,000	$14,000
Labor in finished goods..................	17,000	21,000
Total....................................	$25,000	$35,000

2. Direct labor, 8,050 hours (standard wage rate, $6 an hour; actual wages, $50,232).

3. Labor quantity variance for the year at standard wage rates, $6,300 (unfavorable).

4. The Labor Variances in Inventory account had a $1,000 debit balance on January 1. No entries were made in this account during the year.

a. Compute the standard labor cost of goods sold.

b. Compute the labor cost of goods sold on a Fifo historical cost basis, dividing the variances among labor in process, labor in finished goods, and the labor cost of goods sold. (Suggestion: deal with the quantity variance first. Labor rate and quantity variances were accumulated in two separate accounts during the year.)

c. Prepare a journal entry to close out the year's variances and adjust the inventory accounts to their appropriate year-end balances.

d. Recompute the labor cost of goods sold for the year assuming a Lifo basis of inventory costing and inventorying only the appropriate portion of the labor rate variance.

5. Approximating Fifo cost; New standards; Journal entries. The Schouten Corporation has a basic plan standard costing system in its factory. The factory accounts reflected the following data in 19x1:

	Trial Balance January 1, 19x1		Transactions during 19x1			Trial Balance December 31, 19x1
Materials.....................	43,000	(1)	120,000	(2)	110,400	52,600
Work-in-process:						
Materials...................	12,000	(2)	110,400	(5)	110,000	17,000
		(6)	4,600			
Labor......................	3,000	(3)	31,500	(5)	27,000	6,000
				(7)	1,500	
Overhead..................	6,000	(8)	60,000	(5)	54,000	12,000
Finished goods:						
Materials...................	16,000	(5)	110,000	(9)	106,000	20,000
Labor......................	4,000	(5)	27,000	(9)	27,000	4,000
Overhead..................	8,000	(5)	54,000	(9)	54,000	8,000
Inventory adjustment........	2,000					2,000
Head office..................	90,000			(1)	132,000	324,390
				(3)	33,390	
				(4)	69,000	
Cost of goods sold...........		(9)	187,000			187,000
Overhead summary..........		(4)	69,000			69,000
Overhead absorbed.........				(8)	60,000	60,000
Materials price						
variance...................		(1)	12,000			12,000
Materials quantity						
variance...................				(6)	4,600	4,600
Labor rate						
variance....................		(3)	1,890			1,890
Labor quantity						
variance...................		(7)	1,500			1,500

The inventory account balances in the December 31, 19x1 trial balance measure the standard costs of the inventories on that date. The Schouten Corporation measures its inventories on a Fifo basis for public financial reporting, however. Variances are prorated for this purpose once a year, at their average for the year.

New standard costs were developed for 19x2 and the standard costs of the inventories on hand on December 31, 19x1 were recalculated, using these new standards. The results were as follows:

Raw materials	$57,000
Materials in process	19,000
Labor in process	7,000
Overhead in process	13,300
Materials in finished goods	23,000
Labor in finished goods	5,000
Overhead in finished goods	9,500

a. Identify the standard cost of the materials purchased and the standard cost of the factory's output for the year, cost element by cost element.

b. Calculate separate average variance ratios for materials, labor, and overhead. Remember to calculate separate ratios for price and quantity variances.

c. Prorate all variances, using these ratios, and determine the Fifo cost of goods sold and the year-end Fifo historical cost of the raw materials, work in process, and finished goods inventories.

d. Prepare an entry or entries to close all temporary accounts. (The Head Office account is a permanent account; its balance measures the amount the head office has invested in the factory's inventories.)

e. Prepare an entry to reflect the adoption of new standards for 19x2 and draw up a new trial balance as of January 1, 19x2.

6. Conversion to Lifo; Journal entries. Before closing its books for 19x1, the Schouten Corporation (Problem 5) decided to put the materials content of its inventories (including raw materials, work in process, and finished goods) on Lifo as of January 1, 19x1. All other inventories were to remain on Fifo. None of the January 1, 19x1 balance in the Inventory Adjustment account was to be assigned to the materials components of the opening inventory.

a. Calculate the cost of goods sold with materials on a Lifo basis and labor and overhead on Fifo.

b. Determine the correct December 31, 19x1 balance for the Inventory Adjustment account, after the adjustment to the new standards.

7. Seasonal patterns in overhead variances. In the Travis Paper Company, the principal costs are centered on the paper machines. The company, therefore, attaches great importance to the calculations of machine rates by which manufacturing overhead is assigned to products. Furthermore, the operating executives give considerable attention to the analysis and interpretation of cost figures and in particular to overhead cost variances. In periods of abnormally high or low production, the variances are analyzed to separate controllable from noncontrollable gains or losses.

By running three eight-hour shifts each 24 hours, one of the Travis Paper Company's machines has a normal annual volume of 6,000 hours. An hourly machine rate that will adequately distribute budgeted machine overhead to products at this volume is as follows:

Fixed charges, $61,800/6,000................... $10.30
Variable charges, $98,400/6,000................ 16.40
  Total.. $26.70

During the first three months of 19x1, the machine actually ran 1,490 hours; the first quarter ordinarily provides 30 percent of the year's total production. The overhead account for this machine at the end of the quarter showed the following data:

Machine No. 2 Overhead

Fixed charges	14,485	Fixed charges (1,490 × $10.30)	15,347
Variable charges	23,304	Variable charges (1,490 × $16.40)	24,436
	37,789		39,783
		Overabsorbed balance 1,994	

The costs chargeable to machine no. 2 were:

	Normal Annual Charges	Actual 1st Quarter 19x1
Fixed charges:		
Security and fire brigade...............	$ 1,800	$ 450
Taxes.................................	7,560	1,890
Insurance.............................	4,980	1,245
Depreciation..........................	33,000	8,250
Building repairs.......................	10,460	1,625
Supervision...........................	2,400	600
Accounting and office.................	1,000	250
Laboratory............................	600	175
	$61,800	$14,485
Variable charges:		
Indirect labor.........................	$ 5,400	$ 1,318
Supplies..............................	12,260	3,154
Water.................................	1,620	364
Teaming and yard expense............	6,720	1,520
Stock handling........................	1,980	430
Repairs to machinery..................	8,160	1,880
Power and light.......................	54,220	12,408
Heat..................................	8,040	2,230
	$98,400	$23,304

Determine, insofar as possible, the sources of the $1,994 variance and measure how much of this variance comes from each source. On the basis of your analysis, prepare a brief statement for submission to the general manager.

8. Seasonal variations; Interim reporting. The controller of Navar Corporation wants to issue to stockholders quarterly income statements that will be predictive of expected annual results. He proposes to allocate all fixed costs for the year among quarters in proportion to the number of units expected to be sold in each quarter, stating that the annual income can then be predicted through use of the following equation:

$$\text{Annual income} = \text{Quarterly income} \times \frac{100 \text{ percent}}{\text{Percent of unit sales applicable to quarter}}$$

Navar expects the following activity for the year (in thousands of dollars):

	Units	Average per Unit	Total (000s)
Sales revenue:			
First quarter....................................	500,000	$2.00	$1,000
Second quarter................................	100,000	1.50	150
Third quarter...................................	200,000	2.00	400
Fourth quarter.................................	200,000	2.00	400
Total..	1,000,000		$1,950
Costs to be incurred:			
Variable:			
Manufacturing................................		$0.70	$ 700
Selling and administrative....................		0.25	250
		$0.95	$ 950
Fixed:			
Manufacturing................................			$ 380
Selling and administrative....................			$ 220
			$ 600
Income before taxes...............................			$ 400

a. Ignoring income taxes and assuming that Navar's activities do not vary from expectations, will the controller's plan reach the desired objective? If not, how can it be modified to do so? Explain, using illustrative computations.

b. How should the effect of variations of actual activity from expected activity be treated in Navar's quarterly income statements?

c. What assumptions has the controller made in regard to inventories? Discuss.

(CPA)

23

Control of Project Cost

A LARGE SHARE of the firm's resources are expended on what we have referred to as programmed activities—that is, activities undertaken at management's initiative to meet objectives other than satisfying demands for service imposed on the organization unit from outside. Many of these consist of unique independent programs or projects, and the most important of these are capital expenditures and research and development projects.

Research and development activities are of three types: general research, project research, and product or process development. Development work is ordinarily the closest to commercial exploitation, the most specific, and the least subject to uncertainty about its results. General research, at the other extreme, often has no specific anticipated commercial applications, is not well specified as to expected inputs and outputs, and is characterized by extreme uncertainty as to its benefits.

The purpose of this chapter is to examine the tools available to management for the financial control of research and development projects and other similar activities. There are three control phases —project evaluation and approval, detailed scheduling, and progress review—linked together in the sequence shown in Exhibit 23–1.

PROJECT APPROVAL

The approval of research and development proposals is the most crucial phase in the control process. We need to look at two aspects of this phase:

1. What criteria should be used to evaluate individual proposals?
2. At what stage should these criteria be applied?

Approval Criteria

Project research and development decisions are identical in structure to the capital expenditure decisions we examined in Chapters 14

744

EXHIBIT 23–1

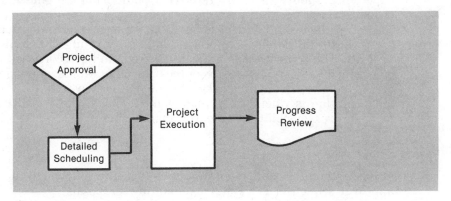

and 15. Management is asked to authorize expenditures now to yield benefits in the future. For this reason, the test to be applied to these decisions is the test we applied to capital expenditure proposals: Is the present value of the expected cash flows positive or negative?

The main trouble with this test is the difficulty of quantifying it. Forecasts of the benefits to be derived from specific programs or projects are subject to considerable error ranges, and the same is often true of forecasts of project costs. Confronted with this uncertainty, management is often tempted to abandon the profitability approach. Instead, research and development budgets are set as total spending limits, tied to some general index of company activity or profitability. Some typical indexes are:

1. Percent of sales.
2. Percent of the pretax profit contribution.
3. Dollars per employee.

The target ratio may be based on the company's own past expenditures or on the activities of its competitors. The base (sales, profit contribution, or employees) may be a current figure or an average covering a number of years.

Rules of thumb like these have one simple advantage—they may remove one source of managerial anxiety. Deciding how much to spend is difficult, and management can never be sure its choices are correct. By using a ratio that has worked in the past or seems to work for competitors, management can push these uncertainties into the background.

The main weakness of budgeting research and development from the top down is that it is likely to lead to neglected opportunities or wasted resources. If research management comes up with more good projects than it can handle within the budget limits, some will have to be deferred or rejected. If promising proposals are scarce, on the other hand, some of the available money will go to projects of dubious merit. In either case, the company loses. Competitive ratios or past experience should serve as reference points, not as guides to decisions.

Even if the overall budget is based on an aggregate ratio, management must still develop preference or priority ratings for individual projects. The work itself is project centered, and someone has to decide which projects get the resources. In other words, management can't avoid project-oriented decisions, no matter how hard it tries. The only question is whether top management makes these decisions or delegates responsibility to research management.

Review of Proposals

Research and development proposals typically go through the same approval sequence as capital expenditure proposals:

Stage 1. Annual budget review.
Stage 2. Specific project approval.
Stage 3. Progress review and reapproval.

We shall discuss the first two of these now, the third in the next section.

Budget review. Once each year, as part of the annual budgetary planning, research management prepares a tentative list of projects and expenditures for the coming year. These budgeted expenditures are usually listed two ways, by project and by object of expenditure:

	Project A	Project B	······	Research Administration
Professional salaries				
Clerical salaries				
Supplies				
Travel				
.				
.				
.				

If the research organization is departmentalized, the budget will also contain an organizational dimension, just as it does for manufacturing and marketing activities.

Some projects in the tentative budget are continuing projects, already approved and under way at the beginning of the year. These are reviewed to see whether they should be continued without change, modified, or discontinued. Others are specific proposals, not yet under way but under study and nearly ready for final decisions.

Most research and development budgets also contain a third element, a forecast of the total expenditures required by projects to be conceived and presented for approval later in the year. Budgeted expenditures in this third category should be relatively small, however. Most research and development projects take months to conceive and plan. Management is generally aware of most of the projects that will mature in time to affect expenditures during the budget period.

Even at this preliminary stage, rough estimates of costs and benefits should be made. This approach has several advantages:

1. It requires management to examine the economic basis for research decisions long before these decisions must be made.
2. It identifies the key variables and assumptions so that they can be analyzed and discussed.
3. It provides a record of management's expectations to serve as a point of reference for future estimates as the project matures.
4. It gives higher management a rough basis for comparing marginal research and development projects with other kinds of expenditure proposals—for plant and equipment, community service, dividends, methods analysis, and so on.

The estimates of costs and benefits at this stage will be very rough. They will also mirror the views of research management or of the operating executives who want the projects undertaken. It is better, however, to have some indication of expected profitability, no matter how rough, than no guidance at all. The advantages cited in the preceding paragraph can't be achieved without them.

Project approval. Inclusion of a project in the annual budget is not necessarily the same as project approval. The decision to initiate a project should not be made until management is ready to make the first expenditures. One reason is that the final project review is management's last chance to avoid spending money. Most research and development costs consist of staff salaries. The decision to initiate a project is also a decision to hire staff or to keep staff on the payroll who would otherwise be released. Once the commitment is made, the money flows out almost automatically.

The second reason is that by delaying approval until this stage, management can use later information, as the diagram in Exhibit 23–2 shows. Later information is at least as good as earlier informa-

EXHIBIT 23–2

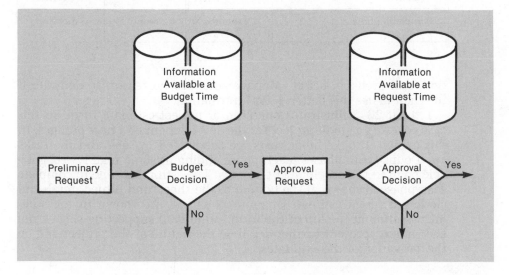

EXHIBIT 23–3

Research Project Estimate

RESEARCH DIVISION
PROJECT ESTIMATE SHEET

Project No.: 16321   Date: 10/15/x0
Project Title: Sandfly Attachment   Type: New Product
Project Supervisor: G. Hill

Completion Estimate 9 Months   Cost Estimate:
                                       Labor and Services $ 8,000
Estimated Annual Profit $30,000   Materials   7,200
                                       Equipment   4,800
                                       Total $20,000

Task	Phase 1, Specifications		Phase 2, Drawings		Phase 3, Prototype	
	Hours	Cost	Hours	Cost	Hours	Cost
Synthesis and analysis	150	$2,400				
Design specifications	25	400				
Breadboarding	50	700				
Layout	25	350				
Parts list			40	$ 400		
Schematics			75	750		
Test specifications			40	400		
Fabrication					150	$1,200
Assembly					50	300
Wiring					25	300
Test					50	800
Total Labor and Services	250	$3,850	155	$1,550	275	$2,600
Materials and purchased parts	$2,000		$ 500		$4,700	
Equipment	$3,000		—		$1,800	
Completion time	4 months		2 months		3 months	

tion, and probably better. Management has no reason to deny itself the right to use this better, later information.

Exhibit 23–3 illustrates one kind of project estimate form, in this case covering a small project for the development of a new product. In this exhibit, project labor costs are subdivided by task and the tasks are grouped into phases, each phase ending at some readily recognizable point in the development process. The estimated time to complete each phase is shown at the bottom of the sheet, and project totals, including a rough estimate of profit potential, are shown in the summary section at the top of the form. Additional supporting sheets, not shown here, present further detail on the nature of the project and on the derivation of the estimates.

DETAILED SCHEDULING

Timing is crucial to the success of research and development projects. Great emphasis is therefore placed on time scheduling and time control. In this section we shall look at four time scheduling devices:

1. Network diagrams.
2. Float diagrams.
3. Departmental resource commitment charts.
4. Uncertainty and the PERT diagram.

Network Diagrams

Every construction project, every research and development project, every consulting assignment can be described as a set of interdependent activities. These activities sometimes can be linked together in a single sequential chain, as in the following diagram for the design, testing, and preparation of production drawings for a new product (Exhibit 23–4).

Few projects are as linear as this. Some activities ordinarily can be performed simultaneously with others, so that the activity diagram takes form of Exhibit 23–5.

Interrelationships of this sort are usually represented in network diagrams. A network diagram is a chart showing the sequential relationships between the constituent tasks required to carry out a project or program, beginning with a single starting point and ending at a single completion point. We can illustrate the network by examining a situation even simpler than those in the two preceding diagrams. Exhibit 23–6 is a typical, though very simple, network. The rectangles represent *events* that occur at specific moments during the course of the project; the connecting lines stand for *activities*, the means of getting from one event to another. Several features of this diagram deserve comment:

1. The direction of progress toward completion of the project is indicated by the arrowheads on the activity lines.
2. The numbers in the event blanks are used to identify the events for computer programming.
3. The numbers on the arrows are the amounts of time required to complete individual activities. (For example, the arrow from

EXHIBIT 23–4

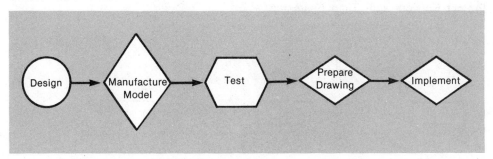

EXHIBIT 23–5

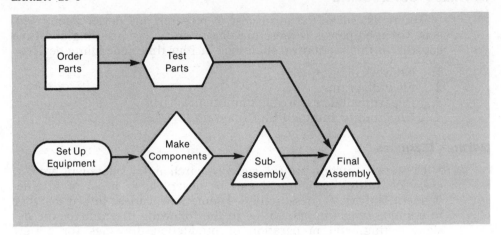

start to event 1 indicates that this activity is expected to take four weeks.)
4. The activities are not numbered, but it is convenient to identify them by the numbers of the events they link together. (For example, the activity linking events 2 and 3 can be referred to as activity 23.)

Some of the relationships in the network are concurrent; others are sequential. For example, two separate sets of activities must be completed independently in order to reach event 2—these are concurrent sets of activities. The activities linking events 0 and 1 and events 1 and 2, on the other hand, are sequential—the second one can't be started until the first one is completed.

Most networks for research and development projects are very large and require high-capacity electronic computers. The networking technique can be applied to simpler tasks without the use of computers, however, both inside and outside the research division.

Critical path. Once the network has been completed, management can estimate the amount of time it will take to complete the project.

EXHIBIT 23–6

Project Network with Time Estimates

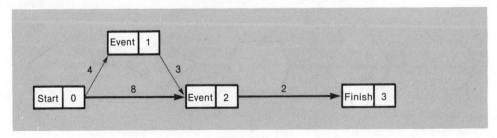

Each activity sequence is known as a *path*. The network in Exhibit 23–6 has two paths:

Path	Time Required
0–1–2–3	$4 + 3 + 2 = 9$
0–2–3	$8 + 2 \quad = 10$

The 0-2-3 path is the *critical path*, the sequence of activities requiring the longest total elapsed time from start to finish. The arrows on this path are heavier than the others.

Calculating slack time. The event blocks in the network diagram can be expanded to show how much slack time any one path contains. This is a two-step process:

Step 1. Enter the *earliest possible start time* for each activity in the lower left corner of the event block, starting at time zero and following the arrows to the right. For block 0, zero is the appropriate number; for block 2, the earliest start time is eight weeks (subpath 0-1-2 can be completed in seven weeks, but we can't get to block 2 until *all* of the first three activities have been completed—this means until after the eight weeks required by activity 02. Event blocks with this information appear as shown in Exhibit 23–7.

Step 2. In the lower right corner of each block enter the *latest possible start time* consistent with a scheduled completion date. These figures are calculated by counting backward from the final block. If ten weeks is the desired completion date, then activity 23 must be started no later than two weeks earlier—that is, eight weeks after the zero date. Event blocks with this information are shown in Exhibit 23–8.

Notice that the two numbers in the block for event 1 are not identical. The difference is known as *slack time*, or slack. Although activity 12 can be started as late as five weeks after the zero date, event 1 is expected to be reached a week earlier. Any path containing an activity that can be started earlier than the latest start date is known as a *slack path*. Slack gives management flexibility. Either activity 01 or activity 12 can be completed a week late without delaying the project's completion date.

EXHIBIT 23–7

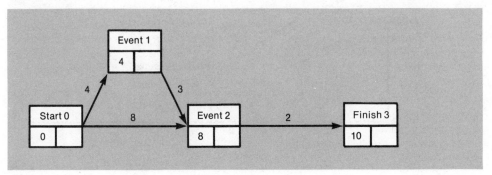

EXHIBIT 23–8

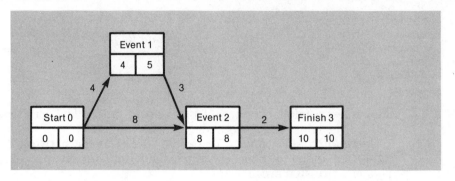

Cost slopes. If the critical path is too long to meet a desired completion date, it may be possible to devote more resources to one or more of the activities on the critical path and thus shorten the total time requirement. Shortening the time required for an activity on one of the slack paths, on the other hand, would not advance the completion date at all.

Management needs to decide whether to shorten the critical path and, if so, which activity or activities to accelerate. These decisions have two variables:

1. The penalty for late completion or premium for early completion of the project.
2. The cost of accelerating the project timetable.

The cost of acceleration depends on the activity management chooses to accelerate. The cost of saving one time unit by adding resources to speed up work on an activity is referred to as a cost slope. By the same token, the amount that would be saved by stretching an activity out is also a cost slope. Both of these are illustrated in Exhibit 23–9. If management shortens this activity by one week, total cost will go up from $5,000 to $6,000. The $1,000 increase is the slope of the total cost line as it moves upward to the left. By spreading the activity

EXHIBIT 23–9

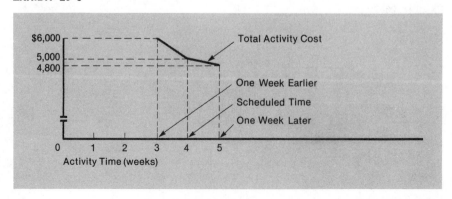

EXHIBIT 23–10

Project Network with Time and Cost Estimates

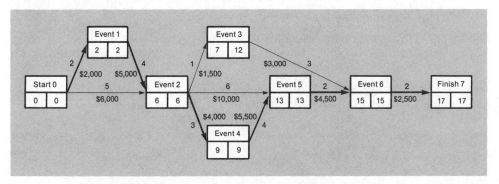

over five weeks instead of four, on the other hand, management could save $200. This is the slope of the cost curve in this segment.

To illustrate this idea more fully, we need a slightly more complex network than the one we have been using. The network in Exhibit 23–10 has ten activities instead of four, and three subpaths containing slack. The dollar figures on the activity arrows are the estimated costs of those activities. The critical path is 17 weeks long.

Suppose this is a development project being carried out for an outside customer. The customer insists that the project be completed in 16 weeks. Otherwise the contract will go to a competitor and the company will lose a $10,000 profit contribution. Management needs to cut a week off the scheduled time if this project is to be undertaken.

The one-week cost slopes for increasing or decreasing estimated time for all activities on the critical path are:

Activity	Cost Penalty to Decrease	Cost Saving If Increased
01	$2,000	$ 0
12	1,000	200
24	1,500	800
45	500	500
56	800	700
67	1,500	100

The cheapest way to gain a week's time is to speed up activity 45 at a penalty cost of $500. Every other activity has a greater penalty. Since the cost of losing the contract is $10,000, the $500 penalty is well worth absorbing.

We hasten to add that estimation of cost slopes is extremely difficult and may be prohibitively expensive. The cost of reducing activity time by one week depends partly on whether the department in which the work is done is already overloaded, and may depend on other factors as well. The number of possible combinations is enormous. The concept is sound, however, and should be applied when the alternatives are clear and few in number.

Dummy activities. All of the activities in Exhibit 23–3 were time consuming activities. Most network diagrams also include one or more activities that take no time at all. These are called dummy activities. They are inserted for either of two reasons:

1. Two events are linked by two or more parallel activities.
2. An activity can't be started until an activity on a different path has been completed.

A dummy activity introduced for the first of these reasons is illustrated in the following diagrams:

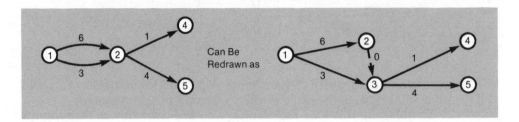

Activity 23 in the right-hand diagram is a dummy activity, and event 3 is a dummy event. (Dummy activities are represented by dashed lines between events.) The main reason for preferring the right-hand diagram is that the amount of time needed to reach event 3 is different from the amount of time needed to reach event 2. The two activities therefore have different latest starting times and different amounts of slack.

The second reason for inserting a dummy activity is illustrated in the following diagram:

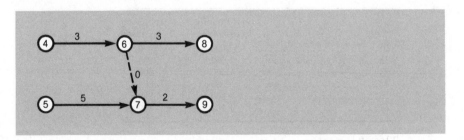

The dummy activity here shows that event 6 must be reached before activity 79 can be started. Events 6 and 7 can't be drawn as a single event, however, because activity 68 can be started even if activity 57 hasn't been completed.

Float Diagrams

Network diagrams like those in the two preceding exhibits make the interdependencies clearly visible and identify the critical path. They have two shortcomings, however: (1) by focusing on events rather than on activities, they don't show the latest possible starting time for the first activity on a slack path; and (2) they aren't keyed to a calendar—that is, they show times, not dates.

Both of these additional bits of information could be added to the network diagram, but we prefer to use a float diagram instead. A float diagram is simply a network in which activities are shown as horizontal bars, proportional to the expected elapsed time, and linkages between activities are shown as dated vertical lines.

The float diagram for our illustrative project is shown in Exhibit 23–11. This shows, for example, that activity 01 must be completed before activity 12, and both 02 and 12 must be completed before 23, 24, or 25 can be started. Activity 24 must be started at the end of week 6 if the project is to be completed at the end of the 17th week.

EXHIBIT 23–11

Float Diagram

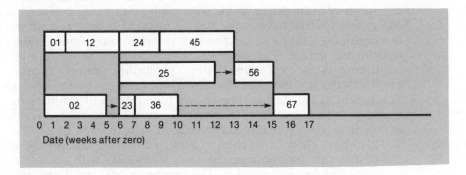

The horizontal dashed lines represent the amount of *float* in the noncritical paths. The amount of float for any activity is calculated from the following formula:

$$\text{Float} = (\text{Latest finish time} - \text{earliest start time}) - \text{activity time}$$

Activity 25, for example, must be finished by the end of thirteen weeks if activity 56 is to be started on schedule. It can be started as early as the end of 6 weeks, when activity 12 is scheduled for completion. Since the time required for activity 25 is 6 weeks, the total amount of float in this activity is one week:

$$\text{Float} = (13 - 6) - 6 = 1 \text{ week.}$$

The length of each of the dashed lines in Exhibit 23–4 identifies the amount of float for *each* of the activities in the bar segment in which it appears. For example, both activity 23 and activity 36 have a five-week float. Our convention is to show the float at the right of each segment, but it could just as well be drawn at the left or even between activities in the segment (between 23 and 36, for example). It shows how much flexibility management has in scheduling the activities in that segment.

Resource Commitment Tables and Charts

The horizontal scale on the float diagram can be keyed to the calendar. Instead of starting from a zero date, we can start from a specific calendar date. This must be done before the final schedule is presented for approval. The research division may have enough resources in the aggregate but not enough of certain key types or at certain peak times. To test this, we must take one additional step: compare resource requirements with the resources available.

Resource availability depends not only on the size of the research organization but also on the other projects in the system at the same time. Certain kinds of labor and occasionally even certain key materials become the scarce resources to be allocated among the projects. If too many projects hit their peak demand at the same time, something will have to give.

Management can use either resource commitment tables or resource commitment charts to identify bottlenecks of this sort. Tables are more convenient to work with and more readily placed on the computer. Charts have more visual impact, however, and we shall use one here. Exhibit 23–12 shows a resource commitment chart for a four-month period. The height of the solid bars shows the tentative requirements for professional time, excluding project A; project A's requirements are indicated by the white area at the top of each bar. The height of the dashed line shows the amount of professional time expected to be available each week. The number of hours over or short is represented by the diagonally shaded area in each bar.

This chart shows two things. First, research time will be slightly out of balance for most of the first 16 weeks, with some weeks of shortage and some of surplus. The shortages and surpluses just about cancel each other out. Second, because of the year-end holidays, pro-

EXHIBIT 23–12

Resource Commitment Chart: Professional Staff Hours

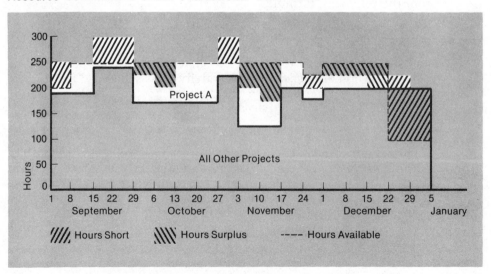

fessional time will be totally inadequate to meet the tentative project schedule for the final two weeks of the year, including the final week of project A.

The first of these can be handled in most cases by trying different schedule combinations to see which one will minimize the cost of schedule adjustments. By starting activity 02 a week late and spreading activities 01 and 12 over a slightly longer period, management could balance the resource requirements for the first four weeks. The cost saving from this stretch-out is $200, but one week on the critical path will be lost. Management can make that up by accelerating activity 45 during the first part of November, when professional time is in surplus. The estimated cost penalty for a one-week speedup in this activity is $500. The net effect of this shift is $300. The question is whether this is a smaller penalty than the penalties from adjustments in other projects.

The second problem is more difficult. No amount of rescheduling within the 18-week period will eliminate the end-of-year time shortage. Management has four alternatives:

1. Add overtime during the first 16 weeks.
2. Add someone to the professional staff.
3. Stretch one of the projects into the next year and accept the penalty for late completion.
4. Discontinue one of the projects.

The resource commitment chart won't help management make this choice, but it does make the need for a choice apparent.

Uncertainty and PERT Time Estimates

All the estimates we have used so far have been single valued—that is, we have assumed that time and cost can be predicted with absolute certainty. Unfortunately, project time and cost estimates are likely to be very uncertain. Management makes firm commitments based on single-valued estimates at its peril.

For example, suppose management is considering a simple, two-phase research project which it expects to complete in 11 months. The time estimates (in months) are:

	Minimum	Most Likely	Maximum
Stage 1	6	8	12
Stage 2	2	3	5
Total	8	11	17

If management's estimates are correct, the program could be completed as early as 8 months or not until 17 months.

Decision trees of the kind we introduced in Chapter 17 can be very useful in displaying the uncertainties inherent in individual research and development projects. For projects with many activities, however, they quickly become unwieldy and confusing. The only feasible approach is to place the entire analysis on a computer. The distribution of possible outcomes then can be approximated by running the computer program many times, using a different combination of estimates each time. This is the simulation technique we referred to in Chapter 17.

The most widely known network technique recognizing uncertainty is PERT (program evaluation and review technique). PERT networks are identical to those we illustrated earlier, with one important exception—four time estimates are provided for each activity instead of one:

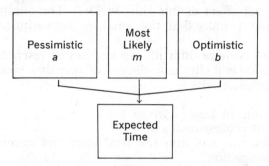

Expected time in PERT networks isn't based on explicit probability estimates. Instead, it is calculated from the following formula:

$$\text{Expected activity time} = t_e = (a + 4m + b)/6$$

For example, the expected time estimate for stage 1 of the two-stage project we mentioned earlier would be calculated as follows:

	Estimated Time	Weight	Weighted Time
Optimistic	6	$\frac{1}{6}$	1
Most likely	8	$\frac{4}{6}$	$5\frac{1}{3}$
Pessimistic	12	$\frac{1}{6}$	2
Expected time			$8\frac{1}{3}$

This is slightly longer than the most likely time (8 months) because the pessimistic estimate (12 months) is farther from the most likely time than the optimistic estimate (6 months).

These expected time estimates are used in just the same way as single time estimates—to identify the critical path and calculate such figures as earliest possible start time, latest possible start time, slack and float. They also allow management to estimate the probability of meeting a target date.

This isn't the place to examine PERT in any detail or to evaluate its limitations. We bring it up mainly as a warning against taking simple network time estimates too literally. The probability of completing a project in the time indicated by these estimates is generally far less than the probability that it will be completed either sooner or later. If precise timing is crucial, management will need to do much more than prepare a single set of time estimates and resource schedules.

PROGRESS REVIEW

The third stage in the control of research and development projects and other unique programmed activities is feedback reporting. Whereas feedback reporting in the factory is most likely to be department oriented, the focus in the research and development organization is on the individual project, for two reasons:

1. The projects are relatively few in number and each one accounts for a substantial share of total activity (the typical job order factory has many jobs, few of them accounting for a major fraction of total activity).
2. First-level control responsibility is assigned to the project manager (no one person has responsibility for a particular job order in the typical factory).

We shall concentrate in this final section on project-oriented progress reporting, leaving department reporting for a few final comments at the end.

Project Reporting

Project costs can be compared with either or both of two benchmarks:

1. The initial project budget.
2. A progress-adjusted budget.

Comparisons with initial budget estimates. One kind of project cost report compares project costs with the amounts originally budgeted for the time period covered by the report. Exhibit 23–13 is a simple example of this type of report. This shows that spending on project No. 16321 in April was $1,540 greater than the amount budgeted and was more than double the budget estimate for the month. On a cumulative basis, actual spending exceeded the budget by $1,480, almost a third of the budgeted amount.

Reports of this kind identify projects on which rates of expenditure are out of line with preestablished schedules, but they ignore one vital element—progress. Project costs have no meaning except in comparison with the progress achieved toward project objectives. Thus Exhibit 23–13 would seem to indicate that project 16321 is running far in excess of its budget, but it may be that resources were available much sooner than had been anticipated and that more progress had been made than had been scheduled originally.

EXHIBIT 23–13

Project Spending Report

RESEARCH DIVISION
MONTHLY PROJECT SPENDING REPORT

Project No.: 16321   Month: April
Project Title: Sandfly Attachment   Supervisor: G. Hill

Start Date: 3/6/x1
Scheduled Completion: 11/30/x1

	This Month			To Date		
	Actual	Budget	Variance	Actual	Budget	Variance
Salaries, professional	$ 800	$ 550	$ (250)	$1,550	$1,000	$ (550)
Salaries, technical	300	220	(80)	900	450	(450)
Laboratory services	15	—	(15)	15	—	(15)
Drafting supplies	25	30	5	95	100	5
Outside services	—	—	—	20	—	(20)
Purchased parts	350	—	(350)	350	—	(350)
Equipment	1,350	500	(850)	3,100	3,000	(100)
Total	$2,840	$1,300	$(1,540)	$6,030	$4,550	$(1,480)

Progress oriented reporting. The cost control comparisons in factory cost reporting contrast two sets of quantities:

	Direct Labor and Materials	Factory Overhead
Actual resources used	Actual Quantities × Standard Prices	Actual Quantities × Actual or Standard Prices
	−	−
Standard resource consumption for the amount of work actually done	Actual Output × (Standard Input Quantities × Standard Prices)	Flexible Budget Allowances for Actual Volume
	=	=
Variances	Quantity Variances	Spending Variances

The existence of activity-based cost and time estimates lets us make this same kind of comparison for research and development projects. Two comparisons are useful:

1. Actual progress versus planned progress.
2. Actual cost versus planned cost for the progress actually achieved.

Comparisons of the first kind tell management whether a project is on schedule, whether one or more slack path activities have been delayed or have run so far over the time estimates that they are now on the critical path, and so on. Comparisons of the second kind indicate whether schedules have been maintained within the anticipated cost limits.

A report in this form for project No. 16321 is presented in Exhibit 23–14. This shows all the activities in phase 1 of this project, but includes budget estimates only for the two activities on which resources were expended during March and April. The first activity, synthesis and analysis, was completed during April. The entire budget allowance for this activity, therefore, appears in the first line of the cumulative budget column at the right. The second activity, preparation of design specifications, wasn't originally scheduled to begin until May, but early completion of the synthesis and analysis stage allowed the design staff to begin work on this activity in April. Some 20 percent of the design work was done in April, and the budget for this portion of the design budget entered in the second line of the report.

As this report shows, total project costs in April were $240 less than the budget provided for. This offset unfavorable variances in March, leaving a cumulative overrun of only $50 for the two months as a whole.

Future-oriented reports. The report in Exhibit 23–14 lists a revised expected completion date, but it says little else about what the future is likely to hold in store for this project. The diagram in Exhibit 23–15 provides this additional information in pictorial form. It directs attention to four aspects of project performance:

1. Cost overrun or underrun to date: total spending minus budgeted spending for the work performed.
2. Expenditure lag or overexpenditure to date: total spending minus budgeted spending.
3. Schedule gain or slippage: expected completion date minus originally scheduled date.
4. Anticipated cost overrun or underrun: expected project cost minus budgeted project cost.

The third and fourth of these aspects focus on the future rather than on the past. Both costs and completion dates are reestimated and compared with the original estimates. In this way the chart can serve as a form of steering control.

Charts like the one in Exhibit 23–15 can be constructed for project segments as well as for the project as a whole, as long as the chart of accounts is subdivided to permit recording of actual costs by segments. In the typical case, the clerical cost of recording project costs

EXHIBIT 23–14

Progress-Adjusted Cost Comparison Report

RESEARCH DIVISION
MONTHLY PROJECT COST REPORT

Project No.: 16321   Month: April
Project Title: Sandfly Attachment   Supervisor: G. Hill

Start Date: 3/6/x1   Scheduled Completion: 11/30/x1
Current Status: Phase 1   Estimated Completion: 10/31/x1

| Activity | Percent Complete | This Month | | | To Date | | |
		Budgeted for Work Done	Actual Cost	(Over-) Under-run	Budgeted for Work Done	Actual Cost	(Over-) Under-run
Synthesis and analysis	100	$1,200	$1,050	$ 150	$2,400	$2,490	$(90)
Design specifications	20	80	90	(10)	80	90	(10)
Breadboarding		not yet started					
Layout		not yet started					
Total labor and services		$1,280	$1,140	$ 140	$2,480	$2,580	$(100)
Materials and purchased parts		500	350	150	500	350	150
Equipment		1,300	1,350	(50)	3,000	3,100	(100)
Total		$3,080	$2,840	$ 240	$5,980	$6,030	$(50)

by individual activities is prohibitive, and so larger groups of activities known as *work packages* are treated as costing units for this purpose.

Using the progress report. The periodic progress reports serve to alert management to actual and anticipated departures from plans so that appropriate adjustments can be made. They can also signal the need to consider discontinuing the project or changing its scope or direction. Reaching a key point in the project network, sometimes referred to as a *milestone,* is one occasion for reviewing a project's rationale; a serious overrun or schedule slippage is another. A large schedule slippage or cost overrun is not necessarily fatal, but it can't be ignored.

The question, of course, is not whether the project has overrun its budget or is behind schedule. The question is how much more money will have to be spent and what is the expected value of the payoff. Both of these factors reflect the future, not the past, and the future appears to be changing constantly. For this reason every project should be reviewed periodically even if the progress reports indicate it is progressing satisfactorily.

EXHIBIT 23–15

Integrated Project Progress Chart

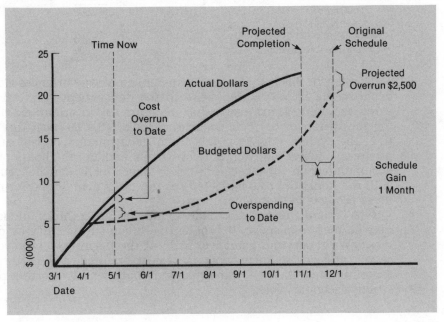

Departmental Performance Review

Departmental cost reports emphasizing differences between departmental budget allowances and total costs are of little value in the control of research and development costs. Most costs are either salaries or are closely related to salaries. Total expenditures for these inputs are controlled by decisions to hire and retain personnel; these, in turn, are the outcome of project approvals. Once the budget is approved, expenditures are likely to conform very closely to the amount budgeted, with few variances of any importance.

Departmental cost reporting can be made more meaningful if it can be integrated with the project performance reports. One approach is to assign to each department the costs and progress of the projects headed by project managers in that department. (Each project is typically the direct responsibility of a project manager.) Progress made by each department is measured by the estimated costs of the work done on its projects' activities during that period. Costs include the department's own costs plus the costs of work done in other departments on the department's projects. The department is credited for the costs of the work it does on other departments' projects. A departmental performance report prepared on this basis would contain the following elements:

Budgeted cost of work done on projects
    headed by departmental personnel............ $14,000
Transfers to other departments.................   1,500
        Total credits.............................. $15,500
Departmental costs........................... $9,900
Transfers from other departments..............   4,800   14,700
        Departmental variance..................... $ 800

The flaw in this is that it may transfer some cost variances from the departments in which they arise to the departments for which the work was done. Management has no summary information, classifying the variances by their department of origin. To meet this objection, the system might provide for a departmental classification of progress achieved on each project. If this is done, the hours or costs accumulated on all projects in each department can be compared with the hours or costs budgeted for the tasks actually performed on those projects in that department.

This second alternative is likely to provide better information, but it may be more expensive, if progress is difficult to identify by department. We repeat the point we made at the beginning, however. Research and development work is project oriented, and performance reporting must have the same focus. Departmental reporting plays a strictly secondary role.

SUMMARY

Research and development activities are project centered, programmed activities. Control is a three-stage process—initial approval, detailed scheduling, and progress review, including implicit or explicit project reapproval.

Research budgets are often set in the aggregate, on the basis of an overall rule of thumb. Budgets set in this way can neglect opportunities or waste funds on low-yield projects. A preferable approach is to regard research and development proposals as a particular kind of capital expenditure proposals with highly uncertain costs and benefits.

The main devices for detailed scheduling are network diagrams and float diagrams, showing the relationships among the various phases of individual projects. These can be used to identify the critical path and the amount of slack or float in the noncritical paths. Adjustments can be made in the critical path to fit the project into a desired time limit. Departmental resource commitment charts can then be used to adapt the overall schedule to the quantities of resources available. A computer is usually necessary to handle networking and scheduling problems of any magnitude, however.

The project networks or activity lists can be used to organize the data for control reporting. Performance reports need to match costs with the amount of progress actually achieved, not the amounts originally budgeted for the calendar period. These reports should be project centered and should include revised estimates of future costs and progress. Serious overruns or schedule slippages on certain projects may even signal difficulties that make it unlikely that further expenditures will have big enough payoffs to justify keeping these projects alive. There is no need to wait for the next budget review date to decide to drop an unpromising project.

KEY TERMS

The most important terms introduced and defined in this chapter are the following:

Cost slope	Overspending/underspending
Critical path	PERT
Earliest start time	Project activities
Float diagram	Project events
Latest start time	Resource commitment chart
Network	Schedule slippage/schedule gain
Overrun/underrun	Slack

INDEPENDENT STUDY PROBLEMS (Solutions in Appendix C)

1. Project planning. The market research manager is preparing to submit a market survey proposal to the marketing vice president. The project will cost $105,000. In the following table of time estimates, each activity is identified by a two-digit number, the first digit denoting the preceding event and the second digit indicating the event that signals the end of the activity:

Activity	Estimated Time (Weeks)
01	1
02	3
03	5
14	2
25	4
35	3
46	6
56	2
57	1
69	4
78	2
89	2

a. Draw a network and trace the critical path.
b. Draw a float diagram.
c. The marketing vice president agrees to the time schedule embodied in the project network, but is not sure the project is worth undertaking. What quantitative estimates would you try to submit to throw light on this decision?

2. Performance report. The management services division of a large public accounting firm would like to be able to offer its clients a new service. A team chosen from the consulting staff has been trying to develop the capability to provide this service. The following network was drawn up when this development project was approved (the numbers on the arrows are estimates of time required, in weeks):

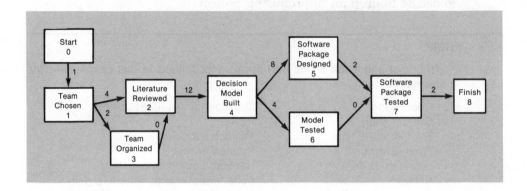

The estimated cost of the project was $200,000, and time and funds for the first eight weeks were budgeted as follows:

Week	Activity	Cost	Milestone to Be Reached
1....................	01	$ 5,000	Team selected.
2....................	{12	6,000	—
	{13	1,000	
3....................	{12	4,000	
	{13	1,000	Team organized.
4....................	12	5,000	—
5....................	12	5,000	Literature summary distributed.
6....................	24	8,000	—
7....................	24	10,000	Preliminary model conference.
8....................	24	7,000	Model type selected.

The total budgeted cost of activity 24 (model construction) was $70,000.

The literature search was completed and the literature summary was distributed at the end of the fourth week. The total cost to that point was $22,000. At that time the project header saw no reason to revise the estimates of the time and costs of the remaining activities.

Work on the construction of the model was begun immediately. It is now the end of the eighth week, and you have the following information:

1. Cost incurred to date: $51,000.
2. Milestone reached, end of eighth week: preliminary model conference.
3. Estimated additional time to complete construction of model: 12 weeks.
4. Estimated future costs to complete construction of model: $65,000.
5. No changes have been made in estimates of time or costs for activities scheduled to take place after the model has been built.

a. Prepare a project performance report covering the first eight weeks.
b. What questions should management ask in reviewing this report? What actions might be taken?

EXERCISES AND PROBLEMS

1. Network diagram: Multiple choice. A construction company has contracted to erect a new building and has asked for assistance in analyzing the project. Using the program evaluation review technique (PERT), the following network has been developed:

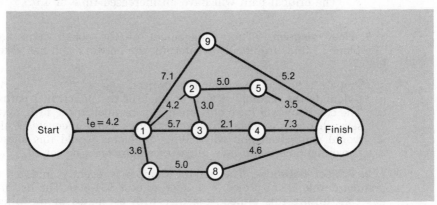

All paths from the start point to the finish point, event 6, represent activities or processes that must be completed before the entire project, the building, will be completed. The numbers above the paths or line segments represent expected completion times for the activities or processes. The expected time is based upon the commonly used, 1–4–1, three-estimate method. For example, the three-estimate method gives an estimated time of 4.2 weeks to complete event 1.

1. The critical path is:
   a. 1–2–5–6.
   b. 1–2–3–4–6.
   c. 1–3–4–6.
   d. 1–7–8–6.
   e. 1–9–6.
2. Slack time on path 1–9–6 equals
   a. 4.3.
   b. 2.8.
   c. 0.9.
   d. 0.4.
   e. 0.
3. The latest time for reaching event 6 via path 1–2–5–6 is
   a. 20.8.
   b. 19.3.
   c. 17.4.
   d. 16.5.
   e. 12.7.
4. The earliest time for reaching event 6 via path 1–2–5–6 is
   a. 20.8.
   b. 16.9.
   c. 16.5.
   d. 12.7.
   e. 3.5.

5. If all other paths are operating on schedule but path segment 7–8 has an unfavorable time variance of 1.9,
   a. The critical path will be shortened.
   b. The critical path will be eliminated.
   c. The critical path will be unaffected.
   d. Another path will become the critical path.
   e. The critical path will have an increased time of 1.9.

(CPA)

2. Float diagram. The management of the construction company (Problem 1) finds it difficult to interpret the network and has asked your help.

a. Prepare a float diagram for this project.
b. Calculate the amount of float on each of the noncritical paths.
c. The company will have only enough personnel in the fifth, sixth, and seventh weeks to engage in two activities simultaneously. Which two would you select, and why? What problems would this shortage of personnel create and how might these problems be solved?

3. Project network. The Villard Company recently initiated a new product development project estimated to cost $31,500. The list of activities constituting this project, together with estimates of the number of weeks each activity would take and the cost to carry it out, is shown in the table below. In this table each activity is identified by a two-digit number, the first digit denoting the preceding event and the second digit indicating the event that signals the end of the activity:

Activity	Estimated Time (weeks)	Estimated Cost
01	2	$ 1,100
12	1	500
23	3	2,500
24	7	3,500
25	2	2,200
34	3	3,300
35	1	400
45	5	4,000
49	3	1,600
56	2	900
67	1	1,200
68	6	4,200
78	2	700
79	4	4,100
89	3	1,300
Total		$31,500

a. Draw a network to represent this project.
b. List the events the critical path passes through and indicate the number of weeks the project was expected to take.

4. Performance reporting. Eight weeks after the Villard Company started its product development project (Problem 3), activities 01, 12, 24, and 25 had been completed and activity 23 was approximately half finished. It was estimated that an additional two weeks and $1,500 would be necessary to finish activity 23. No other estimates had to be revised. As originally approved, the schedule called for completion of activities 01, 12, 23, and 25 in the first eight weeks, with activity 24 to be five-sevenths finished and activity 34 to be two-thirds finished. Costs incurred during the first eight weeks were:

Activity	Amount
01	$1,150
12	250
23	2,400
24	3,000
25	2,500
Total	$9,300

a. Prepare a report summarizing the performance and status of this project at the end of the first eight weeks.

b. What additional information would you find particularly useful at this point?

5. Project network; Cost slopes. Cheerful Calorie Contributors, Inc. operates a chain of ice cream stores. The company has expanded steadily for several years, opening a new store every month, on the average. As a result of this experience, management has been able to develop a fairly precise standard operating procedure for opening a new store. The chief operating officer has drawn up the following description of this procedure:

The first step in opening a store is finding a desirable location in the general area we wish to enter. This generally takes about four days. As soon as we find our location, our engineering department begins drawing plans for the store, including layouts for furniture and for built-in freezers. Plan preparation takes six days.

During this time our real estate department is negotiating rental terms. Since we pay premium rates and obtain virtually every location that we choose, we do not delay the drawing up of the plans for the two days that these negotiations consume.

After terms are negotiated, the lease must be drawn up by our legal department and approved by outside counsel. This process takes six days. We do not actually start installing furniture or freezers until the lease is approved.

When the engineering department completes its plans, they are submitted to the city for approval. This takes seven days. Neither the furniture nor the freezers can be installed before plans are approved by the city.

Furniture can be ordered as soon as plans are completed, since if the city rejects the location, the furniture can be used elsewhere. It takes eight days for furniture to be ordered and delivered. (The ordering process takes one day and delivery is made seven days later.) Installation in the store requires four days.

No ordering time is involved in the case of freezers, since CCC keeps a supply on hand, but building them in and installing and testing the necessary electrical and plumbing facilities takes nine days.

Once the plans have been drawn, the personnel department can identify a manager and hire a staff, a process requiring five days. Then the manager and staff must be trained for six days at CCC's large modern training facility. Once trained, they can begin planning the operation of the store and order the necessary inventory of ice cream and supplies. This process takes four days. The order for the initial inventory can't be placed before the end of the second day; the remaining two days are devoted to drawing up work schedules, arranging for trash collection, and so forth. The staff aren't prepared to take delivery of the inventory until the end of the fourth day of operations planning or the beginning of the day after the last of the freezers and furniture have been installed, whichever comes later. The order for the inventory must be placed at least two days before the desired delivery date. If the facilities aren't ready to receive the inventory at the end of this two-day period, the suppliers will store it on their premises until the CCC premises are ready. It takes one full day to shelve the inventory once it has been delivered.

After freezers, furniture, and inventory are all in place a final pre-opening cleanup is required. This takes two days.

This is the normal procedure, but the company has found it can reduce the time to complete some of these activities by spending more money on them. The following actions are the only possibilities:

Additions	Time Saving
$200................................	One day in installing freezers
$100 (in addition to the $200 above).....	A second day in installing freezers
$150................................	One day in hiring staff
$ 50................................	One day in installing furniture
$120................................	One day in training staff
$175................................	One day in drawing plans
$210 (in addition to the $175 above).....	A second day in drawing plans
$300................................	One day in preopening cleanup

a. Construct a network describing the process, enter the time requirements under the normal procedure, and identify the critical path.

b. How long does the entire process normally take?

c. Which of the time saving options would you recommend if the company wants to reduce total project time by one day? By two days? By three days? Show your calculations.

d. Management is in a great hurry to open its next store. What is the shortest possible time in which the project can be completed? What is the incremental cost of shortening the timetable in this way?

(Adapted from a problem written by Professor John C. Burton)

6. Project network; Supplying missing data. Sangemi, Inc. manufactures industrial parts. It has a sizeable methods engineering department, responsible for finding ways to increase operating efficiency.

One of the company's manufacturing processes suddenly became very unreliable and management halted production. The chief methods engineer has proposed solving this problem by beginning work immediately on the project described in the following network:

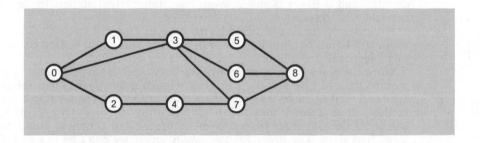

a. Supply the data necessary to fill in the blanks marked by dashes in the accompanying table:

t_o, t_m, t_p = Optimistic, most likely, pessimistic PERT time.
$\qquad t_e$ = PERT expected time.
$\quad$ EST = Earliest start time.
$\quad$ LST = Latest start time.
$\quad$ LFT = Latest finish time.

Activity	t_o	t_m	t_p	t_e	LFT	EST	LST	Slack
—	6	8	10	8.0	14.5	0	6.5	6.5
02	3	3	6	3.5	3.5	0	—	—
03	4	5	—	—	15.5	0	10.0	10.0
13	1	1	1	1.0	—	8.0	—	6.5
24	—	6	11	6.5	10.0	3.5	3.5	—
35	5	6	10	6.5	22.0	9.0	—	6.5
36	2	—	4	3.0	24.0	9.0	21.0	12.0
37	0	0	0	0.0	19.5	9.0	19.5	—
47	7	9	14	9.5	19.5	10.0	10.0	0.0
58	4	4	7	—	26.5	15.5	22.0	6.5
68	1	2	6	2.5	—	12.0	24.0	12.0
78	4	7	10	7.0	26.5	—	19.5	0.0

b. Identify the critical path. What is the project's scheduled completion date?

c. Suppose the required completion date is two time periods earlier than the figure you derived in (b). Which column(s) would be affected by this change?

7. Project performance report; Follow-up decisions. Broadway Contractors, Inc., has a contract to remodel one of the university laboratories. The contract price is $160,000, based on an estimated cost of $130,000. The contract calls for completion of the job in 12 weeks, with a penalty of $10,000 for each week of delay beyond that period. The original network for this project was as follows:

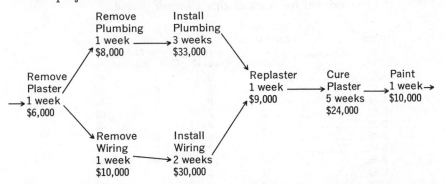

Removal of the old plumbing and removal of the old wiring were scheduled to take place simultaneously, to be followed immediately by the installation of the new plumbing and the new wiring. The job was started on the scheduled date and the following work was done during the first three weeks:

Activity	Cost
Remove plaster...........................	$ 6,200
Remove plumbing.......................	16,000
Remove wiring...........................	9,200
Install wiring (half completed).......................	15,000

Management now estimates that installation of the new plumbing will take four weeks and will cost $40,000. All other cost and time estimates are unchanged.

The project can be speeded up, but only at a cost. The estimated costs of such a speed-up are:

	Additional Expenditures That Would Have to Be Made to Save	
	One Week	Two Weeks
Install plumbing..................	$ 8,000	$19,000
Cure plaster.....................	10,500	22,000

a. Prepare a summary report that will show management the past performance and present status of this contract.
b. Should the company spend additional money to speed up one or more activities? If so, which one(s) and by how much? State your reasons.

8. Resource commitment table. The manager of the methods department of Acme Gear Company is scheduled to begin a new project (project C) next week. It has two projects (A and B) already under way and a straight-time capacity of 200 labor hours a week. Up to 20 hours of overtime are available each week, at a premium of $6 an hour.

When completed, project A is expected to save the company $200 a week in labor costs, project B is expected to save $300 a week, and project C is expected to save $400 a week.

Each activity in one of these projects is assigned a two-digit number. The first digit designates the event immediately preceding this activity; the second digit identifies the following event. The final event in each project is event 9. Only project A is to be completed during the next 13 weeks.

You have the following data about the activities in these three projects to be scheduled for work in this 13-week period.

Project and Activity	Scheduled Start Date, Beginning of Week	Slack (weeks)	Weeks to Complete	Hours Required per Week
A-67..................	1	0	4	40
A-69..................	1	5	5	20
A-78..................	5	0	3	30
A-89..................	8	0	3	60
B-36..................	1	4	7	40
B-45..................	1	0	6	20
B-46..................	1	8	3	60
B-56..................	7	0	5	40
B-67..................	12	0	4	80
C-01..................	1	0	2	80
C-12..................	3	0	3	40
C-13..................	3	3	5	20
C-14..................	3	7	2	40
C-24..................	6	2	4	30
C-25..................	6	0	8	60
C-36..................	8	3	3	40

Work on any activity can be interrupted for a week or more without affecting the total number of hours required for that activity. If an activity has to be scheduled in any week for less than the number of hours normally required for that activity, the lost time must be rescheduled during a week in which that activity is not already scheduled—in no week can any activity be scheduled for more than the number of hours listed in the table.

a. Prepare diagrams showing the portions of the networks for these three projects represented by the activities listed in the table. Indicate which activities are on the critical path in each case.
b. Prepare a resource commitment table for the next 13 weeks.
c. Recommend a set of adjustments that will make it feasible to undertake all three projects. Indicate the criteria you used in making these adjustments.

9. Departmental performance report. The Argus Company's research division has approximately 80 employees, organized as shown in the accompanying table:

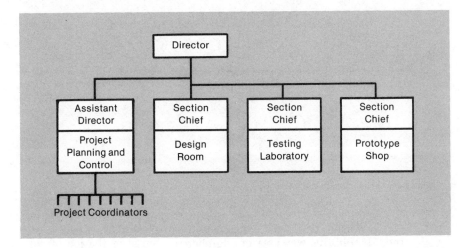

Research proposals are prepared initially in the project planning and control section (PPC). Once a project is approved, an engineer on the PPC staff is assigned to direct that project, evaluate progress, and attempt to keep it on schedule. Line authority over the research staff is vested in the three section chiefs, however.

The project coordinators receive cost and progress reports on their projects every month. In addition, each section chief receives a summary report on cost performance in that section. This is a two-page report, with an overall departmental summary on the first page and an element-by-element comparison on the second. The first-page summary for the testing laboratory for last October showed the following information:

	Budget	Actual	Variance
Project 246..............	$ 4,700	$ 4,650	$ 50
Project 289..............	1,300	3,300	(2,000)
Project 294..............	5,200	3,530	1,670
Total.............	$11,200	$11,480	$ (280)

a. What useful information, if any, would this report give to the section chief in charge of the testing laboratory?
b. What changes would you make in this report to make it more useful to management?

CASE 23–1: SPACE CONSTRUCTORS, INC. (B)*
(Project reporting)

After restudying other elements of the overall construction program, Mr. Alison and Mr. Phillips decided that a ten-week schedule for the construction of the remote control building would be acceptable. They were able to draw the critical path diagram shown in Exhibit 1.

EXHIBIT 1

SPACE CONSTRUCTORS, INC.
Revised Critical Path Diagram for Remote Control Building Project

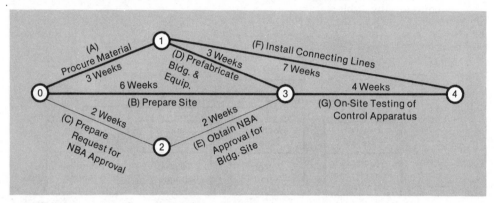

Note: Heavy lines indicate critical paths.

Mr. Alison was field construction supervisor for Space Constructors, Inc. Mr. Phillips was project engineer in charge of the job of constructing a remote control building. This project was an integral part of the work covered by a large construction contract that had been awarded to Space Constructors some months earlier.

Using this information, Mr. Alison and Mr. Phillips agreed on the cost and production schedule summarized in Table 1. "I think that we can meet the ten-week deadline with this schedule," Mr. Phillips said, "but we'll have to watch our progress very closely as we go along. We'll take our first reading at the end of three weeks and see where we stand. If we have to make adjustments, we can make them then."

"I guess that's soon enough," Mr. Alison replied, "but we can't lose sight of the costs on this project. We've gone way over our estimates on those underground installations, and we have to be particularly careful to keep our costs under control on the remaining parts of the contract."

On Monday, October 1, work began on activities A, B, and C. All personnel were scheduled to work a regular five-day week during each of the first three weeks, with no overtime.

At the end of the third week, Mr. Phillips asked each of his project supervisors to report the amount of progress they had made on the ac-

* This case was prepared as a follow-up to "Space Constructors, Inc.," Case No. EA-P380 (copyright 1965 by the President and Fellows of Harvard College). Copyright by l'Institut pour l'Étude des Méthodes de Direction de l'Entreprise (IMEDE), Lausanne, Switzerland. Reproduced by permission.

TABLE 1

SPACE CONSTRUCTORS, INC.
Construction Schedule for Remote Control Building Project

Activity	1	2	3	4	5	6	7	8	9	10	Total
				Cost to Be Incurred During Week							
A.........	$1,667	$1,667	$1,666	—	—	—	—	—	—	—	$ 5,000
B.........	2,333	2,333	2,334	$ 2,334	$ 2,333	$2,333	—	—	—	—	14,000
C.........	1,250	1,250	—	—	—	—	—	—	—	—	2,500
D*........	—	—	—	6,000	6,000	6,000	—	—	—	—	18,000
E.........	—	—	—	4,000	4,000	—	—	—	—	—	8,000
F.........	—	—	—	1,643	1,643	1,643	$1,643	$1,643	$1,643	$1,642	11,500
G.........	—	—	—	—	—	—	2,500	2,500	2,500	2,500	10,000
Total......	$5,250	$5,250	$4,000	$13,977	$13,976	$9,976	$4,143	$4,143	$4,143	$4,142	$69,000

*Crash schedule, providing for maximum permissible amount of overtime work.

tivities under their supervision. The following information reached Mr. Phillips's desk late Monday afternoon, October 22:

Activity	Date Started	Completed as of Oct. 19	Weeks Needed to Complete
A....................	10–1	100%	—
B....................	10–1	33	4
C....................	10–1	100	—
D....................	10–18	10	3

Activity starts and completions were reported routinely to Mr. Phillips, so he already knew that activity A had been completed three days ahead of schedule and that as a result the project supervisor had been able to start activity D two days ahead of schedule. Because of this head start, the amount of overtime work scheduled for activity D had been reduced. No overtime work was performed on any activity during the first three weeks.

Activity F, on the other hand, had not been started early. The necessary personnel had been fully assigned to other projects and the project supervisor had not been able to get them rescheduled. They had reported for work on the remote control building site on Monday, October 22, however, and Mr. Phillips saw no reason why activity F should not be completed on time.

Mr. Phillips also received two reports from his cost accountant. The first of these was the regular weekly cost report for the project, shown in Table 2. The second was a revised set of cost estimates, prepared during the early afternoon by the cost accountant in cooperation with the project supervisors. Expected future costs per week for each activity were:

B.................	$2,500
D.................	5,500
E.................	unchanged
F.................	unchanged
G.................	unchanged

a. · A program of the kind illustrated in Exhibit 1 cannot be implemented unless enough resources of the required kinds can be made available at the dates indicated. How would you use the data summarized in Table 1 to test the feasibility of the proposed construction schedule?

b. Why did Mr. Phillips want a performance report at the end of three weeks? What kinds of decisions did he have to make at that time?

TABLE 2

SPACE CONSTRUCTORS, INC.
Weekly Cost Report for Remote Control Building Project
(week of October 15–19)

	This Week			Cumulative		
Activity	Budgeted Costs*	Actual Costs	(Over) Under	Budgeted Costs*	Actual Costs	(Over) Under
A.............	$1,666	$ 500	$ 1,166	$ 5,000	$ 4,900	$ 100
B.............	2,334	2,300	34	7,000	6,800	200
C.............	....	350	(350)	2,500	2,350	150
D.............	....	1,500	(1,500)	....	1,500	(1,500)
Total...........	$4,000	$4,650	$ (650)	$14,500	$15,550	$(1,050)

* From Table 1.

c. In the light of your answer to question (b), what was wrong with the weekly cost report (Table 2)?

d. Prepare a report or reports that would have told Mr. Phillips what he needed to know about his performance during the first three weeks of the remote control building project.

e. What should Mr. Phillips have done on the basis of the information provided by your report?

24

Divisional Profit Reporting

PROFIT is the main private objective of business firms. Management therefore is held accountable for the amount of profit it is able to generate. This suggests that internal profit reporting for divisions or other segments of the business is likely to be an important feature, perhaps the most important single feature, of any system of financial reporting to management.

We discussed profit contribution reporting to marketing management in Chapter 9. Now it is time to see how profits can be reported to top management. In this chapter we shall examine four related topics:

1. The organizational setting in which divisional profit reporting to management takes place.
2. The purposes internal profit reporting is intended to serve, and the appropriate performance standard for each of these purposes.
3. The form the divisional profit measure should take.
4. Significant measurement problems the accountant will encounter.

THE ORGANIZATIONAL SETTING

Profit performance reports can be issued for any segment of the company's business. A business segment is any portion of the company's business for which both revenues and expenses can be identified. Our attention in this chapter will focus on reports covering business segments that are the particular responsibility of a single manager or group of managers below the chief executive officer level. The organization units responsible for these business segments may be called divisions, or groups, or subsidiary companies, or departments. We shall call them all divisions.

Organizations in which the managers reporting to the chief executive officer are responsible for generating profits in specific business segments are generally referred to as *decentralized* companies. Their major operating divisions are known as profit centers or investment centers. These profit centers or investment centers may be further subdivided into smaller profit centers or investment centers. In this section we shall study five questions:

1. What is a profit center?
2. What is an investment center?
3. Why do companies decentralize?
4. How does a profit center differ from an administered center?
5. What role do service centers play in a decentralized organization?

Profit Centers

The profit center is intended to be very much like an independent business firm. It has four main characteristics:

1. It has a profit objective.
2. Its management has authority to make decisions affecting the major determinants of profit, including the power to choose its markets and sources of supply.
3. Its management is expected to use profit-based decision rules.
4. Its management is accountable to higher management for the amount of profit generated.

The second of these is the only one that gives us any trouble. Top management always reserves certain kinds of authority, particularly over financing and capital expenditures. Divisional autonomy is also limited by the need to have the divisions conform to overall company policies and to coordinate their activities with those of other divisions.

What this says is that decentralization is really a matter of degree rather than a question of either/or (see Exhibit 24–1). Division A in this diagram would be classified as a profit center because it has a large degree of autonomy, but division B is too far down the scale. Locating the dividing line isn't easy, but no division can be a profit center unless the following two kinds of authority are delegated to the division manager:

requirements of a profit center

1. The division must be free to sell most of its output to outside customers.
2. The division must be free to choose the sources of supply for most of the materials and other goods and services it buys.

EXHIBIT 24–1

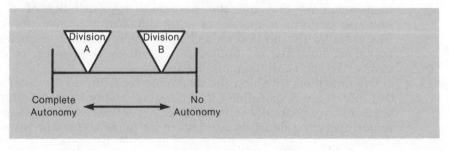

The first of these means that manufacturing divisions can't be classified as profit centers. The sales volume of a manufacturing division is entirely dependent on the number of orders obtained by the marketing division or divisions. This is not within the manufacturing manager's sphere of control. A manufacturing division can be a profit center only if it has an adequate marketing staff of its own, products salable on the outside market, and freedom to sell these products outside the company. Any manufacturing division with these characteristics is not a manufacturing division as that term is usually understood.

The second condition means that marketing divisions can't be classified as profit centers, either. The marketing division exists to market the output of the manufacturing division. The marketing manager can't refuse to promote the manufacturing division's products or services just because better or cheaper substitutes are available from other sources. Any such decision must be made by higher management, with responsibility for both manufacturing and marketing.

The result is that the typical profit center is a division selling a limited number of product lines or serving a specific geographical area. It encompasses both the means of providing goods or services and the means of marketing them. In manufacturing firms factories are the means of providing the goods; in merchandising firms this role is played by the people who buy the merchandise; and in service organizations their counterparts are those who perform the services the customers buy.

Investment Centers

Most profit center managers have some control over the amount of funds invested in the activities of their profit centers. Accounts receivable, inventories, and trade accounts payable are often largely or entirely within the profit center manager's jurisdiction.

To emphasize the manager's responsibility to control the amount invested, these profit centers are sometimes called investment centers. An investment center is a profit center in which the manager has authority to make decisions affecting a significant amount of invested capital.

In addition to their power to influence the amount of working capital required, the investment center managers almost always have some authority to make capital expenditure decisions on their own, without referring the proposals to top management for approval. As we saw in Chapter 14, the maximum amount the manager can approve for any one project is known as the division's *authorization limit*. The larger the unit, or the closer the manager is to the top of the hierarchy, the higher the authorization limit is likely to be. Although each of these expenditures is relatively small, the total may be substantial, and must be controlled.

In practice, almost all profit centers are investment centers, and we shall use the terms interchangeably.

Why Companies Decentralize

The alternative to decentralization is to retain all major decision authority in the company's central headquarters. One way to do this is to organize the company along functional lines, with vice presidents for manufacturing, marketing, and accounting and finance. In such cases only the chief executive officer is in a position to see the profit implications of decisions affecting more than one function.

A firm can also be highly centralized even if its major divisions are organized along market or product lines rather than by function. If all major decisions on prices, sources of supply, marketing strategies, and so forth are made by the chief executive officer, the divisions can hardly be said to be decentralized. The vice presidents in charge are administrators, not managers.

Companies that decentralize do so because centralization of power in either of these two ways seems likely to be counterproductive. Decentralization is intended to increase overall corporate profitability in four ways:

benifits of decent.

1. *Work sharing.* To improve the quality of managerial decisions by dividing the responsibility for decision making among a larger number of executives, thereby allowing each manager to specialize in a particular area with more managerial time and better information available for each decision.
2. *Responsiveness.* To reduce managerial response time by giving decision authority to managers in close, full-time contact with specific products or markets.
3. *Motivation.* To motivate subordinate managers to work toward the company's profit goals by allowing them to identify a portion of the company's profits as the result of their own efforts.
4. *Management development.* To give subordinate managers experience in profit-oriented decision making, to prepare them for greater profit responsibility as they move upward toward the top managerial level.

The advocates of profit decentralization agree that subordinate managers will make some mistakes that the more experienced senior managers might avoid. The underlying assumption, however, has to be that aggregate profit performance will be better than it would be if all profit-oriented decisions were to be reserved for top management. If this assumption isn't valid, the company shouldn't decentralize.

Administered Centers

We maintained earlier that any unit denied the right to choose its sources of supply can't be classified as a profit center. Many such units have substantial decision authority, however. Their managers can set prices, plot marketing strategy, decide how many employees to have, and establish desired inventory levels. Sometimes they even have the power to decide which of the company's products to carry.

The reasons for delegating all this power are the same reasons we listed for companies to decentralize, particularly responsiveness, motivation, and management development. Higher management expects the managers of these units to act like profit center managers.

We call units with these characteristics *administered centers.* They are distinguished from profit centers in that they are captive customers of another unit or units in the company. Sometimes they may also be to some extent captive suppliers to other company units, while producing primarily for their own outside customers.

administered
centers –
captive
customers

The reason these distinctions are important will become apparent when we take up the question of transfer pricing in Chapter 26. Most of the discussion in the rest of this chapter will apply to them just as much as to profit centers. And if calling them profit centers will reinforce the managers' motivation to work toward the company's profit goals, we see no reason for not doing this. We just want to make sure the distinction is recognized when the time comes to set transfer prices.

Service Centers

Many organization units in decentralized companies are classified as service centers. A service center is a unit providing services or support to other units in the organization within the limits set by its capacity and being judged on the quality and cost of the service provided (Exhibit 24–2).

Organization units are classified as service centers for either of two reasons:

1. Most or all of their output is consumed within the organization, so that the unit has little or no access to outside customers (e.g., the controller's department).

2. Top management is unwilling to give the profit center managers the authority to decide how much of the unit's output they are to use or whether they are to use it at all (e.g., a legal department).

Control by service center. Some service centers are extremely important parts of a decentralized organization. When top management

EXHIBIT 24–2

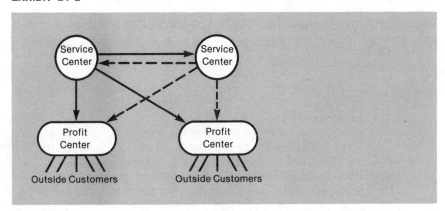

delegates power to the profit center managers, it needs to make sure the managers exercise this power as top management intended. One device to accomplish this is the profit reporting system, as we shall see in a moment. Another is the creation of central staff groups to analyze the budget proposals submitted by the profit center managers, to provide advice and assistance on technical matters, and to keep the lines of communication with the profit centers open.

Central legal staffs, construction specialists, maintenance experts, market research people, accountants, engineers, . . . , the list of potential head office staffers is very long. Top management has to make sure its policies are being observed, and try to make sure the profit center managers don't build today's profits in ways that will weaken the units' long-term competitive position. We pointed out some of the behavioral problems in this arrangement in Chapter 19, but these problems can be solved. They have to be, because there is no workable alternative to at least some of this kind of staff activity.

Quasi-profit centers.   Some service centers provide a limited range of measurable services that can also be bought from outside suppliers. Computer services, printing, art work, and technical advice are typical examples. Management may choose to require some of these to operate as quasi-profit centers, competing with outside suppliers for business within the organization. The objective is to motivate the managers to reduce costs or provide better service.

compete to some extent w/ outside suppliers

One company, for example, has a reproduction shop, performing a wide variety of photographic and printing services for other units within the company. Its "customers" have free access to outside organizations offering the same kinds of services. The shop manager isn't free to solicit business from outside customers, however. The shop is expected to compete with outside suppliers by offering better or faster service at the market price.

The quasi-profit center isn't exactly the mirror image of the administered center. In theory, it can price itself out of the market, or turn down the opportunity to bid on jobs it doesn't like. This seldom happens in practice, however. The main result is to establish a sort of market-based transfer price for the services provided. We'll examine this possibility in detail in Chapter 26.

PURPOSES OF DIVISIONAL PROFIT REPORTING

Management may have any or all of four reasons for wanting reports on divisional profit performance:

1.   To reinforce the managers' *motivation* to contribute to corporate profits.
2.   To help division managers improve the profitability of their divisions' operations (*operations evaluation*).
3.   To help higher management evaluate the desirability of continuing the divisions' activities (*activity evaluation*).
4.   To help higher management evaluate the performance of profit-responsible division managers (*managerial evaluation*).

We shall review each of these, devoting most of our attention to activity evaluation and managerial evaluation, the last two items on the list. We should note in passing, however, that management is not the only party with an interest in divisional profit performance measurement. The Federal Trade Commission line of business program, the Securities and Exchange Commission, and the Financial Accounting Standards Board either now require or soon will require something like divisional profit reporting for external financial reporting. The measurement principles for these purposes are the same as for activity evaluation, modified where necessary to conform to administrative regulations, and therefore do not need to be discussed separately here.

Motivational Reinforcement

As we saw in Chapter 5, budgeting is intended to reinforce the managers' motivation to accept the organization's goals as their own. When managers have responsibility for a portion of their company's profits, budgeting is expected to help them achieve a profit orientation.

Profit reporting has the same objective. Few people can maintain their motivation for long if they never find out how much progress they are making toward the objectives they have set for themselves. Reporting systems are designed in part to provide this kind of reinforcement.

Operations Evaluation

The second purpose of divisional profit reporting is to help the division managers find ways to improve the profitability of the activities they are responsible for. The primary question is whether better operating methods can be found.

To answer this question, management may compare operating results with evaluation standards derived from any of the following five sources:

1. The current profit plan.
2. Historical results.
3. Competitors' performance.
4. Managerial experience.
5. Engineering studies.

This is largely a process of looking for clues. Which products are selling well? Who is buying them? Which costs are higher than planned? Which products are earning less than the industry average? We discussed some of these questions in Chapter 9 and will add to that discussion in the next chapter. For the moment we shall direct our attention to activity evaluation and managerial evaluation.

Activity Evaluation

Activity evaluation is related to operations evaluation but deals with a more fundamental question: Are the division's activities generating enough income to support the resources invested in it?

ROI a key measurement std.

Since investment capital is usually the scarcest of the resources management must deal with, the performance standard for this kind of evaluation must relate the amount of the division's earnings to the amount of invested capital—that is, it should be a *return on investment* standard. Since a decision to continue an activity has the same effect as a decision to invest in it, the appropriate performance standard is the minimum rate of return management is willing to accept for new capital expenditures. This standard should be based on the company's cost of capital and should be the same for all divisions in a given risk category. Management has no reason to regard 8 percent as a satisfactory return on money invested in one division but an unsatisfactory return in another unless the two divisions differ widely in risk.

This kind of analysis can be either prospective or retrospective:

Prospective.   Are this division's activities profitable enough to warrant maintaining or increasing the current investment commitment?

Retrospective.   Are this division's activities profitable enough to support the investments management has already made in the division?

Interpreting these crudely, we might say that prospective analysis attempts to answer the question, Would the company be better off to get rid of the division now? Retrospective analysis attempts to indicate whether the company would have been justified in making these investments in the past if it had had to rely on profits at the current level.

Prospective analysis.   Prospective analysis is simply another form of the disinvestment analysis we explored in Chapter 15. It requires a comparison of the present value of the cash flows from continued operation with the cash flows to be generated by withdrawing from the division's activities now. For example, an analysis based on operating a division for another three years might be diagrammed as in Exhibit 24–3.

The cash flows from immediate withdrawal come from the after-

EXHIBIT 24–3

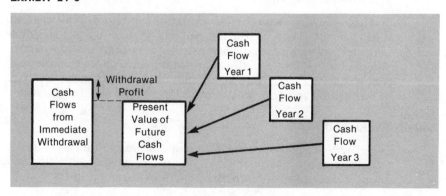

tax liquidation value of the facilities and working capital attributable to the division, less any liquidation costs (employee severance pay, and so on), also adjusted for the tax effects. The cash flows from continued operation are the net receipts the company would lose if it were to drop out of the market now.

Retrospective analysis. Routine divisional profit reports do not and cannot provide these cash flow estimates. Performance reports are by their very nature retrospective, based on observations of actual results. As such, they can play only two roles:

1. To direct top management's attention to divisions, or activities within divisions, that persistently earn less than the target return on investment.
2. To show how viable the division's activities are likely to be on a continuing basis—i.e., are the division's revenues covering all the costs attributable to them; if not, the future is bleak, no matter how favorable the current cash flow relationships.

Managerial Evaluation

The fourth objective of divisional profit reporting is to measure the financial performance of division management. The certainty that managerial profit performance will be evaluated is an essential feature of profit decentralization. Top management can't afford to delegate decision authority without providing some way of finding out how well that authority has been used.

That should be reasonably apparent, but three related issues still need to be resolved:

1. On what basis is management to be evaluated?
2. What criteria should management use in choosing a managerial profit performance standard?
3. Where can a performance standard meeting these criteria be found?

1. The basis of evaluation. The manager plays many roles—coordinator, motivator, troubleshooter, teacher, adviser, regulator, and perhaps even therapist. Managers are likely to be evaluated on how well they play several of these roles. Profit reporting, however, is mainly used to judge how well the manager has controlled revenues, costs, and the amount invested in the division.

We should recognize at the outset that investment control is not achieved primarily through historical comparisons:

1. Most of the division's plant and equipment investment remains substantially unchanged for long periods and is thus not currently controllable.
2. Control over current capital expenditures is achieved by project review and justification procedures that emphasize future expectations rather than past performance; most of these decisions are made at the top management level rather than by the division managers.

Profit center managers do control two parts of the investment flow, however:

1.   Capital expenditures on small projects within the managers' authorization limits.
2.   Investments in working capital.

Auditing the results of even a sample of the small capital expenditure projects would be difficult, probably inconclusive, and prohibitively expensive. Instead, top management ordinarily exercises control by having the division manager build estimates of the total effect of these expenditures into the annual profit plan. These are merged with the many other assumptions and forecasts built into the plan. Profit reporting then indicates how successful management has been in achieving the anticipated results.

Profit center managers generally have greater freedom to invest in working capital than to make new capital expenditures on plant and equipment. One explanation is that working capital investments are assumed to be reversible—if things don't work out, working capital investments can be recovered without loss. Another explanation is that working capital requirements are assumed to flow naturally from the volume of sales and production, with little conscious managerial intervention.

Division managers almost always can control the investment in working capital. They may be able to affect the amount of receivables, for example, by deciding how many slow-paying customers to sell to and by regulating their efforts to collect overdue accounts. They can influence inventory levels by changing reorder points and production quantities. And they can affect the amount of accounts payable to some extent by taking full advantage of suppliers' credit terms.

The managers' success or failure in controlling controllable investments needs to be reflected in the periodic profit performance reports. This is just as much part of profit performance as revenues and operating expenses.

2. Criteria for selecting standards.   Standards to be used in evaluating division managers' profit performance need to meet two major requirements:

1.   Current attainability by competent division managers.
2.   Consistency with the degree of profit controllability.

Both of these are necessary if the managers are to internalize the standards as their own and accept responsibility for achieving them.

Attainability.   Each division is to some extent unique. Profit differences can be created by variations in the age or condition of production facilities; by differences in local wage structures, transportation costs, and raw material prices; by differences in the types of products handled or customers served; or by differences in the degree of competition faced in the marketplace. Each manager's performance should be evaluated in the light of the situation facing the division. This means that the standard must be different from division to division and must be changed from period to period as conditions change.

Controllability. Profit performance should be defined to exclude any variances that are not to some significant extent within the control of the division manager. At the same time, we must recognize that no measure of profit can be a precise reflection of a manager's effectiveness in profit control. Too many other factors enter in. The danger lies in trying to avoid this problem by adopting a profit definition that eliminates so many of the possible sources of variances that the manager is relieved of most profit control responsibilities. No variable is ever completely controllable; controllability always means the ability to influence a cost or revenue within limits.

Variations in divisional sales, for example, are an important aspect of managerial performance even though they may result in large part from changes in general business conditions. Changes in the business environment can and should be considered in evaluating profit performance, but not in calculating the profit figures on which the evaluation is to be based.

3. Developing the standard. For activity evaluation, the relevant profit standard is the rate of return management is willing to accept for new capital expenditures. This is the same for all divisions, or at least for all divisions in the same risk category.

A different standard is appropriate for managerial evaluation. Profit center managers must be held accountable for the amount of invested capital they can control. A uniform standard based on the cost of capital and applicable to all profit centers doesn't do this, however. It violates the attainability criterion.

To illustrate what we mean, let's suppose Ormsby, Inc. uses a 9 percent rate of return as a cutoff rate in its acquisition and capital expenditure decisions. Its transit division is now earning a 3 percent return on investment and management is delighted; its educational division is earning 16 percent, but management is seriously considering removing the division manager for poor profit performance (see Exhibit 24–4).

The manager of the transit division has increased the operating cash flow, has developed bus charter business to reduce idle time, and has far exceeded top management's expectations for this division.

The educational division, in contrast, is earning 16 percent, but its growth is far slower than management had hoped for and slower than other companies in the field have actually achieved. Turnover of personnel is very high, despite high salaries, and most of the cash flow comes from operations that were well established before the present division manager was appointed two years ago.

The only profit standard meeting the attainability criterion is *budgeted performance.* A carefully conceived budget is by definition attainable with good management under expected operating conditions. The budget may be as high or as low as these conditions seem to warrant.

This approach permits the managers to influence the criteria they

EXHIBIT 24-4

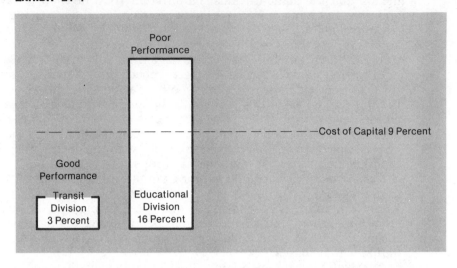

will be judged by. As we pointed out in Chapter 19, this offers the possibility of greater goal congruence. It also offers the division managers an opportunity to make their jobs easier by setting unnecessarily low budgets. Two safeguards are therefore essential:

1. Active top management participation in budget setting.
2. Inclusion of improvement targets in the budgeting process.

A 3 percent return on investment may be good performance for the transit division this year, but no management would be happy maintaining that percentage indefinitely. Recognizing this, top management should judge division managers' performance at least as much by the quality of their budget proposals as by their success in carrying them out.

Top management's acceptance of an operating plan is a two-way commitment, however. It signifies agreement that better performance than planned performance is not reasonably attainable. In evaluating managerial performance, top management should stick to its part of the bargain.

PROFIT, RETURN ON INVESTMENT, AND RESIDUAL INCOME

The second major issue in divisional profit reporting is how the profit figures should be presented. Three main measures are available:

1. Divisional income or profit contribution.
2. Return on investment.
3. Residual income.

Income or Profit Contribution

Profit contribution is often used to measure performance marketing, as we saw in Chapter 9. Divisional profit contribution can be used for the same purpose:

Divisional profit contribution: Divisional revenues less the cost of goods sold and other expenses traceable to the division.

This is relatively simple to measure and contains no allocations of headquarters expenses for people to argue about. The question is whether it meets the needs of activity evaluation or managerial evaluation.

Activity evaluation. To measure divisional profit performance for activity evaluation, we need to relate the amount of profit attributable to the division's activities to the amount of investment devoted to them. Divisional profit contribution clearly reflects neither of these quantities. It overlooks centrally administered costs attributable to the division and doesn't reflect divisional investment at all.

Divisional income may be slightly better on this score. It is calculated by subtracting a portion of headquarters' expenses from the profit contribution figure. Exhibit 24–5, for example, shows one month's income statement for the food division of Ormsby, Inc. Both profit contribution and divisional income are identified on this report. Income taxes are deducted to make the profit figures comparable with the cost of capital.

If the allocations of headquarters' expenses approximate the amount of headquarters' expenses attributable to the division's activities, divisional income will be relevant to activity evaluation. Neither divisional income nor divisional profit contribution reflects divisional investment, however. This means that neither of them is a wholly adequate basis for activity evaluation.

Managerial evaluation. The profit performance measure for managerial evaluation must reflect all the profit determinants the division manager can control. By the same token, it should exclude variances in elements that are not controllable at the division level.

EXHIBIT 24–5

FOOD DIVISION
Divisional Income Statement, March 19xx

	Actual	Planned	Variance
Net sales...........................	$3,495,000	$3,600,000	$(105,000)
Divisional expenses:			
Cost of goods sold...............	$2,169,000	$2,205,000	36,000
Marketing........................	538,000	535,000	(3,000)
Division administration...........	73,000	75,000	2,000
Income taxes.....................	372,000	408,000	36,000
Total division expense........	$3,152,000	$3,223,000	
Profit contribution.................	$ 343,000	$ 377,000	
Head office charges (after taxes)...	173,000	173,000	—
Divisional income.............	$ 170,000	$ 204,000	$ (34,000)

Divisional income fails the first part of this test because it reflects allocations of headquarters' expenses the manager can't control. We can blunt the force of this objection by charging the division amounts equal to the amounts budgeted, thereby removing noncontrollable variances from the divisional profit reports. We discussed this technique in Chapter 8, and Ormsby, Inc. used it to derive the income statement summarized in Exhibit 24–5.

This is only a partial solution, however. Managers tend to quarrel about the amounts allocated, in the belief that top management places a heavy weight on the absolute values of the figures on the bottom line, not just the variances. A manager assigned to improve the division's profit performance may resent seeing the improvements in profit contribution obscured by apparently arbitrary increases in the amounts of allocated headquarters' expenses.

Profit contribution comes out better than divisional income for use in managerial evaluation. It is likely to encompass most of the income statement elements controllable by the division manager. Its main shortcoming is that it ignores the investments under the division manager's control. A division may be able to increase its profit contribution by increasing its investments in inventories and receivables (see Exhibit 24–6). Unless the profit performance measure reflects these investments, it will provide a misleading impression of managerial performance. The manager will get the benefits of the investment with none of the costs.

EXHIBIT 24–6

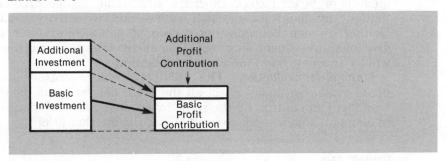

Return on Investment (ROI)

Undoubtedly the most widely known and widely used measure of divisional profit performance is the rate of return on the funds that have been invested in the division, referred to as the *return on investment* (ROI) or *return on capital employed*:

$$\text{Return on investment} = \frac{\text{Profit}}{\text{Investment}}$$

We already know that the food division's income for March was $170,000. Assuming no seasonal influences, this is equivalent to $170,000 × 12 = $2,040,000 a year. The company's net investment

EXHIBIT 24–7

FOOD DIVISION
Net Investment, March 31

Traceable assets:		
Accounts receivable......................		$ 4,192,000
Inventories...............................		3,748,000
Prepayments.............................		59,000
Property, plant and equipment, net........		5,558,000
Total traceable assets.................		$13,557,000
Traceable current liabilities:		
Accounts payable.........................	$2,618,000	
Accruals.................................	274,000	
Total traceable current liabilities........		2,892,000
Net traceable investment....................		$10,665,000
Centrally administered assets:		
Cash......................................		419,000
Other (net)................................		246,000
Divisional net investment...................		$11,330,000

in the division totaled $11,330,000, as shown in Exhibit 24–7. The return on investment in March therefore was:

ROI = $2,040,000/$11,330,000 = 18 percent

Return on investment has a number of advantages over any profit measure that fails to reflect divisional investment:

1. Both the earnings and investment components of the ROI ratio are essential to activity analysis.
2. The impact of capital expenditures can't be audited on a project-by-project basis but does show up in the ROI ratio.
3. Emphasis on the ROI ratio keeps management aware of the need to use assets economically.
4. Similar ratios can be calculated for other parts of the company and other companies in the industry.

ROI measurements have serious shortcomings, however, that suggest they should be used only with caution:

1. Either profit or investment or both may be measured in ways that bias the return on investment figure, leading to faulty invest-ment/disinvestment decisions.
2. Some determinants of return on investment are not controllable by division management, and this reduces the usefulness of ROI-based reports in managerial evaluation.
3. Division management can manipulate the ROI figure by shifting programmed expenditures and even some expenditures on responsive activities from one period to another.
4. Decisions that maximize divisional ROI may be suboptimal.

Measurement difficulties. Many of the defects of ROI arise from the first of these factors, because neither attributable profit nor attributable investment can be measured satisfactorily. These measurement difficulties are so important we shall devote the entire next section to them.

Controllability. Return on investment emerged from the search for a profit measure appropriate to activity evaluation. The allocations of costs and investments for that purpose are irrelevant to managerial evaluation unless two conditions are met:

1. They are proportional to the values of variables division management can control.
2. The allocation formula is known in advance, allowing the division managers to predict the impact of their decisions on the amounts allocated.

For example, suppose the headquarters' staff has concluded that centrally administered cash balances necessary to support divisional operations increase or decrease by 1 percent of any increases or decreases in divisional sales. This relationship can be embodied in an allocation formula to make the division managers consider this as well as other consequences of their decisions affecting sales volume (Exhibit 24–8).

Allocations of this sort don't violate the controllability criterion. Allocations determined by multiplying the companywide ratio of cash to sales by divisional sales each period are another story. If these are used, the amount allocated to a particular division will depend on three factors: (1) divisional sales; (2) sales in the rest of the company; and (3) the effectiveness of cash management by the corporate treasurer's office. The division manager can influence only one of these three.

The usefulness of ROI comparisons in managerial evaluation will vary inversely with the number of allocations based on actual rather than predetermined ratios or amounts. If they are numerous, the variance in the return on investment due to the division manager's performance will be difficult to isolate.

Manipulation of ROI. The third defect of the ROI figure applies to all the measures we are discussing, but it is appropriate to bring it up here because it is usually discussed in an ROI contest. Managers can

EXHIBIT 24–8

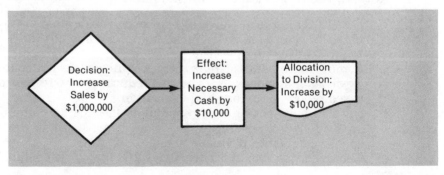

defer expenditures for maintenance, or planning, or research, or management development when market conditions are poor. These actions will cushion the immediate impact on profit of adverse market conditions, but they may place a heavy mortgage on the division's future.

One way to attack this problem is by working closely with division management in developing the budget itself and then questioning very strongly any large "favorable" deviations from budgeted spending on time-shiftable elements. Justification of underspending may be just as important as explaining an overrun. Some manipulation is undoubtedly inevitable, however. Since this is true of any measure we can devise, our only recourse is to recognize the danger and try to be alert to it.

Suboptimization. The fourth danger in the ROI measure is that it may lead managers to apply an invalid decision rule: maximization of the ROI ratio. For example, suppose the manager of the Food Division is authorized to spend up to $500,000 on small projects within the division's authorization limits. The manager is now considering a group of proposals with the following characteristics:

Investment outlay............................ $500,000
Increment in divisional income,
    first year.................................. $ 70,000
Initial rate of return: $70,000/$500,000.......... 14%
Internal rate of return....................... 12%

Each of the projects has an internal rate of return greater than 9 percent, the company's cutoff rate for capital investment proposals.

The usual project review analysis would point to accepting these proposals:

But how will they affect the divisional return on investment?

Before	After
$\frac{\$ 2,040,000}{\$11,330,000} = 18$ percent	$\frac{\$ 2,110,000}{\$11,830,000} = 17.8$ percent

The effect is small, but the direction is clearly downward. If the manager is attempting to maximize the divisional return on investment, the investments won't be made.

Residual Income

The third measure of divisional profit, residual income, is designed to provide the same advantages as return on investment, but without one and perhaps two of ROI's defects.

EXHIBIT 24–9

FOOD DIVISION
Statement of Residual Income, March 19xx

	Actual	Planned	Variance
Net sales............................	$3,495,000	$3,600,000	$(105,000)
Expenses:			
Cost of goods sold..................	$2,169,000	$2,205,000	36,000
Marketing..........................	538,000	535,000	(3,000)
Division administration..............	73,000	75,000	2,000
Income taxes.......................	372,000	408,000	36,000
Investment charges.................	85,000	80,000	(5,000)
Head office charges.................	173,000	173,000	—
Total expenses..................	$3,410,000	$3,476,000	
Residual income.....................	$ 85,000	$ 124,000	$(39,000)

Residual income is defined as divisional income less an investment carrying charge, determined by multiplying divisional investment by an interest rate based on the cost of capital. For example, the Food Division's profit report for March would show the figures summarized in Exhibit 24–9. Residual income is $85,000 smaller than the divisional income figure reported in Exhibit 24–5, the amount of the investment carrying charge. This was calculated as follows:

> Annual rate/12 × Investment = Monthly charge
> 9%/12   × $11,330,000 = $85,000

The variance in this item was $5,000 because the division exceeded its budgeted investment, a fact Exhibit 24–5 ignored.

Advantages of residual income. Using residual income to measure divisional profit has two main advantages over ROI:

1. It states both earnings and investment on the same scale so that a variance in one is comparable with a variance in the other.
2. It is more consistent with decision rules embodying the maximization of present value.

A common scale. Income statement amounts represent flows of economic quantities during a period of time. Balance sheet amounts, however, represent static quantities, at a specific date. Multiplying these static quantities by an interest rate places them on a flow scale. This allows management to make a direct comparison between an investment variance and a variance in a determinant of income. A $1 million inventory variance, for example, would be justified in Ormsby, Inc. by a $7,500 monthly saving in materials costs. The calculation is:

$$9\%/12 \times \$1,000,000 = \$7,500 \text{ a month.}$$

Consistency with managerial decision rules. We saw earlier that the use of ROI may lead to suboptimization in divisions already achieving high ROI ratios. Use of residual income can reduce this danger. In our illustration we had a $500,000 investment bring in $70,000 in new earnings the first year. The investment charges in this situation would be:

Before	*After*
$11,330,000 × 9% = $1,019,700	$11,830,000 × 9% = $1,064,700

Residual income would be as follows:

	Before	*After*
Divisional income..............	$2,040,000	$2,110,000
Investment charge.............	1,019,700	1,064,700
Residual income.........	$1,020,300	$1,045,300

Although the investment will reduce ROI, it will increase residual income. Since the investment is clearly profitable (an internal rate of return of 12 percent), residual income must be a superior performance measure in this case because it produces a signal that is consistent with the managerial decision rule.

Limitations of residual income. Residual income will not solve all of the problems of ROI. First, it is still subject to the measurement problems we shall discuss in the next section. Second, division management can manipulate it by altering the timing of various elements of revenue and expense, just as it can manipulate ROI. Third, although it worked well in our illustration, it can encourage suboptimization in some circumstances. A sound investment with a deferred payoff will depress both the ROI and residual income, as investment goes up and first-year earnings don't. We'll examine this point again in the next section, too. Finally, it doesn't conform to the controllability criterion.

This last limitation is one we can do something about. One way to do this is to classify both income and investment quantities as controllable or noncontrollable, and divide the monthly report into controllable and noncontrollable sections. This would mean two investment charges, one for controllable investments, the other for noncontrollable elements.

Another possibility is a solution we have suggested before: exclude changes in noncontrollable investments from the calculation until the following year when a new budget is made up. For example, if the budget reflects a $1 million investment by top management in new equipment and the actual cost of the equipment is $1.1 million, calculate the investment charge on the $1 million basis until the end of the year.

Under either of these solutions a variance in residual income would be a controllable variance, and this is what we need for managerial evaluation.

METHODS OF HANDLING NONCONTROLLABLE VARIANCES

Report actual amount, adjust budget to eliminate variances.
Report predetermined amount, equal to budget.
Report predetermined rate, equal to budgeted rate.
Report variance below the line, as noncontrollable.

MEASUREMENT PROBLEMS

Divisional profit reports for activity evaluation should reflect the criterion of attributability; those for managerial evaluation should be based on controllability. Ideally, separate reports should be used for these two purposes, but in practice, one set of reports serves both.

In discussing profit reporting systems for these two purposes, we purposely bypassed several difficult measurement issues. We need to review these now, before taking up the analysis of variances from budgeted profit performance in the next chapter:

1. Defining the investment base.
2. Allocating centrally administered assets and expenses.
3. Choosing a depreciation method.
4. Adjusting for changes in resource prices.

Defining the Investment Base

Divisional investment may be defined in many ways. Five possibilities should be listed:

1. *Traceable assets.* All assets identifiable specifically with the division, regardless of their physical location.
2. *Controllable investment.* All assets controllable by division management, less any current liabilities within its jurisdiction.
3. *Total assets.* All assets of the division, including a share of corporate cash and other centrally administered assets.
4. *Net investment.* The division's share of total assets less non-interest bearing current liabilities—i.e., the division's share of the total investment of stockholders and lender creditors.
5. *Stockholders' equity.* The owners' share of the investment in divisional assets.

We used *net investment* figures in our discussion of return on investment and residual income because net investment is more comparable than the others to the cost of capital. It includes all the funds provided to the firm for an interestlike return—i.e., owners' equity, long-term debt, and short-term, interest-bearing debt. It is therefore more suitable for activity evaluation, in which the cost of capital is the relevant performance standard.

Controllable investment would be more suitable for managerial evaluation, but would be totally unsuitable for activity evaluation. It omits many investments attributable to the division but not controllable by division management. Since a single set of reports must serve both purposes, and since noncontrollable variances can be dealt with in other ways, we decided not to use this.

Traceable assets is easier to measure than either of the first two, but is relevant neither to activity evaluation nor to managerial evaluation. It excludes attributable assets that are not directly traceable to the division, includes assets that are traceable but not controllable, and excludes short-term liabilities entirely. Furthermore, if the reports are to be used in operations evaluation, figures based on traceable assets are likely to be noncomparable from division to division and from company to company. For example, one division may handle all its own inventories and receivables, while another uses central billing and warehousing services, thereby burying some of its investment in the common pool.

Total assets is not very different in concept from net investment and is often used in its place. It may distort activity evaluation comparisons, however, because it includes in the investment base varying amounts of assets financed by suppliers and employees, not by investors.

The *equity of the parent company's stockholders* in any division is not measurable. The funds provided to a division can't be identified specifically as debt funds or equity funds. The financing mix is a characteristic of the corporation and is the same for all divisions. Allocating 40 percent debt to one division and 60 percent to another would be arbitrary and meaningless.

A related but very different measurement base is the *equity of the parent company* in a subsidiary. This may be used in measuring the profit performance of subsidiaries in foreign countries or in ventures very dissimilar to the activities of the parent. Automobile company finance subsidiaries are good examples. This is just a way of measuring net investment in these specific situations. The parent company's investment includes parent company equity and debt; the subsidiary's own financing is very separate in that it doesn't affect the parent company's borrowing capacity. Thus the parent company's cost of capital remains a comparable benchmark for parent company investments.

Allocating Centrally Administered Assets and Expenses

Many of the assets that relate to the activities of a specific division can be traced to that division from the organizational account classification. In addition to these, every company has some assets that are administered centrally, either because they are necessary to perform central office or service functions or because central administration represents a more efficient use of resources.

At this juncture we should distinguish between assets that are truly common to more than one division and those that presumably could be traced to specific divisions by a finer subdivision of the account codes. Cash, for example, can never be traced satisfactorily to the operations of individual divisions, whereas it is often possible to identify receivables by division even though billing and accounts receivable operations are performed centrally.

Centrally administered assets of this latter type may be subcoded in the accounts to permit divisional identification. If this step is regarded as excessively costly, at least two solutions are available. First, the percentage distribution might be approximated by sampling techniques; for example, a sample of open customer accounts might be taken to approximate the true distribution of all receivables among divisions. Second, studies might be undertaken to determine the statistical relationship between asset balances and divisional activity. For example, receivables might be found to bear a fixed relationship to sales volume, the exact ratio differing for each division because of differences in terms, collection policies, or industry customs. This second method is likely to be inferior to sampling because statistical relationships frequently get out of date.

Assets and headquarters expenses that are truly common to two or more divisions present a more difficult problem. For some, a statistical relationship can be found, relating these to some measure of divisional volume or capacity. When no such relationship can be found, we must presume the items are not attributable to divisional activities. They therefore have no place in activity evaluation and it is better not to allocate them at all than to use an arbitrary formula.

Choosing the Depreciation Method

Depreciation is neither more nor less relevant in divisional reporting than in corporate financial reporting. Since depreciation presumably measures the cost of one of the resources used to generate divisional revenues, it should be deducted in calculating divisional income for activity evaluation and operations evaluation.

Most depreciation accounting is based on either a straight-line formula or some form of declining-charge depreciation. The most widely used declining charge formulas are the double rate, declining balance and sum-of-the-years'-digits formulas. These formulas may aggravate a problem we mentioned in the preceding section: the effects of some decisions on divisional ROI or residual income in the years immediately following a new investment may be inconsistent with their effects on the present value of the company's cash flows. That is, book depreciation will be very high, thereby reducing net income, just when the book value of the investment is also high. This will reduce the reported rate of return. Take the following five-year investment, for example:

Time	Cash Flows after Taxes	Present Value at 10 Percent	Present Value at 15 Percent
0............................	−$10,000	−$10,000	−$10,000
1............................	− 1,000	− 909	− 870
2............................	+ 1,000	+ 826	+ 756
3............................	+ 5,000	+ 3,755	+ 3,290
4............................	+ 7,500	+ 5,122	+ 4,290
5............................	+ 5,000	+ 3,105	+ 2,485
Net present value...........		+$ 1,899	−$ 49

As the right-hand column shows, the internal rate of return is approximately 15 percent. If depreciation is calculated on a straight-line or declining-charge basis, however, the division will show an increase in investment and a decrease in earnings in the first year. For example, straight-line depreciation of the entire amount would be $2,000 a year. This would be subtracted from the annual cash flow to get annual income. The reported return on investment would be as follows:

Year	Book Value, Beginning of Year	Income	Return on Investment (percent)
1......................	$10,000	−$3,000	−30.0
2......................	8,000	− 1,000	−12.5
3......................	6,000	3,000	50.0
4......................	4,000	5,500	137.5
5......................	2,000	3,000	150.0

A satisfactory return on investment won't be reported until the third year.

The only depreciation formulas that avoid this problem are those that consider the investment charge, otherwise known as *implicit interest*, in calculating the annual depreciation. Implicit interest depreciation on the illustrative investment is calculated as shown in the following table:

(1) Investment, Beginning of Year	(2) Earnings at 15 Percent [(1) × 15%]	(3) Cash Flow (from previous table)	(4) Depreciation [(3) − (2)]	(5) Investment, End of Year [(1) − (4)]
$10,000..............	$1,500	−$1,000	−$2,500	$12,500
12,500..............	1,875	+ 1,000	− 875	13,375
13,375..............	2,006	+ 5,000	2,994	10,381
10,381..............	1,557	+ 7,500	5,943	4,438
4,438..............	666	+ 5,000	4,334	104*

* Rounding error.

The depreciation charges in column (4) are designed to permit the company to report a 15 percent return on investment each year. To do this, however, we'd have to report *negative* depreciation in the first two years. Even if the cash flows are positive in the first year or so, depreciation in those years will still be low or negative.

If management is unwilling to shift to this kind of depreciation, it has only one alternative: to make strong, continuing efforts to separate the activity evaluation and managerial evaluation uses of divisional profit reports. By building the estimated effects of planned capital expenditures into the annual profit plan, and by focusing attention exclusively on variances from the plan, management can keep the effects of temporary reductions in reported return on investment out of the managerial evaluation process.

Adjusting for Changes in Resource Prices

The property, plant and equipment figure in Exhibit 24–7 reflected original historical cost less accumulated depreciation. After a period of inflation, however, long-life property is a mixture of assets acquired at many different price levels. Divisions with an older asset mix are likely to have a lower historical cost investment base and lower depreciation charges than younger divisions and therefore will tend to report a higher return on investment. This may serve to cover up a deteriorating profit situation until price levels stabilize and investment replacement at higher prices begins to make itself felt in lower return-on-investment figures. Measuring the cost of goods sold at historical prices has a similar effect.

The solution to this problem is to base asset figures, depreciation and the cost of goods sold on replacement cost. Most companies in the United States have shied away from doing this, perceiving the benefits to be far less than the costs of measuring replacement cost. Now that the Securities and Exchange Commission is requiring the submission of replacement cost data, the incremental cost of using these figures in the divisional reports is likely to be much smaller.

SUMMARY

Business organizations with more than one clearly identifiable product line or market segment are likely to find it desirable to measure the profit performance of each of these segments. These measurements have some or all of four purposes: (1) to analyze the effectiveness of the methods used to manufacture and market the company's products (operations evaluation); (2) to see whether each segment is earning enough to provide an adequate return on the amount of funds invested in the segment (activity evaluation); (3) to analyze the performance of the managers in charge of this segment (managerial evaluation); and (4) to reinforce the managers' commitment to work toward overall company profit goals (motivational reinforcement).

The third and fourth of these purposes are applicable mainly when the segment is a profit center or investment center in a decentralized company. Decentralization attempts to combine the advantages of large-scale organization with the advantages of flexibility and specialization the small firm has. To implement this idea, top management has to delegate a good deal of authority; internal profit reporting provides the means by which division managers can be held accountable for the exercise of this authority.

Divisional profit performance reports generally encompass both profit and the investment committed to the division's activities, expressed either as a return on investment ratio or as residual income, defined as divisional income less implicit interest on divisional investment. These measures are designed primarily for use in activity evaluation, in which the performance standard is the company's cost of capital. The appropriate measurement concepts are attributable profit and attributable investment.

For managerial evaluation, controllability is the key concept, and the standard must be adapted to fit each division's particular circumstances—budgeted performance is the appropriate standard here, with special effort required to make sure the budget itself reflects strong managerial commitments to company goals. A return on investment standard, applied uniformly to all divisions in all circumstances, is inappropriate for use in managerial evaluation.

None of these measures is perfect. All can be manipulated to some extent; all can lead to some suboptimization. We shall return in the next chapter to see how management can use variance analysis to use reported profit figures more effectively.

KEY TERMS

The more important terms introduced and defined in this chapter are the following:

Activity evaluation	Net investment
Administered center	Operations evaluation
Decentralization	Profit centers
Divisional income	Quasi-profit center
Investment centers	Residual income
Managerial evaluation	Return on investment (ROI)

INDEPENDENT STUDY PROBLEMS
(Solutions in Appendix C)

1. Foreign subsidiary as a profit center. Jacques Dalmas is the managing director of Alifrance, S.A., the French subsidiary of Allen Brands, Inc. Allen Brands owns 100 percent of the voting stock in Alifrance, which sells only products manufactured and distributed by Allen Brands. It has no manufacturing facilities of its own and makes no sales outside France.

Allen Brands bills Alifrance at the regular wholesale prices of the articles shipped. Alifrance pays all taxes, customs duties, and transportation charges on the merchandise it buys from Allen Brands. Mr. Dalmas and his staff decide what prices to charge, which products to offer for sale, how to market them, and how much inventory to carry, all subject to head office approval of the annual profit plan.

a. Is Alifrance a profit center?
b. Should top management consider Alifrance's profit performance in evaluating Mr. Dalmas's managerial performance?

2. Return on investment versus residual income. The investment in division A consists of $200,000 in traceable working capital, $400,000 in traceable plant and equipment, and $100,000 in centrally administered assets, allocated to the division at a rate of one sixth of traceable investment. The budgeted amounts for these three totals were $150,000, $420,-000, and $95,000.

Division A's net income for the year is $63,000, after deducting $30,000 in traceable depreciation, $40,000 in head office charges (allocated to the division at the rate of 5 percent of sales) and income taxes at 50 percent. The budgeted amounts were $70,000, $32,000, $45,000, and 50 percent.

The company estimates that its cost of capital is 12 percent, after taxes.

a. Calculate budgeted and actual return on investment.
b. Calculate budgeted and actual residual income.
c. Discuss the division manager's performance.
d. What action should management take in response to your evaluation of this division's activities, based on the figures supplied here?

EXERCISES AND PROBLEMS

1. Legal department as a profit center. Goldsachs and Merrill is an investment banking firm. It has three divisions organized as profit centers: underwriting, brokerage, and portfolio management. Its legal department, with direct costs of $1 million a year, provides legal services to all three divisions and to corporate management, recommends the use of outside counsel in certain cases, and provides liaison between company personnel and outside counsel working on specific cases or issues.

The costs of outside counsel are assigned to the divisions for which their services are provided. The legal department itself is treated as a service center, its costs being allocated among the three operating divisions in proportion to their revenues, as follows:

Underwriting...........................	$ 300,000
Brokerage.............................	600,000
Portfolio management................	100,000
Total...........................	$1,000,000

The controller of Goldsachs and Merrill has proposed treating the legal department as a profit center. The department would charge the divisions on the basis of a fee schedule similar to those being charged by independent law firms for comparable services. Individual division managers would be free to use outside law firms, set up their own legal staffs, or dispense with legal services entirely.

The controller summed up the arguments for the proposal in the following way: "In the final analysis, it is management that decides whether to initiate lawsuits, whether to defend lawsuits or settle out of court, and how much to spend for legal advice. The functions of the legal department are clearly subsidiary to these responsibilities of management. If this is true at the corporate level, I see no reason why it shouldn't be true at the divisional level as well. I suggest leaving the amount and source of legal services up to the good business judgment of the division managers."

The controller estimates that application of this proposal to this year's legal department activities would have led to the following internal charges:

Underwriting.........................	$ 800,000
Brokerage............................	400,000
Portfolio management................	100,000
Corporate management...............	700,000
Total...........................	$2,000,000

Should the legal division be established as a profit center? Prepare a brief report to support your recommendation.

2. Gross versus net assets. Divisional investment in plant and equipment in the Torrid Tomato Company is measured by the depreciated historical cost of the division's plant and equipment. The manager of the tomato paste division has complained that this is discriminatory because the paste division is a young division, with relatively new assets. Depreciation charges are high and so is the depreciated cost; both of these depress the division's annual ROI. The catsup division, in contrast, has many old facilities, some of them completely amortized. Both depreciated cost and annual depreciation are low. This helps the catsup division maintain a high ROI. The summary figures are:

	Catsup	Paste
Plant and equipment......................	$1,000	$500
Less: Accumulated depreciation.........	800	100
Net plant and equipment...........	$ 200	$400
Working capital...........................	900	300
Net investment......................	$1,100	$700
Revenues.................................	$1,000	$600
Expenses:		
Depreciation...........................	$ 50	$ 80
Other (including taxes)..................	800	436
Net income..............................	$ 150	$ 84
Return on investment....................	13.6%	12%

The paste division manager suggests measuring plant and equipment at its original cost, with no deduction for accumulated depreciation. No depreciation charges would be deducted from divisional revenues. The division manager believes this would deprive the managers of the older divisions of the unfair advantages of having older, more fully depreciated facilities.

a. Recalculate the rate of return on investment for each division on the basis recommended by the manager of the paste division.
b. Which division is more profitable than the other? Explain how you reached this conclusion.
c. What explanation can you give for the concern expressed by the manager of the paste division about the division's low rate of return on investment? Is this a legitimate worry?
d. Would division managers be more likely, less likely, or neither more nor less likely to submit major capital expenditure proposals than they

are now? State the reason(s) supporting your conclusions on this point.

e. What action would you recommend on the proposed measurement change? Why would you recommend this?

3. Depreciation method; Replacement costing.   The top management of the Global Girdle Company is worried that the managers of the more profitable divisions will be reluctant to submit capital expenditure proposals that will depress near-term earnings and ROI. It has adopted two procedures it hopes will reduce the depressing effect of new investment on reported divisional performance:

1. Assets are measured on the basis of replacement cost, less depreciation, and depreciation is calculated on a replacement cost basis.

2. Divisional performance is measured by residual income, not ROI, with an investment charge calculated at 10 percent of average net investment.

Management regards these as partial solutions. It points to the Dandy Dirndl Division, the company's newest. It was formed two years ago to be in a position to capitalize on an opportunity associated with next year's Olympic Games. The initial investment was $120, of which $100 was in assets being depreciated on a straight-line basis over a five-year period and $20 was an investment in working capital. The anticipated cash flows were:

Time	After-Tax Cash Flow
0................	−$120
1................	+ 10
2................	+ 20
3................	+ 60
4................	+ 40
5................	+ 36

The final cash flow includes $20, representing the anticipated liquidation value of the working capital needed to support this division's activities and $16 representing the cash flow from the fifth year's operations. The internal rate of return was expected to be 10 percent, a satisfactory rate for this company.

Dandy Dirndl's income for the second year was reported as follows:

Revenues....................................		$84.0
Expenses:		
Depreciation...............................	$22.0	
Other expenses (including taxes)............	60.0	
Investment charge at 10%..................	7.7	89.7
Residual income (loss)..................		$(5.7)

The estimated facilities replacement cost in the second year was $110. Replacement cost depreciation was 20 percent of this, or $22. Undepreciated replacement cost was 80 percent of replacement cost (new) at the beginning of the year and 60 percent of this at the end of the year, an average of $77 for the year. The investment charge in the income statement was based on this figure.

Top management noted that the negative residual income was not a serious problem in this case because the division was set up as a special venture by top management. The managers of ongoing divisions might hesitate before recommending such investments in their own divisions, however, because they wouldn't like to have their residual income figures depressed.

a.   Why did management expect the two devices it had already adopted to encourage the division managers to submit capital expenditure proposals?
b.   Identify a depreciation method that would not depress residual income in this case, and calculate depreciation for each of the five years using this method on an historical cost basis.
c.   Convert the historical cost depreciation you calculated in answer to (b) to a replacement cost basis, and make a revised calculation of residual income on a replacement cost basis.
d.   Try to suggest some means other than changing the depreciation schedule to deal with this danger and explain how it would work.

4. Calculating net investment. The asset and liability records of the Deutsch Instruments Company show the following account balances (in thousands of dollars):

	Un-distributed	Traceable to		
		Division A	Division B	Division C
Cash....................................	$360	$ 10	$ 20	$ 15
Receivables............................	400	...	....	....
Inventories............................	...	300	450	400
Plant and equipment..................	100	500	1,500	1,000
Allowance for depreciation.............	(40)	(200)	(700)	(300)
Total Assets.....................	$820	$ 610	$1,270	$1,115
Accounts payable......................	$ 30	$ 80	$ 140	$ 100
Accrued liabilities......................	30	20	30	25
Bonds payable.........................	200	...	....	....
Total Liabilities..................	$260	$ 100	$ 170	$ 125

No further divisional identification of undistributed asset balances is possible, but the president of the company has insisted that divisional net profits be expressed as a percentage of divisional investment, including a share of undistributed investment. Further information on company activities for the most recent year follows (in thousands of dollars):

	Division A	Division B	Division C
Net sales............................	$1,500	$2,400	$2,100
Division payroll.......................	400	600	500
Materials received....................	500	800	800
Head office expense distributed......	80	120	100
Division net income..................	150	300	380

Compute net investment for each division and justify the methods you have used in your computations.

5: Allocations of head office expenses. The Ray Manufacturing Company is decentralized in several divisions, including the textile products

	Entire Company		Textile Products	
	Budget	Actual	Budget	Actual
Number of employees...............	5,000	4,600	800	780
Total payrolls......................	$ 3,500,000	$3,175,000	$ 480,000	$ 485,000
Factory payrolls....................	$ 2,400,000	$2,200,000	$ 375,000	$ 365,000
Net sales..........................	$10,000,000	$9,000,000	$1,500,000	$1,600,000

division. The statistical information on page 805 relates to the company as a whole and the textile products division for the month of June. All budget data have been taken from the planning budget for the month.

Actual head office selling and administrative expenses are fully distributed among the divisions each month. All head office expenses are assumed to be fixed with respect to volume. Budgeted and actual head office expenses, together with the relevant allocation bases, were as follows during the month of June:

	Basis	Budget	Actual
Accounting department.................	Employees	$120,000	$115,000
Manufacturing department..............	Factory payrolls	60,000	62,000
Marketing department..................	Net sales	50,000	51,000
Advertising............................	Net sales	200,000	280,000
Executive offices.......................	Total payrolls	70,000	68,000

a. Prepare a budgeted allocation of head office expenses for the textile products division, based on budget data only.

b. Compute the amount of head office expenses to be charged to the division for the month.

c. Compute the variances in the charges for these five items that will appear in the textile products division profit report for the month. What effect do they have on divisional return on investment? What relevance do they have to activity evaluation?

6. Comparison of two divisions. BIG Industries, Inc. is a decentralized, multidivision firm engaged in a variety of businesses. The following data summarize the operations of two of BIG's divisions (Able and Baker) during 19x1:

	Able Division		Baker Division	
	Budget	Actual	Budget	Actual
Net sales.....................................	$100	$110	$300	$280
Cost of goods sold*..........................	40	44	150	150
Selling and administrative expense..........	30	30	80	80
Income before taxes.........................	30	36	70	50
* Including depreciation....................	10	10	12	12

The following figures were taken from the two divisions' statements of financial position at December 31, 19x1:

	Able Division		Baker Division	
	Budget	Actual	Budget	Actual
Current assets...............................	$140	$150	$105	$100
Fixed assets (cost)...........................	218	220	275	275
Accumulated depreciation.................	177	176	25	25
Current liabilities...........................	45	50	55	50

During 19x1 the market conditions facing each division were about what had been expected when the 19x1 budgets were drawn up.

a. Which division is in the more profitable business? Cite figures to support your conclusions and defend the measures you have chosen.

b. Which division manager is doing the better job of running the division? Again cite figures to support your conclusions and defend the measures you have chosen.

(Prepared by Professor Michael Ginzberg)

7. Department as profit center; Feasibility of residual income. The Val-U-Rite Department Store has a number of merchandise departments—cosmetics, jewelry, housewares, and so on—plus a number of service departments—personnel, credit, cashier, accounting, and so forth.

Each merchandise department manager is responsible for the amount of profit generated in his or her department. Each department selects the merchandise that it wishes to stock and sell; the amount of selling space allotted to each merchandise department is determined by the store's top management and varies to some extent from season to season. Selling prices are set by the individual department managers.

The profit report for the housewares department for the month of January showed the following (to narrow the list of issues to be considered, some figures have been omitted):

	Actual	Budget	Variance
Sales revenues	$415,000	$400,000	$15,000
Cost of merchandise sold	249,000	240,000	(9,000)
Gross margin	$166,000	$160,000	$ 6,000
Operating expenses:			
Direct salaries	$ 59,800	$ 60,000	$ 200
Floor space occupied	5,800	5,000	(800)
Receiving and warehousing	9,200	8,000	(1,200)
.	.	.	.
.	.	.	.
.	.	.	.
Total operating expense	$143,000	$138,000	$(5,000)
Departmental margin	$ 23,000	$ 22,000	$ 1,000

The $5,800 in floor space charges was computed by multiplying the number of square feet of floor space in the housewares department by the average cost of owning and operating the store building during January (depreciation, insurance, taxes, heat, light, and so forth).

The $9,200 in receiving and warehousing costs was the sum of two figures: (1) the number of labor hours spent handling housewares merchandise in the receiving and warehousing department during January, multiplied by the average hourly cost of labor and supervision in this department during the month; and (2) the number of cubic feet of storage space occupied by housewares inventories, multiplied by the average cost of operating the warehouse in January (excluding labor and supervision) per cubic foot of warehouse space.

The amount of floor space occupied by the housewares department and the amount of warehouse space occupied by housewares inventories in January were equal to the amounts budgeted for these purposes.

The figures shown in the "budget" column are the amounts included in the budget for January, prepared when the budget for the entire year was drawn up.

a. Is the housewares department a profit center? List the elements in this situation that support your answer to this question. List the elements that would support an opposite answer.
b. Indicate how the January variances in the charges for floor space occupied by the housewares department and for receiving and warehousing are likely to have arisen.
c. Would it be feasible to calculate residual income for the housewares department? Give reasons to support your answer.

8. Managerial evaluation: Residual income. The profit plan of the Dorsey Corporation's Industrial Products Division was summarized as follows (in thousands):

Sales...		$2,000
Less:		
Standard cost of goods sold..........................	$1,400	
Factory cost variances...............................	80	
Selling expense.......................................	300	
Administrative expense...............................	150	
Income taxes at 40%.................................	28	1,958
Net Income...		$ 42

To carry out this profit plan, the division budgeted the following balance sheet totals (in thousands):

Current assets..	$ 600
Fixed assets..	800
Total Assets.......................................	$1,400
Current liabilities....................................	400
Net Investment......................................	$1,000

Actual sales volume for the year amounted to $2.2 million. The standard cost of goods sold was $1.5 million. Divisional selling expenses totaled $290,000 and divisional administrative expenses (excluding allocations of headquarters costs) amounted to $73,000. Factory cost variances amounted to $110,000, unfavorable. Accounts receivable, inventories, and other current assets traceable to the Industrial Products Division totaled $500,000; current liabilities were $380,000. Fixed assets traceable to the division amounted to $780,000.

All goods sold by this division are manufactured in the division's own factory. Selling expenses are all traceable to the division. They do not vary significantly with variations in actual sales.

Budgeted administrative expenses included a charge for the costs of the Dorsey Corporation's central administrative offices. This charge was computed at 4 percent of sales. Central administration costs do not vary in response to changes in sales volume within the year. As the company expands, however, these costs tend to rise and the 4 percent average has been relatively constant for many years.

The budgeted factory cost variances were entirely overhead volume variances.

The budgeted net investment in current assets included $150,000 in cash. Cash balances are administered by the corporate treasurer's office and are allocated among the divisions on the basis of divisional sales.

Budgeted fixed assets included $50,000 as the Industrial Products Division's share of the company's investments in its headquarters offices. All remaining items in the net investment were traceable to the division and administered locally.

Production and sales volumes for the year were identical. The company's target minimum rate of return on investment is 10 percent for all divisions.

a. Prepare a profit report for use in appraising managerial performance in the Industrial Products Division during the year. Use the residual income approach.

b. Prepare a brief description of the principle or principles you followed in (a), referring to items in the report to show how these principles were applied.

c. What additional information would you want to have before evaluating division management's performance for the year?

9. ROI reporting. The following financial report was prepared for the Hepplewhite division of the Duncan Company for the first two months of the 19x1–x2 fiscal year which began on March 1, 19x1 (dollar figures in thousands):

		Comparative Results of Business		
			Two months to April 30	
	Actual, April, 19x1	Budget 19x1	Actual 19x1	Actual 19x0
Sales:				
Product A	$190	$ 500	$ 453	$484
Product B	223	700	522	377
Product C	65	100	132	91
Product D	12	50	28	39
Total sales	$490	$1,350	$1,135	$991
Standard cost of sales:				
Product A	$112	$ 300	$ 266	$312
Product B	107	336	251	183
Product C	38	58	76	44
Product D	6	25	14	22
Total standard cost of sales	$263	$ 719	$ 607	$561
Gross profit on sales	$227	$ 631	$ 528	$430
Expenses:				
Home office commissions	$ 28	$ 66	$ 66	$ 66
Selling	58	128	121	79
Administrative	27	52	61	63
Development	27	77	63	106
Total expenses	$140	$ 323	$ 311	$314
Income before taxes	$ 87	$ 308	$ 217	$116
Taxes at 50%	44	154	109	58
Net Income	$ 43	$ 154	$ 108	$ 58

	Comparative Financial Position		
	2–28–x1	4–30–x1	Change
Assets:			
Cash	$ 16	$ 20	$ 4
Receivables	277	101	(176)
Inventories	2,451	2,324	(127)
Fixed assets—net	1,295	1,291	(4)
Deferred charges—net	19	(67)	(86)
Total assets	$4,058	$3,669	$(389)
Accounts payable	189	94	(95)
Net investment	$3,869	$3,575	$(294)
Return on investment	10.8%	17.5%	+6.7%

1. Home office commissions reflect predetermined payments for central administrative services rendered.

2. Development expenses consist of current research division charges

to projects which have been requested and approved by the Hepplewhite division.

3. Cash balances represent imprest funds only. All payrolls and most payments to vendors are made by the home office.

4. Accounts receivable and accounts payable consist of billings and invoices in transit between Hepplewhite and the home office.

5. All materials, work-in-process, and finished product inventories of the Hepplewhite division, together with plant and equipment listed in the corporate property records as belonging to Hepplewhite, are shown on the Hepplewhite statements. There is no allocation of centrally administered assets. No budgets are prepared for divisional assets and liabilities.

6. No factory cost variances were budgeted in the original profit plan for the first two months. Variances that do arise are classified as deferred charges or credits; deferred charges and credits are reported as a single item on the monthly statements of financial position. Factory flexible budget allowances for March and April amounted to $282,000. Overhead absorbed totaled $308,000, and actual overhead totaled $259,000. Variances in direct materials and direct labor during this period amounted to $14,000 and were unfavorable.

7. All sales were made at budgeted prices. The standard pretax contribution margin is 50 percent of sales for product A, 60 percent for product B, 55 percent for product C, and 50 percent for product D. All expenses other than the cost of goods sold are assumed to be fixed with respect to volume.

a. How well does the return on investment figure, as calculated above, measure the profitability of this division's activities?

b. How well does it measure managerial performance?

c. Prepare a revised report for the two-month period, using a profit contribution format and incorporating any improvements you deem desirable and feasible, given only the information above. Indicate any additional information you would like to have which should be available at little cost.

10. Managerial performance evaluation. George Johnson was hired on July 1, 19x1 as assistant general manager of the Botel Division of Staple, Inc. It was understood that he would be elevated to General Manager of the division on January 1, 19x3, when the then current general manager retired and this was duly done. In addition to becoming acquainted with the division and the general manager's duties, Mr. Johnson was specifically charged with the responsibility for development of the 19x2 and 19x3 budgets. As general manager in 19x3, he was, obviously, responsible for the 19x4 budget.

The Staple Company is a multiproduct company which is highly decentralized. Each division is quite autonomous. The corporation staff approves division prepared operating budgets but seldom makes major changes in them. The corporate staff actively participates in decisions requiring capital investment (for expansion or replacement) and makes the final decisions. The division management is responsible for implementing the capital program. The major device used by the Staple Corporation to measure division performance is Contribution Return on Division Net Investment. The Botel Division budgets presented in the following table were approved by the corporate staff. (The budget is approved in December each year and is not revised, no matter how large the observed departures from the planned results.)

	Actual			Budget	
	19x1	19x2	19x3	19x2	19x3
Sales...	1,000	1,500	1,800	2,000	2,400
Less division variable costs:					
Material and Labor..........................	250	375	450	500	600
Repairs....................................	50	75	50	100	120
Supplies...................................	20	30	36	40	48
Less division managed costs:					
Employee Training..........................	30	35	25	40	45
Maintenance...............................	50	55	40	60	70
Less division committed costs:					
Depreciation...............................	120	160	160	200	200
Rent......................................	80	100	110	140	140
Total.....................................	600	830	871	1,080	1,223
Division net contribution......................	400	670	929	920	1,177
Division investment:					
Accounts receivable.........................	100	150	180	200	240
Inventory..................................	200	300	270	400	480
Fixed assets...............................	1,590	2,565	2,800	3,380	4,000
Less: accounts and wages payable...........	(150)	(225)	(350)	(300)	(360)
Net investment..............................	1,740	2,790	2,900	3,680	4,360
Contribution return on net investment..........	23%	24%	32%	25%	27%

a. Identify Mr. Johnson's responsibilities under the management and measurement program described above.

b. Appraise the performance of Mr. Johnson in 19x3.

c. Recommend to the president any changes in the responsibilities assigned to managers or in the measurement methods used to evaluate division management based upon your analysis.

(CMA)

CASE 24–1: DUNDEE PRODUCTS, INC.

George Dickson would like to take on a new customer, but is worried about his rate of return on investment (ROI). Mr. Dickson is in charge of the Cleveland branch of the Esco division of Dundee Products, Inc., a large conglomerate. Esco is a national distributor of industrial supplies, purchased from a number of manufacturers and sold through a network of 17 regional branches. Most of Dundee's other divisions deal in consumer goods; none of them sells any of its products through the Esco division.

Like the managers of the other branches, Mr. Dickson reports to Frank Corbett, Esco's executive vice president. Each branch is treated as a small profit center and each branch manager has virtually complete discretion over the methods of sales promotion to be used, the products to stock, and the customers to be served within the branch's geographical area. All products are selected from a list supplied by Esco's central purchasing office.

Selling prices are set at Esco's headquarters, but each branch manager can alter the terms of sale to reflect differences in risk and profitability of doing business with different customers. Each branch does its own billing and collection work. The profit performance of the branches and their managers is judged each year on the basis of the rate of return achieved on the investment in the branch, mainly the investment in storage space, the inventories on hand, and the receivables outstanding.

The Profit Plan

Each September, every branch manager submits a tentative profit plan to Mr. Corbett. This plan is a complete summary of the manager's marketing plans, including estimates of the amounts to be spent for field selling, the sales level to be achieved, the costs of warehousing, and the levels of the proposed investments in inventories and receivables. The anticipated first-year effects of proposed investments in physical facilities and equipment are also reflected in this tentative plan.

The proposed profit plans are reviewed critically by Mr. Corbett and his staff, who question the assumptions on which the projections have been based, make sure that alternative plans have been studied carefully, see whether the proposals are within the company's capacity, offer suggestions for improvement, and provide technical help in revising the proposals.

Once Mr. Corbett and the branch managers have come to an agreement, the plans are consolidated into an overall profit plan for the Esco division as a whole. Last-minute adjustments are sometimes made at this stage, but most of the inconsistencies ordinarily have been removed during the staff review.

The profit plans from all of the Dundee divisions are reviewed by corporate staff. Divisional plans are discussed informally as they are being formulated, and as a result relatively few changes are made in the plans after formal submission. The main reason for change at this point is a refusal by top management to fund facilities and equipment proposals at the levels anticipated by the division managers. This requires a reworking of the budgetary proposals in the light of the revised guidelines.

The current profit plan for the Cleveland branch is summarized in the first column of Table 1. Cleveland has been one of the division's most profitable outlets in the past, with rates of return ranging from 17 to 21 percent, but a major expenditure of funds on a new warehouse building and new materials handling equipment has brought the budgeted rate of return down to the 13.6 percent figure shown in Table 1. Even so, this is substantially greater than the 9 percent after-tax figure adopted by Dundee's top management as a minimum profit standard for investments in warehouses and sales offices.

Measurement Methods

For internal reporting, Dundee measures investments in physical facilities at original cost less straight-line depreciation. Inventories in the Esco division are costed on a first-in, first-out (Fifo) basis. Receivables are shown at full face value, less an allowance for uncollectible amounts that is adjusted once a year on the basis of a headquarters staff review of the outstanding account balances.

All payrolls and payments to vendors are processed at Esco's divisional headquarters; the branch managers control only small petty cash accounts and have no direct liabilities of their own. The branch profit plans include a provision for cash and accounts payable, however, based on head office staff estimates of the amounts attributable to each branch's operations. These provisions are calculated from standard formulas, which are also used to compute the amounts shown in the monthly performance reports for each branch.

Investments in facilities and working capital at divisional and corporate

TABLE 1

DUNDEE PRODUCTS, INC.
Esco Division, Cleveland Branch Pro Forma Profit Plan
(dollar figures in thousands)

	Current Plan	Adjusted for Cut-Rate Line*
Net sales......................................	$2,728	$3,740
Cost of goods sold†..........................	1,982	2,792
Gross margin.................................	$ 746	$ 948
Branch expenses‡...........................	264	334
Income before tax............................	$ 482	$ 614
Income tax.................................	265	338
Net income.................................	$ 217	$ 276
Current assets:		
Cash§.......................................	$ 35	$ 50
Accounts receivable........................	253	398
Inventories.................................	702	1,132
Total current assets.......................	$ 990	$1,580
Less accounts payable§.....................	346	431
Net working capital..........................	$ 644	$1,149
Land..	91	91
Buildings (net of depreciation).................	704	704
Equipment (net of depreciation)..............	185	215
Net investment, end of year...................	$1,624	$2,159
Average net investment:		
End of year................................	$1,624	$2,159
Beginning of year..........................	1,572	2,111
Average net investment.....................	$1,598	$2,135
Rate of return (ROI).........................	13.6%	12.9%

* Based on 12 months' operations for comparative purposes.
† Purchase price plus estimated headquarters purchasing department cost.
‡ Including charges for head office services.
§ Based on head office estimates of amounts attributable to this branch.

headquarters are very small, and none of this investment is allocated to the individual branches.

Each branch is charged at predetermined unit prices for head office services such as payroll preparation and vendor payment. In addition, a flat charge of 2 percent of sales is made to cover the average cost of head office administration. Division headquarters charges each branch with the net invoice price of all goods consigned to the branch, plus 1 percent of this amount to cover the cost of the divisional purchasing department, which does all the purchasing for the branches.

The New Opportunity

The operations at the Cleveland branch are proceeding more or less according to plan, and Mr. Dickson expects that when all the results are in at the end of the year he'll be very close to the planned levels of revenue and expense.

His new warehouse was built to meet the company's anticipated growth in the Cleveland area in the next ten years, however, and a good deal of space is currently unused. Reasoning that his method of operation would enable him to offer better warehousing service to local companies with large inventories of nonperishable merchandise than local storage warehouses could provide, Mr. Dickson has spent a considerable amount of time during the past few months looking for one or two such customers.

Preliminary contracts with Cut-Rate Drugs, Inc., a St. Louis-based supplier of cosmetics, proprietary medicines, and other articles typically sold in drug stores, have progressed to such a point that Mr. Dickson has to make up his mind whether to expand into this line of business. Under the proposed arrangement, Cut-Rate would ship its products to the Cleveland warehouse, billing the Esco division on terms of net 30 days. This merchandise would be stored in a separate section of the warehouse.

In accordance with the Cut-Rate method of operation, all store deliveries would be in full case lots. Delivery would be made by four driver-salesmen who would be transferred from the Cut-Rate payroll. Cut-Rate would also lease its local fleet of four delivery vehicles to Mr. Dickson for the duration of the agreement. Mr. Dickson would become responsible for billing the drug stores and collecting the amounts due from them for the merchandise.

"This looks like a natural for us," Mr. Dickson said last week. "Only the sales force would be separate. Otherwise, the operation would be just like what we're doing now with our regular lines. We carry stock, sell, deliver, and collect, and we're pretty good at our job. I see no reason why we shouldn't do just as well with the Cut-Rate line. Our branches in Denver and Atlanta are doing the same sort of thing and seem to be making a go of it.

"The figures seem to bear me out, too. We'd get an extra $59,000 in profit on a $535,000 increase in investment, a rate of return of about 11 percent. The return to the company would be even greater, because our figures reflect the 2 percent surcharge that headquarters skims off the top of all our operations. I can't see how headquarters costs would go up by a penny as a result of this operation.

"The only problem is that our overall rate of return would go down from 13.6 percent to about 12.9 percent on an annual basis. You can see this in the right-hand column of the pro forma budget I gave you this morning [Table 1]. We've already come down from 17 percent as a result of the new warehouse and I don't think I'm going to look very good if I ring in with an even lower rate this year. I think I have a crack at the division manager's job when Frank Corbett retires in a couple of years and I don't want to do anything to rock the boat now. Frank tells me that he'll okay the increase in my inventories and receivables if I want to go ahead, but I'm afraid of that drop in the ROI."

"What kind of commitment would you have to make with Cut-Rate?" the case writer asked. "Could you get out of this easily if it didn't work out the way you expected?"

"Oh, we'd have no problem there. The deal is that either party could cancel the arrangement on six months' notice, and it would take us six months to clean things up anyway. They'd buy back the unsold inventory at book value. The salesmen would go back to Cut-Rate, too, unless they wanted to stay with us and we had room for them."

"What's in it for Cut-Rate? What's wrong with the way they've been operating? I've been taught to be suspicious of people who want to give up part of their business."

"Well, anything's possible, of course, but I think this is on the level. They've been supervising the local sales force from St. Louis, using a local storage warehouse as a transshipment depot. The salesmen are okay, but they've had a lot of trouble with the warehouse. Those people are good at dead storage, but they don't know the first thing about field warehousing. That's our business, and the people at Cut-Rate are pretty sure that we can increase their volume and cut their costs, too. Besides, they have a lot of money tied up in inventories and receivables. We figure that with our controls we can handle the higher volume with a smaller investment. It's unprofitable for them and very profitable for us, and you can't find a better basis for a deal than that."

a. Should Mr. Dickson go ahead with the Cut-Rate venture? Prepare a summary of the calculations and arguments on both sides of these questions.
b. How would you decide whether the Cleveland branch's reported profit or return on investment is satisfactory or unsatisfactory? What profit standards would you adopt in this connection, and where would you get them?
c. Should the measurement system be changed in any way to make it more consistent with the company's objectives? Give reasons to support your suggestions.

25

Profit Analysis

DEVIATIONS from profit plans measure the effects of changes in conditions, poor forecasting, or variations in managerial effectiveness. Since the reasons for these deviations are not always clear, further analysis and explanation are usually necessary.

The main purpose of this chapter is to outline a method that the accountant can use to break the total profit variance into a set of interrelated components. This will be followed by a brief discussion of an alternative approach, focusing on ratios and trends.

PROFIT VARIANCE ANALYSIS

An ideal variance analysis would identify the ultimate or primary cause of each element of the overall profit variance. So much would be attributed to orders lost due to price competition, so much to higher materials prices resulting from an increase in rail freight tariffs, and so on.

Because this ordinarily can be done only for a small part of the total variance, the variance analysis has to focus on intermediate causes or symptoms rather than on the primary causes. Examples of categories into which profit variances ordinarily can be split are:

1. Deviations from budgeted selling prices (sales price variances).
2. Deviations from budgeted physical sales volume (sales volume variances).
3. Deviations from budgeted product sales mix (sales mix variances).
4. Deviations from standard costs and flexible budget allowances (input quantity, input price, and spending variances).

This kind of analysis can be applied to all kinds of organizations. It receives its most complete implementation in manufacturing, however, and for this reason we shall use an illustration of a manufacturing firm in this section. Our immediate purpose will be to describe a method by which the variance from a manufacturing company's planned profit performance can be broken down into the four categories listed on the preceding page. We shall do this by examining four situations of gradually increasing complexity:

1. Calculation of sales price and sales volume variances in a company which manufactures and sells a single product, using variable costing to measure product cost.
2. Calculation of sales price, sales volume, production volume, and factory spending variances in a company which manufactures and sells a single product, using absorption costing.
3. Calculation of sales volume and mix variances when the company manufactures and sells two products, using absorption costing.
4. Analysis of variances in a company which manufactures and sells a large number of products, using absorption costing.

At the end of the section we shall review some of the limitations of this kind of analysis.

Single-Product Firm, Variable Costing

At its simplest, profit variance analysis merely adds two variances—a selling price variance and a sales volume variance—to those already described in previous chapters. For example, the XYZ Company manufactures and sells a single product. The company uses variable costing, and all short-term cost relationships are linear. Budgeted factory costs amount to $120,000 a month plus $3 for each unit produced, and the product sells at a price of $5 a unit. To simplify the presentation, we have assumed that the company has no selling and administrative expenses.

The profit budget appropriate to a normal production and sales volume of 100,000 units a month is as follows:

	Total Amount	Average per Unit
Units sold.....................................	100,000	xxx
Units produced............................	100,000	xxx
Sales revenues............................	$500,000	$5.00
Standard cost of goods sold...............	300,000	3.00
Contribution margin....................	$200,000	$2.00
Fixed manufacturing costs.................	120,000	
Income before taxes....................	$ 80,000	

Sales volume variance. The month of March was expected to be normal in all respects. The budget for the month, therefore, was the same as the budget for a normal month. Actual results for March and the resulting profit variance were as follows:

	Actual	Budget	Variance*
Units sold.....................	90,000	100,000	(10,000)
Units produced................	100,000	100,000	—
Sales revenues................	$450,000	$500,000	$(50,000)
Standard cost of goods sold...	270,000	300,000	30,000
Contribution margin..	$180,000	$200,000	$(20,000)
Fixed manufacturing costs.....	120,000	120,000	—
Income before taxes..	$ 60,000	$ 80,000	$(20,000)

* Brackets will be used in the tables in this chapter to identify unfavorable variances.

The entire profit variance this month was a sales volume variance. It can be computed by multiplying the physical variance in sales volume (10,000 units) by the standard contribution margin per unit:

> Sales volume variance = 10,000 × $2 = $20,000 Unfavorable

Sales price variance. XYZ's management had also budgeted a normal profit for the month of April. The results were even worse than in March:

	Actual	Budget	Variance
Units sold.....................	90,000	100,000	(10,000)
Units produced................	100,000	100,000	—
Sales revenues................	$445,000	$500,000	$(55,000)
Standard cost of goods sold...	270,000	300,000	30,000
Contribution margin..	$175,000	$200,000	$(25,000)
Fixed manufacturing costs.....	120,000	120,000	—
Income before taxes..	$ 55,000	$ 80,000	$(25,000)

Sales volume was the same it had been in March; therefore the sales volume variance once again was $20,000. Fixed factory costs remained the same and no factory cost variances were reported. The difference between March and April was that the company had a sales price variance in April:

Single-Product Firm, Absorption Costing

The ABC Company is exactly like XYZ, except that it uses absorption costing with a normal production volume of 100,000 units a month. At this volume the planned or standard gross margin is $0.80 a unit:

Planned selling price............................		$5.00
Standard product cost:		
Variable...	$3.00	
Fixed: $120,000/100,000..........................	1.20	
Total..		4.20
Standard gross margin...........................		$ .80

We'll identify three different variances for this company:

1. Sales volume variance.
2. Production volume variance.
3. Factory spending variance.

Sales volume variance. The month of May was expected to be normal, and the budget was the same as a budget for a normal month. Actual results for May and the resulting profit variance were as follows:

	Actual	Budget	Variance
Units sold.................................	90,000	100,000	(10,000)
Units produced............................	100,000	100,000	—
Sales revenues............................	$450,000	$500,000	$(50,000)
Standard cost of goods sold..............	378,000	420,000	42,000
Gross margin..............................	$ 72,000	$ 80,000	$ (8,000)
Factory cost variances....................	—	—	—
Income before taxes..................	$ 72,000	$ 80,000	$ (8,000)

The entire profit variance was a sales volume variance. We can verify this by multiplying the physical variance in sales volume (10,000 units) by the standard gross margin per unit:

> Sales volume variance = 10,000 × $.80 = $8,000 Unfavorable

This is $12,000 smaller than the volume variance we calculated for the XYZ Company in similar circumstances. The explanation is that each unit of product sold by ABC absorbs $1.20 of the fixed factory costs.

Production volume variance. The situation in June was different. The budgeted profit was again at its normal level, and actual sales equaled the budgeted amount, but production fell 10,000 units below the budget for the month. The results were as follows:

	Actual	Budget	Variance
Units sold	100,000	100,000	—
Units produced	90,000	100,000	(10,000)
Sales revenues	$500,000	$500,000	—
Standard cost of goods sold	420,000	420,000	—
Gross margin	$ 80,000	$ 80,000	—
Factory cost variances	(12,000)	—	$(12,000)
Income before taxes	$ 68,000	$ 80,000	$(12,000)

The factory cost variance in this case was due entirely to the deviation of production volume from the amount budgeted—that is, it was a production volume variance. We can demonstrate this by comparing the amount of cost budgeted at actual volume with the amount absorbed at this volume:

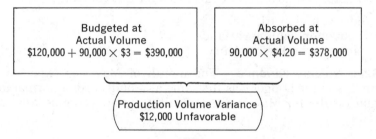

This is the overhead volume variance we encountered in earlier chapters. All other factory cost variances either were zero or canceled each other.

The variance in this case can also be called an *unplanned inventory change variance*. In preparing the budget, management planned to have production equal sales. Inventory was to remain unchanged; all $120,000 in fixed cost was to be assigned to goods finished and placed in inventory. Instead, actual production was 10,000 units less than actual sales. This means that the inventory must have decreased by 10,000 units. As a result, 10,000 × $1.20 = $12,000 in fixed cost was not placed in inventory, as management had anticipated. It went to the income statement because the inventory changed.

Sales and production volume variances combined. Production and sales were again budgeted at 100,000 units in July. Actual production and sales were only 95,000 units. The results were as follows:

	Actual	Budget	Variance
Units sold	95,000	100,000	(5,000)
Units produced	95,000	100,000	(5,000)
Sales revenues	$475,000	$500,000	$(25,000)
Standard cost of goods sold	399,000	420,000	21,000
Gross margin	$ 76,000	$ 80,000	$ (4,000)
Factory cost variances	(6,000)	—	(6,000)
Income before taxes	$ 70,000	$ 80,000	$(10,000)

The sales volume variance is simple to calculate:

Sales volume variance = 5,000 units × $0.80 = $4,000 Unfavorable

---

This accounts for the entire variance in the gross margin.

The production volume variance is also simple to compute. The budgeted production volume was 100,000 units, the normal volume. This means that management budgeted a zero production volume variance for the month. The actual production volume was only 95,000, and the actual production volume variance can be calculated in the usual way:

```
Absorbed:   95,000 × $4.20............................ $399,000
Budgeted: $120,000 + $3 × 95,000...................... 405,000
    Production volume variance....................... $ (6,000)
```

This accounts for the entire factory cost variance for the month.

Since production volume and sales volume were equal, the inventory didn't change. In other words, the production volume variance in this case wasn't the result of an unplanned inventory change, as it was in June. It can be argued, therefore, that this production volume variance was really the result of the departure from planned *sales* volume. Production merely adapted itself to the change in the volume of sales. If this argument is accepted, the two variances can be combined:

```
Variance in gross margin due to reduced sales................. $ (4,000)
Unabsorbed production costs due to reduced sales............   (6,000)
    Total sales volume variance............................ $(10,000)
```

Notice that this is the same result we would get under variable costing. In variable costing we'd have only one variance:

Sales volume variance = 5,000 units × ($5 − $3) = $10,000 Unfavorable

---

This equality will always be true if two conditions are met:

1. Sales and production volumes are identical.
2. All factory cost variances are reported in full on the current income statement.

Budgeted sales and production unequal to normal volume. August was a vacation month. Sales and production were budgeted at 90,000 units. Budgeted and actual results were as follows:

	Actual	Budget	Variance
Units sold.................................	94,000	90,000	4,000
Units produced............................	94,000	90,000	4,000
Sales revenues............................	$470,000	$450,000	$ 20,000
Standard cost of goods sold...............	394,800	378,000	(16,800)
Gross margin..........................	$ 75,200	$ 72,000	$ 3,200
Factory cost variances....................	(7,200)	(12,000)	4,800
Income before taxes...................	$ 68,000	$ 60,000	$ 8,000

   Although sales volume was less than the normal volume of 100,000 units, it was greater than the amount budgeted by 4,000 units. Since the budget is the basis for comparison, we can determine that the sales volume variance was 4,000 units × $0.80 = $3,200, favorable. This accounted for the entire variance in the gross margin.

   When we get to the factory cost variance line in the report, we see something new: a variance from a planned variance. There is nothing mysterious in this. Management knew in advance that production would be less than normal. Knowing this, it was able to prepare a more accurate budget for the month. The $12,000 budgeted factory cost variance was calculated as follows:

Units produced.. 90,000
Absorbed by production: 90,000 × $4.20................. $378,000
Budgeted for budgeted production volume:
   $120,000 + $3 × 90,000............................... 390,000
      Budgeted production volume variance............. $(12,000)

We could get the same result by noting that production volume was 10,000 units less than the amount budgeted, leaving 10,000 × $1.20 = $12,000 in fixed costs unabsorbed.

   The $7,200 actual unfavorable variance in July therefore was good news because it was $4,800 less unfavorable than management had anticipated. We can analyze this as follows:

	Actual	Budget	Variance
Units produced............................	94,000	90,000	4,000
Absorbed by production at $4.20............	$394,800	$378,000	$ 16,800
Budgeted for production:			
$120,000 + $3 × volume....................	402,000	390,000	(12,000)
Volume variance.......................	$ (7,200)	$(12,000)	$ 4,800

An easier method, when costs are assumed to be linear, is to multiply the variance in production volume by the unit fixed cost:

Production volume variance = (94,000 − 90,000) × $1.20 = $4,800 Favorable

For greater precision, this can be labeled the *unplanned production volume variance*. In profit variance analysis we are ordinarily attempting to account for variances from budgeted amounts, not from normal amounts or some other base.

   Once again sales volume and production volume were identical. The inventory remained unchanged. The entire production volume variance can be seen as a result of adapting production volume to the volume of sales:

Variance in gross margin due to increased sales................. $3,200
Unabsorbed production costs due to increased sales............ 4,800
   Total sales volume variance............................... $8,000

Variable costing would lead to the same conclusion. Multiplying the 4,000 unit favorable variance in physical sales volume by the $2 contribution margin yields an $8,000 sales volume variance.

Factory spending variances. Production volume variances are not the only factory variances to appear on the profit report. Materials price and quantity, labor rate and quantity, and overhead spending and efficiency variances all show up, too. For convenience, we shall refer to all of these as *factory spending variances*. If actual factory cost variances in August had totaled $8,200, the factory spending variances would have accounted for $1,000 of the total:

Total factory cost variance	$(8,200)
Production volume variance	(7,200)
Factory spending variances	$(1,000)

This of course would be broken down in great detail, by type and by department, but for profit reporting only the summary figure is necessary.

Variance summary. Budgeted volume in September was back to 100,000 units. Actual results were as follows:

	Actual	Budgeted	Variance
Units sold	95,000	100,000	(5,000)
Units produced	90,000	100,000	(10,000)
Sales revenues	$478,000	$500,000	$(22,000)
Standard cost of goods sold	399,000	420,000	21,000
Gross margin	$ 79,000	$ 80,000	$ (1,000)
Factory cost variances	(14,000)	—	(14,000)
Income before taxes	$ 65,000	$ 80,000	$(15,000)

All four of the variances we have identified so far can be isolated from these figures. The analysis is summarized in Exhibit 25–1. The total variance is the difference between the income figures in the first and last columns. This is broken down in stages—each column is identical to its neighbor except in one element, such as price or volume.

We can make one more subdivision if we wish. The production volume variance can be interpreted as the combined result of two factors: (1) the reduction in sales volume (5,000 units); and (2) an unplanned reduction in inventory (another 5,000 units). The breakdown is simple:

Reduced absorption due to reduced sales volume:	
5,000 × $1.20	$ (6,000)
Reduced absorption due to unplanned reduction	
in inventory: 5,000 × $1.20	(6,000)
Total production volume variance	$(12,000)

We can then combine the first of these with the sales volume variance, as we did in earlier parts of this illustration.

EXHIBIT 25–1

Variance Calculation, Single-Product Firm

| | Standard Prices and Costs | | | Actual Prices, Standard | |
	Budgeted Sales, Budgeted Production	Actual Sales, Budgeted Production	Actual Sales, Actual Production	Costs, Actual Sales, Actual Production	Actual Net Income
Sales revenues..............	$500,000	$475,000	$475,000	$478,000	$478,000
Standard cost of goods sold..	420,000	399,000	399,000	399,000	399,000
Gross margin.................	$ 80,000	$ 76,000	$ 76,000	$ 79,000	$ 79,000
Factory cost variances.........	—	—	(12,000)	(12,000)	(14,000)
Income before taxes.......	$ 80,000	$ 76,000	$ 64,000	$ 67,000	$ 65,000

	Sales Volume Variance	Production Volume Variance	Sales Price Variance	Factory Spending Variance
	5,000 units × $0.80 = $(4,000)	10,000 units × $1.20 = $(12,000)	$478,000 −$5 × 95,000 = $3,000	$(14,000) −$(12,000) = $(2,000)

Effect of the sequence followed. The calculations we made in these analyses are not the only possibilities. The sales volume variance, for example, could just as easily be calculated at $5.03, the average actual price (actual revenues of $478,000 divided by actual sales volume of 95,000 units). The sales volume variance then would be 5,000 units × ($5.03 − $4.20) = $4,150. This might even be a better measure of the effect of the volume deviation on company profit in a given period.

Standard prices are usually used, however, to permit direct comparisons of the volume variances of different time periods. If volume is always measured at the same prices, then any change in the volume variance is the result of a change in volume, not a mixture of price and volume effects. The issue here and the possible solutions are the same as in the calculation of price and quantity variances in factory costs described in Chapter 6.

Two-Product Firm: Sales Mix Variance

In a multiproduct firm or division, profit may vary because high-margin products have increased or decreased their relative share of total volume. The effect of this variation is known as the sales mix variance.

From the analyst's point of view, the sales mix variance is a component of the total of the sales volume variances of all of the products in the line. For example, suppose the ABC Company has two products instead of one. Budgeted and actual data for the month of October are shown in Exhibit 25–2. This shows that the gross margin for the month, $70,000, was $10,000 less than the amount budgeted.

EXHIBIT 25–2

Two-Product Firm: Profit Data for October

	Product A		Product B		Total Amount
	Per Unit	Total	Per Unit	Total	
Budget:					
Units sold.....................		80,000		20,000	
Units produced................		80,000		20,000	
Sales revenues................	$3.75	$300,000	$10.00	$200,000	$500,000
Standard cost of goods sold..	2.85	228,000	9.60	192,000	420,000
Gross margin..................	$0.90	$ 72,000	$ 0.40	$ 8,000	$ 80,000
Actual:					
Units sold.....................		68,000		22,000	
Units produced................		80,000		20,000	
Sales revenues................	$3.75	$255,000	$10.00	$220,000	$475,000
Standard cost of goods sold..	2.85	193,800	9.60	211,200	405,000
Gross margin..................	$0.90	$ 61,200	$ 0.40	$ 8,800	$ 70,000
Variances:					
Units sold.....................		(12,000)		2,000	
Units produced................		—		—	
Sales revenues................		$(45,000)		$ 20,000	$(25,000)
Standard cost of goods sold..		34,200		(19,200)	(15,000)
Gross margin..................		$(10,800)		$ 800	$(10,000)

We can calculate the individual product sales volume variances quite easily, using the variance in units sold and margin per unit from the exhibit:

	Variance in Units Sold	Budgeted Gross Margin	Sales Volume Variance
Product A........................	(12,000)	$0.90	$(10,800)
Product B........................	2,000	0.40	800
Total sales volume variance...			$(10,000)

Production volume, sales price, and factory spending variances were all zero. The sales volume variances accounted for the entire profit variance.

If this were a real company, with only two products, we probably would end the analysis here, reporting two volume variances instead of one. We are using this simple situation to represent a more complex one, however, and for this reason we must go farther.

To break the total of the product sales volume variances down into aggregate mix and volume components, we need two figures:

1. A figure representing the variation in overall physical volume.
2. A measure of the average profitability of one unit of overall volume.

Volume can be measured by (1) the number of units sold; (2) sales revenues at standard prices; or (3) standard product costs. Suppose we use revenues, for example. Since the sales price variance was zero, the difference between budgeted and actual sales is a measure of the change in physical volume in which each product is weighted in proportion to its planned selling price.

From the right-hand column of Exhibit 25–2 we can calculate the budgeted gross margin ratio at the budgeted sales mix:

$$\frac{\text{Budgeted gross margin}}{\text{Budgeted sales revenues}} = \frac{\$\ 80,000}{\$500,000} = 16 \text{ percent}$$

We can use this percentage to calculate an overall volume variance for October:

$$\text{Sales volume variance} = \$25,000 \times 16\% = \$4,000 \text{ Unfavorable}$$

This says that if sales of the two products had stayed in their budgeted proportions, a $25,000 change in volume would have reduced the gross margin by $4,000. In fact, the effect was much greater than that, $10,000. The $6,000 difference was the sales mix variance.

These figures can be derived more systematically by a line-by-line analysis of the income statement. The budgeted gross margin ratio at the budgeted mix was 16 percent; the budgeted standard cost of goods sold therefore was 84 percent of budgeted sales. Applying these ratios to the actual sales volume (at budgeted prices), we get the following volume-adjusted budget for the month:

Sales revenues.................................. $475,000
Standard cost of goods sold at budgeted
  mix (84%)..................................... 399,000
       Gross margin at budgeted mix (16%)....... $ 76,000

These figures have been entered in the middle colume of Exhibit 25–3. Once again, each column differs from its neighbor in only one respect, and this difference provides an explanation for the variance figure shown between the two columns at the bottom of the exhibit.

Variances in Selling and Administrative Expenses

All of our illustrations so far have been based on the assumption that selling and administrative expenses are entirely fixed. We need to modify the analysis if any significant amounts of these expenses are expected to vary with sales.

For example, suppose ABC Company pays its sales representatives commissions amounting to 5 percent of sales. Other selling and ad-

EXHIBIT 25–3

Calculation of Sales Mix Variance

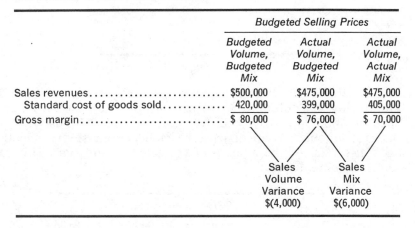

	Budgeted Selling Prices		
	Budgeted Volume, Budgeted Mix	Actual Volume, Budgeted Mix	Actual Volume, Actual Mix
Sales revenues............................	$500,000	$475,000	$475,000
Standard cost of goods sold.............	420,000	399,000	405,000
Gross margin.............................	$ 80,000	$ 76,000	$ 70,000
		Sales Volume Variance $(4,000)	Sales Mix Variance $(6,000)

ministrative expenses are expected to amount to $20,000 a month. Suppose further that operating results in November were as follows:

	Budget	Actual	Variance
Sales revenues.....................	$500,000	$478,000	$(22,000)
Standard cost of goods sold........	420,000	405,000	15,000
Gross margin.................	$ 80,000	$ 73,000	$(7,000)
Selling and administrative expenses........................	45,000	45,500	(500)
Income before taxes.........	$ 35,000	$ 27,500	$(7,500)

Both budgeted and actual sales volumes were the same in November as in October:

	Budgeted (Units)	Actual (Units)
Product A...................	80,000	68,000
Product B..................	20,000	22,000

Sales volume variance. To calculate the sales volume variance, we must first recalculate the budgeted profit margin at the budgeted mix. This is easy because the variable component of selling and administrative expense is unaffected by the product mix—it is a straight 5 percent of sales. The budgeted contribution margin ratio, therefore, is the 16 percent budgeted gross margin ratio, less 5 percent, or 11 percent.

The actual number of units sold, measured at budgeted selling prices, was $475,000:

	Sales Volume	Budgeted Price	Revenues at Budgeted Price
Product A..................	68,000	$ 3.75	$255,000
Product B..................	22,000	10.00	220,000
Total..................			$475,000

This is $25,000 less than the amount originally budgeted ($500,000). Multiplying this difference by 11 percent, we find a sales volume variance of $25,000 × 0.11 = $2,750, unfavorable. This is $1,250 less than the amount we calculated for October, because the reduction in sales also reduced the amount of the sales commission. This can be shown in more detail:

	Budgeted Mix and Prices		Sales Volume Variance
	Budgeted Volume	Actual Volume	
Sales revenues....................	$500,000	$475,000	$(25,000)
Standard cost of goods sold (84%)......................	$420,000	$399,000	21,000
Selling and administrative expenses ($20,000 + 5%).........	45,000	43,750	1,250
Income before taxes........	$ 35,000	$ 32,250	$ (2,750)

Sales price variance. Selling and administrative expenses are also affected in this case by fluctuations in selling prices. If prices are higher than budgeted, sales commissions will be higher; if prices are reduced, sales commissions will fall. Actual sales revenues this month were $478,000, or $3,000 more than was expected, given the actual sales volume. The net variance due to variations in selling prices can be calculated as follows:

	Actual Volume		Sales Price Variance
	At Budgeted Prices	At Actual Prices	
Sales revenues....................	$475,000	$478,000	$3,000
Standard cost of goods sold (84%)......................	$399,000	$399,000	—
Selling and administrative expenses ($20,000 + 5%).........	43,750	43,900	(150)
Income before taxes........	$ 32,250	$ 35,100	$2,850

Spending variance. We can now calculate the spending variance in selling and administrative expenses by adjusting the budget to the actual level of sales:

Budget: $20,000 + 5% × $478,000......... $43,900
Actual.................................. 45,500
    Spending variance................... $(1,600)

The total variance between the amount originally budgeted and the amount spent was $500. We have now accounted for it all:

Effect of variance in sales volume............ $1,250
Effect of variance in selling prices............ (150)
Effect of overspending....................... (1,600)
    Total................................. $ (500)

Multiproduct Firm: Synthetic Index of Volume

Profit variance analysis can be applied to firms far more complex than the ones we have illustrated. When the firm or a division has many products, however, analyzing the profit variance for each product is likely to be too expensive. Instead, profits are analyzed for groups of related products or for individual market areas.

To perform the analysis on this basis, we have to find some way to measure the physical sales volume of the group as a whole. Sometimes the products are similar enough to each other in physical size that a physical unit count will do. A manufacturer of cookies and crackers, for example, may measure volume by the number of cases of products shipped, even though the company manufactures and sells dozens of different varieties of its products. When this is possible, the analysis is no more difficult than the ones we have just illustrated.

The situation unfortunately isn't always this simple. The products in any one grouping are often so different that no meaningful physical measure of total volume is possible. The company may make vacuum cleaners and oil burners, or bowling balls and billiard tables. The usual solution in these cases is to measure the volume of each product by its standard cost or by its budgeted selling price. Total volume is then the total standard cost (or total sales measured at budgeted prices) of all the goods sold during the period.

To illustrate, DEF Company measures volume by what the company calls standard sales dollars, obtained by multiplying the unit sales of each product by its standard selling price. DEF is a merchandising company and does no manufacturing of its own. For this reason it has no production volume variances. To keep the illustration as simple as we can, we shall make two additional simplifying assumptions:

1. No purchase price variances arose in November.
2. Selling and administrative expenses are entirely fixed, and no spending variances arose during November.

This leaves us with three variances to identify: sales price, sales volume, and sales mix.

Budget information. The budget for November showed the following figures:

	Amount	Percent
Standard sales dollars (at standard prices)...........	$300,000	˙100.0
Sales discounts and allowances....................	15,000	5.0
Net sales (at budgeted prices)......................	$285,000	95.0
Standard cost of goods sold......	228,000	76.0
Gross margin..................	$ 57,000	19.0
Selling and administrative expenses.....................	30,000	
Income before taxes.......	$ 27,000	

Actual results. Actual sales totaled $320,000 in November, measured at standard selling prices, but only $295,000 after sales discounts and allowances were taken into consideration. The income statement showed the following:

	Budget	Actual	Variance
Standard sales dollars (at standard prices)................................	$300,000	$320,000	$ 20,000
Sales discounts and allowances.........	15,000	25,000	(10,000)
Net sales.........................	$285,000	$295,000	$ 10,000
Standard cost of goods sold.............	228,000	250,000	(22,000)
Gross margin.......................	$ 57,000	$ 45,000	$(12,000)
Selling and administrative expenses.....	30,000	30,000	—
Income before taxes.................	$ 27,000	$ 15,000	$(12,000)

Income before taxes was $12,000 less than the amount budgeted, and this is the variance we need to analyze.

Sales volume variance. The sales volume variance can be calculated in two steps:

1. Determine the variance in standard sales dollars ($320,000 − $300,000 = $20,000, favorable).
2. Multiply this by the budgeted gross margin ratio ($20,000 × 0.19 = $3,800, favorable).

Sales mix variance. Mix variations can affect profit in many ways. First, if different products have different sales discount and allowance ratios, changes in mix will change the anticipated average revenue deduction from this source. Second, each product has its own standard cost, and variations in mix will affect the average standard cost ratio. Third, in more complex situations than our simple illustration, different products may have different sales commission rates or different effects on administrative expenses.

In this case the mix had no effect on the anticipated discounts and allowances—they were budgeted at 5 percent of standard selling prices for each of the company's products. Selling and administrative expenses were also unaffected by the mix. The only effect was on the cost of goods sold. If the products in the group had been sold in their budgeted proportions, the standard cost of goods sold would have been $243,200 (76 percent of $320,000). Actually, it was $250,000, indicating that the products sold during November had higher cost ratios and lower profit margin ratios, on the average, than the budget had anticipated. The difference between these two figures, $6,800, was the sales mix variance for the month.

Sales price variance. Net sales were budgeted at 95 percent of sales at standard prices. If sales had been at budgeted prices in November, net sales would have been 95 percent × $320,000 = $304,-000. Net sales actually totaled only $295,000. The sales price variance therefore was $304,000 − $295,000 = $9,000, unfavorable.

Sales variance summary. These three variance calculations are summarized in Exhibit 25–4. Again, each variance is measured by the difference between the figures on the bottom line in two adjacent columns. Taken together, these three components account for the $12,000 total profit volume variance for the month.

EXHIBIT 25–4

Sales Variance Summary

	Standard Prices			Actual Prices,
	Planned Volume, Standard Mix	Actual Volume, Standard Mix	Actual Volume, Actual Mix	Actual Volume, Actual Mix
Standard sales dollars...........	$300,000	$320,000	$320,000	$320,000
Sales discounts and allowances....................	15,000	16,000	16,000	25,000
Net sales.......................	$285,000	$304,000	$304,000	$295,000
Standard cost of goods sold........................	228,000	243,200	250,000	250,000
Gross margin....................	$ 57,000	$ 60,800	$ 54,000	$ 45,000
Selling and administrative expenses....................	30,000	30,000	30,000	30,000
Income before taxes..........	$ 27,000	$ 30,800	$ 24,000	$ 15,000

	Sales Volume Variance ($320,000 −$300,000) × 0.19 = $3,800	Sales Mix Variance $54,000 − ($320,000 × 0.19) = $(6,800)	Sales Price Variance $295,000 −($320,000 × 0.95) = $(9,000)
Variances			

Limitations of the Analysis

Useful though it is, this analytical technique suffers from three defects. One of these has already been mentioned. The relative sizes of the various variances depend on the sequence in which they are computed. That is, the size of the volume variance will depend on whether it reflects actual or standard prices, and so on. Confusion can be minimized by adopting a standardized sequence, but the resulting variances give only orders of magnitude and cannot be interpreted literally.

SUMMARY OF VARIANCE CALCULATIONS

Sales volume variance:	(Actual — budgeted sales volume, at budgeted selling prices) X budgeted contribution margin ratio
Sales mix variance:	Actual sales volume, at budgeted selling prices × (budgeted contribution margin ratio — actual contribution margin ratio at budgeted selling and input prices)
Sales price variance:	Actual sales volume × (actual selling prices less price-related deductions from revenues — budgeted selling prices less budgeted price-related deductions from revenues)
Selling and administrative expense spending variances:	Actual expenses — flexible budget allowances for actual volume achieved
Production volume variance:*	Actual overhead volume variance — budgeted overhead volume variance
Factory spending variances:	Actual input costs — budgeted input costs for actual volume achieved.

* Production volume variance can be subdivided into sales volume and inventory change effects.

Second, the profit plan does not necessarily represent what the manager should have been able to accomplish during the period, given the conditions that actually prevailed. In an attempt to deal with this, Demski has provided a model by which the total variance can be divided into two parts, one representing the difference between the original plan and the correct plan in the prevailing circumstances, and the other measuring the difference between the adjusted plan and the actual results.[1] This latter component can then be subjected to the kind of analysis described in this chapter. Although application of this model requires more data than are generally available, the approach represents an improvement over existing practice and deserves efforts to implement it.

The third defect is even more fundamental. Even if the first two defects could be overcome, this analysis does not indicate *why* the price variance is as large or as small as it is or why volume failed to meet the budgeted amounts. In fact, the variances may even be interdependent. Volume may be down because price is too high, the mix may be good because the more profitable product is underpriced, and so on.

All that technical variance analysis can do is provide a convenient summary of symptoms. Identification of the underlying causes then becomes a matter for managerial detective work. The technical breakdown can be very useful, however, in pointing the finger at areas that should be investigated. If the analysis shows that the main problem seems to be the sales mix, management is likely to be much closer to finding a solution than if this information were not available.

Reporting Variances to Shareholders

A small but growing number of companies are including a profit variance analysis of sorts in their published financial statements. The main difference between these and the analyses we have made in this section is that they show the departures from the previous year's reported income rather than from the budgeted figures for the year.

For example, the 1975 annual report for Arthur Andersen & Company contained the following statement: "Approximately 30% of the $53.6 million increase in worldwide fees in fiscal 1975 was due to a 4.5% growth in hours of client service (2.8% in the United States and 9.0% in all other countries). The remainder of this increase was due to higher average hourly billing rates (approximately 8.5% in the United States and 14.7% in all other countries)." Here we have the sales volume and sales price variances all over again, but the base is 1974 results, not the 1975 budget. The analytical technique is the same, and needs no additional illustration.

PROFIT RATIO AND TREND ANALYSIS

A second approach to profit performance reporting is through ratio and trend analysis. At its simplest, this takes the form of a single chart showing the progress of earnings or return on investment from period to period. This kind of chart can have a strong visual impact, and is widely used. It throws little light on the forces that affect reported performance, however. Recognizing this, some companies sup-

---

[1] For descriptions of this model, see Joel Demski, "An Accounting System Structured on a Linear Programming Model," *Accounting Review*, October 1967, pp. 701–12, and "Predictive Ability of Alternative Performance Measurement Models," *Journal of Accounting Research*, Spring 1969, pp. 96–115.

EXHIBIT 25–5

Relationship of Factors Affecting Return on Net Investment

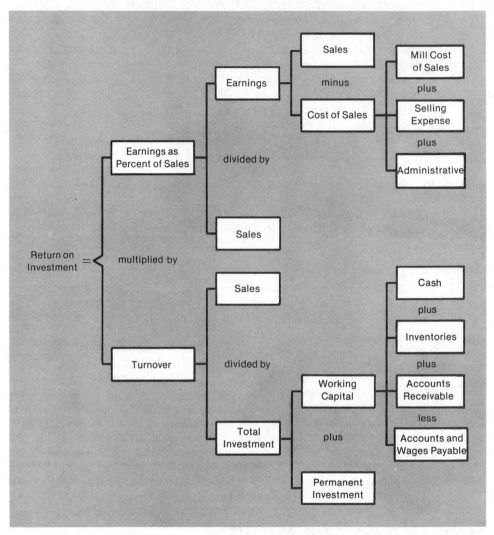

Adapted from E. I. duPont de Nemours & Co., *Executive Committee Control Charts: A Description of the duPont System for Appraising Operating Performance.*

plement the return on investment chart with a series of backup charts, each one dealing with some dimension of performance.

One such chart system is diagrammed in Exhibit 25–5. Each block in this exhibit represents a separate chart or table. The words appearing in the spaces between vertically adjacent blocks describe the relationship between these blocks and the block they are joined to at the left. The basic return on investment (ROI) ratio, for example, can be broken into two component ratios:

$$ROI = \frac{Profit}{Investment} = \frac{Profit}{Sales} \times \frac{Sales}{Investment}$$

A drop in the return on investment ratio that is accompanied by a decline in the earnings percentage has a different meaning from a drop that is accompanied by a reduction in turnover.

A low turnover ratio, for example, may have arisen because total investment increased more rapidly than sales. The increment in investment, in turn, may have been located entirely in the finished goods inventories. Management knows, therefore, that the explanation for the decline in turnover must be sought in the reason for the inventory buildup. By moving farther and farther to the right on this diagram, management can get deeper and deeper into the details of the company's operations. In the process, the major causes of the problem may come to light.

The ratios and other figures used in this system are used by top management to identify favorable and unfavorable trends. While a declining sales margin percentage means nothing in itself, it may be a very bad sign if asset turnover is not increasing at the same time. Unexpected movements revealed in this way initiate a search for explanations, which in turn can trigger management action.

SUMMARY

Comparisons of actual results with the amounts budgeted provide only the crudest of signals to management. The techniques described in this chapter have been developed to provide signals that are more finely tuned.

The most significant of these techniques is profit variance analysis, by which the overall profit variance for a given product line or division is subdivided into portions attributed to departures from budgeted sales volume, sales mix, sales price, production volume, factory spending, and selling and administrative spending.

Another technique is interperiod ratio comparison. Although these comparisons ordinarily ignore planned ratios, and although the various ratios are not independent of each other, this kind of analysis does identify trends that seem to be developing and may help management decide to take action before the need for action otherwise would have become apparent.

KEY TERMS

The most important terms introduced and defined in this chapter are the following:

Factory spending variances	Sales price variance
Inventory change variance	Sales volume variance
Production volume variance	Selling and administrative
Sales mix variance	spending variances

INDEPENDENT STUDY PROBLEMS
(Solutions in Appendix C)

1. Profit variance analysis: Single product. From the information below, compute the amount of the profit variance due to variations in (*a*) selling prices, (*b*) sales volume, and (*c*) other factors, in as much detail as you deem appropriate.

	Budget	Actual
Sales......................................	$60,000	$60,500
Cost of goods sold:		
Direct material...........................	$10,000	$11,200
Direct labor..............................	13,000	14,700
Factory overhead.........................	13,000	14,100
Total cost of goods sold..............	$36,000	$40,000
Gross margin..............................	$24,000	$20,500
Selling and administrative expenses.......	18,000	18,500
Net income................................	$ 6,000	$ 2,000
Units sold................................	10,000	11,000

Additional information: (1) Materials prices and wages were at budgeted levels. (2) Production volume and sales volume were identical. (3) Factory overhead is budgeted at $7,800 plus 40 percent of direct labor cost. (4) Selling and administrative expenses are assumed to be wholly fixed.

2. Sales mix variance. A company sells three products. Sales and cost of goods sold last month were as follows:

	Units Sold	Revenue	Unit Cost
Budget:			
Product X.................	10,000	$20,000	$1.20
Product Y.................	5,000	30,000	4.20
Product Z.................	4,000	20,000	4.00
Total.................	19,000	$70,000	
Actual:			
Product X.................	10,800	$23,100	$1.20
Product Y.................	4,000	23,600	4.20
Product Z.................	5,200	25,500	4.00
Total.................	20,000	$72,200	

a. Calculate the reported gross margin and the total variance in gross margin for the month.

b. Divide this total variance into price, volume, and mix components, using revenues at budgeted selling prices to measure aggregate volume.

c. How would your answer to b) have differed if you had used the number of units sold to measure aggregate volume? Which measure is the correct one?

EXERCISES AND PROBLEMS

1. Profit variance exercises: Nonmanufacturing firms. The exercises in this set are designed to demonstrate different aspects of profit variance analysis. Each one has a lesson that should be noted; they should be solved in sequence.

Exercise A

Company Alpha buys a single commodity at wholesale and sells it at retail. Selling and administrative expenses are entirely fixed. You have the following financial information:

	Budget	Actual
Units sold	1,000,000	900,000
Revenues	$5,000,000	$4,750,000
Cost of goods sold	3,000,000	2,810,000
Gross Margin	$2,000,000	$1,940,000
Selling and administrative expenses	1,000,000	1,045,000
Income before taxes	$1,000,000	$ 895,000

Analyze the variance between budgeted and actual results for the period.

Exercise B

Company Beta buys a commodity at wholesale and sells it at retail. Selling and administrative expenses are expected to vary according to the following formula:

$$\text{Total expenses} = \$800,000 + \$0.20 \times \text{number of units sold}$$

You have the following financial information:

	Budget	Actual
Units sold	900,000	950,000
Revenues	$4,500,000	$5,000,000
Cost of goods sold	2,700,000	2,850,000
Gross Margin	$1,800,000	$2,150,000
Selling and administrative expenses	980,000	1,000,000
Income before taxes	$ 820,000	$1,150,000

Analyze the variance between budgeted and actual results for the period.

Exercise C

Company Gamma buys two commodities at wholesale and sells them at retail. Product X was budgeted to cost $4 this period and sell for $7 a pound, while product Y was budgeted to cost $3 and to sell for $4 a gallon. Selling and administrative expenses were budgeted at $1,500,000 and are entirely fixed.

The income statement for the period showed the following budgeted and actual results:

	Budgeted	Actual
Units sold:		
Product X	600,000 lbs.	550,000 lbs.
Product Y	200,000 gal.	300,000 gal.
Sales revenues	$5,000,000	$4,950,000
Cost of goods sold	3,000,000	3,100,000
Gross margin	$2,000,000	$1,850,000
Selling and administrative expenses	1,500,000	1,510,000
Income before taxes	$ 500,000	$ 340,000

Analyze the variance between budgeted and actual results for this period.

Exercise D

Company Delta buys a large number of items at wholesale and sells them at retail. These items are grouped into two major product lines, X and Y. Selling and administrative expenses are entirely fixed. The following information is taken from the original budget for the period:

	Line X	Line Y	Total
Sales revenues.....................	$3,600,000	$2,400,000	$6,000,000
Cost of goods sold................	2,400,000	1,800,000	4,200,000
Gross margin..................	$1,200,000	$ 600,000	$1,800,000
Selling and administrative expenses........................			1,000,000
Income before taxes...........			$ 800,000

Actual results for the period were as follows:

	Line X	Line Y	Total
Sales revenues....................	$3,370,000	$2,790,000	$6,160,000
Cost of goods sold................	2,340,000	2,070,000	4,410,000
Gross margin..................	$1,030,000	$ 720,000	$1,750,000
Selling and administrative expenses........................			1,040,000
Income before taxes...........			$ 710,000

a. Calculate the following three variances: (1) gross margin variance, line X; (2) gross margin variance, line Y; and spending variance, selling and administrative expenses.

b. Explain why each gross margin variance can't be subdivided into price and volume components and why a mix variance can't be calculated without further information or assumptions.

Exercise E

The facts are the same as in Exercise D, but management has asked you to separate the estimated effects of variations in physical sales volume from the effects of variations in sales mix.

a. Select a surrogate for physical sales volume from the data provided in the problem and use this in preparing a revised variance summary for management's use.

b. How satisfactory is the surrogate you have chosen? What is wrong with it?

Exercise F

The facts are the same as in Exercise D, except that you have the additional information that actual sales, measured at budgeted prices, were as follows:

Line X......................	$3,450,000
Line Y......................	2,800,000
Total..................	$6,250,000

Analyze the variance between budgeted and actual results for the period.

Exercise G

The facts are the same as in Exercise F, but in addition you find that industry sales for line X were at the level forecasted when the budget for this period was adopted, whereas industry sales for line Y were 15 percent greater than their budgeted level. Spot checks of competitors' prices during the year indicated that most of these prices held firm during the year.

Using this information, comment on the company's profit performance for the period.

Exercise H

The facts are the same as in Exercise F, except that selling and administrative expenses are expected to be described by the following formula:

Selling and administrative expense = $700,000 + 5\% \times$ sales revenue

Prepare a revised analysis of the profit variance, using this additional information.

2. Profit variance exercises: Manufacturing firms. The exercises in this set examine the effects of variations in sales and production volume under variable costing and under absorption costing.

Exercise J

Company Theta is a manufacturing firm, making and selling a single product. It has no selling and administrative expenses. All sales are at a price of $5 and manufacturing costs are expected to approximate the following budget formula:

Total cost = $1,000,000 + \$2 \times$ number of units produced

You have the following volume data:

	No. of Units Sold	No. of Units Produced
Normal............................	1,000,000	1,000,000
Budgeted, this period..............	1,000,000	1,000,000
Actual, this period..................	900,000	900,000

Company Theta assigns factory cost to production at standard cost on a variable costing basis. Actual fixed and variable production costs this period total $2,800,000. All production cost variances are classified as expenses of the periods in which they arise.

a. How much of the period's production cost would be assigned to products and how much would be classified directly as expense (1) in the budget drawn up at the beginning of the period, and (2) in the actual records for the period?

b. Prepare a budgeted income statement for the period, the actual income statement and an analysis of the differences between the two.

Exercise K

The facts are the same as in Exercise J, except that the actual production volume is 1 million units and actual production cost is $3 million.

a. Calculate and analyze the profit variance for the period.

b. Prepare an annotated comparison of the results of this analysis with the results of the analysis in Exercise J.

Exercise L

Company Omicron is identical to Company Theta in all respects except that it assigns factory costs to production at standard cost on a full-costing basis. All other facts are the same as in Exercise J.

a. How much of the period's production cost would be assigned to products and how much would be classified directly as expense (1) in the budget drawn up at the beginning of the period, and (2) in the actual records for the period?
b. Prepare a budgeted income statement for the period, the actual income statement, and an analysis of the differences between the two.

Exercise M

The facts are the same as in Exercise L except that the company manufactures 1 million units and actual production cost is $3 million.

a. Prepare a budgeted income statement for the period, the actual income statement, and an analysis of the differences between the two.
b. Compare the results of this analysis with the results of your analyses of Exercises K and L.

Exercise N

Company Omega is a manufacturing firm, making and selling a single product. It has no selling and administrative expenses. All sales are at a price of $5 and manufacturing costs are expected to approximate the following budget formula:

$$\text{Total cost} = \$1{,}000{,}000 + \$2 \times \text{number of units produced}$$

You have the following volume data:

	No. of Units Sold	No. of Units Produced
Normal.............................	1,000,000	1,000,000
Budgeted, this period..............	1,000,000	940,000
Actual, this period.................	850,000	900,000

Company Omega assigns factory costs to production at standard cost on a full-costing basis. Actual production costs this period total $2,875,-000. All production cost variances are classified as expenses of the periods in which they arise.

a. How much of the period's production cost would be assigned to products and how much would be classified directly as expense (1) in the budget drawn up at the beginning of the period, and (2) in the actual records for the period?
b. Prepare a budgeted income statement for the period, the actual income statement, and an analysis of the differences between the two.

3. Profit variance analysis: Nonmanufacturing firm. The ABC Sales Company operates a wholesale outlet. It buys merchandise from two or three manufacturers and sells these goods to retailers. Its planned and actual results for a recent period were as follows:

	Planned	Actual
Selling price per unit...................	$10	$9.50
Sales volume, units....................	50,000	52,000
Cost of goods sold....................	$300,000	$318,000
Selling and administrative cost........	$100,000	$115,000
	+$0.20 a unit	

a. Calculate planned income before taxes for the period.
b. Calculate actual income before taxes for the period.
c. Analyze the difference between (*a*) and (*b*) to measure the effects on net income of deviations in sales volume, selling price, and merchandise purchase prices, and the effect of departures from budgeted selling and administrative expense. Ignore income taxes.

4. Change in sales; Change in production.   A firm has made the following estimates of the percentage of expenses to sales revenue, based on a normal sales volume of $10 million:

Variable manufacturing.....................	30%
Fixed manufacturing.......................	40
Variable selling and administrative.........	15
Fixed selling and administrative............	5
Total expense..........................	90%

Inventory is measured at full absorption cost, based on normal volume. Anticipated sales volume for the current period is $8 million. All production cost variances are taken directly to the income statement as they arise.

a. What would be the effect on net income of increasing sales by $1 million without an increase in production?
b. What would be the effect on net income of increasing production by a quantity of goods that has a sales value of $1 million without an increase in sales?

5. Deviation from expected loss.   Woodbridge, Inc., after several years of profitable operation, showed a loss of $2 million in 19x3, accompanied by a severe cash shortage. Woodbridge seethed with activity as a result: new financial controls were installed, and a new sales manager was hired. By the end of 19x4, the new organization was fully operating and Mr. James Woodbridge, the company's president, was optimistic about the future despite the 19x4 loss of $1.3 million on sales of $5 million.

Looking ahead, Mr. Woodbridge was convinced that the firm could attain a volume of $10 million in a few years, with the following profit results (in thousands):

Sales.............................		$10,000
Variable production costs.........	$5,000	
Fixed production costs............	2,000	
Variable selling costs.............	1,000	
Fixed selling costs................	1,000	9,000
Net income before taxes........		$ 1,000

Variable costs were expected to vary in proportion to changes in physical volume. Standard product costs in the factory were established on the basis of the physical volume required for an annual sales volume of $10 million. All production cost variances were to be taken directly to the income statement for the period in which they arose.

The initial profit budget for 19x5 called for sales of $6.5 million (at standard prices) and a net loss (before taxes) of $400,000. Actual volume for 19x5 was $7 million, also at standard prices. At this volume a loss of $200,000 was budgeted, but the company's cash position had improved so much by the end of 19x5 that Mr. Woodbridge thought the company might have broken even. Therefore, he was aghast when he received the following income statement (in thousands):

Sales (at actual prices).....................		$6,860
Standard cost of goods sold...............	$4,900	
Selling expenses.........................	1,720	
Factory overhead volume variance........	900	
Other factory cost variances...............	30	7,550
Net loss..............................		$ (690)

"What happened?" he gasped. Tell him, in as much detail as possible.

(Prepared by Professor Carl L. Nelson)

6. Ratio decomposition. Pinshaw Enterprises, Inc. is a large manufacturing corporation with operations throughout the United States and in many other countries. It is organized on a product line basis in the United States and on a regional basis abroad. Each of the domestic divisions in the United States is relatively autonomous, with its own manufacturing facilities and its own marketing organization. Profits are reported monthly to management and quarterly to shareholders.

In reviewing the profit performance of each of the company's divisions, management uses a ratio analysis scheme similar to the one described in the final section of this chapter. You have been told that the return on investment in the Able Division fell from 20 percent in the first quarter to 14.7 percent in the second quarter. You are given the following data (in thousands):

	First Quarter	Second Quarter
Sales..................................	$100	$105
Cost of goods sold....................	$ 60	$ 66
Operating expenses....................	20	24
Income taxes..........................	8	6
Total expenses....................	$ 88	$ 96
Net income...........................	$ 12	$ 9
Traceable investment:		
Receivables.........................	$ 50	$ 54
Inventories.........................	60	62
Plant and equipment.................	120	122
Total traceable assets.................	$230	$238
Accounts payable....................	20	25
Net traceable investment..............	$210	$213
Centrally administered assets..........	30	32
Net investment.......................	$240	$245

a. Verify the computation of the return on investment ratios given above.

b. Break the return on investment ratios down into component ratios. Try to explain what has happened, using ratios only.

7. Adequacy of product markup. Van Dyk Corporation distributes cigars, cigarettes, and pipe tobacco to retail outlets. Cigars have the biggest percentage of profit markups, and cigarettes have the smallest. The markups also vary to some extent from brand to brand within each product class, but these variations are relatively small.

Johann van Dyk, the company's president and chief stockholder, is worried. The warehouse seems as busy as ever, the delivery trucks seem to be as heavily loaded, but profits have been close to zero for several months.

Last month was very much like earlier months. Budgeted and actual data for the month were as follows:

	Budget		Actual	
	Cases	Amount	Cases	Amount
Sales:				
Cigars.....................	500	$ 60,000	300	$ 35,000
Cigarettes................	2,125	204,000	2,300	220,000
Pipe tobacco..............	800	24,000	700	22,000
Total.................		$288,000		$277,000
Cost of goods sold:				
Cigars.....................		$ 36,000		$ 22,000
Cigarettes................		163,200		180,000
Pipe tobacco..............		16,800		15,000
Total.................		$216,000		$217,000

Operating expenses are almost entirely fixed within the customary operating range and have been running very close to budget.

Mr. van Dyk thinks that he may have to press the manufacturers for an increase in the spread between the prices he pays and the prices charged the retail dealers. Before doing this, however, he has decided to ask you to analyze last month's figures. Analyze the profit variance for the month and prepare a table summarizing the results of that analysis. What advice would you give Mr. van Dyk?

8. Effect of market factors. The Arsco Company makes three grades of indoor-outdoor carpets. The sales volume for the annual budget is determined by estimating the total market volume for indoor-outdoor carpet, and then applying the company's prior year market share, adjusted for planned changes due to company programs for the coming year. The volume is apportioned among the three grades based upon the prior year's product mix, again adjusted for planned changes due to company programs for the coming year.

Given below are the company budget for 19x3 and the results of operations for 19x3.

	Budget			
	Grade 1	Grade 2	Grade 3	Total
Sales—Units............	1,000 rolls	1,000 rolls	2,000 rolls	4,000 rolls
Sales dollars				
(000 omitted).........	$1,000	$2,000	$3,000	$6,000
Variable expense.......	700	1,600	2,300	4,600
Variable margin........	$ 300	$ 400	$ 700	$1,400
Traceable fixed				
expense..............	200	200	300	700
Traceable margin.......	$ 100	$ 200	$ 400	$ 700
Selling and administrative expense..........				250
Net income.......				$ 450

	Actual			
	Grade 1	Grade 2	Grade 3	Total
Sales—Units..............	800 rolls	1,000 rolls	2,100 rolls	3,900 rolls
Sales—dollars				
(000 omitted)............	$810	$2,000	$3,000	$5,810
Variable expenses........	560	1,610	2,320	4,490
Variable margin...........	$250	$ 390	$ 680	$1,320
Traceable fixed				
expense................	210	220	315	745
Traceable margin.........	$ 40	$ 170	$ 365	$ 575
Selling and administra-				
tive expense................				275
Net income........				$ 300

Industry volume was estimated at 40,000 rolls for budgeting purposes. Actual industry volume for 19x3 was 38,000 rolls.

a. Calculate the profit impact of the unit sales volume variance for 19x3 using budgeted variable margins.

b. What portion of the variance, if any, can be attributed to the state of the carpet market?

c. What is the dollar impact on profits (using budgeted variable margins) of the shift in product mix from the budgeted mix?

(CMA)

9. Supplying missing data. Your superior in the financial analysis department of the Dexter Division of National Brands, Inc. had just started a report to management explaining the division's failure to meet its budget for the third quarter of the current fiscal year when she was called to San Francisco on a more pressing problem. Giving you her partially finished report and the underlying data, she asked you to have it finished upon her return.

She had jotted down the following partial set of conclusions when she was called away:

Increase (or decrease) in sales volume	?	F or U?
Increase in selling prices	?	F
Increase (or decrease) in production volume (can I tell how much was to adjust production to sales and how much was to change the inventory by an amount different from the budgeted change?)	?	F or U?
Increase in manufacturing costs as a result of cost increases or decreased efficiency (can I tell how much for each?)	9,000 U	
Increase in selling and administrative costs as a result of cost increases or decreased efficiency (can I tell how much for each?)	4,800 U	
Difference between budgeted income and actual income	$ 800 U	

Attached to this were the following:

1. Budgeted income statement:

Sales...................................		$500,000
Cost of goods sold—at standard...........		310,000
Gross margin.........................		$190,000
Factory overhead volume variance.........	$ 57,000	
Factory overhead spending		
variance...............................	0	
Other factory variances..................	(8,000)	
Selling and administrative expenses.......	125,000	174,000
Income before income taxes........		$ 16,000

2. Notes on costs and the budget:

   a. We produced more than 200 products, but there is a close relationship among them. As a result, the following percentages of selling price are very representative of the products' standard factory costs:

Material.............................	20%
Labor...............................	10
Overhead............................	32
Total standard cost...............	62%

   b. The budget was based on an increase in the finished goods inventory of $6,200 and no change in the work-in-process inventory.

   c. Factory overhead was budgeted at $210,000 plus 20 percent of direct labor costs.

   d. Standard output required a direct labor cost of $70,000. Because of the expansion program, we were operating far below standard output; hence the large volume variance.

   e. Selling and administrative expenses were budgeted at $100,000 plus 5 percent of sales at actual prices.

3. The actual income statement was:

Sales......................................		$504,000
Cost of goods sold—at standard...........		303,800
Gross margin.........................		$200,200
Overhead volume variance................	$ 54,000	
Overhead spending variance..............	4,000	
Other manufacturing cost variances........	(3,000)	
Selling and administrative expenses........	130,000	185,000
Income before income taxes........		$ 15,200

4. Costs continued their upward climb. In response, we increased our prices by 4 percent in late January. The best guess is that $140,000 in sales were at the old prices; no really hard figures are available because we're still making some shipments at the old prices.

(Prepared by Professor Carl L. Nelson)

10. Comprehensive analysis: Two products. The Moontide Company's Crescent Division manufactures and sells two products. Both products are manufactured in the division's only factory. A full cost standard costing system is in use in this factory.

The Crescent Division operates under an annual profit plan. Each month the division manager receives a report comparing the division's income for the month with that month's share of the annual profit plan. The report for June showed a budgeted income before taxes of $10,000, and actual income of $12,800.

In preparing to analyze the difference between these two figures, you have collected the following information:

1. Profit plan for the month of June:

	Product A	Product B	Total
Units sold..........................	30,000	10,000	
Net sales...........................	$150,000	$100,000	$250,000
Standard cost of goods sold.......	120,000	70,000	190,000
Gross margin...............	$ 30,000	$ 30,000	$ 60,000
Less deductions:			
Selling and administrative			
expenses.....................			$ 32,000
Variances in factory direct			
labor and materials costs......			2,500
Underabsorbed factory			
overhead costs................			15,500
Total deductions............			$ 50,000
Income before taxes.............			$ 10,000

2. Standard product cost per unit (full cost basis):

	A	B
Direct materials...............	$1	$1
Direct labor.....................	1	2
Factory overhead..............	2	4
Total....................	$4	$7

3. Budgeted factory overhead cost for both products combined: $90,000 + (0.5 × standard direct labor cost).
4. Budgeted production volume: Product A, 30,000 units; product B, 10,000 units.
5. Total budgeted selling and administrative expenses for both products combined: $27,000 + 2 percent of net sales.
6. Actual production volume during June: product A, 34,000 units; product B, 9,200 units.
7. Actual factory overhead cost during June: $114,800.
8. Actual profit reported for the month of June:

	A	B	Total
Units sold..........................	36,000	9,000	
Net sales...........................	$181,000	$ 84,000	$265,000
Standard cost of goods sold.....	144,000	63,000	207,000
Gross margin.....................	$ 37,000	$ 21,000	$ 58,000
Less deductions:			
Selling and administrative			
expenses.....................			$ 33,000
Variances in factory direct			
labor & materials costs........			2,200
Underabsorbed factory			
overhead costs................			10,000
Total deductions............			$ 45,200
Income before Taxes.............			$ 12,800

a. Prepare an analysis of the month's operations, indicating insofar as possible the sources of the $2,800 departure from budgeted income before taxes.

b. Without actually making any calculations, explain how the results of your analysis would differ if a variable costing system were in use. Would the total variance be the same or different? Which of the component variances would change in amount?

26

Interdivisional Transfer Pricing

PROFIT CENTERS and other organization units for which profit performance measures must be prepared are not always as independent of the rest of the organization as we may have implied in Chapter 24. They buy from and sell to each other, sometimes in substantial quantities. The prices used to record these transfers are known as transfer prices.

The purpose of this chapter is to see how transfer prices might be set in different situations. Our discussion will be divided into five parts:

1. The criteria by which a proposed transfer pricing system is to be judged.
2. The economic quantities transfer prices might attempt to measure.
3. The ways transfer prices can be determined.
4. The transfer pricing methods that should be used to price transfers between profit centers.
5. The transfer pricing methods that should be used to price transfers from profit centers to administered centers.

CRITERIA FOR TRANSFER PRICING

Transfer prices are likely to affect any or all of the following:

1. The division managers' decisions.
2. Top management's evaluation of the division managers' profit performance.
3. Top management's evaluation of the profitability of each division's activities.
4. The company's taxes and transfers of cash.

In this section we'll develop a selection criterion relating to each of these four. We'll try to demonstrate that the first two of these criteria must be met in all situations. Transfer prices meeting these two criteria may also satisfy the third; if they don't, we'll argue that the activity evaluation criterion may have to be ignored. Finally, we'll explain why management shouldn't try to satisfy the fourth criterion at all in designing a transfer pricing system to serve managerial purposes.

Divisional Resource Allocation Decisions

Goods transferred from one division or subsidiary to another are intermediate *products*. The division the intermediate product is transferred from is the *supplying division;* the division receiving the intermediate product is the *buying division.* The product sold by the buying division is known as the *final product.*

The buying division's immediate objective may be to subject the intermediate product to further processing, to use it in the manufacture of another product, or to offer it for sale. The transfer price measures the revenues the supplying division gets from the transfer; it also establishes part of the buying division's costs. This means it will affect many decisions in the buying division, such as:

Processing. Should the intermediate product be processed, and in what quantity?

Merchandising. Should the final product be sold and, if so, how much marketing effort should be devoted to it?

Pricing. What is the minimum price, and what is the long-term target price for the finished product?

Choosing the source of supply. Should the intermediate product be manufactured by the supplying division or should it be bought outside?

These four kinds of decisions are often interrelated, but the problems encountered in pure processing decisions are typical of them all. In a centralized company, the central decision-making authority can examine the incremental cost of further processing and compare it with the probable increment in sales value of the final product over that of the intermediate product. In a decentralized company, however, the manager of the buying division treats the price at which the intermediate product is transferred as an incremental cost. These relationships are diagrammed in Exhibit 26–1.

This leads to the first criterion for selecting a transfer pricing policy: *the transfer price should lead division management to make the same decisions headquarters management would make if it had the time to study the problem and apply all the data available to the managers of both divisions.* If the transfer price leads to departures from this ideal, it is said to cause suboptimization.

For example, suppose a division can produce only 100 units of product X each month. It can either transfer these units to another division for conversion into product Z or sell them to an outside customer. For some reason a transfer price of $1,100 a unit has been set for product X. The costs and revenues associated with these alternatives are diagrammed in Exhibit 26–2.

EXHIBIT 26–1

Interdivisional Transfer Relationships

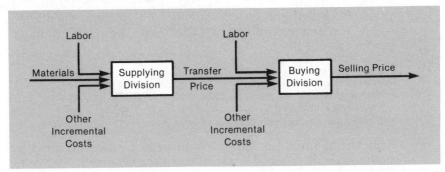

EXHIBIT 26–2

A Processing Decision

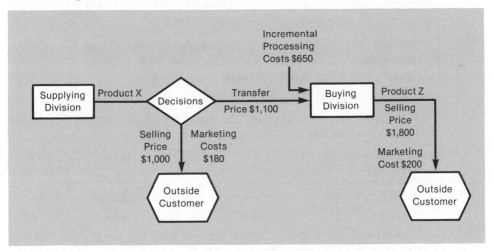

Given all this information, a manager responsible for *both* divisions would decide that the interdivisional transfer would be in the company's interests:

	Sell Product X	Manufacture and Sell Product Z	Difference
Revenues.........................	$1,000	$1,800	$800
Costs:			
Processing.....................	—	$ 650	(650)
Marketing.....................	$ 180	200	(20)
Profit contribution..............	$ 820	$ 950	$130

If decision authority were delegated to the divisions, the manager of the supplying division would be happy to make the transfer. Product X would then bring in $1,100 in revenues, $100 more than the price charged the outside customer, and without spending $180 to sell it. The manager of the buying division, however, wouldn't buy the product at this price:

Estimated revenues................................		$1,800
Estimated costs:		
Materials (product X)...........................	$1,100	
Processing and selling.........................	850	1,950
Estimated processing profit (loss)................		$ (150)

This would force the supplying division to take the next best alternative, sale of product X to the outside customer.

A transfer price of $1,100 would lead to suboptimization because it would lead the supplying division to sell product X to the outside customer. This can be prevented by reducing the transfer price to $820, the product's opportunity cost.

REMINDER: OPPORTUNITY COST

The opportunity cost of using a resource for a specified purpose is the net present value of the cash flows it would generate in its best alternative use.

At this price, the manager of the buying division would reach the profit maximizing solution:

Estimated revenues................................		$1,800
Estimated costs:		
Materials (product X)...........................	$820	
Processing and selling.........................	850	1,670
Estimated processing profit........................		$ 130

All well and good, but suppose we find that the supplying division would incur $900 in incremental costs to manufacture the intermediate product. Now if the transfer price were set at $820, we'd see a different situation:

1. The buying division will have too great an incentive to buy, because the cost to the company will be understated by $80 (the difference between $900 and $820).
2. The supplying division will be unwilling to sell, because its incremental revenues will be $80 less than its incremental costs.

In this case the $820 market value of the intermediate product isn't a valid measure of the sacrifice necessary to provide intermediate products to the buying division. The supplying division would rather not produce at all than to take advantage of this opportunity.

We can now modify our first transfer pricing criterion: *for managerial guidance in decision making, the transfer price charged the buying division should be the incremental cost to the supplying division or the net market value of the intermediate product, whichever is higher.*

Evaluating Managerial Performance

Transfer prices have a second impact, this time on the image of the division and of its management that will be transmitted to top management. When transfers of goods are made, a portion of the revenue of one division becomes a portion of the cost of another. This means that the price at which transfers are made can influence the earnings reported by each division.

For example, suppose a division has budgeted residual income of $210,000 but reports only $116,000, as shown in the following table:

	Actual	Budget	Variance
Sales...............................	$1,600,000	$1,650,000	$(50,000)
Cost of goods sold..................	$1,150,000	$1,100,000	$(50,000)
Divisional overhead.................	235,000	240,000	5,000
Investment carrying charge.........	99,000	100,000	1,000
Total charges..................	$1,484,000	$1,440,000	$(44,000)
Residual income....................	$ 116,000	$ 210,000	$(94,000)

If internal transfers are important, the big profit variance could be due mainly to low transfer prices on the products the division sells to sister divisions or high transfer prices on the products it buys internally.

The danger is that top management will allow the transfer price to influence its appraisal of the division managers' performances, or, which amounts to the same thing, that the division managers will think the transfer price is affecting their performance ratings unfairly. This can lead to dissension and can even defeat the main purpose of profit decentralization by impairing the managers' motivations to produce profits.

This leads to the second transfer pricing criterion: *the transfer pricing system should be designed so that the division managers will regard the transfer prices as fair.* Fairness is a subjective quality, and what one manager regards as fair may seem totally unfair to another. This second principle, therefore, is a statement of a goal, not an absolute quantity.

A corollary of this principle is that the transfer price, or at least the formula for arriving at the transfer price, should be set before the transfer is made rather than afterward. This permits division managers to know in advance what prices they will receive or what prices they will pay for transferred goods. This eliminates one source of uncertainty and permits the division managers to predict more accurately the effects of their decisions on their reported profits.

Divisional Activity Evaluation

Divisional profit reports also play a role in the evaluation of each division's activities, as we saw in Chapter 24. The transfer price can influence this evaluation, just as it can affect the evaluation of the division manager. Getting an acceptable transfer price for this purpose is more difficult, however. We need to examine two different situations:

1. The market value of the intermediate product can be approximated reasonably well.
2. Adequate market value data are unavailable.

Situation 1. Market values are available. The buying and supplying divisions define market value somewhat differently. To the supplying division, market value is the amount the division loses by not selling the intermediate product to an outside customer. To the buying division, market value is the amount it would have to pay to buy an equivalent product from an outside supplier. The reason is that the buying division presumably will seek the lowest cost source of supply. The cost from this source determines the amount of profit attributable to the buying division's activities.

In general, market value and outside purchase cost are assumed to be close enough to each other so that one figure can serve both parties. In these circumstances, we can state the third criterion for a transfer pricing system: *for activity evaluation, the transfer price should approximate the market value of the intermediate product.*

Situation 2. Market values are unavailable. Divisional profit centers often supply other divisions with products that are neither offered for sale nor available on the open market. In these cases the profit from the sale of the final product is the joint result of the two divisions, working together. The two divisions' shares in this joint profit can be approximated by estimating what it would cost the buying division to manufacture the intermediate product, including imputed interest on the investment necessary to support this production. We can fit this into the third criterion by regarding it as a synthetic measure of market value.

This third criterion is likely to conflict with the first two. This is particularly so when the buying division would have to make a substantial investment in facilities to manufacture the intermediate product within the division. In these cases the calculated average cost is likely to be very high, meaning that the supplying division will get most of the joint profit—sometimes even more. This shouldn't be surprising. The reason the buying division gets the intermediate product from the supplying division is that the latter can take advantage of the economies of large-scale production. The intermediate product is likely to be only one of several products processed on the same facilities, and this keeps the cost down. To go it alone, the buying division either would have a good deal of idle production time or would use less efficient equipment. Its costs would be prohibitively high under either of these alternatives.

Conflicts between the third criterion and either or both of the first two can be resolved in either of two ways:

1. Use two sets of transfer prices, one for each purpose.
2. Select a transfer pricing system to meet one purpose, making necessary adjustments whenever divisional profit performance is to be evaluated for the other purpose.

We tend to favor the second of these, subordinating the third criterion to the first two. Activity evaluation takes place relatively infrequently, whereas division managers make resource allocation decisions every day. The first criterion, therefore, is likely to be more important than the third. The infrequency of activity evaluation decisions also leads us to doubt that the creation of a parallel set of transfer prices would be worth its cost. Separate estimates can be prepared for activity evaluation when they are needed rather than all the time.

Fiscal Management

Transfer prices between division or subsidiaries in different tax jurisdictions may affect the amount of taxes the company must pay. Furthermore, when the two parties to a transfer are in different countries, and one of those countries restricts the amount of funds the company can transfer out of the country, the transfer price may affect the amount of cash available for investment and other purposes.

We'll ignore these fiscal variables, and concentrate exclusively on the managerial aspects of transfer pricing. We'll do this for three reasons. First, the rules governing the selection of transfer prices for governmental use are established by governments. The firm ordinarily has some leeway in applying these rules, but the range of choice is relatively limited.

Second, the rules vary from country to country, and this limits our ability to generalize.

Third, and most important, transfer prices meeting governmental requirements are unlikely to satisfy the three criteria we have just established. Taxation and foreign exchange controls are designed to achieve governmental objectives—fewer imports, more taxes, more jobs, and so on. The authorities aren't interested in helping management make decisions or evaluate divisional performance. Management has to apply these criteria, however, and if the governmental rules preclude transfer prices consistent with them, then management should try to find economical and legal ways to maintain two parallel transfer pricing systems.

BASES FOR TRANSFER PRICING

Transfer prices may be based on cost or on the market value of the goods transferred or on some combination of the two. This section will be devoted to descriptions of transfer pricing systems using each of these three measurement bases. We'll defer our analysis and criticism of these systems until later in the chapter.

Cost-Based Systems

Many different kinds of transfer pricing arrangements are based on cost. Two of these are:

1. Standard full cost.
2. Marginal cost.

Standard full cost. Transfer prices in centralized companies aren't intended to affect managerial decisions. Instead, they are designed with one or more of the following three purposes in mind:

1. To transfer accountability for cost control.
2. To identify costs for contract costing.
3. To measure activity performance.

Full manufacturing cost has traditionally been used for these purposes, sometimes with a share of administrative costs added in.

With the advent of decentralization, it was quite natural to use a similar transfer pricing system. For example, suppose a supplying division has a cost budget of $75,000 in fixed costs plus variable costs of $9 for each unit of intermediate product. The normal volume is 25,000 units. A full cost transfer price would be $12 a unit, as in the following diagram:

Marginal cost. The transfer price can also be set equal to the marginal cost of manufacturing the intermediate product. If marginal cost increases as volume increases, the following three-step procedure can be used:

1. Each buying division manager is provided with a schedule representing the marginal costs of each supplying division at various volumes of operations. This provides a basis for calculating the prices the division must pay for additional quantities of the intermediate products.
2. The buying division manager combines this schedule with the division's own schedule of marginal processing costs to determine a composite marginal cost schedule for the final products.
3. The buying division manager calculates the volume at which the marginal revenue from the sale of an additional unit of the final product is just adequate to cover total marginal cost, and places an order for this quantity of the intermediate product.

In more formal terms, this means that the division manager will accept additional orders for the final product as long as the price received exceeds combined marginal cost, assuming that additional orders do not require price reductions on the business already obtainable at higher prices.

EXHIBIT 26-3

Deciding Volume with Marginal Cost Transfer Pricing

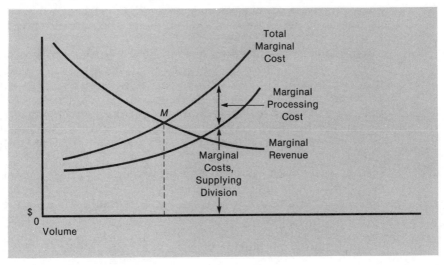

The solution envisioned in this approach is diagrammed in Exhibit 26-3. The marginal revenue and marginal cost curves trace patterns commonly assumed in economic theory: to move to higher and higher volumes, marginal cost increases, and marginal revenue decreases. The optimal production and transfer quantity is identified by the intersection of the marginal revenue and marginal cost lines (point M).

Market Price

If the profit centers were, in fact, independent businesses, any transfer of intermediate products would require a market transaction for which a market price could be recorded. The independent firm is judged on its ability to buy and sell at market and make a profit. If a purchase price is too high, the independent firm will not buy; if its selling prices are too high, it will not sell.

Market price can also be used as the transfer price when a division buys the intermediate products from another division. The idea is to give the supplying division the same incentive to sell to the buying division as it has to supply an outside customer—and to keep the buying division from using the intermediate product unless it can afford to pay as much as an outside customer.

Market price generally means the price at which the intermediate product is sold on the open market. This may be obtained by consulting price catologs, by soliciting bids from outside firms, or by examining published data on completed market transactions.

Combination Methods: Programmed Prices

The third basis for transfer pricing is a combination of the first two. Cost and market can be combined in various ways, but we'll describe only one of them at this point, mathematically programmed prices.

For example, an oil company controls the output of one of its large refineries with the help of a linear programming model. Part of the output of one of the refinery's products is transferred to a nearby petrochemical plant. The linear programming model is solved every quarter for various transfer volumes, and the petrochemical division is given a schedule listing the transfer prices for various quantities. The division manager then decides how much to buy during the quarter.

When the refinery is operating below capacity, the transfer prices represent the marginal cost of serving the petrochemical plant. At full capacity, however, the transfer price is the sale value of the transferred output. Since this is considerably higher than marginal cost, the petrochemical manager will often find it profitable to buy substitute materials from outside sources when the refinery is at capacity.

TRANSFER PRICING MECHANISMS

Transfer pricing methods can be classified not only by the basis on which they are built but also by the mechanisms the company uses to derive them. Transfer prices can be established in either of two ways: by dictation, or by negotiation. When these mechanisms are combined with the bases we described in the preceding section, we get the following set of possible combinations:

Mechanism \ Basis	Cost	Market	Cost or Market
Dictation			
Negotiation			

Before deciding which of these cells are usable, we need to describe each of the two possible transfer pricing mechanisms.

Dictated Transfer Prices

A transfer price that either or both of the parties to the transfer are expected to regard as given may be referred to as a dictated price. We generally think of dictated prices as being imposed on both parties by higher management, but in some cases they may be set by the supplying division or by the buying division, without consultation with the other.

Price dictation can take two forms. In the simpler case, the pricing authority establishes a price, which is then used to record transfers of the intermediate product. In other situations, the price dictator prescribes a pricing formula, such as the following:

Price = 110 percent of standard manufacturing cost

The actual prices are then calculated by inserting the appropriate values of the independent variable or variables.

Negotiated Transfer Prices

The other approach to transfer pricing is to require the parties to deal with each other as they deal with outside customers and suppliers. We call this negotiated transfer pricing.

The negotiation usually begins with a price quotation from the supplying division. From this point any of four routes can be taken: (1) the buying division may accept the price; (2) the buying division may bluff and bargain to get a lower price; (3) the buying division may obtain competing bids and negotiate with each possible supplier to get the best price/service combination; or (4) the buying division may reject the bid and either buy outside or not buy at all, without further discussion of the price. The same sequence can be initiated by a price offer from the buying division.

No matter which of these outcomes takes place, the price can be classified as a negotiated price. The essence of negotiation is in the managers' freedom to accept or reject a price or to initiate a change from the initial bid or offer price. Whether such a change actually takes place is irrelevant.

Independent buyers and sellers sometimes negotiate about the definition of cost, when price is based on cost. The same kind of negotiation can take place between divisions of the same company. Most negotiations focus directly on price, however. The need to negotiate is evidence that the market value of the intermediate product is not known. The purpose of negotiation, in other words, is to establish the market value. What this means is that the "cost" and "cost or market" cells in our transfer pricing matrix are largely empty.

TRANSFER PRICING BETWEEN PROFIT CENTERS

We now have three criteria for choosing a transfer pricing method, three possible bases for transfer pricing, and two mechanisms for setting the price. This leaves us with the only really important question: What method should be used? The answer depends on the status of the two parties to the transfer. Three situations need to be distinguished:

1. Transfers between two service centers or from a service center to a profit center.
2. Transfers between two profit centers.
3. Transfers from a profit center to an administered center.

We covered the first of these situations in Chapter 8 and will deal briefly with the third in the next section. Our attention in this section will be on transfers between profit centers.

Market-Based Negotiated Prices

The only basis for transfer pricing that is fully compatible with profit decentralization is market value. The only way to get the transfer price to approximate market value is through negotiation. These are strong statements, but we can back them up.

The case for negotiated transfer prices. As we said earlier, some form of negotiation is implicit in management's dealings with outside suppliers and outside customers. These negotiations establish the prices at which goods and services are actually exchanged—that is, they determine the market values of these goods and services. The case for extending this process to internal transfer pricing rests on two related arguments:

1. It is consistent with profit decentralization.
2. It is sensitive to variations in opportunity cost.

1. Consistency with profit decentralization. The concept of profit decentralization requires the delegation of decision authority to the division manager. This includes authority to choose the division's sources of supply and to sell the division's products or services in the most profitable markets open to it. Without negotiation, internal transfers are either take-it-or-leave-it decisions or command decisions made by higher management. In either case the division managers' freedom of action is reduced, and this reduces their accountability for profit. Negotiation restores the managers' freedom of action and thereby increases their accountability for profits.

2. Sensitivity to opportunity cost. Part of the division manager's job is to be aware of market conditions affecting the division's operations. Each division manager is expected to make many decisions in which estimates of opportunity cost are crucial. The internal transfer decision is simply one of many.

A simple situation of this kind is illustrated in Exhibit 26–4. This shows a supplying division with average total costs of $17 and some outside customers paying enough to yield $18 a unit after marketing costs are deducted. The shaded area in the block representing the supplying division is the amount of capacity now devoted to filling outside customers' orders—the rest is idle.

The buying division has an opportunity to buy the intermediate product from an outside supplier for $15, and has offered to pay this amount to the supplying division. The situation can be summarized quickly:

The buying division won't buy at a higher price.

It appears that the company will be better off if the transfer takes place (cost will be $13, not $15).

The supplying division will be $2 better off ($15 − $13) if it fills the order than if it lets the capacity stand idle.

In these circumstances it would seem that the two division managers have a mutual interest in reaching agreement on a transfer price. They should fail to agree only if the supplying division's man-

EXHIBIT 26–4

Market Influences on Transfer Pricing Negotiations

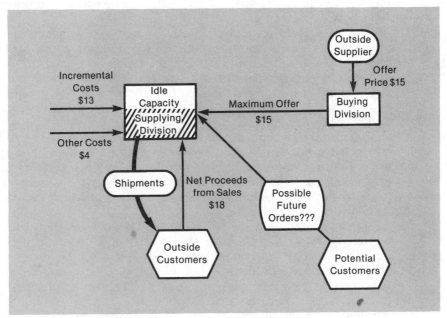

ager estimates that the potential customers in the lower right-hand corner of the diagram are likely to come in with higher priced orders that will fill the division's capacity.

Division managers are paid to exercise their judgment in situations like this. They are expected to be right often enough to justify giving them the authority to make these decisions. The presumption is that the managers will negotiate an agreement if interdivisional transfers seem to be in the company's best interests because both managers will benefit if this is the case.

Necessary conditions for negotiated transfer pricing. These arguments are valid only if four conditions are met:

1. There must be some form of outside market for the intermediate product.
2. Any available market information should be communicated to both parties to the negotiation.
3. Both parties must have freedom to deal outside.
4. Top management must indicate its support of the principle of negotiation.

1. Existence of outside markets. The existence of an outside market for the intermediate product is important in negotiation because it provides both parties with an alternative.

In the absence of an outside market, the bargaining range is likely to be considerably wider because the buying and selling divisions are in the position known to economists as bilateral monopoly—that is, the market for the intermediate product consists of two firms, one buying and one selling, and neither has an outside alternative. Under these conditions the market price is likely to be indeterminate within a fairly wide range.

2. *Access to information.*   Both parties to the negotiation need access to market price information. Dissemination of information relating to the outside market should reduce the bargaining range and permit negotiation to take place in an atmosphere conducive to producing transfer prices that are fair approximations to opportunity cost. Some would even say they need access to internal cost information as well, and for the same reason.

3. *Freedom to buy and sell outside.*   The lack of real freedom to buy or sell outside weakens the effectiveness of negotiation as a means of promoting sound resource allocation. Opportunity costs can't be determined reliably enough unless management has some way to test the market. Freedom to enter the market provides the necessary mechanism.

Freedom to buy outside is particularly important when substantial capacity for the manufacture of the intermediate product exists internally, capacity that would be made idle if the products were to be acquired outside. Paradoxical as this may seem, it is under conditions such as these that it is most important to have internal transfer prices that best reflect the company's opportunity costs. Without buying freedom, transfer prices are less likely to feel the pressure of competitive forces and will remain higher than they should be to guide the managers of the buying divisions in their pricing and output decisions. With their costs kept at artificially high levels, the buying divisions will be unable to accept orders that would prove profitable to the company as a whole.

It should be remembered that freedom to deal outside does not necessarily mean that a substantial volume of purchases will actually be made from outside suppliers when idle internal capacity exists. Freedom must be accompanied by an obligation to negotiate internally. The buying division manager will normally prefer to buy from another unit of the company if the intermediate products are available at competitive prices. On the other side, the supplying division faced with idle capacity should be willing to reduce transfer prices to retain the business as long as some margin remains over the incremental costs of serving the internal customer.

4. *Top management support.*   Strong top management support is essential to reduce the amount of umpiring top management is called upon to do. A system of negotiation can be undermined quickly if top management is ready to step in and arbitrate disputes whenever they arise. Appealing to the umpire is a form of dodging responsibility. Unless top management makes it clear that appeals for arbitration will reflect unfavorably on the executive ability of the negotiators, umpiring is likely to become frequent.

Weaknesses of negotiated transfer pricing.   Negotiated transfer pricing systems are likely to break down if the four conditions we just described aren't met to a reasonable degree. Negotiation has three other disadvantages as well, and these become more and more important as the four conditions become less and less completely met.

The first of these weaknesses is that *negotiation is time consuming*. Although a five-minute telephone call will do the job on occasion, major negotiations can extend over several weeks, backed by extensive staff work.

The second weakness is that *negotiation is a divisive process*. It emphasizes the conflicting interests of the various division managers rather than their mutual interest in the company's prosperity. Although we have said that agreement to transfer internally is in the interest of both parties if the supplying division's opportunity costs are low and the opportunity costs of the buying division are high, the process of reaching this agreement works in the opposite direction.

Finally, if the bargaining range is wide and the volume of transfers is large, *divisional profit will be very sensitive to the division manager's ability as a bargainer*. Wide bargaining ranges and massive transfers are generally found when the conditions required for effective negotiation are poorly met. When this happens, another solution probably should be sought.

Standard Full Cost

Full cost shouldn't be used for transfers between profit centers except as a last resort. The worst defect of full cost as a basis for transfer pricing is that it fails to provide a sound guide to decision making. For example, suppose a division manager is faced with the problem of choosing between an outside vendor and an internal supplying division for all or part of the buying division's requirements of a certain intermediate product. The full cost transfer price is $12, but the product can be obtained from an outside vendor at a delivered price of $10 a unit. Given these conditions, the division manager has a $2 incentive to buy the product outside, other things such as reliability and quality being equal.

But now suppose the internal supplying division is operating at 60 percent of capacity. The opportunity cost of internal transfers is the average variable cost, $9, not the $12 full cost. This means that if the product is bought outside, the supplying division will lose a $3 contribution toward its fixed costs; the loss in total company profit will be $1 a unit.

Top management can prevent this kind of suboptimization in either of two ways: (1) by reducing the transfer price; or (2) by ordering the buying division to buy the product inside at the existing transfer price. Each of these actions will reduce the autonomy of one division or the other. The managers will see their authority reduced and their profit responsibility diluted.

Full cost may have a further distorting effect on executive decisions. As long as a division is operating below capacity—that is, on the relatively flat portion of the average variable cost curve—its management will be willing to produce to satisfy both internal and external demands. Standard full cost will exceed incremental manu-

EXHIBIT 26-5

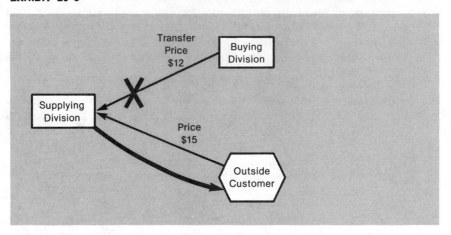

facturing cost, and the supplying division will increase its profit contribution by making the transfer.

The situation will be just the reverse if the supplying division is pressing its capacity limits. Here the manager will be likely to favor the outlet that offers the highest current revenue. At full capacity, market prices for the intermediate product are likely to be higher than average full cost; unless a higher authority intervenes, sales to the outside market are likely to take precedence over internal transfers (see Exhibit 26-5). The full cost transfer pricing system usually breaks down at this point, as top management steps in to ensure the flow of goods to other divisions.

This is just another way of saying that full cost transfer prices are incompatible with the resource allocation objectives of a decentralized company. They do not provide a sound basis on which top management can delegate decision-making authority to division managers—authority over sources of supply and outlets for each division's products. For this reason full cost transfer prices should be restricted to situations in which this authority is not granted, in fact, to companies or divisions that are not decentralized.

Marginal Cost

The shortcomings of full cost transfer pricing have led to suggestions that marginal costs be used instead. The argument for marginal cost transfer pricing is that it will lead the profit center managers to make better decisions than they would under full cost transfer pricing.

The reason for this is that full cost transfer prices will overstate marginal costs unless the supplying division is operating near capacity. The buying division, therefore, is likely to use less of the intermediate product than it would use if a central authority were making the decisions. One way to avoid this kind of suboptimization might be to go to marginal cost pricing.

This is a forceful argument, but it overlooks three important facts:

1. Marginal cost is *indeterminate* when two or more divisions use or sell the same intermediate product.
2. Marginal cost is inapplicable to *capacity rationing*.
3. Marginal cost transfer pricing is *inconsistent with profit decentralization*.

Indeterminacy. The first shortcoming of marginal cost transfer pricing is that the marginal cost of the intermediate product supplied to a buying division is often indeterminate. If marginal cost increases with volume, it will depend on the *total* demands of all the buying divisions and the supplying division's external customers.

Suppose a supplying division and two buying divisions all use a certain intermediate product. If only one of these three divisions is in the market, the marginal cost curve is the segment between 0 and A in Exhibit 26–6. If a second division comes into the market, the marginal cost curve facing *each* of them is the segment between A and B. And if all three are in the picture, the marginal cost curve might be the segment between B and C. In these circumstances, the supplying division can't give *either* of the other divisions a firm schedule of marginal costs. The three divisions must make their decisions jointly, and this generally requires central direction and coordination.

Capacity rationing. Capacity operations place another set of strains on a marginal cost transfer pricing system. When the supplying division is operating at capacity the net revenue available from outside customers often appears to be greater than marginal cost. In theory, this couldn't happen, because the firm would increase its rate of output until marginal cost equaled marginal revenue. In fact, the firm's knowledge of its marginal costs is almost never good enough to extend the cost schedule to this point; or else the firm is unwilling or unable to engage in subcontracting or other high-cost devices to expand its short-run capacity to deliver products.

As a result, when the supplying divisions are operating at capacity, top management may have to permit the division managers to depart from the previously calculated marginal costs or else may have to direct them to divert their production to internal customers at a sacrifice in reported profit. Under the former solution, the marginal cost basis for transfer pricing is acknowledged to be inadequate; under the latter, divisional authority is abrogated.

EXHIBIT 26–6

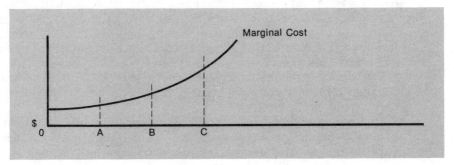

Incompatibility with profit decentralization. We just mentioned that the supplying division manager's authority is likely to be abrogated when operations reach capacity. We also pointed out that divisional autonomy is likely to be diminished when marginal cost is not constant and the intermediate product is used by two or more divisions.

The problem is even more general, however. To make a marginal cost transfer pricing system work, the supplying division must be denied the right to refuse to supply other divisions at these prices. The reason is that marginal cost transfers make internal transfers seem less profitable than external sales. As long as marginal cost is lower than average full cost, the profit reports of supplying divisions qualifying as profit centers will reflect a mixture of "profits" on outside sales and "losses" on internal sales.

Reported losses need have no ill effects on the use of divisional profit statements in the evaluation of managerial performance, provided that evaluation is based on achievement of predetermined goals which have been established in a critical, creative manner. Unfortunately, no matter how intellectually it is committed to this point of view, management often finds it emotionally difficult to accept a low profit figure as evidence of good or satisfactory performance. Furthermore, executive promotion often seems to come faster, the monetary rewards to be greater, and people easier to recruit in divisions with good profit records. A transfer pricing system that division managers feel is unfairly depriving them of these advantages is likely to breed resentment.

The activity evaluation aspect may be even more important, particularly during periods of idle capacity. Here all the profits on internally transferred goods will be lodged in the internal buying divisions, and the supplying divisions may find it correspondingly more difficult to justify capital expenditure proposals.

Variable Cost Plus Retainer

Neither full cost nor marginal cost is consistent with all three of our transfer pricing criteria—short-term decision relevance, fairness, and relevance for activity evaluation. So what does top management do when a supplying division is the only reliable source and the buying division is the only buyer for certain intermediate products?

One possibility is to back off and reclassify the divisions as service centers or administered centers. Management is unlikely to do this, however, if the supplying division sells most of its output to outside customers and the buying division buys most of its other materials from outside suppliers. Management won't allow a small transfer pricing problem to stand in the way if it wants to establish these two divisions as profit centers.

In these circumstances, some companies have turned to a modification of the marginal cost approach. This approach substitutes standard variable cost per unit for marginal cost and adds a monthly

EXHIBIT 26–7

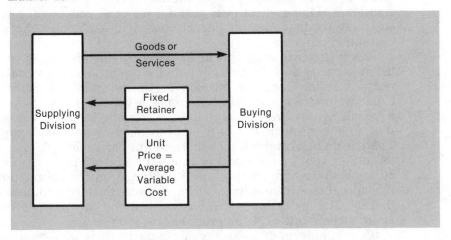

lump-sum retainer to cover the fixed costs and profits of the internal supplier of the intermediate product (see Exhibit 26–7).

The size of the retainer must be set or at least approved by central management, because the intermediate product isn't available on the market. It will typically include a provision for profit to the supplying division. One possible formula is to give the supplying division a profit equal to the amount of imputed interest on the investment attributable to the intermediate product. As long as the supplying division adheres to budgeted performance in other respects, it will report a profit on the intermediate product.

This formula is likely to meet the fairness criterion as long as the total profit margin is wide. If the margin is narrow, however, an imputed interest formula will put most or all of the profit in the supplying division. The manager of the buying division is likely to regard this as less than fair, and top management may wish to work out a different allocation.

The main flaw in this method is that it may bias the activity evaluation process. If the retainer includes a provision for imputed interest, the entire impact of market fluctuations will fall on the buying division. The problem is that the total profit contribution of the final product is the product of the two divisions combined, as we mentioned earlier. In the absence of information on the market value of the intermediate product, management has no way of splitting this profit contribution between the two divisions that will measure the profit attributable to each. In fact, the total profit contribution may even be applicable to *each* division if eliminating either would lead to the loss of the whole profit.

This flaw can't be ignored, but we return to the point we made at the beginning of the chapter, in discussing transfer pricing criteria: the requirements of activity evaluation are often so difficult to satisfy that we must select transfer pricing methods that don't meet them all.

Since we have elected to give primary emphasis to the divisional decision-making and fairness criteria, we can't rule out the variable cost plus retainer method just because it doesn't meet the activity evaluation criterion.

This system will work as long as the supplying division is operating below capacity and the assumption of constant average variable cost remains valid. Once the division begins to press the limits of its capacity, however, something else must be done. For example, suppose a supplying division manufactures a certain intermediate product that is neither sold on the market nor available from outside suppliers. There is no market price. The division has been selling 10 percent of its total output of all products internally and 90 percent to outside customers; the retainer has been established on the assumption that this allocation will continue. During the year the buying division finds that its sales are running ahead of budget, and the manager requests additional quantities of the intermediate product.

If the supplying division has idle capacity, this additional demand can and should be met at standard variable cost. No distortion of the supplying division's profit should result. But if the supplying division is operating at or near capacity, the additional volume for the final product division can be obtained only by diverting capacity from outside sales of other products of the supplying division or by incurring costs in excess of standard variable cost, perhaps by increased subcontracting, increased use of overtime, or use of less productive standby equipment. In this hybrid situation, who makes the decisions and how are these decisions reflected in the transfer prices?

The answers to these questions are not entirely clear, but one solution is worth exploring—require the division managers to negotiate to see if they can agree on a price for the incremental transfers. The supplying division's management will be unwilling to accept any price that will not cover the opportunity costs of increasing deliveries to the buying division:

1. If the increased volume can be reached only by curtailing production of products now being sold outside the company, the supplying division will demand the same dollar markup over variable cost from its internal customer that it would lose by restricting sales to outside customers.
2. If the supplying division can expand its total output, then its management must demand a price that is at least adequate to cover the incremental cost of production by the more costly methods.

The buying division will be willing to pay these higher prices only if the sales value of these additional units is adequate to cover the transfer prices plus any additional costs of further processing and distribution.

This transfer pricing method may seem inconsistent with the profit center concept. In fact, it is the transfer requirement, not the transfer pricing method, that is the inconsistent element. Since the supplying division is the only source of supply, and the buying division is the only customer, the negotiating range is extremely wide. To avoid the dysfunctional effects of negotiation, higher management will have to get into the transfer pricing process. The variable cost plus retainer approach is a method of meeting the three transfer pricing criteria in this situation.

Market in/Cost out

A second alternative when the intermediate product has no immediate market value is one we have labeled the market in/cost out method.[1] In a market in/cost out system, two sets of transfer prices are used, one for the supplying division, the other for the buying division. For example, suppose the supplying division has an average variable cost of $3. The buying division sells the product for $6 after paying $2 to process and market it. The transfer prices would be as follows:

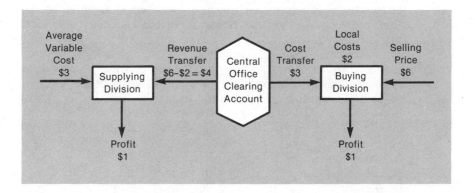

Each division reports the same $1 profit on the transfer.

The purpose of double counting is to emphasize the mutuality of interest of the two divisions. The buying division is really an extension of the supplying division, but management wants its management to work vigorously to expand its profits. This dual transfer pricing system may achieve this.

This mutuality of interest breaks down when the supplying division reaches the limits of its capacity. At this point transfers to the buying division force the supplying division to deny products to its own outside customers. The solution here is not to negotiate, because the buying division has no alternative sources of supply.

Probably the best solution is to maintain the variable cost transfer price for the budgeted transfer volume, with a higher price for any additional quantities, reflecting the current opportunity cost of the supplying division. In this way the buying division's decisions will have to reflect opportunity cost, but its overall profit performance will

[1] A somewhat similar method is supported by Joshua Ronen and George McKinney, III, "Transfer Pricing for Divisional Autonomy," *Journal of Accounting Research* (Spring, 1970), pp. 99–112.

not be undermined. As long as the higher prices are published in advance, this should maintain the impression of fairness which is an essential requirement of any transfer pricing system.

The market in/cost out method may be better for activity evaluation than the variable cost plus retainer method. The presumption is that the total profit contribution of the final product would be lost if *either* division were to discontinue its activities relating to the intermediate product. If this presumption is untrue, then we're back where we were with the variable cost plus retainer method. No routine formula will be able to reflect the attributability of profit to individual divisions without doing serious damage to the other two criteria.

Mathematically Programmed Prices

We started this section with the assertion that negotiation is the best way to derive a transfer price for transfers between two profit centers when both parties have access to viable and visible market alternatives. We followed this with a discussion of various methods that might be used to price transfers of goods or services when outside market alternatives are absent. We found two of these that seemed to satisfy two of our three criteria.

Many writers on transfer pricing reject these propositions. They advocate using mathematical programming to derive transfer prices or transfer pricing schedules for profit centers. We have two objections to this approach. First, it is inconsistent with the profit center concept. It presumes that either the central authority or one of the parties to the transfer gives the other party a transfer pricing formula. Alternative sources of supply are ruled out.

This objection also applies to variable cost plus retainer and the market in/cost out methods. Perhaps programmed prices could be used under the same conditions that make these methods worth considering—that is, when market values of the intermediate product can't be determined by observation or negotiation. We still have our second objection, however. The transfer price is indeterminate if two or more buying divisions use the intermediate product. As we pointed out earlier, this means that the output decisions of the various divisions are interdependent, and a full programming solution would require fully centralized decision making.

To maintain the appearance of decentralized decision making without suboptimization, several writers have advocated an iterative procedure rather than a firm set of predetermined transfer prices.[2] Under this plan the division managers would supply a central analytical staff with preliminary estimates of their output plan and input needs. The

---

[2] William J. Baumol and Tibor Fabian, "Decomposition, Pricing for Decentralization and External Economies," *Management Science*, September 1964, pp. 1–32; Andrew Whinston, "Price Guides in Decentralized Organizations," in W. W. Cooper, H. J. Leavitt, and M. W. Shelly II, eds., *New Perspectives in Organization Research* (New York: John Wiley & Sons, 1964), pp. 405–48; Nicholas Dopuch and David F. Drake, "Accounting Implications of a Mathematical Programming Approach to the Transfer Price Problem," *Journal of Accounting Research*, Spring 1964, pp. 10–24.

central staff would enter these plans into a large-scale linear program and transmit the resulting quantities and transfer prices to the division managers.

Upon receipt of the results of this first run, the division managers would review their initial plans and submit revised estimates to head-quarters. The linear program would be run again with these data and the results would once again be sent to the division managers. By the end of the third or fourth iteration, the divisional plans would approxi-mate the optimal solution and further iteration would become un-necessary.

Whether this procedure would preserve the decentralization pattern or undermine it is a behavioral question for which no data are avail-able. The method would seem to have a positive benefit if the quality of the data considered by the division managers in later iterations were higher than the quality of the data they supplied initially to a central decision staff.

It must be remembered, however, that real decision authority in these situations rests in the supplying division, where the computer program is run. The other division managers may come to regard the iterative process as an unproductive game, taking a good deal of time and energy but played for someone else's benefit. This could reduce the credibility of the entire profit measurement system, and thereby reduce its motivational impact.

PRICING TRANSFERS TO ADMINISTERED CENTERS

Most discussion of transfer pricing focuses on transfers between units that are independent enough to be classified as profit centers. Before leaving the subject, we'd like to examine a slightly different situation—transfers from a profit center to an administered center. We identified the administered center in Chapter 24 as an organiza-tion with the following characteristics:

1. It sells goods mainly to outside customers.
2. It has a profit objective, profit-oriented decision rules, and profit accountability.
3. It obtains a large percentage of its raw materials (or salable merchandise) from other parts of the company and is denied access to other sources of these items.

Sales offices and foreign subsidiaries often fit this description. The third characteristic means that these units aren't profit centers, but the other two characteristics means they are expected to behave like profit centers.

Negotiation isn't a suitable transfer pricing mechanism in these cases. Lacking freedom to buy outside, the administered center has little bargaining power. Negotiation would be a meaningless ritual.

To provide the division manager with guidance in decision making, the transfer price to the administered center should be marginal cost to the supplying division or market value of the intermediate product, whichever is higher. We suggest that any of the three "combination methods" we described in the preceding section can work here:

1. Mathematically programmed prices.
2. Variable cost plus lump-sum retainer.
3. Market in/cost out.

Mathematically programmed prices give the buying division manager the best guidance available for resource utilization decisions, if the inputs to the program are correct. Their main disadvantage is that they tend to locate all the profit on the transferred items in the buying division until the supplying division reaches capacity operations. This defect might be corrected by adding a lump-sum retainer to the transfer price at all volumes below a certain level, which is essentially what the variable cost plus retainer method does.

The market in/cost out method has one great advantage over either of the others—it emphasizes the common interest of both parties in the transfer. Since the administered center is in a sense an extension of the profit center supplying it with intermediate products, identifying the same profit with both units makes a lot of sense.

Whichever method is used, two caveats are necessary to make the transfer pricing system fit the fairness criterion:

1. The pricing formula must be established in advance so the division managers know what to expect.
2. The profit plan benchmark for managerial performance evaluation should be adjusted for any changes in the transfer prices during the budget period.

Mathematically programmed prices, for example, meet the first of these criteria because the formula is known in advance. A programming system doesn't include the adjustment mechanism automatically, however. If mathematical programming is to be used, the fairness criterion requires adjusting the profit plan whenever the program produces a price change.

SUMMARY

Transfer prices on goods or services transferred between profit centers should guide the profit center managers toward decisions that will lead to an economic allocation of resources. They should also be perceived as fair by the profit center managers, so as not to weaken their motivation. Finally, if possible, they should help top management evaluate the profitability of the division's activities. This last criterion may be difficult to implement, however, and in general can be subordinated to the other two.

Transfer prices might be based on cost, or market value, or some combination of the two. They can be dictated by central management or derived by negotiation between the parties. Market-based negotiated prices are the only ones fully consistent with the profit center concept. Other methods should be used only when the conditions necessary for successful negotiation are absent. Mathematically programmed prices, variable cost plus lump-sum retainers, and market in/cost out transfer prices are all worth considering.

Negotiation isn't feasible for transfers from profit centers to administered centers. Market in/cost out transfer prices are appropriate here. The variable cost plus retainer system will also work, and mathematically programmed prices can be used if suitable programs can be developed. Whenever the transfer price is changed during a budget period, however, the fairness criterion requires the budget allowances to be changed, too.

KEY TERMS

The most important terms introduced and defined in this chapter are the following:

Buying division   Negotiated prices
Final product   Programmed prices
Intermediate product   Supplying division
Market in/cost out   Variable cost plus retainer

INDEPENDENT STUDY PROBLEMS
(Solutions in Appendix C)

1. Meeting a competitor's bid. Ballou Corporation, a diversified manufacturing company, has seven main product divisions, each with its own manufacturing facilities and selling most of its output to outside customers. One of these divisions, the Hull Division, manufactures and sells a broad range of industrial chemicals.

Hull Division supplies product X to outside customers and also to the Hingham Division, another of Ballou's seven product divisions. Hingham Division uses product X as a raw material in the manufacture of several products. Hull charges Hingham $1.80 a pound for product X, 10 percent less than it charges its outside customers.

Hingham has been happy with this arrangement for several years, but an outside supplier has just offered to supply a perfectly satisfactory substitute for product X at a firm contract price of $1.60 a pound, delivered at the Hingham factory. The Hingham Division manager has proposed that the interdivisional transfer price of product X be reduced to $1.60 to meet the competing offer; otherwise, the contract will go outside.

You are the assistant controller in the Hingham Division. Your division manager has just given you a copy of Hull division's estimated monthly income statement for product X (dollar totals in thousands):

Sales—outside (100,000 lbs. at $2)		$200
Sales—Hingham (50,000 lbs. at $1.80)		90
Total sales		$290 .
Product-traceable costs:		
Variable manufacturing costs ($0.90 per lb.)	$135	
Sales commissions—outside sales	10	
Depreciation	20	
Other traceable fixed costs	40	205
Product profit contribution		$ 85
Share of divisional fixed costs		60
Income before Taxes		$ 25

The fixed costs traceable to product X wouldn't be reduced if production volume were reduced by a third. The divisional fixed costs, allocated among the division's products at a flat 40 cents a pound, are even stickier. These costs would continue even if Hull Division stopped making product X entirely.

a. Draft a short memorandum, outlining the points Hingham's manager should make in trying to convince Hull's manager to reduce the transfer price.
b. Is negotiation the right way to determine a transfer price in this situation?

2. Transfers to foreign subsidiary. Elsa Corporation is a wholly owned subsidiary of Ballou Corporation, established to market the company's products in other countries in the Western Hemisphere. It handles only Ballou products, including many products manufactured in the Hull Division (see Problem 1). It does no manufacturing of its own.

Elsa has never introduced product X into its markets because in its ordinary uses product X requires support facilities Elsa is in no position to provide. Elsa's manager has found a new use for this product, however, and is convinced the division could sell 20,000 pounds a month at a price of $1.80 a pound. Transportation costs to these markets would amount to 5 cents a pound and incremental local marketing costs would amount to $2,000 a month. Elsa will start marketing product X only if the transfer price is cut to $1.50 a pound.

a. As manager of the Hull Division, would you reduce the transfer price?
b. Is negotiation a good way to reach transfer prices in situations like this? (Ignore any effects the transfer price might have on taxes and customs duties.)

EXERCISES AND PROBLEMS

1. Manufacturing division transfer price. The Apex Machinery Company manufactures and distributes a line of textile machinery and supplies and a line of machinery for nontextile industrial trades. The company's operations are organized as shown in the following chart:

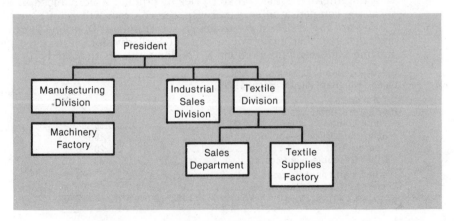

All machinery, including both textile and industrial trades machinery, is manufactured in the machinery factory of the manufacturing division. The textile division manufactures its own supplies in its supplies factory but purchases all its requirements of machinery from the manufacturing division. The machinery is highly technical and cannot be obtained from independent manufacturers.

The management of the Apex Machinery Company wishes to prepare profit reports for each of the company's three divisions, and you have been asked to recommend a transfer pricing system. The manufacturing vice president has suggested that machinery be transferred at standard manufacturing cost plus 10 percent. The industrial sales division has suggested list price less 25 percent, an arrangement that is common among manufacturers' agents in this market. You need not recommend either of these proposals if you feel that some other arrangement would be superior.

2. Profit-splitting transfer price. Professor E. G. Heide recently received the following letter from a former student:

"Dear Professor Heide:

"I found your paper on divisional profit standards very much to the point. We are working on our divisional reporting structure now, and much that you say seems to fit our situation.

"In my limited experience so far, the most difficult aspect of this problem has always been the matter of transfer pricing. I wonder if you could comment on the merit of the following approach which I believe takes into account the effect of below-capacity operation of the supplying division in a market where price and to a large extent market share are constant. This, you will admit, is the case in many industries today, especially where oligopolies exist.

"Consider division A, whose operations can be described as shown on the diagram labeled Figure 1.

"Division B wishes to purchase a quantity M of material produced by division A, whose cost curves are shown and whose output, not counting

FIGURE 1

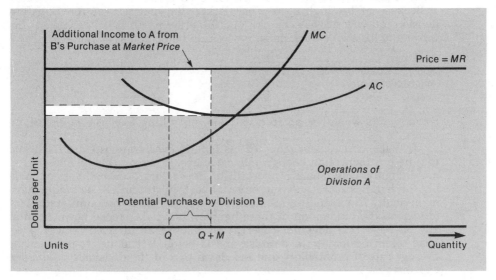

the contemplated interdivisional transfer, is limited to Q, its 'share of market.' A forced purchase of the material at market price by division B would be, in effect, a 'windfall profit' for division A; while purchase at marginal cost would cause division A to lose money. I would suggest that the additional income to A that could result from B's purchase of the material at market cost be divided evenly between A and B, resulting in a transfer price above A's average cost—i.e., a profit to A—and below the market cost, i.e., a saving for B.

"If the purchase price were set at average cost, A's manager would have no incentive to make the transfer of material, while if the price were set at market cost, B might prefer to go 'outside' for marginal reasons like 'service,' and if so, would adversely affect corporate earnings. The 50–50 split could become a matter of company policy, and thus avoid negotiations each time a transfer cost has to be established.

"I look forward to hearing from you."

Draft a reply for Professor Heide's signature.

3. Selecting a source of supply. The Barnaby Corporation was formed two years ago as a merger of two previously independent companies, Dover and Elmsford. These two companies, now Barnaby divisions, have been operated since the merger just as they were before the merger, as if they were still independent businesses. Each has its own sales force and its own production facilities. Interdivisional transactions are rare and the company has never established a transfer pricing policy.

The Dover division now buys 10,000 metal handles a month from the Fowler Company for use on one of its products, a canister-type vacuum cleaner. The Elmsford division recently offered to supply these handles to Dover at a price of 90 cents apiece. The Dover division manager was interested, but not at a 90-cent price. The current purchase price was 82 cents and the Fowler Company had already offered a firm contract for the next year's requirements at this price.

The Elmsford division has a modern, well-equipped factory. Although its equipment is not ideally suited to the production of small items like the Dover handles, labor and materials costs on such items are only a few cents higher than in more suitably equipped plants.

Because of his high costs, Dick Baker, the manager of the Elmsford division, doesn't see how he can cut the price much below 90 cents. According to his own calculations, cost would be 85 cents, as follows:

Materials.......................	$0.55
Labor...........................	0.10
Factory overhead................	0.20
Total........................	$0.85

Because this would be an internal sale, no selling expense would be incurred.

Mr. Baker knows that many of his factory overhead costs are fixed and that he has more than enough idle capacity to take on this business without difficulty. Only about 30 percent of the factory overhead cost of making the handles represents incremental cost. Furthermore, he would have no difficulty in expanding his work force by the small amounts necessary to take on the production of these handles. Mr. Baker feels, however, that any business that does not cover at least its share of fixed factory overhead offers no long-term promise and is better left alone. It reduces the average rate of profitability and ties down part of the division's productive capacity.

The Dover division manager has just decided to continue buying the handles from the Fowler Company at the 82-cent price.

a. On the basis of the data available to you, and ignoring the transfer price, do you believe that the Dover division should buy its handles from the Elmsford division?
b. If you had the power to set the transfer price in this situation, what price would you set?
c. Assuming that the calculations in (a) indicated that Elmsford should supply the handles, should the top management of the Barnaby Corporation step in and order the Dover division to buy them from Elmsford at the transfer price you selected in (b)?

4. Selecting a source of supply. Company B has several product divisions. Each of these has its own manufacturing facilities and sells all or most of its output to outside customers. The company's policy is to allow division managers to choose their sources of supply and, when buying from or selling to a sister division, to negotiate the price just as they would for outside purchases or sales.

One of the company's divisions, division X, buys all of its requirements of its main raw material from division Y. This material is one of several products manufactured in division Y. Until recently, division Y was willing to supply this material to division X at a transfer price of 80 cents a pound, just a few cents more than division Y's estimated incremental cost. Division Y is now operating at capacity, however, and is unable to meet all of its outside customers' demands for this product at a price of $1 a pound. The manager of division has threatened to cut off supplies to division X unless the manager of division X will agree to pay the market price.

The manager of division X is resisting this pressure. The division's budget for the current year was based on an estimated consumption of 1 million pounds of the material each month at a price of 80 cents. Since the division's budgeted income before taxes is only $250,000 a month, a price increase to $1 would bring the division very close to the break-even point.

The company's central purchasing office has found an outside source of an equivalent substitute material at a price of 95 cents, but the manager of division X sees no reason to go outside when a sister division can supply the material at an 80-cent cost. Even if cost were measured at division Y's full manufacturing cost of 88 cents a pound, division X would still be giving division Y a 12-cent profit on every pound and would fall $80,000 a month short of its budgeted profit.

a. Where should division X obtain its materials, from division Y or from the outside supplier? Support your answer with figures from the problem.
b. How, if at all, would your answer to (a) change if division Y had agreed at the beginning of the year to supply up to 1 million pounds a month for 12 months to division X at a fixed price of 80 cents a pound? Explain.
c. Given the company's transfer pricing system, is division X likely to obtain its materials from the source you have recommended in your answer to (a)? Explain.
d. In the light of your answers to (a), (b) and (c), what changes, if any, would you recommend in the transfer pricing system? Give your reasons.

5. Selecting a source of supply. The Gunnco Corporation has several divisions operating as profit centers. Two of these are the Ajax and Defco divisions. Each of these divisions sells most of its output to customers outside the Gunnco group.

Divisional residual income is used in the periodic evaluations of the performance of the divisions and of the division managers. Residual income for each division is calculated by deducting interest at an annual rate of 18 percent on Gunnco's net investment in the division.

The Ajax Division is now operating at capacity, meaning that it could expand its total production and sales volume in the near term only at a very high cost. Defco, on the other hand, is now operating at only 50 percent of its capacity, with many of its production employees either on unpaid furlough or on a short workweek. The division's administrative and clerical staffs have not been cut, with the result that a good deal of administrative capacity is idle.

Defco's manager is actively seeking profitable ways to utilize his idle capacity. A commercial airplane manufacturer has offered to buy 1,000 brake units from Defco, to be delivered during the next 12 months at a price of $52.50 each. Defco could meet this delivery schedule without difficulty. The estimated cost of the brake unit is as follows:

Purchased parts—outside vendors................	$22.50
Ajax electrical fitting No. 1726.....................	5.00
Other variable costs............................	14.00
Fixed overhead and administration...............	8.00
Total cost per unit.........................	$49.50

Management estimates that $5,000 in additional working capital would be required to support this business.

The Ajax fitting required for this brake unit would be supplied by the Ajax Division. This fitting is now being produced and sold to Ajax's outside customers at a price of $7.50 each, and approximately 10,000 of these fittings are likely to be sold this year at that price. Ajax's variable cost of producing fitting No. 1726 is $4.25 each.

Defco could obtain roughly similar fittings from outside suppliers for about $7.50, the same price Ajax charges. If it had to pay this much, however, Defco's profit margin on the brake unit would virtually disappear. Since Defco's manager sees no possibility of getting a higher price for the brake units, he has asked the Ajax manager to supply these fittings at a price of $5 each.

a. As the Ajax Division controller, would you recommend that Ajax supply fitting No. 1726 to Defco at the $5 price? Cite figures and explain your reasoning in two or three well-chosen sentences. (Ignore income taxes.)

b. Suppose Ajax refuses to sell at any price less than $7.50. As the Defco Division controller, would you recommend paying this price? Again cite figures and explain your reasoning.

c. As the Gunnco corporate controller, would you recommend that top management classify this item as one for which the transfer price should be set by top management? Give a brief explanation of your reasoning.

(CMA adapted)

6. Market price transfers: Manufacturing division. A. R. Oma, Inc. manufactures a line of men's perfumes and after-shaving lotions. The manufacturing process is basically a series of mixing operations with the addition of certain aromatic and coloring ingredients; the finished product is packaged in a company-produced glass bottle and packed in cases containing six bottles.

A. R. Oma feels that the sale of its product is heavily influenced by the appearance and appeal of the bottle and has, therefore, devoted considerable managerial effort to the bottle production process. This has resulted in the development of certain unique bottle production processes in which management takes considerable pride.

The two areas (i.e., perfume production and bottle manufacture) have evolved over the years in an almost independent manner; in fact, a rivalry has developed between management personnel as to "which division is the more important" to A. R. Oma. This attitude is probably intensified because the bottle manufacturing plant was purchased intact ten years ago and no real interchange of management personnel or ideas (except at the top corporate level) has taken place.

Since the acquisition, all bottle production has been absorbed by the perfume manufacturing plant. The perfume production division buys all its bottles from the bottle production division. Each division is considered a separate profit center and is evaluated as such. As the new corporate controller, you are responsible for defining the proper transfer prices to use in crediting the bottle production profit center and in debiting the perfume production profit center.

At your request, the bottle division general manager has asked certain other bottle manufacturers to quote prices for the quantities and sizes demanded by the perfume division. These competitive prices are:

Volume (equivalent cases*)	Total Price	Price per Case
2,000,000	$ 4,000,000	$2.00
4,000,000	7,000,000	1.75
6,000,000	10,000,000	1.67

* An "equivalent case" represents six bottles each.

A cost analysis of the internal bottle plant indicates that it can produce bottles at these costs:

Volume (equivalent cases)	Total Cost	Cost per Case
2,000,000	$3,200,000	$1.60
4,000,000	5,200,000	1.30
6,000,000	7,200,000	1.20

(Your cost analysts point out that these costs represent fixed costs of $1,200,000 and variable costs of $1 per equivalent case.)

These figures have given rise to considerable corporate discussion as to the proper value to use in the transfer of bottles to the perfume division. This interest is heightened because a significant portion of a division manager's income is an incentive bonus based on profit center results.

The perfume production division has the following costs in addition to the bottle costs:

Volume (cases)	Total Cost	Cost per Case
2,000,000	$16,400,000	$8.20
4,000,000	32,400,000	8.10
6,000,000	48,400,000	8.07

After considerable analysis, the marketing research department has furnished you with the following price-demand relationship for the finished product:

Sales Volume (cases)	Total Sales Revenue	Sales Price per Case
2,000,000	$25,000,000	$12.50
4,000,000	45,600,000	11.40
6,000,000	63,900,000	10.65

a. The A. R. Oma Company has used market price transfer prices in the past. Using the current market prices and costs, and assuming a volume of 6 million cases, calculate income before taxes for:
   1. The bottle division.
   2. The perfume division.
   3. The corporation.

b. Is this production and sales level the most profitable volume for
   1. The bottle division?
   2. The perfume division?
   3. The corporation?

   Explain your answer.

c. Should the bottle and perfume divisions be treated as separate profit centers? Explain why or why not.

d. In view of your answer to (c), how should the transfer price be set, and what price(s) would you recommend? Explain your reasoning.

(CMA adapted)

CASE 26–1: THE WOLSEY CORPORATION
(Freedom to buy outside)

The Wolsey Corporation established an industrial products division about 15 years ago. Its purpose was to find applications in industrial markets for products and technology that other company divisions had developed successfully for the company's commercial and consumer markets.

In its first 14 years, the industrial products division was required to buy from other company divisions any component part or product that it required and that was manufactured by those divisions for sale to outside customers. For special parts not manufactured by other divisions for sale to outside customers, the industrial products division was required to use internal sources if other divisions had adequate capacity and facilities. As a result, approximately 85 percent of the materials cost in industrial products plants represented parts and processed materials transferred from other divisions. These transfers were made at standard product cost.

Early last year the president of the Wolsey Corporation issued the following directive:

MEMORANDUM TO: Division Managers
SUBJECT: Interdivisional Transfers

1. To place all divisions on a more competitive footing, each division manager is hereby authorized to negotiate with outside vendors for the purchase of all processed materials, component parts, and products now purchased from other divisions of the company, except (a)

products sold directly under the company's brand name without further processing, and (b) components and processed material on Schedule T-146, for which specifications and drawings are classified company confidential.

2. Before any order is placed with an outside vendor for an item currently being supplied from another division, that division must be given a chance to meet the outside price and promised delivery schedule. No such procedure need be followed on orders in amounts of less than $500.

3. Before any order is placed with an outside vendor for a new item, all divisions should be notified and given a chance to bid on the item. This procedure need not be followed for orders amounting to less than $500.

4. Transfers between divisions will continue to be made at standard cost for all items that have not been covered by the negotiations referred to in paragraphs 2 and 3 above. These standard costs are to be approved in all cases by the corporate methods department. Negotiated prices that are less than standard cost will be reported to the accounting department on Form PR-12-60, and do not require review by the corporate staff.

5. The cooperation of all personnel is requested to make this system effective. Each division will keep a record of outside purchases and the savings accomplished thereby.

Shortly after this memorandum was circulated, the president called a meeting of division managers to explain the new procedure and to answer questions that had arisen. The manager of the small machinery division was skeptical. He said, "Does this mean that if I have idle capacity I can be forced to transfer at less than standard cost? It seems to me that that is just the time when I need transfers at standard cost more than ever to help me absorb my overhead." Most of the other division managers were more sympathetic to the new system, although they were not certain exactly how it would work.

Upon his return from this meeting, the manager of the industrial products division instructed the divisional controller to obtain outside quotations on a metal housing used in one of the division's products. This housing was then being cast in the small machinery division's foundry at a standard cost of $22.17 per casting. The castings were then machined to required tolerances in the industrial products division, and the standard cost of this operation was $6.18. Inquiries at local foundries produced a bid from the Gray Foundry Company of $23.75 per casting, plus $175 for the cost of an aluminum pattern. These castings would be produced by a more modern process and would not require any machining in the industrial products division. Annual requirements were expected to average 500 castings.

The manager of industrial products then prepared the following cost estimate and submitted it to the small machinery manager, noting that unless the indicated price could be met, the order would be placed with Gray Foundry:

Cost of outside purchase:
Pattern	$	175
Castings—500 at $23.75		11,875
Total purchase cost	$12,050	
Less: Cost of machining, 500 at $6.18		3,090
Maximum transfer price	$ 8,960	= $17.92 per casting

The manager of the small machinery division exploded when he received this estimate. "This is just what I was afraid of. You don't even know whether these people can live up to their promises and you want me to accept an order at less than cost. How do you expect me to cover my overhead? They are only quoting you this price to get your business, and once you are on the hook, they will raise their prices. As long as I have idle capacity, it is foolish to go outside—the whole company will suffer if you do very much of this. Against my better judgment, however, I'll quote you a price of $19.62. This doesn't cover depreciation on foundry equipment, and it's as low as I can go."

The industrial products manager rejected this offer and placed an initial order for 200 castings with the Gray Foundry Company, whereupon the small machinery manager appealed to the president, claiming that the new system was unworkable and unreasonable.

The president had hoped to avoid participation in disputes of this kind, but since this was the first case he felt that it warranted his attention. A staff assistant was assigned to study the problem and he made the following breakdown of standard costs:

	Variable Cost	Fixed Cost	Total Standard Cost
Casting....................	$17.95	$4.22	$22.17
Machining.................	4.15	2.03	6.18

He also found that materials price variances in the foundry were likely to be unfavorable, amounting to $0.12 per casting.

a. Prepare an analysis that will indicate whether future castings should be acquired from the Gray Foundry Company or from the small machinery division. List any assumptions you had to make in order to reach a conclusion on this question.
b. Would it be possible for the two divisions to find a mutually acceptable transfer price? If so, within what range would this transfer price fall? Show your calculations.
c. Is negotiation appropriate for these castings? Give your reasons.
d. Which features of the company's transfer pricing policy would you change and which ones would you retain? Give your reasons.

CASE 26–2: HOPPIT CHEMICAL COMPANY

The Moorhouse division of the Hoppit Chemical Company has 14 chemical plants located in various parts of the United States. Its profit contribution after deducting all divisional overheads runs about $50 million a year, and in exceptionally good years may even reach $75 million.

The company's Allworth division is much smaller, with only two plants and an annual profit contribution of about $2.5 million. Four years ago, the Allworth division constructed a new plant on a site adjacent to one of the main plants of the Moorhouse division. The idea was to take advantage of a plentiful supply of a chemical known as amalite, a product of the Moorhouse plant. Amalite was made in the Moorhouse plant from the waste residue thrown off by the plant's primary production process.

Before the Allworth plant was built, amalite had been manufactured only intermittently, whenever its market price was high enough to justify the conversion expenditures. The market for amalite had been weak for some time, however, and the Hoppit market research department forecasted that this condition would continue to prevail for many years to come as amalite was gradually displaced by petroleum derivatives in one of its main uses. Under these circumstances, it seemed a good move to build the new plant to convert amalite into another chemical product with a considerably higher market value.

A transfer price system was devised and accepted by the managers of both divisions when the new plant went into production. Under this system, Allworth's management initiated the process each quarter by telling Moorhouse how much amalite it expected to need during the next quarter. The Moorhouse division then quoted a set of prices for different quantities of amalite to be delivered during that quarter. These prices were based primarily on the estimated incremental costs of processing different quantities of Moorhouse waste into amalite. For example, during the first two years the plant was in operation, a typical transfer price schedule was as follows:

Transfers (pounds)	Total Transfer Price
1,000,000 or less..........	$0.40 per lb. (minimum 500,000 lbs.)
1,000,000–2,500,000........	$400,000 + $0.30 per lb. in excess of 1,000,000
More than 2,500,000.......	$850,000 + $0.40 per lb. in excess of 2,500,000

With this schedule in hand, Allworth's management could then decide how much amalite to order from Moorhouse during the next quarter.

The transfer pricing system also provided that transfers would be made at anticipated net market price whenever the Moorhouse plant's capacity for producing amalite was expected to be inadequate to serve all of its outside customers and Allworth too.

The Allworth plant was not completely dependent on Moorhouse amalite for raw materials. It could also use a commercially available product known as flemite. The purchase cost of flemite was considerably higher than the transfer prices prevailing during the first two years of the new plant's operations, however, and flemite was not used. Outside purchases of amalite were impractical for the same reason.

Each year each division manager in the Hoppit Chemical Company is required to prepare a profit plan. In drawing up their plans, the Allworth and Moorhouse managers get together and agree on a forecast of the transfer prices expected to prevail during the coming year. This price schedule is then built into the divisional profit plans for the year.

Shortly after the beginning of the current year, the market price of amalite took a sudden jump to 50 cents a pound, and Moorhouse could sell all it could produce at this price. Moorhouse therefore set 50 cents as the transfer price for the second quarter. Because flemite was available at a price of 45 cents, however, Moorhouse sold most of its amalite on the market and bought flemite to meet its supply commitment to the Allworth plant. Both division managers agreed that this was in the best interest of the Hoppit Chemical Company.

At the same time, however, Mr. C. P. Jones, the Allworth division manager, refused to approve the transfer charge at 45 cents on the ground that this would create a substantial profit variance, amounting to approximately $250,000 a quarter, through no fault of anyone in the Allworth division. As Mr. Jones pointed out, when the plant was constructed he could have signed a long-term contract with outside suppliers of amalite at a price of 40 cents a pound, but he was not allowed by Hoppit's top management to do so. Mr. Jones felt that Moorhouse was under an obligation to continue to supply amalite or a substitute at a price within the range that was forecasted when the plant was built.

Mr. John England, Moorhouse's chief cost analyst and the man responsible for the transfer price calculations, did not agree. "Even if they had signed a contract like that," he said, "we would still have to make our decisions on the basis of current market conditions. If Allworth can't make an incremental profit on the basis of current market prices, then the plant should be shut down until materials prices go back down or selling prices of the Allworth products go up. If we let them have this stuff at 40 cents, the company could be losing as much as 5 cents on every pound they use."

a.   Do you feel that Mr. Jones is justified in asking for a long-term price commitment from Moorhouse, or is Mr. England right in saying that the transfer price should reflect current market conditions?

b.   Should the transfer pricing system be changed, and if so in what way? Can you identify any other defects in the system? Explain your reasoning.

CASE 26–3: AB THORSTEN (D)
(Transfers to foreign subsidiary)*

Anders Ekstrom, managing director of Sweden's AB Thorsten, is apprehensive about the profit position of XL–4, an industrial adhesive product.[1] He is now selling XL–4 at a price of Skr. 1,850 a ton, which is Skr. 300 less than its delivered cost. At the same time, Mr. Gillot, senior vice president of Roget S.A., and Ekstrom's immediate superior in Belgium, is wondering what decision he should take regarding Ekstrom's request that he lower the price at which the Belgian company sells XL–4 to the Swedish company.

AB Thorsten is a wholly owned subsidiary of Roget S.A., one of the largest chemical companies in Belgium. Thorsten buys XL–4 from Roget's Industrial Chemical Products Division, at a transfer price of Skr. 1,700 a ton (Skr. 2,150 with transport costs and import duties). This case describes the problems faced by management as it tries to resolve a conflict arising from this transfer price. It covers a 14-month period, during which the following events took place:

1.   Fourteen months ago, Ekstrom introduced XL–4 to Swedish customers at a price of Skr. 2,500.

2.   Six months ago, after his request for a lower transfer price was turned down, he lowered the price to a more competitive Skr. 2,200.

3.   Two months ago, his request for a lower transfer price again denied, he reduced his selling price a second time, to Skr. 1,850.

Ekstrom now says that he may withdraw XL–4 from the Swedish market if he can't find a way to make it show a profit.

Organization Structure: Roget S.A.

Roget S.A. began operations 40 years ago, manufacturing and selling chemicals in the domestic Belgian market. It has grown steadily, partly

---

* Copyright © 1969, 1977 by l'Institut pour l'Etude des Méthodes de Direction de l'Entreprise (IMEDE), Lausanne, Switzerland. Published by permission.

[1] The letters "AB" and "S.A." are the equivalent designations in Sweden and Belgium of "Corp." or "Inc." in the United States and "Ltd." in the United Kingdom. The title of "managing director" in Sweden and in Britain is approximately the same as that of "president" in the United States.

EXHIBIT 1

ROGET S.A.
Organization Chart

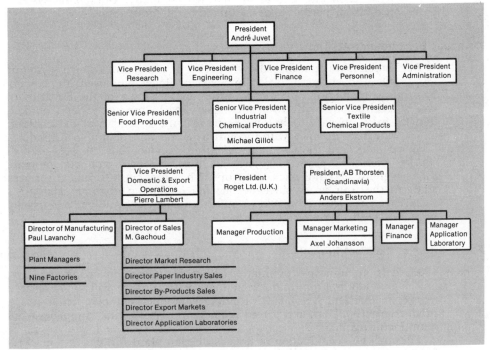

through growth and partly through purchase of companies such as
Thorsten, so that it now produces 208 products in 21 factories. Its organization structure is shown in Exhibit 1.

According to Mr. Juvet, Roget's managing director, "we are organized
on a divisional basis. For example, take the Industrial Chemicals Division,
headed by Mr. Gillot. This is set up as a separate company, and Gillot is
responsible for profits. This concept of decentralization is extended down
to the departments under him—except that they are responsible for profits
on a geographic basis instead of a product basis.

"One of these is the Domestic Department, under Mr. Lambert. This
department sells industrial chemicals throughout Belgium and exports its
products to countries in which we do not manufacture. It has its own
factories to supply both of these markets, and its own .sales force in
Belgium. The Domestic Department, like our other Brussels-based departments, markets most of its export volume through our foreign subsidiaries
and uses independent selling agents only in countries where we don't have
our own personnel.

"Mr. Lambert runs this department on his own. He is responsible for
its profits just as he would be if it were an independent company. In
much the same way, Ekstrom is responsible for the profits made by AB
Thorsten.

"A big company like Roget benefits from this kind of organization. We
must divide the work of management. No man can do it all. Placing re-

sponsibility for profits enables us to measure the result of operations, and is an important means of attracting and motivating top quality executives. Each head of a product division will have more initiative and will work harder if he is in effect head of his own company. Our bonus system, based on division profits, adds to this kind of motivation."

Company Background: AB Thorsten

AB Thorsten was purchased by Roget eight years ago. After a period of low profits and shrinking sales in Sweden, Roget employed Mr. Anders Ekstrom as managing director. A 38-year-old graduate of the Royal Institute of Technology, with 16 years' experience in production and marketing, Ekstrom appears to be an executive with a good deal of ambition and a wide acquaintance with modern financial and planning techniques.

When he joined the company, Ekstrom decided that the best way to restore Thorsten's profitability was to introduce new products, promote them aggressively, and back them up with a first-class technical services staff. In the four years since he became managing director, Thorsten's sales have increased from Skr. 7 million to Skr. 20 million, and profits have increased in even higher ratio.

Early History of the XL–4 Project

XL–4 is an adhesive product used in the paper-converting industry, and one which Ekstrom and his management are sure will enjoy a large market in Sweden. XL–4 is a proprietary product. No competitor has a product exactly like it, and patent protection prevents other suppliers from manufacturing it.

Although total production in Roget's Belgian plant for all other markets is 600 tons a year, Ekstrom's market studies have convinced him that 400 tons a year can be sold to paper companies in Sweden, provided that his customer engineering staff helps customers to modify their own equipment, and that the price can be lowered. He has conclusive evidence that large paper companies can reap significant cost savings due to lower materials handling costs and faster drying times.

Ekstrom and his top manufacturing and sales executives spent six months preparing a feasibility study which proposed building a plant in Sweden to manufacture XL–4, and presented this at a Thorsten board meeting one month later. He states, "we did a complete market study, engineering study and financial study, using discounted cash flows, which showed that we should build a factory in Sweden with a payback period of four years and a rate of return of 15 percent on invested capital. This was presented at a Thorsten board meeting in Stockholm and approved unanimously.[2]

"In our proposal, we suggested an initial selling price of Skr. 2,000 a ton, to be cut to Skr. 1,850 a ton at the end of the first year. We didn't make specific estimates of demand elasticity, but 400 tons represented

---

[2] Swedish law requires that all corporations have two Swedish directors for every foreign director. Thorsten's board is composed of a Swedish banker, a Stockholm industrialist, Mr. Ekstrom, and M. Gillot, a senior vice president of Roget S.A.

50 percent of the market and our cost calculations indicated that a price greater than Skr. 1,850 would keep us from reaching this goal.

"During the next two months, several things happened. First Mr. Gillot informed me that there were objections from Lambert [vice president, Domestic and Export Department], Lavanchy [director of manufacturing in the Industrial and Chemical Products Division] and Gachoud [director of sales in the same division]. I convinced him that we should hold a meeting with all these men in Brussels, but that meeting ended in chaos, with me arguing over and over for the plant in Sweden and the others saying over and over that we would have too many problems in manufacturing, and that we did not have the capabilities and experience in the adhesives industry that they possessed in Belgium. They also had no confidence in my market projection, saying that they didn't think we could sell 400 tons a year. Finally, Mr. Gillot asked the Belgian executives to study the matter further and give him a formal report on whether the plant should be built."

Rejection of the Swedish Proposal

After studying all of the reports on the XL–4 project, Gillot decided not to approve the proposal for a Swedish plant. "I am sorry to inform you," he wrote to Ekstrom, "that your proposal to manufacture XL–4 in Sweden has been rejected. I know that you and your management have done an outstanding job of market research, engineering planning, and profit estimation, and we agree that the plant would be profitable if you had a market of 400 tons and we couldn't supply it from here. This is no time to make this investment, however. First, it seems more profitable for our Belgian plant to make XL–4 and export it to Sweden. We have ample excess capacity to supply 400 tons to Sweden for the next few years. The savings obtainable from using this idle capacity more than offset the disadvantage of paying Swedish import duties. Second, executives in our Domestic Division here are convinced that the product should be made in Belgium where we have the experience and know-how. They are also not sure that you can sell 400 tons a year in Sweden.

"I want you to know, however, that we in Headquarters are most appreciative of the kind of work you are doing in Sweden. This adverse decision in no way reflects a lack of confidence in you or a failure on our part to recognize your outstanding performance as the managing director of one of our most important daughter companies."

Introduction of XL–4 into Sweden

Immediately after this decision, Ekstrom decided to order XL–4 from Roget Domestic and Export Division. "At this point, I decided to prove to them that the market is here. They quoted me a delivered price of Skr. 2,150 a ton (head office billing price of Skr. 1,700, plus Skr. 50 transportation and Skr. 400 import duty).[3] Because of heavy promotion and customer engineering costs (my engineers helping paper companies adapt

---

[3] Some of these figures are actually expressed in Belgian francs. To avoid possible confusion, all figures have been expressed at their Swedish kroner equivalents.

their machinery), I had to have a gross margin of Skr. 350 a ton. This meant I had to sell it for Skr. 2,500." He penciled the following table:

Head office billing price.....................	Skr. 1,700
Shipping cost................................	50
Import duty.................................	400
Delivered cost...........................	Skr. 2,150
Allowance for promotion and	
engineering costs.........................	350
Swedish selling price.......................	Skr. 2,500

"I knew I could never achieve sales of 400 tons a year at this price. It was higher than the prices of other adhesives suitable for this market, and Swedish paper companies are very cost-conscious. I knew we could do some business at this price, however, and this would give our engineers some practical experience in converting customers' equipment to take XL–4. Later on, we could reduce the price and try for the main market.

"I wrote to Mr. Gachoud, director of sales for the domestic and export department in Brussels, showing him the figures, saying that we could eventually reach 400 tons a year in sales, and asking him to reduce the head office billing price. He declined.

"For the next eight months sales were disappointing. At the end of this period, still having faith in our research over the last two years, I decided to lower the price to Skr. 2,200. I hoped that this would induce paper companies to try XL–4 and prove to themselves that it would lower their costs significantly. Of course, this was only Skr. 50 more than my cost, and I could hardly continue permanently on that basis. With me and my company being judged on profits, it is not worth our while to spend all of this time and resources on XL–4 for such a small markup.

"Sales did increase during the next four months, to 150 tons, and I knew I could sell about 200 tons regularly at this price. But I was still intent on proving the market at 400 tons.

"This time I went personally to see Mr. Gachoud in Brussels, and practically demanded that he lower the price of XL–4 exported from Belgium to Sweden. He explained that with a sales volume of 150–200 tons a year in Sweden, sold at an export transfer price of Skr. 1,700, and with strong doubts in his mind that we could ever reach 400 tons a year, he couldn't agree to the reduction.

"At this point I decided to prove that I was right by executing a bold move, backed up by the use of modern financial planning methods. I lowered the price to Skr. 1,850 a ton. I figured that someone in Brussels had to understand my reasoning, if I explained it well enough and backed it up with forceful direct action.

"Please don't get the idea that this was simply a political trick. I wouldn't have done it if I hadn't believed that it would bring in added profits for the group as a whole. I felt sure that volume would go up to 400 tons, and at that rate we would produce a profit contribution of at least Skr. 113,000 a year for the Roget group. This is Skr. 24,000 more than I could hope for at the old price and a volume of 200 tons.

"I showed my calculations to Mr. Gillot after I had decided to go ahead. Here is a little table of figures that I sent to him then [all figures are in Swedish kroner]:

	At 200 tons		At 400 tons	
	Per Ton	Total	Per Ton	Total
Selling price..............................	2,200	440,000	1,850	740,000
Variable Costs:				
Manufacturing (Belgium)...................	930		930	
Shipping (Belgium–Sweden)...............	50		50	
Import duty (Sweden).....................	400		400	
Total variable costs....................	1,380	276,000	1,380	552,000
Factory margin............................		164,000		188,000
Promotional costs.........................		75,000		75,000
Profit contribution to Roget group...........		89,000		113,000

"Let me explain this table. I knew that the Belgian cost accountants used a figure equivalent to Skr. 1,250 a ton as the full cost of manufacturing XL–4. The production people told me, however, that the Belgian plant had enough capacity to supply me with 400 tons of XL–4 a year without additional investment for expansion, and that they could manufacture the additional 400 tons at a variable cost of Skr. 930 a ton. This meant that the fixed costs were sunk costs and I could ignore them. This is why the manufacturing cost figure in the table is Skr. 930.

"Adding in the transportation costs and import duties brings the total variable costs to Skr. 1,380 a ton. My own promotional and engineering costs amounted to about Skr. 130,000 during the first year, but we were already over that hump. They are budgeted for this year at Skr. 75,000 and will go down to Skr. 50,000 a year from now on, mostly for technical services to customers. To avoid an argument, though, I used Skr. 75,000 in the table I sent to Mr. Gillot.

"This gives me the profit contribution of Skr. 113,000 a year that you see at the bottom of the table. This is Skr. 24,000 more than I could have expected at the old price. To me that's conclusive.

"I tell you all this to emphasize that my main motive was to improve our group's profit performance. Even so, I must admit that I still hope to persuade Mr. Gillot to let me build an XL–4 factory in Sweden. That plant will be profitable at a volume of 400 tons and a price of Skr. 1,850, and I suppose that this may have been at the back of my mind, too. If I can show him that the 400 tons is not a Swedish dream, I think he'll go along. It's ridiculous to pay import duties that amount to more than 20 percent of the selling price if you don't have to, and if I could have convinced him on the size of the market 14 months ago, I think I would have had my plant."

In the two months since this last price reduction, sales of XL–4 have increased to a rate of 270 tons a year. Ekstrom feels certain that within another 12 months he will reach the 400-ton level. He also says, however, that he finds himself in a quandary. "The Swedish company is losing Skr. 300 on every ton we sell, plus a great deal of selling and engineering time that could be switched to other products. This is bound to affect the profits of my company when I give my annual report to Mr. Gillot. This is why I quit trying to deal with Gachoud. Last week I wrote to Mr. Gillot, asking him to direct Gachoud to sell me the product at Skr. 1,100. I'm hoping for a reply this week."

The Parent Company's Transfer Pricing Policy

Mr. Gillot has not yet decided what to do with this request. As he says, "Transfer pricing in this company is pretty unsystematic. Each of us division managers is expected to price his own products, and the top management executive committee doesn't interfere. I have the same kind of authority over transfer prices as I have over the prices we charge our independent agents. We've never thought of them as separate problems. I've never been in a situation like this, though, and I want to think it through carefully before I act.

"Our attitude toward transfer pricing is probably the result of the way we operated in foreign markets in the beginning. We developed our export trade for many years by selling our products to independent agents around the world. We still do a lot of business that way. These agents estimated the prices at which they could sell the product and then negotiated with the export sales manager in Brussels for the best price they could get.

"When we began setting up our own daughter companies in our bigger markets, we just continued the same practice. Of course, daughter companies like Thorsten cannot shift to a competing supplier, but they have great freedom otherwise. For example, they can try to negotiate prices with us here at headquarters. This healthy competition within the company keeps us all alert. If they think Belgium is too rigid, they can refuse to market that particular product in their home country. Or, if they can justify building their own manufacturing plants, they can make the product themselves and not deal with the Belgian export department at all."

A Norwegian Example

Head office practices have resulted in head office billing prices that vary widely from market to market. In some cases, outside agents are able to obtain products at lower prices than Roget charges to its own subsidiaries. Ekstrom particularly wanted to tell the case writers about a Norwegian example. XL–4 is sold in Norway through an independent agent. This agent sells XL–4 to his customers at the equivalent of Skr. 1,290 plus Norwegian import duty. He persuaded Gachoud to sell him XL–4 at a price of Skr. 1,225, thus in effect giving him an agent's commission of Skr. 65 a ton. Roget also agreed to pay the shipping costs to Norway, amounting to Skr. 52 a ton. This meant that Roget received only Skr. 1,173 a ton to cover manufacturing and administrative costs and provide a profit margin. This was less than the average full cost of production in Belgium (Skr. 1,250) and Skr. 527 less than the Skr. 1,700 price at which Roget billed AB Thorsten.

"At one point," Ekstrom says, "I even thought of buying my XL–4 through the Norwegian agent. But then I realized this would be destructive warfare against Belgium. The total profits of the Roget group of companies would be less by the amount of the Norwegian agent's commission. I would be blamed for this when Lambert or Gillot reported it to the Executive Committee."

Other Factors to Consider

Division managers' performance in Roget S.A. was judged largely on the basis of the amount of profit they were able to generate on product sales, including both sales to agents and sales to subsidiary companies.

The managing board relied on this to induce the division managers to work for greater company profits.

The performance of the daughter company managers was appraised in much the same way. Ekstrom, for example, knew that group management in Brussels judged his performance on the basis of the amount of profit reported on AB Thorsten's income statement. Because of his success in the past four years, Roget's managing board gave him a good deal more freedom than the managers of any of the other subsidiaries enjoyed, but this happy state of affairs would come to an end if Thorsten's reported profits began to slide.

Gillot says that he must also consider three other factors before reaching a decision. First, Ekstrom's profit analysis must be evaluated. Second, Ekstrom's feelings of responsibility as head of the Swedish company must not be destroyed. Finally, he must review the points made by Lambert and Gachoud. Gillot says that Lambert told him, "If Ekstrom decides to take advantage of company rules and discontinues selling XL–4 in Sweden, we can certainly find an independent agent in Sweden to handle it. That's one bridge we'll never have to cross, though. Ekstrom will never push it that far. He believes in introducing new products as the key to his success. If we stand fast, he will simply raise the price back to a level that is profitable for both of us."

Taxes and foreign exchange regulations had no bearing on M. Gillot's decision. Income tax rates in Belgium were about the same as in Sweden, and no restrictions were placed on Thorsten's ability to obtain foreign exchange to pay for imported goods or pay dividends. In fact, Roget's top management insisted that each daughter company play the role of good citizen in its own country, by measuring taxable income on the same basis as that used by management in the evaluation of the subsidiary's pretax profit performance. No attempt was to be made to divert taxable income from one country to another.

* * * * *

At the present time, both Ekstrom on the one hand, and Lambert and Gachoud on the other, are waiting for Mr. Gillot to settle the transfer pricing question and let them know his decision.

a. Should Mr. Ekstrom have introduced XL–4 into Sweden? (This question should be examined both from Mr. Ekstrom's viewpoint and from the Roget point of view.)
b. Should Mr. Gachoud have lowered the price?
c. Why did Mr. Gachoud and Mr. Ekstrom fail to agree?
d. Is negotiation the best means of arriving at a transfer price in this situation? Can you suggest a better way?

Appendixes

appendix A

Compound Interest Tables
for Present Value Calculations[1]

THE TABLES in this appendix contain the multipliers or conversion factors necessary to convert cash flows of one or more periods into their equivalent values at some other point in time. The basic explanation of the reasons for conversion is given in Chapter 14; only the mechanical details of how the numbers in the tables should be used are explained here. If more extensive tables or specialized tables are needed, they can be found in readily available financial handbooks or can be derived from fairly simple computer programs.

Table 1. Present Value of $1

Each figure in Table 1 is the present value on a given reference date of $1 to be paid or received n periods later. To obtain the present value of any sum:

1. Select a date to serve as a reference date.
2. Determine the number of periods (n) between the reference date and the date on which the cash is to be paid or received.
3. Determine the interest rate (r) at which amounts are to be discounted.
4. Find the figure from Table 1 corresponding to these values of n and r.
5. Multiply the cash sum by this figure.

For example, to find the present value of $10,000 to be received five years from now, discounted at a compound annual rate of 8 percent, multiply $10,000 by the number 0.681 from the 8 percent

---

[1] The term interest is often used to mean the lenders' compensation for the use of their money. It is used here in a different sense, as an annual rate of return on capital. This capital may come from either lenders or owners. The available synonyms are too awkward to use in an introductory explanation.

column of Table 1. This says that $6,810 invested now at 8 percent will grow to $10,000 in five years if the interest is left on deposit and reinvested each year at 8 percent interest.

Extending Table 1

Table 1 can be extended easily to provide multipliers for any number of periods. The procedure is simple:

1. Select the column for the desired interest rate.
2. From this column select any two or more multipliers for which the number of periods adds up to the number of periods (n) for which a multiplier is needed.
3. Multiply these multipliers.

For example, the present value of $1 twenty years after the reference date at 5 percent compounded annually can be calculated in many ways. Three of these are:

Multiplier for ($n = 10$) × multiplier for ($n = 10$) = 0.614 × 0.614 = 0.377
Multiplier for ($n = 5$) × multiplier for ($n = 15$) = 0.784 × 0.481 = 0.377
Multiplier for ($n = 1$) × multiplier for ($n = 19$) = 0.952 × 0.396 = 0.377

Why does this work? Suppose the company expects to receive $1 20 years from now. Multiplying it by the discount factor for $n = 10$ brings it to its present value *at a point ten years from now*, $0.614. That amount is not the present value today, however. It is the future value ten years from now. The present value today of any sum ten years in the future can be calculated by discounting it for ten years— in other words, by multiplying $0.614 by 0.614.

Table 2. Present Value of an Annuity of $1 per Period

The present value of a series of cash flows can always be determined by using the multipliers in Table 1. For example, a series of three payments of $10,000 each, the first one a year from now, the second a year later, and the third a year after that, has a present value at 8 percent, compounded annually, as follows:

Years after Reference Date	Cash Flow	Multiplier at 8 Percent (Table 1)	Present Value at 8 Percent
1......................	$10,000	0.926	$ 9,260
2......................	10,000	0.857	8,570
3......................	10,000	0.794	7,940
Total..............			$25,770

Doing this for a large number of periods would be time consuming. Table 2 has been developed for use whenever the cash flows in a series are identical each period (an *annuity*). The multipliers in Table 2 for a three-year annuity at 8 percent is 2.577. Multiplying this by the amount of the annuity, $10,000, produces a present value of $25,770, identical to the figure we derived above. *Each multiplier in Table 2 is merely the sum of the multipliers in Table 1* for periods 1 through n.

Converting Table 2 to Earlier Equivalents

The multipliers in Table 2 are used to calculate the present value of a series of cash payments on a reference date exactly one period prior to the date of the first payment. To find the present value at a still earlier reference date, the present value of the annuity can be multiplied by the multiplier from Table 1 for the number of additional years desired.

For example, the present value at 8 percent of a ten-year, $10,000 annuity is:

$$\$10,000 \times 6.710 = \$67,100$$

Suppose, however, that the first payment in this annuity is five years from now and that we want to know its present value as of today. The $67,100 figure is the present value *one year before the first payment is made*, or four years from now:

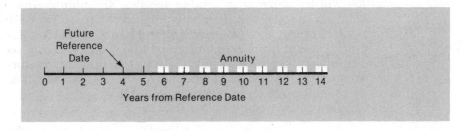

The present value today, therefore, can be obtained by multiplying $67,100 by the four-year multiplier from Table 1:

$$\$67,100 \times 0.735 = \$49,318$$

The same figure can be derived in a different way. A 10-year annuity starting 5 years from now is the same as a 14-year annuity minus the first four payments. The multiplier in Table 2 for 14 years at 8 percent is 8.244 and the multiplier for 4 years is 3.312. The appropriate multiplier, therefore, is:

$$8.244 - 3.312 = 4.932$$

Multiplying this by the $10,000 annuity produces a present value of $49,320, which differs only by an insignificant rounding error from the answer we derived earlier.

Finding Equivalent Annuities

It is sometimes useful to find the annuity that is equivalent to a given present sum. This is a simple arithmetic operation, once the present sum and the interest rate are known. The formula for the present value of an annuity can be expressed as:

$$\text{Present value} = \text{Table 2 multiplier} \times \text{annuity}$$

Turning this equation around, we find:

$$\text{Annuity} = \text{Present value} \div \text{Table 2 multiplier}$$

The ten-year annuity that is equivalent at 8 percent interest to a present sum of $100,000 is:

$$\text{Annuity} = \$100,000/6.710 = \$14,903$$

In other words, anyone who wants to buy a ten-year annuity of $14,903 a year in an 8 percent market will have to pay $100,000 for it.

The Compounding Interval

The present value of a cash flow is affected by the length of the compounding interval, the length of time between two successive dates on which interest is added to an invested sum. At an 8 percent interest rate, $10,000 will grow to $10,800 in a year if interest is compounded annually. If the compounding interval is six months, however, then one half of the annual interest (4 percent of $10,000, or $400) will be added at the end of the first six months. Interest in the second six months will then be 4 percent $\times$ $10,400 = $416. The future value at the end of one year will be $10,400 + $416 = $10,816. The future value multiplier therefore will be 1.0816 instead of 1.08.

The compounding interval also affects the discount factors. The more frequently interest is compounded, the less money has to be invested to built up to a given sum n years later.

In Chapter 14 we demonstrated that

$$P = F_n/(1 + r)^n$$

If we cut the compounding interval in half, this becomes:

$$P = F_n \frac{1}{\left(1 + \dfrac{r}{2}\right)^{2n}}$$

Because only half of the interest is earned each period, r has to be cut in half; because the calculation is made twice as often, n has to be multiplied by 2. This can be restated in general terms by letting m represent the number of compounding intervals per year:

$$P = F_n \frac{1}{\left(1 + \dfrac{r}{m}\right)^{mn}}$$

If m/r is represented by the letter k, this becomes:

$$P = F_n \frac{1}{\left(\left(1 + \dfrac{1}{k}\right)^k\right)^{rn}}$$

As the length of the compounding interval $(1/m)$ becomes shorter, k becomes larger. As k approaches infinity, the quantity $[1 + (1/k)]^k$ approaches the limit e, which is the base of the so-called natural logarithms. In other words, with an infinitely short compounding interval, the present value formula becomes:

$$P = F_n \left(\frac{1}{e^{rn}}\right)$$

Strictly speaking, the compounding interval should correspond to the interval at which cash flows can be used. For example, if cash is reinvested monthly, then the compounding interval should be one month. If it is reinvested daily or hourly, then continuous compounding is appropriate. The difference is really very small, however, and annual compounding is usually accurate enough for use in capital expenditure analysis.

TABLE 1

Present Value of $1 Received or Paid in a Lump Sum (discounted once each period for *n* periods)

n	5%	6%	7%	8%	9%	10%	11%	12%	13%	14%	15%	20%	25%	30%	40%
1. .	0.952	0.943	0.935	0.926	0.917	0.909	0.901	0.893	0.885	0.877	0.870	0.833	0.800	0.769	0.714
2. .	0.907	0.890	0.873	0.857	0.842	0.826	0.812	0.797	0.783	0.769	0.756	0.694	0.640	0.592	0.510
3. .	0.864	0.840	0.816	0.794	0.772	0.751	0.731	0.712	0.693	0.675	0.658	0.579	0.512	0.455	0.364
4. .	0.823	0.792	0.763	0.735	0.708	0.683	0.659	0.636	0.613	0.592	0.572	0.482	0.410	0.350	0.260
5. .	0.784	0.747	0.713	0.681	0.650	0.621	0.593	0.567	0.543	0.519	0.497	0.402	0.328	0.269	0.186
6. .	0.746	0.705	0.666	0.630	0.596	0.564	0.535	0.507	0.480	0.456	0.432	0.335	0.262	0.207	0.133
7. .	0.711	0.665	0.623	0.583	0.547	0.513	0.482	0.452	0.425	0.400	0.376	0.279	0.210	0.159	0.095
8. .	0.677	0.627	0.582	0.540	0.502	0.467	0.434	0.404	0.376	0.351	0.327	0.233	0.168	0.123	0.068
9. .	0.645	0.592	0.543	0.500	0.460	0.424	0.391	0.361	0.333	0.308	0.284	0.194	0.134	0.094	0.048
10. .	0.614	0.558	0.508	0.463	0.422	0.386	0.352	0.322	0.295	0.270	0.247	0.162	0.107	0.073	0.035
11. .	0.585	0.527	0.475	0.429	0.388	0.350	0.317	0.287	0.261	0.237	0.215	0.135	0.086	0.056	0.025
12. .	0.557	0.497	0.444	0.397	0.356	0.319	0.286	0.257	0.231	0.208	0.187	0.112	0.069	0.043	0.018
13. .	0.530	0.469	0.415	0.368	0.326	0.290	0.258	0.229	0.204	0.182	0.163	0.093	0.055	0.033	0.013
14. .	0.505	0.442	0.388	0.340	0.299	0.263	0.232	0.205	0.181	0.160	0.141	0.078	0.044	0.025	0.009
15. .	0.481	0.417	0.362	0.315	0.275	0.239	0.209	0.183	0.160	0.140	0.123	0.065	0.035	0.020	0.006
16. .	0.458	0.394	0.339	0.292	0.252	0.218	0.188	0.163	0.142	0.123	0.107	0.054	0.028	0.015	0.005
17. .	0.436	0.371	0.317	0.270	0.231	0.198	0.170	0.146	0.125	0.108	0.093	0.045	0.023	0.012	0.003
18. .	0.416	0.350	0.296	0.250	0.212	0.180	0.153	0.130	0.111	0.095	0.081	0.038	0.018	0.009	0.002
19. .	0.396	0.331	0.277	0.232	0.194	0.164	0.138	0.116	0.098	0.083	0.070	0.031	0.014	0.007	0.002
20. .	0.377	0.312	0.258	0.215	0.178	0.149	0.124	0.104	0.087	0.073	0.061	0.026	0.012	0.005	0.001
21. .	0.359	0.294	0.242	0.199	0.164	0.135	0.112	0.093	0.077	0.064	0.053	0.022	0.009	0.004	0.001
22. .	0.342	0.278	0.226	0.184	0.150	0.123	0.101	0.083	0.068	0.056	0.046	0.018	0.007	0.003	0.001
23. .	0.326	0.262	0.211	0.170	0.138	0.112	0.091	0.074	0.060	0.049	0.040	0.015	0.006	0.002	
24. .	0.310	0.247	0.197	0.158	0.126	0.102	0.082	0.066	0.053	0.043	0.035	0.013	0.005	0.002	
25. .	0.295	0.233	0.184	0.146	0.116	0.092	0.074	0.059	0.047	0.038	0.030	0.010	0.004	0.001	
30. .	0.231	0.174	0.131	0.099	0.075	0.057	0.044	0.033	0.026	0.020	0.015	0.004	0.001		
35. .	0.181	0.130	0.094	0.068	0.049	0.036	0.026	0.019	0.014	0.010	0.008	0.002			
40. .	0.142	0.097	0.067	0.046	0.032	0.022	0.015	0.011	0.008	0.005	0.004	0.001			
45. .	0.111	0.073	0.048	0.031	0.021	0.014	0.009	0.006	0.004	0.003	0.002				
50. .	0.087	0.054	0.034	0.021	0.013	0.009	0.005	0.003	0.002	0.001	0.001				

$$P = F_n(1 + n)^{-n}$$

TABLE 2

Present Value of an Annuity of $1 a Period for *n* Periods, Received or Paid as a Series of Lump Sums at the End of Individual Periods (discounted once each period for *n* periods)

n	5%	6%	7%	8%	9%	10%	11%	12%	13%	14%	15%	20%	25%	30%	40%
1..	0.952	0.943	0.935	0.926	0.917	0.909	0.901	0.893	0.885	0.877	0.870	0.833	0.800	0.769	0.714
2..	1.859	1.833	1.808	1.783	1.759	1.736	1.713	1.690	1.668	1.647	1.626	1.528	1.440	1.361	1.224
3..	2.723	2.673	2.624	2.577	2.531	2.487	2.444	2.402	2.361	2.322	2.283	2.106	1.952	1.816	1.589
4..	3.546	3.465	3.387	3.312	3.240	3.170	3.102	3.037	2.974	2.914	2.855	2.589	2.362	2.166	1.849
5..	4.329	4.212	4.100	3.993	3.890	3.791	3.696	3.605	3.517	3.433	3.352	2.991	2.689	2.436	2.035
6..	5.076	4.917	4.767	4.623	4.486	4.355	4.231	4.111	3.998	3.889	3.784	3.326	2.951	2.643	2.168
7..	5.786	5.582	5.389	5.206	5.033	4.868	4.712	4.564	4.423	4.288	4.160	3.605	3.161	2.802	2.263
8..	6.463	6.210	5.971	5.747	5.535	5.335	5.146	4.968	4.799	4.639	4.487	3.837	3.329	2.925	2.331
9..	7.108	6.802	6.515	6.247	5.995	5.759	5.537	5.328	5.132	4.946	4.772	4.031	3.463	3.019	2.379
10..	7.722	7.360	7.024	6.710	6.418	6.145	5.889	5.650	5.426	5.216	5.019	4.192	3.571	3.092	2.414
11..	8.306	7.887	7.499	7.139	6.805	6.495	6.207	5.938	5.687	5.453	5.234	4.327	3.656	3.147	2.438
12..	8.863	8.384	7.943	7.536	7.161	6.814	6.492	6.194	5.918	5.660	5.421	4.439	3.725	3.190	2.456
13..	9.394	8.853	8.358	7.904	7.487	7.103	6.750	6.424	6.122	5.842	5.583	4.533	3.780	3.223	2.468
14..	9.899	9.295	8.745	8.244	7.786	7.367	6.982	6.628	6.302	6.002	5.724	4.611	3.824	3.249	2.477
15..	10.380	9.712	9.108	8.559	8.061	7.606	7.191	6.811	6.462	6.142	5.847	4.675	3.859	3.268	2.484
16..	10.838	10.106	9.447	8.851	8.313	7.824	7.379	6.974	6.604	6.265	5.954	4.730	3.887	3.283	2.489
17..	11.274	10.477	9.763	9.122	8.544	8.022	7.549	7.120	6.729	6.373	6.047	4.775	3.910	3.295	2.492
18..	11.690	10.828	10.059	9.372	8.756	8.201	7.702	7.250	6.840	6.467	6.128	4.812	3.928	3.304	2.494
19..	12.085	11.158	10.336	9.604	8.950	8.365	7.839	7.366	6.938	6.550	6.198	4.844	3.942	3.311	2.496
20..	12.462	11.470	10.594	9.818	9.129	8.514	7.963	7.469	7.025	6.623	6.259	4.870	3.954	3.316	2.497
21..	12.821	11.764	10.836	10.017	9.292	8.649	8.075	7.562	7.102	6.687	6.312	4.891	3.963	3.320	2.498
22..	13.163	12.042	11.061	10.201	9.442	8.772	8.176	7.645	7.170	6.743	6.359	4.909	3.970	3.323	2.498
23..	13.489	12.303	11.272	10.371	9.580	8.883	8.266	7.718	7.230	6.792	6.399	4.925	3.976	3.325	2.499
24..	13.799	12.550	11.469	10.529	9.707	8.985	8.348	7.784	7.283	6.835	6.434	4.937	3.981	3.327	2.499
25..	14.094	12.783	11.654	10.675	9.823	9.077	8.422	7.843	7.330	6.873	6.464	4.948	3.985	3.329	2.499
30..	15.372	13.765	12.409	11.258	10.274	9.427	8.694	8.055	7.496	7.003	6.566	4.979	3.995	3.332	2.500
35..	16.374	14.498	12.948	11.655	10.567	9.644	8.855	8.176	7.586	7.070	6.617	4.992	3.998	3.333	2.500
40..	17.159	15.046	13.332	11.925	10.757	9.779	8.951	8.244	7.634	7.105	6.642	4.997	3.999	3.333	2.500
45..	17.774	15.456	13.606	12.108	10.881	9.863	9.008	8.283	7.661	7.123	6.654	4.999	4.000	3.333	2.500
50..	18.256	15.762	13.801	12.233	10.962	9.915	9.042	8.305	7.675	7.133	6.661	4.999	4.000	3.333	2.500

$$P = A\left[\frac{1 - (1 + r)^{-n}}{r}\right]$$

appendix B

Cost Accounting Standards
for Contract Costing

THE DEFINITION of "cost" for contract costing purposes is a matter for the contracting parties to agree on before a contract is signed.

For contracts with the U.S. government or its agencies, the government for generations has supplied the definitions by requiring adherence to various kinds of regulations, most notably the Armed Services Procurement Regulations (ASPR). Individuals or firms wishing to use cost figures in their contractual dealings with the federal government generally must accept these definitions. The alternative is to withdraw from competition for this kind of business, a route that many potential contractors have taken at one time or another.

Concerned that the existing regulations allowed contractors too much flexibility in defining cost, the U.S. Congress asked the General Accounting Office (GAO) to study the feasibility of establishing uniform cost accounting standards for negotiated defense contracts. The GAO concluded that such standards were feasible and the Congress passed Public Law 91–379, establishing the Cost Accounting Standards Board (CASB). This law was signed by the president on August 15, 1970, funds were appropriated, and the board was organized formally in January 1971. It issued its first standard on February 29, 1972.

In this appendix we shall outline the structure and role of the Cost Accounting Standards Board, the basic measurement concepts it has adopted, and the standards it issued during its first five years.

ORGANIZATION STRUCTURE OF THE CASB

The CASB, or CAS Board, is responsible to the Congress, not to the executive branch of the federal government. The board has five members, with the comptroller general of the United States as chairman. The comptroller general appoints the other four members—two from the accounting profession, one from industry, and one from the federal government. Board members are appointed for four-year terms and serve on a part-time basis.

The board is assisted by a sizable professional staff, headed by an executive secretary. The staff carries out research, develops and tests proposed cost accounting standards, and analyzes data supplied to the board.

THE BOARD'S OBJECTIVES AND RESPONSIBILITIES

The objective of the Cost Accounting Standards Board is "to achieve uniformity and consistency in the cost-accounting principles followed by defense contractors and subcontractors under Federal contracts."[1]

Each major contractor is required to file a Disclosure Statement with the board, describing its cost accounting system in considerable detail. These disclosure statements are used by the board and its staff to identify areas in which standards appear to be necessary.

The board is responsible for setting cost accounting standards to be used in measuring the costs assignable to contracts subject to the requirement to conform to the board's standards. The board has defined a Cost Accounting Standard in the following terms:

> A Cost Accounting Standard is a statement formally issued by the Cost Accounting Standards Board that (1) enunciates a principle or principles to be followed, (2) establishes practices to be applied, or (3) specifies criteria to be employed in selecting from alternative principles and practices in estimating, accumulating, and reporting costs of contracts subject to the rules of the Board.[2]

The board does not negotiate contracts, nor does it decide what costs are *allowable*—that is, reimbursable by the federal government. The board's statement continues:

> Allocability is an accounting concept affecting the ascertainment of contract cost; it results from a relationship between a cost and a cost objective such that the cost objective appropriately bears all or part of the cost. To be charged with all or part of a cost, a cost objective should cause or be an intended beneficiary of the cost.
>
> Allowability is a procurement concept affecting contract price and in most cases is expressly provided in regulatory or contractual provisions. . . . The use of Cost Accounting Standards has no direct bearing on the allowability of individual items of cost which are subject to limitations or exclusions set forth in the contract or are otherwise specified by the government or its procuring agency.[3]

In other words, a cost may be allocable (assignable) to a contract, but it is not a determinant of contract price unless the regulations or the particular contracts permit it to be classified as an allowable cost.

---

[1] Defense Production Act of 1950 (as amended by Public Law 91–379), section 719, paragraph (g).

[2] Cost Accounting Standards Board, *Statement of Operating Policies, Procedures and Objectives* (Washington, D.C.: March 1973), p. 1.

[3] Ibid., pp. 2–3.

APPLICABILITY OF THE STANDARDS

The Congress established the applicability of the standards in the following terms:

> Such promulgated standards shall be used by all relevant Federal agencies and by defense contractors and subcontractors in estimating, accumulating, and reporting costs in connection with the pricing, administration and settlement of all negotiated prime contract and subcontract national defense procurements with the United States in excess of $100,000, other than contracts or subcontracts where the price negotiated is based on (1) established catalog or market prices of commercial items sold in substantial quantities to the general public, or (2) prices set by law or regulation.[4]

A promulgated standard becomes effective automatically 60 days after it is transmitted to Congress unless during that time both Houses of Congress pass a concurrent resolution disapproving it.

BASIC MEASUREMENT CONCEPTS

Shortly after issuing its first standards, the board outlined its basic approach to the measurement of contract cost. It made three basic points:

1. Contract cost is to be based on full costing.
2. The primary criterion for assigning costs to contracts is traceability.
3. For costs not readily traceable to individual contracts, the board intends to provide a hierarchy of criteria to be applied sequentially —that is, apply the topmost criterion in the hierarchy first; if that fails, go to the second; etc.

The following excerpts from the board's statement convey the essence of the board's position:

> Cost accounting for negotiated Government contracts has long been on the basis of full allocation of costs, including general and administrative expenses and all other indirect costs. The allocation of all period costs to other products and services of the period is not a common practice either for public reporting or for internal management purposes; yet this has long been the established cost principle for costing defense procurement. The Board will adhere to the concept of full costing wherever appropriate. . . .
>
> As an ideal, each item of cost should be assigned to the cost objective which was intended to benefit from the resource represented by the cost or, alternatively, which caused incurrence of the cost. To approach this goal, the Board believes in the desirability of direct identification of costs with final cost objectives to the extent practical. . . .
>
> Costs not directly identified with final cost objectives should be grouped into logical and homogeneous expense pools and should be allocated in accordance with a hierarchy of preferable techniques.[5]

---

[4] Public Law 91–379.

[5] *Statement of Operating Policies,* pp. 16–17.

The board then stated its preference for systems based on the application of the following sequential hierarchy of techniques:

1. First, try to get a measure of average cost per unit of *activity* in the supporting function—e.g., cost per square foot to allocate a pool of the costs of owning and operating a warehouse.
2. If that is not practical, try to use cost per unit of *output* of the supporting function—e.g., allocate the costs of an employment office by using the average cost per employee hired.
3. If neither of these is practical, then use a measure of the *activity* of the functions *receiving* the service, provided that this measure of activity seems to vary in proportion to the amount of service received.
4. Finally, if none of these measures can be found, allocate the pooled cost as a percentage of some measure of the *entire activity being managed*—e.g., allocate the president's salary and similar costs to factories in proportion to the total costs assigned to those factories by direct identification or other methods.

THE OVERALL STRUCTURE OF THE STANDARDS

The CASB has never set forth an explicit overall cost accounting structure that its standards will eventually describe. It has preferred to allow the structure to emerge gradually, to reveal itself bit by bit as each subsequent standard is issued. This has the advantage of giving the board greater flexibility because it has no public commitment to a single structure.

The diagram in Exhibit B–1 is based on an analysis of the first four standards governing the assignment of costs to contracts, and on a review of projects the board's staff has in process or in prospect. It shows three basic levels of cost accumulation: the home office, the segment, and the final cost objectives. The costs of the home office are divided among the segments it serves and administers. The costs of the segments are then divided among the final cost objectives. Home office costs fall into three categories; segment costs are of five different types. Each of these may be subdivided further.

The board's problem is to devise a set of standards (*a*) to identify the three streams of costs flowing in at the left of the exhibit, and (*b*) to govern the ways these costs are channeled to the final cost objectives.

THE STANDARDS ISSUED BY THE BOARD

The standards, rules and regulations of the CAS Board are contained in Title 4, Chapter III, Code of Federal Regulations. Each standard constitutes a Part of Title 4, identified by a three-digit number, starting with 401. Part 400 is reserved for definitions of technical terms, and is revised each time a new standard is issued.

The standards are numbered sequentially, and the sequence provides little guidance to the interrelationships among them. The fol-

EXHIBIT B-1

Implicit Structure of Cost Flows in Cost Accounting Standards

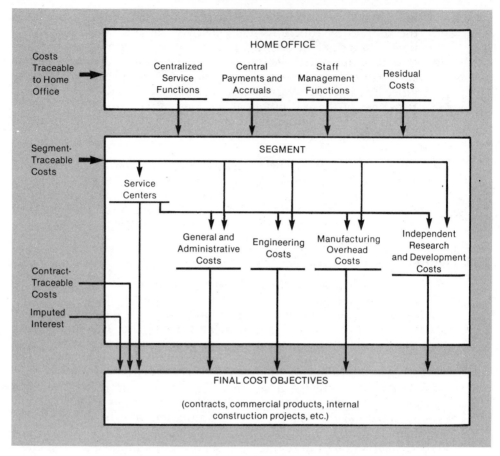

lowing classification system is unofficial and imperfect, but may be of some help to someone approaching these standards for the first time:

A. System constraints:
CAS 401. Consistency in estimating, accumulating, and reporting costs.
CAS 402. Consistency in allocating costs incurred for the same purpose.
CAS 405. Accounting for unallowable costs.
CAS 406. Cost accounting period.
B. Assigning costs to accounting periods:
CAS 404. Capitalization of tangible assets.
CAS 408. Accounting for costs of compensated personal absence.
CAS 409. Depreciation of tangible capital assets.
CAS 411. Acquisition costs of material.

CAS 412.   Composition and measurement of pension cost.
CAS 415.   Accounting for the costs of deferred personal compensation.
C.   Assigning costs to cost objectives within the period:
CAS 403.   Allocation of home office expenses to segments.
CAS 407.   Use of standard costs for direct materials and direct labor.
CAS 410.   Allocation of business unit general and administrative expenses to final cost objectives.
CAS 414.   Cost of money as an element of the cost of facilities capital.

In this section we shall describe the first two sets of standards very briefly, reserving most of our limited space for the four standards in the third group.[6]

Constraining Standards

CAS 401 requires the contractor to accumulate and report costs on the same bases it uses in preparing cost estimates for contract bidding purposes. This is to prevent a contractor from bidding low on the basis of one cost accounting system and then charging higher amounts to the government, based on some other system.

CAS 402 forbids double counting: ". . . each type of cost is [to be] allocated only once and on only one basis to any contract or other cost objective. . . . All costs incurred for the same purposes, in like circumstances, are either direct costs only or indirect costs only with respect to final cost objectives."

CAS 405 provides that unallowable costs be identified and excluded from amounts billed or claimed.

CAS 406 requires the contractor to use the same cost accounting period for accumulating costs in indirect cost pools as it uses in establishing the allocation bases for those pools. In general, the cost accounting period must be the fiscal year, but the standard recognizes a number of situations in which some other period may be used.

Standards for Assigning Costs to Periods

The standards for assigning costs to periods are generally similar to those the contractor would use for external financial reporting. These are more detailed than the constraining standards, but they can be summarized almost as briefly for our purposes:

CAS 404 requires the contractor to capitalize the costs of tangible capital assets, with a written capitalization policy specifying the characteristics an expenditure must have if it is to be regarded as the cost of a tangible capital asset. The standard also prescribes a set of guidelines the capitalization policy must observe.

CAS 408 has two main requirements: "(*a*) The costs of compen-

---

[6] This list includes all standards issued prior to January 1, 1977. No standard was issued bearing the number 413.

OFFICIAL DEFINITIONS OF KEY TERMS
(FROM CAS 400)

Allocate. To assign an item of cost, or a group of items of cost, to one or more cost objectives. This term includes both direct assignment of cost and the reassignment of a share from an indirect cost pool.

Business unit. Any segment of an organization, or an entire business organization which is not divided into segments.

Cost objective. A function, organizational subdivision, contract or other work unit for which cost data are desired and for which provision is made to accumulate and measure the cost of processes, products, jobs, capitalized projects, etc.

Final cost objective. A cost objective which has allocated to it both direct and indirect costs, and, in the contractor's accumulation system, is one of the final accumulation points.

Home office. An office responsible for directing or managing two or more, but not necessarily all, segments of an organization. . . . An organization which has intermediate levels, such as groups, may have several home offices which report to a common home office. An intermediate organization may be both a segment and a home office.

Indirect cost pool. A grouping of incurred costs identified with two or more objectives but not identified specifically with any final cost objective.

Segment. One of two or more divisions, product departments, plants, or other subdivisions of an organization reporting directly to a home office, usually identified with responsibility for profit and/or producing a product or service. . . .

---

sated personal absence shall be assigned to the cost accounting period or periods in which the entitlement was earned. (*b*) The costs of compensated personal absence for an entire cost accounting period shall be allocated pro rata on an annual basis among the final cost objectives of that period."

CAS 409 provides for the assignment of depreciation charges to cost accounting periods and provides a set of broad criteria to be applied in calculating annual depreciation charges. Boiled down to their essentials, the main provisions are:

1. The depreciable amount is original cost minus estimated residual value.

2. The depreciable amount is to be spread over the asset(s)' useful life.
3. The depreciation pattern must reflect the pattern of asset service consumption (e.g., straight line if the services are likely to be consumed in equal annual amounts).
4. Gains or losses on disposal are to be assigned to the periods in which disposals take place.

CAS 409 also provides instructions for assigning depreciation costs to cost objectives within the period. The main provisions are:

1. Direct charges to cost objectives can be made only if depreciation charges are calculated on a usage basis.
2. Depreciation within an organization unit providing chargeable services to other cost objectives is to be included as part of the chargeable costs of that organization unit.
3. Other depreciation charges are to be included in appropriate indirect cost pools.

CAS 411 requires that inventory cost be defined as net delivered cost and that an inventory costing method be chosen and used consistently for each type of materials. It permits the contractor to charge individual contracts directly only for materials purchased specifically for those individual contracts.

CAS 412 provides that pension costs can be accrued only to the extent they are accompanied by current payments or by binding commitments to make future payments. These costs include the normal cost of the period, the current amortization of the unfunded prior service liability and interest on the unfunded liability, and an adjustment for actuarial gains or losses.

CAS 415 requires the use of accrual accounting to assign the costs of deferred compensation to cost accounting periods. (Deferred compensation includes future payments of cash, other assets, or shares of the contractor's stock during some limited period of time.) The cost is to be recognized in the period in which the contractor incurs an obligation to compensate an employee at a later time. Cost is to be measured by the present value of the future amounts to be paid by the contractor.

Standards for Assigning Costs to Cost Objectives

Although the standards in the second group include a few provisions governing the assignment of costs to cost objectives within a period, only four of the standards issued in the first five years are concerned primarily with intraperiod cost allocation—CAS 403, 407, 410, and 414. Because these standards are the only ones to fall directly within the realm of cost accounting proper, we shall examine them in slightly greater detail than was appropriate for the other ten standards.

CAS 403: Allocation of home office expenses to segments. Home office expenses consist mainly of (*a*) the costs of centralized service functions (including staff management functions), (*b*) central payments and accruals, and (c) residual expenses. (Note: the word *expense* is used by the CAS Board to describe an operating cost; this may not equal the amount reported as an expense on the company's income statement, our usual definition of this term.)

Centralized service functions are "functions which, but for the existence of a home office, would be performed or acquired by some or all of the segments individually. Examples include centrally performed personnel administration and centralized data processing."

If these costs can be traced directly to a specific segment, they must be charged to that segment. If they are not traceable to a segment, the standard prescribes a hierarchy of allocation bases:

First priority:	A measure of the *activity* of the organization unit performing the function (labor hours, machine-hours, etc.)
If that can't be found, then second priority:	A measure of the *output* of the supporting function (number of printed pages in a print shop, number of orders processed in an order department, etc.)
If neither of these can be found, then third priority:	A surrogate for the beneficial or causal relationship underlying the service function's costs. These are generally measures of the activity of the segments receiving the service (number of personnel, labor hours, etc.).

Central payments and accruals are those which, but for the existence of the home office,[7] would be accrued or paid by the individual segments. Common examples are group insurance costs, local property taxes, and payrolls paid by a home office on behalf of its segments.

The standard provides that these are to be assigned directly to individual segments if they can be traced to those segments. Otherwise, they are to be assigned to segments "using an allocation base representative of the factors on which the total payment is based."

Residual expenses are all those not falling in either of the first two categories. A typical example is the salary of the chief executive officer. They are to be allocated to the segments on a base representing the segments' total activity. The standard prescribes a formula to be used for this purpose, if the amount exceeds specified limits.

The main ambiguity in this standard centers on the term, *beneficial.* As used in cost accounting, a beneficial relationship can be said to exist if the performance of the service function is *necessary to* the operation of the segment. No other interpretation makes sense.

CAS 407. Standard costs for direct materials and direct labor. This standard authorizes contractors to use standard cost to measure the

---

[7] The standard uses the phrase "but for the existence of a number of segments." We think our wording more clearly conveys the meaning of the standard.

consumption of direct materials and direct labor, provided that three conditions are met:

1. Standard costs are entered into the books of account.
2. Standard costs and variances are accumulated separately for each production unit with homogeneous inputs or outputs.
3. The accounting treatment of standards and variances is described in writing and is consistently followed.

The standard provides a number of restrictions on the use of standard costs. Separate labor rate standards, for example, must be set for each homogeneous group of workers or for each crew working as an integral team. Materials price variances must be accumulated separately for each homogeneous group of materials. When the price variances are segregated at the time of purchase, they must be spread pro rata at least once a year between materials inventory and the production units to which the materials were issued. Labor cost variances must also be accumulated by production unit.

The effect of these requirements is to make contract cost approximate the historical cost of the labor and materials inputs. The homogeneity requirement means that variances will be matched fairly closely with the standard inputs they relate to. Large variance pools are allocated in proportion to standard costs.

CAS 410. Allocation of general and administrative overheads to final cost objectives. Although the board's explanation of standard 410 occupied six pages in the *Federal Register* (April 16, 1976, pp. 16135–41), the standard itself took up only four pages. It is basically very simple, containing only two essential provisions:

1. Each business unit is to have a single pool of general and administrative costs and this is to be allocated directly to final cost objectives.
2. General and administrative costs of any business unit are to be allocated by means of a cost *input* basis.

The second of these two provisions is the more controversial. "Cost input" may mean all the operating costs of the business unit other than general and administrative costs, or it may mean costs other than materials, or it may mean a single cost element, such as direct labor. The standard means that general and administrative costs can't be allocated as a percentage of sales revenues. General and administrative costs therefore are likely to be assigned to contract work in process before it is ready for delivery to the government.

CAS 414. Imputed interest on facilities capital. This standard plows new ground. For the first time, imputed interest is recognized as an *essential* element of contract cost. The standard requires the following:

1. Interest is to be imputed to individual contracts.
2. The amount to be imputed is to be based on the amount of *facilities* used to support work on individual contracts. (Investments in working capital are specifically excluded from the provisions of this standard.)

3. The interest rate is to be based on an average of long-term commercial borrowing rates calculated periodically by the secretary of the treasury.
4. Imputed interest assignable to an indirect cost pool is to be allocated to final cost objectives in proportion to the number of "allocation base units" (direct labor hours, and so on) identified with the contract.

To implement this standard, the contractor must assign the costs of facilities to individual business units. The standard provides a form to be used to make this calculation. The main criterion, as usual, is traceability of the investment to the business unit and to the specific overhead cost pools within this business unit. For facilities not traceable to individual overhead cost pools, the costs are to be allocated "on any reasonable basis that approximates the actual absorption of depreciation or amortization of such facilities." In other words, imputed interest is to parallel the depreciation allocation.

appendix C

Solutions to Independent Study Problems

Chapter 2

2–1.   The new ventures make the enterprise more complex. Management will need control information by department (president's office, sales, and controller's office), by product line (glue and findings), and by customer group (shoe trade and furniture manufacturers). Which of these segments deserves more emphasis? Which of them deserves less, or even deserves to be dropped? Which of the department heads is performing well? Which one is performing poorly?

One student provided the following additional account codes to accumulate data management might use to try to answer these questions:

President's office..........................	100
Sales department..........................	200
Sales manager...........................	210
Shoe trades—general......................	220
Shoe trades—glue........................	221
Shoe trades—findings....................	222
Furniture trades—general.................	230
Furniture trades—glue....................	231
Controller's office..........................	300

The object of expenditure accounts should also be reviewed to see whether they will provide the amount of detail management will need.

2–2.   *a.* Cost of job No. 423:

> Burden rate = $900,000/100,000
>   = $9 a direct labor hour

Materials.........................	$ 800
Labor............................	400
Overhead ($9 × 60)...............	540
Total...........................	$1,740

911

b.

```
Actual overhead................ $106,000
Absorbed overhead (10,000 × $9)   90,000
    Underabsorbed overhead.....  $ 16,000
```

2–3.   *a.*

```
Materials (21,000 × $0.66)................. $13,860
Materials returned (800 × $0.66)..........    (528)
Labor (2,000 × $668).....................   13,360
Overhead.............................      8,000
    Total................................  $34,692
```

$$\text{Unit cost} = \frac{\$34,692}{9,800} = \$3.54$$

b.

```
Work-in-Process ............................ 34,692
    Materials Inventory ......................           13,860
    Wages  Payable  .........................           13,360
    Factory Overhead Absorbed ..............            8,000
Materials Inventory .........................    528
    Work-in-Process .........................              528
Finished Goods ............................. 34,692
    Work-in-Process .......................              34,692
```

2–4.   The amount to be charged to the job is 41 hours at $8 an hour, or $328. The overtime premium is a function of the total load on the production facilities. It is not specifically related to the M227.

An economist might suggest that the entire 41 hours should be imputed a cost of $12 an hour, on the grounds that the company could have avoided 41 hours of overtime premium by rescheduling its other work. In other words, doing job M227 caused the company to spend 41 × $12 = $492. This is not the kind of cost calculation that is made to support routine entries in the job cost sheets, however.

2–5.   *a.*

Raw Material and Stores

Bal.	12,650	(2)	7,250
(1)	4,500	Bal.	9,900
Bal.	9,900		

Work-in-Process

Bal.	8,320	(6)	12,650
(2)	6,320		
(3)	3,300		
(5)	4,950	Bal.	10,240
Bal.	10,240		

Finished Goods

Bal.	11,100	(8)	14,500
(6)	12,650	Bal.	9,250
Bal.	9,250		

Accounts Payable, Etc.

		(1)	4,500
		(4)	2,700
		(7)	1,835

Accrued Payroll

	(3)	7,780

Cost of Goods Sold

| (8) | 14,500 | |
| (11) | 560 | |

Factory Overhead Summary

(2)	930	(10)	5,510
(3)	1,880		
(4)	2,700		

Factory Overhead Absorbed

| (10) | 5,510 | (5) | 4,950 |
| | | (11) | 560 |

Selling and Admin. Expense

| (3) | 2,600 | |
| (7) | 1,835 | |

Accounts Receivable

| (9) | 19,350 | |

Sales Revenue

| | (9) | 19,350 |

b.

ACE APPLIANCE COMPANY
Statement of Income for the Month Ended October 31

Sales...		$19,350
Cost of goods sold (Schedule A)....................		15,060
Gross margin..		$ 4,290
Selling and administrative expenses................		4,435
Net Income (Loss)...................................		$ (145)

Schedule A: Cost of Goods Sold

Direct materials.....................................		$ 6,320
Direct labor...		3,300
Factory overhead absorbed.........................		4,950
Total factory costs charged to production........		$14,570
Less: Increase in work in process:		
Work in process, October 31........................	$10,240	
Work in process, October 1.........................	8,320	(1,920)
Cost of goods finished..............................		$12,650
Add: Decrease in finished goods:		
Finished goods, October 1...........................	$11,100	
Finished goods, October 31.........................	9,250	1,850
Cost of goods sold..................................		$14,500
Add: Underabsorbed overhead.......................		560
Cost of goods sold (adjusted)......................		$15,060

Chapter 3

3–1.

Output Rate	Average Total Cost	Average Fixed Cost	Average Variable Cost	Marginal Cost
1	$11.00	$10.00	$1.00	$1.00
2	6.00	5.00	1.00	1.00
3	4.33	3.33	1.00	1.00
4	3.50	2.50	1.00	1.00
5	3.00	2.00	1.00	1.00
6	2.67	1.67	1.00	1.00
7	2.43	1.43	1.00	1.00
8	2.25	1.25	1.00	1.00
9	2.22	1.11	1.11	2.00
10	2.30	1.00	1.30	3.00

3–2.   Differential cost is the effect of the decision on total cost:

Total cost if the service is provided: 25 × $14,000	$350,000
Total cost if the service is not provided: 10 × $15,500	155,000
Differential cost	$195,000

The proposal should be approved.

3–3.   The only relevant figure is opportunity cost, reflecting the cash flows Ms. Smith will receive in the future. None of the past prices is relevant to this decision because Ms. Smith can do nothing now to change them. The $6 figure was an opportunity cost in 19x5. Her decision not to sell then was the same as a decision to buy 200 shares at that price at that time. It no longer has any more relevance, however, than the $15 and $20 historical purchase prices. Even the $8 figure has no relevance because the $10 tender offer makes that the effective floor under the market price —it can't go lower as long as the tender offer is in effect, and it will go higher only if enough shareholders believe that the stock is worth more than $10.

3–4.   Differential costs of making the parts:

	Part 104	Part 173	Part 221
Direct materials	$216	$ 460	$110
Direct labor	240	780	240
Factory overhead:			
Indirect labor (20%)*	48	156	48
Indirect materials (5%)*	12	39	12
Service charges (5)*	12	39	12
Total	$528	$1,474	$422
Differential purchasing costs:			
Purchase price	$480	$1,400	$400
Purchasing and handling	100	100	100
Total	$580	$1,500	$500
Advantage of manufacturing	$ 52	$ 26	$ 78

    * These are the rates of increase as direct labor cost goes from $10,000 to $11,500 and from $11,500 to $13,000. For example, indirect labor goes up by $300 for a $1,500 increase in direct labor cost, an average of 20 percent.

In each case, manufacturing is cheaper than purchasing. The company should continue to manufacture all three of these parts, at least for the time being.

Chapter 4

4–1.   *a.*

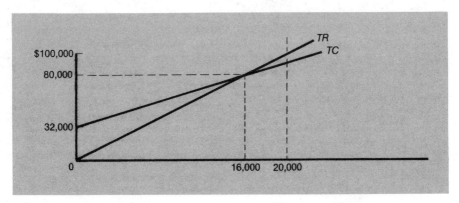

b.

Break-even point: $32,000/($5 − $3) = 16,000$ units
Margin of safety: $20,000 − 16,000 = 4,000$ units

Anticipated profit:
Revenues at $5...............................	$100,000
Variable costs at $3..........................	$ 60,000
Fixed costs...................................	$ 32,000
Income before taxes......................	$ 8,000

c.

(1)   Break-even point: $32,000/($5.50 − $3) = 12,800$ units
        Margin of safety: $18,000 − 12,800 = 5,200$ units

Anticipated profit:
Revenues at $5.50.............................	$99,000
Variable costs at $3..........................	$54,000
Fixed costs...................................	32,000
Income before taxes......................	$13,000

(2)   The effect of the price increase is to increase the spread between total cost and total revenue at any given volume. When volume is measured in physical units, as it is in this case, this increased spread is reflected in the profit-volume chart as a steeper slope for the total revenue line. The revised chart is shown at the top of the next page.

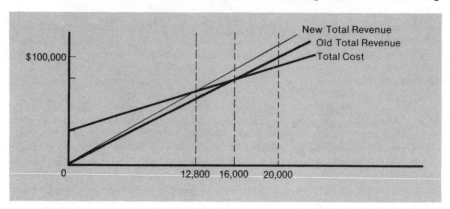

(3)   Operating leverage has decreased because the ratio of fixed cost to contribution margin per unit is now smaller than it was before, but the sensitivity of profit to a unit change in volume is greater than before.

(4)

Profit target: $1.1 \times \$13,000$ $14,300
Total fixed costs 32,000
     Needed contribution margin $46,300

Crossover volume $= \$46,300/\$2.50 = 18,520$ units

    d.

(1)   Break-even point: $\$36,000/(\$4.60 - \$3) = 22,500$ units
(2)   This would increase the operating leverage dramatically as fixed costs would increase and the contribution margin rate would fall. The sensitivity of profit to a unit change in volume would be less, however.

(3)

Profit target: $1.1 \times \$8,000$ .... $ 8,800
Total fixed cost 36,000
     Needed contribution margin $44,800

Crossover point $= \$44,800/\$1.60 = 28,000$ units

4–2.   a. Absorption costing overhead rates:

Department A: $\$25,000/5,000 = \$5$ a direct labor hour
Department B: $\$60,000/10,000 = \$6$ a pound

Job order costs:

	Job 1	Job 2
Direct materials	$2,400	$ 4,800
Direct labor:		
Department A	1,620	900
Department B	420	280
Overhead:		
Department A at $5	900	500
Department B at $6	2,880	9,000
Total	$8,220	$15,480
Unit cost	$13.70	$15.48

b. Variable costing overhead rates:

Department A: $15,000/5,000 = $3 a direct labor hour
Department B: $20,000/10,000 = $2 a pound

Job order costs:

	Job 1	Job 2
Direct materials......................	$2,400	$4,800
Direct labor:		
Department A......................	1,620	900
Department B......................	420	280
Overhead:		
Department A at $3.................	540	300
Department B at $2.................	960	3,000
Total............................	$5,940	$9,280
Unit cost............................	$9.90	$9.28

c. Variable unit cost of job 2 is less than that of job 1; full cost was greater for job 2 than for job 1. The main reason is that job 2 used much more of department B's capacity than job 1 and department B has a much higher proportion of fixed costs than department A. Total profit is thus much more sensitive to variations in sales of product Y (job 2) than to variations in sales of product X.

4–3.   *a.* The first step is to calculate the average contribution margin at the assumed mix:

	Units	Revenue	Contribution Margin
Product A.............	30,000	$150,000	$60,000
Product B.............	40,000	100,000	30,000
Total............		$250,000	$90,000

Average = 90/250 = 36 percent

The *break-even sales volume* is obtained by dividing this average into the fixed costs:

$72,000/0.36 = $200,000

Units of A: 150/250 × $200,000 + $5   = 24,000 units
Units of B: 100/250 × $200,000 $2.50 = 32,000 units

Margin of safety:

Actual sales:	
Product A: 30,000 × $5....................	$150,000
Product B: 40,000 × $2.50.................	100,000
Total sales.........................	$250,000
Break-even volume.......................	200,000
Margin of safety......................	$ 50,000

Anticipated profit = $90,000 − $72,000 =$18,000

b. New volume and contribution margin:

	Units	Revenue	Contribution Margin
Product A..............	40,000	$200,000	$ 80,000
Product B.............	32,000	80,000	24,000
Total..............		$280,000	$104,000
Fixed costs...........			81,700
Profit.............			$ 22,300

c. Average contribution margin at the new mix: $104,000/$280,000 = 37.14 percent.

$$\text{Break-even sales volume} = (\$72,000 + \$9,700)/.3714 = \$220,000$$

d. The two main assumptions are that as volume drops sales of the two products will drop proportionally and fixed costs will remain at $81,700. Either of these assumptions can be challenged.

4-4.   a.

	1st Quarter	2nd Quarter
Sales...	$300,000	$450,000
Cost of goods sold..................................	220,000	330,000
Gross margin..	$ 80,000	$120,000
Less:		
Selling and administrative expenses................	$ 25,000	$ 27,000
Underabsorbed overhead............................	.....	36,000
Total deductions..............................	$ 25,000	$ 63,000
Profit...	$ 55,000	$ 57,000
Ending inventory...................................	$110,000	$ 44,000

b.

	1st Quarter	2nd Quarter
Sales...	$300,000	$450,000
Cost of goods sold..................................	100,000	150,000
Gross margin..	$200,000	$300,000
Less:		
Selling and administrative expenses................	$ 25,000	$ 27,000
Fixed overhead....................................	180,000	180,000
Total deductions..............................	$205,000	$207,000
Profit (loss)..	$ (5,000)	$ 93,000
Ending inventory...................................	$ 50,000	$ 20,000

c.

	Full Costing	Variable Costing
Sales...	$450,000	$450,000
Cost of goods sold..................................	330,000	150,000
Gross margin..	$120,000	$300,000
Less:		
Selling and administrative expenses................	$ 27,000	$ 27,000
Fixed costs.......................................	...	180,000
Total deductions..............................	$ 27,000	$207,000
Profit...	$ 93,000	$ 93,000
Ending inventory...................................	$110,000	$ 50,000

Chapter 5

5–1. *a.*

	Division A	Division B	Division C	Total
Profit Plan:				
Sales revenues............................	$1,000	$3,000	$2,100	$6,100
Divisional expenses:				
Cost of goods sold........................	$ 650	$1,650	$1,260	$3,560
Marketing...............................	150	500	300	950
Administrative..........................	150	300	200	650
Total.................................	$ 950	$2,450	$1,760	$5,160
Division profit contribution.................	$ 50	$ 550	$ 340	$ 940
Headquarters expenses.....................				400
Net income..............................				$ 540
Cash Budget:				
Revenues................................	$1,000	$3,000	$2,100	$6,100
Less: Increase in receivables..............	10	200	50	260
Collections.............................	$ 990	$2,800	$2,050	$5,840
Cost of goods sold.......................	$ 650	$1,650	$1,260	$3,560
Add: Inventory increase....................	50	100	50	200
Purchases..............................	$ 700	$1,750	$1,310	$3,760
Less: Increase in payables.................	15	50	80	145
Payments to suppliers....................	$ 685	$1,700	$1,230	$3,615
Division marketing costs...................	150	500	300	950
Division administration (expense less depreciation).............................	145	285	180	610
Total division disbursements..........	$ 980	$2,485	$1,710	$5,175
Division cash flow.........................	$ 10	$ 315	$ 340	$ 665
Central administration......................				$ 390
Equipment purchases......................				130
Dividends................................				350
Total head office disbursements..........				$ 870
Net decrease in cash......................				$ (205)

b.

Anticipated cash balance: $290 − $205......................	$ 85
Minimum cash balance: 5% × $6,100.......................	305
Cash shortage..	$220

Since the company has only a $100 line of credit, the proposed plan is not financially feasible.

Chapter 6

6–1.   *a.* Preparing a diagram like this is almost always a good way to begin problems of this sort:

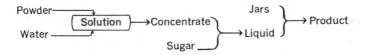

b. One way is to trace a pound of powder through to the end:

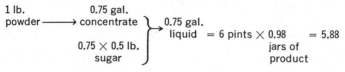

Powder/jar = 1 lb./5.88 = 0.170/jar
Sugar/jar = 0.375 lb./5.88 = .064/jar
Jars/jar = 1,005/1,000 = 1.005 jars/jar

c. Standard materials cost:

Powder: $0.80/lb. × 0.170.................................. $0.136
Sugar: $0.25/lb. × 0.064.................................. 0.016
Jars: $2.40/doz. × 1.005/12............................ 0.201
    Standard materials cost/jar.......................... $0.353 per pint jar

6–2.   *a. Materials*

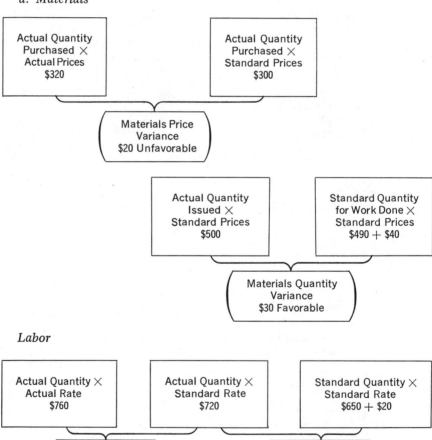

b. This means that some of the work on completed products was done last month. This means that this month's performance was worse than we thought:

Materials quantity variance:
Input.. $500
Output: $490 + $40 − $100......................... 430
Materials quantity variance...................... $ 70 Unfavorable

Labor quantity variance:
Input.. $720
Output: $650 + $20 − $10.......................... 660
Labor quantity variance......................... $ 60 Unfavorable

6–3.   *a.*

Materials				**Materials in Process**				**Labor in Process**		
Bal.	1,000	(4)	500	(4)	500	(6)	490	(5)	720	(6)	650
(3)	300			(7)	30					(7)	50
Bal. 800				Bal. 40				Bal. 20			

Materials Price Var.				**Labor Rate Variance**				**Accounts Payable, etc.***		
(3)	20	(8)	20	(5)	40	(9)	40			(3)	20
										(5)	760

Finished Goods		**Materials Quantity Variance**				**Labor Quantity Variance**		
(6)	1,140	(10)	30	(7)	30	(7)	50	(11)	50

* Any account or accounts can be used to record the payables; this aspect of these transactions is not part of cost accounting.

b.

Materials				**Work-in-Process**				**Finished Goods**	
Bal.	1,000	(4)	518	(4)	518	(6)	1,214	(6)	1,214
(3)	320			(5)	760				
Bal. 802				Bal. 64					

Variance Summary				
(8)	MPV	20	(10) MQV	30
(9)	LRV	40		
(11)	LQV	50		
Bal. 80				

(4) Materials issued = $1,000 + $320 − $802 = $518
(6) Goods finished = $518 + $760 − $43 − $21 = $1,214

Chapter 7

7–1.   *a.* Overhead rate = ($12,000 + $8,000)/10,000 = $2 a pound.

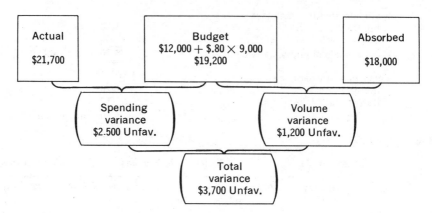

The number of units of product is ignored in this situation, because overhead costs vary with the amount of materials used rather than with the output of the product. A meaningful performance standard for overhead cost must reflect this relationship.

    b. This calls for an adjustment of the flexible budget:

Fixed cost: $12,000 × 1.02................... $12,240
Variable cost: $0.80 × 1.05 × $9,000........   7,560
   Revised budget........................ $19,800

Now we have a three-part breakdown of the total overhead variance:

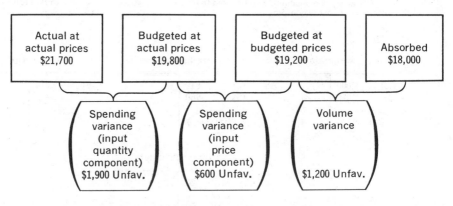

    c. A fixed cost is not necessarily noncontrollable. The department head has the responsibility to supervise and coordinate the department's activities, even those that are not affected by the volume of business done. In this case, we can see the following:

    Cleaning labor: Fixed, but controllable.
    Depreciation: Fixed, noncontrollable.

Materials handling labor: Variable, controllable.

Royalty: Variable, controllable through control of materials usage; if royalty were based on production output, it would be variable but noncontrollable.

7–2.   *a.*

	Month 4			Month 5		
	Budget	*Actual*	*Variance*	*Budget*	*Actual*	*Variance*
Controllable:						
Nonproductive time.........	$1,000	$ 800	$ 200	$ 750	$1,200	$(450)
Other indirect labor.........	4,000	3,700	300	3,500	3,600	(100)
Operating supplies..........	600	650	(50)	450	430	20
Total controllable.........	$5,600	$5,150	$ 450	$4,700	$5,230	$(530)
Noncontrollable:						
Depreciation................	2,000	2,100	(100)	2,000	2,150	(150)
Building service charges....	700	770	(70)	700	730	(30)
Total.....................	$8,300	$8,020	$ 280	$7,400	$8,110	$(710)

b. Only the first three overhead cost items listed are likely to be of any significance in evaluating the cost control performance of the department supervisor, and of these nonproductive time and other indirect labor have the greatest impact. Depreciation and building service charges are noncontrollable and have no bearing on managerial evaluation in this department.

c. Labor costs did not go down with decreasing volume. There are many possible reasons for this. This may merely be a time lag—management may have decided not to cut the labor force to meet the volume reduction in the hope that volume would recover quickly. This should be examined more critically if volume continues at these newer and lower levels. We cannot ignore any one month's reports, but we need to examine them in the context of a longer period of time. Even two months is likely to be too short a period for random forces to have averaged themselves out.

The other item in which the variance has increased is depreciation, and this should be labeled as noncontrollable.

d.

Overhead rate = $4,700/4,000 + $3,600/4,000

$$= \quad \$1.175 \quad + \quad \$.90 \qquad = \$2.075/\text{DLHr.}$$

Volume variance:

Month 4: zero

Month 5:

$$\$1.175 \times (4,000 - 3,000) = \$1,175 \text{ Unfav.}$$

Or:

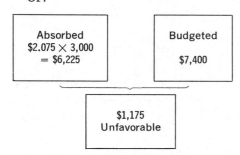

The main significance is to identify the charge against profits due to low volume, a charge not reflected in product cost.

Chapter 8

8–1.   *a.* Dept. S charging rate $= \dfrac{\$2,000}{20,000} + \$0.20 = \$0.30/\text{service unit}$

Component of departmental overhead rates:

Dept. 1: 1,000 × \$0.30/10,000.................... \$0.03/direct labor hour
Dept. 2: 5,000 × \$0.30/ 8,000.................... \$0.1875/direct labor hour
Dept. 3: 8,000 × \$0.30/20,000.................... \$0.12/machine-hour
Dept. 4: 6,000 × \$0.30/15,000.................... \$0.12/direct labor hour

Cost of S service included in cost of 1,000 units of product A:

Dept. 1: \$0.03 × 10.................................... \$ 0.30
Dept. 2: \$0.1875 × 20................................   3.75
Dept. 3: \$0.12 × 100.................................   12.00
Dept. 4: \$0.12 × 5....................................   0.60
    Total... $16.65

b. Cost of S service included in cost of 1,000 units of product A under variable costing:

Dept. 1: no department S cost because departmental
            consumption of S service is fixed............ —
Dept. 2: \$0.20 × ⅝ × 20............................. \$ 2.50
Dept. 3: \$0.20 × 8/20 × 100..........................   8.00
Dept. 4: \$0.20 × 6/15 × 5............................   0.40
    Total... $10.90

8–2.   *a.*

Step 1:   Allocate building costs (\$5,000):

Office	Storeroom	Maintenance	Able	Baker
750	500	250	2,000	1,500

Step 2:   Allocate office costs, including share of building costs (\$6,370 + \$750):

Hours spent in building and office departments should not be included in the allocation base because the building department's costs have already been allocated and the office department can't allocate costs to itself. The allocation base therefore is 8,900 labor hours, and the allocation is:

Storeroom	Maintenance	Able	Baker
240	400	4,480	2,000

Step 3:   Allocate storeroom costs (\$2,260 + \$500 + \$240):

Maintenance	Able	Baker
150	1,050	1,800

Step 4:   Allocate maintenance costs (\$6,000 + \$250 + \$400 + \$150):

Only 400 maintenance hours enter into the calculation. The 10 hours used in the office must be ignored because that department's costs have already been allocated. The allocation is:

Able	Baker
2,550	4,250

The cost distribution sheet now shows the following:

	Building	Office	Storeroom	Maintenance	Able	Baker
Direct overhead...	$ 5,000	$ 6,370	$ 2,250	$ 6,000	$ 2,770	$ 3,100
Allocations:						
Building.........	(5,000)	750	500	250	2,000	1,500
Office..........		(7,120)	240	400	4,480	2,000
Storeroom.......			(3,000)	150	1,050	1,800
Maintenance....				(6,800)	2,550	4,250
Total.........					$12,850	$12,650
Normal volume (direct labor hours)..........					5,000	2,000
Overhead rate.....					2.57	$6.325

b.

	Able	Baker	Service
Direct overhead...............	$2,770	$3,100	$19,630
Direct labor hours.............	5,000	2,000	7,000
Overhead rate.................	$0.554	$1.55	$2.804

c.

	Job 123	Job 321
Allocation method:		
Able at $2.57 an hour............	$12.85	$ 5.14
Baker at $6.325 an hour..........	12.65	31.62
Total......................	$25.50	$36.76
Direct apportionment:		
Able at $0.554 an hour...........	$ 2.77	$ 1.11
Baker at $1.55 an hour...........	3.10	7.75
Service at $2.804 an hour........	19.63	19.63
Total......................	$25.50	$28.49

8–3.　　a.

Dept. A: $\dfrac{\$12,000}{6,000 \text{ units}} = \$2/\text{unit}$

Dept. B: $\dfrac{\$18,000}{8,000 \text{ units}} = \$2.25/\text{unit}$

Dept. C: $\dfrac{\$20,000}{12,000 \text{ units}} = \$1.67/\text{unit}$

b.

	Dept. A	Dept. B	Dept. C	Production
Direct charges............	$12,000	$18,000	$20,000	xxx
Allocations:				
Service dept. A..........	(12,000)	1,800	1,200	$ 9,000
Service dept. B..........		(19,800)	2,949	16,851
Service dept. C..........			(24,149)	24,149

Charging rates:
　Department A: $12,000/8,000 = $1.50/service unit
　Department B: $19,800/9,400 = $2.1064/service unit
　Department C: $24,149/12,000 = $2.0124/service unit

c.

Dept. A = $2.0788/unit
Dept. B = $2.2146/unit
Dept. C = $1.6510/unit

Computations:

$$\text{Rate}_A = \frac{\$12,000 + 600 \times \text{Rate}_B + 2,000 \times \text{Rate}_C}{8,000} \tag{1}$$

$$\text{Rate}_B = \frac{\$18,000 + 1,200 \times \text{Rate}_A + 1,000 \times \text{Rate}_C}{10,000} \tag{2}$$

$$\text{Rate}_C = \frac{\$20,000 + 800 \times \text{Rate}_A + 1,400 \times \text{Rate}_B}{15,000} \tag{3}$$

$$8,000\ \text{Rate}_A = 12,000 + 600 \times \text{Rate}_B + 2,000 \times \text{Rate}_C \tag{1}$$
$$\text{Rate}_A = 1.5 + 0.075\ \text{Rate}_B + 0.25\ \text{Rate}_C \tag{1a}$$

Substituting this in equations (2) and (3):

$$10,000\ \text{Rate}_B = 18,000 + (1,800 + 90\ \text{Rate}_B + 300\ \text{Rate}_C)$$
$$+ 1,000\ \text{Rate}_C$$
$$9,910\ \text{Rate}_B = 19,800 + 1,300\ \text{Rate}_C \tag{2a}$$
$$15,000\ \text{Rate}_C = 20,000 + (1,200 + 60\ \text{Rate}_B + 200\ \text{Rate}_C)$$
$$+ 1,400\ \text{Rate}_B$$
$$14,800\ \text{Rate}_C = 21,200 + 1,460\ \text{Rate}_B \tag{3a}$$

Solving (2a) for Rate_B:

$$\text{Rate}_B = \frac{19,800}{9,910} + \frac{1,300}{9,910}\ \text{Rate}_C$$

Substituting in (3a):

$$14,800\ \text{Rate}_C = \$21,200 + \frac{1,460 \times 19,800}{9,910} + \frac{1,460 \times 1,300}{9,910}\ \text{Rate}_C$$
$$\underline{\text{Rate}_C = \$1.6510/\text{unit}}$$

Substituting this in (2a):

$$9,910\ \text{Rate}_B = 19,800 + (1,300 \times \$1.6510)$$
$$\underline{\text{Rate}_B = \$2.2146/\text{unit}}$$

Substituting in (1a):

$$\text{Rate}_A = \$1.5 + 0.075 \times \$2.2146 + 0.25 \times \$1.6510$$
$$\underline{\text{Rate}_A = \$2.0788/\text{unit}}$$

8–4.   *a.* Department M should be charged for department S services because those services are measurable and controllable.

The best basis for the charge is actual consumption, multiplied by a predetermined rate. The rate can be either full cost or variable cost. The full cost rate is $45,000/10,000 = $4.50 an hour. The variable cost rate is $2.50 an hour. The charge for February would be:

Full cost: 1,100 × $4.50 = $4,950
Variable cost: 1,100 × $2.50 = $2,750

Ideally, the company would want to supplement the charge for variable costs with a capacity charge, representing the ratio of department M's demand to total demand at the peak time. We don't have this—we only know that the department uses 10 percent of *normal* service volume, and on this basis $2,000 in fixed cost would be allocated.

b. The variance on department M's report:

		Full Cost Basis	Variable Cost Basis
Budget..............	900 hours	$4,050	$2,250
Actual...............	1,100 hours	4,950	2,750
Variance.........	200 hours	$ (900)	$ (500)

There would be no variance in the fixed cost capacity charge in the variable cost system.

c. The department S variance:

Budget at 8,000 hours:
8,000 × $2.50 + $20,000............... $40,000
Actual................................. 42,000
Spending variance.............. $(2,000)

But departmental accounts will show a larger amount if full costing is used:

Charge out: 8,000 × $4.50............. $36,000
Actual............................... 42,000
Total undistributed............... $(6,000)

The extra $4,000 is a volume variance.

Chapter 9

9–1. *a.* The first step is to separate the fixed and variable components of the cost of goods sold. Since the total cost of goods sold went up by 10 percent, the variable portion also must have gone up by 10 percent, from $290 to $319. Knowing this, we can construct the report very easily:

	Budget		Actual		Variance
Sales.........................		$500		$550	$ 50
Variable expenses:					
Cost of goods sold..........	$290		$319		(29)
Sales commissions..........	10		11		(1)
Delivery.....................	14	314	16	346	(2)
Contribution margin........		$186		$204	$ 18
Product advertising...........		11		11	—
Profit contribution.........		$175		$193	$ 18

b. Since this is to be a profit contribution report, since fixed factory overheads are not traceable to individual products, and since the volume variance arises in most cases from under- or overabsorption of fixed costs, no portion of the volume variance should be assigned to either product.

c. If management insists on full allocation, our answer must be different, but it should not be to endorse the present system. This serves to saddle product A with more than half of the volume variance, even though production of product A was greater than the amount budgeted.

If we want to quantify this point, we need to identify the amount of fixed overhead absorbed. We start with two facts:

1. $290 of the budgeted cost of goods sold was variable cost.
2. $100 of the budgeted cost of goods sold was overhead cost.

Putting these together, we find that standard factory cost ($350) included $60 in fixed overhead, $40 in variable overhead, and $250 in direct labor and direct materials. Since production of A increased by 10 percent, the amount of fixed overhead absorbed also went up by 10 percent, to $66. Other things being equal, a *favorable* volume variance of $6 should be assigned to product A if profit reporting is to be on a full-cost basis. This means that product B must have been responsible for an unfavorable volume variance amounting to $36 and that's how it should be reported.

d. An effort might be made to convince management that "full allocation" means allocation of all costs originally budgeted. If that is successful, lump-sum allocations can be made for all nontraceable fixed costs. Failing that, very little can be done, except for the adjustment of the volume variance described in (*c*). One common suggestion to minimize the damage done by these arbitrary allocations is to allocate in proportion to profit contribution. This will maintain the *relative* profitability of the two lines in their proper proportions.

e. Product A seems to be in good shape. Its sales are up 10 percent and so is its profit contribution. The marketing manager may even see this as evidence of market strength that ought to be exploited even more vigorously than now.

The main problem seems to be with product B. Its production and sales seem to be only 60 percent of their budgeted levels (absorption of $90 of factory overhead instead of $150). As a result, product A is assigned a much bigger share of factory variances and selling and administrative expenses. Management should devote its efforts to product B.

Chapter 10

10–1.

	Department A		Department B	
	Materials	*Processing*	*Materials*	*Processing*
Cost divisors:				
Finished.............................	90	90	85	85
Ending inventory.....................	60	20	45	30
Moving average divisors...........	150	110	130	115
Beginning inventory.................	50	15	40	20
Equivalent production.............	100	95	90	95
Total cost............................$105		$399	$450*	$570
Unit cost, this month.................$1.05		$4.20	$5	$6

* Transferred from department A: 90 units × $5—the $5 is taken from the table below.

Costs to be distributed:				
In process, 6/1......................	$ 45	$ 41	$213	$150
Charged to department.............	105	399	450	570
Total...........................	$150	$440	$663	$720
Moving average divisors, department A				
(from above).......................	150	110		
Moving average costs,				
department A.......................	$ 1	$ 4		
Fifo unit costs,				
department B.......................			$ 5	$ 6
Costs distributed:				
In process, 6/30....................	$ 60	$ 80	$225	$180
To department B....................	90	360		
To finished goods...................			438*	540*
Total.........................	$150	$440	$663	$720

*Determined by subtracting ending inventory from total cost.

10–2.   *a.*

	Materials		Processing	
	With Spoilage	Without Spoilage*	With Spoilage	Without Spoilage*
Finished.............................	82,000	87,000	82,000	87,000
Ending inventory......................	10,000	10,000	5,000	5,000
Moving average divisors.............	92,000	97,000	87,000	92,000
Beginning inventory....................	4,000	4,000	2,000	2,000
Equivalent production................	88,000	93,000	85,000	90,000

* Spoilage = Beginning inventory (4,000) + units received (93,000) − units transferred (82,000) − ending inventory (10,000) = 5,000

The second set of divisors is not called for in instruction (a), but since we'll need them in (c) we have calculated them here for convenience.

b. In calculating current unit costs, the costs of the beginning inventory are irrelevant and the equivalent production divisors should be used.

	Total Cost	Divisor	Unit Cost
Materials.......................	$ 81,840	88,000	$0.93
Labor...........................	61,200	85,000	0.72
Other processing...............	45,900	85,000	0.54
Total.......................	$188,940		$2.19

c. To calculate the effect of lost units, we need to calculate unit cost as if no units had been lost, and then subtract these from the figures in (b):

	Total Cost	Divisor	Unit Cost	Effect of Lost Units
Materials.......................	$ 81,840	93,000	$0.88	$0.05
Labor...........................	61,200	90,000	0.68	0.04
Other processing...............	45,900	90,000	0.51	0.03
Total.......................	$188,940		$2.07	$0.12

d.

	Materials	Processing	Total
Total cost to be distributed:			
In process, 1/1..................	$ 2,800	$ 1,650	$ 4,450
Current costs....................	81,840	107,100	188,940
Total.......................	$84,640	$108,750	$193,390
Divisors [from (a)].................	92,000	87,000	
Moving average unit cost..........	$0.92	$1.25	
Costs distributed:			
Goods transferred (82,000)........	$75,440	$102,500	$177,940
In process, 1/31 (10,000)..........	9,200	6,250	15,450
Total.......................	$84,640	$108,750	$193,390

Chapter 11

11–1.   *a.* Step 1. Calculate the value of the output:

Product	Unit Price	Completion Costs	Net Value per Unit	Total Value
A..................	$ 6.20	$0.90	$5.30	$ 5,300
B................	3.80	0.80	3.00	6,000
C................	10.00	2.52	7.48	18,700
Total...............				$30,000

Step 2. Calculate the net cost:

Cost $21,500 − by-product value $500 = $21,000

Step 3. Calculate the cost/value ratio:

$21,000/30,000 = 70 percent

Step 4. Allocate the joint costs:

Product	Value	70 Percent	Joint Cost per Unit	Completion Cost per Unit	Total Unit Cost
A..................	$ 5,300	$ 3,710	$3.71	$0.90	$4.61
B..................	6,000	4,200	2.10	0.80	2.90
C..................	18,700	13,090	5.236	2.52	7.756

Cost of by-product D is $0.05. Deducting this value from the joint costs is equivalent to assigning 5 cents of the costs to each unit of the by-product.

b. Total number of physical units (excluding by-product): 5,500

Unit cost: $21,000/5,500 = $3.82 a unit.

This would not be acceptable because it would indicate that product B was produced at a loss. Since the production decision is based on total cost and total revenue, it is impossible to lose money on any one without losing money on them all as long as forecasted conditions materialize.

11–2.   *a.* The 40-cent figure was irrelevant. If management accepts the proposal, it must give up the sale of product Y—in other words, it must sacrifice the revenues from this source. These revenues measure the opportunity cost of the new product. On these grounds, the Y-Plus proposal should be rejected:

Revenue............................	$ 1.30
Less: Incremental processing....... $0.80	
Opportunity cost............. 0.60	1.40
Processing loss..................	$(0.10)

b. To get 20,000 pounds of Z, the factory will have to process 30,000 pounds of materials. Materials and variable processing costs amount to 30 cents a pound. The other calculations are:

Additional materials and variable processing costs: 30,000 × $0.30............................	$ 9,000
Additional revenues from Z: 20,000 × $0.35........	7,000
Additional revenue needed from Y.............	$ 2,000
Current revenues from Y.........................	60,000
Minimum revenues needed from Y.............	$ 62,000
Production of Y: 100,000 + 10,000 lbs..............	110,000
Average price of Y.........................	$0.564

If the price of Y falls as far as $0.564 a pound, the company will be no better off than it is now.

c. Since processing costs will be unaffected, the margin for the purchase of materials must come from the revenues:

	New Material	Present Material
Y:.................	120,000 × $0.60 = $ 72,000	$ 60,000
Z:.................	180,000 × $0.45 = 81,000	90,000
Total.........	$153,000	$150,000

This means that the company can afford to pay up to $3,000 more for the new materials, or $63,000.

The maximum price is $63,000/300,000 = $0.21 a pound.

Chapter 12

12–1. *Step 1. Identify all the traceable items.* These items are sales, cost of sales, sales salaries, sales commissions, sales discounts and allowances, sales travel, regional office expenses, freight and delivery, and local advertising. The cost of goods sold can be stated either at attributable cost or at full cost, since we are concerned only with the relative profitability of the various regions. We prefer the attributable cost calculation because it provides a more complete picture of the region's contribution to the corporate well-being. Attributable factory costs consist of the variable costs (75 percent of the normal amount) and 60 percent of the fixed overhead (60 percent of 25 percent = 15 percent), a total of 90 percent of normal unit cost.

Step 2. Apply formulas for customer defaults and for divisible repetitive service functions. They are payroll, order processing, packing and shipping, credit review, cashier, and general accounting.

Step 3. Ignore the other costs. These cannot be identified clearly with individual sales regions. This is just as true of marketing management expenses as of other common expenses. Managerial time allocations say very little about attributability, particularly when the staffs are this small.

Step 4. Summarize the calculations in a table, as follows:

	Region A	*Region B*	*Region C*	*Total*
Sales:				
Product X..........................	$ 10,000	$ 5,000	$ 50,000	$ 65,000
Product Y..........................	80,000	140,000	70,000	290,000
Product Z..........................	10,000	10,000	20,000	40,000
Total..........................	$100,000	$155,000	$140,000	$395,000
Customer defaults....................	500	775	700	1,975
Discounts and allowances............	1,000	2,000	4,000	7,000
Net sales......................	$ 98,500	$152,225	$135,300	$386,025
Cost of goods sold				
(90% of full cost):				
Product X at $3.60..................	$ 7,200	$ 3,600	$ 36,000	$ 46,800
Product Y at $5.40..................	43,200	75,600	37,800	156,000
Product Z at $ .90..................	4,500	4,500	9,000	18,000
Total cost of sales............	$ 54,900	$ 83,700	$ 82,800	$221,400
Gross margin......................	$ 43,600	$ 68,525	$ 52,500	$164,625
Regional expenses:				
Sales commissions.................	$ 5,000	$ 7,750	$ 7,000	$ 19,750
Sales salaries.....................	5,000	6,000	8,000	19,000
Sales travel.......................	3,000	3,000	2,000	8,000
Regional office....................	4,000	4,500	5,000	13,500
Freight and delivery................	2,000	2,400	1,650	6,050
Advertising.......................	1,000	1,000	1,000	3,000
Allocated charges:				
Payroll............................	180	192	240	612
Order processing...................	1,920	2,160	3,600	7,680
Packing and shipping..............	1,500	1,800	3,300	6,600
Credit review......................	1,200	1,320	2,400	4,920
Cashier...........................	1,000	1,100	1,500	3,600
General accounting................	1,400	1,540	2,100	5,040
Total........................	$ 27,200	$ 32,762	$ 37,790	$ 97,752
Attributable profit....................	$ 16,400	$ 35,763	$ 14,710	$ 66,873
Percent of sales...................	16.4%	23.1%	10.5%	
Nonattributable expenses:				
Manufacturing (10% of full cost).....				$ 24,600
Marketing division salaries.........				10,000
National advertising...............				5,000
Other marketing....................				12,000
Corporate management.............				20,000
Total......................				$ 71,600
Income (loss) before taxes...........				$ (4,727)

Chapter 13

13–1.   *a.* The company's objective is to make a profit. Ignoring fixed costs, which aren't specified in the problem and would be irrelevant in any case, profit is equal to $5 for each unit of product A sold plus $8 for each unit of product B. Expressed in mathematical form, the objective function is:

$$\text{Profit} = \$5A + \$8B$$

The first constraint is that only 3,000 hours of department X time are available. Each unit of product A requires 2 hours in this department, and each unit of product B needs 1 hour. These relationships can be expressed as an inequality:

$$2A + B \leq 3,000$$

The inequality for department Y can be calculated and expressed in the same way:

$$2A + 4B \leq 6,000$$

The other constraints are that sales of neither product can exceed 2,000 units and that negative sales volumes are not admissible. We can express these constraints in two separate inequalities:

$$2,000 \geq A \geq 0$$
$$2,000 \geq B \geq 0$$

b. Construction of the departmental constraint lines:

$A = 0, B = 3,000$	$B = 0, A = 1,500$ (Dept. X)
$A = 0, B = 1,500$	$B = 0, A = 3.000$ (Dept. Y)

Slope of the isoprofit lines:

$$A = 0, B = 5 \qquad B = 0, A = 8$$

Drawing the graph:

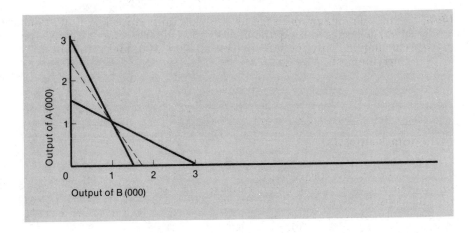

The optimal solution is to produce 1,000 units of each product, for a total contribution margin of $13,000:

		Contribution Margin	
	No. of		
Product	Units	Per Unit	Total
A.....................	1,000	$5	$ 5,000
B.....................	1,000	8	8,000
Total			$13,000

An alternative approach is to start with a tentative solution (e.g., $B = 0$, $A = 1,500$, using all the capacity of department X), and then see whether profit can be improved by substituting (e.g., one unit of B can be obtained by sacrificing half a unit of A, for a profit gain of $8 − $2.50). This substitution uses up three hours of department Y's idle time, and 1,000 of these substitutions are possible. The optimal solution is as computed above.

    c. If the contribution margin of product A rises beyond $16, the optimal solution will be to manufacture no product B. If it falls below $4, the optimal solution will be to manufacture no product A. Between these two values, the optimal decision will be the same.

13–2.   *a.*

$$\text{EOQ} = \sqrt{\frac{2 \times 10{,}000 \times 36}{.2 \times \$2.50}} = 1{,}200 \text{ units}$$

    b. Average inventory = 1,200/2 = 600 units

Carrying cost	= 0.2 × $2.50 × 600 =	$300
Number of orders = 10,000/1,200 = 8⅓		
Processing costs	= 8⅓ × $36	= 300
Total cost		$600

    c. Average usage = 10,000/50 = 200 units a week

Reorder level = 3 × 200 = 600 units

13–3.   *a.* The maximum usage level is 800 units a week, 200 units above the average usage during the reorder period. Therefore, we need to make calculations only for safety stocks of 200, 100, and zero units. Carrying costs:

0 units:	$ 0
100 units × 0.2 × $2.50	50
200 units × 0.2 × $2.50	100

Stockout costs:

Safety Stock	Units Short per Order Period	Probability Percent	Expected Number of Units Short	Number of Orders per Year	Stockout Costs at $1
0...............	100	0.20	20		
	200	0.10	20		
			40	8⅓	$333
100...............	100	0.10	10	8⅓	83
200...............	0	—	0	—	0

The total cost is $333 with a zero safety stock, $133 with a 100-unit safety stock, and $100 with a 200-unit safety stock. In this case a 200-unit safety stock is optimal.

    b. At $0.75 a unit, a 200-unit stock-out level remains optimal. Total costs at a 100-unit level would be $62.50 + $50 = $112.50, or $12.50 more than at the 200-unit level.

    At $0.50, the optimal solution would be a 100-unit safety stock (total cost $91.67). At $0.10, a zero safety stock would be appropriate (total costs only $33.33 instead of $58.33 with a 100-unit safety stock).

Chapter 14

These simple exercises have two objectives: (1) to provide an opportunity to practice the calculations described in the chapter; and (2) to demonstrate the impact of differences in the timing and duration of cash flows on different measures of project value.

The average annual cash inflow in each exercise is $1,750, but present value ranges from a small negative sum to +$3,310 and the internal rate of return varies from 9.7 percent to 15.6 percent.

14–1.   Present value and internal rate of return:

	Time	Cash Flow	10 Percent Factor	PV at 10 Percent	PV at X Percent	Internal Rate of Return
a.					12%	
	0.............	−$10,000	1.000	−$10,000	−$10,000	
	1–10.........	+ 1,750/yr.	6.145	+ 10,754	+ 9,888	
	Net PV......			+$ 754	−$ 112	11.7%
b.					15%	
	0.............	−$10,000	1.000	−$10,000	−$10,000	
	1–10.........	+ 1,500/yr.	6.145	+ 9,217	+ 7,529	
	1–5..........	+ 500/yr.	3.791	+ 1,896	+ 1,676	
	Net PV......			+$ 1,113	−$ 795	12.9%
c.					11%	
	0.............	−$10,000	1.000	−$10,000	−$10,000	
	1–5..........	+ 1,500/yr.	3.791	+ 5,686	+ 5,544	
	6–10.........	+ 2,000/yr.	2.354	+ 4,708	+ 4,386	
	Net PV......			+$ 394	−$ 70	10.8%
d.					9%	
	0.............	−$10,000	1.000	−$10,000	−$10,000	
	1–10.........	+ 1,350/yr.	6.145	+ 8,296	+ 8,665	
	10...........	+ 4,000	0.386	+ 1,544	+ 1,688	
	Net PV......			−$ 160	+$ 352	9.7%
e.					15%	
	0.............	−$10,000	1.000	−$10,000	−$10,000	
	1–15.........	+ 1,750/yr.	7.606	+ 13,310	+ 10,232	
	Net PV......			+$ 3,310	+$ 232	
					20%	
	0.............	−$10,000			−$10,000	
	1–15.........	+ 1,750/yr.			+ 8,181	
	Net PV......				−$ 1,819	15.6%

Payback period:

a.   10,000/1,750 = 5.7 years (6 years if payments come in annually).
b.   10/000/2,000 = 5 years
c.   6.25 years (7 years with annual payments).
d.   10,000/1,350 = 7.4 years (8 years with annual payments).
e.   10,000/1,750 = 5.7 years (6 years with annual payments).

Average return on investment:

	Average Cash Flow	Average Depreciation	Average Income	Average Investment*	Average Return (percent)
a.	1,750	1,000	750	5,000	15%
b.	1,750	1,000	750	5,000	15
c.	1,750	1,000	750	5,000	15
d.	1,350	600	750	7,000	10.7
e.	1,750	667	1,083	5,000	21.7

* These averages are halfway between the initial investment and the end-of-life salvage value. If the beginning-of-year book values are averaged and straight-line or declining charge depreciation is used, average investment will be smaller and the average return will be greater.

14–2.   The key to the solution of most investment problems is to locate the cash flows on a time scale. As we pointed out in the chapter, most analysts simplify the analysis by assuming that each cash flow takes place either at the beginning or at the end of a year. In this case no such assumption is necessary—the timing of the cash flows is described in precise terms. If we take the date of the first payment to the trustee as the zero date, we can construct the following diagram:

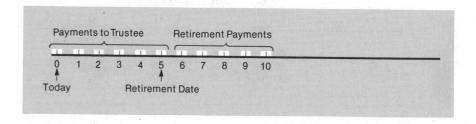

Retirement annuity for years 6 to 10:

This is equivalent to the difference between a ten-year annuity and a five-year annuity. The multipliers from Table 2 in Appendix A are:

$$6.710 - 3.993 = 2.717$$

Payments to the trustee:

By putting these on a time scale, we can see that six payments are called for, not five. The annuity tables cover series of cash flows in which the first payment comes one period after the zero date. The five-year annuity factor therefore covers all but the first payment. The discount factor for the first payment is 1,000. Therefore the annuity factor is $3.993 + 1,000 = 4.993$.

The series of annual payments (X) has a present value of $4.993X$.

The problem is solved by finding the X with a present value equal to the present value of the retirement payments:

$$4.993X = \$54,340$$
$$X = \$10,883.24$$

Chapter 15

15-1.   *a.*

	Gross	Tax	Net
Purchase price....................	$50,000	—	$ 50,000
Training........................	10,000	$ (4,000)	6,000
Investment credit.................	.....	(3,500)	(3,500)
Salvage (old machine).............	(8,000)	(4,800)	(12,800)
Incremental outlay..............	$52,000	$(12,300)	$ 39,700

b.

Gross cash savings before tax.................	$ 6,800
Tax depreciation:	
New: 30% of $50,000........................ $15,000	
Old....................................... 3,000	
Increased depreciation.....................	(12,000)
Taxable saving...............................	$ (5,200)
Tax reduction at 40%.........................	(2,080)
After-tax incremental cash savings...........	$ 8,880

15-2.   *a.*

Initial outlay:		
Cost of machine..................................		−$50,000
Less: Sale value of old machine..................	$10,000	
Tax reduction on retirement loss		
on old machine..........................	10,000	+ 20,000
Net initial outlay................................		−$30,000
Present value at 10% of after-tax future cash		
savings (see table below).......................		+ 68,566
Net present value............................		+$38,566

Calculation of discounted cash flows:

(1)	(2) Net Book Value	(3) Tax	(4) Depre- ciation	(5) Increase	(6)	(7)	(8) After- Tax	(9) Present Value
Years Hence	of New Machine	Depre- ciation	on Old Machine	in Depre- ciation	Taxable Income	Income Tax	Cash Flow	at 10 Percent
1..........	$50,000	$10,000	$ 3,750	$ 6,250	$ 13,750	$ 6,875	$ 13,125	$11,931
2..........	40,000	8,000	3,750	4,250	15,750	7,875	12,125	10,015
3..........	32,000	6,400	3,750	2,650	17,350	8,675	11,325	8,505
4..........	25,600	5,120	3,750	1,370	18,630	9,315	10,685	7,298
5..........	20,480	4,096	3,750	346	19,654	9,827	10,173	6,317
6..........	16,384	3,277	3,750	− 473	20,473	10,237	9,763	5,506
7..........	13,107	3,277	3,750	− 473	20,473	10,237	9,763	5,008
8..........	9,830	3,277	3,750	− 473	20,473	10,237	9,763	4,559
9..........	6,553	3,277	—	3,277	16,723	8,361	11,639	4,935
10..........	3,276	3,276	—	3,276	16,724	8,362	11,638	4,492
Total.........		$50,000	$30,000	$20,000	$180,000	$90,000	$110,000	$68,566

(3) 20% of (2) through year 6, then straight line amortization of remaining book value for the last four years.
(4) 12.5% of $30,000 (remaining book value).
(5) Col. 4 − Col. 3.
(6) $20,000 cash flow less increase in depreciation (col. 5).
(7) 50% of col. 6.
(8) $20,000 less col. 7.
(9) Col. 8 × Table 1, Appendix A.

b. The rate lies between 30 and 40 percent and must be approximated by interpolation. The calculations are:

Year	30 Percent Factor	PV at 30 Percent	40 Percent Factor	PV at 40 Percent
0....................	1.000	−$30,000	1.000	−$30,000
1....................	0.769	+ 10,093	0.714	+ 9,371
2....................	0.592	+ 7,178	0.510	+ 6,184
3....................	0.455	+. 5,153	0.364	+ 4,122
4....................	0.350	+ 3,740	0.260	+ 2,778
5....................	0.269	+ 2,737	0.186	+ 1,892
6....................	0.207	+ 2,021	0.133	+ 1,298
7....................	0.159	+ 1,552	0.095	+ 927
8....................	0.123	+ 1,201	0.068	+ 664
9....................	0.094	+ 1,094	0.048	+ 559
10....................	0.073	+ 850	0.035	+ 407
Net PV..............		+$ 5,619		−$ 1,798

$$\text{Rate of return} = 30\% + \frac{5,619}{5,619 + 1,798} \times 10\% = 37.6\%$$

Chapter 16

16–1.

Price	Sales (Units)	Sales Revenues	Fixed Costs	Variable Costs	Total Costs	Profit Margin
$0.75	100,000	$75,000	$11,000	$62,500	$73,500	$ 1,500
0.80	90,000	72,000	11,000	55,400	66,400	5,600
0.85	80,000	68,000	11,000	48,700	59,700	8,300
0.90	70,000	63,000	10,000	42,300	52,300	10,700
0.95	60,000	57,000	10,000	36,100	46,100	10,900
1.00	50,000	50,000	10,000	30,000	40,000	10,000

The most profitable price is $0.95 per unit.

16–2.   *a.*

	West Coast	Midwest
Sales.........................	$32.50	$44.00
Variable costs:		
Materials....................	$18.70	$18.70
Labor.......................	3.00	3.00
Variable overhead...........	3.30	3.30
Freight......................	....	1.50
Commissions...............	....	2.20
Total variable cost........	$25.00	$28.70
Contribution margin..........	$ 7.50	$15.30

The indications are that the company could increase its profit by $7.50 × 1,000 = $7,500 − $1,500 a month, or $6,000. All present fixed costs can be charged against existing sales in making this decision.

b. One factor that definitely should be considered is whether the West Coast distributors would reship the products to distributors in the Midwest. The delivered cost in the Midwest would be $39.50. This is substantially less than the price now quoted to Midwest dealers, but whether it is low enough to tempt the West Coast distributors to set up a clandestine distribution outlet in the company's present market areas is not clear. The West Coast distributor would be unlikely to risk the loss of a franchise on which a good deal of promotional effort has been exerted, unless, of course, West Coast operations are unprofitable.

It is fairly certain that reshipment by West Coast dealers is unlikely, nor is it likely that ultimate industrial purchasers who having consuming plants in both areas would find it profitable to buy in the West and reship to the Midwest. There may be some questions on these points in the edges of the company's sales territory, but the issue is probably not serious.

Another problem is how to react to complaints by Midwest retailers when they hear of the lower West Coast retail price. There is probably no Robinson-Patman problem because this is in the nature of a trade discount, and the areas are noncompeting, but dealers might exert pressure to get a reduction in the $44 price.

A more fundamental question, of course, is whether the company could go into the West Coast and perform the distribution function more economically—or whether the product would sell as well at $44 as at $42.50 on the West Coast. If either of these questions can be answered affirmatively, the justification for giving the West Coast distributor a special price disappears. This illustrates the point that pricing is not an isolated decision problem. Pricing decisions are intermingled with decisions on a wide range of marketing issues, and can't be ignored.

16–3. The company's pricing strategy in the past has not been a classic skimming pricing strategy—the government has ways of keeping profit margins slim. Three of the features of a skimming pricing situation have been present, however: (1) a relatively low sales volume, (2) achieved in a relatively price-insensitive sector of the market in which (3) product quality is highly important.

The company may choose to retain this strategy, but it has a number of risks. First, total reliance on a single customer is almost always risky. Second, total reliance on a single product is even riskier. Macronaut is vulnerable both to larger companies with extensive research laboratories and other bright young technicians coming in with new ideas, just as Macronaut did originally. Third, the lack of growth prospects may discourage the company's most dynamic employees, making it even more vulnerable to competition. Fourth, small scale denies the company access to the economies available from the latest technology.

These risks constitute the main argument for shifting to a penetration pricing strategy. These are strengthened by the presence of a huge, price sensitive market and the availability of the technology to penetrate it. But a penetration pricing strategy has its own risks. Management may not be able to adapt to such a sudden change in its way of doing business. Furthermore, the company may become even more vulnerable to market fluctuations once it has expanded its fixed costs.

Cost is a crucial element in strategy formation, although obviously not the only one. One question is whether the company can make money if the penetration pricing strategy is effective—this calls for good estimates of cost at normal operating volume. A second question is the relative importance of fixed costs. A high fixed cost ratio means high operating leverage—the higher the leverage the greater the risk and the greater the opportunity. If management fails to ask these questions, it cannot deal rationally with the main strategic issues.

Chapter 17

17–1.   *a.*

Probability	.1	.2	.3	.2	.15	.05	
No. Demanded	10	11	12	13	14	15	Expected
No. Produced							Value
10	10	10	10	10	10	10	10.0
11	8	11	11	11	11	11	10.7
12	6	9	12	12	12	12	10.8
13	4	7	10	13	13	13	10.0
14	2	5	8	11	14	14	8.6
15	0	3	6	9	12	15	6.75

b. Expected value is maximized at a volume of 12 units.

c. The maximum possible gain is associated with production of 15 units. The minimum possible loss is associated with production of ten units. Although no actual loss takes place, this is the best solution in the worst possible state of nature, and this is what this decision rule means.

17–2.   *a.*

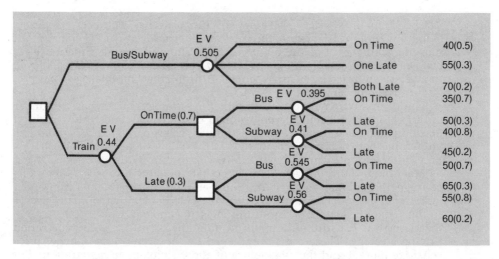

b. The expected values have been entered above the event nodes in the decision tree. Ms. Green can minimize her travel time by taking the train and then the bus. The bus is better than the subway whether the train is late or on time.

c. To answer this, tabulate the possible times on the train/bus combination, one for each possible branch:

Time (minutes)	Probability	Cumulative Probability
35	$0.7 \times 0.7 = 0.49$	0.49
50	$0.7 \times 0.3 = 0.21$	0.70
50	$0.3 \times 0.7 = 0.21$	0.91
65	$0.3 \times 0.3 = 0.09$	1.00

If she leaves home just before 8:10, she will reach the office on time 91 percent of the time.

Chapter 18

18-1.   *a.* The first step in this problem is to adjust January–June power costs for the rate increase:

January:	$1,000 × 1.1.....................	$1,100
February:	1,100 × 1.1.....................	1,210
March:	1,300 × 1.1.....................	1,430
April:	1,200 × 1.1.....................	1,320
May:	1,200 × 1.1.....................	1,320
June:	1,100 × 1.1.....................	1,210

Then, let $y =$ cost and $x =$ machine-hours.

x	y_o (adj.)	xy	x^2
3,500	1,100	3,850,000	12,250,000
4,200	1,210	5,082,000	17,640,000
4,900	1,430	7,007,000	24,010,000
4,400	1,320	5,808,000	19,360,000
4,300	1,320	5,676,000	18,490,000
3,800	1,210	4,598,000	14,440,000
3,300	1,090	3,597,000	10,890,000
4,100	1,280	5,248,000	16,810,000
4,700	1,400	6,580,000	22,090,000
3,800	1,210	4,598,000	14,440,000
3,000	1,080	3,240,000	9,000,000
4,000	1,230	4,920,000	16,000,000
Σ = 48,000	14,880	60,204,000	195,420,000

The normal equations can be solved to yield the following estimating equation:

$$\text{Power costs} = \$440 + \$0.20 \text{ x machine-hour}$$

b. The formula for r^2 is:

$$r^2 = 1 - \frac{\Sigma(y_o - y_c)^2}{\Sigma(y_o - \bar{y})^2}$$

y_c	$y_o - y_c$	$(y_o - y_c)^2$	$y_o - \bar{y}$	$(y_o - \bar{y})^2$
1,140	−40	1,600	−140	19,600
1,280	−70	4,900	− 30	900
1,420	10	100	+190	36,100
1,320	—	—	+ 80	6,400
1,300	20	400	+ 80	6,400
1,200	10	100	− 30	900
1,100	−10	100	−150	22,500
1,260	20	400	+ 40	1,600
1,380	20	400	+160	25,600
1,200	10	100	− 30	900
1,040	40	1,600	−160	25,600
1,240	−10	100	− 10	100
Σ = 14,880	—	9,800	—	146,600

$$r^2 = 1 - \frac{9,800}{146,600} = 0.933$$

The formula for the standard error is:

$$s_e = \sqrt{\frac{\Sigma(y_o - y_c)^2}{n - 2}}$$

$$s_e = \sqrt{9{,}800/10} = \$31.30$$

c.

Volume	Cost Forecast
2,500	$ 940
4,000	1,240
5,500	1,540

d. This is a highly reliable estimating formula with a high coefficient of determination and very narrow confidence interval. At a volume of 4,000 machine-hours, for example, the 95 percent confidence interval is $\pm 1.96 \times \$31.30 = \pm\$61.35$. We can be 95 percent certain that the true value lies between $1,178.65 and $1,301.35.

This may seem like a wide range, but actual data seldom yield ranges this narrow.

We must be much more cautious about the predicted cost at the extreme volumes, however. None of the actual observations was even close to either of these volumes and we have no assurance that the relationship extends this far.

18–2.   a.

Average cost decreases by 10 percent every time the cumulative total production doubles. Therefore:

Average cost of first 200 units = 0.9 × average cost of
first 100 units

Average cost of first 400 units = 0.9 × average cost of
first 200 units

Average cost of first 800 units = 0.9 × average cost of
first 400 units

Combining these, we find that the average cost of the
first 800 units = 0.9 × 0.9 × 0.9 × $100 = $72.90
Total cost = 800 × $72.90 = $58,320

b.

Average cost of the first 1,600 units = 0.9 × $72.90 = $65.61
Total cost of 1,600 units = 1,600 × $65.61 = $104,976
Additional cost of 2nd 800 units = $104,976 − $58,320
= $46,656, or $58.32/unit

c.

Because this increase will not increase cumulative production to twice some figure we already have, we need to use the formula given in the chapter:

Average cost = $10,000 × 9^s where $s = \dfrac{-0.0458}{0.301} = -0.15216$

Log av. cost = log 10,000 − 0.15216 log 9
= 4 − 0.1452 = 3.8548

Average cost = $71.5833/unit

Total cost = 900 × $71.5833 = $64,425

Incremental cost = $64,425 − $58,320 = $6,105 or $61.05/unit

Chapter 20

20–1.   *a.*

(1)	Materials	123,000	
	Purchase Price Variance	8,000	
	Accounts Payable		131,000
(2)	Materials in Process	140,000	
	Materials		140,000
(3)	Materials Quantity Variance	12,000	
	Materials		12,000
(4)	Materials	8,000	
	Materials Quantity Variance		8,000
(5)	Labor in Process	80,000	
	Labor Quantity Variance	5,600	
	Payroll Cost Summary		85,600
(6)	Accrued Wages Payable	79,500	
	Cash		79,500
(7)	Payroll Cost Summary	83,600	
	Accrued Wages Payable		83,600*
(8)	Finished Goods	198,900	
	Materials in Process		122,400
	Labor in Process		76,500
(9)	Labor Rate Variance	2,000	
	Payroll Cost Summary		2,000
(10)	Cost of Goods Sold	183,500	
	Finished Goods		183,500

* Amount paid + $8,100 increase in Accrued Wages Payable.

	Materials				**Materials in Process**		
(1)	123,000	(2)	140,000	(2)	140,000	(8)	122,400
(4)	8,000	(3)	12,000				

	Labor in Process				**Purchase Price Variance**		
(5)	80,000	(8)	76,500	(1)	8,000		

	Materials Quantity Variance				**Labor Quantity Variance**		
(3)	12,000	(4)	8,000	(5)	5,600		

	Payroll Cost Summary				**Accrued Wages Payable**		
(7)	83,600	(5)	85,600	(6)	79,500	Bal.	8,200
		(6)	79,500			(7)	83,600
		(9)	2,000				

Finished Goods			Labor Rate Variance	
(8) 198,900	(10) 183,500	(9) 2,000	

Cost of Goods Sold	
(10) 183,500	

b. Four-wall inventory accounts [numbers in parentheses refer to the entries in (*a*)]:

(1) Materials in Inventory 123,000
 Purchase Price Variance 8,000
 Accounts Payable 131,000

(2) No entry.
(3) Same as in (*a*).
(4) Same as in (*a*).

(5) Labor in Inventory 80,000
 Labor Quantity Variance 5,600
 Payroll Cost Summary 85,600

(6) (7) Same as in (*a*).
(8) No entry.
(9) Same as in (*a*).

(10) Cost of Goods Sold 183,500
 Materials in Inventory 115,200
 Labor in Inventory 68,300

Materials in Inventory			Labor in Inventory	
(1) 123,000	(3) 12,000	(5) 80,000	(10) 68,300
(4) 8,000	(10) 115,200		

The variance accounts and the Payroll Cost Summary, Accrued Wages Payable, and Cost of Goods Sold accounts are the same as in part (*a*).
c. The supplemental requisitions and the time tickets would have to be coded by cause as the variances occurred. A list of major causes would be given to the supervisor or clerk, who would mark the document whenever one of these causes arose.

20–2. *a.* The control limits were breached, both by the mean and by the range:

$$\bar{X} = 59$$
$$R = 19$$

The presumption is that the operation was out of control.
b. Control limits can be developed and used in this way only for highly repetitive activities in which one set of operations is very much like any other. If many products are manufactured, process variability must re-

late solely to the process, not to the characteristics of individual products. In other words, the variance must not be influenced by the product mix.

It is also unlikely that many operations will be so homogeneous that the individual observations in a sample will be comparable to each other. In the Appendix to Chapter 20, all batches were of identical size and required the same operation. This condition is rare in multiproduct operations.

Chapter 21

21–1.   *a.* Because overhead costs vary with *actual* machine-hours, a three-variance system should be used:

Actual..	$21,750	
Budget at actual hours..........................	21,500	
Spending variance.............................		$ 250 U.
Budget at standard hours.......................	22,000	
Machine efficiency variance....................		500 F.
Standard.......................................	20,000	
Volume variance..............................		2,000 U.
Total variance............................		$1,750 U.

Note: U. = unfavorable.
      F. = favorable.

b. This now requires a two-variance analysis. The volume variance remains the same, but the spending variance is $250, and favorable:

Actual..	$21,750	
Budget at standard hours.....................	22,000	
Spending variance.......................	$ 250 F.	

21–2.

Actual labor cost....................................	$57,000	
Actual labor hours at standard rates.................	56,000	
Labor rate variance...............................		$1,000 U.
Actual labor hours at standard rates, standard mix		
(9,000 hours × $6.50)............................	58,500	
Labor mix variance................................		2,500 F.
Standard labor cost................................	59,000	
Labor performance variance.......................		500 F.
Total labor variance............................		$2,000 F.

21–3.   *a.* Calculation of total direct labor variance:

Actual labor cost.............................	$16,800	
Standard labor cost...........................	15,000	
Total variance............................	$ 1,800 U.	

List of likely causes of variance:

   Rates
   Materials usage
   Other

Analysis:

Actual hours × actual rates: 3,200 × ?.................. $16,800
Actual hours × standard rates: 3,200 × $5.............. 16,000
    Labor rate variance................................ $ 800 U.
Required hours × standard rates: 2,300 × 1½ × $5...... 17,250
    Labor performance variance.......................   1,250 F.
Standard hours × standard rates: 1,000 × 3 × $5........ 15,000
    Effect of materials quantity variance...............   2,250 U.
       Total variance.................................. $1,800 U.

Check figure:

Materials quantity variance = 2,300 − 2,000 = 300 lbs.
Effect = 300 × 1½ × $5 = $2,250

b. Calculation of total overhead variance:

Actual overhead cost........................... $11,100
Standard overhead cost.........................   9,000
    Total overhead variance..................... $ 2,100 U.

List of likely causes:

Spending (overhead input price and quantity).
Effect of materials quantity variance.
Effect of labor performance variance.
Volume.

Analysis:

Actual.. $11,100
Budget at actual hours: $7,200 + $3,200.................. 10,400
    Spending variance................................. $ 700 U.
Budget at required hours: $7,200 + $3,450............... 10,650
    Effect of labor performance variance................   250 F.
Budget at standard hours: $7,200 + $3,000............... 10,200
    Effect of materials quantity variance................   450 U.
Standard (absorbed)....................................   9,000
    Volume variance....................................   1,200 U.
       Total variance.................................. $2,100 U.

Check figures:

Effect of MQV: 300 lbs × 1½ hours × $1 = $(450)
Effect of LPV: 250 hours × $1 = $250
Effect of volume: 200 units (below normal volume of 1,200) × $6 (fixed cost)
         = $(1,200)

21–4.   a.

Materials Inventory				Purchase Price Variance	
Bal.	11,400	(3)	6,000	(2)	450
(2)	5,400				
		Bal.	10,800		
Bal.	10,800				

Matls. in Process.—Dept. I

Bal.	2,400	(6a)	900
(3)	6,000	(6b)	3,000
(8)	300	(6c)	3,600
		Bal.	1,200
Bal.	1,200		

Payroll Cost Summary

(4a)	14,200	(4b)	14,000

Labor in Process—Dept. I

Bal.	1,600	(6a)	2,400
(4b)	14,000	(6b)	6,000
(9)	1,800	(6c)	4,000
		Bal.	1,400
Bal.	1,400		

Overhead in Process—Dept. I

Bal.	2,400	(6a)	3,600
(7)	18,300	(6b)	9,000
		(6c)	6,000
		Bal.	2,100
Bal.	2,100		

Overhead Summary—Dept. I

(5)	25,500	(10)	23,000*
		(11)	2,500

Overhead Absorbed—Dept. I

(12)	22,100*	(7)	18,300
		(13)	3,800

Matls. Qty. Var.—Dept. I

		(8)	300

Overhead Spending Var. —Dept. I

(11)	2,500

Ov. Lab. Eff. Var. —Dept. I

(10)	23,000*	(12)	22,100*

Labor Qty. Var. —Dept. I

		(9)	1,800

Overhead Volume Var.—Dept. I

(13)	3,800

Matls. in Process—Dept. II

(6a)	6,900
(6b)	18,000
(6c)	13,600

Payables, etc.

(2)	5,850
(4)	14,200
(5)	25,500

* Budget at actual hours: $16,000 + $2 \times 3,500 = $23,000
Budget at standard hours: $16,000 + $2 \times 3,050 = $22,100

Entries (10) and (12) may be omitted, but they facilitate the breakdown of the overhead variance. Entries (4a) and (4b) may be combined as a single entry.

b.

Materials price variance.............................	$ (450)
Labor rate variance.................................	(200)
Materials quantity variance.........................	(300)
Labor quantity variance.............................	1,800
Overhead spending variance........................	(2,500)
Overhead labor efficiency variance..................	(900)
Overhead volume variance..........................	(3,800)
Total variance................................	$(6,350)

Chapter 22

22–1.   *a.* Our first task is to calculate the standard materials cost of goods sold. The first step in this calculation is to find the standard materials cost of the work done during the year. The materials issued had a standard cost of $30,000, but $5,000 of this was a quantity variance. Therefore, the standard materials cost of the work done was $30,000 − $5,000 = $25,000. We can adjust this for the changes in inventories to get the standard materials cost of goods sold:

Standard materials cost of work done..............	$25,000
Decrease in work-in-process......................	1,100
Decrease in finished goods.......................	1,000
Standard materials cost of goods sold.............	$27,100

The second task is to prorate the quantity variance. Assuming that materials quantity variances are proportional to standard costs, the variance ratio is $5,000/$25,000 = 20 percent. Applying this ratio to ending work-in-process and finished goods inventories:

To work-in-process: $5,000 × 20%.................	$ 1,000
To finished goods: 7,000 × 20%....................	1,400
Total variance to inventories..................	$ 2,400
Remainder, to cost of goods sold..................	$ 2,600

Since this is a Fifo system, the materials cost of goods sold includes the $900 favorable materials quantity variance assigned to the January 1 inventory, and the $2,600 unfavorable variance for this year. The full calculation is:

Standard materials cost of goods sold.............	$27,100
Materials quantity variance:	
From prior year..................................	(900)
From this year...................................	2,600
Fifo historical materials cost of goods sold.........	$28,800

b.

The inventory variance account now has a $900 credit balance. It should have a $2,600 debit balance. The clearest way to make the adjustment is through the two following entries:

Materials Quantity Variance in Inventory	900	
Cost of Goods Sold		900
To transfer the opening balance		

Materials Quantity Variance in Inventory	2,400	
Cost of Goods Sold	2,600	
Materials Quantity Variance		5,000
To prorate the materials quantity variance for the year		

Chapter 23

23–1.   *a.*

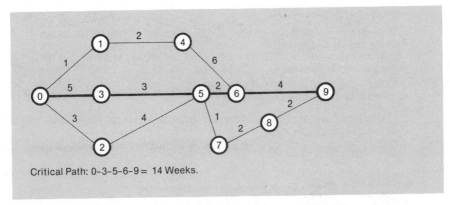

Critical Path: 0–3–5–6–9 = 14 Weeks.

b.

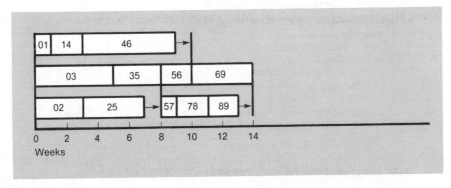

c. What management wants is an estimate or estimates of the cash flows emerging as a result of the market survey. The survey may be in preparation for the introduction of a new product, or for a change in some element of the marketing mix, or to identify a market opportunity. The project will be successful if it provides data that change management's plans and thereby improve the company's cash flows. The question is how probable this is, and what the cash costs and payoffs will be. This is an excellent place to draw a decision tree with this information.

23–2.   *a.* We have less detail than we would usually expect to find. Our report therefore has to be very condensed. We can start with some calculations:

	First 4 Weeks	Second 4 Weeks	Total
Budgeted cost of work done:			
Activity 01...............................	$ 5,000	—	$ 5,000
Activity 12...............................	20,000	—	20,000
Activity 13...............................	2,000	—	2,000
Activity 24...............................	—	$18,000	18,000
Total................................	$27,000	$18,000	$45,000
Budgeted expenditures..................	22,000	30,000	52,000

Report on cost performance:

	First 4 Weeks	Second 4 Weeks	Total
Actual costs..............................	$22,000	$29,000	$51,000
Budgeted cost of work done..............	27,000	18,000	45,000
Budgeted expenditures...................	22,000	30,000	52,000
Spending variance.......................	5,000 F.	11,000 U.	6,000 U.
(Over)/underexpenditure.................	—	1,000	1,000

Report on schedule slippage to date:

Preliminary model conference held one week late—one week behind schedule on the critical path.

Revision of forecasts:

Cost of activity 24:	
Incurred to date......................................	$29,000
Future spending......................................	65,000
Total...	$94,000
Original estimate.....................................	70,000
Estimated overrun..............................	$24,000
Schedule in weeks, activity 24:	
Early start...	− 1
Elapsed time to date...............................	4
Estimated time to complete...........................	12
Revised schedule from originally scheduled start....	15
Original time estimate................................	12
Estimated schedule slippage.....................	3

We have to find ways to present these figures effectively. Revised float diagrams or cumulative expenditure/progress charts are often useful.

b. The crucial questions are the same as those management must have posed when it approved the project in the first place: (1) what are the potential payoffs; and (2) what are the probabilities associated with each?

The costs incurred to date are sunk costs, but the difficulties encountered in constructing the model may lead management to question the validity of the revised estimates of incremental time and costs. It is also possible, though unlikely, that management now has a better estimate of the market potential of the new service. If so, the cost/benefit comparison will have to be based on revised estimates of both costs and benefits.

The main possible actions here are to continue the project, replace the project leader, or discontinue the project. The choice will depend on the

estimated future cash flows and probabilities and on management's appraisal of the reasons for the difficulties encountered to date.

Chapter 24

24–1.   *a.* Alifrance is not a profit center because it controls neither the
source of its merchandise nor the prices paid for it. It controls almost
every determinant of profit other than source and purchase price, however, and therefore is quite far along the continuum between a centrally
controlled unit and a completely autonomous unit. It falls into the category we have described as administered centers.

   b. Because Mr. Dalmas has control over many of the determinants of
profit, profit performance should be one of the key indicators of his
managerial ability. The question of what price to set on the merchandise
transferred should not affect this evaluation, however. We shall take up
this question in Chapter 26.

24–2.   *a.*

	Budgeted	Actual
Income..................................	$ 70,000	$ 63,000
Investment.............................	665,000	700,000
Return on investment....................	10.5%	9.0%

   b.

Income..................................	$ 70,000	$ 63,000
Investment charge at 12%................	79,800	84,000
Residual income (loss)...............	$ (9,800)	$(21,000)

   c. Neither the ROI figures nor the residual income figures are relevant
to managerial evaluation because of the changes in the allocated amounts
and the changes in traceable investments and depreciation, none of
which is controllable in any meaningful sense of the word. Using budgeted amounts to replace the actual amounts reported for these elements,
we can calculate a revised residual income figure as follows:

Working capital (actual).............................		$200,000
Traceable plant and equipment (budgeted)............		420,000
Allocated investments (budgeted).....................		95,000
Adjusted investment............................		$715,000
Income as reported.....................................		$ 63,000
Less: Change in depreciation.........................	$2,000	
Change in allocations...........................	5,000	(7,000)
Add: Tax on the changes.............................		3,500
Adjusted income................................		$ 59,500
Carrying charge (12% × $715,000).....................		(85,800)
Adjusted residual income (loss)..................		$(26,300)

This indicates that the division manager's performance was actually a
good deal worse than the initial comparisons indicated. One problem is
that investment in working capital exceeded the plan by $50,000. Sales
volume was $100,000 less than the budgeted amount (evidenced by

the decrease in the allocation of head office costs), so this factor can't account for the increase in working capital. Furthermore, the decrease in sales volume was accompanied by a $10,500 after-tax decrease in divisional income (from $70,000 to $59,500). The sources of this decrease should be investigated to see how much of it was within the division manager's control.

d. The figures don't permit the calculation of residual income or ROI on an attributable basis because the formulas don't measure attributability. The ratio of profit contribution to traceable investment is 13.8 percent ($63,000 income plus 50 percent of $40,000 in head office charges, divided by $600,000 traceable investment). This indicates that the division may be paying its way. If a study finds that attributable costs and investments in the head office are large enough to push the division's attributable return on investment substantially below 12 percent, then top management should analyze the division's incremental cash flows, both now and in the future when major capital investments are being considered. The purpose: to find out whether withdrawal would be desirable.

Chapter 25

25–1.   Budgeted profit margin per unit:

Sales..		$6.00
Direct materials..............................	$1.00	
Direct labor..................................	1.30	
Variable overhead............................	0.52	
Fixed overhead...............................	0.78	3.60
Profit margin.............................		$2.40

Variance summary:

Increased sales volume: 1,000 × $2.40*..............	$ 2,400 F.
Increased production volume*......................	780 F.
Reduced selling price: 11,000 × $0.50..............	5,500 U.
Materials quantity variance.......................	200 U.
Labor quantity variance...........................	400 U.
Overhead spending variance.......................	420 U.
Overhead labor efficiency variance.................	160 U.
Selling and administrative expense variance........	500 U.
Total variance..................................	$ 4,000 U.

* These two figures would be combined in a variable costing system, and can be reported as a single figure if the change in production volume is assumed to be the effect of the change in sales volume.

25–2.   *a.*

	(1)	(2)	(3)	(4)	(5)	(6)	(7)
		Budgeted Results			Actual Results		
Product	Reve-nues	Cost of Goods Sold	Gross Margin	Reve-nues	Cost of Goods Sold	Gross Margin	Profit Variance (6) − (3)
X.......	$20,000	$12,000	$ 8,000	$23,100	$12,960	$10,140	$2,140 F.
Y.......	30,000	21,000	9,000	23,600	16,800	6,800	2,200 U.
Z.......	20,000	16,000	4,000	25,500	20,800	4,700	700 F.
Total.......	$70,000	$49,000	$21,000	$72,200	$50,560	$21,640	$ 640 F.

b. Step 1: Calculate actual sales at budgeted prices and isolate the selling price variance:

Product	Units Sold	Budgeted Price	Calculated Revenue	Actual Revenue	Selling Price Variance
X.............	10,800	$2	$21,600	$23,100	$1,500 F.
Y.............	4,000	6	24,000	23,600	400 U.
Z.............	5,200	5	26,000	25,500	500 U.
Total...........	20,000		$71,600	$72,200	$ 600 F.

Step 2: Calculate the budgeted margins for the actual sales volumes and compare these figures with the budgeted margins for the budgeted sales volumes—to determine the sales volume variance for each product:

Product	Calculated Revenue	Cost of Goods Sold at Budgeted Unit Costs	Calculated Gross Margin	Budgeted Gross Margin	Sales Volume Variance
X..............	$21,600	$12,960	$ 8,640	$ 8,000	$ 640 F.
Y..............	24,000	16,800	7,200	9,000	1,800 U.
Z..............	26,000	20,800	5,200	4,000	1,200 F.
Total..............	$71,600	$50,560	$21,040	$21,000	$ 40 F.

Step 3: Because the $40 total of the three sales volume figures results from a combination of sales volume and sales mix variations, calculate the budgeted average gross margin per sales dollar and use this to calculate the sales mix variance:

$$\frac{\text{Budgeted gross margin}}{\text{Budgeted revenues}} = \frac{\$21,300}{\$70,000} = 30\%.$$

Budgeted gross margin..................	$21,000	
Calculated revenues × budgeted percent ($71,600 × 0.3)...............	21,480	
Sales volume variance..................		$480 F.
Sum of calculated gross margins for individual products...................	21,040	
Sales mix variance.....................		440 U.

Variance summary:
Selling price...........................	$600 F.	
Sales volume.........................	480 F.	
Sales mix.............................	440 U.	
Total...............................	$640 F.	

c. The budgeted gross margin per unit was $21,000/19,000 units = $1.105. Using this instead of the 30% contribution margin ratio produces the following analysis:

Budgeted gross margin...........................	$21,000	
Actual units sold × budgeted margin per unit (20,000 × $1.105)......................	22,100	
Sales volume variance...........................		$1,100 F.
Sum of actual calculated gross margins for individual products...........................	21,040	
Sales mix variance.............................		1,060 U.

This isn't necessarily more correct than the analysis in (b). This method simply weights low priced units more heavily than the method used in (b). Since the number of units increased more sharply than revenues, the volume variance appears larger here than in (b). If management measures its market penetration by the number of units sold rather than by sales dollars, then this method will meet management's needs better than the method used in (b).

Chapter 26

26-1.   *a.* The memorandum should stress the following points:

1. If the alternative is idleness, the only incremental costs may be the variable costs of 90 cents a pound, and this is far less than the proposed transfer price. Hull's profit will be 70 cents greater for every pound of X it processes for the Hingham division. Without these 50,000 pounds, product X would show a loss of $20,000 after deducting its share of division fixed costs; with this production, the net profit figure would be $15,000. This can be summarized in the following schedules for the Hull division:

	If Hingham Buys from Hull @ $1.60	If Hingham Buys Outside
Sales—outside (100,000 lbs.)	$200,000	$200,000
Sales—Hingham (50,000 lbs.)	80,000	—
Total sales	$280,000	$200,000
Product-traceable costs:		
Variable mfg. costs	$135,000	$ 90,000
Sales commissions	10,000	10,000
Depreciation	20,000	20,000
Other traceable costs	40,000	40,000
Total traceable costs	$205,000	$160,000
Product profit contribution	$ 75,000	$ 40,000
Share of division fixed costs	60,000	60,000
Income before taxes	$ 15,000	$(20,000)

2. If the Hull division will retain idle workers on the payroll to avoid losing a skilled work force, the incremental cost could be even less than 90 cents a pound because some labor costs would be sunk.
3. Even if the traceable fixed costs increase in steps, it is unlikely that these could be high enough to make an incremental loss. At the present volume they average only 27 cents a pound.
4. The Hull division manager should recognize a longer term problem— if cheaper substitutes are available, this may indicate a serious competitive weakness for the long run.

b. Some economists establish such a strict set of necessary conditions for the use of negotiation that they are almost never met. If you are willing to use the criteria established in this chapter, however, negotiation should be appropriate here. Hull has access to outside customer markets; Hingham has access to outside suppliers. If Hull were busy, the company might even be better off to have Hingham buy outside. If profit decentralization is to mean anything, we must rely on the division managers to identify situations of this type.

26–2.   *a.* The same arguments favoring a $1.60 transfer price for the Hingham division (Problem 1) support granting the $1.50 transfer price, unless Hull division is operating so close to capacity it would incur substantial cost penalties or opportunity costs to meet Elsa's demands.

b. Elsa division is an administered center, responsible for profits but with no choice of supplier. In these circumstances, the manager has little bargaining power, and the market value of the intermediate product is unknown to either party. Average variable cost plus retainer, market in/cost out, or even a decomposition solution—each of these would be established by top management decree—would be more appropriate than negotiation. Since decomposition requires a more highly structured decision situation than we're likely to see very often, one of the other two methods should be pressed.

Index

Index

This book has been set in 10 and 9 point Primer, leaded 1 point. Part numbers are 42 point Helvetica Bold and part titles are 24 point Helvetica. Chapter numbers are 48 point Bulmer and chapter titles are 18 point Helvetica. The size of the maximum type page is 31 picas by 47½ picas.